CASSELL

DICTIONARY OF

CLASSICAL
MYTHOLOGY

CASSELL
DICTIONARY OF
CLASSICAL
MYTHOLOGY

Jenny March

CASSELL

To my dear family

to Len, Alex, Robbie and Felicity,

and to Jessica, Rosanna, Tom, Joe, William,

Sam, Jenny and Rachel – my other *magnum opus*

This edition first published in the UK 1998 by
Cassell
Wellington House, 125 Strand, London WC2R 0BB

Copyright © Dr Jennifer R. March 1998

The right of Dr Jennifer R. March to be identified as the author of this work has been asserted
by her in accordance with the Copyright, Designs and Patents Act 1988

Distributed in the United States by
Sterling Publishing Co. Inc. 387 Park Avenue South
New York, NY 10016, USA

British Library Cataloguing-in-Publication Data
A catalogue record for this book is available from the British Library

ISBN 0-304-34626-8

Designed by Gwyn Lewis
Cartography by Lovell Johns Limited

Printed and bound in Great Britain by the Bath Press, Bath

CONTENTS

PREFACE

I have long had a passion for Greek myths, so when a letter came four years ago from Cassell, asking whether I would like to write their Dictionary of Classical Mythology, I had no hesitation in replying with a resounding 'Yes!'. At the time I had no real idea of quite what a massive project I was taking on, nor of how it would dominate my life, especially in its final stages. But I have never – or at least never for long – regretted that initial happy response.

I must express my warm thanks to a number of people. To Nigel Wilcockson, who originally commissioned this book. To Susan Woodford, who valiantly read my manuscript and offered many useful comments (but is in no way responsible for any deficiencies remaining). To my husband, Len, who supported me throughout in all manner of ways, and who gave invaluable help with such intricacies as the computer-generation of genealogies. To everyone at Cassell who saw the book through the press, and particularly to Sarah Chatwin and Richard Milbank, who were unfailingly cheerful and helpful to an anxious author through the final stages of publication.

I thank my friends for their encouragement, and for their patience with my absence, physical and mental. I thank especially Barbara Goward, who cheered and supported me when, at times, I felt that I would never be finished; and Phyllis Pitt, who first taught me Greek, and from whom a card arrived at a particularly low moment saying that now the end must be in sight (though it wasn't, for I was running late), and adding, 'I think of Odysseus, coming home to Ithaca.' I carried on, my courage renewed.

And finally I thank my family, who have borne with me through it all, and who are always there for me, as I for them, on and on without end. To them I dedicate this book.

Jenny March
September 1998

INTRODUCTION

For centuries people have spoken of the Greek myths as of something to be rediscovered, reawoken.
The truth is, it is the myths that are still out there waiting to wake us and be seen by us,
like a tree waiting to greet our newly opened eyes.

Roberto Calasso, *The Marriage of Cadmus and Harmony*

Myths were at the heart of ancient Greek life and culture. They held a central place in poetry at public and private festivals, and were told and retold by the poets, changing and developing as time went by, and from the sixth century BC onwards forming the subject of gripping dramas played out on the tragic stage. But these myths were more than mere stories. To the Greeks they were history, telling of real people in the real past; and a man's genealogy, often originating from a divine mythical ancestor, showed his place in the world and his relation to the great heroes of myth[1]. Myths too were portrayed in the visual arts: on wall paintings, now all lost, in sculptures, and above all on the pots that were an integral part of everyday life, since Greek vase-painters were (luckily for us) the most prolific illustrators of myth. Even the physical world – rivers, springs, woods, mountains, the very earth itself – was alive with divine presences; and in the time of Homer, whose *Iliad* and *Odyssey* give us our first recorded myths, the gods still walk among men.

In due course the Romans adopted the Greek myths, often making their own unforgettable adaptations (think of Virgil's Dido, or of some of the brilliant metamorphoses in Ovid), though on the whole adding few new myths of their own. This body of Greek and Roman myths, the 'Classical Mythology' of our title, covers the widest range of human experience. Compare, for instance, the bloody violence of Atreus and his kin with the simple goodness of Philemon and Baucis, or the comic fate of Midas with the tragic fate of Pentheus, or the very different loves and lusts shown in the myths of Admetus and Alcestis, of Tereus, of Hero and Leander, of Myrrha, or of Ceyx and Alcyone. Small wonder, then, that classical myths have lived on, becoming an inspiration for creative artists of all kinds down the centuries to our own day. In recent years there has been a tremendous resurgence of interest in this mythology, so this book has been written both as a cele-bration of a vital and fascinating subject, and as a key to the world of classical myth for anyone wishing to delve more deeply into its many delights.

My aim has been to retell the myths as readably as possible, detailing any major variants and including, where appropriate, translations from ancient writers to give life to my narrative. The illustrations too have been chosen to give visual immediacy to the words, by showing how ancient artists perceived their gods and heroes[2]. In the text, where relevant, I touch on a myth's use in ancient art and on its influence in the postclassical arts. I also supply many references, so that readers may, if they wish, go back to the original literary sources[3], and I give suggestions for further reading, occasionally at the end of an entry, and more generally in the Bibliography at the end of the book. For clarity I also include in the end matter two maps of the ancient world, a list of the ancient sources and their chronology, a detailed list of the illustrations, and a few of the more important genealo-gies. The spelling of ancient names is always a thorny problem, and my own solution has been to adopt the most familiar current usage.

A word should be said on how to approach the cross-references within each entry, signalled by SMALL CAPITALS. These will give more information (including source refer-ences) about the character under discussion, and/or useful background to his/her story. To take just a few examples from the entry on Patroclus: more information can be found from MENOETIUS (2) about Patroclus' child-hood, from ACHILLES about Patroclus' relationship with his dearest comrade and the traumatic effect on Achilles of his death, and from SARPEDON about Patroclus' defeat in battle of his mightiest victim; while HECTOR and APOLLO will simply give a greater understanding of the mortal and the god who were involved in Patroclus' death.

This book has been a long time in the making, far

more than the four years of actual writing. In a sense it goes back some forty years to a time when, in my impressionable teens, I was moved by Gilbert Murray's translation of Euripides' *Trojan Women*, and specifically by the speech of Andromache here quoted in my own translation (closer to the Greek, though perhaps less emotive than Murray's) in the article on Astyanax. At that moment I knew beyond a doubt that I had to learn Greek. I should like to think that this book also may spur some readers towards the joys of Greek or Latin, and of making contact for themselves with the endless riches of classical literature. But if I simply succeed in bringing some of these incomparable myths to life for the reader, I shall rest content.

1 The question of how far the myths are based on fact is a difficult one, and there is no generally agreed answer, nor ever likely to be. My own feeling is that many of the myths have a core of truth. Yes, a Trojan War (of a kind) did take place.

2 Readers who wish to pursue this subject further will find in *LIMC* (see Bibliography) a complete illustrated catalogue of myths in classical art.

3 These citations are not intended to be complete, and refer, almost invariably, to the easily accessible works of ancient literature commonly found in translation, or in the Loeb Classical Library which gives Greek and Latin texts with facing translations. If readers wish to pursue a matter further among the scholia or less accessible authors, they might begin by looking up any reference to Apollodorus, using the Loeb edition which has translation and footnotes by Sir J. G. Frazer (see Bibliography). This will very often give pointers to the less familiar sources. Another great help will be Timothy Gantz's *Early Greek Myth* (again, see Bibliography), where the author traces the chronology of myths as they appear in ancient art and literature.

A

Abantes *see* ELEPHENOR.

Abas (1)
A king of Argos, the son of LYNCEUS (1) and Hypermestra. He married Aglaia, daughter of Mantineus, and had twin sons, ACRISIUS and PROETUS, who fought each other even in their mother's womb and grew up to fight over the rule of Argos. Eventually they divided the land of Argos between them, with Acrisius ruling at Argos and Proetus at Tiryns.

[Apollodorus 2.2.1.]

Abas (2)
Son of the famous seer MELAMPUS and Iphianassa, the daughter of Proetus. Abas had two children, a son, Coeranus, who became the father of another seer, POLYIDUS, and a daughter, Lysimache, who married TALAUS.

[Apollodorus 1.9.13; Pausanias 1.43.5.]

Abas (3)
The man who gave his name to the Abantes tribe in Euboea. He was the father of CHALCODON and the grandfather of ELEPHENOR, who led the Abantes to the Trojan War.

Abderus
A son of HERMES from Opuntian Locris in central Greece who was loved by HERACLES. He was killed by the man-eating mares of DIOMEDES (1) when left to guard them by Heracles, who then founded the city of Abdera in Thrace in memory of his lover.

[Apollodorus 2.5.8.]

Acacallis
A daughter of MINOS, king of Crete, and PASIPHAE. When Acacallis (called Acalle by Apollodorus) became pregnant by APOLLO, her father banished her to Libya where she bore the god a son, Amphithemis, also called Garamas. The Cretans claimed that she also bore a son to HERMES called Cydon, after whom the Cretan city of Cydonia was

named; though the people of Tegea in Arcadia said that Cydon was the son of Tegeates and emigrated from Tegea to Crete. According to another legend Acacallis also bore a son, MILETUS, to Apollo, but from fear of her father's anger she abandoned the infant in a forest. He was guarded and suckled by wolves until he was found by shepherds, who took him in and brought him up.

[Apollonius, *Argonautica* 4.1489–94; Apollodorus 3.1.2; Pausanias 8.53.2; Antoninus Liberalis, *Metamorphoses* 30.]

Academus
An Attic hero who helped the DIOSCURI to recover their sister HELEN when she was carried off from Sparta by Theseus. Academus told them that Helen was hidden at Aphidnae in Attica, and for this he was honoured by the Dioscuri for the rest of his life. In historical times there were many occasions when the Spartans invaded Attica and devastated the country, but spared the spot where Academus was worshipped, a grove near the river Cephissus about a mile north-west of Athens. This was named Academeia ('the Academy') after him, and it was here that Plato and his followers later taught.

[Plutarch, *Theseus* 32, *Cimon* 13; Diogenes Laertius 3.7–8.]

Acamas (1) and Demophon
Sons of THESEUS and PHAEDRA. Acamas' name was given in historical times to one of the tribes of Athens. When MENESTHEUS usurped the throne of Athens from Theseus, the brothers took refuge with ELEPHENOR, king of the Abantes in Euboea. They later accompanied him to the TROJAN WAR in the hope of rescuing their grandmother AETHRA, who had been taken to Troy as Helen's slave. It was said that before the fighting began, Acamas went on an embassy with Diomedes to demand the return of Helen. LAODICE (1), an unmarried daughter of King Priam, fell in love with him and took him as her lover. She bore him a son, Munitus, who was brought up during the war years by Aethra.

Fig. 1 Acamas and Demophon lead away their grandmother, Aethra, after the fall of Troy.

When Troy at last fell to the Greeks, Acamas and Demophon took their grandmother home again to Athens (fig. 1) and reclaimed their kingdom. Munitus went with them, but was killed by a snake-bite while hunting with his father in Thrace. During the brothers' rule, according to Euripides' *Children of Heracles*, they defended Heracles' family against the persecutions of the tyrant EURYSTHEUS.

Another legend gives a different ending to the story. While in Thrace, Acamas (or in some sources Demophon) married Phyllis, a Thracian princess, who brought her father's kingdom to the marriage as dowry. After a while Acamas wished to go home again, and despite his wife's entreaties he set off, promising to return to her within a certain time. As he left, Phyllis gave him a casket, telling him that it contained objects sacred to the Great Mother, Rhea, and adding that he must never open it unless he gave up all intention of ever coming back to her. Time passed and Acamas did not return. Eventually Phyllis abandoned all hope of seeing her dear husband again and killed herself. Acamas, meanwhile, had settled in Cyprus. One day he opened the casket, and what he saw inside terrified him so much that he leapt on his horse and galloped wildly away. He was thrown, and died by falling on his own sword.

Another sad story, told of Phyllis and Demophon, is found in Servius' commentary on Virgil (*Eclogues* 5.10).

Once again Phyllis was deserted after marriage. She hanged herself in grief and was turned into a leafless almond tree; but one day Demophon returned. Learning of his wife's suicide and metamorphosis, he put his arms around the tree in sorrow and kissed it. At once it burst into leaf; so leaves, which had previously been called *petala*, were ever after called *phylla*. Hyginus (*Fabula* 59) says that when Phyllis died of love, trees grew on her grave, and every year at the time of her death they mourned her as their leaves withered and fell.

[Epic Cycle, Proclus' summary of the *Sack of Troy*; Euripides, *Hecuba* 122–9; Apollodorus, *Epitome* 1.18, 1.23, 5.22, 6.16–17; Plutarch, *Theseus* 35; Pausanias 1.5.2, 1.17.6, 10.10.1, 10.25.8, 10.26.2; Quintus of Smyrna, *Sequel to Homer* 13.496–543; Virgil, *Aeneid* 2.262; Ovid, *Heroides* 2.]

Acamas (2)

A Trojan, son of ANTENOR and Theano, who, together with his brother Archelochus and AENEAS, led the Dardanian contingent in the TROJAN WAR. When Archelochus was killed by AJAX (1), Acamas avenged his brother by killing the Boeotian Promachus. Soon afterwards Acamas was himself killed by MERIONES.

[Homer, *Iliad* 2.819–23, 12.98–100, 14.458–89, 16.342–4.]

Acamas (3)

The leader of Troy's Thracian allies in the TROJAN WAR, killed by AJAX (1).

[Homer, *Iliad* 2.844–5, 6.5–11.]

Acarnan see ALCMAEON.

Acastus

Son of PELIAS, king of Iolcus, and Anaxibia. He married Astydameia (sometimes called Hippolyte), by whom he had three daughters, LAODAMEIA (2), Sterope and Sthenele, and a number of sons. Against his father's wishes, Acastus sailed with JASON and the ARGONAUTS, and on their return, after the sorceress MEDEA had engineered Pelias' death, he succeeded to the throne of Iolcus. In honour of his father, Acastus held great funeral games at which many of the Greek heroes competed. He later went on the CALYDONIAN BOARHUNT; here his fellow-Argonaut PELEUS accidentally killed Eurytion, then came to Iolcus to be purified of blood-guilt by his friend. Unfortunately, Astydameia fell in love with Peleus and tried to seduce him, and when he rejected her advances she accused him to her husband of trying to rape her. Acastus, unwilling to kill the man whom he had purified, took him hunting on Mount Pelion in the hope that there he would meet his death, and even stole his sword while he was asleep, leaving him alone and defenceless against the wild Centaurs. But Peleus was saved by the kindly Centaur

Cheiron and so lived to take his revenge: he sacked Iolcus with the help of Jason and the DIOSCURI, then killed Astydameia and marched his army into the city between the severed halves of her corpse. In some versions he killed Acastus as well. When Peleus was an old man, this deed was avenged when either Acastus or his sons drove him out of his kingdom of Phthia.

[Pindar, *Nemean* 4.54–60, 5.25–36; Euripides, *Alcestis* 732–3, *Trojan Women* 1126–8; Apollonius, *Argonautica* 1.321–3; Apollodorus 1.9.16, 1.9.27, 3.12.2–3, 3.13.7–8, *Epitome* 6.13.]

Acca Larentia

The wife of the shepherd, Faustulus, who found the abandoned twins, ROMULUS AND REMUS, being suckled by a she-wolf and adopted them. Because *lupa* can mean both 'she-wolf' and 'prostitute', some writers rationalised the boys' legend by claiming that Acca Larentia herself had saved their lives by suckling them.

A very different story is told of her by Plutarch (*Moralia* 272f–273b). The keeper of HERCULES' temple at Rome once invited his god to a game of dice. When Hercules won, the temple servant rewarded him with a fine dinner and the services of Larentia, the most beautiful prostitute in Rome, for a night. In the morning, on Hercules' advice, she made advances to the first man she met on leaving the temple – a wealthy Etruscan named Tarrutius – and became his wife. He left her all his money, and she in turn bequeathed her estate to the Roman people.

Acestes or Aegestes

Son of the Sicilian river-god Crinisus and a Trojan mother. Acestes entertained AENEAS and his comrades in Sicily during their travels, and it was while staying with him that Aeneas celebrated his father Anchises' funeral games. When he sailed onwards, Aeneas left behind some of his companions to people the newly founded city of Acesta (later Segesta), named after his host.

[Virgil, *Aeneid* 1.195–7, 549–60, 5.35–778.]

Achaeans see ACHAEUS.

Achaeus

Ancestor of the Achaeans, and brother of ION, the ancestor of the Ionians. Achaeus and Ion were the sons of the Thessalian XUTHUS and Creusa, daughter of King ERECHTHEUS of Athens. At the time of Xuthus' death, they were living in Aegialus (the Coastland) in the northern Peloponnese. Ion and Achaeus then separated. Ion stayed

in Aegialus, married the king's daughter and eventually became king himself, calling his people Ionians. Achaeus returned to southern Thessaly, from which Xuthus had long ago been driven out, and with the help of allies from Athens and Aegialus he recovered the Thessalian throne. The land was called Achaea after him and his people the Achaeans. Many generations later the Achaeans drove the Ionians out of Aegialus, which was now also renamed Achaea. Homer uses the name Achaean in the broader sense of all the Greeks who fought against Troy.

[Pausanias 7.1.2–9.]

Achates

As Patroclus is to Achilles in Homer's *Iliad*, so Achates is to AENEAS in Virgil's *Aeneid*: his loyal friend and henchman, so often referred to as *fidus Achates* ('faithful Achates') that this term has come to mean a devoted companion.

Achelous

The name of the greatest of all Greek rivers and its god. The Achelous is situated in north-western Greece on the borders of Acarnania and Aetolia, rising in central Epeirus and flowing into the Ionian Sea. Its modern name is the Aspropotamo. Homer calls it the 'prince of rivers' (*Iliad* 21.194), and certainly it was the most important in cult and legend. Like all river-gods, Achelous was the son of OCEANUS and Tethys, and he himself was the father of the SIRENS, of Calirrhoe, the second wife of ALCMAEON, and of

Fig.2 **Heracles wrestles with the river-god Achelous, grasping him by the horn.**

the nymphs of two famous springs, Peirene at Corinth and Castalia at Delphi.

At the mouth of the Achelous lie the Echinades Islands. These had originally been five nymphs who forgot to honour the great river-god in their festivities. In his anger he swept them away and they were transformed into islands. Another island, a little apart from the rest, was especially dear to Achelous, for this had once been a lover of his, a mortal woman called Perimele. After she was seduced by the river-god, her indignant father flung her from a cliff into the sea, but Achelous caught her and held her up as she swam. In answer to his prayers she was changed into an island by Poseidon.

Achelous wished to marry DEIANEIRA, the daughter of Oeneus, king of Calydon, and he wooed her in three monstrous manifestations. 'He came in three shapes to ask my father for my hand', says Deianeira in Sophocles' *Women of Trachis* (10–17), 'now manifest as a bull, now a shimmering, coiling snake, now with a man's body and a bull's head, and from his shaggy beard flowed streams of water from his springs. Expecting a suitor like that, I was always praying, poor creature, that I might die before ever I came near his bed.' But another suitor appeared, the mighty HERACLES, and wrestled with Achelous for Deianeira's hand. The river-god changed his shape unavailingly and Heracles vanquished him, breaking off as he did so one of the god's horns. To recover this, Achelous gave in its place the horn of AMALTHEIA, who had once been the nurse of Zeus. Vase-paintings of the combat show Achelous as a centaur-like figure with bull's horns, or a human-faced bull or (in one case: fig.2) fish with the horn prominent.

[Hesiod, *Theogony* 340; Apollodorus 1.3.4, 1.7.10, 1.8.1, 2.7.5, 3.7.5; Pausanias 2.2.3, 3.18.16, 8.24.9–11, 8.38.9–10, 10.8.5; Ovid, *Metamorphoses* 8.547–9.88.]

Acheron

The River of Woe in the Underworld (though it was sometimes imagined as a marshy lake); and by extension the name often given to the Underworld itself (*see* HADES (2)). The Acheron, rather than the Styx, was sometimes seen as the boundary of Hades across which the aged ferryman CHARON rowed the souls of the dead. Its name suggests the pain (*achos*) caused by the deaths of loved ones. There was a River Acheron in Thesprotia, in southern Epeirus, which ran underground and was thought to lead to the Underworld. On the banks of the river was an Oracle of the Dead, where the souls of the departed could be called for consultation.

The river-god was the father of ASCALAPHUS (1) by one of the nymphs of the Underworld, Gorgyra or Orphne. Sophocles' Antigone, when she is about to die, laments

(810–16) that she has had no wedding, no bridal song, but must now take Acheron for her bridegroom.

Pausanias (10.28.1) describes Polygnotus' painting of the Acheron at Delphi: a river with reeds growing in it, and with fishes dim and shadowy in its depths. The Acheron is one of Milton's 'four infernal rivers' in *Paradise Lost*: 'sad Acheron of sorrow, black and deep'.

[Homer, *Odyssey* 10.513–4; Herodotus 5.92.7; Euripides, *Alcestis* 439–44; Apollodorus 1.5.3; Pausanias 1.17.5; Virgil, *Aeneid* 6.107, 295; Ovid, *Metamorphoses* 5.538–41.]

Achilles

The greatest of the Greek heroes who fought at Troy. His anger with AGAMEMNON, the main theme of the *Iliad*, was an anger which almost lost the Greeks the war and which brought about the death of Achilles' beloved comrade PATROCLUS, of the great Trojan warrior HECTOR, and finally of Achilles himself. He was a popular figure with ancient artists, and the various episodes of his life are frequently depicted on vase-paintings.

1. THE EARLY YEARS

Achilles was the son of PELEUS, king of Phthia in Thessaly, and the sea-goddess THETIS. When Achilles was born, Thetis tried to make him immortal by burning away the mortality inherited from his father. She put him in the fire at night and anointed him with ambrosia during the day. But one night Peleus caught her in the act of putting their son in the fire and angrily interfered. So Thetis forsook both baby and husband and went back to live in the sea with the Nereids. A late version of the myth said that Thetis dipped the baby Achilles in the River Styx, gripping him by the heel and making him completely invulnerable except for the heel by which she held him. An arrow-shot in that one, weak heel would eventually bring about his death (hence the expression 'Achilles' heel' for a vulnerable spot).

With Thetis once more living in the sea, Peleus gave Achilles to be reared and educated by CHEIRON, the wise and kindly Centaur who lived on Mount Pelion (fig.39). Cheiron instructed his young charge in hunting, medicine and music, and fed him on the entrails of lions and wild boars to instil in him strength and courage. Achilles also learnt to become fleet of foot, so swift that he could overtake a deer: *podarkes Achilleus*, Homer calls him, 'swift-footed Achilles'. Later he returned to his home in Phthia, where his father Peleus had taken in two refugees who would be important figures in Achilles' life: PHOENIX (3), who helped to bring him up and later accompanied him to Troy, and Patroclus, who became his dearest friend and inseparable companion (fig.109), and whose death at Troy would lead to his own. Meanwhile, events were taking place that would inexorably bring about the TROJAN WAR: the beautiful HELEN of Sparta was wooed by many suitors, each of whom took an oath to defend the marriage rights of her chosen husband if the need ever arose – which it did, when Helen eloped with PARIS to Troy.

Thetis, with her divine foreknowledge, was well aware of the approach of the war. She also knew that Achilles was fated to die if he went to fight at Troy; so she dressed him as a girl and sent him instead to live with the women at the court of LYCOMEDES, king of the island of Scyros. The secret, however, was in some way betrayed, and when the Greeks were marshalling troops for the war ODYSSEUS went to the island and tricked Achilles into revealing his identity. Once unmasked, Achilles went eagerly to war, taking with him fifty ships from Phthia, even though, unlike the other Greek leaders, he had taken no oath of loyalty that forced him to fight. He left behind him a son, NEOPTOLEMUS, born of Lycomedes' daughter, Deidameia.

2. THE TROJAN WAR

The Greeks mustered their fleet and set sail, but they lost their way, landing in Mysia far to the south of Troy. The king of the country was TELEPHUS, a son of Heracles, and he and his countrymen drove the pillaging Greeks back to their ships, though not before Telephus himself had been wounded in the thigh by Achilles. The Greeks, realising their mistake, sailed back to Argos, followed by

Telephus, who had learnt from an oracle that his wound could be cured only by the one that had caused it. Odysseus pointed out that the oracle meant the spear itself, and not the man wielding it, so Achilles rubbed some rust from his spear into the wound and Telephus was soon cured. In return for this favour, he agreed to show the Greeks the way to Troy.

The fleet now became weather-bound at Aulis. The seer CALCHAS foretold that the angry goddess Artemis must be appeased by the sacrifice of Agamemnon's virgin daughter IPHIGENEIA, so she was lured to Aulis on the pretext of marriage with Achilles, a situation movingly dramatised in Euripides' *Iphigeneia at Aulis*. Achilles knew nothing of this ruse and tried to save the girl's life, but she chose to help the Greek army by going willingly to death. She was killed, the winds blew once again, and the Greek fleet sailed.

When they put in at the island of Tenedos, Thetis warned Achilles that he must on no account kill its king, TENES, else he himself would die at the hands of the god APOLLO, Tenes' father. Despite her warning, Achilles killed the king and would later pay the price. He paid more heed to his mother's caution that he must not be the first to land at Troy, since an oracle had predicted that the first man to touch Trojan soil would be the first to die. It was

Fig.3 Two heralds lead Briseis away from Achilles, who sits in his tent, muffled in grief.

PROTESILAUS who took the initiative and leapt ashore, dying at the hands of Hector, the son of King PRIAM of Troy and leader of the Trojan forces.

For nine years the Greeks besieged Troy, fighting the Trojans and sacking the neighbouring cities (fig.145). Many fell victim to Achilles. He killed CYCNUS (3), king of Colonae, strangling him with the thongs of his own helmet since he had been made invulnerable to weapons by his father Poseidon. He ambushed and killed TROILUS, son of King Priam (fig.4), it being said that Troy was destined never to fall if Troilus reached the age of twenty. He killed EETION, king of Thebe in the Troad, and his seven sons. He sacked Lyrnessus, a city near Troy, and won for himself the beautiful captive BRISEIS. This brings us to the events of Homer's *Iliad*, in the tenth year of the war.

3. ACHILLES IN THE ILIAD

> Sing, Muse, the wrath of Peleus' son, Achilles,
> the accursed wrath that brought countless sorrows
> to the Greeks, hurled down to Hades the souls
> of many brave heroes, and left their corpses a prey
> for the dogs and all the birds ...

Thus begins the *Iliad*, the very first word in the Greek being *menin*, 'wrath', the anger of Achilles that will reverberate through the whole work, until it is finally eased to acceptance and compassion in his meeting with Priam and the ransoming of Hector's body.

This anger, Homer tells us, is set in motion by a violent quarrel between Achilles and Agamemnon, the leader of the expedition, who has been forced to give up his concubine CHRYSEIS to appease Apollo. Agamemnon says that in recompense he will take the war-prize of some other man, maybe Achilles himself, and the angry Achilles responds to this injustice by threatening to leave Troy and take his ships and men home to Phthia. Agamemnon, furious in his turn, replies (1.177–86):

> Always strife is dear to you, and wars and battles,
> and though you are very strong, that is a god's gift.
> Go home then with your ships and your comrades,
> be king over the Myrmidons. I care nothing for you,
> nothing for your anger. But here is my threat to you:
> Since Phoebus Apollo has taken away my Chryseis
> ... I shall come myself to your hut and take away
> the fair-cheeked Briseis, your prize, and you will learn
> how much greater I am than you.

Achilles feels himself dishonoured and reacts by refusing to fight any more, warning Agamemnon that he will regret the loss of his best warrior (1.240–4): 'I swear that there will come a time when a longing for Achilles will be felt by the sons of the Achaeans, by every one of them', cries Achilles, 'and on that day, for all your sorrow, you

will be able to do nothing to help, when many of them drop and die before man-slaughtering Hector. Then you will eat your heart out in anger that you did no honour to the best of the Achaeans.' He retires to his tent, and when Briseis is taken from him he goes alone to the sea shore and weeps (fig.3).

His mother Thetis hears his sorrow and comes to him from the deeps of the ocean. He asks her to intercede for him with Zeus, requesting the great god to help the Trojans so that the Greeks will feel the lack of their supreme warrior. She does so and Zeus nods his agreement.

Battle continues for some days, with the Trojans driving the Greeks back towards their ships in an assault led by Hector. The Greeks, deeply concerned, hold a council where Agamemnon publicly announces that he was wrong to shame Achilles by taking his war-prize from him. He will give back Briseis, together with many other fine gifts: seven tripods, ten talents of gold, twenty cauldrons, twelve horses, and seven women of Lesbos, with yet more gifts when Troy is conquered, and even the hand of one of his own daughters in marriage with a great dowry. An embassy of three men – Odysseus, AJAX (1) and old Phoenix – goes to Achilles' tent to tell him what Agamemnon offers if only he will come back and fight.

Achilles welcomes his three friends kindly and serves them food and drink, but he refuses to return to battle, even when Odysseus outlines the bounty that Agamemnon is promising. Indeed, Achilles has become disenchanted with the whole war (9.318–27):

> Fate is the same for the man who holds back
> and the man who fights his best. In one honour
> are held both the cowards and the brave.
> Death still comes to the man who does nothing,
> as well as the man who does much. I win nothing
> for suffering heart-sorrow and forever risking
> my life in war. As a bird brings in her beak
> to her unfledged chicks whatever she can catch,
> while she herself suffers, such was I as I lay
> through many nights unsleeping, and spent
> full many bloody days in battle ...

Still full of anger and wounded pride, he rejects Agamemnon's gifts (9.378–87):

> Hateful to me are his gifts. I value them
> no more than a splinter of wood. Not if he gave
> ten times or twenty times as much to me
> as he has now, and offers more besides ...
> not even if his gifts numbered as sand or dust,
> not even so would Agamemnon persuade me,
> until he has paid full price for the outrage

he has done me, grieving my heart.

He says that his mother has told him that he has a choice of two destinies: either a long and obscure life at home, or death at Troy and everlasting glory. Therefore he will return home immediately, since his life is worth more than all the spoils of Troy.

Now old Phoenix tries to win him over, and succeeds in persuading him to put off until morning his decision as to whether he will sail home or stay at Troy. Finally Ajax appeals to him on the grounds of friendship, and he relents a little more: he will stay at Troy, but will not return to battle until the Trojans fire his huts and ships. So Achilles' stern resolve not to fight any more has indeed been softened by his friends, but his pride and outraged honour do not allow him to relent enough to avoid tragedy. The price that he must pay will be a terrible one.

The Greeks now fare ever worse in battle as the Trojans beat them right back to their ships, breaching their defence-wall and attacking with fire. In these desperate straits Patroclus begs Achilles to lend him his armour and let him lead out his men, the MYRMIDONS, to battle, even if he himself is not willing to fight. Achilles gives in. He warns his friend to do no more than beat back the Trojans from the ships, but Patroclus goes too far and is killed by Hector. Achilles, overwhelmed by grief and remorse, now realises the price that he must pay for his anger and pride. Yet he is determined to avenge Patroclus and slaughter his killer, even though his mother, who with her Nereids has come to mourn with him, warns him that his own death is fated to come soon after Hector's. Achilles answers her resolutely (18.98–116):

> Then let me die directly, since I was not there
> to stand by my friend when he was killed. And now
> far from the land of his fathers he has died,
> without me there to keep him from destruction.
> Now, since I shall not go back to my native land,
> since I was no light of safety to Patroclus, nor
> to my other comrades killed by mighty Hector
> in their numbers, but sit here beside my ships,
> a useless burden on the good earth ...
> now I shall go, to find the killer of that dear life,
> Hector. And I shall accept my own death
> whenever Zeus and the other immortal gods
> wish to bring it about.

Achilles is at last eager to fight again, his hurt pride no longer an issue and his anger against Agamemnon as nothing compared to the greater rage that he now feels towards the Trojans in general, and Hector in particular. He stands in front of the Greek ships and three times shouts a great war-cry, at which the Trojans scatter in panic. Then, since Achilles' own armour, borrowed by Patroclus, has been seized by Hector, Thetis has splendid new armour made for her son by HEPHAESTUS (fig. 141). Achilles' men too hurry to arm themselves for battle (19.357–68):

> As when thick snowflakes flutter from the sky,
> cold beneath the blast of the north wind
> born in the bright heaven, so now in their numbers
> were carried out from the ships the helmets, gleaming
> bright, the bossed shields, the plated corselets
> and the ashen spears. The shining went up to heaven,
> and all around the earth laughed with the flash of bronze,
> while a thunder rose from beneath the feet of the men.
> And in their midst Achilles armed himself to fight.
> A gnashing came from his teeth, his eyes flashed
> brilliant fire, and into his heart there came
> unbearable grief. Raging at the Trojans he donned
> the gifts of the god, wrought by Hephaestus' toil.

His immortal horses XANTHUS and Balius are yoked to his chariot, and now, at last, Achilles returns to the battle-field.

His driving urge is to reach and kill Hector, but he slaughters a multitude of Trojans as he goes (20.490–4):

> As inhuman fire rages through the deep glens
> of a dry mountain, and the forest burns to its depths,

Fig.4 **Achilles kills the young Troilus.**

and the blustering wind drives on the flames
in all directions, so Achilles swept everywhere
with his spear like some god, harrying Trojans
as they died, and the black earth ran with blood.

Many Trojans flee into the River SCAMANDER, and Achilles leaps in after them to continue his massacre. A son of Priam, LYCAON (2), begs for his life, but he too is killed, as is ASTEROPAEUS. Finally the river-god Scamander, enraged at having his streams congested with corpses, hurls his waters in great waves out on to the land and pursues Achilles, threatening him with death. And he would have been killed, had not Hera sent Hephaestus to dry up Scamander's turbulent flood with fire.

AGENOR (2), with the help of Apollo, withstands Achilles long enough for all the Trojans left alive to escape into Troy – all except Hector, who staunchly remains outside the city walls to face his enemy. When he sees Achilles' terrifying appearance, Hector at first runs from him in fear; but at last he turns, and fights, and dies. Still raging, Achilles maltreats his corpse, fastening it by the ankles to his chariot and dragging it in the dust behind him.

Achilles slaughters twelve Trojan captives on Patroclus' funeral pyre, then holds funeral games in honour of his friend, offering many rich prizes to the contestants. But even with Patroclus given full burial rites and Hector dead, Achilles still burns with anger. For eleven days he continues to drag his enemy's corpse in the dust behind his chariot, driving round Patroclus' tomb, until on the twelfth day the gods in pity intervene and send King Priam by night to the Greek camp, to beg for the return of his son's body (fig. 122). Achilles sees the old man, so like his own father, grieving the loss of his great son just as Achilles himself grieves the death of his dear friend, and is moved to pity. At long last his anger is over. The two enemies, a Greek and a Trojan, weep together in friendship, then share food together in peace, and sleep. In the early morning Priam returns to Troy with the body of Hector.

4. AFTERMATH

The *Iliad* ends with the burial of Hector, and Achilles still alive. But because his death is fated to come soon after Hector's, we know that soon he must die. We learn a little more about the last days of his life from other fragmentary epics. He killed the Amazon queen PENTHESILEIA, who had come to help Priam; but the story goes that, even as he delivered the fatal blow, their eyes met and he fell in love with his victim (fig. 113). He then killed the commoner THERSITES for jeering at him. He killed the great MEMNON, king of the Ethiopians and another Trojan ally.

This was probably Achilles' greatest triumph, though it was to be followed almost immediately by his own death, when he routed the Trojans and rushed after them into Troy. Here he was killed by Paris and Apollo, with Paris shooting an arrow and Apollo guiding it to the fatal spot.

A bloody struggle took place over his body, but at last he was carried from the battlefield by the Great Ajax (fig. 12) while Odysseus fought off the Trojans from the rear. From Agamemnon's words in Homer's *Odyssey* (24.15–94) we know something about Achilles' funeral rites. At his death, his mother came with her Nereids out of the sea and for seventeen days, along with the nine MUSES and the whole Greek army, all weeping, mourned his loss. On the eighteenth day his funeral pyre was lit. At dawn on the following day his ashes were laid alongside those of Patroclus in a golden urn, made by Hephaestus and given to Thetis by Dionysus. The remains of the two friends were laid to rest with those of ANTILOCHUS, another dear comrade, and a grave mound was heaped high over them on a jutting headland there by the Hellespont.

Even after his death, Achilles still influenced other people's lives. Odysseus and the Great Ajax argued as to which of them deserved his splendid armour, and when the Greeks awarded it to Odysseus, Ajax committed suicide (fig. 11). After the fall of Troy, POLYXENA, daughter of Priam, was sacrificed in honour of Achilles, as his share of the spoils from Troy's destruction (fig. 120).

In Homer's *Odyssey* (11.467–540), Odysseus meets the shade of Achilles in Hades, in company with Patroclus, Antilochus and the Great Ajax. Odysseus tries to console Achilles for his death by speaking of the authority he holds among the dead, and he replies unforgettably (489–91): 'I would rather be alive and toiling as serf to another man, one with no land and nothing much to live on, than be king over all the perished dead.' But in later tradition, Achilles was said to live on with Patroclus and other heroes, all immortalised, on *Leuke*, the White Island, lying in the Black Sea at the mouth of the Danube. It was occasionally said that after death he married Helen, or MEDEA, or Iphigeneia.

Achilles was the hero most admired by Alexander the Great, and it was said that Alexander slept with a copy of the *Iliad* beneath his pillow. He too, like Achilles, died young.

[Epic Cycle, Proclus' summary of the *Aethiopis*; Sophocles, *Philoctetes* 334–5; Euripides, *Hecuba* 387–8, *Andromache* 655; Apollodorus, *Epitome* 3.16–17, 3.20–6, 3.29–33, 4.1, 4.6–5.7; Pausanias 3.19.11–13, 3.24.10–11; Virgil, *Aeneid* 6.56–8; Ovid, *Metamorphoses* 12.598–611; Statius, *Achilleid*. S. Schein, *The Mortal Hero* (1984).]

Acis

The name of a river near Mount Etna on the island of Sicily, and its god. Acis began life as the son of FAUNUS and the river-nymph Symaethis. He became the lover of the sea-nymph Galatea, and it was she who turned him into a river when he was killed by his jealous rival POLYPHEMUS (2).

Acoetes

When the young DIONYSUS was kidnapped by the crew of a Tyrrhenian pirate ship, the helmsman Acoetes sensed that he was no ordinary mortal and tried to defend him. Dionysus avenged himself on the rest of the crew by turning them into dolphins, but Acoetes was spared their fate and became an ardent follower of the god. In Ovid (*Metamorphoses* 3.572–700), as the leader of the MAENADS at Thebes, Acoetes tells his story to PENTHEUS, who is doing his utmost to keep the worship of Dionysus out of his city.

Acontius

A beautiful youth from the island of Ceos who fell in love with Cydippe, the daughter of a noble Athenian, at a festival of Artemis on Delos. Realising that he had no hope of winning Cydippe as his wife by straightforward means, he threw before her a quince on which he had inscribed the words 'I swear by the sanctuary of Artemis to marry Acontius'. The girl picked up the fruit and innocently read aloud what was written upon it, then threw it away; but the goddess had heard her vow. At home again in Athens, Cydippe's father tried three times to marry her to a man of his choice, and three times she fell so ill that the wedding had to be postponed. Finally he consulted the Delphic Oracle and was told that, since his daughter had promised herself to another man, Artemis was punishing her with illness each time she was on the point of committing perjury. Cydippe related the story of the quince, and her father at last gave her to Acontius as his bride.

[Ovid, *Heroides* 20, 21, *Tristia* 3.10.73.]

Acrisius

Son of Abas, king of Argos, and Aglaia, and twin-brother of PROETUS. The boys fought each other even in their mother's womb and grew up to be still violently antagonistic to each other. After Abas' death they fought over the kingdom, until Acrisius drove Proetus out and took the throne of Argos. Later Proetus returned with an army provided by his father-in-law, Iobates, and the twins then divided the Argolid between them, agreeing that Acrisius should rule Argos and Proetus Tiryns.

Acrisius married Eurydice, the daughter of Lacedaemon, king of Sparta. She bore him a daughter, DANAE. When he enquired of an oracle how he might get a son, he was told simply that a son of Danae would one day kill him, so he shut his daughter up in an underground bronze chamber to keep her away from men. But he reckoned without the great god Zeus, who came to Danae through a chink in the roof of her chamber as a shower of golden rain. In due course she gave birth to a son, PERSEUS. Acrisius shut mother and baby up in a chest (fig. 45) which he threw into the sea, but it drifted safely to the island of Seriphos where the outcasts were given refuge. Perseus grew up to perform heroic exploits, the high point of his achievements being the slaying of the Gorgon Medusa.

Perseus eventually returned to Argos with Danae and his wife Andromeda, hoping to be reunited with his grandfather, but Acrisius heard of his impending arrrival. Remembering all too clearly the oracle, he left Argos in fear of his life. He went to Larissa, and here too came Perseus to compete in the funeral games held by the local king, Teutamides, in honour of his father. The oracle was fulfilled when a discus thrown by Perseus accidentally struck and killed Acrisius.

[Apollodorus 2.2.1–2, 2.4.1, 2.4.4; Pausanias 2.16.1–3, 2.23.7, 2.25.7.]

Actaeon

Son of ARISTAEUS and AUTONOE, and grandson of CADMUS, king of Thebes. Actaeon was a skilled huntsman whose tragic fate was to be turned into a deer by ARTEMIS, or to have a deerskin thrown over him by the goddess, and then to be torn to pieces by his own hounds. Various motives are given for this agonising death. The earliest, said to have been found in the lyric poet Stesichorus, was that Zeus was angry with Actaeon for wooing his aunt SEMELE, the beautiful mortal whom Zeus himself desired. Other versions said that Actaeon had angered Artemis by boasting that he was a better hunter than she, or by wishing to marry her. But the most familiar version of his fate was that Artemis was angry because he chanced to see her bathing naked with her nymphs. The goddess splashed him with water and transformed his body into that of a stag, though his mind remained the same and he was able to realise the full horror of his fate. He fled into the forest, where his own hounds gave tongue and pursued him while he galloped before them in terror. At last they dragged him down. They tore at him while his friends urged them on, all the while looking round for Actaeon himself and lamenting that he was not there to see this triumphant capture. Only when the life was at last torn out of him was the anger of Artemis appeased. The hounds, finding that their beloved master had disappeared, sought him everywhere, howling in grief, until the Centaur CHEIRON took pity on them and made a statue of Actaeon, so lifelike that they were comforted.

The death of Actaeon is a popular subject in ancient art from the sixth century BC, with Artemis almost always shown in attendance (fig. 5). In earlier pictures he sometimes wears a deerskin (as he did apparently in Stesichorus); the first vases on which he sprouts antlers are after the middle of the fifth century. Artemis surprised while bathing appears first in Pompeian paintings. Actaeon's story was even more popular among postclassical artists, and he has been painted by Cranach, Titian, Veronese, Rubens, Rembrandt, Claude, Tiepolo and Gainsborough, among very many others. In *Twelfth Night* Orsino likens himself to Actaeon (I. i. 19–23):

> O, when mine eyes did see Olivia first …
> That instant was I turn'd into a hart,
> And my desires, like fell and cruel hounds,
> E'er since pursue me.

[Euripides, *Bacchae* 337–40; Apollodorus 3.4.4; Diodorus Siculus 4.81.3–5; Pausanias 9.2.3–4; Lucian, *Dialogues of the Gods* 18; Ovid, *Metamorphoses* 3.138–252.]

Actaeus

The first mythical king of Attica, which was originally named Acte or Actaea after him, though he was by no means such an important figure to the Athenians as CECROPS (1), his son-in-law and successor.

[Apollodorus 3.14.1–2; Pausanias 1.2.6.]

Admetus

Son of PHERES (1), king of Pherae in Thessaly. Admetus was one of the ARGONAUTS and took part in the CALYDONIAN BOARHUNT, and while he was still young his father resigned the throne to him. He won so great a reputation for justice and hospitality that when APOLLO, as a punishment for killing the Cyclopes, was forced by Zeus to spend a year in servitude to a mortal, it was to Admetus' home that he came, to serve as a herdsman. Admetus treated Apollo so well that the god made all his cows bear twins. He also helped Admetus to win the hand of his chosen bride, ALCESTIS, the beautiful daughter of Pelias, king of Iolcus. She had so many suitors that her father set an apparently impossible test to decide between them, saying that he would give her to whoever could yoke a boar and a lion to a chariot. Apollo harnessed the beasts and Admetus drove the chariot to Pelias. Alcestis became his.

At his marriage Admetus forgot to sacrifice to ARTEMIS and the angry goddess filled the bridal chamber with snakes. Apollo once again intervened to help, advising Admetus to appease Artemis with sacrifices. The god won for his friend an even greater boon from the FATES. He made them drunk, then persuaded them to agree that Admetus would be reprieved from his fated day of death, so long as he could find someone willing to die in his place. Admetus felt sure that one of his aged parents

Fig. 5 **Actaeon is killed by his own hounds, while Artemis looks on.**

would be only too happy to sacrifice themselves for their own son. On the contrary, they were quite unwilling to do so, and finally his wife Alcestis agreed to die for him.

The outcome is movingly dramatised in Euripides' *Alcestis*. Several happy years of marriage have passed, children have been born, but now at last the fated day of death has arrived. THANATOS, the implacable god of death, comes to take Alcestis to the Underworld. The paradox is that although Admetus now lives on because of the self-sacrifice of his loving wife, he finds that, with Alcestis dead, he no longer wants to go on living. 'I think my wife's fate is happier than my own,' he says, 'even though it may not seem so. No pain will ever touch her now, and she has ended life's many troubles with glory. But I, who have escaped my fate and ought not to be alive, shall now live out my life in sorrow. Now I understand ... whenever I come indoors, the loneliness will drive me out again when I see my wife's bed, and the chair in which she used to sit, now empty, the floor in every room unswept, the children clinging round my knees and crying for their mother, the servants lamenting the beloved mistress they have lost' (935–49).

But the situation is saved by HERACLES, who visits Pherae on his way to catch the man-eating mares of Diomedes. Admetus, still hospitable even in his deepest grief, takes him in without telling him that Alcestis is dead. Heracles learns the truth from a servant, then waits for Thanatos at Alcestis' tomb and wrestles with him until Death gives up his victim. Heracles brings Alcestis back to the living, and husband and wife are reunited. Admetus is only too happy to accept ordinary mortal existence once more.

The best-known of Admetus' and Alcestis' children is EUMELUS (2), who led a contingent from Pherae to fight in the Trojan War. Homer says that his horses, once belonging to Admetus, were the fastest horses at Troy, so it is no surprise to find Admetus himself taking part in the chariot-race in artistic representations of the funeral games of Pelias. These included the chest of Cypselus, according to Pausanias, who also tells us that the Amyclae throne depicted Admetus yoking the lion and the boar to his chariot.

[Homer, *Iliad* 2.711–15, 763–7; Aeschylus, *Eumenides* 723–8; Apollodorus 1.8.2, 1.9.14–16, 3.10.4; Pausanias 3.18.16, 5.17.9.]

Adonis

A god of vegetation and fertility, introduced into Greece from Cyprus or Assyria and akin to the Babylonian Tammuz, a consort of the Great Goddess. His name probably stems from the Semitic title Adon, 'Lord'. He was sometimes said to be the son of PHOENIX (2) and Alphesiboea, or of CINYRAS, king of Cyprus, and his wife Metharme, the daughter of Pygmalion. But in the usual tradition he was born of an incestuous union between Cinyras (or sometimes Theias, king of the Assyrians) and his own daughter MYRRHA (or Smyrna). Myrrha, passionately desiring her father, went to his bed in the darkness and he took her in, not knowing who she was. After many nights of enjoying her, he at last brought in a lamp that he might see her face. Realising the truth, he tried to kill her, but she fled far away from the palace. She wandered the world in sorrow, until eventually the gods took pity on her, transforming her into a myrrh tree and her tears into drops of myrrh. The goddess of childbirth brought forth the baby Adonis from the tree trunk, and the nymphs laid him on the soft grass and bathed him in his mother's tears. In one version, Adonis was born when a wild boar gored the trunk of the myrrh tree with its tusks, an event that was thought to presage his death, since he would ultimately be killed by the slash of a boar's tusks.

The baby was so beautiful that APHRODITE wanted him for herself, so she secretly hid him in a chest and gave him to PERSEPHONE to keep for her. But Persephone too was taken by his beauty and refused to give him up. They took their dispute to Zeus, who decreed that Adonis should spend a third of the year with each goddess and have the remaining third for himself. He always chose to spend his own third of the year with Aphrodite. In another version, Zeus referred the dispute to the muse Calliope (*see* MUSES). She decreed that Adonis should spend half the year with each goddess, which so enraged Aphrodite that she punished Calliope by inducing the Thracian women to kill her son ORPHEUS. In both versions, the time that Adonis spent in the arms of Aphrodite was the living, burgeoning time of spring and summer. His disappearance from the earth marked the harvesting of the crops, and his time in the arms of Persephone was the dead, winter period when seed lay dormant below the earth.

In Ovid's version of the story, Aphrodite fell in love with Adonis only when he grew to be a beautiful young man. She became his constant companion, and because like most young men he was a passionate huntsman, she too learnt to enjoy hunting, roaming forests and mountains with her skirts kilted up to her knees, just like ARTEMIS, and urging on the hounds. But she only pursued creatures safe to hunt, like the hare or the deer, and she warned Adonis against the wild boars and wolves and lions, who were always ready to turn and attack their pursuers. Unfortunately he paid too little heed to her advice, for one day he roused a wild boar from its lair and struck it with his spear. The boar easily dislodged the weapon, then went for Adonis, slashing him deep in the groin with its tusk. Aphrodite heard from afar the groans of the dying boy and rushed to him. Inconsolable, she decreed that his death would thereafter be lamented every year, and she made the blood-red anemone spring from his blood as an everlasting token of her grief.

It was elsewhere said that Adonis' death was also the origin of the red rose, for as Aphrodite hurried to her dying love she pricked her foot on a white rose. Stained with her blood, it was ever afterwards red. The wild boar was sometimes said to be Aphrodite's husband HEPHAESTUS or her lover ARES in disguise, jealous because of her affair with Adonis. Yet another instigator of Adonis' death was in some versions Artemis, for in Euripides' tragedy *Hippolytus* this goddess promises to avenge HIPPOLYTUS (2) by killing one of Aphrodite's favourites (1420–2), and certainly Apollodorus says (3.14.4) that Adonis was killed by the boar 'through the anger of Artemis'.

Adonis' festival, the *Adonia*, was widely celebrated every year, his cult being particularly popular with women. His followers mourned his death by planting 'gardens of Adonis', seeds set in shallow soil that sprang up quickly and as quickly died, symbolising the brief life of the god. Mourning for his death was followed by rejoicing at his rebirth. Byblos in Phoenicia was especially sacred to him, and the nearby river of Adonis was each year stained with blood at the time of his death.

Adonis appears with Aphrodite in ancient art from the late fifth century BC. His myth has been tremendously popular in the postclassical arts, particularly in painting, which usually depicts Aphrodite restraining him from the hunt, or mourning his death. There are versions by Tintoretto, Titian, Veronese, Rubens, van Dyck, Poussin, Giordano, and Boucher, among very many others. Shakespeare's *Venus and Adonis*, probably his first published work, is based on Ovid's account of Adonis' death, with once again the anemone springing up from his blood. Venus plucks the flower and addresses it as she puts it in her bosom:

> Here was thy father's bed, here in my breast;
> Thou art the next of blood, and 'tis thy right.
> Lo, in this hollow cradle take thy rest;
> My throbbing heart shall rock thee day and night;
> There shall not be one minute in an hour
> Wherein I will not kiss my sweet love's flow'r.

[Hesiod, *Catalogue of Women* fr. 139; Apollodorus 3.14.3–4; Ovid, *Metamorphoses* 10.300–739.]

Adrasteia

A Cretan nymph, daughter of Melisseus. She and her sister Ida received the baby ZEUS from RHEA (1), then brought him up in safety, far away from his cannibalistic father, Cronus. The CURETES (1) guarded the cave in which the child was hidden, dancing around the entrance and clashing their shields and spears so as to drown his infant cries. The nymphs fed him on milk from the she-goat AMALTHEIA, and Adrasteia made him a beautiful ball to play with, all blue and gold. When thrown in the air, it flamed through the sky like a star.

[Apollonius, *Argonautica* 3.132–8; Apollodorus 1.1.6–7.]

Adrastus (1)

A king of Argos and the leader of the famous expedition of the SEVEN AGAINST THEBES. He was the son of TALAUS and Lysimache, and he married Amphithea, the daughter of his brother Pronax. He had by her two sons, Aegialeus and Cyanippus, and three daughters, Argeia, Deipyle and Aegialeia. He was driven out of Argos in a feud with the seer AMPHIARAUS and took refuge in Sicyon, where he inherited the throne from his grandfather POLYBUS (1); but in due course he became reconciled with Amphiaraus, and the seer married his sister ERIPHYLE (to his later cost). Adrastus returned to Argos, where he became king.

One fateful night two visitors came to his palace seeking shelter: Oedipus' son POLYNEICES, exiled from Thebes, and Oeneus' son TYDEUS, driven out of Calydon. Adrastus was awakened by the two young men fighting for possession of a bed in the palace porch, and at once he was reminded of an oracle that said he must yoke his daughters in marriage to a lion and a boar. Either the two men were fighting like wild beasts; or they had on their shields the emblems of a lion (Polyneices) and a boar (Tydeus); or they were clad in the skins of those animals; or the creatures were symbols of their homelands, the lion standing for the lion-bodied Sphinx of Thebes and the boar for the Calydonian Boar. Whatever the reason, Adrastus remembered the oracle and married his daughters to the young men, Argeia to Polyneices and Deipyle to Tydeus. He then agreed to help his new sons-in-law to recover their lost kingdoms, and first of all Thebes.

Despite prophecies of doom from Amphiaraus, a powerful army of seven champions and their followers was raised and they set out on their disastrous expedition. All the leaders lost their lives except for Adrastus, who was saved by the swiftness of his divine horse AREION. He returned to Argos, and ten years later organised a second attack on Thebes when the sons of the Seven, the EPIGONI, marched to avenge their fathers. This time the attack was a success and the walls of Thebes

20

were razed. Of the attackers, only Adrastus' son Aegialeus was killed, and Adrastus died of grief on the way home.

[Homer, *Iliad* 2.572, 14.119–25, 23.344–7; Aeschylus, *Seven against Thebes*; Herodotus 5.67; Euripides, *Phoenician Women* 406–23, *Suppliant Women* 131–61; Apollodorus 1.9.13, 3.6.1–3.7.3; Pausanias 2.6.6, 8.25.8.]

Adrastus (2)

A son of POLYNEICES and Argeia who, according to Pausanias (2.20.5), was one of the EPIGONI.

Aeacus

The first king of Aegina. He was the son of ZEUS and the nymph AEGINA, daughter of the river-god Asopus, and was born on the island then named Oenone but later renamed by him after his mother. When he grew to manhood and was grieved by his solitude, Zeus transformed all the island's ants (*myrmekes*) into men and women. Aeacus called his new people the MYRMIDONS.

He married ENDEIS, who was probably the daughter of the kindly Centaur Cheiron, and had by her two sons, PELEUS and TELAMON. Both of these were great heroes in their own right and became the fathers of even mightier sons: Peleus the father of ACHILLES, and Telamon the father of AJAX (1). Aeacus also had by the Nereid Psamathe a son, PHOCUS (1), so named because his mother had changed herself into a seal (*phoke*) in trying to avoid intercourse with Aeacus. When his two legitimate sons killed their half-brother, he banished them. It was sometimes said that Aeacus had a fourth son, MENOETIUS (2).

According to some accounts, Aeacus helped Apollo and Poseidon to build the walls of Troy for LAOMEDON. When the work was complete, three snakes tried to leap on to the ramparts. Two of these at once fell dead, but the third succeeded, and at the very part of the wall that Aeacus had built. Apollo interpreted this omen as meaning that Troy would be taken by Aeacus' descendants – as indeed it was, first by Heracles with the help of Telamon, and later by the Greek army under the leadership of Agamemnon, which included Achilles and his son NEOPTOLEMUS, and the Great Ajax.

Aeacus was renowned for his justice and wisdom. When Zeus was angry with PELOPS for dismembering the body of his enemy, Stymphalus, and for scattering the pieces over the land, he inflicted on Greece a prolonged drought. In another version, the god was angry because of the murder of ANDROGEOS. Whichever the reason, it was Aeacus who was chosen by oracles to intercede with Zeus for deliverance. He did so, and even as he prayed the blessed rain began to fall. Even after his death he was honoured for his justice, for he kept the keys of HADES (2),

and along with MINOS and RHADAMANTHYS became a judge of the souls of the dead.

[Hesiod, *Theogony* 1003–5, *Catalogue of Women* frr. 205, 212a; Pindar, *Olympian* 8.30–47, *Nemean* 8.7–8, *Isthmian* 8.21–4; Aristophanes, *Frogs* 464–78; Plato, *Gorgias* 524a, *Apology* 41a; Apollodorus 3.12.6; Pausanias 1.39.6, 2.29.2–, 6–10; Ovid, *Metamorphoses* 7.517–660.]

Aedon ('Nightingale')

Daughter of PANDAREOS and wife of Zethus, joint ruler of Thebes with his brother AMPHION. Aedon had only one son, and she so much envied the many children born to her sister-in-law NIOBE (2), Amphion's wife, that she tried during the night to kill Niobe's eldest son in his sleep. In the darkness she mistook his bed and killed her own son, Itylus. Distraught at what she had done, she begged the gods to turn her into a nightingale and they answered her prayer. As a bird she could sing out her never-ending sorrow for her dead son, and this is why the nightingale sings both day and night. (For a different myth about the nightingale, *see* TEREUS.)

[Homer, *Odyssey* 19.518–24; Pausanias 9.5.9.]

Aeetes

Son of HELIOS the Sun-god and the Oceanid Perse (or Perseis) and brother of PASIPHAE and the enchantress CIRCE. Aeetes was the cruel and ruthless king of barbarian Colchis, at the eastern end of the Black Sea. Here he lived in his capital of Aea in a splendid palace of bronze built by HEPHAESTUS. He was married to the Oceanid Eidyia and had two daughters, Chalciope and MEDEA, and a son, APSYRTUS, who was sometimes said to have been born of a Caucasian nymph, Asterodeia.

When the flying ram with the fleece of gold set PHRIXUS down at Aea, Aeetes welcomed him and gave him the hand of his daughter Chalciope in marriage. In gratitude for his safe landing, Phrixus sacrificed the wondrous ram to Zeus and gave its fleece to the king. Aeetes hung it in an oak tree in a grove of ARES and set a sleepless dragon to guard it. Years later Jason and the ARGONAUTS arrived in Aea, after a long and arduous journey, in their quest for the Golden Fleece. Aeetes promised the Fleece to Jason if he successfully completed certain seemingly impossible tasks. With the help of Medea's sorcery Jason did so, but Aeetes went back on his word and refused him the Fleece. Jason, once again helped by Medea, stole the Fleece and fled; and it was Medea who delayed her furious father's pursuit by murdering her little brother, Apsyrtus, and strewing his dismembered body over the sea. Aeetes stopped to gather up the pieces, then turned back to bury them at a place he named Tomi ('cuttings').

Aeetes was later deposed by his brother Perses, but on

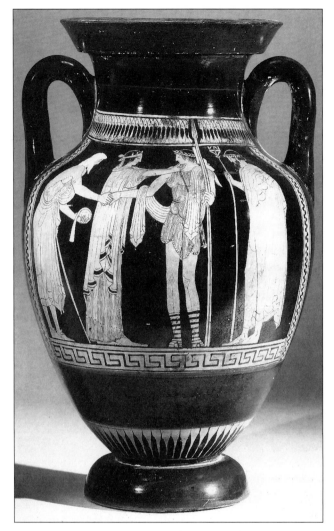

Fig.6 Old Aegeus greets Theseus, while his mother Aethra affectionately strokes his chin. Poseidon looks on.

Medea's eventual return from Greece the usurper was killed either by Medea or by her son (*see* MEDUS (1)) and Aeetes regained his throne.

[Homer, *Odyssey* 10.135–9; Hesiod, *Theogony* 956–62; Herodotus 1.2; Apollonius, *Argonautica* 2.1140–4.240; Apollodorus 1.9.1, 1.9.23–4, 1.9.28, *Epitome* 7.14; Diodorus Siculus 4.45.1–4.48.4.]

Aegaeon

One of the HUNDRED-HANDERS, called Briareos by the gods but Aegaeon by mortals.

Aegestes *see* ACESTES.

Aegeus

Son of PANDION (2), the deposed ninth king of Athens, and brother of NISUS (1), PALLAS (2) and LYCUS (4) (though some claimed that Aegeus was really the son of Scyrius, ruler of the island of Scyros, and had merely been adopted by Pandion). After their father's death, the brothers marched against Athens and drove out the sons of Metion who had usurped Pandion's throne. Aegeus now became king of Athens.

He married twice, but neither marriage produced children, so he asked the Delphic Oracle what he must do to cure his childlessness. 'Loose not the jutting neck of the wineskin, best of men, until you come again to the city of Athens', proclaimed the Oracle, meaning that he should not have intercourse with a woman until he returned home, and implying that the next time he did so, the union would bear fruit. But Aegeus was at a loss to understand, so he broke his journey at Troezen to consult its king, PITTHEUS, who had a reputation for wisdom. Pittheus realised at once what the oracle meant, and since he wished to have a grandchild with Aegeus' royal blood in its veins, he encouraged his guest to get drunk, then enticed him into sleeping with his daughter, AETHRA. In the morning Aegeus departed, after hiding a sword and a pair of sandals under a great rock. He told Aethra that if she bore a son, who on reaching manhood could lift the rock, she should send him with these tokens of recognition to Athens. In the course of time Aethra did indeed bear a son, THESEUS, though many said that his father was the god Poseidon.

Aegeus gave refuge in Athens to the sorceress MEDEA, who had fled from Corinth after murdering her children by Jason. She married her benefactor and bore him a son, MEDUS (1). When Theseus, grown to maturity, came to Athens bearing the tokens of recognition, Medea realised at once that he was Aegeus' son and resolved to dispose of him before he could make himself known to his father. She filled Aegeus' mind with suspicions of the young stranger and induced him to send Theseus to capture the deadly MARATHONIAN BULL. Theseus returned triumphant, and now Medea persuaded Aegeus to serve him a cup of poison. Just as the unsuspecting youth was about to drink, Aegeus recognised the sword that he was carrying and dashed the cup from his lips. Father and son joyously made themselves known to each other. Medea fled from Athens for ever. The lost *Aegeus* plays of both Sophocles and Euripides dramatised Theseus' arrival in Athens and his near-death at Medea's hands.

Soon afterwards, Theseus sailed for Crete with the tribute of seven youths and seven girls, the payment to King Minos for the death of his son ANDROGEOS, who were to be fed to the Minotaur in the Labyrinth. Theseus planned to dispatch the monster, and promised his father that if he survived he would change his ship's black sail of mourning for a white or scarlet sail. He killed the Minotaur and sailed triumphantly home, but he forgot to change the black sail. Aegeus, eagerly watching for his son's ship from a headland, flung himself in despair into the sea that has ever afterwards borne his name, the Aegean. Another version has it that he watched from the Acropolis, from the lofty bastion at the western end where the little temple of Athena Nike now stands, and from there he flung himself down to his death on the rocks below. Fraser (*Apollodorus: The Library*, vol. 2, p. 137) comments on his vantage point:

> It commands a wonderful view over the ports of Athens and away across the sea to Aegina and the coast of Peloponnese, looming clear and blue through the diaphanous Attic air in the far distance. A better look-out the old man could not have chosen from which to watch, with straining eyes, for the white or scarlet sail of his returning son.

See also fig. 6.

[Euripides, *Medea* 663–758; Apollodorus 1.9.28, 3.15.5–3.16.1, *Epitome* 1.5–11; Diodorus Siculus 4.61.4, 4.61.6–7; Plutarch, *Theseus* 3, 12–17, 22; Pausanias 1.5.3–4, 1.22.5, 1.39.4.]

Aegialeia

Either the daughter of ADRASTUS (1), who led the expedition of the Seven against Thebes, or of his son AEGIALEUS (2). She married her cousin (or nephew) DIOMEDES (2), and while he was away fighting at Troy became the mistress of Cometes, the son of his comrade Sthenelus.

[Homer, *Iliad* 5.410–15; Apollodorus 1.8.6, 1.9.13, *Epitome* 6.9.]

Aegialeus (1)

A son of INACHUS, the Argive river-god, and the brother of IO, who was loved by Zeus.

[Apollodorus 2.1.1; Pausanias 2.5.6.]

Aegialeus (2)

The eldest son of ADRASTUS (1), and perhaps the father of AEGIALEIA, who married Diomedes. Aegialeus was the only one of the EPIGONI to die in the second expedition against Thebes, killed by LAODAMAS, the son of Eteocles. His body was carried to Pagae in Megaris and buried there.

[Pausanias 1.44.4, 9.5.13.]

Aegimius

Son of DORUS and king of the Dorians. When, because of a boundary dispute, he and his people were at war with the Lapiths, led by CORONUS, Aegimius called for the help of HERACLES, offering him a share of the land of Doris. Heracles came to his aid, killing Coronus and other Lapiths, and the war was soon won, but he refused any immediate reward. The Dorians, however, later allied themselves with his descendants, the HERACLIDS, in their successful invasion of the Peloponnese. Aegimius' two sons, Pamphylus and Dymas, were killed in the fighting, and they, together with Heracles' son Hyllus, gave their names to the three Dorian tribes, the Hylleis, the Pamphyli and the Dymanes.

[Pindar, *Pythian* 1.62–5; Apollodorus 2.7.7, 2.8.3; Diodorus Siculus 4.37.3–4, 4.58.6.]

Aegina

Daughter of the river-god ASOPUS. ZEUS carried her off and ravished her on the island of Oenone, where in the fullness of time she bore him a son, AEACUS. Asopus, meanwhile, hunted everywhere for his lost daughter. He was finally helped by SISYPHUS, who had seen the abduction and now promised to tell what he knew, in return for a spring of fresh water for his city of Corinth. The river-god at once granted him the spring of Peirene, and Sisyphus told him of Zeus' iniquity (though Zeus duly punished this disclosure). Intent on saving his daughter, the angry Asopus pursued her abductor but was driven back to his own river by Zeus' thunderbolts, so had no choice but to leave Aegina on Oenone. Aeacus later renamed the island after his mother. According to Pindar, she married Actor and was mother to another son, MENOETIUS (2), who became the father of PATROCLUS.

Depictions of Aegina pursued by Zeus occur first in ancient art in the fifth century BC. In historical times, coal could be found in the river Asopus and was thought to be the result of Zeus' attack on the angry river-god.

[Pindar, *Isthmian* 8.17–23, *Nemean* 8.6–12; Apollodorus 1.9.3, 3.12.6; Pausanias 2.5.1–2; Ovid, *Metamorphoses* 6.113.]

Aegipan ('Goat-Pan')

A rather vague figure who may have been PAN himself, or else the son of ZEUS and a nymph Aex ('she-goat'). Aegipan helped Zeus in his fight to win supreme power as king of the Olympians, after his enemy, the monstrous TYPHON, had made him helpless by cutting off the sinews of his hands and feet. Aegipan, along with HERMES, stole the sinews from the she-dragon Delphyne, who had been set to guard them, and fitted them once again to Zeus. With his strength recovered, he was able to pursue and overcome Typhon, finally hurling Mount Etna on top of the monster and crushing him beneath it. As thanks for his help, Aegipan was immortalised in the stars as the constellation Capricorn.

[Apollodorus 1.6.3.]

Aegisthus

Son of THYESTES, and the instrument of his revenge on his hated brother ATREUS, who had killed Thyestes' other sons, and cooked and served them up for their father to eat. According to Aeschylus (*Agamemnon* 1583–1606), Aegisthus was only a baby when Atreus killed the other boys, and was apparently (for the text is somewhat corrupt) the youngest boy of three. So here two boys were murdered, and Thyestes took the baby Aegisthus with him into exile. Another version, found in Hyginus (*Fabula* 88) but as far as we can tell based on a lost tragedy by Sophocles, has Aegisthus as the incestuous son of Thyestes' daughter Pelopia. Thyestes had learnt that he would get revenge on Atreus if he had a child by his own daughter, so he raped Pelopia. Soon afterwards she married Atreus, now king of Mycenae, who knew neither her true parentage nor that she was pregnant. In due course the baby was born and Pelopia abandoned him in the wilds to die, but some shepherds saved him and gave him to be suckled by a she-goat. When Atreus heard about the boy he took him in, named him Aegisthus because of the goat (*aix, aigos*) and brought him up as his own son.

Years later Thyestes fell into the hands of Atreus, who instructed Aegisthus, now grown up, to kill him. But Aegisthus learnt that Thyestes was his real father and killed Atreus instead, thus avenging the deaths of his brothers. Thyestes became king of Mycenae in Atreus' place, but was later driven out by Tyndareos, king of

Sparta, who put Atreus' son AGAMEMNON on the throne. When Agamemnon led the Greek expedition to the Trojan War, his wife CLYTEMNESTRA and Aegisthus became lovers, and on Agamemnon's return home ten years later, together they killed him. Aegisthus then ruled the kingdom securely for some years, until he and Clytemnestra were in turn killed in revenge by her and Agamemnon's son, ORESTES. During their years together they had a daughter, ERIGONE (2), and a son, ALETES.

This myth proved a popular subject in fifth-century BC tragedy. Three extant tragedies deal with Orestes' revenge on his mother and Aegisthus: Aeschylus' *Libation Bearers* (the second play in his *Oresteia* trilogy), and the *Electra* plays of Sophocles and Euripides. In Aeschylus, Aegisthus is a blustering weakling, an almost insignificant figure when compared with the powerful and awe-inspiring Clytemnestra. In Sophocles, both Clytemnestra and Aegisthus are completely unsympathetic figures, vicious and tyrannical, and fully deserving of their fate at Orestes' hands. Only in Euripides are they depicted with any kind of sympathy. Here Aegisthus is shown acting as a warm and welcoming host to Orestes, who kills him when he is turned away, trusting and vulnerable, by smashing his backbone with a butcher's cleaver.

Orestes' murder of Aegisthus (unlike that of Clytemnestra) is a favourite subject in ancient art. Usually Aegisthus is shown sitting on a throne or a chair (fig. 7), sometimes with a lyre as though playing to himself, relaxed and unaware of any danger, when Orestes rushes in with his murderous sword. Sometimes Clytemnestra is shown, restrained by a servant (fig. 135), but swinging a double axe and doing her best to leap to her lover's defence (fig. 8). Reminiscent of this are her words in Aeschylus when she hears the outcry at the murder of Aegisthus: 'Bring me quick, somebody, an axe to kill a man!' (*The Libation Bearers*, 889). But never, in art or literature, is she able to save her lover.

Aegyptus *see* DANAUS.

Aello *see* HARPIES.

Aeneas

The legendary founder of the Roman race and the national hero of Rome. Although Aeneas is best known from Virgil's *Aeneid*, he also had a vigorous existence in early Greek myth. He was the son of APHRODITE and the Trojan prince ANCHISES, and thus a descendant of TROS

Fig. 7 **Orestes, supported by Chrysothemis, kills Aegisthus. For the reverse of the vase, see fig. 135.**

and a member of the junior branch of the royal house of Troy. He was born on Mount Ida and brought up by NYMPHS until, at five years old, he was taken to his father's care. He married CREUSA (3), a daughter of King PRIAM of Troy, who bore him a son, ASCANIUS.

1. AENEAS AT TROY

Aeneas became an ally of Priam in the TROJAN WAR, leading the Dardanian contingent along with two sons of the Trojan elder Antenor, Archelochus and ACAMAS (2). In the *Iliad* Aeneas is second only to the Trojan leader, HECTOR, and fights bravely and effectively in defence of Troy. He takes part in two important duels: DIOMEDES (2) fights and wounds him (fig.9), but he is saved by the intervention of, first, Aphrodite, and then APOLLO (5.166–453); and he fights with ACHILLES, almost fatally, but POSEIDON intervenes and transports him far away to the edge of the battle. The god explains to the other divinities that Aeneas is destined to survive the war, and that he and his descendants will rule over the Trojans (20.75–350).

After Homer there developed the legend of Aeneas' escape from Troy. Vase-paintings from the sixth century BC show him carrying his old father on his back, and accompanied by his little son Ascanius, as he flees from his ruined city to safety (fig.35). The story of his voyage to Italy was well established by the third century, and when Pyrrhus led the Italian Greeks against Rome in 280 BC, he saw himself as a descendant of Achilles making war on a colony of Troy. Long before Virgil's time, Aeneas was acknowledged as the man who led the remnants of the Trojans from Troy, becoming the ancestor of a line of kings who ruled for generations in the city of Alba Longa, and from whose stock came Rhea Silvia, the mother by Mars of ROMULUS, the founder of Rome. But it is Virgil who creates the canonical story of Aeneas and his Trojan followers, of their long wanderings from Troy, and of the war they fought on their arrival in Italy.

Although the *Aeneid* is set largely in pre-Roman Italy and continually looks ahead to the world of Rome, its events, lasting seven years, take place in the same legendary time as Homer's *Odyssey*: ODYSSEUS is still on CALYPSO's island, and will be there for some years yet, when Aeneas reaches his destination in Italy. Virgil portrays Aeneas as dutiful (*pius*), compassionate and brave, an admirable leader and a devoted father and son. He recounts Aeneas' story from the time of the appearance of the WOODEN HORSE, the stratagem by which the Greeks secretly entered Troy and attacked the Trojans from

within, to his victory over the Latins, which will make possible the foundation of a new 'Troy' in Italy.

At the fall of his city, Aeneas fights desperately but unavailingly alongside a small band of followers, and becomes a horrified witness of all the bloody carnage that takes place, especially NEOPTOLEMUS' butchery of the Trojans, with POLITES (1) dying in front of his parents' eyes, and Priam slaughtered on his own altar. He sees HELEN hiding in the palace and is ready to kill her for causing this disastrous war, but his mother Venus (Aphrodite) intervenes and begs him to save his family. He returns home, resolved to lead them to safety. At first old Anchises refuses to go with him, but when the gods send three signs – Ascanius' head lit with flame, a crash of thunder, and a falling star – the old man is convinced and hesitates no longer. Taking with him his household gods, the Penates, Aeneas carries Anchises on his back and leads Ascanius by the hand. Creusa follows behind, but on the way through the burning city she is lost. Aeneas rushes back to search for her, but encounters only her ghost, who reassures him that the gods wish him to leave Troy without her and to found a new kingdom in Italy.

2. THE JOURNEY TO ITALY

On Mount Ida Aeneas musters his followers and builds a fleet. At last they set sail with twenty ships. They land in Thrace, intending to found a city there, but they inadvertently disturb the grave of POLYDORUS (3), a son of Priam, whose spirit warns them to leave this cruel land

Fig.8 Clytemnestra, with axe, runs to defend her lover Aegisthus.

Fig.9 **Diomedes, supported by Athena, attacks Aeneas, who falls backwards towards his anxious mother, Aphrodite.**

where he himself was treacherously murdered. They perform funeral rites to give him peace, then depart. On Delos, ANIUS gives them hospitality, and they learn from the oracle of Apollo that they must seek out their 'ancient mother'. 'For there', says Apollo, 'the house of Aeneas, and his sons' sons, and their sons who come after them will rule over all the world' (3.97–8). Anchises takes this to mean Crete, home of their ancestor TEUCER (1). They reach the island and begin to build a city, but a plague afflicts them, and Aeneas is told by the Penates that the oracle referred, not to Crete, but to the land of Italy, the home of their ancestor DARDANUS.

They set sail once again. Thrown off course by a storm, they land on the Strophades Islands, where they find themselves powerless against the monstrous HARPIES, who swoop down on them and snatch up their food. Celaeno, the Harpies' leader, predicts that they will found a city only after they have been driven by hunger to eat their own tables.

Landing in Epeirus, they find ruling there a fellow-Trojan, the seer HELENUS, now married to Hector's widow, ANDROMACHE. From his prophetic knowledge, Helenus warns them of the dangers of their long voyage, and tells them to found their city where they find a white sow lying with her thirty piglets. They sail to Sicily, avoiding the dangers once posed to Odysseus by the monster SCYLLA (1) and the whirlpool CHARYBDIS, though seeing in the distance the terrible Cyclops, POLYPHEMUS (2), who caused him so much affliction. They put in at Drepanum, and here Anchises dies and is buried.

On leaving Sicily they head for Italy, but Juno (HERA), intent on foiling their plan to found a new Troy, commands the guardian of the winds, AEOLUS (2), to send a storm that will wreck their fleet. The ships are scattered and driven far off course, but Neptune (Poseidon) calms the winds and the Trojans come safely to Libya. They are welcomed by DIDO, the queen of Carthage, who at the instigation of Venus quickly falls in love with Aeneas and is encouraged to yield to her passion by her sister ANNA. While out hunting, Aeneas and Dido take shelter in a cave during a violent storm. There they consummate their love. Now the lovers live only for each other and Aeneas forgets all about his quest, until reminded of his destiny by Mercury (HERMES) and urged to sail once more for Italy. Unwillingly, but obediently, he departs. Dido, inconsolable, kills herself.

As the Trojans sail away, they see Carthage glowing from the flames of Dido's funeral pyre, and although they know nothing of her death, they are filled with foreboding. A storm drives them once more to Sicily. Here they are welcomed by their compatriot ACESTES and hold funeral games in Anchises' honour, a year on from his death. The Trojan women, weary of wandering and goaded by Juno, set fire to some of the ships in the hope of staying in this friendly land, so Aeneas allows the oldest and frailest of his followers to stay behind in the newly founded city of Acesta. He sets out once more with the others after sacrificing to his half-brother ERYX. During the journey, the helmsman, PALINURUS, falls asleep and is lost overboard.

3. AENEAS IN ITALY

At last they land in Italy. They find the body of MISENUS, unjustly killed by Triton, and bury him with full honours. Aeneas consults the SIBYL of Cumae, begging to go down to the Underworld to meet his father once again. Following her instructions, he picks the GOLDEN BOUGH as an offering for Proserpina (Persephone), then with the Sibyl he passes through her cave by Lake Avernus and makes the fearful descent. On the shore of the river Styx they see the souls of the unburied dead, who have to wait for a hundred years before crossing to Hades. At the sight of the Golden Bough, the ferryman CHARON willingly takes Aeneas and the Sibyl across the river. The Sibyl puts the monstrous guard-dog CERBERUS to sleep with a drugged honey-cake, so they easily gain entry to the land of the dead. Here Aeneas sees Dido among those who died of love, but she turns away from him without even a word. Among the valiant warriors, he encounters his kinsman DEIPHOBUS and hears of his ghastly death at the fall of Troy. In Elysium he finds Anchises, who predicts for him the future greatness of Rome and shows him the souls of great Romans to be born in the years to come. Comforted and encouraged, Aeneas returns to the upper world and sails with his followers to their destined home.

They land in Latium, and there on the banks of the river Tiber they eat a scant meal. So hungry are they that they also eat the thin, wheaten bread which they are using as platters, and Ascanius points out that the prediction of the Harpy Celaeno has now been fulfilled. Jupiter (Zeus) thunders three times and spreads in the heavens a burning cloud, confirming that they have at last found their new home.

The king of Latium is the aged LATINUS, married to AMATA and with a marriageable daughter, LAVINIA. The king of the Rutulians, TURNUS, wishes to marry Lavinia and is supported by Amata. But Latinus has heard from an oracle that his daughter must marry someone from overseas, and not a native Italian. When he hears of Aeneas' arrival he is very willing to accept him as his son-in-law, but the hostile Juno once more interferes, sending the Fury Allecto to stir up violent animosity to the Trojans in both Amata and Turnus. Hostilities are triggered off between Latins and Trojans when Ascanius wounds a pet stag belonging to Silvia, the royal herdsman's daughter. These soon develop into full-scale war. Latinus keeps apart from the fighting, but Turnus, filled with a lust for battle against the foreigners, recruits allies. He asks the exiled Greek Diomedes for support, and is refused; but many allies flock to join him, including MEZENTIUS, an exiled Etruscan king, the virgin-warrior CAMILLA, leader of the Volscians, AVENTINUS, a son of Hercules, and CAECULUS, the founder of Praeneste.

Aeneas, anxious and disheartened, is encouraged in a dream by the god of the River Tiber. In the morning he finds, just as the god promised, the white sow prophesied by Helenus lying on the riverbank with her thirty piglets, a sign that on this spot Ascanius will found a city thirty years later, and will call it Alba Longa ('Long White') after the sow. On the god's instructions, Aeneas rows up the Tiber to Pallanteum, a city on a hill that will later be the Palatine Hill of Rome, and asks its king, the Arcadian EVANDER, to be his ally. Evander welcomes him, and although he himself is too old to fight, he entrusts his dear son PALLAS (4) to Aeneas and provides a large contingent of cavalry for his war with the Latins. Aeneas is also aided by the Etruscan king TARCHON, who becomes his ally out of hatred for the exiled Mezentius, and by Venus, who has new and splendid armour made for her son by Vulcan.

While Aeneas is away, Turnus and his army advance on the Trojan camp. They try to fire the ships, but these have been made from the pines of Mount Ida, haunt of the Phrygian goddess Cybele. She turns the ships into nymphs and they swim far away. The Rutulians besiege the camp, and during the night NISUS (2) and Euryalus try to get through their lines to summon Aeneas. They slaughter many of the sleeping enemy, but are themselves killed, even as Nisus courageously tries to save his comrade.

When Aeneas returns with his reinforcements, Turnus attacks. Pallas leads his men into the thick of the battle and is killed by Turnus himself, who now wears his belt as a battle spoil. Aeneas, full of grief for his young ally, rages through the enemy ranks seeking revenge, but Juno has lured Turnus away from the battlefield to safety. Aeneas wounds the Etruscan king Mezentius, then reluctantly kills his son Lausus, who tries to save his father. The grief-stricken Mezentius mounts his faithful horse, Rhaebus, for a last attack on Aeneas, but both horse and rider are killed.

Twelve days of peace follow, during which the dead are buried. In the battle that follows, Camilla and her Volscian cavalry fight valiantly, but Camilla is killed and her troops routed. Discouraged, the Latins beg Turnus to make peace. He resolves to meet Aeneas in single combat to settle the issue, despite the efforts of Latinus and Amata to dissuade him. Before the duel can take place, the Latins are incited to fight again by Turnus' sister, JUTURNA, and the two armies join battle. Aeneas is wounded by an arrow, but is quickly healed by Venus. He attacks the Latins' city with fire, and Amata, thinking that Turnus must be dead, hangs herself. At last the decisive duel takes place. Aeneas wounds Turnus in the thigh, and is about to spare his life when he sees that he is wearing Pallas' belt as a battle spoil. Overcome with fury, he plunges his sword full into Turnus' heart.

The *Aeneid* ends with the death of Turnus, but we know that Aeneas now made peace with the Latins and married Lavinia, founding the city of Lavinium in her name and ruling over a union of Latins and Trojans. Lavinia bore him a second son, Silvius, after his death. Aeneas was rewarded with immortality.

[Homer, *Iliad* 2.19–23, 5, 12–13, 15–17, 20; *Homeric Hymn to Aphrodite*; Hesiod, *Theogony* 1008–10; Xenophon, *On Hunting* 1.15; Apollodorus, *Epitome* 3.32, 3.34, 4.2, 5.21; Dionysius of Halicarnassus 1.44–64, 1.72; Pausanias 1.12.1–2, 2.23.5, 3.22.11, 8.12.8; Livy, 1.1–3; Ovid, *Metamorphoses* 13.623–14.622, *Heroides* 7. W. A. Camps, *An Introduction to Virgil's Aeneid* (1969); J. N. Bremmer and N. M. Horsfall, *Roman Myth and Mythography* (1987), pp. 12–24.]

Aeneid *see* AENEAS.

Aeolus (1)

The ancestor of the Aeolians. He was the son of HELLEN and the nymph Orseis, and the brother of DORUS and XUTHUS. It was traditionally said that Hellen divided the Greek lands among his three sons, and as a result Aeolus ruled Thessaly, calling his people Aeolians after himself. He married Enarete and had a large and influential family: seven sons, CRETHEUS, SISYPHUS, ATHAMAS, SALMONEUS, Deion, Magnes and Perieres, and five daughters, CANACE (1), ALCYONE (2), Peisidice, Calyce and Perimede. A later tradition said that he had a daughter, MELANIPPE (1), by Hippo, the daughter of the Centaur Cheiron, and was grandfather to AEOLUS (3) and Boeotus. *See also* AEOLUS (2).

[Hesiod, *Catalogue of Women* fr. 9; Apollodorus 1.7.3; Pausanias 10.8.4.]

Aeolus (2)

Son of Hippotas, and king of the floating island of Aeolia, traditionally identified with one of the Lipari Islands north of Sicily. Aeolus had a wife and twelve children, six sons who were married to six daughters, and they all lived happily together on their island paradise, completely free from care. To this island came ODYSSEUS and his men, and for a month they were feasted royally by Aeolus and his family. Then came the time to leave, and Aeolus was able to help Odysseus since he had been made guardian of the winds by Zeus. He kept them in a cave on his island and could release them as he wished or as some god instructed, just as once before, on Hera's command, he had helped the ARGONAUTS with a gentle wind for their homeward voyage. Now he gave to Odysseus all the boisterous winds sewn up in a leather bag, leaving outside only the gentle West Wind to blow him safely back to Ithaca. All went well for nine days of sailing, until on the tenth day Ithaca was in sight. Then, fatally, Odysseus went to sleep and his men opened the leather bag, sure that it contained treasure. At once the winds burst out and swept the ship violently all the way back to Aeolia. Odysseus appealed to Aeolus to help him once more, but Aeolus turned him away, feeling that it would be unwise to help a man who was obviously so bitterly hated by the gods.

In the *Aeneid*, Virgil describes Aeolus' home (1.51–9).

... Aeolia, where the storm-clouds have their home, a place teeming with furious winds from the south. Here Aeolus is king, and in a vast cavern he controls the brawling winds and the roaring storms, keeping them curbed and fettered in their prison. Resentfully they rage from door to door in the mountainside, protesting loudly, while Aeolus sits in his high citadel, sceptre in hand, taming their arrogance and controlling their fury. But for him, they would snatch up the land, the sea, the very depths of the sky, and sweep them all through space.

Juno commands Aeolus to whip up winds that will overwhelm and sink Aeneas' ships as he sails from Troy, and he obeys her (81–7):

He struck the butt of his spear against the side of the hollow mountain and the winds came streaming out, rushing through the opening he had made, and blew a hurricane over all the earth. They swept down on the sea at once, the east wind, and the south wind, and the stormy wind from Africa, stirring it up from its bottommost depths and rolling great waves to the shores. Now men were shouting and ropes shrieking ... .

All ends well, however, for Neptune intervenes, angry that his authority over the sea has been usurped, and calms the storm.

This Aeolus is often confused with AEOLUS (1), most notably by Euripides in his lost tragedy *Aeolus* and by Ovid. From fragments of Euripides' play, we learn that Aeolus had six sons and six daughters, one son of whom, Macareus, committed incest with his sister Canace. When she became pregnant, he proposed to his father that all six sons marry their six sisters. Unfortunately Canace was not allotted to him, and when Aeolus learnt about the rape and pregnancy, it seems that he sent Canace a sword with which she killed herself. Macareus too committed suicide. In Ovid's version of Canace's tragic story, she gave birth to her baby in secret, but Aeolus discovered the truth when he heard the infant's cries. Once again he sent his daughter a sword, and he threw the baby to the dogs.

[Homer, *Odyssey* 10.1–75; Apollonius, *Argonautica* 4.761–9; Plutarch, *Moralia* 312c–d; Ovid, *Heroides* 11.]

Aeolus (3)

Son of Poseidon and MELANIPPE (1), the daughter of AEOLUS (1).

Aepytus (1)

A king of Arcadia, son of ELATUS (1) and grandson of ARCAS. He died, bitten by a snake, while hunting near Mount Cyllene and was buried where he fell. Pausanias was very keen to see his grave since it is mentioned in Homer, and he reports (8.16.3) that it was 'a mound of earth, not very large, surrounded by a circular base of stone'. Aepytus was the guardian of EVADNE (1).

[Homer, *Iliad* 2.603–11; Pausanias 8.4.4, 8.4.7.]

Aepytus (2)

The name sometimes given to CRESPHONTES (2).

Aerope

Daughter of CATREUS, king of Crete. When Catreus learnt from an oracle that he would be killed by one of his own children, he gave his daughters Aerope and Clymene to NAUPLIUS (1), the navigator and slave-trader, to be sold overseas. In another version, Aerope was caught by her father in the arms of a lover and given to Nauplius to be drowned. The outcome in both versions was the same: Nauplius, disobeying Catreus, married Clymene himself and spared Aerope, giving her as wife to ATREUS (or in some versions Atreus' son PLEISTHENES). She gave birth to the Atreidae, AGAMEMNON and MENELAUS.

She was not, however, a faithful wife. She committed adultery with Atreus' brother, Thyestes, which led to a tragic feud between the two men. She secretly gave Thyestes the lamb with the golden fleece owned by Atreus, which won her lover the throne of Mycenae in her husband's place. But Zeus demonstrated his support for Atreus' claim to the throne by reversing the course of the sun, making it rise in the west and sink in the east. At this great portent, Atreus once more took the throne. He banished Thyestes, and when he later learnt of Aerope's adultery, he drowned his unfaithful wife, as well as taking a hideous and bloody revenge on his brother.

[Hesiod, *Catalogue of Women* frr. 194–5; Sophocles, *Ajax* 1295–7; Euripides, *Orestes* 11–18, *Helen* 390–2, (lost) *Cretans*; Apollodorus 3.2.1–2, *Epitome* 2.10–12.]

Aesacus

Son of PRIAM, king of Troy, either by his first wife Arisbe, daughter of Merops, or by the nymph Alexirhoe, daughter of the river-god Granicus. Aesacus was a seer, and some say that it was he (rather than Cassandra, as in the usual account) who interpreted the pregnant Hecuba's ominous dream of a firebrand, predicting that her baby, if allowed to live, would grow up to bring destruction on Troy (*see* PARIS and THYMOETES). Apollodorus (3.12.5) tells us that Aesacus married the nymph Asterope, daughter of the river-god Cebren, adding that when she died he mourned for her and was transformed into a bird. Ovid (*Metamorphoses* 11.749–95) fills in some details of this brief and tantalising summary. In his version, Cebren's daughter was called Hesperia. She was unmarried, though Aesacus was in love with her and often pursued her through the woods. Always she escaped until one day, as he was chasing her, she was bitten on the foot by a snake and died. Filled with remorse he flung himself from a cliff into the sea, but the sea-goddess TETHYS pitied him and would not let him drown. He was turned by her into a water-bird, a diver, and spent all his days flying up and dashing himself down into the waves, forever seeking the death he longed for.

Aesculapius

The Roman name for ASCLEPIUS.

Aeson

The eldest son of CRETHEUS, king of Iolcus, and TYRO. On his father's death Aeson should have inherited the throne, but this was usurped by his half-brother PELIAS, son of Tyro and Poseidon. Aeson's wife was usually said to have been Alcimede, daughter of Phylacus, though Apollodorus names her as Polymede, daughter of Autolycus. They had a son, JASON, but from fear of Pelias they said that the boy had been born dead, then secretly sent him to be brought up by the wise Centaur CHEIRON.

When Jason grew up, he came back to Iolcus and was sent by Pelias to fetch the Golden Fleece. The expedition was long and arduous (*see* ARGONAUTS), and eventually Pelias thought himself safe from Jason's return and free to kill his family. Aeson, when he saw death coming, asked to take his own life, then died by drinking bull's blood, which the ancients thought to be poisonous. Aeson's wife too committed suicide, calling down curses upon the wicked Pelias. She left an infant son, Promachus, but Pelias killed him too.

A happier outcome was accorded to Aeson by the author of the Epic Cycle's *Returns* (now lost, bar fragments) and by Ovid. Both said that he lived to see Jason come home again, and was magically restored to youth by the sorcery of MEDEA.

[Homer, *Odyssey* 11.259; Pindar, *Pythian* 4.106–15, 120–3; Apollonius, *Argonautica* 1.45–7; Apollodorus 1.9.11, 1.9.16, 1.9.27; Diodorus Siculus 4.50.1; Ovid *Metamorphoses* 7.162–3, 251–93.]

Aethalides

The herald of the ARGONAUTS. He was a son of HERMES by Eupolemeia, the daughter of Myrmidon, and the half-brother of Erytus and Echion. Hermes granted Aethalides an undying memory that stayed with him even after death. He then lived alternately in the Underworld and on earth, where he inhabited a new body from time to time, one of which was said to have been that of the philosopher Pythagoras.

[Apollonius, *Argonautica* 1.51–6, 641–52.]

Aether ('brightness')

The personification of the upper air, where the light was thought to be brighter and clearer than in the air immediately surrounding the earth. Aether was born, according to Hesiod (*Theogony* 124–5), of the first sexual union in creation, that of EREBUS (Darkness) and NYX (Night), as was his sister HEMERA (Day).

Aethon *see* ERYSICHTHON.

Aethra

Daughter of PITTHEUS, king of Troezen, and mother of the great hero THESEUS. She was wooed by BELLEROPHON, but before their marriage could take place he was exiled from his home at Corinth for killing a man, so it came to nothing. Instead she was made pregnant with Theseus by AEGEUS, king of Athens. Having gone to Delphi to enquire about the childlessness of his marriage, Aegeus called at Troezen to consult Pittheus about the Oracle's reply. Pittheus, who wished to have a grandchild with Aegeus' royal blood in its veins, encouraged his guest to get drunk, then enticed him into sleeping with Aethra. In the morning Aegeus left for Athens, but before he departed he hid a sword and a pair of sandals under a great rock, telling Aethra that if she bore a son, who on reaching manhood could lift the rock, she should send him with these tokens of paternity to Athens.

Since Theseus was often said to be the son of POSEIDON, various explanations were given as to how this came about: either this was a story invented by Pittheus to save his daughter's credit; or Poseidon visited Aethra on the same night as Aegeus; or Aethra was inspired in a dream by Athena to cross to the neighbouring island of Sphaeria, where Poseidon came to her, and the name of the island was thereafter changed to Hiera, 'Holy Island', on which Aethra set up a temple to Athena Apaturia, 'the Deceitful'. But whether his father was mortal or god, Theseus was born to Aethra, and when grown to manhood he lifted the rock and carried sword and sandals to Aegeus in Athens, eventually succeeding to his throne.

Theseus and his friend Peirithous later abducted the young and beautiful HELEN of Sparta to be Theseus' wife. They left her at Aphidnae in Attica, in the charge of Aethra, while they set off down to Hades to abduct Persephone as wife for Peirithous. Meanwhile, in their absence Helen's two brothers, the DIOSCURI, came to her rescue. They captured Aphidnae and carried their sister back to Sparta, but they also took Aethra, who was made Helen's slave. She even accompanied Helen to Troy when she later eloped with PARIS, staying there with her through all the long years of the TROJAN WAR. During this time she brought up her great-grandson, Munitus, who had been born to Laodice, the daughter of Priam (*see* ACAMAS (1)). When Troy at last fell to the Greeks, Aethra's grandsons, Acamas and Demophon, took her home again to Attica.

Aethra is depicted in various scenes in ancient art from about 500 BC. She is shown pursued by Poseidon, or rescued from Troy by her grandsons (fig. 1); and in a scene unique to art, she is apparently threatened by Theseus with a sword while she supplicates him for mercy. But if 'Aethra' is labelled correctly (it should perhaps read 'Medea'), it may be that Theseus is merely showing his mother the sword hidden by Aegeus and telling her of his intention to seek out his father, while she is begging him to stay at home with her and keep away from all the potential dangers of such an expedition (and indeed these turned out to be many).

See also fig. 6.

[Homer, *Iliad* 3.144; Euripides, *Suppliants* 1–7; Apollodorus 3.10.7, 3.15.7, *Epitome* 1.23, 5.22; Plutarch, *Theseus* 3 and 6; Pausanias 1.41.4, 2.31.9, 2.33.1–2, 5.19.3, 10.25.7–8; Quintus of Smyrna, *Sequel to Homer* 13.496–543.]

Aetna

A Sicilian nymph who gave her name to Mount Etna, a mountain over 10,000 feet in height and Europe's highest active volcano, situated near the eastern coast of Sicily. Various stories were told to explain its fiery activities: crushed everlastingly beneath it was either the Giant ENCELADUS or the monster TYPHON, or it contained the forge of the smith-god HEPHAESTUS, manned by the one-eyed Giants, the CYCLOPES.

Aetolus

Son of ENDYMION, the king of Elis, who made his three sons, Aetolus, Epeius and Paeon, run a race to determine who would inherit the throne. Epeius won, but died without male issue and was succeeded by Aetolus. Unfortunately Aetolus was exiled after accidentally killing a certain Apis (possibly the king of Argos) by running him over with a chariot at the funeral games of Azan. Aetolus went to the land of the Curetes around the river Achelous, where he killed his hosts and named the land Aetolia after himself. He married Pronoe and had two sons, Calydon and Pleuron, after whom the two chief cities of Aetolia were named.

[Apollodorus 1.7.6–7; Pausanias 5.1.4–5, 5.1.8.]

Afterlife *see* HADES (2); ELYSIUM.

Agamedes *see* TROPHONIUS.

Agamemnon

Son of ATREUS, king of Mycenae, and AEROPE (or occasionally said to be son of their son PLEISTHENES, who died young), and brother of MENELAUS. Agamemnon and Menelaus together were commonly called the Atreidae. On Atreus' death they were expelled from Mycenae by Thyestes, but were later brought back by TYNDAREOS, king of Sparta, and Thyestes in his turn was driven out. Agamemnon then became king at Mycenae, dominating the whole of the Argolid (though one variant tradition has him king of Amyclae, near Sparta), while Menelaus took over the throne of Sparta from Tyndareos, having married his daughter, the beautiful HELEN. Agamemnon married a second daughter of Tyndareos, CLYTEMNESTRA, though according to one tradition she was already married to Tantalus, son of Thyestes, and had a son by him. Agamemnon murdered both Tantalus and the boy, then took Clytemnestra for himself. The fruits of their union were four children who grew up to play a dramatic part in the fates of their parents: three daughters, IPHIGENEIA (in Homer called Iphianassa), ELECTRA (3) (originally called Laodice) and CHRYSOTHEMIS, and a son, ORESTES.

When PARIS carried Helen off to Troy, Agamemnon helped Menelaus to muster a large army to fetch her back by force. He himself became commander-in-chief, taking with him a hundred ships, the largest single contingent. At Aulis the fleet became weather-bound, and the seer CALCHAS declared that the angry goddess Artemis must be appeased by the sacrifice of Agamemnon's virgin daughter, Iphigeneia. She was lured to Aulis on the pretext of marriage with ACHILLES, and there she was killed. The winds blew once again and the Greek fleet sailed onwards, with all apparently well; but Iphigeneia's death would be a major factor in Clytemnestra's subsequent hatred of Agamemnon, leading to his murder when he returned home triumphant at the end of the ten-year-long TROJAN WAR.

The events of the *Iliad* take place in the last year of the war. Homer depicts Agamemnon as a man of personal valour, a brave and effective warrior, but also a far from ideal leader since he is irresolute and easily discouraged. Three times he proposes that he and his men give up the war and sail home, once – inspired by a dream (*see* DREAMS) – simply to test the spirits of the army, but the other times in all seriousness, and he has to be rallied and supported by ODYSSEUS, DIOMEDES (2) and old NESTOR. Moreover it is his ill-judged quarrel with Achilles, the greatest warrior of all his men, that brings death to many of the Greeks and almost loses them the war. The dispute comes about when Agamemnon is forced by Apollo's anger to give back his war-prize and concubine, CHRYSEIS, to her father, Apollo's priest Chryses. Displeased by his loss of status, Agamemnon unwisely decides to replace her by taking Achilles' war-prize, BRISEIS. Achilles withdraws to his tent, full of the wrath that will determine the rest of the *Iliad*'s action and lead to tragedy, both for himself and for the rest of the Greeks. At the end of the *Iliad*,

HECTOR, the greatest of the Trojan warriors, is dead, and the war is about to enter its final phase.

Eventually the Greeks entered Troy by using the stratagem of the WOODEN HORSE. They sacked the city by night, killing the Trojan men and carrying off the women and children as slaves. Now, with King PRIAM dead and the wealth and pride of Troy brought to nothing, great renown fell to Agamemnon as leader of the victorious expedition. For this he was famous throughout antiquity; but famous also for the sordid death that he met on his return home. His sorry fate is recounted in the *Odyssey* by Menelaus and Nestor, and also by the shade of Agamemnon himself in Hades. In his absence from Mycenae, Clytemnestra took his cousin AEGISTHUS as her lover; then on Agamemnon's return home at the end of the long war, together they murdered him. For a year a watchman had been looking out for his arrival, so when at last he landed, kissing the earth with joy to be back in his own country, his murderers were ready for him. Aegisthus invited him to a banquet, then set upon him and his followers with a band of twenty armed men, killing him as he feasted 'as a man strikes down an ox at the manger' (4.535), while Clytemnestra killed his Trojan captive CASSANDRA, the daughter of Priam. Eight years later Agamemnon was avenged by his son Orestes, who killed both Aegisthus and Clytemnestra.

This whole saga of death and revenge became a favourite one with later authors, particularly the tragedians of the fifth century BC who retold it with various changes and elaborations. Aeschylus in his *Agamemnon*, for instance, develops Clytemnestra into a powerful and awe-inspiring figure who quite alone kills Agamemnon, pinioning him in a robe while he is unarmed and vulnerable in his bath. The tragedians also developed the

Fig. 10 **Death of Agamemnon, trapped in a net-like garment. Aegisthus has stabbed him once and is about to strike again, while Clytemnestra follows him and a daughter cries in alarm.**

role of Agamemnon's daughter Electra in the final vengeance (a development that would prove important for modern reworkings of the legend). Agamemnon in his role of army-leader plays a part in tragedies about the Trojan War, such as Sophocles' *Ajax* and Euripides' *Hecuba*; and it is in this role that he is usually depicted in the visual arts from the seventh century BC onwards, in a variety of scenes relating to the war at Troy (fig. 137). One famous vase, however, known as the Boston Oresteia Krater (fig. 10), shows Agamemnon enveloped in the deadly robe, while Aegisthus attacks him with a sword and Clytemnestra follows on wielding an axe.

In the nineteenth century, Heinrich Schliemann, excavating the shaft graves at Mycenae, found a beaten gold funerary mask and (so the legend goes) telegraphed to King George of the Hellenes, 'I have gazed upon the face of Agamemnon'. In fact the 'Mask of Agamemnon', which can be seen in the National Museum at Athens, dates from a period some centuries earlier than the Homeric king. Perhaps the last word should be given to Horace (*Odes* 4.9): 'Many brave heroes lived before Agamemnon, but on all alike, unwept and unknown, eternal night lies heavy since they lack a divine poet.'

[Homer, *Iliad* 1.1–326, 2.1–454, 4.148–97, 9.9–161, 10.1–24, 14.27–136, 19.40–275, *Odyssey* 3.141–50, 247–312, 4.512–37, 11.404–53, 24.96–7, 199–202; Pindar, *Pythian* 11.17–37; Pausanias 2.16.6, 2.18.2, 2.22.2–3; Seneca, *Agamemnon*. A. J. N. W. Prag, *The Oresteia: Iconographic and Narrative Tradition* (1985).]

Aganippe

Daughter of the river-god Permessus, and nymph of the spring named Aganippe on Mount Helicon in Boeotia. This spring was sacred to the MUSES and was believed to inspire with poetry all those who drank from it.

[Pausanias 9.29.5; Virgil, *Eclogues* 10.12.]

Agapenor

Son of ANCAEUS (1), and king of Tegea in Arcadia at the time of the TROJAN WAR. After the sons of Phegeus had killed ALCMAEON, they carried off Arsinoe, his wife and their own sister, and gave her as a slave to Agapenor, falsely accusing her of Alcmaeon's murder. But Alcmaeon's sons too came to Agapenor's house and killed the sons of Phegeus, thus avenging their father's death.

Agapenor was one of HELEN's suitors, so bound by the common oath to defend the marriage rights of her chosen husband, he went to fight at Troy. He led the Arcadian contingent of sixty ships, provided by Agamemnon. He survived the war, and on his journey home his fleet was driven by a storm to Cyprus. Here he settled, founding Paphos and building a sanctuary of Aphrodite at Old Paphos.

[Homer, *Iliad* 2.603–14; Apollodorus 3.7.6, 3.10.2, *Epitome* 3.11, 6.15; Pausanias 8.5.2.]

Agave

Daughter of CADMUS, king of Thebes, and HARMONIA; sister of AUTONOE, INO and SEMELE. Agave married Echion, one of the Sown Men (the original inhabitants of Thebes), and bore him a son, PENTHEUS, who was brought to his death by the god DIONYSUS. Euripides' tragedy *The Bacchae* gives the most familiar and moving version of the legend. Because Agave, Autonoe and Ino refuse to believe that their sister Semele bore Dionysus to Zeus, they are driven mad by Dionysus and sent to revel as MAENADS on Mount Cithaeron. Here they tear Pentheus to pieces under the delusion that he is a mountain lion, and it is Agave herself, as leader of the maenads, who is the first to lay violent hands on him. She carries his head home in triumph, still believing it to be that of a lion, until Cadmus gently brings her back to sanity and grief.

[Hesiod, *Theogony* 975–8; Apollodorus 3.4.2–3, 3.5.2.]

Agdistis

A Phrygian name of CYBELE.

Agelaus

The labourer who saved the infant PARIS.

Agenor (1)

Son of POSEIDON and LIBYA, and twin-brother of BELUS. While Belus stayed in Africa and ruled the Egyptians, Agenor migrated to Phoenicia and became king of Tyre or Sidon. He married Telephassa (or Argiope), who bore him a daughter, EUROPA, and several sons, CADMUS, PHOENIX (2), CILIX, PHINEUS (2) and THASUS. (The genealogies are somewhat confused, and some of these children are sometimes given different fathers – Europa, for instance, is sometimes called the daughter of Phoenix instead of his sister. But they all seem to be descended from Agenor.) When Europa was carried off by Zeus, Agenor sent his sons out into the world to find her, and their mother went too. They were never to return home. When at last, after wandering far over the earth, they gave up their unsuccessful quests, they all chose to settle elsewhere.

[Herodotus 2.44, 4.147, 6.46–7, 7.91; Apollonius, *Argonautica* 2.178, 237, 240; Apollodorus 1.9.21, 2.1.4, 3.1.1, 3.4.1; Pausanias 5.25.12.]

Agenor (2)

A brave son of the Trojan elder ANTENOR. In Homer's *Iliad*, when ACHILLES is about to storm through the gates of Troy, Agenor has the courage to withstand him and saves the

Trojans who are desperately trying to flee to safety within the city. He knows that Achilles will probably kill him, but nevertheless stands firm (21.573–80):

> Just as a leopard comes out of her deep thicket
> to face the man who is hunting her, and has no fear
> nor any thought of flight when she hears the baying
> of his hounds, and even though he is too quick for her
> and throws or strikes with his spear, yet even then,
> stuck through with the shaft, she does not lose her courage
> until she has fought or died; so noble Agenor
> refused to flee before he had fought Achilles.

Agenor challenges Achilles and throws his spear, striking him on the leg without piercing his armour, then is spirited away by APOLLO before Achilles himself can let fly a more deadly cast. The god then disguises himself as Agenor and lures Achilles into giving chase, thus allowing the Trojans to escape safely into Troy – all except HECTOR, who now waits alone outside the city for his own fatal confrontation with Achilles.

Ages of man

Hesiod was the first to speak of earlier races of men who lived in happier ages than ours (*Works and Days* 109–201). The first was a golden race who lived a peaceful and idyllic life under the rule of CRONUS:

> They lived like gods, with carefree hearts, remote from toil and grief. Nor did wretched old age beset them, but with hands and feet ever the same they took their joy in feasting, far from all ills, and they died as if overcome by sleep. All good things were theirs, for the fruitful earth of its own accord put forth its plentiful harvest without stint, while they enjoyed a life of peace and ease in abundance, rich in flocks and loved by the blessed gods.

After this Golden Age, a silver race was created, who were so foolish and neglectful of the gods that Zeus destroyed them. Next came a race of bronze, so dedicated to warfare that they destroyed themselves; then the race of heroes who lived in the heroic age (the subjects of our Greek myths), many of whom fought at Thebes and Troy. Fifthly and finally came a race of iron, Hesiod's race and our own: 'And men never rest from toil and misery by day, nor from perishing by night; and the gods shall lay harsh trouble upon them ...'

The concept of the Golden Age has been inspirational to artists from ancient times onwards, and indeed nostalgia for an idealised past and pessimism about a worsening future seems almost inherent to the human condition.

Aglaea *see* GRACES.

Aglaurus (1) (Sometimes **Agraulus**)

Daughter of Actaeus, the first king of Athens. She married the earth-born CECROPS (1), who inherited her father's kingdom, and bore him a son, Erysichthon, and three daughters, AGLAURUS (2), Herse and Pandrosus.

Aglaurus (2) (Sometimes **Agraulus**)

Daughter of CECROPS (1), the second king of Athens, and AGLAURUS (1). She was loved by ARES and bore him a daughter, Alcippe (*see* HALIRRHOTHIUS), and according to some she bore Ceryx to HERMES; but she is most famous for her tragic end, when she and her sisters Herse and Pandrosus, disobeying ATHENA's instructions, opened the chest containing the baby ERICHTHONIUS (1). What they saw inside caused them to hurl themselves from the Acropolis to their deaths.

Ovid tells a different story in which the girls lived on after prying into Athena's secret. Hermes fell in love with Herse when he saw her returning home from the festival of Athena, so he went to her house to woo her. Here he was intercepted by Aglaurus, who promised to further his suit if he fetched her a fortune in gold. Meanwhile Athena, angry with Aglaurus for disobediently opening the chest, afflicted the girl with jealousy of her sister's good fortune. When Hermes returned, Aglaurus barred his way to Herse's room, so the god opened the door with his wand and turned Aglaurus to stone that was stained black by her dark thoughts. Ovid says no more of Hermes' union with Herse, but other sources say that she bore the god a son, CEPHALUS (1), who was loved by Eos.

Both Aglaurus and Pandrosus were worshipped in independent sanctuaries on the Acropolis.

[Euripides, *Ion* 20–4, 260–74; Apollodorus 3.14.2–3, 3.14.6; Pausanias 1.2.6, 1.18.2, 1.27.2, 1.38.3; Ovid, *Metamorphoses* 2.552–65, 708–832.]

Agrius (1)

One of the GIANTS. In the battle of the Gods and the Giants, Agrius and his brother Thoas were killed by the FATES with brazen clubs.

Agrius (2)

Son of Porthaon and Euryte, and brother of OENEUS, king of Calydon. In old age Oeneus had no sons left alive to defend him and was deposed by the sons of Agrius. They imprisoned the old man and gave his kingdom to their father; but Oeneus was avenged by his grandson DIOMEDES (2), who came secretly to Calydon and killed most of Agrius' sons. The only survivors were THERSITES and Onchestus, who later ambushed Oeneus as he was passing through Arcadia and killed him. Agrius took his own life.

[Apollodorus 1.7.10, 1.8.5–6.]

Agrius (3)

Son of Odysseus and the enchantress CIRCE.

Ajax (1)

Son of TELAMON, king of Salamis, and Eriboea (or Periboea); half-brother of TEUCER (2), and known as the Great Ajax to differentiate him from AJAX (2), son of Oileus. His name, Aias in Greek, was said to derive from the eagle (*aietos*) which appeared as a good omen when, before his birth, Telamon's friend HERACLES prayed to Zeus that Telamon might have a brave son. It was sometimes said that Heracles wrapped the new-born baby in the skin of the NEMEAN LION that he was wearing. Wherever it touched the infant, his skin became as invulnerable as the skin of the lion. Only one vital spot on his left side was missed.

Ajax was one of the many suitors of HELEN, offering as his wedding gifts great flocks of sheep and oxen raided from neighbouring lands. Bound by the oath taken by all the suitors to defend the marriage rights of Helen's chosen husband, he later followed MENELAUS and AGAMEMNON to the TROJAN WAR, taking twelve ships as his contribution to the expedition.

Two pieces of ancient literature give us a very clear picture of this great hero: the *Iliad* of Homer and Sophocles' tragedy *Ajax*, neither of which sees him as invulnerable, but simply as an extraordinary mortal of immense strength and courage. In the *Iliad* we see Ajax fighting at Troy during the tenth year of the war. He is physically huge, towering head and shoulders over the other Greeks, and he carries a massive shield, seven ox-hides thick and covered with bronze. He is a tremendously powerful warrior, the greatest of the Greeks after ACHILLES, and the bulwark of the army when Achilles stays in his tent refusing to fight.

Ajax fights a duel with HECTOR, the greatest Trojan warrior (fig. 64), and comes close to killing him before darkness falls and puts an end to the contest. They exchange gifts, Hector giving a sword and Ajax a sword-belt. Later they have a second confrontation where again Ajax has very much the better of it, felling Hector with a rock. But perhaps we see Ajax at his finest when he defends the Greek wall and ships from the Trojan assault, keeping the enemy off long enough for PATROCLUS to lead out the Myrmidons and put them to flight. One by one the other Greek leaders have been wounded and put out of action, but Ajax fights on relentlessly until finally, pushed back on to the ships by the Trojans, he strides up and down the decks, encouraging his men, beating off the attackers with a huge pike, sweating, weary, fully believing that he is going to die, but nevertheless ready to battle on until he drops. What is more, he is the only one of the great Iliadic heroes who never has a god to help him. From beginning to end, all that he achieves comes from his own tremendous powers.

Ajax is a close friend of Achilles, and although in the *Iliad* he is shown as a man of action rather than words, he is one of the three Greeks chosen to go on an embassy to Achilles to persuade him back into the fighting. But in fact Ajax' words, brief and to the point and appealing to Achilles on friendship's grounds, have more effect than the far lengthier persuasions of ODYSSEUS and PHOENIX (3).

When Patroclus is killed by Hector and stripped of his armour, Ajax covers his naked corpse with his own great shield and prevents the Trojans from dragging it off (17.132–7):

> Ajax covered Patroclus with his broad shield,
> standing fast like a lion defending his young,
> one who, in leading his little ones through the forest,
> comes upon huntsmen. He glares, fierce in his strength,
> and draws down his brows, hooding his eyes.
> Even so did Ajax protect the hero Patroclus.

Later he takes part in Patroclus' funeral games, where he draws a wrestling match with Odysseus, strength against cunning, comes second in the weight-throwing, and is beaten by DIOMEDES (2) in a close combat fight with spears. By later authors he was said to have won the discus-throwing at the funeral games of Achilles.

Other epics told of later events in Ajax' life. These are now lost, but enough fragments are left for us to piece together the story. When Achilles was killed, it was Ajax who carried the body of his friend off the battlefield

Fig. 11 **Ajax resolutely prepares for death, fixing his sword firmly in the earth.**

while Odysseus held off the Trojans. Then came a dispute as to who should receive Achilles' armour, with both Ajax and Odysseus staking their claims. In various epic versions, the dispute was settled by the Trojans' saying which of the two they thought the better warrior: either Trojan prisoners were asked for their verdict, or Trojan women were overheard talking on the walls of Troy. In later tragedy, a vote was held among the Greek warriors. But the outcome was always the same: Odysseus was awarded the arms, and Ajax, full of rage because he believed that they should have been his (as indeed – or so it seems from the literature left to us – they should have been), decided to kill the Greek leaders to avenge this slight to his honour. But ATHENA sent him mad; and instead of killing men he slaughtered the flocks which were to feed the army. When his madness left him and he realised what he had done, full of shame and despair he fell on his sword.

It is this last part of Ajax' life which Sophocles dramatises in his *Ajax*. When the play opens Ajax has already killed the animals, and we see him both triumphant in his madness when he thinks that he has slain his enemies, and then sunk into despair when he wakes to sanity and reality. Surrounded by bloody carcases, he cries in anguish (364–76):

> Do you see me, the bold, the valiant,
> the one who was fearless in deadly war,
> and now formidable to tame and trusting beasts?
> What mockery! What shame! ...
> I let my enemies go, and fell
> on horned cattle and splendid flocks
> of goats, shedding their dark blood.

He decides that the only course left is to kill himself: 'Honour in life or honour in death is the only choice for a man of any nobility', he says (479–80); and since after what he has done there is no more chance of honour in life, then he must die. His concubine, TECMESSA, the mother of his little son EURYSACES, does her utmost to dissuade him, but his heart is resolute, even though he lulls her fears and those of his men with what sound like reassurances that he will learn to live with what fate has dealt him: this Ajax, unlike Homer's, is a man of words and poetry as well as of deeds (669–77):

> Even harsh and mightiest strengths give way.
> Snow-packed winter yields to fruitful summer.
> The vault of endless night at last gives place
> to dawn's white horses kindling radiant light.
> The dread winds' breath slackens and lulls to rest
> the sounding sea. Even all-powerful sleep
> in time must loose his captive. Must not I,
> then, likewise learn to yield?

But left alone, Ajax, still cursing his enemies, makes his last prayers to the gods and falls on the very sword given him by Hector after their duel – a reminder, in a death brought about by shame and dishonour, that he was once a great hero.

When his body is discovered (fig. 136), Menelaus and Agamemnon want to throw it out to be eaten by the dogs and birds; but Teucer, determined that Ajax shall be buried, defends it until Odysseus steps in and persuades Agamemnon that it is not right to harm 'the bravest man, except Achilles, of all that came to Troy' (1340–1). The play ends with Ajax' body ceremoniously carried out for burial with full honours.

In Homer's *Odyssey*, Odysseus meets the shade of Ajax in Hades and speaks conciliatory words to him, begging him to forget his bitterness over the award of Achilles' arms. But Ajax refuses to speak, and stalks away in haughty silence (11.563–4): 'He made no answer, but went off after the other ghosts of the perished dead, into the darkness.'

In Ovid's later version, on the spot where Ajax' blood fell on the ground the hyacinth (which also commemorates the death of HYACINTHUS) sprang up, its petals marked with the letters AI, in Greek the first two letters of Ajax' name and also of the word meaning 'alas'. It was said by Pausanias (1.35.4) that after the wreck of Odysseus' ship during his wanderings, Achilles' arms were washed ashore at Ajax' tomb in the Troad. So Ajax did, in the end, receive his rights.

As far as we can tell from fragments, Aeschylus produced an Ajax-trilogy, the plays being *The Award of the Arms*, *The Thracian Women* and *The Women of Salamis*. Certainly we know that, unlike Sophocles', his Ajax was invulnerable but for one weak spot, for when he tried to kill himself his sword bent, until a goddess (Athena?) showed him the vulnerable place. Scenes from Ajax' life were popular among Greek vase-painters, especially Ajax playing dice with Achilles (fig. 145) or carrying his corpse off the battlefield (fig. 12), the argument and voting over Achilles' arms, and Ajax' suicide. He was a particular favourite with the great painter/potter Exekias, whose depiction of Ajax quietly and resolutely preparing for death (fig. 11) is one of the most arresting vase-paintings of antiquity.

In historical times, Ajax was the eponymous hero of the tribe Aiantis, one of the ten tribes of Athens, and had a hero-cult also in several other places, including Salamis and the Troad. Before the battle of Salamis in 480 BC the Greeks invoked his aid, along with that of his father Telamon and the other sons of Aeacus; and after their victory they dedicated to Ajax one of three Phoenician triremes, offered in gratitude to the gods, in Salamis itself.

tingent of forty ships (2.527–35). His men were light-armed troops, with bows and slings instead of the usual heavy arms (13.712–8), while he himself was lightly armoured in a linen corselet (2.529). He was physically very unlike his namesake, being small and fleet of foot, but was said to surpass all the Greeks in the use of the spear (2.530) and to be the most successful in pursuit of a fleeing enemy (14.520–2). He fought well in all the great battles described in the *Iliad*, often alongside the Great Ajax, with Homer repeatedly referring to the two of them together as the Aiantes (Ajaxes).

In character too Ajax was very different from his greater namesake, being on occasion arrogant and quarrelsome, as when he is grossly insulting to the respected IDOMENEUS during the chariot-race at Patroclus' funeral games (23.473–81). It seems appropriate, when himself afterwards competes in the foot-race, that ATHENA should make him slip on some ox-dung and get a mouthful of it, to the great amusement of all the onlookers, so that he comes second to Odysseus. Homer gives us the delightful picture of the loud-mouthed Ajax receiving a great ox as second prize while still spitting out the dung that brought him down (23.740–84). But there are serious undertones here too, for his insolence and subsequent fall are perhaps a foreshadowing of the ultimate folly that will bring him to death.

The lost epic *The Sack of Troy* told how CASSANDRA, the Trojan prophetess and daughter of King Priam, took refuge during the capture of the city at a statue of Athena. Ajax dragged her away from the image to which she was clinging (this was to become a favourite scene in archaic and classical art) and raped her, while the statue turned away its eyes in horror at his crime (figs. 27 and 35). The Greeks, appalled at this great sacrilege, wanted to stone Ajax, but he escaped death by taking refuge at Athena's altar.

His fate, however, caught up with him and brought disaster on the rest of the Greeks, since Athena resolved that he should be punished for his crime, and his comrades too because they had made him pay no penalty. With the help of ZEUS and POSEIDON she wrecked the Greek ships when they sailed away from Troy. In Euripides' *Trojan Women*, a dialogue between Athena and Poseidon, just as the Greeks are preparing to sail, predicts the horrors to come (48–97). Zeus has promised Athena a storm, and now she asks the sea-god to play his part too. 'Zeus will send forth rains and endless hail and great, dark storms', she tells him, 'and he promises me the fire of his thunderbolt to smite the Greek ships and set them ablaze. Then you, for your part, make the Aegean rage with surging waves and whirlpools. Fill the Euboean Gulf with corpses. Then the Greeks may learn henceforth to

Fig.12 *Above*: **Artemis, Mistress of the Animals.** *Below*: **Ajax carries the body of Achilles from the battlefield.**

[Homer, *Iliad* 2.557–8, 7.181–305, 9.622–42, 12–16.123, 23.700–849; Hesiod, *Catalogue of Women*, fr. 204; Herodotus 5.66, 8.64, 121; Pindar, *Isthmian* 6.41–54; Apollodorus 3.10.8, *Epitome* 5.4–7; Plutarch, *Themistocles* 15; Pausanias 1.5.1–2, 5.19.2, Ovid, *Metamorphoses* 12.624 13.398. Jennifer R. March, 'Sophocles' *Ajax*: the Death and Burial of a Hero', *BICS* 38 (1991–93), 1–36.]

Ajax (2)

Son of Oileus, the Locrian king, and known as the Lesser Ajax to differentiate him from AJAX (1), the son of Telamon. This Ajax too was one of the suitors of HELEN, and he too followed Agamemnon and Menelaus to the TROJAN WAR, taking with him, according to Homer's *Iliad*, a large con-

reverence my altars and respect all other gods.'

'It shall be so,' replies Poseidon. 'I shall stir up the wide Aegean, and the shores of Mykonos, the Delian reefs, Scyros, Lemnos and Cape Caphareus will all be filled with the bodies of many dead.'

During the god-driven storm, Athena herself hurled a thunderbolt at Ajax' ship and sank it, but Ajax himself swam safely away and hauled himself out on to a rock called Gyrae. Here, however, his rash insolence finally destroyed him when he uttered one arrogant boast too many, as Homer describes (*Odyssey* 4.502–11):

> Ajax would have escaped his doom, though hated
> by Athena, had he not thrown out a reckless,
> boastful word, saying that he had eluded
> the great sea's depths, even against the will
> of the gods; and Poseidon heard him loudly boasting.
> At once in his sturdy hands he seized his trident
> and struck at the Gyrae rock and broke it in two.
> Part of it stayed where it was, but a fragment fell
> in the sea, just where Ajax sat when he spoke
> his foolish boast. It carried him down and deep
> in the boundless, surging sea. So Ajax died ...

In historic times the Locrians, in expiation of Ajax' sacrilege, sent two virgins each year to serve as priestesses in Athena's temple at Troy. This practice continued, it was said, for a thousand years.

[Apollodorus, *Epitome* 5.22–3, 6.5–6, 6.20–2; Strabo 13.1.40; Plutarch, *Moralia* 557d.]

Alalcomeneus

The man who gave his name to the town of Alalcomenae in Boeotia, where the local inhabitants claimed that ATHENA had been brought up. The very same story of human intervention in a quarrel between Zeus and Hera was told of Alalcomeneus as of CITHAERON (1).

[Plutarch, *On the Festival of Images at Plataea* 6; Pausanias 9.3.4, 9.33.5.]

Alba Longa *see* ASCANIUS.

Alcaeus (1)

Son of PERSEUS and Andromeda. By Astydameia, the daughter of PELOPS, he had two children, AMPHITRYON and Anaxo. Alcaeus' grandson HERACLES was often called Alcides after him.

[Apollodorus 2.4.5.]

Alcaeus (2) *see* STHENELUS (2).

Alcathous (1)

Son of PELOPS, the king of Pisa in Elis, and Hippodameia. Alcathous won the throne of Megara by his valour.

Evippus, the son of Megareus, king of Megara, was one of the many slain by the lion of Cithaeron that was ravaging the land, so Megareus promised that whoever killed the beast would win the hand of his daughter, Evaechme, and succeed to the rule of the kingdom. Alcathous killed the lion and won both wife and kingship (though according to Apollodorus 2.4.9–10, it was Heracles who destroyed the lion). He built a temple to APOLLO and ARTEMIS in gratitude for his achievement, and rebuilt the walls of Megara which had been destroyed by the Cretans during the reign of NISUS (1). It was said that Apollo helped Alcathous with the work on the walls, and that the god rested his lyre on a certain stone which ever afterwards, if struck with a pebble, reverberated with a sound like a lyre. The traveller Pausanias saw the stone, and thought it a marvel.

Alcathous had three daughters, Periboea who married TELAMON, Automedousa who married IPHICLES, and Iphinoe; and two sons, Ischepolis and Callipolis. Ischepolis was killed at the CALYDONIAN BOARHUNT, and it was Callipolis who was the first to hear the sorry news. He ran to tell his father, whom he found preparing a fire to sacrifice to Apollo. Callipolis flung the logs from the altar, thinking the sacrifice inauspicious at such a moment, and Alcathous killed him for his apparent impiety by striking his head with one of the logs, learning too late the reason for his son's impetuous action. He was purified of the murder by the seer Polyidus, but this could not bring him back his sons, and on his death the kingdom passed to his grandson, AJAX (1).

[Pindar, *Isthmian* 8.67; Pausanias 1.41.3–6, 1.42.1–6, 1.43.4–5.]

Alcathous (2)

Son of Porthaon and Euryte. He is notable only for his death, killed either by his nephew TYDEUS, or as one of the victims in the deadly chariot-race which OENOMAUS set for his daughter Hippodameia's suitors.

Alcestis

The beautiful daughter of PELIAS, king of Iolcus, and Anaxibia. She had many suitors, but was finally won by ADMETUS, king of Pherae and a favourite of Apollo. The god helped him to win his chosen bride, and even gained for him a reprieve from his fated day of death, as long as he could find someone willing to die in his place. It was Alcestis who chose to die that he might live. The outcome is dramatised in Euripides' play *Alcestis*, where she dies as promised, but is won back to the living by HERACLES, who wrestles with THANATOS (Death) and takes his victim from him. In another version recorded by Plato (*Symposium* 179b–d), the gods so admired Alcestis' courage that they themselves sent her back from Hades.

Since our first preserved account of Heracles' saving her is to be found in Euripides, it may be that Heracles' wrestling-match with Death was his own innovation.

Alcestis as the model wife and the story of her love and loyalty have been inspirational in the postclassical arts, particularly in the fields of drama and opera. Gluck's opera *Alceste* is largely modelled on Euripides' play, but has Alcestis rescued by Apollo.

Alcides

The name by which HERACLES, grandson of ALCAEUS (1), was often known.

Alcimede

Daughter of PHYLACUS, wife of AESON, and mother of JASON, the hero who won the Golden Fleece.

Alcinous

King of the Phaeacians on the *Odyssey*'s fantasy-island of SCHERIA, where ODYSSEUS is shipwrecked on his way home to Ithaca. Alcinous is married to ARETE and they have five sons and a daughter, NAUSICAA, who is the first person to meet Odysseus when he is cast up by the sea. She gives him food and drink and clothing and brings him home to her parents' palace. They welcome him kindly, and it is to them that he tells in the course of a banquet the long tale of his wanderings, brought about by the wrath of POSEIDON (*Odyssey* Books 9–12). They give Odysseus many rich gifts and provide a ship to take him home to Ithaca, despite an earlier prophecy that such help to strangers would one day earn them Poseidon's wrath. The god is indeed angry at their interference, and when their ship returns to Scheria he turns it to stone and roots it to the bottom of the sea.

Alcippe

A daughter of Ares raped by HALIRRHOTHIUS.

Alcithoe

One of the three daughters of MINYAS who refused to worship Dionysus and were turned into bats.

Alcmaeon

Son of the seer AMPHIARAUS and his treacherous wife ERIPHYLE, and brother of Amphilochus. Eriphyle, bribed by Polyneices with the beautiful necklace of his ancestress Harmonia, forced Amphiaraus to go on the doomed expedition of the Seven against Thebes, even though they both knew that he would never return. Before he left home for the last time, he charged his sons Alcmaeon and Amphilochus to avenge him. Ten years later a second expedition was mustered and the EPIGONI marched against Thebes. The two brothers took part, persuaded by Eriphyle who once again had been bribed, this time by

Polyneices' son Thersander with Harmonia's beautiful robe. But this second expedition, led by Alcmaeon himself, was a resounding success. The brothers returned safely home and Alcmaeon, on the instructions of Apollo's oracle at Delphi, killed Eriphyle. Amphiaraus was avenged.

According to Apollodorus, some said that Amphilochus helped his brother to do the deed; but we hear nothing more of this, nor of its consequences for Amphilochus. The consequences for Alcmaeon, however, were severe: he was pursued by his mother's FURIES, as was Orestes after the murder of Clytemnestra, and went mad. Leaving Argos, he went first to stay with his grandfather Oecles in Arcadia, then on to Psophis, where King Phegeus took him in and purified him. Alcmaeon married Phegeus' daughter Arsinoe (or Alphesiboea) and gave her Harmonia's robe and necklace, recovered from Eriphyle on her death. But he was still maddened by the Furies, and the land of Psophis became barren because it harboured a matricide, so once more he consulted the Delphic Oracle. He was told to seek further purification from the river-god ACHELOUS and to find a land that had not been in existence at the time of his mother's murder. He wandered far, staying for a while with Oeneus at Calydon, and visiting the Thesprotians, who drove him out of their land. According to one of Euripides' lost tragedies, at some stage in his wanderings he had two children by MANTO, the daughter of Teiresias. But at last he arrived at the mouth of the river Achelous. Here he discovered new land formed by alluvial deposits, so he settled there as the oracle had instructed, and Achelous not only purified him but married him to his daughter Callirhoe ('fair-flowing'). She bore Alcmaeon two sons, Acarnan, after whom the land was named Acarnania, and Amphoterus.

All was now well – until Callirhoe heard of the magnificent robe and necklace of Harmonia and wanted them for herself, threatening that she would leave Alcmaeon if he did not give them to her. So away he went reluctantly back to Psophis, where he lied to Phegeus, saying that he would be cured of his madness only if he dedicated the gifts at Delphi. Phegeus believed him and handed them over, but one of Alcmaeon's servants confessed his master's true purpose. Phegeus ordered his sons (Pronous and Agenor, or Temenus and Axion) to kill Alcmaeon. They did so, burying him in a grove of cypress trees.

Alcmaeon's first wife Arsinoe protested violently, so her brothers clapped her in a chest and took her to Tegea, where they gave her as a slave to the king, Agapenor, falsely accusing her of Alcmaeon's murder. Meanwhile Callirhoe, hearing of her husband's death, prayed to Zeus to make her sons grow up quickly, that they might lose no time in avenging him. Zeus, who loved her, granted her prayer and at once the boys became men. They too came to Agapenor's house and there killed the sons of Phegeus (and presumably freed Arsinoe, though it is not recorded); then going on to Psophis they killed Phegeus and his wife as well. At the command of Achelous, they dedicated the robe and necklace of Harmonia at Delphi, and now at last the beautiful objects could cause no more harm among men.

Pausanias, who saw Alcmaeon's tomb in its bleak upland valley in Psophis, says that the cypresses surrounding it were so tall that even the nearby mountain was overshadowed by them, but the local people refused to cut them down since they were sacred to Alcmaeon. Fraser adds (*Apollodorus: The Library*, vol. 1, p. 385): 'A quiet resting-place for the matricide among the solemn Arcadian mountains after the long fever of the brain and the long weary wanderings.'

[Thucydides 2.102.5–6; Apollodorus 1.8.6, 3.6.2, 3.7.2–7; Pausanias 8.24.7–10; Ovid, *Metamorphoses* 9.407–17.]

Alcmene

Daughter of ELECTRYON, king of Mycenae; wife of AMPHITRYON; mother by ZEUS of HERACLES and by Amphitryon of IPHICLES. Alcmene's seduction by Zeus is one of the great god's most famous affairs. Alcmene, a girl of exceptional beauty, was married to Amphitryon, but she refused to consummate their marriage until he had avenged the deaths of her eight brothers, killed by the Taphians during a cattle raid. Not surprisingly, her husband set off with alacrity on an expedition against the Taphians, and was on the point of arriving home, triumphant and laden with booty, when Zeus saw his moment. He came to Alcmene disguised as Amphitryon and recounted the victory over the Taphians. Delighted to hear of it and completely taken in, she welcomed him to her bed. Zeus even prolonged the night to three times its usual length by persuading the Sun-god HELIOS not to rise for three days, so that he might enjoy Alcmene to the full.

As soon as Zeus left, Amphitryon himself arrived and was amazed to find, when he went to his wife's bed, that she knew all about his victory and was sure that she had already slept with him. Bewildered, he consulted the blind seer TEIRESIAS and was told what Zeus had done. Several vase-paintings exist illustrating Amphitryon's

reaction and may well have been inspired by the *Alcmene* of Euripides (fig. 13): Alcmene has taken refuge at an altar, around which Amphitryon has piled wood for a fire that he is lighting (presumably he has come to believe that his wife was seduced by some mortal lover). But Zeus intervenes, sending thunderbolts to discourage Amphitryon and rain to put out the fire. Faced with this divine intervention, Amphitryon forgave his wife, and in the course of time she gave birth to twins, Zeus' son Heracles and Amphitryon's son Iphicles, though not without more troubles (*see* EURYSTHEUS and GALANTHIS).

After Heracles' death, Alcmene and his children were persecuted by Eurystheus. When finally Eurystheus was killed, his head was taken to Alcmene who, in an ecstasy of triumph, gouged out his eyes with weaving-pins. Amphitryon was by now dead too, and it was said that she married the Cretan lawgiver RHADAMANTHYS.

The comic possibilities of Amphitryon's cuckolding by Zeus have appealed to dramatists of all ages, with famous comedies by Plautus, Molière, John Dryden (with music by Purcell) and Jean Giraudoux.

See also fig. 78.

[Homer, *Iliad* 14.323–4, *Odyssey* 11.266–8; Hesiod, *Shield of Heracles* 1–56; Pindar, *Isthmian* 7.5–7; Apollodorus 2.4.5–8, 2.8.1; Pausanias 5.18.3.]

Fig. 13 Alcmene sits on an altar and cries to Zeus for help, while Amphitryon (*right*) and Antenor light a pile of wood stacked in front. Clouds pour down water to douse the flames.

Alcon

A Cretan archer, so skilled with his bow that when a snake wrapped itself around his sleeping child, he shot the snake without harming the child. A similar story is told of another Alcon, an Athenian, and father of the Argonaut Phalerus.

[Apollonius, *Argonautica* 1.95–100; Virgil, *Eclogues* 5.11 and Servius *ad loc.*; Valerius Flaccus, *Argonautica* 1.398–401.]

Alcyone (1)

Daughter of the Titan ATLAS and Pleione, and thus one of the seven PLEIADES. She bore to POSEIDON two sons, HYRIEUS, the father of Nycteus and Lycus, and Hyperenor, and a daughter, Aethusa, the mother of Eleuther by Apollo.

[Apollodorus 3.10.1.]

Alcyone (2)

A daughter of AEOLUS (1) and Enarete. She was married to Ceyx, the son of the morning star, and both were turned into birds. One version of their story, found in Apollodorus (1.7.3–4), says that in their arrogance Ceyx and Alcyone called themselves ZEUS and HERA, until Zeus punished them with transformation, Alcyone into a kingfisher and Ceyx into some kind of sea-bird, perhaps a gannet or a tern. But Ovid (*Metamorphoses* 11.410–748) tells a more romantic story about the pair, who loved each other devotedly. One day Ceyx sailed away to consult an oracle, despite Alcyone's strong premonition of disaster – which turned out to be justified, for during the voyage his ship was wrecked and he drowned. Meanwhile Alcyone, eagerly awaiting his return, kept sacrificing to Hera for his safety until at last the goddess took pity on her ignorance and hope, sending her a dream in which MORPHEUS told her the truth of her husband's death by drowning. Overcome with grief, Alcyone awoke and rushed to the seashore, where she saw Ceyx' body washed towards her. The gods took pity on her inconsolable sorrow and transformed them both into halcyons, kingfishers, that they might carry on living together and loving each other. Every winter they mated, and the gods calmed the sea for seven days – the Halcyon Days – while Alcyone brooded peacefully over her nest, floating on the sea, and hatched her eggs.

Alcyone (3)

Daughter of Idas and MARPESSA, renamed Cleopatra by Homer.

Alcyoneus

One of the GIANTS. Apollodorus (1.6.1) tells us that he and his brother PORPHYRION were the strongest of them all, and that Alcyoneus himself was even immortal so long as he remained within the land of his birth, Phlegrae in Thrace, later called Pallene. In the battle between the Gods and the Giants, HERACLES, the only mortal taking part, shot Alcyoneus with an arrow, but when the giant fell on his native ground he began to revive. On Athena's advice, Heracles dragged him beyond the bounds of Pallene and he died.

Apollodorus adds that Alcyoneus stole the cattle of HELIOS, the Sun-god, from Erytheia. Pindar calls him a 'herdsman', and says that he was 'huge as a mountain' (*Isthmian* 6.32); but he appears to regard the combat leading to the giant's death as an isolated one, and with mortals, since Heracles was helped by TELAMON: 'They killed the mighty warrior,' he says, 'though not before he had hurled a rock and destroyed twelve chariots, and twice that number of heroic horsemen riding within them' (*Nemean* 4.25–30). Yet another variant seems to appear in Greek art, where Alcyoneus is shown reclining, and often even asleep, as Heracles approaches him, suggesting that here Heracles takes advantage of his slumber to kill him. But here, too, cattle are involved, for sometimes a herd of cows is shown nearby.

Alecto or Allecto *see* FURIES.

Aletes

Son of AEGISTHUS and CLYTEMNESTRA, and thus half-brother to ORESTES, ELECTRA (3), IPHIGENEIA and CHRYSOTHEMIS. Hyginus (*Fabula* 122) recounts a story, sounding like a lost tragedy, whereby Aletes seized the throne of Mycenae after hearing a false report that Orestes had been killed by the Taurians. Electra went to Delphi to get confirmation of this news and there met Orestes himself with Iphigeneia. At first, failing to recognise her brother, Electra almost killed Iphigeneia because she believed her responsible for Orestes' death. Then, reunited, the three returned to Mycenae, where Orestes killed Aletes and would have killed his sister ERIGONE (2) too, had not Artemis carried her off to be a priestess in Athens.

Alexander *see* PARIS.

Alexandra *see* CASSANDRA.

Aloadae *see* OTUS.

Aloeus

Son of POSEIDON and CANACE (1). *See* OTUS.

Alope

Daughter of CERCYON, the evil king of Eleusis. We know her sad story from Hyginus (*Fabula* 187), though Euripides wrote a tragedy *Alope*, now lost, which may well lie behind Hyginus' narrative. Alope became pregnant by

POSEIDON, but she was afraid of her father's anger and so kept her condition a secret. Even more fearful when her son was at last born, she dressed him in warm clothes and abandoned him in the countryside. He lived, suckled by a mare no doubt sent by Poseidon, until he was found by a shepherd. This man gave him to another shepherd, but they quarrelled over the ownership of the fine clothes that the baby was wearing. Unable to settle the matter, they asked Cercyon to arbitrate. Unfortunately he recognised the clothes as his daughter's work and the truth came out. He locked Alope away to die, then exposed the baby for a second time. Once again it was suckled by a mare until found by shepherds, and this time the boy was saved and successfully brought up. He was called Hippothoon ('horse-swift') – a name recalling both the mare that saved him and his father Poseidon, god of horses.

In due course Cercyon was killed by THESEUS, and when Hippothoon asked to be made ruler of Eleusis in his place, Theseus granted his request. One of the ten tribes of Athens was named after Hippothoon.

[Pausanias 1.5.2, 1.39.3.]

Alpheius

The name of the largest river in the Peloponnese and its god. The Alpheius, rising in Arcadia and flowing past Olympia, was like all rivers the offspring of OCEANUS and Tethys. It was one of the rivers diverted by Heracles to cleanse the dung-filled stables of AUGEAS, but the river-god also has a far more romantic story associated with him. Alpheius fell in love with the nymph Arethusa when she bathed in his waters, but she fled from his embrace, even as far away as Sicily. Here, on the island of Ortygia at the entrance to the bay of Syracuse, she was turned by Artemis into the spring called Arethusa. But Alpheius did not give up his love. He flowed beneath the sea all the way to Ortygia and there mingled his waters with those of the spring.

Strabo (6.2.4) expresses a natural disbelief in the possibility of this phenomenon physically occurring, but reports the claim that a cup thrown into the Alpheius reappeared in the spring of Arethusa on Ortygia, and that the spring was discoloured as a result of the sacrifices of oxen at Olympia.

[Homer, *Iliad* 5.541–9; Hesiod, *Theogony* 338; Pausanias 5.7.1–3; Virgil, *Aeneid* 3.692–6; Ovid, *Metamorphoses* 5.572–641.]

Alphesiboea (1)

An Asian nymph who was passionately loved by DIONYSUS, but long refused to yield to his desires. One day he was inspired to transform himself into a tiger. Alphe-siboea fled in terror, and when she found her escape blocked by the great River Sollax, she was only too happy to entrust herself to the god if he would carry her across to safety. She bore him a son, Medus, who gave his name to the Medes; and the name of the river was changed to the Tigris.

Alphesiboea (2)

The name given by Pausanias (8.24.8) to the daughter of Phegeus and first wife of ALCMAEON, usually called Arsinoe.

Alseids *see* NYMPHS.

Althaea

The daughter of THESTIUS, and the wife of OENEUS, king of Calydon, by whom she had several sons and daughters, the best known being MELEAGER, DEIANEIRA and GORGE, though Meleager was sometimes said to be the son of ARES, and Deianeira the daughter of DIONYSUS. When Meleager was born, Althaea was told by the FATES that he would live only until a log, then burning on the hearth, was completely consumed. Hastily she quenched the flames and put the log safely away in a chest. Many years later, when Meleager had killed two of her brothers in the fight that followed the Calydonian Boarhunt, she took the log out again and angrily flung it into the fire. It burnt to ashes, and her son died. She killed herself in despair.

Althaemenes

The son of CATREUS, king of Crete. When an oracle fore-told that Catreus would be killed by one of his own children, Althaemenes emigrated with his sister Apemosyne to Rhodes. Here he founded a town called Cretinia, named in memory of his homeland, and also a shrine of Atabyrian Zeus on the top of Mount Atabyria from which, on a clear day, Crete could be seen. Soon after-wards he murdered his sister: she was desired by HERMES, but when the god pursued her she ran too fast for him, so he spread fresh hides in her path on which she slipped and fell. There he raped her. She told Althaemenes what had happened, but he refused to believe her and kicked her to death.

When Catreus grew old, he wanted to bequeath his kingdom to his son, so he came to Rhodes to find him. On landing, however, he and his men were taken for pirates and attacked by some cowherds. Althaemenes appeared, but failing to recognise his father he killed him with a javelin, thus fulfilling the old oracle. When he realised his victim's identity, he prayed to the gods and was swallowed up by the earth.

[Apollodorus 3.2.1–2.]

Amaltheia

Amaltheia was either the goat on whose milk the infant ZEUS was fed when his mother RHEA (1) took him for safety to Crete, far away from his cannibalistic father, Cronus, or the nymph who owned the goat that suckled the god. From one of the goat's horns flowed ambrosia and from the other nectar. Zeus later gave one of the horns in thanks to the nymphs who had reared him, at the same time ordaining that it would produce whatever food and drink they might wish for. This was the original *cornu copiae*, the 'Horn of Plenty'. Out of gratitude Zeus also immortalised the goat in the sky as the star Capella, 'little she-goat', in the constellation Auriga.

[Callimachus, *Hymn* 1.46–8; Apollodorus 1.1.6–7, 2.7.5; Diodorus Siculus 5.70; Ovid, *Fasti* 5.111–28.]

Amarynceus

The son of Pittius, a Thessalian immigrant to Elis. After Heracles had been refused his payment for cleaning out the 'Augean Stables', he marched against AUGEAS, the king of Elis, who gave Amarynceus a share of the kingdom in return for military help. Amarynceus had a son, Diores, who became one of the leaders of the Elean contingent to the Trojan War and was killed by the Thracian leader Peirus. Perhaps Amarynceus is most famous for the funeral games held in his honour at Buprasium. Old NESTOR tells of his own outstanding performance there: he won the boxing, the wrestling, the spear-throwing and the footrace, and was beaten only in the chariot-race by the MOLIONES.

Fig. 14 Theseus *(left)* fights the Amazons.

[Homer, *Iliad* 2.615–24, 4.517–26, 23.629–45; Pausanias 5.1.10–11.]

Amata

Wife of LATINUS, the king of Latium, and mother of Lavinia. Of all her daughter's many suitors, Amata wished her to marry TURNUS, the young king of the Rutulians, but an oracle had warned that she should marry a foreigner. So when AENEAS arrived in Italy, Latinus was happy to accept him as a husband for Lavinia. The Fury Allecto, sent by Juno, stirred up mad hostility to the strangers in both Amata and Turnus, then caused a needless quarrel between Latins and Trojans that led to a bloody war. Eventually Turnus and Aeneas agreed to settle the outcome by single combat, despite Amata's desperate attempt to dissuade Turnus from such a course of action. When she falsely believed her favourite dead, distraught with grief and guilt she hanged herself. Soon afterwards Turnus was indeed killed by Aeneas, who then married Lavinia.

[Virgil, *Aeneid* 7.52–8, 341–405, 12.54–80, 593–611.]

Amazons

A mythical race of female warriors who lived by hunting and delighted in war. Their home was rather vaguely located to the east or north-east of Greece, at the outer reaches of the known world. There they lived apart from men, though for purposes of procreation they would copulate occasionally with males from neighbouring tribes. Naturally they reared only the female infants born to them. Their name, supposedly meaning 'breastless' (*maza*, 'breast'), was said to derive from their custom of amputating the right breast to facilitate their use of weapons during battle (the left breast was needed to suckle their daughters). But there is no trace of this physical singularity in ancient art, where Amazons are an immensely popular subject from the seventh century BC, both in vase-painting and sculpture, and are often depicted with their (intact) right breast exposed. They usually appear in scenes of conflict (fig.14), fighting with spears and bows, and sometimes axes. Battles between Amazons and victorious Greeks were often seen as symbolising the triumph of the values of civilisation over the forces of barbarism.

A number of legends tell of Greek heroes fighting and overcoming the Amazons. BELLEROPHON conquered them as one of the three fearsome tasks set for him by Iobates. HERACLES, as his ninth Labour for Eurystheus, fought them while fetching the girdle of HIPPOLYTE (1). His companion THESEUS carried off the Amazon queen and later had the whole tribe of Amazons march against Athens (*see* ANTIOPE (2)). PENTHESILEIA led an army of Amazons to assist King Priam in the Trojan War, and killed many Greeks before she was in turn killed by Achilles, who fell in love with her even as he delivered the fatal wound.

[Homer, *Iliad* 3.184–9, 6.186; Herodotus 4.110–17; Apollodorus 2.3.2, 2.5.8; Diodorus Siculus 2.45–6, 3.53–5, 4.28, 17.77; Pausanias 1.15.2, 1.17.2, 1.25.2, 4.31.8, 5.11.7, 7.2.7–8; Virgil, *Aeneid* 11.648–63. D. von Bothmer, *Amazons in Greek Art* (1957); W. B. Tyrrell, *Amazons: A Study in Athenian Mythmaking* (1984); J. Blok, *The Early Amazons* (1995).]

Amor

The Roman name for EROS, god of Love.

Ampelus

A beautiful youth loved by DIONYSUS, who gave him a vine laden with grapes as a token of his love. The vine hung from the branches of an elm tree, and the unfortunate boy fell to his death while picking the fruit. In another version he died when gored by a wild bull. Dionysus named the vine (*ampelos*) after him, that he might be remembered for ever when his fruits brought joy to men.

[Nonnus, *Dionysiaca* 10.175–12.397; Ovid, *Fasti* 3.409–14.]

Amphiaraus

A famous seer, son of Oecles and Hypermestra and descendant of the great seer MELAMPUS. On the resolution of a quarrel with ADRASTUS (1), Amphiaraus married Adrastus' sister ERIPHYLE, and both men agreed that she would have the right to settle any future dispute between them. For many years no dispute arose, but this calm state of affairs changed when Adrastus began to organise the expedition of the SEVEN AGAINST THEBES, in a bid to win the throne of Thebes for Polyneices, the exiled son of Oedipus. Through his prophetic skills Amphiaraus knew that the expedition was doomed to disaster, and that none of its leaders except Adrastus would live to return, so he was reluctant to support the cause and tried to discourage all the other warriors from doing so. Polyneices now asked Eriphyle for her support, bribing her with the beautiful necklace that had belonged to his ancestress Harmonia. Eriphyle greedily took the necklace and forced Amphiaraus to join the expedition. True to his old agreement with Adrastus, he did so, but not before he had charged his two sons, ALCMAEON and Amphilochus, to avenge his expected death.

On the army's journey to Thebes, Amphiaraus interpreted another portent of doom when the baby Opheltes was killed at Nemea. The subsequent attack on Thebes turned into a disaster when its leaders, one by one, were killed. As his comrade TYDEUS lay dying, Amphiaraus divined that Athena was about to give him the gift of immortality, and since the seer still resented Tydeus for helping to initiate the calamitous expedition, he cut off the head of the dead Theban Melanippus and gave it to the dying man. Tydeus at once began to gnaw on his enemy's brains, a sight so barbaric that the disgusted goddess withheld her intended gift and allowed her former favourite to die. Amphiaraus himself fled, driven from the battlefield by his charioteer, Baton or Elato, and hotly pursued by the Theban Periclymenus. The seer was about to be speared in the back when Zeus, taking pity on him, split open the earth ahead of him with a thunderbolt. Amphiaraus was swallowed up, chariot, charioteer, horses and all, and in this fashion he descended to the Underworld, where he was said to live on, still fully alive and immortalised by Zeus.

Pausanias, travelling in the second century AD, saw the seer's famous oracular shrine at Oropus, between Attica and Boeotia, where dreams were interpreted and the sick healed. He also saw not far from Thebes the place where, so it was said, Amphiaraus disappeared into the earth. It was a small enclosure, with pillars in it on which no bird ever sat, and with fresh grass which no beast, tame or wild, would ever graze.

[Homer, *Odyssey* 11.326–7, 15.243–8; Pindar, *Olympian* 6.12–17, *Pythian* 8.38–55, *Nemean* 9.13–27; Herodotus 1.46, 1.52, 8.134; Aeschylus, *Seven Against Thebes* 568–625; Sophocles, *Electra* 837–48; Euripides, *Phoenician Women*

1109–12, *Suppliant Women* 925–7; Apollodorus 1.8.2, 1.9.13, 3.6.2–6; Pausanias 1.34.1–5, 2.23.2, 8.2.4, 9.8.3, 9.19.4.]

Amphictyon

The fourth mythical king of Athens. He was either the son of DEUCALION (1) and Pyrrha, or else sprung from the earth of Attica. He married a daughter of the ruling king, CRANAUS, and subsequently deposed his father-in-law. He himself ruled for twelve years before being deposed by ERICHTHONIUS (1).

[Apollodorus 1.7.2, 3.14.6; Pausanias 1.2.5–6, 10.8.1–2.]

Amphilochus (1)

Younger son of the seer AMPHIARAUS and his treacherous wife ERIPHYLE, and brother of ALCMAEON. Amphilochus was one of the EPIGONI who marched against Thebes and captured the city ten years after a similar expedition had brought their fathers to death. As for the rest of his history, he is frequently confused with his nephew AMPHILOCHUS (2). He (or his nephew) was one of the suitors of HELEN and fought in the TROJAN WAR. On his return from the war, he was dissatisfied with the situation in his homeland of Argos, so he founded another Argos on the Ambracian Gulf in southern Epeirus. He accompanied the seer CALCHAS to Colophon, where a famous contest took place between Calchas and the greater seer MOPSUS (1). Amphilochus and Mopsus jointly founded Mallus in Cilicia, but unfortunately their rivalry over the kingdom brought about their deaths. They afterwards shared a famous oracle there.

[Thucydides 2.68.3; Apollodorus 3.6.2, 3.7.2, 3.7.7, 3.10.8, *Epitome* 6.2, 6.19; Pausanias 1.34.3, 2.18.4–5, 3.15.8.]

Amphilochus (2)

Son of ALCMAEON and Teiresias' daughter MANTO, and brother of Tisiphone. According to Apollodorus (3.7.7), one of Euripides' two lost tragedies *Alcmaeon* told how Alcmaeon gave his two children to be brought up by CREON (1), the king of Corinth. Tisiphone grew up to be very beautiful, so Creon's jealous wife sold her as a slave. She was bought, quite unrecognised, by Alcmaeon himself, who then went to Corinth and recovered Amphilochus.

For the rest of Amphilochus' history, *see* AMPHILOCHUS (1).

Amphimachus

Son of Cteatus, one of the Siamese twins known as the MOLIONES, and grandson of POSEIDON. Amphimachus led one of the Elean contingents of ten ships to the TROJAN WAR, where he was killed by HECTOR. The Great Ajax saved his corpse from the Trojans, and the Lesser Ajax, angry at Amphimachus' death, hewed off the head of Imbrius and flung it like a ball to land at Hector's feet. Poseidon too

was angered by his grandson's death, and avenged himself on the Trojans by stirring up the Greeks to fight mightily against them.

[Homer, *Iliad* 2.615–24, 13.184–209.]

Amphinomus

In Homer's *Odyssey*, Amphinomus is the son of Nisus, from Doulichium, and is one of the Suitors, the young men who have invaded ODYSSEUS' house during his long absence, carousing at his expense and hoping to marry his wife PENELOPE. Amphinomus is the least obnoxious of them: he tries to dissuade the others from following ANTINOUS' suggestion to murder TELEMACHUS, and is best-liked by Penelope because of his good sense (16.394–405). When Odysseus comes home to the palace disguised as a beggar, Amphinomus is friendly towards him, and Odysseus advises him to leave before disaster falls, warning him as clearly as he can that there is likely to be bloodshed because of the Suitors' behaviour (18.118–50). But Amphinomus stays. He is the third Suitor to die in the general massacre, killed by Telemachus (22.89–94).

Amphion and Zethus

Twin sons of ZEUS and ANTIOPE (1). Their mother gave birth to them on Mount Cithaeron while she was travelling as a captive of her uncle, LYCUS (1). He left the babies abandoned on the mountainside and returned with Antiope to Thebes, but a herdsman found the boys and took them home to his cottage. There they grew up. Eventually they were reunited with Antiope, who had spent many wretched years enslaved to Lycus' wife Dirce. They avenged their mother's miseries by tying Dirce to a wild bull so that she was torn and trampled to death, a fate that she herself had intended for Antiope. They also killed Lycus, or drove him out of Thebes where he had been ruling as regent for the young LAIUS, son of Labdacus. Laius now found a home with Pelops, the king of Pisa in Elis, and Amphion and Zethus took over the joint rule of Thebes.

Although they were twins, their natures were very different. Zethus was a down-to-earth man, skilled in the practical pursuits of agriculture, cattle-breeding and war. Amphion was a brilliant musician, playing so beautifully on his lyre, given him by HERMES, that animals and birds and even stones followed him. Each of the brothers used his own particular skill when they came to build walls around Thebes, with Zethus' strength and practical ability paying dividends, but Amphion's musicianship even more so, for when he played his lyre the stones fitted themselves into place of their own accord. Amphion had married NIOBE (2), daughter of the Lydian Tantalus, and had not only learnt the Lydian mode of music but had added three new strings to the four that his lyre already possessed. Now the brothers gave their city-walls seven gates, one for each lyre-string; and their city, previously known as Cadmeia after its founder, CADMUS, was renamed Thebes after Zethus' wife Thebe (although another tradition named his wife as AEDON – see below).

Both brothers died in grief. Amphion's marriage to Niobe was blessed with many children, but Niobe rashly boasted that she was superior to the goddess Leto, who had only two offspring, and the offended goddess sent APOLLO and ARTEMIS to earth to avenge the insult. Apollo killed the couple's sons and Artemis their daughters. Niobe returned to Lydia where the gods turned her into a rock on Mount Sipylus, with tears of everlasting sorrow flowing down her face. Amphion died: either he was killed along with his sons, or he committed suicide from grief, or he tried to take vengeance on Apollo and was shot by the god while attacking his temple. Zethus died of a broken heart when his wife accidentally killed their son. With both brothers dead, Laius returned from Pisa to take the throne of Thebes.

In the *Odyssey*, Homer records a slightly different tradition about the brothers: that Amphion was the son of Iasus and ruled Orchomenus in Boeotia, and that Zethus was married to a daughter of Pandareos, Aedon, who killed their son Itylus by mistake and was turned into a nightingale.

[Homer, *Odyssey* 11.260–5, 283–4, 19.518–24; Apollonius, *Argonautica* 1.735–41; Apollodorus 3.5.5–6; Pausanias 6.20.18, 9.5.6–9, 9.8.4, 9.17.2–5.]

Amphissus *see* DRYOPE.

Amphithemis *see* ACACALLIS and CAPHAURUS.

Amphitrite

A sea-goddess, daughter of NEREUS and Doris and thus one of the NEREIDS. She was the wife of POSEIDON, god of the sea, and lived with him in his glorious golden palace beneath the waves. When Poseidon first wooed her, she fled from him into the sea, so he sent all the sea-creatures, his servants, to seek her. A dolphin was the first to find her, and pleaded so persuasively for his master that she gave in and married him. She bore Poseidon a son, the merman TRITON, and daughters, the nymphs RHODE and Benthesicyme. Out of gratitude to the dolphin, the god immortalised him in the stars as the constellation Delphinus.

Amphitrite usually appears in myth as a personification of the sea, as when Homer, in the *Odyssey*, speaks of 'the waves of Amphitrite' (3.90), of 'the great swell of dark-eyed Amphitrite' (12.60), and of sea-monsters 'like

Fig. 15 **Poseidon, holding a trident, sits with his queen, Amphitrite.**

those that famous Amphitrite fosters in such numbers' (5.422). She does, however, play a small part in the myth of THESEUS. Bacchylides (*Ode* 17) recounts how Minos threw his ring into the sea, challenging Theseus to fetch it back and thus prove that Poseidon was his father. Undaunted, Theseus leapt into the sea and was taken by dolphins to Poseidon's palace. Here Amphitrite gave him a crimson cloak and set on his head a garland, dark with roses, that had been given to her on her marriage by APHRODITE herself.

In ancient art Amphitrite is usually depicted in the company of Poseidon (figs. 15 and 121). On the François Krater the pair attend the wedding of Peleus and Thetis, riding together in the second chariot behind Zeus and Hera. Amphitrite is a popular subject also in the postclassical arts, usually in stylised sea-triumphs.

[Hesiod, *Theogony* 243, 252–4, 930–3; Apollodorus 1.2.7, 1.4.5, 3.15.4; Pausanias 1.17.3.]

Amphitryon

Son of Alcaeus and Astydameia, and grandson of PERSEUS. Amphitryon married ALCMENE, the daughter of his uncle ELECTRYON who had been king of Mycenae since Perseus' death. But Electryon decreed that the marriage must not be consummated until vengeance had been taken on the Taphians (also called the Teleboans) for stealing his cattle and killing his sons, Alcmene's brothers. First, however, Amphitryon recovered the cattle and brought them safely back to Mycenae. Unfortunately, as he was returning them to the king, one of the cows charged and he

Fig. 16 Amycus has been bound to a rock by the Dioscuri, one of whom (no doubt Polydeuces) holds a strigil, a reference to the boxing match in which Amycus was defeated.

threw a club at her, which rebounded and killed Electryon himself. STHENELUS (1), Electryon's brother, then seized the throne and banished Amphitryon, who went with Alcmene and Electryon's bastard son, LICYMNIUS, to Thebes, where he was purified of his unintentional manslaughter by CREON (2).

The deaths of Alcmene's brothers had still to be avenged, and Creon agreed to help if Amphitryon first got rid of the TEUMESSIAN VIXEN, a fierce fox, fated never to be caught, that was preying cruelly on the people of Thebes. Amphitryon called for the aid of a famous hunting dog belonging to CEPHALUS (2): Laelaps, a hound that was fated never to miss its quarry. The inescapable hound ran after the uncatchable fox until Zeus ended the everlasting pursuit by turning both animals to stone.

After this success, Creon helped Amphitryon in his vengeance on the Taphians. Together with a few other allies they made a triumphant raid on the islands, helped by the treachery of the king's daughter, Comaetho, who had fallen in love with Amphitryon (*see* PTERELAUS). Returning to Thebes, laden with booty, Amphitryon at last had the right to consummate his marriage with Alcmene. Zeus, however, had pre-empted him, and in due course Alcmene gave birth to twin boys: HERACLES, the mightiest of all the mortal sons of Zeus, and IPHICLES, the son of Amphitryon. When they were only eight months old it became clear which of the pair was the son of the god: two huge snakes crawled into the boys' bed,

at which Iphicles screamed in terror, while Heracles grasped the snakes and strangled them with his baby hands (fig. 78). Some say that Hera sent the snakes because of her hostility to Heracles, others that Amphitryon did so to find out which of the children was his own son.

For the rest of his life Amphitryon lived at Thebes. At one time he led the Thebans to victory in battle against the Euboeans, killing their leader, Chalcodon. Amphitryon is a character in Euripides' tragedy *The Madness of Heracles*, where LYCUS (2) has in Heracles' absence usurped the throne of Thebes by killing Creon. He is on the very point of killing Amphitryon, together with Heracles' wife and three children, when Heracles returns and kills the usurper. In his hour of triumph, Heracles is tragically driven mad by Hera and himself kills his wife and children. Amphitryon almost becomes a victim too, but Athena halts Heracles by striking him unconscious with a rock. In fact Amphitryon met a courageous death on the battlefield while he was fighting with Heracles against ERGINUS (1) and the Minyans.

See also fig. 13.

[Hesiod, *Shield of Heracles* 79–89; Pindar, *Nemean* 1.33–72; Herodotus 5.59; Apollodorus 2.4.5–11; Pausanias 8.15.6, 9.17.3, 9.19.3.]

Amphoterus *see* ALCMAEON.

Amulius

A king of Alba Longa who usurped the rule from his elder brother Numitor. He then murdered Numitor's sons, and tried to kill his grandsons, ROMULUS AND REMUS. Instead they grew up to kill Amulius himself and to restore the rule to Numitor.

Amyclas *see* LACEDAEMON.

Amycus

A king of the Bebrycians, and the son of POSEIDON and a nymph, Melia. He was a savage man, in the habit of challenging all visitors to his land to a boxing contest (which in the ancient world was a much more violent, bloody and deadly affair than its modern equivalent). He always won, and always killed his opponent. He met his match, however, when the ARGONAUTS came to his country and for one last time he uttered his challenge. This was willingly taken up by one of the DIOSCURI, the expert boxer Polydeuces, whose skill and suppleness defeated his opponent's huge size and brute strength. After a hard fight, Polydeuces killed Amycus with a shattering blow to the head. (Apollodorus says implausibly that the fatal blow was to the elbow.)

According to Theocritus, Amycus survived and was

persuaded to mend his ways. Castor and Polydeuces met him by a spring, but he would not allow them to drink until they had boxed with him. They agreed that the winner might do what he liked with the loser, then Polydeuces beat Amycus soundly. He contented himself with making Amycus promise never again to abuse strangers. This version may go back to the fifth century BC and Sophocles' satyr play *Amycus*, since artistic representations of this period and later show Amycus being tied up by Polydeuces, suggesting a non-fatal resolution of their conflict (fig. 16).

[Apollonius, *Argonautica* 2.1–97, 754–95; Theocritus 22.27–134; Apollodorus 1.9.20, 2.5.9.]

Amymone

One of DANAUS' fifty daughters. When Danaus arrived in the Argolid in his flight from Aegyptus, he sent his daughters out into the arid land to find water. As Amymone searched, she happened to throw her javelin at a deer. She missed, but hit a sleeping SATYR. He leapt up and tried to rape her, and she was saved only by the sudden appearance of POSEIDON, who flung his trident and drove the satyr away (satyrs were as cowardly as they were lustful), then took the girl for himself. Afterwards the god tore his trident from the rock and out flowed a spring of water, thereafter called the spring of Lerna, and also Amymone after the girl. So she found her water and returned to her father successful in her quest. She was also pregnant by Poseidon, and bore a son, NAUPLIUS (1), who became a famous seaman. Aeschylus' (lost) satyr play *Amymone*, which followed the Danaid trilogy, told her story.

[Apollodorus 2.1.4; Strabo 8.6.8; Pausanias 2.37.1 and 4; Lucian, *Dialogues of the Sea-gods* 8; Propertius 2.26.45–50.]

Amyntor

Son of Ormenus and king of Eleon or Ormenium, at the foot of Mount Pelion. His son, PHOENIX (3), quarrelled irrevocably with Amyntor after sleeping with his father's favourite concubine, and left his home and country for ever. Amyntor also had a daughter, Astydameia, whom HERACLES wanted to marry. Amyntor refused because Heracles was already married to Deianeira, but he raped the girl anyway and she had a son, Ctesippus. Pindar says that she bore him TLEPOLEMUS. Heracles also killed Amyntor himself when the king took arms and tried to stop him passing through his territory.

Amyntor was the original owner of the famous boar's tusk helmet, stolen from him by the master-thief AUTOLYCUS and later passed to Odysseus, who wore it during his night-time spying expedition into the Trojan camp with Diomedes.

[Homer, *Iliad* 9.447–84, 10.260–71; Pindar, *Olympian* 7.20–38; Apollodorus 2.7.7, 2.7.8, 3.13.8; Diodorus Siculus 4.37.4.]

Amythaon

Son of CRETHEUS, king of Iolcus, and TYRO. He married Idomene, the daughter of his brother Pheres, and the couple migrated from Thessaly to Pylos in Messenia where they brought up their two sons, MELAMPUS (who became a famous seer) and Bias. Amythaon and his sons supported JASON in his bid to reclaim the throne of Iolcus from the usurper PELIAS.

[Homer, *Odyssey* 11.258; Pindar, *Pythian* 4.124–6; Apollodorus 1.9.11; Pausanias 5.8.2.]

Anaxarete

A Cypriot princess, descended from the line of Teucer, who according to Ovid (*Metamorphoses* 14.698–758) was loved by a humble man named Iphis. She, however, was a cruel and arrogant girl, and she mocked him callously until at last he was driven to hang himself from the lintel of her door. On the day of his funeral procession, she climbed to the top of the house to look down on the street from her windows, and as soon as she saw Iphis, dead of love for her and lying on his bier, the life left her body and she was turned to stone, to match the hardness of her heart.

Anaxibia (1)

Daughter of Bias and Lysippe, and wife of PELIAS, king of Iolcus.

Anaxibia (2)

Daughter, according to Hesiod, of PLEISTHENES and Cleolla, and sister of the Atreidae, AGAMEMNON and MENELAUS. She married STROPHIUS, king of Phocis, and was the mother of PYLADES.

[Hesiod, *Catalogue of Women* fr. 194; Pausanias 2.29.4.]

Ancaeus (1)

Son of LYCURGUS (2), king of Arcadia. Ancaeus sailed with the ARGONAUTS, dressed in a bearskin and armed with a two-headed axe, and because of his great strength he was chosen to row next to the mighty HERACLES. His grandfather Aleus, afraid that he would be killed on the expedition, tried to stop him setting out by hiding his weapons in the depths of the corn-store. But Ancaeus survived all the hardships and perils, acquitting himself well, and returned safely home.

He also went on the CALYDONIAN BOARHUNT; but here he was not so fortunate, for as he rushed at the huge boar, swinging his great axe, the beast gored him in the groin and he died. He left behind him a son, AGAPENOR, who led the Arcadian forces to the Trojan War. In ancient art Ancaeus (though here spelt Antaeus) appears first in the François Krater's depiction of the Boarhunt, lying dead beneath the enormous boar (fig. 34), and after this he becomes a standard figure in such scenes.

[Homer, *Iliad* 2.603–14; Bacchylides, *Ode* 5.115–20; Apollonius, *Argonautica* 1.161–71, 396–400, 2.118–21; Apollodorus 1.8.2, 3.9.2; Pausanias 8.4.10, 8.45.2, 8.45.4–7; Ovid, *Metamorphoses* 8.315–407.]

Ancaeus (2)

Son of POSEIDON and Astydameia, the daughter of Phoenix, and king of the Leleges on Samos, the island named after his wife Samia, daughter of the river-god Maeander. He was often confused with ANCAEUS (1). Like ANCAEUS (1) he sailed with the ARGONAUTS, and being an able steersman he took over the helm on the death of TIPHYS. Again like ANCAEUS (1) he survived the expedition, only to be killed by a boar. He owned a vineyard planted some years previously, but a seer had warned him that he would never live to taste the wine from it. Now safely home again, he filled a cup with wine and lifted it to his lips, reproaching the seer as he did so for his false prophecy. The seer replied, 'There is many a slip 'twixt the cup and the lip!', and at that very moment a servant cried out that a wild boar was ravaging the vineyard. Ancaeus leapt up, his wine still untasted, and ran to drive off the beast with his spear. The boar gored him to death, and the seer's saying became proverbial.

[Apollonius, *Argonautica* 1.185–9 (and the scholiast on 1.185), 2.851–98; Apollodorus 1.9.23; Pausanias 7.4.1.]

Anchinoe

Daughter of the river-god Nile and wife of BELUS.

Anchises

Son of CAPYS (1), king of Dardania, and Themiste; and great-grandson through both his parents of TROS. Ancient literature gives us two vivid but very different images of Anchises. The first, found in the *Homeric Hymn to Aphrodite*, is of the young prince, tending his cattle on Mount IDA; he is so beautiful that APHRODITE herself falls in love with him. She has all too often inflicted helpless love on the other gods and goddesses, but now by the contrivance of Zeus it is her turn to be tormented with desire for a mortal. She comes to Anchises pretending to be a mortal girl, the daughter of the Phrygian king Otreus, who has been carried to Ida by Hermes and is now ready for marriage. Joyfully Anchises takes her to his bed. After their union she drifts sweet sleep over him, and only when he awakes does she reveal her true identity. At once Anchises is full of fear, certain that now he will be punished, and he turns away his face and begs the

goddess to have mercy on him. She reassures him, saying that she will bear him a son, AENEAS, who will be reared by the mountain-NYMPHS. When the boy is five years old she will bring him to his father, and all will be well so long as Anchises never names his son's real mother, but says that he is a nymph's child.

It happened as Aphrodite predicted, except that years later, while drunk, Anchises told his great secret and was punished: either Zeus blinded him or lamed him with one of his thunderbolts. So when the Trojan War took place Anchises could not fight, and it was Aeneas who led the Dardanian contingent in support of King PRIAM. He took with him two of his father's splendid horses, surreptitiously bred from the divine horses that Zeus had once given to Tros, in recompense for Ganymede.

The second image, found most notably in Virgil's *Aeneid* (but depicted in ancient art from the sixth century BC), is of the old and helpless Anchises whom Aeneas carries on his shoulders, through the fire and slaughter of fallen Troy, to safety (fig. 35). Anchises then accompanies his son and the Trojan survivors as far as Drepanum in Sicily. There he dies and is buried. But Aeneas sees his dear father once more when he meets his shade among the blessed spirits in the Underworld. Anchises tells him of the future glories of Rome and shows him the souls of some of the great Romans to be born in the years to come. Three times Aeneas tries to take his dead father in his arms, but three times the shade melts in his hands, as light as the winds, as fleeting as a dream.

[Homer, *Iliad* 2.819–21, 5.260–72, 13.427–33, 20.230–40; Hesiod, *Theogony* 1008–10; Xenophon, *On Hunting* 1.15; Apollodorus 3.12.2, *Epitome* 5.21; Diodorus Siculus 7.4; Pausanias 8.12.8–9; Virgil, *Aeneid* 1.617–18, 2.634–804, 3.707–15, 6.106–17, 679–899.]

Andraemon *see* GORGE.

Androgeos

Son of MINOS, king of Crete, and PASIPHAE, and himself king of Paros in the Cyclades. He was a fine athlete, and when he visited Athens he won many victories at the Panathenaic festival. Unfortunately this led to his death, though there are several versions of how it came about. In one version his defeated rivals ambushed and killed him. In another AEGEUS, the king of Athens, was so impressed by his prowess that he sent him against the MARATHONIAN BULL, the very bull that had coupled with Pasiphae to produce the MINOTAUR and was now plaguing the inhabitants of Attica. Despite Androgeos' athletic ability, he was no match for the beast and it gored him to death. (It was eventually killed by Theseus.) According to a third version, Androgeos became friends with the sons of PALLAS (3), and Aegeus, fearing an alliance that might threaten his rule, had him assassinated. Whatever the cause of his death, the result was always the same: his father Minos wanted vengeance, so he claimed tribute from Athens of seven youths and seven girls, to be taken to Crete and periodically fed to the Minotaur in the Labyrinth. Androgeos was survived by his two sons Alcaeus and STHENELUS (2).

[Apollodorus 3.1.2, 3.15.7; Diodorus Siculus 4.60.4–5; Pausanias 1.1.2, 1.1.4, 1.27.10.]

Andromache

Daughter of EETION, king of Thebe in the Troad. During the TROJAN WAR her father and seven brothers were killed by Achilles, and her mother too died soon afterwards. Andromache was married to HECTOR, the son of Priam and Hecuba and the leader of the Trojans, and was the mother of his one son, ASTYANAX. In one of the most famous scenes of Homer's *Iliad* (6.390–502) she goes with her baby son to the tower at Troy's Scaean Gate, and there Hector finds her when he comes briefly back into the city from the battlefield. Full of fear for him, she begs him not to carry on risking his life in battle. She cannot bear to lose him since, with the rest of her family dead, he is father, mother and brother to her, as well as husband. He replies that, come what may, he is honourbound to fight. The couple laugh together over their little son before Hector goes once more to battle. Andromache returns to the house where she and the rest of the women mourn for Hector, quite sure that he will not return alive from the fighting.

When Hector is killed, Andromache does not at once hear the news of his death (22.440–72):

> She was weaving at her loom inside their high house
> a double cloak, crimson and covered with flowers.
> She called through the house to her lovely-haired maids
> to set on the fire a great cauldron, and heat warm water
> for Hector, for when he came home out of the fighting,
> poor innocent, not knowing the time for baths had passed
> and he was dead, killed by Achilles and grey-eyed Athena.
> But now she heard mourning and wailing from the walls,
> her limbs shook and the shuttle fell from her hand ...
> she ran from the house like a mad woman, her heart
> leaping in fear, and her maidservants ran with her.
> Then when she came to the tower and the crowd of men,
> she stood on the wall, staring, and saw her husband
> being dragged in front of the city, roughly dragged
> by galloping horses towards the ships of the Greeks.
> Black night covered her eyes and she fell backwards,
> breathing out her life and throwing far away
> her shining headdress – the netted cap, the woven

> head-band, and the veil once given to her
> by golden Aphrodite, on that day when
> shining-helmeted Hector led her forth
> from the house of Eetion ...

When Priam brings Hector's body back from Achilles, Andromache holds her husband's head in her arms and laments over him (24.725–45):

> ... Your people are grieving for you through all the city,
> Hector, you have left for your parents pain and mourning
> beyond all words. But for me above all there is left
> bitter sorrow, for you did not die in your bed
> and hold out your arms to me, saying to me
> some memorable word that I could hold in my heart
> through all the nights and days of my long weeping.

At the sack of Troy, Astyanax was killed and Andromache given as slave and concubine to Achilles' son, NEOPTOLEMUS – events most powerfully dramatised in Euripides' tragedy *The Trojan Women*. Euripides' *Andromache* deals with her new life in Neoptolemus' house, where she has borne him a son, Molossus. She and her child are being persecuted by his wife, HERMIONE, who, being childless herself, jealously wants them dead. Hermione is abetted by her father MENELAUS, and the two together almost succeed in their murderous aims. Andromache, seeing death apparently inevitable, says (453–6), 'Death is less terrible to me than you might think, for I died long ago, when my poor city of Troy was sacked, when my great Hector died.' Nevertheless she and her son are saved by PELEUS, Neoptolemus' aged grandfather, who arrives in time to prevent their murder.

Molossus lived to be the ancestor of the Molossians. Andromache married HELENUS, the brother of Hector, either when Neoptolemus was killed at Delphi (Euripides), or when he married Hermione (Virgil, *Aeneid* 3.294–348). She bore Helenus a son, Cestrinus. In the *Aeneid*, AENEAS comes to Epeirus, where Helenus is king, and finds that he and Andromache are living in a new city which they have named Pergamum, after Troy. According to Pausanias (1.11.1–2), Andromache had three children by Neoptolemus, Molossus, Pielus and Pergamus, and on Helenus' death she went with Pergamus, the youngest, to Mysia, where he conquered Teuthrania and founded Pergamum. In Pausanias' time, Andromache still had a shrine at Pergamum.

Occasionally Andromache is seen in ancient art in scenes of Troy, but she was more frequently an inspiration to postclassical artists, particularly in the fields of opera and drama following Racine's seminal tragedy *Andromaque*. She has become a symbol of all women who suffer loss in war.

Andromeda

Daughter of CEPHEUS (1), king of the Ethiopians, and CASSIOPEIA, and wife of PERSEUS. When the vain Cassiopeia boasted that she was more beautiful than the NEREIDS, they complained to POSEIDON, who sent a flood and a sea-monster to destroy the land. An oracle predicted that deliverance would come only if Andromeda were sacrificed to the monster, so Cepheus was forced by his people to chain his daughter to a rock on the sea-shore and leave her to be devoured. At this critical point Perseus flew by on his winged sandals, returning from his task of cutting off the Gorgon Medusa's head. He fell in love with Andromeda on sight, and her father agreed that if he saved her, he might have her hand in marriage. So he killed the sea-monster and set Andromeda free. But she had been betrothed to Cepheus' brother, Phineus, who now tried to stop her marrying her rescuer. In a pitched battle, Perseus uncovered Medusa's head, the sight of which could turn a mortal to stone, and lithified Phineus and all his supporters. The wedding could now take place.

The site of Andromeda's rescue by Perseus was some-times said to be Joppa, on the eastern Mediterranean coast, and certainly at Joppa the marks left by her fetters on the rocks near the sea were still being pointed out in the first century AD. There was also near Joppa a spring whose water ran red because, they said, it was here that Perseus washed his bloody hands after slaying the sea-monster. All the main participants in this drama were after their deaths immortalised as constellations – Perseus, Andromeda, Cassiopeia, Cepheus and Cetus (the sea-monster) – and this may have been foretold in Euripides' lost tragedy, *Andromeda* (412 BC). Sophocles too wrote a (now lost) *Andromeda*. Her rescue by Perseus was a popular scene in ancient vase-painting from the sixth century BC (fig. 17), and several frescoes of the scene were found at Pompeii. It was even more popular in post-classical art, with paintings by Piero di Cosimo, Titian, Veronese, Rubens, Tiepolo, Delacroix and Burne-Jones, among many others. Perseus is sometimes shown with Bellerophon's winged horse Pegasus, rather than flying by means of his own winged sandals.

[Herodotus 7.61; Apollodorus 2.4.3–5; Josephus, *The Jewish War* 3.420; Pausanias 4.35.9; Ovid, *Metamorphoses* 4.663–5.249.]

Anius

King of Delos and priest of APOLLO at the time of the Trojan War. He was the son of Apollo and Rhoeo, the daughter of STAPHYLUS (1). When Rhoeo was pregnant, her father did not believe that her baby had been fathered by a god, so he imprisoned her in a chest and flung it into the sea. It floated safely to Delos, the very island where Apollo himself had been born. Here Rhoeo bore her child and placed him on the altar of Apollo, charging the god to look after him if he acknowledged him as his son. The god did so, and gave the boy the gift of prophecy. Anius grew up to be Apollo's priest and king of the island. According to Virgil, he gave hospitality to AENEAS and old Anchises on their escape from the ruins of Troy.

Anius married Dorippa and had a son, who became king of the island of Andros, and three daughters. The girls were called the *Oinotrophoi*, the Winegrowers, because they received from DIONYSUS the power to produce at will, either from the ground or simply by touch, wine, corn and olive oil, after which they were named: Oeno (*oinos*, wine), Spermo (*sperma*, seed), and Elais (*elaia*, olive). It was said that the Greek expedition to the

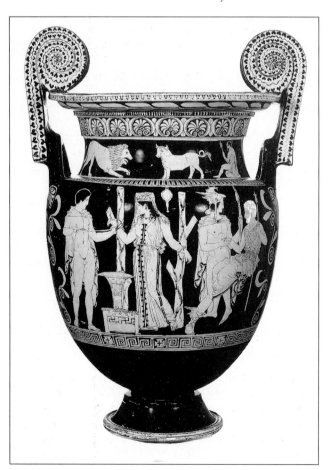

Fig. 17 **Andromeda is tied up for sacrifice to the sea-monster, while Perseus bargains with her father, Cepheus, for her hand in marriage in return for killing the creature.**

Trojan War, led by AGAMEMNON, landed on Delos, and Anius – who knew from his gift of prophecy that the war would not be over until the tenth year – offered to let the Greeks stay on the island for nine years, during which time his daughters would provide for them all. This hospitable offer was refused and the Greeks sailed on, though taking with them plentiful supplies. Later, however, when the war dragged on and food stores grew low, Agamemnon sent either PALAMEDES or MENELAUS and ODYSSEUS to fetch Anius' daughters. In some accounts the girls came to Troy and carried on supplying the army satisfactorily; but according to Ovid the girls fled. Overtaken by an armed force sent by Agamemnon, they prayed to Dionysus for protection and he turned them into white doves. This, says one commentator, is why down to this day it is deemed a sin to harm a dove on Delos.

[Apollodorus, *Epitome* 3.10; Diodorus Siculus 5.62.1–2; Virgil, *Aeneid* 3.80–3; Ovid, *Metamorphoses* 13.632–74.]

Anna and Anna Perenna

A Roman goddess about whom Ovid tells three stories (*Fasti* 3.523–696), one of which identifies Anna with an old woman who provided food for the Roman plebeians, during a period of political troubles, when they left Rome and went to live for a while on the Sacred Mountain. He also identifies her with DIDO's sister Anna, who supported Dido in her passion and grief over AENEAS and mourned deeply for her on her suicide. Anna fled from Carthage, eventually arriving in Latium where Aeneas was now ruling. Recognising her, he welcomed her and wept over Dido's sad death, then took Anna into his household. Unfortunately his wife Lavinia was jealous of this link with her husband's past, and Anna, warned in a dream, fled from the palace at dead of night. In the darkness she was swept away by the river Numicius. The next day they all searched for her, following her tracks to the river bank, and there she appeared to them, announcing that she was now a nymph with the name Anna Perenna, signifying eternity. They spent the day in celebration, and this was the origin of the goddess' annual festival.

In old age Anna was persuaded by MARS to act as his go-between in his pursuit of MINERVA. Anna knew that the virgin goddess would never succumb, but she fed Mars on false hopes and eventually herself took Minerva's place in an assignation with the god by night. Only when he lifted her veil did he recognise her, and the angry words that he uttered were said to be the origin of the ribald songs sung at Anna's festival.

Antaeus

A giant, the son of POSEIDON and GAIA (Earth), and king of Libya, who forced all foreigners coming to his country to

Fig. 18 **Heracles wrestles with Antaeus, watched by various unidentified women.**

wrestle with him. Because his strength was constantly renewed while he stayed in contact with the earth, his mother, he seemed to be invincible, and always defeated and killed his opponents. He used the skulls of his victims to roof his father Poseidon's temple. When HERACLES came to Libya, on his way to fetch the golden apples of the Hesperides, he too was forced to wrestle with Antaeus. Heracles soon discovered the giant's secret and lifted him from the earth, then crushed him to death high in the air.

There are about thirty representations of Heracles wrestling with Antaeus in late sixth and early fifth century BC art, but they all seem to depict an ordinary wrestling match (fig. 18), with not one of them showing the giant lifted into the air. The first visual evidence of Heracles lifting him from the ground is a Tarentine coin of the third century BC, and the first written source stating that Antaeus drew his strength from the earth is Ovid.

[Pindar, *Isthmian* 4.52–5; Apollodorus 2.5.11; Ovid, *Ibis* 393–5, *Metamorphoses* 9.183–4.]

Anteia

The name that Homer gives to Stheneboea, wife of PROETUS.

Antenor

A Dardanian, and one of the most respected of King PRIAM's council of elders at Troy. After HELEN had eloped with PARIS, her husband MENELAUS and ODYSSEUS came as envoys to Troy in the hope of recovering her by peaceful means. Antenor gave them hospitality during their visit, then intervened to save their lives when certain more aggressive Trojans, bribed by Paris, said that Menelaus should be killed (*see* ANTIMACHUS). The two Greeks left Troy with their lives, but without Helen, and the TROJAN WAR began. We see something of Antenor's conciliatory nature in the *Iliad*, where he advocates that Helen should now be returned to Menelaus (7.345–53) so that the war, now in its tenth year, may be brought to an end. His advice is ignored.

Antenor and his wife Theano, the priestess of Athena at Troy, had many sons, including Archelochus and ACAMAS (2), who with Aeneas led the Dardanian contingent in the war. Troy finally fell to the Greeks when they entered the city by means of the WOODEN HORSE, and now Antenor's earlier kindness to Menelaus and Odysseus won its reward. His son Helicaon, wounded during the night battle, was recognised by Odysseus and carried safely out of the fighting, and his son Glaucus was similarly recognised and rescued. Moreover his house was spared in the general sack of the city, for Agamemnon hung a leopard-skin over the door as a sign to the Greek warriors that it should remain unharmed. In Polygnotus' famous painting of the Sack of Troy, Antenor's house was shown with the leopard-skin over the door. He himself was standing outside with his family, while a donkey was being loaded with household goods ready for the long journey away from their now ruined city. Traditions vary as to where Antenor settled. Some say that he founded Cyrene in Libya, others that he led a colony of Enetians to the head of the Adriatic, where the people were thenceforth called Venetians and he himself founded Patavium (later Padua).

[Homer, *Iliad* 3.148–9, 203–24, 262–3, 6.297–311, 11.122–42; Pindar, *Pythian* 5.80–7; Apollodorus, *Epitome* 3.28–9, 3.34, 5.21; Strabo 13.1.53; Pausanias 10.26.7–8, 10.27.3–4; Livy 1.1; Virgil, *Aeneid* 1.242–9.]

Anthemoessa

The island of the SIRENS.

Anticleia

Daughter of AUTOLYCUS; wife of LAERTES; and mother of ODYSSEUS (Homer says by Laertes, but later writers say by SISYPHUS, who seduced her after Autolycus stole his cattle) and of a daughter, Ctimene. Anticleia died while Odysseus was fighting at Troy, in one version killing herself when NAUPLIUS (1) lied to her that her son was dead. In the *Odyssey*, Odysseus learns of her death only when he meets her shade in the Underworld. She explains that she died out of grief at his absence (11.202–3): 'It was care and longing for you and your gentleness, glorious Odysseus, that took the sweet life from me.' Three times he tries to take his dead mother in his arms, but three times her

shade flutters from his hands like a shadow or a dream, because 'this is the way of mortals, when they die'.

[Homer, *Odyssey* 11.84–9, 152–224, 15.363; Pausanias 10.29.8.]

Antigone (1)

One of the four children born of OEDIPUS' incestuous marriage to his mother JOCASTA, and thus the sister of ISMENE, Eteocles and POLYNEICES. In ancient literature, Antigone is known almost exclusively from Greek tragedy. She first appears in Aeschylus' *Seven Against Thebes* (467 BC), where she and Ismene lament the deaths of their brothers. In Sophocles' *Oedipus the King*, the two girls, here very young, come on stage at the end of the play (in non-speaking parts) to be with their broken, blinded father. At the end of Euripides' *Phoenician Women*, Antigone leads Oedipus into exile. In Sophocles' *Oedipus at Colonus*, Antigone has looked after her father for many years while he wandered in exile, a blind outcast, and now they reach Athens and the place of Oedipus' final, triumphant release from his sufferings when he is taken to the gods. But it is in Sophocles' seminal *Antigone* that she achieves her definitive character, enduring and inspirational, as the voice of individual conscience and family loyalty in defiance of law and state.

When the play opens, Polyneices and Eteocles have just killed each other in the battle that has raged around Thebes. CREON (2), now ruling, has decreed that Eteocles, the defender of the city, will be given honourable burial, while the corpse of the attacker Polyneices, the enemy of his country, will be left lying in the plain as a prey for the birds. The penalty for disobedience to this decree will be death. But to Antigone both men are her brothers, regardless of their political actions, and both equally deserve burial, so she resolves to bury Polyneices herself. She tries to persuade her timid sister Ismene to help her, but Ismene has not the courage. 'Do what you please', says Antigone (71–7), 'but I shall bury him. And if I die in doing it, that will be fine. I shall lie, convicted of a righteous crime, a loved sister beside a loved brother ... But if you so choose, you must dishonour what the gods hold dear.'

So quite alone Antigone scatters on her brother's body the earth that will suffice for token burial. She is captured and brought to Creon, and despite the threat of death hanging over her she proclaims the eternal validity of her principles in defiance of Creon's edict (450–69):

Your edict did not come from Zeus, and Justice who dwells with the gods below made no such law for mankind. I did not think your orders strong enough to outrun the gods' unwritten and unfailing laws, you being only a man. Those laws are not of today, nor yesterday, but everlasting ... I knew that I should have to die, of course, even without your edicts. And if I am to die before my time, so much the better ... For me to meet my fate will be no pain. But if I had let my mother's son lie there unburied, then I'd have cause to grieve as now I grieve not.

So Antigone is walled up alive in a tomb, with Creon persisting in carrying out his threat of death even though he is told that he is wrong, first by his son, HAEMON, who is betrothed to Antigone, and then by the blind seer TEIRESIAS. Only when the Chorus of Theban elders remind Creon that never yet has Teiresias made a false prophecy does he change his mind. He goes to set Antigone free, stopping on the way to bury Polyneices. By the time he gets to the tomb it is too late: Antigone has hanged herself, and Haemon now kills himself in front of his father. Even Creon's wife Eurydice takes her own life when she hears of her son's death. Creon is left alive, and alone, to suffer the tragic results of his stubbornness.

Euripides' lost tragedy *Antigone* was very different, for here Antigone and Haemon had a son called Maeon. Too little of the play is left to be sure of the plot, but it may well be connected with a story in Hyginus (*Fabula* 72). Antigone, with the help of Polyneices' widow Argeia, succeeds in dragging her brother's unburied body on to the funeral pyre of Eteocles. Caught in the act, she is handed over by Creon to Haemon, who is told to execute her. But Haemon saves her and lodges her with some shepherds, pretending that she is dead. She bears him a son, Maeon. Years later Maeon comes to Thebes to take part in some games and Creon recognises him as a descendant of the Sown Men, the original inhabitants of Thebes, by a birthmark. Realising the truth, Creon is so angry that Haemon kills both Antigone and himself. Probably the earlier (and happier) part of the story is the one used by Euripides. The traveller Pausanias (9.25.2) was shown the place at Thebes where Antigone was said to have dragged the body of Polyneices towards Eteocles' burning pyre.

Interesting though these variants are, it is Sophocles' version, with its conflict of principles and Antigone's heroic stance, that has been of perennial interest and inspiration to thinkers and creative artists down the centuries.

[Apollodorus 3.7.1; Seneca, *Phoenician Women*; Statius, *Thebaid* 12. George Steiner, *Antigones* (1984).]

Antigone (2)
First wife of PELEUS.

Antigone (3)
Daughter of LAOMEDON, king of Troy. She was very proud of her hair and boasted that it was lovelier than HERA's. The angry goddess turned her hair into snakes, but later the gods took pity on the girl and transformed her into a stork, after which snakes became her prey.

[Virgil, *Georgics* 2.320; Ovid, *Metamorphoses* 6.93–7.]

Antilochus
The eldest son of NESTOR, king of Pylos. He went with his father and his brother THRASYMEDES to fight in the TROJAN WAR and took a prominent part in the fighting, often alongside his brother. It was Antilochus who broke the news of PATROCLUS' death to ACHILLES, and the two friends wept together. Afterwards Antilochus became Achilles' closest comrade in Patroclus' place. He took part in the funeral games, coming second in the chariot-race and third in the footrace; but his own death was soon to follow. MEMNON, king of the Ethiopians, brought a large army to help the Trojans and himself killed many Greeks. One of his victims was Antilochus, rushing to save his father whose chariot foundered when Paris shot and killed one of the horses. Achilles, raging with anger and grief at the death of his dear friend, came swiftly up to avenge him, and after a hard-fought duel killed Memnon. Then he himself died, for he routed the Trojans and rushed after them into Troy, where he was killed by Paris and Apollo. Antilochus' ashes were laid to rest beside those of Achilles and Patroclus, and over them was piled a huge grave mound, one to be seen from afar, on a jutting headland there by the Hellespont. The spirits of the three friends were said to live immortally on *Leuke*, the White Island, lying in the Black Sea at the mouth of the Danube.

[Homer, *Iliad* 5.565–89, 13.545–65, 15.568–91, 16.317–29, 17.377–83, 673–701, 18.1–34, 23.287–613, 740–97, *Odyssey* 3.111–12, 24.72–84; Epic Cycle, Proclus' summary of the *Aethiopis*; Pindar, *Pythian* 6.28–42; Pausanias 3.19.13; Quintus of Smyrna, *Sequel to Homer* 2.243–344.]

Antimachus
A rich Trojan. After HELEN had eloped with PARIS, her husband MENELAUS came with ODYSSEUS to Troy in the hope of recovering her by peaceful means. Antimachus was the most vocal of those Trojans who had been bribed by Paris to oppose the return of Helen, and he even went so far as to urge that Menelaus be murdered on the spot. The two Greeks were saved by the Trojan elder ANTENOR and they returned safely home, but Helen remained with Paris in Troy. Antimachus paid for his greed, however, for his sons were killed in the ensuing war, Hippomachus by Leonteus, and Peisander and Hippolochus by AGAMEMNON, even though they offered rich treasure from their father if they were allowed to live. Agamemnon, recalling past events, scorned any thought of ransom and slew them pitilessly.

[Homer, *Iliad* 11.122–47, 12.188–9.]

Antinous

In Homer's *Odyssey*, Antinous is the ringleader of the Suitors, the young men who have invaded ODYSSEUS' house during his long absence, carousing at his expense and hoping to marry his wife PENELOPE. They all behave outrageously, but Antinous is the most brutal and insolent of them all. He is the instigator of the plot to kill TELEMACHUS (4.660–74). Later, when Odysseus comes to the palace disguised as an old beggar, Antinous strikes him with a footstool (17.405–88) and incites the (genuine) beggar IRUS to fight him (18.1–116). He is justifiably Odysseus' first victim after the stringing of the great bow (22.8–21):

> He aimed a painful arrow straight at Antinous,
> who was about to lift a fine two-handled goblet
> made of gold, holding it in his hands to drink
> his wine, with no thought in his heart of death.
> Who would think that one man, alone among
> many men at their feasting, however strong,
> could inflict on him the dark fate of death?
> Odysseus aimed and shot him through the throat,
> and the point of the arrow ran straight through
> his soft neck. He slumped to one side, the cup
> fell from his hand, and a thick jet of mortal blood
> gushed from his nostrils. With a sharp jerk of his foot
> he kicked the table from him, and knocked the food
> to the floor, bread and roast meat all spoiled.

In the pitched battle that follows, Odysseus and his three allies massacre the rest of the Suitors. Antinous' father, EUPEITHES, is the leader of the Ithacans who attack Odysseus and his allies in an unsuccessful attempt to avenge their sons' deaths.

Antiope (1)

According to Homer, Antiope was the daughter of the river-god ASOPUS; but she was later usually said to be the daughter of NYCTEUS, the regent of Thebes during Labdacus' childhood. Her story was dramatised in Euripides' famous tragedy *Antiope*, now for the most part lost, although its plot can be largely reconstructed from fragments. Antiope grew up to be so beautiful that even ZEUS desired her, so he came to her in the guise of a satyr and raped her, leaving her pregnant with twins. She fled from her father's anger to Sicyon, where the king, EPOPEUS (1), gave her refuge and married her. Nycteus killed himself from shame and grief, charging his brother LYCUS (1) with the task of punishing Epopeus and Antiope. Lycus marched against Sicyon and subdued it, killing Epopeus and taking Antiope away captive. On the way back to Thebes she gave birth to twin sons at Eleutherae on Mount Cithaeron. Lycus left them in a cave to die, but a

herdsman found them and took them home to his cottage. There they grew up. The herdsman named them AMPHION AND ZETHUS.

On his return to Thebes, Lycus gave Antiope as a slave to his wife Dirce, who kept her imprisoned and treated her cruelly for many years. One day Antiope's bonds were miraculously loosened and she escaped. She went to the herdsman's cottage and begged her sons to take her in, but they did not recognise her and turned her away. Alone and unprotected, she was recaptured by Dirce, who was worshipping Dionysus on Mount Cithaeron. Dirce, in her maenadic state, was about to tie Antiope to a wild bull when Amphion and Zethus saved her, having been told by the herdsman that this was indeed their mother. They tied Dirce to the bull in her place and she was torn and trampled to death by the maddened beast. Her body was flung into the stream that was then named Dirce after her.

Dionysus was angry at this death suffered by one of his worshippers, so he punished Antiope by sending her mad. She wandered through Greece until she came at last to Phocis. Here PHOCUS (2) cured her and made her his wife. At their deaths they were buried together in a grave at Tithorea.

[Homer, *Odyssey* 11.260–5; Apollodorus 3.5.5, 3.10.1; Pausanias 2.6.1–4, 9.17.4–6, 9.25.3; Ovid, *Metamorphoses* 6.110–11; Propertius 3.15.11–42; Hyginus, *Fabulae* 7 and 8.]

Antiope (2)

An AMAZON queen. Antiope is the name most commonly given to the leader of the Amazons whom THESEUS carried off to Athens (fig. 139), though she is sometimes called Hippolyte. The rest of the Amazons marched against Athens and encamped in the city itself, but they were vanquished in a fierce battle and most of them were killed. Antiope bore Theseus a son, HIPPOLYTUS (2). Theseus later married Phaedra, the daughter of King Minos of Crete, and during the wedding celebrations Antiope, feeling herself rejected and dishonoured, led out her Amazons in arms, threatening to kill the assembled guests. Instead it was Antiope who was killed, either by Theseus, or by his men, or accidentally by her fellow-Amazon PENTHESILEIA.

[Aeschylus, *Eumenides* 685–90; Apollodorus, *Epitome* 1.16–17, 5.1–2; Plutarch, *Theseus* 26–8; Pausanias 1.2.1, 1.38.9, 1.41.7, 2.32.9, 5.11.4; Quintus of Smyrna, *Sequel to Homer* 1.18–26.]

Antiphus

Son of PRIAM and HECUBA who, with his half-brother Isus, was captured by ACHILLES on Mount Ida while they watched their sheep. Achilles released them for ransom, but later AGAMEMNON caught them in battle and killed them savagely, stripping them of their armour. There was no one to help them, for the rest of the Trojans were in full flight (*Iliad* 11.113–21):

As a lion easily crushes the young of a swift deer,
invading their lair and seizing them in his strong teeth,
and tears the gentle life from them, and even if
their mother is very near, she can do nothing to help,
for terrible shivers of fear are on her too,
and swiftly she dashes away through trees and thick
woodland, sweating and striving to escape the spring
of the mighty beast; so there was not one among
the Trojans who could save these two from death,
but they themselves were fleeing in fear from the Greeks.

Apemosyne *see* ALTHAEMENES.

Aphareus

Son of Perieres and Perseus' daughter Gorgophone. On his father's death, he and his younger brother Leucippus ruled Messenia jointly. Aphareus married his half-sister Arene (his mother's daughter by her second husband, Oebalus) and named his new capital after her. She bore him two famous sons, IDAS and Lynceus, though Idas was sometimes said to be the son of POSEIDON.

Aphareus provided safe refuge for LYCUS (4) when Aegeus drove him out of Athens. He also gave refuge to NELEUS when he was driven out of Iolcus by Pelias, providing him with a great deal of land along the sea-coast. Here Neleus settled in Pylos and made it one of the most flourishing cities in the Greek world. Since Leucippus had only daughters, and Aphareus' sons Idas and Lynceus were killed by the DIOSCURI, leaving no sons of their own, the kingdom of Messenia passed after Aphareus' death to Neleus' son NESTOR.

[Apollodorus 1.9.5, 3.10.3, 3.10.4; Pausanias 4.2.4–7, 4.3.1–2.]

Aphrodite

One of the twelve great Olympian deities, Aphrodite was the Greek goddess of erotic love, the giver of beauty and sexual attraction, identified by the Romans with VENUS. There are two versions of her birth. To Homer she was the daughter of ZEUS and DIONE. To Hesiod she was born when CRONUS, son of Uranus and Gaia, hacked off his father's genitals and flung them into the sea. They were carried over the waves, and from the foam (*aphros*) that gathered round them was born radiant Aphrodite. She came ashore either on Cythera (an island south of the Peloponnese) or at Paphos in Cyprus, and her epithets Cythereia, Paphian and Cyprian evoke these places.

Literature from Homer onwards celebrates the power of love and the dominion of Aphrodite. Her longest

Fig. 19 **The Venus de Milo.**

Homeric Hymn begins: 'Tell me, Muse, the deeds of golden Aphrodite, the Cyprian, who stirs up sweet desire in the gods, and overcomes the tribes of mortal men, and the birds that fly in the air, and all the creatures that live on dry land and in the sea.' The only living beings immune to her influence were the three virgin goddesses ATHENA, ARTEMIS and HESTIA. Everyone else, mortal and immortal alike, was open to the power and pain of love. Sappho begins her famous *Hymn to Aphrodite* with the words, 'Richly-enthroned, immortal Aphrodite, daughter of Zeus, weaver of wiles, I pray you, Lady, break not my spirit with heartache or grief.' In the *Iliad*, when HERA wishes to draw Zeus' attention away from the battlefield, she has only to borrow a love-charm from Aphrodite to make herself so overpoweringly attractive that Zeus cannot restrain his desire to make love to her.

Aphrodite herself was married to the crippled smith-god, HEPHAESTUS, but she bore him no children and was an unfaithful wife. Her regular lover was the war-god, ARES. The bard Demodocus in the *Odyssey* (8.266–366) recounts Hephaestus' reaction to their affair. He was told about it by the Sun-god, HELIOS, who sees all things on his daily journey through the sky and so had spotted the lovers lying together. Hephaestus determined to get his revenge. He fashioned a magical, invisible net over his marriage-bed, then pretended to go on a journey to Lemnos. Naturally the lovers took this opportunity to go to bed together, but in the midst of their passion the net descended, catching them in its snare. Hephaestus at once came in, calling all the other gods to witness the humiliation of the naked and helpless pair. The goddesses stayed away out of modesty, but all the gods came and laughed their fill, with Hermes confessing to Apollo that to be in bed with golden Aphrodite would be worth a far greater penalty. Poseidon at last persuaded the angry Hephaestus to release the lovers, on the understanding that Ares would pay a fine. Ares went off to Thrace and Aphrodite to her sacred precinct on Cyprus, where her wounded dignity was soothed by the GRACES. She later punished Helios for telling Hephaestus of her affair by making him fall helplessly in love with a mortal woman, Leucothoe, the daughter of the Persian king Orchamus. Her father buried her alive for succumbing to the Sun-god's desire, and although Helios tried his utmost to bring her back to life, he tried in vain.

Aphrodite bore several children to Ares: a daughter, HARMONIA, who married the mortal CADMUS, and two sons, the warrior-twins PHOBOS and Deimos, who accompanied their father on the battlefield. Their most famous son, EROS, the god of love, was in early myth not their son at all: according to Hesiod, Eros was one of the primal entities, born at the beginning of time, and was present at Aphrodite's birth to welcome her to the world, thereafter becoming her constant companion. Only in later writers (first in Simonides, fr. 575) is he the son of Aphrodite herself and Ares. Once Ares went to bed with EOS, the goddess of Dawn, and Aphrodite was so angry that she punished Eos by condemning her to be forever falling in love with one mortal after another.

Aphrodite bore children to other lovers. She all too often inflicted helpless love on the other gods, so Zeus made her fall in love with the Trojan prince, ANCHISES, that she might know what it was like to be tormented with desire for a mortal. She went to Anchises on Mount IDA, where he was tending his cattle. Pretending to be an ordinary mortal, she seduced him into bed. She bore him a son, AENEAS. According to late accounts, she bore the fertility god PRIAPUS to Dionysus, the bisexual HERMAPHRODITUS to Hermes, and the Sicilian king ERYX to

either Poseidon or the Argonaut Butes. She also had a passionate affair with the beautiful young huntsman ADONIS, and grew so infatuated with him that she abandoned her normal occupations and took up hunting instead, following the hounds through forests and mountains, with her skirt kilted up to her knees, just like Artemis. When her lover was killed by a wild boar, she made the blood-red anemone spring from his blood as an everlasting token of her grief.

Aphrodite would often interfere in mortal concerns, aiding lovers and punishing those who rejected love. She helped Hippomenes to win the love of ATALANTA, and Jason to win the love of MEDEA; she made DIDO fall in love with Aeneas and give him refuge in Carthage. Most famously of all, she won the love of the beautiful HELEN of Sparta for PARIS, prince of Troy, as a reward for judging Aphrodite the most beautiful goddess in the JUDGEMENT OF PARIS (fig. 81). After this Aphrodite naturally favoured the Trojan side in the Trojan War. In the *Iliad*, we see her helping her favourite, Paris, by breaking his chinstrap when he is about to be defeated by Menelaus in a duel, and sweeping him in a cloud back to his own bedroom. She then forces the recalcitrant Helen to go to bed with him. She later intervenes to help her son Aeneas against DIOMEDES (2), who wounds her, scratching her hand, so that she rushes back to OLYMPUS to be comforted by her mother, Dione.

Aphrodite punished anyone who dishonoured her, especially by rejecting love. Such a one was HIPPOLYTUS (2), the son of Theseus, so she made his stepmother PHAEDRA fall hopelessly in love with him. At Phaedra's death, Theseus cursed his son, and Poseidon sent a bull from the sea to terrify Hippolytus' horses. They overturned his chariot and dragged him to his death. Aphrodite also punished TYNDAREOS for neglecting her by making three of his daughters betray their husbands: Helen ran off to Troy with Paris, Timandra deserted Echemus for Phyleus, and Clytemnestra took a lover, Aegisthus, while her husband Agamemnon was away commanding the Greek force at Troy, and she and her lover killed him on his return. When the Lemnian women failed to honour Aphrodite, the goddess punished them by afflicting them all with a vile smell (*see* HYPSIPYLE). She punished MYRRHA for neglecting her rites by making her fall in love with her own father, Cinyras. The goddess even intervened when GLAUCUS (3) kept his prize mares from mating, so as to improve their performance on the race-track: she made his maddened mares tear him to pieces and devour him.

The principal myth of Aphrodite depicted in ancient art, from about 460 BC, is her birth. Pausanias (5.11.8) tells us that Eros receiving the goddess, as she rose from the sea, was one of the myths portrayed by Pheidias on the base of Zeus' throne at Olympia. She was a favourite subject of sculpture, her two most famous statues being the Aphrodite of Melos (Venus de Milo) of the second century BC (fig. 19), now in the Louvre, Paris (probably the most famous female nude of all time); and the Aphrodite of Cnidos by Praxiteles, of about 350 BC, showing a modest Aphrodite about to enter her bath, now lost, and known to us only from coins and many Roman copies. She is very popular in postclassical art, where she is often accompanied by Eros, by the Graces, and by doves, her sacred birds. Aphrodite Anadyomene ('rising') is a favourite subject; she takes part in riotous sea-triumphs; and she often keeps company with Ares or visits Hephaestus at his forge.

See also figs. 9, 65 and 108.

[Homer, *Iliad* 2.819–21, 3.373–447, 5.311–430, 14.187–224, 21.416–33, 22.468–72, 23.184–91, *Odyssey* 8.266–36, 4.259–64, 20.67–78; Hesiod, *Theogony* 188–206, 975, 986–91; *Homeric Hymn to Aphrodite*, nos. 5, 6, 10; Pindar, *Pythian* 4.213–23; Herodotus 1.105, 1.131, 1.199, 3.8, 4.59, 4.67; Apollodorus 1.3.1, 1.3.3, 1.4.4, 1.9.17, 3.4.2, 3.9.2, 3.12.3, 3.14.3–4, *Epitome* 3.2, 4.1–2; Pausanias 1.14.7, 1.19.2, 2.34.12, 5.18.5, 7.23.2, 9.31.2, 10.26.1; Virgil, *Aeneid passim*. W. Burkert, *Greek Religion* (1985), pp. 152–6.]

Apis

Son of PHORONEUS and the nymph Teledice, and one of the earliest inhabitants of Argos. Like his father he ruled the whole Peloponnese, calling it Apia after himself (it was later given its final name by Pelops). Unfortunately Apis' rule was so tyrannical that he was deposed by Thelxion and Telchis, and dying childless (accidentally killed, it was sometimes said, by AETOLUS) he was succeeded by ARGUS (2), the son of his sister Niobe by Zeus. Aeschylus, however, shows Apis in a kindlier light, saying that he was a seer and physician, the son of APOLLO, who came from Naupactus and purified the Peloponnese of monstrous snakes and plagues.

Apis was also the name of the Egyptian bull-god of Memphis, sacred to Osiris, who was identified by the Greeks with EPAPHUS. But Apollodorus seems to conflate the Argive Apis and the Egyptian bull-god, for he says that Apis after his death was deified and called Sarapis – who was an Egyptian god combining the attributes of Apis and Osiris.

[Aeschylus, *Suppliant Women* 260–70; Herodotus 2.153, 3.27, 3.28; Apollodorus 1.7.6, 2.1.1–2; Pausanias 2.5.7, 5.1.8.]

Fig. 20 **Apollo and Heracles fight for possession of the Delphic tripod.**

Apollo

One of the twelve great Olympian gods. Apollo (so called by both Greeks and Romans) was the god of prophecy and divination, the patron of music and the arts, and the leader of the MUSES. Like his half-brother HERMES, he was associated with the care of flocks and herds. Known from Homer onwards as Phoebus Apollo, the Shining One, he came to be seen during the fifth century BC as a sun-god, and was sometimes identified with the Sun-god HELIOS; but only much later did this identification become standard. He was the god of healing, often called PAEON (1); and also the archer-god whose arrows could bring plague and death. Homer calls him 'Lord of the silver bow' and Apollo the 'Far-shooter'. The beginning of the *Iliad* splendidly portrays this awesome god in action, when he brings plague on the Greeks because Agamemnon has slighted his priest, Chryses (1.44–53):

> Angered in his heart he strode from the peaks of Olympus,
> carrying on his shoulders his bow and covered quiver,
> and the shafts clashed on the shoulders of the angry god,
> moving in fury. He came as night comes down.
> Settling far from the ships he let fly an arrow,
> and terrible was the clash that rose from his silver bow.
> First he killed the mules and the running dogs,
> then shot his piercing arrows against the men, and
> the funeral pyres burned thick and kept on burning.
> For nine days the shafts of the god fell on the army … .

Apollo was the son of ZEUS and LETO and the twin-

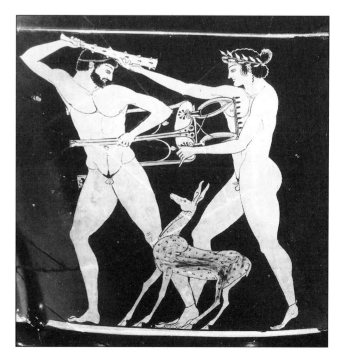

brother of ARTEMIS, born on the island of DELOS after Leto had wandered through many lands, in search of a place for her labour. The *Homeric Hymn to Apollo* recounts the early days of the young god. As soon as he was born, he was fed with nectar and ambrosia, then at once sprang up to stride forth into the world, with his first words declaring his three major concerns (131–2): 'The lyre and the curved bow shall ever be my special care, and I shall prophesy to men the infallible will of Zeus.' He travelled over the earth, seeking a place to found his oracular shrine. His first choice was Haliartus in Boeotia, but the local nymph, TELPHUSA, had no wish to share with him, so she persuaded him to travel onwards to Mount Parnassus. Here he chose the ideal spot, at Delphi, but found that it was the lair of a monstrous she-dragon, later called PYTHON, who was plaguing the surrounding countryside and ravaging the flocks. He did battle with the great serpent and shot her dead, and thereafter the place was named Pytho because her carcase rotted away (*pyth-*) in the sun beside the sacred spring. He himself was called

Pythian Apollo. Now the place was his, for the establishment of his DELPHIC ORACLE. In the form of a dolphin, he diverted a shipload of Cretans sailing to Pylos and brought them to Delphi to be his priests. Later it was said that he founded the Pythian Games to commemorate the dead Python, and that his prophetess at Delphi was known as the Pythia in her memory. His victory over the serpent symbolises the triumph of the Olympian god of light over the chthonian forces of darkness, and his Oracle became the most important in Greece. Apollo shared his rule with his half-brother DIONYSUS, who resided at Delphi during the winter months while Apollo was away, living with the HYPERBOREANS in the far north.

Apollo became close friends with his half-brother Hermes. On the very day that he was born, Hermes was up to mischief, stealing fifty of Apollo's cattle and driving them backwards so as to confuse the trail. Apollo nevertheless guessed the culprit and angrily accused the infant of the theft, but was appeased when Hermes presented him with the lyre that he had just invented, using a tortoise shell for the sounding board and sheep gut for the seven strings. This became Apollo's special instrument, and the two gods were ever afterwards firm allies.

Apollo's half-brother HERACLES once visited Delphi, to ask the Oracle how he might be cured of the disease that had afflicted him since his murder of Iphitus. The Pythia refused to answer, so Heracles seized the sacred tripod and threatened to set up an oracle of his own. Apollo tried to wrest the tripod from him (fig.20, a favourite scene in ancient art), and peace was restored only after Zeus hurled a thunderbolt between his two sons. But on another occasion Heracles did Apollo a favour, when he fought CYCNUS (2), son of the war-god Ares, who had roused Apollo's anger by murdering travellers bringing offerings to the god's shrine at Pagasae, in Thessaly. Heracles fought and killed Cycnus, despite Ares' support for his son; and Apollo, still resentful about his lost offerings, made the river Anaurus flood its banks and blot out Cycnus' grave.

Like all the gods, Apollo was quick to avenge slights to his honour. The satyr MARSYAS challenged him to a musical contest, Apollo on the lyre and the satyr on the pipes, and when Apollo won he flayed Marsyas alive. On another occasion he held a musical contest with the goat-god PAN. The judge was the mountain-god Tmolus, who pronounced Apollo the winner. But an onlooker, the Phrygian king MIDAS, disagreed, and the furious Apollo

Fig.21 **Apollo, from the west pediment of the Temple of Zeus at Olympia, where he oversees the battle of the Lapiths and Centaurs.**

took his revenge by giving Midas asses' ears. The god even killed his own grandson, EURYTUS (1), the king of Oechalia, for having the presumption to challenge him to an archery contest. Other victims of Apollo's wrath were the giants OTUS and Ephialtes, who tried to climb to OLYMPUS; and with his sister Artemis he punished two wrongs done to Leto, killing the giant TITYUS, who had tried to rape her, and shooting the children of NIOBE (2) when she boasted that she had far more children than Leto, Apollo killing the boys and Artemis the girls.

Apollo had a number of children by mortal women, many of whom were graced with their father's special skills. The great healer ASCLEPIUS was his son, in the usual version by Coronis. Apollo carried off the huntress CYRENE when he saw her wrestling with a lion, and she bore him ARISTAEUS, skilled in prophecy and healing. The god lay with CHIONE (2), the daughter of Daedalion, on the same day as Hermes, and she bore the famous thief Autolycus to Hermes, and PHILAMMON, an accomplished musician, to Apollo. He was also the father of the famous seer Iamus by EVADNE (1), and of the priest-seer ANIUS by Rhoeo; and was sometimes said to be the father of the musicians ORPHEUS and LINUS, the seer MOPSUS (2), Hecuba's son TROILUS, and TENES , king of Tenedos. Apollo raped DRYOPE, who bore him Amphissus; and in one tradition he raped Creusa, the daughter of Erechtheus, king of Athens, and was the father of ION, the ancestor of the Ionians.

Despite these many mortal children, Apollo was often unlucky in love. He vied with Poseidon for the love of HESTIA, the goddess of the hearth, but she rejected both of them, swearing a vow of eternal chastity. He pursued DAPHNE, only to have her turned into a laurel tree as he reached out to grasp her. He was ready to fight with the mortal Idas for the love of MARPESSA, but Zeus intervened and allowed her to make her own choice, at which she chose Idas because she knew that he would grow old along with her, while Apollo would abandon her when her beauty faded. He gave CASSANDRA prophetic powers in return for her favours, but she changed her mind and rejected him; so he left her with the power to foretell the future truly, but condemned her to the fate of never being believed. Another prophetess, the SIBYL of Cumae, asked to live for a thousand years as a reward for her favours; but she forgot to ask for perpetual youth, and as time passed she shrivelled away to a withered husk. To win SINOPE's love, Apollo promised to give her whatever she desired, and she cunningly asked to remain forever a virgin. He loved two youths, HYACINTHUS and CYPARISSUS, both of whom returned his love; but both died tragically, Hyacinthus by an accidental blow from a discus, and

Cyparissus of grief over the death of his pet stag.

Even Apollo's love for Coronis, who bore him Asclepius, had a tragic ending, for she preferred a mortal, Ischys, since (like Marpessa) she believed that the god would tire of her when her beauty faded. A crow, left by Apollo to guard Coronis, saw her making love with Ischys and flew excitedly to the god to report the girl's infidelity. Apollo cursed it, turning it black when it had previously been white – since when all crows have been black. (For another story about Apollo and the crow, *see* CORVUS.) Artemis killed Coronis, but Apollo saved Asclepius, snatching the baby from her dead body as it was burning on the funeral pyre.

Asclepius too came to a sad end, killed by Zeus' thunderbolt for using his medical skills to bring mortals back to life. Apollo took revenge for the death of his son by killing the CYCLOPES who had fashioned the deadly thunderbolt; and Zeus in turn punished this deed by making Apollo serve a mortal, ADMETUS, for a year as his herdsman. Admetus treated Apollo so well that the god rewarded him in several ways: by making all his cows bear twins, by helping him to win the hand of his chosen bride, Alcestis, and by reprieving him from his fated day of death, so long as he could find someone willing to die in his place.

Apollo helped ALCATHOUS (1) to build the walls of his city, Megara; and together with Poseidon he built the walls of Troy for LAOMEDON. When Laomedon refused the promised payment, Apollo sent a plague on the land and Poseidon a sea-monster, which would have devoured the king's daughter, Hesione, if Heracles had not saved her. Laomedon nevertheless got his deserts, for he also refused to pay Heracles the promised reward, and Heracles killed him and his sons, and sacked Troy.

Laomedon's treachery was enough to make Poseidon support the Greek side in the Trojan War; but Apollo became the most powerful ally of the Trojans. In the *Iliad* we see him in action, helping his favourites, and most memorably of all during PATROCLUS' great onslaught against the Trojans. Apollo disarms him, striking off his helmet, shield and breastplate, and splintering his spear. Patroclus stands helpless and bewildered, then is wounded by Euphorbus and killed by Hector. An even more famous victim of the god, though later than the events chronicled in Homer, was ACHILLES: he was killed by an arrow shot from Paris' bow and guided to the fatal spot by Apollo.

Apollo's oracle at Delphi played an important role in myth as well as in historical reality. Perhaps its most famous mythical pronouncement was to OEDIPUS, telling him that he would kill his father and marry his mother, a prophecy that was realised precisely because Oedipus, in ignorance of his true parentage, tried to avoid fulfilling it. The Oracle also instructed Agamemnon's son, ORESTES, to kill his mother Clytemnestra and her lover Aegisthus, to avenge their murder of Agamemnon on his return home from Troy. The results of this prediction are famously dramatised in fifth-century BC tragedy, and Apollo himself is a character in two of the plays that treat the subject: in Aeschylus' *Eumenides* he defends Orestes against the charge brought against him by his mother's FURIES, and in Euripides' *Orestes* he appears as *deus ex machina*. But on the whole he cuts no very noble figure in drama, particularly in Euripides, who has the DIOSCURI openly denounce his oracular instruction to Orestes at the end of his *Electra*, and who is indirectly critical of the god's callous treatment of Creusa in his *Ion*.

In ancient art Apollo is young, almost always beardless and often naked, the epitome of youthful male beauty. His attributes are the lyre and the bow. Perhaps the finest depiction of the austere and rational god is the sculpture on the west pediment of the temple of Zeus at Olympia, where he oversees the violent battle between the Lapiths and the CENTAURS, a guarantor of final order and serenity (fig. 21). He is a popular figure in post-classical art, often depicted with his sister Artemis, or as *Mousagetes*, leader of the Muses, or in his role as sun-god, driving his sun-chariot through the sky, and sometimes accompanied by EOS, goddess of Dawn.

See also figs. 26 and 58.

[Homer, *Iliad* 1.603–4, 7.17–43, 452–3, 9.555–64, 16.698–857, 21.435–78, 538–611, 22.6–20, 358–60, 24.31–76, *Odyssey* 8.223–8, 11.305–20, 15.243–53; *Homeric Hymn to Hermes*; Hesiod, *Theogony* 94–5, 918–20, *Shield of Heracles* 68–9, 477–80; Pindar, *Pythian* 3.1–67, 9.1–70; Aeschylus, *Agamemnon* 1202–12; Euripides, *Alcestis* 1–71, *Iphigeneia among the Taurians* 1234–58; Callimachus, *Hymn* 2, 4; Apollodorus 1.3.2–4, 1.4.1–2, 1.6.2, 1.7.8–9, 1.9.11, 1.9.14–15, 2.4.11, 2.5.9, 2.6.2, 3.5.6, 3.10.1–4, 3.12.5, *Epitome* 3.10, 3.23–6, 5.3, 5.18, 6.3; Pausanias 1.3.4, 1.30.3, 1.42.2, 1.43.7–8, 2.7.7, 2.26.4–7, 2.30.3, 2.33.2, 3.21.8, 5.14.8, 5.18.2, 8.30.3–4, 9.10.5–6, 10.5.5–12, 10.13.7; Ovid, *Metamorphoses* 1.438–567, 2.535–632, 676–86, 6.204–66, 10.106–219, 11.146–215, 301–45, 14.129–53. W. Burkert, *Greek Religion* (1985), pp. 143–9; Jon Solomon (ed.), *Apollo: Origins and Influences* (1994).]

Apsyrtus

Son of AEETES, king of Colchis, and brother of MEDEA. He was brutally murdered by Medea, when she fled from home with Jason and the ARGONAUTS after helping them to win the Golden Fleece. There are three versions of Apsyrtus' death, perhaps the best known being that re-

corded by Apollodorus (1.9.23–4). Here Apsyrtus was still a child when Medea set sail on the *Argo*. She took him with her as a hostage, and when Aeetes, following in hot pursuit, drew near and Medea feared capture, she murdered her little brother and dismembered him, strewing his fragmented body over the sea. Aeetes stopped to gather up the pieces, then turned back to give them honourable burial at a place that he named Tomi ('cuttings'). Medea and Jason escaped.

Sophocles, in his lost tragedy *Women of Colchis*, apparently had Medea murder Apsyrtus in Aeetes' house before she fled with Jason, and this is also the case in Euripides' *Medea* (1334–5), although we know no further details of this version. In the third version by Apollonius (*Argonautica* 4.303–481), Apsyrtus was a full-grown man who commanded the Colchian fleet that pursued Jason and Medea. He and his men intercepted the *Argo* at the mouth of the Danube and Medea lured him to a meeting on a nearby island. Jason, waiting in ambush, killed him, then ritually cut off his victim's hands, feet, nose and ears to prevent his ghost from taking vengeance for the murder, and licked and spat out his blood in an attempt to remove blood-guilt. Later Jason and Medea visited the enchantress Circe on Aeaea (4.559–91, 659–752). She welcomed them and willingly purified them, but when she learnt the nature of their treacherous crime she drove them from her island in horror.

Aquarius (The Water-carrier)

A constellation immortalising GANYMEDE, who was loved by Zeus and carried up to Olympus to be his cupbearer.

Aquila (The Eagle)

A constellation immortalising the eagle who carried GANYMEDE up to Olympus to be Zeus' cupbearer.

Arachne

A young Lydian woman, the daughter of Idmon of Colophon. She was of humble origin, but her skill at weaving made her famous throughout Lydia, and even the nymphs from the countryside around came for the pleasure of watching her at work. She was so proud of her skill that she challenged ATHENA (Minerva), goddess of crafts, to a weaving contest. The goddess came to her disguised as an old woman and warned her of her folly, but Arachne scorned her advice. Even when Athena resumed her own shape, the girl was undismayed. The contest began. Athena wove a tapestry depicting herself and Poseidon competing for the patronship of Athens, and four other scenes showing the fates of presumptuous mortals who had dared to compete with the gods. Arachne countered these with depictions of the disguises and deceptions effected by the gods in their various – usually discreditable – love affairs. Her work was perfect, and Athena tore it to pieces in fury, then attacked the girl with her shuttle. Arachne could not endure this, and was about to hang herself when Athena took pity on her and changed her into a spider, who could carry on weaving in peace. To this day her descendants still weave their webs.

[Ovid, *Metamorphoses* 6.5–145.]

Arcadia

The wild and mountainous central region of the Peloponnese, birthplace of HERMES and realm of the goat-god PAN. The name Arcadia derives from ARCAS, the son of CALLISTO who was loved by Zeus and turned into a bear, and its early myths include the savage tale of LYCAON (1) and his fifty wicked sons, punished for eating human flesh. Later, under the initial influence of Theocritus and Virgil, it became idealised as the setting for pastoral poetry and song, a place of NYMPHS and shepherds, SATYRS and demigods, all living an idyllic life of rustic simplicity. This pastoral ideal has ever since been tremendously influential in the arts, especially in poetry and painting. The Latin tag *et in Arcadia ego*, familiar from seventeenth-century pastoral painting, is often taken to mean 'I too once lived in Arcady', but is more probably a grim reminder of mortality, referring to death and meaning 'I [Death] am found even in Arcadia'.

Arcas

The king who gave his name to ARCADIA. He was the son of ZEUS and CALLISTO, who had been raped by the god and transformed into a bear. In one version of the myth the pregnant Callisto, in bear-form, was hunted and killed by Artemis, and the baby Arcas was snatched from her womb as she died and given to MAIA (1), the mother of Hermes, to be brought up. In another version, Callisto gave birth to her son before becoming a bear, and the boy was brought up by her father LYCAON (1), the king of Arcadia. He, together with his sons, was later punished by Zeus, either for child-sacrifice or for cooking and serving human flesh. It was sometimes said that Arcas was the victim. If so, then Zeus reassembled his son and restored him to life.

Arcas became king of Arcadia and taught his people the arts he had learnt from TRIPTOLEMUS: how to grow corn, to make bread, and to weave clothes. He married the nymph Erato, and she bore him three sons, ELATUS (1), Apheidas and Azan, who succeeded jointly to the rule and divided the kingdom among themselves. Arcas' life on earth ended when he met his mother once again, but failed to recognise her in her bear-form. Either he saw a bear wandering into a forbidden sanctuary of Zeus, and

pursued her, or he came face to face with a bear while out hunting, who seemed to recognise him and eagerly came near, but he was afraid and drew back his spear to kill her. However the meeting came about, Zeus stayed Arcas' hand and carried mother and son to the stars. Here he made them immortal, Callisto as the constellation the Great Bear (Ursa Major), and Arcas, in the nearby constellation Boötes, as the brilliant star Arcturus, 'Bear-guardian', forever following his mother through the night sky.

[Apollodorus 3.8.2, 3.9.1; Pausanias 8.4.1–4, 8.9.3–4, 8.36.8, 10.9.5–6.]

Archelochus *see* ACAMAS (2).

Archemorus

The name given to Opheltes, son of Lycurgus (*see* HYPSIPYLE).

Areion

A divine horse, fabulously swift, the offspring of POSEIDON *Hippios* (Horse Poseidon) and DEMETER. When Demeter was wandering the earth, seeking her lost daughter Persephone, Poseidon saw her as she was passing through Arcadia and was filled with desire for her. To escape his amorous attentions, she changed herself into a mare and hid among the horses of a local king, Oncius, but the god became a stallion and mounted her. She bore two offspring, the horse Areion and a daughter, DESPOINA.

Areion ran with Oncius' herds until the king gave him to HERACLES, who later gave him to ADRASTUS (1), king of Argos. Areion carried Adrastus on the expedition of the SEVEN AGAINST THEBES, even saving his master's life by galloping him off the battlefield to safety when the other champions had been killed.

[Homer, *Iliad* 23.346–7; Apollodorus 3.6.8; Pausanias 8.25.4–10.]

Areithous *see* LYCURGUS (2).

Arene *see* APHAREUS.

Ares

Ares was one of the twelve great Olympian gods, and the Greek god of war. He was relatively little worshipped by the Greeks, but his Roman equivalent, MARS, was a very important god, second only to JUPITER (ZEUS). While ATHENA presided over the disciplined and rational use of war to protect the community, Ares stood for the blood-lust and mindless frenzy of battle, delighting in the blood and slaughter, and relishing all the tumult, confusion and horror of war. His sons PHOBOS (Terror) and Deimos (Fear) often accompanied him on the battlefield, as sometimes did ERIS (Strife) and the war-goddess ENYO (1).

Not surprisingly Ares was an unpopular god, both on

Fig. 22 Heracles kills Cycnus, whom Ares tries to defend.

earth and on OLYMPUS. In the *Iliad* Zeus says to him (5.890–1): 'To me you are the most hateful of all the gods who live on Olympus, for always strife is dear to your heart, and wars, and battles.' This being a war poem, Ares naturally plays a large part, but despite his warlike nature he is not very successful in combat. He supports the Trojan side, and the Greek hero DIOMEDES (2), inspired by Athena, has no trouble in wounding him, at which the sorry war-god flees bellowing up to Olympus to complain to Zeus (5.835–909). Later Ares attacks Athena, and she, surprised that he would even try his strength against her, sends him sprawling to the ground with a blow from a great stone (21.391–433). Homer also has Dione tell the strange story of Ares being shut in a bronze jar for thirteen months by the twin giants OTUS and Ephialtes. At the end of that time he was rescued in a state of great exhaustion by HERMES (5.385–91). Hesiod recounts how Ares fought on the side of his son, the brigand CYCNUS (2), against HERACLES, who killed Cycnus and wounded Ares in the thigh. The war-god had to be lifted into his chariot and driven back to Olympus by Phobos and Deimos.

Ares was the son of Zeus and HERA. He himself was not married, but he had many liaisons, most famously with APHRODITE, wife of HEPHAESTUS, the crippled smith-god. Hephaestus caught the lovers in the act by trapping them beneath a magical, invisible net, then called in the other gods to witness their humiliation. Poseidon at length persuaded Hephaestus to release them on the understanding that Ares would pay a fine. Ares disappeared off to Thrace – a favourite country of his, full of warlike peoples – while Aphrodite went to her sacred precinct on Cyprus.

Aphrodite bore Ares four children, EROS, the god of love, the warrior twins Phobos and Deimos, and a daugh-

ter, HARMONIA, who married the mortal CADMUS at a wedding attended by all the gods. Ares had many other famous children, who often inherited their father's belligerent and disruptive nature. They include the brigand Cycnus, who cut off the heads of passing strangers and used them to build a temple to his father; DIOMEDES (1), king of the Thracian Bistones, who was devoured by his own man-eating horses; OENOMAUS, king of Elis, who forced the suitors of his daughter Hippodameia to run a deadly chariot-race with him; the Amazon queen PENTHESILEIA; the Thracian king TEREUS, who unwittingly ate his own son, Itys; PHLEGYAS, the violent king of Orchomenus; and ASCALAPHUS (2) and Ialmenus, who led the Minyans from Orchomenus to the Trojan War. Ares was sometimes said to be the father of MELEAGER, the mighty hero who killed the Calydonian Boar, and of PARTHENOPAEUS, son of the huntress Atalanta, who fought at Thebes.

Ares also had a daughter, Alcippe, by the Athenian princess AGLAURUS (2). Alcippe was raped by Poseidon's son HALIRRHOTHIUS, and for this Ares killed him. The god was then charged with murder by Poseidon and tried by a tribunal of the other gods, but was acquitted. This, the first-ever trial for the shedding of blood, was held on the hill to the west of the Acropolis, ever after known as the Areopagus (the 'Hill of Ares'), on which murder trials were held in historical times.

Ares plays a small part in the myths of others. The dragon that Cadmus killed before he founded Thebes lurked near a spring sacred to Ares and was sometimes said to be his son. To atone for the slaughter of the dragon, Cadmus had to serve the god for eight years. Later, during the expedition of the Seven against Thebes, MENOECEUS (2) sacrificed himself to Ares to save the city from destruction. The belt belonging to the Amazon queen HIPPOLYTE (1), which Heracles had to fetch as his ninth Labour for Eurystheus, had been given to her by Ares as a symbol of her power. The Golden Fleece, the motive for the long and arduous journey of Jason and the ARGONAUTS to Colchis, was hung in an oak tree in a grove sacred to Ares and guarded by a sleepless dragon. And when SISYPHUS tricked Thanatos (Death) and tied him up, so that no mortal could die, it was Ares who was sent to deal with the situation. He released Thanatos and handed Sisyphus over to him to meet his death (though the great trickster managed to avoid his fate).

In ancient art Ares appears as a bystander in scenes with the other gods (fig. 80); and the only myth popularly depicted, in which he is a key figure, is his son Cycnus' fight with Heracles (fig. 22). But he and Aphrodite are frequently depicted together, often caught in the net of Hephaestus, in postclassical paintings.

[Homer, *Iliad* 2.511–16, 4.439–45, 5 *passim*, 13.298–303, 516–25, 15.110–42, 20.47–53; *Homeric Hymn to Ares*; Hesiod, *Theogony* 921–3, 933–7, *Shield of Heracles*; Apollodorus 1.4.4, 1.7.4, 1.7.7, 1.8.2, 1.9.16, 2.5.8–9, 2.5.11, 3.4.1–2, 3.5.5, 3.9.2, 3.14.2, 3.14.8, *Epitome* 2.5, 5.1; Pausanias 1.21.4, 1.28.5, 5.7.10, 5.18.5, 5.22.6, 8.44.7–8, 8.48.4, 9.36.1, 9.37.7. W. Burkert, *Greek Religion* (1985), pp. 169–70.]

Arete

Wife of ALCINOUS, king of the Phaeacians, and mother by him of five sons and a daughter, NAUSICAA. In the *Odyssey*, they live on the fantasy-island of SCHERIA, where ODYSSEUS is shipwrecked on his way home to Ithaca. Arete seems to have a great deal of power in the land, for Nausicaa advises Odysseus that Arete is the person to whom he must first appeal for help, 'and if she has friendly thoughts towards you in her heart, then there is hope that you will see your dear ones again, and will come to your strong-built house and the land of your fathers' (6.313–5). Athena repeats this advice, adding of Arete that 'the people look upon her as a god, and greet her with their words as she walks about the city. She has no lack of fine intelligence, and she resolves the quarrels of those to whom she is well-disposed, even among men' (7.71–4).

Arete gives Odysseus her support, as a generation earlier she had helped MEDEA: in the *Argonautica*, when Jason and Medea come to the island (called Drepane by Apollonius), hotly pursued by the angry Colchians, Arete is deeply moved by Medea's pleas not to be sent back to her father, Aeetes. Alcinous' considered judgement is that if she is still a virgin, she must return to her father, but if not, then she must stay with Jason. On hearing this, Arete immediately arranges for the couple to consummate their love, thus saving Medea from the punishment awaiting her in Colchis.

[Homer, *Odyssey* 6–8, 13.1–187; Apollonius, *Argonautica* 4.982–1222; Apollodorus 1.9.26.]

Arethusa

A nymph loved by the river ALPHEIUS.

Argeia (1)

Daughter of ADRASTUS (1) and Amphithea. She married Oedipus' son POLYNEICES, who was killed in the fateful expedition of the Seven against Thebes. Their son THERSANDER later marched against Thebes with the Epigoni, and when the city was taken he became king. In one version of the myth, Argeia helped her sister-in-law ANTIGONE (1) to lift Polyneices' unburied body on to the funeral pyre of his brother Eteocles.

Argeia (2) *see* AUTESION.

Argeius *see* LICYMNIUS.

Arges *see* CYCLOPES.

Argonauts

The heroes who sailed with JASON on the ship *Argo* in quest of the Golden Fleece, a famous expedition 'of interest to all men', according to its first brief mention in Homer (*Odyssey* 12.69–72). PELIAS, king of Iolcus in Thessaly, hoped to rid himself of the threat to his throne posed by Jason, the legitimate heir, by sending him to fetch the golden fleece of the flying, talking ram that had carried PHRIXUS to Colchis, a distant land at the eastern end of the Black Sea ruled over by AEETES, son of the Sun-god Helios. The Fleece was hung in an oak tree in a grove sacred to the war-god, ARES, and guarded by a dragon that never slept. Pelias was convinced that Jason would never return alive from such a dangerous quest.

The ship for the long voyage, the *Argo*, was built by ARGUS (4) under the direction of the goddess ATHENA, and fitted into its prow had a miraculous speaking beam from Zeus' sacred oak at DODONA. Jason invited about fifty of the bravest heroes in Greece to accompany him. Lists of the crew differ, but the most important names from the varying accounts include the mighty HERACLES and his squire HYLAS; the great Athenian hero, THESEUS; ORPHEUS, the world's finest musician; the swift-flying sons of Boreas, ZETES and Calais; the DIOSCURI, Castor and Polydeuces; IDAS and Lynceus, the sons of Aphareus; the seers IDMON and MOPSUS (1); a son of Poseidon, EUPHEMUS, who was so swift-footed that he could run over the sea without getting his feet wet; ANCAEUS (1), the son of Lycurgus; the helmsman, TIPHYS; the Lapith, POLYPHEMUS (1); Neleus' son PERICLYMENUS (2), who had the power to change his shape; PELEUS and TELAMON, the sons of Aeacus; AUGEAS, famous for his 'Augean Stables'; MELEAGER, who later killed the Calydonian Boar; ADMETUS, Pheres' son from Pherae; Argus, who built the ship; and Pelias' son ACASTUS. Pindar's *Pythian* 4 (fifth century BC) gives our first – fairly brief – account of the expedition, but our fullest and best-known version is Apollonius' late epic (third century BC), the *Argonautica*.

1. THE JOURNEY TO COLCHIS

The expedition set sail under favourable auspices. The first port of call was Lemnos. At this point in time the island was ruled by a queen, HYPSIPYLE, and inhabited only by women, since some years previously they had massacred all their menfolk. Now, keen to have more sons, they took the Argonauts into their homes and beds. Naturally Jason fell to Hypsipyle's lot. In due course, he and his men sailed on, but the women's purpose was achieved and Lemnos was repopulated. Hypsipyle herself had two sons by Jason, Euneus, who was ruling Lemnos at the time of the Trojan War, and Thoas.

On the suggestion of Orpheus, the Argonauts next put in at Samothrace, where they celebrated the mysteries of the CABIRI to ensure the safety of their journey. Passing through the Hellespont, they were welcomed hospitably by CYZICUS, the young king of the Doliones. Here a race of giants called the *Gegeneis*, 'Earthborn', each with six huge arms, attacked the ship and were killed by the crew, led by the invincible Heracles. The *Argo* put to sea once more, but unfortunately it was blown by a storm back to the land they had just left. The Doliones attacked them by night, thinking they were pirates, and in the darkness Cyzicus was killed by Jason. Only in the morning light did they all realise their tragic error. Cyzicus' young wife, Cleite, hanged herself from grief.

Off the coast of Mysia Heracles broke an oar, so they put ashore for him to cut a new one. Meanwhile his young lover Hylas went to fetch water, but the nymph of the spring was so entranced by Hylas' beauty that she dragged him down with her into the water. Polyphemus heard his cry of fear and rushed to his aid, but too late to see what had happened. He ran to tell Heracles, who spent the whole night raging through the woods, bellowing for Hylas, but to no avail. In the morning the Argonauts set sail without noticing that three of their crew were missing. When they realised their mistake, Zetes and Calais persuaded them not to turn back (for

which Heracles later punished them with death); then the sea-god GLAUCUS (1) rose from the waters and instructed them to carry on regardless.

They arrived next in the land of the Bebrycians, ruled by AMYCUS, a savage king who challenged all comers to box with him, then killed them. He issued his usual challenge to the Argonauts, which was taken up by the expert boxer Polydeuces. This time Amycus himself died, his head crushed by a ferocious blow behind the ear. The fighting now became general, but the Bebrycians were soon routed.

Their next port of call was at Salmydessus in Thrace, where they found the blind seer-king PHINEUS (2) almost dead of starvation, a victim of the monstrous HARPIES who had been flying down and snatching his food. The men laid out a feast and lured down the Harpies once again, but when they flew away, Zetes and Calais sped in pursuit of them. They flew until the Harpies were exhausted, and their sister IRIS promised that they would never trouble Phineus again. In gratitude for his deliverance, Phineus helped the Argonauts by foretelling the dangers of the rest of their voyage, particularly the hazards of the SYMPLEGADES, the Clashing Rocks at the northern end of the Bosphorus, guarding the entrance to the Black Sea. These rocks were forever on the move, and clashed together with such force that any ship caught between them was utterly destroyed. As they approached them, the Argonauts followed Phineus' instructions: first Euphemus launched a dove whose fate would foretell the crew's destiny. She flew safely between the rocks, with just the tips of her tail-feathers caught in their rocky jaws. Now it was the turn of the *Argo*, and the crew rowed desperately through, urged on by Euphemus. A great wave held them back just at the danger-point, but at the last moment the goddess Athena intervened, giving the ship a heave that sent her through the rocks as they crashed together, leaving only the tip of her stern-ornament caught between them. Once the Symplegades had been overcome in this way, their danger to men was gone, for they were now immovably locked together and rooted in one spot for ever.

Now the worst of the Argonauts' journey was behind them as they sailed over the open water of the Black Sea. They were welcomed by LYCUS (3), king of the Mariandyni in Mysia, a people who had long been at war with the Bebrycians. Delighted to hear of Amycus' death, Lycus

Fig. 23 **Jason reaches up for the Golden Fleece, which is guarded by a small serpent. Athena stands by in support. To the right is the *Argo* and one of the other Argonauts.**

entertained the Argonauts royally. But they suffered two losses in his land, for here the seer Idmon was killed by a wild boar, and the helmsman Tiphys died of a sickness. When they put to sea, Tiphys' place at the helm was taken by ANCAEUS (2), and Lycus' son Dascylus joined the crew. Bypassing the land of the AMAZONS, they came alongside the Island of Ares, where a flock of birds attacked them by dropping their feathers, sharp as arrows. The Argonauts locked their shields over their heads and scared away the birds with a ferocious din. Landing on the island, they encountered the four sons of Phrixus – Argus, Phrontis, Melas and Cytorissus – who had been shipwrecked here on their voyage back to Greece after their father's death in Colchis. Now they joined the Argonauts, telling them about the dangers that awaited them in Colchis.

2. WINNING THE GOLDEN FLEECE

Soon after this, the Argonauts sailed up the river Phasis and reached their destination, anchoring at Colchis' capital city of Aea. Guided by the sons of Phrixus, Jason went with Telamon and Augeas to Aeetes' palace, hoping to persuade him to hand over the Fleece peaceably. Now the goddess HERA took a major part in the action, since she wished to destroy her old enemy Pelias, and needed Jason to succeed in his quest and return to Iolcus with Aeetes' daughter MEDEA. Hera and Athena enlisted the help of APHRODITE, who bribed her son EROS to shoot one of his inescapable arrows into Medea and make her fall in love with Jason. Eros did so, and as soon as Medea set eyes on the handsome stranger, she burned with love for him.

Aeetes was sure that the Greeks had come to kill him and seize his throne, but he pretended compliance, saying that he would willingly hand over the Fleece if Jason would perform certain apparently impossible tasks: he must yoke two bronze-hooved, fire-breathing bulls and plough a field, then sow the ground with teeth from CADMUS' dragon and kill the host of armed men who would spring from the earth. Jason was despondent, but Medea, urged on by her sister Chalciope, gave him a magic salve that for one day would make him invulnerable. In return he promised to marry her if she came to Greece. He followed Medea's instructions, enlisting the aid of HECATE and anointing his body and weapons with the magic salve. Full of strength and confidence, he was now ready to face Aeetes' test.

At dawn he strode out to meet the great bulls, and for all their ferocity and fire, he yoked them forcibly to the plough. He tilled the soil and sowed the dragon's teeth, and when the armed men sprang from the earth, he followed Medea's advice and flung a boulder among

them. They fought among themselves, while he hacked at them with his sword. As the sun sank from the sky, the field was strewn with dead bodies and Jason stood triumphant.

Aeetes had no intention of giving him his promised reward, so during the night the king plotted treachery against the Greeks. Meanwhile Medea, afraid of her father's anger, fled to Jason's camp. From here she led him to the dense grove of Ares where the dragon guarded the Golden Fleece. With drugs and incantations she put the serpent to sleep, and Jason lifted from the sacred oak the object of his long quest (fig. 23). He carried it, shimmering with a golden radiance, back to the *Argo*. Now they rowed with all speed down the River Phasis, taking Medea with them. As the next day dawned, Aeetes' ships were already streaming in pursuit.

3. THE JOURNEY HOME

The Colchian fleet was led by Aeetes' son, APSYRTUS. (In other versions of the myth, Apsyrtus was only a child at the time of Medea's flight. She took him with her, then murdered him and strewed the fragments of his dismembered body over the sea to delay Aeetes' pursuit. Accounts differ too as to the Argonauts' return route: for instance they might sail up the river Phasis to the great river of OCEANUS, and round again into the Mediterranean; or over the continent of Europe by river-routes, and into the Baltic, then down through the Straits of Gibraltar; or they might return by the way they had come. The following route given by Apollonius is unique.)

The Colchian fleet divided up in an attempt to block all escape routes. The Argonauts, rather than return home the way they had come, sailed up the Ister (Danube) and down the branch thought to flow into the Adriatic Sea. At the river mouth they found that a part of the fleet led by Aeetes' son, Apsyrtus, had forestalled them. Apsyrtus, a reasonable man, was willing to let Jason keep the Fleece, since Aeetes had promised it to him; but he insisted that Medea be left behind. Rather than face this fate, she was quite prepared to resort to murder, so she lured her brother to a meeting on one of the nearby islands, and Jason, waiting in ambush, killed him.

The *Argo* tried to sail southwards down the Adriatic, but was blown north again by a contrary wind, and the speaking plank announced that Zeus demanded Jason and Medea be purified of Apsyrtus' murder by the enchantress CIRCE, Aeetes' sister. She lived on the island of Aeaea on the west coast of Italy, so they now sailed up the Eridanus (Po) and down the Rhone into the Tyrrhenian Sea. Circe welcomed them on Aeaea and purified them, but only then did she learn the nature of their crime. She drove them from her island in horror.

Sailing southwards, the Argonauts passed the island of the SIRENS, the singing enchantresses who lured men to their deaths. But the crew were kept safe by Orpheus, who played his lyre to drown out the Sirens' fatal song. Only BUTES (3) succumbed to the magic of their singing and leapt into the sea to swim to them, but he was saved by Aphrodite and carried away to Sicily. Hera now called on the sea-goddess THETIS and the NEREIDS to help the *Argo* speed swiftly onwards. They guided the ship safely past the twin perils of SCYLLA and CHARYBDIS and between the Wandering Rocks.

Sailing eastwards over the Ionian Sea, the *Argo* landed on SCHERIA (Drepane/Corfu), the island of the Phaeacians. King Alcinous welcomed them warmly, but soon afterwards a fleet of Colchian ships sailed in with a demand for Medea's return. Medea pleaded with the queen, ARETE, to save her, and she did so: since Alcinous judged that if Medea was still a virgin, she should be returned to her father, and if not, she should stay with Jason, Arete arranged at once that the couple should consummate their love that very night. A sacred cave became their nuptial chamber and the Golden Fleece their marriage-bed.

Setting sail again, the Argonauts were blown off course across the sea to Libya. The *Argo* was carried far inland by a tidal wave and left stranded in the desert. For nine days the men carried their ship until they reached Lake Tritonis. Nearby was the garden of the HESPERIDES, recently visited by Heracles, who had killed the snake,

Ladon, and taken the golden apples. He had also created a spring of water from a rock, and here the Argonauts were able to quench their parching thirst. In this land they lost two more of their comrades: the seer Mopsus died, bitten by a snake, and Canthus was killed by CAPHAURUS, a Libyan shepherd, when he tried to steal some sheep to feed the crew.

They buried their comrades and launched the *Argo* on Lake Tritonis. Now the sea-god TRITON came to help them, disguised as a local king, Eurypylus. He presented Euphemus with a clod of earth as a gift of friendship, then reverting to his true form he swam beside the ship and guided it safely back to the Mediterranean. Nearing Crete, they were pelted with rocks by the bronze man, TALOS (1), who was invulnerable except for one weak spot near his ankle. Medea put a spell on him, and he grazed his ankle on a sharp rock. The vital fluid that filled his single vein drained out, and he died. Euphemus dropped the clod of earth into the sea north of Crete, where it became the island of Calliste, later to be known as Thera and colonised by Euphemus' descendants. After a final stop on the island of Aegina, the *Argo* sped on the final lap of its long journey and arrived safely back in Iolcus. Joyfully the Argonauts stepped ashore.

Thus ends Apollonius' *Argonautica*, but this is not quite the end of the saga. Jason gave the Fleece to Pelias, but he did not enjoy his prize for long, since Medea, sent here by Hera for just this purpose, brought about his death by her magic: she turned an old ram into a lamb by cutting it up and boiling it with herbs in a cauldron, then persuaded Pelias' daughters likewise to rejuvenate their ageing father. They killed him and cut him up and boiled him, and that was the end of him. Jason fled with Medea to Corinth, and here dedicated the *Argo* to Poseidon. Years later Jason was killed when a beam, falling from the rotting carcass of the once glorious ship, fell on him and crushed him to death.

Various episodes of Jason's quest are depicted in ancient art, such as the defeat of Amycus (fig. 16), the death of Talos, Phineus and the pursuit of the Harpies. (fig. 63) Most intriguing of all is a red-figure cup by Douris (*c.* 480 BC), showing a huge dragon apparently regurgitating a naked Jason. Nearby is a vigilant Athena and the tree with the Fleece hanging in it (fig. 24). No source has survived to tell us how Jason got inside the dragon in the first place. Pindar's *Pythian* 4 has Jason kill

Fig. 24 Jason in the jaws of the dragon that guards the Golden Fleece, hanging in a tree. Athena, holding an owl, looks on.

the monster (though we do not know how), rather than have Medea put it to sleep; so it may be that in the early version of the myth, Jason leapt inside its jaws and entered its belly, then wounded it mortally from within, in the same way that Heracles killed the sea-monster threatening HESIONE.

[Apollodorus 1.9.16–26; Diodorus Siculus 4.40–53; Ovid, *Metamorphoses* 7.1–158; Valerius Flaccus, *Argonautica*. Tim Severin, *The Jason Voyage: The Quest for the Golden Fleece* (1985); B. K. Braswell, *A Commentary on the Fourth Pythian Ode of Pindar* (1988); Richard Hunter, *The Argonautica of Apollonius: Literary Studies* (1993); James J. Clauss, *The Best of the Argonauts* (1993).]

Argus (1)

A monster known as Argus *Panoptes* – All-seeing Argus – because he had multiple eyes. Either he had an extra eye in the back of his head, or two eyes both front and back, or many eyes all over his body; and he never closed all his eyes in sleep at any one time (hence the modern expression 'Argus-eyed', meaning keen-sighted or vigilant). Apollodorus briefly mentions various exploits of Argus, saying for instance that he killed a bull that was ravaging Arcadia and clad himself in its hide, despatched a satyr that was stealing cattle, and slew the monster ECHIDNA while she slept. But Argus is best-known as the guardian of IO.

When Io, desired by Zeus, was turned into a cow, HERA set Argus to guard her so that Zeus would have no chance of fulfilling his passion. Zeus, undeterred, sent HERMES to despatch Io's unsleeping guardian, but Argus had tied her to an olive tree in the groves of Mycenae and was watching her day and night, so at first not even Hermes could draw near. Finally the god achieved his purpose either by killing Argus from a distance with a great stone, or (according to Ovid) by disguising himself as a goatherd, then lulling the hundred watchful eyes to sleep with stories and music from his panpipes. He then struck off Argus' head. To mark this deed, Hermes was ever afterwards called *Argeiphontes*, 'Slayer of Argus'; and Hera set Argus' many eyes into the tail of her royal bird, the peacock. In ancient art, Argus appears on a number of red-figure vases from the late sixth century BC, often depicted naked, his body covered with eyes (fig. 77). Hermes' weapon is usually a sword. Io is often a bull.

[Aeschylus, *Suppliant Women* 303–5, *Prometheus Bound* 566–74; Euripides, *Phoenician Women* 1113–18; Apollodorus 2.1.2–3; Ovid, *Metamorphoses* 1.622–723; Pliny, *Natural History* 16.239.]

Argus (2)

Son of ZEUS and NIOBE (1), the daughter of Phoroneus, and the first child to be born from a union of Zeus with a mortal woman. He gave his name to the kingdom of Argos.

[Apollodorus 2.1.1–2; Pausanias 2.16.1. 2.22.5.]

Argus (3)

The eldest of the four sons of PHRIXUS who helped the ARGONAUTS to win the Golden Fleece and escape from Colchis. He is sometimes confused with ARGUS (4) and called the builder of the *Argo*.

Argus (4)

The man who built the *Argo* under the direction of ATHENA. He became one of the ARGONAUTS, though nothing is known of his part in the subsequent adventures.

[Apollonius, *Argonautica* 1.18–19, 111–12, 226, 321–6, 527; Apollodorus 1.9.16; Diodorus Siculus 4.41.3.]

Argus (5) ('Swift')

In Homer's *Odyssey* (17.290–327), Argus is the old dog of ODYSSEUS who joyfully recognises his master on his return home after twenty years' absence. Too weak to get to his feet, he wags his tail in greeting, and dies.

Ariadne

Daughter of MINOS, king of Crete, and PASIPHAE. In Knossos the master-craftsman DAEDALUS built her a dancing-floor. When THESEUS arrived from Athens to kill the MINOTAUR, housed in the Labyrinth, Ariadne fell in love with him. She provided him with a ball of thread that guided him safely out of the Labyrinth once the Minotaur was dead, then fled with him to escape her father's anger. Theseus had promised to marry her and take her with him to Athens, but on the island of Dia, later called Naxos, he abandoned her – some say from choice, others on the command of the gods – and Ariadne awoke in the morning to find herself alone and to see her lover's ship speeding into the distance. But she was not desolate for long. The god DIONYSUS arrived in his chariot drawn by panthers, accompanied by his revelling entourage of satyrs and maenads, and he carried Ariadne off to be his wife, giving her the gift of immortality. As a wedding present he also gave her a golden crown, made by Hephaestus, that was later set among the stars as the Corona Borealis. Ariadne bore him four sons, OENOPION, STAPHYLUS (1), THOAS (1) and Peparethus.

A different version is found in Homer, who mentions briefly that Ariadne was killed by ARTEMIS on Naxos because of some accusation made by Dionysus. We know no more of this, but perhaps Ariadne had been promised to Dionysus, then was punished for her infidelity with Theseus (as Coronis was killed by Artemis for her infidelity to Apollo). Plutarch records other variants, such as

Fig.25 **Ariadne with Dionysus and two of their children.**

Oenopion and Staphylus being the sons of Theseus, not Dionysus; and Theseus taking Ariadne when pregnant to Cyprus, where she died before her child was born.

The theme of Ariadne's abandonment by Theseus and her rescue by Dionysus appears frequently in ancient art (fig.25) and literature, but was to prove even more inspirational for postclassical artists, in literature, the fine arts and music, especially opera.

[Homer, *Iliad* 18.590–2, *Odyssey* 11.321–5; Hesiod, *Theogony* 947–9; Apollodorus 3.1.2, *Epitome* 1.8–10; Diodorus Siculus 4.61.5; Plutarch, *Theseus* 20; Pausanias 1.20.3, 2.23.7–8, 5.19.1, 10.29.3–4; Catullus 64.50–206; Ovid, *Metamorphoses* 8.172–82, *The Art of Love* 1.527–64, *Fasti* 3.459–516, *Heroides* 10.]

Aries (The Ram)

A constellation commemorating the golden ram that carried PHRIXUS to Colchis. Phrixus sacrificed the ram to Zeus and took off its golden fleece, or else the ram itself gave him its fleece before flying off into the sky. (This wondrous fleece would later be the motive for the long and arduous journey of Jason and the ARGONAUTS.) The paleness of this cluster of stars is said to be because the ram no longer wears his fleece of gold.

Arimaspians *see* GRIFFIN.

Arion

A Greek poet and singer who lived around the end of the seventh century BC and was the most distinguished musician of his day. He was born at Methymna on the island of Lesbos, but spent much of his life at the court of Periander, the tyrant of Corinth. He was thus a historical figure, but the traditions surrounding him are partly mythical. Herodotus (1.23–4) tells his story. Arion left Corinth for a while to travel to Italy and Sicily, where he made a great deal of money from his musicianship. Eventually wishing to return home again, he hired a Corinthian ship to carry him from Tarentum to Corinth. The villainous crew, however, hatched a plot to throw him overboard and steal his money. When Arion learnt of their intention in mid-voyage, he offered them all his money in return for his life. This the sailors refused to accept, but they granted his request to sing one last song before dying. Arion dressed in his full professional costume and sang a hymn to Apollo, then leapt overboard. But he did not drown, for a nearby dolphin, who had been enchanted by his music, took him on its back and carried him all the way to Taenarum in the Peloponnese. From there Arion travelled overland, reaching Corinth ahead of the ship, and told Periander what had happened. When the ship arrived, Periander questioned the crew, who assured him that they had left Arion alive and well in Italy. At this Arion himself came in, wearing the very clothes in which they had seen him last. The terrified crew admitted their guilt and were crucified by Periander. Herodotus adds that Arion out of thankfulness made an offering in the temple at Taenarum of a small bronze figure of a man on a dolphin, and the traveller Pausanias records (3.25.7) that he saw such a one there in the second century AD. Apollo immortalised the dolphin who had carried Arion to safety by placing him in the stars as the constellation Delphinus.

'What sea, what land knows not Arion?', asks Ovid (*Fasti* 2.83–90). 'By his song he would halt the running waters. Often the wolf in pursuit of the lamb stood still at his voice, often the lamb would stop in its flight from the ravening wolf. Often hares and hounds have lain in one shelter, and the deer on the rock has stood next to the lioness. The chattering crow has sat at peace with the owl, and the dove beside the hawk.'

Arisbe *see* MEROPS (2).

Aristaeus

Son of APOLLO and the nymph CYRENE. Apollo had been smitten with love when he saw Cyrene wrestling with a lion on Mount Pelion, so he carried her off to Libya and made her queen of the city named after her. In due course their son Aristaeus was born, also called *Agreus* (Hunter) and *Nomios* (Herdsman). He was taken from his mother and brought up by GAIA (Earth) and the HORAE, goddesses of the Seasons, or by the wise and kindly Centaur CHEIRON. He learnt the arts of healing, prophecy and hunting, and also many country pursuits valuable to man, including beekeeping, shepherding, olive-growing and cheesemaking.

Aristaeus fell in love with the beautiful dryad Eurydice, the wife of ORPHEUS, but he inadvertently brought about her death when, fleeing to escape his attentions, she was bitten by a snake. The dryads avenged her death by killing all Aristaeus' bees. In despair he journeyed to the River Peneius where his mother was living and appealed to her for help. She sent him to the sealherding sea-god PROTEUS, who had to be caught and bound, then held tightly through all his shape-changing, until at last he gave in and became willing to offer his wise advice. He explained why the bees had died, and on returning home Aristaeus carried out a propitiatory sacrifice to the dryads of four bulls and four cows. He returned nine days later and found the carcases alive with new swarms of bees.

Aristaeus married AUTONOE, the daughter of Cadmus, king of Thebes. Their son, ACTAEON, grew up to be a skilled huntsman, but was torn to pieces by his own hounds at the instigation of Artemis. Aristaeus, grief-stricken, left the Greek mainland for ever. He went to the island of Ceos that was beset by heat and plague, and brought the cooling Etesian winds (*see* ERIGONE (1)). He also went to Sardinia and to Sicily, teaching the arts of agriculture wherever he went. After his death he was worshipped as a god.

[Hesiod, *Theogony* 977; Pindar, *Pythian* 9.1–70; Apollonius, *Argonautica* 2.500–27; Diodorus Siculus 4.81.2; Pausanias 8.2.4, 10.17.3–4, 10.30.5; Virgil, *Georgics* 4.315–558.]

Aristodemus

Son of ARISTOMACHUS, brother of TEMENUS (2) and CRESPHONTES (1), and one of the HERACLIDS who planned the final and successful assault on the Peloponnese. Unfortunately, before they could set out, Aristodemus himself was killed, either by a thunderbolt, or by an arrow from APOLLO, or by the sons of PYLADES and Electra, whose cousin Tisamenus' kingdom at Argos was first at risk. Aristodemus left a widow, Argeia, and twin sons, Eurysthenes and Procles. The boys went in their father's place on the expedition, accompanied by their uncle and guardian, THERAS. When lots were drawn to divide the conquered territory, they won the rule of Sparta and later established there the dual kingship.

[Herodotus 4.147, 6.52; Apollodorus 2.8.2; Pausanias 2.18.7, 3.1.5–7, 4.3.4–5.]

Aristomachus

Son of Cleodaeus, grandson of HYLLUS, and great-grandson of Heracles. He was killed during an abortive attempt by the HERACLIDS to conquer the Peloponnese, but his sons TEMENUS (2) and CRESPHONTES (1) later succeeded where he had failed. A third son, ARISTODEMUS, was killed before the final invasion could take place.

Arruns

The killer of the virgin-warrior CAMILLA.

Arsinoe (1)

Daughter of LEUCIPPUS (1), king of Messenia, and sometimes said to be the mother by Apollo of ASCLEPIUS, the god of healing.

Arsinoe (2)

Daughter of Phegeus, king of Psophis, and first wife of ALCMAEON. Pausanias (8.24.8) calls her Alphesiboea.

Arsippe

One of the three daughters of MINYAS who refused to worship Dionysus and were turned into bats.

Artemis

One of the twelve great Olympian deities, identified by the Romans with Diana. Herself a virgin huntress, Artemis was the goddess of hunting, and of women, particularly at time of childbirth; and as *Potnia Theron* ('Mistress of the Animals', fig.12) was the mistress of the whole of wild nature and the protector of all young living things. As Aeschylus puts it (*Agamemnon* 140–3), she was 'kind to the playful cubs of fierce lions, delighting in the suckling young of every wild creature that roams the fields'. She was the daughter of ZEUS and LETO and the twin-sister of APOLLO, born on the island of DELOS after Leto had wandered through many lands, seeking a place for her labour. Sometimes it was said that Artemis was born first, then acted as midwife for Apollo. Brother and sister were together the two great archer-deities, whose unerring arrows brought death in their train. In the battle of the Gods and the GIANTS, Apollo slew Ephialtes, with Heracles' help, while Artemis shot Gration. In their relationships with mortals, Artemis in particular was a divinity who often dealt out punishment and death.

Mother and children were always devoted to each other and mutually protective. When the giant TITYUS tried to rape Leto, brother and sister together killed him, and he was punished with eternal torment in Hades because of his crime. They also shot the sons and daughters of NIOBE (2) when she boasted that she had far more children than Leto, Apollo killing the boys and Artemis the girls. Artemis killed Apollo's lover Coronis when she was unfaithful to him, even though pregnant by him with ASCLEPIUS; but the baby was saved, snatched from Coronis' body as she was burning on her funeral pyre. In the *Iliad*, we see Leto and her children supporting the

Trojan cause. For all Artemis' great power, she is treated humorously by Homer. When she comes face to face with Hera in the battle of the gods in Book 21, Hera scolds her and boxes her ears, spilling all her arrows. Artemis rushes up to OLYMPUS and sits on her father's knee, crying like a little girl.

Artemis was believed to roam the mountains and forests with a band of attendant nymphs, all of them delighting in the hunt and vowed to a determined chastity. If this was violated, they would be sternly punished. When CALLISTO was raped by Zeus, one of the versions of her tragic fate, quite apart from being transformed into a bear, was death at Artemis' hands. Procris, shunning all men, joined Artemis' band for a time after she had been deceived by her husband, CEPHALUS (2). When she left to go back to her husband, she was given two gifts by the goddess, a hound called Laelaps who always caught his prey, and a javelin that always hit its mark. The javelin brought about Procris' own death at Cephalus' hands.

A male devotee of Artemis was HIPPOLYTUS (2), the son of Theseus. Hippolytus was so chaste, and so devoted to the goddess, that he completely ignored the worship of APHRODITE, who avenged her slighted honour by bringing him to death. Artemis took him to Italy as the minor deity VIRBIUS. Another of her companions was the giant hunter ORION, but he too died. It was sometimes said that Artemis herself killed him, either intentionally (for a whole variety of reasons), by shooting him or by sending a giant scorpion against him; or unintentionally, because she wanted to marry him and the jealous Apollo tricked her into shooting him. This last is the only instance in myth of Artemis, the eternal virgin, being moved by sexual passion.

Many mortals were punished by the goddess. ACTAEON offended her, either by boasting that he was a better hunter than she, or by wishing to marry her, or by seeing her naked in her bath. She transformed him into a deer and had him torn to pieces by his own hounds (fig. 5). When OENEUS, king of Calydon, forgot to sacrifice to her, she sent a huge boar against the land, which led to the famous CALYDONIAN BOARHUNT and the death of Oeneus' son, Meleager. When ADMETUS forgot to sacrifice to Artemis at his marriage to Alcestis, she filled the bridal chamber with snakes. She drove BROTEAS mad when he paid her no honours, whereupon he threw himself into a fire, thinking that he was invulnerable, and was burnt to death. The giants OTUS and Ephialtes offended her by presuming to woo both her and Hera, but Artemis killed them by a trick: she turned herself into a deer and ran between them, and when they each flung a spear at her, they struck each other and died. At the beginning of the Trojan War, Artemis was angry with the Greek leader, Agamemnon (again, for a variety of reasons) and demanded the sacrifice of his virgin daughter, IPHIGENEIA, before winds would come to take his fleet to Troy. In some versions, Artemis saved the girl at the moment of death, substituting a deer on the altar in her place, and taking her to be her priestess in the land of the Taurians. In one version of ARIADNE's death on Naxos, it was Artemis who killed her because of an accusation made by Dionysus. When CHIONE (2) foolishly boasted that she was more beautiful than Artemis, the angry goddess shot her dead.

Artemis was sometimes conflated with other divinities: with the Cretan goddess BRITOMARTIS; with EILEITHYIA,

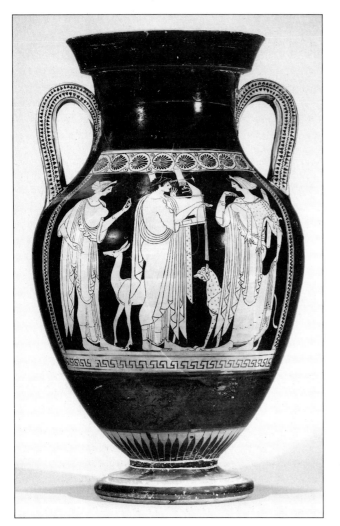

Fig. 26 *From left to right*: Leto, Apollo, Artemis.

the goddess of childbirth; with the moon-goddess SELENE, so that Artemis too was known as Phoebe; and with the goddess of the night, HECATE, who was sometimes called Artemis of the Crossroads. Artemis herself was widely worshipped throughout the ancient world. One of her most famous places of cult was at Brauron, in Attica, where little girls in yellow dresses served her as *arktoi*, bears, and performed a bear dance at her annual festival, the *Brauronia*. The great temple of Artemis at Ephesus, one of the Seven Wonders of the World, contained a celebrated statue covered with what are assumed to be multiple breasts, perhaps to mark the goddess' connection with childbirth.

Artemis appears frequently in ancient art, carrying bow and arrows, and often wearing animal skins or accompanied by animals, especially deer (fig. 26, 38, 64 and 108). She is a very popular figure in postclassical art, often depicted with Apollo, or in her role as goddess of the hunt, or resting or bathing after the hunt, with or without her attendant nymphs.

[Homer, *Iliad* 6.428, 9.533–60, 19.59–60, 20.31–40, 70–1, 21.468–513, 24.602–9, *Odyssey* 5.121–4, 6.102–9, 11.171–3, 576–81, 15.478, 18.202–4, 20.60–3, 80–1; *Homeric Hymn to Artemis*, nos. 9 and 27; Hesiod, *Theogony* 918–20; Euripides, *Hippolytus, Iphigeneia at Aulis*; Callimachus, *Hymn* 3; Apollodorus 1.4.1–5, 1.6.2, 1.7.4, 1.8.2, 1.9.15, 2.5.3, 3.4.4, 3.5.6, 3.8.2, *Epitome* 2.2, 2.10, 3.21–2; Pausanias 2.7.7–8, 3.18.15, 8.3.6, 8.27.17, 8.53.1–3, 9.2.3, 9.19.1, 9.19.6–7. W. Burkert, *Greek Religion* (1985), pp. 149–52.]

Ascalabus

A boy who was punished for laughing at the goddess DEMETER. When Demeter was searching long and wearily for her daughter Persephone, she stopped at the door of a cottage to ask for a drink. The old woman who lived there gave her some barley water, and she gulped it down so thirstily that the woman's cheeky son, Ascalabus, laughed at her and taunted her for being greedy. The offended goddess threw the dregs over him and he was changed into a spotted lizard. His mother wept, putting out her hand to touch the little creature, but it fled away in fear and she never saw it again.

[Ovid, *Metamorphoses* 5.446–61.]

Ascalaphus (1)

Son of the Underworld river-god ACHERON by one of the Underworld nymphs, Gorgyra or Orphne. When PERSEPHONE ate pomegranate seeds on her visit to Hades, Ascalaphus was the only witness. He told of what he had seen, and because this meant that Persephone could not now return permanently to her mother DEMETER on Olympus, but would have to spend part of each year in the Underworld, Demeter punished Ascalaphus by putting a huge rock on top of him. When HERACLES came down to Hades to fetch CERBERUS, he rolled the rock away, but Demeter, still angry with the boy, turned Ascalaphus into an owl. In Ovid's version of the myth, it was Persephone herself who punished him. She flung water from the river Phlegethon into his face, and once again he was turned into an owl.

[Apollodorus 1.5.3, 2.5.12; Ovid, *Metamorphoses* 5.533–50.]

Ascalaphus (2)

Son of ARES and Astyoche, the daughter of Actor, who lay in secret with the god in an upper room of her father's house. She bore two sons, Ascalaphus and Ialmenus, both of whom grew up to sail with the ARGONAUTS, to become suitors of the beautiful HELEN, and to lead the Minyan contingent of thirty ships to fight in the TROJAN WAR. Ialmenus survived the war but Ascalaphus was killed by DEIPHOBUS. 'The powerful spear was driven through his shoulder', says Homer (*Iliad* 13.519–24), 'and falling in the dust he clawed at the ground with his hands. But mighty Ares of the great voice, sitting beneath golden clouds on the heights of Olympus, had as yet no idea that his son had fallen in the cruel conflict.' On learning the sad news, Ares put on his armour and would have thundered off to the battlefield in his chariot, seeking revenge, had not Athena reminded him of how wrathful Zeus would be if he interfered, adding (15.138–41): 'So give up your anger over your son. Already some man, better than he in might and strength of hand, has been killed, or soon will be killed. It is hard to keep safe all the children of men.'

[Homer, *Iliad* 2.511–16, 15.110–42; Apollodorus 1.9.16, 3.10.8; Strabo 9.2.42; Pausanias 9.37.7.]

Ascanius

In the usual version of his myth, recounted by Virgil in the *Aeneid*, Ascanius was born in Troy, the son of AENEAS and his first wife CREUSA (3), and thus the grandson on his mother's side of King PRIAM of Troy, and on his father's side of the goddess Venus (APHRODITE) and ANCHISES. (Livy mentions an alternative tradition in which Ascanius was Aeneas' son by his second wife, the Italian princess LAVINIA.) At the end of the Trojan War, Ascanius escaped from burning Troy with his father and grandfather (fig. 35). They sailed with a band of surviving Trojans to Italy, though Anchises died on the long journey. In Latium Aeneas soon established a friendly relationship with the local king, Latinus, but unfortunately Ascanius wounded a pet stag belonging to Silvia, the royal herdsman's daughter, while he was out hunting (7.476–530). This triggered off hostilities between Latins and Trojans which soon developed into full-scale war. Aeneas eventually brought the war to a successful conclusion by killing the Latins' commander, Turnus, in single combat. He then married Latinus' daughter, Lavinia, and ruled over a union of Trojans and Latins, founding a city called Lavinium. After Aeneas' death, Ascanius took over the rule, and thirty years after the establishment of Lavinium founded Alba Longa, the city that preceded Rome as capital. In due course he was succeeded by Silvius, Aeneas' son by Lavinia. Ascanius was also called Iulus by Latin writers, and the Julian family later claimed descent from him, and thus from his divine grandmother Venus.

[Diodorus Siculus 7.5.3–8; Dionysius of Halicarnassus 1.65–70; Pausanias 10.26.1; Livy 1.3.1–6; Virgil, *Aeneid passim*.]

Asclepius

The god of healing, born a mortal and, like Heracles, deified after death. He was the son of APOLLO, but there is some disagreement as to who his mother was. Sometimes she was said to be the Messenian Arsinoe, daughter of Leucippus; but in the usual version she was the Thessalian Coronis, daughter of Phlegyas. Apollo made Coronis pregnant; but she preferred Ischys, the son of Elatus, for she was all too aware (like Marpessa in similar circumstances) that the god would tire of her when her beauty faded, whereas the mortal Ischys would, in the nature of things, grow old along with her. So she planned to marry her mortal lover, even against her father's wishes. But a crow, left by Apollo to guard Coronis, saw the young couple making love and flew excitedly to the god to report the girl's infidelity. The angry god cursed the crow, turning it black when it had previously been white – since when all crows have been black. He sent his sister ARTEMIS to kill Coronis, but he saved her baby, snatching him from her body as it was burning on the funeral pyre. He gave this son of his, Asclepius, to be reared by the wise Centaur CHEIRON, who educated the boy and taught him the arts of medicine.

The people of Epidaurus told a rather different tale. Coronis gave birth to Asclepius while she was visiting the area with her father. She abandoned the baby on Mount Myrtium, but he lived, suckled by one of the goats that pastured there and guarded by the watch-dog of the herd. One day the baby was found by the goatherd, Aresthanas, who realised that the child was divine when he saw lightning flashes playing around his body. He piously turned away, leaving the infant to the protection of his father Apollo.

When Asclepius grew up, the fame of his healing powers spread over all the land. He married Epione and had two sons, MACHAON AND PODALEIRIUS. They both learnt from their father the arts of medicine, which they put into practice when they accompanied the Greek army to Troy. He also had several daughters who were all personifications of one aspect or another of healing, including Hygieia, the personification of health.

Unfortunately Asclepius' superb medical skill brought about his own death. Athena had given him two kinds of blood from the GORGON Medusa: one destroyed life, but the other could restore life to the dead, and when Asclepius made use of it, thus encroaching on the gods' preserve, Zeus struck him down with a thunderbolt. Various names are given of the men whom the good doctor raised from the dead, including HIPPOLYTUS (2), CAPANEUS, LYCURGUS (precise identity uncertain), TYNDAREOS, HYMENAEUS and GLAUCUS (2), but the result was always the same, and Asclepius was killed for his presumption. Apollo avenged the death of his son by killing the CYCLOPES who had fashioned Zeus' thunderbolt, then was punished in his turn by Zeus, who forced him to serve a mortal (Admetus) for a year.

Asclepius' oldest sanctuary in Greece was at Tricca in western Thessaly, but the principal centre of his cult was at Epidaurus in the Peloponnese. Here people seeking cures slept in the temple overnight to await visitation from the god. Snakes were sacred to Asclepius and were present at his many shrines, regularly assisting in the cures. Following a plague in 293 BC, his worship was taken to Rome by a snake embodying the god, which swam ashore and chose its own abode. Here he was worshipped under the name Aesculapius, his cult being modelled on that of Epidaurus. In art, he is shown carrying a staff with a snake coiled around it, and his eternal symbol in the heavens is the constellation Ophiuchus, the Serpent-holder.

[Homer, *Iliad* 2.729–33, 4.218–9, 11.518; *Homeric Hymn to Asclepius*; Pindar, *Pythian* 3.8–58; Apollodorus 3.10.3–4; Diodorus Siculus 4.71, 5.74.6; Strabo 9.5.17; Pausanias 2.26.3–10, 2.27.2, 4.3.2, 4.31.12, 8.25.11; Lucian, *Dialogues of the Gods* 15; Ovid, *Metamorphoses* 2.534–632, 15.533–46, 626–744, *Fasti* 6.746–62.]

Asia *see* IAPETUS.

Asius (1)

In Homer's *Iliad*, the younger brother of HECUBA, wife of King PRIAM of Troy, and thus the uncle of their son HECTOR. Apollo takes Asius' likeness when he urges Hector on to fight the Greek hero PATROCLUS (16.715–25).

Asius (2)

In the *Iliad*, Asius is the son of Hyrtacus, king of Percote in the Troad, and the leader of a contingent of Trojan allies. His son Phaenops is HECTOR's dearest guest-friend and lives in Abydos. Asius is proud of his chariot and the 'huge and fiery horses' that brought him to Troy, and against the advice of POLYDAMAS he rashly takes them into the thick of the Trojan attack on the wall protecting the Greek ships. 'Poor fool,' says Homer (12.113–5), 'for he was not going to escape the evil fates, nor ever again go back from the ships to windy Troy, delighting in his horses and chariot.' Soon afterwards he is killed by IDOMENEUS with a spear-cast to his throat (13.389–93):

> He fell, as when an oak tree falls, or a white poplar,
> or a tall pine, which carpenters in the mountains
> have hewn down with whetted axe to be a ship-timber.
> So he lay outstretched, in front of his horses
> and chariot, roaring and clutching at the bloody dust.

His charioteer is killed by ANTILOCHUS, and his precious horses taken as booty for the Greeks.

[Homer, *Iliad* 2.835–9, 12.108–74, 17.583–4.]

Asopus

A river-god identified with two Greek rivers of that name, one flowing through Sicyon into the Gulf of Corinth and one through Boeotia into the Aegean Sea. All rivers were thought to be the children of OCEANUS and Tethys, though Apollodorus (3.12.6) says that for Asopus alternative parents were sometimes given: POSEIDON and Pero or ZEUS and EURYNOME. Asopus married Metope, a daughter of the River Ladon, and had by her two sons, Ismenus and Pelagon, and twenty daughters, many of whom were loved by various gods, including CORCYRA, SALAMIS, THEBE and SINOPE. But his most famous daughter was AEGINA, who was carried off by Zeus with Asopus himself in hot pursuit.

[Pindar, *Olympian* 6.84–5, *Isthmian* 8.17–20; Diodorus Siculus 4.72.1–5; Pausanias 1.35.2, 2.5.1–3, 2.12.4, 2.15.1, 2.15.3, 5.22.6, 9.1.1–2, 9.20.1, 9.26.6.]

Assaracus

Son of TROS, king of Dardania, and Callirhoe, daughter of the river-god SCAMANDER. Assaracus, succeeding his father, stayed in the city of Dardania on the slopes of Mount Ida, while his brother ILUS founded Ilium (Troy) nearer the coast. Assaracus was the progenitor of the Romans, since he married Hieromneme, daughter of the river-god SIMOEIS, and had by her a son, CAPYS (1), who became the grandfather of AENEAS.

[Homer, *Iliad* 20.231–40; Apollodorus 3.12.2.]

Asteria

Daughter of the Titans COEUS and PHOEBE (1) and mother, by PERSES (1), of the goddess HECATE. To escape capture by the amorous ZEUS, Asteria turned herself into a quail (*ortyx*) and jumped into the sea. Here an island appeared, named Asteria or Ortygia ('Quail Island'). It was later renamed Delos and would offer a haven to Asteria's sister LETO, pregnant with Apollo and Artemis.

[Hesiod, *Theogony* 404–12; Pindar, *Paian* 5.40–2; Apollodorus 1.2.2, 1.2.4, 1.4.1; Callimachus, *Hymn* 4.36–40, 197–316; Ovid, *Metamorphoses* 6.108; Pliny, *Natural History* 4.66.]

Asterion

A river of Argos and its god (*see* INACHUS).

Asterius (1)

The Cretan king (sometimes called Asterion), son of Tectamus, who married EUROPA after her union with Zeus and brought up her three sons by the god, MINOS, RHADAMANTHYS and SARPEDON, as his own. He and Europa had a daughter, Crete, but no sons, so on his death Minos took over the rule of the island.

Asterius (2)

A son of Minos' wife Pasiphae, by a bull, was also called Asterius, but he was better known as the MINOTAUR.

Asteropaeus

In the *Iliad*, Asteropaeus is one of the greatest of the Trojan allies and the only hero who succeeds in wounding (albeit slightly) the mighty ACHILLES. During their encounter Asteropaeus, being ambidextrous, throws two spears at once, one of them striking Achilles' shield, the other grazing him on the forearm and drawing a gush of blood. Achilles in his turn throws and misses, and his spear drives deep into the river-bank. Asteropaeus is courageously striving to wrench it free, even as Achilles leaps forward and strikes him in the belly with his great sword. He flings Asteropaeus' corpse into the river SCAMANDER where the uncaring fish tear at his flesh.

[Homer, *Iliad* 12.101–7, 21.139–204.]

Asterope *see* STEROPE (1).

Astraeus ('starry')

One of the TITANS, son of the Titan CRIUS and of EURYBIA, the daughter of Pontus and Gaia. By EOS, the goddess of Dawn, Astraeus was father of the winds, BOREAS, NOTUS, EURUS and ZEPHYRUS, and of all the stars.

[Hesiod, *Theogony* 375–82.]

Astyanax

The little son of HECTOR, son of King PRIAM of Troy, and ANDROMACHE. He had been named Scamandrius by his father, but Astyanax ('lord of the city') by everyone else, because Hector was the mainstay of Troy in the face of

Fig. 27 Neoptolemus kills Priam, swinging the body of the old king's little grandson, Astyanax, like a club. To the left, Ajax is about to rape Cassandra.

the Greek attack. In Homer's *Iliad* (6.399–502), Andromache comes to the gates of Troy with Astyanax, 'a little child, only a baby, the beloved son of Hector, lovely as a star shining'. Here Hector finds her when he comes briefly back from the battlefield, and Andromache begs him not to carry on risking his life in the fighting, but to stay in Troy within the safety of the city walls. He replies that he is honour-bound to go out and fight. Then follows one of the most famous scenes in ancient literature, when the baby cries in fright at his father's fearsome helmet (6.466–74):

> Glorious Hector held out his arms to his son,
> but the baby shrank back crying against the breast
> of his fair-girdled nurse, scared at the sight of his father,
> frightened by the bronze and the horse-hair crest
> that he saw nodding dreadfully at the top of his helmet.
> His beloved father laughed, and his lady mother,
> and at once glorious Hector took from his head
> the helmet, and laid it shining upon the ground,
> and kissed his son, and rocked him in his arms.

Hector prays for his son's future (6.476–81):

> Zeus and you other gods, grant that my son
> may be like me, pre-eminent among the Trojans,
> as strong and brave as I am, a mighty ruler of Troy.
> And let them say, as he comes back out of the fighting,
> 'He is better by far than his father.' And let him kill
> his enemy, and carry home the bloody spoils,
> and bring joy to the heart of his mother.

But this prayer will not be fulfilled, for Hector will be killed by Achilles, and Troy will fall, and Hector's little son will be murdered by the Greeks.

When Hector is dead, Andromache foresees this fate for their child as she laments over her husband's body (24.725–37):

> My husband, you died young, and left me a widow
> in your house, and the child is only a baby
> who was born to you and me, ill-fated. I think
> he will never grow up, for before then this city
> will be sacked top to bottom, for you, its defender,
> are dead, you who protected the city and kept
> the women and little children safe from harm,
> women who soon will go in the hollow ships,
> and I along with them. And you, my child,
> must follow me, and there do shameful work,
> toiling for a hard master. Or else some Greek
> will take you by the arm and hurl you from the tower
> to painful death, angry that Hector once killed
> his brother, or his father, or his son.

Astyanax' death was narrated in the Epic Cycle, now almost all lost; but we know from fragments that, when Troy was captured by the Greeks, he was flung from the walls by NEOPTOLEMUS (*Little Iliad*) or ODYSSEUS (*Sack of Troy*). But these are brief references only, and for a full and moving depiction of the child's death we turn to Euripides' tragedy *The Trojan Women*. Here it is Odysseus who urges that Astyanax must be killed, for if he is left alive he may, when he becomes a man, take vengeance for his father's death and the destruction of his city. The news that he must die is brought to Andromache, who grieves for her little son's fate (749–60):

> Child, you cry. Do you know your death is coming?
> Why do your little hands clutch and cling to my gown,
> like a young bird come to nestle under my wings?
> And Hector will not come. He will not come,
> great spear in hand, back from the earth to save you,
> nor will his kinsmen, nor all the power of Troy.
> A deathly fall from the walls will break your neck
> and choke your breath, with none to pity you.
> Little one, here in my arms, your mother's darling,
> how sweet the smell of your skin! All for nothing
> this breast nursed you, you in your baby shawls,
> all for nothing now my toil, my weary labour ...

She herself can do nothing to protect her son, for she is carried off to be the concubine of Neoptolemus. Astyanax is killed, flung from the walls of Troy, then carried on his father's great shield to his grandmother, HECUBA. She in turn laments his fate, mourning over his broken body (1173–93):

Poor little head, how cruelly your father's walls,
the towers built by Apollo, have rent your curls
that once your mother so often tended and kissed,
and now your blood grins out from the broken bones ...
What could a poet write of you on your grave?
'This child the Greeks once killed because they feared him.'
Words to bring everlasting shame on Greece.
Now you have lost all that your father had,
but one thing you shall keep, his shield of bronze
in which to sleep ...

And Astyanax is dressed and carried out for burial, with Hector's shield for his coffin.

In archaic and classical art, Astyanax' death is often linked with the death of Priam: the old king has taken refuge at an altar, and Neoptolemus attacks him, swinging the body of the child like a club (fig. 27, cf. fig. 123). Pausanias (10.25.9) tells us that Polygnotus' painting at Delphi of the sack of Troy showed Priam dead but Astyanax still alive, a child at his mother's breast in the Greek camp. Hector's farewell to Andromache and Astyanax became one of the most popular episodes from the *Iliad* in the postclassical arts.

Astydameia

The wife of ACASTUS, king of Iolcus. (*See also* PELEUS.)

Astyoche (1)

Daughter of the river-god SIMOEIS, and wife of ERICHTHONIUS (2), king of Dardania.

Astyoche (2) *see* PHYLAS (1).

Astyoche (3) *see* EURYPYLUS (2).

Astyoche (4) *see* ASCALAPHUS (2).

Atalanta

A famous huntress. There seem originally to have been two Atalantas, one a Boeotian whose father was Schoeneus, the son of Athamas, and whose husband was Hippomenes; and one an Arcadian, whose father was Iasus (or Iasius, or Iasion), the son of Lycurgus, and whose husband was her cousin Melanion. But their stories were so frequently confused, even by early writers, that it is simpler to treat them as a single Atalanta.

When Atalanta was born, her father abandoned her in the wilds because he wanted only male children. A she-bear chanced on the crying infant and suckled her until she was found by some hunters. They adopted her and brought her up. Grown to womanhood, she too became an expert hunter, interested only in manly pursuits and with no desire for marriage. When two Centaurs, Rhoe-cus and Hylaeus, tried to rape her, she shot and killed them both. It was even sometimes said that she joined the expedition of the ARGONAUTS, though according to Apollonius, Jason refused to enlist her because he thought the presence of a woman in the *Argo*, among so many men, would cause conflict. But she certainly took part in the funeral games for Pelias, where she wrestled with PELEUS, and won; and she hunted with many great heroes, including MELEAGER, prince of Calydon, in the CALYDONIAN BOARHUNT (figs. 34 and 89) Meleager fell in love with the beautiful huntress, and was delighted when she drew first blood by shooting the boar in the back with an arrow. When he himself finally killed the huge beast, he presented Atalanta with the trophies of the hunt, the head and hide of the boar, as an acknowledgement of her skill. Unfortunately this roused resentment among the other hunters, and Meleager's uncles took the spoils away from her. Enraged, Meleager killed them, but then was killed in turn by his mother Althaea, angry at the deaths of her brothers. At some point in her life, and possibly by Meleager, Atalanta had a son (*see* PARTHENOPAEUS).

The most famous part of Atalanta's legend is the deadly race she set her would-be suitors. In some way she was reunited with her parents, and her father tried to persuade his newly discovered daughter that she should choose a husband. But Atalanta would have none of it, either because she wished to remain a virgin, or because an oracle had warned her to shun marriage. Confident in the speed of her feet, she swore that she would never marry unless her husband could first beat her in a footrace. Suitors might run against her, but only on the understanding that if they lost, they would at once be killed. In spite of this, many men were moved by her beauty to risk their lives. And they were given every chance: they had a head start and ran naked, while Atalanta ran fully clothed and armed. But always she caught up with them before they reached the finishing line and speared them as they ran – until, that is, one final suitor tried his luck and was helped by APHRODITE.

Hippomenes (or Melanion) saw the beautiful Atalanta and determined to win her, but unlike her other suitors he had the wit to invoke Aphrodite's aid on his behalf. Ovid says that the goddess brought him three golden apples from Cyprus, where there grew in her sacred field a wondrous tree, its leaves and branches bright with crackling gold. Some say that the apples came from the garden of the HESPERIDES. But whatever their source, Hippomenes started his race armed with the means of Atalanta's defeat. Three times he threw down an apple as they raced, and three times she lost precious ground as she ran aside to pick it up. The third time Aphrodite intervened to make the apple heavier, and with a final burst of speed the joyful Hippomenes passed the winning post. And so he married his love, who in the end seems happily to have given up her freedom.

But the marriage met unusual difficulties. One day the couple, overcome with passion, made love in a sacred precinct (of Zeus or CYBELE), and for this sacrilege they were transformed into lions. After this they roamed the wild forests, or drew the chariot of Cybele (fig. 43). It is worth quoting Fraser (*Apollodorus: The Library*, vol. 1, p. 401) on their punishment: 'The reason why the lovers were turned into a lion and a lioness for their impiety is explained by the ancient mythographers to be that lions do not mate with each other, but with leopards, so that after their transformation the lovers could never repeat the sin of which they had been guilty. For this curious piece of natural history they refer to Pliny's *Natural History*; but all that Pliny ... appears to affirm on this subject is, that when a lioness forgot her dignity with a leopard, her mate easily detected and vigorously punished the offence (*NH* 8.43). What would have happened if the lion had similarly misbehaved with a leopardess is not mentioned by the natural historian.' So perhaps the mythographers were mistaken, and we may more happily imagine the lovers zestfully living out their lives in the freedom of their animal forms.

In ancient art Atalanta is shown at the Calydonian Boarhunt (first on the François Krater, paired with Melanion) and as an athlete at the funeral games for Pelias; but thanks to Ovid's stirring account, the episode of the footrace also caught the imagination of postclassical artists, as well as her exploits with Meleager. She has been painted by Veronese, Guido Reni, Rubens, Jordaens and Poussin, among many others.

[Hesiod, *Catalogue of Women* frr. 72–6; Apollonius, *Argonautica* 1.769–73; Apollodorus 1.8.2–3, 1.9.16, 3.9.2; Diodorus Siculus 4.41.2; Pausanias 3.24.2, 5.19.2, 8.35.10, 8.45.2; Ovid, *Metamorphoses* 8.270–525, 10.560–704, *The Art of Love* 2.185–92; Propertius 1.1.9–10; Hyginus, *Fabula* 185.]

Ate

The daughter of ERIS (Strife). Ate was the personification of Delusion, clouding the minds of her victims and causing them to commit acts of blind folly. In the *Iliad*, Agamemnon claims that he was overcome by Ate when he quarrelled with Achilles and took away his concubine Briseis, just as Zeus' mind was clouded by Ate, at the time of his son Heracles' birth, when Hera tricked him into swearing that the child born on that very day would rule over all those around him. Hera then held back the birth of Heracles, at the same time bringing forward EURYSTHEUS' birth prematurely, so that it was he who won

the position of power that Zeus had intended for his son, while Heracles became his servant. Zeus in anger flung Ate from Olympus, commanding her never to return. She landed on the hill in Phrygia on which ILUS built Troy. From that time on Ate lived among men. But Zeus later sent among men too his daughters the *Litai* – 'Prayers' for forgiveness, and thus 'Apologies' – whose task was to follow in Ate's wake, and help to heal the troubles she caused among deluded humanity.

[Homer, *Iliad* 9.503–14, 19.85–136; Hesiod, *Theogony* 226–30; Apollodorus 3.12.3.]

Athamas

A son of the powerful Thessalian king AEOLUS (1) and his wife Enarete, and himself king of the wealthy city of Orchomenus in Boeotia. He is credited with three wives and perhaps eight children, but his family life was far from happy. By his first wife, Nephele, he had a son and a daughter, PHRIXUS and Helle, but for some unspecified reason Nephele left him. He then married INO, the daughter of Cadmus, king of Thebes, and had by her two sons, Learchus and Melicertes. Ino was jealous of her stepchildren and plotted against them, even to the extent of almost achieving Phrixus' death. But a wondrous ram with a fleece of gold flew in, sent by Nephele, and carried off Phrixus and Helle to safety. Helle was drowned in the sea named the Hellespont after her and Phrixus settled in Colchis, so Athamas lost them both.

Next his sons Learchus and Melicertes came to grief. Athamas and Ino were driven mad by HERA, to punish them for looking after the baby DIONYSUS. While mad, Athamas mistook Learchus for a deer and shot him dead. Ino threw Melicertes into a cauldron of boiling water, then leapt into the sea with her dead child in her arms. She too perished. After this, Athamas was banished from Orchomenus. He asked the Delphic Oracle where he should settle and was told to find a place where animals shared their food with him. He wandered through Thessaly until he came across some wolves devouring a sheep. They ran off at his approach, leaving him the half-eaten carcase, so here he decided to settle. He called the place Athamantia and took a third wife, Themisto, daughter of the Lapith king Hypseus. She bore him four sons, Leucon, Erythrius, Schoeneus and Ptous. For a tragic version of this marriage, *see* INO.

In old age, Athamas' sorrows about the loss of his first children were somewhat eased by unexpected events. Herodotus (7.197) tells us that an oracle named him as scapegoat for the Thessalian city of Achaea, and he was on the point of being sacrificed to Zeus when his grandson Cytissorus, Phrixus' son, arrived from Colchis and saved him. (One of Sophocles' two lost tragedies called *Athamas* seems to have had a plot similar to this, though here Athamas was saved by HERACLES.) Unfortunately this brought down the wrath of the gods on Cytorissus' descendants, for in each generation the eldest son was obliged to keep out of the city Council Chamber, otherwise he would be sacrificed. According to Pausanias (9.34.6–8), Athamas was welcomed back to Orchomenus by King Andreus, where Phrixus' son Presbon, or even perhaps Phrixus himself, came to him from Colchis.

[Apollodorus 1.9.1–2, 3.4.2–3; Diodorus Siculus 4.47; Strabo 9.5.8; Pausanias 1.44.7, 7.3.6, 9.23.6, 9.24.1, 9.34.5–9; Ovid, *Metamorphoses* 4.416–542, *Fasti* 3.853–76.]

Athena or Athene

One of the twelve great Olympian deities, and one of the three virgin goddesses of OLYMPUS. Athena was the Greek goddess of war and of handicrafts, identified by the Romans with Minerva. As war-goddess, she presided over the disciplined and rational use of war to protect the community. She is regularly depicted in art fully armed, with helmet, aegis (a goatskin cape, fringed with snakes, and often decorated with the Gorgon's head), spear and shield (fig. 28). Not surprisingly, she fought mightily in the battle of the Gods and the GIANTS: she killed and flayed Pallas, then used his tough skin as a shield; and she pursued Enceladus when he fled westward, then flung the island of Sicily on top of him.

As the goddess of handicrafts, she presided not only over women's work of spinning and weaving, but also over men's skills, such as carpentry, metalworking and pottery-making. In this capacity, she is often said to have been involved in the skilled projects of mortals. She helped EPEIUS (2) to build the Wooden Horse, and ARGUS (4) to build the *Argo*, installing in the ship a speaking plank from Dodona. She also invented the *aulos*, the double pipe, but threw her instrument away in disgust when she saw her face as she played, distorted by puffed and swollen cheeks, unflatteringly reflected in water. The satyr MARSYAS picked up her pipes and learnt to play them – to his cost, for he challenged Apollo to a musical contest and was flayed alive when he lost.

Athena was born from the head of ZEUS (fig. 51). When Zeus' first wife, METIS, was pregnant with their first child, a daughter, Zeus learnt that she was destined to bear, as second child, a son who would be king of gods and men. Zeus had already deposed his own father, Cronus, and was unwilling to suffer the same fate himself, so he swallowed his pregnant wife to forestall the birth of this mighty son. When the time came for their daughter to be born, HEPHAESTUS split Zeus' head with an axe and out sprang Athena, fully armed, and shouting her war-cry

Fig. 28 **Athena, goddess of war.**

that resounded throughout heaven and earth. Thus she was in a sense a reincarnation of *metis*, 'intelligence', and was seen as the personification of wisdom. She was known as *glaukopis* Athena, the meaning of which is uncertain, but 'owl-faced' is a possibility (or 'grey-eyed', or 'flashing-eyed'). Certainly in art she is often portrayed with that wise bird, an owl, on her shoulder, and her owl also appears on the reverse side of Athenian coins bearing her helmeted head. (For her epithet 'Pallas' Athena, *see* PALLAS (1).)

On the whole Athena had benevolent relationships with mortals. She could punish wrongs if need be: she blinded TEIRESIAS for seeing her bathing naked, but she gave him various benefits in reparation, including the art of prophecy. She also punished ARACHNE for presuming to challenge her to a weaving contest, then took pity on her and changed her into a spider, who would go on weaving for ever. But she is more usually seen as standing by her mortal favourites in support and encouragement. She helped PERSEUS (fig. 114) in his expedition to cut off the head of the deadly Gorgon Medusa (*see* GORGONS). She intended to grant immortality to her favourite TYDEUS as he lay dying, and changed her mind only when she saw him gnawing on the brains of his dead enemy, Melanippus. She helped BELLEROPHON to tame the winged horse, Pegasus, on which he would attack the monstrous Chimaera. In art she watches and supports her favourite HERACLES in hundreds of depictions of his various dangerous exploits (figs. 38, 60, 72 and 96). Most famously of all, she is the constant friend and adviser of the wily ODYSSEUS throughout Homer's *Odyssey*. She intercedes with the gods to free him from the nymph CALYPSO, and thereafter helps him to achieve his long journey home to Ithaca and his victory over the arrogant Suitors.

Throughout the *Iliad* she is a strong supporter of the Greeks in the Trojan War (not surprisingly, given her resentment of the Trojans ever since the JUDGEMENT OF PARIS went against her). Of particular note is her intervention in Book 4, when she tempts PANDARUS to shoot at Menelaus and thus break the temporary truce, setting in motion the last stage of the war that will lead to the destruction of Troy. In Book 5 she assists DIOMEDES (2) in his heroic achievements in battle against the Trojans, even helping him to wound the war-god, ARES, himself. And in Book 22 she impersonates DEIPHOBUS, so as to lure Hector to his death at the hands of Achilles. The Trojans are not aware that she sides so resolutely with the Greeks, and she remains the goddess of the Trojan citadel. HECUBA, queen of Troy, beseeches Athena to ward off disaster from her city, offering the goddess a beautiful robe of fine workmanship: 'But Pallas Athena turned away her head from her', says Homer (6.311).

The Trojans also owned a statue of Athena, the PALLADIUM, believed to have the power of keeping safe the city that possessed it. The Greeks stole it before Troy could fall. But although Athena supported the Greeks, this did not stop her from punishing them at the end of the war for the rape of the Trojan prophetess Cassandra by AJAX (2). With the help of Poseidon, she sent violent storms that wrecked the Greek fleet off Cape Caphareus and brought death to many, including Ajax himself.

Athena was widely worshipped throughout the Greek world and was adopted as the protectress of many cities. But she had a very special connection with Athens, which is even reflected in her name (though the precise relationship between place and goddess is much debated and impossible to define). She vied with Poseidon for the patronship of the city during the reign of CECROPS (1), and both demonstrated their divine powers, Poseidon by creating a well of sea-water on the Acropolis, Athena by planting an olive tree. Athena's gift was judged the greater benefit, and thereafter she was Athens' special patron. She was even, in a sense, the ancestor of the Athenians through their fifth king, ERICHTHONIUS (1), born as the result of the smith-god Hephaestus' uncontrollable lust for her: he did his best to ravish her against her will, and in the struggle his semen fell on her thigh. She wiped it off with a scrap of wool, which she threw to the ground. From where it fell, Erichthonius was born of the earth, and Athena became his foster-mother (fig. 53).

She was worshipped on the Acropolis, where between 447 and 438 BC the Athenians built the Parthenon (*parthenos*, virgin) in her honour. Inside was the huge and famous statue of Athena, in gold and ivory, created by the great artist and sculptor Pheidias. Although it has been lost, we know a great deal about its appearance from Pausanias' description (1.24.5–7) and from small Roman copies. Pheidias also made a colossal bronze statue of Athena that stood on the Acropolis. We know from Pausanias (1.28.2) that the crest of Athena's helmet and the tip of her spear could be seen from the sea, the bronze catching the sunlight, as soon as Cape Sounion was passed.

See also figs. 23, 24, 35, 58, 64, 80, 81, 94 and 95.

[Homer, *Iliad* 4.68–140, 9.390, 10.277–95, 14.178–9, 15.410–12, 22.167–363, *Odyssey* 13.221–310; Homeric *Hymn to Aphrodite* 7–15; Hesiod, *Theogony* 886–900, 924–6; Pindar, *Olympian* 7.35–8, 13.63–82; Aeschylus, *Eumenides* 736–8; Apollodorus 1.3.6, 1.4.2, 1.6.1–2, 1.9.16, 2.1.4, 2.4.1–3, 2.5.6, 2.7.1, 3.4.1–2, 3.6.7–8, 3.12.3, 3.14.1, 3.14.6, *Epitome* 3.2, 5.22–23, 6.5–6, 6.20–2; Pausanias 1.24.1–7, 8.26.6–7, 9.33.7; Ovid, *Metamorphoses* 6.1–145. W. Burkert, *Greek Religion* (1985), pp. 139–43.]

Atlantis

A mythical island that lay in the Atlantic Ocean beyond the PILLARS OF HERACLES, first mentioned in literature in two dialogues of Plato and perhaps invented by him. According to Plato, in prehistoric times the people of Atlantis ruled over much of Europe and North Africa until, in an attempt to enslave the rest of the world, they were defeated by the various free nations led by the Athenians. Violent earthquakes and floods then assailed the island and it sank overnight beneath the ocean, never to be seen again. 'Lost Atlantis' has since captured the popular imagination. Speculations abound as to its location and fate, the most widespread hinging on the cataclysmic eruption in the late Bronze Age of the volcanic island of Thera (now Santorini).

[Plato, *Timaeus* 24e–25d, *Critias* 108e–109a, 113b–121b; Strabo 2.3.6. J. Luce, *The End of Atlantis* (1969); E. Ramage (ed.), *Atlantis: Fact or Fiction* (1978); P. Forsyth, *Atlantis* (1980).]

Atlas ('very enduring')

One of the TITANS, the son of IAPETUS and an Oceanid, Clymene or Asia; father by the Oceanid Pleione of the PLEIADES and the goddess-nymph CALYPSO, and by the Oceanid Aethra of Hyas and the HYADES. Because of his defiance of Zeus in the Titans' revolt against the Olympians, Atlas was condemned to hold up the sky for all eternity. This he did at the far ends of the earth, near the garden of the HESPERIDES, either by supporting the sky directly on his head and hands (fig. 29), or by bearing the weight of the pillars which held the sky up from the earth. Only once was he ever relieved of his burden, when HERACLES came to steal the Hesperides' golden apples for Eurystheus. Heracles offered to hold the sky for him if only he would fetch the apples from the Hesperides' garden, so Atlas happily relinquished his load while he went to pick the golden fruit (fig. 72). In fact he planned never to take up his burden again, but Heracles tricked him by asking for a moment's reprieve, pretending that he wanted to make himself more comfortable with a padded cushion for his head. The dull-witted giant took back the sky, never again to set it down.

Another legend explains how he was turned into Mount Atlas, the highest peak in the Atlas range of north-west Africa. He had been warned that one day a son of Zeus would come and steal the golden apples; so when PERSEUS, son of Zeus and Danae, passed by and asked for hospitality, Atlas turned him away. Perseus showed him the head of the Gorgon Medusa (*see* GORGONS), which turned him into the huge mountain high enough and strong enough to support the sky with all its stars.

Atlas holding up the sky occurs in art from the sixth century BC. In Hellenistic and Roman art he strains to support the globe. The Titan about to hand his great burden over to Heracles was the subject of one of the panels painted by Panaenus around Pheidias' great statue of Zeus at Olympia. In the Middle Ages, Atlas was believed to have taught men astrology because of his association with the sky and the stars. His name has entered modern parlance in two ways: it was used for a volume of maps after he was depicted with the world on his back in a six-teenth-century 'atlas' by the Flemish geographer Mercator; and in architecture an 'atlas' (plur. atlantes) is a column

in the form of a male figure, used to support a roof or crossbeam (the male counterpart of a caryatid). Because of his never-ending burden, Atlas has become a symbol of endurance.

[Homer, *Odyssey* 1.51–4; Hesiod, *Theogony* 507–20, 744–50; Pindar, *Pythian* 4.289–90; Aeschylus, *Prometheus Bound* 347–20, 425–30; Herodotus 4.184; Euripides, *Ion* 1–4, *The Madness of Heracles* 403–7; Apollodorus 1.2.3, 2.5.11, 3.10.1; Diodorus Siculus 3.60.2; Pausanias 3.18.10, 5.11.5–6, 5.18.4; Virgil, *Aeneid* 4.246–51; Ovid, *Metamorphoses* 4.631–62.]

Atreidae

The name commonly given to the sons of Atreus, AGAMEMNON and MENELAUS.

Atreus

Atreus and his brother THYESTES, the eldest and most famous sons of PELOPS and Hippodameia, were destined to a tragic and bloody feud with one another, perhaps because of the curse of MYRTILUS on Pelops and his family, perhaps because of the curse of Pelops himself on his own children after their murder of CHRYSIPPUS. In Homer's *Iliad* alone there seems to be harmony between the brothers, in the peaceful transition of power from one to another by means of the ancient and hallowed royal sceptre (2.100–8). In every other account they are at each other's throats, vying for the kingship of Mycenae. Their story is one of adultery, cannibalism, incest and murder.

Until the death of Eurystheus, king of Mycenae, Atreus and Thyestes shared the rule of Midea, given to

Fig. 29 Atlas holds up the sky, covered with stars, while Prometheus, bound to a column, is attacked by the eagle that daily consumes his liver.

them by their brother-in-law STHENELUS (1). Atreus married AEROPE, the daughter of Catreus, king of Crete, and she bore him two famous sons, AGAMEMNON and MENELAUS. (Some accounts say that she married an otherwise unknown son of Atreus called PLEISTHENES, and had her sons by him. Even in this version, however, Atreus still brought up Agamemnon and Menelaus, for it seems that he married Aerope after Pleisthenes died young.) The two brothers are frequently referred to as the Atreidae, the 'sons of Atreus'.

Aerope, however, proved to be an unfaithful and treacherous wife. She took Thyestes as her lover, and she secretly gave him the golden lamb which won him the throne of Mycenae. There are two stories about this lamb, both linking it with the kingship. In one version it was provided by HERMES, as a way of causing trouble in revenge for the death of his son Myrtilus, and it gave its possessor the right to the throne. Atreus had owned it and had become king, but when Aerope gave it to Thyestes, he was able to take the throne in his brother's place. In the second version, ARTEMIS caused the lamb to be born after Atreus had vowed to sacrifice to her the best of his flock, but when he saw the lamb he ignored his vow, and killed it, and put it in a chest. Once Thyestes was in possession of the lamb through Aerope's treachery, he declared in public that the throne should belong to whoever owned such an animal. Atreus, of course, agreed, thinking himself the owner – whereupon Thyestes produced the lamb and was made king.

Whichever way he gained the kingship, Thyestes' rule was short-lived, for Atreus had the mightiest of supporters in the great god ZEUS. To demonstrate his championship of Atreus' claim to the throne, Zeus reversed the course of the sun, making it rise in the west and sink in the east. At this miraculous proof of divine approval, Atreus once more became king. He drove Thyestes into exile, and when he later learnt of Aerope's infidelity, he punished his treacherous wife by drowning her. He also took a hideous revenge on his brother. First he summoned him back to Mycenae, pretending an attempt at reconciliation. He then invited him to a feast, the main dish of which consisted of Thyestes' own sons, killed and cut up and stewed. Thyestes ate heartily, and at the end of the meal asked for his sons to be brought in. Atreus presented him with their heads and hands and feet, telling him that what he did not see, he already had, and then banished him once more. Some writers, including Seneca and Sophocles, said that it was at this point that the sun reversed its direction, in horror at the appalling feast. Thyestes left, cursing Atreus and all his house, and vowing revenge.

He enquired of an oracle how he might get that revenge, and was told to have a child by his own daughter. The outcome is related by Hyginus (*Fabula* 88), which as far as we can tell is based on a lost Sophoclean tragedy. In Sicyon Thyestes came across his daughter, Pelopia, acting as priestess in rites to Athena, and when she undressed to wash the blood of sacrifice from her robe, he raped her. Before he fled away, quite unrecognised by her, she seized his sword. Shortly after this, Atreus came to Thesprotia, where he met Pelopia, believing her to be the daughter of the king, Thesprotus. The king did nothing to disabuse him, nor did he tell him that Pelopia was pregnant. Atreus married the girl, and when she gave birth to a baby son, she cast him out to die. He was saved, however, by shepherds, who gave him to be suckled by a she-goat. When Atreus heard about the boy, he found him and brought him up as his own son, naming him AEGISTHUS because of the goat (*aix, aigos*).

Years later Atreus' sons Agamemnon and Menelaus came across Thyestes at Delphi and captured him, taking him back with them to Mycenae. Atreus flung him into prison and told Aegisthus, now grown up, to kill him. Aegisthus was about to run him through with his sword when Thyestes recognised it as his own weapon, lost on the night of the rape, and found out that it had originally come from Pelopia. He begged to see her, and when she came to his prison he told the truth about Aegisthus' conception. Appalled to learn of her incest, she seized the sword and killed herself. Aegisthus was now unwilling to murder the man who had turned out to be his real father, but he took the bloody sword to Atreus and pretended that he had done so. Atreus, overjoyed at the supposed death of his old enemy, went down to the seashore to offer sacrifices in thanksgiving to the gods. Aegisthus followed, and there killed him.

Thyestes then took the throne once more and banished Agamemnon and Menelaus. They were later brought back to Mycenae by TYNDAREOS, who drove Thyestes out and made Agamemnon king. Thyestes spent the rest of his days in Cythera. His curse on the house of Atreus was further realised, many years later, when Agamemnon was killed on his return from Troy by Aegisthus and Clytemnestra, who were in turn killed by Agamemnon's son, ORESTES.

This bloody myth was a most potent source of inspiration for the fifth-century BC tragedians. Many plays have been lost, all bar fragments, but we know that Sophocles wrote an *Atreus* and a *Thyestes in Sicyon*, plus one (possibly two) *Thyestes* plays, and that Euripides wrote a *Cretan Women* and a *Thyestes*. As for extant tragedies, these often contain substantial references to the myth, as, for instance, Euripides' *Electra* 699–746, where the chorus sing of Aerope betraying Atreus by giving Thyestes the golden lamb, and of Zeus reversing the course of the sun and the stars in support of Atreus. But perhaps the most memorable dramatisation that we possess is Aeschylus' *Oresteia* trilogy, where Thyestes' curse on the house of Atreus forms a bloody and violent background to the bloody and violent events enacted on and off stage – the murder of Agamemnon by Clytemnestra with the support of Aegisthus, the murder of Clytemnestra and Aegisthus by Orestes, and the pursuit of Orestes by the Furies, raging at the murder of his mother.

The so-called 'Treasury of Atreus' at Mycenae is the largest circular-vaulted tholos tomb in Greece, with its main chamber being 14.60 metres in diameter, and its lofty vault almost 13.50 metres high. It must be the greatest known engineering achievement of the Mycenaean age, but it is unlikely that it has anything to do with Atreus.

[Aeschylus, *Agamemnon* 1191–3, 1219–22, 1583–1611; Euripides, *Orestes* 812–18, 995–1012; Apollodorus, *Epitome* 2.10–15; Dio Chrysostom 66.6; Pausanias 2.16.6, 2.18.1; Seneca, *Thyestes*.]

Atthis

Daughter of CRANAUS who gave her name to Attica.

Attis

The young male consort of the Phrygian mother-goddess CYBELE.

Auge

Daughter of Aleus, king of Arcadia, and his niece Neaera, and the mother of TELEPHUS by HERACLES. Auge's story has a number of different versions, and was particularly popular in fifth-century tragedy. The Hesiodic *Catalogue of Women* (fr. 165) gives a unique version of events, saying that Teuthras, king of Teuthrania in Mysia, received Auge as a daughter, and that she was made pregnant by Heracles while on his way to fetch the man-eating mares of Diomedes. But more usually her encounter with Heracles occurs at home in Arcadia. Here she was a virgin priestess in the temple of Athena at Tegea, and Heracles either seduced or raped her when he was passing through the area. In one version (used by Apollodorus, 2.7.4, 3.9.1) she bore a son, but kept his birth a secret and hid him in the temple precinct. He was found by Aleus after oracles pronounced that the shrine was polluted. The angry king exposed the baby on Mount Parthenion and gave Auge to the navigator and slave-trader NAUPLIUS (1), either to be drowned, or to be sold overseas. Nauplius, however, took pity on her and gave her to Teuthras in Mysia, who married her. In another version (used by Sophocles in his lost

Aleadae), Auge was given to Nauplius while still pregnant. She gave birth to her son on the way down to the sea, then was forced to leave him behind before being once again taken to Mysia. In all versions the baby survived, suckled by a doe until found and brought up by shepherds. On reaching manhood, Telephus enquired at Delphi about his parents, and an (unusually) unequivocal reply sent him to Mysia. Here he was reunited with his mother and adopted by Teuthras, eventually succeeding him to the throne of Teuthrania.

Another version said that Auge and her baby were put by Aleus in a chest and thrown into the sea. In due course they once again ended up safely in Mysia with Teuthras: this seems to have been the plot of Euripides' lost *Auge*. A quite different story is found in Hyginus (*Fabulae* 99, 100), quite possibly the plot of another lost tragedy (perhaps Sophocles' *Mysians*). Here Auge is adopted by Teuthras as his daughter. Once again Telephus, on reaching manhood, goes to Mysia to find his mother, but of course he does not recognise her, and after helping Teuthras to defend his kingdom, he accepts the king's offer of his adopted daughter's hand in marriage. Auge wants none of it, however, and on her wedding night she tries to kill her young husband with a sword. The gods send a huge snake that crawls between them, and Auge in terror confesses her murderous intention. Telephus is about to punish her with death when she calls on Heracles to protect her, and he learns that she is his long-lost mother.

[Diodorus Siculus 4.33.7–12; Strabo 13.1.69; Pausanias 8.4.9, 8.47.4, 8.48.7, 8.54.6, 10.28.8.]

Augeas or Augeias

A king of Elis in the Peloponnese, usually said to be a son of HELIOS, the Sun-god, but sometimes a son of Poseidon or Phorbas. He sailed with the ARGONAUTS, but his main claim to fame was as the owner of the 'Augean stables', the cleansing of which formed HERACLES' fifth Labour for Eurystheus (see LABOURS OF HERACLES). Augeas had many herds of cattle which he kept in stables that had never been cleaned, and Heracles' task was to clear up all the dung in a single day. He made a bargain with Augeas that, if he succeeded, the king would reward him with a tenth part of his herds. He then broke openings through the walls of the stables and diverted the rivers Alpheius and Peneius to flow through the yards and buildings, sweeping them clean. Augeas, however, refused to pay the agreed reward. His son PHYLEUS, who had witnessed the agreement, supported Heracles' claim, and the king, in a rage, banished both Heracles and his own son. Eurystheus made matters worse by refusing to count this as one of the Labours, on the grounds that it had been performed with a view to payment.

Years later Heracles returned to Elis with an army and marched against Augeas, who in turn raised a force of Eleans under the leadership of Eurytus and Cteatus, the sons of his brother Actor and known as the MOLIONES. After suffering an initial defeat, Heracles ambushed and killed the Moliones at Cleonae, then captured the city of Elis, putting Augeas and his sons to death. He recalled Phyleus from refuge in Dulichium and made him king of Elis. In another tradition, Aegeas died naturally of old age and was paid hero's honours in Elis for centuries after his death.

The cleansing of the Augean stables proved of little inspiration to artists – perhaps not surprisingly, since it was a Labour with no worthy adversary and no hint of danger – although it occurs regularly among representations of the whole cycle of the twelve Labours. Its first depiction is on a metope of the temple of Zeus at Olympia, where Heracles breaches the stable walls with a long crowbar. The term 'Augean stables' has become proverbial, referring to anything thoroughly filthy or corrupt.

[Homer, *Iliad* 2.629, 11.698–702; Pindar, *Olympian* 10.26–42; Apollonius, *Argonautica* 1.172–5; Apollodorus 2.5.5, 2.7.2; Diodorus Siculus 4.13.3, 4.33.1–4; Pausanias 5.1.9–5.3.3, 5.4.2.]

Auriga (The Charioteer)

A constellation representing the driver of a four-horse chariot, and variously identified in antiquity as PHAETHON (2), the son of Helios, the Sun-god, who borrowed his father's sun-chariot for a day and was burnt to death by a thunderbolt from Zeus; or HIPPOLYTUS (2), the son of Theseus, who died in a fall from his chariot, when Poseidon sent an immense bull from the sea to terrify his horses; or MYRTILUS, the famous charioteer of Oenomaus, who betrayed his master and was murdered as a result of his treachery; or ERICHTHONIUS (1), an early Attic hero and king of Athens, who was credited with the invention of the four-horse chariot.

Aurora

The Roman name for EOS, goddess of Dawn.

Autesion

A king of Thebes, son of TISAMENUS (2) and great-grandson of Polyneices. Autesion was hounded by the Furies of his ancestors LAIUS and OEDIPUS, so on the advice of an oracle he left the throne of Thebes to Damasichthon and joined the Dorian invaders of the Peloponnese, the HERACLIDS. His daughter Argeia was married to the Heraclid leader ARISTODEMUS, and his son THERAS became guardian of her twin sons, Procles and Eurysthenes, when Aristodemus

was killed. The boys eventually ruled Sparta, establishing there the dual kingship.

[Apollodorus 2.8.2; Pausanias 4.3.4, 9.5.15–16.]

Autolycus

A famous thief and liar. According to Homer, HERMES (who was the god of thieves) gave Autolycus his deceitful skills in return for sacrifices, but a later tradition makes Hermes his father by CHIONE (2), the daughter of Daedalion, and thus able to pass all his skill at deceit and trickery directly on to his son.

Autolycus lived near Mount Parnassus with his wife Amphithea. They had sons, and a daughter, ANTICLEIA, who married Laertes and was the mother of ODYSSEUS. It was Autolycus who gave Odysseus his name, and it was while staying at his grandfather's house and boarhunting with Autolycus' sons that Odysseus received a tusk wound in his leg, leaving the scar by which, many years later, the nurse Eurycleia recognised him on his return to Ithaca after the Trojan War. Apollodorus credits Autolycus with another daughter, Polymede, who married Aeson and was the mother of JASON. He also tells us that it was Autolycus who taught HERACLES to wrestle.

Many were Autolycus' thefts, including the celebrated boar's tusk helmet from AMYNTOR that was later worn by Odysseus during the night-time spying expedition into the Trojan camp. But his especial skill was in stealing animals, for he possessed magical abilities which could make things vanish, or change their colour or their markings. Many were the flocks and herds that he made his own, giving their real owners no chance of identifying them, as when he stole cattle from EURYTUS (1), king of Oechalia, and it was Heracles who fell under suspicion. But Autolycus finally met his match in SISYPHUS, king of Corinth, who was as great a trickster as he. As usual Autolycus stole cattle, transforming them so that they would not be recognised, but Sisyphus suspected the truth when he noticed that his herds were gradually diminishing, while those of Autolycus kept increasing. He outwitted the master-thief by fixing lead tablets to his animals' hooves inscribed with the words 'stolen by Autolycus'. He then had but to follow their tracks and reclaim his beasts. It was said that the two rogues became friends, and that Sisyphus seduced Autolycus' daughter Anticleia, with the result that he, rather than her husband Laertes, was often said to be the father of the wily Odysseus.

Autolycus' name has become synonymous with roguery, and is used by Shakespeare for his ballad-monger and peddler in *The Winter's Tale*. Here Autolycus is the original 'snapper-up of unconsidered trifles', who, 'having flown over many knavish professions ... settled only in rogue' (IV.iii).

[Homer, *Iliad* 10.266–71, *Odyssey* 19.392–466; Apollodorus 1.9.16, 2.4.9, 2.6.2; Ovid, *Metamorphoses* 11.301–17.]

Automedon

In the *Iliad*, Automedon is the comrade and charioteer of ACHILLES. He also drives Achilles' horses for PATROCLUS when he goes into his final, fatal battle. Then, being a considerable warrior in his own right, he kills the Trojan Aretus to gain some sort of vengeance for the death of his friend. 'Now I have put from my heart a little of my grief for Patroclus' death, even though the man I killed was not as great as he was', he says, before climbing back into his chariot 'with his hands and his feet all bloody, like a lion after devouring a bull' (17.538–42).

After Achilles' death Automedon fought alongside his son, NEOPTOLEMUS, when they took part in the capture of Troy.

[Homer, *Iliad* 9.209, 16.148, 472–6, 864–7, 17.426–542, 19.392–7, 23.563–5, 24.473–5, 574–5, 625–6; Virgil, *Aeneid* 2.476–8.]

Automedousa

Daughter of ALCATHOUS (1), king of Megara, and Evaechme. Automedousa married IPHICLES, the half-brother of Heracles, and bore a son, IOLAUS, who became Heracles' faithful companion and charioteer.

Autonoe

Daughter of CADMUS, king of Thebes, and HARMONIA; sister of AGAVE, INO and SEMELE. Autonoe married ARISTAEUS and bore him a son, ACTAEON. The boy grew up to be a skilled huntsman, but was torn to pieces by his own hounds at the instigation of Artemis.

Autonoe, Agave and Ino refused to believe that Semele had been the mother of the god DIONYSUS by Zeus.

Dionysus punished them by driving them mad, sending them to revel as MAENADS on Mount Cithaeron. Here, in a bacchic frenzy, they tore Agave's son PENTHEUS apart, believing him to be a mountain lion.

Pausanias (1.44.5) reports that the tomb of Autonoe was to be seen in the village of Erenea, near Megara. She had left Thebes because of her great grief over the death of Actaeon and the other tragedies of the house of Cadmus.

[Hesiod, *Theogony* 975–8; Euripides, *Bacchae* 1121–36; Apollodorus 3.4.2–4.]

Aventinus

In Virgil's *Aeneid* (7.655–69), Aventinus is one of TURNUS' allies against AENEAS. He is the son of Hercules (HERACLES) and a priestess named Rhea, conceived on Hercules' journey home after stealing Geryon's cattle, and named Aventinus because he was born on the Aventine Hill, later part of Rome. He flaunts his parentage by displaying on his shield the HYDRA OF LERNA, fringed with a hundred snakes, and by wearing a lionskin with its scalp serving as a helmet, just as his father wore the pelt of the NEMEAN LION.

Avernus

A lake near Naples and Cumae, in ancient times thought to be one of the entrances to HADES (2). Close by was the cave through which AENEAS descended to the Underworld in the company of the Cumaean SIBYL. Avernus was said to derive its name from the Greek *aornos*, 'without birds', since its deadly vapours made it a place over which no bird could fly and survive. The name was also used for the Underworld itself. In the famous words of the Sibyl (Virgil, *Aeneid* 6.126–9): 'Easy is the descent to Avernus: the door of black Dis stands open night and day. But to retrace your steps and escape back to the upper air, that is the task, that is the labour.'

B

Bacchus *see* DIONYSUS.

Balius *see* XANTHUS.

Bateia

Daughter of TEUCER (1), the first king of the Troad, and wife of the immigrant DARDANUS who succeeded him. She thus became the mother of the Trojan race.

Battus (1)

An old man who saw HERMES, on the very day that he was born, stealing Apollo's cattle. Hermes bribed the old man with a cow to say nothing of what he had seen, and he replied that a stone would more readily tell of the theft than he. A little while later the god returned, in disguise, to test Battus, offering him a cow and a bull if he could tell him anything about the stolen cattle. Tempted by the double reward, the old man told what he knew, so Hermes transformed his betrayer, very appropriately, into a stone.

[Ovid, *Metamorphoses* 2.679–707.]

Battus (2)

The founder of the Theran colony of Cyrene in Libya. He was the son of a Theran nobleman, Polymnestus, and a direct descendant in the seventeenth generation of the Argonaut EUPHEMUS. Battus had been afflicted with a stammer ever since he was a child, and eventually he went to consult the Delphic Oracle about his defective speech. He was told that he must found a city in Libya. Full of doubt he returned home and did nothing. But misfortunes began to afflict the Therans, until at last they too consulted the Oracle. Once again the reply came that Battus must be despatched to found a city in Libya, so the Therans sent him off together with a party of colonists.

Battus and his men sailed as far as the Libyan coast, but not knowing what to do next, they returned to Thera. The Therans refused to let them land, resolutely driving them away with shouts and missiles until they set off once more for Libya. At first they settled on an island near the Libyan coast, but when this settlement failed to prosper, a third enquiry at Delphi elicited the reminder that they had not yet colonised Libya itself. They next settled for six years at a pleasant spot on the mainland coast, then the Libyans led them further west to what they promised would be an even better place. Here Battus and his men founded Cyrene, a colony that prospered so well that men flocked from all over Greece to live there. Thus Battus fulfilled the destiny that had been implicitly promised to his ancestor Euphemus, when he was presented by the sea-god Triton with a clod of earth, symbolising the future sovereignty in Libya of his descendants.

As for Battus' stammer, he one day encountered a lion in the desert and let out a yell of terror, which had two happy results: the lion fled, and Battus found that he could now at last speak normally.

[Pindar, *Pythian* 4.59–63; Herodotus 4.150–160; Pausanias 10.15.6–7.]

Baubo *see* IAMBE.

Baucis *see* PHILEMON.

Bellerophon or Bellerophontes

Son of GLAUCUS (3) and Eurymede (or Eurynome), though sometimes said to be the son of POSEIDON. Bellerophon had to leave his native Ephyra (later Corinth) because he accidentally killed a man. Various names are given to his victim, one of them being Bellerus, hence Bellerophon's own name, meaning Bellerus-killer. He went to the palace of PROETUS, king of Tiryns, where the king's wife Stheneboea (called Anteia by Homer, who first tells this story) fell in love with him and tried to seduce him. But Bellerophon would have none of her. Rejected and vengeful, hoping that Proetus would kill him, she claimed that he had tried to rape her, but the king hesitated to kill a guest. Instead he sent him to IOBATES, king of Lycia and father of Stheneboea, with a sealed letter containing instructions to kill the bearer ('dire, life-destroying symbols' is how Homer describes the letter, in his only reference to writing). For nine days Iobates feasted Bellerophon and only on the tenth day opened the letter. He too had scruples about killing his guest directly, so instead he set him three fearsome tasks that would have been quite sufficient to destroy any ordinary man. The first task was to kill the monstrous CHIMAERA who was ravaging Lycia and who, as Apollodorus says (2.3), was more than a match for many men, let alone one (fig.30). She met her own match, however, in Bellerophon. Returning from this task, he was sent to fight single-handed against the tribe of the SOLYMI, and then against the AMAZONS. From both battles he returned triumphant. Finally the king sent the best of his Lycian men to ambush him, but Bellerophon killed them all. Recognising that his guest must be of divine descent, Iobates gave him half his kingdom and the hand of his daughter, Philonoe, in marriage. She bore him three children, HIPPOLOCHUS, ISANDER and LAODAMEIA (1).

Homer makes no mention of the winged horse PEGASUS, but in all later accounts Bellerophon accomplished his tasks by flying high on Pegasus and attacking his enemies from above. Bellerophon saw the wondrous horse by the spring of Peirene, and asked the seer POLYIDUS for advice on how to tame him. Told to sleep for a night on the altar of Athena, Bellerophon dreamed that the goddess gave him a golden bridle and instructed him to sacrifice a white bull to Poseidon, Tamer of Horses. When he awoke he found the golden bridle beside him and lost no time in sacrificing a white bull. When he now approached Pegasus, the horse willingly accepted the bridle and Bellerophon mounted easily on his back. From this vantage point he tackled the deadly tasks set him by Iobates. In art we see him mounted on Pegasus and attacking the Chimaera from the early decades of the seventh century BC onwards (fig. 110), in the earlier representations confronting the monster head-on, later flying above her. Vase-paintings from about 420 BC depict the fatal letter, either Proetus handing it over to Bellerophon, or Iobates receiving it.

According to Euripides' lost play *Stheneboea*, Bellerophon used Pegasus to take vengeance on the woman who had tried to have him killed: he persuaded her to mount his horse with him, then flew out over the sea and threw her down to her death. His later fate was

Fig.30 **The raging Chimaera, wounded by Bellerophon.**

dramatised in Euripides' lost tragedy *Bellerophon*, and cleverly parodied in Aristophanes' comedy *Peace*. He tried to ride Pegasus up to Olympus, the home of the gods; but ZEUS, in anger at his presumption, sent a gadfly to sting his winged steed, and Pegasus threw him back to earth again. He survived the fall, reappearing onstage in Euripides' play, crippled and in rags. Homer says that, 'hated by all the gods, he wandered alone over the Aleian plain, eating his heart out and keeping far away from the trodden paths of men' (*Iliad* 6.200–2). His death is unrecorded.

[Homer, *Iliad* 6.154–202; Hesiod, *Catalogue of Women* fr. 43a; Pindar, *Olympian* 13.60–92, *Isthmian* 7.44–7; Pausanias 3.18.13. C. Collard, M. J. Cropp and K. H. Lee, *Euripides: Selected Fragmentary Plays* I (1995), pp. 79–120.]

Bellona

A Roman goddess of war, similar to the Greek ENYO (1) but with a more important cult, just as the Roman god of war, MARS, had a more important cult than his Greek equivalent, ARES. Like Enyo, Bellona played little part in myths and was more a personification of the bloody spirit of warfare.

Belus

Son of POSEIDON and LIBYA, and twin-brother of AGENOR (1). His name is the Hellenised form of the Levantine *Baal* and the Babylonian *Bel*, both of which mean 'lord'. While Agenor migrated to Phoenicia and became king of Tyre or Sidon, Belus stayed in Africa and ruled the Egyptians. He married Anchinoe, daughter of the river-god Nile, who bore him twin sons, Aegyptus and DANAUS, fathers in their turn respectively of fifty sons and fifty daughters. (According to some, Belus fathered CEPHEUS (1) and PHINEUS (1) too.) Aegyptus' fifty sons married Danaus' fifty daughters, forty-nine of whom murdered their husbands on their wedding night. Despite this, Belus was the ancestor of royal lines and many great heroes through his single surviving grandson Lynceus and his granddaughter Hypermestra. Belus was also the name of DIDO's father.

[Herodotus 7.61; Apollodorus 2.1.4; Virgil, *Aeneid* 619–22.]

Benthesicyme *see* EUMOLPUS.

Bia

Daughter of the Titan PALLAS (2) and the Oceanid STYX. Bia was the personification of Might. She and her two brothers Zelus (Aspiration) and Cratos (Power) and her sister NIKE (Victory) were the constant companions of ZEUS, an honour accorded them after they and their mother supported Zeus in his battle with the TITANS. Bia and Cratos are characters in Aeschylus' tragedy *Prometheus Bound*, where at the beginning of the play they compel HEPHAES-

TUS to chain PROMETHEUS to a rock, as Zeus' punishment for stealing fire and giving it to mankind.

[Hesiod, *Theogony* 383–403.]

Bias *see* MELAMPUS.

Boeotus

Son of MELANIPPE (1).

Boötes (The Ploughman)

A constellation near URSA MAJOR, the Great Bear, which is also known as the Plough or the Wagon. Two identities are given to the Ploughman. Either he was Icarius, the Attic farmer who introduced Dionysus' gift of wine to his neighbours (*see* ERIGONE (1)). Or he was Philomelus, a son of IASION (1) and DEMETER, who unlike his rich brother PLUTUS was only a poor farmer. With his small store of money Philomelus bought two oxen, then invented the plough to prepare the earth for grain, his mother's gift to mankind. Demeter was so pleased with her inventive son that she immortalised him among the stars.

Boreadae

The name commonly given to ZETES and Calais, the twin sons of Boreas, the North Wind.

Boreas

The violent North Wind and its god. He was the son of EOS, goddess of Dawn, and the Titan Astraeus, and his home was in Thrace to the north of Greece. He brought the icy blasts of winter and was often contrasted with his gentler brothers ZEPHYRUS, the West Wind, and Notus, the South Wind. He was also closely associated with horses, and took the form of a stallion to father twelve colts, swift as the wind, on the beautiful mares of ERICHTHONIUS (2), king of Troy. But he is best-known for his abduction of Oreithyia, a daughter of Erechtheus, king of Athens. At first he pleaded for her favour, relying on persuasion, but all in vain. So then, bristling with rage, he reverted to his normal violent temper, and swooped upon her while she was dancing on the banks of the Ilissus. He swept her up in a cloud of wind and carried her off to Thrace, where she bore him two winged sons, ZETES and Calais, and two daughters, CLEOPATRA (1) and CHIONE (1). Thereafter the Athenians saw Boreas as their relative by marriage, and Herodotus (7.189) tells us that they called on him for help in 480 BC when threatened with invasion by the Persian fleet. The ships were duly scattered and defeated by the North Wind, as had happened on a similar occasion twelve years earlier. 'Now I cannot say if this was really why the Persians were caught at anchor by the storm-wind,' says Herodotus with typical caution, 'but the

Athenians are quite positive that, just as Boreas helped them before, so Boreas was responsible for what happened on this occasion also. And when they went home they built the god a shrine by the river Ilissus.'

The popularity in Athens of the myth of Oreithyia's abduction, both before and after the Persian War, is shown by its frequent depictions on vase-paintings. Boreas is usually depicted bearded and winged, and clad in a short pleated tunic, while his hair is shaggy, and sometimes frosted and spiky (fig. 31). On the chest of Cypselus he was shown with serpents' tails instead of feet. Aeschylus dramatised the myth in his (lost) satyr play *Oreithyia*. Late accounts make Boreas the lover of the nymph PITYS, and the father, by different mothers, of two sons, BUTES (1) and Lycurgus.

[Hesiod, *Theogony* 378–80, 869–71, *Works and Days* 504–35; Simonides fr. 534; Pindar, *Pythian* 4.179–83; Plato, *Phaedrus* 229cd; Apollonius, *Argonautica* 1.211–223; Apollodorus 3.15.1–3; Diodorus Siculus 5.50.1–5; Pausanias 1.19.5, 5.19.1, 8.27.14, 8.36.6; Ovid, *Metamorphoses* 6.675–721.]

Briareos

One of the HUNDRED-HANDERS, called Briareos by the gods but Aegaeon by mortals.

Briseis

ACHILLES' concubine in the *Iliad*, a minor character but a key figure, since it is the loss of Briseis that causes Achilles' fateful wrath and lies behind all the resultant action of the poem. When, in the tenth year of the Trojan War, AGAMEMNON is forced to give up his own concubine, CHRYSEIS, he bolsters his hurt pride by taking Briseis away from Achilles, who retires to his tent in anger and thereafter refuses to fight (fig. 3). As a result, many people will die, including Achilles' beloved comrade PATROCLUS, killed by the greatest warrior on the Trojan side, Hector. Hector too will die, killed in revenge by Achilles; as will Achilles himself, since his death is fated to come soon after Hector's.

Achilles won Briseis when he sacked Lyrnessus, a town near Troy, killing her husband and three brothers. She is promised to him in marriage (19.297–9) and he loves her dearly, calling her his 'dear wife' (9.336) and saying, once she has been taken from him, 'any man loves the woman who is his, and cares for her, just as I loved this one from my heart, even though I won her by my spear' (9.342–3). She loves him in return, and when the heralds come to take her from Achilles to Agamemnon, she goes with them unwillingly (1.348). Agamemnon, however, does not sleep with her, as he later swears when, after Patroclus' death, Achilles is ready to fight again and the two men make their peace. Briseis is thus returned untouched to

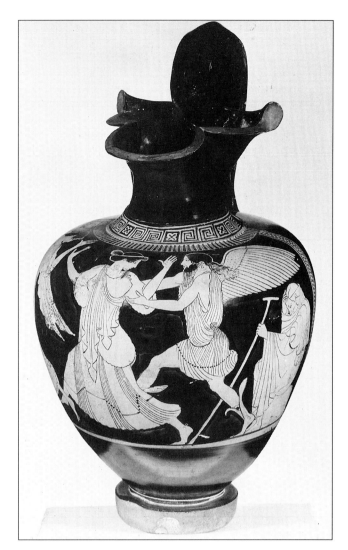

Fig. 31 Boreas abducts Oreithyia, while her father, Erechtheus, sits grieving.

Achilles (fig. 122), and he is given many other rich gifts in appeasement for his earlier loss.

Our last sight of Achilles in the *Iliad* is, appropriately, as he sleeps with Briseis (24.675–6). Moved by compassion for Priam, he has returned Hector's body to the old king, and now, his anger at last over, 'Achilles slept in the corner of his strong-built tent, and the lovely Briseis lay by his side'.

[Homer, *Iliad* 1.181–7, 318–48, 2.688–94, 9.328–45, 19.246–302; Quintus of Smyrna, *Sequel to Homer* 3.551–81; Ovid, *Heroides* 3.]

Britomartis

A Cretan goddess similar to ARTEMIS. She was born the daughter of ZEUS and a Cretan woman called Carme, and grew up to be a virgin huntress, very dear to Artemis. MINOS, the king of Crete, fell in love with her and tried to win her, but she resolutely fled from him. For nine months he pursued her over plains and mountains until, just as he was about to seize her, she flung herself in desperation from a cliff into the sea. She was caught in the nets of some fishermen, and Artemis made her a goddess. After this she was also called Dictynna, supposedly meaning 'Lady of the Nets' (*dictys*, 'net'), though this title may instead refer to the Cretan Mount Dicte, associated with her cult. She was also worshipped on the island of Aegina under the title of Aphaea.

[Callimachus, *Hymn* 3.189–205; Diodorus Siculus 5.76.3–4; Pausanias 2.30.3, 3.14.2, 8.2.4, 9.40.3.]

Brontes *see* CYCLOPES.

Broteas

Son of TANTALUS (1). He was said to have carved the ancient rock-hewn image of CYBELE, the Phrygian Mother-goddess, which is still to be seen on the side of

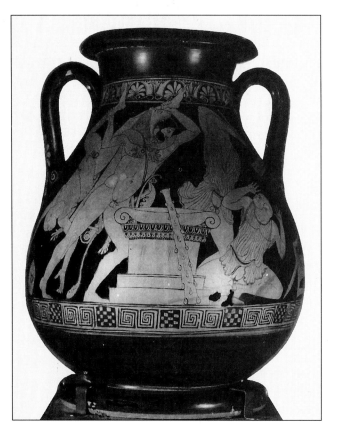

Mount Sipylus about three hundred feet above the plain. He was a hunter, but he paid no honours to ARTEMIS and so she drove him mad. He threw himself into a fire, believing that he was invulnerable and that even fire could not hurt him, and perished in the flames.

[Apollodorus, *Epitome* 2.2; Pausanias 3.22.4.]

Busiris

A king of Egypt, son of POSEIDON by Lysianassa, the daughter of Io's son EPAPHUS. After a nine-year famine, Busiris consulted Phrasius, a seer from Cyprus, who said that famine would be averted if he sacrificed a foreigner to Zeus every year. Busiris began by sacrificing Phrasius himself, then carried on killing any foreigner who came to the country. When HERACLES travelled through Egypt, on his way to fetch the golden apples of the Hesperides, he too was caught and dragged to the sacrificial altar, but he burst his bonds and killed Busiris, together with his son and many attendants.

Busiris was the subject of a lost satyr-play by Euripides. Ancient vase-paintings have some lively depictions of this episode (fig. 32), with Busiris killed at his own altar and Egyptian attendants either flung around by Heracles or fleeing in terror. Herodotus tells the story, adding his own rationalistic comments (2.45):

> The Greeks tell many unbelievable stories. One silly one is the story which they tell about Heracles, of how, when he came to Egypt, the Egyptians crowned him with a wreath and took him in solemn procession to be sacrificed to Zeus. He submitted quietly until they began the ritual of the sacrifice at the altar, but then he at last resisted and killed them all. Now the Greeks in saying this seem to me to be completely ignorant of Egyptian character and customs. For it is against their religion to kill animals for sacrifice, except geese and sheep and such bulls and bull-calves as are deemed suitably clean. So would they be likely to sacrifice humans? Besides, if Heracles was, as they say, one man on his own, how would he kill tens of thousands of people? And now may the gods and the heroes forgive me for saying these things!

[Apollodorus 2.5.11.]

Butes (1)

A son of BOREAS who plotted against his half-brother, Lycurgus, and was exiled from Thrace. He went to Naxos, where he and his followers lived by piracy. Since there

Fig. 32 Heracles kills the Egyptian king Busiris at his altar.

were no women on their island, they often seized women on their piratical expeditions and carried them home. In a raid on Drius in Phthiotis, Butes raped Coronis, a worshipper of DIONYSUS, and in answer to her prayers, the god punished Butes by striking him with madness. He flung himself into a well and drowned.

[Diodorus Siculus 5.50.1–5.]

Butes (2)

Son of PANDION (1), king of Athens, and Zeuxippe, and twin-brother of ERECHTHEUS. He married his brother's daughter, Chthonia. When Pandion died, Erechtheus took the throne and Butes received the priesthoods of ATHENA and POSEIDON. After his death Butes was worshipped as a hero in the Erechtheum on the Acropolis.

[Apollodorus 3.14.8–3.15.1; Pausanias 1.26.5.]

Butes (3)

An ARGONAUT, the son of Teleon. While the *Argo* was sailing past the island of Anthemoessa on which lived the SIRENS, the singing enchantresses who lured men to their deaths, ORPHEUS played his lyre to drown out their fatal song. Butes, however, jumped overboard and began to swim towards the singers, but before he reached the island and certain death, APHRODITE snatched him safely from the water. She took him to Cape Lilybaeum on the western tip of Sicily, modern Marsala, where she bore him a son, ERYX. Here Butes had a hero-cult after his death.

[Apollonius, *Argonautica* 1.95, 4.891–921.]

Byblis and Caunus

The twin daughter and son of MILETUS and a nymph, Cyanea, daughter of the river-god Maeander. When they grew up, Byblis fell in love with her brother and after much anguish confessed her passion, doing her best to seduce him. Appalled and angry, he left his home city of Miletus for ever and founded the city of Caunus in southern Caria. Byblis was overcome with longing for her brother. She went mad and roamed over many lands, seeking him to no avail. At last, too tired to go further, she lay on the ground despairing, and wept so unceasingly that the nymphs in their pity turned her into a spring of water that would never run dry.

[Ovid, *Metamorphoses* 9.451–665.]

C

Cabiri

Minor divinities of the northern Aegean Sea and adjacent mainlands, often confused with the CORYBANTES or the CURETES (1). Their mysteries were celebrated on Lemnos, Imbros and Samothrace in particular, and they also had a cult at Thebes. They are rather obscure figures, for their number is uncertain (from two to seven) and also their parentage, though their father was most commonly said to be HEPHAESTUS. Aeschylus wrote a play called *Cabiri*, now lost and about which we know virtually nothing, except that the ARGONAUTS visited the Cabiri and became drunk. Certainly in Apollonius' *Argonautica* (1.915–21) the Argonauts, on the instructions of Orpheus, put in at Samothrace to celebrate the Cabiri's mysteries, so that they might sail onwards in greater safety.

[Herodotus 2.51, 3.37; Strabo 10.3.7, 10.3.19–1; Athenaeus 10.428f.]

Cacus

A fire-breathing monster, the son of VULCAN, who lived in a cave in the Aventine Hill on the future site of Rome. To the terror of all who dwelt nearby he lived on human flesh, afterwards nailing the heads of his victims to the doors of his cave. But he was finally overcome by HERCULES, as EVANDER recounts in the *Aeneid* (8.193–272). When Hercules was driving home the cattle he had stolen from GERYON, he stopped to pasture them in the region of Cacus' lair. The monster spotted the splendid beasts and slyly stole eight of them, four bulls and four cows, dragging them back to his cave by their tails so as to leave no tracks pointing to their place of concealment. He almost got away with his theft undetected, but when Hercules at last made to move on, his cattle began to low plaintively at leaving their lush pastures, and a single cow, from deep in the cave, lowed in reply. Full of rage, Hercules dashed up the mountain in pursuit. 'Never before', says Evander, 'had anyone seen Cacus afraid, never before had there been terror in his eyes. But now

he fled back to his cave swifter than the wind, with fear lending wings to his feet.' Once in his refuge he blocked the doorway with a vast immovable boulder, so that Hercules had to tear off the top of the mountain to get at his quarry. The monster vomited fire and smoke at his pursuer, while Hercules bombarded him from above with branches of trees and rocks the size of millstones. At last, losing all patience, Hercules leapt down into the cave, aiming for the spot where the smoke boiled thickest. Gripping hold of Cacus he strangled him. For ridding the district of its scourge he was honoured ever after.

[Strabo 5.3.3; Dionysius of Halicarnassus 1.39–40; Livy 1.7.4–15; Propertius 4.9.1–20; Ovid, *Fasti* 1.543–82, 5.643–52.]

Cadmus

The legendary founder of Thebes. He was the son of the Phoenician king AGENOR (1) and his wife Telephassa, and thus the brother of EUROPA, who was carried off to Crete by Zeus in the form of a bull. Because her family knew nothing of what had happened, Agenor sent his sons off in different directions to seek for their lost sister. None of them found her. Cadmus, accompanied by his mother, at first settled in Thrace, but when she died he went on to Delphi to consult the Oracle. He was told not to be concerned about his sister, but to follow a cow that had a white mark like the orb of the full moon on both flanks, going wherever she led him. He must found a city where she lay down to rest. Cadmus travelled through Phocis before he found the prophesied cow, then was led through the whole of Boeotia before the animal at last sank to the ground in weariness. This, then, was to be the site of his city.

Wishing to sacrifice the cow to ATHENA, Cadmus sent some of his companions to draw water from a nearby spring, called the Spring of ARES, not realising that it was guarded by a monstrous dragon said to be the offspring of Ares himself. According to Ovid (*Metamorphoses* 3.32–45):

It had a wonderful golden crest, its eyes flashed fire, its body was all puffed up with poison, and a three-forked tongue flickered from a triple row of teeth ... It was as huge as the Serpent that lies between the two Bears in the sky.

Not surprisingly it killed most of the men, but was then in turn, after a terrible fight, killed by the valiant Cadmus. Athena appeared, and on her advice he sowed some of the dragon's teeth in the ground (the rest were given by the goddess to AEETES, king of Colchis). At once armed men sprang from the earth and Cadmus in fear flung a stone among them. Each thinking that he was being attacked by the others, they turned and fought each other until only five survived. These were Echion, Udaeus, Chthonius, Hyperenor and Pelorus, who came to be known as the *Spartoi*, the 'Sown Men'.

To atone for the slaughter of Ares' dragon, Cadmus had to serve the god for eight years; but at the end of that time he became king of his city, built in the place where the cow first lay down to rest. It was called Cadmeia (later Thebes), and Zeus honoured Cadmus by giving him HARMONIA, the daughter of Ares and Aphrodite, as his bride. All the gods attended the wedding and brought gifts, celebrating this union of divinity and mortal, just as they would later come to the marriage of the sea-goddess Thetis to the mortal Peleus. Cadmus and Harmonia had a son, POLYDORUS (1), and four daughters, AUTONOE, INO, SEMELE and AGAVE. The Sown Men became the ancestors of the principal Theban families, and one of them, Echion, married Cadmus' daughter Agave.

Despite the auspicious beginnings of Cadmus' marriage to Harmonia, the couple were forced to suffer much grief from the fates of their family. Semele was loved by Zeus, but was burnt to death in the flame of her lover's thunderbolt. Ino was driven mad by Hera for looking after Semele's infant son, the god Dionysus, and while mad killed her own child and herself (though she was then transformed into the sea-deity Leucothea). Two of Cadmus' grandsons were torn to pieces because of the anger of the gods, ACTAEON, the son of Autonoe, by his own hounds, and PENTHEUS, the son of Agave, by his own mother.

A rather peculiar end is recorded for Cadmus and Harmonia. After Pentheus' tragic death they left Thebes for ever, going to live among the Encheleans, an obscure barbarian tribe of Illyria in north-western Greece. Here, riding in an ox-cart, Cadmus led his people to victory in wars against other tribes and finally ruled over the whole of Illyria. It was said that a son, Illyrius, was born to him. At the end of their lives both Cadmus and Harmonia were transformed into snakes (this was particularly odd,

but was perhaps seen as an honour, since the souls of heroes were thought to live on in the bodies of benevolent snakes), and were sent by Zeus to live for ever in the Elysian Fields. Their tomb could be seen in Illyria.

Cadmus was honoured as a hero at both Thebes and Sparta, and throughout Greece as the man who introduced the Greek alphabet from Phoenicia. He appears occasionally in art, both ancient and postclassical. There is a particularly horrifying painting, 'Two Followers of Cadmus Devoured by the Dragon', by Cornelis van Haarlem in London's National Gallery.

[Euripides, *Phoenician Women* 818–27, 931–52; Apollonius, *Argonautica* 517–18; Apollodorus 3.1.1, 3.4.1–2, 3.5.4; Diodorus Siculus 4.2.1–3, 5.58.2–3; Pausanias 3.15.8, 3.24.3, 9.5.1–3, 9.10.1, 9.12.1–3; Ovid, *Metamorphoses* 3.3–137, 4.563–603. R. B. Edwards, *Kadmos The Phoenician* (1979).]

Caeculus

The founder of the Italian city of Praeneste. In Virgil's *Aeneid* (7.678–90) Caeculus leads his people in support of TURNUS in the war against AENEAS and the Trojans; and Servius, commenting on the passage, tells Caeculus' story. He was conceived when a spark flew from the fire into his mother's lap, so he was said to be a son of the fire-god VULCAN. His mother abandoned him, but some girls found him lying near the hearth of Jupiter's shrine, and because the infant seemed to be blinded (*caecus*) by the fire, he was called Caeculus. He was brought up among shepherds, and later with a group of comrades founded the new town of Praeneste. He invited the neighbourhood to the celebration of public games, and when they were assembled he urged them to settle in his community, adding weight to his appeal by declaring that he was a son of Vulcan. They scoffed at his claim, so he called on his father to give them a sign and at once the whole assembly was surrounded by a wall of flame. Seeing this miracle, the people flocked to become members of Caeculus' new town.

[J. N. Bremmer and N. M. Horsfall, *Roman Myth and Mythography* (1987), pp. 49–62.]

Caeneus

Caeneus was originally a female, Caenis, the daughter of the Lapith chieftain ELATUS (2). Her story is told most vividly by Ovid (*Metamorphoses* 12.169–535). She was famous for her beauty, but rejected all her many suitors. One day, when she was wandering over a lonely part of the seashore, POSEIDON came out of the sea and raped her. Afterwards he offered her as a reward whatever she might wish, and she chose to become a man, so that she might never again have to undergo such an outrage. The god granted her wish, adding the gift of invulnerability, and

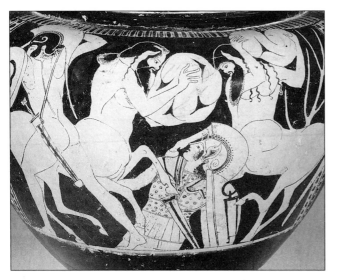

Fig. 33 The Centaurs hammer Caeneus into the ground, here using rocks.

Caenis became Caeneus. He married and had a son, CORONUS, who sailed with Jason and the Argonauts.

Caeneus became a leader of the LAPITHS, and during the famous battle of the Lapiths and the CENTAURS, at the wedding of Peirithous and Hippodameia, he killed several of the monstrous creatures. They did their utmost to kill him too, using swords and spears against his invulnerable body, but all to no avail. Finally they struck him with the trunks of fir trees until he was hammered into the ground (fig. 33). But now he was once more transformed: from the mass of tree trunks piled over his body, a yellow bird flew upward, soaring into the clear air.

[Homer, *Iliad* 1.263–4, 2.746; Hesiod, *Catalogue of Women*, fr. 87; Apollonius, *Argonautica* 1.57–64; Apollodorus, *Epitome* 1.22; Virgil, *Aeneid* 6.448–9.]

Calais *see* ZETES.

Calchas

The seer who accompanied the Greek army to the TROJAN WAR. The advice and predictions that he gave during many crucial episodes of the long war often had far-reaching consequences. When ACHILLES was nine years old, Calchas, who saw the war approaching, foretold that Troy could not be taken without him; so his mother disguised him as a girl and sent him to live among the daughters of King LYCOMEDES of Scyros, resulting in the birth of NEOPTOLEMUS. Achilles was recruited by the Greeks after Odysseus penetrated his disguise. At Aulis, Calchas predicted the length of the coming war when a snake climbed a plane tree and devoured a mother sparrow and her eight babies, and was then turned into stone by Zeus: he said this meant that the war would last for nine years, and that in the tenth year Troy would be taken. When the fleet was later becalmed at Aulis, the seer interpreted another portent which meant that Artemis was angry, and that Agamemnon's virgin daughter IPHIGENEIA would have to be sacrificed to appease the goddess. Iphigeneia's death was one of the motives for CLYTEMNESTRA's murder of Agamemnon when he returned home at the end of the war.

In the tenth year of the war, a plague ravaged the army, and Calchas explained to the Greeks its cause: Apollo was angry because Agamemnon had refused to give back his concubine CHRYSEIS to her father Chryses, Apollo's priest (1.68–100). To put an end to the plague Agamemnon gave up Chryseis, but took Achilles' own prize of honour, BRISEIS, to replace her. This led to Achilles' wrath, and to the deaths of many great heroes, Greek and Trojan alike, including Patroclus and Hector, and later Achilles himself.

After Achilles' death, Calchas was involved in various events which brought the war to an end. He foretold that Troy could not be taken unless the Greeks possessed the bow and arrows of Heracles. These were with PHILOCTETES on Lemnos, so Odysseus led a mission to fetch Philoctetes to Troy. Calchas also advised the Greeks to capture the Trojan seer HELENUS, who could – and did – tell them under what other conditions Troy would be captured. Finally, after Odysseus had conceived the idea of the WOODEN HORSE to get warriors into Troy by stealth, Calchas urged the Greeks to build it. The horse was built and Troy was sacked. The Greeks paid less attention to the seer when he told them that Athena was angry because of Cassandra's rape by AJAX (2). Despite his warning, many of them put to sea, and many were killed in the subsequent god-sent storms.

Calchas met his own death at Colophon, soon after the end of the war. It was predicted that he would die if he ever met a seer better than himself; this turned out to be MOPSUS (2), son of Manto and grandson of the great Theban seer, Teiresias. Calchas challenged Mopsus to say how many figs were borne by a certain fig tree, and he gave what proved to be the right answer. Mopsus in turn challenged Calchas to say how many piglets a pregnant sow was carrying. He said that there were eight, but Mopsus said that he was wrong, and that she was carrying nine, all males, which would be born the next day at the sixth hour. It happened as he had said, and Calchas died of a broken heart.

[Homer, *Iliad* 2.300–30; Aeschylus, *Agamemnon* 104–257;

Apollodorus 3.13.8, *Epitome* 5.8–10, 6.2–4; Strabo 14.1.27; Quintus of Smyrna, *Sequel to Homer* 12.3–10.]

Callidice

A queen of Thesprotia who played a part in ODYSSEUS' life after the events recounted by Homer in the *Odyssey*. In his journeyings after he had killed the Suitors on Ithaca, Odysseus came to Thesprotia where Callidice urged him to stay with her, promising him the rule of the kingdom. He married her and they had a son, Polypoetes. During Callidice's lifetime Odysseus stayed in Thesprotia, but when she died he handed over the kingdom to his son and returned to Ithaca.

[Epic Cycle, Proclus' summary of the *Telegony*; Apollodorus, *Epitome* 7.34.]

Calliope *see* MUSES.

Callirhoe

Several mythical women have the name Callirhoe, meaning 'Fair-flowing', and they all have watery connections.

Callirhoe (1)

A daughter of OCEANUS and Tethys. To CHRYSAOR, son of the Gorgon Medusa, Callirhoe bore triple-bodied GERYON.

Callirhoe (2)

A daughter of the river-god SCAMANDER, and wife of the Trojan king TROS.

Callirhoe (3)

A daughter of the river-god ACHELOUS, and second wife of ALCMAEON.

Callirhoe (4)

A girl loved by Coresus, a priest of DIONYSUS at Calydon. When Callirhoe rejected Coresus' advances he complained to his god, and Dionysus responded by afflicting the people of Calydon with madness. They appealed to the oracle at Dodona and were told that the angry god was demanding the sacrifice of Callirhoe, or of a willing substitute, before the madness could be lifted. It was of course the task of Coresus, as priest, to carry out the sacrifice. The girl was led to the altar, but at the last moment, overcome by love, Coresus plunged the knife into his own breast. Seeing him lying dead, Callirhoe was stricken with pity and remorse, and she cut her own throat, dying beside a spring that ever afterwards bore her name.

[Pausanias 7.21.1–5.]

Callisto ('most beautiful')

Either a nymph, or the daughter of LYCAON (1), king of Arcadia. Ovid tells the most familiar version of her story (*Metamorphoses* 2.409–531). She was a huntress in the mountains of Arcadia, vowed to chastity, and a favourite companion of ARTEMIS. 'But a favourite is never a favourite for long,' adds Ovid cynically (416). ZEUS saw Callisto one day as she was resting in the woods. At once he desired her, and approached her disguised as Artemis. In her ignorance she welcomed him warmly, and only when he was kissing her did she realise that this was no goddess. By then it was too late, for Zeus went on to rape her even though she struggled against him with all her strength. He left her pregnant.

The months passed, and one hot day Artemis persuaded all her companions to undress and bathe in a cool stream – all but Callisto, who naturally shrank from revealing her condition. But she had no choice, for her friends stripped the clothes from her, and the goddess, realising the truth, in fury banished her. Rejected by them all, Callisto left their company in disgrace. But worse was to come. She gave birth to a son, ARCAS, and this made HERA so angry and jealous that she punished the innocent girl cruelly. She caught Callisto by the hair and flung her to the ground (477–85):

> And when the girl stretched out her arms to beg for mercy, they began to bristle with coarse black hairs, and her hands curved round, tipped with crooked claws, and turned into feet. Her face, which just now Zeus had praised, was disfigured by wide gaping jaws. And lest she might win sympathy with her prayers and imploring words, her powers of speech were taken from her, and only an angry threatening growl, terrifying to hear, came harshly from her throat. She was now a bear, but still her mind remained as it was ...

For fifteen years she lived in the wilds, afraid of humans and wild beasts alike and forever grieving her fate. Then one day her son Arcas came face to face with her in the woods. She seemed to recognise him, but he shrank back in fear from this beast that gazed at him so fixedly. Eagerly she tried to approach him, but he did not know her and drew back his spear to thrust and kill. Then Zeus, after ignoring Callisto's long misery for all too many years, at last took pity on her and stayed her son's hand. The god caught up mother and son and carried them into the sky, where he immortalised them among the stars. Callisto became the constellation Arctos, the Great Bear (Ursa Major), and Arcas became the brilliant star Arcturus, 'Bear-guardian', forever following his mother through the night sky. This, however, made Hera even angrier, and she begged the sea-gods OCEANUS and Tethys never to allow her rival's constellation to sink for rest into the waters of Ocean that surrounded the earth.

This is why the Great Bear never sets, but revolves eternally around the Pole Star, high in the heavens.

Other versions of the myth vary its details. Sometimes Callisto was turned into a bear by Artemis, angry that her companion had broken her vow of chastity, sometimes by Zeus himself, to try and hide his infidelity from Hera. Sometimes Callisto was hunted and killed by Artemis, either out of anger, or to please Hera; and sometimes she died before her baby was born, and he was snatched from her womb by Zeus, or Hermes, and given to Maia to bring up. Sometimes Callisto in her bear-form wandered unknowingly into a forbidden sanctuary of Zeus, or was chased into it by Arcas, and because such a violation was punishable by death, mother and son were once again rescued by Zeus and transported to the heavens. But the essence of the story remains the same: Callisto was raped by Zeus; she bore a son and was parted from him; she was turned into a bear and as a bear was hunted and killed, or almost killed; and at the end of her misery she was rewarded with immortality in the stars.

In ancient cult there is a connection between Callisto's myth and the worship of Artemis, for the goddess was served in her cult at Brauron in Attica by little girls in yellow dresses who were known as her 'bears', and who performed a bear dance at her annual festival the *Brauronia*.

Callisto's poignant story was popular in the postclassical arts, particularly in painting, with versions by Titian, Rubens, Rembrandt, Claude, Boucher and Fragonard, among many others.

[Euripides, *Helen* 375–80; Apollodorus 3.8.2; Pausanias 1.25.1, 8.3.6–7; Ovid, *Fasti* 2.155–92.]

Calydonian Boarhunt

One of the great exploits of the ancient world in which many famous heroes of the generation before the Trojan War participated. When OENEUS, king of Calydon, forgot to pay due sacrifice to ARTEMIS, the angry goddess sent a gigantic wild boar that ravaged the countryside, destroying crops and killing cattle and men. 'His eyes glared with a bloody fire,' says Ovid (*Metamorphoses* 8.284–9):

> His neck was stiff and hairy, his hide was covered with bristles that stuck straight out like spears. He squealed harshly, hot foam streaming over his broad shoulders, and his tusks were as long as an elephant's. Flames came out of his mouth, and the leaves were burnt up by his breath.

Oeneus' son MELEAGER gathered a large band of the best men from all over Greece to despatch the boar, including the DIOSCURI, Castor and Polydeuces; IDAS and Lynceus, the sons of Aphareus; the great Athenian hero, THESEUS,

and his friend PEIRITHOUS; JASON, the leader of the Argonauts; ADMETUS from Pherae; the Arcadians ANCAEUS (1) and CEPHEUS (2); IPHICLES, the half-brother of Heracles; the two sons of Aeacus, PELEUS and TELAMON; EURYTION (1), the king of Phthia; Pelias' son ACASTUS; the seer AMPHIARAUS; and the huntress ATALANTA. Once they were all assembled, the famous Boarhunt began.

Several lost their lives, including Ancaeus, gored in the groin as he was poised to strike the boar with his axe, and Eurytion, accidentally killed by Peleus. Meleager had fallen in love with the beautiful Atalanta, so he was delighted when she drew first blood by shooting the boar in the back with an arrow. He himself finally killed the huge beast and presented Atalanta with the trophies of the hunt, the head and hide of the boar, as an acknowledgement of her skill. But in the fight that followed the Boarhunt, he tragically lost his life.

The Calydonian Boarhunt is a popular theme in Archaic art, appearing first on the François Krater, where most of the participants, including dogs, are named (fig. 34). Meleager and Peleus, side by side, face the enormous boar, with Atalanta and Melanion behind them, while beneath the boar Ancaeus (though here spelt Antaeus) and a disembowelled dog lie dead. After this Ancaeus becomes a standard figure in such scenes, and Atalanta too is often prominent (cf.fig.89).

Pausanias records that the boar's tusks had been preserved in Athena's temple at Tegea in Arcadia, but that Augustus had taken them to Rome, where one was still to be seen, and was about three feet long. Pausanias himself saw the hide of the boar at Tegea, though by then it was rotted by age and had lost all its bristles.

[Homer, *Iliad* 9.529–99; Bacchylides, *Ode* 5.93–154; Apollodorus 1.8.2–3; Diodorus Siculus 4.34; Pausanias 3.18.15, 8.45.3, 8.45.5–7, 8.46.1, 8.46.5, 8.47.2; Ovid, *Metamorphoses* 8.267–546.]

Calypso ('Concealer')

The nymph and goddess, daughter of the Titan ATLAS, who in the *Odyssey* lives on the lush and beautiful island of OGYGIA. Here ODYSSEUS is washed up on his journey home from Troy, and Calypso, falling in love with him, keeps him there as her lover for seven years while all the time he longs to return home to rocky Ithaca, his homeland. 'She keeps the grieving, unhappy man with her', explains ATHENA to the other gods, soliciting their aid for Odysseus, 'and she keeps on charming him with soft and flattering words to make him forget Ithaca. But Odysseus, longing to catch sight of even the smoke rising up from his own country, wants only to die' (1.55–9). The immortal and ageless Calypso even offers to make him immortal too, if only he will stay with her for ever, but Odysseus, despite the delights of the goddess' bed, chooses rather to go home to his mortal and ageing wife Penelope.

At the end of these seven years the gods, urged by Athena, intervene to release Odysseus. Zeus sends HERMES to tell Calypso that she must let Odysseus go, and sadly she bows to the inevitable. She provides Odysseus with tools and materials to construct a raft. When it is finished, she dresses him in fine clothing, gives him food and water and wine, and sends him on his way with a fair wind. He sails to Scheria, the land of the Phaeacians, and Homer says no more of Calypso left alone on Ogygia. It is Hesiod (*Theogony* 1017–8) who tells us that she has had two sons, Nausithous and Nausinous, by Odysseus; and Propertius who describes the aftermath of her lover's leaving (1.15.9–16):

> She wept to the lonely waves, and many days
> she sat grieving his loss, her hair unkempt,
> and many times cried out to the cruel sea,
> and while she never again would see his face,
> still she grieved, recalling long hours of joy.

The West Indian ballad-form calypso probably derives its name from this mythological figure: from 'Calypso' to 'island nymph', to 'West Indian island', to 'calypso'.

[Homer, *Odyssey* 1.13–15, 48–59, 5.13–281, 7.244–69; Apollodorus, *Epitome* 7.24; Ovid, *The Art of Love* 2.125–42.]

Camenae

Roman goddesses identified with the MUSES. They had a sacred spring, meadow and grove near the Porta Capena at Rome.

Camilla

In the *Aeneid*, Camilla is a virgin-warrior of the Volsci tribe and one of TURNUS' allies against AENEAS. When she was a baby, her father Metabus was driven from his throne because of his savagery. With his infant daughter in his arms he fled into exile, hotly pursued by his enemies, until he found his way blocked by the flooded River Amasenus. Swiftly he lashed the baby to his spear, dedicated her to DIANA, then flung her over the torrent to safety before swimming across himself, just in time to escape his pursuers. He brought up his daughter on the lonely mountains, feeding her on milk from wild mares, dressing her in a tiger skin, and teaching her to hunt and fight. She grew up a favourite with Diana, chaste and courageous, and so fleet of foot that she could run over the standing corn without crushing it, or over the surface of the sea without wetting her feet.

Virgil relates how she joins Turnus in his war against Aeneas, riding like the AMAZONS with one breast exposed at the head of her cavalry, a band of picked warrior-women aglitter with bronze. She kills many of the enemy before she herself is brought down by the Etruscan Arruns, a spear lodged in her naked breast. At once Arruns flees, more terrified than anyone when he sees what he has done. He is like a wolf who has killed a shepherd or a great bull, says Virgil, then flees to the woods in fear, his quivering tail tucked under his belly for comfort. And Arruns is right to be afraid, for Diana sends down the nymph Opis to avenge her favourite, and she shoots him dead with an arrow.

[Virgil, *Aeneid* 7.803–17, 11.432–3, 498–868.]

Canace (1)

Daughter of AEOLUS (1) and Enarete. She had five sons by POSEIDON: Hopleus, Nireus, Epopeus, Triops and Aloeus, the nominal father of the giants OTUS and Ephialtes.

[Apollodorus 1.7.3–4.]

Canace (2)

Daughter of AEOLUS (2), the ruler of the winds. She committed incest with her brother Macareus and came to a tragic end.

Fig. 34 **The Calydonian Boarhunt, as depicted on the François Krater. In front of the great Boar are Meleager and Peleus, behind the Boar are the Dioscuri. Ancaeus (here spelt *Antaios*) lies dead beneath.**

Cancer (The Crab)

A constellation immortalising the giant crab that attacked Heracles when he was trying to kill the HYDRA OF LERNA.

Canens ('Singing')

A nymph of Latium, the daughter of JANUS and Venilia. She was very lovely, but her voice was lovelier still, so beautiful that her singing could move rocks and trees, soothe wild beasts, and stay the rivers in their courses. She had many suitors, but chose to marry the handsome and athletic PICUS, son of Saturn and king of Latium. One day he left her singing and went off to hunt wild boars in the woods. Here the enchantress CIRCE saw him and at once fell in love with him. She created a phantom boar that led him far into the forest until he was quite lost, and there she appeared to him and begged for his love; but all to no avail, for he refused to be untrue to his beloved Canens. The rejected sorceress turned him into a woodpecker, then found his hunting companions and turned them into wild beasts of many kinds.

Canens, waiting in vain for her husband, went anxiously in search of him. For six days and six nights she roamed the countryside without food or sleep, and at last, worn out with grief and wandering, she lay down by the River Tiber. Here she wasted away, weeping and singing her sorrow, until she vanished into thin air.

[Ovid, *Metamorphoses* 14.310–434.]

Canis Major and Canis Minor

Two constellations, the Greater Dog and the Lesser Dog. Canis Major is the hound that forever follows the great hunter ORION up the night sky. It includes the brilliant Dog Star, Sirius, 'the Scorcher', so called because its appearance marked the season of greatest heat in Greece. 'When the thistle is in flower', says Hesiod in his *Works and Days* (582–8), 'and the singing cicada sits in a tree, pouring down his shrill music thick and fast from under his wings, in the season of wearying heat, then goats are plumpest and wine is sweetest; women are most lustful, but men are weakest, because Sirius parches their head and knees, and their skin is dried out from the heat.'

Canis Minor is Maera, the faithful dog belonging to the Attic farmer Icarius, who was so grieved at his master's death that he jumped into a well and drowned (*see* ERIGONE (1)).

Capaneus

Son of Hipponous and Astynome, a sister of ADRASTUS (1), king of Argos. Capaneus was one of the heroes who took part in Adrastus' expedition of the SEVEN AGAINST THEBES, with his shield bearing the device of a naked man carry-ing fire and the words 'I shall burn this city'. During the battle he began to scale the walls of Thebes on a long ladder, boasting that not even the lightning of Zeus could stop him now, but as he crested the ramparts he was blasted to death by a thunderbolt.

When the bodies of the defeated were being burned prior to burial, Capaneus' wife EVADNE (2) flung herself into his funeral pyre. Their son STHENELUS (3) was one of the Epigoni who avenged their fathers' deaths. Some said that Capaneus was restored to life by the healer ASCLEPIUS.

[Homer, *Iliad* 2.564; Aeschylus, *Seven Against Thebes* 422–51; Sophocles, *Antigone* 127–38, *Oedipus at Colonus* 1318–19; Euripides, *Phoenician Women* 1129–33, 1172–86, *Suppliant Women* 496–9, 860–71; Apollodorus 3.6.3, 3.6.7, 3.10.3; Pausanias 9.8.7.]

Caphaurus

A Libyan shepherd, son of Amphithemis (also known as Garamas) and a nymph of Lake Tritonis, and thus the grandson of Apollo and Acacallis. Caphaurus killed the ARGONAUT Canthus when he tried to steal some of his sheep to feed his hungry comrades, but was in turn killed in revenge by the other Argonauts. They then took all his sheep.

[Apollonius, *Argonautica* 4.1485–1501.]

Capricorn (The Goat)

A constellation immortalising AEGIPAN (who may have been the god PAN under another name) for the help he gave to Zeus against the monster TYPHON.

Capys (1)

Son of ASSARACUS and Hieromneme, daughter of the river-god SIMOEIS. He ruled in Dardania and married his cousin Themiste, daughter of ILUS, king of Troy. Their son was ANCHISES, their grandson AENEAS.

[Homer, *Iliad* 20.239; Apollodorus 3.12.2.]

Capys (2)

A Trojan who suspected that the WOODEN HORSE was some trick of the Greeks. He wanted to throw it into the sea, or set fire to it, or bore holes in its hollow belly and probe for hiding places; but unfortunately for the Trojans his opinion was overridden. The Wooden Horse was dragged into Troy, and during the night the Greek warriors hiding within it came out and sacked the city. After the fall of Troy, Capys accompanied AENEAS to Italy, where it was said that he founded the city of Capua.

[Virgil, *Aeneid* 2.35–9, 10.145.]

Cardea *see* CARNA.

Carmentis *see* EVANDER.

Carna or Cardea

A Roman goddess who presided over door hinges. In Ovid's version of her myth (*Fasti* 6.101–68) Carna was a nymph, dedicated to virginity, who would trick any amorous pursuer by sending him ahead of her into a shady cave, promising to follow him and enjoy the delights of love; instead of which she would escape by hiding in the forest. She was finally outwitted by JANUS, the god with two faces. As usual, she directed him to a cave, but with the eyes in the back of his head he spotted her just as she was hiding behind a rock. He caught her before she could escape and had his way with her. In return he appointed her the protector of door hinges, giving her a branch of flowering hawthorn that would keep out all evil spirits. She especially protected infants in their cradles from vampires, thought to attack them by night and suck their blood.

Carnabon *see* TRIPTOLEMUS.

Cassandra

Daughter of PRIAM, king of Troy, and HECUBA. Both she and her twin brother HELENUS were famous for their gift of prophecy, but Homer makes no mention of Cassandra's prophetic powers: to him she is simply the most beautiful of Priam's daughters, loved by Othryoneus, who had become one of Priam's allies in the Trojan War on the understanding that he would marry Cassandra when the hostilities were over. But he was killed by Idomeneus in the tenth year of the war, so despite his

Fig. 35 **Ajax is about to drag Cassandra away from the statue of Athena, to which she is clinging for sanctuary, and rape her. To the left, Aeneas lifts his old father, Anchises, on to his back while his son, Ascanius, leads the way out of fallen Troy.**

long years of fighting he had no joy of his love. At the end of the *Iliad*, it is Cassandra, anxiously watching from the heights of Troy, who first sees Priam bearing home the body of HECTOR.

There are two stories in later tradition of how Cassandra won her gift of prophecy. According to one account found in the scholia, she and Helenus were left as infants in the temple of Thymbraean APOLLO. There they fell asleep, and as they slept the god's sacred serpents licked their ears and mouths. From that hour they possessed prophetic powers. Better known is the second story, where Apollo fell in love with Cassandra and promised to teach her the art of prophecy in return for her sexual favours. She agreed and Apollo fulfilled his promise; but she then went back on her word and rejected the god's advances. He left her with the power to foretell the future truly, but turned the blessing into a curse by condemning her to the fate of always being disbelieved. Thus Cassandra often appears as a prophet of doom, forewarning of terrible events but having her warnings unheeded. When PARIS, who had been abandoned on Mount Ida as a baby, returned to Troy when grown to manhood, he was at first unrecognised by everyone except Cassandra. She predicted that he would bring disaster on the city, but his parents none the less welcomed him back into the family. Again, when Paris was about to visit King Menelaus of Sparta, Cassandra warned of the disastrous consequences that would follow. Paris ignored her, and brought on Troy the long and bloody Trojan War when he returned home with Menelaus' wife, the beautiful Helen. Finally, at the end of ten years of war when the Greeks left the WOODEN HORSE outside the city, Cassandra foretold that it was a trick and would bring calamity on the Trojans; but still they dragged it inside the city walls, and when night fell were massacred by the Greeks who had been hidden inside the horse's hollow body.

During the capture of the city, while the Greeks were killing and looting, Cassandra took refuge at a statue of Athena. But AJAX (2) dragged her away and raped her, while the statue turned away its eyes in horror at his crime. Because of this sacrilege, Athena punished the Greeks by wrecking their ships on the journey home. COROEBUS (2), son of the Phrygian king Mygdon, who had recently come to Troy in the hope of marrying Cassandra, saw the Greeks dragging her away by her hair from Athena's precinct and was killed as he tried to save her. She was given to AGAMEMNON as his concubine, and on his return home to Mycenae his wife CLYTEMNESTRA killed them both. This is most memorably dramatised in Aeschylus' tragedy *Agamemnon*, where Cassandra, before going into the palace to her certain death, sings of the horrors that have already polluted the house of ATREUS and foretells its bloody future, which will include Agamemnon's murder and her own. As ever, she is not believed.

Pausanias (2.16.6–7) reports that at Mycenae was the tomb of Teledamus and Pelops, twin sons of Cassandra and Agamemnon, who were murdered by Aegisthus after the slaughter of their parents. He adds that Cassandra was buried near Amyclae, where she had a shrine under the name of Alexandra (3.19.6). A favourite scene in ancient art is that of Cassandra being dragged by Ajax away from the image of Athena, during the fall of Troy (figs. 27 and 35). Cassandra's name has become synonymous with all prophets of doom.

[Homer, *Iliad* 13.361–82, 24.697–706, *Odyssey* 11.421–3; Epic Cycle, Proclus' summary of the *Cypria* and the *Sack of Troy*; Pindar, *Pythian* 11.17–22; Aeschylus, *Agamemnon* 1035–1330; Euripides, *Trojan Women* 308–461; Apollodorus 3.12.5, *Epitome* 5.17, 5.22–3, 6.23; Pausanias 1.15.3, 3.26.5, 5.11.5, 5.19.5, 10.26.3, 10.27.1; Virgil, *Aeneid* 2.246–7, 341–6, 3.182–7.]

Cassiopeia

Wife of CEPHEUS (1), king of the Ethiopians, and mother of ANDROMEDA. When the vain Cassiopeia boasted that she was lovelier than the NEREIDS, they complained to Poseidon, who sent a flood and a sea-monster to destroy the land. An oracle predicted that deliverance would come only if Andromeda were sacrificed to the monster, but she was rescued by PERSEUS. Cassiopeia at her death was turned into a constellation, one of the most easily recognisable in the night sky, where she is imagined as sitting on a chair – but for much of the time upside down, to give her a lesson in humility.

Castalia

The name of a spring at Delphi and its nymph, the daughter of the river-god ACHELOUS.

Castor *see* DIOSCURI.

Catreus

Son of MINOS, king of Crete, and PASIPHAE, and father of a son, ALTHAEMENES, and three daughters, Apemosyne, AEROPE and CLYMENE (3). When an oracle foretold that one of his children would kill him, Althaemenes and Apemosyne emigrated to Rhodes, and Catreus gave Aerope and Clymene to NAUPLIUS (1), the navigator and slave-trader, to be sold overseas. Many years later Catreus, having grown old, went to Rhodes to find his son since he wished to bequeath him his kingdom. On landing at a deserted spot he was attacked by cowherds, who thought that he and his men were pirates. He tried to tell them who he was, but the barking of the dogs drowned his words and the cowherds stoned him until Althaemenes appeared. Not recognising his father, Althaemenes hurled a javelin and killed him, thus fulfilling the old oracle. When he learnt what he had done, he prayed to the gods and was swallowed up by the earth. Catreus was taken back to Crete and was buried there by his grandson MENELAUS, the son of his daughter Aerope. It was while Menelaus was performing these rites that Paris ran off with his wife Helen, thus setting in motion the Trojan War.

[Apollodorus 3.1.2, 3.2.1–2, *Epitome* 3.3.]

Caunus *see* BYBLIS.

Cebriones

In the *Iliad*, Cebriones is a bastard son of King PRIAM of Troy and the brave charioteer of HECTOR. He is killed by PATROCLUS, who then fights Hector over Cebriones' body (16.756–61):

> Like two lions who, on a high mountain,
> both of them hungry, and both of high courage,
> fight together over a dead deer, just so
> above Cebriones these two, urgent for battle,
> Patroclus, son of Menoetius, and glorious Hector,
> were eager to tear each other with ruthless bronze.

Greeks and Trojans join in the battle, fighting with spears and arrows and stones around Cebriones, while all the while (775–6):

> ... he lay in the whirling dust,
> a mighty man mightily brought down,
> his horsemanship all forgotten.

[Homer, *Iliad* 8.318, 11.521–37, 12.88–92.]

Cecrops (1)

Technically the second mythical king of Attica, inheriting the rule from the first king Actaeus, whose daughter Aglaurus he had married. But to the Athenians Cecrops was far more important than his father-in-law and was regarded as their archetypal ancestral figure. Said to be sprung from the earth, he had the body of a man and the tail of a snake, which is how he is normally depicted in vase-paintings of Athenian scenes. He had by Aglaurus one son, Erysichthon, who predeceased him, so he was succeeded on his death by CRANAUS, another Athenian sprung from the earth. Cecrops also had three daughters: AGLAURUS (2), who bore Alcippe to ARES, Herse, who bore Cephalus to Hermes, and Pandrosus (for their sad end, *see* ERICHTHONIUS (1)).

The famous court of the Areopagus, where murder trials were held in historical times, was said to have been founded in Cecrops' reign, when Ares was tried for killing HALIRRHOTHIUS because he had raped the god's daughter Alcippe. Cecrops is also credited with recognising the supremacy of ZEUS among the gods, with establishing monogamous marriage, writing and funeral rites, and with putting an end to human sacrifice. The contest between ATHENA and POSEIDON for the possession of Attica was another famous event that took place while Cecrops was king. To demonstrate their divine powers, Poseidon struck the Acropolis with his trident and produced a well of sea-water, while Athena planted an olive tree on the hill, taking Cecrops as the witness of her deed. Athena's creation was judged the greater benefit, so the country became hers and she named the city Athens after herself. Poseidon in anger sent a flood to cover Attica.

The west pediment of the Parthenon at Athens depicted Athena and Poseidon contesting the right to be patron of the city. When Pausanias was at Athens (second century AD), he was shown within the Erechtheum the olive tree planted by Athena, the print of Poseidon's trident on a rock, and the well of sea-water produced by the god which, he records, gave forth the sound of waves when the south wind blew.

[Herodotus 8.55; Euripides, *Ion* 1163–4; Apollodorus 3.14.1–2, 3.14.5; Strabo 9.1.16; Pausanias 1.2.6, 1.24.5, 1.26.5, 1.27.2, 8.2.2–3; Ovid, *Metamorphoses* 6.70–82.]

Cecrops (2)

The eighth mythical king of Athens, son of ERECHTHEUS and Praxithea. Although he was their eldest son, he was chosen king at his father's death by his brother-in-law XUTHUS, who had been appointed judge to decide which of Erechtheus' sons should succeed him. Having made his choice, Xuthus was driven out of Athens by Cecrops' disappointed brothers. Cecrops married Metiadusa and had a son, PANDION (2), who succeeded him.

[Apollodorus 3.15.1, 3.15.5; Pausanias 1.5.3, 7.1.2, 9.33.1.]

Cedalion

A servant of HEPHAESTUS at the god's forge on Lemnos. He guided the blind ORION towards the sunrise until the rays of the Sun-god restored his sight.

Celaeno (1)

Daughter of the Titan ATLAS and Pleione, and thus one of the seven PLEIADES. She bore a son, Lycus, to POSEIDON, who made him immortal and took him to dwell in the Islands of the Blest.

[Apollodorus 3.10.1.]

Celaeno (2) *see* HARPIES.

Celeus

The king of Eleusis to whom Demeter taught her secret rites, the Eleusinian Mysteries (*see* METANEIRA).

Centaurs

A race of wild creatures, part horse and part man, the offspring of IXION's son Centaurus when he copulated with wild Magnesian mares on the slopes of Mount Pelion. In art they are usually depicted with the body and legs of a horse, and growing from their shoulders the torso, head and arms of a man. They lived in the mountains and forests of Thessaly, feeding on raw flesh, and had natures to match their monstrous forms: as a race they were savage, brutal and lascivious, with the exception of two Centaurs with different parentage, the wise and humane CHEIRON and the civilised and hospitable PHOLUS.

The Centaurs are best known for their famous battle with the LAPITHS, another Thessalian tribe, men who were as civilised as the Centaurs were savage. Hostilities began when Ixion's son PEIRITHOUS became king of the Lapiths on his father's death, and the Centaurs claimed a share in the rule because Ixion was their grandfather. This first dispute, however, was settled peaceably, and when Peirithous married Hippodameia he invited the Centaurs to the wedding. All went well at first while the Centaurs, who were unused to wine, drank milk; but soon they smelled the fragrant wine and grabbed it, swilling it down greedily. Before long they became drunken and

Fig. 36 A Lapith fights a Centaur on one of the metopes from the Parthenon.

randy. They seized the Lapith women – one of them, EURYTION (2), even tried to carry off the bride – and a violent and bloody battle broke out. Both sides had many casualties. Many Centaurs fell to Peirithous' Athenian friend THESEUS. One of the Lapith fatalities was CAENEUS, who had been made invulnerable by Poseidon, but the Centaurs killed him by hammering him into the ground with pine trunks (fig. 33). Finally, however, the Lapiths were the victors. This battle is a favourite subject in ancient art, perhaps depicted most powerfully in sculpture, such as on the Parthenon metopes (fig. 36), the west pediment of the Temple of Zeus at Olympia, and the frieze from the Temple of Apollo at Bassae. It seems to have symbolised the triumph of Greek civilisation over bestiality and the forces of barbarism. (It is not such a popular subject in postclassical art, though there is a large and famous depiction of the battle by Piero di Cosimo in London's National Gallery.)

The Lapiths drove the Centaurs out of Thessaly and into the Peloponnese, where they next encountered HERACLES, who was on his way to catch the Erymanthian Boar. They were attracted by the smell of wine while he was being entertained by the civilised Centaur Pholus on Mount Pholoe, so they galloped up, armed with rocks and pine-branches, to quaff their now favourite drink (fig. 116). A fight broke out, during which Heracles shot some of the Centaurs dead with his unerring arrows, tipped with fatal venom from the HYDRA OF LERNA. The rest he pursued as far as Malea in the southern Peloponnese, where they took refuge with the kindly Centaur Cheiron. Heracles, still angry, shot at them and killed Elatus, but to his sorrow the arrow passed through his victim and struck Cheiron, eventually bringing him to death.

After this sad accident, Heracles returned to Mount Pholoe only to find the result of another. In his absence Pholus had pulled an arrow from one of the Centaurs' corpses, wondering that so small an object could kill so large a creature, and had accidentally let it fall on his foot. So he too had died, and Heracles was left with the sad task of burying his friend before going on his way to find the Erymanthian Boar.

The surviving Centaurs dispersed to various places. Some went to Mount Malea; some went to Eleusis where Poseidon gave them secret refuge on a mountain. Eurytion went back to Pholoe, and was later killed by Heracles for trying to force Mnesimache, the daughter of Dexamenus, king of Olenus, into marriage. NESSUS went to the river Evenus, where he acted as ferryman to travellers wishing to cross the water. When Nessus tried to rape Heracles' wife DEIANEIRA as he ferried her across the stream, Heracles saved her by shooting the Centaur. But Nessus avenged himself on his killer, for as he lay dying he persuaded the credulous Deianeira that the blood from his wound would act as a powerful love-charm if ever she needed one. She gathered some up, not realising that mixed with the blood was the Hydra's deadly venom. Years later she used it when she thought that she had lost Heracles' love to his new concubine, Iole. When Heracles dressed himself in a robe smeared with the 'love-charm', the poison ate into his flesh and he died in agony. At last Nessus had his revenge.

[Homer, *Iliad* 1.262–72, 2.740–4, *Odyssey* 21.295–304; Hesiod, *Shield of Heracles* 178–90; Pindar, *Pythian* 4.21–48; Apollodorus 2.5.4, *Epitome* 1.20–2; Diodorus Siculus 4.69–70; Plutarch, *Theseus* 30; Pausanias 3.18.10; Ovid, *Metamorphoses* 12.210–535. R. Osborne, in S. Goldhill and R. Osborne (eds), *Art and Text in Ancient Greek Culture* (1994), pp. 52–84.]

Centaurus

Son of IXION and progenitor of the CENTAURS.

Cephalus (1)

Son of HERMES and Herse, the daughter of Cecrops, second king of Athens (*see* AGLAURUS (2)). The amorous EOS, goddess of Dawn, fell in love with Cephalus and carried him off to live on Olympus. She bore him a son, Phaethon, who was taken by Aphrodite to be an attendant in her temple. Pausanias reports that Eos' abduction of Cephalus was depicted on the Amyclae Throne and on an acroterion of the Stoa Basileios in Athens. Several red-figure vase-paintings portray Eos pursuing Cephalus. Postclassical art often shows Eos gazing at the sleeping Cephalus, or carrying him off in her chariot, with paintings by Poussin and Boucher, among others.

In later myth, and first of all in Ovid, this Cephalus was conflated with CEPHALUS (2), son of Deion and husband of Procris.

[Hesiod, *Theogony* 986–91; Apollodorus 3.14.3; Pausanias 1.3.1, 3.18.12.]

Cephalus (2)

Son of Deion, king of Phocis, and Diomede, daughter of Xuthus; he was married to Procris, daughter of Erechtheus. The most familiar story of their tragic love is found in Ovid (*Metamorphoses* 7.672–862). EOS, goddess of Dawn, fell in love with Cephalus soon after his marriage to Procris and carried him off, much against his will; but she grew so annoyed by his continuing passionate attachment to his young wife that she sent him home again. To gain revenge on the couple she inspired Cephalus with the idea of disguising himself and testing Procris' fidelity. She helped him in his unfortunate course of action by altering his appearance. Completely disguised, he made advances to his own wife, offering countless gifts to win her over. For a long time Procris stayed firm and faithful, but when he promised her a vast fortune in return for a night in her bed, she finally gave in. At this Cephalus revealed his true identity and reproached her with her infidelity. Overcome by shame, and distrustful of all men because of her husband's deceitful trick, she ran away and lived in the mountains, devoting herself to hunting as a follower of ARTEMIS. After a time the penitent Cephalus found her and begged her to forgive him, which at last she did. The reunited couple returned home and spent some years together in great happiness.

Procris, however, had not come empty-handed from the mountains: she brought with her two gifts from Artemis, a hound called Laelaps that could not fail to catch its prey, and a javelin that could not miss its mark. These gifts she passed on to Cephalus. He took the hound to get rid of the TEUMESSIAN VIXEN, a fierce fox, fated never to be caught, preying cruelly on the people of Thebes. When Cephalus sent Laelaps in pursuit of her, Zeus solved the dilemma of an inescapable hound chasing an uncatchable fox by turning both animals to stone. So the infallible hound served a good purpose; unlike the unerring javelin, which brought only tragedy in its wake.

Cephalus went hunting each dawn, quite alone, since his javelin was all that he needed to kill as many animals as he chose. At the end of his hunting, when he was hot and tired, he would lie in the shade and call on a breeze, 'Aura', to come and cool him. Some busybody at last reported this to Procris, who thought that Aura must be a nymph with whom her husband was in love. In her unhappiness, and hoping still that she might be mistaken, she followed him the next morning when he went off to hunt. He made his kill, then as usual lay down and called on Aura to come and soothe him. Procris, overhearing, moaned in sorrow, and Cephalus, thinking that some wild creature was hiding in the bushes, threw his javelin towards the sound. Procris cried out in pain as the javelin found its mark, and Cephalus, recognising the voice of his dear wife, ran to her. She died in his arms.

Apollodorus (3.15.1) draws a quite different picture of Procris, making her an utterly faithless wife. She went to bed with a certain Pteleon after he had bribed her with a golden crown. When Cephalus discovered her infidelity she ran away to King MINOS of Crete, who tried to seduce her. His wife Pasiphae, however, angry because of his promiscuity, had drugged him in such a way that, whenever he had intercourse with a woman, he ejaculated snakes and scorpions, and she died. Procris wanted to possess the hound and javelin (in this version, once given to EUROPA by Zeus and passed down to Minos) which Minos promised her in return for her favours. So she drugged him in her turn to prevent any harm coming to her, then went to bed with him. She took the hound and javelin home, where she was reconciled with Cephalus. The couple went hunting together and Procris was killed, her death in this version being the result of a simple hunting accident. Cephalus was tried in the Athenian court of the Areopagus and condemned to everlasting exile. Elsewhere (2.4.7) Apollodorus says that Cephalus went with AMPHITRYON on a successful raid against the Taphians, and was rewarded with the gift of a large island which he renamed Cephallenia. Pausanias (10.29.6) adds that Cephalus married a second wife, CLYMENE (2), daughter of Minyas, and had a son, Iphiclus.

The tragic outcome of the love of Cephalus and Procris is a theme rarely found in ancient art, but thanks to the moving story told by Ovid it becomes a popular subject in the postclassical arts, particularly in painting, which includes a (possible) *Death of Procris* by Piero di Cosimo in London's National Gallery, and in music and dance. The names of Cephalus and Procris are garbled to Shafalus and Procus in the Pyramus and Thisbe episode of Shakespeare's *A Midsummer Night's Dream*.

[Apollodorus 1.9.4; Ovid, *The Art of Love* 3.687–746.]

Cepheus (1)

King of the ETHIOPIANS. His parentage is uncertain, since his father is given as either BELUS or PHOENIX (2); but he was certainly husband of CASSIOPEIA and father of ANDROMEDA, who was saved from sacrifice to a sea-monster by PERSEUS (fig. 17). Cepheus was succeeded by PERSES (3), son of Perseus and Andromeda, and when he died he was immortalised in the stars as the constellation Cepheus.

Cepheus (2)

Son of Aleus and Neaera, and king of Tegea in Arcadia. He sailed with the ARGONAUTS, together with his brother Amphidamas and their nephew ANCAEUS (1), and went on the CALYDONIAN BOARHUNT with Ancaeus. HERACLES asked Cepheus and his twenty sons to join the expedition against HIPPOCOON and his sons at Sparta, but Cepheus refused, fearing that Tegea would be attacked by Argive enemies in his absence. So Heracles handed over to Cepheus' daughter, Sterope, a lock of the GORGON's hair in a bronze jar, once given to him by Athena, telling the girl that she had only to hold this up three times from the city walls for any approaching enemy to be put to flight. Thus reassured, Cepheus joined Heracles' expedition. Tegea did indeed remain safe, but in the battle at Sparta Cepheus and all his sons were killed.

[Apollonius, *Argonautica* 1.161–71; Apollodorus 2.7.3, 1.8.2.]

Cephissus (1)

A river in Argos and its god. *See* INACHUS.

Cephissus (2)

A river in Boeotia and its god, the father of the beautiful NARCISSUS.

Cerberus

The monstrous dog who guarded the entrance to the Underworld, ensuring that those who entered never left. 'With his tail and ears he fawns on those who enter,' says Hesiod (*Theogony* 770–3), 'though he will not let them go back out again, but lies in wait and devours anyone he catches going out of the gates.' He was the offspring of TYPHON and ECHIDNA, and thus brother to other famous monsters, the HYDRA OF LERNA, the CHIMAERA, and ORTHUS, the hound of Geryon. Hesiod describes him as 'unmanageable, unspeakable Cerberus who eats raw flesh, the hound of Hades with a voice of bronze, fifty-headed, bold and strong' (310–12). But he was more usually said to have only three heads; and in art, for practical reasons, he is usually shown with two or three, and occasionally just one. He was also described as having a serpent for a tail and snake heads sprouting from his body.

In the last and most difficult of his twelve Labours (*see* LABOURS OF HERACLES), HERACLES had to bring Cerberus up from the Underworld. HADES gave him permission to do so on condition that he used no weapons; so Heracles mastered the hound by brute strength, even though bitten by the serpent-tail, then carried him off to show to Eurystheus before returning his captive to Hades. In art Heracles is shown confronting Cerberus, or leading him away, sometimes accompanied by Athena and/or Hermes. On two Caeretan hydriai, Eurystheus hides in terror in his great jar (*see* NEMEAN LION), and here from a truly fearsome Cerberus, three-headed and embellished with snakes (fig. 37).

Cerberus plays a part in the stories of two other heroes who visited the Underworld: ORPHEUS had to charm him with music when he went to seek Eurydice; and the Sibyl of Cumae, while helping AENEAS to get past him, threw him a honey-cake steeped in soporific drugs – hence the expression 'a sop for Cerberus', meaning to give a bribe, to quieten a troublesome person. Ovid describes the hound's visit to the upper world, and how he struggled madly, turning his eyes away from the daylight and the bright sunshine and filling the air with his furious

Fig. 37 **Heracles delivers three-headed Cerberus to the terrified Eurystheus, who has taken refuge in a great jar.**

barking. His spittle, shed in rage from his three mouths, spattered the ground and took root, giving rise to the aconite plant from which is produced deadly poison. With this MEDEA later tried to kill THESEUS.

[Apollodorus 2.5.12; Pausanias 3.18.13; Virgil, *Aeneid* 6.417–5; Ovid, *Metamorphoses* 7.408–19.]

Cercopes

Two brothers captured by HERACLES while he was serving OMPHALE as a slave; captured at Ephesus, says Apollodorus (2.6.3), while Herodotus locates them in mainland Greece near Thermopylae (7.216). Perhaps they had no fixed abode, for a fragment of an early epic called *Cercopes* describes them as 'liars and cheats, well versed in all kinds of mischief, complete rogues', and adds: 'Far over the earth they wandered, forever deceiving men as they travelled.'

Their mother warned them against a certain *Melampygos*, 'Blackbottom', who turned out to be Heracles although they realised this fact too late. They found him sleeping and tried to rob him of his arms, but he awoke and caught them, tying them up by their heels to a pole that he carried over his shoulders. From this position they recognised their assailant, from his tanned and hairy buttocks, as the *Melampygos* against whom their mother had warned them, but quite undaunted they amused him so much with ribald jokes at his expense that he let them go. Their encounter with Heracles is found in only very late literary sources, along with varying accounts of their names and parentage, but is depicted in art from the early sixth century BC, with several representations of the two Cercopes suspended from a pole hung over Heracles' shoulder.

Other writers tell of an entire tribe of Cercopes, some of whom Heracles killed and others he brought alive to Omphale; while Ovid says that, because of their mischievousness, they were turned into monkeys by Zeus and sent to live on Pithecusae (Monkey) Island near the Bay of Naples, now Ischia.

[Diodorus Siculus 4.31.7; Ovid, *Metamorphoses* 14.90–100.]

Cercyon

One of the many evil-doers dispatched by the young THESEUS on his journey from Troezen to Athens (fig.140). Cercyon, a son of POSEIDON, was the king of Eleusis, and forced all passers-by to wrestle with him against their will. He killed every one of his opponents until he came up against Theseus, who lifted him high in the air and threw him violently to the ground. This time it was Cercyon who died.

After Theseus had come into power at Athens, he made Hippothoon, Cercyon's grandson, the king of Eleusis. For

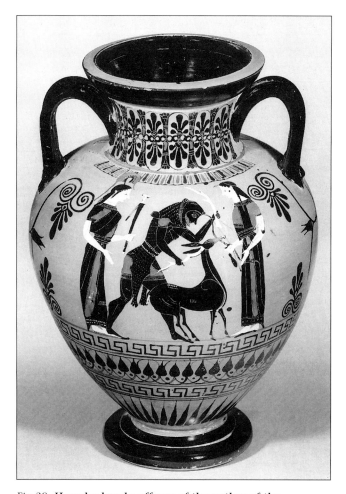

Fig. 38 **Heracles breaks off one of the antlers of the Ceryneian Hind, while Athena *(left)* and Artemis look on.**

Cercyon's cruel treatment of his daughter, Hippothoon's mother, *see* ALOPE. Pausanias saw Alope's grave near the spot still known in his day as the 'wrestling ground of Cercyon'.

[Bacchylides, *Ode* 18.26–7; Apollodorus, *Epitome* 1.3; Diodorus Siculus 4.59.5; Plutarch, *Theseus* 11; Pausanias 1.14.3, 1.39.3.]

Ceres *see* DEMETER.

Ceryneian or Cerynitian Hind

The third Labour (*see* LABOURS OF HERACLES) which HERACLES performed for Eurystheus was to capture the hind with the golden horns, sacred to ARTEMIS and named after either Mount Ceryneia or the river Cerynites. According to Apollodorus (2.5.3), Heracles pursued the hind for a whole year, starting from Oenoe on the border between Arcadia and the Argolid, and ending at the River Ladon in Arcadia. Here he wounded the weary deer with an arrow just as she was about to swim across the stream. He put her across his shoulders and carried her alive to Mycenae, on his way meeting Artemis and Apollo. The angry goddess would have taken the deer from him, but he explained his subservience to Eurystheus and she allowed him to continue on his way.

Pindar says that TAYGETE, one of the Pleiades, had dedicated the hind to Artemis, after the goddess had transformed her for a time into a deer to escape the attentions of Zeus. In this version Heracles pursued the hind to the far north and the land of the HYPERBOREANS. According to Callimachus, the goddess found five golden-horned hinds, larger than bulls, at Parrhasia in Arcadia, four of which she captured and harnessed to her chariot. But the fifth escaped, and with the guidance of HERA took refuge on Mount Ceryneia, thus becoming a Labour for Hera's enemy Heracles.

Euripides has a version quite different from any other, in which the hind was a pest that plundered the countryside, then was killed by Heracles and dedicated by him to Artemis. In the rest of ancient literature, and always in ancient art, the hind is captured alive. A few representations in art, however, hint at a slightly different ending: Heracles is shown grasping the horns of the beast, and on a black-figure neck-amphora (London B231, fig. 38) he has broken off one of them. This just possibly suggests a version of the myth where he brings back only the horns of the hind and not the whole animal.

[Pindar, *Olympian* 3.28–32; Euripides, *The Madness of Heracles* 375–9; Callimachus, *Hymn to Artemis* 98–109.]

Cestrinus

Son of ANDROMACHE by Helenus.

Ceto

A sea-monster, the daughter of Pontus (Sea) and GAIA (Earth). Ceto's name in the Greek suggests any large inhabitant of the sea. She bore to her brother, the ancient sea-god PHORCYS, the GRAEAE, the GORGONS, the monster ECHIDNA, and LADON, the snake who guarded the apples of the Hesperides.

[Hesiod, *Theogony* 238, 270–336.]

Cetus

A constellation representing the sea-monster killed by Perseus. *See* ANDROMEDA.

Ceyx (1)

Son of PHOSPHORUS, the morning star (*see* ALCYONE (2)).

Ceyx (2)

King of Trachis, often conflated with CEYX (1), the husband of Alcyone. Ceyx is connected in various ways with HERACLES, his friend to whom he gave shelter and hospitality. Indeed, Ceyx' palace is the setting for Sophocles' tragedy *The Women of Trachis*: here DEIANEIRA awaits the return of her husband Heracles, and here the tortured Heracles is carried, dying from the poisoned robe that she has sent him.

Ceyx was the father of a son, Hippasus, and a daughter, Themistonoe. Hippasus died while helping Heracles to attack Oichalia; and Themistonoe was married to CYCNUS (2), who was killed by Heracles and then given funeral honours by Ceyx. After Heracles' death Ceyx sent his friend's children to Athens and the protection of the powerful Theseus (or his sons), since he himself felt too weak to oppose the cruel EURYSTHEUS.

[Hesiod, *Shield of Heracles* 350–6, 472–6; Apollodorus 2.7.6–7, 2.8.1; Diodorus Siculus 4.57; Pausanias 1.32.6.]

Chalciope (1) *see* PHRIXUS.

Chalciope (2) *see* THESSALUS (2).

Chalcodon

Son of ABAS (3), and king of the Abantes of Euboea. He led his people against Thebes, where he was killed by AMPHITRYON and buried near Teumessus on the road to Chalcis. His son, ELEPHENOR, took forty ships from Euboea to fight in the Trojan War.

[Homer, *Iliad* 2.536–45; Pausanias 9.19.3.]

Chaos

A dark intangible element, the very first thing that came into being according to the Greek creation myth, closely followed by GAIA (Earth), TARTARUS and EROS. No idea of confusion or disorder is implied by the Greek name, rather Chaos was a yawning space, a kind of primeval void. Out of Chaos were born EREBUS and NYX (Night).

[Hesiod, *Theogony* 116–23.]

Chariclo (1)

A nymph, the mother of TEIRESIAS, and a favourite companion of ATHENA. One day, in the heat of noon, the goddess and the nymph were bathing in a spring on Mount Helicon, when Teiresias, hot and weary from the hunt, came there to drink. Quite inadvertently he saw Athena naked, and at once she cried out in anger and struck him blind. To Chariclo's anguished laments, the goddess replied that any mortal who saw a deity without their consent must be thus punished, and moreover Teiresias was getting off lightly compared with ACTAEON, who would soon lose his life for a similar transgression. In reparation for Teiresias' blindness, Athena gave him the gift of prophecy, the power to understand the speech of birds, and a staff with which he could guide himself as well as if he still had his sight. She also promised him a long life, and after his death the retention of his mental powers undimmed among the dead.

[Callimachus, *Hymn* 5.57–133; Apollodorus 3.6.7.]

Chariclo (2)

The wife of the wise Centaur CHEIRON.

Charioteer *see* AURIGA.

Charis, Charites *see* GRACES.

Charon

The aged ferryman of HADES (2), who carried the shades of the dead in his boat across the rivers ACHERON or STYX to their final abode in the Underworld. It was customary to bury the dead with a coin in their mouths as payment for Charon, his regular fee being one obol. Virgil gives a memorable description of him (*Aeneid* 298–301): 'a dreaded ferryman, frightful and foul, his chin covered with unkempt hoary hair, his fierce eyes lit with fire, and a filthy cloak hanging from a knot on his shoulder.' We see him in action in Aristophanes' comedy *The Frogs* (180–270), where he is brusque, churlish and abusive as he conveys Dionysus across Acheron to Hades. Dionysus has to do his own rowing while Charon steers.

Our first extant picture of Charon in ancient art is on a black-figure vase of about 500 BC. Pausanias tells us (10.28.1–2) that he was painted by Polygnotus in his famous picture of the Underworld at Delphi. Charon is frequently portrayed on white-ground funerary lekythoi, dressed as a labourer and standing with a punt-pole at the stern of his boat. Often HERMES leads the dead person towards him. T. S. Eliot in *The Hollow Men* refers to Charon's fee: 'A penny for the Old Guy.'

[R. H. Terpening, *Charon and the Crossing: Ancient, Medieval and Renaissance Transformations of a Myth* (1985).]

Charybdis

The giant whirlpool which, with the sea-monster SCYLLA (1), posed a double danger to sailors passing through a narrow sea-channel traditionally thought to be the Straits of Messina. In Homer's *Odyssey*, the enchantress CIRCE warns ODYSSEUS that three times each day Charybdis sucks down the sea-water and casts it out again, bringing certain destruction to any ship that she catches and death to all its crew. So at all costs Odysseus must avoid Charybdis, even if this means risking the dangers posed by Scylla, since this monster with her six heads will manage to kill only six of his men as they pass. Odysseus

does as Circe advises, keeping well away from Charybdis, and later he describes the awesome sight of her (12.236–43):

> Terrible was the way she sucked down the sea's water,
> and when she spewed it up, the whole sea would boil
> in turbulence, like a cauldron on a big fire, and high spray
> spattered the tops of the rocks on both sides.
> But when again she sucked down the sea's salt water,
> the turbulence showed all the inside of the sea,
> and around it the rock roared terribly, and the ground
> showed dark with sand at the ocean bottom,
> and pale fear seized upon my comrades.

Later, when Zeus has wrecked Odysseus' ship and killed all his men to punish them for eating the cattle of Helios, Odysseus himself is driven by the winds back to Scylla and Charybdis on a makeshift raft. He manages to avoid the attentions of Scylla, but his raft is sucked down by Charybdis and he survives only by clinging to the fig tree that overhangs the whirlpool. Hours later Charybdis spews up the remains of the raft, and Odysseus escapes by hauling himself on to a spar and paddling away with his hands.

Cheiron

One of the CENTAURS, but unlike his fellows, who were descended from Ixion's son Centaurus, Cheiron was the immortal son of the Titan CRONUS and the Oceanid PHILYRA. Cronos, intent on deceiving his jealous wife Rhea, transformed himself into a horse to mate with Philyra, and this was why Cheiron was born a Centaur, part man, part horse. His nature, too, differed from that of the other Centaurs, for while they were savage and brutal (apart from the hospitable Pholus), Cheiron was kindly and humane, and one of the wisest of living beings. He was skilled in archery, medicine, hunting and the arts, especially music, and for this reason many of the great heroes were sent as children to his cave on Mount Pelion to be reared and educated by him. Among his pupils were ACHILLES, JASON, ASCLEPIUS, ARISTAEUS and ACTAEON.

Cheiron was married to a nymph, Chariclo, and they had two daughters, HIPPO and Endeis. (Ovid adds a third, Ocyrhoe, who had the gift of prophecy and foretold her father's eventual death.) One of Endeis' sons by Aeacus was PELEUS, and Cheiron was greatly involved with the fortunes of this grandson. He saved Peleus' life when Acastus hid his sword and abandoned him on Mount Pelion, hoping that the Centaurs or wild beasts would kill him. He also encouraged Peleus to win the sea-goddess Thetis for his bride, and their wedding took place at Cheiron's cave on Pelion. Here all the gods came, bringing gifts. Cheiron himself gave Peleus a stout ash spear, which Achilles would later use at Troy. Finally, the Centaur reared Achilles when Thetis deserted her husband and son and went back to live in the sea. These scenes from Peleus' life were popular in ancient art, and vase-paintings from the seventh century BC show Cheiron approaching to save Peleus on Pelion, standing by while he wrestles with Thetis, attending the couple's wedding (as does his wife Chariclo), and receiving the young Achilles (fig. 39). Cheiron's difference from the usual savage Centaurs is often emphasised by the vase-painters' giving him human rather than equine forelegs and by dressing him in elegant robes.

Cheiron also played a part in other myths. He predicted to Apollo, who had seen CYRENE wrestling with a lion and had fallen in love with her, that the god would carry her off to Libya and make her queen of a great city. When Actaeon was turned into a deer by Artemis and torn to pieces by his own hounds, Cheiron comforted them for the loss of their beloved master by making a statue of him so lifelike that they believed it to be him.

Cheiron met his end, despite being immortal, when Heracles was attacking the other Centaurs. He was accidentally shot by one of Heracles' arrows, which were tipped with the Hydra's deadly venom and always caused a mortal wound. But the arrow could not kill the immortal Cheiron, even though his agony was so great that he longed to die. At last the Titan PROMETHEUS offered himself to Zeus to be made immortal in the Centaur's place, and Cheiron, relieved to be spared eternal suffering, willingly succumbed to death. He still achieved an immor-

tality, however, for Zeus set him in the stars as the constellation Sagittarius.

[Homer, *Iliad* 4.218–9, 11.830–2; Hesiod, *Theogony* 100–2; Pindar, *Pythian* 3.1–7, 4.102–5, 9.29–66, *Nemean* 3.43–58, 4.60–1, *Isthmian* 8.41–5; Apollonius, *Argonautica* 1.554–8, 2.510, 2.1229–42; Apollodorus 1.2.4, 2.5.4, 2.5.11, 3.4.4, 3.13.3–6; Pausanias 3.18.12, 5.5.10, 5.19.8–9; Ovid, *Metamorphoses* 2.630–54.]

Chimaera ('She-goat')

A monster, killed by BELLEROPHON riding on the winged horse PEGASUS, and described by Hesiod (*Theogony* 319–25) as 'breathing invincible fire, a great and terrible creature, swift of foot and strong. She had three heads, one of a fierce-eyed lion, the second of a goat, and the third of a snake, a mighty serpent. The lion was at the front, the snake at the rear, and the goat in the middle breathing out a great blast of blazing fire.'

This is clear enough, especially when we see the Chimaera depicted on vase-paintings from the early decades of the seventh century BC, with the goat's head growing out of the middle of her back and her tail ending in a snake's head (fig.110, cf. fig.30). What is not so clear from Hesiod is the creature's genealogy: her parents were either ECHIDNA and TYPHON, or the HYDRA OF LERNA and an unnamed father (the pronoun at 319 being ambiguous), and she may – or may not – have given birth to the SPHINX and the NEMEAN LION with ORTHUS, the hound of Geryon, as her mate (the pronoun at 326 being similarly ambiguous). There is no agreement among later writers to clarify the matter. Homer provides a further tantalising piece of information, saying that the Chimaera was reared by a Lycian called Amisodarus to be an evil for many men (*Iliad* 16.328–9); but nothing more about this do we know, although Apollodorus (2.3.1) adds, hardly surprisingly, that the monster devastated the land and destroyed livestock.

Postclassical Chimaeras developed into all kinds of fantastic beasts, often winged, and from these has come our own word 'chimera', meaning a wild fancy.

Chione (1)

Daughter of BOREAS, the North Wind, and Oreithyia. She had by POSEIDON a son, EUMOLPUS, but to save her reputation she flung the baby into the sea. Poseidon rescued him, and gave him to his daughter Benthesicyme to bring up in Ethiopia.

[Apollodorus 3.15.2–4.]

Fig. 39 Peleus brings the young Achilles to be reared and educated by the Centaur Cheiron.

Chione (2)

The daughter of Daedalion, a fierce and war-loving man. Chione at fourteen was so beautiful that she had countless suitors, and even the gods HERMES and APOLLO desired her when they chanced to see her one day. While Apollo deferred his enjoyment of her love until night-time, coming to her after dark disguised as an old woman, Hermes put her magically to sleep there and then and took his pleasure of her at once. In the fullness of time she bore twin sons, each taking after the god who had fathered him: AUTOLYCUS became an expert thief like the crafty Hermes, and PHILAMMON an accomplished musician like Apollo.

Unfortunately Chione allowed the favour shown her by the gods to go to her head, and she foolishly boasted that she was more beautiful than ARTEMIS. At this the angry goddess shot her dead with an arrow. Daedalion was so grieved by his daughter's death that he flung himself from the summit of Mount Parnassus, but Apollo saved him and changed him into a hawk, a bird with the same fierce and courageous nature as the man. He lived on, still suffering, and by preying on other birds he caused others to suffer too.

[Ovid, *Metamorphoses* 11.291–345.]

Chloris (1)

A daughter of AMPHION and NIOBE (2), and the only one to survive the attack by Apollo and Artemis. It was said that her name had originally been Meliboea, but she was renamed Chloris ('Pale Woman') when she turned pale with fear at the slaughter of her brothers and sisters. She married NELEUS, king of Pylos, who chose her for her surpassing beauty and gave many gifts to win her. She bore him a daughter, Pero, and twelve sons including NESTOR and PERICLYMENUS (2). Nestor was the only one of her sons to survive the attack on Pylos by Heracles.

[Homer, *Odyssey* 11.281–97; Apollodorus 1.9.9, 3.5.6; Pausanias 2.21.9, 5.16.4.]

Chloris (2)

A nymph loved by ZEPHYRUS, the West Wind. He carried her off and she became the goddess of flowers and spring, FLORA, transformed at his touch just as the cold earth is transformed in spring at the touch of the warm west wind.

Chrysaor

Son of POSEIDON and the Gorgon Medusa (*see* GORGONS), born together with the winged horse PEGASUS from Medusa's neck after PERSEUS cut off her head. Chrysaor married the Oceanid Callirhoe and fathered triple-bodied GERYON. Chrysaor's name means 'Golden Sword', and Hesiod calls him 'great' and 'stouthearted'; but of his nature we know no more than this. We might have expected him to be of monstrous shape, since he is born of the line of PHORCYS and CETO, a family prone to monsters – and indeed his own son is monstrous – but on the rare occasions that Chrysaor appears in ancient art, he seems normal enough.

[Hesiod, *Theogony* 281, 979; Apollodorus 2.4.2, 2.5.10.]

Chryseis

The daughter of Chryses, priest of APOLLO on the island of Chryse, not far from Troy, and a key figure in Homer's *Iliad* since it is she who sets in motion the events which lead to the wrath of ACHILLES, the linchpin of the action (1.1–492). She has been captured by the Greeks and awarded as war-prize to King AGAMEMNON; and when Chryses brings ransom gifts and begs to have her back, the king angrily drives the old man away. Because of this slight to his priest, Apollo comes to earth and strikes the Greek camp with plague. For nine days men die, but on the tenth day the Greeks hold an assembly, during which the seer CALCHAS explains the reason for the plague and Apollo's anger. Agamemnon is forced to return Chryseis to her father, but displeased by this loss of status, he replaces her by taking away Achilles' war-prize, BRISEIS. Achilles withdraws to his tent, full of the wrath that will determine the rest of the *Iliad*'s action until he comes at last, after pain and loss and suffering, to acceptance and peace.

According to a very late story told only by Hyginus (*Fabulae* 120–1), Chryseis had a son by Agamemnon but claimed that the child was Apollo's. She named him Chryses after her father. Years later, when ORESTES and IPHIGENEIA came to the house of Chryses while fleeing from Thoas, king of Tauris, Chryses the younger wanted to hand them back to their enemy. But the truth came out that really he was Agamemnon's son, and thus half-brother to Orestes and Iphigeneia, so he helped them instead to kill Thoas and return to Greece. This sounds so like a fifth-century recognition play that it is tempting (but entirely speculative) to think that it may have been the plot of Sophocles' lost *Chryseis*.

In medieval times, Chryseis' name was corrupted to Cressida and she was made the lover of TROILUS.

Chryses *see* CHRYSEIS.

Chrysippus

The beautiful young son of PELOPS, king of Pisa in Elis, and a nymph, and the victim of the first homosexual abduction among mortals. He was carried off to Thebes by LAIUS, a guest of Pelops who had been teaching Chrysippus to drive a chariot and had fallen in love with the boy. Chrysippus killed himself in shame by falling on his sword, and Pelops, who had loved his son dearly, laid a curse on Laius that led to his death, since Zeus ordained that as punishment Laius would be killed by his own son (*see* OEDIPUS). One of the reasons later given for the SPHINX' assault on the Thebans was their failure to punish Laius for his unlawful passion.

Another version of Chrysippus' death said that he was killed by his half-brothers ATREUS and Thyestes, the legitimate sons of Pelops and Hippodameia, because they and their mother were afraid that Pelops, from affection, would make him his heir. When Pelops discovered the murder he exiled the two killers and proclaimed another powerful and effective curse, that they and their race might die at each other's hand (*see* ATREUS).

The first certain appearance of Chrysippus' abduction by Laius was in Euripides' lost tragedy *Chrysippus*; but in fact there are few references to it in what we have left of ancient literature and art. Nevertheless it played a crucial part in myth, because of the profound effects on the legends of Thebes and Mycenae made by the curses of the angry and grieving Pelops.

[Apollodorus 3.5.5, *Epitome* 2.10.]

Chrysothemis

Daughter of AGAMEMNON and CLYTEMNESTRA, and sister of ORESTES, ELECTRA (3) and IPHIGENEIA. Her first, brief mention comes in Homer (*Iliad* 9.145), but it is in Sophocles' *Electra* that she comes to her most vivid life. In this play Electra, faithful to the memory of her dead father, constantly shows her overwhelming hatred of his two murderers, Clytemnestra and Aegisthus, and they in turn force her into a life little better than that of a slave. Chrysothemis serves as a foil to Electra's courage and integrity, since she is the prudent daughter who is too fond of the material advantages in being a princess of Mycenae to risk losing them by any display of active hostility. 'I know this much', she says to Electra (332–40):

I too am grieved at our situation, so much so that if I could find the strength I would show them what I think of them. But as it is, it seems best to me to lower my sails in time of trouble ... The right course is not as I say, but as you have chosen; yet if I am to live in freedom, I must obey our masters in everything.

She constantly urges caution, and denounces as folly Electra's plan to kill Aegisthus, refusing to dare anything that might put her comfortable life at risk.

See also fig. 7.

Chthonius

One of the SOWN MEN of Thebes.

Ciconians or Cicones

A tribe living in south-western Thrace who were allies of PRIAM in the Trojan War. In the *Odyssey* (9.39–61), ODYSSEUS encounters the Ciconians after leaving Troy to sail home to Ithaca. He and his men sack their city of Ismarus, killing all the men except for MARON, priest of Apollo, and capturing their women and possessions. But against Odysseus' advice his men linger too long, eating and drinking and sacrificing cattle, so that Ciconian reinforcements are able to come from inland. 'They came at morning, as many as flowers in spring, or leaves,' says Odysseus. 'They fought their battle there by the swift ships ... and when the sun passed over to the time for the unyoking of oxen, then at last the Ciconians turned back the Greeks and overcame them, and out of each ship six of my strong-greaved comrades were killed.'

The tribe was still in existence in classical times, when Herodotus (7.110) reports them as being on Xerxes' route into Greece during the Persian Wars.

[Homer, *Iliad* 2.846, 17.73.]

Cilix

Son of AGENOR (1). He travelled in search of his abducted sister, EUROPA, and when his quest failed, he settled in south-eastern Asia Minor where he gave his name to Cilicia. Sometimes he was said to be the father of THASUS, rather than his brother.

Cilla *see* THYMOETES.

Cinyras

A rich king of Cyprus at the time of the Trojan War. When the Greeks were recruiting support for their expedition against Troy, MENELAUS, ODYSSEUS and TALTHYBIUS went to Cyprus and asked Cinyras to join them. He gave them a richly decorated breastplate as a present for the absent AGAMEMNON, and swore on oath that he would send fifty ships. When the time came he did indeed launch fifty ships, but only one, commanded by the son of Mygdalion, was of use: the other forty-nine were made of clay, and manned by a clay crew, so they dissolved beneath the waves. But Cinyras had kept his oath.

His family background is much disputed. He may have been born a Cypriot, the son of Paphos, Pygmalion's daughter by the statue he had made, after whom the Cypriot city of Paphos was named. Or, as the son of the Syrian Sandocus, a descendant of EOS and TITHONUS, he may have emigrated from Cilicia to Cyprus, and there married Metharme, the daughter of Pygmalion, who bore him several children, including the beautiful ADONIS. But the more usual tradition is that Adonis was Cinyras' son by his own daughter (*see* MYRRHA).

Either Cinyras killed himself when he found out about his incest with Myrrha; or he lived to a great and prosperous old age as a priest of Aphrodite. He was succeeded by TEUCER (2), the son of Telamon, who had settled in Cyprus and married one of Cinyras' daughters after his father banished him from Salamis.

[Homer, *Iliad* 11.19–28; Pindar, *Pythian* 2.15–17, *Nemean* 8.18; Apollodorus 3.14.3–4, *Epitome* 3.9; Pausanias 1.3.2, 2.29.4; Tacitus, *Histories* 2.3.]

Circe

A powerful enchantress who could – and often did – turn human beings into animals. She was the daughter of the Sun-god HELIOS and the Oceanid Perse (or Perseis), and thus the sister of AEETES, the king of Colchis who owned the Golden Fleece, and of PASIPHAE, the mother of the Minotaur. Circe lived on the island of Aeaea, which was located by Homer in the far east, but was later identified by the ancients as Monte Circeo on the west coast of Italy, thought once to have been an island.

Circe is most famous for the interlude described in the *Odyssey*, where she detains ODYSSEUS for a year as her lover, on his journey home from Troy to Ithaca. When he and his men land on her island, exhausted and disheartened by their horrific encounter with the LAESTRYGONIANS, they find that the only sign of life is a column of smoke rising up from some habitation deep in the forest. Odysseus sends out a scouting party, led by his brother-in-law EURYLOCHUS, who are all very fearful of what they may find. They come to Circe's gleaming home, around which prowl huge lions and wolves, fearsome beasts, who unexpectedly wag their tails and fawn on the strangers. Inside the house they hear Circe singing sweetly. Eurylochus has the sense to suspect danger, so he waits outside when the rest of his party are welcomed indoors by the enchantress. She gives them wine to drink, flavoured with barley and cheese and honey but mixed with a magical drug. Having drunk it they are all turned into pigs, with the heads and voices and bristles of swine, but keeping their human intelligence. Eurylochus, the only one to escape, flees back to the ship and tells the whole sad story to Odysseus.

Odysseus, never for long at a loss, valiantly sets off to confront Circe. On his way he is met by HERMES, who supplies him with a plant called moly that will make him proof against Circe's charms. Once more she gives her new guest the drugged wine, but this time Odysseus, instead of becoming a pig, rushes at her with a drawn sword. The defeated goddess suggests that they retire to bed and the pleasures of love, and so they do, once Circe has sworn a solemn oath not to harm Odysseus. Afterwards, on Odysseus' insistence, she turns all his men back into human beings (10.388–99, with Odysseus telling the story):

> Circe walked on out through the hall, staff in hand,
> and opening the doors of the pigsty she drove them out,
> looking like nine-year old hogs. They stood facing her,
> and she went among them, anointing each of them
> with some other drug. The bristles, grown on them
> from the harmful drug that Circe had supplied,
> fell away from them and they turned once more into men,
> but younger and taller and handsomer than before.
> They recognised me and clasped me by the hand,
> and lovely weeping overtook us all, and the house
> echoed terribly to the sound. Even the goddess had pity.

Odysseus and his men stay with the enchantress for a

Fig. 40 **Circe drops her bowl of magic potion as Odysseus advances on her with drawn sword. Behind him are two victims of Circe's enchantments, a pig and a donkey.**

year, feasting on unlimited food and wine. At the end of that time they sail onwards, but not before Circe has instructed Odysseus to go to Hades to consult the spirits of the dead, and has given him valuable advice about the dangers of his journey home.

It was later said that Circe had sons by Odysseus: Agrius, LATINUS, and TELEGONUS, who grew up to kill his unrecognised father by accident. Circe plays a part in other myths too. She received the ARGONAUTS on their journey home with the Golden Fleece, purifying Jason and her niece MEDEA for the treacherous murder of APSYRTUS; though when she learnt the nature of their crime she drove them from her island in horror. She turned PICUS, the son of Saturn, into a woodpecker for refusing her love. And when the sea-god GLAUCUS (1) went to her for a potion to win the love of the beautiful nymph SCYLLA (1), Circe fell in love with him herself. He rejected her, so she turned Scylla into a hideous monster who haunted the Straits of Messina, preying on sailors.

In ancient art from the sixth century BC onwards, Circe appears with Odysseus and the men whom she has turned into animals (fig. 40) – not just pigs, but lions, dogs, roosters, sheep. She was later frequently allegorised by moralists as a symbol of brute pleasure, the pursuit of which turns men into beasts.

[Homer, *Odyssey* 10.133–574, 12.1–150; Hesiod, *Theogony* 956–7, 1011–14; Apollonius, *Argonautica* 3.311–13, 4.559–91, 659–752; Apollodorus 1.9.1, 1.9.24, *Epitome* 7.14–18; Ovid, *Metamorphoses* 13.966–14.71, 14.248–440.]

Cithaeron (1)

An early king of Plataea in Boeotia who gave his name to the nearby Mount Cithaeron. ZEUS and HERA quarrelled during his reign and Hera went off in dudgeon to Euboea, refusing to be appeased. Zeus asked Cithaeron for advice, since at that time he was the cleverest man on earth. He advised Zeus to make a wooden statue of a woman, and covering it with a cloak to draw it along in an ox-cart, circulating the rumour that this was his new bride Plataea, the daughter of Asopus. Zeus did so; and as soon as Hera heard the news she rushed up angrily to the cart and tore the cloak from the statue. Realising her deception, she began to laugh, and she and Zeus were reconciled. To commemorate this reconciliation, a festival called the Daedala was instituted, so called because the name *daidala* was given to wooden images.

[Pausanias 9.1.2, 9.3.1–8.]

Cithaeron (2), Mount

A mountain range separating Boeotia and Attica, said to have been named after CITHAERON (1). The northern slopes of the range are not far from Thebes, and Cithaeron is the site of many key legendary events, particularly in the Theban cycle of myths. Here the baby OEDIPUS was abandoned to die, only to be saved, growing up far from Thebes, and returning as a man to kill his father and marry his mother. Here ACTAEON was torn to pieces by his own hounds at the command of the implacable goddess Artemis. Here ANTIOPE (1) bore twin sons, Amphion and Zethus, who were abandoned at birth, like Oedipus; but they too lived, and grew up to be reunited with their mother, when they killed her persecutor, Dirce, by tying her to a wild bull so that she was torn and trampled to death. Here PENTHEUS met his fate, torn to pieces by the MAENADS, their leader his own mother, Agave; and perhaps it is this legend, and Euripides' powerful tragedy *The Bacchae*, that gives us our most vivid image of the mountain. Here Cithaeron broods over Thebes, a place of retribution for the unfortunate Pentheus, though he does not know it. Here the maenads are waiting to punish him for his rejection of their god Dionysus, and here he goes, with pleasure and excitement, pathetically unaware of the fate ahead of him. At last the women fall savagely upon him, tearing him limb from limb, until Cithaeron echoes and re-echoes with their cries, Pentheus shrieking in agony and the maenads howling in triumph.

Cithaeronian Lion *see* ALCATHOUS (1) and THESPIUS.

Clashing Rocks *see* SYMPLEGADES.

Cleio or **Cleo** *see* MUSES.

Cleite *see* CYZICUS.

Cleitus

Son of Mantius, and grandson of the seer MELAMPUS. Because of his beauty, Cleitus was snatched up by the amorous EOS, goddess of Dawn, to live among the immortals.

[Homer, *Odyssey* 15.249–51.]

Cleopatra (1)

Daughter of BOREAS, god of the North Wind, and Oreithyia. She married PHINEUS (2), the king of Salmydessus in Thrace, and bore him two sons; but he married a second wife (Cleopatra having died or been abandoned) and the boys were cruelly blinded.

Cleopatra (2)

Daughter of Idas and MARPESSA, and wife of MELEAGER.

Clymene (1)

Daughter of OCEANUS and Tethys. According to Hesiod (*Theogony* 507–12) she married the Titan IAPETUS and was mother by him of ATLAS, MENOETIUS (1), PROMETHEUS and

EPIMETHEUS. According to Ovid (*Metamorphoses* 1.750–2.366) she was married to the Ethiopian king Merops and was mother, by the Sun-god HELIOS, of PHAETHON (2) and the Heliades.

Clymene (2)

A daughter of MINYAS. She was usually thought to be the wife of PHYLACUS, and mother by him of IPHICLUS (1) and Alcimede, the mother of JASON. Pausanias, however, says (10.29.6) that she married Phylacus' brother CEPHALUS (2) after the death of his wife Procris, and bore Iphiclus to him. According to Apollodorus (3.9.2) she was the mother of ATALANTA by the Arcadian king, Iasus.

Clymene (3)

Daughter of CATREUS, king of Crete. When Catreus learnt from an oracle that he would be killed by one of his own children, he gave his daughters Clymene and AEROPE to NAUPLIUS (1), the navigator and slave-trader, to be sold overseas. Nauplius, however, gave Aerope as wife to either Atreus or Pleisthenes, and married Clymene himself. She bore him three sons, PALAMEDES, OEAX and Nausimedon.

[Apollodorus 2.1.5, 3.2.1–2.]

Clymenus (1) *see* HARPALYCE (2).

Clymenus (2)

A son of Presbon, and grandson of PHRIXUS, who was king of Boeotian Orchomenus, and was probably the Clymenus mentioned by Homer (*Odyssey* 3.452) as the father of NESTOR's wife Eurydice. He was killed in a brawl at Onchestus and avenged by his son ERGINUS (1).

Clytemnestra

Daughter of TYNDAREOS and LEDA, and sister or half-sister of HELEN and the DIOSCURI, Castor and Polydeuces. (Although accounts differ as to exactly who fathered these four children, Clytemnestra and Castor were usually said to be the mortal children of Tyndareos, and Helen and Polydeuces the immortal children of Zeus.) Clytemnestra was the wife of AGAMEMNON, king of Mycenae; though according to one tradition she first married Tantalus, son of Thyestes, and had a son by him. Agamemnon murdered both Tantalus and the boy, then took Clytemnestra for himself. The couple had four children who grew up to play a dramatic part in the fates of their parents: three daughters, IPHIGENEIA, ELECTRA (3) and CHRYSOTHEMIS, and a son, ORESTES.

When the Trojan War was set in motion by Helen's elopement to Troy with Paris, Agamemnon became commander-in-chief of the Greek forces. On his instructions, Clytemnestra brought Iphigeneia to Aulis, supposedly to

Fig. 41 **Clytemnestra bares her breast and appeals for mercy to her son, Orestes, as he is about to kill her. A Fury, with snakes in her hair and hands, looks down from above.**

marry Achilles; but instead Agamemnon sacrificed his daughter to raise winds to take the Greek fleet to Troy (a deed movingly dramatised in Euripides' *Iphigeneia at Aulis*). Clytemnestra never forgave him. During his absence she took his cousin AEGISTHUS as a lover, and on her husband's return home after the ten-year war they murdered him, along with his Trojan captive, CASSANDRA. Years later Orestes, encouraged by Electra, avenged his father's murder by killing both Clytemnestra and Aegisthus.

The legend was a favourite with poets from Homer onwards and was given a variety of treatments, but it is in fifth-century tragedy that it comes fully into its own, with the Clytemnestra of Aeschylus' *Oresteia* trilogy (*Agamemnon, Libation Bearers, Eumenides*, 458 BC) dominating the extant literature that deals with the story. Prior to Aeschylus, Aegisthus and Clytemnestra were, as far as we can tell, joint partners-in-crime in Agamemnon's murder, with Aegisthus taking the dominant role (fig. 10); but in the *Agamemnon*, Aegisthus' part in the murder has dwindled into relative insignificance and he has become a blustering weakling who appears onstage only at the end of the play. It is Clytemnestra, the woman with the heart of a man (10–11), who has nursed her rage and grief down the long years since Iphigeneia's death and now kills Agamemnon with a fierce joy, netting him in a robe while he is unarmed and vulnerable in his bath. She is a powerful and awe-inspiring figure, needing no one's help to kill her treacherous husband. Alone she greets Agamemnon on his return from Troy, and persuades him to walk into the palace over the crimson carpet that her servants lay down for him (905–11): 'Now, my beloved,' she cries, 'step down from your chariot, and let not your foot, my lord, sacker of Troy, touch the earth. Servants, what are you waiting for? You have been told to strew the ground where he must walk with tapestries. Let there be spread before the house he never expected to see, where Justice leads him in, a crimson path.' And on Clytemnestra's command down flow the tapestries, red as blood, symbol of all the blood that Agamemnon shed at Troy, of the blood that he shed when he killed Iphigeneia, of his own blood about to be shed. And he walks over the blood-red tapestries into the palace, to his death.

Quite alone too Clytemnestra kills him, along with his concubine Cassandra. Agamemnon's death cries are heard inside the palace, then the doors open to disclose Clytemnestra standing, exultant, over the bodies of her victims (1381–92):

> That he might not escape nor ward away his death, like one who catches fish I cast around him a net with no way out, a vast and deadly wealth of robes. I struck him twice, and with two great cries he buckled at the knees and fell. When he was down I struck a third blow, a thank-offering to Zeus, lord of the Underworld, saviour of corpses. Thus he fell and belched out his life, and as he died he poured forth his blood and spattered me with a dark and crimson rain, and I rejoiced as the sown corn rejoices, drenched with god-given showers when buds break forth in Spring.

Although Aeschylus' creation may be seen as the archetypal Clytemnestra, Sophocles and Euripides too present memorable dramatisations of her character in their *Electra* plays. Both make her the more prominent figure in the vengeance, while increasing the relative importance of Aegisthus once again. In Sophocles she is depicted as a truly evil woman: she rejoices in the murder of her husband; she is cruel to Electra; she would earlier have killed Orestes if Electra had not saved him; and in the play she gloats when she believes him dead, since she may now suppose herself safe for ever from retribution. Euripides treats her more sympathetically, making her well-inten-tioned towards Electra and somewhat regretful about all that has happened; but despite this she still must die, the victim of Orestes' vengeance for his murdered father.

When the time comes for her death at Orestes' hands, in Aeschylus' *Libation Bearers* she pleads with him for her life, and when this is unavailing threatens him with pursuit by her FURIES. In the third play of the trilogy, the *Eumenides*, her ghost stirs up the Furies to a relentless hounding of her son (fig. 58), although after Orestes' trial and acquittal they are finally appeased. In the two other tragedians, Clytemnestra simply pleads in vain for her life; while Euripides (though not Sophocles) makes the Furies a consequence of her murder.

Clytemnestra appears occasionally in ancient art from the seventh century BC (fig. 8), though usually in scenes where she herself is not the main character, such as Orestes' murder of Aegisthus (figs. 7 and 135). Depictions of her own death are rare (figs. 41 and 105). Pausanias records that both Clytemnestra and Aegisthus were buried outside the walls of Mycenae, since they were deemed unworthy of a place within it near to Agamemnon himself.

[Homer, *Iliad* 1.113–15, *Odyssey* 11.409–53, 24.199–202; Apollodorus, *Epitome* 2.16, 3.22, 6.9, 6.23–25; Pausanias 2.16.7, 2.18.2, 2.22.3. J. R. March, *The Creative Poet* (1987), pp. 81–98.]

Clytie

A lover of HELIOS, the Sun-god.

Clytius *see* GIANTS.

Cocalus *see* DAEDALUS.

Cocytus

The River of Lamentation in the Underworld, a branch of the Styx flowing into the Acheron. On its banks the souls of the unburied dead were said to wander for a hundred years before being allowed to cross into HADES (2). In the living world there was a river Cocytus in Thesprotia, near the Acheron that was thought to descend into the Underworld itself, which Pausanias (1.17.5) describes as 'a most unlovely stream'.

The Cocytus is one of Milton's 'four infernal rivers' in *Paradise Lost*: 'Cocytus, nam'd of lamentation loud / heard on the rueful stream'.

[Homer, *Odyssey* 10.513–14; Virgil, *Aeneid* 6.296–7, 317–30.]

Codrus

The last fully empowered Athenian king. He was the son of Melanthus and a descendant of NESTOR, king of Pylos in Messenia. When the HERACLIDS invaded the Peloponnese, Melanthus and many Messenians were driven out of their homeland and settled in Attica. Here Melanthus supplanted Thymoetes, the last of the kings of the line of

Theseus, and himself became king of Athens. His son Codrus married an Athenian girl and in due course succeeded his father to the throne.

During Codrus' reign the Peloponnesians invaded Attica, having been promised victory by an oracle so long as the Athenian king was spared. They took great care not to injure Codrus, but he learnt of the prediction and resolved to sacrifice himself for his country. Disguising himself as a woodcutter, he picked a quarrel with some enemy soldiers and was killed. When they found out what they had done, the Peloponnesians marched home again, convinced because of the oracle that there was no point in prolonging the hostilities, since they were sure to be defeated. Because no one was thought worthy to succeed so noble a king, royal power began to be limited in the rule of Codrus' lame son, Medon, leading to the replacement of monarchy by archonship. Codrus' other sons emigrated and settled in Ionia.

[Herodotus 5.65; Strabo 9.1.7, 14.1.3; Pausanias 1.19.5, 1.39.4, 2.18.8–9, 7.1.9, 7.2.1–3, 7.25.2.]

Coeus

One of the TITANS, son of Uranus (Heaven) and GAIA (Earth). By his sister-Titan PHOEBE (1) he was father of LETO and ASTERIA.

[Hesiod, *Theogony* 134, 404–10.]

Comaetho (1)

A priestess of ARTEMIS at Patrae in Achaea. Although the beautiful Comaetho and Melanippus, the most handsome youth of the district, were deeply in love with each other, their parents refused to let them marry. Despite this opposition their passion took its course, for they would meet in secret and make love in the temple of Artemis. The virgin goddess, angry at this sacrilege, sent plague and famine on the land, until at last the people consulted the Delphic Oracle. On the Oracle's instructions, they at once sacrificed Comaetho and Melanippus to appease Artemis, then every year thereafter the most beautiful girl and youth in Patrae. This custom continued for many generations until, again on the instructions of the Oracle, the practice ended when a strange king came to the land, bringing a strange god. The king was EURYPYLUS (1) and the god was Dionysus.

[Pausanias 7.19.]

Comaetho (2) *see* PTERELAUS.

Cometes *see* STHENELUS (3).

Copreus

A son of PELOPS, who killed an otherwise unknown man named Iphitus and fled to Mycenae where his nephew EURYSTHEUS was ruling. Eurystheus gave him refuge and employed him as a herald to take his commands to HERACLES, whose strength and courage so alarmed the king that he was afraid to meet him face to face.

Since Copreus was employed in such a way, as a lackey to a coward, it is no surprise to find that he was viewed as a generally despicable character. Homer mentions the death of his son Periphetes at Hector's hands, adding that to a base father had been born a far superior son. In Euripides' *Children of Heracles*, Copreus comes as Eurystheus' envoy to the Athenians to demand that they expel the Heraclids. He is presented as a cruel and insolent bully.

[Homer, *Iliad* 15.638–43; Apollodorus 2.5.1.]

Corcyra or Cercyra

A nymph, daughter of the river-god ASOPUS, who was loved by POSEIDON and carried off by him to the island afterwards named Corcyra (now Corfu) in her honour. She bore the god a son, Phaeax, who gave his name to the Phaeacians. *See* SCHERIA.

[Apollonius, *Argonautica* 4.566–71; Diodorus Siculus 4.72; Pausanias 2.5.2, 5.22.6.]

Coresus *see* CALLIRHOE (4).

Coroebus (1)

A hero buried at Megara. Psamathe, the daughter of Crotopus, king of Argos, was loved by APOLLO and bore the god a son called LINUS. In terror of her father she abandoned the baby in the wild, where it was torn to pieces by dogs. Apollo, angry at the death of his son, sent a monster called Poene ('Punishment') who preyed on the children of the Argives, snatching them up and carrying them off, until Coroebus took it upon himself to kill her. Apollo then sent a plague on the city, so Coroebus went to Delphi to submit to whatever punishment the god wished on him for killing Poene. He was told by the Oracle not to return to Argos, but to carry a sacred tripod from the sanctuary, and where it fell from his hands he was to settle and build a temple to Apollo. He carried the tripod as far as Mount Geraneia, and there built a temple to the god and founded the town called Tripodisci ('Little Tripods'). Pausanias saw Coroebus' grave in the market-place of Megara, surmounted by statuary depicting Poene's death. 'These are the oldest stone images I am aware of having seen among the Greeks', he says.

[Pausanias 1.43.7–8, 2.19.8.]

Coroebus (2)

Son of Mygdon, king of Phrygia. King PRIAM of Troy had once been Mygdon's ally in a battle against the AMAZONS, so the Phrygian king later supported Priam during the Trojan War. Towards the end of the war, Mygdon's son Coroebus went to fight for Priam in the hope of marrying his daughter CASSANDRA, but instead he was killed during the fall of Troy, rushing to save his promised bride when he saw the Greeks dragging her away by her hair from Athena's precinct. His killer is variously named as Peneleos or Diomedes or Neoptolemus.

[Homer, *Iliad* 3.184–9; Euripides, *Rhesus* 539; Pausanias 10.27.1; Virgil, *Aeneid* 2.341–6, 403–8, 424–6.]

Corona Borealis

A constellation. *See* ARIADNE.

Coronides

Daughters of the giant hunter ORION whose names were Metioche and Menippe. After their father was taken to the stars, the girls were brought up by their mother, while ARTEMIS taught them how to weave and APHRODITE granted them great beauty. When a plague came upon the city of Orchomenus and many died, an oracle declared that the gods would be appeased and the plague ended only if two virgins sacrificed themselves voluntarily. A servant took this news to Metioche and Menippe as they were weaving at their loom, and at once the two girls stabbed themselves to death with their shuttles. The plague ceased, and HADES (1) and PERSEPHONE took pity on the girls and immortalised them among the stars as two fiery comets.

[Ovid, *Metamorphoses* 13.681–99; Antoninus Liberalis, *Metamorphoses* 25.]

Coronis (1)

Daughter of PHLEGYAS and mother by APOLLO of ASCLEPIUS, the god of healing.

Coronis (2) *see* BUTES (1).

Coronus

One of a family of Lapith warriors. He was the son of CAENEUS, the Lapith chieftain who began life as a woman. Coronus sailed with the ARGONAUTS, and later led the Lapiths against the Dorians in a dispute over the boundaries of their land. He was killed by Heracles, who had come to help the Dorians (*see* AEGIMIUS). Coronus' son Leonteus led forty ships to the Trojan War and fought there valiantly, sharing the command with his comrade POLYPOETES (1).

Corvus (The Crow)

A constellation, set close to the constellation Crater (The Bowl). The crow was APOLLO's bird, and one day the god sent him to a spring to fill a drinking bowl with water.

Near the spring the crow saw a fig tree loaded with fruit, not quite ripe enough to eat, and forgetting all about his task the greedy bird settled down to wait for the fruit to ripen. Several days later, pleasurably full of figs, the crow suddenly remembered his master's command. Hurriedly he filled the bowl with water and flew back to Apollo, but the displeased god set both the crow and the bowl among the stars as a warning to others. For the reason why crows, originally white, are now black, *see* ASCLEPIUS.

[Hyginus, *Poetic Astronomy* 2.40.]

Corybantes

Sons of APOLLO and one of the MUSES, Thalia, who became the male attendants of CYBELE, the Phrygian goddess identified by the Greeks with RHEA (1), wife of Cronus and mother of Zeus. Together with the CURETES (1) they protected Zeus, when he was a baby, by dancing around the Cretan cave in which he was concealed, clashing their shields and spears so as to hide his infant cries from his cannibalistic father Cronus. Perhaps the drum (mentioned by Euripides) which they invented and gave to Rhea served the same purpose.

[Euripides, *Bacchae* 120–34; Apollodorus 1.3.4; Diodorus Siculus 3.55.9, 5.49; Strabo 10.3.7, 10.3.19.]

Corybas *see* IASION (1).

Corythus

The son of PARIS and the nymph OENONE. Corythus grew up to be even more handsome than his father, and after Paris had deserted his wife for the beautiful HELEN, Oenone sent the boy to Troy in the hope of stirring up trouble. She succeeded, for Helen was attracted to him, and Paris in his jealousy killed him.

Cottus *see* HUNDRED-HANDERS.

Crab *see* CANCER.

Cranaus

The third mythical king of Athens. When the great CECROPS (1) died without male issue, Cranaus, as the most powerful of the Athenians, succeeded him. Like his predecessor, he was said to be sprung from the earth of Attica. By his Spartan wife, Pedias, he had daughters, among them Atthis, who died young and gave her name to Attica. It was said that during Cranaus' reign the Great Flood took place. Cranaus married one of his daughters to AMPHICTYON, who was either the son of Deucalion or else sprang from the earth of Attica. The ungrateful Amphictyon deposed his father-in-law and took the throne in his place.

[Apollodorus 1.7.2, 3.14.5; Strabo 9.1.18; Pausanias 1.2.6.]

Crataeis

Mother of SCYLLA (1).

Crater (The Bowl)

A constellation. For two explanations of its presence among the stars, *see* CORVUS and MASTUSIUS.

Cratos ('Power') *see* BIA.

Creation *see* GAIA.

Creon (1) ('Ruler')

A king of Corinth. He plays a small part in the legend of ALCMAEON, for he brought up the two children, AMPHILOCHUS (1) and Tisiphone, whom Alcmaeon had fathered on Manto, the daughter of the seer Teiresias. But Creon is better known for his part in the legend of JASON and MEDEA. He welcomed them to Corinth when they fled from Iolcus, after the murder of old King Pelias. Ten peaceful years passed, during which Medea bore Jason two or three children. At the end of that time, he cast off Medea and married Creon's daughter GLAUCE (sometimes called Creusa), which aroused in Medea an unquenchable fury and lust for revenge. These events are powerfully dramatised in Euripides' tragedy *Medea*. Creon is afraid that Medea, in her rage, may harm his daughter, so he orders her banishment. Medea begs to stay in Corinth just one more day, to provide for her children, and Creon gives in – unwisely, for that single day will be enough for Medea to bring about the deaths of both Glauce and Creon himself. Medea sends a poisoned robe and coronet to the princess, who puts them on in great delight, then dies in agony as her flesh is burnt up by the poison. Creon, distraught with grief, gathers her into his arms, and he too dies, his flesh welded immovably to the deadly robe.

[Apollodorus 1.9.28, 3.7.7; Diodorus Siculus 4.54; Seneca, *Medea*.]

Creon (2) ('Ruler')

A ruler of Thebes on several occasions. He and his sister JOCASTA were the children of Menoeceus, a descendant of the 'Sown Men', the original inhabitants of Thebes. When Creon's brother-in-law, LAIUS, was killed on a journey to Delphi, Creon took over the rule of the city. The SPHINX was at that time preying on the Thebans, asking her famous riddle and snatching up and devouring anyone who failed to answer it. In one version, Creon's son HAEMON was a victim. Creon decreed that whoever answered the riddle correctly, and thus rid them of the Sphinx, would win the rule of the kingdom and marry Laius' widow Jocasta. OEDIPUS, a stranger form Corinth, arrived in Thebes and solved the riddle. The defeated Sphinx killed herself and Oedipus married Jocasta, who was (unknown to anyone) his own mother. They had years of happy marriage and four children, before at last the truth came out and they realised that they were mother and son. Jocasta hanged herself and Oedipus put out his eyes, then wandered in exile, an outcast, accompanied by his daughter ANTIGONE (1). Now Creon ruled Thebes for a second time, until Oedipus' sons, Eteocles and POLYNEICES, should come of age.

The brothers grew up to fight over the rule of the city. There are differing accounts as to how they attempted to resolve the matter, but the end result was always the same: Eteocles, supported by Creon, ruled Thebes, while Polyneices, exiled from his homeland, set about winning the throne by violence. Together with his father-in-law, Adrastus, he brought together an army of seven champions and their followers for the famous expedition from Argos of the SEVEN AGAINST THEBES. During this war Creon lost two more sons, MEGAREUS (2) and MENOECEUS (2); and both Eteocles and Polyneices lost their lives when they fought each other in single combat. For the third time Creon ruled Thebes.

He buried Eteocles with honour, but he decreed that the traitor Polyneices should be left lying in the plain as a prey for the birds. Anyone who tried to bury him would die. When Antigone was discovered scattering on her brother's body the earth that would suffice for token burial, Creon punished her by walling her up alive in a tomb. There she committed suicide. Creon was forced by an Athenian army led by THESEUS to allow the burial of the Argive dead, then carried on ruling Thebes as regent for Eteocles' young son, Laodamas.

Earlier in his life Creon had purified AMPHITRYON after he accidentally murdered his father-in-law, Electryon, and had helped him in his war with the Taphians. Amphitryon for his part had aided Creon by getting rid of the fierce TEUMESSIAN VIXEN that was preying on Thebes. Years later Creon married his daughter MEGARA to HERACLES, the son of Zeus and Amphitryon's wife Alcmene. In Creon's old age, Thebes was invaded by LYCUS (2), who killed Creon himself and usurped the rule. Heracles avenged Creon by killing Lycus, but in a fit of madness he also murdered Megara and the children she had borne him. According to a late account in Statius, Creon was killed by Theseus in a battle over the burial of the Argive dead.

Creon is a prominent figure in extant Greek tragedy. In Sophocles' *Oedipus the King*, he is a cautious, reasonable and unambitious man, who none the less takes over the rule when Oedipus blinds himself in despair, having discovered that he has killed his father and married his mother. In Sophocles' *Oedipus at Colonus*, Creon tries to force the exiled Oedipus to return to Thebes, since he knows from an oracle that the old man's presence will bring victory in the coming war between Eteocles and Polyneices. Here Creon is a cruel and violent character who even has Antigone and ISMENE abducted to achieve his own ends (though he is overcome and driven away by Theseus). He is more sympathetic in Euripides' *Phoenician Women*, where he has to suffer the grief of his son Menoeceus' death, a willing self-sacrifice that will bring victory to Thebes during the attack by the Seven. But it is Sophocles' *Antigone* that gives our fullest depiction of Creon. When the play opens, Eteocles and Polyneices are recently dead and Creon has just decreed that no one shall bury the traitor Polyneices, on pain of death. However misguided Creon may be, he is acting from good intentions and, he fully believes, in the interests of Thebes – to him the most important consideration. 'The man who considers a friend more important than his own country', he says (182–3), 'I count him as nothing.' So when Antigone is caught giving her brother token burial, Creon is sure that he is right to carry out his threat of death and to wall her up alive in a tomb. But he should not bury the living, any more than he should leave unburied the dead. His son Haemon, who is betrothed to Antigone, tells him how wrong he is, and that the whole city censures his action; but he refuses to listen. The blind seer TEIRESIAS tells him that the gods disapprove and are rejecting all Theban sacrifices; but Creon still stands firm. Only when the Chorus of Theban elders remind him that never yet has Teiresias prophesied falsely does he yield. But he is too late: he buries Polyneices and goes to free Antigone, but by the time he gets to the tomb Antigone has hanged herself. Haemon, discovering her body, kills himself in front of his father; even Creon's wife Eurydice takes her own life when she hears of her son's death. Creon is left alive, and alone, to mourn the chain of disaster and bereavement caused by his own obstinacy.

[Apollodorus 2.4.6–7, 2.4.11, 3.5.8–3.7.1; Pausanias 1.39.2, 9.5.13, 9.10.3; Statius, *Thebaid* 12.677–781.]

Cresphontes (1)

Son of ARISTOMACHUS, brother of TEMENUS (2) and ARISTODEMUS, and one of the HERACLIDS who invaded and conquered the Peloponnese. Cresphontes, Temenus, and the two young sons of the dead Aristodemus, Procles and Eurysthenes, agreed to decide the ownership of the three chief regions by drawing lots, the first to have the Argolid, the second Sparta and Laconia, and the third Messenia. Cresphontes wanted Messenia and won it by a trick: when the others threw pebbles into a pitcher of water, he threw in a clod of earth, so that his lot dissolved

and the other two lots were drawn out first. So Temenus received the Argolid and the sons of Aristodemus Laconia, while Cresphontes won the land he wanted. He married Merope, the daughter of Cypselus, king of Arcadia, and had three sons by her. He and his two eldest sons were killed by rebels, but his youngest son, named either Cresphontes or Aepytus, survived. He was brought up by Cypselus, and in due course he returned to Messenia, avenged his father, and recovered the throne (*see* CRESPHONTES (2)).

[Sophocles, *Ajax* 1283–7; Apollodorus 2.8.4–5; Pausanias 2.18.7, 3.1.5, 4.3.3–8, 4.5.1, 8.5.6, 8.29.5.]

Cresphontes (2)

Son of the Heraclid CRESPHONTES (1) and Merope. His legend was dramatised in Euripides' *Cresphontes*, and although the play has been lost, his story can be recovered from fragments and from Hyginus' *Fabula* 137. When his father and brothers were killed by Polyphontes, another Heraclid and the leader of the rebels, the young Cresphontes was saved by his mother Merope and brought up by her father Cypselus, the king of Arcadia. Polyphontes, meanwhile, had seized the throne and forced Merope to marry him, but he was always fearful of her son growing up to take revenge, so he promised a large reward to anyone who would kill Cresphontes. Just as he feared, the boy grew up and returned to Messenia to avenge his father and brothers. Quite unrecognised, he went to Polyphontes, saying that he himself had killed Cresphontes and claiming the reward. Polyphontes, with no idea of the deception, gave him hospitality, but while the boy was asleep Merope, believing that he had indeed killed her son, approached with an axe to murder him. (This scene probably occurred onstage in Euripides' play.) Luckily Cresphontes was recognised in time by an old servant, and mother and son were reunited. Together they plotted revenge on Polyphontes: pretending to be reconciled to the death of her son, Merope suggested a sacrifice in thanks for Cresphontes' supposed death to which the young stranger would be invited. The joyful king agreed. During the ceremony, at which Cresphontes was given a weapon to kill the sacrificial victim, he killed Polyphontes instead, thus regaining his father's throne and kingdom.

In later versions of the myth, Cresphontes was renamed Aepytus after his great-grandfather, the father of Cypselus. Pausanias says that he gained so fine a reputation for his wise rule that his descendants were given the name of Aepytidae instead of Heraclids. His son Glaucus succeeded him.

[Apollodorus 2.8.5; Pausanias 4.3.6–9. C. Collard, M. J. Cropp and K. H. Lee, *Euripides: Selected Fragmentary Plays* I (1995), pp. 121–47.]

Cressida *see* TROILUS.

Cretan Bull

The seventh of the LABOURS performed by HERACLES for Eurystheus was to go to Crete and capture the bull, sent by Poseidon, that had fathered the Minotaur on Pasiphae. The god grew angry when MINOS failed to sacrifice the bull to him, so he made it savage, and Heracles had to fight hard to subdue it. He then rode on its back across the sea to the Peloponnese. Having shown it to Eurystheus, he set it free and it made its way to Attica. There it became the MARATHONIAN BULL, and plagued the inhabitants until it was killed by Theseus.

In ancient art Heracles is shown attacking the bull, usually with his club, or wrestling with it (fig. 42), or occasionally driving it back to Eurystheus.

[Apollodorus 2.5.7, 3.15.7; Diodorus Siculus 4.13.4; Pausanias 1.27.9–10; Quintus of Smyrna, *Sequel to Homer* 6.236–40.]

Crete *see* ASTERIUS (1).

Cretheus

Son of AEOLUS (1) and Enarete, and brother of SALMONEUS whose daughter TYRO he married. He had by her three sons, AESON, PHERES (1) and AMYTHAON. He was the founder and first king of Iolcus in Thessaly, from which Aeson's son JASON set sail in the *Argo*.

Creusa (1)

The youngest daughter of ERECHTHEUS, king of Athens, and Praxithea. She married XUTHUS, and was the mother by him of ION and ACHAEUS, the ancestors of the Ionians and Achaeans, though in one tradition Ion was her son by the god APOLLO.

Creusa (2)

Another name for GLAUCE, daughter of Creon, king of Corinth, who was murdered by Medea.

Creusa (3)

A daughter of PRIAM, king of Troy, and HECUBA. She married AENEAS, leader of the Dardanian allies of the Trojans, and bore him a son, ASCANIUS (Iulus). In Virgil's account of the fall of Troy, when Aeneas and his family were escaping from the burning city, Creusa became somehow separated from the party and vanished. This to Aeneas was the cruellest blow of all. He rushed back into Troy to search for her, only to see her ghost rise before him. She

reassured him that it was the gods' will that he should leave Troy without her and found a new kingdom in Italy. Three times in his sorrow he tried to clasp her in his arms, but three times her phantom escaped him, as weightless as the winds, and faded away.

[Apollodorus 3.12.5; Pausanias 10.26.1; Virgil, *Aeneid* 2.736–95.]

Crisus *see* PANOPEUS.

Crius

One of the TITANS, son of Uranus (Heaven) and GAIA (Earth). By EURYBIA, daughter of Pontus (Sea) and Gaia, he was father of the Titans ASTRAEUS, PALLAS (2) and PERSES (1).

[Hesiod, *Theogony* 134, 375–7.]

Croesus

The last king of Lydia, *c.* 560–546 BC, proverbial for his great wealth. Soon after his death, his fate became the stuff of legend (*see* HYPERBOREANS).

Cronus

The youngest and wiliest of the TITANS, son of Uranus (Heaven) and GAIA (Earth), according to Hesiod's account of creation in his *Theogony*. Uranus, who hated all his children, forced them back inside Gaia's womb until, in agony, she appealed to her children for help. Only Cronus had the courage to do as she wished. Armed with a sickle of adamant he lay in wait for his father, and when Uranus next came to lie with Gaia, Cronus hacked off his genitals and flung them into the sea. He then released his brothers and sisters from inside their mother.

Uranus' power was gone and Cronus was now the

Fig. 42 **Heracles wrestles to subdue the Cretan Bull, while Iolaus holds his weapons.**

king of the gods, but he soon became as brutal and tyrannical as his father, imprisoning his brothers the CYCLOPES and the HUNDRED-HANDERS in TARTARUS. He married his sister RHEA (1) who bore him five children, HESTIA, DEMETER, HERA, HADES (1) and POSEIDON, but because he had learnt from Gaia that he was destined to be overthrown by his own son, Cronus swallowed each baby as it was born. When Rhea was pregnant with her sixth child she turned to her mother for help. So Gaia rescued ZEUS when he was born, hiding him in Crete and handing over to Cronus a stone wrapped in swaddling clothes in place of the baby (fig. 126). Cronus noticed nothing amiss and swallowed the stone.

Zeus was reared in secret, and when he grew to maturity, helped either by Gaia or METIS, he induced Cronus to disgorge the children he had swallowed. First to be vomited up was the stone that had been substituted for the divine infant, and this was set in the earth at Delphi as a wonder for mortals. Then came Zeus' brothers and sisters. Aided by the freed Cyclopes and Hundred-handers, they fought together with Zeus against Cronus and some of his brother Titans. After a long and desperate struggle Cronus was defeated and deposed. Zeus, reigning in his place, imprisoned his father and the hostile Titans in the depths of Tartarus. The Hundred-handers were appointed to guard them.

According to a different tradition, Cronus' rule was a blessed Golden Age in which men lived with carefree hearts like gods, without toil or grief, without even old age, and spent their lives constantly feasting on all the good things produced in abundance by the earth. (It is this aspect of Cronus that links him with his Roman counterpart, SATURN.) One tale tells how he fathered the Centaur CHEIRON on PHILYRA, the daughter of Oceanus, transforming himself into a horse to mate with her so as to deceive the jealous Rhea. When Cronus no longer reigned in Olympus, he became ruler of ELYSIUM, where the souls of heroes honoured by the gods lived after death.

Both traditions about Cronus are reflected in postclassical art. Perhaps the best-known painting of Cronus is Goya's horrific *Saturn Devouring One of His Children* in the Prado, Madrid. By a confusion between Cronus' name and the Greek word for time, *chronos*, he is sometimes seen as Time personified, and is depicted as old Father Time, complete with scythe.

[Homer, *Iliad* 8.478–81, 14.203–4, 271–9; Hesiod, *Theogony* 137–8, 155–82, 453–506, 617–735, *Works and Days* 109–20, 169–73; Pindar, *Olympian* 2.68–77; Apollonius, *Argonautica* 2.1229–42; Apollodorus 1.1.3–1.2.1; Pausanias 5.7.6–10, 8.8.2–3, 8.36.2–3, 10.24.6.]

Croton

The man who gave his name to Croton in southern Italy. When HERACLES was returning to Mycenae with the cattle of GERYON, his tenth Labour for Eurystheus, Croton gave him hospitality. A neighbour, Lacinius, tried to steal the splendid cattle, so Heracles fought and killed him, but also accidentally killed his host in the struggle. In expiation Heracles built Croton a fine tomb and prophesied that in time to come a famous city would rise, bearing his name.

[Diodorus Siculus 4.24.7; Ovid, *Metamorphoses* 15.9–59.]

Crow *see* CORVUS.

Cteatus

One of the Siamese twins known as the MOLIONES.

Ctimene

Daughter of LAERTES and ANTICLEIA, and younger sister of ODYSSEUS. She married EURYLOCHUS.

[Homer, *Odyssey* 10.441, 15.363–4.]

Cupid

The Roman name for the Greek EROS, god of Love. For the most famous of his myths, *see* PSYCHE.

Curetes (1)

Minor Cretan divinities who protected the great god ZEUS when he was a baby. He was given by his mother RHEA (1) to the Cretan nymphs, ADRASTEIA and Ida, who brought him up in safety, far from his cannibalistic father, Cronus. The Curetes guarded the cave in which the child was hidden, dancing around the entrance and clashing their shields and spears so as to drown his infant cries. It seems that they had the gift of prophecy, for they later advised King Minos of how he could find his lost son GLAUCUS (2). They were finally killed by Zeus himself, angry because they had stolen Epaphus, his son by IO, to please the jealous HERA.

The Curetes' name is derived from *kouroi*, 'young men'. Bronze shields found in the cave on Mount Ida, where Zeus was said to have been reared, suggest that human *kouroi* ritually enacted the part of the divine Curetes and performed dances in honour of the god. The Curetes were often associated with the CORYBANTES, the male attendants of the Phrygian goddess Cybele, who was identified by the Greeks with Zeus' mother Rhea.

[Callimachus, *Hymn* 1.51–3; Apollodorus 1.1.6–7, 2.1.3, 3.3.1; Diodorus Siculus 5.65, 5.70.2–4; Strabo 10.3.7, 10.3.11; Pausanias 4.31.9, 4.33.1, 5.7.6, 8.37.6; Ovid, *Fasti* 4.207–14.]

Curetes (2)

An Aetolian tribe. *See* MELEAGER.

Cyane ('Blue')

A Sicilian water-nymph who gave her name to a famous spring and pool near Syracuse. Cyane saw HADES (1) abducting PERSEPHONE in his chariot and, rising from her pool, she tried to block their path. Hades in fury hurled his royal sceptre into the depths of the waters, opening up a road down to his kingdom in the Underworld. Through the yawning crater hurtled the chariot, and Cyane was left alone to grieve for the fate of Persephone, and for the contempt that Hades had shown for her own dear pool. She grieved so much that she wasted entirely away with weeping, dissolving into her own waters until nothing else remained of her. When DEMETER came by, searching for her lost daughter, Cyane could no longer speak to tell her what she knew, so instead she showed Persephone's belt floating on the surface of her pool, a silent token of her friend's fate.

[Ovid, *Metamorphoses* 5.409–77.]

Cybele

The great Phrygian mother-goddess, identified by the Greeks with RHEA (1), wife of CRONUS and mother of the gods, though occasionally also with DEMETER. Cybele was a goddess of fertility and the mistress of wild nature, her chief sanctuary being on the Phrygian Mount Dindymus at Pessina, where her sacred image in stone was believed to have fallen from heaven. From here her cult spread over the whole of the Greek world, and later into the Roman world too when (traditionally in 204 BC) the Romans brought the goddess' sacred stone from Pessina to Rome and built her a temple on the Palatine Hill. Cybele was associated in myth and cult with a young male consort, Attis, whose story centred on his self-castration. Her priests too were eunuchs, who in a state of religious ecstasy castrated themselves in ritual commemoration of Attis' self-mutilation and death.

The story of Cybele's love for Attis has many variants, such as the following Phrygian version. Where ZEUS' semen fell upon the ground while he slept, Cybele (also known as Agdistis) was born, with both male and female sex organs. The gods castrated this hermaphrodite creation, and from the severed male genitals there sprang an almond tree. From its fruit the nymph Nana, daughter of the river-god Sangarius, conceived Attis. When her son was born she abandoned him, but a he-goat miraculously suckled the baby, who grew into a beautiful youth. Cybele, now all female, fell in love with him so jealously that to prevent him marrying another she drove him mad, and in his frenzy he castrated himself, and died.

In another version, Attis was in love with a wood nymph, Sagaritis, whom Cybele killed in a jealous rage by

Fig. 43 The goddess Cybele in her chariot drawn by lions.

cutting down the tree in which she lived. Mad with grief, Attis again castrated himself. He died at the foot of a pine tree, and from his blood violets grew. Some say that he was transformed into a pine, and that this tree was made sacred to him.

Cybele is portrayed in art wearing a turreted crown and seated on a throne flanked by lions, or riding in a chariot drawn by lions (fig. 43). (In Greek myth, her lions were sometimes said to be the huntress ATALANTA and her lover Hippomenes in animal-form.) She was accompanied by revelling MAENADS and her male attendants, the CORYBANTES, who produced her celebratory music with the clash of cymbals and the sound of pipes and drums.

[*Homeric Hymn* 14; Apollonius, *Argonautica* 1.1092–1152; Diodorus Siculus 3.58.1–3.59.8; Pausanias 7.17.9–12, 7.20.3; Lucretius 2.594–643; Catullus 63; Virgil, *Aeneid* 6.784–90, 10.215–55; Ovid, *Metamorphoses* 10.102–5, 686–704, 14.530–55, *Fasti* 4.179–244. M. Vermaseren, *Cybele and Attis* (1977).]

Cychreus

Son of POSEIDON and SALAMIS, daughter of the river-god Asopus. Cychreus was the first king of the island that he named Salamis after his mother; here he gave refuge to TELAMON when he was exiled from Aegina, and left him the kingdom when he himself died childless.

His legend associates him in various ways with snakes. Some said that he won the rule of Salamis through killing a snake that was ravaging the island; others that he himself had reared the snake, and that it was driven out by a certain Eurylochus, then went to the nearby mainland at Eleusis where the goddess DEMETER welcomed it as one of her attendants. After his death Cychreus was honoured as a guardian hero of Salamis, buried on the island with his face to the west. He was also worshipped in Athens, and it was said that when the Athenians were fighting the Persians in the naval battle of Salamis (480 BC), Cychreus appeared to the Athenians in the form of a snake, bringing his aid and blessing. Certainly the Athenians won a splendid victory.

[Apollodorus 3.12.6–7; Diodorus Siculus 4.72.4; Strabo 9.1.9; Plutarch, *Solon* 9, *Theseus* 10; Pausanias 1.35.2, 1.36.1.]

Cyclopes ('round-eyed')

Giants with a single eye in the middle of their foreheads. According to Hesiod there were three of them, Brontes (Thunderer), Steropes (Lightner) and Arges (Vivid), and they were the sons of Uranus (Sky) and GAIA (Earth), born after the TITANS and just before their monstrous brothers the HUNDRED-HANDERS. Gaia induced her son Cronus to castrate and overthrow Uranus, after which Cronus reigned supreme. But he feared the power of his brothers the Cyclopes and the Hundred-handers, so he imprisoned them in TARTARUS.

He was right to fear them. In time his own children, led by his youngest son ZEUS, rebelled against him; and Zeus released both Cyclopes and Hundred-handers to help him in his war against his father and the rest of the Titans. The Cyclopes provided Zeus with thunder and lightning and thunderbolt, and they made a trident for POSEIDON and a cap of invisibility for HADES. Armed with these weapons, the gods defeated the Titans and threw them into Tartarus. Now Zeus reigned supreme, and the Cyclopes carried on forging the great god's thunderbolts until finally they were killed by APOLLO, enraged because they had fashioned the bolt that slew his son ASCLEPIUS. Apollo was punished in his turn by Zeus, who forced him to serve a mortal (Admetus) for a year.

Many monumental works were attributed by the ancients to the Cyclopes (giving us the adjective 'Cyclopean') including the Lion Gate at Mycenae and the immense walls of both Mycenae and Tiryns, so huge that it seemed impossible they could have been built by mortal hands. The forges of the Cyclopes were thought to be under the volcanic Mount Etna in Sicily, thus giving rise to its fiery activities. Virgil describes an underground cavern near Sicily, beneath an island of smoking rocks that rose sheer from the sea, where many smiths worked under the direction of HEPHAESTUS, fashioning equipment for the gods – thunderbolts for Zeus, a chariot for ARES, armour for ATHENA – and their vast cavern resounded with the constant clanging of hammers on anvils.

Perhaps the most famous Cyclops is Homer's POLYPHEMUS (2), who has a traumatic encounter with ODYSSEUS and his men on their journey home from Troy.

Homer's Cyclopes are a race of shepherds, still gigantic, still with a single eye, but here dwelling in a world of men, on an island that was later identified with Sicily. Their parentage too seems to be different from that of Hesiod's Cyclopes, for Polyphemus at least is the son of Poseidon and the nymph Thoosa. He is a murderous savage, and when Odysseus and his men are trapped in his cave, he eats six of them before the wily Odysseus can evolve the plan of making him drunk and then blinding him. They eventually escape from the cave, once the blinded Cyclops had pulled away the great boulder from its entrance, by clinging to the undersides of his sheep as they go out to pasture. It will be Poseidon's anger at the blinding of his son that will keep Odysseus, for all too many weary years, away from his longed-for Ithaca.

[Homer, *Odyssey* 9.105–566; Hesiod, *Theogony* 139–46, 501–6; Euripides, *Cyclops* 296–7; Callimachus, *Hymn* 3.46–86; Apollodorus 1.1.2, 1.1.4–5, 1.2.1, 2.2.1, 3.10.4; Strabo 8.6.11; Pausanias 2.2.1, 2.16.5, 2.25.8, 7.25.6; Virgil, *Aeneid* 8.416–53, *Georgics* 4.170–5.]

Cycnus

There are a number of different heroes with the name Cycnus, meaning 'swan', and their legends recount how several of them became transformed into swans.

Cycnus (1)

A musician king of the Ligurians in Italy. He was a relative of PHAETHON (2), the son of Helios the Sun-god, and loved the boy dearly. When Phaethon borrowed his father's sun-chariot for a day and was hurled by Zeus' thunderbolt to his death in the Eridanus river, Cycnus mourned him unceasingly, wandering the river-banks and singing of his loss, until the gods took pity on him and turned him into a swan. While he lived, remembering Zeus' thunderbolt, he chose as his element water, the very antithesis of fire. Shunning the dangerous skies, he haunted lakes and rivers and marshes. When at last he grew old and it was time for him to die, he left the earth and became the constellation Cygnus, singing as he flew towards the stars. Swans have ever afterwards sung songs, 'swan songs', when they are about to die.

[Pausanias 1.30.3; Virgil, *Aeneid* 10.189–93; Ovid, *Metamorphoses* 2.367–80.]

Cycnus (2)

Son of the war-god ARES, and bloodthirsty like his father, for he enjoyed waylaying travellers who brought offerings for APOLLO's shrine at Pagasae, in Thessaly, and challenging them to single combat. When he killed his victims, as he always did, he cut off their heads and used these gory trophies to build a temple to his father. He finally met his match – as did so many who preyed violently on their fellow men – in the great HERACLES. Cycnus barred that hero's path and issued his usual challenge, which Heracles, incited by an angry Apollo, was only too happy to take up. The two met in single combat, with Ares standing by to support his son (fig. 22). This time it was Cycnus who was killed. Heracles also wounded Ares when the god rushed to avenge his son, but on the advice of Athena he did not pursue his advantage and Ares escaped to Olympus; though some say that the two fought until Zeus flung a thunderbolt to separate them. CEYX (2), the king of Trachis and father-in-law of Cycnus, gave the dead brigand funeral honours; but Apollo, angry because of all his lost offerings, made the river Anaurus flood its banks and blot out Cycnus' grave.

[Hesiod, *Shield of Heracles* 57–480; Pindar, *Olympian* 10.15–16; Euripides, *Heracles* 391–3; Apollodorus 2.5.11, 2.7.7; Plutarch, *Theseus* 11; Pausanias 1.27.6, 3.18.10.]

Cycnus (3)

A son of POSEIDON, and an ally of the Trojans in their war against the Greeks. His father had made his body invulnerable to human weapons, so when Cycnus tried to oppose the Greek landing in the Troad, ACHILLES attacked him with spear and sword to no avail, then at last forced him to the ground and throttled him with his own helmet thongs. Achilles was preparing to strip the armour from his conquered foe when he saw that it was empty, for Poseidon had turned his son into a swan.

[Epic Cycle, Proclus' summary of the *Cypria*; Pindar, *Olympian* 2.81–3; Aristotle, *Rhetoric* 2.22.12; Apollodorus, *Epitome* 3.31; Ovid, *Metamorphoses* 12.71–145.]

Cycnus (4)

Son of Poseidon and king of Colonae near Troy (*see* TENES).

Cycnus (5)

Son of APOLLO and Hyrie. Cycnus lived with his mother at Tempe, near Pleuron in Aetolia, and was loved by Phyllius, but he treated his lover very capriciously. To satisfy Cycnus' demands, Phyllius tamed wild birds and even a savage lion, giving them as presents to the boy, but always his affection was scorned. Finally he was ordered to tame a wild bull, and did so; but because his love had been spurned so often, he refused Cycnus this last gift. The boy was wildly indignant, and shouting that his lover would be sorry for this, he flung himself off a cliff. Everyone believed that he had fallen to his death, but instead he was transformed into a swan, floating in the air on snowy wings. His mother Hyrie, not knowing that he had been saved, melted away with weeping and was turned into the lake that bears her name.

[Ovid, *Metamorphoses* 7.371–81.]

Cydippe *see* ACONTIUS.

Cydon *see* ACACALLIS.

Cygnus (The Swan)

A constellation commemorating either the form that Zeus took when he fathered Helen on LEDA or NEMESIS, or one or another of the heroes named CYCNUS.

Cynthia, Cynthius *see* DELOS.

Cyparissus

A beautiful boy from the island of Ceos. Like Hyacinthus, he was loved by APOLLO and returned the god's love, and like Hyacinthus too he died tragically. He had a pet stag, sacred to the nymphs, that was tame and surpassingly beautiful. He would lead it to water or to fresh grass, and hang wreaths of flowers on its antlers, and even ride upon its back. But one summer's day, as the stag was sleeping, stretched out in the shade, Cyparissus threw his hunting-spear and accidentally killed it. Filled with grief, he longed only to die, and all the comfort that Apollo could offer was unavailing. The boy begged as a last gift from the gods that he might go on mourning for ever, so Apollo transformed him into a cypress tree, the symbol of eternal grief.

[Ovid, *Metamorphoses* 10.106–42.]

Cypselus (1)

The king of Arcadia at the time when the Peloponnese was conquered by the HERACLIDS, led by Cresphontes, Temenus, and the two sons of Aristodemus. To win an alliance that would safeguard his kingdom, Cypselus married his daughter Merope to Cresphontes, who acquired Messenia as his portion of the Peloponnese (*see* CRESPHONTES (1)). When rebels killed Cresphontes and his two eldest sons and usurped the throne of Messenia, Cypselus brought up the surviving youngest son to avenge his father and regain the kingdom (*see* CRESPHONTES (2)).

Cypselus (2)

A Corinthian, the son of Eetion and the father of Periander, one of the Seven Sages, and as such a historical rather than a mythical figure, living in the seventh century BC. But the story of his infancy is legendary. After his birth, his mother saved him from the family of the Bacchiadae, then rulers of Corinth, by hiding him in a cedarwood chest, and it was said that he was given the name of Cypselus from the Corinthian term for chests, *kypselidai*. He grew up to oust the Bacchiadae from their long-established rule and to become tyrant of Corinth himself. Cypselus or his grateful descendants dedicated at Olympia the chest that saved him. In the second century

AD the traveller Pausanias saw the chest in the temple of Hera. He gives a long description of the many mythological scenes that decorated it, with figures in ivory, gold and wood (5.17.5–5.19.10).

Cyrene

A nymph and huntress, daughter of Hypseus, king of the Lapiths, and mother of ARISTAEUS by APOLLO. The god's

encounter with Cyrene is described by Pindar (*Pythian* 9.1–70). One day he saw her on Mount Pelion, wrestling with a huge lion (fig. 44), and fell in love with her beauty and prowess. Calling the wise Centaur CHEIRON, he asked who she was, and Cheiron, realising that Apollo was dissembling, teased him a little:

> Do you ask, lord, the girl's birth? You who know the appointed end of all things, and all the ways that lead there. You know how many leaves the earth puts forth in spring, you know how many grains of sand in the sea and the rivers are driven before the waves and the rushing winds. You know what will be, and why it will be – all this you see clearly.

The Centaur then predicted that Apollo would carry Cyrene off to Libya, and make her queen of a city named after her – and this is exactly what the god did, bearing her away in his golden chariot.

Cytorissus

One of the four sons of PHRIXUS who helped the ARGONAUTS to win the Golden Fleece and escape from Colchis. In later years he rescued his grandfather ATHAMAS from sacrifice as a scapegoat.

Cyzicus

King of the Doliones, a Mysian tribe living on the southern shores of the Propontis, who traced their origins back to Poseidon. When the ARGONAUTS came to his land on their journey to Colchis to win the Golden Fleece, Cyzicus was still a very young man, recently married to Cleite, the daughter of Merops, king of Percote, and they had as yet no children. Cyzicus entertained the Argonauts hospitably and on the following day they set sail once again. But they met a storm, and during the night were unwittingly blown back to the land they had just left. The Doliones attacked them, mistaking them for pirates, and in the pitched battle that followed Cyzicus was killed by Jason. In the morning light both sides realised their tragic error. For three days they all mourned the young king, then buried him with full funeral honours. His city was named Cyzicus in his memory. Cleite hanged herself from grief, and the many tears shed for her by the woodland nymphs were turned into a spring, named Cleite in her everlasting honour.

[Apollonius, *Argonautica* 1.936–1077.]

Fig.44 **The huntress Cyrene with a lion.**

D

Dactyls ('Fingers')

The Dactyls were sorcerers and smiths; but beyond this one known particular, they are surrounded by obscure and conflicting traditions. Their number was uncertain, for they were said to be sometimes five, sometimes ten, sometimes far more (in one case fifty-two: thirty-two who cast spells and twenty who dissolved them). Their place of origin was uncertain, since they were located on both Mount Ida in Crete and Mount Ida in Phrygia, near Troy, in both cases being known as the 'Idaean Dactyls'. Thus they are associated sometimes with RHEA (1) and identified with the CURETES (1), who guarded the infant Zeus in Crete, and sometimes with the Phrygian goddess CYBELE and confused with the CORYBANTES.

[Apollonius, *Argonautica* 1.1125–31; Strabo 10.3.7, 10.3.22; Diodorus Siculus 5.64.3–7, 17.7.5; Pausanias 5.7.6–5.8.1, 5.14.7, 8.31.3, 9.19.5.]

Daedalion

Son of Phosphorus, the Morning Star (*see* CHIONE (2)).

Daedalus ('Ingenious')

A brilliant inventor and master-craftsman. He was an Athenian, either the grandson or great-grandson of King ERECHTHEUS, and his father was appropriately named as either Eupalamus, 'skilful', or Metion, 'knowledgeable'. Daedalus was forced to leave Athens after murdering his nephew, PERDIX, and went to the court of MINOS, king of Crete. When Pasiphae lusted for the bull that Poseidon sent from the sea, Daedalus built for her the hollow wooden cow, realistically covered with hide, inside which Pasiphae crouched so that the bull might couple with her. When she gave birth to the monstrous MINOTAUR, a man with the head of a bull, Minos commissioned Daedalus to build the Labyrinth, a vast underground maze in which the creature could be shut away for ever.

The Minotaur was fed on human flesh, for Minos claimed from Athens, in recompense for the death of his son Androgeos, a tribute (either annually or every nine years) of seven youths and seven girls, who were sent into the Labyrinth to feed the monster. This maze had been so cleverly devised by Daedalus that anyone going in would be quite unable to find the way out again – until, that is, Daedalus himself took a hand in the matter. When the Athenian hero THESEUS came as one of the seven sacrificial youths, but with the intention of killing the Minotaur and putting an end to this ghastly tribute, Minos' daughter ARIADNE fell in love with him. For her sake Daedalus provided a ball of thread that would show Theseus the way back out of the Labyrinth. Theseus duly killed the Minotaur and made his escape by following the thread, then left Crete, taking Ariadne with him.

Minos was so angered by Daedalus' treachery that he imprisoned him in the Labyrinth, together with his little son ICARUS, born to him from one of the palace slave girls. But the clever Daedalus was never at a loss, and now he fashioned wings of wax and feathers with which they flew to freedom. Sadly, despite warnings from his father, Icarus flew so near the sun that the wax of his wings melted in the heat, and he fell to his death in the sea below. Daedalus escaped to Sicily and took refuge at the court of Cocalus, king of Camicus. Minos, still bent on revenge, searched for him everywhere, taking with him a spiral seashell and promising a great reward to anyone who could pass a thread through it. He believed (and quite rightly) that no one but the clever Daedalus would be able to solve the problem, as indeed he did when Minos brought the shell to Camicus. Daedalus (perhaps remembering Theseus' escape from the Labyrinth) bored a hole in the shell, then tied a thread to an ant and induced it to pass through the spiral. Cocalus gave the threaded shell to Minos, who at once demanded that he surrender Daedalus to him. The king promised to do so. But that night Minos, while in his bath, was killed by Cocalus' daughters. They had grown so fond of Daedalus, delighting in their clever guest's artistic skill, that they did not want to lose him, so they scalded Minos to death with boiling water (some say pitch), flooding it through a system of pipes installed by Daedalus himself.

Daedalus' name became synonymous with ingenuity and fine craftsmanship. The ancients saw evidence of his work in many remarkable buildings and art works throughout the Greek world, and even in Egypt. He is mentioned first by Homer (*Iliad* 18.590–2) as the maker of a dancing-floor for Ariadne at Knossos. Virgil (*Aeneid* 6.14–33) says that he built Apollo's great temple at Cumae, adorning it with scenes depicting the birth and death of the Minotaur. 'And you too, Icarus', adds Virgil, 'would have had a great part in this splendid work, but for Daedalus' grief. Twice he tried to shape your fall in gold, and twice his hands, a father's hands, dropped helpless.'

Daedalus as symbol of the creative artist has remained important into the twentieth century, as when James Joyce chose the name Stephen Dedalus for his hero in *A Portrait of the Artist as a Young Man* and for one of his three chief characters in *Ulysses*, both to a large extent modelled on Joyce himself. The earlier novel ends with an invocation to Daedalus: 'Old father, old artificer, stand me now and ever in good stead.'

[Apollodorus 3.15.8, *Epitome* 1.8–15; Diodorus Siculus 1.61, 1.97.5–6, 4.30.1, 4.76.1–79.2; Pausanias 1.21.4, 1.27.1, 2.4.5, 7.4.4–7, 8.35.2, 8.53.8, 9.11.4–5, 9.39.8, 9.40.3–4; Ovid, *Metamorphoses* 8.152–262.]

Danaans and Danaids *see* DANAUS.

Danae

Daughter of ACRISIUS, king of Argos, and Eurydice. Acrisius was warned by an oracle that Danae would give birth to a son who would kill him, so to keep her away from all contact with men he imprisoned her in a bronze, underground chamber. (The earliest source of the popular later notion that the prison was a bronze tower seems to be Horace, *Odes* 3.16.) This chamber, however, had a small aperture for light and air, and despite her imprisonment she became pregnant when ZEUS came to her as a shower of golden rain, pouring down into her lap. She gave birth to a son, PERSEUS. Acrisius refused to believe that the father was Zeus, so he shut mother and baby in a wooden chest and threw it into the sea. Protected by Zeus, the chest drifted to the island of Seriphos where it was caught in the fishing nets of Dictys, brother of the local king, Polydectes. Dictys took Danae and her baby into his home, and there Perseus grew to manhood. Then Polydectes fell in love with Danae. Finding that Perseus was a hindrance in his attempts to woo her, he contrived to have him sent off to fetch the head of the Gorgon Medusa. The sight of this monster could turn a man to stone, so Polydectes was certain that Perseus would not survive.

He was wrong, for in due course Perseus returned triumphant from his mission. Finding that his mother and Dictys had taken refuge at the gods' altars to escape persecution by Polydectes, he went into the palace where the king and his companions were feasting. He showed them Medusa's head and turned them all into stone. Making Dictys king in Polydectes' place, he took his mother back to Argos. He himself went on to Larissa, where he fulfilled the oracle given before his birth by

Fig. 45 Acrisius, afraid that baby Perseus will grow up to kill him, urges his daughter, Danae, into the chest in which she and her son will be flung to their (supposed) deaths in the sea.

accidentally killing his grandfather, Acrisius, while throwing the discus at the games given by the local king.

According to Virgil, Danae went to Italy where she founded the city of Ardea. One of her descendants there was TURNUS, king of the Rutulians and great rival of Aeneas.

Danae's story has always been an inspiration for artists. Both Sophocles and Euripides wrote tragedies, now lost, about the events surrounding Perseus' birth, Sophocles a *Danae* and an *Acrisius* and Euripides a *Danae*, while Euripides' lost *Dictys* seems to have told of Polydectes' persecution of Danae. So probably did Aeschylus' lost *Polydectes*, while his fragmentary satyr play the *Netdrawers* treats Danae's arrival on Seriphos. Simonides wrote a lyric poem of which a few poignant fragments remain of Danae's lament to her baby within the wooden chest (fr. 543):

... When, in the wrought chest,
the blowing wind and the swelling sea
struck her with fear, her cheeks wet
she put her loving arms round Perseus
and said, 'My child, what trouble is mine.
But you sleep sound, your little heart
at peace as you lie on comfortless
bronze-nailed wood, drowsing in the unlit night,
the black dark. You care nothing
for the deep spray of the swelling sea
above your head, nor the roaring wind,
as you lie there, your pretty face
bright in the crimson shawl.
If this danger were danger to you,
your tiny ear would hear my words.
But as it is, I tell you, sleep,
my baby, and let the sea sleep,
and let our endless suffering sleep ...'

In Greek art there are vase-paintings from the early fifth century BC of Danae receiving the golden rain, or of her and Perseus with the chest (fig. 45). She was a popular subject for painters in the Renaissance and later, and there are several paintings of her by Titian alone, and others by Coreggio, Tintoretto, Rembrandt, Rubens, Boucher and Klimt, to name but a few. Tennyson refers to Danae in *The Princess*:

Now lies the Earth all Danae to the stars,
And all thy heart lies open unto me.

[Apollodorus 2.4.1–5; Virgil, *Aeneid* 7.371–2, 408–13.]

Danaus

Son of BELUS and Anchinoe, and twin-brother of Aegyptus. Both brothers had children by many wives, Danaus fifty daughters, known as the Danaids, and Aegyptus fifty

sons. Belus, who ruled a vast empire centred on the kingdom around the Nile, settled Danaus in Libya and Aegyptus in Arabia. But Aegyptus was not content with this, so he conquered the tribe of the Melampodes ('Black-feet') and named the land Egypt after himself. He then offered his fifty sons in marriage to Danaus' fifty daughters, but Danaus believed that his brother had now set his sights on stealing Libya, so on the advice of ATHENA he built a ship (the first man to do so, it was said), and with his fifty daughters sailed away to Argos, the birth-place of his ancestress IO. On his journey he put in at Lindos, on the island of Rhodes, and there dedicated a temple to Athena in gratitude for her help.

On arriving in Argos, Danaus claimed the kingdom from the ruling king, Gelanor, on the basis of his descent from Io, but Gelanor disputed the claim and the two of them debated the matter in the Argive assembly. The people were moved to vote for Danaus because of an omen: on the morning of the judgement, a wolf came from nowhere and attacked a herd of Argive cattle, killing the leading bull, which was interpreted as meaning that the outsider should prevail. So Danaus won the kingdom and founded a sanctuary of APOLLO *Lykeios* (meaning 'wolf-god' in this interpretation of the word). His people were named *Danaoi*, Danaans, the general name for the Greek nation in Homer and later poets. He also brought water to Argos, which had been a dry land as a result of POSEIDON's anger, ever since the time when the sea-god and HERA had both claimed overlordship of the country. INACHUS and other river-gods had judged the dispute in favour of Hera, so in revenge Poseidon had dried up all their springs. Danaus now showed his people how to dig wells, and Poseidon himself created the spring of Lerna out of love for the Danaid AMYMONE.

In Aeschylus' tragedy *The Suppliants*, the first play in his Danaid trilogy, the situation is rather different. Danaus arrives in Argos with his fifty daughters, hotly pursued by the fifty sons of Aegyptus, eager for marriage. The reluctant Danaids beg PELASGUS, the king of Argos, for protection from their pursuers. At first he demurs, but then agrees when all the girls threaten to hang themselves from the city altars. Sadly the two following plays, *The Egyptians* and *The Danaids*, are lost, but the general outcome is well known from many other accounts. Danaus was forced to agree to the marriages and allotted each of his daughters to one of their cousins. He gave a great feast to celebrate the weddings, but secretly presented each girl with a dagger and instructed them all to murder their husbands during the night. Forty-nine of them obeyed. The eldest Danaid, Hypermestra, spared her husband Lynceus, either because she loved him or because he had respected her virginity. He escaped to nearby Lyrceia and there lit a fire-signal to let her know that he was safe. Danaus punished Hypermestra with imprisonment and even put her on trial for her disobedience, but the Argive court acquitted her. Perhaps in Aeschylus this was through the intervention of APHRODITE, for we know that the goddess had a role in the third play, *Danaids*, and made a speech in favour of love and sexual union, through which all life is nurtured and renewed.

The other forty-nine Danaids hacked off their husbands' heads and took them to their father as proof of their obedience, then gave the bodies full funeral honours near the walls of the city and buried the heads at Lerna. At the command of Zeus, Athena and Hermes purified the girls of their murders. Danaus then had the task of finding new husbands for his daughters among the young men of Argos, who were understandably disinclined to choose such doubtful brides. So he promised to give them away, without requiring the customary bride-gifts in exchange, as prizes for whoever would run for them in footraces, the winner to take his pick, and so on, until all the girls were chosen. Eventually they all remarried.

Lynceus was later reunited with Hypermestra and reconciled with his father-in-law, though one tradition said that to avenge his brothers he killed Danaus and the forty-nine murdering Danaids. He took the throne of Argos on Danaus' death, and he and Hypermestra had a son, Abas, through whom they were the generators of a splendid royal line that included the great heroes PERSEUS and HERACLES. The fate of the other Danaids was not so happy: after their deaths they were punished for their crime in the Underworld, forced to spend all eternity drawing water into leaking vessels that had to be forever refilled.

[Aeschylus, *Prometheus Bound* 855–69; Pindar, *Pythian* 9.111–16, *Nemean* 10.1–6; Herodotus 2.182; Euripides, *Orestes* 871–3; Apollodorus 2.1.4–2.2.1; Strabo 1.2.15, 8.6.8–9; Pausanias 2.16.1, 2.19.3–7, 2.20.6–7, 2.21.1–2, 2.25.4, 2.38.4, 3.12.2, 7.21.13, 10.10.5; Horace, *Odes* 3.11.21–52; Ovid, *Heroides* 14. E. Keuls, *The Water-carriers in Hades* (1974).]

Daphne ('Laurel')

A nymph loved by APOLLO. She was the daughter of a river-god, either Ladon in Arcadia or Peneius in Thessaly, and was a virgin huntress like ARTEMIS. Two stories are told of her. Pausanias (8.20.2–4) relates how Leucippus, the son of Oenomaus, king of Pisa in Elis, fell in love with Daphne, but had no hope of winning her by a normal courtship since she avoided all contact with men. So he disguised himself as a girl, braiding his long hair and dressing in women's clothes, and told Daphne that he

was the daughter of Oenomaus and would like to hunt with her and her band of women. She accepted his companionship and the two became close friends, particularly since his prowess at the hunt won her admiration. Apollo, who himself desired Daphne, became jealous, and one day he inspired all the women with a sudden and strong desire to bathe in the river Ladon. Leucippus alone was unwilling, so the women undressed themselves, then stripped off his clothes too, despite his reluctance. When they realised his imposture, they angrily attacked him with their hunting spears and daggers, and killed him.

The second and more famous story is related by Ovid in his *Metamorphoses* (1.452–567). Apollo, an unerring archer whose special weapon was the bow, once imprudently derided EROS' prowess at archery, and the Love-god took his revenge by inflicting on Apollo the pains of an unrequited passion. He let fly two of his potent arrows. The first, sharp and golden, the kind that kindles love, pierced Apollo to the very marrow of his bones, and he fell violently in love with Daphne. The second arrow, blunt and tipped with lead, the kind that repels love, pierced Daphne herself. It caused her to shun the entire male sex, instilling in her a desire to remain a virgin for the rest of her days, even though she had a multitude of suitors because of her great beauty. So when Apollo pursued her, she ran from him, swifter than the wind's breath. But the god, inspired by love, ran faster still, and was just about to catch hold of her when they drew near the banks of her father's river, the Peneius. Daphne, in desperation, prayed to her father for help, and the river-god acted at once (1.548–65):

> Her prayer was scarcely ended when her limbs grew numb and heavy, her soft breasts were covered in delicate bark, her hair became leaves, her arms branches, and her swift feet were rooted into the ground, while her head became a treetop. Nothing of her was left, except her grace, her shining.
>
> Apollo loved her, even as a tree. He put his hand where he had hoped and felt her heart still beating under the new bark. Embracing the branches as though they were still limbs he kissed the wood, but even as wood she shrank from his kisses. Then the god said, 'Since you can never be my bride, my tree at least you shall be. The laurel will henceforth adorn my hair, my lyre, my quiver ... and just as my head is always young and my hair never shorn, so may you also wear forever the crowning glory of leaves that never fade or fall.'

A laurel crown became the prize for the victor at the Pythian Games in honour of Apollo, and has been a symbol of victory ever since.

Daphne's story becomes enormously popular in the postclassical arts, particularly the fine arts, with paintings by Pollaiuolo, Tintoretto, Veronese, Poussin and Rubens, among many others, and Bernini's famous statue-group of Apollo and Daphne now in the Borghese Gallery in Rome.

Daphnis

A legendary Sicilian herdsman who was said to have been the inventor of pastoral poetry. He was the son of a nymph, who left him at his birth in a grove of laurel trees (*daphne*) from which he was named. He was brought up among shepherds. They taught him their skills, and he was a favourite of HERMES (or even his son) and of APOLLO and ARTEMIS. PAN taught him to play the pipes.

He grew to be a beautiful youth and was passionately loved by a nymph (her name varies), who made him swear eternal fidelity to her, on pain of blindness if he ever broke his oath. Unfortunately the king's daughter fell in love with him and contrived to make him drunk, then went to bed with him. He was duly blinded by the nymph and spent the rest of his life singing mournful songs about his unhappy fate. According to Theocritus he died of love, when Aphrodite grew angry with him for refusing to love anyone, then punished him with an unquenchable passion that eventually killed him.

Another version reports a happier outcome. Daphnis loved a nymph called Pimplea, and when she was carried off by pirates he searched the world for her. He eventually found her in Phrygia, now one of LITYERSES' slave girls. This king forced all comers to compete with him at harvesting, and when they inevitably lost, he beheaded them and bound their bodies in a corn stook. Daphnis would have suffered the same fate, but HERACLES came by and took his place, beating and killing Lityerses. He then gave the kingdom to Daphnis and Pimplea.

[Theocritus, *Idylls* 1.64–142, 8; Parthenius, *Love Romances* 29; Diodorus Siculus 4.84; Aelian, *Historical Miscellany* 10.18.]

Dardanus

The son of ZEUS and ELECTRA (2), daughter of Atlas, and according to Homer Zeus' favourite of all his sons by mortal women. He was the ancestor of the Trojan kings. According to the Greek tradition, he came from his birthplace, Samothrace, to the Troad, where TEUCER (1) welcomed him and gave him land and the hand of his daughter, Bateia, in marriage. Dardanus founded a city, Dardania, then on Teucer's death became king of the whole country and changed the name of the people from Teucrians to Dardanians. He was succeeded by his son, ERICHTHONIUS (2). His grandson, TROS, gave his name to Troy and the Trojans.

According to Virgil's *Aeneid*, Dardanus was born in Italy, and for this reason AENEAS too made his home there, since he had been told by Apollo to settle in the homeland of Dardanus: 'For there', said Apollo (3.97–8), 'the house of Aeneas, and his sons' sons, and their sons who come after them, will rule over all the world.'

[Homer, *Iliad* 20.215–30, 304–5; Apollodorus 3.12.1–2; Virgil, *Aeneid* 3.84–171, 7.205–11, 8.134–7.]

Dares

The wealthy priest of HEPHAESTUS at Troy. Dares had two sons, Phegeus and Idaeus, who fought in the TROJAN WAR. The Greek hero DIOMEDES (2) killed Phegeus, and would have killed Idaeus too, had not Hephaestus intervened and carried him to safety, so that Dares might not be left completely desolate. This was the god's only intervention in the fighting during the war.

[Homer, *Iliad* 5.9–24.]

Dascylus *see* LYCUS (3).

Daunus (1)

Son of Pilumnus and king of the Rutulians of Ardea in Latium. By his wife Venilia he was the father of Aeneas' rival, TURNUS, and of the water-nymph JUTURNA.

[Virgil, *Aeneid* 10.74–6, 12.22, 223.]

Daunus (2)

King of Apulia in Italy. He gave refuge to the Greek hero DIOMEDES (2) after the Trojan War.

Death *see* THANATOS.

Deianeira

Daughter of OENEUS, king of Calydon, and ALTHAEA (though she was sometimes said to be the daughter of DIONYSUS); sister of the great hero MELEAGER; second wife and killer of the even greater hero HERACLES. The fateful meeting between these two heroes that led to the marriage of Heracles and Deianeira occurred in Hades, when Heracles travelled there to fetch the hellhound Cerberus for King Eurystheus. Bacchylides describes their encounter in his *Ode* 5. The shade of Meleager tells Heracles about the killing of the Calydonian Boar and the war with the Curetes that followed, then of how he himself died at the hands of his mother Althaea. Heracles, full of pity, says that he would like to marry the sister of such a hero, and Meleager tells him of Deianeira, young and unversed in love, whom he has left behind in the palace of Oeneus. Heracles listens with pleasure, little knowing that this choice of wife will inexorably set in motion events leading to his own death, since Deianeira will in the course of time kill him by sending him a poisoned robe.

Fig. 46 Heracles rescues Deianeira from Nessus.

Our first full depiction of Deianeira comes in Sophocles' tragedy *The Women of Trachis*. Before Sophocles' staging of her story, Deianeira seems to have been seen as a bold-hearted and aggressive woman, with hints of this earlier character appearing in comments such as that of Apollodorus (1.8.1): 'She drove a chariot and practised the arts of war.' It is also likely that this earlier Deianeira deliberately murdered Heracles out of jealousy and rage at his infidelity, with full knowledge of what her poisoned robe would do to him. But in Sophocles everything is quite different, for his Deianeira is a gentle, timid and loving woman, who during the course of the play unintentionally kills Heracles with the robe out of a desire to win back his love. She and Heracles have been married for many years and have had several children, including a son, HYLLUS, who takes part in the action of the play. From Deianeira we learn how Heracles once won her as his wife by wrestling with her other suitor, the river-god ACHELOUS, while she sat watching in dread lest this monstrous being might turn out to be her husband. But Heracles was the victor, so all was well. She also tells of a later and even more fateful past event. Early in their marriage, she and Heracles had to cross the River Evenus where the Centaur NESSUS acted as ferryman. Heracles was able to wade across the river alone, but he gave his wife to be carried on the back of the Centaur. Nessus tried to rape Deianeira, so Heracles shot him with one of his unerring arrows poisoned with the HYDRA OF LERNA's blood. Nessus, dying, and hoping to get revenge on his murderer at some future date, told the credulous Deianeira to gather some blood from around the arrow-wound, assuring her that it would act as a potent love-charm if it were ever needed. She did so, not realising that mixed with the Centaur's blood was the Hydra's fatal venom.

Now, during the course of the play, Heracles is about to return home triumphant after sacking the city of Oechalia, and he sends ahead of him a group of slaves that includes his new concubine IOLE. Deianeira, knowing herself to be an ageing woman, and afraid that Heracles will no longer love her now that he has the young and beautiful Iole, at last takes out the 'love-charm' from its hiding place. She smears it on a fine robe, which she gives to the herald LICHAS to take to her husband, hoping in this way to win back his love. Heracles, who is preparing to sacrifice on Cape Cenaeum in Euboea, at once puts on the robe (often called the 'shirt of Nessus'). Soon the poison begins to eat into his flesh like acid. In his torment, seizing Lichas by the foot, he flings him to his death on a rock projecting from the sea, and is then himself carried home in his death agonies. Hyllus has no idea of Deianeira's good intentions, so when he brings the news to his mother, he curses her bitterly for his father's murder. Deianeira, with the terrible knowledge that she has caused the death of her beloved husband and is now hated by her son, in utter despair kills herself.

Deianeira with Nessus is a popular subject in art from the seventh century BC (fig. 46), although Heracles is depicted almost invariably as killing the Centaur with his great club or sword rather than by an arrow-shot as in Sophocles. The subject was also one which inspired many postclassical artists, including Cranach, Veronese, Rubens, Jordaens, Giordano and Picasso. The agony of Heracles in the poisoned robe provided poets with an allusion for unendurable pain: in Shakespeare's *Antony and Cleopatra* Mark Anthony, whose family claimed descent from Heracles (also known as Alcides after his grandfather Alcaeus), cries out when all is lost (IV. xii. 43–7):

> The shirt of Nessus is upon me. Teach me,
> Alcides, thou mine ancestor, thy rage.
> Let me lodge Lichas on the horns o' th' moon,
> And with those hands that grasp'd the heaviest club
> Subdue my worthiest self.

[Hesiod, *Catalogue of Women* fr. 25; Bacchylides, *Ode* 16; Diodorus Siculus 4.38; Apollodorus 2.7.5–8; Nonnus, *Dionysiaca* 35.89–91; Ovid, *Metamorphoses* 9.101–33, *Heroides* 9; Seneca, *Hercules on Oeta*. J. R. March, *The Creative Poet* (1987), pp. 47–77.]

Deidameia

Daughter of LYCOMEDES, king of Scyros; and mother of NEOPTOLEMUS by ACHILLES, who made her pregnant while he was living among the women at Lycomedes' court disguised as a girl. Apollodorus (*Epitome* 6.12–13) says that after the Trojan War Neoptolemus married Deidameia to the Trojan prophet HELENUS.

Deimos *see* PHOBOS.

Deino *see* GRAEAE.

Deioneus *see* IXION.

Deiphobus

A son of PRIAM, king of Troy, and HECUBA. In the *Iliad* Deiphobus is one of the more powerful Trojan warriors, and is said to be HECTOR's favourite brother. ATHENA impersonates him to lure Hector to his death: in Deiphobus' likeness she urges Hector on to fight Achilles, saying that they will stand fast against him side by side. But at a crucial point in the battle Hector finds himself alone, and all too late realises the truth, and that now he must die (22.297–301):

> So the gods have indeed summoned me to death.
> I thought the hero Deiphobus was standing close by me,
> but he is inside the walls, and Athena was tricking me.
> And now evil death is right at my side, no longer
> far away, and there is no way out.

Deiphobus is still alive at the end of the *Iliad*, and we learn from later sources that he and HELENUS argued as to who should marry HELEN after PARIS was killed. It was Deiphobus who won her. On the night of Troy's capture, he went with Helen to examine the WOODEN HORSE while the Greeks were still hiding silently within it; and when later they poured out to attack the Trojans, Deiphobus' house was the prime target of MENELAUS and ODYSSEUS. Helen, having treacherously removed all her husband's weapons, now let Menelaus and his men into the house. Deiphobus was dragged from his bed by the avenging Greeks, killed and savagely mutilated. AENEAS later erected a cenotaph for him on the shore of Cape Rhoeteum.

[Homer, *Iliad* 12.94, 13.156–64, 402–16, 445–539, 22.233–4, *Odyssey* 4.276, 8.517–20; Apollodorus, *Epitome* 5.9; Virgil, *Aeneid* 6.494–547.]

Deiphontes

Son of Antimachus and a descendant of Heracles. The Heraclid leader TEMENUS (2), ruler of the Argolid, thought so highly of Deiphontes that he married him to his favourite daughter, Hyrnetho, and made him his chief adviser. This made Temenus' own sons afraid that they might be disinherited, so they killed their father and seized the throne. Deiphontes and Hyrnetho fled to Epidaurus, where for a time they found safe refuge with King Pityreus. But Temenus' sons still felt aggrieved with Deiphontes, so they tried to hurt him by persuading Hyrnetho to leave him. She refused, for she loved her husband and had borne him three sons and a daughter, and was even now pregnant with her fifth child. So her brothers kidnapped her, and handled her so roughly when Deiphontes tried to rescue her that both she and her baby died. Deiphontes buried her in an olive grove at Epidaurus, where cult honours were later paid to her. He himself was made king by the Argives in preference to Temenus' sons.

[Apollodorus 2.8.5; Pausanias 2.19.1, 2.23.3, 2.26.1–2, 2.28.3–7.]

Deipyle

Daughter of ADRASTUS (1) and wife of TYDEUS.

Deipylus *see* POLYDORUS (3).

Delos

A small island in the Cyclades, famous as the birthplace of APOLLO and ARTEMIS (*see* ASTERIA and LETO). The later epithets of Cynthius and Cynthia for the divine brother and sister were derived from the island's Mount Cynthus. Delos had connections with the HYPERBOREANS, and was the home of ANIUS, priest-king and son of Apollo, at the time of the Trojan War.

Delphic Oracle

The most important oracle in Greece, situated on the southern slopes of Mount Parnassus and presided over by APOLLO, who had established himself there by killing a guardian serpent called PYTHON. In Apollo's temple stood the *omphalos* marking the centre of the earth, once determined by Zeus when he released two eagles, one from the eastern bounds of the earth and one from the west. They met at Delphi. Oracles, given by a priestess, the Pythia, in a state of trance and interpreted for the enquirer by priests, were renowned for their ambiguity – although the Delphic pronouncement that is probably the most famous of all mythical oracles, telling OEDIPUS that he would kill his father and marry his mother, was entirely clear, but misleading.

[H. W. Parke and D. E. W. Wormell, *The Delphic Oracle* (1956); J. Fontenrose, *The Delphic Oracle* (1978); S. Price, in P. E. Easterling and J. V. Muir (eds) *Greek Religion and Society* (1985), pp. 128–54; R. Parker, in P. Cartledge and F. D. Harvey (eds), *Crux* (1985), pp. 298–326.]

Delphinus (The Dolphin)

A constellation commemorating both the dolphin that found AMPHITRITE for Poseidon, and the dolphin that saved the poet and singer ARION from drowning.

Delphyne

A dragon, half-serpent, half-woman. When the monster TYPHON fought with Zeus and cut out the sinews of his hands and feet, he hid them in a bearskin and set Delphyne to guard them in the Corycian cave in Cilicia. Somehow Hermes and Aegipan succeeded in stealing them and refitting them to the helpless god, and Zeus recovered his strength. Apollonius (*Argonautica* 2.705–7) says that Delphyne was killed by Apollo at the foot of Parnassus, but this may be a confusion with the snake Python.

Demeter

Demeter, one of the twelve great Olympian gods, was the Greek goddess of corn and thus the great sustainer of life for men and beasts alike. She was identified by the Romans with Ceres. One of the six children of the Titans CRONUS and Rhea, she was swallowed and later regurgitated by her cannibalistic father. To her brother ZEUS she bore a daughter, PERSEPHONE, also known as Kore ('the Girl'), with whom she was closely associated in Greek cult, the two of them often being called simply 'the Two Goddesses', or even 'the Demeters'. Mother and daughter frequently appear together in ancient art, often holding torches and wearing crowns, sometimes holding sceptres and stalks of grain.

The principal myth of Demeter concerns Persephone's abduction by HADES (1), the god of the Underworld, and her own long search for her beloved daughter. The story is first told in the *Homeric Hymn to Demeter*. Hades' desire to have Persephone for his wife was supported by Zeus, but because Demeter would have been violently against the match, he could not openly woo his chosen bride. Instead he snatched her up one day as she was gathering flowers, speeding with his chariot out of a chasm in the earth and carrying her down into his realm below. While she could still see the light of the sun, Persephone cried out for her mother, and Demeter, hearing her, sped towards the sound as swift as a bird. But she was too late, for Persephone had disappeared. For nine days and nights Demeter wandered the earth with flaming torches in her hand, seeking her daughter. On the tenth day she met the goddess HECATE, who had also heard Persephone's cries, and together they went to the Sun-god HELIOS, who sees all things on his daily journey across the sky. They asked him what he knew. He told them of the abduction, adding that it had Zeus' approval and reassuring Demeter that Hades was a worthy husband for her daughter; but Demeter was so angry that she deserted OLYMPUS and the dwellings of the gods, and went to live among mortals disguised as an old woman.

In her wanderings she came to Eleusis in Attica, where the wife of King Celeus, METANEIRA, took her into her home as nurse to her baby son, Demophon. The goddess' spirits were cheered by the jokes of the old serving woman, IAMBE, and she laughed for the first time since the loss of her daughter. In gratitude for the kindness shown her, Demeter began to make her infant charge immortal, secretly burning away his mortal part in the fire each night, and anointing him with ambrosia each day. But one night Metaneira interrupted her and cried out, horrified at seeing her little son in the fire. At once Demeter rebuked her soundly and reassumed her divine splendour. Telling Metaneira what the Eleusinians must do to regain her favour, she left the house. Celeus and his people built the goddess a great temple, and here she lived for a whole year, still shunning Olympus. Now in her grief she made the whole earth barren. No corn would grow and a great famine afflicted mankind, so that Zeus feared there would soon be no men left to sacrifice to the gods. He sent IRIS as his messenger to Demeter, ordering her to Olympus, but she refused to come. He sent all the gods, one by one, to offer her gifts and plead with her, but still she refused. At last he saw that he would have to bring Persephone back from Hades, so HERMES fetched her up to the light of day (fig. 47). But before she left, Hades secretly gave her pomegranate seeds to eat.

Mother and daughter were reunited with great joy; but because Persephone had eaten while in the Underworld, she could not leave it completely and was obliged to spend four months of every year with Hades. These were the months when winter gripped the land and the seed lay dormant within the earth. For the rest of the year, the spring and summer months of life and growth and harvest, Persephone lived joyously with her mother. Demeter, accepting this compromise, now made the earth bring forth rich harvests once again. She returned to Eleusis, and provided the Eleusinian TRIPTOLEMUS (fig. 142) with a supply of corn and a chariot drawn by winged dragons. In this he flew over all the earth, scattering Demeter's corn and teaching the people the arts of agriculture. She also taught the Eleusinians – including EUMOLPUS, the ancestor of the priestly clan of the Eumolpidae – the new and secret rites, known as the Eleusinian Mysteries, that would be performed for many centuries in her honour.

Later tradition added further incidents to Demeter's myth. During her long search for her daughter, an Athenian called PHYTALUS gave her hospitality and she rewarded him with the gift of the first fig tree. She also stopped at a cottage to ask an old woman for a drink and was given some barley water. She gulped it down so thirstily that the woman's cheeky son, ASCALABUS, taunted her with being greedy. She threw the dregs of the drink over him and turned him into a lizard. According to some, she transformed Persephone's companions at the time of her abduction into the SIRENS. She also turned ASCALAPHUS (1), who disclosed the fact that Persephone had eaten pomegranate seeds while in the Underworld, into an owl. When Tantalus served his son PELOPS in a stew to the gods, testing their omniscience, they all knew what had happened and refused to eat, except for Demeter. In her grief for Persephone she absentmindedly ate part of Pelops' shoulder. But all was well, for the gods brought the boy back to life and Demeter gave him a new shoulder made of ivory. Not so happy was the sorry fate which the impious ERYSICHTHON suffered. Demeter punished him for cutting down trees in her sacred grove by afflicting him with such a raging, insatiable hunger that he eventually died by gnawing away at his own flesh.

Demeter had other children apart from Persephone. She lay with IASION (1), the son of Zeus and Electra, in a thrice-ploughed field in Crete, and bore him a son, PLUTUS, 'Wealth', who symbolised the wealth and good fortune, both vegetable and mineral, that springs from the earth. It was sometimes said that she bore Iasion a second son, Philomelus, who invented the plough to prepare the earth for grain. This so pleased Demeter that she set him in the stars as the constellation BOÖTES. She also bore two children to POSEIDON, who mated with her in the form of a stallion, after she had transformed herself into a mare in a vain attempt to escape his amorous attentions. One of these children was the divinely swift horse, AREION, and the other a daughter, DESPOINA.

Demeter was widely worshipped throughout the ancient world. Her best-known place of cult was Eleusis, where the greatest of all mystery cults, the Eleusinian Mysteries, were celebrated. There is evidence for at least eighteen centuries of continuous worship, from Mycenean times until the sanctuary was destroyed in AD 395. Although the details of the rites were successfully kept secret, it seems that they centred around Demeter's search for her lost daughter, and Persephone's return and reunion with her mother, symbolising both the rebirth of the crops in spring, and the mystic rebirth of the initiates after death. Also celebrated as part of the ritual was the youthful god Iacchus, a rather obscure deity often identified with Dionysus.

Demeter's festival of the Thesmophoria, attended only by women, took place in the autumn, near to the time of sowing, with ceremonies intended to promote fertility. It is delightfully burlesqued in Aristophanes' comedy *Women Celebrating the Thesmophoria*. Demeter was occasionally

Fig. 47 **Persephone, accompanied by Hermes, emerges from the Underworld, and Hecate, carrying torches, leads her to her waiting mother, Demeter.**

identified with the Phrygian mother-goddess CYBELE; and sometimes with the Egyptian goddess ISIS, who also sought far and wide for a lost loved one.

[Homer, *Iliad* 5.499–502, *Odyssey* 5.125–8; Hesiod, *Theogony* 453–506, 912–14, 969–74; Euripides, *Helen* 1301–68; Apollodorus 1.1.5–1.2.1, 1.5.1–3, 2.1.3, 2.5.12, 3.6.8, 3.12.1, 3.14.7; Diodorus Siculus 5.2–5, 5.68–9; Pausanias 1.14.1–3, 1.37.2, 1.38.5, 2.5.8, 2.11.3, 2.35.4, 8.15.1–4, 8.25.2–7, 8.37.1–10, 8.42.1–13. N. J. Richardson, *The Homeric Hymn to Demeter* (1974, 1979); W. Burkert, *Greek Religion* (1985), pp. 159–61.]

Demodocus

In Homer's *Odyssey* (Book 8), Demodocus is the bard at the court of ALCINOUS, king of the Phaeacians, on SCHERIA, the mythical island visited by ODYSSEUS in his wanderings. Demodocus is blind, just as Homer himself was reputed to be. 'The Muse loved him greatly', says Homer (8.63–4), 'and she gave him both good and evil. She robbed him of his eyes, but gave him the gift of sweet song.'

At a feast in the palace, Demodocus sings of the TROJAN WAR which, although recent, has already entered the bardic repertoire. The subject that he chooses is a quarrel between Odysseus and Achilles. Odysseus weeps at the song and at his sad memories of the war, and Alcinous wonders why, for as yet his guest has gone unrecognised. The banquet is followed by games, and here Demodocus sings of the love-affair between Ares and APHRODITE, and of how Hephaestus trapped the two lovers in a magical net. Later, at another feast, Odysseus sends the bard a special portion of meat and a request to sing once again of the Trojan War, this time the story of the WOODEN HORSE and the fall of Troy. Demodocus does so, and once more Odysseus weeps. Afterwards he at last reveals his identity, thus acknowledging the part that he himself played in the events sung by the bard.

Demophon (1) *see* METANEIRA.

Demophon (2)
Son of Theseus and Phaedra (*see* ACAMAS (1)).

Demophon (3) *see* MASTUSIUS.

Despoina ('Mistress')
Daughter of POSEIDON *Hippios* (Horse Poseidon) and DEMETER. When Demeter was wandering the earth, seeking her lost daughter PERSEPHONE, Poseidon saw her as she was passing through Arcadia and was smitten with love for her. She changed herself into a mare to escape his amorous attentions, hiding among the horses of a local king, Oncius. But the god became a stallion and mounted her. She bore two offspring, Despoina and the divinely swift horse AREION.

Despoina was worshipped in Arcadia, along with a Titan called Anytus, who was said to have brought her up, and with her mother Demeter. Pausanias tells us that Despoina was merely a cult title, while her real name was too sacred to be mentioned except during her secret rites, and was thus known only to initiates. Her worship seems to have been distinct from that of Kore/Persephone, but was perhaps related to it, for all fruits were offered to Despoina except the pomegranate, the consumption of which had condemned Persephone to spend part of each year in Hades.

[Pausanias 8.25.4–10, 8.37.1–10, 8.42.1–6.]

Deucalion (1)
The Greek Noah, survivor of the Great Flood. Son of the Titan PROMETHEUS, he married Pyrrha, the daughter of Epimetheus and PANDORA. When ZEUS decided to destroy the human race with the Flood because of man's wickedness, Prometheus told Deucalion to build an ark and stock it with food. The Flood came, and Deucalion and Pyrrha floated in their ark for nine days and nights until it came to rest on the summit of Mount Parnassus. At last the rain ceased. They disembarked and made a thanks-offering to Zeus for their preservation. But now, as the only mortals left alive, it was their task to repopulate an empty world. On Zeus' instructions, brought to them by HERMES, they picked up stones from the earth and threw them over their shoulders. Deucalion's stones were transformed into men and Pyrrha's into women. In Ovid's ver-

sion, the same instructions were given to them by the goddess THEMIS, though in oracular form: she told them to throw behind them the bones of their mother, and while Pyrrha was alarmed at the thought of such impiety, Deucalion realised that these obscure words referred to their mother the Earth, and that her bones must be stones.

Deucalion and Pyrrha had several children of their own, most notably HELLEN, who gave his name to the Hellenes.

[Pindar, *Olympian* 9.42–53; Apollodorus 1.7.2; Pausanias 1.18.7; Ovid, *Metamorphoses* 1.125–415.]

Deucalion (2)
Son of MINOS and PASIPHAE, and Minos' heir as king of Crete. Deucalion was the father of IDOMENEUS, who led the Cretan contingent to the Trojan War.

[Homer, *Iliad* 13.451–4; Apollodorus 3.1.2, 3.3.1.]

Dexamenus
A king of Olenus in Achaea who gave hospitality to HERACLES. The Centaur EURYTION (2) was trying to force Dexamenus' daughter, Mnesimache, into marriage, so Heracles intervened and killed the would-be bridegroom. Dexamenus also had twin daughters, Theronice and Theraephone, who married the Siamese twins known as the MOLIONES.

[Apollodorus 2.5.5; Pausanias 5.3.3.]

Dia (1) *see* IXION.

Dia (2) *see* DRYOPS.

Diana
Ancient Italian goddess of wild nature, of hunting and the moon (*see* SELENE), and of women, particularly at the time of childbirth. She was early identified with the Greek goddess ARTEMIS. Diana's most famous cult-centre in Italy was in a grove at Aricia, on the shores of Lake Nemi which was known as Diana's Mirror. Here she was worshipped in association with the nymph EGERIA and the male god VIRBIUS, the priest being a runaway slave who had killed his predecessor (*see* GOLDEN BOUGH).

[Catullus 34.]

Dicte, Mount
A mountain towards the east of Crete where, in a cave, the infant ZEUS was said to have been reared, far away from his cannibalistic father, Cronus. (The Cretan Mount Ida is also accorded this honour.) The monstrous HARPIES were said to live in a cave deep on Dicte. The Cretan goddess Dictynna (BRITOMARTIS) was probably thus named because of her worship here.

Dictynna *see* BRITOMARTIS.

Dictys *see* DANAE.

Dido

The founder and first queen of Carthage. Dido, whose Phoenician name was Elissa, was the daughter of a Phoenician king of Tyre, Belus (or Mutto), and was married to her wealthy uncle Sychaeus (or Sicharbas). Her wicked brother Pygmalion, now king of Tyre, murdered Sychaeus out of greed for his riches. Dido escaped with her sister ANNA and a band of followers and fled to Libya. A native king, Iarbas, sold her a piece of land as large as could be encompassed by a bull's hide, so she cut the hide into such thin strips that, tied together, they encircled enough territory to build her city, Carthage. The city prospered and grew, until Iarbas was alarmed by its potential power. He pressed Dido to marry him, threatening to attack Carthage if she refused. She pretended to agree, but rather than succumb to him she built a pyre, as though for a sacrifice, and leapt into the flames.

Virgil took this legend for his *Aeneid* and transmuted it into what has become the classic version of Dido's tragedy. When AENEAS lands on the coast of Carthage, his mother, VENUS, takes him to Dido's new city, then sends her son Cupid (EROS) to inspire Dido with love. The queen welcomes Aeneas, and at a banquet given in his honour he tells of his adventures and of the fall of Troy. Dido falls deeply in love with him, and is encouraged to yield to her passion by her sister Anna. Virgil likens Dido to a deer, shot by a shepherd in the woods, that runs away far over the wooded slopes of Mount Dicte, while all the time, lodged in her side, is the arrow that will bring her death. While out hunting, Dido and Aeneas take shelter in a cave during a violent storm and there they consummate their love. 'That day was the beginning of her death', says Virgil (4.169–70), 'and the beginning of all her sufferings.'

Now Dido and Aeneas have no thought but for each other, until at last JUPITER sends down MERCURY to remind Aeneas of his destiny and to urge him to sail for Italy. Against his will, and despite all Dido's pleas, he departs, obedient to the call of fate. Anna unknowingly helps Dido to prepare for death by having a pyre built, supposedly so that she can destroy everything reminiscent of her lost lover. But Dido climbs on top of the pyre and kills herself with Aeneas' sword. Her dying curse on the Trojans will be fulfilled in the historical wars between Rome and Carthage. The pyre is lit, and its flames rising over the city and lighting the sky are seen by the departing Trojans. Although they know nothing of Dido's death, their hearts are filled with foreboding.

When Aeneas goes down to the Underworld, accompanied by the Sibyl of Cumae, he sees the shade of Dido wandering among the dead with the wound in her breast still fresh. Weeping for her fate, he swears to her that he left Carthage against his will, but in hatred and bitterness she moves away, without a look, without a word, to rejoin her first husband, Sychaeus, in the shadows.

Although Aeneas' determined abandonment of his love in response to the call of duty would have been understood and appreciated by a Roman audience, Dido's love and death have made her a sympathetic heroine to romanticists of all ages, and her love affair with Aeneas has been a tremendously inspirational subject in music, drama, literature and the visual arts.

[Virgil, *Aeneid* 1.335–756, 4.1–705, 6.450–76; Ovid, *Heroides* 7.]

Diomedes (1)

Son of ARES and king of the Bistones, a very warlike tribe of Thrace. Diomedes owned four mares which he kept tethered to bronze mangers with iron chains. He fed them with human flesh. HERACLES' eighth Labour (*see* LABOURS OF HERACLES) for Eurystheus was to capture these fierce mares, and to tame them he fed them either with the stable-lad or with Diomedes himself. After this they were cured of their man-eating tastes. Heracles took them back to Eurystheus, who dedicated them to Hera and bred from them. Their descendants were said to have lived on to the time of Alexander the Great.

Apollodorus (2.5.8) gives a rather different version of

Fig.48 Heracles with one of the man-eating horses of Diomedes. A man's head and arm hangs from the horse's mouth.

the story: Heracles overpowered the grooms, then drove the mares down to the sea. Here he left them in the charge of his young lover, Abderus, while he himself fought off the pursuing Bistones and killed Diomedes. But the mares dragged Abderus to his death, so Heracles founded the city of Abdera in his memory before taking the captive animals on to Eurystheus. The king let them go and they wandered to Mount Olympus, where they were killed by wild animals.

For all its dramatic potentialities, this Labour is very rarely depicted in ancient art (fig. 48).

[Euripides, *Alcestis* 483–98, *The Madness of Heracles* 380–5; Diodorus Siculus 4.15.3–4; Pausanias 3.18.12; Quintus of Smyrna, *Sequel to Homer* 6.245–8; Ovid, *Metamorphoses* 9.194–6.]

Diomedes (2)

One of the most famous of the heroes who fought at Troy. His father was TYDEUS, who was killed in the expedition of the Seven against Thebes; and his mother was Deipyle, the daughter of ADRASTUS (1), king of Argos, who led the Seven. Diomedes took part in the successful attack on Thebes made by the EPIGONI, when the sons of the Seven marched against the city to avenge their fathers. He married Aegialeia, who was either the daughter or the granddaughter of Adrastus.

Diomedes' grandfather was OENEUS, the king of Calydon, who in old age was deposed by the sons of his brother, Agrius. They imprisoned Oeneus and gave his kingdom to their father; but Diomedes came secretly to Calydon and killed most of Agrius' sons, thus regaining the kingdom. By this time Oeneus was too old to rule, so he handed the throne of Calydon over to Andraemon, the husband of his daughter Gorge, and went with Diomedes back to the Peloponnese. However the two surviving sons of Agrius, Thersites and Onchestus, ambushed the old man as he was passing through Arcadia and killed him. Diomedes buried his grandfather in the Argolid at Oenoe, the town named after him.

Diomedes had been one of the unsuccessful suitors of HELEN, so at the beginning of the TROJAN WAR, bound by the oath taken by all the suitors to protect the marriage rights of her chosen husband, he sailed to Troy with eighty ships from the Argolid, and with STHENELUS (3) and EURYALUS (1) as his subordinates. The *Iliad* recounts events during the tenth and final year of the war, with Homer depicting Diomedes as one of the greatest of the Greek warriors. Book Five sees him in triumphant battle-action, inspired by the war-goddess herself, ATHENA (2–8):

> She gave him strength and courage, to be conspicuous
> among the Greeks and win the glory of valour.

> She made unwearying fire blaze from his shield
> and helmet, like the autumn star that beyond all stars
> rises brilliant from bathing in the stream of Ocean:
> such was the fire she made blaze from his head and
>   shoulders,
> urging him into the midst of the throng of battle.

He creates havoc in the Trojan ranks (87–94):

> He stormed across the plain like a winter-swollen
> torrent in spate, sweeping away the dykes
> in its swift flood, one that the strong-built dykes
> and the walls of fruitful vineyards cannot hold back,
> or stay its sudden rise when the rain of Zeus
> falls heavy, and many are the lovely works of men
> that fall beneath it. Like these the massed battalions
> of Trojans were scattered by Diomedes, and many
> as they were they could not stand against him.

He is shot in the shoulder by PANDARUS, but retires for only a moment while his comrade Sthenelus pulls out the arrow, then returns to the fighting with his zest for battle even greater than before (135–43):

> His heart before had raged to fight the Trojans,
> but now a tripled fury seized him, as of a lion
> that a country shepherd, guarding his fleecy sheep,
> grazed as he leapt the fence of the fold, and has not
> killed him, but only stirred up the lion's strength
> and cannot help his flock, but the lion enters
> the fold and the forsaken sheep flee in fear,
> then lie strewn on each other in heaps, when he
> in fury leaps out again from the deep yard:
> raging so did mighty Diomedes fight the Trojans.

He not only kills Trojans, including the man who wounded him, Pandarus, but he even attacks the gods themselves. When APHRODITE comes to help her son AENEAS, who has been felled by a great stone, Diomedes wounds her in the wrist so that she flees in pain up to Olympus. APOLLO takes over the care of Aeneas, and three times Diomedes surges forward to kill him (fig. 9), three times the god batters back his bright shield. When for the fourth time Diomedes comes on as if he were more than human, then Apollo orders him to give way, and he obeys. But later he comes across the war-god ARES on the battlefield, stripping a corpse, and once more with the help of Athena attacks him, wounding him in the belly. Ares bellows as loud as nine thousand men, or ten thousand, when they forge forward into battle. Then he too flees in pain up to Olympus.

Diomedes encounters the Trojan hero GLAUCUS (4) on the battlefield, but they discover that their families share a bond of guest-friendship, so instead of fighting they clasp hands and pledge their own friendship by exchanging armour. 'But Zeus took away the wits of Glaucus', adds Homer (6.234–6), 'since he exchanged with Diomedes, son of Tydeus, golden armour for bronze, giving for nine oxen's worth the worth of a hundred.' (So a 'Diomedean exchange' has come to mean one in which the benefit is all on one side.) When one of NESTOR's horses is shot by PARIS, Diomedes saves the life of the old man, taking him up into his own chariot. Together the two pursue HECTOR and come close to killing him, until Zeus flings a thunderbolt in front of their horses to warn them off. Later Diomedes goes, with ODYSSEUS, on a night-raid to the Trojan camp, where he murders the Trojan spy DOLON (fig. 50) and butchers thirteen sleeping Thracians, including their leader RHESUS (fig. 127). Soon after this he is shot in the foot by Paris, but belittles his wound (11.388–95):

> Now you have grazed the flat of my foot and boast
> for no reason. I care no more than if a woman
> or a witless child had struck me, for blunt is the dart
> of a weak and worthless man. Far different it is
> if a man is struck by me, touched only a little,
> for the sharp edge suddenly lays him lifeless;
> and his wife has cheeks torn with grief, his children
> are fatherless, while his blood stains the earth
> and he rots away, more birds than women around him.

But despite his boast, Diomedes has been put out of battle-action for the rest of the *Iliad*. He does, however, carry on offering shrewd advice to the Greek war-council; and he later takes part in the funeral games for Patroclus, where he wins the chariot-race (we see him racing his horses on the François Krater, though here Odysseus is in the lead), and has rather the better of it when he fights in armour with AJAX (1).

Diomedes was often linked with Odysseus in other events that took place during the war. In one version of the treacherous murder of PALAMEDES, it was said that Diomedes and Odysseus drowned him while he was fishing, in another that they lowered him down a well where they claimed to have found gold, then threw stones down on top of him until he was dead. Diomedes was also involved in various events towards the end of the war which, according to prophecy, ensured that Troy would fall. He was often said to have gone with Odysseus to fetch PHILOCTETES from Lemnos, and in one version to fetch NEOPTOLEMUS from Scyros. Together Diomedes and Odysseus slipped into Troy by night and stole from the citadel Athena's sacred image, the PALLADIUM, on which the safety of the city depended.

Diomedes was one of the warriors in the WOODEN HORSE, the stratagem by which the Greeks entered Troy. Once the city had fallen he journeyed safely home to Argos, arriving on the fourth day after setting sail. There, however, he found that his wife Aegialeia had become the mistress of Sthenelus' son, Cometes, to whom he had entrusted the affairs of his household. She had been spurred to infidelity either by Aphrodite, angry because Diomedes had wounded her at Troy, or by NAUPLIUS (1), eager to avenge the murder of his son Palamedes. Diomedes left Argos for ever and went to Italy, where he settled in Apulia with King Daunus, marrying his daughter Evippe and founding several cities including Argyripa (Arpi). According to the Roman poets, the prince of the Rutulians, TURNUS, sought Diomedes' aid against the Trojan invader Aeneas, but Diomedes refused, on the grounds that he had no wish to offer any more offense to Venus (Aphrodite), Aeneas' mother. It was said that when Diomedes died (the scholia add that he was killed by Daunus), his companions, lamenting him, were changed into birds. The descendants of these birds carried on guarding his shrine on the island where he was buried, named Diomedeia after him. In some accounts he was made immortal after his death.

Despite his depiction by Homer as a noble hero of all-round excellence, Diomedes has never been an especially inspirational figure for artists, either ancient or postclassical. In Chaucer and Shakespeare, he is the 'Diomed' who wins Cressida from Troilus.

[Homer, *Iliad* 2.559–68, 4.365–421, 6.119–236, 8.78–171, 10.219–579, 11.368–400, 14.109–34, 23.262–513, 798–825, *Odyssey* 3.180–2; Pindar, *Nemean* 10.7; Apollodorus 1.8.5–6, 3.7.2–3, 3.10.8, *Epitome* 5.8, 5.13, 6.1; Strabo 6.3.9; Pausanias 2.25.2, 2.30.10, 10.31.2; Virgil, *Aeneid* 8.9–17, 11.225–95; Ovid, *Metamorphoses* 14.457–513.]

Dione

A rather obscure goddess, with various sources naming her as a TITAN, daughter of Uranus (Heaven) and Gaia (Earth), or an OCEANID, daughter of Oceanus and Tethys, or a NEREID, daughter of Nereus and Doris. Homer and certain others make Dione the consort of ZEUS and mother of APHRODITE, in contrast to Hesiod's account of Aphrodite's birth from the sea-foam that gathered around the severed genitals of Uranus. Thus Dione may well have once been an important goddess, especially as her name seems to be the feminine form of Zeus. Certainly Hesiod names Dione, along with other important deities, at the beginning of his *Theogony* (17) as one of the goddesses whom the poem will celebrate; and the *Homeric Hymn to Apollo* (93) has Dione as one of the 'principal goddesses' present at the birth of Apollo. She was worshipped at DODONA in Epeirus, reputedly the oldest Greek oracle, where she had a cult as Naïa alongside Zeus Naïos.

[Homer, *Iliad* 5.370–417; Hesiod, *Theogony* 353; Euripides, *Helen* 1098; Apollodorus 1.1.3, 1.2.7, 1.3.1.]

Dionysus or Bacchus

One of the twelve great Olympian gods, Dionysus was the god of wine and intoxication, of ritual madness and ecstatic liberation from everyday identity. Homer calls him a 'joy for mortals' (*Iliad* 14.325) and Hesiod 'he of many delights' (*Theogony* 941). He introduced wine to men, says Euripides, 'which, when they drink their fill, banishes the sufferings of wretched mortals, and brings forgetfulness of each day's troubles in sleep. There is no other cure for sorrow ... ' (*Bacchae* 278–83). He was also the god of the theatre and impersonation, the mask being the symbol of the transformation of identity. His revelling train of ecstatic followers were SATYRS and Silens, led by old SILENUS, and NYMPHS and MAENADS, all celebrating the god's rites with wine and music, song and dance, and sometimes, in their ecstasy, tearing animals to pieces (*sparagmos*) and eating the flesh raw (*omophagia*). He was identified by the Greeks with the Orphic god ZAGREUS, and as such was the giver of blessed immortality, by the Romans with Liber, and by the Egyptians with Osiris. Dionysus was once thought to be a latecomer to the Greek pantheon, a foreign god imported into Greece from Thrace or Phrygia whose cult was met with violent resistance; but the discovery of several Mycenean Linear B tablets, dated at around 1250 BC and confirming his status as a divinity, has disproved this theory.

Dionysus was the twice-born son of ZEUS and SEMELE, snatched prematurely from his mother's womb when she was burnt to death by Zeus' thunderbolt, then stitched into his father's thigh until he could be born full-term. HERMES carried the infant to be brought up by INO and Athamas, who dressed him as a girl to hide him from the ever-jealous HERA. But eventually she learnt the truth and punished Ino and Athamas by driving them mad. They killed their own two sons: Athamas shot Learchus, and Ino flung Melicertes into a cauldron of boiling water, then leapt into the sea with him in her arms and drowned. Mother and son were transformed by Dionysus into the sea-deities Leucothea and Palaemon.

While Dionysus was still a child, Zeus turned him into a kid to elude Hera and took him to the nymphs of Mount Nysa (variously located) for safety. They brought him up in a cave and later became part of his revelling entourage. They were sometimes said to be the HYADES, and were later rewarded with immortality among the stars.

When he grew to manhood, Dionysus was driven mad by the still hostile Hera and wandered the world, through Egypt and Syria to Phrygia, where he was cured by Rhea/CYBELE. He travelled on, even as far as India, before returning to Greece, spreading his worship and dispensing knowledge of the vine and its pleasures. Some men welcomed him, such as OENEUS, king of Calydon, who was given a vine by Dionysus, perhaps in gratitude for his enjoyment of Oeneus' wife, Althaea. The god also gave a vine to an Attic farmer, Icarius, who shared its glorious wine with his neighbours. Unfortunately they grew drunk and thought that he had bewitched them, so they clubbed him to death. When his daughter ERIGONE (1) found his body, she hanged herself, and even their dog, Maera, jumped into a well and drowned. But Dionysus avenged the deaths of his followers and immortalised them in the stars as the constellations Virgo and Boötes. He granted a wish to the Phrygian king, MIDAS, in gratitude for saving his jovial companion, old Silenus. Midas asked that all he touched might turn into gold, but when he found out the drawbacks of such a doubtful boon, he fervently begged Dionysus to take it from him.

Other myths tell of the god persecuting those who refused to recognise his divinity. LYCURGUS (1), king of the Edonians in Thrace, was blinded, or driven mad, or torn asunder by wild horses, or devoured by panthers. The daughters of PROETUS, king of Tiryns, were driven mad and roamed wildly over the countryside, divesting themselves of their clothes, until they were cured by MELAMPUS. The daughters of MINYAS, king of Orchomenus in Boeotia, were terrified by the god into tearing one of their children

Fig. 49 **Dionysus, holding wine cup and vine branch, revels with maenads.**

into pieces, and were themselves turned into bats. Most famous of all is the myth of PENTHEUS, the young king of Thebes, who was torn to pieces by his own mother. Dionysus was indeed a god with a dual nature, a god 'most terrible and most gentle to mortals' (*Bacchae* 861).

One of the *Homeric Hymns* (7) to Dionysus recounts how the young god was kidnapped by pirates, hoping to get a high ransom for him. But in mid-ocean a miracle occurred: wine ran streaming through the ship, and vines and ivy grew from the mast and sail. A bear appeared on the deck, and the god became a lion and sprang upon the pirate captain. The terrified sailors leapt overboard and were transformed into dolphins (which is why dolphins, having once been human themselves, have ever since been friendly to men). The only one to be spared was the helmsman (later named ACOETES), who had spoken out against the pirates' plans and now became an ardent follower of Dionysus.

Dionysus became reconciled with Hera, for when her son HEPHAESTUS trapped her on a golden throne, held fast by invisible fetters, it was the wine god who saved her. Making Hephaestus drunk, he brought him up to OLYMPUS on the back of a mule and persuaded him to set his mother free (fig.67). In the battle of the Gods and the GIANTS, Dionysus killed Eurytus with his thyrsus, the magical wand made from a fennel rod with a bunch of ivy leaves attached to the tip. (Both of these scenes were popular in ancient art.) He descended into the Underworld to fetch his mother Semele up to Olympus (fig.131), where she was made immortal and renamed Thyone. He also brought ARIADNE up to Olympus as his bride (fig.25), after she had been abandoned by Theseus. She bore him four sons, OENOPION, STAPHYLUS (1), THOAS (1) and Peparethus. The goddess APHRODITE bore him the rustic god PRIAPUS. Dionysus shared the home of his half-brother APOLLO, residing at Delphi on Mount PARNASSUS during the winter months, while Apollo was among the Hyperboreans.

Dionysiac festivals were held over the whole Greek world, with Athens alone holding seven each year. These included the dramatic festivals of the City Dionysia, the Rural Dionysia and the Lenaea, at which the image of Dionysus, as god of the theatre, was carried in to watch the performances put on in his honour. In two very different plays from the late fifth century BC, Dionysus himself takes part, becoming a richly comic character in Aristophanes' *Frogs*, and in Euripides' *Bacchae* the sinister, smiling god who orchestrates Pentheus' destruction. In ancient art, Dionysus is depicted most frequently of all the gods. He is easily identified by his attributes of drinking vessel and ivy wreath, and sometimes the thyrsus. He

often appears as god of wine, accompanied by his ecstatic followers (fig. 49) and sometimes by panthers or snakes. Until about 430 BC, he is depicted as a bearded, ivy-wreathed man, often wearing a deerskin or panther-skin; while after 430 he is usually youthful, beardless, and naked or half-naked.

[Homer, *Iliad* 6.130–43, 14.323–5, *Odyssey* 11.321–5, 24.73–7; *Homeric Hymns* nos. 1, 7, 26; Hesiod, *Theogony* 940–2, 947–9; Herodotus 2.48–9, 2.146; Sophocles, *Antigone* 1115–54; Euripides, *Cyclops*; Apollodorus 1.3.2, 1.6.2, 1.8.1, 1.9.12, 1.9.16, 2.2.2, 3.4.2–3.5.3, 3.14.7, *Epitome* 1.9, 3.10; Diodorus Siculus 3.67–74, 4.2–5, 4.25.4, 5.75.4–5; Pausanias 2.37.5, 3.18.11, 3.24.3–4, 5.19.6, 10.4.3; Lucian, *Dialogues of the Gods* 3, 12, 22; Nonnus, *Dionysiaca*; Horace, *Odes* 2.19. W. F. Otto, *Dionysus: Myth and Cult* (1965; German original, 1933); W. Burkert, *Greek Religion* (1985), pp. 161– 7; T. H. Carpenter, *Dionysian Imagery in Archaic Greek Art* (1986); T. H. Carpenter and C. A. Faraone (eds), *Masks of Dionysus* (1993); Albert Henrichs, 'Dionysus', *The Oxford Classical Dictionary* (1996).]

Diores *see* AMARYNCEUS.

Dioscuri

The 'Heavenly Twins' Castor and Polydeuces (Latin: Castor and Pollux). They were the sons of LEDA, either by ZEUS or by her mortal husband TYNDAREOS, and the brothers or half-brothers of HELEN and CLYTEMNESTRA. Although accounts differ as to exactly who fathered these four children, Castor and Clytemnestra were usually said to be the mortal children of Tyndareos, and Helen and Polydeuces the immortal children of Zeus.

Castor was renowned for his skill at horsemanship (though both brothers rode swift white horses), while Polydeuces excelled at boxing. Like all the great heroes of their generation, they went on the CALYDONIAN BOARHUNT and sailed with Jason and the ARGONAUTS to fetch the Golden Fleece. During the voyage, Polydeuces' boxing expertise was brought into play when he killed AMYCUS, the brutal king of the Bebrycians (fig. 16). They also helped PELEUS to destroy the city of Iolcus in punishment for the attempt made by its king, Acastus, to kill him. Later when their sister Helen was abducted by Theseus and Peirithous, and left in the charge of Theseus' mother AETHRA at Aphidnae in Attica, the Dioscuri came to her rescue. Told by ACADEMUS their sister's whereabouts, they captured Aphidnae and took her back to Sparta, along with Aethra who was made Helen's slave.

The most important story involving Castor and Polydeuces concerns the quarrel with their cousins IDAS and Lynceus, the sons of Aphareus. This quarrel led to a fight that brought death to three out of the four. Sometimes the dispute was said to be over HILAEIRA AND PHOEBE, the daughters of Leucippus (brother to both Tyndareus and Aphareus), who were thus their cousins too. Idas and Lynceus were betrothed to these girls, but the Dioscuri seized them, perhaps on their very wedding day, and carried them off to Sparta. Both girls gave birth to sons: Hilaeira bore Anaxis (or Anogon) to Castor, and Phoebe bore Mnasinous (or Mnesileos) to Polydeuces. The other reason for the quarrel – and this seems to have been the older version – was a disagreement over cattle. Proclus mentions that in the *Cypria* the Dioscuri stole their cousins' cattle; Pindar, in his *Nemean* 10, simply says, 'Idas was in some way angered about his cattle' (60); but in Apollodorus we find a delightfully detailed story (3.11.2). The four cousins together stole a great herd of cattle from Arcadia, and it was given to Idas to divide the booty. He cut a cow into four, saying that half the booty would go to whoever ate his share of the meat first, and the rest to whoever ate his share second. Before they knew where they were, Idas, who was a prodigious trencherman, had himself eaten both his own and his brother's share, and had driven off all the cattle to his home in Messenia. In revenge for this (to them) unfair dealing, the Dioscuri marched against Messenia and recovered the cattle, taking much else besides. They then lay in wait for Idas and Lynceus.

For an account of the fatal battle, we go back to Pindar. Lynceus, who was gifted with vision so acute that he could see even through solid objects, ran to the top of Mount Taygetus and from there, scanning the country-side below, he saw Castor and Polydeuces hidden in a hollow oak tree. He and Idas were thus able to take the Dioscuri by surprise, and Idas mortally wounded Castor by stabbing through the tree with his spear. Polydeuces leapt out and pursued the brothers to the tomb of their father Aphareus, where they turned and in desperation flung the tombstone at their pursuer. Undeterred, Polydeuces killed Lynceus with his spear while Zeus hurled a thunderbolt at Idas. With both cousins dead, Polydeuces returned to Castor who was now on the point of death too. Weeping, Polydeuces begged Zeus to allow him to die with his brother, and the god responded by allowing Castor to share the immortality to which Polydeuces had been born: thenceforth the brothers spent alternate days in the Underworld with the shades, and on Olympus with the gods. Zeus also placed them in the stars as the constellation Gemini, the Twins.

The Dioscuri appear onstage as *dei ex machina* at the end of Euripides' tragedies *Electra* and *Helen*. In ancient art they are depicted in a variety of scenes, such as at the Calydonian Boarhunt (they approach the boar side by side on the François Krater, fig. 34), at home with their

parents, and as Argonauts. They are also shown seizing the daughters of Leucippus, which became the most popular of their adventures to be treated in the postclassical arts.

Castor and Polydeuces were the special patrons of sailors, to whom they appeared as St Elmo's fire, the luminous phenomenon sometimes seen playing round the masts of ships in a storm. It was said that one ball of fire was a bad omen, while two balls of fire were a sure sign of the Dioscuri's protective presence. The Lesbian poet Alcaeus refers in a hymn to this aspect of the twin gods:

> You who journey the wide earth
> and all the sea on swift horses,
> easily delivering men
> from freezing death;
>
> you leap to the peaks of their sturdy ships
> and shine out brilliant from afar,
> bringing light to the black vessel
> in the grievous night ...

They were important gods in their native Sparta, and also at Rome after they appeared and fought on the Roman side against the Latins at the battle of Lake Regillus of about 496 BC, and then took the news of the resounding victory to Rome. The temple of Castor and Pollux in the Forum, three columns of which still stand, was erected to commemorate this event. As horsemen they were the patrons of the *equites*, the Roman order of knights.

[Homer, *Iliad* 3.236–44, *Odyssey* 11.298–304; *Homeric Hymns* 17 and 33; Hesiod, *Catalogue of Women* fr. 24; Pindar, *Pythian* 11.61–4, *Nemean* 10.49–90; Theocritus 22.137–213; Apollodorus 1.8.2, 1.9.16, 3.10.6–7, 3.11.2, 3.13.7, *Epitome* 1.23; Diodorus Siculus 8.32; Pausanias 1.18.1, 2.22.5, 3.13.1, 3.17.3, 3.18.11, 3.18.14, 3.26.3, 4.31.9, 5.17.9, 5.19.2; Lucian, *Dialogues of the Gods* 25; Ovid, *Metamorphoses* 8.301–2, 372–7, *Fasti* 5.699–720; Pliny, *Natural History* 2.101. W. Burkert, *Greek Religion* (1985), pp. 212–13.]

Dirae *see* FURIES.

Dirce *see* ANTIOPE (1).

Dis *see* PLUTO.

Dius *see* OXYLUS.

Dodona

A city in Epeirus, the site of a famous oracle of ZEUS dating from very ancient times, where the goddess DIONE was worshipped alongside him. Oracular responses emanated from the rustling leaves of a sacred oak or from doves sitting in the tree. The speaking plank in the *Argo* came from an oak at Dodona.

[Homer, *Iliad* 16.233–5, *Odyssey* 14.327–8; Herodotus 2.55; Apollonius, *Argonautica* 1.527; Pausanias 10.12.10.]

Dolius

In the *Odyssey*, Dolius is an old servant of ODYSSEUS on Ithaca. He remains faithful to his master during his long absence, as do six of his sons; but his son MELANTHIUS and his daughter MELANTHO both betray Odysseus' interests by siding with the Suitors. Both suffer a painful death for their treachery. Dolius and his six loyal sons fight alongside Odysseus in his final battle with the relatives of the dead Suitors.

[Homer, *Odyssey* 24.386–411, 492–532.]

Dolon

Son of Eumedes, a Trojan herald. In the *Iliad*, when recounting Dolon's ill-fated spying expedition among the Greeks (10.299–464), Homer describes him as 'ugly, but swift of foot, and the only son among five sisters' – this last probably meant as disparagement, suggesting, as the ancient commentators point out, that he is a sissy. Certainly he is greedy, for he offers to go and spy on the Greeks by night, not out of patriotism, but for the reward promised by Hector of Achilles' chariot and immortal horses. Dolon wears a wolfskin as camouflage and a cap of weasel skins, and these perhaps symbolise his unattractive character, for both animals had a bad reputation.

He is also ineffectual, for he is captured almost at once by ODYSSEUS and DIOMEDES (2), who are on a similar expedition (fig. 50). Gibbering with terror, he promises them a rich ransom if they will only let him go, then proceeds to tell them all he knows about the Trojan camp and the position of the Trojan allies. He even points out the newly arrived contingent from Thrace, led by RHESUS.

But this is all to no avail, for Diomedes cuts off his head in the midst of his pleas for life.

In the extant Greek tragedy *Rhesus* (traditionally said to be by Euripides, but probably not), Dolon is portrayed in a rather better light, although he still utilises the wolf skin, actually disguising himself as a wolf and creeping through the Greek camp on all fours (208–15).

Dolphin *see* DELPHINUS.

Dooms *see* KERES.

Doris

Daughter of OCEANUS and Tethys, and mother by the sea-god NEREUS of the fifty (occasionally in later accounts a hundred) NEREIDS.

Dorus

The ancestor of the Dorians. He was the son of HELLEN and the nymph Orseis, and the brother of AEOLUS (1) and XUTHUS. It was traditionally said that Hellen divided the Greek lands among his three sons, and as a result Dorus ruled the region north of Delphi and Parnassus, calling his land Doris and his people Dorians after himself. The Dorians later allied themselves with the descendants of Heracles, the HERACLIDS, after Dorus' son AEGIMIUS had been helped by Heracles to win a war against the Lapiths. Dorians and Heraclids together invaded and settled in the Peloponnese.

Euripides, in his play *Ion* (1589–91), made Dorus the

Fig. 50 **Odysseus and Diomedes capture Dolon, dressed in a wolf's skin.**

son of Xuthus and Creusa, the daughter of ERECHTHEUS, king of Athens, thereby enhancing the status of the Athenians by making the Dorians their descendants. This innovation could also, perhaps, be seen as a deprecatory comment on the Peloponnesian War (431–404 BC), which was at that time in progress between Athens (Ionians) and Sparta (Dorians).

[Hesiod, *Catalogue of Women* fr. 9; Herodotus 1.56; Apollodorus 1.7.3; Strabo 8.7.1.]

Draco (The Serpent)

A constellation commemorating LADON, the giant serpent who guarded the golden apples of the Hesperides.

Dreams

Dreams, the thousand sons of HYPNOS (Sleep), are often personified in ancient literature. Sent by the gods, they visit dreamers in sleep, usually taking the form of a person known to them, then give advice or comfort as a waking companion might. Dreams can be deceptive, like the false Dream that Zeus sends to Agamemnon in the *Iliad* when Achilles is refusing to fight. Taking the form of old Nestor, the Dream tells Agamemnon that Zeus bids him to arm his men, since on this very day he will take Troy; whereas Zeus really intends the Trojans to beat back the Greeks to their ships, killing many, so that they will realise to the full how much they need Achilles' fighting presence. All Dreams come to mortals through the 'Gates of Sleep', the deceptive Dreams passing through a gate of ivory, and true Dreams through a gate of polished horn.

Ovid envisages the Dreams living with their father in a dark and misty cavern in the land of the Cimmerians. LETHE, the river of forgetfulness, flows with a gentle murmuring through the cave, and at its entrance poppies shed drowsiness. All around is a great stillness, and here Hypnos and his thousand sons sleep. When a Dream is needed, he wakes and flies on his swift wings in seconds to anywhere on earth. Ovid mentions three of the Dreams by name. MORPHEUS is skilled at taking human form (*morphe*) and is able to imitate anyone to perfection, while Phantasos specialises in inanimate objects. The third Dream, called Icelos by the gods but Phobetor ('Terrifier') by men, assumes the form of monsters.

[Homer, *Iliad* 2.1–40, *Odyssey* 19.560–7; Virgil, *Aeneid* 6.893–8; Ovid, *Metamorphoses* 11.592–649.]

Dryads *see* NYMPHS.

Dryas *see* LYCURGUS (1).

Dryope

A daughter either of DRYOPS, or of EURYTUS (1), king of Oechalia. Of all the women in Oechalia Dryope was the loveliest, so beautiful that APOLLO desired her when he saw her dancing with the nymphs in the woods. To get closer to her, he turned himself into a tortoise which the delighted girls petted. Soon he found himself in Dryope's lap. At once he turned himself into a snake, and when the rest of the nymphs fled in terror, he raped Dryope, leaving her pregnant. She kept this a secret and soon afterwards married the mortal Andraemon, but in due course she gave birth to Apollo's son, Amphissus. The boy grew up to found a city named after him, Amphissa, and there to build a temple to Apollo. Dryope would often meet her old companions, the nymphs, nearby, and one day they carried her off and made her one of themselves. In her place they left a tall black poplar and a spring.

In Ovid's version, Dryope's story is recounted by her half-sister IOLE. One day, when Amphissus was not yet a year old, Dryope was wandering near a lake with her baby in her arms when she saw a lotus tree covered with bright red blossoms. She picked some of the flowers for the infant to play with, but unfortunately this tree was no normal tree: it had once been a nymph, Lotis, whose transformation had saved her from the amorous intentions of PRIAPUS. Now the tree's branches trembled and its plucked blossoms began to bleed. The terrified Dryope tried to run away, but found that her own feet were rooted to the ground and that she too was slowly becoming a lotus tree. She had just time to make her farewells, and to beg her husband to look after their little son, before the creeping bark spread and shrouded her.

[Antoninus Liberalis, *Metamorphoses* 32; Ovid, *Metamorphoses* 9.327–923.]

Dryops

A son either of the river-god Spercheius, or of APOLLO by Lycaon's daughter Dia, who hid her new-born baby in a hollow oak tree (*drus*, hence his name). He grew up to rule over the Dryopes, named after him, in the area of Mount Parnassus. Two generations after Dryops, in the reign of Phylas (or Laogoras), HERACLES made war on the Dryopes because the king had violated Apollo's sanctuary at Delphi. Heracles killed Phylas and took his people to Delphi as an offering to Apollo. From there, on the god's instructions, they were taken to the Peloponnese. At first they settled at Asine in the Argolid, then were driven out by the Argives and founded a new Asine in Messenia.

Dryops' daughter, who was perhaps called Penelope, was the mother of the rustic god PAN. Another daughter, according to a late legend, was DRYOPE.

[*Homeric Hymn to Pan* 33–4; Apollodorus 2.7.7; Diodorus Siculus 4.37.1–2; Strabo 8.6.13; Pausanias 4.34.9–11; Antoninus Liberalis, *Metamorphoses* 32.]

E

Eagle *see* AQUILA.

Earth *see* GAIA.

Echemus

The king of Arcadia who succeeded LYCURGUS (2). He married Timandra, daughter of Tyndareos and Leda, and had by her a son, Laodocus, before she deserted him for Phyleus, king of Dulichium. When, after the death of Eurystheus, HYLLUS led the HERACLIDS in an attempt to invade the Peloponnese, Echemus offered himself as champion of the defending Arcadian forces and killed Hyllus in single combat. The Heraclids then withdrew.

[Herodotus 9.26; Diodorus Siculus 4.58; Pausanias 1.41.2, 1.44.10, 8.5.1, 8.45.3, 8.53.10.]

Echetus

A king of Epeirus proverbial for his cruelty. He blinded his daughter with bronze pins for having a love affair, then shut her up in a dungeon and forced her to spend her life grinding bronze grain. In Homer's *Odyssey*, the brutal suitor ANTINOUS forces IRUS the beggar to fight the disguised ODYSSEUS by threatening to hand him over to Echetus. 'And he', says Antinous, 'will cut off your nose and your ears with the pitiless bronze, and tear off your testicles and give them raw for the dogs to feed on' (18.86–7). Later Antinous uses a similar threat to Odysseus himself (21.307–9), still not realising his identity. Antinous will be the first suitor to be killed by Odysseus, and it will be his henchman, the goatherd MELANTHIUS, who will suffer the very fate that he himself is so ready to threaten – though at the hands of Odysseus' supporters rather than Echetus.

[Apollonius, *Argonautica* 4.1092–5.]

Echidna ('Snake')

A monster, said by Hesiod (*Theogony* 295–32) to be the daughter of PHORCYS and CETO. He describes her as half beautiful woman and half huge, speckled snake, death-less and ageless, dwelling in a cave under the earth and living on raw flesh. She mated with the terrible monster TYPHON to produce other monstrous beings: ORTHUS, the two-headed watchdog of Geryon, CERBERUS, the many-headed guard dog of the entrance to Hades, the snaky HYDRA OF LERNA, and possibly (the pronoun at 319 being ambiguous) the fire-breathing CHIMAERA with her three heads. Possibly too (the pronoun at 326 being similarly ambiguous) Echidna mated with her son Orthus to produce two more fearsome beasts, the SPHINX and the NEMEAN LION. Apollodorus makes Typhon and Echidna the parents of the Chimaera, the Sphinx, the eagle that devoured PROMETHEUS' liver, PHAEA, the Sow of Crommyon, and LADON, the snake who guarded the golden apples of the Hesperides; while Typhon alone is named as parent of the Nemean Lion. He also says that Echidna herself was the daughter of TARTARUS and GAIA (as, in Hesiod's account, was Typhon), and that she was in the habit of carrying off passers-by, until she was caught asleep one day and killed by all-seeing ARGUS (1).

[Apollodorus, 2.1.2, 2.3.1, 2.5.1, 2.5.11, 3.5.8, *Epitome* 1.1; Pausanias 3.18.10.]

Echinades *see* ACHELOUS.

Echion (1)

One of the SOWN MEN who sprang from the dragon's teeth at Thebes. He married AGAVE, the daughter of Cadmus, and had by her a son, PENTHEUS, who was Cadmus' successor to the throne of Thebes before being destroyed by Dionysus.

[Apollodorus 3.4.1–2, 3.5.2.]

Echion (2)

One of the ARGONAUTS. Echion and his twin brother Erytus (sometimes Eurytus or Eurytion) were sons of HERMES by Antianeira, the daughter of Menetes, and half-brothers of AETHALIDES. They came from Alope in Thessaly to join the

Argo's crew. They also went on the CALYDONIAN BOARHUNT, where Echion threw the first spear at the boar, but missed.

[Pindar, *Pythian* 4.179–80; Apollonius, *Argonautica* 1.57–8; Ovid *Metamorphoses* 8.311, 345–6.]

Echo

A NYMPH of Mount Helicon. When HERA tried to catch ZEUS making love to the nymphs on the mountainside, Echo often detained her with an endless flow of chatter until the nymphs had a chance to escape. Hera, realising what was happening, grew very angry and punished Echo by making it impossible for her to say anything of her own volition. She could only repeat the last words spoken by others.

The god PAN loved Echo, but she rejected him. One story says that it was his long pursuit of her that turned her into an echo, another that the spurned and vindictive god maddened some shepherds, who ripped her to pieces. But she is most famous for being one of the many lovers of the beautiful but cold youth NARCISSUS. Her love unrequited, she wasted away until only her plaintive voice was left. Then in turn Narcissus himself wasted away when he conceived a vain passion for his own reflection in a woodland pool. Echo, even though angry at his treatment of her, still grieved for him. When he sighed 'Alas', so did she; when he cried aloud for the love he loved in vain, she echoed 'In vain'; and when he sighed his last farewell, 'Farewell', she replied. Worn out by his hopeless love, he laid down his head on the grass by the pool, and died. The wood nymphs all mourned for him, and Echo re-echoed their laments.

[Longus, *Daphnis and Chloe* 3.23; Nonnus, *Dionysiaca* 2.117–9; Ovid, *Metamorphoses* 3.356–510.]

Eetion

In Homer's *Iliad*, Eetion is a king of Thebe in the Troad, an ally of Troy in the Trojan War, and the father of ANDROMACHE, wife of Hector. She tells of Eetion's death at ACHILLES' hands (6.414–24):

> It was godlike Achilles who killed my father
> and sacked the strong-built city of the Cilicians,
> Thebe of the high gates. He killed Eetion,
> but honouring him in his heart, he did not strip his
>   armour:
> he burnt him on a pyre in all his elaborate war-gear,
> and built him a burial mound. The mountain nymphs,
> daughters of shield-bearing Zeus, grew elms around it.
> And my seven brothers who lived there in the palace
> they all in one day went down to the house of Hades,
> slaughtered together by swift-footed, godlike Achilles,

while tending their white sheep and their lumbering oxen.

Achilles freed Eetion's wife on payment of a ransom, but with all her family lost to her, soon she too died.

Egeria

An Italian water-nymph worshipped at DIANA's grove at Aricia, on the shores of Lake Nemi near Rome, and at Rome itself in a grove sacred to the CAMENAE near the Porta Capena. She was either the wife or mistress of NUMA POMPILIUS, the mythical second king of Rome renowned for his wisdom; certainly she was his constant adviser, instructing him in all matters of statecraft and religion. When he died, she hid herself away at Aricia, weeping so much in her despair that Diana turned her into a spring of everlasting water.

[Strabo 5.3.12; Livy 1.21.3; Virgil, *Aeneid* 7.761–77; Ovid, *Metamorphoses* 15.482–551, *Fasti* 3.273–6; Juvenal 3.11–12.]

Egypt

The land around the River Nile. The country was said to have been named after Aegyptus, the son of Belus (*see* DANAUS), and was the scene of many Greek myths. Here IO came in the form of a cow, maddened by a gadfly sent by the jealous Hera; and here, at the end of Io's long wanderings, her son by Zeus, Epaphus, was born. Here the young PHAETHON (2) grew up, who was later blasted to earth by Zeus' thunderbolt when he was driving his father's sun-chariot across the sky. Here lived King BUSIRIS, who tried to sacrifice the mighty Heracles but was himself put to death on his own altar. Here lived the ancient, sealherding sea-god PROTEUS, who could change his shape and prophesy the future, as he did for Menelaus on his long journey home from Troy. And here, according to one unorthodox legend, the beautiful HELEN stayed throughout the Trojan War, while only a phantom Helen went with Paris to Troy.

Eidothea

Daughter of the ancient sea-god PROTEUS. In Homer's *Odyssey*, she takes pity on MENELAUS when he is stranded on the island of Pharos, off Egypt, on his way home from Troy, and explains what he must do to get back to Sparta (4.349–570).

In Euripides' *Helen*, Eidothea's name is changed to Theonoe: Proteus is here king of Egypt and has had by the Nereid PSAMATHE (1) two children, Theonoe (once called Eido) and a son, Theoclymenus. HELEN has been staying with Proteus in Egypt for the duration of the Trojan War, but when the play opens the war is over and Proteus is dead, succeeded on the throne by his son. Theoclymenus is a very different king from his kindly father: he has been trying to force Helen to marry him, despite her resistance, and is in the habit of killing all Greek visitors on the chance that they may be her real husband, Menelaus. When Menelaus himself arrives on his way home from the war, he and Helen are joyfully reunited. The sympathetic Theonoe helps them to trick Theoclymenus and escape from Egypt. At the end of the play the DIOSCURI intervene to save Theonoe from her angry brother, explaining that everything has happened by the will of Zeus. Theoclymenus renounces his anger and wishes Helen well.

Eileithyia

The goddess who presided over childbirth, often associated by the Greeks with ARTEMIS and known to the Romans as Lucina (*see also* JUNO). Homer speaks of *Eileithuiai* in the plural as well as the singular, making them appropriately the daughters of HERA, the goddess who presided over marriage. To Hesiod, Eileithyia (singular) was the daughter of ZEUS and Hera and the sister of HEBE and ARES. It seems that she had to be physically present for a birth to be accomplished, for when LETO, pregnant with Apollo and Artemis, was in labour on the island of Delos, Hera out of jealousy kept Eileithyia close by on Olympus so that she would not hear of Leto's distant sufferings and deliver her of her child. Leto was racked with pains for nine days and nights, until the other goddesses sent IRIS to fetch Eileithyia, offering her an enormous necklace strung with golden threads if she would come. As soon as she set foot on Delos, Apollo at last was born.

Again because of Hera's jealousy, Eileithyia held back the birth of Alcmene's son Heracles, so that EURYSTHEUS might be born first and win the power promised by Zeus. In Ovid's version, Eileithyia was finally tricked by Alcmene's slave-girl GALANTHIS into allowing the birth to take place, and she punished the poor girl by turning her into a weasel (*gale* in Greek).

Eileithyia was worshipped in many places throughout the Greek world and from very early times. Her name has been found on several Linear B tablets. When her cave sanctuary at Amnisos on Crete (mentioned in the *Odyssey*) was excavated some seventy years ago, evidence was found of continuous cult use from the third millennium BC to the fifth century AD. In Greek art Eileithyia is often depicted in scenes of divine birth from archaic times onwards (fig.51).

[Homer, *Iliad* 11.269–72, 16.187–8, 19.95–133, *Odyssey* 19.188; *Homeric Hymn to Apollo* 97–116; Hesiod, *Theogony* 921–3; Pindar, *Olympian* 6.41–2, *Nemean* 7.1–4; Apollodorus 1.3.1; Pausanias 1.18.5, 2.22.6, 3.14.6, 3.17.1, 6.20.2–6, 8.21.3, 9.27.2; Ovid, *Metamorphoses* 9.280–323.]

Eioneus *see* IXION.

Fig.51 **Eileithyia attends the birth of Athena from the head of Zeus.**

Elatus (1)

One of the three sons of ARCAS, king of Arcadia. He received Mount Cyllene as his share of his father's kingdom, but he later emigrated to Phocis, where he founded Elatea. His wife Laodice, the daughter of Cinyras, bore him several sons, including STYMPHALUS and AEPYTUS (1).

[Apollodorus 3.9.1; Pausanias 8.4.2–6.]

Elatus (2)

A LAPITH chieftain, the father of three children more famous than himself: the Argonaut POLYPHEMUS (1); Ischys, the mortal lover of Coronis who bore ASCLEPIUS to Apollo; and CAENEUS, who began life as a woman but was granted a sex-change by Poseidon.

Electra (1)

Daughter of OCEANUS and Tethys. She married the Titan THAUMAS, and bore IRIS and the HARPIES.

[Hesiod, *Theogony* 265–9.]

Electra (2)

Daughter of the Titan ATLAS and Pleione, and thus one of the seven PLEIADES. ZEUS desired her and carried her off to Olympus. Here she clung for refuge to the PALLADIUM, but Zeus simply threw it from heaven to earth, where it became a sacred object at Troy. He then had his way with Electra and she bore him two sons, DARDANUS, the ancestor of the Trojan kings, and IASION (1). Some say that the faintest star in the constellation of the Pleiades is Electra, hiding her face in mourning for the death of Dardanus and the destruction of Troy.

[Apollodorus 3.10.1, 3.12.1–3; Ovid, *Fasti* 4.177–8.]

Electra (3)

Daughter of AGAMEMNON and CLYTEMNESTRA, and sister of ORESTES, IPHIGENEIA and CHRYSOTHEMIS. Homer makes no mention of Electra: in the *Iliad* (9.145), Agamemnon's three daughters are named Chrysothemis, Laodice and Iphianassa, though it was later said that Electra was in fact Homer's Laodice, but renamed because she was for so long unwedded (Greek, *alektra*). Her legend comes into its own in fifth-century tragedy, where she plays a central role in Orestes' vengeance on Clytemnestra and her lover Aegisthus for the murder of Agamemnon. Electra's first appearance is in Aeschylus' *Libation Bearers*, a play named after the Chorus who come with Electra to offer libations at the tomb of Agamemnon. Here she is reunited with Orestes, and together they invoke Agamemnon's ghost to support them in the vengeance. But Electra herself plays no part in the killings. The focus here is mainly on Orestes, and it is he alone (though supported by the presence of his friend PYLADES) who kills first Aegisthus, and then Clytemnestra.

In Sophocles and Euripides, Electra's role is developed further. In Sophocles' *Electra*, the main focus of the play is Electra herself, steadfast and enduring, passionately grieving her father's murder and passionately set on revenge. At the time of Agamemnon's death she rescued Orestes, then an infant, from the murderers, who would have killed him too if they had had the chance, and she sent him to be brought up in safety at the court of STROPHIUS, king of Phocis. Now she longs for him to return. When she is given a false report of his death, she is quite prepared to kill Aegisthus alone and unaided once she learns that her sister Chrysothemis is unwilling to help her, but in fact it does not come to this: Orestes himself returns to take the necessary revenge. But Electra stands guard when her brother goes indoors to kill Clytemnestra, and at the first death-cry of her mother she shouts 'Strike, if you have the strength, a second blow'. She then enthusiastically helps to entrap Aegisthus so that he too can meet his fate.

In Euripides' *Electra* she is even more active in the vengeance. Here she has been married off to a poor farmer to ensure that she will bear no son with a claim to the throne, but she is still a virgin since her husband, respecting her noble birth, refuses to take advantage of her. She is mad for revenge on her father's killers, while Orestes in this play is weak and indecisive, altogether unhappy about killing his mother. Electra is the dominant figure, planning how to kill Clytemnestra and driving Orestes on to do so, then even grasping the sword with him when his own nerve fails at the crucial moment of murder. Afterwards she is as full of remorse as before she was full of lust for revenge. In Euripides' *Orestes* the murders are behind them, and she acts as the faithful nurse for her mad brother, devoted to his welfare and abetting him and Pylades in their attacks on Helen and Hermione.

Of all these plays, it is perhaps Sophocles' tragedy that presents for us the quintessential Electra, mourning Agamemnon and longing for the return of Orestes. She sings (103–118):

> Never shall I cease my dirges and painful laments, as long as I look on the bright rays of the stars and on this light of day. No, like the nightingale, slayer of her young, I will cry aloud, for all to hear, sorrows without end before my father's doors. O house of Hades and Persephone, Hermes of the Underworld and hallowed Curse, and Furies, holy daughters of the gods, who look upon all those who die unjustly and those who have their marriage-beds defiled: come, help me, avenge my father's murder and send my brother home.

And again (164–86):

> On and on without end I wait for him, living my sad life forever without a child, without a husband, drowned in tears, bearing this fate in which my sorrow finds no end ... For me the best part of my life has already passed away in hopelessness, and I have no strength left.

But her grief is at its deepest when she hears the false news of Orestes' supposed death, and holds in her hands the urn which she believes contains his ashes (1126–30):

> O last memorial of the life of Orestes, the dearest of men to me, how far from the hopes with which I sent you forth do I receive you home! For now you are nothing carried in my hands, but I sent you off from home, child, radiant ...

Now she wants only to die (1165–70):

Receive me to this little room of yours, nothing to nothing, that with you below I may live for all the time to come. For when you were on earth I shared all with you equally, so now I long to die and share your grave. For I see that the dead no longer suffer pain.

Her move from despair to joy, when she learns that the man standing beside her is in fact the living Orestes himself, gives us one of the most moving recognition scenes in extant Greek tragedy.

As to Electra's future after the vengeance, she married Pylades and went with him to Phocis, where she had two sons by him, Medon and Strophius. In ancient art there is no certain representation of Electra before the beginning of the fifth century BC, where she is present at the murder of Aegisthus. Later her meeting with Orestes at Agamemnon's tomb becomes popular.

Electra, like Antigone, is one of the great female figures of Greek myth and has proved a powerful influence on later works. Richard Strauss' opera *Elektra* has as its libretto a play by Hugo von Hofmannsthal, based on Sophocles' *Electra*. Eugene O'Neill's *Mourning Becomes Electra* is a retelling of the *Oresteia* set in nineteenth-century New England. Modern psychology has given the name 'Electra complex' to a girl's fixation on her father and jealousy of her mother, the counterpart of Freud's Oedipus complex. There is even a hint of the Electra complex in ancient tragedy, for in Euripides' *Electra*, Clytemnestra says to Electra (1102–4): 'My child, love for your father is in your nature. This happens sometimes. Some children belong to their fathers, while others love their mothers more.'

Electryon

The son of PERSEUS and Andromeda who succeeded to the throne of Mycenae on his father's death. He married Anaxo and had by her a daughter, ALCMENE, who became the mother of HERACLES, and nine sons. He also had a tenth son, LICYMNIUS, by a Phrygian woman called Midea. All Electryon's legitimate sons perished in a single day, when the six sons of PTERELAUS, descended from Electryon's brother Mestor, came with a band of Taphians to claim a share of the kingdom. When the king ignored their claim they set about raiding his cattle, and of his sons only Licymnius survived the battle that followed. All but one of Pterelaus' sons were also killed. The Taphians who were left alive sailed off with the cattle, but AMPHITRYON, who was betrothed to Alcmene, went after them and brought the cattle safely back to Mycenae. Unfortunately, as he was returning them to the king, one of the cows charged and Amphitryon threw a club at her, which rebounded and killed Electryon himself. STHENELUS

(1), the brother of the dead king, then seized the throne and banished Amphitryon, who nevertheless avenged the deaths of Electryon's nine sons.

[Apollodorus 2.4.5–6.]

Elephenor

Son of CHALCODON and king of the Abantes of Euboea. He was one of the suitors of HELEN, so bound by the common oath to defend the marriage-rights of her chosen husband, he took forty Euboean ships to fight in the TROJAN WAR. He also took with him ACAMAS (1) and Demophon, the two sons of his friend Theseus, who had taken refuge with him from Menestheus, the usurping king of Athens. Towards the end of the war, Elephenor was killed by AGENOR (2) while trying to drag away the corpse of Echepolus to strip its armour.

Homer says that the Abantes' hair was long at the back and cropped close at the front, apparently to prevent an enemy grabbing it, and he describes them as 'nimble spearmen, eager to pierce with out-thrust spear the corslets on the chests of their enemies' (*Iliad* 2.542–4). On their way home after the sack of Troy, those of Elephenor's men who had survived were driven off course and shipwrecked off the coast of Epeirus, where they founded the city of Apollonia.

[Homer, *Iliad* 2.536–45, 4.457–72; Hesiod, *Catalogue of Women* fr. 204; Apollodorus, *Epitome* 6.15b; Plutarch, *Theseus* 5, 35.]

Elpenor

In Homer's *Odyssey*, Elpenor is the youngest member of ODYSSEUS' crew, a man 'not very powerful in battle nor quite all there in his mind' (10.552–3). On the hot summer night before Odysseus is to leave CIRCE's island of Aeaea, on a visit to the Underworld, Elpenor sleeps on the roof of the enchantress' palace to keep cool. In the morning, still groggy from sleep and wine, he blunders off the edge and breaks his neck. When Odysseus arrives in the Underworld, he meets Elpenor's shade, who begs him to return to Aeaea and give his body proper burial. This in due course Odysseus does (12.8–15), exactly as Elpenor requests. 'Burn me with all the armour I have', he says (11.74–8), 'and heap up a gravemound for me by the shore of the grey sea, for an unhappy man, so that those to come will know of me. Do this for me, and set on top of my grave the oar that I used to row with, in the time when I was alive and among my comrades.'

Elysium or Elysian Fields

The dwelling place of a few privileged mortals after death, where through the favour of the gods they lived for ever in blissful ease. Elysium is first mentioned by Homer as the future home of MENELAUS: because he is the son-in-law of Zeus, he will win a blessed eternal life there, instead of descending at his death to HADES (2). Homer's Elysium is near the stream of Ocean at the ends of the earth, ruled over by RHADAMANTHYS, and never sees snow, or harsh winter, or rain. Hesiod calls this happy land the Islands of the Blest, ruled over by CRONUS, and he emphasises (naturally, hard-working farmer that he was) a life of ease where the earth gives forth harvest three times a year of its own accord. Pindar too speaks of a world without labour and without tears, a land of eternal sunlight, of golden fruit and flowers, of meadows red with roses, where men have unending leisure to enjoy sports, or games, or music. His Islands of the Blest are ruled by both Rhadamanthys and Cronus, and he names CADMUS, PELEUS and ACHILLES as mortals who share their blissful existence. These islands were later identified with Madeira or with the Canaries.

Later writers make Elysium a particular part of Hades, isolated from the area where the shades of ordinary mortals lived a dreary life after death, as does Virgil in *Aeneid* Book 6, where AENEAS meets his father ANCHISES in the Underworld. For Virgil, Elysium is the place where the good soul rests before being reborn. But Pausanias locates the abode of the blessed within the known world, on the White Island, near the mouth of the Danube. Here a certain Leonymus saw, living in eternal bliss, the shades of Achilles, PATROCLUS, ANTILOCHUS, the two AJAXES, and HELEN.

[Homer, *Odyssey* 4.561–8; Hesiod, *Works and Days* 167–73; Pindar, *Olympian* 2.56–83, fr. 129; Diodorus Siculus 5.19–20; Pausanias 3.19.11–13.]

Emathion

Son of EOS, goddess of Dawn, and the mortal TITHONUS, and brother of MEMNON. We know little more about him, except that he was king of Arabia and killed by HERACLES during his quest for the golden apples of the Hesperides.

[Hesiod, *Theogony* 984–5; Apollodorus 2.5.11.]

Empusa

A bogey-woman who, like other spectres and phantoms that filled the night with terrors, was one of HECATE's retinue. She was said to have one donkey's leg and one leg made of bronze, and to be able to change her form at will. She would turn herself into a beautiful girl and lure young men to her bed, then drink their blood until they died. The way to get rid of her was to insult her loudly, at which she would flee shrieking.

[Aristophanes, *Frogs* 292–5, *Assemblywomen* 1056–7.]

Enceladus

One of the GIANTS. In the battle between the Gods and the Giants he fled from ATHENA, but she pursued him and flung the island of Sicily on top of him. Crushed everlastingly beneath it, he lived on. 'The story goes', says Virgil (*Aeneid* 3.578–82), 'that the body of Enceladus, half burnt up by the thunderbolt, lies crushed beneath this great mass, and mighty Etna stands on top of him, breathing out flame from her bursting furnaces. And every time he turns wearily from one side to the other, the whole of Sicily quakes and growls and wreathes the sky with smoke.'

Endeis

Wife of AEACUS and mother of PELEUS and TELAMON. She may have induced her sons to kill their half-brother, PHOCUS (1). Some ancient writers (such as Apollodorus 3.12.6) say that her father was the evil SCIRON whom Theseus slew, but in the scholia she is said to be the daughter of the wise and humane Centaur CHEIRON. One of these names is most likely a simple mistake, and probably Sciron, in view of the family of great heroes that were born of Aeacus and Endeis. That Cheiron seems the likelier father is borne out by the great involvement that the Centaur had in the fortunes of Peleus and his son ACHILLES.

Endymion

The son of Aethlius, son of Zeus, and of Calyce, daughter of AEOLUS (1). Endymion was king of Elis and had three sons, EPEIUS (1), AETOLUS and PAEON (2), whom he made run a race to determine his successor to the throne. Epeius won. According to one tradition, Endymion was taken by Zeus to Olympus, where he fell in love with HERA in the shape of a cloud and was cast into Hades for pursuing her. But his most famous legend is his relationship with the Moon-goddess, SELENE. Because of his surpassing beauty Selene fell in love with him, and according to Pausanias she bore him fifty daughters. Zeus allowed Endymion to choose his own fate, and he chose to sleep for ever, remaining always young. He slept in a cave on Mount Latmus, in Caria, and here every night Selene would visit him and gaze upon his beauty, or else awaken him to fulfill her desires.

Endymion's romantic legend proved, not surprisingly, to be very influential in the postclassical arts. 'The moon sleeps with Endymion' became a literary commonplace, and he was painted by Titian, van Dyck, Poussin, Rubens, Giordano and Boucher, among many others, with his lover variously named as Selene, Diana, Phoebe, Luna and Cynthia.

[Hesiod, *Catalogue of Women* fr. 245a, *Great Ehoiae* fr. 260; Apollonius, *Argonautica* 4.57–8; Apollodorus 1.7.5–6; Pausanias 5.1.3–5, 5.8.1; Lucian, *Dialogues of the Gods* 19.]

Enipeus

A Thessalian river and its god, according to Homer (*Odyssey* 11.239) 'the most beautiful of all the rivers that flow over the earth'. TYRO fell violently in love with him and would often wander his river-banks. One day Poseidon assumed the form of Enipeus and made love to her, concealing her with a great wave of water. She bore him twin sons, Pelias and Neleus.

Enyalius ('Warlike')

A god of war. In literature, from Homer on, Enyalius was simply an epithet of the war-god ARES, but in cult the two were distinct, though Enyalius had no mythology of his own and seems to have been little more than a personification of war. At Sparta youths sacrificed puppies to him. Here also his cult statue stood in fetters, the idea being that he could never leave the city, if bound, so his valour would always remain with the Spartans.

[Homer, *Iliad* 13.512–25, 17.210–11, 259, 18.309, 20.69; Pausanias 3.14.9, 3.15.7, 5.18.5.]

Enyo (1)

A goddess of war whom we first meet in the *Iliad* (5.333, 590–5). She accompanied ARES into battle, but had no mythology of her own and was little more than a personification of bloody war. The Romans identified her with their goddess of war, BELLONA.

Enyo (2) *see* GRAEAE.

Eos

The goddess of Dawn, known to the Romans as Aurora. 'She shines upon all who live on earth, and upon the immortal gods living in the wide heaven', says Hesiod (*Theogony* 372–3); while Homer calls her 'rosy-fingered' and 'saffron-robed', epithets derived from the colours of the dawn sky. She was thought to provide not just the early light of dawn, but the light of day as well, accompanying the Sun-god HELIOS on his journey through the sky and driving her two-horse chariot drawn by Lampus, 'Bright', and Phaethon, 'Shiner'. She was the daughter of the Titans HYPERION and Theia, and sister of Helios and SELENE (the Moon). She married her cousin, Astraeus. To him she bore all the stars, most notably the morning and evening stars, PHOSPHORUS and HESPERUS, and the winds BOREAS, EURUS, NOTUS and ZEPHYRUS. She also, however, had several mortal loves whom she seized and carried off, perhaps because APHRODITE condemned her to be always falling in love as a punishment for going to bed with Aphrodite's own lover, ARES. Eos snatched up CLEITUS to

live among the gods because of his beauty. She fell in love with the giant hunter ORION and carried him off to Ortygia (Delos), but the gods were jealous of his favoured status and he was killed by Artemis. She seized CEPHALUS (1) and took him up to live among the gods, where she bore him a son, Phaethon. But perhaps her most notable love affair was with TITHONUS, whom she carried off to her home in Ethiopia in the farthest East. She loved him so much that she had Zeus grant him immortality, but she had forgotten to ask that he might remain for ever young. As time went by he slowly withered away to a dry husk, which yet could never die. Eos had two sons by him, MEMNON and EMATHION, who became kings, respectively, of Ethiopia and Arabia. Memnon took a large army to fight at Troy, where he was killed in a duel by Achilles, despite Eos' pleas to Zeus that he might be the victor. The dew that falls at dawn is said to be tears of grief from the still inconsolable mother for her dead son (fig.90).

In art Eos is usually winged. From the sixth century BC she appears, together with Achilles' mother, THETIS, in scenes concerned with Memnon's death. The two mothers watch Zeus weighing the souls of their sons, or gaze anxiously at the duel itself. There are many representations of Eos pursuing a youth; and in both ancient and postclassical art she is often shown with chariot and horses, bringing in the day (fig.52). Eos, as bearer of light and conqueror of the darkness of night, is often seen as an allegory of enlightenment.

[Homer, *Odyssey* 5.121–4, 15.249–51, 23.246; Hesiod, *Theogony* 371–82; Apollodorus 1.4.4–5.]

Eosphorus *see* PHOSPHORUS.

Fig.52 Eos rides her dawn-chariot from the sea.

Epaphus

The son of ZEUS and IO. After Io, in the form of a cow, was stung by a gadfly sent by the angry and jealous HERA, she wandered far over the earth until at last she came to Egypt. Here she recovered her human form and gave birth to Epaphus beside the Nile, naming him for the touch (*epaphe*) of Zeus by which she had conceived him. Hera was still angry, so on her instructions the CURETES (1) stole the child. Io searched for her son, until at last she found him in Syria. She took him back to Egypt and there married the Egyptian king, Telegonus. The Curetes were punished by Zeus with death.

Epaphus succeeded his stepfather to the throne of Egypt and married Memphis, daughter of the river-god Nile. He named the great city of Memphis after her, and they had two daughters, LIBYA, who gave her name to the neighbouring country, and Lysianassa, the mother of BUSIRIS. Epaphus, whom Aeschylus calls 'the calf born of Zeus', was identified by the Greeks with the Egyptian bull-god Apis, and Io with the Egyptian goddess Isis.

[Aeschylus, *Suppliants* 40–8, 312–15, *Prometheus Bound* 846–52; Herodotus 2.153, 3.27, 3.28; Apollodorus 2.1.3–4.]

Epeius (1)

Son of ENDYMION, king of Elis, and brother of Aetolus and Paeon. He won the footrace held by his father to determine the succession to the Elian throne, then named his people the Epeians after himself. He died without male issue and was succeeded by Aetolus.

[Pausanias 5.1.4–5, 5.1.8.]

Epeius (2)

The better-known Epeius was the son of PANOPEUS, and went with the Greeks to the TROJAN WAR. In the *Iliad* he is never named as a participant in the battle scenes, and himself freely admits that he is a poor warrior. But he is a champion boxer, and at the funeral games for Patroclus he fells his opponent EURYALUS (1) with a single blow. He prefaces his fight with the kind of boasting familiar from heavyweight boxers of our own day: 'I'm the greatest! ... I tell you this, and I'll do it too: I'll smash his skin open and break his bones, and his friends had better stay around to carry him off after I've murdered him.' But despite his dire threats, he behaves decently to his opponent, setting him on his feet again after knocking him down. Later he performs so badly in the weight-throwing contest that all his comrades laugh at him. Despite his boxing skill, he is not a heroic figure, and it was later said by the lyric poet Stesichorus that he was a water-carrier for AGAMEMNON and MENELAUS, and that ATHENA pitied his hard toil.

Epeius' chief claim to fame was that he built the WOODEN HORSE with the help of Athena.

[Homer, *Iliad* 23.664–99, 826–41, *Odyssey* 8.492–515; Stesichorus, *The Sack of Troy* fr. 200.]

Ephialtes (1) *see* GIANTS.

Ephialtes (2) *see* OTUS.

Epicasta

Homer's name for JOCASTA.

Epigoni ('After-born')

The sons of the heroes who took part in the expedition of the SEVEN AGAINST THEBES. This first attack on Thebes, led by ADRASTUS (1), had been a bid to win the throne for Oedipus' son Polyneices, but it had turned into a disaster, with all its leaders killed except Adrastus himself. Ten years later, encouraged by Adrastus, the Epigoni rallied to avenge their fathers, then made a second and successful attack on the city. The warriors at the head of the army were Aegialeus, son of Adrastus, THERSANDER, son of Polyneices, DIOMEDES (2), son of Tydeus, ALCMAEON and AMPHILOCHUS (1), sons of Amphiaraus, STHENELUS (3), son of Capaneus, Promachus, son of Parthenopaeus, EURYALUS (1), son of Mecisteus, and Polydorus, son of Hippomedon; while Pausanias mentions two other sons of Polyneices, Adrastus and Timeas, and the scholia add Medon, son of Eteoclus. The young men consulted the Delphic Oracle, which promised them victory if they made Alcmaeon their leader. At first he and Amphilochus were loath to take part in the expedition, but were persuaded to do so by their mother ERIPHYLE, after she had been bribed by Thersander with the beautiful robe of his ancestress Harmonia (just as ten years before she had been bribed by Polyneices with Harmonia's necklace, and persuaded her husband Amphiaraus to war, even though she knew that he would never return).

Under the leadership of Alcmaeon the army marched on Thebes. The Thebans came out to meet them, led by Laodamas, son of the dead Eteocles, and were routed at a town called Glisas. It was usually said that the only one of the Epigoni to die, killed by Laodamas, was Aegialeus, just as his father Adrastus had been the only one to survive the first expedition. Laodamas himself was killed by Alcmaeon. The Thebans fled within the walls of their city, then on the advice of the old, blind seer TEIRESIAS they stole away under cover of night. (It was sometimes said that Laodamas survived and led his defeated people to a new home in Illyria.) The Epigoni entered the city in triumph. They razed its walls and pillaged it, sending a part of their booty to Apollo at Delphi. This included Teiresias' daughter MANTO as a thank-offering, since they had vowed that, if they took Thebes, they would dedicate to the god the 'fairest of the spoils'. Thersander now took the throne that his father Polyneices had been so eager to win, but Thebes would never again have the strength that once it had. Homer, describing the Greek forces that went to the Trojan War, mentions only 'lower Thebes' and not the great citadel.

The rest of the Epigoni returned to Argos, but on the journey Adrastus died of grief for his dead son Aegialeus.

[Homer, *Iliad* 4.405–10; Pindar, *Pythian* 8.39–55; Herodotus 5.61; Apollodorus 3.7.2–7; Diodorus Siculus 4.66; Pausanias 2.20.5, 9.5.13–14, 9.8.6–7, 9.9.4–5, 9.19.2, 10.10.4.]

Epimetheus

Son of the Titan IAPETUS and of an Oceanid, Clymene or Asia. His name, significantly, means 'afterthought', while that of his brother PROMETHEUS means 'forethought'. The wise Prometheus warned him never to accept any gift from Zeus, but Epimetheus forgot all about this when Zeus sent him the first woman, the beautiful PANDORA. Desiring to possess such loveliness he took her as his bride, and only too late did he realise that she was cunning and deceitful as well as beautiful. Moreover she opened the lid of a great jar and let loose among men all the sorrows and sicknesses of the world. Thus Pandora was responsible for mankind's miseries, but so too was Epimetheus because of his gullibility.

[Hesiod, *Theogony* 507–616, *Works and Days* 47–105; Apollodorus 1.2.3, 1.7.2.]

Epistrophus *see* IPHITUS (2).

Epopeus (1)

Epopeus was a king of Sicyon and Corinth, and the father of MARATHON; but his main claim to fame was for marrying ANTIOPE (1), the daughter of Nycteus, regent of Thebes. Either Epopeus gave Antiope refuge when she was pregnant by Zeus and fleeing from her father's anger, or he carried her off himself. Either way, the result was a war between Thebes and Sicyon in which Epopeus was killed. In one version, Nycteus led the Thebans and was defeated, though both he and Epopeus were mortally wounded during the battle. In another, Nycteus committed suicide and left it to his brother, Lycus, to lead the Thebans against Sicyon. Lycus was victorious and killed Epopeus, then led Antiope captive back to Thebes.

[Apollodorus 1.7.4, 3.5.5; Pausanias 2.1.1, 2.3.10, 2.6.1–4, 2.11.1.]

Epopeus (2) *see* NYCTIMENE.

Erato *see* MUSES.

Erebus ('Darkness')

The darkness of the Underworld. In Hesiod's creation myth, Erebus and his sister NYX (Night) were born of CHAOS, the primeval void. Then Erebus mated with Nyx – the very first sexual union – to produce AETHER (Brightness) and HEMERA (Day). Erebus has little character of his own, and his name is most commonly used simply as a synonym for the Underworld.

[Homer, *Iliad* 8.368, 16.326–7, *Odyssey* 10.528, 11.37; Hesiod, *Theogony* 123–5.]

Erechtheus

The seventh mythical king of Athens, though he was often confused with his grandfather, ERICHTHONIUS (1), and the two may well have been originally one and the same. Homer, for instance, says (and this could well describe Erichthonius) that Erechtheus was born from the earth, brought up by ATHENA and installed in her sanctuary, and there worshipped by the Athenians with sacrifices of bulls and rams. Later tradition makes him the son of PANDION (1) and Zeuxippe, with a brother, BUTES (2), and two sisters, Procne and Philomela, who were tragically transformed into birds (*see* TEREUS). When Pandion died, Erechtheus became king and Butes the priest of Athena and Poseidon.

Erechtheus married Praxithea and had several sons, including CECROPS (2), who succeeded him, Metion, Pandorus and Orneus. He also had many daughters, of whom Apollodorus names four: Oreithyia, who was carried off by BOREAS, the god of the North Wind (fig. 31), Procris, who married CEPHALUS (2), Creusa, who married XUTHUS, and Chthonia, who married her uncle Butes. But according to Euripides' tragedy *Erechtheus*, now lost apart from fragments, there were three unmarried daughters who sacrificed themselves for their city when Athens was at war with neighbouring Eleusis. Erechtheus learnt that only the sacrifice of one of his daughters would make Athens victorious, so one of them was chosen, and died, while the others killed themselves, true to an oath they had all taken to die together. The Eleusinians were defeated and their leader EUMOLPUS, son of Poseidon, killed. (The chronology is odd, since Eumolpus was usually said to be a grandson of Oreithyia.) But Poseidon was angry at the death of his son, so unfortunately for Athens Erechtheus also died, slain by a blow from the god's trident and engulfed in the earth.

Erechtheus' temple on the Acropolis at Athens, the Erechtheum, dating from the late fifth century BC and in antiquity housing the holy olive-wood statue of Athena, has always been famous for its south porch, supported by caryatids. Pausanias records that within the Erechtheum were three altars, one of Poseidon and Erechtheus, one of Butes, and one of Hephaestus, and also the physical evidence of the contest between Athena and Poseidon for the right to be the patron of Athens (*see* CECROPS (1)).

Fig. 53 Gaia lifts the baby Erichthonius into the arms of Athena, while Hephaestus looks on.

[Homer, *Iliad* 2.546–51, *Odyssey* 7.78–81; Euripides, *Ion* 275–82; Apollodorus 1.7.3, 1.9.4, 3.14.8, 3.15.1, 3.15.4–5; Pausanias 1.5.3, 1.26.5–1.27.4, 1.38.3, 2.25.5. C. Collard, M. J. Cropp and K. H. Lee, *Euripides: Selected Fragmentary Plays* I (1995), pp. 148–94.]

Ereuthalion *see* LYCURGUS (2).

Erginus (1)

Son of CLYMENUS, king of the Minyans of Boeotian Orchomenus. Clymenus was mortally wounded by a stone thrown by a Theban called Perieres, the charioteer of Menoeceus, at a festival of Poseidon at Onchestus. With his dying breath he urged his son to avenge him. Becoming king in his father's place, Erginus marched on Thebes, killed a good many Thebans, and finally made a treaty with them whereby they agreed to send him a tribute of a hundred head of cattle every year for twenty years. Thus was Clymenus avenged.

This happy state of affairs was changed, however, by the intervention of HERACLES. As he was returning home from killing the lion of Cithaeron, he came across Erginus' heralds travelling to Thebes to demand the annual tribute. He cut off their ears and noses and hands, hung these round their necks, and told them to take that tribute back to their master. The furious Erginus once more marched on Thebes, but this time against an army led by Heracles, who was fighting with weapons given to him by the goddess ATHENA. Erginus was killed and his men put to flight. Heracles then compelled the people of Orchomenus to pay tribute to the Thebans of two hundred head of cattle every year.

Another tradition had Erginus survive, spending long years in toiling to recover his prosperity, and eventually growing old and childless and lonely. He consulted the Delphic Oracle and was told to fit a new tip to his ploughshare; so he married a young wife and had two sons, TROPHONIUS and Agamedes, who became famous master-builders.

[Apollodorus 2.4.11; Diodorus Siculus 4.10.3–5; Pausanias 9.37.1–4.]

Erginus (2)

An ARGONAUT, usually said to be a son of POSEIDON, hailing from Miletus, though Pindar calls him a son of Clymenus and thus conflates him with Erginus (1). He was a fine seaman, for on the death of the helmsman TIPHYS, Erginus, along with several others, volunteered to take the helm in his place, though it was Ancaeus who was chosen. When the Argonauts held athletic contests on the island of Lemnos, Erginus won the footrace in bronze armour, thus amazing the Lemnian women who had previously mocked his grey hairs.

[Pindar, *Olympian* 4.19–28, *Pythian* 4.253; Apollonius, *Argonautica* 1.185–9, 2.896; Apollodorus 1.9.16.]

Erichthonius (1)

The fifth mythical king of Athens, often confused with his grandson ERECHTHEUS. Although in one version of his legend Erichthonius was said to be the son of the smith-god HEPHAESTUS and Atthis, the daughter of Cranaus, the more usual tradition makes him the offspring of Hephaestus and (in a sense) ATHENA, though born from the earth (fig. 53). Athena visited the smith-god's workshop to ask him to make her some weapons, but on seeing her he lost all thought of his craft, afflicted with a fit of uncontrollable passion. The virgin-goddess was determined not to submit and fled, but in spite of his lameness the god caught her and did his best to ravish her. In the struggle his semen fell on her thigh. Athena in disgust wiped it off with a scrap of wool, which she threw on the ground. Where it fell, GAIA (Earth) produced a child and gave him to Athena, who called him Erichthonius (from either *eris*, strife, or *erion*, wool, and *chthon*, earth). She put him in a chest and entrusted it to the three daughters of CECROPS (1), AGLAURUS (2), Herse and Pandrosus, forbidding them to open it. The girls were naturally full of curiosity, and although sources differ as to exactly who opened the chest (sometimes it was one of them, sometimes two, sometimes all three) the result was the same: the chest was opened and the girls paid the price of their disobedience. Terrified by what they saw inside, either a snake coiled round the baby, or the baby himself formed as half-child and half-serpent, they went mad and flung themselves from the Acropolis on to the rocks below. Some say the snake killed them.

Athena herself brought up the child on the Acropolis. When he reached manhood he drove out AMPHICTYON, who had usurped the throne of Athens from Cranaus, and himself became king. During his reign Erichthonius promoted the cult of Athena, setting up her ancient wooden image on the Acropolis and instituting the Panathenaea, her principal festival. He married the Naiad Praxithea and had a son, PANDION (1), who succeeded him as king. Erichthonius was said to have invented the four-horse chariot, perhaps out of a desire to hide his serpent feet, and as such was immortalised in the stars on his death as the constellation Auriga (the Charioteer).

[Euripides, *Ion* 20–4, 260–74; Apollodorus 3.14.6; Pausanias 1.2.6, 1.14.6, 1.18.2, 1.24.7, 1.27.2, 3.18.13; Virgil, *Georgics* 3.113–14; Ovid, *Metamorphoses* 2.552–65.]

Erichthonius (2)

Son of DARDANUS and Bateia, daughter of TEUCER (1), the first king of the Troad. Erichthonius succeeded his father as king of Dardania and married Astyoche, daughter of the river-god SIMOEIS. Their son was TROS, who gave his name to Troy, the Troad and the Trojans. Erichthonius became, according to Homer, the richest of all mortal men. His wealth lay in his horses. Indeed, Troy was always famous for its horses: Tros was given some marvellous steeds by Zeus in recompense for the loss of his son GANYMEDE; and it was for these that Heracles agreed to save LAOMEDON's daughter Hesione from the sea-monster, and then sacked Troy when her father reneged on his promise. A frequent epithet in Homer of both the Trojans in general, and the great Trojan hero Hector, is 'horse-taming', and their home is called 'land of fine horses', reflecting the fame of their steeds on the plains of windy Troy. But Erichthonius' horses were particularly wondrous (*Iliad* 20.221–9):

> Three thousand mares had he, that fed on the grasslands,
> mares that joyed in their young foals. And as they grazed,
> Boreas, the North Wind, desired them, and made himself
> into a dark-maned stallion, and coupled with twelve mares,
> and they, conceiving, bore to him twelve young horses.
> These, when they frisked across the grain-giving land,
> would run along the topmost ears of corn, not breaking
> them,

> and again, when they sported over the wide sea's waves,
> would gallop above the crests of the salt grey breakers.

[Homer, *Iliad* 20.215–41; Apollodorus 3.12.2.]

Eridanus

A mythical river and its god, and like other rivers the son of OCEANUS and Tethys. The location of the Eridanus is uncertain. It seems to have been situated rather vaguely in the far west or north, though ancient writers with their imprecise knowledge of geography usually identified it either with the Po or the Rhone. The blazing corpse of PHAETHON (2) fell into the Eridanus when he was hurled from Helios' sun-chariot by a thunderbolt from Zeus. Here his sisters, the Heliades, came to mourn his death, weeping for so long and so unceasingly on the riverbanks that they were turned into poplar trees, and their tears into amber. After Phaethon's death the Eridanus was commemorated as a constellation, its stream of stars flowing far through the sky to the west of Orion.

[Hesiod, *Theogony* 338; Herodotus 3.115.]

Erigone (1)

The daughter of an Attic farmer called Icarius. She and her father welcomed the god DIONYSUS to Attica, and in return he gave them the gift of a vine branch and taught them how to make wine. Wishing to share the pleasures of this glorious boon, Icarius gave some of his wine to a group of shepherds, but because they drank it unwatered they soon became tipsy. Unfortunately they thought that Icarius had bewitched them, so they clubbed him to death and buried him under a tree. When Erigone was searching everywhere for him, his dog Maera led her to the grave and dug away the loose earth. Seeing her father dead, she hanged herself from the tree; and the dog, also overcome by sorrow, jumped into a well and drowned.

Dionysus, angry at the unavenged deaths of his followers, sent a madness on Athenian girls that made them, like Erigone, hang themselves from trees, until the Delphic Oracle explained the cause of this phenomenon. At once the murderous shepherds were sought out and hanged, and the Athenians instituted an annual festival at the time of the grape harvest, the *Aiora* ('Swinging'), during which girls swung on ropes suspended from trees with their feet resting on small platforms: this is how swings were invented. Dionysus also immortalised his followers by putting Icarius in the sky as the constellation Boötes, Erigone as Virgo, and the faithful dog Maera as Canis Minor, the Lesser Dog.

In another version, the murderers fled from Attica and took refuge on the island of Ceos. They were nevertheless hunted down, for the Dog-star rose, bringing scorching heat and causing a plague among the islanders in vengeance for the murder of Icarius. When the wise ARISTAEUS, son of Apollo and Cyrene, was sent to the island by his father's oracle, he propitiated the Dog-star by putting the murderers to death. He also offered sacrifices to Zeus, who responded by sending the Etesian winds to cool the island and bring the plague to an end. Ever since then, the Etesian winds have cooled the whole of Greece for forty days from the Dog-star's rising.

[Apollonius, *Argonautica* 2.500–27; Apollodorus 3.14.7; Diodorus Siculus 4.82; Athenaeus 14.618e; Nonnus, *Dionysiaca* 47.34–255; Ovid *Metamorphoses* 6.125.]

Erigone (2)

Daughter of AEGISTHUS and CLYTEMNESTRA. She is linked with her half-brother ORESTES in several contradictory ways. According to one version, Orestes would have killed her, along with her brother ALETES, had not Artemis carried her off to be a priestess in Athens. Various sources said that it was Erigone who brought Orestes to trial on the Areopagus because of his matricide, then hanged herself in disappointment when he was acquitted. A third story said that she was the mother of Orestes' bastard son Penthilus. It may well have been this Erigone who was the subject of Sophocles' lost tragedy of the same name, for the lost *Erigona* by the Roman poet Accius certainly mentioned Aegisthus and Orestes, and it presumably had a Greek original.

[Apollodorus, *Epitome* 6.25; Pausanias 2.18.6.]

Erinyes *see* FURIES.

Eriphyle

Daughter of TALAUS and Lysimache, and sister of ADRASTUS (1), king of Argos. From the time of Homer onwards, she was renowned as a treacherous wife who brought about the death of her husband, the seer AMPHIARAUS, because of her greed. When Adrastus was organising the expedition of the Seven against Thebes, in a bid to win the throne of Thebes for Oedipus' son Polyneices, Amphiaraus was unwilling to take part because he foresaw that it was doomed to disaster and that he himself, if he joined, would never return. Polyneices now bribed Eriphyle, offering her the beautiful necklace of his ancestress Harmonia in return for her support. She took the necklace and forced Amphiaraus to join the expedition, even though she too knew that she would never see him again. Before he left for Thebes, he charged their two sons, ALCMAEON and AMPHILOCHUS (1), to avenge him.

The attack was an utter failure. None of the leaders, apart from Adrastus, survived. Ten years later a second expedition was organised, when the Epigoni, the sons of the heroes who had fallen at Thebes, set out to avenge their fathers' deaths. Once more Eriphyle was bribed, this time by Polyneices' son Thersander and with the gorgeous robe that had once belonged to Harmonia. She took the robe and persuaded her sons to go on the expedition, but this time the attack on Thebes was a success and both victims of her treachery lived to see that she was dealt her just deserts. Alcmaeon killed her, then was driven mad by her FURIES.

Scenes from the story of Eriphyle's treachery appear in ancient art from the sixth century BC (fig.118), especially the moment of Amphiaraus' departure from Thebes. Pausanias (5.17.7–8) graphically describes the dramatic depiction of such a scene on the chest of Cypselus. In front of his house, bidding Amphiaraus goodbye, stands an old woman carrying the infant Amphilochus, Eriphyle holding the necklace with which she was bribed, her daughters Eurydice and Demonassa, and a naked Alcmaeon. Baton is driving Amphiaraus' chariot, and Amphiaraus himself already has one foot in the chariot, 'and with his sword drawn is turned towards Eriphyle in such a transport of anger that he can scarcely keep himself from striking her'.

Eris

The goddess of Strife. For the most part she is little more than a personification of discord, as when we see her in action during battle scenes in the *Iliad*. Homer describes her as 'Strife incessantly raging, sister and comrade of murderous Ares, who at first holds her head low, but thereafter strides the earth with head rearing to heaven. And now she moved through the throng of battle, casting evil strife in their midst and ever increasing men's sorrow' (4.440–5). In the *Theogony* (223–32), Hesiod makes Eris the daughter of NYX (Night) and the mother of many personified abstractions as disagreeable as herself: she bore Toil, Neglect, Famine, Pain, Battles, Conflicts, Bloodshed, Slaughter, Quarrels, Lies, Pretences, Disputes, Lawlessness, Oath and Delusion (ATE), with only the last having any distinct mythological identity. But in the *Works and Days* (11–24) Hesiod speaks of two quite separate Strifes, the first pernicious, fostering war and conflict, and the second a spirit of emulation, put among men by Zeus to instil in them a healthy competitive instinct that can help them to success.

Eris plays one crucial role in myth as the instigator of the JUDGEMENT OF PARIS and thus of the whole TROJAN WAR.

[Homer, *Iliad* 5.518, 740, 11.3–14, 73, 18.535, 20.48; Hesiod, *Shield of Heracles* 148, 156; Apollodorus, *Epitome* 3.1–3.]

Eros

The Greek god of love, called by the Romans Cupid or Amor. According to the creation myth of Hesiod's *Theogony*,

Eros was one of the primal entities, born at the beginning of time out of CHAOS, the dark and primeval void, together with GAIA (Earth) and TARTARUS. He is a fundamental cosmic force, omnipotent over mortals and gods alike: 'the most beautiful of the immortal gods, he melts the limbs, and overpowers the reason and the careful plans in the breasts of all gods and all men' (120–2). He was present at the birth of APHRODITE, goddess of love, and thereafter became her constant companion (192–202). Only in later writers (first in Simonides, fr. 575) is he the son of Aphrodite herself and the war-god, ARES.

Eros is not personified in Homer, though in passages where the word *eros*, sexual love, is used, his effect on gods and men is clear: he 'overwhelmed the heart' of both Paris and Zeus (*Iliad* 3.442, 14.294), and when the Suitors looked at Penelope, 'their knees went slack, their hearts were enchanted with passion, and all of them prayed to lie in her bed beside her' (*Odyssey*, 18.212–13). The Archaic lyric poets give us memorable images of Eros' violent impact on body and mind. From Sappho: 'Eros shook my heart, like a wind falling on mountain oaks' (47), and 'Once again Eros melts my limbs and spins me round, bitter-sweet creature, irresistible' (130). From Anacreon (413): 'Once again Eros, like a blacksmith, has struck me with his great axe, and has plunged me into an icy mountain torrent.' From Ibycus (287):

> Once again Eros looks at me meltingly from under his dark eyelids, and with all his enchantments flings me into the inescapable nets of Aphrodite. How I tremble at his onset, like a prize-winning horse, now old, who is put once again in the chariot-yoke and goes all unwilling to the race.

The bow and arrows with which Eros pierces his victims and takes them captive are first mentioned by Euripides.

Eros was widely worshipped in antiquity. In Greek art he appears first as a beautiful winged youth (fig. 54), but in Hellenistic times and later he is depicted by both poets and artists as a mischievous infant, with a torch that could inflame love and a quiver full of inescapable arrows. These were said to be of two kinds: sharp and tipped with gold to kindle love, and blunt and tipped with lead to repel love (*see* DAPHNE). He played tricks on men and gods, and his mischief often had serious, even tragic, consequences. Sometimes Eros becomes a plurality of Erotes. For his own love affair, *see* PSYCHE.

[Sophocles, *Antigone* 781–800, *Women of Trachis* 441–4; Euripides, *Iphigeneia at Aulis* 543–51, *Medea* 627–34, *Hippolytus* 1268–82; Apollonius, *Argonautica* 3.119–66, 275–98, 4.445–51; Pausanias 1.30.1, 5.11.8, 9.27.1–4, 9.31.3; Virgil, *Aeneid* 1.657–722; Ovid, *Metamorphoses* 1.452–76, 5.362–84; Horace, *Odes* 2.8.13–16.]

Erymanthian Boar

The fourth of the Labours (*see* LABOURS OF HERACLES) performed by HERACLES for Eurystheus was to bring back alive the ferocious boar that lived on Mount Erymanthus in Arcadia and ravaged the land of Psophis. Heracles ousted the boar from its lair with his shouts, then chased it far through the mountains. Finally, by driving the exhausted beast into deep snow, he caught it, and carried it across his shoulders back to Eurystheus in Mycenae.

This exploit of Heracles was frequently depicted in Greek art, with the most popular scene being the delivery of the boar to Eurystheus. The terrified king hides in his great jar (*see* NEMEAN LION), while Heracles looms above him and lifts the boar high, preparing to ram it down on top of him (fig. 57). Pausanias (8.24.5) reports that the boar's tusks were preserved in a sanctuary of Apollo at Cumae in Campania.

[Apollonius, *Argonautica* 1.127; Apollodorus 2.5.4; Diodorus Siculus 4.12.1–2.]

Erysichthon

Son of Triops, and sometimes called Aethon, 'Fiery',

Fig. 54 **Eros pursues Atalanta.**

because of his insatiable appetite. He was an impious man, so when he needed some timber to build a banqueting-hall, he did not hesitate to cut down the trees in DEMETER's sacred grove. Here there was one huge, old oak, towering high above all the other trees, and even this Erysichthon attacked with his axe. As the blade cut into the wood, blood began to flow from the nymph (*see* NYMPHS) who lived inside the tree, but the ruthless man refused to stop. When a bystander objected, Erysichthon lopped off his head. The tree fell, and all the nymphs who had often danced beneath it begged Demeter to punish its destroyer. While he was asleep, the goddess sent on Erysichthon an insatiable hunger, so that when he woke he could think of nothing but food. He ate and ate, and the more he ate, the more he longed to eat. He used up all his worldly wealth buying food, and still he was afflicted with a ferocious appetite. At last, to raise more money, he sold his daughter Mestra into slavery. She prayed to her old lover POSEIDON to help her, and the god granted her the power of metamorphosis. Turning into a fisherman, she escaped, then became herself once again. Because of this lucky gift, her father thereafter often sold her as a slave to raise money for food, and each time she changed her shape and went free, ready to be sold again. But even this was not enough, and finally Erysichthon began to gnaw at his own flesh, feeding his body by eating it away, and so died.

[Callimachus, *Hymn* 6.24–115; Athenaeus 10.416b; Ovid, *Metamorphoses* 8.738–878.]

Erytheia

An island in the far west, beyond the PILLARS OF HERACLES and the great river of Ocean (*see* OCEANUS), and thus in the region beyond human knowledge where anything strange and wonderful might be found. Here triple-bodied GERYON kept his cattle before Heracles stole them.

Here also Menoetes herded the cattle belonging to HADES, and HELIOS the Sun-god pastured his cattle before they were stolen by the Giant Alcyoneus.

Erytus *see* ECHION (2).

Eryx

A son of APHRODITE, either by POSEIDON or by the Argonaut BUTES (2). Eryx was a king in western Sicily, with a city and a mountain named after him. On the summit of the mountain he founded a famous sanctuary for the worship of his mother. When HERACLES was driving the cattle of GERYON from Erytheia, in the far west, back to Mycenae, a bull broke loose from the herd and swam to Eryx' territory in Sicily. Leaving the rest of the herd in the care of Hephaestus, Heracles followed. Eryx challenged him to a wrestling match, staking his own kingdom against Geryon's splendid herd. Heracles, accepting the challenge, brought Eryx down in three consecutive falls and killed him. Heracles handed the kingdom over to the inhabitants, telling them that one of his descendants would one day take possession. This prediction was fulfilled when the Spartan Dorieus founded a colony there in the historical era.

AENEAS, son of Aphrodite and thus Eryx' half-brother, visited Sicily on his journey from Troy and honoured Eryx with sacrifices.

[Herodotus 5.41–8; Apollodorus 2.5.10; Diodorus Siculus 4.23.2, 4.83.1; Pausanias 3.16.4–5, 4.36.4; Virgil, *Aeneid* 5.410–14, 772–3.]

Eteocles *see* POLYNEICES.

Eteoclus

Son of IPHIS (1) and one of the SEVEN AGAINST THEBES. He was killed either by Leades or Megareus, the son of Creon. His son, Medon, was one of the EPIGONI who avenged their fathers' deaths.

[Aeschylus, *Seven Against Thebes* 457–80; Euripides, *Suppliant Women* 871–80; Apollodorus 3.6.3–4, 3.6.8.]

Ethiopians (Greek, *Aithiopes*, 'Burnt-faces')

Ethiopia was known to Greek historians and geographers as a land south of Egypt, but the Ethiopia of mythology was far less well defined. According to Homer, the Ethiopians lived at the ends of the earth beside the river of Ocean (*see* OCEANUS), some at the sunrise and some at the sunset, and their feasts were shared with the gods. Their proximity to the burning Sun-god as he approached the earth accounted for their dark skins; though it was

Fig. 55 **Memnon with his two black Ethiopian squires, one of whom is named Amasis.**

also said that they were burnt black when Helios' son PHAETHON (2) lost control of his father's sun-chariot and drove it too near the earth. Perhaps the most famous of the Ethiopians was their mighty king MEMNON, son of Eos, goddess of Dawn (fig. 55). He came from the east to fight at Troy and was slain by the even mightier Achilles. Cepheus was another famous Ethiopian king: he was the father of ANDROMEDA, the princess saved from a sea-monster by Perseus, and the site of this Ethiopia was often thought to be on the eastern Mediterranean coast.

[Homer, *Iliad* 1.423–4, 23.205–7, *Odyssey* 1.22–6, 5.282–3; Aeschylus, *Prometheus Bound* 807–9.]

Etna, Mount *see* AETNA.

Euchenor

A rich and noble Corinthian, son of the seer POLYIDUS, who knew that Euchenor was destined either to die at home of a painful illness, or to fight at Troy and be killed by the Trojans. Euchenor (like Achilles himself, given the choice of death and glory at Troy, or a long but unsung life peacefully at home) chose to fight. Euchenor (again like Achilles) was shot and killed by PARIS.

[Homer, *Iliad* 13.663–72.]

Eudorus

Son of HERMES and Polymele, the daughter of Phylas. Hermes' ardour was fired by the sight of the beautiful Polymele, dancing with a group of girls in honour of Artemis, so he crept secretly into her bedroom by night and made love to her. After she had borne him a son, Eudorus, she married Actor's son Echecles, and the boy was brought up with great affection by his grandfather, Phylas. Eudorus fought in the TROJAN WAR as captain of one of the five battalions of MYRMIDONS under ACHILLES.

[Homer, *Iliad* 16.179–86.]

Eumaeus

In the *Odyssey*, Eumaeus is ODYSSEUS' faithful swineherd on Ithaca (fig. 102). He was of royal birth, the son of Ctesius, king of the island of Syria, but while still a child was given by a treacherous slave-girl to Phoenician sailors, who sold him to Odysseus' father LAERTES. Thereafter he served the family well, remaining loyal to Odysseus' interests throughout his long absence during and after the Trojan War, and doing his best to keep his pigs out of the hands of the greedy Suitors. When Odysseus returns to Ithaca disguised as a beggar, he goes first of all to Eumaeus' hut and is given generous food and shelter by the swineherd. Here too he reveals his identity to his son TELEMACHUS.

Odysseus later makes himself known to Eumaeus and

to the faithful cowherd Philoetius, who greet the return of their beloved master with tears of joy. They help Odysseus and Telemachus to kill the Suitors, and then the twelve serving-women who have been sleeping with the enemy. They also punish the treacherous goatherd MELANTHIUS by mutilating him and leaving him to die. Finally, when the families of the dead Suitors attack in a vain attempt to get their revenge, Eumaeus and Philoetius fight staunchly alongside Odysseus and his other supporters, until Athena separates the warring parties and re-establishes peace among the Ithacans.

[Homer, *Odyssey* 13–17, 20–2, 24.]

Eumelus (1) *see* TRIPTOLEMUS.

Eumelus (2)

Son of ADMETUS and Alcestis, and husband of Icarius' daughter Iphthime. He led eleven ships from Pherae and Iolcus to the TROJAN WAR, taking with him his father's fine horses which were the swiftest of all those at Troy. With these he would have won the chariot-race at Patroclus' funeral games, if ATHENA had not smashed his chariot yoke, intervening to help DIOMEDES (2). Later Eumelus was more fortunate, winning the chariot-race at Achilles' funeral games. He was one of the warriors in the WOODEN HORSE, and returned home safely after the war.

[Homer, *Iliad* 2.711–15, 763–7, 23.288–565, *Odyssey* 4.795–8; Apollodorus, *Epitome* 5.5.]

Eumenides ('Kindly Ones')

A euphemistic name for the FURIES.

Eumolpus ('Sweet Singer')

Son of POSEIDON and Chione, the daughter of Boreas and Oreithyia. To save her reputation Chione flung her baby into the sea, but Poseidon saved him and gave him to Benthesicyme, his daughter by Amphitrite, to bring up. Benthesicyme was married to an Ethiopian king who later gave Eumolpus one of his two daughters in marriage. She bore a son, Ismarus. Eumolpus was banished, together with his son, when he tried to rape his sister-in-law. He found a home with Tegyrius, a king of Thrace, who married his daughter to Ismarus; but Eumolpus was banished once again when he was caught plotting against the king. This time he settled in Eleusis, where he made many friends. Tegyrius recalled him to Thrace when Ismarus died and they were reconciled, so much so that on the death of the king Eumolpus succeeded to the throne. When war broke out between Eleusis and Athens, the Eleusinians called on him for help and he invaded Attica with a horde of Thracians. This was the situation dramatised in Euripides' lost tragedy *Erechtheus*, where Eumolpus claimed Attica in the name of his father

Poseidon, who had himself unsuccessfully claimed it against Athena (*see* CECROPS (1)). According to Euripides, Eumolpus led his Thracians against the army of ERECHTHEUS, king of Athens, and was killed in battle. But Poseidon was angry at the death of his son and so Erechtheus also died, slain by a blow from the god's trident and engulfed in the earth.

Eumolpus was the ancestor of the priestly Eleusinian clan of the Eumolpidae, and was also associated, along with Celeus and TRIPTOLEMUS, with the foundation of the Eleusinian Mysteries. In the *Homeric Hymn to Demeter* (154, 475) he is named as one of the leading citizens of Eleusis to whom DEMETER taught her rites. It was he who initiated HERACLES into the Mysteries after purifying him for killing the Centaurs. In ancient art he appears on several pots together with Triptolemus.

[Euripides, *Phoenician Women* 852–7; Apollodorus 2.5.12, 3.15.4; Pausanias 1.5.2, 1.27.4, 1.38.3, 2.14.2. C. Collard, M. J. Cropp and K. H. Lee, *Euripides: Selected Fragmentary Plays* I (1995), pp. 148–94.]

Euneus

Son of JASON and HYPSIPYLE. When he and his brother Thoas grew up, they saved their mother from slavery at the court of Lycurgus, king of Nemea, and took her home to Lemnos. Euneus was king of Lemnos at the time of the Trojan War and supplied the Greek army with wine. When Achilles captured LYCAON (2), one of Priam's sons, Euneus bought him from Patroclus in return for a richly engraved drinking-bowl of silver. This was later awarded as a prize at Patroclus' funeral games.

[Homer, *Iliad* 7.467–75, 14.230, 21.40–1, 23.740–9.]

Eunomus

Son of Architeles, and relative and cupbearer to OENEUS, the king of Calydon. During a banquet at the palace, Eunomus caused HERACLES some trivial annoyance when he was serving him, and Heracles, with no intention of serious damage, hit the boy. Such was his strength, however, that Eunomus dropped dead. Heracles went into exile, even though Architeles forgave him the accidental homicide.

[Apollodorus 2.7.6; Diodorus Siculus 4.36.2–3; Pausanias 2.13.8; Athenaeus 9.410f–411a.]

Eupeithes

In the *Odyssey*, Eupeithes is an Ithacan noble whom ODYSSEUS once protected from his angry countrymen after he joined the Taphians in a pirate raid on the Thesprotians, allies of the Ithacans. Despite this favour, Eupeithes allowed his son ANTINOUS to become one of the Suitors, the young men who invaded Odysseus' house during his long absence, carousing at his expense and hoping to marry his wife Penelope. Indeed, Antinous was the most cruel and insolent of them all, and was deservedly the first to be killed by Odysseus on his return. After he and the rest of the Suitors had been massacred, Eupeithes led an attack on Odysseus and his allies in an unsuccessful attempt to avenge their deaths. He was killed by Odysseus' old father LAERTES.

[Homer, *Odyssey* 16.424–32, 24.417–525.]

Euphemus

A son of POSEIDON by Europa, the daughter of Tityus. He was one of the ARGONAUTS, and so swift-footed that he could run across the swell of the sea without getting his feet wet. When the *Argo* approached the Clashing Rocks, it was Euphemus who launched the dove whose fate would foretell the crew's destiny: she flew safely through the narrow strait, catching only the tips of her tail-feathers between the rocks as they crashed together, just as the Argonauts would row desperately through, urged on by Euphemus, and escape with only the tip of the *Argo*'s stern-ornament caught between the rocky jaws.

When the Argonauts were stranded at Lake Tritonis in Libya, carried far inland by a tidal wave, the sea-god TRITON appeared to them, disguised as the local king Eurypylus, and presented a clod of earth to Euphemus as a gift of friendship. This clod symbolised the future sovereignty in Libya of Euphemus' descendants. After Triton had guided the *Argo* safely back into the Mediterranean, Euphemus dropped the clod of earth into the sea north of Crete (or it was washed overboard), and here it grew into the island named Calliste. In later years, Euphemus' descendants were among the companions of THERAS who colonised Calliste and renamed it Thera. Finally, a seventeenth-generation descendant of Euphemus, BATTUS (2), led a party of Therans back to Libya where he founded the glorious city of Cyrene.

[Pindar, *Pythian* 4.19–56; Apollonius, *Argonautica* 1.179–84, 2.531–90, 4.1550–62, 1731–64; Pausanias 5.17.9.]

Euphorbus

Son of the Trojan elder PANTHOUS and a key figure in Homer's *Iliad*, not because he is one of the greatest warriors, but because he is the man who gives PATROCLUS his first wound before HECTOR delivers the second and fatal blow. Euphorbus makes his spear-thrust; but although he is a brilliant athlete and has already killed twenty men in battle, he does not dare to confront Patroclus again, wounded though he is, so he snatches out his spear and runs away (16.806–15). He comes against MENELAUS, and in trying to avenge the death of his brother, HYPERENOR (2), is himself killed (17.50–60):

He thudded to the ground, his armour clashing upon him,
and his hair, lovely as the Graces, was wet with blood,
those braided locks bound tight with silver and gold.
Like some young olive tree that a man makes thrive
in a lonely place, and gives it generous water,
so it grows in beauty, and the breezes from all sides
shake it, and it breaks into thick, pale blossom;
but then a sudden wind coming in a great storm
uprooted it and laid its length on the ground, like this
was Panthous' son, Euphorbus of the strong ash spear,
when Menelaus killed him and stripped his armour.

The traveller Pausanias (2.17.3) reports that, in the
second century AD, the shield which Menelaus took from
Euphorbus at Troy was still to be seen as a votive offering
at the Argive temple of Hera.

Euphorion

In late classical tradition, the son of the shades of ACHILLES
and HELEN.

Euphrosyne *see* GRACES.

Europa

Although Europa was thought by some earlier poets
(including Homer) to be the daughter of PHOENIX (2), she
was later more usually said to be the daughter of the
Phoenician king, AGENOR (1). ZEUS saw the beautiful Europa
gathering flowers near the seashore with her friends and
was filled with desire for her. He changed himself into a
beautiful bull, white as untrodden snow and with horns
shining like jewels, and ambled about among the girls.
When Europa saw how mild and gentle he was, she fed
him flowers and played with him. She stroked him, and
hung fresh garlands on his horns. When he lay down, a
benign snowy white bull on the yellow sand, with all fear
gone she climbed upon his back. At once he leapt up and
plunged into the sea, carrying her far out into the ocean.
Her friends never saw her again.

Zeus carried Europa over the sea to Crete and there
coupled with her. She bore him three sons, MINOS,
RHADAMANTHYS and SARPEDON (although Homer knows
Sarpedon as the son of Laodameia, daughter of
Bellerophon). Zeus was said to have given four presents
to Europa: the bronze man, TALOS (1), who walked on his
untiring feet three times a day round Crete and got rid of
strangers; a necklace made by Hephaestus, later given by
Europa to Cadmus, and by him to his bride HARMONIA; a
javelin that never missed its mark (*see* CEPHALUS (2)); and
LAELAPS, a hound that never missed its quarry. Europa
married Asterius, the king of Crete, and bore him a
daughter named Crete, while he brought up her sons by
Zeus as his own family.

Fig. 56 Europa seduced by Zeus in the guise of a bull.

Aeschylus' lost tragedy *Carians* seems to have treated
Europa's fortunes later in life, when she was waiting for
news of Sarpedon, fighting at Troy. 'It is for my son that
I fear', she says in one fragment, 'lest, raging with his
spear, he may do and suffer some terrible evil.' Almost
certainly an announcement of his death would have
arrived during the course of the play. An early Apulian
bell-krater by the Sarpedon Painter shows Europa in
tragic costume, seated on a throne in the midst of what
looks like stage architecture, while HYPNOS (Sleep) and
THANATOS (Death) fly towards her carrying the body of
the dead Sarpedon. Elsewhere in ancient art, Europa carried off by the bull is a favourite subject from the sixth
century BC (fig. 56). It was also very popular among postclassical painters, with versions existing by Titian (with a
particularly benign bull), Tintoretto, Veronese, Rubens,
Rembrandt and Claude, among many others.

Europa gave her name to the continent of Europe –
appropriately, since the Minoan civilisation that flourished on Crete, taking its name from Europa's son Minos,
was the first great civilisation in European history. The
bull whose form Zeus took to abduct her is commemorated in the stars as the constellation Taurus.

[Homer, *Iliad* 14.321–2; Hesiod, *Catalogue of Women* frr. 140–1;
Bacchylides, *Ode* 17.29–33; Apollonius, *Argonautica* 4.1643;
Apollodorus 2.5.7, 3.1.1–2, 3.4.2; Ovid, *Metamorphoses*
2.836–75, 6.103–7.]

Eurus

The East Wind and its god. Presumably he was, like the other winds, the son of EOS, goddess of Dawn, and the Titan Astraeus, even though Hesiod does not mention him by name in this genealogy in his *Theogony* (378–80). Unlike his brothers BOREAS (the North Wind) and ZEPHYRUS (the West Wind), Eurus has no particular mythological story associated with him.

Euryale *see* GORGONS.

Euryalus (1)

Son of MECISTEUS and one of the EPIGONI who conquered Thebes. He also sailed with the ARGONAUTS. With DIOMEDES (2) and STHENELUS (3) he led the Argive contingent of eighty ships to fight in the TROJAN WAR. In the funeral games for Patroclus he had the courage to stand against the mighty EPEIUS (2) in the boxing contest, but was felled by a single blow.

[Homer, *Iliad* 2.559–68, 6.20–8, 23.653–99; Apollodorus 1.9.13, 1.9.16, 3.7.2–3.]

Euryalus (2) *see* NISUS (2).

Eurybates

A herald who went with ODYSSEUS from Ithaca to the TROJAN WAR. Twice Eurybates was sent on official duty to ACHILLES' tent: when Agamemnon decided to commandeer Achilles' concubine Briseis, it was Eurybates, together with TALTHYBIUS, who reluctantly went to fetch her (fig. 3). He also, with Odius, accompanied the embassy sent by Agamemnon to try and persuade the angry Achilles back into battle. Homer describes him as 'round-shouldered and swarthy, with thick, curly hair'.

[Homer, *Iliad* 1.318–48, 2.182–4, 9.163–78, *Odyssey* 19.244–8.]

Eurybia

Daughter of Pontus (Sea) and GAIA (Earth). She bore ASTRAEUS, PALLAS (2) and PERSES (1) to the Titan CRIUS. Hesiod, for some unknown reason, says that she had a heart of adamant in her breast.

[Hesiod, *Theogony* 239, 375–7.]

Eurycleia

The devoted old slave in ODYSSEUS' household who nursed both him and his son TELEMACHUS. Odysseus' father LAERTES once bought her for twenty oxen (a goodly sum, since the usual price seems to have been four oxen). He valued her as highly as his own wife ANTICLEIA, but never slept with her for fear of his wife's anger. Eurycleia, like EUMAEUS the swineherd, is one of the humble characters in the *Odyssey* who have remained completely loyal to the household in Odysseus' long absence, and who

play an important part in his return.

Eurycleia is the chief female servant in the palace and is so well trusted that she has been put in charge of Odysseus' treasure house. She is a delightful character, robust and outspoken, and passionately concerned with the welfare of the family. When Odysseus comes home to the palace disguised as a beggar, Eurycleia is set by PENELOPE to wash his feet, and in so doing she recognises her master from an old scar on his leg once made by the tusk of a wild boar (19.467–75):

> The old woman, with the scar in the palms of her hands,
> knew it as she touched it, and she let his foot go.
> His leg fell on the basin, and the bronze vessel rang
> and tipped to one side, and the water spilled on the floor.
> Joy and pain seized her at once, and her eyes
> were filled with tears, and her lusty voice was checked.
> Taking him by his chin, she said to Odysseus: 'Yes,
> dear child, you really are Odysseus, I did not
> know you before, not till I had touched my master.'

She is about to cry to Penelope the happy news of his return when Odysseus stops her mouth with his hands, for the time has not yet come for his wife to know of his presence.

Eurycleia abets the killing of the Suitors by barring the doors to shut them in, and when they have all been slaughtered she begins to raise the cry of triumph, until once again Odysseus silences her. She tells him which of the serving-women have been disloyally sleeping with the Suitors, and these are put to death. Finally she exultantly takes the news of Odysseus' return and the Suitors' massacre to Penelope, and husband and wife are joyfully reunited.

[Homer, *Odyssey* 1.427–35, 2.337–81, 4.742–57, 19.357–505, 20.128–59, 21.380–7, 22.394–497, 23.1–84.]

Eurydice (1) *see* ORPHEUS.

Eurydice (2)

Wife of ACRISIUS, king of Argos, and mother of DANAE.

Eurydice (3)

Wife of ILUS, king of Troy, and mother of LAOMEDON.

Eurydice (4)

Wife of CREON (2), regent of Thebes, and mother of HAEMON.

Euryganeia

In fifth-century BC tragedy, OEDIPUS unwittingly married his own mother, Jocasta, and had four children by her; but in earlier epic, they discovered their incest before any children were born and Jocasta hanged herself from shame. Oedipus then married Euryganeia, the daughter of Hyperphas, and it was she who bore him his four children. She was thus alive to suffer the fateful conflict between her two sons, Eteocles and POLYNEICES, over the rule of Thebes, and is probably the unnamed mother of the warring boys in the long papyrus fragment of Stesichorus in Lille (PLille 76a, b, c; fr. 222b). Pausanias speaks of a painting by Onasias showing Euryganeia 'bowed with grief because of the fight between her children'.

[Apollodorus 3.5.8; Pausanias 9.5.10–11.]

Eurylochus

In the *Odyssey*, Eurylochus is ODYSSEUS' brother-in-law, married to his sister Ctimene, and is the second-in-command of his ship. He leads the scouting party to CIRCE's palace on Aeaea, though he has the sense to suspect danger and to wait outside when the rest of his party are welcomed indoors by the enchantress. Thus when they are turned into pigs by her magic potion, he is able to get safely away and take the sorry news back to the ship. Odysseus, with the help of Hermes, counters Circe's magic, but even now Eurylochus is loath to go anywhere near the enchantress, and it is only fear of his captain's anger that makes him return.

Unfortunately he is less aware of danger when the ship later approaches the island of Thrinacia, for it is he who forces Odysseus to land there, and he who persuades his shipmates to kill and eat the sacred cattle of the Sungod HELIOS, despite the solemn warnings earlier given by the seer Teiresias. Zeus, in anger, sends a violent storm against them once they put to sea again. The ship breaks up, and only Odysseus, who took no part in the sacrilege, survives to tell the tale (12.417–19):

> My men were thrown into the water, and bobbing like sea-crows were carried away by the waves from around the black ship, and the god took away their homecoming.

[Homer, *Odyssey* 10.203–448, 12.270–419.]

Eurymachus

In the *Odyssey*, Eurymachus is the son of the Ithacan noble Polybus. He is one of the two leading Suitors, the young men who have invaded ODYSSEUS' house during his long absence, carousing at his expense and hoping to marry his wife PENELOPE. Eurymachus insults Odysseus when he comes home to his palace, disguised as an old beggar, and throws a footstool at him. The seer THEOCLYMENUS (1) predicts disaster for the Suitors, but Eurymachus mocks him and calls him insane. When retribution at last comes, and Odysseus begins by killing the worst of the Suitors, ANTINOUS, Eurymachus at first pleads on their behalf. When this is to no avail he urges them all to fight, and is himself the second to be killed. The disloyal maid

MELANTHO, who had been his mistress, is hanged.

[Homer, *Odyssey* 2.177–207, 18.349–98, 20.359–70, 21.245–55, 22.44–88.]

Eurynome

Daughter of OCEANUS and Tethys, and mother by ZEUS of the GRACES and, according to some, of the river-god ASOPUS. In the *Iliad*, where HEPHAESTUS is married to one of the Graces and so has Eurynome for his mother-in-law, he relates how she, together with THETIS, saved him when he was flung from the heights of heaven by Hera. He lived with them for nine years, working as a smith.

According to an obscure tradition found in Apollonius, Eurynome was the most ancient of the goddesses, ruling over Olympus with her consort Ophion until, after a violent struggle, they were supplanted, he by CRONUS and she by RHEA (1), and fell into the river of Ocean. Eurynome had an ancient sanctuary at Phigalia in Arcadia, where her wooden image had the head and torso of a woman and the tail of a fish.

[Homer, *Iliad* 18.394–405; Hesiod, *Theogony* 358, 907–11; Apollonius, *Argonautica* 1.503–7; Apollodorus 3.12.6; Pausanias 8.41.4–6.]

Eurypylus (1)

Son of Evaemon who led forty ships from Thessaly to the TROJAN WAR. In the *Iliad* Eurypylus kills several Trojans, but is finally put out of action with an arrow wound in his leg by PARIS. Limping back to the Greek camp he meets PATROCLUS, who has been learning from Nestor how disastrously the Greeks are faring in battle and who now tends Eurypylus' wound. It is this encounter which helps to bring about Patroclus' death, for it moves his pity for all his beleaguered comrades, reinforcing his decision to dress in Achilles' armour and beat back the Trojans.

Eurypylus survived the war, and in the division of the spoils after the sack of Troy he won as his portion a chest in which there was an ancient image of DIONYSUS, made by Hephaestus and once given by Zeus to DARDANUS, the ancestor of the Trojan kings. When Eurypylus saw the image he was stricken with madness. Going in a rare moment of lucidity to consult the Delphic Oracle, he was told that he must settle in a land where he found a people making a strange sacrifice. The winds took his ship to Patrae in Achaea, and he realised that the oracle had been fulfilled when he saw a beautiful girl and youth about to be sacrificed to Artemis, an annual custom there ever since a sacrilege was committed by COMAETHO (1) and Melanippus. Moreover the people of Patrae had been instructed by an oracle that they might put an end to the cruel annual rite when a strange king came to their land, bringing a strange god; and when Eurypylus arrived, bearing the image of Dionysus, they too recognised the fulfilment of the oracle. The annual sacrifice was ended and Eurypylus settled in Patrae, completely cured of his madness.

[Homer, *Iliad* 2.734–7, 5.76–83, 6.36, 11.575–95, 806–48, 15.390–404; Pausanias 7.19.1–10.]

Eurypylus (2)

Son of TELEPHUS, king of Teuthrania, and Astyoche. His mother refused to let him fight in the TROJAN WAR, but her brother, King PRIAM of Troy, overcame her scruples with the gift of a golden vine, made by Hephaestus and once given by Zeus to Tros in recompense for the loss of his son GANYMEDE. Eurypylus then led a large Mysian force to Troy, where he fought valiantly, killing several Greeks including PENELEOS and MACHAON, until he was himself killed by Achilles' son NEOPTOLEMUS.

[Homer, *Odyssey* 11.519–21; Epic Cycle, Proclus' summary of the *Little Iliad*; Apollodorus, *Epitome* 5.12; Pausanias 9.5.15, 10.27.2; Quintus of Smyrna, *Sequel to Homer* 8.128–220.]

Eurysaces ('Broad-shield')

Son of AJAX (1) and TECMESSA, born to them at Troy and named after his father's most characteristic weapon, the huge shield seven hides thick and covered with bronze. At the time of Ajax' suicide, Eurysaces was still only a small child. In Sophocles' *Ajax*, which deals with the hero's madness and death, Ajax shows the boy the bloody remains of all the animals he has killed while mad, saying, 'Lift him up, lift him to me. For he will not be afraid to see this fresh-shed blood, if he is indeed a true son of his father' (545–7). Nor is Eurysaces afraid; and it may be that Sophocles was pointing a contrast between his stoutness of heart and the fear which

ASTYANAX, son of the Trojan hero Hector, displayed in a famous scene in Homer's *Iliad* (6.466–73) when he shrank in terror from his father's plumed helmet.

Before killing himself, Ajax entrusted his son to the care of his half-brother TEUCER (2), who after the fall of Troy returned to Salamis where his father TELAMON was king, taking the boy with him. When Telamon died, Eurysaces became king of Salamis.

In historical times, the Athenians claimed that Eurysaces had handed Salamis over to Athens and had become an Athenian citizen. Certainly he had a hero-cult in Athens, and eminent Athenians such as Miltiades, Cimon and Alcibiades claimed descent from him.

[Plutarch, *Solon* 10; Pausanias 1.35.1–3.]

Eurystheus

Son of STHENELUS (1) and Nicippe, grandson of PERSEUS, and great-grandson of ZEUS. His destiny from birth was bound up with that of the great hero HERACLES. Homer tells how Eurystheus, instead of Heracles, became king of all the Argolid, including Mycenae and Tiryns, because of the goddess HERA's interference with their births (*Iliad* 19.95–133): when Heracles, Zeus' mightiest son, was about to be born to ALCMENE, Zeus rashly boasted that on that very day would be born a child of his own lineage who would grow up to rule over all those around him. Hera, angry and jealous of this child by a mortal woman, craftily made Zeus swear that this would indeed be so. She then came down to earth from Olympus, and with the help of the birth-goddess, EILEITHYIA, held back the birth of Heracles, at the same time bringing forward Eurystheus' birth prematurely at seven months. Triumphant she returned to Olympus:

> And she announced to Zeus, son of Cronos: 'Father Zeus, lord of the bright lightning, I have a message for your heart. Today is born a great man who will rule over all the Argives: Eurystheus, son of Sthenelus and of the line of Perseus, your own descendant. He is not unfit to be lord over the Argives.' So she spoke, and a bitter sorrow struck him deep in his heart ... and forever he would grieve when he saw his dear son labouring at one of his shameful tasks for Eurystheus.

These tasks were the twelve great LABOURS OF HERACLES, performed while he served Eurystheus for twelve years. In the *Odyssey* (11.617–26), the ghost of Heracles in Hades laments his harsh fate, that even though he was the son of the great god Zeus, it was ever his miserable lot on

Fig.57 **Eurystheus hides in a great jar as Heracles prepares to ram down the Erymanthian Boar on top of him.**

earth to serve a much lesser man than himself; and indeed Eurystheus is generally depicted as cowardly or cruel. When Heracles returned to Mycenae with the result of his first Labour, the huge Nemean Lion, the king was so terrified that he had a huge bronze jar set in the earth as a refuge from danger. He ordered Heracles never to enter the city again, but to leave his trophies outside the gates. From this point on, Eurystheus gave him no direct commissions, but sent his commands through a herald, COPREUS. In ancient art, the terrified Eurystheus is shown hiding in his great jar while Heracles delivers the fruits of two of his Labours, the Erymanthian Boar (fig. 57) and (rarely) Cerberus (fig. 37).

Even after Heracles' death and apotheosis, Eurystheus continued to persecute his children, the HERACLIDS. With their grandmother Alcmene, they fled for refuge to Ceyx, king of Trachis, but he was afraid to help them because Eurystheus was threatening war. They came to Athens, still with their persecutor and an armed force in pursuit, where King Theseus, or his sons Acamas and Demophon, accepted their appeal for help. The Athenians duly defeated the Argive army. Eurystheus was killed, either by Heracles' old henchman IOLAUS, or by Heracles' son Hyllus at the Scironian Rocks on the Isthmus of Corinth. Hyllus then cut off the king's head and brought it to Alcmene, Heracles' mother, who gouged out the eyes with weaving-pins. According to Euripides' play *The Children of Heracles*, Eurystheus was captured alive by Iolaus but Alcmene insisted on his death. Because this was against the wishes of the Athenians, Eurystheus promised that, if they interred him in Attic soil, his body would protect their land from invasion. He was buried towards the north-east of Attica, his body at Pallene/Gargettus and his head at Trycorithus.

[Pindar, *Pythian* 9.79–81; Euripides, *Children of Heracles* 1026–37; Apollodorus 2.4.12–2.5.12, 2.8.1; Strabo 8.6.19.]

Eurytion (1)

Son or grandson of Actor and king of Phthia, where PELEUS took refuge after the murder of PHOCUS (1) and was purified of blood-guilt either by Actor or by Eurytion. Peleus was also given a third of the kingdom, and the hand in marriage of Eurytion's daughter Antigone, who bore him a daughter, Polydora. Eurytion and Peleus sailed with the ARGONAUTS and went together to the CALYDONIAN BOARHUNT. Here Peleus accidentally killed his father-in-law with a spear-cast aimed at the boar.

[Apollonius, *Argonautica* 1.71–4; Apollodorus 3.13.1–2.]

Eurytion (2) (also Eurytus)

One of the CENTAURS who rioted drunkenly at the wedding of Peirithous and Hippodameia, and even tried to carry off the bride. He later fought HERACLES at the cave of PHOLUS. Heracles finally killed Eurytion to save Mnesimache, the daughter of DEXAMENUS, king of Olenus, from a forced marriage with the Centaur.

[Homer, *Odyssey* 21.295–304; Apollodorus 2.5.4, 2.5.5.]

Eurytion (3)

The cowherd of GERYON, king of Erytheia. HERACLES killed both Eurytion and the dog ORTHUS when he stole Geryon's cattle (fig. 60).

Eurytus (1)

Son of MELANEUS, the son of APOLLO, and Stratonice. Eurytus was king of Oechalia, a city variously located in either Thessaly, Messenia or Euboea, and had four sons, Iphitus, Clytius, Toxeus and Deion (or Deioneus), and a beautiful daughter, IOLE. A late legend makes him the father of DRYOPE. As grandson of the archer-god Apollo, Eurytus was naturally a famous archer, and it was he, some said, who trained HERACLES in the use of the bow. According to Homer, Eurytus was so proud of his skill that he challenged Apollo to an archery contest and was killed by the god for his presumption. His great bow passed on his death to his son Iphitus, and was later given by Iphitus to ODYSSEUS when the two young men met and became friends. It was with this bow that Odysseus eventually slew the Suitors, the young men who had invaded his home on Ithaca to woo his wife, Penelope.

A more familiar version of Eurytus' death makes it the result of a feud with Heracles. Eurytus promised to marry his daughter Iole to whoever could beat him and his sons in an archery contest. Heracles took up the challenge and won the contest, but against Iphitus' wishes Eurytus refused to honour his word: he was afraid that Heracles might go mad and kill any children he had by Iole, just as he had killed his children by MEGARA. Heracles left Oechalia in anger. Soon afterwards twelve of Eurytus' mares went missing, either taken by Heracles out of spite, or stolen by the arch-thief AUTOLYCUS and sold to Heracles. Iphitus, confident that Heracles was innocent, went in search of the mares (or cattle, according to Apollodorus). Having invited Heracles to help him find the beasts, he stayed as his guest at Tiryns. Heracles took him up to the top of the palace walls and in a fit of rage hurled him down to his death. In expiation for this crime, Heracles was forced by the gods to serve the Lydian queen Omphale as a slave for either one or three years.

Some years later, after Heracles had married DEIANEIRA, he returned to Oechalia with an army, determined on revenge. He sacked the city and killed Eurytus and his surviving sons, then carried off Iole as his concubine. This deed brought about his own death, for Deianeira sent him a robe smeared with the blood of the Centaur Nessus, believing it to be a love-charm that would win back his love, when in fact it was a deadly poison that ate into his flesh like acid.

The Samian epic poet Creophylus wrote a *Capture of Oechalia*, now lost; but the aftermath of Heracles' fateful revenge is dramatised in Sophocles' extant tragedy *The Women of Trachis*. The famous archery contest is an occasional subject of ancient vase-paintings.

[Homer, *Iliad* 2.729–33, *Odyssey* 8.223–8, 21.11–33; Hesiod, *Catalogue of Women* fr. 26; Sophocles, *Women of Trachis* 252–80, 476–8; Apollonius, *Argonautica* 1.86–9, 2.114–16; Apollodorus 2.4.9, 2.4.11, 2.6.1–3, 2.7.7; Diodorus Siculus 4.31.1–3; Pausanias 4.2.2–3, 4.33.5.]

Eurytus (2) *see* GIANTS.

Eurytus (3) *see* MOLIONES.

Eurytus (4) *see* EURYTION (2).

Euterpe *see* MUSES.

Euthymus

Son of either the god of the River Caecinus, in the toe of Italy, or the mortal Astycles. He was a famous boxer, several times winning the crown for boxing at the Olympic Games. On his return to Italy he settled at Temesa, where he found the town plagued by the ghost of POLITES (2), one of Odysseus' comrades. Polites had raped a local girl when drunk and the inhabitants had stoned him to death. After this his angry ghost haunted the town, killing old and young indiscriminately, until the Delphic Oracle advised the townspeople to propitiate him by building a temple and sacrificing every year the most beautiful girl in Temesa. This they did, until the time of Euthymus' arrival. He found the annual sacrifice to Polites' ghost about to take place, but he fell in love with the intended victim and resolved to save her. Dressed in armour, he awaited the ghost, and when it appeared he attacked it and drove it into the sea. It disappeared for ever and Euthymus married the girl he had saved. He lived to a ripe old age, and instead of dying disappeared in mysterious circumstances.

[Pausanias 6.6.4–10.]

Evadne (1)

Daughter of POSEIDON and a Spartan nymph, Pitane, whose father was the river-god Eurotas. Pitane gave Evadne to be brought up by Aepytus, a king of Arcadia. Evadne too grew up to be beautiful and to be seduced by a god, in her case APOLLO. When she found that she was pregnant, she tried to keep it a secret from her guardian, but he discov-

ered the truth. Angry and worried, he went to the Delphic Oracle for advice. There he was told that Apollo was the father of the child, who would be a boy and was destined to become a great prophet. Now easy in his mind, Aepytus returned home. Evadne, meanwhile, had given birth to her son. Not daring to take him home, she had abandoned him in a thicket, but the gods sent two snakes who fed the baby with honey. Five days later Aepytus and Evadne found him alive and well, lying in a bed of violets; so they took him home called him Iamus, 'child of the violets'.

[Pindar, *Olympian* 6.27–74.]

Evadne (2)

Daughter of IPHIS (1). She was married to CAPANEUS, one of the warriors in the expedition of the SEVEN AGAINST THEBES. When he was killed she threw herself into his funeral pyre, an action dramatised in a daring coup de théâtre by Euripides in his tragedy *Suppliant Women* (985–1071). 'To die a death with the one you love is the sweetest death of all', she cries from high above the pyre, 'and this may the gods grant me!' Her old father cannot reach her physically and tries to dissuade her from dying, but fails. 'I let my body go', she says. 'My end is a grief to you, but to me, and to my husband with me in the fire, a joy.' And with this, she falls into the flames.

Evander

Son of HERMES and an Arcadian nymph, Themis or Nicostrate, the daughter of the River Ladon. In Greece Evander was a minor deity worshipped in Arcadia and associated with PAN. In Roman legend his mother was identified with the prophetic Roman goddess Carmentis, and Evander himself was thought to have been the first settler on the future site of Rome. Having led a small colony from Arcadia, he founded a new city on a hill near the Tiber, naming it Pallanteum after his home town. The hill was later called the Palatine. HERCULES visited Evander and aided him by killing the fire-breathing monster, CACUS, who lived on human flesh.

When AENEAS came to Pallanteum, seeking allies in his war with the Latins, Evander was an old man, too old himself to fight; but he entrusted his beloved son PALLAS (4) to Aeneas, sending with him a large contingent of cavalry. Pallas was killed by TURNUS, and it was to avenge his death that Aeneas later slew Turnus pitilessly when he had him at his mercy.

[Dionysius of Halicarnassus 1.31; Pausanias 8.43.2, 8.44.5; Livy 1.5.1–2; Virgil, *Aeneid* 8.51–369, 455–519; Ovid, *Fasti* 1.461–586, 5.91–100.]

Evenus *see* MARPESSA.

F

Fates (Greek, *Moirai*; Latin, *Parcae* or *Fata*)

The goddesses who appointed the deaths of mortals. Hesiod, in his *Theogony* (217–22), says that they were the daughters of NYX (Night), though later he calls them daughters of ZEUS and THEMIS and sisters of the HORAE (901–6). They were three in number and were named Clotho ('the Spinner'), Lachesis ('the Apportioner') and Atropos ('the Inevitable'). Their names reveal their particular tasks: Clotho spun the thread of a man's life, Lachesis measured it out to its allotted length, and Atropos cut it off when the time for death was come.

Even the gods, it seems, were subject to the decrees of the Fates. In the *Iliad* (16.433–61), Zeus knows that his beloved son SARPEDON is destined to die at the hands of Patroclus, and – much as he grieves – he does nothing to save him. All he can do is to mark his son's death by raining blood down on the battlefield, then have his body carried by Sleep and Death for honourable burial in his homeland of Lycia. Twice Zeus weighs in his golden scales the fates of heroes (HECTOR and ACHILLES, Greeks and Trojans) to discover what is ordained, and in each case one fate (Hector, the Greeks) comes down heavier, signifying death (22.209–13, 8.69–74). In the *Odyssey* (3.236–8), Athena explains to Telemachus that a man's death is fixed: 'Death comes to everyone alike, and not even the gods can fend it away from a man they love, when the destructive doom of death lays a man low and overpowers him.' In one instance, however, the Fates were tricked by APOLLO into changing a man's allotted destiny. When it came time for Apollo's favourite ADMETUS to die, the god made the Fates drunk, then persuaded them to reprieve Admetus from his appointed day of death, so long as he could find someone willing to die in his place.

The Fates played only an occasional part in mythological events. They helped Zeus in the battle of the Gods and the GIANTS by killing the Giants Agrius and Thoas. They helped him again in his contest with the monster TYPHON by persuading Typhon to eat fruit which, they assured him mendaciously, would strengthen him. Zeus won the contest and Typhon ended up crushed beneath Mount Etna. Only once did the Fates communicate directly with mortals about their destiny. When MELEAGER was born, they appeared to his mother Althaea and told her that her son would live until a log, then burning on the hearth, was completely burnt away. Althaea immediately quenched the flames and put the log away in a chest, keeping it safe for many years. Only when Meleager angered her by killing her brothers did she take the log from its safe hiding place and throw it into the fire. The log burnt to ashes and Meleager died.

In Catullus' long poem (64) about the wedding of PELEUS and THETIS, the Fates sing the marriage song and spin their thread, telling the fate of Achilles. They attend the wedding on the François Krater and on the Sophilos dinos in the British Museum. In the postclassical arts they are often depicted spinning the destinies of men; and Milton, in his *Lycidas*, gives a memorable image of Atropos' fated task:

> Comes the blind Fury with the abhorréd shears
> And slits the thin-spun life.

[Homer, *Iliad* 13.602, 18.119, 20.127–8, 24.49, 209–10, *Odyssey* 7.197–8; Hesiod, *Shield of Heracles* 258–63; Pindar, *Pythian* 4.145–6; Aeschylus, *Eumenides* 723–8, 956–67, *Prometheus Bound* 515–8; Euripides, *Alcestis* 10–14; Aristophanes, *Frogs* 448–53; Apollodorus 1.3.1, 1.6.2–3, 1.8.2, 1.9.15; Pausanias 2.11.4, 8.42.3, 10.24.4. B. C. Dietrich, *Death, Fate and the Gods* (1967).]

Faunus

Italian god of the wild forests and protector of flocks, who was identified with the Greek pastoral god PAN. Faunus was one of the early kings of Latium, being the son of PICUS, the grandson of SATURN, and the father, by the water-nymph Marica, of LATINUS, king of the Latins when AENEAS arrived in Italy. Faunus was an oracular god, who could reveal the future through dreams or supernatural voices in sacred groves, as he does to Latinus in Virgil's *Aeneid* (7.45–103), warning him that he should marry his daughter Lavinia not to a Latin but a foreigner. Faunus' name is given in the plural to the fauns (*fauni*), wild woodland creatures who were part-man and part-goat, identified with the Greek SATYRS.

Faustulus

The shepherd who found the abandoned twins ROMULUS AND REMUS, and with his wife ACCA LARENTIA brought them up.

Flood *see* DEUCALION (1).

Flora

An ancient Italian goddess of flowers and spring. According to Ovid, she was originally a nymph named Chloris who was loved by the West Wind, ZEPHYRUS. At his kiss she was transformed into Flora, and breathed out flowers that spread over all the earth, just as the cold earth in spring is warmed by the gentle West Wind into blossoming.

Being a fertility goddess, Flora was able to help JUNO when she grew annoyed with Jupiter for producing Min-

erva from his own head, without the need of a female. Flora gave Juno a magical herb at whose touch she became pregnant. She gave birth to MARS, the Roman god of war.

Flora was painted by many postclassical artists, most famously by Botticelli, who depicts Ovid's myth in his *Primavera*, with Chloris fading in Zephyrus' grasp and becoming the radiant, queenly Flora.

[Ovid, *Fasti* 5.183–37.]

Fortuna

The Roman goddess of fate, chance and luck, identified with the Greek goddess TYCHE.

Furies (Greek, *Erinyes*; Latin, *Furiae* or *Dirae*)

Goddesses of retribution who exacted punishment for murder and other serious crimes, particularly of kin against kin, and who guarded the established order of the world. Hesiod says that they were born (appropriately) from an act of violence of son against father: from the drops of blood that fell on GAIA, the Earth, when Cronus hacked off the genitals of Uranus. Thus they belong to the oldest generation of divinities, more ancient and more primitive than the Olympian gods. Aeschylus makes them the daughters of NYX (Night), which is also appropriate to the aura of dread that surrounded them. They were later said to be three in number, and to be named Alecto, Megaera and Tisiphone. They were also given the propitiatory names of *Eumenides*, 'Kindly Ones', and *Semnai*, 'Revered Ones'.

We see the Furies in action as the Chorus of Aeschylus' *Eumenides*, the third play in his tragic trilogy the *Oresteia*, where they have mercilessly maddened ORESTES and pursued him to Delphi for the murder of his mother, CLYTEMNESTRA. In the opening scene of the play, the

Fig. 58 Orestes, flanked by Athena and Apollo, takes refuge from the Furies at Delphi. The busts in the top corners represent Clytemnestra and Pylades.

Pythia comes out of Apollo's sanctuary on her hands and knees, so appalled by the horrendous sight of the Furies inside that she is quite unable to stand. They are depicted as disgusting, loathsome creatures, repulsively dressed in black, wreathed in snakes, crawling on all fours to scent their prey, whining and howling like dogs; and indeed tradition had it that, at the first performance of the play, the appearance of the Furies was so terrifying that women in the audience fainted and suffered miscarriages. Orestes is sent for trial to the homicide court on the Areopagus in Athens, with Apollo acting as his advocate and the Furies as his prosecutors. When the jury's votes turn out to be equal, Athena gives the casting vote in Orestes' favour and he is acquitted. The play ends with the Furies conciliated by a new cult at Athens, in which they are honoured in their new role as beneficent powers.

Another famous matricide pursued by the Furies and hounded into madness was ALCMAEON, though in his case we are not so fortunate as to have any extant tragedy dramatising his plight. We also see the Furies, in many places in ancient literature, extracting vengeance for crimes apart from matricide. In Homer, for instance, they torment OEDIPUS after the suicide of his mother, Epicaste; they hear Althaea's prayers and curses when her son MELEAGER kills her brother; they fulfil Amyntor's curse on his son, PHOENIX (3), by ensuring that he has no children of his own; and they punish those who swear false oaths. They came to be seen as goddesses who not only exacted vengeance on earth for crimes committed, but also punished sinners after death, torturing and terrifying the shades of the dead in the Underworld. In art they are usually depicted as winged, their hair entwined with snakes, and carrying torches and scourges (figs. 41, 58, 73 and 88).

[Homer, *Iliad* 9.453–56, 566–72, 19.87, 259–60, 418, 21.412–14, *Odyssey* 2.135, 11.279–80, 15.234, 17.475, 20.77–8; Hesiod, *Theogony* 182–7, 472–3; Pindar, *Olympian* 2.38–42; Apollodorus 1.1.4; Pausanias 1.28.6, 2.11.4; Virgil, *Aeneid* 6.570–2, 7.324–6, 12.845–8; Ovid, *Metamorphoses* 4.451–511.]

G

Gaia or Ge

The Earth, and the primordial goddess of the Earth. According to the Greek creation myth of Hesiod's *Theogony*, Gaia was the first goddess to be born after CHAOS, the dark primeval void, came into being. She was followed by TARTARUS, with his dim realms far below the earth, and by EROS, the god of sexual love. Without a mate Gaia bore Uranus (Sky), the Mountains, and Pontus (Sea); then Uranus mated with his mother and she bore the TITANS: OCEANUS, COEUS, CRIUS, HYPERION, IAPETUS, THEIA, RHEA (1), THEMIS, MNEMOSYNE, PHOEBE (1), TETHYS, and last of all CRONUS. Next Gaia bore to Uranus the three one-eyed giants, the CYCLOPES (Brontes, Steropes and Arges), and the three HUNDRED-HANDERS (Briareos, Cottus and Gyges), monstrous giants each with a hundred arms and fifty heads. But Uranus hated his children so much that he pushed them back into the womb of their mother the Earth, until Gaia was overwhelmed with the pain of it. She begged her sons to help her, but they were all afraid – except for Cronus, who took from her a great sickle of adamant and lay in wait for his father. Uranus came with the night, and as he lay over Gaia, Cronus reached out and hacked off his genitals, flinging them far away into the sea. Drops of blood were scattered over Gaia, and from these were born the Erinyes (FURIES), the GIANTS, and the Meliads (NYMPHS of ash trees). The severed genitals were carried over the waves, and from the foam (*aphros*) that gathered around them was born APHRODITE, the goddess of love. Cronus released his brothers and sisters from inside their mother. Gaia later mated with another of her sons, Pontus, bearing five more children, NEREUS, THAUMAS, PHORCYS, CETO and EURYBIA.

Cronus now reigned supreme, but fearing the power of his brothers, the Hundred-handers and the Cyclopes, he imprisoned them in Tartarus. He learnt from Gaia that he was destined to be overthrown by his own son, so he swallowed all the children that his sister Rhea bore him as soon as they were born. Rhea in her sorrow turned to

her mother for advice, and Gaia saved the last of Rhea's children, ZEUS, by hiding him safely in Crete and giving Cronus a stone wrapped in swaddling clothes instead of the baby. Cronus was deceived and swallowed the stone.

When Zeus grew to maturity he set out to recover his brothers and sisters and to overthrow his father. With the help of Gaia (or of METIS) he induced Cronus to disgorge his children, then battled against his father in a war lasting ten years. Some of the Titans fought alongside Cronus, while Zeus was supported by his now regurgitated brothers and sisters, and by the Cyclopes and Hundred-handers whom he had freed from Tartarus on the advice of Gaia. At last he was victorious, overthrowing Cronus just as Gaia had predicted. She now advised the other gods to choose him as their ruler, and he reigned supreme. But he imprisoned his father and the hostile Titans in the depths of Tartarus, and this made Gaia angry. She stirred up her offspring, the Giants, to fight against Zeus and the other gods, a rebellion that ended in defeat. She also mated with Tartarus and bore the gigantic monster TYPHON as a final challenge to Zeus' power, but Zeus overcame him and flung him into Tartarus. Thereafter Gaia accepted her grandson's supremacy as king of the gods. She even helped him when his first wife Metis was pregnant, telling him that Metis' second child was destined, like Zeus himself, to overthrow his father. Zeus followed Cronus' example and swallowed Metis, and in due course brought forth her daughter ATHENA from his own head. When he married his sister HERA, Gaia attended the wedding and gave Hera the golden apples of the HESPERIDES.

Many other children are sometimes credited to Gaia, such as the monster ECHIDNA, the giant TITYUS, and TRIPTOLEMUS, who transmitted Demeter's gifts of grain and agriculture among mortals. Gaia also produced the huge scorpion that killed ORION when he boasted that he would hunt down all the animals on earth. The Athenian king ERICHTHONIUS (1) was also said to be earth-born, grown from the semen that HEPHAESTUS spilt on the ground when he tried to rape Athena. The scene of Erichthonius' birth sometimes appears on Attic vases, where Gaia, depicted as a women emerging from the earth, hands over the baby to Athena (fig.53). She is also sometimes present in scenes showing the battle of the Gods and the Giants, again depicted as a woman rising from the earth (fig.66).

Gaia had prophetic powers and was closely associated with a number of oracles. It was said that APOLLO's Oracle at Delphi had been originally hers, and that it was she who set there as guardian the huge snake, PYTHON, which Apollo later killed. She was worshipped as a fertility goddess at shrines in many parts of Greece, though she tended as time went by to be superseded by the Olympian gods, as happened at Delphi. In Rome she was identified with Tellus or Terra.

[Homer, *Odyssey* 11.576; Hesiod, *Theogony* 116–200, 233–9, 453–506, 820–2, 881–5; Aeschylus, *Eumenides* 1–11; Apollodorus 1.1.1–5, 1.2.1, 1.2.6, 1.3.6, 1.5.2, 1.6.1–3, 2.1.2, 2.5.11, 3.8.1; Pausanias 1.2.6, 1.14.3, 1.22.3, 5.14.10, 7.25.13, 8.25.8–10, 10.5.5–7, 10.6.6.]

Galanthis

The slave girl of ALCMENE who, according to Ovid (*Metamorphoses* 9.280–323), helped her mistress at the birth of Heracles. EILEITHYIA, the goddess of childbirth, was on Hera's instructions holding back the birth by sitting outside the bedroom door, with legs crossed and fingers intertwined, murmuring spells. For seven days and seven nights Alcmene was in painful labour, and all to no avail. Then Galanthis tricked Eileithyia by suddenly announcing that the baby had been born. The goddess leaped to her feet in astonishment, loosening her clasped hands, and in that moment of inattention Heracles was at last born. Eileithyia punished Galanthis by turning her into a weasel (*gale* in Greek).

Pausanias (9.11.3) gives a somewhat different version of events, in which the birth was delayed by witches, and it was Historis, the daughter of Teiresias, who tricked them in a similar fashion to Galanthis.

Galatea (1) ('milk-white')

A NEREID, daughter of the sea-god NEREUS and the Oceanid Doris, living in the seas off Sicily. She was ardently wooed by the monstrously ugly Cyclops, POLYPHEMUS (2), but she loathed him quite as much as she adored the handsome Acis, the young son of Faunus and the river-nymph Symaethis. One day she was lying in her lover's arms when Polyphemus found them, and in a jealous rage

heaved up a huge chunk of the mountainside and flung it at them. Acis was crushed beneath it, but Galatea escaped and turned her lover into a river that would ever afterwards bear his name.

In the postclassical arts, Galatea often becomes a shepherdess or a milkmaid, a development originating in the pastoral settings of her story in the poetry of Theocritus, Virgil and Ovid. In painting she is a popular subject for sea-triumphs, elaborate compositions with sea-horses, cupids, Tritons and other Nereids, with famous versions existing by Raphael, Cambiaso and Giordano, among many others.

[Homer, *Iliad* 18.45; Hesiod, *Theogony* 250; Lucian, *Dialogues of the Sea-gods* 1.]

Galatea (2)

The name given to PYGMALION's statue that came to life.

Ganymede(s)

A Trojan prince, usually said to be the son of TROS and Callirhoe, daughter of the river-god SCAMANDER, though occasionally son of one of the other Trojan kings. According to Homer, Ganymede, because of his great beauty, was snatched up by the gods to be ZEUS' cupbearer on Olympus. There seems to be no sexual element in this early myth, but in later versions Zeus' interest in Ganymede becomes erotic and it is Zeus himself who

Fig.59 **The young Ganymede, rolling a hoop, holds a cock, a love-gift from Zeus.**

chooses to kidnap the boy. This was a popular scene on vase-paintings in the fifth century BC, many of them depicting also a cockerel, which was a favourite love-gift from a man to the boy he desired (fig. 59). In literature there are several versions of the abduction itself. In early myth Ganymede was carried off by a whirlwind, but later he was snatched up by an eagle, either a servant of Zeus bringing the boy to his master, or Zeus himself in disguise. Zeus sent HERMES to give Tros the glad news that his son would be forever immortal among the gods. He also recompensed him for his loss, either with some marvellous horses (which were later promised to Heracles as a reward for saving Hesione, *see* LAOMEDON), or with a golden vine wrought by Hephaestus (later used to inveigle EURYPYLUS (2) into going to the Trojan War, and to his death). Zeus immortalised Ganymede among the stars as the constellation Aquarius, and near him the eagle as Aquila; but for all the favouritism that he showed the boy, it did nothing in the end to help Troy: Zeus still allowed the city to be sacked by the Greeks.

The erotic interpretation of the myth appealed particularly to Roman poets, and from the Latin version of Ganymede's name comes our word 'catamite'. The allegorisers and moralists of the Renaissance read into the myth something more spiritual, seeing Ganymede as the symbol of the innocent soul ascending to heaven and finding its joy in God. But throughout the Middle Ages and the Renaissance, and later, Ganymede was also a symbol of homosexual love. His abduction was a favourite subject among artists, and was drawn or painted by (among many others) Correggio, Michelangelo, Rubens, Rembrandt and Tiepolo. Tennyson describes a picture of the rape in appealingly sensuous fashion in *The Palace of Art*:

> ... Or else flush'd Ganymede, his rosy thigh
> Half-buried in the Eagle's down.

But it was Rembrandt who saw the full horror of the abduction, painting Ganymede in the grip of the eagle as a terrified struggling child.

[Homer, *Iliad* 5.265–7, 20.231–5; *Homeric Hymn to Aphrodite* 202–17; Epic Cycle, *Little Iliad* fr.7; Pindar, *Olympian* 1.40–5; Euripides, *Trojan Women* 821–3; Apollodorus 2.5.9, 3.12.2; Lucian, *Dialogues of the Gods* 8; Virgil, *Aeneid* 1.28, 5.250–7; Ovid, *Metamorphoses* 10.152–61.]

Ge *see* GAIA.

Gelanor *see* DANAUS.

Gemini (The Twins)

A constellation immortalising the DIOSCURI, Castor and Polydeuces.

Geryon

Son of CHRYSAOR and the Oceanid Callirhoe, and according to Hesiod (*Theogony* 981) the strongest of all men – not surprisingly, since although Hesiod calls him merely three-headed, elsewhere in literature and art he is in fact triple-bodied, with his three forms joined at the waist. Usually in art he has three torsos and three pairs of legs, but just occasionally the tripling is from the waist up and he has only one pair of legs.

He lived on an island called Erytheia, 'the red land', located as its name suggests in the far west, the place of the setting sun, beyond the river of Ocean (*see* OCEANUS). Here he kept great herds of cattle, guarded by his herdsman, Eurytion, and his two-headed hound, ORTHUS. The tenth of the Labours performed by HERACLES (*see* LABOURS OF HERACLES) was to steal these herds and to bring them back to Eurystheus. Clearly Geryon would be a formidable opponent, with Heracles needing to overcome each of his three torsos individually before he could defeat the whole; but the location of Erytheia would also prove problematic, since he would need to find some way of crossing the river of Ocean encircling the earth. This he did by borrowing the bowl belonging to the Sun-god, HELIOS, in which the Sun sailed each night along Ocean, away from his setting in the west, to reach the east in time to bring the morning light to the world. Heracles dared to draw his bow at the Sun, who in admiration of his audacity lent him his great golden bowl. In this Heracles sailed to Erytheia, although not without incident, since Ocean sent huge waves to rock the bowl until Heracles frightened him into calm with his drawn bow.

The dog Orthus attacked Heracles as he approached the pasturing herds of cattle, so he killed it, and then the herdsman Eurytion, who was following close behind. But he was seen by another herdsman, MENOETES, who was tending the cattle belonging to Hades and now warned Geryon of the assault. So just as Heracles was driving away the herds, Geryon attacked him by the River Anthemus. After a fierce combat, Geryon was killed. Heracles loaded the cattle into the bowl and sailed away across Ocean. Returning the bowl to Helios, he herded the cattle overland to Mycenae, where Eurystheus sacrificed them to Hera.

Ancient art has depictions of Heracles sailing in the bowl of the Sun (fig.69), as well as many examples of the combat from the seventh century BC onwards, showing Heracles attacking Geryon with bow or sword or club (fig. 60). An early account of this Labour was given in a long and detailed poem, the *Geryoneis*, by the lyric poet Stesichorus, mostly, but fortunately not entirely, lost, for we possess a number of tantalising papyrus fragments which yet tell us a good deal about this early version of the myth. Geryon here is not only triple-bodied, with three torsos and six hands and feet, but has wings. Interestingly, the situation is seen from his point of view, and he seems to be shown as a sympathetic and apparently innocent defender of his own property in face of attack. His mother pleads with him not to risk his life; but he is determined to withstand Heracles, arguing that either he himself is immortal and ageless, in which case he cannot be harmed, or, if he is mortal, then it is better, as Chrysaor's son, to die a noble death now than to wait for hateful old age. A few lines describing the fatal combat survive. It seems that Heracles attacked one of Geryon's heads with a club, while he tackled another by knocking off the helmet, perhaps with a stone, then shooting Geryon with one of his arrows poisoned with the blood of the Hydra:

> ... it cut through the flesh and bone ... straight to the crown of his head, and stained his breastplate and bloody limbs with crimson gore. And Geryon drooped his neck to one side, like a poppy that suddenly sheds its petals, spoiling its tender beauty ...

[Hesiod, *Theogony* 287–94, 979–83; Pindar, fr.169a; Aeschylus, *Agamemnon* 870–3; Herodotus 4.8; Apollodorus 2.5.10; Pausanias 3.18.13, 5.19.1; Quintus of Smyrna, *Sequel to Homer* 6.249–55; Virgil, *Aeneid* 6.289.]

Giants

The Greek myths tell of many giants, but the creatures called simply Giants, *Gigantes*, were the sons of GAIA, the Earth, born from the drops of blood that fell on her when Cronus hacked off the genitals of his father, Uranus. The place of their birth was said to be Phlegrae on the peninsula of Pallene in Thrace. They were monstrous beings of invincible strength and hideous aspect, wild of hair, with huge bodies terminating in snaky coils instead of legs.

The Giants are famous for their war with the Olympian gods, known as the *Gigantomachia*. Gaia was angry because ZEUS had flung her children, the TITANS, into Tartarus, so she stirred up the Giants to rebellion. They demonstrated their hostility by hurling huge rocks and flaming trees at the heavens. Faced with this threat, the gods prepared for battle, our most detailed account of which is found in Apollodorus (1.6.1–3). An oracle had predicted that the gods alone would never kill the Giants, but that if they had the help of a mortal, the Giants would die. Gaia, learning of this, produced a magic herb that would protect her sons from all comers, mortal or god. Zeus countered her efforts by forbidding the Sun and the Moon and the Dawn to bring light to the earth, then himself plucked the herb and destroyed it. He sent ATHENA to summon the aid of the mortal HERACLES.

The strongest of the Giants, ALCYONEUS and PORPHYRION, were dealt with first. Heracles shot Alcyoneus with an

Fig.60 **Heracles fights three-bodied Geryon. The two-headed dog, Orthus, lies dead beneath. Behind Heracles, Athena chats to Iolaus near the dying Eurytion, while the woman behind Geryon is probably his grieving mother, Callirhoe.**

arrow, but when the Giant fell on his native earth he began to revive. On Athena's advice Heracles dragged him beyond the bounds of Pallene and he died. Zeus inspired Porphyrion with lust for HERA, then when he tried to rape her felled him with a thunderbolt. Heracles finished him off with one of his arrows. Ephialtes was slain by two arrows, one from APOLLO in his left eye and one from Heracles in his right eye. DIONYSUS killed Eurytus with his thyrsus. Clytius and Mimas were burnt to death, Clytius by HECATE's infernal torches and Mimas by missiles of red-hot metal hurled by HEPHAESTUS. ENCELADUS fled westward but Athena flung the island of Sicily on top of him, since when his fiery breath has blazed forth from Mount Etna. She also killed and flayed Pallas and used his tough skin as a shield. POSEIDON pursued Polybotes through the sea to Cos, then broke off a piece of the island and flung it on top of him, crushing him beneath what then became the island of Nisyros. HERMES, wearing the cap of invisibility that belonged to HADES, killed Hippolytus. ARTEMIS slew Gration. The FATES, fighting with clubs of bronze, killed Agrius and Thoas. The rest of the Giants were felled by Zeus' thunderbolts and finished off by Heracles' arrows as they lay dying. Thus the gods, with a mortal's help, were victorious over the Giants, and Gaia, angrier than ever, gave birth to the even more fearsome monster TYPHON.

The Gigantomachy is often confused with the Titanomachy, the war of the Titans with the Olympian gods, and also with the attempt on Olympus made by the gigantic Aloadae, OTUS and Ephialtes. Other giants are sometimes mentioned, whose immense size and prodigious strength entitle them to the term. Homer speaks of a savage race of giants and their king, Eurymedon, who once lived. Another race of giants, each with six huge arms and called by Apollonius the *Gegeneis*, 'Earthborn', were killed by Heracles and the ARGONAUTS on their voyage to Colchis. The Arcadians claimed that a small group of giants, led by Hopladamus, protected RHEA (1) from Cronus when she was pregnant with Zeus. Other famous giants were the hunter ORION, immortalised in the night sky, and TITYUS, who suffered eternal punishment in Hades, his vast bulk sprawled over two acres while two vultures continually tore at his liver. For the three giants Cottus, Briareos and Gyges, each with a hundred arms, *see* HUNDRED-HANDERS; and for their one-eyed giant brothers, *see* CYCLOPES.

The Gigantomachy was popular with ancient artists from the mid-sixth century into Roman times (fig. 66). The Giants are first depicted simply as warriors and only later as snake-legged monsters. The battle is a powerful subject in sculpture, the most famous renderings being those on the frieze of the Archaic treasury of the Siphnians at Delphi (Giants as armed warriors) and on the Hellenistic altar of Zeus at Pergamum (Giants with snaky tails). Euripides, in his *Ion* (205–18), describes scenes from the battle depicted on the west pediment of Apollo's temple at Delphi.

[Homer, *Odyssey* 7.58–60; Hesiod, *Theogony* 182–7; Pindar, *Nemean* 1.67–9; Euripides, *The Madness of Heracles* 177–80; Apollonius, *Argonautica* 1.940–1010; Diodorus Siculus 5.71.2–6; Pausanias 1.25.2, 8.29.1–4, 8.32.5, 8.36.2.]

Glauce

The daughter of CREON (1), king of Corinth, also known as Creusa. JASON married her, casting off his first wife MEDEA, the barbarian sorceress who had helped him to win the Golden Fleece. The outcome is powerfully dramatised in Euripides' tragedy *Medea*. Overcome with jealous rage and lust for revenge, but pretending friendship, Medea sends her rival a beautiful robe and coronet, both steeped in deadly poison. Glauce, quite unsuspecting, puts them on. At first she is entranced by her appearance, but soon the poison turns to flame, and robe and coronet consume her with a fierce fire. 'And the flesh dropped from her bones like resin from a pine torch', says the servant who reports her death. But this is not the extent of Medea's revenge. Creon, in an agony of grief, takes his daughter's corpse in his arms, crying, 'I wish I might die with you, child.' And die he does. He has his fill of lamentation, holding her to him; but when at last he tries to put her down and stand up, he finds that he is stuck fast to the robe, 'as ivy clings to laurel shoots', and in struggling to free himself, he too is killed, the frail flesh ripped from his bones.

Pausanias (2.3.6) reports that at Corinth there was a well called the Well of Glauce, so named because in her agony she threw herself into it.

[Euripides, *Medea* 1136–1221; Apollodorus 1.9.28; Diodorus Siculus 4.54.]

Glaucus (1)

A sea-god. He was born a mortal, living in the Boeotian city of Anthedon, but even as a mortal he passionately loved the sea and spent all his days near it, fishing with nets or with rod and line. One day he laid out his catch on some particularly verdant grass, only to see each fish come to life and wriggle back into the sea. Anxious to find out what magic properties the grass possessed, he ate some and was seized with an overwhelming desire to abandon the land and take to the sea for ever. He plunged beneath the waves and the sea-gods received him as one of themselves, cleansing him of any last traces of mortality. He found that he had taken on a new form: he now had a beard, tinted green like old bronze, the tail and fins of a fish, and long hair that covered his broad shoulders and streamed down his back.

Glaucus fell in love with the nymph SCYLLA (1), but she rejected his advances. He went to the enchantress CIRCE for a love-potion. Unfortunately Circe fell in love with him herself. When he repulsed her, the jealous enchantress poisoned the water of the pool in which the nymph bathed. When she next slipped into the water, she was turned into a monster that ever after preyed on sailors.

Like other sea-deities, Glaucus had prophetic powers. Euripides says that it was he who advised MENELAUS on his homeward journey, rather than the Old Man of the Sea, PROTEUS, who is familiar in that role from the *Odyssey*. Glaucus also advised the ARGONAUTS, and was thought to come to the rescue of sailors in storms.

[Euripides, *Orestes* 362–9; Apollonius, *Argonautica* 1.1310–28; Pausanias 9.22.6–7; Athenaeus 7.296–97c; Ovid, *Metamorphoses* 13.898–14.69.]

Glaucus (2)

Son of MINOS, king of Crete, and PASIPHAE. As a small child, Glaucus was chasing a mouse when he fell into a storage-jar full of honey and was drowned. His distraught father searched everywhere for him, but unavailingly, so he called in seers to help him. Now Minos had in his herds a miraculous cow that changed colour every four hours, from white, to red, to black, and he was told by the CURETES (1) that the man who offered the best comparison for this cow's colour would also be able to find the lost boy. The seer POLYIDUS likened the cow to the fruit of the mulberry tree, which is first white, then turns red, and finally ripens to black. So Minos told him to find Glaucus. The seer, rightly interpreting the omen of an owl (*glaux*) perched near the storage-room and being plagued by bees, found the boy's drowned body in the honey-jar. But now Minos wanted his son brought back to life, and he ordered the seer to be shut up with the corpse until this was done. At first Polyidus was completely at a loss. Then he saw a snake slithering towards the boy's body and killed it, fearing that it meant harm. To his amazement, a second snake appeared, carrying a herb which it put on the dead snake's body, bringing it back to life. Polyidus lost no time in using the herb on Glaucus, and at once the boy too revived and was restored to his joyful parents.

Before Polyidus left Crete, Minos made him teach Glaucus the art of divination. The seer complied, but just as he was leaving the island he told the boy to spit into his mouth. Glaucus did so and forgot all that he had learnt. According to another version of the legend, Glaucus was brought back to life by the healer ASCLEPIUS.

[Apollodorus 3.1.2, 3.3.1–2, 3.10.3; Hyginus, *Fabula* 136.]

Glaucus (3)

Son of SISYPHUS, king of Corinth, and Merope. He married Eurymede (or Eurynome) and fathered sons, including the monster-killer BELLEROPHON, though sometimes the boy was said to be the son of Poseidon. Glaucus is most famous for the manner of his death: he took part in the chariot-race at the funeral games of Pelias, running a team of mares that he kept at Potniae in Boeotia, and when he lost the race his maddened mares tore him to pieces and devoured him. Various reasons are given for their frenzy: either the water they had drunk from a well at Potniae had turned them wild; or Glaucus had been feeding them on human flesh to make them more aggressive; or he had kept them from mating to improve their performance, and Aphrodite, feeling herself scorned, turned them against their master. Whatever the reason, Glaucus died hideously, and for generations thereafter his ghost, known as Taraxippus, haunted the stadium of the Isthmian Games at Corinth, scaring the horses when they raced.

[Homer, *Iliad* 6.154–5; Hesiod, *Catalogue of Women* fr. 43 (a); Apollodorus 1.9.3, 2.3.1; Pausanias 6.20.19.]

Glaucus (4)

Son of Hippolochus and great-grandson of GLAUCUS (3), who with his cousin SARPEDON led the Lycian contingent of PRIAM's allies in the TROJAN WAR. Glaucus met his death at the hands of AJAX (1) in the tenth year of the war, while they were fighting for the corpse of ACHILLES. But he is best remembered for his earlier encounter on the battlefield at Troy with the Greek leader DIOMEDES (2). The two were about to fight in single combat when they found that their families shared a bond of guest-friendship: Diomedes' grandfather Oeneus had once entertained Glaucus' grandfather Bellerophon, and at parting they had exchanged gifts to mark their friendly relationship. Now Diomedes and Glaucus did the same, clasping hands and pledging their friendship by exchanging armour. 'But Zeus took away the wits of Glaucus', adds Homer (6.234–6), 'since he exchanged with Diomedes, son of Tydeus, golden armour for bronze, giving for nine oxen's worth the worth of a hundred.'

[Homer, *Iliad* 2.876–7, 6.119–236, 12.309–32, 387–91, 16.476–501, 17.140–68; Herodotus 1.147; Apollodorus, *Epitome* 5.4.]

Glaucus (5) *see* ANTENOR.

Golden Apple *see* JUDGEMENT OF PARIS.

Golden Bough

The magical bough, growing in a sacred grove near

Cumae, that AENEAS was told by the SIBYL to pluck, to gain him entrance to the Underworld (Virgil, *Aeneid* 6.125–211). Virgil's fourth-century commentator, Servius, associates this bough with the cult of the goddess DIANA at Aricia, where a runaway slave could fight and kill the priest, then take his place, if he first broke off a bough from a particular tree in Diana's sacred grove. This legend of ritual killing was the inspiration for the title, *The Golden Bough*, of Sir James Frazer's monumental work on comparative religion and mythology, published between 1890 and 1915. The golden bough has often been seen as a symbol of wisdom and initiation.

Golden Fleece

The fleece of the flying, talking ram, offspring of Poseidon and THEOPHANE, that saved PHRIXUS and Helle from the wiles of their wicked stepmother, Ino. When Phrixus landed safely in Colchis, he sacrificed the ram to Zeus in gratitude for his salvation. He gave its fleece to the king, AEETES, who hung it in an oak tree in a grove of Ares and set a sleepless dragon to guard it (figs. 23 and 24). It would in ·due course be the motive for the long and arduous journey of Jason and the ARGONAUTS: the quest for the Golden Fleece. The ram was immortalised in the stars as the constellation ARIES.

Gordius

A Phrygian king, the father of MIDAS. Gordius was born a poor peasant, but a divine portent promised him a kingly future when an eagle flew down while he was ploughing and settled on the yoke of his oxen, staying there all day. This portent came true during a period of civil disturbance in Phrygia, when an oracle foretold that a king would arrive, riding in a cart, who would bring peace to the land. Just as the Phrygians were discussing the oracle in assembly, Gordius arrived, riding in a cart with his wife and son, Midas. At once the people made him (or Midas) their king, naming their city Gordium in Gordius' honour. He dedicated his cart to Zeus, its pole coupled ingeniously to the yoke with a rope of bark, and another oracle declared that whoever could undo the fastening would be lord of all Asia. The complicated knot defied all attempts to untie it until Alexander the Great arrived. He solved the problem by simply cutting through the fastening with his sword, since when 'cutting the Gordian knot' has become proverbial for resolving a difficulty by drastic action.

[Plutarch, *Alexander* 18; Arrian, *Anabasis of Alexander* 2.3.]

Gorge

One of the daughters of OENEUS, king of the Aetolians of Calydon, and Althaea. When her brother MELEAGER was killed, Gorge was spared the fate of being turned into a guinea-hen which some of her sisters suffered. She married Andraemon and had by him a son, THOAS (3), who led the Aetolian contingent to the Trojan War. According to Apollodorus (1.8.5), it was sometimes said that Gorge, instead of Oeneus' second wife Periboea, was the mother of his son TYDEUS, because it was Zeus' will that Oeneus should fall in love with his own daughter.

Gorgons

Three monstrous daughters of PHORCYS and CETO, and sisters of the GRAEAE. The Gorgons were named Stheno, Euryale and Medusa, and lived in the far west, beyond the river of Ocean (*see* OCEANUS). Their heads were entwined with writhing snakes, they had great tusks like a boar, hands of bronze and wings of gold, and the sight of them could turn a man to stone. Stheno and Euryale were immortal, but Medusa was mortal and killed by PERSEUS. Polydectes, king of Seriphos, wishing Perseus dead, sent him off on what he believed to be a fatal quest, to fetch Medusa's head. Perseus found his way to her distant land with the help of ATHENA and HERMES, flying on winged sandals and armed with a curved sword of adamant, a bag, and a cap of darkness which made the wearer invisible. He found the Gorgons asleep, and by averting his gaze, and looking only at their reflection in Athena's shield of polished bronze, he cut off Medusa's head. She had been pregnant by POSEIDON, and now from her severed neck leapt two offspring, the winged horse, PEGASUS, and CHRYSAOR. Perseus thrust her head into his bag – later he would use it against his enemies – and flew away. Stheno and Euryale did their best to pursue him, but because he was wearing the cap of darkness they were bound to fail. They returned to mourn their dead sister, and Pindar tells us that Athena invented the mournful music of the *aulos*, the double pipe, from the sound of their sad lament.

Perseus returned to Seriphos, flying above Libya where drops of blood from Medusa's severed head fell to the ground and became deadly snakes, with which Libya now abounds. In due course he gave the Gorgon's head to Athena and she put it in the middle of her *aegis*, a goatskin cape fringed with snakes, or on her shield, as a threat to her enemies. She gave some of Medusa's blood to ASCLEPIUS, the god of healing, and while blood from veins on the Gorgon's left side brought only harm to man, that from veins on her right side could raise the dead. According to Euripides, Athena gave two drops of the blood, again one of them a deadly poison and one a powerful medicine for healing, to Erichthonius. To Heracles she gave a lock of the Gorgon's hair in a bronze jar, and this was later used to keep Tegea safe (*see* CEPHEUS (2)).

Gorgons were very popular subjects in ancient art. In the earliest versions they are very ugly, with snaky hair, staring eyes, fearsome grins and lolling tongues, boar's tusks, and a striding gait (fig. 61). Later, however, Medusa can be beautiful (fig.114), and indeed Apollodorus tells us that Athena helped Perseus in his mission because the Gorgon once presumed to compare her own loveliness with that of the goddess. According to Ovid, her hair was her particular beauty, so Athena turned it into a mass of snakes as a punishment for having intercourse with Poseidon in her temple.

The image of the Medusa head has been a powerful influence in the postclassical arts, particularly in literature, in, for instance, Iris Murdoch's novel *A Severed Head*, where the heroine is a Medusa-figure, and in poetry. In modern Greek lore, Gorgons have become sea-spirits, double-tailed mermaids who haunt the Aegean, singing sweetly.

[Homer, *Iliad* 5.738–42; Hesiod, *Theogony* 270–81; Pindar, *Pythian* 12.6–27; Euripides, *Ion* 989–1017; Apollodorus 2.4.3, 3.10.3; Pausanias 3.18.11, 5.18.5; Ovid, *Metamorphoses* 4.614–20, 770–803.]

Graces (Greek, *Charites*; Latin, *Gratiae*)

Minor goddesses, the personifications of beauty, charm and grace, and also of favour and gratitude for favour. Hesiod makes them three in number, the daughters of ZEUS and the Oceanid EURYNOME, and names them Aglaea (Splendour), Euphrosyne (Gaiety) and Thalia (Festivity). He adds that Aglaea was married to HEPHAESTUS. Homer reflects a different tradition, for in the *Iliad* Hephaestus' wife is called simply Charis (Grace), while in the *Odyssey* and elsewhere she is Aphrodite; and he says that the youngest Grace was Pasithea, whom HERA promised to give in marriage to HYPNOS (Sleep), as a bribe to persuade him to help her by lulling Zeus to sleep. On the whole, however, the Graces played little individual part in myths. As a group they appear frequently in literature and art in contexts of joy or festivity, as the companions of the MUSES, since they were fond of poetry, song and dance, or as attendant upon some god; and they are often associated with Aphrodite and EROS as creators of the love bond between men and women: 'From their glancing eyes', says Hesiod, 'flows love that melts the limbs' strength, and beautiful is their gaze from beneath their brows' (*Theogony* 910–11). So in art they are suitable attendants at marriages, and we see them, for instance, on the François Krater at one of the most famous weddings in myth, that of the mortal Peleus to the goddess

Thetis. In early art they are always clothed, but in Hellenistic times and later they are frequently nude. Here they are popularly depicted as an interlaced group of three, a model that found its way into Renaissance art, perhaps most famously in Botticelli's *Primavera*.

[Homer, *Iliad* 5.338, 14.263–76, 18.382–3, *Odyssey* 8.362–7, 18.192–4; Hesiod, *Theogony* 64–5, 907–11, 945–6; Pindar, *Olympian* 14.3–17; Apollodorus 1.3.1; Pausanias 3.18.9–10, 5.11.7, 6.24.6–7, 9.35.1–7.]

Graeae

The three daughters of PHORCYS and CETO, and sisters of the three GORGONS. Their names were Enyo, Pemphredo and Deino, though Hesiod names only the first two, 'fine-robed Enyo and saffron-robed Pemphredo' (*Theogony* 270–3). He calls them 'fair of cheek' and says that they were named Graeae, 'Old Women', simply because they were white-haired from birth. When they later play a part in the legend of PERSEUS they seem to live up to their name rather better, for here they were blind and toothless, apart from a single eye and a single tooth which they shared among themselves, passing them around as needed. Perseus wished to find out from them the

Fig.61 **The Gorgon Medusa.**

whereabouts of certain nymphs, who could help him in his quest to fetch the head of the Graeae's sister, the Gorgon Medusa, but the Graeae were naturally loath to give any assistance. So Perseus stole from them their single eye and tooth, until they were forced in their helplessness to tell him what he wanted. He then returned the eye and tooth, though in Aeschylus' lost tragedy *The Children of Phorcys*, he threw the eye into Lake Tritonis.

In ancient art the Graeae are depicted as sometimes young and lovely, sometimes old and ugly. Perseus' theft of the eye occurs first on vases at about 425 BC.

[Apollodorus 2.4.2.]

Gratiae *see* GRACES.

Gration *see* GIANTS.

Griffin or Gryphon
A fabulous beast with the head and wings of an eagle and the body and hind quarters of a lion, a conception that seems to be eastern in origin. Aeschylus calls the griffins 'the sharp-toothed hounds of Zeus that have no bark' (*Prometheus Bound* 804). They were thought to live at the northern limits of the world, next to the HYPERBOREANS, and to guard hoards of gold from their warlike and greedy neighbours, the one-eyed Arimaspians, who stole the gold at every opportunity. (Herodotus declines to believe that the Arimaspians were one-eyed: *see* 3.116, 4.13, 4.27).

The legend was familiar to Milton (*Paradise Lost* ii.943–7):

> As when a gryphon, through the wilderness
> With winged course, o'er hill or moory dale
> Pursues the Arimaspian, who by stealth
> Had from his wakeful custody purloin'd
> The guarded gold ...

[Pausanias 1.24.5–6.]

Gyes or **Gyges** *see* HUNDRED-HANDERS

H

Hades (1)

King of the Underworld, which itself is often called simply Hades (*see* HADES (2)). He was one of the six children of the Titans CRONUS and Rhea, swallowed and later regurgitated by his cannibalistic father. When the sons of Cronus divided the universe among themselves after their father's defeat, they kept the earth and Olympus as common property, while ZEUS took the heavens as his domain, POSEIDON the seas, and Hades the misty darkness of the Underworld. Here he ruled over the souls of the dead, a grim and sinister god, but in no sense evil or Satanic, just as his kingdom bore no resemblance to the Christian Hell. He was called euphemistically Pluto, 'Rich one', because of all the riches that come from the earth (fig. 117). The Romans too adopted this title, and also called him Dis, a contraction of *dives*, 'rich', and Orcus. He was given a wide variety of epithets, such as *Stugeros*, 'Hateful', *Klumenos*, 'Renowned', *Polydektes* and *Polydegmon*, 'Receiver of Many', *Polyxeinos*, 'Host to Many', *Eubouleus*, 'Good Counsellor'; and he was also known as *Zeus Katachthonios*, 'Zeus of the Underworld', this last emphasising his absolute power over his realm. Just occasionally he gave permission for a dead person to return to earth, as he did for PROTESILAUS, SISYPHUS, and ORPHEUS' wife Eurydice.

Hades' main myth is his abduction of PERSEPHONE, the beautiful daughter of the goddess DEMETER, to be his queen. With Zeus' approval he came up to earth and seized her while she was gathering flowers, then carried her in his four-horse chariot down to his shadowy domain. He planned to keep her there forever, but Demeter grieved so deeply for her lost daughter that she made the whole earth barren, and Zeus was obliged to intervene and have Persephone brought back to the light of day. But because Hades had induced her to eat pomegranate seeds while she was with him, she could not leave the Underworld completely and had to spend part of every year there (either four or six months) as Hades'

wife (fig. 62), while the rest of the year was spent with her mother. The marriage was childless. We hear from Ovid of Hades' mistress, MENTHE, whom jealous Persephone trampled underfoot and transformed into the mint plant.

Hades possessed a cap of darkness that conferred invisibility on the wearer. This he would sometimes lend to others: to ATHENA, for instance, when she wished to be unseen by ARES on the battlefield; or to HERMES, who wore it during the battle of the Gods and the GIANTS, and with its help slew the Giant Hippolytus; and it was borrowed by PERSEUS on his expedition to cut off the Gorgon Medusa's head. Hades also owned flocks of cattle guarded by his herdsman MENOETES, who once encountered HERACLES when he went down to Hades to fetch the guard-dog CERBERUS. Heracles killed one of Hades' cows, so Menoetes challenged him to a wrestling match, only to have his ribs broken. Hades too was wounded when one of Heracles' poisonous arrows struck him painfully in the shoulder. He had to leave his realm and travel up to Olympus, where he was healed by Paeon.

Hades had very little cult, since his jurisdiction was confined to the souls of the dead and he had no interest in the living. He appears in ancient art much less frequently than the other major gods.

[Homer, *Iliad* 5.394–402, 844–5, 9.457, 15.187–93, 20.61–7; Hesiod, *Theogony* 453–506, 850; Apollodorus 1.1.5–1.2.1, 2.7.3; Strabo 3.2.9; Pausanias 5.20.3, 6.25.2–3.]

Hades (2)

The Underworld, the subterranean land of the dead, ruled by the god HADES (1) and his queen PERSEPHONE. It was a chill and sunless place, watered by five rivers, the STYX, ACHERON, COCYTUS, PHLEGETHON and LETHE. HERMES escorted the dead souls down to the boundary of the Underworld, the Acheron or the Styx. If they had received proper burial, the aged ferryman CHARON carried them across the waters in his boat, charging a fee of one obol for his trouble. The gates were guarded by the

Fig. 62 Hades, holding a cornucopia, lies on a couch next to his queen, Persephone.

fearsome watchdog CERBERUS, who wagged his tail for new arrivals, but devoured all those who tried to leave again. The souls lived a shadowy existence on the Plain of Asphodel. In Homer's *Odyssey* (11.467–540), ODYSSEUS meets the shade of ACHILLES there, and tries to console him for his death by speaking of the authority he holds among the dead. Achilles replies unforgettably (489–91): 'I would rather be alive and toiling as serf to another man, one with no land and nothing much to live on, than be king over all the perished dead.'

According to later writers, ELYSIUM was a part of Hades, where a few blessed mortals, through the favour of the gods, lived an afterlife of blissful ease. There was also a place of punishment for wrongdoers: TARTARUS. Here the TITANS were guarded by the HUNDRED-HANDERS. Here SISY-PHUS continually pushed his great stone uphill, only to have it roll down again. IXION turned on his wheel of fire. The giant TITYUS was tied down, sprawling over two acres, while two vultures gnawed at his liver. TANTALUS (1) suffered perpetual and unappeasable hunger and thirst. And the daughters of DANAUS forever tried to draw water into leaking vessels, that had always to be refilled. The judges of the dead were AEACUS, who also kept the keys of the kingdom, RHADAMANTHYS and MINOS.

Homer puts the entrance to Hades in the far west, beyond the river of Ocean, but there were believed to be

entrances within the known world, at Taenarum in the southern Peloponnese, at the Alcyonian Lake at Lerna, in Argos, and at Lake Avernus, near Naples. A few privileged mortals visited Hades while still living and escaped safely back to earth. Odysseus travelled to the edge of the Underworld, to seek advice from the shade of the seer Teiresias about his journey home to Ithaca. HERACLES went down to fetch Cerberus as one of his Labours for Eurystheus. AENEAS descended to meet the shade of his father Anchises, who told him of the future greatness of Rome. PSYCHE had to fetch a day's supply of Proserpina's store of beauty for Venus. ORPHEUS descended, hoping – and failing – to win back to life his dead wife Eurydice. These all made the journey safely back to the daylight again. But when THESEUS and PEIRITHOUS went to the Underworld, planning to abduct Persephone, they were trapped by Hades in seats from which they had no power to move. Theseus was eventually rescued by Heracles, on his quest for Cerberus, but Peirithous stayed fixed firmly in his seat for ever.

[Homer, *Iliad* 23.71–4, *Odyssey* 10.488–540, 11 *passim*, 24.1–204; Lucian, *Dialogues of the Dead*; Virgil, *Aeneid* 6. E. Vermeule, *Aspects of Death in Early Greek Art and Poetry* (1979).]

Haemon

Son of CREON (2), ruler of Thebes, and Eurydice. Early epic places Haemon in the generation of Oedipus, for he was said to be a victim of the SPHINX, and his son MAEON was one of the Thebans who ambushed Tydeus just before the expedition of the Seven against Thebes. But the fifth-century tragedians place him later, making him the husband or lover of Oedipus' daughter ANTIGONE (1).

This last is the situation in Sophocles' famous tragedy *Antigone*. Here, in the aftermath of the attack on Thebes by the Seven, Creon has declared Polyneices a traitor and refused him burial, while Antigone, in defiance of Creon's edict, insists on giving last rites to her brother. When she is caught red-handed, Creon has her sealed up alive in a tomb. Haemon, who is betrothed to Antigone, pleads with his father for leniency, but Creon rages at his son for siding against him. Finally, after he learns from the blind seer Teiresias that the gods are rejecting all Theban sacrifices, Creon gives in, but too late: he buries Polyneices, then goes to the tomb to release Antigone, only to find that she has hanged herself. Haemon is with her, having just discovered her body, and the Messenger reports his reaction (1231–41):

With wild eyes, the boy glared at his father, wordlessly spat in his face, then drew his two-edged sword. His father jumped back to evade him and he missed his aim. Then the wretched boy, enraged with himself, pressed his body against the sword and drove half its length into his side. Still living, he clasped the girl in a feeble embrace and coughed out a sharp jet of blood that sprinkled her white cheek. He lies, a corpse enfolding a corpse, achieving his marriage rites, poor boy, in the house of Hades.

Nor is this the whole tragedy for Creon: his wife Eurydice has heard this news of Haemon's death and now commits suicide too, so Creon is left alive at the end of the play, desolate, to mourn the chain of tragedies brought about by his obstinacy.

[Homer, *Iliad* 4.394; Euripides, *Phoenician Women* 944–6, 1635–8, 1672–9; Apollodorus 3.5.8.]

Halirrhothius

An Athenian, the son of POSEIDON and a nymph called Euryte, whose death was said to have brought about the founding of the famous homicide court in Athens, the Areopagus. Halirrhothius raped Alcippe, the daughter of the war-god ARES and Cecrops' daughter AGLAURUS (2), and to punish this crime Ares killed him. The war-god was then charged with murder by Poseidon and tried by a tribunal of the other gods, but was acquitted. This, the first-ever trial for the shedding of blood, was held on the hill to the west of the Acropolis, thereafter known as the Areopagus (the 'Hill of Ares'), on which murder trials were held in historical times.

[Euripides, *Electra* 1258–63, *Iphigeneia in Tauris* 945–6; Apollodorus 3.14.2; Pausanias 1.21.4, 1.28.5.]

Halitherses

In Homer's *Odyssey*, Halitherses is the wise seer who correctly predicted, when ODYSSEUS went to Troy, that he would be away for twenty years, then after much suffering would come home, alone and unrecognised. Now, in the twentieth year, he foresees that Odysseus is about to return and bring retribution on the Suitors of his wife PENELOPE, who have invaded his home and are constantly eating up his substance. The seer warns the Suitors they had better beware (2.146–76), but they ignore him – to their cost, for Odysseus kills them all. Halitherses next warns the Suitors' kinsmen not to seek revenge on Odysseus and his followers, for he sees that such an attack will be futile; but once again he is ignored (24.451–62).

Hamadryads *see* NYMPHS.

Hare *see* LEPUS.

Harmonia

Daughter of ARES and APHRODITE. She married the mortal CADMUS, king of Thebes, and the gods honoured the couple by attending their wedding and bringing gifts, just as they did at the marriage of the sea-goddess Thetis with the mortal Peleus. Two significant gifts given to Harmonia, either by the gods or by Cadmus, were a necklace made by HEPHAESTUS and a beautiful robe, both of which became prized family heirlooms. (Later used as bribes in time of war, they always brought bloodshed in their train: *see* ALCMAEON.) The traveller Pausanias saw on the Amyclae Throne a depiction of the gods bearing wedding gifts. He reports that in his day (the second century AD) the market-place in Thebes was believed to be where Cadmus' house had stood, and the Thebans would point out the ruined bridal-chamber of Harmonia and the very spot where the MUSES sang at her wedding.

[Hesiod, *Theogony* 933–7, 975–8; Pindar, *Pythian* 3.88–103; Apollodorus 3.4.2; Pausanias 3.18.12, 9.12.3.]

Harpalyce (1)

Daughter of Harpalycus, a Thracian king. Her mother died when Harpalyce was an infant, so her father brought her up on the milk of cows and mares, and later taught her the arts of hunting and war. She was so fleet of foot that she could outrun horses, or the swift current of the Hebrus, the principal river of Thrace. She fought alongside her father in battle, on one occasion saving his life, and when at last he died she lived by brigandage, raiding the herds and flocks of the neighbourhood. She was finally caught in a snare by shepherds, and killed. She was given cult honours after her death in the form of a mock battle at her tomb.

[Virgil, *Aeneid* 1.314–20; Hyginus, *Fabula* 193.]

Harpalyce (2)

The daughter of Clymenus, a king of Argos or Arcadia. He gave Harpalyce in marriage to Alastor, a son of Neleus, but then abducted her because he was in love with her himself, and lived with her incestuously. Only after she gave birth to a son, who was also her brother, did she take her revenge. She killed the baby, then cut up his flesh and served it to her father at a feast. Some say that Clymenus, on discovering what he had eaten, killed his daughter and then himself; others that he hanged himself, but the gods took pity on Harpalyce and transformed her into an owl.

[Parthenius, *Love Romances* 13; Nonnus, *Dionysiaca* 12.71–5.]

Harpies ('Snatchers')

Winged female monsters, goddesses of the storm-winds who snatched people away so that they were never seen again. According to Hesiod (*Theogony* 265–9) there were two of them, daughters of the Titan THAUMAS and the Oceanid Electra, and thus sisters of IRIS, the messenger of the gods. Their names reflect the swift and sudden nature of their attacks: Aello ('Storm') and Ocypete ('Swift-flying'). 'On their swift wings', says Hesiod, 'they keep pace with the blasts of the winds and the birds, hurling themselves through the high air.' Homer knows of a Harpy called Podarge ('Fleetfoot') who mated in the form of a mare with the West Wind, ZEPHYRUS, and brought forth XANTHUS and Balius, the immortal horses of Achilles who ran like the winds. Later writers add the Harpy Celaeno ('Dark', like the storm-clouds).

In the *Odyssey*, Odysseus' disappearance is so complete and unaccountable that Telemachus puts it down to seizure by the Harpies (1.241), and Penelope wishes that she could be carried out of the world, just as the Harpies snatched away the daughters of PANDAREOS and gave them as servants to the Furies (20.61–78). But the Harpies are best known for their torment of the blind Thracian king PHINEUS (2), the fullest account being in Apollonius' *Argonautica* (2.164–499). Phineus was constantly plagued by the Harpies, the 'hounds of Zeus', who snatched up most of his food and left a loathsome stench over what little they left him. When the ARGONAUTS visited him on their way to Colchis and the Golden Fleece they found him almost starved to death, but Phineus was now hopeful, for he knew that two of their company, ZETES and Calais, were destined to save him from his persecutors. In return for their help, he agreed to foretell the dangers of the Argonauts' voyage. So the next time the Harpies swooped down to snatch up Phineus' food, Zetes and Calais were standing by. Apollonius says:

> As soon as the old man touched his meal, the Harpies without warning darted from the clouds like sudden storms or flashes of lightning, swooping down and screaming in their lust for food. The heroes cried out when they saw them, but the Harpies devoured everything, and with a cry flew off far across the sea, leaving behind an unbearable stench.

Zetes and Calais were the winged sons of Boreas, the North Wind, and the swiftest men on earth. Now they sped in pursuit of their prey, their swords drawn. This would have been the end of the Harpies, had not Iris intervened: pursued and pursuers reached the Floating Islands (*Plotai*), traditionally identified as the Echinades in the Ionian Sea, and here Iris told the Boreadae to spare her sisters, promising that they would never trouble Phineus again. Zetes and Calais turned and went back to their comrades, after which the islands were renamed the Strophades, the 'Islands of Turning'. The Harpies went to Crete, where they settled in a deep cave on Mount Dicte.

Apollodorus (1.9.21) records a less happy version in which pursuers and pursued both perished, it being fated that the Harpies would die at the hands of the Boreadae, and that the Boreadae would die if they ever failed to catch whoever was fleeing from them. During the pursuit one Harpy fell into the River Tigres in the Peloponnese and drowned, after which the river was renamed the Harpys, while the second Harpy outflew her pursuers, but died of exhaustion when she reached the Strophades. According to Virgil, the Harpies lived on, settling in the Strophades, and here AENEAS and the Trojans encountered them on their way to Italy. Twice the monsters snatched their food, and the mens' swords were powerless against them. Celaeno, the leader, predicted that the Trojan wanderers would found a city only after they had been driven by hunger to eat their own tables.

In ancient art the Harpies are depicted as winged women (fig.63) or, like the Sirens, as birds with the faces of women. Pausanias saw the Boreadae driving them away from Phineus on both the Chest of Cypselus (5.17.11) and the Amyclae Throne (3.18.15). The term harpy has come to mean a cruel, rapacious person. To quote W. M. Thackeray's *The Virginians* (ch. xviii): 'Was it my mother-in-law, the grasping, odious, abandoned, brazen harpy?' [Homer, *Iliad* 16.148–51; Apollonius, *Argonautica* 2.176–499; Virgil, *Aeneid* 3.209–67.]

Hebe

The goddess of Youth, known to the Romans as Juventas. She was the daughter of ZEUS and HERA, and thus the sister of ARES and EILEITHYIA. When the great hero HERACLES was made a god after his life of toil on earth, Hebe was given to him as his new, immortal wife, symbolising his own now eternal youth. In the *Iliad* we see her administering to the other gods on OLYMPUS: she acts as cupbearer and pours nectar (4.2–3), she helps Hera to harness her divine horses and chariot (5.722–32), and she bathes Ares after he has been wounded by Diomedes (5.905). In Euripides'

Fig.63 **Winged Harpies persecute old, blind Phineus.**

Children of Heracles (847–58), Hebe renews the youth of Heracles' now aged nephew IOLAUS, so that he can go into battle against Eurystheus in defence of Heracles' children.

Hebe appears occasionally in ancient art (fig. 67), primarily in scenes of Heracles' arrival on Olympus. Since she was the goddess of youthful beauty, she was a popular subject for portraits of gentlewomen in postclassical art during the seventeenth and eighteenth centuries.

[Homer, *Odyssey* 11.601–4; Hesiod, *Theogony* 921–3, 950–5; Apollodorus 1.3.1.]

Hecale

The old woman who gave THESEUS shelter when he was on his way to capture the ferocious MARATHONIAN BULL. She treated him kindly, and promised to sacrifice to Zeus in thanksgiving if he returned safely the next day from his encounter with the beast. He did so, but found Hecale dead. Because of her kindness and hospitality, Theseus instituted a local ceremony to honour her memory.

[Callimachus, *Hecale* (fragmentary); Plutarch, *Theseus* 14.]

Hecate

An Underworld goddess connected with sorcery and black magic, though for Hesiod, who first mentions her, she seems to have had no such sinister associations. He makes her the daughter of PERSES (1) and ASTERIA (and thus the first cousin of APOLLO and ARTEMIS), and declares that ZEUS honoured her above all other deities. He mentions no association with the Underworld, but praises her as a powerful goddess with dominion over earth, sea and sky, who could bring innumerable blessings to men, and wealth and success in all their various endeavours, if she so wished.

She was sometimes identified with Artemis, and also closely associated with DEMETER, who was occasionally said to be her mother. Hecate helped Demeter in her search for her lost daughter, PERSEPHONE (fig. 47), and after the reunion of mother and daughter she became Persephone's attendant. In the battle of the Gods and the GIANTS she killed Clytius with her torches. By the fifth century BC she had become the more familiar and menacing figure who was associated with magic and witchcraft, ghosts and creatures of the night. Sorceresses such as MEDEA invoked her name as one who made spells more powerful. She was worshipped at crossroads (good locations for magic), where dishes of food were put out for her every month to mark the rising of the new moon. She made her fearful appearances on earth in the dark of night, accompanied by packs of barking hell-hounds. As SELENE or Artemis/Diana represent the moonlit splendour of night, so Hecate represents its darkness and terrors.

Though in ancient art she can be portrayed with a single face, she is often represented with three faces or three bodies. On the altar of Zeus at Pergamum, where she and her dog are attacking a snake-tailed Giant, she has a single body, three heads and three pairs of arms. In Shakespeare's *Macbeth* she makes two brief appearances to direct the three witches: she berates them for making prophecies to Macbeth without her knowledge ('I, the mistress of your charms, / the close contriver of all harms'), then joins with them in bringing him to destruction.

[Hesiod, *Theogony* 404–52; *Homeric Hymn to Demeter* 25–61, 438–40; Euripides, *Helen* 569–70, *Ion* 1047–50, *Medea* 395–7; Apollonius *Argonautica* 3.477–8, 528–30, 1035–41, 1207–24, 4.827–9; Pausanias 1.43.1, 2.30.2; Virgil, *Aeneid* 4.511, 609, 6.247, 564.]

Hector

The eldest son of PRIAM, king of Troy, and HECUBA, though he was sometimes said to be the son of APOLLO. He was the husband of ANDROMACHE and the father of ASTYANAX, and the greatest of the Trojan champions. Although he deplored PARIS' irresponsible seduction of Helen which plunged Troy into the protracted TROJAN WAR, nevertheless it was Hector who killed PROTESILAUS, the first Greek to set foot on Trojan soil, and he remained the bulwark of the Trojan army until his death in the tenth year of the war.

In the *Iliad*, Homer depicts Hector as noble and compassionate, much loved by his fellow-Trojans, and makes him a key figure in the action of his epic. When ACHILLES retires from battle, full of wrath because his concubine Briseis has been taken from him by Agamemnon, it is Hector whom he names as the Trojan fighter who will bring the greatest suffering to the Greeks, now that their own finest warrior is off the battlefield (1.240–4): 'I swear that there will come a time when a longing for Achilles will be felt by the sons of the Achaeans, by every one of them', he says to Agamemnon, 'and on that day, for all your sorrow, you will be able to do nothing to help, when many of them drop and die before man-slaughtering Hector. Then you will eat your heart out in anger that you did no honour to the best of the Achaeans.' When Achilles still refuses to fight, even after many losses have been sustained by the Greeks, it is Hector who kills his dearest comrade PATROCLUS when he goes into battle in his friend's place. After this, when Achilles re-enters the fighting to avenge Patroclus, slaughtering countless Trojans, it is his slaying of Hector that is the climax of his revenge. And in the final book of the *Iliad*, it is Priam's recovery of Hector's body from Achilles that leads to the supremely moving scene of pity and reconciliation between enemies with which Homer ends his epic.

Hector first appears leading the Trojans out to battle

(2.807–18). He reproaches his brother Paris for being afraid to fight MENELAUS, who is eager to do battle with the man who stole his wife, then arranges the truce and the indecisive single combat between the two of them (3.38–120). He takes a major part in the fighting of Books 5 and 6, so that even the mighty DIOMEDES (2) quails before him (5.590–606). Here occurs one of the most famous scenes of the *Iliad* (6.369–502), when Hector goes back into the city to arrange for offerings to be made to the gods, then meets Andromache and Astyanax on the city walls. Andromache begs him not to carry on risking his life in battle, and his reply shows his sense of duty that keeps him fighting in what seems to be a hopeless war (6.441–9):

> I would be ashamed before the Trojans
> and the Trojans' wives, with their trailing dresses,
> if like a coward I skulk away from the fighting.
> My spirit will not let me, for I have learnt
> always to be brave and to fight in the forefront,
> winning great glory for myself, and for my father.
> But this I know well in my mind and in my heart:
> the day will come when sacred Ilium shall perish,
> and Priam, and the people of Priam of the strong ash spear.

So Hector returns to battle, and there he challenges any Greek hero to single combat. At first the Greeks are hesitant, which underlines Hector's excellence as a warrior; but finally he is met by AJAX (1) in a duel that is inconclusive, although Ajax has the better of it before night stops the contest. They part in friendship with an exchange of gifts, Hector giving a sword and Ajax a sword-belt

(7.44–312). Sophocles would later make dramatic use of these gifts in his *Ajax*, where Ajax kills himself by falling on the sword, and Hector is dragged to his death while lashed to a chariot with the sword-belt.

In Book 8 Hector drives the Greeks back to their camp by the ships and bivouacs with his men on the plain. In the long battle of Books 11 to 17 he takes a prominent part, leading the main attack against the fortifications of the Greek camp. A fierce fight between Greeks and Trojans develops around the ramparts, and finally Hector breaks through the gates by hurling a huge stone and smashing them open (12.462–71):

> Then glorious Hector leapt inside, his face
> like the onset of night. He gleamed in fearful bronze
> that girded his skin, and brandished two spears.
> No one but a god could have come against him
> and stopped him as he burst through the gates,
> his eyes blazing with fire. Turning, he shouted
> to the mass of Trojans to climb over the wall,
> and they obeyed his order. Some climbed the wall
> and others poured in through the strong-built gates,
> The Greeks fled in fear among their hollow ships,
> and the clamour rose unceasing.

During the battle Hector is felled by a stone flung by the Great Ajax (14.402–20), but Apollo restores his strength and urges him back to the fighting, to which he goes with enthusiasm (15.263–70):

As when a horse, stabled and corn-fed at the manger,
breaks his rope and gallops in thunder over the plain
to where he likes to bathe in a sweet-flowing river,
exulting. He holds his head high and his mane
streams over his shoulders; knowing his splendour,
he is carried on swift knees to his loved pastures.
So Hector lightly moved his feet and knees, urging
his horsemen, when he heard the voice of the god.

He leads his men against the Greek ships, and after a mighty battle succeeds in setting fire to one of them. At this, Patroclus takes Achilles' place, and with his friend's blessing, and clad in his armour, he leads out the MYRMI-DONS. He beats back the Trojans from the ships, then carries on fighting and killing until he is himself slain by Hector with the help of Apollo (16.712–863). Despite the efforts of the Greeks, Hector strips Patroclus of his armour, then himself puts it on. Achilles appears and three times gives a great shout that has the Trojans scattering in panic (18.207–38). Even so, Hector is full of confidence, and he again bivouacs with his men on the plain, even though this is against the advice of POLYDAMAS. He will live to regret his folly when all too many of his fellow-Trojans are killed.

On the following day Hector's last moments are at hand, for Achilles rejoins the battle, appearing in new armour made by Hephaestus. He slaughters vast numbers of Trojans in his lust for revenge, all the while seeking Hector, the slayer of his beloved friend. He kills POLYDORUS (3), another son of Priam, and Hector tries to avenge his brother, knowing full well that Achilles is the better man and likely to kill him: 'I know that you are brave', he says, 'and that I am far weaker than you. But all this rests on the knees of the gods, and I may yet, even though I am weaker, rob you of life with a cast of my spear, since my weapon too has before now been found sharp' (20.434–7). He lets fly his spear, which through Athena's intervention drops harmlessly to the ground. He is now at Achilles' mercy, but Apollo delays the fatal moment by shrouding Hector in a thick mist, and Achilles tries to reach him in vain before once again creating carnage among the Trojans.

The surviving Trojans flee back into their city, all except Hector, who alone stands his ground outside the walls and waits for Achilles, even though his parents beg him to come inside the city to safety. He is determined to atone for his folly in keeping his men out too long on the plain, and thus causing much unnecessary loss of life. Achilles approaches, brandishing his terrible spear, his armour blazing like a great fire or the shining sun, and the terrifying sight is too much for Hector: he turns and flees, and Achilles pursues him. They run round Troy,

past the two well-springs 'near which are fine broad washing-troughs made of stone, where the Trojans' wives and their lovely daughters used to wash their bright clothes, in the old days, when there was peace, before the coming of the Greeks' (152–6) – a pathetic reminder of a peace now forever lost, since Hector is about to be killed, and without Hector, the city's champion, Troy must fall, and the Trojan women be taken into slavery. On Olympus, Zeus weighs the fates of the two men in his golden scales and Hector's is the heavier, sinking down towards Hades.

Three times the two adversaries run around Troy, until Athena intervenes and tells Achilles to halt. She then takes the form of DEIPHOBUS, another of Priam's sons, and deceives Hector into thinking that his brother has come to his aid. Hector stands firm, faces Achilles, and fights. When he suddenly finds Deiphobus gone, he realises that the gods have been deceiving him. His death is near and there is no way out. 'Now my fate is upon me', he says, 'but at least let me not die without a struggle, ingloriously, but in doing some great deed which men in the future will hear of' (303–5). He goes bravely into his final combat (316–12):

He drew his sharp sword, huge and sturdy,
from by his side, and gathering himself he swooped
like a high-flying eagle, who darts to the plain
through the dark clouds to seize a tender lamb
or a cowering hare; even so Hector swooped,
swinging his sharp sword, and Achilles rushed
at him, his heart within him full of savage wrath.

They meet, and Achilles drives a spear into Hector's throat, wounding him mortally. With his dying breath, Hector prophesies Achilles' own death at the hands of Paris and Apollo. He also begs that his body be returned to Priam, but Achilles, still overcome with rage and hatred, bitterly rejects his plea (345–54):

Do not entreat me, you dog, by knees or parents.
I only wish that my wrath and fury might drive me
to hack your flesh away and eat it raw, for the evil
that you have done to me. So no one can ward off
the dogs from your head, not if they bring here
and set before me ten times and twenty times
the ransom, and promise even more; not if
Priam, son of Dardanus, should offer your weight
in gold; not even so shall your lady mother
lay you on the death-bed and mourn her son.
No, the dogs and birds shall utterly devour you.

Hector dies and Achilles maltreats his corpse, fastening it with thongs to his chariot and dragging it in the dust behind him. When the Trojans look down and see that their defender is dead, their cries of grief echo and re-echo through the city. 'It was as if the whole of towering Troy had been torched, and was burning top to bottom', says Homer (410–11) – a true vision of what now must happen.

Achilles' rage and his refusal to give up his victim for burial continue for eleven days, but the gods pity Hector and keep his body safe from harm, however much Achilles maltreats it. On the twelfth day they intervene to arrange that Hector be ransomed. Priam comes to the Greek camp by night, bringing gifts, to beg for the return of his son (24.189–676), and at last Achilles' wrath is eased and replaced by pity. They weep together, then Achilles accepts Priam's gifts and gives him back his son. The two enemies eat together in peace, and sleep. Then Priam returns to Troy. There is an eleven-day truce in which Hector can be given the full honours of death, and the *Iliad* ends with his funeral, the burial of a noble Trojan (784–804):

> For nine days they gathered piles of wood,
> but when the tenth dawn brought its light to men,
> they carried out brave Hector, their tears falling,
> and set his body on a towering pyre, and lit it.
> When rosy-fingered dawn appeared next day,
> the people collected round glorious Hector's pyre.
> And when they had assembled there together,
> they first with gleaming wine put out the burning,
> wherever fire still had strength, then his friends
> and brothers gathered his white bones, mourning,
> tears pouring down cheeks. They took the bones
> and laid them in a golden urn, shrouding them
> in soft crimson robes, and straightway set it
> in a hollow grave, piling on huge stones
> laid close together. Quickly they heaped a mound,
> with look-outs set on every side, for fear
> the well-greaved Achaeans might soon attack.
> Having piled the grave-mound they went back,
> and met together and held a glorious feast
> in the palace of Priam, the god-ordained king.
> Such was the funeral of Hector, tamer of horses.

Pausanias (9.18.5) says that the Thebans fetched Hector's bones from Troy and buried them at Thebes, where they worshipped him as a hero. In ancient art, Hector is depicted from the seventh century BC onwards, setting out to battle, fighting Ajax (fig. 64) or one of the other heroes, meeting his death at Achilles' hands, or having his body dragged or ransomed (fig. 122). In the postclassical arts, Hector's farewell to Andromache and Astyanax became one of the most popular episodes from the *Iliad*. In Shakespeare's *Troilus and Cressida*, Hector is a noble man

ignobly killed, while unarmed, by Achilles, and his death brings the play to a bitter close (V. x. 22):

> Hector is dead; there is no more to say.

Hecuba or Hecabe

The chief wife of PRIAM, king of Troy, and mother by him of many sons (nineteen, according to Homer), including HECTOR, PARIS, TROILUS, DEIPHOBUS, HELENUS, POLYDORUS (3) and POLITES (1), and daughters, including CASSANDRA, POLYXENA, LAODICE (1), CREUSA (3) and Ilione. She herself was the daughter of Dymas, king of Phrygia, or of Cisseus.

When Hecuba was pregnant with Paris, she had an ominous dream in which she brought forth a firebrand that set light to Troy and destroyed the whole city. This was interpreted as meaning that her baby would grow up to bring utter destruction on Troy, so when Paris was born he was given to a shepherd to be abandoned in the wilds. But the boy lived, and when grown up he returned to Troy, where he was recognised and welcomed back into the family. He later carried off the beautiful HELEN, wife of King Menelaus of Sparta, which set in motion the TROJAN WAR and did indeed, ten years later, bring destruction on Troy.

In the *Iliad* we see Hecuba, a noble and pathetic figure, suffering the effects of this war on her family and city. She beseeches ATHENA to ward off disaster from Troy, offering the goddess a beautiful robe of fine workmanship: 'But Pallas Athena turned away her head from her', says Homer (6.311). In a memorable scene just before Hector fights Achilles, Hecuba begs her son to come to safety inside the walls of Troy, rather than meet Achilles in single combat. She lays bare her bosom, appealing to him by the breast that fed him as an infant; but all to no avail. Hecuba must watch from the city walls as her son fights Achilles, and dies; and with Hector dead, there is no real hope left for Troy.

In the *Aeneid*, Virgil gives a harrowing description of the sack of the city by the Greeks. Old Priam buckles on the armour of his youth, intending to fight, but Hecuba, gathered with her daughters round the altar 'like doves driven down by a dark storm' (2.516), begs him to seek refuge with them. Together they helplessly watch their son Polites, wounded by NEOPTOLEMUS, die in front of their eyes, then Neoptolemus drags Priam through pools of his son's blood before slaughtering him too. Hecuba, bereft of most of her family, lives on.

The sorrows of Hecuba in the aftermath of the war are powerfully dramatised in the *Trojan Women* of Euripides, where the women, with their menfolk dead, are at the mercy of their Greek captors. Hecuba laments that with her own eyes she has seen her sons killed by the Greeks, her daughters dragged away captive, her husband slaughtered at the household altar. Now she herself is to become the slave of the hated ODYSSEUS, while her daughter Cassandra will be the concubine of Agamemnon, and her daughter-in-law ANDROMACHE of Neoptolemus. Already her daughter Polyxena has been sacrificed at Achilles' grave, and during the play her little grandson ASTYANAX is flung to his death from the walls of Troy. At the end of the play the city is put to the torch, and the women leave for captivity to the sound of Troy's towers falling.

Euripides' *Hecuba* focuses even more closely on the old queen's suffering. Here Polyxena is put to death within the course of the play; but more grief is still to come for Hecuba, when she finds that Polydorus, her only surviving son, is dead at the hands of the Thracian king Polymestor, murdered by his guardian for the gold he had with him. Now she is overcome by a fury for vengeance and she lures Polymestor and his two little sons into her tent, where she and her serving women stab the boys to death and gouge out Polymestor's eyes with their brooches. Her blinded victim predicts her end: that on the ship carrying her to Greece she will be transformed into a bitch with eyes of fire and will plunge into the sea to her death. The nearby headland will be called 'Bitch's Grave', *kynos sema* (Cynossema, in the Thracian Chersonese), and will act as a landmark for future sailors. In Ovid's version, Hecuba's transformation occurs while she is being stoned by Polymestor's countrymen. Cynossema is said still to re-echo with her mournful howling.

Hecuba's name, like that of Priam, has become a symbol for someone who suffers the mutability of fortune, as in a well-known verse from the *Carmina Burana*:

The king sits at the top,
Let him beware of a fall;
For beneath the wheel we read
'This is Queen Hecuba'.

Hecuba's sorrows are the subject of the First Player's impassioned speech in Hamlet, which provokes *Hamlet's* retort:

What's Hecuba to him or he to Hecuba
That he should weep for her?

[Homer, *Iliad* 6.251–311, 16.718, 22.79–92, 405–9, 430–6, 24.193–227, 283–301, 747–60; Apollodorus 3.12.5, *Epitome* 5.23; Pausanias 10.27.2; Virgil, *Aeneid* 2.506–58, 7.319–20, 10.704–5; Ovid, *Metamorphoses* 13.422–575; Seneca, *Trojan Women*. Judith Mossman, *Wild Justice* (1995).]

Helen

'Helen of Troy', 'the face that launched a thousand ships', and the most beautiful woman that ever lived. She was the daughter of ZEUS, and her mother is usually said to be LEDA, the wife of TYNDAREOS, king of Sparta. Zeus in the form of a swan seduced Leda, after flying to her for protection from a pursuing eagle. Helen was then born from an egg. From the same, or a second, egg were born Castor, Polydeuces (the DIOSCURI) and CLYTEMNESTRA – Castor and Clytemnestra were usually said to be the mortal children of Tyndareos, while Polydeuces and Helen were the immortal children of Zeus. Another tradition has NEMESIS as Helen's mother, who also produced an egg after Zeus, as a swan, mated with her in the form of a goose. A shepherd found the egg in a wood and presented it to Leda. To keep it safe she put it in a chest, and when in due course Helen hatched from it, Leda brought her up as her own daughter. Helen's egg, whether that of Nemesis or Leda's own, was seen by the traveller Pausanias in the second century AD, hanging by ribbons from the roof of a temple at Sparta (3.16.1).

1. THE EARLY YEARS

While Helen was still young (seven, ten, or twelve, according to differing versions) she was abducted by THESEUS and PEIRITHOUS, both of whom had resolved to marry a daughter of Zeus. They drew lots for Helen and Theseus won her. They left her in the charge of his mother, AETHRA, at Aphidnae in Attica while they set off together down to Hades, intending to abduct Persephone as wife for Peirithous. In their absence, Helen's two brothers Castor and Polydeuces came to her rescue. They captured Aphidnae and took their sister back to Sparta, along with Aethra who was made Helen's slave. Usually Helen was thought to return home still a virgin, but some said that she gave birth to IPHIGENEIA, who was more commonly known as the daughter of Agamemnon and Clytemnestra.

When Helen came of an age to marry, suitors from all over Greece gave bride-gifts to Tyndareos in the hope of winning her hand. The fragmentary list of suitors given in the Hesiodic *Catalogue of Women* includes THOAS (3), PODARCES (1), PROTESILAUS, AJAX (1) (who promised great gifts of sheep and oxen rustled from his neighbours), ELEPHENOR, IDOMENEUS, MENESTHEUS, ODYSSEUS (who gave no gifts because he thought that he had no chance of winning Helen), ALCMAEON and AMPHILOCHUS (1), the two sons of Amphiaraus, and MENELAUS – who proved to be the chosen husband because he gave the most gifts. Agamemnon was not a suitor, for he was already married to Clytemnestra; nor was ACHILLES, who was too young. Apollodorus (3.10.8) gives a list of thirty-one names. In general we can assume that all the Greek leaders named in the *Iliad* would have tried for Helen's hand, since Tyndareos, afraid of making enemies by choosing one suitor above the rest, made them all swear an oath to defend the rights of Helen's chosen husband in the event of any rival trying to abduct her. They willingly took the vow, standing on the severed pieces of a sacrificed horse, says Pausanias (3.20.9), so as to make the oath all the more binding. Thus, when PARIS later carried Helen off to Troy, the ex-suitors were all bound by this common oath to follow Agamemnon and Menelaus in their attempt to recover her, and to risk their lives in the TROJAN WAR.

This, of course, was all some way in the future, for Helen married Menelaus and bore him a daughter, HERMIONE. Homer knows only of this one child, but other sources also mention a son, NICOSTRATUS. Meanwhile, the JUDGEMENT OF PARIS took place, and in due course (when Hermione was nine, says Apollodorus) Paris, prince of Troy, arrived in Sparta, eager to win the love of Helen, the most beautiful woman in the world, who had been promised to him by APHRODITE as his reward for choosing her as the loveliest goddess. For nine days Menelaus entertained Paris, while he responded by giving gifts to Helen. On the tenth day, after telling Helen to supply their guests with anything they might need, Menelaus sailed to Crete to bury his grandfather, Catreus. Influenced by Aphrodite, Helen succumbed to Paris' charms and went to bed with him. The couple eloped, taking with them a great deal of property belonging to Menelaus. There are differing accounts of their journey to Troy: either it lasted a long time, while they delayed in Phoenicia and Cyprus so as to avoid pursuit; or they reached Troy in three days, with a fair wind and calm sea. Once in Troy they formally celebrated their marriage.

2. HELEN AT TROY

When Menelaus came home from Crete and found Helen gone, he reminded her old suitors of their oaths to support him, and with the help of his brother Agamemnon he gathered a large army to fetch his wife back by force. When this had all been mustered, Menelaus and Odysseus led an embassy into Troy to demand Helen's return. This approach failed and the war began in earnest. It was to last for nine years, with Troy being captured and destroyed in the tenth. In the *Iliad*, we see Helen in Troy during this tenth and final year. She now regrets her action in coming there with Paris: 'I wish that evil death had been my choice', she says to Priam, 'when I came here, following your son, forsaking my house and family, my beloved child and my dear friends. But that did not happen, which is why I waste away with weeping' (3.173–6). When Paris returns from his abortive duel with Menelaus, Helen exclaims, 'So you have come back from the fighting. How I wish that you had died there, beaten under by the stronger man, who used to be my husband' (3.428–9). But despite comments like this, she

is still in sexual thrall to Paris. He says to her, 'Let us go to bed and find pleasure in love, for never so much before has passion enfolded my heart, not even when I first took you from lovely Sparta, carrying you off in the sea-faring ships, and lay with you in love on a rocky island. Not even then did I love you as much as now and sweet desire overcome me' (3.441–6). And Helen says no more, but goes with him to bed. This was indeed one of the great love stories of all time, and Helen was right to say that the two of them 'would in time to come be the subject of song for men of future generations' (6.357–8).

In the final stages of the war, Greek envoys went to fetch Philoctetes from Lemnos and he came to Troy, bringing with him the great bow and the deadly arrows that had once belonged to Heracles. With these he shot and killed Paris. Now, with Paris dead, his two brothers DEIPHOBUS and HELENUS argued as to who should marry Helen, and it was Deiphobus who became her third husband – though not for long, since he was killed during the sack of Troy, after Helen had betrayed him by taking away his weapons while he slept and letting Menelaus and his men into the house to murder him. By this time Helen was eager for the Greeks to be victorious so that she might return home with her first husband. As for Menelaus himself, his first reaction was an attempt to kill his wife for her infidelity (fig. 65); but when he saw the beauty of her naked breasts once more, his drawn sword fell from his hand (fig. 91) and he willingly forgave her. In Stesichorus' *Sack of Troy* (fr. 201) the Greeks in general had a similar reaction: they were on the point of stoning her to death when they saw her face, and their stones dropped to the ground. Always her beauty had this effect. The old men on the walls of Troy, seeing her approaching, had said, 'No one could blame the Trojans and the well-greaved Achaeans if, for so long a time, they suffer pain and hardship for a woman such as this. She looks terribly like the immortal goddesses' (*Iliad* 3.156–8).

3. HOME FROM TROY

So Helen, reunited with Menelaus, returned with him to Sparta. In the *Odyssey*, the couple are portrayed at home once more in their palace when TELEMACHUS comes to visit them in quest of Odysseus, and they reminisce to him about the last days of the war. Helen recounts how she recognised Odysseus when he went on a spying mission into Troy, disguised as a beggar, and they talked together about the destruction of the city. 'My heart was happy', says Helen, 'since by now I had changed my mind and I wanted to go home again. I was sorry for the madness which Aphrodite inflicted on me when she took me to Troy, away from my own dear country, forsaking my child and my marriage and my husband' (4.259–63).

This strong pro-Greek feeling seems to be contradicted somewhat by the story which Menelaus tells in response, of how Helen had walked three times around the WOODEN HORSE, trying to trick the Greeks inside into giving themselves away as she imitated in turn the voices of their wives. This seems at first puzzling behaviour from a woman who, by her own admission, wanted the Greeks to be victorious. But the story may be as it is because its purpose is to show how resourceful Odysseus was in a crisis, since he kept the Greeks silent when Helen spoke and thus saved their lives. Furthermore, Menelaus says that some pro-Trojan god must have made her do it; and it may be that in retrospect, with Helen safely back home in his possession, he could be proud and amused by her old cleverness.

Certainly, in the *Odyssey*'s depiction of Helen once more at home in Sparta, she seems every inch the good housewife and hostess. She spins, she eases her guests' sorrows with drugs put into their wine and with her storytelling, and she gives Telemachus as a parting gift a beautiful robe for his bride to wear on their wedding day. She seems full of contentment to be home again and at her first husband's side once more. Indeed, this gentle, sunset picture of Helen, some twenty years or more after her flight to Troy with Paris, is very much in harmony with Homer's warm and sympathetic portrayal of her in the *Iliad*, where she is sorry for what she has done and longs for her old home and family.

4. LATER ACCOUNTS

Later writers were not so generous to Helen, however, and she was bitterly blamed for setting in motion the Trojan War by her infidelity, and for causing the deaths of so many Greeks. Hostility to Helen thus runs through much of what we have left of fifth-century tragedy, such as Aeschylus' *Agamemnon*, where the Chorus sing of Helen stepping lightly through the gates of Troy, bringing to the Trojans her dowry, death (403–8). When they welcomed her as Paris' bride, they little realised that they were bringing into their midst a lion cub, sweet and loving at first, who as time passed would reveal its true nature and repay those who cherished it with blood and death (717–49). Helen, says Aeschylus, was suitably named, for 'hel' in Greek means 'destroyer', and Helen did indeed bring death and destruction to men, to ships, to cities (681–98).

There was also, however, a quite different literary tradition, which made Helen entirely innocent of the Trojan War by saying that she did not, after all, go to Troy with Paris. This version began with Stesichorus, who, the story goes, was blinded after recounting in a lyric poem the usual tale of Helen's infidelity and flight. Realising that

Fig. 65 **Menelaus threatens Helen with a sword while Aphrodite *(right)* protects her.**

Helen's anger was the cause of his blindness, he then composed a recantation beginning, 'That story is not true. You did not sail in the well-benched ships, nor did you come to the citadel of Troy', and claiming that it was merely a phantom resembling Helen that ran off with Paris. As soon as the poem was complete, Stesichorus regained his sight. Unfortunately only the slightest fragments of this poem are left to us, but we do have an entire play by Euripides on this very theme, his *Helen*. Here the phantom was the work of Hera, angry because she had been passed over in the 'Judgement of Paris'. Paris was completely deceived by the phantom Helen and took it off to Troy, whereupon the Trojan War took place as usual. Meanwhile the real Helen was taken by HERMES to Egypt, where she was left in the guardianship of the kindly Egyptian king, PROTEUS. When the play opens, the war is over, Proteus has died, and his son Theoclymenus, the new king, is trying to force marriage on Helen. Menelaus arrives on his journey home from the war and is understandably bewildered at meeting a second Helen. Eventually matters are straightened out and husband and wife are happily reunited after their long years apart. By some clever plotting they succeed in escaping from the persecutions of the cruel Theoclymenus, and at the end of the play they sail joyfully away to Sparta, to their peaceful, sunset years together.

One unique version, also by Euripides, denies Helen and Menelaus their final, quiet years in Sparta. In his

Orestes, Orestes and Pylades try to kill Helen on the very day of her return to Sparta with Menelaus, but she is snatched up into the sky by Apollo and made immortal, to be, like her brothers, a guardian for sailors (1629–43). In the usual tradition, however, Helen and Menelaus lived contentedly at Sparta until their deaths, after which they were buried nearby at Therapnae. Helen was made immortal, since she was the daughter of Zeus – indeed, no other mortal woman could claim Zeus as a father: always, apart from Helen, he fathered sons. Menelaus too was made immortal, according to Proteus in the *Odyssey* (4.561–9) because Helen was his wife and he was thus son-in-law to Zeus. (Small wonder that so many suitors competed for Helen's hand, quite apart from her beauty.) Another variant said that after death the soul of Helen was blissfully united with that of Achilles on *Leuke*, the White Island that lay in the Black Sea at the mouth of the Danube. Here they were eternal lovers. According to a late account, they were even said to have had a son, Euphorion.

In historical times there were many shrines to Helen, but most importantly she was worshipped as a goddess at Sparta and Therapnae, her temple there being on the site of a Mycenean palace shrine. She was also worshipped on the island of Rhodes under the title of Helen *Dendritis*, 'Helen of the Tree'. One tale said that she was actually hanged from a tree there, a fate brought on her by POLYXO (2) as revenge for the death of her husband Tlepolemus in the Trojan War. This story was most likely invented to explain a cult practice of hanging Helen's image in a tree.

Helen does of course appear in art; but because her supreme beauty challenges depiction, and must be the more potent for being left to the imagination, it is no surprise to find that hers is a predominantly literary tradition. Rupert Brooke offers a cynical view of her later years in *Menelaus and Helen*:

So far the poet. How should he behold
    That journey home, the long connubial years?
He does not tell you how white Helen bears
Child on legitimate child, becomes a scold,
Haggard with virtue. Menelaus bold
    Waxed garrulous, and sacked a hundred Troys
'Twixt noon and supper. And her golden voice
Got shrill as he grew deafer. And both were old.
Often he wonders why on earth he went
    Troyward, or why poor Paris ever came.
Oft she weeps, gummy-eyed and impotent;
    Her dry shanks twitch at Paris' mumbled name.
So Menelaus nagged; and Helen cried;
And Paris slept on by Scamander side.

But more usually Helen is seen as the quintessential symbol of female beauty and sexual attraction. A few words can often bring home her loveliness more powerfully than any detailed description, as in Marlowe's famous 'Was this the face that launch'd a thousand ships, /And burnt the topless towers of Ilium?' (*Doctor Faustus*); or when Shakespeare's Troilus remarks, on hearing the din of battle, 'Helen must needs be fair, /When with your blood you daily paint her thus' (I. i. 89–90); or in Thomas Nashe's awareness of beauty's brief life in his *In Time of Pestilence*:

Beauty is but a flower
Which wrinkles will devour;
Brightness falls from the air;
Queens have died young and fair;
Dust hath closed Helen's eye.
I am sick, I must die.
    Lord, have mercy on us.

[Homer, *Iliad* 3.121–447, 6.313–58, 24.761–76, *Odyssey* 4. 81–5, 120–305, 15.56–181; Epic Cycle, Proclus' summaries of the *Cypria*, the *Little Iliad,* and the *Sack of Troy*; Herodotus 2.113–20; Thucydides 1.9; Euripides, *Andromache* 590–631, *Electra* 1278–83, *Trojan Women* 860–1059, *Iphigeneia at Aulis* 49–85, *Cyclops* 177–86; Isocrates, *Helen*; Apollodorus 3.10.7–3.11.1, *Epitome* 3.1–6, 3.28, 5.9, 5.13, 5.19, 5.21, 6.29; Plutarch, *Theseus* 31; Pausanias 2.22.6–7, 3.18.15, 3.19.9–3.20.1, 3.24.10; Virgil, *Aeneid* 2.567–603. John Pollard, *Helen of Troy* (1965); M. L. West, *Immortal Helen* (1975).]

Helenus

Son of PRIAM, king of Troy, and HECUBA, and twin brother of CASSANDRA. Both he and Cassandra had the gift of prophecy, given them as children, when snakes licked their ears as they slept in the Thymbraean sanctuary sacred to Apollo. Both knew the disastrous consequences for Troy that would follow PARIS' intended visit to King Menelaus at Sparta, and both tried to dissuade him from going. Paris ignored them, and brought on Troy the long and bloody TROJAN WAR when he returned home with Menelaus' wife, the beautiful HELEN.

Helenus fought bravely in the war and often gave advice to his brother HECTOR, the leader of the Trojan forces; though it would seem from the events recounted in the *Iliad*, even though Homer calls Helenus 'by far the best of the augurs' (6.75), that he had no realisation that Troy's fall was near. This would change, for he was later able to tell the Greeks exactly what was needed for them to take the city.

After Paris was killed, Helenus quarrelled with his brother DEIPHOBUS as to who would now marry Helen. When Deiphobus won her, Helenus left Troy in dudgeon and went to live on Mount Ida. On the advice of the Greek seer Calchas, Odysseus captured him and took him to the Greek camp. Here he revealed to them the oracles, known only to himself, foretelling how they could take Troy: they must steal the PALLADIUM, the image of Athena, from her Trojan temple; they must bring the bones of PELOPS to Troy; and they must have fighting with them both NEOPTOLEMUS, the son of Achilles, and PHILOCTETES, who owned the great bow and arrows of the mighty Heracles. These conditions were fulfilled, the Greeks built the WOODEN HORSE, and Troy fell.

In gratitude for his advice, the victorious Greeks spared Helenus' life. He went with Neoptolemus from the ruins of Troy, warning him to travel by land and thus saving him from the great storm, sent by Poseidon at Cape Caphareus, which wrecked most of the Greek fleet. They settled in Epeirus, and on Neoptolemus' death Helenus married his concubine, ANDROMACHE, who had once been the wife of Hector. She bore Helenus a son, Cestrinus. In Virgil's *Aeneid* (3.294–491), AENEAS comes to Epeirus where Helenus is king, and finds that he and Andromache are living contentedly in a new city which they have named Pergamum, after their dearly loved Troy. Helenus, from his prophetic knowledge, gives Aeneas encouraging advice about his journey to Italy and predicts a prosperous outcome. Apollodorus alone says that Helenus married Neoptolemus' mother Deidameia.

[Homer, *Iliad* 6.72–101, 7.44–53, 13.576–600, 24.249; Sophocles, *Philoctetes* 604–13, 1337–42; Apollodorus 3.12.5, *Epitome* 5.9–10, 5.23, 6.12–13; Pausanias 1.11.1–2, 2.23.6, 5.13.4; Ovid, *Metamorphoses* 15.437–52.]

Heliades

The daughters of HELIOS, the Sun-god. Although Helios had a number of daughters, the term Heliades seems to have been restricted to those who were the sisters of PHAETHON (2). When Phaethon was killed by a thunderbolt from Zeus while driving his father's sun-chariot through the sky, his body fell into the River Eridanus. His grieving sisters journeyed there, and wept so long and so unceasingly on the banks of the river that they were turned into poplar trees, and their tears into amber.

Helicaon *see* ANTENOR.

Helicon, Mount

A mountain in Boeotia, celebrated as a favourite haunt of the MUSES. On its slopes was the village of Ascra, the home of the poet Hesiod, who tells how the Muses came to him and gave him the gift of song, while he was tending his sheep on the mountainside (*Theogony* 1–34). Two famous springs, sacred to the Muses, were on Helicon: HIPPOCRENE and AGANIPPE, both of which were believed to inspire with poetry all those who drank from them.

Helios

The Sun and its god, known as Sol to the Romans. He was the son of the Titans HYPERION and Theia, and the brother of SELENE (Moon) and EOS (Dawn). By day he brought light to the world by driving his four-horse sun-chariot across the sky from east to west (fig. 66). By night he sailed in a great golden bowl back to his home in the east, floating along the river of Ocean that encircled the earth.

When Zeus divided the world between the various gods, Helios was away driving his chariot through the sky, so initially he was given no portion. But when the island of Rhodes came into being and Helios saw it rising in beauty from the sea, he claimed it as his own. The nymph of the island, RHODE, bore him seven sons; and three of his grandsons gave their names to the three chief cities of Ialysos, Cameiros and Lindos. Rhodes was an important centre for the worship of Helios, and each year the islanders threw into the sea a chariot and four horses for use by the god, to replace the weary steeds who had been toiling every day for a whole year to bring light to the world. The famous Colossus of Rhodes, one of the Seven Wonders of the World, was a huge statue of Helios at the entrance to Rhodes harbour. He also had territory in Corinth, once disputed with POSEIDON. Briareos, one of the HUNDRED-HANDERS, was called in as arbitrator, and he awarded the citadel of Acrocorinth to Helios and the Isthmus to Poseidon.

Helios was married to the Oceanid Perse (sometimes called Perseis), who bore him several children: AEETES, the ruthless king of Colchis who owned the Golden Fleece; PERSES (2), who for a time deposed Aeetes; PASIPHAE, the mother of the Minotaur; and the enchantress CIRCE. AUGEAS, the king of Elis who owned the 'Augean Stables' was also sometimes said to be their son. Helios also had several mistresses, one of whom was the Oceanid Clymene, wife of the Ethiopian king Merops. She bore Helios several daughters, known as the HELIADES, and a son, PHAETHON (2), who begged to borrow his father's sun-chariot for a day and to drive it on its fiery journey. Helios yielded to his son's pleas, but in Phaethon's inexperienced hands the horses raced out of control and set fire to much of the earth. To save it from complete destruction, Zeus killed Phaethon with a thunderbolt. His body fell into the River Eridanus, and his grieving sisters wept so long and so unceasingly on its banks that they were turned into poplar trees, and their tears into amber.

As a god who on his daily journey saw and heard everything, Helios was often called upon to witness oaths. He was able to tell DEMETER, searching everywhere for her lost daughter Persephone, that she had been

Fig. 66 Helios, in his sun-chariot, brings in the light of day while Giants prepare to storm Olympus. Their mother, Gaia, rises from the earth in their support.

abducted by Hades. He also spotted Ares' love affair with APHRODITE and relayed the news to the goddess' husband, Hephaestus, who trapped the lovers beneath a wondrous net and called all the gods to witness the spectacle. But this had an unfortunate result for Helios, since Aphrodite wanted revenge. She made him fall helplessly in love with a mortal woman, Leucothoe, the daughter of the Persian king Orchamus. Helios came to Leucothoe's room disguised as her mother, Eurynome, but once inside he returned to his true form and ravished the girl, who was overcome by his magnificence. This caused bitter jealousy in an old flame of the Sun-god's, Clytie, who still loved him and wanted him for herself. She spread abroad the story of Leucothoe's seduction until it came to Orchamus' ears. Deeply angry, he buried Leucothoe alive. She died, crushed by the weight of earth, and although Helios tried his utmost to uncover her body and bring her back to life, he tried in vain. Stricken with grief, he transformed her into the tree that gives frankincense. Clytie too suffered, for now Helios hated her. She wasted away in sorrow, sitting alone on the ground and every day gazing on the Sun-god as he passed across the sky. When she died, she became the heliotrope, whose flower turns to follow the course of the sun from morning to evening.

Helios occasionally plays a part in the myths of others. He restored the sight of the blinded giant ORION. He himself may have blinded the seer-king PHINEUS (2). He lent his granddaughter MEDEA a chariot, drawn by dragons, to escape from Corinth after she had murdered her children

(fig. 88). When Thyestes stole the kingship of Mycenae from ATREUS, Zeus made the Sun-god travel backwards in the sky, rising in the west and sinking in the east, to demonstrate his support for Atreus' claim to the throne. Zeus also persuaded Helios not to rise for three days at the time of his seduction of ALCMENE, so that his night with the beautiful mortal might be three times its usual length. When Heracles journeyed to Erytheia, in the far west, to fetch the cattle of GERYON as his tenth Labour for Eurystheus, Helios lent him his great golden bowl in which to cross the river of Ocean (fig. 69).

Helios too once had cattle on Erytheia, but these were stolen by the giant ALCYONEUS. He also had cattle pastured on the island of Thrinacia (usually identified as Sicily), milk-white beasts with horns of gold. They were tended by Lampetie and Phaethusa, his daughters by his mistress Neaera. When some of these cattle were eaten by ODYSSEUS' crew, on their long journey home from the Trojan War, Helios demanded that Zeus punish the offenders. He even threatened to leave the earth and take his light down among the dead men in Hades if nothing were done. So when the men put to sea after six days of feasting on the sacred meat, Zeus sent a violent storm against them. The ship broke up and only Odysseus, who had taken no part in the sacrilege, survived.

One of Helios' titles was Phoebus ('Shining'), and during the fifth century BC APOLLO, likewise called Phoebus, developed into a sun-god and was sometimes identified with Helios; but only much later did this identification become standard. Pausanias (8.29.4) records a tradition that the first men, of huge size, were created in India, generated by the Sun's warmth on the earth while it was saturated with moisture. 'And what other land', he asks, 'is likely to have brought men into being either before India, or of greater size, seeing that even today India still breeds beasts monstrous in their peculiar appearance and monstrous in size.'

[Homer, *Iliad* 3.277, 19.259, *Odyssey* 8.270–1, 12.127–41, 260–419; *Homeric Hymn to Demeter* 22–7, 62–89; Hesiod, *Theogony* 371–4, 956–62; Pindar, *Olympian* 7.54–76; Apollonius, *Argonautica* 4.964–69; Apollodorus 1.2.2, 1.4.3, 1.9.1, 1.9.25, 2.5.10–11, *Epitome* 2.12; Pausanias 2.1.6, 2.3.10, 2.4.6, 8.29.4; Ovid, *Metamorphoses* 1.750–2.380, 4.169–270.]

Helle *see* PHRIXUS.

Hellen

The son of DEUCALION (1), the Greek Noah, and his wife Pyrrha, though he was sometimes said to be the son of ZEUS. He gave his name to the Hellenes. To Homer, the Hellenes were simply a tribe living in Thessaly, who sent ships to Troy under the leadership of ACHILLES; but the name soon came to be applied to the whole Greek race, i.e. to everyone who shared the Greek language and culture. By the nymph Orseis Hellen had three sons, AEOLUS (1), DORUS and XUTHUS, from whom sprang the four branches of the Hellenes. Aeolus was the ancestor of the Aeolians, Dorus of the Dorians, and the two sons of Xuthus, ION and ACHAEUS, of the Ionians and the Achaeans. It was traditionally said that Hellen divided the Greek lands among his three sons, and that Aeolus succeeded his father where he ruled in Thessaly, while the other two sons moved away and settled in different areas of Greece.

[Homer, *Iliad* 2.681–5; Hesiod, *Catalogue of Women* fr. 9; Thucydides 1.3; Apollodorus 1.7.2–3; Strabo 8.7.1.]

Hemera

The personification of the Day, and its goddess. She was born, according to Hesiod, of the first sexual union in creation, that of EREBUS (Darkness) and NYX (Night), as was her brother AETHER (Brightness). Hesiod adds that mother and daughter would twice a day greet each other on the bronze threshold of TARTARUS, the deepest and darkest part of the Underworld, as they went about their business of bringing night and day to the cosmos, once when Hemera emerged as Nyx entered, and again when Hemera returned as her mother was leaving. But Hemera was often identified with EOS, the goddess of Dawn, who was thought to provide not just the early light of dawn, but the light of day as well as she accompanied the Sun-god Helios on his journey through the sky.

[Hesiod, *Theogony* 124–5, 744–57; Pausanias 1.3.1.]

Hemithea *see* TENES.

Hephaestus

Hephaestus, one of the twelve great Olympian gods, was the Greek god of fire and metalworking, identified by the Romans with Vulcan. Either the son of ZEUS and HERA, or born of Hera alone after a quarrel with Zeus, he was crippled from birth. Hera was so ashamed of her son's deformity that she flung him out of OLYMPUS. He fell down into the great river of Ocean (*see* OCEANUS), but was saved by the sea-goddess THETIS and the Oceanid EURYNOME. For nine years he lived in a cave by the ocean, practising his smith's craft and making intricate jewellery for his benefactresses. When his skill grew great enough, he took

revenge on his cruel mother by sending her a beautiful golden throne, with invisible fetters that held her fast as soon as she sat down. The other gods begged Hephaestus to come to Olympus and release her, but he resolutely refused. Only when DIONYSUS made him drunk and brought him up to heaven on the back of a mule (a favourite scene in ancient art) did he yield and set his mother free.

He must have forgiven Hera, for he tried to defend her when Zeus hung her from Olympus, with anvils tied to her feet, as a punishment for her vindictive persecution of Heracles. Zeus responded to Hephaestus' intervention by picking him up by the leg and flinging him a second time from Olympus. This time he fell through the air for a whole day before landing at sunset on the island of Lemnos. Half-dead, he was tended by the inhabitants and ever afterwards had a special affection for the island, which in historical times was his chief cult-centre in the Greek world. He returned to Olympus once again, apparently bearing no resentment against Zeus. In the battle of the Gods and the GIANTS, Hephaestus fought valiantly on Zeus' side, killing Mimas by hurling at him missiles of red-hot metal; and it was he who acted as midwife to Zeus at the birth of ATHENA, splitting open the great god's cranium with his blacksmith's axe.

As the divine master-craftsman, Hephaestus made many objects of magical beauty and intricacy, including the palaces of the gods themselves in gold and bronze, gold-wheeled tripods that moved of their own accord,

Fig.67 **Hephaestus, on a mule, is brought back to Olympus by Dionysus. A satryr playing pipes leads the procession. Hera, bound fast to her throne by invisible fetters, is fanned by (?) her daughter Hebe.**

golden robots that attended him in his forge on Olympus, immortal gold and silver dogs to guard the palace of Alcinous on the island of SCHERIA, the fearsome aegis of Zeus, and the famous golden necklace of HARMONIA. At Thetis' request, he made splendid armour for her son ACHILLES, just as, in Roman myth, his equivalent Vulcan made fine armour for AENEAS at the request of his mother, Venus. He also fashioned the two punishments sent by Zeus on the Titan PROMETHEUS: the first woman, PANDORA, who let loose miseries on mankind, and the chains with which the Titan was bound to his rock, at the mercy of the eagle who continually tore at his liver.

The *Iliad* well illustrates three different aspects of Hephaestus. In Book 18 Homer vividly depicts the master-craftsman, with his huge, hairy torso and spindly legs, at work in his forge, sweating and puffing over his anvil. He makes the marvellous armour requested by Thetis for Achilles, and most notably the famous ornate shield, in gold and silver, bronze and tin, decorated with a multitude of intricate pictures. In Book 1 we see the comical aspect of the crippled smith-god, as he tries to make peace after a quarrel between Zeus and Hera. He puffs and bustles about, pouring wine, so that all the gods laugh at him and harmony is restored. Finally, Book 21 presents the powerful and fearsome god of fire, when Hephaestus comes, on Hera's command, down to the plain of Troy to dry up the floods of the river SCAMANDER. He scorches the river-god with flame until his waters seethe and boil and he begs for mercy.

As god of fire, Hephaestus was thought to have not only a workshop on Olympus, but forges elsewhere in the world, especially beneath the volcanic Mount Etna in Sicily. Here the one-eyed giants, the CYCLOPES, worked under his direction, and the mountain resounded with the noise of their hammering, and quaked and smoked from the ceaseless fiery activity. In Hesiod's *Theogony*, Hephaestus is married to Aglaia, the youngest of the GRACES, and in Homer's *Iliad* simply to Charis (Grace). In the *Odyssey* his wife is APHRODITE, the goddess of love. Here Homer famously recounts how he was cuckolded by ARES, the god of war. But Hephaestus had his revenge by trapping the lovers beneath a magical, invisible net, and calling in all the other gods to witness the humiliation of the naked and helpless pair. He had few children (none at all by his wives). They include the wicked PERIPHETES, killed by Theseus, the lame Argonaut Palaemonius, and the obscure CABIRI. He also became the father of the Athenian king ERICHTHONIUS (1) when he tried to rape Athena (fig. 53). He was thus the ancestor of the Athenians, and Athens in historical times was an important centre for his cult. His temple, built in the mid-fifth century, still stands above the Athenian Agora.

In ancient vase-painting Hephaestus appears in a variety of scenes: returning to Olympus (fig. 67), delivering Achilles' armour to Thetis (fig. 141), and present at gatherings of the gods and (with axe) at the birth of Athena, a scene also depicted on the East pediment of the Parthenon. He often wields an axe or blacksmith's tongs, and sometimes wears a brimless workman's hat and tunic. In the postclassical arts he seems to have appealed most strongly to painters, and the smith-god in his forge, often visited by Aphrodite, is a very popular scene. But Milton makes verbal magic of his fall from Olympus in *Paradise Lost* (1.742–6):

> ... from Morn
> To Noon he fell, from Noon to dewy Eve,
> A Summers day; and with the setting Sun
> Dropt from the Zenith like a falling Star,
> On Lemnos th' Aegaean Ile ...

[Homer, *Iliad* 1.571–608, 2.426, 5.9–24, 9.468, 14.338–9, 15.309–10, 18.368–617, 21.328–82, *Odyssey* 7.91–4, 8.266–366; *Homeric Hymn to Hephaestus*, *Homeric Hymn to Apollo* 316–20; Hesiod, *Theogony* 570–2, 927–9, 945–6, *Works and Days* 60–71; Pindar, *Olympian* 7.35–8; Aeschylus, *Prometheus Bound* 1–81, 365–9; Apollonius, *Argonautica* 1.202–6, 850–60; Apollodorus 1.3.5–6, 1.4.3–4, 1.6.2, 3.14.6, 3.16.1; Lucian, *Dialogues of the Gods* 11, 13, 17, 21; Pausanias 1.20.3, 2.31.3, 3.17.3, 3.18.13, 3.18.16, 5.19.8; Virgil, *Aeneid* 8.416–54. W. Burkert, *Greek Religion* (1985), pp. 167–8.]

Hera

One of the twelve great Olympian deities, Hera was the sister and wife of ZEUS, and the queen of heaven. She was the goddess of marriage and childbirth, identified by the Romans with Juno. As one of the six children of the Titans CRONUS and Rhea, she was swallowed and later regurgitated by her cannibalistic father, then was brought up by OCEANUS and TETHYS at the far ends of the earth. Here she married Zeus. GAIA (Earth) put forth a tree, in a western garden beyond the sunset, bearing the golden apples of the HESPERIDES as a marriage-gift.

Hera bore Zeus three children: ARES, the god of war, EILEITHYIA, the goddess of childbirth, and HEBE, the goddess of youth. Their fourth child, the smith-god HEPHAESTUS, was sometimes said to have been born of Hera alone. He was crippled from birth, and Hera was so ashamed of his deformity that she flung him out of OLYMPUS. He fell into the ocean and was saved and brought up by Thetis and Eurynome, so he lived to take his revenge on his cruel mother. He sent her a beautiful golden throne, with invisible fetters attached, that held her fast as soon as she sat down. Appealed to by the other gods, he resolutely refused to release her. Only under the influence of wine from DIONYSUS did he at last set his mother free (fig. 67). It was sometimes said that Hera bore the monstrous TYPHON to be Zeus' most dangerous enemy, though the creature was more usually said to be the offspring of Gaia.

Hera was worshipped throughout the Greek world. Festivals commemorating her sacred marriage with Zeus took place in many parts of Greece. The Argives believed that she bathed once a year in the spring of Canathus, at Nauplia, and recovered her virginity. At Stymphalus, in Arcadia, she was said to have been brought up by an early king, TEMENUS (1), and was worshipped there as Child, Wife and Widow, this last referring to the time when she returned to Stymphalus after one of her frequent quarrels with Zeus. The reconciliation of Zeus and Hera after one of those quarrels was commemorated in Boeotia at a festival called the Daedala (*see* CITHAERON (1)).

Despite her importance as a goddess of cult, particularly for women, in literature and myth Hera is most often presented as a deity with a capricious and vindictive nature. She was continually jealous of Zeus' many infidelities and often persecuted both his loves and the children that resulted from his liaisons, most famously of all HERACLES, the son of Zeus and ALCMENE. Hera delayed his birth, so that EURYSTHEUS might be born first and win Heracles' birthright. She sent snakes into Heracles' cradle to kill him, but the fearless infant, heroic even then, strangled them. She afflicted him throughout his life with endless hardships, even personally nurturing the NEMEAN LION and the HYDRA OF LERNA to be his enemies, and (surely her worst piece of vindictiveness) driving him mad so that he killed his wife and children. Her endless persecution so riled Zeus that at one time he suspended her from Olympus, her hands bound with a golden chain, and with anvils tied to her feet. When, at the end of his laborious life, Heracles himself became a god, Hera at last made her peace with him and gave him her daughter Hebe as his wife.

Hera caused SEMELE's death by suggesting that she ask Zeus to appear to her in all his godlike glory. He came to her as the great storm-god, lord of the lightning, and she was burnt to ashes. But her baby Dionysus was saved and was given a home with INO and Athamas. When Hera found out, she punished them both by driving them mad, and they killed their own two children, Learchus and Melicertes. She tried to deny LETO, pregnant by Zeus with Apollo and Artemis, any place to give birth. She punished CALLISTO by turning her into a bear, or by sending Artemis to kill her. She sent on her Argive priestess IO, who had been turned into a cow (perhaps by Hera herself), a stinging gadfly to torment her and drive her far over the earth. When Io at last gave birth to her son by Zeus, Epaphus, Hera sent the CURETES (1) to steal him, and Io had once again to wander the earth in search of him.

Naturally, as the protector of marriage, Hera had no lovers herself. Some, however, did their best to attempt her virtue. In the battle of the Gods and the GIANTS, Zeus inspired Porphyrion with lust for Hera, then felled him with a thunderbolt when he attempted to rape her. The mortal IXION also tried to rape her, and when she told Zeus what had happened, he fashioned a cloud (Nephele) in her likeness and put it in Ixion's bed. Ixion ravished the cloud, whereupon Zeus punished him by binding him to the four spokes of an ever-turning wheel of fire (fig. 80). A similar story was told of ENDYMION, who was cast into Hades for his crime.

Hera was herself ever ready to punish offences committed against her by mortals. When the JUDGEMENT OF PARIS (fig. 81) went against her, and the Trojan prince Paris chose APHRODITE as more beautiful than Hera or ATHENA, both rejected goddesses sided firmly with the Greeks in the consequent Trojan War. In the *Iliad* we see them intervening to help their favourites. Perhaps most memorable is Hera's seduction of Zeus, when she wishes to draw his attention away from the battlefield (14.153–353). She borrows a love-charm from Aphrodite, and this makes her so overpoweringly attractive that Zeus cannot restrain his desire to make love to her. 'Never before have I wanted anyone so much', he says, 'not when I loved Ixion's wife, not when I loved Danae, not when I loved ...', and so he goes on, tactlessly chronicling his many infidelities. Hera puts up with it, for she is achieving her aim. In Virgil's *Aeneid* also, Hera's resentment against the Trojans endures in her persecution of the Trojan AENEAS, during his long journey away from Troy.

Hera blinded TEIRESIAS for siding against her, and with Zeus, in an argument as to whether a man or a woman felt the greatest sexual pleasure. She made the daughters of PROETUS mad because they showed disrespect to her. When Side, the wife of the giant hunter ORION, claimed to rival her in beauty, she cast her into Hades. She took away from ECHO all speech, other than the ability to repeat what others had just said, to punish her for giving Zeus' lovers a chance to escape by distracting Hera with constant chatter. She sent the monstrous SPHINX on Thebes, because the Thebans had dishonoured her, as goddess of marriage, when they failed to punish LAIUS for his abduction of Chrysippus. It is true that she helped JASON and the ARGONAUTS, but even here her aid was motivated more by enmity against PELIAS, who had slain his stepmother, Sidero, on the very altars of Hera's

Fig. 68 The 'Farnese Hercules'. Heracles rests, weary from his long Labours.

precinct, and had otherwise dishonoured the goddess through his long life.

In ancient art Hera often carries a sceptre or wears a crown (fig. 124). Her royal bird was the peacock, its tail decorated with the many eyes of All-seeing ARGUS (1) after his death at the hands of Hermes. The oldest and most important Greek temples were dedicated to her. The two best-known were on the island of Samos (sixth-century BC, and one of the largest temples in Greece), and her Argive temple, between Argos and Mycenae. In the *Iliad* (4.51–2) Hera names Argos as one of her three favourite cities, the other two being Mycenae and Sparta. It was said that Hera vied with POSEIDON for the patronship of

Argos, and that the river-gods INACHUS, Cephissus and Asterion were made judges of the dispute. They chose in favour of Hera, and the furious Poseidon responded by drying up their waters. In the Argive Heraion there was a colossal ivory and gold statue of Hera on her throne, fashioned by the great sculptor Polycleitus and famous for its beauty, but now familiar only from its depictions on Argive coins. Pausanias (2.17.3–4) says that on her crown were depicted the GRACES and the HORAE, and in one hand she held a pomegranate, in the other a sceptre. On the sceptre was seated a cuckoo, the bird whose form Zeus took to seduce Hera before their marriage: he was ever a master of successful disguise, and Hera caught the enchanting bird to be her pet. ('This story and suchlike tales about the gods I relate without believing them', says the rational Pausanias, 'but I relate them nonetheless.')

[Homer, *Iliad* 1.536–611, 4.5–67, 5.392–4, 711–92, 888–909, 8.198–211, 350–484, 15.12–150, 19.96–133, 20.113–55, 309–17, 21.327–81, 418–34, 24.55–76; *Homeric Hymn to Apollo* 92–101, 305–55, *Homeric Hymn to Hera*; Hesiod, *Theogony* 326–32, 453–506, 921–9; Pindar, *Nemean* 1.33–72; Herodotus 3.60; Apollodorus 1.1.5, 1.3.1, 1.3.5, 1.4.1, 1.4.3, 1.6.2, 1.7.4, 1.9.8, 1.9.16, 1.9.22, 1.9.25, 2.1.3–4, 2.2.2, 2.4.8, 2.4.12, 2.5.9–11, 2.7.7, 3.4.3, 3.5.1, 3.5.8, 3.6.7, 3.7.1, 3.13.5, *Epitome* 3.2–4. 6.29; Pausanias 1.18.5, 1.20.3, 2.13.3, 2.15.4–5, 2.17.1–7, 2.36.2, 2.38.2–3, 8.22.1–2, 9.2.7–9.3.8; Lucian, *Dialogues of the Gods* 9, 18. W. Burkert, *Greek Religion* (1985), pp. 131–5; J. V. O'Brian, *The Transformation of Hera* (1993).]

Heracles

The greatest of all Greek heroes, a man of superhuman courage, prowess and fortitude; a man also of violent passions and of hearty and unashamed appetites, with a tremendous voracity for food, wine and sex. Often known as *Alexikakos*, 'averter of evil', he lived an arduous life of toil and hardship, purging the world of monsters and evildoers, and was rewarded after death with immortality among the gods. In Homer, Odysseus sees Heracles' shade in the Underworld, a lonely and awesome figure (*Odyssey* 11.605–12), lines no doubt written before Heracles' apotheosis became an established part of his legend:

> Around him the dead cried out like frightened birds
> fleeing in every direction. Like dark night he came,
> holding his bow uncovered, an arrow on the bowstring,
> glaring round him fiercely, forever about to shoot.
> A fearsome sword-belt lay across his chest,
> a golden baldric emblazoned with wondrous works,
> bears and wild boars, and lions with flashing eyes,
> conflicts, and battles, and deaths, and slayings of men.

1. THE EARLY YEARS

Heracles was born in Thebes, the son of ZEUS and

ALCMENE, the wife of AMPHITRYON. The great god seduced Alcmene in the guise of her own husband, just before Amphitryon himself came to her bed. She bore twin sons, Heracles to her divine lover, and IPHICLES to her mortal husband. Even in babyhood it became clear which of the boys was the god's child, for when two snakes crawled into their bed, Iphicles cried out in terror, while Heracles seized the snakes and strangled them (fig. 78). Some said that Amphitryon had put the snakes there to find out which boy was his own son; others that they were sent by HERA, angry at Zeus' infidelity with Alcmene. Certainly Hera would persecute Heracles with implacable anger throughout his life, which seems at first hardly to accord with the usual interpretation of his name as meaning 'Glory of Hera'. But it is true to say that most of his ordeals were occasioned by Hera's spite, and that the overcoming of those ordeals necessarily brought glory not only to himself, but also (though less directly) to the goddess who initiated them. In youth Heracles was also called Alcides after his putative grandfather, Alcaeus.

As Heracles grew up, he was instructed by experts in all the usual skills. He was taught to drive a chariot by Amphitryon, to wrestle by AUTOLYCUS, to shoot with the bow by EURYTUS (1), and to fence by Castor, one of the DIOSCURI. The famous musician LINUS taught him to play the lyre; but one day the master struck out in irritation at his inexpert pupil and Heracles retaliated, killing Linus with his own lyre (fig. 85).

By his eighteenth year Heracles had become a magnificent specimen of manhood, ready to begin on his adult life of toil and glory. Chronology varies in the ancient accounts of his life, and what follows here is the sequence of events recorded by Apollodorus (2.4.8–2.7.8), with slight adaptations. Minimal details of each of Heracles' exploits are given, so to gain the fullest appreciation of his epic life-story, the reader should follow up the cross-references.

The first of his many and dangerous exploits, according to Apollodorus, was the slaying of the vicious lion that was preying on the flocks of Mount Cithaeron. For fifty days Heracles hunted it, and for fifty nights he stayed with THESPIUS, the king of Thespiae. Thespius was full of admiration for him, and since he wanted to have as many grandchildren as possible by such a hero, he sent his fifty daughters to Heracles' bed, either over fifty nights, or seven nights, or even just one night. Heracles fathered sons on them all, and twins on the eldest and the youngest.

It was at this time in his life that the famous 'Choice of Heracles' took place. Xenophon (*Memorabilia* 2.1.20–34) records the legend as originating from the sophist Prodicus, a contemporary of Socrates. Heracles came to a parting of the ways and was confronted by two beautiful women. One of them, Vice, offered him the easy path of pleasure and indolence, and the other, Virtue, the long and hard path of duty and labour for mankind. After careful thought Heracles chose the path of Virtue.

On the way back to Thebes from Thespiae, Heracles encountered the heralds of ERGINUS (1), king of the Minyans of Boeotian Orchomenus, who were travelling to Thebes to collect an annual tribute. He lopped off their ears and noses and hands, hung these round their necks, and sent them back to their master. The furious Erginus led out an army, but Heracles killed him and vanquished his followers, then imposed on Orchomenus twice the tribute that the Thebans had been obliged to pay.

CREON (2) rewarded him with marriage to his daughter MEGARA, who bore Heracles several children; but Hera later afflicted Heracles with madness and he killed his children, and perhaps Megara too. Returning to sanity, he went back to Thespius for purification, and to the Delphic Oracle for advice. He was told to go to Tiryns and to serve its king, EURYSTHEUS, for twelve years as expiation for his crime. He must carry out all tasks imposed on him by the king, and their completion would earn him immortality. These tasks became the famous twelve LABOURS OF HERACLES. He was well equipped, for he possessed a bow and arrows given him by Apollo, a sword by Hermes, a golden breastplate by Hephaestus, horses by Poseidon, and a robe by ATHENA; he himself cut a great club at Nemea.

2. THE LABOURS

The first Labour was to bring Eurystheus the skin of the NEMEAN LION, a monstrous beast that was terrorising the foothills of Nemea in the Argolid. Its pelt was invulnerable to weapons, so Heracles choked it to death with his bare hands and skinned it with its own claws (fig. 96). Eurystheus was terrified when he saw the size of the beast, so he had a great bronze jar set in the earth to serve as his hiding place if Heracles should come near again, and from now on he employed a herald, COPREUS, to carry all his instructions for future Labours. Heracles ever afterwards wore the lion's pelt as a trophy of his first great task, with the beast's scalp serving as a helmet.

His second Labour was to kill the HYDRA OF LERNA, a many-headed serpent that grew two heads for every one destroyed. He finally killed it with the help of his nephew IOLAUS, who throughout his life would be his faithful companion and charioteer, accompanying him on his Labours and his many expeditions. Now, as soon as Heracles cut off each of the Hydra's heads, Iolaus cauterised the neck-stump with a firebrand so that no more heads could grow; and in this way the creature slowly died (fig. 74). Heracles cut open the Hydra's body and took its poisonous blood. This deadly venom applied to his arrow-tips would in the future kill many of his enemies, and finally, inadvertently, Heracles himself.

For his third Labour Heracles had to capture the CERYNEIAN HIND, a deer with golden horns that was sacred to Artemis. He pursued his quarry for a whole year, and finally wounded the weary deer with an arrow just as she was about to swim across the River Ladon. Now he could catch her and carry her back to Mycenae (fig. 38). His fourth Labour was to capture the ferocious ERYMANTHIAN BOAR that was plaguing Psophis in Arcadia. Passing over Mount Pholoe, he was entertained by the civilised Centaur PHOLUS with roast meats and wine; but the smell from the open jar of wine attracted the other CENTAURS, who galloped up to share it (fig. 116). A pitched battle broke out, in which Heracles killed many of the beasts and pursued the rest as far as Malea in the southern Peloponnese, where they took refuge with the kindly Centaur CHEIRON. Heracles, to his sorrow, inadvertently killed Cheiron with one of his deadly arrows; and when he returned to Mount Pholoe he found that Pholus too was dead, having accidentally let another of the arrows fall on his foot. Heracles sadly buried his friend, then went on his way to find the Erymanthian Boar. Driving it through drifts of deep snow until he was able to capture the exhausted beast, he carried it back to Mycenae. Eurystheus once again hid in his great jar (fig. 57).

Heracles' fifth Labour was rather different, for he was told to cleanse the stables of AUGEAS, king of Elis, who had many herds of cattle. The stables were deep with the dung of years, so Heracles diverted the rivers Alpheius and Peneius to flow through them, sweeping away all the filth. The king had promised to reward him with a tenth part of his herds, but once the job was done he went back on his word, despite the protestations of his son, Phyleus. In a rage, he banished both Phyleus and Heracles (to his own eventual undoing). Heracles visited DEXAMENUS, the king of Olenus in Achaea, and aided his host by killing the Centaur Eurytion, who was trying to force the king's daughter, Mnesimache, into marriage. The sixth Labour was to get rid of the vast flocks of STYMPHALIAN BIRDS that infested the woods around Lake Stymphalus in Arcadia. Heracles scared them from their coverts with a bronze rattle, then shot them as they flew into the air (fig. 134).

His remaining Labours took him much further afield. For his seventh Labour he travelled to Crete to capture the CRETAN BULL (fig. 42), then rode on its back across the sea to the Peloponnese. Next he went to Thrace to capture the man-eating mares of DIOMEDES (1) as his eighth Labour. On his journey he stayed with ADMETUS, king of Pherae in Thessaly, where he brought back his host's wife, Alcestis, from the dead. Arriving in Thrace, he tamed the vicious mares by feeding them with the flesh of their own master (fig. 48). Unfortunately Heracles' young lover, ABDERUS, was killed during this exploit, so Heracles founded the city of Abdera in his memory before taking the mares on to Eurystheus.

Heracles' ninth Labour was to fetch the belt of HIPPOLYTE (1), queen of the Amazons, who lived around the River Thermodon off the Black Sea. He took with him a shipload of allies, including TELAMON and (some say) THESEUS. On his journey he touched at the island of Paros, where two of his men were killed by the inhabitants, so he took the king's sons, Alcaeus and STHENELUS (2), in their place. In Mysia, he stayed with LYCUS (3), the king of the Mariandyni, and helped him in battle against the barbarous Bebrycians. Arriving among the Amazons, Heracles believed at first that Hippolyte's belt would be an easy acquisition, for the queen promised to give it to him. But his old enemy Hera thought this far too simple a victory, so she stirred up the other women, saying that their queen had been abducted. The Amazons attacked, and Heracles, suspecting treachery, killed Hippolyte and took her belt, then with his men fought and overcame the Amazon army.

Fig. 69 **Heracles rides across the sea in the great golden bowl belonging to the Sun-god Helios.**

On his way home he touched at Troy, where LAOMEDON was king. Finding the city beset by a sea-monster, and the king's daughter HESIONE about to be devoured, he undertook to save her, on condition that Laomedon reward him with the divine horses once given by Zeus in exchange for Ganymede. The king agreed, so Heracles killed the sea-monster and saved the girl. But the treacherous Laomedon went back on his word and refused to hand over the horses (to his later cost). Heracles left Troy empty-handed, vowing revenge. On the journey back to Mycenae, he subjugated the Thracians on Thasos and gave the island to the Parians, Alcaeus and Sthenelus, as their kingdom.

For his tenth Labour Heracles had to fetch the cattle of GERYON from the island of Erytheia in the far west, beyond the river of Ocean. Passing through Libya, he set up the PILLARS OF HERACLES on either side of the Straits of Gibraltar to mark how far he had travelled. Wearied by the heat he threatened the Sun with his bow, and the Sun-god HELIOS, in admiration of his audacity, lent him the great golden bowl in which he himself sailed each night from west to east. Heracles travelled in this to Erytheia (fig. 69), and there killed the guard-dog ORTHUS, the herdsman Eurytion, and triple-bodied Geryon himself (fig. 60), before herding the cattle into the bowl and sailing back to Europe, landing at Tartessus in Spain. He returned the bowl to Helios and now proceeded on foot. Various adventures are recorded of his journey back to Greece. Passing through Liguria in southern France, he was attacked by a large force of warlike natives who tried to rob him of his cattle. He shot at them until he ran out of arrows, then, forced to his knees, he called in desperation to Zeus, who rained down stones from the sky. Still on his knees, Heracles pelted his enemies until they retreated. The stones still lie thickly on the plain west of Marseilles (Strabo 4.1.7).

In a forest-land north of the Black Sea, he fathered SCYTHES and two more sons on a woman who was a snake from the waist downwards. In Italy, on the future site of Rome, he killed the monster CACUS for stealing some of the cattle. When a bull broke loose from the herd at Rhegium, Heracles followed it to Sicily and there wrestled with ERYX, who also had designs on his fine beasts, and killed him. Before he finally delivered the cattle to Eurystheus, Hera intervened once again and afflicted them with a gadfly. They scattered as far as the mountains of Thrace, so Heracles had the trouble of collecting them all over again. Some he was unable to find and these went wild. This was the origin of the wild cattle of Thrace.

His eleventh Labour was to fetch the golden apples of the HESPERIDES, growing in a western garden beyond the sunset, at the far ends of the earth where ATLAS held up the sky. Having forced the sea-god NEREUS to tell him the way to the land of the Hesperides, he had a number of adventures on the long and difficult journey. He shot the eagle that tormented the Titan PROMETHEUS. He slew Emathion, the king of Arabia. He killed BUSIRIS, the king of Egypt, who tried to sacrifice him to Zeus (fig. 32). In Libya he wrestled with the giant ANTAEUS, lifting him high in the air and crushing him to death (fig. 18). Finally he came to the place where the Titan Atlas was holding up the sky. In one version, acting on advice given him by Prometheus, he offered to take over Atlas' burden while the Titan fetched the apples for him (fig. 72). In another, he fetched the apples himself, perhaps killing the giant snake, LADON, who guarded the tree with the golden fruit.

His twelfth and final Labour was to bring the hellhound CERBERUS up from the Underworld. First he was initiated into the Eleusinian Mysteries by Eumolpus and purified of his killing of the Centaurs. Then accompanied by Hermes he descended through the entrance at Taenarum in the southern Peloponnese, and it was perhaps here that he wounded HADES (1), the lord of the dead, in an incident mentioned by Homer (*Iliad* 5.394–402), when one of Heracles' poisonous arrows struck Hades painfully in the shoulder, and he had to travel up to Olympus to be healed by Paeon. When the shades of the dead saw Heracles, they fled in terror, all but MELEAGER and Medusa (see GORGONS). He drew his sword against Medusa, but Hermes explained that she was merely an empty phantom. Meleager related the sad story of his death, and when Heracles, moved by compassion, said that he would like to marry the sister of such a hero, Meleager named DEIANEIRA, who would indeed become Heracles' wife, but would also bring about his death.

Heracles next came across Theseus and PEIRITHOUS, held fast in their seats as punishment for attempting to seize Persephone, the queen of Hades, as Peirithous' bride. Heracles took Theseus' hand and raised him up, free to return to earth; but when he tried to raise Peirithous, the ground quaked and he was forced to let go. He lifted the huge rock that Demeter had put on top of ASCALAPHUS (1) to punish his tale-telling; then sacrificed one of the cows belonging to Hades as blood for the ghosts. Their herdsman, MENOETES, challenged him to a wrestling match, but Heracles broke his ribs, and might have done worse had not Persephone intervened to have the herdsman spared. Hades agreed that Heracles might take Cerberus back to earth, on condition that he mastered the hound without using weapons. He did so, clasping the monstrous beast in his strong arms until it yielded, then carried it off to show to Eurystheus, who once again hid in his great jar (fig. 37). Now Heracles returned his captive to the Underworld, and his Labours for Eurystheus were at an end.

3. LATER EXPLOITS

Heracles decided to marry again, and took part in an archery competition to win the hand of IOLE, the beautiful daughter of Eurytus, king of Oechalia. Heracles won, but Eurytus refused to give him Iole, afraid that he might again go mad and kill any children he had by her. Heracles returned to Tiryns in anger and soon afterwards, when Eurytus' son Iphitus visited him in friendship, he took him up to the top of his palace walls and in a fit of rage hurled him down to his death.

Wishing to be purified of his crime, Heracles went to NELEUS, king of Pylos in Messenia, who turned him away out of friendship towards Eurytus. Heracles now became afflicted with a disease because of the murder, so he consulted the Delphic Oracle for a cure. The Pythia refused to answer him, so in a great rage Heracles seized the sacred tripod, threatening to set up an oracle of his own. Apollo tried to wrest the tripod from him (fig. 20), and peace was restored only after Zeus hurled a thunderbolt between the two of them. The Pythia now told Heracles that to be cured he must be sold and serve as a slave for three years.

OMPHALE, the queen of Lydia, bought him (fig. 104), and during his period of servitude he performed many courageous feats: he killed the brigand SYLEUS, captured the CERCOPES, killed a great snake that was plaguing the land, and sacked the city of Omphale's enemies, the Itoni. It was also during this time that the voyage of the ARGONAUTS, to fetch the Golden Fleece from Colchis, took place. Heracles' part in the expedition is rather anomalous, for he was by far the greatest of the heroes on board, and yet the expedition was traditionally captained by JASON. Our most detailed source, Apollonius' *Argonautica*, gets over this difficulty by having Heracles unanimously elected as captain, but stepping down in favour of Jason; then getting left behind part way through the voyage while he sought for his lost lover HYLAS.

Once Heracles' servitude to Omphale was over he decided to settle some old scores. First he mustered an army and sailed to Troy to take revenge on Laomedon. Aided by his friend, Telamon, he captured the city and killed Laomedon and most of his sons, leaving PRIAM to rule Troy. As he sailed away, Hera sent great storms against him which drove him south to the island of Cos, where he and his men were attacked by the natives, thinking they were pirates. Zeus was so angry at Hera's continued persecution of his son that he suspended her from Olympus with anvils tied to her feet. But Heracles came from Cos to Phlegrae in Thrace and gave indispensable help to the gods in their victorious battle against the GIANTS.

Next he took revenge on Augeas for failing to pay him the agreed fee for cleaning the Augean stables. He suffered an initial defeat by Augeas' army, led by the Siamese twins known as the MOLIONES. But, undeterred, Heracles ambushed and killed the twins at Cleonae, then captured Elis, putting Augeas and his sons to death. He recalled Phyleus from exile, making him king in his father's place, and founded the Olympic Games at Elis. Next he marched against Pylos, to exact revenge on Neleus for his refusal to purify him of Iphitus' murder. In battle he slaughtered Neleus and eleven of his twelve sons, Nestor being the only survivor because he was away in Gerenia. Next to suffer was HIPPOCOON and his twelve or twenty sons. They had fought on the side of Neleus, and had moreover murdered Heracles' cousin Oeonus for throwing a stone at their dog. Heracles now attacked Sparta, aided by CEPHEUS (2), the king of Tegea, and killed Hippocoon and all his sons. On his way past Tegea he either raped or seduced the priestess of Athena, AUGE, and fathered on her TELEPHUS, who later became the king of Mysia and was said to be, of all Heracles' sons, the one most like his father.

Heracles now went to Calydon where Oeneus was king and married his daughter Deianeira, after wrestling with her other suitor, the river-god ACHELOUS (fig. 2). Over the years she bore Heracles several children, including HYLLUS and MACARIA. Heracles aided his father-in-law by marching with the Calydonians against the Thesprotians and subduing Ephyra, of which PHYLAS (1) was king; there he lay with Phylas' daughter, Astyoche, and became the father of TLEPOLEMUS.

When Oeneus' cupbearer EUNOMUS was accidentally killed by Heracles, he and Deianeira left Calydon and settled with CEYX (1), the king of Trachis. On the journey there they had to cross the River Evenus, and Heracles entrusted Deianeira to the Centaur NESSUS, who acted as ferryman (figs. 46 and 99). Nessus tried to rape her, so Heracles shot him with one of his arrows steeped in the Hydra's venom. On the instructions of the dying Centaur, the credulous Deianeira gathered up some of his blood, believing it to be a love-charm. She kept it carefully for years, in case it might ever be needed.

While in Trachis, Heracles aided his host by fighting the Dryopes, and he fought with AEGIMIUS against the Lapiths. He killed CYCNUS (1), son of the war-god ARES, in single combat (fig. 22), and even wounded Ares himself. Finally he raised an army to take vengeance on Eurytus for refusing him the hand of Iole. He slaughtered Eurytus and all his sons, then took Iole as his concubine and sent her with other prisoners back to Trachis. When Deianeira saw the lovely young girl and realised what she meant to Heracles, she decided that the time had come to use Nessus' 'love-charm'. She smeared it on a fine robe and sent it to Heracles at Cape Cenaeum in Euboea, where he was sacrificing to Zeus in thanks for his triumph. He put on his wife's fine gift, and soon the poison began to eat into his flesh like acid. Seizing the herald LICHAS, who had innocently brought him the robe, he flung him to his death in the sea. When Deianeira heard from her bitter and accusing son Hyllus just what she had done, she killed herself in despair.

4. DEATH AND APOTHEOSIS

Heracles, in agony, had a funeral pyre built on Mount Oeta and mounted it, ready for death. No one was willing to set light to the pyre, but at that moment POEAS passed by, looking for his sheep. He agreed to light it, and Heracles rewarded him with his great bow and unerring arrows, which were later given to PHILOCTETES. The pyre burned and a clap of thunder broke from heaven. Heracles was taken up to Olympus and made immortal among the gods. Reconciled with Hera, he married her daughter HEBE, the goddess of youth. Zeus set in the stars the constellation named after Heracles, depicting him as a kneeling man and commemorating his battle with the Ligurians, when in desperate straits he was brought to his knees, but still fought on.

With such a life of effort and dedication, and a death that led to immortality, it is not surprising that Heracles came to be closely linked with the Christian saints, and even to be seen as symbolically related to Christ. One of Ronsard's most famous *Hymnes* is *l'Hercule Chrestien*, in which he draws many parallels between Heracles and Jesus, from their birth, threatened by the snakes and Herod's soldiers, to their death on Oeta and Calvary. Milton also sees many links between the two, most famously in his description of the fall of Satan in *Paradise Regained* (4.562–71), where Christ's defeat of Satan is compared to Heracles' victory over the giant Antaeus.

Heracles appears in several Attic dramas of the fifth century BC. Euripides dramatises his tragic madness in *The Madness of Heracles*, and Sophocles his death at Deianeira's hands in *The Women of Trachis*. In Sophocles' *Philoctetes* the divine Heracles appears at the end of the play to direct Philoctetes and Neoptolemus to Troy.

Heracles was a comic character in many satyr plays and comedies, now lost but for fragments. But he appears in a comic role in Aristophanes' *Frogs*; and Euripides' *Alcestis* unites his comic and serious sides, depicting him both as a rowdy drunkard and as the compassionate and valiant hero who saves Alcestis from death. He was a tremendously popular figure in ancient vase-painting, almost always to be recognised by his lion-skin, club and bow, and usually bearded, though towards the end of the fifth century BC and into the fourth he is often beardless. The east pediment of the temple of Aphaea on the island of Aegina, now in Munich, depicts Heracles' sack of Troy. It is incomplete, but we have a fine Heracles drawing his bow, with his head framed by the jaws of the Nemean Lion (fig. 70). The famous Farnese Hercules, in the Museo Nazionale in Naples, shows the weary hero leaning on his club at the end of his long Labours (fig. 68).

[Consecutive narratives of Heracles' life can be found in Apollodorus 2.4.8–2.7.8 and Diodorus Siculus 4.9–4.39. Other references, too numerous to mention here, may be found in the cross-referenced entries. See also G. K. Galinsky, *The Heracles Theme* (1972).]

Fig. 70 **Heracles, the jaws of the Nemean Lion framing his face, draws his great bow during the sack of Troy, depicted on the east pediment of the Temple of Aphaea on Aegina. See also fig. 83.**

Heraclids

The descendants of HERACLES and DEIANEIRA. EURYSTHEUS, who had persecuted Heracles in life, continued to persecute his children after his death. With their grandmother ALCMENE they took refuge with Ceyx, king of Trachis; but he felt himself too weak to oppose the cruel Eurystheus, so he sent them to Athens and the protection of the powerful Theseus, or his sons. Eurystheus pursued with an Argive army. On learning from oracles that Athens would prevail only if a virgin of noble family were sacrificed to Persephone, Heracles' daughter MACARIA willingly offered herself. The Athenians duly defeated the Argive army and Eurystheus was killed, either by Heracles' son HYLLUS or by his nephew and charioteer IOLAUS.

Although Heracles had been born at Thebes in Boeotia, he would have ruled Mycenae and Tiryns, the kingdom of his forefathers, but for Eurystheus, and he had always regarded these cities as his rightful home. Now Hyllus led the other Heraclids in an attempt to re-establish themselves in the Peloponnese. They captured many cities, but after a year a plague broke out and an oracle proclaimed that their invasion had been premature. They withdrew, then obediently waited for three years when the Delphic Oracle instructed them to return only at 'the third harvest'. Unfortunately the Oracle meant not three years but three generations, so their next attack was a failure and Hyllus was killed in single combat by a Pelo-

ponnesian champion, ECHEMUS, the king of Arcadia. Once again the Heraclids withdrew.

Fifty or a hundred years later the three sons of Aristomachus – CRESPHONTES (1), TEMENUS (2) and ARISTODEMUS – once more consulted the Oracle and grasped the true meaning of 'the third harvest'. Another expedition was launched. After various initial difficulties, including the death of Aristodemus, struck by lightning, the Heraclids set out for the last time to conquer the Peloponnese, accompanied by their allies, the Dorians (*see* AEGIMIUS) and taking as their guide OXYLUS, 'the three-eyed one'. This time the invasion, known as the 'Return of the Heraclids', was successful. Its leaders then drew lots for the kingship of the three chief Peloponnesian regions. Cresphontes won Messene by a trick. Temenus drew Argos, whose king TISAMENUS (1), the son of Orestes, had been killed in battle. The two sons of Aristodemus, Procles and Eurysthenes, drew Sparta and established there the dual kingship, which lasted until the end of the third century BC.

[Herodotus 9.26; Thucydides 1.12.3; Euripides, *The Children of Heracles*; Apollodorus 2.8; Diodorus Siculus 4.57–8; Pausanias 1.32.6, 2.7.6, 2.18.7–19.2, 3.1.5–9, 4.3.3–8, 8.5.1, 8.5.6, 10.38.10.]

Hercules

The Roman name for HERACLES. Hercules shared the mythology of his Greek counterpart, though with various minor Roman additions, the best-known being that of his destruction of the fire-breathing monster CACUS.

Hermaphroditus

Son of HERMES and APHRODITE, and named after both of them. He is first mentioned by Diodorus Siculus (4.6.5), who seems to suggest that he was bisexual from birth; but his more familiar legend has his bisexuality originating from fusion with the nymph Salmacis and occurs first in Ovid (*Metamorphoses* 4.285–388). Hermaphroditus was brought up by nymphs in the caves of Mount Ida, but as soon as he was fifteen he set out to see the world, travelling even as far as Lycia and Caria. Here he came to a beautiful pool where lived the nymph Salmacis. As soon as she set eyes on the handsome youth, she was overcome with desire for him. She propositioned him, but he, knowing nothing yet of love, brusquely repulsed her. She pretended to go away, then watched as he stripped to swim in her pool. As soon as he was in the cool water, she plunged in with him and clung to him passionately. He struggled violently against her embraces, but she prayed

Fig. 71 **Hermes with a satyr and a deer.**

to the gods that they might be united for all time. Her prayer was granted and the two bodies became one flesh, half-man and half-woman. Hermaphroditus in his turn prayed to his divine parents that any other man who bathed in the pool should become similarly weak and effeminate, a half-man, and this prayer too was granted. The pool was still said to have this power in the time of Strabo (14.2.16).

Hermaphrodites, with female breasts and proportions but male genitals, were popular in ancient art, particularly in the Hellenistic period. Many Roman copies of Greek statues exist, the best known showing sensuously reclining bisexual figures.

Hermes

One of the twelve great Olympian gods, Hermes was the gods' herald and messenger, identified by the Romans with Mercury. He was the son of ZEUS and the Pleiad MAIA (1), born at dawning in a deep and shadowy cave on Mount Cyllene in Arcadia. The *Homeric Hymn to Hermes* recounts the first deeds of this god who was 'wily and charming, a thief, a cattle-rustler, a bringer of dreams, a spy by night, a watcher at the door ...' (13–15). As soon as he was born, he was ready for mischief. At noon he sprang from his cradle, and finding a tortoise outside the cave he created the first lyre, using the shell for a sounding board and sheep gut for the seven strings. For a time he was content to make marvellous music with his new instrument, but all the while trickery was brewing in his heart. At evening he set off to steal the cattle of APOLLO. He found the god's herds pasturing in the mountains of Pieria and carried off fifty cows, driving them backwards so as to confuse the trail, and masking his own footprints with sandals made of brushwood. Near the River Alpheius he halted and built a fire. There he sacrificed two of the cows, dividing the meat into twelve portions for the gods but eating none himself, much as he would have liked to. Then leaving the rest of the cattle behind, he returned to his mother's cave and crept innocently back into his cradle.

In the morning, Apollo set off on the trail of his stolen cows. An old man (called BATTUS (1) in later accounts) told the god that he had seen a child driving them off, and Apollo, with his powers of prophecy, now knew who the culprit was. He went angrily to Maia's cave (235–42):

And when the little son of Zeus and Maia saw Apollo in a rage about his cattle, he snuggled down inside his fragrant baby-clothes; and as the deep embers of tree-stumps are covered over with wood ash, so Hermes cuddled down when he saw the Far-Shooter, drawing

his head and hands and feet together into a little space, like a newborn baby seeking the sweetness of sleep, even though in fact he was wide awake.

After searching the cave and finding nothing, Apollo demanded to know where his cattle were, threatening that he would cast Hermes down to Hades and make him the ruler of all the babies there. Hermes innocently denied all knowledge of the theft, even claiming not to know what cows were, but Apollo was not convinced. He took the infant up to Olympus and told the story to Zeus. Despite Hermes' protestations of innocence, Zeus ordered him to show Apollo where he had hidden the cattle. He did so, then to avert Apollo's anger he took up his lyre and played so enchantingly that the god wanted the instrument for himself. They made a bargain: Apollo would keep the lyre and Hermes would become divine keeper of herds. The two became firm friends.

Hermes had many functions among both gods and men. He frequently brought messages from Olympus down to earth, as when he came to tell the nymph CALYPSO that she must release Odysseus and let him return to his homeland of Ithaca, or to tell Aeneas that he must linger no longer in Carthage, enjoying the love of DIDO. He was a helper to both gods and heroes. When the gigantic monster TYPHON cut the sinews from Zeus' hands and feet and set the she-dragon Delphyne to guard them, Hermes, with the help of Aegipan, stole them and refitted them to the helpless god. He rescued Ares after he had been shut in a bronze jar for thirteen months by the giants OTUS and Ephialtes. With Zeus he visited the hospitable peasants PHILEMON and Baucis and transformed their lives. He carried the baby Dionysus to Athamas and INO and persuaded them to rear him (to their cost). He gave Odysseus a magical plant called moly to make him proof against the wiles of the enchantress CIRCE. He gave PERSEUS a scimitar of adamant with which to cut off the Gorgon Medusa's head.

Hermes himself was no lover of violence, though when he had to fight in the battle of the Gods and the GIANTS, he killed Hippolytus while wearing Hades' cap of invisibility. He also had to kill ARGUS (1) for Zeus, whose love IO had been turned into a cow and was being guarded day and night by All-seeing Argus (fig. 77). This deed, it was said, earned Hermes the title of *Argeiphontes*, 'Slayer of Argus'.

As god of travellers, Hermes acted as guide and escort to both men and gods. He led the goddesses Hera, Athena and Aphrodite to Mount Ida for the JUDGEMENT OF PARIS; and he guided PRIAM to Achilles' tent in the Greek camp, where the old king begged for the body of his son, Hector, to be returned for burial. He also led the souls of the dead down to Hades, as in the *Odyssey* (24.1–14) he accompanies the souls of the dead Suitors. In this role he was known as Hermes *psychopompos*, 'conductor of souls'. He could even guide them back to earth again, as when he returned Persephone from Hades to her grieving mother DEMETER (fig. 47), or when he brought back Protesilaus for just one day to his widow LAODAMEIA (2).

Crafty and full of trickery himself, Hermes was suitably the god of thieves and merchants. As the patron of athletic contests, his statue was often erected in gymnasia. He was the god of flocks and herds, especially concerned with their fertility; and in art he is often shown carrying a ram over his shoulders. In general he brought prosperity and luck to men. Statues of Hermes known as *hermae*, 'herms', were set up at the roadside, at crossroads and outside houses: rectangular stone pillars, topped with a bearded head of the god and with an erect phallus on the front, they were believed to bring good fortune. A lucky find, a windfall, was known as a *hermaion*, a 'gift of Hermes'.

He had no wife, but had many children by many mistresses. He was the father of the pastoral goat-god PAN by the daughter of Dryops, and of EUDORUS by Polymele, the daughter of Phylas. Aphrodite bore him the bisexual HERMAPHRODITUS. MYRTILUS, the charioteer of Pelops, was Hermes' son, and his murder so angered the god that he sent to Pelops' descendant, ATREUS, the golden lamb that brought so much bloodshed in its train. He fathered CEPHALUS (1) on Herse, the daughter of Cecrops, and he turned to stone Herse's greedy sister AGLAURUS (2) who tried to stand in his way. He lay with CHIONE (2), the daughter of Daedalion, on the same day as Apollo, and she bore Philammon, an accomplished musician, to Apollo, and the famous thief AUTOLYCUS to Hermes. He was the father of the Argonauts Erytus, ECHION (2) and AETHALIDES; and of ABDERUS, who was killed by the man-eating mares of Diomedes. He raped Apemosyne, the daughter of Catreus, king of Crete, but she bore him no child, for she was kicked to death by her brother ALTHAEMENES.

Hermes appears very frequently in ancient art and is easily recognised by his herald's staff, the caduceus (*kerykeion*), and by his wide-brimmed traveller's hat (sometimes winged) and winged sandals (fig. 71). He appears in Aeschylus' *Prometheus Bound* (941–1079) and Euripides' *Ion* (1–81); and Sophocles' (incomplete) satyr play *Searching Satyrs* dramatises the first day of his life, with the invention of the lyre and the theft of the cattle, famously updated in Tony Harrison's *Trackers of Oxyrhynchus*.

See also figs. 25, 75 and 80.

[Homer, *Iliad* 20.31–40, 21.497–501; Pindar, *Olympian* 6.78–9, *Pythian* 2.10; Apollodorus 3.10.2; Diodorus Siculus 5.75.1–3; Lucian, *Dialogues of the Gods* 11; Pausanias 9.22.1–2. W. Burkert, *Greek Religion* (1985), pp. 156–9.]

Hermione

The only daughter of MENELAUS and HELEN. At the age of nine she was abandoned by her mother, who ran off with Paris, prince of Troy, thus setting in motion the Trojan War. According to Homer, Menelaus betrothed Hermione to Achilles' son NEOPTOLEMUS while away fighting at Troy, and the wedding was celebrated on his return home at the end of the war. The marriage, however, was childless.

We gain our fullest depiction of Hermione from Euripides' tragedy *Andromache*, where she comes to vivid life in the violent bitterness and jealousy that she feels because she is barren. She blames this on spells cast by ANDROMACHE, the concubine that Neoptolemus has won at Troy and by whom he has had a son, Molossus. Aided by Menelaus, she almost succeeds in having Andromache and Molossus put to death, before they are rescued in the nick of time by old PELEUS, Neoptolemus' grandfather. Terrified of her husband's anger, Hermione tries time and again to kill herself. 'When she tried to hang herself', says her old nurse (811–16), 'the servants told to watch her barely managed to stop her, or to snatch a sword she had found and take it away. She is full of remorse, and knows very well that what she did was wrong. I'm just worn out with trying to stop her hang herself.' Hermione is hysterical with fear, until Agamemnon's son ORESTES arrives and saves her from Neoptolemus' wrath. In this version of the myth, Menelaus betrothed his daughter to Orestes before the war began, but then changed his mind and promised her to Neoptolemus if he would help to capture Troy (966–81). So now to escape her husband's vengeance, Hermione thankfully flees with Orestes to Sparta and there marries him after Neoptolemus' death (here brought about at Delphi by Orestes himself).

Euripides gives a rather different version in his *Orestes*. In this play, where Hermione is briefly held hostage for Orestes' safety, Apollo prophecies that she will indeed marry Orestes, but never Neoptolemus, since he will be killed first (1652–7). Traditions agree, however, that Hermione bore Orestes a son, TISAMENUS (1), who united the kingdoms of Argos and Sparta before falling to the Heraclids.

[Homer, *Odyssey* 4.1–14; Apollodorus, *Epitome* 3.3, 6.14, 6.28; Pausanias 2.18.6; Virgil, *Aeneid* 3.327–32; Ovid, *Heroides* 8.]

Hero and Leander

Ill-fated lovers who lived on opposite sides of the narrow Hellespont (Dardanelles). Hero was a priestess of

Aphrodite at Sestos, on the European shore, and each night she would light a lamp in the window of the tower in which she lived, to guide Leander as he swam across to her from Abydos. He stayed with her until daybreak and then swam home again. In this way they met and made love through many summer nights. But winter came, with its stormy weather, and still Hero lit the lamp, and still Leander braved the treacherous seas. Then one night, during a violent storm, the lamp was blown out by the wind and Leander, losing his way among the dark and heaving waves, was drowned. Next morning Hero looked down and saw his body washed up on the shore. In her grief she flung herself from the tower, falling to her death beside her lover.

The story most likely originated in an Alexandrian poem, but in extant literature we come across it first in Virgil (*Georgics* 3.258–63) and Ovid (*Heroides* 18 and 19). Its fullest treatment is in the poem *Hero and Leander* by Musaeus, probably of the late fifth or early sixth century AD. The myth proved of great inspiration to postclassical artists: to painters, including Rubens and Turner, and most of all to poets. In May 1810 Lord Byron, wishing to repeat Leander's achievement, himself swam from Sestos to Abydos:

> ...'Twere hard to say who fared the best:
>> Sad mortals! thus the Gods still plague you!
> He lost his labour, I my jest;
>> For he was drowned, and I've the ague.

A. E. Housman characteristically saw Hero and Leander's love as symbolising the transient nature of happiness:

> By Sestos town, in Hero's tower,
>> On Hero's heart Leander lies;
> The signal torch has burned its hour
>> And sputters as it dies.
> Beneath him in the nighted firth,
>> Between two continents, complain
> The seas he swam from earth to earth
>> And he must swim again.

Herse ('Dew') *see* AGLAURUS (2).

Hesione

Daughter of King LAOMEDON of Troy. When Laomedon refused to pay Apollo and Poseidon their agreed wage for building the walls of Troy, the gods in fury sent a plague and sea-monster to ravage the land. Oracles foretold that they would be appeased only if Hesione were sacrificed to the monster, so her father had her chained to the rocks near the sea. There she waited to be devoured. But HERACLES arrived in Troy and offered to save the girl on condition that he be rewarded with Laomedon's divine

horses. The king agreed and Heracles killed the monster: according to Hellanicus, he leapt into the jaws of the beast and entered its belly, then destroyed it from within. Laomedon, however, refused to keep to his bargain, so Heracles sailed away threatening vengeance. In due course he returned with an army. He captured Troy, killing Laomedon and most of his sons. He gave Hesione as the prize for greatest valour to his ally, TELAMON, who had been the first to breach the city walls. Hesione was allowed to choose one of the Trojan captives to be set free, so she chose her brother Podarces, ransoming him with her veil, after which his name was changed to PRIAM (reputedly from the Greek verb *priamai*, 'to buy') and he took over the rule of Troy.

Hesione bore Telamon a son, TEUCER (2), who was to play a heroic part on the Greek side in the Trojan War.

[Homer, *Iliad* 5.638–51, 20.144–8 and schol. 20.146 (Hellanicus); Sophocles, *Ajax* 1299–1303; Apollodorus 2.5.9, 2.6.4; Ovid, *Metamorphoses* 11.211–17.]

Hesperides ('Daughters of evening')

Singing NYMPHS who lived in a western garden beyond the sunset, on an island at the far ends of the earth where ATLAS held up the rim of the sky (though Apollodorus locates the garden in the far north near the HYPERBOREANS, and Apollonius in Libya near the Atlas Mountains). In this garden grew the golden apples which GAIA (Earth) once put forth as a marriage-gift for Zeus and Hera. The Hesperides, helped by the giant serpent LADON, guarded the tree bearing these apples from the daughters of Atlas, who were in the habit of pilfering the golden fruit. Hesiod calls the Hesperides the daughters of NYX (Night). Their number varies in literature and art from two to seven.

HERACLES' eleventh Labour (*see* LABOURS OF HERACLES) was to fetch the golden apples for Eurystheus. He wrestled with the sea-god NEREUS to find out the way to the land of the Hesperides, and came at last to the place where Atlas stood, supporting the sky. Heracles offered to hold up the sky for him if he would fetch the apples from the Hesperides' garden, so Atlas with pleasure relinquished his load and did as Heracles asked. On his return, unwilling to take up his weary burden again, he said that he would himself deliver the apples to Eurystheus; but Heracles tricked him by asking for a moment's reprieve while he put a padded cushion on his head. Once Atlas was holding up the sky again, Heracles at once seized the fruit and made good his escape. After Eurystheus had seen the apples they were returned to the Hesperides by Athena, since the sacred fruit could not be possessed by a mortal.

In some accounts Heracles himself confronted and

Fig. 72 **Atlas brings the golden apples of the Hesperides to Heracles, who holds up the heavens, with a little help from Athena.**

with now one, now the other, holding up the sky or carrying the apples. On the metopes from the temple of Zeus at Olympia, Atlas brings the apples while Heracles holds up the sky, with a little help from Athena (fig. 72). Elsewhere Heracles tackles the serpent; but there are also peaceful scenes in which he is entertained by the Hesperides, who themselves pick the apples and give them to him. South Italian art shows the Hesperides alone in their garden, with one of them usually giving the snake something to drink.

[Hesiod, *Theogony* 215–7, 275, 333–5, 517–20; Sophocles, *Women of Trachis* 1090–1100; Euripides, *The Madness of Heracles* 394–9, *Hippolytus* 742–51; Apollonius, *Argonautica* 4.1384; Apollodorus 2.5.11; Diodorus Siculus 4.26.2–4; Ovid, *Metamorphoses* 4.630–62; Seneca, *The Madness of Hercules* 530–2.]

Hesperus

The evening star (i.e. the planet Venus), by early tradition the son of EOS, the Dawn, and the Titan Astraeus, but later said to be son or brother of ATLAS. Hesperus was carried away by a great wind when he climbed to the summit of Mount Atlas to watch the stars, disappearing without trace. Men believed that he had been transformed into the kindly evening star that brings the quiet night. Homer names him once (*Iliad* 22.317–8):

> A star moves among stars in the darkening night,
> Hesperus, the loveliest star in the sky.

In later arts, Hesperus is sometimes – appropriately – associated with wedding songs or with HYMEN, the god of marriage. A few lines of Sappho, addressing Hesperus, survive, which may have been part of a marriage hymn (fr. 104a):

> Hesperus, bringing all that the bright dawn scattered,
> you bring home the sheep, you bring home the goat,
> you bring home the child to its mother.

[Diodorus Siculus 3.60.]

Hestia

The goddess of the hearth and its fire (known to the Romans as VESTA), and thus a divinity central to every home. She was the daughter of CRONUS and Rhea, both the first- and last-born, since Cronos swallowed each of his children at their moment of birth, then later was forced to disgorge them. Hestia, the first-born, was the first to be swallowed and the last to be disgorged.

She was wooed by POSEIDON and APOLLO, but instead of marrying she renounced sexual love and swore an oath of eternal chastity. Zeus, in compensation, granted her special honours, for as goddess of the hearth she was worshipped in every household and in all the temples of

killed the serpent before taking the apples with his own hands. Apollonius (*Argonautica* 4.1383–1449) describes how the ARGONAUTS found the snake killed and the Hesperides mourning its death at the brutal hands of Heracles:

> The snake lay fallen by the trunk of the apple tree. Only the tip of his tail was still twitching, but from his head to the end of his dark spine he lay lifeless. Where the arrows had left in his blood the sharp venom of the Lernaean Hydra, flies wilted and died on the festering wounds. Nearby, the Hesperides made shrill lament, their silvery arms flung over their golden heads ... 'That most heartless man took away the life of our guardian snake and carried off the golden apples of the goddesses. Bitter is the grief he has left to us.'

After its death the serpent was immortalised in the sky as the constellation Draco, curling between the Great and Little Bears, and right next to it is Heracles himself, with raised club.

Ancient art from the sixth century BC depicts both versions of the story: Heracles and Atlas are shown together,

the gods. While other gods travelled the world, Hestia remained quietly on OLYMPUS and so played no part in the stories of mythology, but we should never forget her importance as goddess of hearth and home, and her very real power. As her *Homeric Hymn* (29.1–6) puts it:

> Hestia, you have won an eternal home and the greatest of honours in the high dwellings of all, both immortal gods and men who walk the earth. Glorious is your privilege and your praise. For without you men can have no feasts, and to you the sweet wine is poured both first and last.

Although she plays no part in the myths, we see Hestia in ancient art in the procession of the gods at the wedding of Peleus and Thetis. On the François Krater, for instance, she is portrayed next to Chariclo, the wife of Cheiron the Centaur, and in Sophilos' two depictions of the scene next to her sister Demeter.

[Hesiod, *Theogony* 453–506; *Homeric Hymn to Aphrodite* 21–32; Pindar, *Nemean* 11.1–7; Pausanias 5.14.4.]

Hieromneme

Daughter of the river-god SIMOEIS, and wife of ASSARACUS.

Hilaeira and Phoebe

Daughters of LEUCIPPUS (1), king of Messenia, so they were known as the Leucippides, though they were sometimes said to be the daughters of APOLLO. They were carried off by the DIOSCURI and had sons by them: Hilaeira bore Anaxis (or Anogon) to Castor, and Phoebe bore Mnasinous (or Mnesileos) to Polydeuces. In Pausanias' time the sisters had a sanctuary at Sparta, where their priestesses were young girls also called Leucippides (3.16.1).

Himeros

The personification of desire. He was present with EROS at the birth of APHRODITE and accompanied her to OLYMPUS, thereafter becoming a member of her train; and his home among the gods was (appropriately) near that of the MUSES and the GRACES.

[Hesiod, *Theogony* 64, 201.]

Hippasus (1)

Son of Leucippe, one of the three daughters of MINYAS who refused to worship Dionysus. To appease the angry god, Hippasus was torn to pieces by his mother and her sisters.

Hippasus (2) *see* CEYX (2).

Hippo or Hippe

Daughter of the Centaur CHEIRON and Chariclo. She was seduced by AEOLUS (1) on Mount Pelion and became pregnant, but was ashamed to tell her parents of her condi-tion. When the time of her baby's birth drew near, she fled into the forest. Her father came in search of her while she was in labour, and she prayed to the gods to hide her by turning her into a horse. Artemis took pity on her and ensured that her baby, MELANIPPE (1), was born in secret. The goddess then put Hippo in the stars as the constellation Hippos, the Horse, usually identified with Pegasus. A fragment from Euripides' lost tragedy *Wise Melanippe* says that Hippo was a seer, so Zeus turned her into a horse to stop her prophesying divine secrets and then immortalised her as a constellation. Her daughter Melanippe was brought up by Aeolus.

Hippocoon

A king of Sparta, son of Oebalus and the nymph Bateia, and brother or half-brother of TYNDAREOS and ICARIUS (2). Tyndareos succeeded to the throne of Sparta, but Hippocoon drove him into exile and took over the rule. He had many sons, twelve or twenty (the Hippocoontids), but they all came to an unfortunate end for incurring the anger of the mighty HERACLES. He had plenty of motives for anger, for Hippocoon had refused to purify him for the murder of Iphitus, then with his sons had fought on the side of NELEUS in his great battle against Heracles. Above all, the Hippocoontids had killed Heracles' cousin Oeonus, the son of Licymnius, for as he was passing their palace a Molossian hound rushed out at him, and when he threw a stone at the dog, they too rushed out and clubbed him to death. Heracles mustered an army and marched against Sparta, where he killed Hippocoon and all his sons, then restored Tyndareos to the throne.

[Apollodorus 2.7.3, 3.10.4–5; Diodorus Siculus 4.33.5; Pausanias 2.18.7, 3.1.4–5, 3.15.1–9, 3.19.7, 8.53.9.]

Hippocrene

The 'Horse's Spring' on Mount Helicon, created when the winged horse PEGASUS struck the ground with his hoof. Around this Spring the MUSES danced, and its water was said to bring poetic inspiration to all who drank from it. Thus Keats in his *Ode to a Nightingale*:

> O for a beaker full of the warm South,
> Full of the true, the blushful Hippocrene,
> With beaded bubbles winking at the brim,
> And purple-stained mouth;
> That I might drink, and leave the world unseen,
> And with thee fade away into the forest dim.

There was another, less famous, Horse's Spring at Troezen, created by Pegasus in just the same way.

[Hesiod, *Theogony* 1–8; Strabo 8.6.21; Pausanias 9.31.3, 2.31.9; Ovid, *Metamorphoses* 5.254–68.]

Hippodameia (1) *see* PELOPS.

Hippodameia (2) *see* PEIRITHOUS.

Hippolochus

Son of BELLEROPHON, and father of GLAUCUS (4) who led the Lycian army at Troy.

Hippolyte (1)

A queen of the AMAZONS living around the river Thermodon off the Black Sea. As the ninth of his Labours for Eurystheus (*see* LABOURS OF HERACLES), Heracles had to fetch Hippolyte's belt at the request of the king's daughter, Admete. The belt, given to the Amazon queen by ARES, was a symbol of her power. Heracles set sail, taking with him a band of allies including TELAMON and (some say) THESEUS. At first Hippolyte received him kindly and promised him the belt, but in the eyes of HERA this seemed far too easy a victory. Disguising herself as an Amazon, the goddess stirred up the other women by saying that their queen had been abducted. The Amazons charged on horseback down to Heracles' ship, and he, assuming treachery, killed Hippolyte and took her belt, then with his comrades fought and overcame the Amazon army. According to Apollonius, no blood was shed, for Heracles ambushed and captured Melanippe, Hippolyte's sister, and the queen ransomed her back with her belt.

The combat of Heracles and his friends with the Amazons enjoyed tremendous popularity in ancient art, appearing on nearly four hundred vases. Interestingly, Heracles' own opponent, when named, is usually Andromache.

[Pindar, *Nemean* 3.38–9; Euripides, *The Madness of Heracles* 408–18; Apollonius, *Argonautica* 2.966–9; Apollodorus 2.5.9; Diodorus Siculus 16.1–4; Pausanias 5.10.9, 5.11.4; Quintus of Smyrna, *Sequel to Homer* 6.240–5.]

Hippolyte (2) *see* ANTIOPE (2).

Hippolyte (3)

A variant name for the wife of ACASTUS. *See also* PELEUS.

Hippolytus (1)

One of the GIANTS, killed in the battle between the Gods and the Giants by HERMES, wearing Hades' cap of invisibility.

Hippolytus (2)

Son of the great Athenian hero THESEUS and his Amazon queen ANTIOPE (2). Hippolytus' legend is bound up with that of Theseus' later wife PHAEDRA, who fell in love with her young stepson. In what seems to have been the traditional story, Phaedra was a shameless woman who set out to seduce him. He rebuffed her and she, afraid of the consequences and desiring revenge for the slight, de-

clared to Theseus that he had tried to rape her. Theseus cursed his son, calling on POSEIDON to kill him, and the god answered his prayer by sending a bull raging from the sea to terrify Hippolytus' horses (fig. 73). The poor youth was tossed from his chariot, entangled in the reins and dragged to his death (his name means 'torn apart by horses'). Phaedra hanged herself.

Hippolytus' story is best known, however, from Euripides' version of the myth in his powerful tragedy *Hippolytus*. Here Hippolytus is a chaste youth, in fact so totally chaste, and so devoted to the virgin goddess ARTEMIS, that he completely ignores the worship of the love-goddess APHRODITE. It is she who punishes him by forcing the virtuous Phaedra to fall in love with him, well knowing that this will bring her enemy to death, and Phaedra too, innocent though she is. Phaedra struggles to overcome her passion in silence, but eventually she is too weak to keep her love secret any longer, so she tells her nurse what ails her. The nurse, anxious to ease her mistress' sufferings, reveals her love to Hippolytus, and he responds to these well-meant overtures with bitter rage against women in general and Phaedra in particular (616–68): 'Zeus', he begins,

> why did you create and put on earth with men so vile and worthless a thing as woman? If you wanted to propagate the human race, you didn't have to do it through women. Better that men should buy children from you, paying at your temples in gold or iron or bronze, each man what he could afford. Then they could live in freedom in their own homes, without women. Women are a great curse to men ...

Hippolytus' misogynistic attack on Phaedra seems all the more outrageous because she is essentially innocent of all his charges. And yet he is honourable enough to keep his stepmother's secret when Theseus returns, to find his wife dead and a letter accusing Hippolytus of rape. Theseus curses his son, ordering him into exile, then prays to Poseidon to kill him. Poseidon sends the bull from the sea. The dying boy is carried onstage, and Theseus too late finds out the truth from Artemis.

It was said by certain later writers that the healer ASCLEPIUS brought Hippolytus back from the dead. Refusing to forgive his father, he went to Aricia in Italy. Here he became king and dedicated a precinct to Diana (Artemis) on the shores of Lake Nemi near Rome, becoming the minor god VIRBIUS. At Troezen, the usual location of Phaedra's passion and Hippolytus' death, it was the custom in historical times for girls to dedicate a lock of hair to Hippolytus on their marriage, and Troezenians believed him to have been immortalised in the stars as the constellation Auriga (the Charioteer).

[Apollodorus 3.10.3, *Epitome* 1.18–19; Pausanias 1.22.1–3, 2.27.4, 2.32.1–4, 2.32.10; Seneca, *Phaedra*.]

Hippomedon

There is some uncertainty about Hippomedon's parentage, for either he was the son of TALAUS and Lysimache, and thus the brother of ADRASTUS (1), king of Argos; or he was the son of Adrastus' brother Aristomachus or of his sister, and thus Adrastus' nephew. What is certain is that he went with Adrastus on the fateful expedition of the SEVEN AGAINST THEBES and died there, killed either by Ismarus or Hyperbius. His son Polydorus was one of the EPIGONI who later avenged their fathers' deaths.

[Aeschylus, *Seven Against Thebes* 486–520; Sophocles, *Oedipus at Colonus* 1317–18; Euripides, *Phoenician Women* 1113–18, *Suppliant Women* 881–7; Apollodorus 3.6.3, 3.6.6, 3.6.8; Pausanias 2.20.5, 2.36.8, 10.10.3.]

Hippomenes *see* ATALANTA.

Hippothoon *see* ALOPE.

Horae

Goddesses of the Seasons. They were the daughters of ZEUS and THEMIS, and sisters of the FATES. Hesiod makes them three in number and gives them names with ethical connotations, Eunomia ('Good Order'), Dike ('Justice') and Eirene ('Peace'), reflecting their function as goddesses of order who maintained the stability of society. In Athens their names referred to the effects of the seasons and their function as goddesses of fruitful nature: Thallo ('Blooming', Spring), Auxo ('Increase', Summer) and Carpo ('Fruiting', Autumn).

In the *Iliad* the Seasons guard the cloud-gates of OLYMPUS: twice they open them to let Hera and Athena through on their way down to earth, and they take charge of the chariot and horses when the goddesses return. In one of the shorter *Homeric Hymns* to APHRODITE (6.5–13), they welcome the goddess at her birth, clothe and adorn her, then escort her to Olympus, where they themselves often go to dance with the gods. Thereafter, like the GRACES, they are often depicted as her companions, and are seen in contexts of joy and festivity, such as the births or marriages of the gods. Their earliest appearance in ancient art is at the wedding of Peleus and Thetis on the François Krater. In Hellenistic times they become four in number, and from this period on they often appear in Graeco-Roman and postclassical art as the seasons of the year, with appropriate attributes. The orderly procession of the seasons was seen as proof of the divine order of the world.

[Homer, *Iliad* 5.749–51, 8.393–5, 433–5; *Homeric Hymn to Apollo* 194–6; Hesiod, *Theogony* 901–6, *Works and Days* 74–5;

Fig. 73 A bull rises from the sea in front of Hippolytus' chariot, while a Fury brandishes a torch and an old man looks on in alarm.

Pindar, *Olympian* 13.6–8, *Pythian* 9.54–65; Pausanias 3.18.10, 5.11.7, 9.35.2; Ovid, *Metamorphoses* 2.116–18.]

Hundred-handers

Three brothers, giants, the children of Uranus (Sky) and GAIA (Earth), called Briareos (also Aegaeon), Cottus and Gyges (or Gyes). Hesiod describes their terrible forms (*Theogony* 148–56):

> They were huge and strong beyond all telling. From their shoulders sprang a hundred arms, terrible to behold, and each had fifty heads upon his shoulders, growing from sturdy bodies. Boundless and powerful was the strength that lay in their mighty forms. All those that were born of Earth and Sky were the most fearsome of children, and they were hated by their own father from the first ...

Uranus hated them so much that he pushed them back into the womb of their mother the Earth, until at last Gaia, overcome by the pain of it, induced their brother CRONUS to castrate his father and overthrow him. Cronus then reigned supreme, but he was afraid of the power of the Hundred-handers and their brothers the CYCLOPES, so he imprisoned them in TARTARUS.

He was right to fear them. In time his own children, led by his youngest son ZEUS, rebelled against him. Zeus released the Hundred-handers and Cyclopes, and they helped him to a tremendous victory over his father and the rest of the TITANS. Cronus in his turn was deposed by his son. Zeus imprisoned the Titans in Tartarus and gave the task of guarding them to the Hundred-handers, who remained his faithful allies. When the other gods later revolted from Zeus and tried to put him in chains, THETIS hurried to fetch Briareos, the mightiest of the three brothers. He came up to Olympus, and his terrifying presence was quite enough to quell the rebellious gods into submission. He was also called in to decide a dispute between his father-in-law POSEIDON (he was married to Poseidon's daughter Cymopoleia) and the Sun-god HELIOS over the ownership of Corinth. He awarded the citadel of Acrocorinth to Helios and the Isthmus to Poseidon.

[Homer, *Iliad* 1.396–406; Hesiod, *Theogony* 617–735, 807–19; Apollodorus 1.1.1–1.2.1; Pausanias 2.1.6, 2.4.6; Virgil, *Aeneid* 10.565–8.]

Hyacinthus

Usually said to be the son of Amyclas, king of Sparta, and Diomede, though occasionally son of the Macedonian king Pierus and the Muse Clio. Hyacinthus was a beautiful youth, and much loved: by the bard THAMYRIS (the first instance, so it was said, of homosexual love among mortals), by the god of the West Wind, ZEPHYRUS, and by the god APOLLO. Hyacinthus favoured Apollo but died tragically of his love, for one day, when boy and god were throwing a discus to one another, Apollo's unsuccessful rival Zephyrus, out of jealous spite, deflected the discus with a gust of his wind. Apollo made his throw and the discus swerved, hitting Hyacinthus on the head and killing him at once. Apollo tried and failed to revive him, so in his grief he transformed the blood that flowed from his lover's mortal wound into a dark blue flower, the 'hyacinth', a type of iris or lily. In this way the god gave Hyacinthus a kind of immortality, for the flower was born again every spring, and on its petals were marks that read '*ai ai*' ('alas!'), forever recalling Apollo's great cry of grief at his lover's death. The god also promised that the hyacinth, by these same marks on its petals, would one day commemorate one of the bravest of heroes. This would be AJAX (1), son of Telamon.

After his death Hyacinthus was worshipped at Amyclae and honoured every year at Sparta by the important and very ancient three-day festival of the Hyacinthia. Pausanias saw his tomb at Amyclae below an image of Apollo. He also saw Hyacinthus depicted on the Amyclae Throne (late sixth century BC), being escorted up to Olympus by various gods and portrayed as a bearded, mature man, not as the young and beautiful boy of the later romantic story and of later art.

[Euripides, *Helen* 1465–75; Apollodorus 1.3.3, 3.10.3; Pausanias 3.1.3, 3.19.3–5; Lucian, *Dialogues of the Gods* 16; Ovid, *Metamorphoses* 10.162–219.]

Hyades ('Rainers')

Daughters of the Titan ATLAS and the Oceanid Aethra; sisters of Hyas and half-sisters of the seven PLEIADES. The number of the Hyades ranges in different accounts from two to seven. When their brother Hyas was killed while out hunting, either by a lion or a boar or a snake, the girls died of grief for him, and the Pleiades died in turn from mourning their half-sisters. Zeus out of pity immortalised them all in the night sky, and now the star cluster Hyades lies close to that of the Pleiades in the constellation Taurus. The Hyades were also said to have been the nurses of the young DIONYSUS on Mount Nysa, and this is sometimes given as another reason for their place among the stars.

[Homer, *Iliad* 18.486; Hesiod, *Poetic Astronomy* fr.291; Apollodorus 3.4.3; Ovid, *Fasti* 5.163–82.]

Hyas *see* HYADES.

Hydra of Lerna

A monster, the offspring of ECHIDNA and TYPHON, and possibly the mother of the CHIMAERA (Hesiod, *Theogony* 313–19, with the pronoun at 319 being ambiguous). HERA herself had nurtured the Hydra in her anger against HERACLES, whose second Labour for Eurystheus (*see* LABOURS OF HERACLES) was to kill the monster. It was a poisonous, many-headed serpent, with the number of its heads varying in art and literature from just a few to a hundred, although the sceptical Pausanias (2.37.4) would reduce them to one. It lived in the swamps of Lerna near Argos and ravaged the nearby countryside, killing the flocks.

Heracles forced it to come out of its lair near the spring of Amymone by shooting at it with burning arrows, but he then found that whenever he destroyed one head, two grew in its place. A giant crab added further difficulties by siding with the Hydra and pinching Heracles' foot, so he killed it. Hera, however, was so pleased with its efforts that she immortalised it in the stars as the constellation Cancer. Heracles finally killed the Hydra with the help of his nephew IOLAUS, who cauterised the neck-stumps with a firebrand as soon as Heracles had cut off the heads. Apollodorus (2.5.2) says that one of the (here, nine) heads was immortal, and this one Heracles chopped off and buried beside the road from Lerna to Elaeus, putting a heavy rock on top of it. He also says that Eurystheus refused to count this victory as one of the Labours on the grounds that help had been needed from Iolaus.

Heracles cut open the dead body of his victim and took its poisonous blood, which ever afterwards he used as venom on his arrow-tips. This would in future years kill many of his enemies, but it would also eventually bring about his own death when his wife DEIANEIRA mistakenly gave him a robe impregnated with the poisoned blood of the Centaur Nessos, killed by one of these arrows.

There are many depictions of the killing of the Hydra in ancient art. In early representations its heads are cut with a sword or sickle, clubbed, or even, rarely, shot with arrows, and only from the later sixth century BC do we see fire used to cauterise the severed necks (fig. 74). Quintus of Smyrna gives a vivid description of the scene as depicted on the shield of Eurypylus (*Sequel to Homer* 6.212–19):

> There was wrought the dreadful many-headed Hydra
> flickering its tongues. And of its fearsome heads
> some lay dead on the ground, but many more
> were budding from its necks, while Heracles
> and Iolaus, refusing to give in, toiled on:
> Heracles lopped the fierce heads with swift
> and jagged sickle, while Iolaus seared each neck
> with glowing iron, and bit by bit the creature died.

This is the Labour of Heracles which has been of greatest inspiration to postclassical artists, both painters and sculptors. The Hydra's name has also entered modern parlance, with a 'hydra-headed problem' being one that presents fresh difficulties as fast as one is overcome.

[Sophocles, *Women of Trachis* 573–4, 714–18; Euripides, *Heracles* 419–21, *Ion* 194–200; Diodorus Siculus 4.11.5–6; Pausanias 3.18.13, 5.17.11; Virgil, *Aeneid* 6.803, 8.299–300; Ovid, *Metamorphoses* 9.69–74.]

Hygieia

The personification of health, and (not surprisingly) a daughter of ASCLEPIUS, the god of healing.

Hylas

The beautiful son of Theiodamas, king of the lawless Dryopes. When HERACLES was passing through the land, he picked a quarrel with Theiodamas, demanding one of the two bulls with which he was ploughing a field. Theiodamas refused, so Heracles fought and killed him, then carried off Hylas. The boy became his squire and lover, accompanying him on the voyage of the ARGONAUTS. When Heracles broke an oar near the Mysian coast, they put ashore for him to cut a new one. Meanwhile Hylas went off to draw water from a local spring called Pegae. The nymph of the spring saw him in the moonlight and was so moved by his beauty that, when he reached out to dip his pitcher in the stream, she dragged him down with her into the water. The only person to hear his cry of fear as he fell was the Argonaut POLYPHEMUS (1), who rushed to his aid. Finding no trace of the boy, he assumed that he had been carried off by wild beasts or bandits. He ran to tell the sorry news to Heracles, who was wild with grief at

his loss and went raging through the woods all night, bellowing for his dear companion. It was said that Hylas answered his call three times before he sank out of sight for ever. Morning came, and the rest of the Argonauts set sail without noticing that three of their crew were missing.

When Heracles at last gave up hope of finding Hylas he departed, threatening to lay waste the land if the local Mysians did not continue the search once he was gone. To ensure their compliance, he took as hostages boys from noble families and settled them at Trachis. For centuries the Mysians sacrificed annually to Hylas at the spring where he had disappeared; three times the priest called him by name, and three times an echo came in reply.

[Apollonius, *Argonautica* 1.1207–1357; Theocritus, *Idyll* 13.36–75; Apollodorus 1.9.19, 2.7.7; Strabo 12.4.3; Antoninus Liberalis, *Metamorphoses* 26; Propertius 1.20.5–32.]

Hyllus

The eldest son of HERACLES and DEIANEIRA. As Heracles lay dying from the poisoned robe sent to him by Deianeira, he instructed Hyllus, when he came of age, to marry IOLE (the indirect cause of his death) so that no other man might have her. Hyllus unwillingly agreed to do so. Once Heracles was dead, leaving his children unprotected from the persecutions of his enemy EURYSTHEUS, they at first took refuge with Ceyx, king of Trachis. But when Eurystheus threatened him with war, he was afraid to help them any further, so they fled to Athens, still with their persecutor and an armed force in pursuit, and begged for help. The Athenians defeated the Argive army and Eurystheus was killed. In one version it was Hyllus himself who killed him, then cut off his head and brought it to his grandmother, ALCMENE. In a vindictive fury, she gouged out the eyes with weaving-pins.

Hyllus married Iole, who bore him a son, Cleodaeus. In due course Hyllus led the other HERACLIDS in an attempt to re-establish themselves in the Peloponnese, obediently waiting for three years when the Delphic Oracle instructed them to await 'the third harvest'. Unfortu-

Fig. 74 **Heracles, bitten in the ankle by a crab, attacks the Hydra of Lerna with a club. Iolaus, using a sickle, has a fire ready for cauterising.**

nately the Oracle meant three generations, so the attack was a failure and Hyllus was killed in single combat by a Peloponnesian champion, ECHEMUS, the king of Arcadia. Hyllus' name was later given to one of the three Dorian tribes, the Hylleis.

Hyllus is a character in Sophocles' tragedy *The Women of Trachis*, where Deianeira sends the fatal robe to Heracles, smeared with what she believes to be a love-charm that will win back his love from Iole, but is in fact a deadly poison. Hyllus knows nothing of her motives and sees only the results of her gift: his father dying in agony as the poison eats into his flesh like acid. He tells his mother what she has done, sparing her nothing and bitterly condemning her. Speechless and despairing, she goes indoors to kill herself. Too late Hyllus learns of her good intentions and deeply reproaches himself for his hasty anger. The final scene of the play is a dramatic and moving confrontation between Hyllus and his tortured, dying father, as Heracles, surmounting his agony, directs his son to arrange his funeral pyre and to marry Iole.

[Herodotus 8.131; Apollodorus 2.7.7–2.8.2; Diodorus Siculus 4.57; Strabo 9.4.10; Pausanias 1.41.2–3, 1.44.10, 3.15.10, 4.2.1, 8.5.1, 8.53.10.]

Hymen or Hymenaeus

The god who presided over marriage. Such cries as *hymen o hymenaie* were a traditional part of the Greek wedding song (called the *hymenaeus*), and perhaps began as mock laments for the bride's hymen, about to be broken; but they came to be seen as invocations to a deity, Hymen. Various myths were invented to explain his connection with marriage, such as the following Attic version. Hymenaeus was a beautiful Athenian youth, so lovely and delicate of feature that he might be taken for a girl. He fell in love, but being of humble origins he was too poor to marry the girl of his heart, who was far richer and nobler than he. Eventually he won her by a deed of valour. One day, when he had followed his love and her friends to a festival of Demeter at Eleusis, the girls were all carried off by pirates, and Hymenaeus too, mistaken for a girl. At last they came to a distant and desolate country, where the weary brigands lay down to rest. While they slept, Hymenaeus killed them. He returned to Athens, where he promised to bring all the girls safely back home so long as he could marry the girl of his choice. His bargain was accepted, and the marriage turned out to be a very happy one. In memory of his story, his name was invoked at every wedding to bring good luck to the newly married pair.

Other stories were told to account for his association with marriage: he was a fine musician who sang the bridal hymn at the marriage of DIONYSUS and ARIADNE, but sud-denly lost his voice; or he was a young man who died on his wedding day. None, however, are early. Apollodorus names him as one of the mortals brought back to life by the healer ASCLEPIUS. In art Hymenaeus is shown as a beautiful young man carrying a bridal torch.

[Euripides, *Trojan Women* 310–25; Apollodorus 3.10.3.]

Hyperboreans

A mythical people living, as their name suggests, at the northern limits of the world, 'beyond the North Wind', the region from which BOREAS sends his icy blasts. According to Pindar, theirs was an earthly paradise where they lived untouched by disease or old age or strife, spending their days in song and dance and sacrifice, and worshipping their god APOLLO. Here he came every year to spend the winter months with his favoured people.

No ordinary mortal could reach their land, only the greatest of heroes. Here PERSEUS came during his quest for the Gorgon Medusa. Here HERACLES came in pursuit of the CERYNEIAN HIND; then returned to ask the gift of an olive tree, which he planted in the precinct of Zeus at Olympia so that its leaves might be a crown of prowess for victors in the Games. Here also, it was said, Croesus was transported by Apollo, as a reward for his piety towards Delphi, after Zeus had sent rains to quench the pyre that would otherwise have incinerated him.

The Hyperboreans had connections both with Delphi, the principal site of Apollo's worship, and with Delos, the birth-place of their god. Pausanias reports (10.5.9) that Apollo's second temple at Delphi, made from beeswax and feathers, was sent to their land. In historical times, the straw-wrapped offerings to Apollo which reached Delos, passing through the hands of a long chain of real-life intermediaries, were said to have come in the first place from the Hyperboreans.

[Pindar, *Olympian* 3.11–34, *Pythian* 10.29–46; Bacchylides, *Ode* 3.23–62; Herodotus 4.13, 4.32–6; Diodorus Siculus 2.47; Pausanias 1.4.4, 1.18.5, 1.31.2, 5.7.7–10, 10.5.7–9.]

Hyperenor (1)

One of the 'SOWN MEN' who sprang from the dragon's teeth at Thebes.

Hyperenor (2)

Son of the Trojan elder PANTHOUS and a warrior at Troy. MENELAUS killed him when he was yet newly married, then killed his brother EUPHORBUS when he tried to avenge his death.

[Homer, *Iliad* 14.516–9, 17.9–60.]

Hyperion

One of the TITANS, the son of Uranus (Sky) and GAIA (Earth). He married his sister-Titan, Theia (also called

Euryphaessa), who bore HELIOS (Sun), SELENE (Moon) and EOS (Dawn). Often, however, Hyperion ('he who travels above') is simply another name for the Sun-god, Helios.

Keats, in his unfinished *Hyperion*, makes Hyperion the last of the Titans, about to be deposed by the young Olympian sun-god, Apollo. Hamlet compares his dead father to his mother's new husband, Claudius, as 'Hyperion to a satyr'.

[Homer, *Odyssey* 1.24; Hesiod, *Theogony* 134, 371–4.]

Hypermestra (1)

One of the fifty daughters of DANAUS who married their fifty cousins, the sons of Aegyptus; and the only one who did not murder her new husband (Lynceus) on the wedding night.

Hypermestra (2)

Daughter of THESTIUS; wife of Oecles; and mother of the famous seer AMPHIARAUS.

Hypnos

The personification of Sleep, called Somnus by the Romans. Hypnos, like his twin brother THANATOS (Death), was the son of NYX (Night). He is usually seen as little more than an abstraction, but he plays a part in the action of the *Iliad* during HERA's 'Deception of Zeus', when she wishes to have ZEUS lulled to sleep, so that he

will not notice Poseidon intervening on the battlefield to help the Greeks. She meets Hypnos in Lemnos and explains what aid she requires of him, but Hypnos at first refuses, saying that he was almost thrown into the sea by Zeus the last time that he did such a thing, and he has no wish to risk another such punishment. He gives in, however, when Hera bribes him with the promise of marriage to one of the GRACES, Pasithea, whom he has long loved. He goes with Hera to Mount Ida where Zeus is looking down on the battle, then waits in a nearby pine tree in the likeness of a mountain owl, while Hera makes love with Zeus among the flowers below in the midst of a golden cloud. Their passion over, Hypnos drifts a sweet sleep over Zeus, then hurries to spur Poseidon on to help the Greeks.

Later in the *Iliad*, Hypnos and his brother Thanatos carry the body of SARPEDON away from the Trojan battlefield and home to Lycia. This scene is depicted in ancient art, most famously on the calyx krater by Euphronios (fig. 75). The brothers were also shown as children (one white, the other black) in the arms of their mother Nyx on the chest of Cypselus. Hypnos alone occurs in

Fig. 75 **Hypnos *(left)* and Thanatos lift the body of Sarpedon, supervised by Hermes.**

scenes where Heracles is about to kill the sleeping giant ALCYONEUS. Ovid gives a powerful description of Hypnos' dwelling in the land of the Cimmerians: a dark and misty cavern, with LETHE, the river of forgetfulness, flowing through it; at the doors poppies shedding drowsiness, and all around a still silence. Here the god sleeps, surrounded by his thousand sons, the DREAMS.

[Homer, *Iliad* 14.225–362, 16.666–83; Pausanias 2.31.3, 5.18.1; Ovid, *Metamorphoses* 11.592–649.]

Hypsipyle

Hypsipyle played a part in two major myths, the journey of the ARGONAUTS and the expedition of the SEVEN AGAINST THEBES. She was the daughter of Thoas, son of Dionysus and Ariadne and king of the island of Lemnos. The Lemnian women failed to honour APHRODITE, so the goddess punished them by afflicting them all with a vile smell. After this their menfolk brought home captive women from neighbouring Thrace and had sex only with them. The neglected women retaliated by murdering their husbands and the concubines, then in fear of retribution they massacred the rest of the male population too. The only man to survive was Thoas, the king: he was secretly hidden by Hypsipyle, then set adrift in a chest which safely reached the island of Oenoe. Hypsipyle then ruled Lemnos as queen.

This was the situation when JASON and the Argonauts sailed in on their way to Colchis. The women were by now starved of male companionship and wished to repopulate the island with more children; moreover they had lost their repulsive smell. They took the crew of the *Argo* as lovers. Hypsipyle naturally took Jason, and had at least one son by him, EUNEUS, though a second son is often mentioned and named variously as Thoas, Nebrophonus or Deipylus.

After the Argonauts had sailed onwards towards Colchis, the Lemnian women found out that Hypsipyle had spared her father. She was sold into slavery, either by the women, angry at her treachery to their cause, or by pirates who captured her when she fled in fear from Lemnos. Purchased by Lycurgus, the king of Nemea, she became the nurse of his baby son, Opheltes. One day she encountered the seven champions on their journey north to attack Thebes. The Seven asked for water and she showed them the way to a spring, meanwhile leaving the baby lying on a bed of parsley. They returned to find the child dead, bitten by a snake that had coiled itself around his little body. The seer AMPHIARAUS foretold that this was an omen signifying the failure of their expedition, so they killed the snake and buried the child under the name of *Archemoros*, 'Beginner of Doom'. In his honour they founded the Nemean Games, at which the judges wore dark-coloured clothing in mourning for Opheltes and the victor was rewarded with a crown of parsley.

Euripides dramatised this death of Opheltes in his partially preserved play *Hypsipyle*, at the end of which Hypsipyle's two sons, Euneus and Thoas, rescued her from slavery and took her back to Lemnos. Pausanias (2.15.3) saw the grave of Opheltes at Nemea.

[Homer, *Iliad* 7.467–75, 14.230, 21.41, 23.740–9; Bacchylides, *Ode* 9.10–18; Herodotus 6.138; Apollonius, *Argonautica* 1.609–909; Apollodorus 1.9.14, 1.9.17, 3.6.4, *Epitome* 1.9; Ovid, *Heroides* 6; Statius, *Thebaid* 5.486–753.]

Hyrie *see* CYCNUS (5).

Hyrieus

Son of POSEIDON and the Pleiad ALCYONE (1). He was the founder and ruler of the Boeotian city of Hyria, where a famous treasury was built for him by TROPHONIUS and Agamedes. Apollodorus says in one passage (3.10.1) that Hyrieus married the nymph Clonia and was the father of LYCUS (1) and NYCTEUS, though elsewhere (3.5.5) he calls them the sons of Cthonius, one of the Sown Men of Thebes.

A different and late tradition makes Hyrieus a poor beekeeper and farmer, who grew old and impotent while still childless. One day, when entertaining ZEUS, POSEIDON and HERMES in his cottage, he was asked by the appreciative gods what gift he most desired. He said that he would like a son, so on their instructions he sacrificed and skinned a bull. The gods then urinated on the hide and covered it with soil. Nine months later, to Hyrieus' great joy, his son ORION was born from the earth.

[Ovid, *Fasti* 5.493–536.]

Hyrtacus

King of Percote in the Troad, and an ally of King PRIAM of Troy. Two of his sons went to fight in the Trojan War, ASIUS (2) and NISUS (2).

I

Iacchus

An obscure deity celebrated at the Eleusinian Mysteries (*see* DEMETER).

Ialmenus *see* ASCALAPHUS (2).

Iambe

An old serving woman in the household of Celeus, king of Eleusis, into which DEMETER was welcomed during her long hunt for her lost daughter Persephone. The goddess sat immersed in silent grief until Iambe, cheering her distraught spirits with lewd jokes, made her laugh. This was said to be the origin of the jokes ritually made at the Thesmophoria, the women's festival in honour of Demeter. Iambe was believed to have given her name to iambic poetry.

In another version, Demeter's hosts were Dysaules and his wife Baubo, and it was Baubo who cheered the visitor by pulling up her skirts and exposing herself, much to the goddess' delight.

[*Homeric Hymn to Demeter* 192–205; Apollodorus 1.5.1; Diodorus Siculus 5.4.6; Clement of Alexandria, *Exhortation to the Greeks* 2.17.]

Iamus

The son of APOLLO and EVADNE (1), who was himself a great seer, and founded a famous family of seers, the Iamidae.

Iapetus

One of the TITANS, and the son of Uranus (Heaven) and GAIA (Earth). By an Oceanid, either Clymene or Asia, he was the father of the second-generation Titans PROMETHEUS, EPIMETHEUS, ATLAS and MENOETIUS (1). After the defeat of the Titans by Zeus, Iapetus was cast into the depths of TARTARUS, and here, says Homer, he sits for ever in the gloomy dark, far from the delights of sun and winds.

[Homer, *Iliad* 8.478–81; Hesiod, *Theogony* 132–6, 507–11; Apollodorus 1.2.3.]

Iarbas *see* DIDO.

Iasion (1) or Iasius

Son of ZEUS and ELECTRA (2), the daughter of Atlas. According to Homer and Hesiod, Iasion was loved by the goddess DEMETER and lay with her in a thrice-ploughed field in Crete. The fruit of their union was PLUTUS, 'Wealth', symbolising the riches that come from the earth; but despite this happy outcome, Zeus killed Iasion for his presumption by blasting him with a thunderbolt. For a second son, Philomelus, said to have been born to Iasion and Demeter, *see* BOÖTES.

Later writers had Iasion live on: in Ovid, Demeter regrets the grey hairs of her lover as he grows old; and Diodorus says that Iasion married the Phrygian goddess CYBELE, had by her a son, Corybas, and was finally made immortal.

[Homer, *Odyssey* 5.125–8; Hesiod, *Theogony* 969–74; Apollodorus 3.12.1; Diodorus Siculus 5.48.3–49.5, 5.77.1–2; Ovid, *Metamorphoses* 9.422–3.]

Iasion (2) or Iasius or Iasus *see* ATALANTA.

Icarius (1) *see* ERIGONE (1).

Icarius (2)

The genealogy of Icarius and his more famous brother TYNDAREOS is in doubt, for their father may have been Perieres or Oebalus, and their mother Gorgophone or Bateia. Tyndareos became king of Sparta, but he and Icarius were driven out by their brother or half-brother HIPPOCOON (although in one version Icarius himself helped to expel Tyndareos). Eventually Hippocoon and his many sons aroused the wrath of HERACLES and all were killed by him, whereupon Tyndareos regained his throne. Icarius married the nymph Periboea, who bore him two daughters – Iphthime, who married EUMELUS (2), and PENELOPE – and five sons.

Icarius' main claim to fame is as the father of Penelope, the wise and faithful wife of ODYSSEUS and the heroine of the *Odyssey*. Either Odysseus wooed Penelope with the support of her uncle Tyndareos, or Icarius made her many suitors run a footrace to decide between them, and Odysseus won. Even then her father was loath to let her go. He tried unavailingly to persuade Odysseus to settle in Sparta, then begged Penelope to stay with him, and even followed the chariot in which the bridal pair drove off, still beseeching her. Odysseus finally told her to choose between her father and her husband, at which she modestly veiled her face in silence, a gesture that formed part of the wedding ritual. Icarius, realising that she had made her choice, now let her go, and at that very place dedicated an image of Modesty.

[Homer, *Odyssey* 2.52–4, 132–3, 4.797, 15.15; Apollodorus 1.9.5, 3.10.3–6, 3.10.9; Pausanias 3.1.4, 3.12.1, 3.20.10–11, 8.34.4.]

Icarus

Son of the supreme inventor and craftsman DAEDALUS, borne to him by a slave-girl while he was living at the court of MINOS, king of Crete. When Theseus came to Crete to kill the Minotaur, Daedalus provided the thread that helped him to escape from the Labyrinth once the deed was done. This enraged Minos so much that he imprisoned Daedalus himself in the Labyrinth, and Icarus with him. But this was no lasting impediment to such a brilliant inventor, and Daedalus fashioned wings of wax and feathers in which he and his young son could fly to freedom. While fitting these ingenious wings to Icarus, he gave him careful instructions on how to fly safely: he must keep midway between earth and heaven, neither too low, where the sea-spray might weigh down his wings, nor too high, where the flaming sun might scorch them. When they took off, Daedalus watched his son as anxiously as any parent bird its fledgling.

All went well as they flew far out over the ocean, but at last Icarus was fatally overtaken by the joy of flying freely through the air. Letting his wings lift him higher and higher he soared towards the sun, until he came so close that the wax of his wings melted in the heat, the feathers parted and he plummeted headlong into the sea below, still calling for his father as the waters engulfed him. The stricken Daedalus retrieved his son's body and buried it on a nearby island, ever afterwards called Icaria, just as the sea was renamed the Icarian Sea in honour of the dead boy and still bears his name.

The rational Pausanias (9.11.4–5) suggests that the 'wings' that Daedalus made were in fact ships' sails, as yet unknown to the men of those times, an invention with which he hoped to take advantage of a favourable wind and outsail the fleet of Minos, powered only by oars. Daedalus' ship, he adds, sailed on safely, but Icarus' ship overturned because he was a clumsy helmsman. Despite such rationalisation, it is the notion of genuine flight that has captured the imagination of later artists. Ovid writes of the people who may have watched Daedalus and Icarus as they flew across the sky (*Metamorphoses* 8.217–20):

> Perhaps some fisherman, wielding his quivering rod,
> or a shepherd leaning on his crook, or a ploughman
> resting on his plough handle caught sight of them and
> stood stupified, thinking these must be gods who
> could fly through the air.

When Peter Brueghel the Elder painted *The Fall of Icarus*, he put in the fisherman, the shepherd and the ploughman, but showed them all going about their work quite indifferent to the tiny figure of Icarus disappearing into the sea: as the proverb says, no plough stops for the man who dies. The myth has always been a potent source of inspiration for artists and has had many different interpretations, but with Icarus' flight remaining a powerful symbol of man's soaring aspirations. As the eighteenth-century French poet Phillippe Destouches writes:

> Le ciel fut son désir, la mer son sépulture:
> Est-il plus beau dessein ou plus riche tombeau?

And W. B. Yeats echoes the glory and exhalation of Icarus' flight to the sun in *An Irish Airman Foresees His Death*:

> Nor law, nor duty bade me fight,
> Nor public men, nor cheering crowds,
> A lonely impulse of delight
> Drove to this tumult in the clouds;
> I balanced all, brought all to mind,
> The years to come seemed waste of breath,
> A waste of breath the years behind
> In balance with this life, this death.

[Apollodorus, *Epitome* 1.12–13; Diodorus Siculus 4.77.5–9; Strabo 14.1.19; Ovid, *Metamorphoses* 8.183–235.]

Ida

A Cretan nymph (*see* ADRASTEIA).

Ida, Mount

The name of two famous mountain ranges, one in central Crete and the other in the Troad, south east of Troy. A cave on the Cretan Ida (or, in another version, on the Cretan Mount Dicte) was where the infant ZEUS was said to have been reared, far away from his cannibalistic father, Cronus. The Trojan Ida was the site of APHRODITE's union with the mortal ANCHISES, as described in the *Homeric Hymn to Aphrodite*. Here she saw Anchises tending his cattle and was seized with desire for him (68–74):

> So she came to Ida of the many springs,
> the home of wild beasts, and went straight
> to his dwelling across the mountain. After her
> came grey wolves and bright-eyed lions,
> bears and swift leopards, eager for deer,
> all of them fawning on her. And seeing them
> she was glad in her heart, and put desire
> in their breasts, so that two and two they mated,
> all through the shadowy groves.

Here on Ida she lay with Anchises, and here their son AENEAS was born. The slopes of the Trojan Ida saw also many events crucial to the history of Troy: here the baby PARIS, son of Priam and Hecuba, was left to die, because they knew that he was fated to bring destruction on the city. He survived, and married the nymph OENONE, then lived a rural life on the mountain as a herdsman until fate took him back to Troy. Here on Ida he judged the beauty contest between the three goddesses – Hera, Athena and Aphrodite – and in choosing Aphrodite set in motion the long and bloody TROJAN WAR. At the end of ten years' fighting, the Trojan seer HELENUS was captured on Ida by Odysseus, and revealed to the Greeks the oracles, known only to himself, foretelling how they could take Troy. And it was the slopes of Ida that provided the wood to build the WOODEN HORSE, the stratagem by which the Greeks finally entered Troy and bloodily sacked the city, razing it to the ground.

Idaea (1)

A nymph of Mount IDA near Troy, who bore to the river-god SCAMANDER a son, TEUCER (1), the ancestor of the Trojan kings.

[Apollodorus 3.12.1.]

Idaea (2)

The second wife of PHINEUS (2), and cruel stepmother to his two sons by his first marriage to Cleopatra.

Idaeus (1)

One of King PRIAM's heralds during the Trojan War. Idaeus, driving a wagon drawn by mules, accompanied Priam by night into the enemy camp to ransom the body of Hector from Achilles, carrying rich gifts to persuade him to mercy and at dawn returning to Troy with Hector's body. Homer's powerful description of this journey must have moved Virgil, for in the *Aeneid* (6.485) he places Idaeus among other brave warriors in the Underworld, 'still keeping hold of Priam's chariot, still keeping hold of his arms'.

[Homer, *Iliad* 3.245–58, 7.273–86, 381–97, 24.265–718.]

Idaeus (2) *see* DARES.

Idas and Lynceus

Sons of APHAREUS, king of Messenia, and Arene, though Idas was also said to be the son of POSEIDON. Idas had a voracious appetite and was one of the strongest men of his generation, while Lynceus was gifted with vision so acute that he could see even through solid objects. Like all the great heroes of their day, they joined the voyage of the ARGONAUTS to win the Golden Fleece, and they went on the CALYDONIAN BOARHUNT.

Idas married MARPESSA after winning her from her father Evenus in a chariot-race, using horses given him by his father Poseidon. He even drew his bow against the god APOLLO, who also desired her (fig. 76). Zeus intervened and told Marpessa to choose which of the two she preferred. She chose Idas, since he would grow old with her, while Apollo was likely to abandon her when her beauty faded. She and Idas had a daughter called Alcyone (renamed Cleopatra by Homer). Marpessa must have loved her chosen husband, for when Idas later died fighting the DIOSCURI in a quarrel over cattle, Marpessa killed herself from grief. Lynceus too died in the combat. Pausanias saw the grave of Idas and Lynceus at Sparta, though he thought it more likely that they would have been buried in Messenia.

[Apollodorus 1.8.2, 1.9.16, 3.10.3; Pausanias 3.13.1, 4.2.7.]

Fig. 76 Idas draws his bow to defend Marpessa from Apollo, who is shown on the reverse.

Idmon ('The knowing one')

Son of APOLLO, though his mortal father was Abas. Idmon was one of the ARGONAUTS, and since he was a seer, he was able to predict for his comrades a successful conclusion to their quest for the Golden Fleece, even though they would meet countless obstacles on the long journey. He also knew that he himself was fated to die if he joined the expedition, but still he did so, that he might win a glorious reputation. His death occurred while the Argonauts were among the Mariandyni, on the southern shore of the Black Sea: he was killed by a wild boar, one so immense and deadly that it terrified the nymphs of the marshland where it lived. His comrades mourned his passing for three days, then on the fourth day they buried him with lavish honours and crowned his burial mound with wild olive.

[Apollonius, *Argonautica* 1.139–45, 435–49, 2.815–50; Apollodorus 1.9.23.]

Idomeneus

A king of Crete, son of Deucalion and grandson of MINOS. He was one of the suitors of HELEN, so bound by the oath which all the suitors took to defend the marriage-rights of her chosen husband, he led the Cretan contingent of eighty ships to the TROJAN WAR, with his nephew MERIONES as his second-in-command.

He is an important figure in the *Iliad*, older than most of the other Greek leaders, but a great warrior, staunch and courageous on the battlefield (13.470–6):

> No childish fear gripped hold of Idomeneus,
> but he stood firm, like some great mountain boar
> who, trusting in his strength, stands up
> to a great rabble of men coming against him
> in a lonely place. He bristles up his back,
> and his eyes shine with fire; he grinds his teeth
> in his longing to fight off the dogs and men.
> Thus did spear-famed Idomeneus stand firm,
> and he would not give way ...

He is one of the nine warriors who volunteer to fight in single combat against the mighty HECTOR, and he supports MENELAUS in the rescue of PATROCLUS' corpse.

He was later said to be one of the warriors in the WOODEN HORSE. After Troy fell he sailed safely home to Crete, together with those of his men who had survived the fighting. Diodorus says that he was buried in Crete, sharing a tomb at Knossos with Meriones, and that the Cretans held the two heroes in special renown, offering up sacrifices to them and calling on their aid in times of war. But Apollodorus relates an unhappy homecoming for him which led to exile from his country. His wife Meda, influenced by NAUPLIUS (1), had taken a certain

Leucus as a lover. He killed both Meda and her daughter, then seized control of ten Cretan cities. When Idomeneus returned home to Crete, Leucus drove him into exile. Virgil says that he was exiled to Sallentinum in Calabria, at the south-eastern extremity of Italy; but it is Servius, the commentator on Virgil, who is our main source for another story about Idomeneus' return to Crete. Caught in a storm on his journey home, he vowed that if he arrived safely he would sacrifice to Poseidon the first living creature that he met on landing. This turned out to be his own son, who was waiting to welcome him. When Idomeneus offered him up to fulfil his vow, a plague broke out, and the people of Crete, believing this to be a divine judgement, banished their king.

Several operas, mostly of the eighteenth century, have taken Idomeneus as their subject, the most famous being Mozart's first operatic masterpiece, *Idomeneo, re di Creta* (1781), set in Crete at the homecoming of Idomeneus. The king has promised to sacrifice the first person to greet him, who of course turns out to be his own son, Idamante. When he tries to escape fulfilling his vow, Crete is ravaged by storms and a terrible monster. As the sacrifice is finally about to take place, Neptune appears and releases Idomeneus from his promise, as long as he yields the throne to his son. All ends with rejoicing.

[Homer, *Iliad* 2.645–52, 3.230–3, 4.251–72, 7.161–9, 13.306–519, 17.258–9, 605–25, 23.450–98, *Odyssey* 3.191–2; Apollodorus, *Epitome* 6.10–11; Diodorus Siculus 5.79; Quintus of Smyrna, *Sequel to Homer* 1.247–8, 4.284–92, 5.134–8, 6.539–44, 12.320; Virgil, *Aeneid* 3.121–2, 400–1, 11.264–5.]

Iliad *see* ACHILLES.

Ilione *see* POLYDORUS (3).

Ilus

Son of TROS, king of Dardania, and Callirhoe, daughter of the river-god SCAMANDER. Ilus' brother ASSARACUS stayed in the city of Dardania on the slopes of Mount Ida, while Ilus himself founded a new city nearer the coast after he won the wrestling match at games held by the king of Phrygia. Ilus' prize consisted of fifty youths and fifty girls, but the king, in obedience to an oracle, added to these a dappled cow, telling Ilus that he must found a city wherever the cow first lay down. Ilus followed the cow, which eventually lay down on a hill, sacred to the goddess ATE, which rose from the broad plain between Mount Ida and the sea. Here he built his city, naming it Ilium after himself. Its other name was after his father, Tros: it was called TROY.

When Ilus prayed for a sign of approval from Zeus, the

PALLADIUM, a wooden image of ATHENA, miraculously fell from the sky. At the spot where it landed, Ilus built Troy's great temple of Athena to house the statue. It was believed that as long as the Palladium was kept safely there, Troy would never fall.

Ilus married Eurydice and had by her two children, a son, LAOMEDON, who succeeded him as king of Troy, and a daughter, Themiste, who married her cousin CAPYS (1), son of Assaracus, and in due course became the grandmother of AENEAS. Ilus' tomb on the Trojan plain became a familiar landmark near Troy.

[Homer, *Iliad* 10.415, 11.166–7, 371–2, 20.231–6; Apollodorus 3.12.1–3.]

Inachus

The chief river of Argos and its god, offspring of OCEANUS and Tethys, and ancestor of the Argive kings. When POSEIDON and HERA both claimed overlordship of the land, Inachus and the two smaller Argive rivers Cephissus and Asterion judged the dispute in favour of Hera. Poseidon, aggrieved at their decision, immediately dried up their waters, and ever since then Argos has frequently suffered from drought, with its rivers flowing only after rains.

By his half-sister the Oceanid Melia, Inachus had two sons, PHORONEUS and Aegialeus, and a daughter, the beautiful IO, who was loved by Zeus and turned into a cow, to Inachus' grief.

[Aeschylus, *Prometheus Bound* 589–673; Apollodorus 2.1.1, 2.1.4; Pausanias 2.15.4–5, 2.22.4; Ovid, *Metamorphoses* 1.583–7, 639–66.]

Ino

Daughter of CADMUS, king of Thebes, and HARMONIA, and sister of SEMELE, AGAVE and AUTONOE. Ino became the second wife of ATHAMAS, king of Orchomenus, and persecuted her two step-children by his previous marriage (*see* PHRIXUS). She herself had two sons by Athamas, Learchus and Melicertes, but they came to a sad end. She and her husband took in the baby DIONYSUS, born of Zeus' union with Semele but left motherless when she was burnt up by the great god's thunderbolt. They dressed him as a girl to hide him from HERA, who was always jealous of Zeus' love-children; but eventually Hera learnt the truth and punished Ino and Athamas by driving them mad. Athamas, thinking that Learchus was a deer, hunted him and shot him dead. Ino flung Melicertes into a cauldron of boiling water, then leapt into the sea, carrying her dead child in her arms, and drowned. But some good came out of tragedy, for a dolphin carried the body of Melicertes ashore where it was found by his uncle SISYPHUS, king of Corinth, who then founded the Isthmian

Games in his honour; and Dionysus transformed Ino and Melicertes into the sea-deities Leucothea ('White Goddess') and Palaemon. They lived with the NEREIDS and came to the aid of sailors in distress. In the *Odyssey* (5.333–462) it is Ino-Leucothea who saves ODYSSEUS by lending him her shawl to buoy him up while he swims to safety on the island of Scheria. In Rome, Ino-Leucothea was identified with Mater Matuta, and Palaemon with Portunus, the god of harbours.

According to Hyginus (*Fabula* 4), a rather different story was dramatised by Euripides in his (now lost) tragedy *Ino*. Here Ino deserted Athamas and their two sons, running off to join the MAENADS in Dionysiac revels. (So this is perhaps the point in Ino's life when Euripides envisaged the events of his tragedy *The Bacchae* occurring, where Ino and her sisters tear the young king of Thebes, PENTHEUS, to pieces.) With Ino gone, Athamas now married a third wife, Themisto, who bore him two sons, Sphincius and Orchomenus. Some years later Ino returned, but Athamas kept her identity a secret and employed her as a nurse for the children. Themisto then decided to kill Ino's two sons and confided her plan to the 'nurse', telling her to cover Ino's children that night with black covers, Themisto's with white. Ino, of course, did just the opposite and Themisto in the darkness killed her own two sons. When she found out what she had done, she took her own life.

[Pindar, *Olympian* 2.28–30; Euripides, *Medea* 1282–9, *Bacchae* 1129–30; Pausanias 1.42.7, 1.44.7–8, 2.1.3, 4.34.4; Ovid, *Metamorphoses* 4.416–542, *Fasti* 6.489–550.]

Io

Daughter of the Argive river-god INACHUS and the Oceanid Melia (or of Iasus or Piren, descendants of Inachus). Famous dynasties, including the royal houses of Argos and Thebes, were descended from her. She was the virgin-priestess of HERA at Argos, and was so beautiful that ZEUS himself desired her. He sent her seductive dreams, suggesting she come and lie with him in the meadows of Lerna, but she was afraid and confessed her dreams to her father. Perplexed, he consulted the oracles at Delphi and Dodona, only to be told that he must drive his daughter out of home and country, or else his whole race would be blotted out by Zeus' thunderbolts. In great sadness Inachus obeyed. Io was transformed by Zeus or Hera into a cow, then was driven far through the world by a stinging gadfly, sent by Hera to stop her resting long enough for Zeus to make love to her.

Ovid tells a rather different story. Zeus told the girl to come with him into the woods, and when she ran from him in fear, he darkened the earth with clouds and had his way with her. Hera, looking down from Olympus, saw the unnatural clouds over Argos and at once suspected

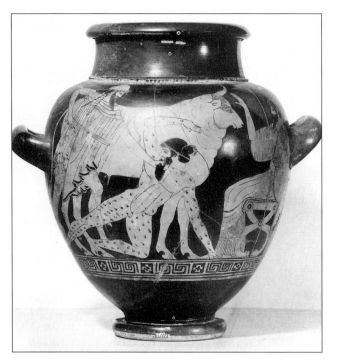

Fig. 77 **Hermes attacks Argus, whose body is covered with eyes. Zeus, seated, looks on, lifting his hand to caress Io, who is depicted as a bull.**

some misbehaviour by her husband. Coming to investigate, she dispersed the clouds and found Zeus in the company of a beautiful white cow, for he had sensed his jealous wife's approach and had swiftly transformed the unfortunate girl. Hera, still suspicious, asked to have the cow as a present – a request that Zeus could not reasonably refuse – then set hundred-eyed ARGUS (1) to guard her. When Io tried to speak, she was terrified by the lowing sound that came from her lips, and terrified too by the sight of her horns and gaping jaws reflected in her father's river. Inachus did not recognise her until she wrote her sad story in the dust with her hoof. All-seeing Argus drove her away, and Inachus, overcome with grief, hid himself in a cave at the source of his river, weeping for his beloved daughter and swelling his streams with his tears.

Now Zeus took pity on the girl and sent HERMES to kill Argus (fig. 77): no mean feat, for he had to lull all those watchful eyes to sleep at the same time before striking off the monster's head. But still Io was in torment, for Hera sent the gadfly to drive her over all the earth. In Aeschylus' tragedy *Prometheus Bound*, she comes to the rocky crag where PROMETHEUS is chained. The Titan predicts her

future and the tortuous route of her wanderings. She will cross the channel that divides Europe from Asia, and it will ever afterwards be called the Bosporus ('Cow's-ford') after her. She will visit the lands of the Scythians, the AMAZONS, the GRAEAE and the GORGONS, the GRIFFINS and the one-eyed Arimaspians, the dark-skinned ETHIOPIANS; and she will come at last to Egypt.

Here in Egypt, her wanderings complete, she recovered her human form and gave birth to EPAPHUS beside the Nile, naming him for the touch (*epaphe*) of Zeus by which she had conceived him. Hera was still angry and sent the CURETES (1) to steal the child. For this they were killed by Zeus. Io once more wandered the earth, now in search of her son, until at last she found him in Syria. She took him back to Egypt and there married the Egyptian king, Telegonus. She was worshipped there as the goddess ISIS, and Epaphus as the bull-god Apis. Epaphus was the ancestor of DANAUS, who with his fifty daughters returned to Argos.

[Aeschylus, *Prometheus Bound* 561–886, *Suppliant Women* 40–57, 291–324, 531–89; Herodotus 1.1, 2.41; Apollodorus 2.1.3; Pausanias 1.25.1, 2.16.1, 3.18.13; Lucian, *Dialogues of the Gods* 7; Ovid, *Metamorphoses* 1.583–750.]

Iobates

A king of Lycia, with whom PROETUS took refuge when he was driven out of Argos by his brother Acrisius. Iobates married his daughter Stheneboea to Proetus, then sent an army to help him regain his kingdom. Thereafter Proetus ruled at Tiryns and Acrisius at Argos. Later, at Proetus' request, Iobates took in BELLEROPHON and tried unavailingly to have him killed, but then relented and married him to his second daughter, Philonoe. On his death he bequeathed his kingdom to Bellerophon. Sophocles wrote a tragedy *Iobates*, now lost, but presumably on the subject of Iobates' dilemma when confronted with a guest whom his son-in-law wanted killed.

[Apollodorus 2.2.1, 2.3.1–2.]

Iolaus

Son of IPHICLES, the half-brother of HERACLES, and Automedousa. Iolaus became the charioteer and faithful companion of his uncle Heracles, valiantly accompanying him on his Labours for EURYSTHEUS (*see* LABOURS OF HERACLES) and his many expeditions (figs. 42, 60 and 96). He was particularly helpful in the battle with the HYDRA OF LERNA: this monster grew two heads whenever one was cut off, and was finally defeated only when Iolaus cauterised its neck-stumps with a firebrand as soon as Heracles had cut off its heads (fig. 74). Iolaus' part in this exploit was so great that Eurystheus afterwards refused to consider it as one of the Labours. Iolaus was also renowned for his skill as charioteer: he won the chariot-race at the first Olympian Games established by Heracles, and was depicted on the Chest of Cypselus as a victor in the chariot-race at the funeral games of Pelias. In one version of the myth, after Heracles had tragically murdered his children in a fit of madness, he ended his marriage to their mother, MEGARA, and gave her instead to Iolaus.

When Eurystheus continued to persecute Heracles' children after their father's death and apotheosis, Iolaus did his utmost to protect them. He is a character in Euripides' *Children of Heracles* where, now an old man, he prays to HEBE and Zeus that for just one day he may be young again to go into battle against Eurystheus, and thus take vengeance on their persecutor. His prayer is granted. Completely rejuvenated, he pursues and captures his old enemy, bringing him back in chains (847–66). According to Pindar, he even cut off Eurystheus' head. Pausanias says that Iolaus colonised Sardinia, taking with him Athenian settlers and Heracles' children by the fifty daughters of King THESPIUS.

[Pindar, *Pythian* 9.78–83, *Nemean* 3.36–9; Apollodorus 2.4.11, 2.5.2, 2.6.1, 2.7.6; Pausanias 1.19.3, 1.29.5, 1.44.10, 5.8.3–4, 5.17.11, 7.2.2, 8.14.9, 8.45.6, 9.23.1, 9.40.6, 10.17.5.]

Iole

The beautiful daughter of EURYTUS (1), king of Oechalia, who indirectly brought about the death of the great hero HERACLES. Her father promised her hand in marriage to whoever could beat him and his sons in an archery contest. Heracles did so, but Eurytus refused to honour his word, afraid that Heracles might go mad and kill any children he had by Iole, just as he had killed his children by MEGARA. Some years later, after he had married DEIANEIRA, Heracles returned to Oechalia with an army, determined on revenge. He sacked the city and killed Eurytus and his sons, then carried off Iole as his concubine. The tragic sequel is dramatised in Sophocles' *Women of Trachis*, where Iole appears as a non-speaking character. When Deianeira realises that the lovely young slave girl is to share her husband's bed, she sends Heracles a robe smeared with the blood of the Centaur Nessus, believing it to be a love-charm that will win back his love, when in fact it is a deadly poison. Heracles dons the robe and the poison eats into his flesh like acid. Deianeira kills herself when she finds out what she has unwittingly done, and Heracles, dying, instructs his son HYLLUS to marry Iole so that no other man shall have her. Hyllus unwillingly agrees to do so.

[Apollodorus 2.6.1, 2.7.7; Diodorus Siculus 4.31.1–2.]

Ion

The ancestor of the Ionians. There are two very different versions of his origin: in both his mother was Creusa, the daughter of ERECHTHEUS, king of Athens, but his father was in one version the mortal XUTHUS, son of Hellen, and in the other the god APOLLO. In the first version, recorded by Pausanias (7.1.2–5), Xuthus went from his birthplace in Thessaly to Athens, where he married Creusa and had two sons by her, Ion and ACHAEUS. When King Erechtheus died, Xuthus was appointed judge to decide which of his sons should succeed him. He chose the eldest son, Cecrops, whereupon the other sons of Erechtheus drove him out of Athens. With his own two sons he settled in Achaea in the northern Peloponnese, then called Aegialus (the Coastland), and lived there until his death. Ion and Achaeus then separated, Achaeus returning to Thessaly and Ion preparing to fight for the rule in Aegialus. He gathered armies to make his attack but was forestalled by the king, Selinus, who offered to marry him to his daughter Helice and to make him his heir. Ion accepted, and when he took over the rule on Selinus' death he renamed the people Ionians after himself. Later the Athenians asked him to lead them in their war with Eleusis and he returned to Athens. Under his generalship the Athenians were victorious, but Ion himself was killed and buried in Attica. Many generations later the Ionians were driven out of Aegialus by the Achaeans, but were allowed to settle in Attica because of Ion's connections there. After this Aegialus was renamed Achaea.

The second and better-known version is that found in Euripides' play *Ion*. Here Ion was born to Creusa after she was raped by Apollo. Afraid of her parents' anger, she sorrowfully abandoned her baby in a cave under the Acropolis, but Apollo had the boy brought to his temple at Delphi by Hermes. Here Ion was found by Apollo's priestess. She brought him up in the god's service while all the time he believed himself an orphan. Creusa meanwhile married Xuthus, who became king of Athens on the death of Erechtheus; but for many years the couple had no children. Now in the play they come to Delphi to consult the oracle about their childlessness, which is a source of pain to both of them, but particularly to Creusa, who is torn apart with longing for a child and with sorrow for her lost son.

Xuthus consults the oracle and is told that the first person he meets on leaving the temple will be his son. He meets Ion, who at first believes that this stranger joyfully greeting him as his son is mad; but eventually matters are straightened out and they assume that Ion must be the illegitimate result of some youthful indiscretion. Both agree that they must tell the news to Creusa with great tact. But before they can do so, Creusa learns from her servants that Xuthus is intending to bring into the family a bastard son, who will in due course supplant the line of Erechtheus on the throne of Athens. She tries to murder Ion, sending a servant with poison for Ion's wine at a celebratory feast given by Xuthus. The wine is spilt, and when Ion sees a dove drink it and die in agony, he realises that it was poisoned. Forcing the truth from the servant, he goes to kill Creusa, but the priestess intervenes, bringing out the basket in which Ion was found as a baby. Creusa recognises it at once. Mother and son are finally reunited with great joy: she has her son back again, and he has at last the mother he never knew and always missed. Xuthus remains content in the belief that he is Ion's father, and the family return in great happiness to Athens.

[Herodotus 7.94, 8.44; Apollodorus 1.7.3; Pausanias 1.31.3, 2.14.2, 7.1.2–9.]

Iphianassa (1)

One of the three daughters of PROETUS, king of Argos, who were driven mad by the gods and cured by the seer MELAMPUS.

Iphianassa (2)

A daughter of Agamemnon and Clytemnestra according to Homer (*Iliad* 9.145). She is later usually identified with IPHIGENEIA, though the Epic Cycle's *Cypria* differentiates between the two of them.

Iphicles

Son of ALCMENE and twin brother of the great hero HERACLES, but conceived of a different father. Alcmene was visited in the same night by Zeus and by her lawful husband AMPHITRYON, and in due course Heracles was born of Zeus and Iphicles of Amphitryon. Even while they were babies the difference in the boys' paternity was obvious, for when two huge snakes crawled into their bed (sent either by Hera, angry at Zeus' infidelity with Alcmene, or by Amphitryon, to find out which boy was his own), Iphicles screamed with terror like any normal human child, while Heracles seized the snakes and strangled them (fig.78).

Iphicles married Automedousa, the daughter of Alcathous, and had by her a son, IOLAUS, who shared most of Heracles' Labours. Two other children of theirs were killed by Heracles in his madness. According to a tale found only in the Hesiodic *Shield of Heracles* (87–94), Iphicles left his home and family and went to serve his brother's harsh taskmaster, King EURYSTHEUS, to his own later regret; but more usually he was seen as a loyal companion to Heracles on his exploits and a fine warrior in his own right: he took part in the CALYDONIAN BOARHUNT; won the hand of his second wife, the youngest daughter

of Creon, king of Thebes, after fighting with Heracles against ERGINUS (1) and the Minyans; and finally died while fighting alongside his brother, either against HIPPOCOON and his sons, or against King AUGEAS and the Eleans where he was killed by the Siamese twins the MOLIONES. The traveller Pausanias saw the tomb of Iphicles at Pheneus in Arcadia, where he was still honoured as a hero in the second century AD.

[Apollodorus 1.8.2, 2.4.8, 2.4.11–12, 2.7.3; Pausanias 8.14.9–10.]

Iphiclus (1)

The son of PHYLACUS, King of Phylace, and CLYMENE (2), famous for his running. In the speed of his feet he rivalled the winds, and could pass so swiftly over a field of corn that the stalks did not bend beneath his weight. In Homer's *Iliad* (23.629–42), when old NESTOR boasts about his youthful prowess and his superlative achievements at the funeral games of Amarynceus, it is Iphiclus whom he names as the man he defeated in the footrace; and Pausanias reports (5.17.10) that in the footrace at the splendid funeral games of Pelias, depicted on the chest of Cypselus, Iphiclus was shown as the winner.

Iphiclus was one of the ARGONAUTS, who were led by his nephew Jason, the son of his sister Alcimede. He himself had two sons, PODARCES (1) and PROTESILAUS, but only after he had been cured of impotence by MELAMPUS.

[Hesiod, *Catalogue of Women* 62; Apollonius, *Argonautica* 1.45–8.]

Iphiclus (2)

A son of THESTIUS. He accompanied his nephew MELEAGER, the son of his sister Althaea, on the voyage of the *Argo*, but was later killed by him in the fighting that followed the CALYDONIAN BOARHUNT.

[Bacchylides, *Ode* 5.124–35; Apollonius, *Argonautica* 1.190–201; Apollodorus 1.7.10.]

Iphigeneia

Eldest daughter of AGAMEMNON and CLYTEMNESTRA, and sister of ORESTES, ELECTRA (3) and CHRYSOTHEMIS (though occasionally said to be the daughter of THESEUS and HELEN, then given to her aunt Clytemnestra to be brought up). She is probably to be identified with the Iphianassa mentioned by Homer, just as she is given a variant name, Iphimede, in Hesiod.

It was Iphigeneia's death that allowed the TROJAN WAR to take place. When the Greek fleet was mustered at Aulis, ready to sail to Troy, it was held back by contrary winds, or by no winds at all, because of the anger of ARTEMIS. Various reasons were given for her wrath. Either Agamemnon had shot a stag, perhaps in the goddess' sacred grove, and had boasted that he was a finer hunter than Artemis herself. Or he had broken a vow to give to the goddess the most beautiful thing born in the year of Iphigeneia's birth – which had been the girl herself. Or his father ATREUS had promised Artemis the finest animal in his flocks, then had failed to give her the golden lamb. Whatever the cause of the goddess' wrath, the seer CALCHAS announced that she would be appeased only by the sacrifice of Agamemnon's virgin daughter Iphigeneia. The girl was brought to Aulis on the pretext of marriage with ACHILLES, and there sacrificed. The winds blew favourably, the fleet sailed, and the Trojan War was fought for ten long years.

Homer knows nothing of the sacrifice, which is first mentioned in the Epic Cycle. In most versions Artemis substituted a deer for Iphigeneia on the sacrificial altar, snatching the girl away to be her priestess in the land of the Taurians, in the Cimmerian Chersonese (Crimea). This is the version followed by Euripides in his *Iphigeneia at Aulis*. He movingly depicts Agamemnon's despair at the need for his daughter's death; Clytemnestra's anger when she finds out the real reason why she and Iphigeneia have been brought to Aulis; the valour of Achilles, who resolves to save the frightened young girl, at whatever cost; and the courage of Iphigeneia herself, who finally decides to offer herself willingly for sacrifice in order to save the expedition. She says to her father (1552–60):

> I am here at your bidding, but for my homeland, and for the whole of Greece, I willingly give my body, to be led to the goddess' altar and there sacrificed, if this is her decree. From what I do, may you prosper, and win victory, and return safe home. Then let no Argive lay a hand on me: silent, unflinching, will I offer my throat.

And so she does. But at the crucial moment, at the very stroke of the knife, Iphigeneia is gone, and on the altar in her place is a deer in its death throes.

For the happy outcome, dramatised in Euripides' play *Iphigeneia among the Taurians*, when nearly twenty years later Iphigeneia's brother came to the land where she was priestess of Artemis, *see* ORESTES. Iphigeneia returned to Greece and became a priestess of Artemis at Brauron. After her death she had sanctuaries in several places, including Brauron and Megara, where the locals claimed that she had died. She was sometimes identified with Artemis, sometimes distinct from her. According to Herodotus (4.103), in the fifth century BC the Taurians were still performing human sacrifice to a virgin goddess, whom they identified with Iphigeneia. It was sometimes said that she was made immortal and, further, that she married Achilles and lived with him forever on *Leuke*, the White Island.

Fig. 78 **The infant Heracles strangles the snakes, while the terrified Iphicles reaches out for his mother. Amphitryon raises his sword to strike the snakes, but his help is unnecessary.**

A different version of Iphigeneia's death is memorably dramatised in Aeschylus' tragedy *Agamemnon*, where she was not saved by Artemis. The sacrifice at Aulis took place as usual at the beginning of the war and is harrowingly described by the Chorus – Iphigeneia was gagged, lifted horizontal over the altar so that her throat was bare to the knife, and though she could not speak, her eyes begged for pity – but here there was no substitution, no deer, and Iphigeneia is simply a child, dead. Clytemnestra has nursed her rage and grief down all the long years since her daughter's murder, and now on Agamemnon's return home at the end of the war, she can at last have her revenge. With a fierce and pitiless joy she kills the murderer of her child.

[Homer, *Iliad* 9.145; Epic Cycle, Proclus' summary of the *Cypria*; Hesiod, *Catalogue of Women* fr. 23; Apollodorus, *Epitome* 2.10, 3.21–2; Pausanias 1.33.1, 1.43.1, 2.22.6–7, 2.35.1, 3.16.7–11, 7.26.5, 9.19.6–7; Antoninus Liberalis, *Metamorphoses* 27; Ovid, *Metamorphoses* 12.24–38.]

Iphimedeia *see* OTUS.

Iphinoe

One of the three daughters of PROETUS, king of Argos, who were driven mad by the gods and cured by the seer MELAMPUS, though in one version of the legend Iphinoe died during the cure.

Iphis (1)

Son of the Argive king Alector. Iphis was asked by POLYNEICES, the son of Oedipus, how the seer AMPHIARAUS might best be induced to join the expedition of the SEVEN AGAINST THEBES. Iphis advised him to bribe Amphiaraus' wife, Eriphyle, with the beautiful necklace of Harmonia. Polyneices did so and Eriphyle forced her husband to march against Thebes. Unfortunately Iphis' son ETEOCLUS and his son-in-law CAPANEUS were both killed in the expedition, and his daughter EVADNE (2) flung herself into her husband's funeral pyre in grief. Iphis bequeathed his kingdom to his grandson, STHENELUS (3).

[Apollodorus 3.6.2–3, 3.7.1; Pausanias 2.18.5, 10.10.3.]

Iphis (2) *see* ANAXARETE.

Iphis (3)

Iphis was the daughter of Ligdus, a poor man of Phaistos in Crete, and Telethusa. Ligdus wished for a son, so when Telethusa was pregnant with their first child he told her that, if it turned out to be a girl, the baby could not be allowed to live. In due course a girl was born, but Telethusa, inspired by the goddess ISIS in a dream, pretended that she was a boy. She was named Iphis, a name common to both boys and girls, and for thirteen years the fond mother kept her secret and brought up her daughter as a son. At the end of that time Ligdus betrothed the supposed youth to Ianthe, the most beautiful girl in Phaistos, and the pair fell in love. Ianthe, who knew nothing of Telethusa's deception, longed for their marriage with unalloyed pleasure; but poor Iphis was torn apart with what she felt to be her unnatural love for a member of her own sex. Telethusa too was in a frenzy of anxiety, and kept finding excuses to postpone the wedding ceremony. At last it could be put off no longer, and the desperate mother appealed to Isis once more for help. The goddess, taking pity on her, turned her daughter into a boy, and the now joyful Iphis married his Ianthe.

[Ovid, *Metamorphoses* 9.666–797.]

Iphitus (1)

Son of EURYTUS (1), king of Oechalia, who was treacherously murdered by HERACLES.

Iphitus (2)

A king of Phocis who entertained JASON when he went to consult the Delphic Oracle about his quest for the Golden Fleece. Iphitus then joined the ARGONAUTS on their voyage. His two sons, Schedius and Epistrophus, led the Phocian contingent of forty ships to the Trojan War. Epistrophus returned safely home when the war ended, but Schedius was killed by Hector and only his bones were taken back to Phocis. The tomb of the two brothers was seen there by Pausanias.

[Homer, *Iliad* 2.517–26, 17.306; Apollonius, *Argonautica*

1.207–10; Apollodorus 1.9.16; Pausanias 10.4.2, 10.36.10.]

Iphitus (3)

A man of Elis killed by Pelops' son COPREUS, who was then forced to flee to Mycenae where he became the despised lackey of King Eurystheus.

Iphthime

Daughter of ICARIUS (2), sister of PENELOPE, and wife of EUMELUS (2).

Iris

A goddess, daughter of the Titan THAUMAS and the Oceanid Electra, and sister of the HARPIES. She was sometimes said to be married to ZEPHYRUS, the West Wind. *Iris* is the Greek for 'rainbow', the phenomenon which seems to connect heaven and earth; so Iris, as the personification of the rainbow, was seen as the link between gods and men. She frequently appears in her role of gods' messenger in Homer's *Iliad* (she is not mentioned in the *Odyssey*, and here her role of messenger is taken by HERMES). Usually it is ZEUS who gives her instructions, sometimes HERA, and since she is as fleet of foot as the winds, she can swiftly act as intermediary between gods and men, or between the gods themselves. Two very different images in ancient literature depict Iris in action. In Homer, where the rainbow portends war or storm (17.547–50), she goes down to Troy, 'as when out of the clouds the snow or the hail fly cold, driven by the blast of the North Wind born in the bright air, so swiftly in her eagerness flew Iris' (15.170–2). In the *Aeneid* Virgil paints a radiant image of her, sent down to earth by Juno to help Dido to her death: 'Iris flew down on her saffron wings, bathed in dew, and spreading all her colours over the sky opposite the sun' (4.700–2).

Iris appears as a character in Euripides' tragedy *The Madness of Heracles*, where she accompanies Lyssa ('Madness') down to earth to afflict Heracles, and in a comic role in Aristophanes' comedy *The Birds*. She is a popular figure in vase-painting, where she plays a variety of roles (fig. 79), acting as cupbearer to the gods, for instance, or escorting them to the wedding of Peleus and Thetis. Almost always she is shown with wings, and indeed Homer calls her 'golden-winged' as well as 'wind-footed' and 'storm-footed'. Her name survives as the name of a flower and of the coloured part of the eye, and in 'iridescent' – 'shimmering with the colours of the rainbow'.

[Homer, *Iliad* 2.786–807, 3.121–40, 5.352–69, 8.397–425, 11.185–210, 15.143–217, 18.165–202, 23.192–225, 24.77–99, 143–88; *Homeric Hymn to Apollo* 102–14; Hesiod, *Theogony* 265–6, 780–7; Apollonius, *Argonautica* 2.283–300, 4.753–79; Callimachus, *Hymn* 4.228–39.]

Irus

In Homer's *Odyssey*, Irus is an Ithacan beggar 'famous for his ravening stomach and his incessant eating and drinking' (18.2–3). His real name is Arnaeus, but he has been renamed after IRIS, the messenger of the gods, because he often carries messages for the Suitors, the young men who have invaded ODYSSEUS' palace in his long absence. When Odysseus at last returns, himself disguised as a beggar, Irus sees him as unwelcome competition and decides to fight him, thinking him old and weak. 'How the old varmint runs on when he talks', he says, 'just like some old oven-woman. I could think up something nasty for him: hit him with both hands, and knock all the teeth out of his jaws on to the ground, as if he was some wild pig eating the crops. Come on, tuck up your clothes, so that everyone can see us do battle' (18.26–31). So Odysseus tucks up his rags, displaying a broad and strong body. At this Irus completely changes his tune, but he is forced to fight by ANTINOUS, the most brutal of the Suitors, and Odysseus fells him with a single blow.

Isander

A son of BELLEROPHON who was killed fighting the Solymi.

[Homer, *Iliad* 6.203–4.]

Ischys

Son of ELATUS (2) and lover of Coronis (*see* ASCLEPIUS).

Isis

A great Egyptian goddess whose cult and myth were widespread in the Graeco-Roman world. She was the sister-wife of Osiris and mother of Horus. Seth, the god of darkness, killed Osiris and scattered his dismembered body throughout Egypt, but Isis sought for all the pieces and his body was finally reassembled. She was identified by the Greeks with IO, who wandered the world in the form of a cow and gave birth to her son by Zeus, Epaphus, beside the River Nile; and also DEMETER, who sought far and long for her daughter Persephone, abducted by Hades and taken unwillingly to the Underworld.

[F. Solmsen, *Isis among the Greeks and Romans* (1979).]

Islands of the Blest *see* ELYSIUM.

Ismene

One of the four children born of OEDIPUS' incestuous marriage to his mother JOCASTA, and thus the sister of ANTIGONE (1), Eteocles and POLYNEICES. Like Antigone, Ismene is known almost exclusively from Greek tragedy.

She first appears in Aeschylus' *Seven Against Thebes* (467 BC), where both sisters lament the deaths of their brothers. In Sophocles' *Oedipus at Colonus*, where Oedipus and Antigone are wandering in exile and have reached Athens, Ismene brings news of the situation at Thebes and of CREON (2)'s aggressive intentions towards them. But she is best known from Sophocles' *Antigone*, where she acts as a foil to her fearless and determined sister, just as Chrysothemis does to Electra in his *Electra*. In the *Antigone*, Ismene is the cautious and timid sister, who sympathises with Antigone's resolution to bury their brother Polyneices in defiance of Creon's edict, but feels herself too weak to take any part in the deed.

> We must remember that we are women and are not meant to fight against men; remember too that we are ruled by those who are stronger, and so must obey this decree, and other things even more painful. ... I shall obey those in authority, for there is no sense in actions that exceed our powers (61–8).

Later in the play, after Antigone has given Polyneices token burial by sprinkling his body with earth, her defiance of Creon's edict is discovered and Ismene is willing to die with her sister. But Antigone will have none of it. 'Don't try to share my death', she says, 'and don't lay claim to something you had no hand in' (546–7). So Antigone dies alone.

Isus *see* ANTIPHUS.

Italus

The hero who gave his name to Italy, though his identity is very uncertain. Virgil (*Aeneid* 1.533–4) calls him a king of the Oenotrians, Thucydides (6.2) a king of the Sicels, an Italian tribe who later invaded Sicily, and an Italus was sometimes said to be a son of TELEGONUS and Penelope. There are several other possibilities.

Fig. 79 **Satyrs attempt to rape Iris.**

Ithaca

One of the loveliest of the Greek islands, situated between Cephallenia and the mainland of Acarnania; but also one of the most famous of all mythological sites, since it was the homeland of ODYSSEUS and the place to which he longed to return through all his enforced wanderings. 'A rough place', he himself said of it, 'but it breeds good children', and added that there was no sweeter place on earth (*Odyssey* 9.27–8).

Some critics have found certain aspects of Homer's picture inconsistent with the reality of modern Ithaca, and have tried to locate Odysseus' homeland elsewhere. But on balance there seem to be sufficient similarities between Homer's descriptions and the actual island of Ithaca to make it likely that he intended this to be the home of his hero. A cave near Polis Bay has yielded evidence of cult activity from Mycenean to Roman times and (more specifically) the remains of twelve fine geometric tripods which recall the ones brought home by Odysseus from Scheria (13.13–15, 217–8, 363–71).

[W. B. Stanford and J. V. Luce, *The Quest for Ulysses* (1974), ch. 4; Tim Severin, *The Ulysses Voyage* (1987), ch. 13.]

Itylus *see* AEDON.

Itys *see* TEREUS.

Ixion

One of the four great sinners (along with SISYPHUS, TANTALUS (1) and TITYUS) who after death endured eternal punishment for their transgressions on earth. Ixion, a Thessalian king (his parentage is much disputed) and the ruler of the Lapiths, was the Greek Cain, the first mortal to shed a kinsman's blood. He married Dia, the daughter of Deioneus or Eioneus, promising his father-in-law bride-gifts and inviting him to collect them. When Deioneus arrived, he fell into a pit of fire prepared by Ixion and perished. Yet evil though this murder was, it was not the crime for which Ixion was eternally punished – more was yet to come.

No mortal was willing to purify Ixion of so terrible a deed, but at last ZEUS had pity on him. Taking him up to Olympus, he purified him and cured him of the madness that had beset him after the murder. Ixion repaid his benefactor by trying to rape HERA. When she told Zeus what had happened, he fashioned a cloud (Nephele) in her likeness and put it in Ixion's bed to test the truth of her story. Ixion ravished the cloud, whereupon Zeus punished him by crucifying him on the four spokes of an ever-turning wheel of fire (fig.80). Sometimes this wheel was thought to revolve around the world in the sight of men, to teach them the dangers of ingratitude to benefactors; but usually it was located in TARTARUS. Sometimes the wheel was said to be covered with snakes. What is certain is that Ixion's punishment was eternal. Ixion bound to his wheel is depicted occasionally in ancient art, first in the early fifth century BC.

From her union with Ixion, the cloud produced a child, Centaurus, who in turn copulated with wild Magnesian mares on the slopes of Mount Pelion. From these were born the CENTAURS, part man and part horse, a race of savage and brutal beasts. Ixion also had a son, PEIRITHOUS, by Dia, though according to Homer the boy was fathered on her by Zeus. Perhaps Ixion pursued Hera in retaliation for the god's seduction of his wife.

[Homer, *Iliad* 14.317–8; Pindar, *Pythian* 2.21–48; Aeschylus, *Eumenides* 717–8; Sophocles, *Philoctetes* 676–80; Apollonius, *Argonautica* 3.61–3; Apollodorus, *Epitome* 1.20; Diodorus Siculus 4.69; Lucian, *Dialogues of the Gods* 9; Virgil, *Georgics* 3.37–9, 4.484; Ovid, *Metamorphoses* 4.461, 9.124, 10.42, 12.504–6.]

Iynx

A nymph who, by her spells, captured the affections of ZEUS either for herself or for IO. The jealous HERA turned Iynx into a wryneck, a shy woodland bird that in the mating season has a curious writhing movement of its neck thought to attract its mate. For this reason it was used in love-charms, spreadeagled on a wheel and revolved to the chanting of spells, thus, it was thought, attracting the person whose love was desired.

[Pindar, *Pythian* 4.213–17; Theocritus, *Idyll* 2.]

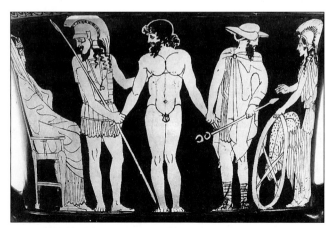

Fig.80 Ares and Hermes present the captured Ixion to Hera, while Athena holds the wheel to which he will be bound.

J K

Janus

The ancient Roman god of gateways and doorways (*ianuae*). He presided over all beginnings, which the Romans believed crucial to the success of any undertaking, and he gave his name to the first month of the year, January. Appropriately for such a god, he had two faces, one looking forwards and one backwards, just as every door looks two ways. This useful attribute helped him in his amorous pursuit of the elusive nymph CARNA, to whom he gave power over door hinges as a reward for her favours. He was the father of TIBERINUS, who gave his name to the River Tiber, and of the nymph CANENS, who married Picus. Janus with his two faces was often the image chosen for Roman republican coins.

[Livy 1.19.1–4; Virgil, *Aeneid* 7.180, 607–15, 8.355–8; Ovid, *Metamorphoses* 14.332–4, *Fasti* 1.63–288, 6.101–30.]

Jason

The hero who captained the *Argo* on the quest for the GOLDEN FLEECE. He was the son of AESON and Alcimede (or Polymede). In the usual version of the myth, Aeson should have become king of Iolcus on the death of his father, Cretheus, but the throne was usurped by his half-brother, PELIAS. At Jason's birth his parents, fearing for his life, told Pelias that their baby had been born dead, then secretly sent him to be brought up by the wise Centaur CHEIRON on Mount Pelion. Pelias, meanwhile, ruled on, though he knew from an oracle that he must beware of a man, coming from the country and wearing a single sandal, by whom he was destined to die.

When he grew to manhood, Jason returned to Iolcus to claim his heritage. He arrived wearing only one sandal, for he had lost the other while he was carrying the goddess HERA, disguised as an old woman, across the flooded river Anaurus. Hera hated Pelias because he had often dishonoured her, and in this way she marked Jason as the instrument of her enemy's destruction, from then onwards aiding him in all his tribulations until the day of Pelias' death. Pelias recognised his danger as soon as he saw Jason, so he asked him what he would do if he knew from an oracle that a certain man would kill him. Jason, perhaps inspired by Hera, replied that he would send such a man to fetch the Golden Fleece from King AEETES of Colchis. Thus he sealed his own fate. Pelias at once ordered him to set off on this quest, convinced that he could never return.

In Pindar's version, Jason was supported on his arrival in Iolcus by all his kinsmen: not only his father, but his uncles, PHERES (1) and AMYTHAON, and their sons. Jason claimed the throne from Pelias, but offered to let him keep the land and flocks that he had seized. Pelias gave a smooth reply, pretending that the spirit of the dead PHRIXUS, the original owner of the Golden Fleece, kept haunting his dreams, ordering him to fetch the Fleece from Colchis. Since he himself was too old, Jason must go on his behalf. He promised that on the successful completion of this quest, he would hand over the throne to Jason.

Whichever the motivation for Pelias' command, Jason, eager for glory, swiftly prepared for the adventure. ARGUS (4) built the ship *Argo* under the direction of Athena, and Jason invited the bravest heroes in Greece to accompany him. Joyfully they set sail. Pelias watched them go, and even though his own son ACASTUS was on board, he rejoiced that he would never more be troubled by the threat posed by Jason to his throne and life. He little knew that this was but the first move in Hera's elaborate plan for his destruction.

For the long expedition, beset by dangers, *see* ARGONAUTS. On the way to Colchis, Jason fathered two sons, EUNEUS and Thoas, on the Lemnian queen HYPSIPYLE. Once in Colchis, he succeeded in winning the Golden Fleece (figs. 23 and 24), helped by Aeetes' daughter, the sorceress MEDEA, who was another of Hera's instruments in her plan for Pelias' death. Jason returned to Iolcus with Medea as his bride. Here he found that Pelias had exterminated his family: Aeson, seeing death coming, had asked to take his own life, then had drunk bull's blood, believed by the ancients to be poisonous. Jason's mother had also killed herself, and his infant brother, Promachus, had been killed by Pelias.

Pelias was about to meet his own fate through the witchcraft of Medea, who persuaded his own daughters to kill him: she showed them how she could rejuvenate an old ram by cutting it up and boiling it in a cauldron with magic herbs. When it emerged as a lamb, they were persuaded that she could restore the youth of their ageing father as well. So they killed Pelias, and cut him up and boiled the pieces – and that was the end of him.

Despite the death of the usurper, Jason did not become king of Iolcus. After the brutal murder of Pelias, Acastus became king and held splendid funeral games for his father, while Jason and Medea fled from Iolcus and took refuge with CREON (1), the king of Corinth. Jason later went with other heroes of his generation on the CALYDONIAN BOARHUNT; and he returned to Iolcus once more to help his friend PELEUS gain revenge on Acastus, who had tried to engineer Peleus' death. With the help of the DIOSCURI, Jason and Peleus sacked the city and killed Acastus' wife, Astydameia, and perhaps Acastus too.

Medea bore Jason children, sometimes named as MEDUS (1) and Eriopis, or THESSALUS (1), Alcimenes and Tisander, or – most commonly – MERMERUS and Pheres. They were usually said to have died, killed either by the Corinthians or by Medea herself, either intentionally or unintentionally. In the version made famous by Euripides' tragedy *Medea*, Jason deserted Medea and married GLAUCE, King Creon's daughter. Medea murdered the new bride and her father; but to get the greatest possible revenge on her treacherous husband, she also killed her two sons by him, because this was the deed that would bring him the greatest pain. She escaped to Athens in a dragon-chariot sent by her grandfather, the Sun-god Helios, while Jason was left alone, his life in ruins around him (fig.88). It was sometimes said that he killed himself in despair, but he was more usually said to have been crushed to death by a beam, falling from the rotting carcase of his old ship, the *Argo*.

There is only a brief mention of Jason and his quest in Homer (*Odyssey* 12.69–72), where already he is called 'dear to Hera'. Our first description of him is in Pindar's *Pythian* 4, where he strides into Iolcus, clad in a leopard-skin and brandishing two spears, his long hair flowing down his back. Sadly, there is no epic version of his story preserved from the archaic period, so we have lost any

clear picture of what would no doubt have been the early Greek conception of him, the heroic achiever of seemingly impossible tasks, like Bellerophon or Heracles. The next major depictions of him that survive are very different: in Euripides' *Medea* (431 BC) he has lost all trace of his early heroism, becoming a selfish and obtuse man, concerned with materialistic values and his own social standing; and in Apollonius' late epic, the *Argonautica* (third century BC), he has become almost a travesty of an epic hero, often timid and confused, and easily prone to doubts and despair, a man who cannot succeed without the help of others, mortal and divine.

[Hesiod, *Theogony* 992–1002; Apollodorus 1.8.2, 1.9.16–28, 3.13.7; Diodorus Siculus 4.40–53; Pausanias 2.3.6–11, 5.17.9–10; Ovid, *Metamorphoses* 7.1–397, 8.302, *Heroides* 6, 12; Seneca, *Medea*.]

Jocasta

Daughter of the Theban Menoeceus and sister of CREON (2), called Epicasta by Homer. She was the renowned mother (and later wife) of OEDIPUS, whom she bore to her husband LAIUS, king of Thebes. Because an oracle had predicted that if he had a son, that son would kill him, Laius pinned the baby's ankles together and sent him to be abandoned in the wilds of Mount Cithaeron. The child was saved and taken to Corinth by a herdsman, where he was adopted by the childless king and queen, Polybus and Merope. They called him Oedipus ('Swollen Foot') because of the wounds in his feet, and brought him up to believe that he was their true son.

Many years later, a second oracle warned Oedipus that he was destined to kill his father and marry his mother, so he left Corinth for ever. On the road he met his father and killed him in a brawl, neither recognising the other. He then went on to Thebes, where the monstrous SPHINX was ravaging the city and devouring anyone who failed to answer her riddle correctly. Oedipus gave the right answer, and was rewarded with the kingship of Thebes and the hand of his mother Jocasta in marriage – again, neither recognising the other. In the most familiar version of the myth, found in fifth-century BC tragedy, Oedipus and Jocasta had two sons, Eteocles and POLYNEICES, and two daughters, ANTIGONE (1) and ISMENE. In the epic version the children were born of a second wife (*see* EURYGANEIA).

Eventually the truth came out and – in the usual version of the myth – at this point Oedipus blinded himself and Jocasta hung herself in shame and anguish. Euripides gives a different version in his tragedy *Phoenician Women*. Here Oedipus blinded himself when the incest became known, but Jocasta chose not to commit suicide, and she

is alive in the play to try and make peace between her two sons who are fighting over the rule of Thebes. She fails, and they fight and kill each other. It is only now that she kills herself, and from grief rather than shame (1455–9):

> And when their mother saw them dead, it was more than she could bear. She snatched up a sword that lay beside the corpses and did a fearful thing: right through her throat she thrust the iron blade, and now she lies between her beloved sons, with a lifeless arm embracing each.

[Homer, *Odyssey* 11.271–80; Sophocles, *Oedipus the King*; Apollodorus 3.5.7–9; Seneca, *Phoenician Women*.]

Jove *see* JUPITER.

Judgement of Paris

This was the origin of the TROJAN WAR. When the mortal Peleus married the sea-goddess Thetis, all the other gods attended the wedding and brought gifts, except, that is, for the unpopular ERIS (Strife). She was not invited, but appeared nevertheless and out of spite threw into the gathering a golden apple (the 'Apple of Discord') in-

Fig. 81 The Judgement of Paris. Hera, Athena and Aphrodite approach Paris as he sits on Mount Ida, looking after his sheep.

scribed with the words 'for the fairest'. The three goddesses HERA, ATHENA and APHRODITE all claimed it, and to settle the dispute Zeus told Hermes to take them to PARIS, the son of King Priam of Troy, who was tending flocks on Mount Ida, and to let him decide between them. They all offered Paris bribes: Hera offered him imperial power, Athena victory in battle, and Aphrodite the love of the most beautiful woman in the world, HELEN, wife of King Menelaus of Sparta. Paris awarded the apple to Aphrodite, and as his reward, during a visit to Sparta, he won the love of Helen and carried her off to Troy. Menelaus and his brother Agamemnon led a vast Greek force to Troy to regain Helen, and this was the beginning of the ten-year-long Trojan War during which the three goddesses took sides: Aphrodite naturally supported Paris and the Trojans, while the rejected Hera and Athena never forgave Paris and were staunch upholders of the Greek cause.

The Judgement of Paris is a popular scene in Greek art

from the seventh century BC (fig. 81). Sometimes Paris is shown on the point of running away in fear at the approach of the goddesses – a sound instinct, since the consequent war was to bring about his death, the deaths of his family, and the destruction of his city. The scene has also been an inspiration for many later painters, including Cranach, Rubens, Claude, Watteau, Cezanne and Renoir.

[Homer, *Iliad* 24.27–30; Epic Cycle, Proclus' summary of the *Cypria*; Euripides, *Trojan Women* 924–34, *Andromache* 274–92, *Iphigenia at Aulis* 573–89; Apollodorus, *Epitome* 3.1–3; Lucian, *The Judging of the Goddesses*; Pausanias 3.18.12, 5.19.5. T. C. W. Stinton, *Euripides and the Judgement of Paris* (1965).]

Juno

An ancient and important Italian goddess, the wife of JUPITER, and together with Jupiter and Minerva one of the three great deities of the Capitoline Triad. The goddess of marriage and, as Juno Lucina, of childbirth, Juno was early identified with the Greek HERA, adopting her characteristics and mythology. But Juno has one Roman myth, recounted by Ovid (*Fasti* 5.231–58). She was annoyed with Jupiter for producing Minerva from his own head without the need of a female, so the goddess FLORA gave Juno a herb at whose touch she at once became pregnant. She gave birth to MARS, the Roman god of war. (In Greek myth, Hera is also the mother of the war-god, Ares. But his father is Zeus, the Greek equivalent of Jupiter; and the child that Hera bears without male assistance is Hephaestus, the god of fire.)

Jupiter or Jove

The sovereign divinity of the Romans from early times, with supreme power over gods and men. Originally a sky-god and responsible for the weather, he was particularly associated with rain and storms. His weapon was the thunderbolt. His temple, the centre of the state cult, was on the Capitol at Rome and was shared with two other great Roman divinities, his wife JUNO and daughter MINERVA. He was identified with the Greek king of the gods, ZEUS, and adopted Zeus' mythology as his own.

Juturna

A water-nymph, daughter of Daunus, king of the Rutulians of Ardea in Latium. She was desired by JUPITER, and after he had his way with her – not without difficulty (*see* LARA) – he rewarded Juturna with immortality and with rule over springs and rivers. In the *Aeneid*, she does her best during the war between Latins and Trojans to save her beloved brother TURNUS from Aeneas, disguising herself as Turnus' charioteer Metiscus and driving him to safety. When he insists on fighting Aeneas in single combat, she restores to him his lost sword, made by Vulcan. Finally a Fury, sent by Jupiter, warns her to leave Turnus to his fate and unwillingly she obeys. Lamenting his now certain death and her own immortality, she plunges back into the depths of her river.

[Virgil, *Aeneid* 12.134–886; Ovid, *Fasti* 2.585–604.]

Juventas

The Roman goddess of Youth, identified with the Greek goddess HEBE.

Keres (Dooms, singular Ker)

Female death-spirits who, according to Hesiod, were the children of NYX (Night), along with other powerful abstract forces such as Fate, Death, Sleep, Strife and Old Age. The Hesiodic *Shield of Heracles* describes the Keres in action on the battlefield (248–57):

> The black Dooms, gnashing their white teeth, grim-eyed, fierce, bloody, terrifying, fought over the men who were dying, for they were all longing to drink dark blood. As soon as they caught a man who had fallen, or one newly wounded, one of them clasped her great claws around him and his soul went down to Hades, to chilly Tartarus. And when they had satisfied their hearts with human blood, they would throw that one behind them, and rush back again into the battle and the tumult.

A Ker who was dragging a corpse by the feet through the fighting 'had on her shoulders a cloak, red with the blood of men, and terribly she glared and loudly she bellowed' (159–60). The Ker that Pausanias saw depicted on the Chest of Cypselus had 'teeth as cruel as those of a wild beast and fingernails bent like talons' (5.19.6).

Sometimes the word is used in the sense of 'fate', for ACHILLES had a choice of two *keres*, either a long and obscure life at home, or death at Troy and everlasting glory. And when Achilles and HECTOR were about to fight to the death, Zeus weighed the *keres* of both heroes in his scales to find out which of them was fated to die: Hector's *ker* was the heavier, so he was abandoned to his destiny.

[Homer, *Iliad* 9.410–16, 18.535–8, 22.208–13, 365; Hesiod, *Theogony* 211–12, 217–22; Euripides, *Electra* 1252–3; Apollonius, *Argonautica* 4.1665–70.]

L

Labdacus

A king of Thebes. He was the son of Polydorus by Nycteis, and the grandson of CADMUS, the founder of Thebes. Polydorus died while Labdacus was still a child, and NYCTEUS, the boy's maternal grandfather, ruled Thebes as regent. On Nycteus' death, his brother LYCUS (1) became regent until Labdacus himself was old enough to take the throne. The young man waged an unsuccessful war over boundaries against PANDION (1), king of Athens, then he too died young. Apollodorus tells us that he perished thinking similar thoughts to those of PENTHEUS, which suggests that Labdacus, like Pentheus, opposed the worship of Dionysus and was torn apart by MAENADS, but no other author either clarifies or confirms Apollodorus' vague and sinister statement. Labdacus left a one-year-old son, LAIUS, so Lycus once more became regent of Thebes.

[Apollodorus 3.5.5, 3.14.8; Pausanias 2.6.2, 9.5.4–5.]

Labours of Heracles

The twelve Labours that HERACLES had to perform as an act of expiation for killing his own children, and in some accounts his wife MEGARA as well, in a fit of madness sent on him by Hera. For twelve years, proclaimed the Delphic Oracle, he must serve EURYSTHEUS, king of the Argolid, by carrying out whatever tasks the king imposed on him. Their accomplishment would earn him immortality. The canonical number of these Labours seems to have been set at twelve as early as the fifth century BC, perhaps under the influence of the twelve metopes depicting them on the temple of Zeus at Olympia (c. 460). There is some slight disagreement as to the order in which the Labours were performed, but the following is the order given by Apollodorus (2.4.12–2.5.12). Heracles must (1) kill the NEMEAN LION and bring back its pelt, (2) kill the HYDRA OF LERNA, (3) bring back the CERYNEIAN HIND with the golden horns, (4) capture the ERYMANTHIAN BOAR, (5) clean the stables of AUGEAS in a single day, (6) get rid of the STYMPHALIAN BIRDS, (7) capture the CRETAN BULL, (8) bring back the man-eating mares of DIOMEDES (1), (9) acquire the belt of the Amazon HIPPOLYTE (1), (10) steal the cattle of GERYON from Erytheia, (11) fetch the golden apples from the garden of the HESPERIDES, and (12) bring CERBERUS up from Hades. Thus the first six Labours took place in the Peloponnese, the next two in remoter parts of the Greek world, and the last four at the far ends of the earth, even including the Underworld.

Heracles' Labours are immensely popular subjects in ancient art, with some much more so than others. The Nemean Lion is by far the favourite exploit, followed by the battle with the Amazons, with the Lernean Hydra, the Erymanthian Boar and Cerberus also popular; while depictions of the Stymphalian Birds are infrequent, and of the Augean Stables and the mares of Diomedes very rare. In the postclassical arts the Lernean Hydra has been the most inspirational exploit, followed by the Nemean Lion and the quest for the apples of the Hesperides.

Labyrinth

The maze-like prison in which the MINOTAUR was housed.

Lacedaemon

The mythical ancestor of the Spartans. He was the son of ZEUS and the Pleiad TAYGETE, and married Sparta, the daughter of the Laconian king Eurotas, from whom he inherited the kingdom. He renamed the country after himself, and its principal city after his wife. She bore him a son, Amyclas, who gave his name to Amyclae, near Sparta, and was the father of HYACINTHUS, loved by Apollo; and a daughter Eurydice, who married Acrisius and was the mother of DANAE, loved by Zeus.

[Apollodorus 3.10.3; Pausanias 3.1.1–3, 3.20.2, 9.35.1.]

Lacinius *see* CROTON.

Ladon

The snake who helped the HESPERIDES to guard the golden

apples. Hesiod makes him the offspring of PHORCYS and CETO, and calls him 'the fearful serpent who guards the golden apples in a secret region of the dark earth, at the far edge of the world' (*Theogony* 333–6). Here he is named simply *ophis*, 'snake', and it is Apollonius who first names him Ladon (*Argonautica* 1396–8). Apollodorus (2.5.11) makes him the offspring of TYPHON and ECHIDNA, and adds that he had a hundred heads and many different voices. He also calls him immortal. Ladon, nevertheless, was sometimes said to have been killed by HERACLES in his quest for the golden apples, but he was finally immortalised in the sky as the constellation Draco, curling between the Great and Little Bears and with Heracles, club raised, right next to him.

Laelaps

A hound that was fated never to miss its quarry. It was given to Procris, wife of CEPHALUS (2), either by King Minos of Crete in return for sexual favours, or by Artemis after Procris had hunted in the mountains as a devotee of the goddess. Procris presented the hound to her husband, who took it to catch the TEUMESSIAN VIXEN, a fearsome fox that was ravaging Thebes and was, moreover, fated never to be caught. Hound ran off in pursuit of fox, the one inescapable, the other uncatchable, until Zeus resolved the problem by turning both animals to stone.

Laertes

Son of Arceisius, and in the *Odyssey* father of ODYSSEUS, though after Homer it was said that Laertes' wife, ANTICLEIA, was already pregnant by Sisyphus when Laertes married her. He and Anticleia also had a daughter, Ctimene (15.363–4). In his youth and strength Laertes sailed with the ARGONAUTS, but when we meet him in the *Odyssey* he is a very old man, who long years since has yielded the rule of Ithaca to his son and gone into retirement. Like his wife, he has suffered greatly during Odysseus' twenty-year absence. Anticleia has died of grief, but Laertes lives on, enduring a life of poverty and hardship. When Odysseus meets his mother's shade in Hades, she tells him of the old man's sufferings, adding, 'There he lies in sorrow, while the grief swells in his heart as he longs for your homecoming, and harsh old age had come upon him' (11.195–6).

In Odysseus' absence, Laertes has been too old and feeble to protect PENELOPE from the Suitors' excesses, but for a time she was able to use him as an excuse to put off their proposals of marriage, saying that they must wait until she had finished weaving the old man's shroud. Every day she wove more, then every night she unpicked what she had woven during the day. For three years she deceived the Suitors before they discovered her trick

(19.137–156), long enough still to be free when Odysseus at last returns.

Laertes too survives long enough to see his son return and kill the Suitors. In the final battle of the *Odyssey*, when the families of the dead Suitors attack Odysseus and his supporters, Laertes fights valiantly alongside his son and his grandson, TELEMACHUS. Athena breathes great strength into the old man, and he kills EUPEITHES, the leader of the attackers and the father of Antinous, the most rampant of the Suitors (23.489–548).

Laestrygonians

In Homer's *Odyssey* (10.80–132), the Laestrygonians are a race of man-eating giants living in a city called Telepylos, once founded by Lamus, a son of Poseidon. ODYSSEUS and his men moor their ships in a quiet harbour surrounded by tall cliffs, and he sends three scouts to spy out the land. They meet a girl who turns out to be the daughter of the local king, Antiphates. She leads them to her father's house (as Odysseus narrates):

> but when they went into the splendid palace, they found
> a woman as big as a mountain peak, who filled them with
>   terror.
> At once she called from the assembly famous Antiphates,
> her husband, who planned a ghastly death for them
> and prepared for his dinner by snatching up one of my
>   comrades ...

The two other scouts run back to the ships, followed by the whole population – 'thousands of them, not like men, but giants' – who stand on the cliffs and smash the ships below with boulders, spearing the men like fish and carrying them off for eating. Only Odysseus' ship, moored at the entrance to the harbour, manages to escape.

Laius

A king of Thebes, the father of the parricide OEDIPUS. Laius was the son of LABDACUS and the great grandson of CADMUS, founder of Thebes. Labdacus ruled the city for only a short time, dying young when Laius was only one year old. He left his baby son in the care of a regent, LYCUS (1), who was later either killed or driven out by AMPHION and Zethus. They jointly took over the throne of Thebes, while the young Laius was given a home by PELOPS, the king of Pisa in Elis. There he grew to manhood. He taught Pelops' illegitimate son, the beautiful CHRYSIPPUS, to drive a chariot and fell in love with the boy. When Amphion and Zethus died, Laius returned to Thebes to claim the throne, carrying Chrysippus off with him. This was said to be the first homosexual abduction among mortals. Chrysippus killed himself in shame by falling on his sword, and Pelops, who had loved his son dearly, laid a curse on Laius. This would lead to his death, since Zeus ordained that as punishment Laius would be killed by his own son. It also brought disaster to Thebes, for one of the reasons later given for the SPHINX' assault on the city was the anger of HERA, as goddess of marriage, because of the Thebans' failure to punish Laius for his unlawful passion.

Laius became king of Thebes and married JOCASTA, the daughter of Menoeceus. When they remained childless, Laius consulted the Oracle at Delphi for advice, but was given instead the horrifying prediction that if he had a son, that son would kill him. For a time he kept away from his wife's bed, but one night, drunk on wine, he lay with Jocasta, and in the course of time she bore him a son. Before the baby was three days old, Laius pinned his ankles together and had him taken from his mother, with instructions that he be cast out to die on Mount Cithaeron. Although Laius never knew it, his son was saved and taken by a herdsman to Corinth, where he was adopted by the childless king and queen, Polybus and Merope, and was named Oedipus ('Swollen Foot') because of the wounds in his feet.

Years later, Laius went once again to consult the Delphic Oracle, either to ask for advice about the monstrous Sphinx who was ravaging Thebes, or because he had heard sinister omens suggesting that his predicted fate was almost upon him. On the way to Delphi in his chariot, he met a young man at a narrow place where three roads met and tried to force him off the road, even striking him with his goad. The young man – who was, unknown to him, his own son Oedipus – struck back in anger and killed him, then killed most of his servants. The bodies were found by Damasistratus, the king of Plataea, who buried them in the middle of the place where the three roads met, piling unhewn stones on top of their graves.

[Sophocles, *Oedipus the King*; Apollodorus 3.5.5–8; Pausanias 9.2.4, 9.5.5–9, 9.26.2–4, 10.5.3–4.]

Lamia ('Devourer')

A beautiful Libyan woman loved by ZEUS. Every time she gave birth to a child, it was murdered by Zeus' jealous wife HERA, until at last Lamia went mad with grief. In despair, and deeply envying the happiness of every mother more fortunate than herself, she took to snatching and eating their children. She turned into a monster with a hideous face, which had the added peculiarity of removable eyes that she took out whenever she wanted

to go to sleep. Lamia became a nursery bogey-woman, a child-eating ogress used by Greek mothers and nurses as a threat to encourage good behaviour in children.

[Aristophanes, *Wasps* 1035, *Knights* 693, *Peace* 757; Diodorus Siculus 20.41.3–6; Strabo 1.2.8.]

Lampetie

Daughter of the Sun-god HELIOS.

Lamus *see* LAESTRYGONIANS.

Laocoon (1)

A Trojan priest who (rightly) tried to prevent the people of Troy from taking the WOODEN HORSE into their city. In the tenth year of the Trojan War the Greeks set fire to their camp and sailed away from Troy, leaving behind them a huge wooden image of a horse which appeared to be an offering to Athena, but which in fact was hollow and contained a body of armed warriors, the pick of the Greek fighting force. This was the means by which they hoped to gain entry to Troy. Laocoon suspected that this was the case and warned his people against the horse as strongly as he could, but was disregarded. His story is dramatically told by Virgil (*Aeneid* 2.40–56, 199–233). He gives his warning (which includes the much-quoted

Fig.82 Laocoon and his sons in their death agonies, strangled by the snakes.

words, 'I fear the Greeks, especially when they bear gifts', 49), then casts his great spear into the horse's side. The image booms and echoes, sounding suspiciously hollow, but at that moment the Greek SINON, pretending to be a deserter, comes on the scene and persuades the Trojans that the horse is a genuine offering to Athena. Their belief in Sinon's words is strengthened when they see what happens next to Laocoon and his two sons. He is sacrificing a huge bull to Poseidon when suddenly (203–24):

> There came over the calm water from Tenedos two snakes, forging through the sea in great coils and making side by side for the shore. They breasted the waves, their blood-red crests towering high, and the rest of their bodies drove through the water behind, their backs wreathing mighty spirals through the sounding foam of the sea. And now they were on land. Their eyes were blazing and blood-shot, and they hissed as they licked their lips with darting tongues ... They made straight for Laocoon, and first the snakes twined round the bodies of his two young sons, devouring their poor little limbs. Next, when Laocoon grabbed his sword and hastened to the rescue, they seized him and bound him in their huge and scaly coils, twice round his middle, twice round his throat, their heads and necks towering over him. He struggled frantically to wrench open the knots, his priestly bands drenched with filth and black venom, and his terrible cries rose to the sky, like the bellowing of a wounded bull that flees from the altar, shaking from its neck the axe that has struck awry.

Thus Laocoon died, and traditions vary as to what offence he had committed to warrant such a punishment. In one version, APOLLO was angry because Laocoon was his priest and yet had married and had children; in another because he had had intercourse with his wife in the god's sacred precinct. Whatever the real cause, the Trojans now firmly believed that he had been punished for defacing the offering to Athena with his spear, and they dragged the horse into their city. When night came, they were massacred by the Greeks.

In art, Laocoon is best known for the statuary group in the Vatican Museum that depicts him and his two sons in their death agonies, strangled by the snakes (fig. 82). It was in the palace of the Emperor Titus in the time of Pliny, who declared (*Natural History* 36.37) that it surpassed all other works of painting and sculpture.

Laocoon (2)

One of the ARGONAUTS, the son of OENEUS, king of Calydon, by a slave-woman. Although Laocoon was quite old,

he was sent on the voyage of the *Argo* to protect his young half-brother MELEAGER, who was still a boy.

[Apollonius, *Argonautica* 1.190–4.]

Laodamas

Son of Eteocles, king of Thebes, and grandson of Oedipus. He was only a boy when his father was killed in the attack of the SEVEN AGAINST THEBES, so CREON (2) ruled as regent until Laodamas grew up. When the sons of the Seven, the EPIGONI, attacked Thebes, Laodamas took command and was defeated. Some say that he was killed by Alcmaeon after himself killing Aegialeus, the son of Adrastus, others that on the night of the battle he escaped and led his defeated people to a new home in Illyria.

Laodameia (1)

The daughter of BELLEROPHON. According to Homer (*Iliad* 6.196–206) she bore the great hero SARPEDON to ZEUS, and was later killed by ARTEMIS in anger. Later writers make Sarpedon the son of Zeus and EUROPA, the daughter of Agenor.

Laodameia (2)

Daughter of ACASTUS and wife of PROTESILAUS, king of Phylace, who was the first warrior to leap ashore when the Greek ships landed at Troy, only to be killed by Hector. Laodameia was inconsolable at his death. In some accounts she even had a statue made in her husband's likeness, either of wood or wax or bronze, and took it with her to bed for comfort. Seeing her great grief, the gods took pity on her, and HERMES brought Protesilaus back to earth for a few hours. On his return to Hades, Laodameia killed herself so that she might go with him. Euripides wrote a tragedy *Protesilaus*, now lost, on this theme, in which the couple had been married for only one day when the summons came for the expedition to Troy. Here it was Protesilaus who, after his death, appealed to the gods to let him have just one more day with his young wife; and here, too, Laodameia killed herself when he was taken to Hades for the second time.

Laodice (1)

According to Homer, Laodice was the most beautiful of the many daughters of PRIAM, king of Troy, and HECUBA. She was married to Helicaon, the son of Antenor. When Troy fell to the Greeks, she stretched her hands to heaven and prayed that the earth might swallow her up before she was taken as a slave. There and then, in the full sight of everyone, a chasm opened in the ground and she disappeared from view, never to be seen again.

A later legend said that Laodice, while still unmarried, had fallen in love with ACAMAS (1), the son of Theseus,

when he came with Diomedes to Troy before the Trojan War to seek the return of Helen. Laodice went to bed with Acamas, and in due course bore him a son, Munitus. She handed the baby over to his great-grandmother AETHRA, the mother of Theseus, who brought the child up during the ten-year-long war. At the fall of Troy, Munitus left the city with his father, but was killed by a snake-bite while hunting in Thrace.

[Homer, *Iliad* 3.121–4, 6.252; Apollodorus, *Epitome* 5.23; Plutarch, *Theseus* 34; Pausanias 10.26.7–8; Quintus of Smyrna, *Sequel to Homer* 13.544–54.]

Laodice (2)

One of the daughters of Agamemnon and Clytemnestra, mentioned by Homer (*Iliad* 9.145) but later renamed ELECTRA (3).

Laomedon

A king of Troy, son of ILUS and Eurydice, and father of several children, including TITHONUS, PRIAM (who was at first called Podarces) and HESIONE. Laomedon was famous for his treachery to both gods and mortals, a failing which would bring him to a violent end.

APOLLO and POSEIDON built the walls of Troy for him, either because they wanted to test his reputation for bad faith, or because they had to serve a mortal for a whole year as a punishment for rebellion against Zeus. But Laomedon refused to pay them the agreed wage. It was sometimes said that the gods were helped by a mortal, AEACUS, because Troy was fated to be captured, and if the walls had been built by the gods alone, the city would have been impregnable. Homer gives a slightly different version of events (*Iliad* 21.441–57) and a vivid picture of the treacherous and violent king: Poseidon reminds

Fig. 83 A fallen warrior, usually identified as Laomedon, from the east pediment of the Temple of Aphaea on Aegina depicting Heracles' sack of Troy. See also fig. 70.

Apollo of how they both served Laomedon for a year, Poseidon building the walls of Troy and Apollo tending the king's cattle in the wooded glens of Mount Ida:

> But when the changing seasons brought round the glad time for payment, then outrageous Laomedon robbed us of all our wage and sent us away with menaces, threatening to bind us hand and foot and to sell us as slaves in far-off islands. He even said he would peel off our ears with a cleaver. So we went away with rage in our hearts, angry about our wage which he promised and would not pay.

To punish Laomedon, Apollo sent a plague on the land, and Poseidon a sea-monster that preyed on the people. Oracles foretold that salvation from these calamities would come only if the king gave his daughter Hesione to be devoured by the monster. He chained her to the rocks near the sea; but HERACLES arrived in Troy and promised to kill the monster, on condition that Laomedon would reward him with the divine horses once given by Zeus in exchange for GANYMEDE. Once again, however, the king went back on his agreement, for when the monster was dead and Hesione saved, he refused to hand over the horses. Heracles left Troy empty-handed, vowing revenge.

In due course he returned to Troy with an army, and with the help of TELAMON, who was the first to breach the walls, he captured the city. He killed Laomedon and all his sons, except for Tithonus, who had previously been carried off by Eos, and Priam, who alone had advised Laomedon to honour his agreement. Heracles gave Hesione to Telamon as his concubine and left Priam to rule Troy. Laomedon was buried at the Scaean Gate. It was said that Troy would be safe as long as his grave remained undisturbed, but it was destroyed by the Greeks during the Trojan War, which ended with the capture of Troy.

The east pediment of the temple of Aphaea on the island of Aegina, now incomplete, depicts Heracles' sack of Troy, with the magnificent bearded warrior collapsing in the left corner usually taken to be Laomedon (fig.83).

[Homer, *Iliad* 5.638–51, 6.23–4, 7.452–3, 20.144–8, 237–8; Pindar, *Olympian* 8.30–33; Apollodorus 2.5.9, 2.6.4, 3.12.3–5, *Epitome* 3.24; Diodorus Siculus 4.32.1–5, 4.49.3–7; Strabo 13.1.32; Ovid, *Metamorphoses* 11.194–217.]

Laothoe

In Homer's *Iliad*, Laothoe is one of the wives of PRIAM, king of Troy, and mother by him of two sons, LYCAON (2) and POLYDORUS (3), both of whom are killed by Achilles.

Lapiths

A Greek tribe living in northern Thessaly. They were most famous for their victorious battle against the CENTAURS, frequently depicted in ancient art, where the Lapiths represented the virtues of civilisation triumphing over the forces of barbarism and bestiality. Famous Lapiths were IXION, one of the four great sinners who suffered eternal punishment after death; Ixion's son PEIRITHOUS, who led the Lapiths in their famous battle with the Centaurs that broke out during his wedding with Hippodameia; CAENEUS, an invulnerable Lapith leader, born a girl, who was killed when the Centaurs hammered him into the ground; Caeneus' son CORONUS, who led the Lapiths against the Dorians in a dispute over the boundaries of their land and was killed by Heracles; and POLYPOETES (1), son of Peirithous, and Leonteus, son of Coronus, who led forty ships to Troy and were formidable warriors in the Trojan War.

Lara

A nymph of Latium, daughter of the river Almo, a tributary of the Tiber, who was punished by JUPITER for being a chatterbox. Jupiter had amorous designs on the nymph JUTURNA, who constantly fled from him, so he asked all her sister-nymphs to help him by keeping firm hold of her when next he pursued her. They all agreed to help except for Lara, who chattered to Juturna and even to JUNO about what was afoot. The wrathful Jupiter tore out her tongue and handed her over to MERCURY to be taken down to Hades, where she could spend the rest of time

silent, among the silent dead. On the long journey Mercury raped her in a grove, and she bore him twin sons, the Lares, guardian spirits of the household and the state.

[Ovid, *Fasti* 2.583–616.]

Lares *see* LARA.

Latinus

The man who gave his name to Latium and the Latins. Hesiod says that he was a son of Odysseus and Circe, and king of the Tyrrhenians (Etruscans); others that he was the son of Heracles or Telemachus. But according to the most familiar version of his myth, found in the *Aeneid*, he was the son of FAUNUS and the water-nymph Marica, and thus the great-grandson of SATURN. When AENEAS arrived in Italy with his Trojan followers, he found Latinus ruling Latium, now an ineffectual old man. His wife AMATA wanted to marry their only child, Lavinia, to TURNUS, king of the Rutulians; but Latinus had been warned by an oracle not to give his daughter to a native from Italy, but to someone coming from overseas, so he was happy to accept Aeneas as her husband. Dissension arose, however, when the Fury Allecto, sent by Juno, stirred up a quarrel between Latins and Trojans. Latinus was powerless to prevent the bloody war that followed, but he kept apart from the fighting, and when finally Aeneas killed Turnus in single combat, Latinus made peace with the Trojans and celebrated the marriage of Lavinia and Aeneas that would link the two peoples. Livy records another tradition in which Latinus was killed while fighting on the side of Aeneas against Turnus and the Rutulians.

[Hesiod, *Theogony* 1011–16; Strabo 5.3.2; Dionysius of Halicarnassus 1.43, 1.57–60, 1.72; Livy 1.1.5–1.2.3; Virgil, *Aeneid* 7–12.]

Lausus *see* MEZENTIUS.

Lavinia

Daughter of LATINUS, king of Latium, and AMATA. She married AENEAS, who founded the city of Lavinium in her name. Their son, Silvius, was born after his father's death and was the ancestor of the Alban royal house of Silvii. It was sometimes said that Lavinia, fearing the jealousy of ASCANIUS, Aeneas' son by his first wife, fled into the woods to give birth.

[Diodorus Siculus 7.5.8–9; Dionysius of Halicarnassus 1.70; Livy 1.3; Virgil, *Aeneid* 6.760–6, 12.193–4.]

Leander *see* HERO.

Learchus *see* INO.

Leda

A daughter of the Aetolian king THESTIUS, and wife of TYNDAREOS, king of Sparta. She is most famous for being loved by ZEUS, who seduced her in the guise of a swan, flying into her arms for protection from a pursuing eagle. The result of their union was an egg, from which was born the beautiful HELEN – 'Helen of Troy '– over whom the Greeks and Trojans warred for ten long years. From the same, or a second, egg were born Castor and Polydeuces (the DIOSCURI), and CLYTEMNESTRA. Although accounts differ as to exactly who fathered these four children, Castor and Clytemnestra were usually said to be the mortal children of Tyndareos, and Helen and Polydeuces the immortal children of Zeus. Leda also had other daughters by Tyndareos: TIMANDRA, PHILONOE (2), and PHOEBE (3). Homer knows nothing of the egg, and when Odysseus sees Leda in the Underworld, she is mentioned as mother only of the Dioscuri.

Another tradition had NEMESIS as Helen's mother, who also produced an egg after Zeus mated with her as a swan, while she took the form of a goose. A shepherd found the egg in a wood and took it to Leda, who kept it carefully in a chest until it hatched. She then brought Helen up as her own daughter. Whoever the mother of the egg may have been, Pausanias records (3.16.1) that it was still to be seen in his time, hanging by ribbons from the roof of a temple at Sparta. Zeus put the constellation Cygnus, the Swan, in the night sky to commemorate the form that he took when he fathered Helen.

Leda with the swan (fig. 84), or with the egg, were popular subjects in ancient art from about 450 BC, but it was in the postclassical arts, particularly painting and literature, that Leda and the Swan became an especially potent source of inspiration. Among the many who have painted them are Leonardo da Vinci, Michelangelo, Coreggio, Tintoretto, Veronese, Rubens, Boucher and Delacroix. In Spenser's *Faerie Queene* (3.II.32) Leda's rape, depicted in the tapestry of 'Cupid's Wars', is powerfully described:

> Whiles the proud Bird, ruffing his fethers wyde
> And brushing his faire brest, did her invade,
>
> She slept; yet twixt her eyelids closely spyde
> How towards her he rusht, and smiled at his pryde.

But perhaps it is W. B. Yeats, in his *Leda and the Swan*, who captures most memorably, in a few words, the significance of this moment of union, from which Helen was to be born:

> A sudden blow: the great wings beating still
> Above the staggering girl, her thighs caressed
> By the dark webs, her nape caught in his bill,
> He holds her helpless breast upon his breast ...
>
> A shudder in the loins engenders there
> The broken wall, the burning roof and tower
> And Agamemnon dead ...

[Homer, *Odyssey* 11.298–300; Hesiod, *Catalogue of Women* frr. 23a and 176; Euripides, *Helen* 6–21, 213–16, 256–9; Apollodorus 3.10.5–7.]

Lemnian Women *see* HYPSIPYLE.

Leo (The Lion)

A constellation commemorating the NEMEAN LION killed by Heracles.

Leonteus

A Lapith warrior, the son of CORONUS, and the grandson of the famous Lapith leader CAENEUS, who began life as a woman. *See* POLYPOETES (1).

Lepus (The Hare)

A constellation. The Hare was put among the stars by HERMES to celebrate its fleetness of foot, and now forever keeps its distance from the great hunter ORION as they move through the night sky.

Fig.84 Zeus, in the form of a swan, rapes Leda.

Lethe

The River of Forgetfulness in the Underworld. The souls of the dead drank its waters to make them forget their earthly lives. Ovid mentions Lethe as a river running through the dark and misty cavern of HYPNOS (Sleep), where its murmuring flow invites slumber. One of the preliminary rituals in consulting the oracle of Trophonius at Lebadea in Boeotia was to drink from the spring called Lethe.

Byron in *Don Juan* sees the ability to forget, symbolised by Lethe, as an essential part of life:

> And if I laugh at any mortal thing,
>   'Tis that I may not weep; and if I weep
> 'Tis that our nature cannot always bring
>   Itself to apathy, for we must steep
> Our hearts first in the depths of Lethe's spring
>   'Ere what we least wish to behold will sleep:
> Thetis baptised her mortal son in Styx;
>   A mortal mother would on Lethe fix.

[Plato, *Republic* 10.621a; Pausanias 9.39.8; Virgil, *Aeneid* 6.703–15; Ovid, *Metamorphoses* 11.602–4.]

Leto

Daughter of the TITANS Coeus and Phoebe, and known to the Romans as Latona. 'She was always gentle', says Hesiod (*Theogony* 406–8), 'mild to men and to the immortal gods, gentle from the beginning, the kindest in all Olympus.' She was one of the earliest loves of ZEUS and bore to him the two great archer-deities, APOLLO and ARTEMIS. When the time of their birth came near, Leto wandered through many lands, seeking a place for her labour, but no land dared let her rest because they feared the wrath of HERA, who was always violently hostile to Zeus' loves. Finally Leto came to DELOS, then a floating island, but afterwards secured to the sea-bed. Delos gladly agreed to receive her when she promised that Apollo would build a glorious temple there for his worship; but even now Leto was not free from Hera's anger. The jealous goddess kept EILEITHYIA, who presided over childbirth, close by her on Olympus so that she would not hear of Leto's distant sufferings and deliver her of her child. Leto was racked with pains for nine days and nights, until at last the other goddesses sent IRIS to fetch Eileithyia, offering her an enormous necklace strung with golden threads if she would come and end Leto's long labour. The *Homeric Hymn to Apollo* relates how the first child, Apollo, was born (115–19):

> As soon as Eileithyia, goddess of childbirth, set foot on Delos, Leto's time was come and she strove to bring forth her child. She clasped her arms around a palm tree, kneeling on the soft meadow while the earth laughed for joy beneath, and the child leaped forth to the light.

Some say that Artemis was born first, then served as midwife in the birth of Apollo. In another version the snake PYTHON, knowing through his oracular powers that he was fated to perish at the hands of Leto's son, pursued the pregnant goddess, intent on killing her. So Zeus had BOREAS, god of the North Wind, carry her to POSEIDON, who took her to Ortygia ('Quail Island', created when Leto's sister ASTERIA turned herself into a quail and jumped into the sea to escape capture by the amorous Zeus). Because Hera had decreed that Leto's children might not be born in any place where the sun shone, Poseidon made a great wave curl over the island and hide it from the sun's light. There Apollo and Artemis were born and the island was renamed Delos.

Leto was a devoted mother to her children (fig. 26). She often hunted with Artemis, and the two of them persuaded Zeus to immortalise the giant hunter ORION as a constellation. Together with Apollo and Artemis, Leto sided with the Trojans in the Trojan War. They, for their part, were always ready to take revenge for any slight or hurt done to their mother. Apollo avenged Python's pursuit of her by shooting the huge snake dead. When TITYUS tried to rape her, brother and sister together killed him and he endured eternal torment in Hades for his crime. They also shot the sons and daughters of NIOBE (2) when she boasted that she was superior to Leto in the number of her children. But Leto herself could sometimes be driven to vengeful anger: soon after her children's birth she was travelling with them in Lycia when, hot and weary, she tried to quench her thirst at a lake. Some peasants not only refused to let her drink, but threatened and insulted her, so she turned them into frogs. This episode is particularly popular in postclassical art, with paintings by Tintoretto, Rubens and Giordano among many others.

[Homer, *Iliad* 5.447–8, 20.38–40, 21.497–504; Hesiod, *Theogony* 404–7, 918–20; *Homeric Hymn to Apollo* 1–18, 25–126; Apollodorus 1.2.2, 1.4.1, 3.5.6, 3.10.4; Ovid, *Metamorphoses* 6.157–381; Hyginus, *Fabula* 140.]

Leucippe

One of the three daughters of MINYAS who refused to worship Dionysus. To appease the angry god, Leucippe's son Hippasus was torn to pieces by the three women, who were then turned into bats.

Leucippides *see* HILAEIRA AND PHOEBE.

Leucippus (1)

Son of Perieres and Perseus' daughter Gorgophone. On his father's death, he and his elder brother APHAREUS ruled

Messenia jointly. Leucippus had three daughters, HILAEIRA AND PHOEBE, known as the Leucippides, who were carried off by the DIOSCURI, and Arsinoe, who was said by some to be the mother of ASCLEPIUS by Apollo.

[Apollodorus 1.9.5, 3.10.3, 3.10.4; Pausanias 3.12.8, 4.2.4, 4.3.1–2.]

Leucippus (2)

Son of OENOMAUS, king of Pisa. Leucippus disguised himself as a girl to win the love of DAPHNE, but was killed by her female companions when his ruse was discovered.

Leucothea ('White Goddess')

The name given to INO when she became a sea-goddess.

Leucothoe

A mistress of HELIOS, the Sun-god.

Leucus *see* IDOMENEUS.

Liber

Roman god of fertility and wine, identified with the Greek DIONYSUS. He was worshipped together with Ceres and Libera, who were identified with DEMETER and PERSEPHONE, though Ovid says that Libera was the deified ARIADNE.

[Ovid, *Fasti* 3.510–12, 713–90.]

Libya

The daughter of EPAPHUS and Memphis (and thus the granddaughter of ZEUS) who gave her name to the land of Libya. By POSEIDON she had twin sons, BELUS and AGENOR (1), who became kings of Egypt and Phoenicia, and a third son, Lelex, who left Egypt and became king of Megara in mainland Greece.

[Apollodorus 2.1.4; Pausanias 1.39.6, 1.44.3.]

Lichas

The herald who in good faith carried the robe, poisoned with the blood of the Centaur Nessus, from DEIANEIRA to his master HERACLES, who was preparing to sacrifice on Cape Cenaeum in Euboea. When Heracles put on the robe and the poison began to bite into his flesh like acid, he seized Lichas by the foot, and hurled him to his death on a reef projecting from the sea. It was later said that Lichas' body was transformed into a sea-swept rock, and that the three Lichades Islands off Euboea were named after him.

[Sophocles, *Women of Trachis*; Apollodorus 2.7.7; Strabo 9.4.4.]

Licymnius

The bastard son of ELECTRYON, king of Mycenae, by a Phrygian slave-woman called Midea, and the only one of his sons to escape massacre by Taphian raiders. When Electryon himself was killed, Licymnius went to live with AMPHITRYON and ALCMENE in Thebes. In due course he married Amphitryon's sister Perimede. She bore him three sons, Oeonus, Argeius and Melas, who with their father were firm and valued supporters of their cousin HERACLES. Oeonus was clubbed to death by the sons of HIPPOCOON for throwing a stone at their savage dog, so Heracles avenged him by marching against Sparta and killing every one (twelve or twenty) of the boy's murderers. Argeius and Melas died in Heracles' expedition against EURYTUS (1), king of Oechalia. Licymnius himself, after fighting with the HERACLIDS in Argos, was killed in his old age, either accidentally or in anger, by Heracles' son TLEPOLEMUS.

[Homer, *Iliad* 2.661–3; Pindar, *Olympian* 7.27–30; Apollodorus 2.4.5–6, 2.7.3, 2.7.7, 2.8.2; Diodorus Siculus 4.38, 4.57–8; Pausanias 2.22.8, 3.15.4.]

Linus

A famous musician, whose name and story derived from the ancient Linus-song, a lament with the refrain *ailinon*, 'alas for Linus'. This was interpreted as a mournful song in honour of one Linus, around whose name various sad stories grew. He was often said to be the son of one of the MUSES, Calliope or Urania, which was a fair guarantee of fine musicianship; and in one version of his legend he was killed by APOLLO because he rivalled the god in his musical skill. Pausanias tells of a Linus, son of Apollo by Psamathe, the daughter of King Crotopus of Argos: in terror of her father, Psamathe abandoned the baby in the wild, where he was torn to pieces by dogs. A third Linus was the music teacher of HERACLES. One day he struck out in irritation at his inexpert pupil and Heracles retaliated, killing Linus with his own lyre (fig.85).

Once Linus was dead, mourning for him spread throughout the Greek world and beyond.

[Homer, *Iliad* 18.569–72; Herodotus 2.79; Apollodorus 1.3.2, 2.4.9; Diodorus Siculus 3.67.1–2; Pausanias 1.43.7, 2.19.8, 8.18.1, 9.29.6–9.]

Lityerses

The name of an ancient reapers' song and of the man whose story lay behind it. Lityerses, a bastard son of King MIDAS of Phrygia, was renowned for preying on passing travellers and forcing them to compete with him at harvesting. Always he won. When his victims flagged, he whipped them, and in the evening he beheaded them and bound their bodies in a corn stook, singing his reaping song as he did so.

The shepherd DAPHNIS promised to be a victim like all the rest. After searching the world for his lost love Pimplea, carried off by pirates, Daphnis found her among

Lityerses' slave girls. He too was challenged to a reaping contest, but HERACLES came by and took his place. This time it was Lityerses who was beaten and beheaded. Heracles flung his body into the River Maeander and gave his kingdom to Daphnis and Pimplea.

[Theocritus, *Idylls* 10; Pollux, *Onomasticon* 4.54; Athenaeus 10.415, 14.619.]

Lotis *see* DRYOPE *and* PRIAPUS.

Lotus-eaters or Lotophagi

A mythical people living on the fruit of the lotus plant, which induces forgetfulness and makes those who eat it lose all desire to return home. In Homer's *Odyssey* (9.82–104), ODYSSEUS and his men come to their land on the journey home from Troy. The scouts who go ashore and eat of the lotus have to be dragged back to the ships by force and tied down, so great is their desire to stay with the Lotus-eaters.

Herodotus (4.177) locates the Lotus-eaters on the Libyan coast, adding that they made wine as well as food from the lotus plant. In the arts, it was only after Tennyson's seminal poem *The Lotus-eaters* that they captured the popular imagination and became a source of

Fig.85 Heracles attacks his music teacher, Linus, with part of a broken stool, while the other students mill about in dismay.

inspiration for artists. The sensuous lure of his island is irresistible:

> There is sweet music here that softer falls
> Than petals from blown roses on the grass,
> Or night-dews on still waters between walls
> Of shadowy granite, in a gleaming pass;
> Music that gentlier on the spirit lies,
> Than tir'd eyelids upon tir'd eyes;
> Music that brings sweet sleep down from the blissful skies.
> Here are cool mosses deep,
> And thro' the moss the ivies creep,
> and in the stream the long-leaved flowers weep,
> And from the craggy ledge the poppy hangs in sleep.

Nor do Tennyson's mariners resist. The poem ends:

> Surely, surely, slumber is more sweet than toil, the shore
> Than labour in the deep mid-ocean, wind and wave and oar;
> Oh rest ye, brother mariners, we will not wander more.

Lucifer *see* PHOSPHORUS.

Lucina *see* EILEITHYIA.

Luna *see* SELENE.

Lycaon (1)

An early king of Arcadia, the son of PELASGUS either by the Oceanid Meliboea or by the nymph Cyllene. He had a daughter, CALLISTO, who was raped by ZEUS and bore a son called ARCAS, then was transformed (by Zeus or by Hera or by Artemis) into a bear. He also had fifty sons by several wives. There are two divergent stories about him, both concerning murder and the eating of human flesh. In one version, Lycaon was a virtuous king but his sons were wicked. Zeus came down to earth disguised as a poor man, to test for himself the rumours he had heard of their impiety. They gave him hospitality, but among the meat that they served him were the intestines of a murdered child. Zeus in fury upset the table – since when the place has been called Trapezus (*trapeza*, table) – and blasted Lycaon and his sons with thunderbolts, all except for Nyctimus, the youngest. He was saved by GAIA and later took over the rule of the kingdom. Some said that it was the impiety of Lycaon's sons which caused Zeus to destroy most of the human race with the Great Flood.

In the other version, Lycaon himself was as bad as his sons. He set human meat before Zeus (perhaps the flesh of a slave, or perhaps even the flesh of the god's own son Arcas), or else he sacrificed a human child on the altar of Lycaean Zeus, a worship that he himself had established. Once again Zeus sent his thunderbolts against Lycaon's family, but Lycaon himself he transformed into a wolf (*lykos*). It was said that from this time onwards, whenever a man tasted human flesh at sacrifices to Lycaean Zeus in Arcadia, he was turned into a wolf, but at the end of nine years, if he had meanwhile abstained from eating human flesh, he became a man again; if not, he remained a wolf until he died. Thus Lycaon's story is one version of the werewolf tradition.

[Hesiod, *Catalogue of Women* frr. 161–4; Plato, *Republic* 565d–e; Apollodorus 3.8.1–2; Pausanias 8.2.1–6, 8.3.1, 8.3.6–7; Ovid, *Metamorphoses* 1.192–243; Pliny, *Natural History* 8.80–3.]

Lycaon (2)

A son of PRIAM, king of Troy, and LAOTHOE. His death at ACHILLES' hands is one of the most memorable scenes in Homer's *Iliad* (21.34–127). Achilles had caught him once before while he was cutting young fig branches to make rails for his chariot, but on that occasion he sold him as a slave to King EUNEUS of Lemnos, gaining in return for him a fine mixing-bowl of silver (23.740–7). A family friend, Eetion of Imbros, bought Lycaon from Euneus and he eventually returned to Troy. There for eleven days he took delight in his home and family, but now on the twelfth day Achilles catches him once more, unarmed, on the banks of the River SCAMANDER. But Achilles now is not as he was in the old days, before his beloved comrade PATROCLUS was killed by HECTOR. In those days he preferred to ransom or sell his captives. Now, having lost Patroclus, he is full of a fury for revenge, passionate to kill as many Trojans as he can, and above all Hector. Lycaon goes down on his knees, pleading for his life and clutching the spear that may kill him, but even as he does so he knows that his pleas are useless. 'This time death will come to me here', he says, 'for I think there is no way I can escape your hands, now that a god has brought me to them'; but still he adds, 'Do not kill me, for I was not born of the same mother as Hector, who killed your comrade gentle and brave' (92–6). Achilles replies that he has changed since Patroclus was slain: 'Now there is no one who shall escape death if the gods send him into my hands in front of Troy, not one of all the Trojans, and least of all the sons of Priam' (103–5). But his killing of Lycaon is no mere brutal murder, for Achilles knows that he himself will die too, just as Lycaon now must die, and he is deeply aware of their shared humanity. 'Friend', he calls Lycaon, even as he kills him (106–19):

'So, friend, you die also. Why all this lamentation?
Patroclus too is dead, who was better by far than you.
Do you not see what kind of a man I am,
in beauty and stature, the son of a noble father,
and my mother a goddess? Yet even over me
hangs death and mighty fate. And there shall come
a dawn, or an evening, or a noonday, when some man
will take my life in the fighting, whether it be
with a cast of his spear or an arrow from his bow.'
So he spoke, and Lycaon's strength and spirit
collapsed. He let go of the spear and sat back,
both arms outspread, and Achilles, drawing
his sharp sword, struck his collar-bone by the neck,
and the two-edged sword sank full in. He dropped
to the ground, face down, and lay full length,
and out flowed his dark blood, soaking the earth.

Lycomedes

King of the island of Scyros at around the time of the Trojan War. He played a significant part in the legends of both THESEUS and ACHILLES. He gave refuge to Theseus, who had ancestral land on Scyros and went there after MENESTHEUS banished him from Athens. But Lycomedes, while pretending friendship, treacherously murdered his guest by pushing him off a cliff, either because he feared his reputation, or out of a desire to please Menestheus.

Achilles' sojourn on Scyros began when his mother THETIS, knowing that he was fated to die if he fought in the Trojan War, dressed him as a girl and sent him instead to live with the women at Lycomedes' court. The secret was in some way betrayed, and when the Greeks were marshalling troops for the war ODYSSEUS went to Scyros, determined to penetrate Achilles' disguise and recruit him to the Greek army. Once in the palace, Odysseus laid out a collection of feminine trinkets mixed with military weapons, and while the women eagerly pounced on the fripperies, Achilles gave himself away by reaching for the arms. In another version, he was at first too wily to be taken in by Odysseus' ploy, but then a call to arms was sounded on a bugle, and Achilles, thinking that an enemy was at hand, tore off his girls' clothes and seized spear and shield. Either way, once unmasked he went eagerly to war, although he did not survive the fighting at Troy – just as Thetis had foreseen. He left a son, however, for while on Scyros he had made Lycomedes' daughter Deidameia pregnant. Lycomedes named their child Pyrrhus and brought him up in his father's absence. In due course the boy too went to the war, when he was renamed NEOPTOLEMUS.

The earliest evidence for the tale of Achilles among the women on Scyros is a (fifth-century BC) painting by Polygnotus (Pausanias 1.22.6). We know from a papyrus fragment that Euripides dramatised this story in his lost tragedy *The Scyrians*, in which Lycomedes himself was taken in by Achilles' disguise and was at first quite unaware that his young visitor was in fact male. In postclassical arts the episode on Scyros was a popular subject, particularly in opera, and also in the fine arts where we have paintings by Rubens, van Dyck, Claude, Poussin and Tiepolo, among many others.

[Sophocles, *Philoctetes* 243; Apollodorus 3.13.8, *Epitome* 1.24; Plutarch, *Theseus* 35; Pausanias 1.17.6, 10.26.4.]

Lycurgus (1)

Son of Dryas and king of the Edonians in Thrace. When the god DIONYSUS was introducing his worship into Greece, Lycurgus (like PENTHEUS) was one of the mortals who opposed him and was duly punished for his impiety. His story first occurs in Homer (*Iliad* 6.130–40), who says that he pursued Dionysus and his nurses with an ox-goad, terrifying them so much that the god dived into the sea, taking refuge with THETIS. Lycurgus was blinded by Zeus in punishment and soon after died, hated by all the gods. According to Apollodorus (3.5.1), Lycurgus drove out the god – who again took refuge with Thetis – and imprisoned his train of MAENADS and SATYRS. These were suddenly released by a divine miracle and Dionysus punished Lycurgus by driving him mad. In his madness he struck his son Dryas dead with an axe, believing that he was chopping at a grapevine. After cutting off his son's ex-

tremities, he regained his sanity, but soon after died when, at the command of the god, his people put him to death: he was torn asunder by wild horses. Hyginus has yet another version (*Fabula* 132) in which Lycurgus became drunk and tried to rape his own mother, then killed his wife and son, and finally cut off his own foot, believing it to be a vine. Dionysus then had him devoured by panthers.

Aeschylus wrote a (lost) tetralogy on the legend of Lycurgus, and he appears occasionally on ancient vase-paintings, slaughtering his wife or son.

Lycurgus (2)

Son of Aleus and Neaera, and king of Arcadia. He is the subject of one of old NESTOR's reminiscences in the *Iliad* (7.132–57): Lycurgus was notorious for killing, by treachery instead of in fair fight, a warrior called Areithous, who was also nicknamed 'mace-man' from his habit of fighting with a great iron mace. Lycurgus caught him on a narrow path where his mace could get no swing, then speared him through the middle. He took the splendid armour of his victim and himself used it in war until he grew old, when he passed it on to his squire Ereuthalion. Dressed in this armour, Ereuthalion rashly offered to take on anyone in single combat, but the only one brave enough to accept his challenge was (unsurprisingly) Nestor – who fought him and killed him: 'He was the biggest and the strongest man I ever killed', says Nestor, 'with his great bulk sprawling this way and that.'

Lycurgus outlived all his sons (the most famous of these being ANCAEUS (1), who was killed by the Calydonian boar). He was succeeded on the throne of Arcadia by ECHEMUS, the grandson of his brother Cepheus.

[Apollodorus 3.9.1–2; Pausanias 8.4.10–8.5.1.]

Lycurgus (3)

Son of Pheres and king of Nemea; father of Opheltes/Archemorus (*see* HYPSIPYLE).

Lycurgus (4) *see* BUTES (1).

Lycus (1)

A ruler of Thebes. His origins are a little uncertain: he and his brother NYCTEUS were the sons either of Chthonius, one of the 'Sown Men' of Thebes, or of Hyrieus and the nymph Clonia, and were exiled from Euboea (perhaps a Boeotian town called Euboea) after killing PHLEGYAS, the king of Orchomenus in Boeotia. They moved from Euboea to Hyria, and from there to Thebes. Now Lycus' story becomes much clearer, and is tied in with that of ANTIOPE (1), the daughter of Nycteus.

Antiope became pregnant by Zeus and fled from her

father's anger to Sicyon, where she married the king, Epopeus. Nycteus either died in battle with Epopeus, or he killed himself from shame and sorrow, charging Lycus with the task of punishing both Antiope and Epopeus. Lycus led an army against Sicyon, killed the king and carried Antiope off captive. On the journey back to Thebes, she gave birth to twin sons on Mount Cithaeron. Lycus forced her to abandon them on the mountainside, but they were found by a herdsman who brought them up, calling them AMPHION AND ZETHUS.

Lycus gave Antiope as a slave to his wife Dirce, who kept her imprisoned and treated her cruelly for many years. For much of that time Lycus ruled Thebes. At first he acted as regent for the young LABDACUS, Nycteus' grandson. In due course Labdacus came of age and took the throne, but he died young, and Lycus once again became regent, this time for Labdacus' one-year-old son LAIUS. He finally lost his rule when Amphion and Zethus grew up and avenged their mother's sufferings. They tied Dirce to a wild bull which tore and trampled her to death, a fate that she herself had intended for Antiope. Then either they killed Lycus or drove him from the city. Laius found a home with Pelops, the king of Pisa in Elis, and Amphion and Zethus took over the joint rule of Thebes.

[Apollodorus 3.5.5, 3.10.1; Pausanias 2.6.1–4, 9.5.4–6, 9.16.7.]

Lycus (2)

A descendant of Lycus (1). Euripides introduces him into his powerful tragedy *The Madness of Heracles*, where Lycus has in Heracles' absence usurped the throne of Thebes by killing CREON (2) and is on the point of killing Heracles' wife MEGARA, his children, and his father AMPHITRYON. Heracles returns at the last moment and kills the evil Lycus, then in a fit of madness sent by Hera kills his wife and children as well. When he returns to sanity and grief, he finds the courage to go on living, enduring the terrible knowledge of what he has done.

Lycus (3)

Son of Dascylus and king of the Mariandyni in Mysia, a people who were for a long time in a state of war with the barbarous Bebrycians. HERACLES, on his way to fetch the belt of Hippolyte, queen of the Amazons, fought on behalf of the Mariandyni, killing many Bebricians including their king, Mygdon, and winning for his hosts a great deal of territory. Much of this land was later regained by the Bebrician king AMYCUS, a savage man who was in the habit of challenging all visitors to his land to a boxing contest. He always won, and always killed his opponent, until he was himself killed by the expert boxer Polydeuces when the ARGONAUTS came to his country. When

Lycus learnt the good news of his enemy's death, he warmly welcomed the Argonauts and entertained them royally. He even sent his son Dascylus with them in the *Argo*.

[Apollonius, *Argonautica* 2.138–42, 720–850; Apollodorus 1.9.23, 2.5.9.]

Lycus (4)

One of the four sons of PANDION (2), king of Athens. They united in driving out the sons of Metion, who had deposed their father. They then divided the kingdom between themselves, with AEGEUS as eldest son taking the throne. Lycus later left Athens, perhaps banished for taking part in the rebellion led by the sons of PALLAS (3), though traditions vary as to where he settled. In one version he went to Messenia, taking with him the rites of Demeter and Persephone, and was given refuge by APHAREUS. Here he developed prophetic powers and became famous for his oracles. In another version he went to the land of the Termilae in southern Asia Minor, where the Cretan exile SARPEDON was ruling, and the country was later named Lycia after him. He was also said to have given his name to the Lyceum at Athens. The Athenian clan of the Lycomedae, who were priests of Demeter and Persephone, claimed him as their ancestor.

[Herodotus 1.173; Apollodorus 3.15.5–6; Strabo 12.8.5, 14.3.10; Pausanias 1.19.3, 4.1.6–9, 4.2.6, 4.20.4.]

Lycus (5) *see* CELAENO (1).

Lynceus (1)

When the fifty sons of Aegyptus were married to the fifty daughters of his twin-brother DANAUS, king of Argos, forty-nine of the bridegrooms had their heads cut off by their brides on their wedding night. Lynceus alone was spared by his wife, Hypermestra. He was later reconciled with his father-in-law, the instigator of the murders, and took the throne of Argos on his death. He himself was succeeded by Abas, his son by Hypermestra.

Lynceus (2) *see* IDAS.

Lyncus

A king of Scythia who was turned into a lynx. *See* TRIPTOLEMUS.

Lyra (The Lyre)

A constellation commemorating the instrument used by the supreme musician ORPHEUS.

Lysippe

One of the three daughters of PROETUS, king of Argos, who were driven mad by the gods and cured by the seer MELAMPUS.

M

Macareus

A son of AEOLUS (2) who committed incest with his sister Canace, with tragic results.

Macaria ('Blessed')

The daughter of HERACLES and DEIANEIRA who voluntarily sacrificed herself to save the HERACLIDS from their persecutor, EURYSTHEUS. She appears for the first time in Euripides' *Children of Heracles*. Here Demophon and Acamas, sons of Theseus and kings of Athens, agree to fight in support of Iolaus and the Heraclids against Eurystheus and his army. Both sides prepare for war. Demophon then learns from oracles that Athens will prevail only if a virgin of noble family is sacrificed to Persephone. Macaria willingly offers herself. 'I am ready to give myself in sacrifice and die', she says (501–32):

> For what can we say, when Athens is prepared to face great danger for our sake, if we ourselves lay this burden on their shoulders, and then shrink back from death when we have power to bring them victory? Never! We should deserve contempt if we, born of the great Heracles, show ourselves cowards ... Lead me to the place where I must die. Garland me and perform the rite, if so you will. Defeat your enemies. Willingly, with no hesitation, I offer my life and pledge myself to death for my brothers' sake.

Eurystheus was defeated and killed, and his persecution of Heracles' children ended, because of Macaria's self-sacrifice. Pausanias (1.32.6) tells us that a spring of water at Marathon was named Macaria in her honour.

Machaon and Podaleirius

Sons of the great healer ASCLEPIUS and themselves famous healers, having learnt the arts of medicine from their father. According to the *Iliad*, they accompanied the Greek army to Troy, taking with them thirty ships from western Thessaly and serving during the TROJAN WAR as both war-

riors and army physicians. Machaon treated the wounded MENELAUS, and was later himself wounded by PARIS, a cause of especial concern to the Greeks since 'a healer is a man worth many men' (11.514).

According to later writers, Machaon was said to be a surgeon (perhaps his name, similar to *machaira*, 'knife', plays some part in this idea) and Podaleirius a specialist in medicine. One or other of the brothers healed the terrible wound of PHILOCTETES, who then returned to the fighting and killed Paris. Machaon was killed either by the Amazon PENTHESILEIA or by Telephus' son EURYPYLUS (2). His bones were taken back to Greece by NESTOR and buried at Gerenia, where a sanctuary with healing powers was established. Podaleirius survived the war and travelled overland from Troy, calling at Delphi where he enquired of the Oracle where he should settle. 'In a city where, if the sky should fall, you will suffer no harm', came the reply. So he settled in Caria in southern Asia Minor, in an area ringed with high mountains.

[Homer, *Iliad* 2.729–33, 4.193–219, 11.506–21, 832–5; Sophocles, *Philoctetes* 133–4; Apollodorus 3.10.8, *Epitome* 5.1, 5.8, 6.2, 6.18; Pausanias 2.11.5, 2.23.4, 2.38.6, 3.26.9–10, 4.30.3.]

Maenads ('frenzied women')

Followers of DIONYSUS, also known as Bacchae or Bacchants ('women of Bacchus'), who celebrated the god's rites in a state of ecstatic frenzy with music, song and dance. They wore fawnskins and wreathes of ivy, oak, or bryony, and sometimes they girdled themselves with snakes. They carried the thyrsus, the magical wand of the god, made from a fennel rod with a bunch of ivy leaves attached to the tip, and sometimes torches or branches of oak or fir. Both ancient and postclassical art provide plenty of visual images of maenads enjoying their bacchanals, an ever-popular theme (figs. 49 and 86). From ancient literature we get a dramatic picture of maenads in miraculous action, both peaceful and violent, from Euripides' tragedy *The*

Bacchae. Up on Mount Cithaeron they handle snakes and suckle wild animals. At a touch they draw springs of water and wine and milk from rocks and earth, while from their thyrsi flow streams of sweet honey. But when enraged, they are inspired with tremendous physical strength: they uproot trees, and tear cattle or other animals to pieces (*sparagmos*), devouring the flesh raw (*omophagia*). Their thyrsi become dangerous weapons against an enemy, while their own bodies are impervious to iron and fire. The climax of their violence is the bloody murder and rending of PENTHEUS. For other myths in which maenads figure, *see* LYCURGUS (2), ORPHEUS and MINYAS.

Maeon

A Theban warrior, the son of HAEMON. With Polyphontes, the son of Autophonus, he led the fifty men sent by the Thebans to ambush TYDEUS, just before the expedition of the SEVEN AGAINST THEBES. Tydeus killed forty-nine of them, including Polyphontes, but he spared Maeon in obedience to portents from the gods. When Tydeus himself was later killed in the attack on Thebes, Maeon buried him. In Euripides' lost tragedy *Antigone*, Maeon was a son of Haemon and ANTIGONE (1), who in Sophocles' extant play of the same name are merely betrothed, and die before they can marry.

[Homer, *Iliad* 4.385–98; Apollodorus 3.6.5; Pausanias 9.18.2.]

Maia (1)

The eldest daughter of the Titan ATLAS and Pleione, and thus one of the seven PLEIADES. Maia lived alone in a deep and shadowy cave on Mount Cyllene in Arcadia, but still ZEUS saw her and desired her. At dead of night, when his wife HERA was fast asleep, he often slipped away from Olympus and made love to Maia in her cave. There in the course of time she bore him a son, the god HERMES. The delightful *Homeric Hymn to Hermes* tells how this precocious baby, on the very evening of the day of his birth, left his cradle and travelled to Pieria, where he stole fifty head of Apollo's cattle. Returning home again he slipped back into his cradle, pulling his swaddling clothes over him and pretending to be a weak and innocent new-born infant, but Maia was not deceived. 'Where have you come from at this hour of the night, all covered in shamelessness?' she cried, '... Your father got you to be a great worry to mortal men and to the immortal gods' (155–61). Nor, later, was Apollo deceived.

In one version of CALLISTO's story, after she was killed

through Hera's jealousy, Zeus gave her baby son ARCAS to be brought up by Maia.

[Hesiod, *Theogony* 938–9; *Homeric Hymn to Hermes* 1–19; Apollodorus 3.8.2, 3.10.1–2.]

Maia (2)

An Italian spring goddess after whom the month of May was named.

Manes

Roman spirits of the dead, worshipped collectively as *di manes*. By extension the name *manes* was given by poets both to the realm of the dead, the Underworld, and to the gods of the Underworld.

[Virgil, *Aeneid* 3.565, 10.39, 11.181, *Georgics* 1.243; Ovid, *Fasti* 2.609.]

Manto

Daughter of the blind Theban seer TEIRESIAS, and herself gifted with prophetic (mantic) powers. When Thebes was captured by the EPIGONI, led by ALCMAEON, the son of Amphiaraus, they sent Manto as a thank-offering to APOLLO at Delphi, for they had vowed that, if they took the city, they would dedicate to the god 'the fairest of the spoils'. Teiresias went with his daughter, but died on the journey. According to Apollodorus, one of Euripides' two tragedies *Alcmaeon* (now lost) told how Manto bore two children, Amphilochus and Tisiphone, to Alcmaeon, presumably while she was still at Delphi. Their father gave

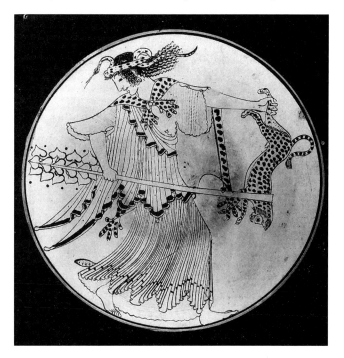

Fig. 86 **A revelling maenad carrying a thyrsus and a small leopard.**

them to be brought up by Creon, king of Corinth (*see* AMPHILOCHUS (2)). Later, at the command of Apollo, Manto went with other Theban prisoners to found a colony in Asia Minor. They came to Clarus, near Colophon, where they were captured by Cretans who were trying to win the land from the local Carians. The Cretan leader Rhacius married Manto and she bore him a son, MOPSUS (2), though the boy was sometimes said to be the son of Apollo. Mopsus too became a famous seer and succeeded in driving the Carians out of the country.

Diodorus Siculus (4.66.5–6) calls Manto Daphne, adding that she became famous for her poetry and that Homer took some of his best lines from her.

[Apollodorus 3.7.4, 3.7.7, *Epitome* 6.3; Pausanias 7.3.1–2, 9.10.3, 9.33.2.]

Marathon

Son of EPOPEUS (1), the king of Sicyon (then Asopia) and Corinth (then Ephyra). Marathon took refuge in Attica to escape his father's violence and lawlessness, then on Epopeus' death returned to his homeland and divided it between his two sons Sicyon and Corinthus, renaming the cities after them. He himself was honoured as a hero in Athens. He gave his name to the town and the plain of Marathon in Attica, where the decisive defeat of the Persians by the Athenians took place in 490 BC. In the time of the traveller Pausanias (second century AD), the plain still resounded by night with the echoes of horses neighing and men fighting.

[Pausanias 1.32.4, 2.1.1.]

Marathonian Bull

The wild bull that ravaged the plain of Marathon and was captured by THESEUS. This was originally the CRETAN BULL, once given by Poseidon to MINOS. It was captured by Heracles as his seventh Labour for Eurystheus and taken to

Mycenae. From there it escaped and made its way to Attica, where it soon became a plague to the inhabitants. Theseus tackled it knowing that it had already claimed Minos' son ANDROGEOS as victim, but he himself mastered the ferocious beast (figs. 87 and 140) and took it back to Athens. He drove it alive through the city for all to see, before sacrificing it to Apollo.

[Apollodorus, *Epitome* 1.5; Diodorus Siculus 4.59.6; Plutarch, *Theseus* 14.]

Maron

The priest of Apollo at Ismarus, the city of the CICONIANS in south-western Thrace which ODYSSEUS and his men sacked during their return from Troy. But Odysseus spared Maron, together with his wife and child. In return the priest gave him seven talents of gold, a mixing bowl of silver, and, most important, twelve jars of the strong, honey-sweet wine with which he later befuddled POLYPHEMUS (2) so that he and his men might escape the Cyclops' murderous hospitality.

According to Homer, Maron was the son of Euanthes; but to Euripides he was the son of DIONYSUS and companion of SILENUS.

[Homer, *Odyssey* 9.196–211; Euripides, *Cyclops* 141–3.]

Marpessa

The daughter of Evenus, son of Ares and Demonice. Marpessa had many suitors, whom Evenus always challenged to a chariot-race, promising to bestow her on anyone who could beat him. He always won, then cut off the heads of his vanquished competitors and nailed them to the walls of his house. One day IDAS came from Messenia to woo Marpessa. He was known as the son of Aphareus, king of Messenia, but his real father was Poseidon, and his chariot was drawn by horses given him by the god. With such horses Idas easily won his race against Evenus, then carried off Marpessa. Evenus pursued them, but had no chance of catching them with his merely mortal horses. When at last he came to the River Lycormas in Aetolia, he gave up in despair. He killed his horses and drowned himself in the river, which was renamed the Evenus after him.

Idas took his bride back to Messenia, but here also the god APOLLO came with designs upon the beautiful Marpessa. He seized her, and Idas drew his bow against the god, ready to fight for his bride (fig. 76). But Zeus came between them, telling Marpessa to choose which suitor she preferred. She chose Idas because she knew that he would grow old along with her, while Apollo

Fig. 87 **Theseus captures the Marathonian Bull.**

would abandon her when her beauty faded. Certainly she loved her chosen husband, for when Idas later died while fighting the DIOSCURI in a quarrel over cattle, Marpessa killed herself from grief.

Idas and Marpessa had a daughter whom they named Alcyone after the kingfisher (a bird believed to have a plaintive cry), in memory of Marpessa's sorrowful weeping when Apollo seized her. Alcyone married the great hero MELEAGER. In the *Iliad*, when old Phoenix tells Meleager's story to ACHILLES in the hope of persuading him back into battle, Homer changes Alcyone's name to Cleopatra, perhaps to give his parable greater persuasive power by echoing the name of Achilles' dear comrade PATROCLUS.

[Homer, *Iliad* 9.553–64; Simonides fr. 563; Apollodorus 1.7.7–9; Pausanias 4.2.7; 5.18.2.]

Mars (also known as **Mavors**, **Mamars**, **Marmar**, **Mamers**, **Maris**)

The Italian war-god, second in importance only to the sovereign deity Jupiter. Mars' festivals took place in March, the month named after him, and October. He was identified with the Greek god of war, ARES, and adopted Ares' mythology as his own. But the story of Mars' birth is unique to Roman myth. He was born to Jupiter's wife, JUNO, after she became pregnant at the touch of a magic herb, given her by Flora, the goddess of spring. He himself was the father of twin sons, ROMULUS AND REMUS, by Rhea Silvia, a Vestal Virgin. The wicked ruler Amulius had the infants thrown into the river Tiber, but under Mars' protection the basket in which they lay floated safely to shore. Here a she-wolf, hearing their cries, came and suckled them, and a woodpecker (*see* PICUS) fed them scraps of food. Both creatures were sacred to Mars. Finally they were taken in by a shepherd and his wife, Faustulus and Acca Larentia, and grew up to be the founders of Rome.

Another uniquely Roman myth is the comic tale of Mars' association with the aged goddess Anna Perenna (*see* ANNA). Mars desired the virgin goddess Minerva (ATHENA), and he persuaded Anna to act as his go-between. Anna knew that Minerva would never succumb to him, but she gave him every encouragement to think the opposite, and finally herself took Minerva's place, heavily veiled, once he believed she had consented. Mars came eagerly to claim her favours, only to discover beneath the veil the old crone Anna.

Marsyas

One of the Phrygian SATYRS. Athena invented the music of the *aulos*, the double pipe, in imitation of the sad lament made by the GORGONS at the death of their sister Medusa. But when she saw her face, distorted by puffed and swollen cheeks, unflatteringly reflected in water as she played, she threw her new instrument away in disgust. Marsyas found the pipes and was enchanted with their music. At last he became so expert a performer that he challenged APOLLO to a musical contest. They agreed that the MUSES should be the judges, and that the victor might do whatever he liked with the loser. Then Marsyas played his pipes and Apollo his lyre, both performing equally well. Finally Apollo played his lyre upside down and challenged the satyr to do the same – which was impossible – so Apollo was adjudged the winner. The price that he exacted from Marsyas was an agonising death: he hung him on a tall pine tree and flayed him alive. The tears of all the woodland creatures who loved the satyr became the River Marsyas, a tributary of the Maeander and the clearest river in Phrygia.

In historical times the skin of Marsyas could still be seen exhibited at Celaenae in southern Phrygia. According to Pausanias (2.7.9), his discarded pipes reputedly floated away down the river Marsyas and eventually reappeared in the Asopus, where a shepherd found them and dedicated them to Apollo in a temple at Sicyon, though by Pausanias' time they had been burnt in a temple fire.

Marsyas was a popular subject in ancient art, beginning with Myron's bronze statue group of the mid-fifth century BC, now lost, but known to us from Roman copies, showing Marsyas with Athena. Marsyas first appears with Apollo on red-figure vases of the latter part of the fifth century. He was also a popular subject in postclassical art, and we have paintings by Raphael, Tintoretto, Titian, Claude, Velázquez and Tiepolo, and sculptures by Rodin and Bourdelle.

[Herodotus 7.26; Xenophon, *Anabasis* 1.2.8; Apollodorus 1.4.2; Diodorus Siculus 3.59; Plutarch, *Alcibiades* 2; Pausanias 1.24.1, 2.22.8–9, 10.30.9; Ovid, *Metamorphoses* 6.382–400, *Fasti* 6.695–710; Pliny, *Natural History* 5.106, 16.240.]

Mastusius

A nobleman of Elaeus in the Thracian Chersonese whose story, told by Hyginus in his *Poetic Astronomy* (2.40), is said to have been taken from a work by Phylarchus, a Greek historian of the third century BC. Demophon, the king of Elaeus, learnt from an oracle that a plague threatening his land could be averted only if he sacrificed each year a virgin of noble birth. Each year he drew lots for the victim, but he never included the names of his own daughters. Mastusius, when the time came for the name of his daughter to be included in the draw, protested against the unfairness of the king – only to find that his daughter was immediately taken for sacrifice without even the formality of lot-drawing. He pretended to accept this cruelty calmly, but privately he resolved to avenge his child, and with interest. He invited Demophon and his daughters to a sacrifice, knowing that the king would arrive late, then killed the girls when they came ahead of their father. When the king himself arrived, Mastusius served him a bowl of wine mixed with their blood and he unwittingly drank from it. On learning the truth, Demophon had Mastusius flung into the harbour, together with the bowl, which was set among the stars as the constellation Crater.

Mecisteus

Son of TALAUS and Lysimache, and brother of ADRASTUS (1), king of Argos. Mecisteus took part in Oedipus' funeral games at Thebes and defeated all the Thebans in the boxing match. Later, as one of the SEVEN AGAINST THEBES, he was killed by MELANIPPUS (2). His son EURYALUS (1) was one of the Epigoni who avenged their fathers' deaths.

[Homer, *Iliad* 2.565–6, 23.677–80; Herodotus 5.67.3; Apollodorus 1.9.13, 3.6.3, 3.7.2; Pausanias 2.20.5, 9.18.1.]

Meda *see* IDOMENEUS.

Medea

Daughter of AEETES, the king of barbarian Colchis, and the Oceanid Eidyia, and thus the granddaughter of HELIOS the Sun-god. Medea, like her aunt CIRCE, was an enchantress.

1. MEDEA IN COLCHIS

When JASON came with the ARGONAUTS to Colchis in quest of the Golden Fleece, Medea fell in love with him at sight and helped him to complete the seemingly impossible tasks set him by Aeetes. She gave Jason a magic salve that would keep him invulnerable for a whole day, and with the help of this he yoked two bronze-footed, fire-breathing bulls and ploughed a field, then sowed dragon's teeth in the furrows and killed the armed men who sprang up from the soil. Knowing that Aeetes had no intention of surrendering the promised reward of the Golden Fleece, Medea helped Jason to steal it by drugging the unsleeping dragon that guarded it night and day. In fear of her father's anger and reassured by Jason's promise to marry her, she fled with him in the *Argo* back to Iolcus.

Aeetes' Colchian fleet soon pursued them. In one version, Medea murdered her little brother APSYRTUS and strewed the fragments of his dismembered body over the sea to delay Aeetes' pursuit. In another, Apsyrtus was a grown man and himself led the hunt for the fugitives. When he and his men intercepted the *Argo*, Medea tricked him into meeting her; and Jason, waiting in ambush, leapt out and killed him. The immediate threat of pursuit was now over, but their long journey back to Iolcus was beset by many difficulties. On the island of

Scheria they had one final encounter with the Colchians, who demanded that Medea be returned to her father. Aided by the queen, ARETE, Jason hastily made Medea his wife, thus overriding the Colchians' claim.

Medea was later involved in more murders on Jason's behalf: on Crete she used her sorcery to kill the bronze man TALOS (1), who guarded the island; and back in Iolcus, where Jason was the rightful heir to the throne, she famously persuaded the daughters of the usurping king, PELIAS, to kill their father.

2. MEDEA IN IOLCUS

Medea applied her magic arts to an old ram with dramatic results, vividly described by Ovid (*Metamorphoses* 7.312–21):

> A woolly ram, worn out with untold years, was dragged in, his horns curling round his hollow temples. Medea cut his scraggy throat with her Thessalian knife, barely staining the blade with his scanty blood. She plunged his carcass into a bronze pot, throwing in with it magic herbs of great potency. These made his body shrink and burnt away his horns, and with his horns, his years, until a thin bleating was heard from within the pot. While they were all marvelling at the sound, out jumped a lamb and ran frisking away, in search of some udder to give him milk.

Pelias' daughters were so impressed that they readily killed their old father and boiled his mangled body, fully believing that he would have his youth renewed. Medea, of course, omitted the appropriate herbs, and that was the end of Pelias. In one version, she used her sorcery to a good purpose and rejuvenated Jason's father, AESON; but in the usual version he was already dead when Jason returned home, done away with, together with his wife and infant son, by the wicked Pelias.

3. MEDEA IN CORINTH

Medea and Jason fled from Iolcus and found refuge with CREON (2), the king of Corinth. Ten years passed peaceably in which they had either two or three children. Then Jason deserted Medea and married Creon's daughter, GLAUCE. The terrible revenge that Medea took for this betrayal is powerfully dramatised in Euripides' tragedy *Medea*. The new bride dies in agony, killed by a poisoned robe and coronet sent her, in feigned goodwill, by Medea. Creon dies too, embracing his dead daughter until he too is overcome by the poison. Medea also kills her two sons by Jason. In earlier versions of the myth, the children died: either they were killed by the Corinthians, or by Creon's family, who put about the rumour that Medea herself had killed them; or they were unintentionally killed by Medea while trying to make them immortal. But

Euripides makes Medea choose to kill them, since this is the greatest pain that she can inflict on her treacherous husband; and it may well be that this was the playwright's own innovation to the myth.

Even though his Medea commits such a horrendous deed, Euripides creates in her a character with whom it is easy to empathise, a woman very definitely wronged by a selfish, self-satisfied and insensitive Jason. He puts into her mouth a long and justly famous monologue, in which she agonises as to her right course of action and whether she can really bring herself to kill her own sons (1021–80). Even when the princess and Creon are dead of her poison, and the time has come for the boys to die, Medea's last words before she kills them show clearly that, by gaining the ultimate revenge on Jason, she is hurting herself quite as much. They also show in a strange and memorable way the reaction of a loving mother: the children are bound now to die, since the Corinthians will insist on revenge for their murdered king and princess, so her sons' kindest death is by the hand of the mother who bore them (1236–50):

> My course of action is clear: to kill my children with all speed and then leave this land; not delay and give my children over to be killed by another and less loving hand. They are bound to die in any case, and since they must, then I shall kill them, I who bore them. Come, my heart, steel yourself. Why do I put off doing the terrible deed that must now be done? Come, wretched hand, take the sword, take it; go forward to the point where life turns into grief. No cowardice, no memories of your children, how dear they were, how your body gave them birth. For this one brief day forget your children – and then mourn them. For even though you kill them, yet they were dear ...

So in the end, Medea – in a way – kills her sons out of love.

At the end of the play she escapes in a chariot drawn by winged serpents, sent her by her grandfather Helios, the Sun-god: a tremendously effective *coup de théâtre*, and probably also Euripides' own innovation. Vengeance accomplished – at whatever cost to herself – Medea gloats over the broken and grieving Jason down below. 'You don't know yet what grief is', she says to him, 'wait till you're old.'

Fig. 88 Overseen by two Furies, Medea rides off in a dragon-chariot sent by her grandfather, the Sun-god Helios. Her two sons lie dead on an altar below, mourned by two servants, while Jason looks helplessly up at his departing wife.

4. MEDEA IN ATHENS

Medea took refuge with AEGEUS, king of Athens, and bore him a son, MEDUS (1). When THESEUS, Aegeus' son by AETHRA, came to Athens to make himself known to his father, he was recognised by no one except Medea. She, by her magic powers, guessed who he must be and determined to get rid of him. She persuaded Aegeus that the young stranger was a threat, so he sent Theseus to deal with the deadly Marathonian Bull that was plaguing the land, believing that he would never return alive. Theseus returned triumphant with the captured bull, so now Medea persuaded Aegeus to poison him at a feast. At the last moment, Aegeus recognised the sword that Theseus was carrying as his own, once left with Aethra, and he dashed the cup of poison from his son's lips. Father and son were joyously reunited, and Medea fled from Athens for ever.

5. AFTERMATH

She went with Medus to Colchis, where she found that her father Aeetes had been deposed by his brother PERSES (2). Either she or Medus killed Perses and restored the throne to Aeetes. Presumably Medea lived out her life in Colchis. Nothing is known of her death – if indeed she was thought to have died at all, for in Hesiod's *Theogony* (992–1002) she is listed among a catalogue of goddesses who slept with mortal men and is clearly conceived as a divine being. In the lyric poets Ibycus (fr. 291) and Simonides (fr. 558) she was apparently said to have married ACHILLES in the Elysian Fields.

Various scenes from Medea's myth occur in ancient

art. The death of Pelias is a popular subject, often with the ram in the cauldron and Medea looking on (fig. 112); she also kills her children, and flies in the dragon-chariot (fig. 88), and appears with Theseus. According to Pausanias (5.18.3) she was depicted on the Chest of Cypselus, enthroned between Aphrodite and Jason, with the caption 'Jason marries Medea, as Aphrodite commands'. The events at Aeetes' court were dramatised in Sophocles' lost *Colchian Women*, and the death of Pelias in Euripides' lost *Daughters of Pelias* and perhaps Sophocles' lost *Root-cutters*. Medea's myth has also proved inspirational in the postclassical arts. Corneille dramatised her story in 1634, using Seneca's *Medea* as a model; and in 1693 Charpentier composed the first of many operas about Medea. In Anouilh's drama *Medée* (1946), Medea commits suicide in the flames of her children's funeral pyre after she has murdered them. Maria Callas famously played Medea in Pasolini's powerful cinematic version of her myth.

[Hesiod, *Theogony* 956–62; Pindar, *Pythian* 4; Herodotus 1.2, 7.62; Apollonius, *Argonautica* 3–4; Apollodorus 1.9.16, 1.9.23–8, *Epitome* 5.5; Plutarch, *Theseus* 12; Pausanias 2.3.6–11, 8.11.2–3; Ovid, *Metamorphoses* 7.1–424, *Heroides* 12; Seneca, *Medea*. James J. Clauss and Sarah Iles Johnston (eds), *Medea: Essays on Medea in Myth, Literature, Philosophy and Art* (1997).]

Medeius *see* MEDUS.

Medon (1) *see* CODRUS.

Medon (2)
Son of ETEOCLUS and one of the EPIGONI.

Medon (3)
The bastard son of Oileus, king of Locris, by Rhene, and thus the half-brother of AJAX (2). Medon was exiled to Phylace for killing the brother of Oileus' wife, Eriopis, and from there went to fight in the TROJAN WAR. When PHILOCTETES was bitten by a snake and left behind on Lemnos, Medon took command of his seven ships. He was killed in battle by AENEAS during the last year of the war.

[Homer, *Iliad* 2.716–28, 13.693–700, 15.332–6.]

Medon (4)
In the *Odyssey*, Medon is ODYSSEUS' herald on Ithaca. Although he is forced to serve the Suitors, he remains loyal to his master and tells PENELOPE about their plot to kill TELEMACHUS. When Odysseus returns home and massacres the Suitors, he spares Medon's life

[Homer, *Odyssey* 4.675–714, 22.352–80.]

Medon (5)
One of the two sons of PYLADES and ELECTRA (3), his brother being Strophius.
[Pausanias 2.16.7.]

Medus (1) or **Medeius**
Son of the sorceress MEDEA. According to Hesiod, his father was JASON and he was brought up, like many other Greek heroes such as Achilles, by the wise and kindly Centaur CHEIRON. But later writers make him Medea's son by AEGEUS, king of Athens. After Medea's failed attempt to murder Theseus, she fled from Athens for ever, taking Medus with her. She went back to her birthplace, Colchis, and there found that her father AEETES had been deposed by his brother Perses. Either she or Medus killed Perses and restored the throne to Aeetes. A dramatic version of this part of the myth, found in Hyginus (*Fabula* 27), may well go back to a lost Greek tragedy. Here, Medus arrives in Colchis ahead of his mother. Perses has heard that he will be killed by a descendant of Aeetes, so he imprisons Medus, even though he claims that he is Hippotes, son of King Creon of Corinth. As a result, the country is hit by famine. Medea arrives, pretending to be a priestess of Artemis, and on learning that Perses has in his hands the son of her old enemy, Creon, she promises to put an end to the famine by sacrificing the boy. In the midst of her rituals she recognises her son and hands him the sacrificial sword. Medus turns on Perses and kills him, and Aeetes is avenged.

From Colchis Medus travelled east, where he conquered a great deal of territory and gave his name to the Medes. He died leading his army against the Indians.

[Hesiod, *Theogony* 1000–2; Apollodorus 1.9.28; Diodorus Siculus 4.55.7–4.56.1; Strabo 11.13.10; Pausanias 2.3.8.]

Medus (2)
Another Medus said to have given his name to the Medes was the son of ALPHESIBOEA (1).

Medusa *see* GORGONS.

Megaera *see* FURIES.

Megapenthes (1)
Son of PROETUS and Stheneboea. He inherited the throne of Tiryns from his father, but later exchanged it with PERSEUS for the throne of Argos.

Megapenthes (2)
Bastard son of MENELAUS by a slave-woman, Pieris or Tereis, born after HELEN had run away to Troy with Paris, and so named ('great grief') because of the sorrow felt by Menelaus at being abandoned by his wife. When Menelaus

returned to Sparta after the Trojan War, he married Megapenthes to the daughter of the Spartan Alector. Pausanias says that Megapenthes, with his brother Nicostratus, drove Helen out of Sparta after Menelaus' death and she died in Rhodes (*see* POLYXO (2)). The Spartan throne passed to Orestes.

[Homer, *Odyssey* 4.10–12; Apollodorus 3.11.1; Pausanias 2.18.6, 3.19.9.]

Megara

Daughter of CREON (2), ruler of Thebes, who gave her in marriage to HERACLES as his reward for defeating Erginus and the Minyans. The marriage was a happy one and the couple had children (between two and eight according to varying sources). But it ended in tragedy when Heracles murdered both children and wife in a fit of madness, powerfully dramatised in Euripides' *Madness of Heracles*. Here the evil Lycus has in Heracles' absence usurped the throne of Thebes by killing Creon. He is on the very point of killing Megara, the three children, and Heracles' father AMPHITRYON when Heracles returns. He easily despatches Lycus, but IRIS and Lyssa (Madness) arrive, sent by Hera, to drive him mad, and he slays wife and children as well. It was usually said to be because of this terrible act that Heracles was condemned to perform his twelve Labours (*see* LABOURS OF HERACLES), although according to Euripides the madness and tragic murders occurred after his Labours were complete.

According to one version of the myth Megara survived the massacre, but Heracles, afraid of having more children by her because of the fate that had befallen the others, put an end to their union and married her to his nephew and faithful companion, IOLAUS.

[Homer, *Odyssey* 11.269–70; Pindar, *Isthmian* 4.61–4; Apollodorus 2.4.11–12; Diodorus Siculus 4.10.6, 4.31.1; Pausanias 1.41.1, 9.11.2, 10.29.7; Seneca, *The Madness of Hercules*.]

Megareus (1)

A king of Onchestus in Boeotia who helped NISUS (1), king of Megara, in his war with MINOS, king of Crete. Some said that Megareus was killed by Minos, but the Megarians themselves claimed that he survived Nisus and married his daughter Iphinoe, then succeeded him on the throne of Megara. During Megareus' reign, his land was ravaged by the bloodthirsty lion of Cithaeron and many were slain, including his own son Evippus. Megareus promised, to whoever killed the beast, the hand of his daughter, Evaechme, and the rule of the kingdom after his death. ALCATHOUS (1), a son of Pelops, slew the lion and won both wife and kingship.

[Apollodorus 3.15.8; Pausanias 1.39.5–6, 1.41.3–5, 1.42.1.]

Megareus (2)

A son of CREON (2), ruler of Thebes. He defended the Neistan gate against ETEOCLUS in the attack of the SEVEN AGAINST THEBES. He is mentioned in Sophocles' tragedy *Antigone*, though in rather vague terms and linked with some deed of nobility. It has sometimes been assumed that he sacrificed himself to save his city, as did Creon's son MENOECEUS (2).

[Aeschylus, *Seven Against Thebes* 457–80; Sophocles, *Antigone* 993, 1058, 1191, 1303.]

Meges

Son of PHYLEUS and king of Dulichium. He was one of the suitors of HELEN, and later led forty ships to fight in the TROJAN WAR. A good warrior, he survived the war, but was drowned in a shipwreck off Cape Caphareus on his way home (*see* AJAX (2)).

[Homer, *Iliad* 2.625–30, 5.69–75, 10.110, 175, 13.691–2, 15.302, 518–45, 16.313, 19.239; Apollodorus 3.10.8, *Epitome* 6.15a.]

Melampodes ('Black-feet')

A tribe in North Africa, conquered by Aegyptus, who then named their land Egypt after himself (*see* DANAUS).

Melampus ('Black-foot')

One of the greatest of Greek seers, who founded an important family of prophets. He was the son of AMYTHAON and Idomene, and the brother of Bias, living at Pylos in Messenia. Melampus saved the young of some snakes killed by his servants, looking after them until they were fully grown. Because of his kindness, the snakes licked his ears one night as he slept, thus giving him the art of divination. After this he could understand the language of birds and animals, so could learn the future from them and foretell it to men. He also met APOLLO one day by the River Alpheius, and the god gave him the ability to interpret the signs at sacrifices.

Bias fell in love with Pero, the beautiful daughter of NELEUS, king of Pylos. She had many suitors, so her father said that he would give her to the man who brought him the splendid cattle of Phylacus, king of Phylace in Thessaly. These were guarded by a fearsome and unapproachable dog. Bias asked for his brother's help, which Melampus promised to him, prophesying that he himself would be caught while trying to steal the cattle and would be imprisoned for a year, but at the end of that time the cattle would be his. It fell out as he said, and Melampus was caught by Phylacus and imprisoned. When nearly a year had passed, he heard woodworms talking in the roof of his cell, saying that the wood of the main beam had been almost eaten through. He demanded to be moved to another cell, and when shortly afterwards the roof of the first cell collapsed, Phylacus was so impressed by his prophetic powers that he consulted him about the impotence of his son, IPHICLUS (1). Melampus promised to cure Iphiclus in return for the cattle. Having sacrificed two bulls he summoned the birds, and learnt from an old vulture that once, when Phylacus was castrating rams, Iphiclus had been terrified by the bloody knife, so his father had stuck the knife in a sacred oak tree. Bark had since grown around the knife, but if it were now retrieved, and the rust scraped off and given to Iphiclus in a drink for ten days, he would have a son. Melampus did exactly as the vulture advised, and in due course Iphiclus had two sons, Podarces and Protesilaus.

Melampus drove the cattle to Neleus at Pylos, thus winning the hand of Pero for Bias. She bore Bias several children, including TALAUS. For a time both brothers continued to live in Messenia, but they later moved to Argos, the kingdom of King PROETUS. The three daughters of the king, Lysippe, Iphinoe and Iphianassa, had been driven mad, either by DIONYSUS because they would not accept his rites, or by HERA because they showed disrespect to her. In their frenzy they roamed over the whole countryside in a wild and unseemly fashion, divesting themselves of their clothes; in one version of the myth, they imagined themselves to be cows. Melampus offered to cure them in return for a third of the kingdom. Proetus refused his offer, but then the girls became madder than ever, and the madness spread to the rest of the Argive women. They all abandoned their homes, even killing their own children, and went roaming through mountains and forests. At this Proetus accepted Melampus' offer, but too late, for now the seer had raised his price and was demanding two thirds of the kingdom, a third for himself and a third for Bias. Proetus gave in, fearing that the price would become even higher, and Melampus effected his promised cure by taking a band of strong young men with him and chasing the girls down from the mountains with shouts and frenzied dancing. During the pursuit Iphinoe died, but her two sisters and the rest of the women were purified and restored to sanity. Proetus in gratitude gave his two surviving daughters in marriage to the seer and his brother, Melampus marrying Iphianassa, and Bias (Pero presumably having died) Lysippe. Melampus and Iphianassa had three sons, Abas, Mantius and Antiphates (the grandfather of AMPHIARAUS), and Bias and Lysippe a daughter, Anaxibia, who married PELIAS, king of Iolcus.

[Homer, *Odyssey* 11.287–97, 15.225–55; Pindar, *Paean* 4.28–30; Herodotus 2.49, 9.34; Apollodorus 1.9.11–13, 2.2.2; Diodorus Siculus 4.68.3–5; Pausanias 2.18.4, 4.36.3, 5.5.10, 8.18.7; Virgil, *Eclogues* 6.48–51; Ovid, *Metamorphoses* 15.322–8.]

Melaneus

Son of APOLLO and a nymph, Pronoe. He was a notable archer, and after marrying Stratonice, a daughter of Porthaon who was carried off to be his wife by Apollo, he fathered the even more famous archer EURYTUS (1). He founded Oechalia, a city variously located in either Thessaly, Messenia or Euboea.

Melanion *see* ATALANTA.

Melanippe (1)

Daughter of AEOLUS (1), the king of Thessaly, and HIPPO, and thus the granddaughter of the founder of the Hellenic race, HELLEN, and of the wise and humane Centaur CHEIRON. She was brought up by Aeolus and grew to be extraordinarily beautiful, so lovely that the god POSEIDON desired her. She bore him twin sons, AEOLUS (3) and Boeotus.

Melanippe was the heroine of two tragedies by Euripides, now lost, but about which we know a great deal from fragments and other sources. *Wise Melanippe* told of the events surrounding the birth of her twin boys. Her father was away when they were born, and just before his return she hid them in a cowshed. There some of the cowherds saw them being watched over by the bull and suckled by one of the cows, and they mistook the infants for cow-born monsters. They took them to Aeolus, who decreed that the babies must be burnt – and we are not sure exactly what happened from this point on in the play. But we do know that the boys survived, to become in the course of time the ancestors of the Aeolian and Boeotian Greeks. As for Melanippe, there is some evidence to suggest that her mother Hippo appeared onstage in her horse-form, so perhaps she saved her daughter from Aeolus' wrath.

Hyginus tells the story of Melanippe's later life in his *Fabula* 186, which reflects to a greater or lesser extent the plot of Euripides' *Captive Melanippe*. According to Hyginus, when the twins were born Aeolus blinded and imprisoned Melanippe, then cast out the babies to die. But they survived, suckled by a cow until they were found and taken in by herdsmen. The men gave the infants to Theano, the wife of Metapontus, king of Metapontium in Italy, who was at that time childless, though later she bore two sons of her own. When the four boys grew up, Metapontus favoured the elder pair, so Theano urged her own sons to kill them and secure the kingdom for themselves. They tried to do so during a hunting expedition, but Poseidon intervened to help his sons and it was Theano's boys who were killed. The

Fig. 89 The Calydonian Boarhunt, with Meleager spearing the boar.

queen committed suicide and Melanippe's sons returned to the herdsmen who had originally saved them. Here they learnt from Poseidon of their true parentage and their mother's incarceration, so they killed Aeolus and set Melanippe free. The god restored her sight, and her sons took her to Metapontium and told Metapontus the whole story. He adopted the two boys and married Melanippe, so all ended happily for her. Euripides' play must have differed from this at least to some extent, since we know, for instance, that it was the brothers of the queen (who seems here to be called Siris) who tried to kill Melanippe's sons on a hunting expedition and were themselves killed; but his general storyline was no doubt similar. Indeed, this type of plot was one of Euripides' favourites: sons separated from their mother in infancy, who grow up to rescue her from tribulation and to be joyfully reunited with her.

[Diodorus Siculus 4.67; Strabo 6.1.15; Pausanias 9.1.1. C. Collard, M. J. Cropp and K. H. Lee, *Euripides: The Fragmentary Plays* I (1995), pp. 240–80.]

Melanippe (2)

Sister of the Amazon queen HIPPOLYTE (1).

Melanippus (1) *see* COMAETHO (1).

Melanippus (2)

Son of Astacus, and one of the Thebans who defended their city against the attack of the SEVEN AGAINST THEBES. Pausanias (9.18.1) calls him 'one of the very best of the warriors of Thebes'. He killed MECISTEUS and dealt TYDEUS a mortal wound before being killed in turn by his victim, though some say that he was killed by AMPHIARAUS. Cer-

tainly Amphiaraus cut off Melanippus' head and gave it to the dying Tydeus, who savagely gulped down his enemy's brains, disgusting the goddess Athena so much that she withheld from him the gift of immortality that she had planned to give him.

[Aeschylus, *Seven Against Thebes* 407–16; Apollodorus 1.8.6, 3.6.8.]

Melanippus (3)

Son of THESEUS and Perigune, the daughter of SINIS the Pine-bender. Melanippus was a noted runner and won the footrace at the second celebration of the Nemean Games, held by the Epigoni.

[Plutarch, *Theseus* 8; Pausanias 10.25.7.]

Melanthius

In the *Odyssey*, Melanthius is the son of ODYSSEUS' old and faithful servant DOLIUS. He is Odysseus' goatherd on Ithaca, but unlike the swineherd EUMAEUS and the cowherd Philoetius, both of whom remain faithful to their master, he betrays him and sides with the rapacious Suitors, as does his sister MELANTHO. He insults and kicks Odysseus when he comes home disguised as a beggar, and even after he learns his master's identity, he tries to help the Suitors by bringing them weapons in the final, fatal battle. Eumaeus and Philoetius tie him up and leave him locked in the storeroom, then when all the Suitors have been massacred, they punish him for his treachery by

Fig. 90 Eos mourns over the body of her dead son, Memnon.

cutting off his nose, ears, hands, feet and genitals, and throwing them to the dogs. He is left to die.

[Homer, *Odyssey* 17.204–59, 20.172–84, 22.135–200, 473–7.]

Melantho

In the *Odyssey*, Melantho is the daughter of ODYSSEUS' old and faithful servant DOLIUS. She is one of PENELOPE's maids, but unlike her loyal father she treacherously sides with the Suitors, and even becomes the mistress of one of them, EURYMACHUS. She is insolent to Odysseus when he returns home disguised as a beggar, as is her brother MELANTHIUS. After the massacre of the Suitors, she and the other eleven maids who have slept with the enemy are hanged for their treachery (22.468–73):

> As long-winged thrushes or doves fly into a snare
> set for them in a thicket, trying to get to their nests,
> but a dreadful bed receives them; so the women's heads
> were strung in a row, nooses around their necks, that all
> might die a ghastly death. They kicked with their feet
> for a little while, but not for very long.

[Homer, *Odyssey* 18.320–42, 19.65–95, 22.424–73.]

Melanthus

King of Athens and father of CODRUS.

Melas *see* LICYMNIUS.

Meleager

Son of OENEUS, king of the Aetolians of Calydon, and ALTHAEA, though he was sometimes said to be the son of ARES. Meleager was one of the great heroes of Greek mythology, even though he plays only a small part in the ancient literature that has chanced to survive. He sailed with Jason and the ARGONAUTS, and won the javelin contest at the funeral games for PELIAS; but he is chiefly known as the great hero of the CALYDONIAN BOARHUNT (figs. 34 and 89). The story of this is first found in the *Iliad* (9.529–99). When Oeneus forgot to sacrifice to ARTEMIS, the angry goddess sent a huge wild boar to ravage the country; so Meleager gathered a large band of huntsmen and hounds from all over Greece to accompany him on the famous Boarhunt. He himself finally killed the boar. Artemis, still angry, next stirred up strife between the Aetolians and the Curetes over the head and hide of the boar, which led to a violent battle. All went well for the Aetolians while Meleager was fighting and they had the upper hand. But when his mother called on the FURIES and cursed him for killing her brother, he retired from battle in anger and refused to fight any more. With Meleager out of action, the Curetes attacked Calydon more and more violently, and he was offered gifts by the elders and begged by his father, his mother and his sisters to return to battle. He still refused, and only when entreated by his wife Cleopatra (*see* MARPESSA) did he go and fight, but then too late to receive the promised gifts. No mention is made here of how Meleager died, but in other early versions, the lost epic *Minyas* and the Hesiodic *Catalogue of Women*, he died a typical epic death, killed by APOLLO who was fighting in support of the Curetes.

In later legend the manner of Meleager's death changes to one better known and far more pathetic. Just after his birth, his mother Althaea was told by the FATES that he would live until a log, then burning on the hearth, was completely burnt away. Althaea immediately quenched the flames and put the log away in a chest, keeping it safe for many years. Then came the Boarhunt. During the ensuing fight over the spoils, Meleager killed Althaea's brothers, either accidentally, or in anger because they had taken away from the great huntress ATALANTA, with whom he was in love, the boar's hide that he had presented to her. At this his angry mother took the log from its safe hiding place and threw it into the fire. As soon as it was burnt up, Meleager died. Althaea killed herself in remorse. His sisters mourned for him and were transformed into guinea-hens (*Meleagrides*), except for two of them: GORGE, who married Andraemon, and DEIANEIRA, who later married HERACLES as a result of his fateful meeting with the shade of Meleager in the Under-world. When all the other shades fled in terror at sight of the fearsome mortal, Meleager courageously stood his ground. He told Heracles of his sad fate and mentioned his sister Deianeira, thus setting in motion events that would finally lead to Heracles' own death.

[Homer, *Iliad* 2.642; Bacchylides, *Ode* 5.93–154; Aeschylus, *Libation Bearers* 602–11; Apollodorus 1.8.2–3; Diodorus Siculus 4.34, 4.48; Pausanias 10.31.3–4; Ovid, *Metamorphoses* 8.270–525. J. R. March, *The Creative Poet* (1987), pp. 29–46.]

Melia *see* INACHUS.

Meliads *see* NYMPHS.

Melicertes *see* INO.

Melpomene *see* MUSES.

Memnon

Son of EOS, goddess of Dawn, and the mortal TITHONUS, and said to be very beautiful, for Odysseus accounted him the handsomest man he had ever seen (*Odyssey* 11.522). He was king of the Ethiopians. Wearing armour made by HEPHAESTUS (fig. 55), he led a large army to the Trojan War in support of his uncle, King PRIAM. The great Hector, mainstay of Troy, was by now dead at the hands of ACHILLES, and Memnon's arrival brought fresh hope to the dispirited Trojans. In a tremendous battle he killed many Greeks, including ANTILOCHUS, who died while saving the life of his old father, Nestor. Achilles came swiftly up to avenge his friend's death, and he and Memnon fought a great duel while their two mothers, the goddesses Thetis and Eos, pleaded with Zeus for their sons' lives. Finally Memnon was killed – probably Achilles' greatest triumph, though it was to be followed almost immediately by his own death, when he routed the Trojans and rushed after them into Troy. Here he was killed by Paris and Apollo.

Eos, grief-stricken, carried Memnon's body from the battlefield and asked Zeus to show her son some special honour. Zeus either made him immortal, or changed the smoke from his funeral pyre into birds which circled the pyre and then, separating into two groups, fought and killed each other, falling into the flames as offerings to the hero's soul. Ever afterwards fresh flocks of birds, called *Memnonides*, came once a year to Memnon's tomb, and fought again and died again in his honour.

Many ancient writers say that Suza was the city of Memnon. From here he marched north-westwards to Troy, erecting as he went several great memorial pillars to mark his route. These, Herodotus tells us (2.106), caused him to be confused with Sesostris, ruler of Egypt. Memnon had other connections too with Egypt: there was a Memnoneion at both Thebes and Abydos, and the 'Colossus of Memnon' was the name given to one of the two huge, seated statues at Thebes which mark the position of the now-vanished mortuary temple of Amenhotep III. This colossus was said to emit a musical note when struck by the rays of the rising sun, as though Memnon were greeting his mother's light.

We know a little about the two tragedies, now lost, which Aeschylus wrote on the subject of Memnon. The *Memnon* brought him to fight at Troy, and probably included the death of Antilochus. The *Psychostasia* told of Memnon's fatal duel with Achilles, and in this play Zeus weighed the souls (*psychai*) of the two heroes to decide who should die, while Eos and Thetis, one each side of the scales of Zeus, pleaded for the life of their sons. Though this might sound like a particularly dramatic Aeschylean invention, it cannot be so, for the scene occurs in vase-painting from about 540 BC. Memnon's final combat with Achilles was also a popular theme in archaic and classical art, and a famous red-figure cup by Douris shows the mourning Eos with her son's body in her arms (fig. 90). The morning dew is said to be the tears shed by the still inconsolable Eos in grief for her dead son.

[Homer, *Odyssey* 4.187–8; Hesiod, *Theogony* 984–5; Epic Cycle, Proclus' summary of the *Aethiopis*; Pindar, *Pythian* 6.28–42; Herodotus 5.53, 54; Apollodorus 3.12.3, *Epitome* 5.3; Diodorus Siculus 2.22; Strabo 15.3.2; Pausanias 1.42.3, 3.18.12, 5.19.1, 10.31.7; Quintus of Smyrna, *Sequel to Homer* 2.100–666; Ovid, *Metamorphoses* 13.576–622; Pliny, *Natural History* 10.74.]

Memphis

Daughter of the river-god Nile and wife of EPAPHUS.

Menelaus

Son of ATREUS, king of Mycenae, and AEROPE (or occasionally said to be son of their son PLEISTHENES, who died young), and brother of AGAMEMNON. Menelaus and Agamemnon together were commonly called the Atreidae. On Atreus' death they were expelled from Mycenae by Thyestes, but were later brought back by TYNDAREOS, king of Sparta, and Thyestes in his turn was driven out. Agamemnon then took the throne. Tyndareos gave two of his daughters to the Atreidae: Agamemnon married CLYTEMNESTRA, and Menelaus married the beautiful HELEN, after competing for her hand with suitors from all over Greece. He took over the rule of Sparta from Tyndareos, who abdicated in his favour. Helen bore him a daughter, HERMIONE, and according to some accounts a son, NICOSTRATUS. Menelaus later had a son, MEGAPENTHES (2), by a slave-woman.

Fig. 91 Menelaus, intending to kill his wife, Helen, for her infidelity, pursues her as she flees to an altar for sanctuary, but is overcome by passion at the sight of her beautiful body and drops his sword.

When Hermione was nine years old, PARIS, prince of Troy, visited Sparta and was royally entertained for nine days by Menelaus. The king then sailed for Crete to bury his grandfather, CATREUS. In his absence Paris won Helen's love, already promised to him by Aphrodite for choosing her as the most beautiful goddess in the JUDGEMENT OF PARIS. Paris carried Helen off to Troy, along with a great many rich treasures from the palace. When Menelaus returned and found his wife gone, with the help of Agamemnon he mustered a large army to fetch her back by force. Agamemnon was made commander-in-chief. Before war began in earnest, however, Menelaus and ODYSSEUS led an embassy to Troy to ask for Helen to be peacably returned. They were entertained, and their lives protected, by the Trojan ANTENOR, but their request was refused and they were forced to return to Greece without Helen. The resultant TROJAN WAR lasted for nine years, with Troy being captured and destroyed in the tenth.

The *Iliad* recounts events during this tenth and final year, and here we see Menelaus in action. He has brought sixty ships as his contribution to the expedition (2.581–90), and Homer depicts him sympathetically as a kindly and considerate man, as well as a good and valiant warrior. He fights a duel with Paris for the possession of Helen and would have won, had not Aphrodite covered Paris in a thick mist and spirited him away (3.15–382).

Certainly Menelaus comes across as the better man, for Homer likens him, on seeing Paris, to 'a lion that is glad when he comes upon a mighty carcase, in his hunger finding the body of an antlered stag or a wild goat, and he eats it eagerly, even though swift hounds and strong young men run at him' (23–6); while Paris, on seeing Menelaus (fig. 108), is like 'a man who recoils when he sees a snake in the mountain glens, and trembling seizes his limbs, and he moves backwards, and pallor seizes his cheeks' (33–5). But because of Aphrodite's intervention, the duel is unfinished.

Menelaus is also willing to take on the mighty HECTOR in single combat, even though it most likely means his own death (7.94–121), and he kills or wounds many of the Trojan enemy; but perhaps his finest hour is when he defends the corpse of PATROCLUS (17.1–8):

> When Patroclus went down in battle to the Trojans
> he was seen by Atreus' son, warlike Menelaus,
> who came through the ranks of fighters, helmeted
> in shining bronze, and bestrode his body. As over
> a first-born calf the mother cow stands lowing,
> she who has known no children before this,
> so over Patroclus stood fair-haired Menelaus,
> and held his spear and round shield in front of him,
> raging to kill any man who might come against him.

AJAX (1) comes to help him, while a pitched battle breaks out between Greeks and Trojans. Hector succeeds in stripping Patroclus' armour, but Menelaus and Ajax, fighting magnificently, save his body and carry it back to the Greek ships.

In the closing stages of the war, Paris was killed by Philoctetes and Helen married another son of Priam, DEIPHOBUS. Now, however, she was eager for the Greeks to take Troy so that she could go home again with her first husband. On the night of Troy's capture, when the WOODEN HORSE, full of Greek warriors including Menelaus, was brought into the city, she took away Deiphobus' weapons while he slept and let Menelaus and his men into the house to murder him. Menelaus would have killed his wife too for her infidelity, but when he saw her beauty once more, his sword dropped from his hand and he forgave her. So husband and wife, reunited, set sail for Sparta. Their journey home lasted eight years, during which they encountered storms and wandered to many lands, gathering rich possessions as they went. Finally they were becalmed off Egypt, and Menelaus sought help from PROTEUS, the Old Man of the Sea, who told him how to get safely home again. Having made appropriate sacrifices to the gods, they swiftly sailed back home with a favourable wind.

In the usual tradition, Menelaus and Helen spent their

remaining years quietly together at Sparta. The *Odyssey* (4.1–624) gives a warm depiction of their domestic contentment when TELEMACHUS visits them, seeking for news of Odysseus. After their death they were buried nearby at Therapnae, and both were made immortal by Zeus.

Menelaus is a prominent figure in fifth-century tragedy, appearing as a major character in several plays. He is treated sympathetically in Euripides' *Helen*, where it is only a phantom Helen who went with Paris to Troy, while the real Helen stayed with Proteus in Egypt. Here, in the course of the play, she is joyfully reunited at last with her husband and they sail home to Sparta. In other plays, however, Menelaus is depicted as less than heroic. He is a weak character in Euripides' *Trojan Women* and *Orestes* and despicable in his *Iphigeneia at Aulis*, meanminded and vindictive in Sophocles' *Ajax*, and downright brutal and treacherous in Euripides' *Andromache*. This is all a far cry from the Menelaus familiar from Homer.

Menelaus is not a very frequent subject of ancient art, although the scene of his recovery of Helen, where he advances on her with drawn sword (fig. 65), or drops his weapon on seeing her (fig.91), is quite popular. It was also depicted on the chest of Cypselus, where, says Pausanias (5.18.3), 'Menelaus, wearing a breastplate and carrying a sword, advances to kill Helen'.

[Homer, *Odyssey* 3.276–302; Apollodorus 3.10.8–3.9.1, *Epitome* 2.15–6.1, 6.29; Pausanias 3.18.16.]

Menestheus

Son of Peteos and great-grandson of ERECHTHEUS. When THESEUS, king of Athens, was in Hades with his comrade PEIRITHOUS, Menestheus stirred up the people of Athens against him, sowing discontent. There was reason enough for the people to resent Theseus, for he had abducted the young and beautiful HELEN from Sparta and hidden her at Aphidnae, and now her brothers, the DIOSCURI, had invaded Attica to recover her. They took her home and the country was restored to peace; but when Theseus returned to earth (Peirithous was not so lucky), he found that Menestheus had been made king of Athens in his place. Theseus' sons, ACAMAS (1) and Demophon, had already fled for refuge to Elephenor, king of the Abantes in Euboea, and now Theseus himself took refuge with Lycomedes, king of the island of Scyros. But Lycomedes, while pretending friendship, treacherously murdered Theseus by pushing him off a cliff, either because he feared his reputation, or out of a desire to please Menestheus.

Menestheus was later one of Helen's suitors, and true to his oath to defend the marriage rights of her chosen husband, he led fifty Athenian ships to the TROJAN WAR.

Some say that he died at Troy, others that he was one of the warriors in the WOODEN HORSE, and that after Troy fell he became king of the island of Melos, since Acamas and Demophon had by then reclaimed the rule of Athens. [Homer, *Iliad* 2.546–56, 4.327–8, 12.331–74; Apollodorus 3.10.8, *Epitome* 1.24, 3.11, 6.15b; Plutarch, *Theseus* 32–35; Pausanias 1.1.2, 1.17.5–6, 1.23.8, 2.25.6.]

Menesthius *see* POLYDORA.

Menestratus

A young man of Thespiae in Boeotia who killed a dragon that was ravaging his city. Zeus had commanded that every year a youth, chosen by lot, should be offered to the dragon, and every year this sacrifice was duly made, until one year the lot fell on Menestratus' lover, Cleostratus. Menestratus resolved to save his city and his beloved by offering himself in his place. He made himself a breastplate of bronze, covered in hooked spikes, then gave himself up to the dragon, who devoured him and died.

[Pausanias 9.26.7–8.]

Menoeceus (1)

A descendant of the SOWN MEN who sprang from the dragon's teeth at Thebes. He was the father of CREON (2), who became ruler of Thebes, and of JOCASTA, the mother and wife of OEDIPUS.

Menoeceus (2)

Grandson of MENOECEUS (1) and son of CREON (2) and Eurydice. According to Euripides' tragedy *The Phoenician Women*, during the expedition of the SEVEN AGAINST THEBES Menoeceus voluntarily sacrificed himself to bring victory to his city (and his noble act may well have been the playwright's own innovation, since Euripides developed the figure of the self-sacrificing hero or heroine in several of his tragedies). The blind prophet TEIRESIAS predicted that Thebes could be saved only by the sacrifice to the War-god ARES of a virgin male, descended from the 'Sown Men'. The only young man who answered that description was Menoeceus. Creon tried to persuade him to leave Thebes and Menoeceus agreed to do so, then secretly climbed to the top of the city. Thrusting his sword into his throat, he plunged down from the battlements. The Thebans went into battle against the enemy and were victorious.

[Euripides, *Phoenician Women* 903–1018, 1090–2; Apollodorus 3.6.7; Pausanias 9.25.1.]

Menoetes

The herdsman who guarded the cattle belonging to HADES

253

(1). Twice HERACLES encountered him while performing his Labours. When he stole the cattle of GERYON from Erytheia, it was Meneotes who warned Geryon of his approach; and when he killed one of Hades' cows on his journey to fetch CERBERUS from the Underworld, Menoetes challenged him to a wrestling match, and had his ribs broken for his pains before PERSEPHONE intervened to have him spared.

[Apollodorus 2.5.10, 2.5.12.]

Menoetius (1)

Son of the Titan IAPETUS and an Oceanid, Clymene or Asia. In the battle of the gods and the Titans, ZEUS smote Menoetius with a thunderbolt and hurled him down to TARTARUS.

[Hesiod, *Theogony* 510; Apollodorus 1.2.3.]

Menoetius (2)

Son of Actor and AEGINA, and one of the ARGONAUTS. He was the father of PATROCLUS, and we learn from the *Iliad* that he lived at Opous in Locris until Patroclus as a child accidentally killed a friend, the son of Amphidamas, in anger over a dice game. Menoetius took Patroclus to his nephew PELEUS' house in Phthia and gave him to be brought up with ACHILLES, who would be Patroclus' life-long comrade. When the young men set out together to the Trojan War, Achilles tried to comfort Menoetius for his son's leaving by saying that he would bring Patroclus back from the war in glory (18.324–8, a 'futile promise' says Homer). Menoetius at that time offered his son advice which defines the relationship of the two comrades (11.786–9): 'My child, Achilles is higher-born than you are, but you are the elder; and yet in strength he is by far the greater. You must speak sound words to him and advise him well and guide him.' Yet it would be Patroclus' advice to his friend that would bring about his own death, and thus Achilles' death too.

Given the above parentage, Menoetius was the half-brother of Achilles' grandfather AEACUS; but a Hesiodic fragment makes him the son of Aeacus and thus the brother of Achilles' father Peleus, in which case Patroclus and Achilles would have been cousins.

[Homer, *Iliad* 16.2–47, 23.82–90; Hesiod, *Catalogue of Women* fr. 212a; Apollodorus 1.9.16.]

Mentes

Leader of the Taphians and an old friend of ODYSSEUS. Athena took his likeness in order to persuade Odysseus' son TELEMACHUS to leave Ithaca and seek for news of his long-departed father.

[Homer, *Odyssey* 1.105–323.]

Menthe (or Minthe)

A beautiful nymph whom HADES (1) took as his mistress. The jealous PERSEPHONE, hearing of their affair, trampled Menthe underfoot, and the unhappy nymph was turned into the aromatic plant garden-mint. Its leaves, when trodden on, fill the air with fragrance.

[Strabo 8.3.14; Ovid, *Metamorphoses* 10.728–30.]

Mentor

An Ithacan of noble birth and an old friend of ODYSSEUS, who was left to look after his household when Odysseus himself went to fight at Troy. Athena in Mentor's likeness did much to encourage TELEMACHUS in his father's absence, and later to support Odysseus in the battle with the Suitors and to bring peace between him and the Ithacans. Mentor's name has become synonymous with a wise and faithful guide.

[Homer, *Odyssey* 2.225–95, 2.399–3.379, 22.205–40, 24.503–48.]

Mercury

Roman god of merchants and travellers, identified with the Greek god HERMES and having the same attributes of caduceus, winged hat and winged shoes. He fathered on the nymph LARA the Lares, guardian spirits of the Roman household and state. In the astrological beliefs of the Middle Ages, those born under the influence of the planet Mercury were thought to have a 'mercurial' temperament, lively, ingenious and volatile. The element mercury (quicksilver) was given his name because of his imagined quickness of movement.

Meriones

Son of Molus, who was the bastard son of Deucalion, king of Crete. In the *Iliad*, Meriones is second-in-command to IDOMENEUS, his uncle and the leader of the eighty-ship contingent from Crete to the TROJAN WAR. Meriones performs well on the battlefield, fighting with both spear and bow, and is one of the nine warriors who volunteer to fight in single combat against the mighty HECTOR. When ODYSSEUS and DIOMEDES (2) go by night on a spying expedition to the Trojan camp, Meriones supplies Odysseus with a bow and a sword, as well as the celebrated boar's tusk helmet. He helps MENELAUS to rescue the corpse of PATROCLUS from the Trojans, helps to gather timber for Patroclus' funeral pyre, and competes in three events at his funeral games, the chariot-race, the archery contest, which he wins, and the javelin-throwing.

He was later said to be one of the warriors in the WOODEN HORSE; and when Troy fell he sailed with Idomeneus safely back to Crete. He shared a tomb with him at Knossos, and the Cretans held the two heroes in special renown, offering up sacrifices to them and calling on their aid in times of war.

[Homer, *Iliad* 2.645–52, 5.59–68, 7.161–9, 10.260–71, 13.156–68, 246–329, 650–1, 17.258–9, 23.110–13, 351, 859–83, 884–97, *Odyssey* 3.191–2; Diodorus Siculus 5.79; Quintus of Smyrna, *Sequel to Homer* 12.320.]

Mermerus and Pheres

Sons of JASON and MEDEA. In the most familiar version of the myth, famous from Euripides' tragedy *Medea*, both boys were killed by their mother to avenge Jason's deserting her and marrying GLAUCE, the daughter of Creon, king of Corinth. According to Pausanias (2.3.6–7), the Corinthians stoned the boys to death because they had carried Medea's fatal gifts to Glauce. As a result of this outrage, the children's spirits haunted Corinth, killing the townspeople's babies. Finally the Corinthians, advised by an oracle, set up a statue of Terror and made a yearly sacrifice to Medea's children, in honour of whom their own children would cut their hair and wear black clothes. This custom continued until Corinth was taken by the Romans. Pausanias (2.3.9) also records an otherwise unknown story taken from the (lost) epic *Naupactia*, in which Mermerus was killed by a lioness while out hunting.

Merope (1)

Daughter of the Titan ATLAS and Pleione, and thus one of the seven PLEIADES. She married SISYPHUS, the king of Corinth, and bore him four sons including GLAUCUS (3), the father of Bellerophon. The faintest star in the constellation of the Pleiades was said to be Merope, hiding her face in chagrin at being the only one of the sisters to marry a mere mortal.

[Apollodorus 1.9.3, 3.10.1; Ovid, *Fasti* 4.175–6.]

Merope (2) *see* ORION.

Merope (3)

Wife of Polybus and foster-mother of the baby OEDIPUS.

Merope (4) *see* CRESPHONTES (2).

Merops (1)

An Ethiopian king who married the Oceanid Clymene and was stepfather to PHAETHON (2), her son by the Sun-god Helios.

Merops (2)

A king of Percote in the Troad, the fate of whose children brought him great sorrow. His daughter Cleite was married to CYZICUS, the young king of the Doliones in Mysia, but before they could have children he was accidentally killed by the Argonauts. Cleite hanged herself from grief.

Another daughter of Merops, Arisbe, was the first wife of Priam and bore him a son, AESACUS, but Priam, wishing to marry Hecuba, gave Arisbe to Hyrtacus. Aesacus tried to drown himself for love, but was turned into a water-bird, a diver.

Merops had two sons, Adrestus and Amphius. Being a skilled seer, he tried to stop them from fighting in the Trojan War because he knew that they would die. He tried in vain, and they were killed at Troy by DIOMEDES (2).

[Homer, *Iliad* 2.828–34, 11.328–34; Apollonius, *Argonautica* 1.974–7, 1063–9; Apollodorus 3.12.5.]

Mestra *see* ERYSICHTHON.

Metabus *see* CAMILLA.

Metaneira

The wife of Celeus, king of Eleusis, and mother of four daughters and a late-born son, Demophon. The *Homeric Hymn to Demeter* (96–304) tells how the goddess DEMETER, in her long hunt for her daughter PERSEPHONE, came in the guise of an old woman to the house of Celeus at Eleusis. Here, sad at heart, she rested in the shade of an olive-tree, near the Maiden Well from which the women drew their water. The king's daughters came to the well, greeting her courteously, and she told them that she was seeking domestic work of some kind. They took her home to their mother Metaneira, who welcomed her warmly and made her the nurse of baby Demophon. He flourished under Demeter's care and she secretly set about making him immortal: she began to burn away his mortal part by putting him in the fire at night, and anointing him with ambrosia during the day. But one night Metaneira caught her in the act of putting her baby in the fire and cried out in alarm. The angry goddess dropped the child to the ground and rebuked Metaneira. Revealing her divine identity, Demeter told her what the Eleusinians must do to win back her favour, then left the house. Celeus and his people built a great temple to the goddess at Eleusis, and she taught them the new and secret rites that would be performed for many centuries in her honour, the Eleusinian Mysteries. As for Demophon, he grew and flourished, and even though he had not gained immortality, throughout his life he enjoyed the glory of having been nursed by a goddess in his infancy.

Later versions offer minor variations to this early story. Apollodorus (1.5.1–2), for instance, says that Demophon was burnt up by the fire, and that TRIPTOLEMUS, the mortal whom Demeter chose to transmit her gift of grain and agriculture to the world, was the eldest son of Celeus and Metaneira. Ovid (*Fasti* 4.502–60) identifies the child whom Demeter tried to make immortal as Triptolemus

Fig. 92 The captured Silenus is brought to Midas, whose regal bearing as he sits on his throne is somewhat marred by his asses' ears.

himself. The traveller Pausanias (1.39.1–2) saw at Eleusis the very well at which Demeter rested and calls it the 'Flowery Well'.

Metapontus *see* MELANIPPE (1).

Metis ('Intelligence')

A daughter of OCEANUS and Tethys, and the first wife of ZEUS. According to one version of the legend, it was Metis who helped Zeus to overcome his father, CRONUS, by giving him an emetic that caused him to vomit up all the children he had earlier swallowed. These were Zeus' brothers and sisters, and with their aid Zeus now waged war against his father, eventually deposing him and ruling in his place. He then married Metis, even though she transformed herself into many different shapes to avoid his embraces. When she was pregnant, Zeus learnt from his grandparents Uranus (Heaven) and GAIA (Earth) that, once Metis had given birth to the daughter now in her womb, she was destined to bear a son who would be king of gods and men. So the great god, unwilling to lose his supreme power, deceived his wife with wily words and swallowed her. He thus forestalled the birth of the son who would have overthrown him, and at the same time assimilated into himself Metis' powers of practical wisdom. When the time came for their daughter to be born, HEPHAESTUS split Zeus' head with an axe and out leapt ATHENA, fully armed.

[Hesiod, *Theogony* 358, 886–900, 924–9; Apollodorus 1.2.1, 1.3.6. M. Detienne and J.-P. Vernant, *Cunning Intelligence in Greek Culture and Society* (1978).]

Mezentius

In the *Aeneid*, Mezentius is the Etruscan king of Caere, a cruel and bloodthirsty tyrant who has been expelled by his people and is now an ally of TURNUS, king of the Rutulians and enemy of AENEAS. Mezentius is wounded in battle by Aeneas, and while he struggles to get away, his son Lausus leaps to intervene and saves his life. Aeneas kills Lausus, and Mezentius returns to the battlefield on his horse Rhaebus, his faithful companion through many campaigns, determined either to avenge his son and carry back the head of his killer, or to die with his horse in the attempt. He gallops in a circle round Aeneas and hurls three spears, all in vain; then Aeneas throws his own spear and hits Rhaebus in the head. The horse rears and throws his rider, then falls, pinning Mezentius to the ground. Aeneas can now kill him at leisure, and Mezentius dies with courage, begging only to be buried with his son.

According to other sources, Mezentius survived the war and was later defeated by Aeneas' son, ASCANIUS, after which the Etruscans and Latins were firm allies.

[Dionysius of Halicarnassus 1.64–5, 2.5.5; Livy 1.2.3–6, 1.3.4; Virgil, *Aeneid* 7.647–54, 8.478–503, 9.581–9, 10.762–11.16; Ovid, *Fasti* 4.877–900.]

Midas

A king of Phrygia, the son of GORDIUS. According to Ovid, when Phrygian peasants captured an old, drunken man and brought him to their king, Midas at once recognised him as SILENUS, the oldest and wisest of DIONYSUS' revelling companions. Midas gave the old man rich hospitality for ten days, and on the eleventh day took him back to his god. Dionysus in gratitude granted Midas one wish, and Midas, not the most far-seeing of mortals, asked that all he touched might turn into gold. His wish granted, he went away rejoicing, finding that everything he touched – twigs, stones, earth, ears of corn, apples – did indeed become gold. But all too soon he regretted his wish. Even his food and drink changed into unconsumable metal and he could do nothing to ease his hunger and thirst. At last he begged Dionysus to take away his ill-chosen gift, and the god told him to wash in the River Pactolus, near Sardis. Midas did so, and washed off his wondrous 'golden touch' into the river which has ever afterwards had golden sand.

Midas showed his lack of common sense once again when APOLLO and PAN held a musical contest. The judge was the mountain-god Tmolus, who pronounced Apollo the winner; but Midas foolishly intervened, saying that the decision was unjust. The furious Apollo transformed the ears that had obviously listened so stupidly into asses' ears, long, twitching, and covered with grey and bristling hair. Midas, disfigured and mortified, tried to hide these shameful ears under a turban, but one person in the world was bound to find out his humiliating secret: his barber saw the ears when he cut the king's hair. The barber longed to pass on this fascinating piece of news, but dared not, yet could not stay absolutely silent. So he dug a hole deep in the ground and whispered into it Midas' unhappy secret. He filled up the hole and went quietly away. But a thick carpet of reeds grew there and betrayed what their earth had been told, for every time a breeze ruffled them they whispered, 'Midas has asses' ears.' You can still hear them.

Midas was reputedly the first foreigner to send tributes to Apollo's shrine at Delphi. Herodotus reports that his royal throne stood there and was 'well worth seeing' (1.14). Midas with his asses' ears appears, together with Silenus (fig. 92), on late fifth-century red-figure vase-paintings, and the ears are mentioned by Aristophanes (*Wealth* 286–7). Earlier sixth-century scenes show the capture of Silenus, some of them clearly reflecting another story about Midas: that the king deliberately caught the old man by lacing the fountain at which he used to drink with wine, after which the drunken Silenus shared his wisdom with the king. In postclassical art Midas has been painted by, among many others, Poussin, Veronese, Rubens and Tiepolo, although the contest of Apollo and Pan is sometimes confused with that of Apollo and the satyr Marsyas. It may well be that the story of Midas and his asses' ears inspired Shakespeare's scene of Bottom with his ass's head in *A Midsummer Night's Dream*.

[Herodotus 8.138; Xenophon, *Anabasis* 1.2.13; Pausanias 1.4.5; Ovid, *Metamorphoses* 11.85–193.]

Miletus

The son of APOLLO and one of his human loves, Areia, or ACACALLIS, or Deione. Miletus, living in Crete, grew into a beautiful youth and was loved by the three sons of Zeus and Europa, MINOS, SARPEDON and RHADAMANTHYS. They quarrelled over him, although the boy himself preferred Sarpedon. The result of their conflict was that Minos stayed ruling in Crete while the others journeyed to different lands. Miletus went to Caria, where the city of Miletus was named after him. By the nymph Cyanea he had a son and daughter, Caunus and BYBLIS.

[Apollodorus 3.1.2; Pausanias 7.2.4–11; Ovid, *Metamorphoses* 9.441–53.]

Milky Way

The long, luminous band of light that crosses the night sky, composed of the innumerable stars of our own galaxy (*galact-*, milk) so distant that they are indistinguishable to the eye as separate points of light. It was said to have been formed from the milk of the goddess HERA. She was tricked into suckling the baby HERACLES, son of her husband Zeus by the beautiful mortal, Alcmene; but when she discovered that this was the child of her hated rival, she tore her breast from his mouth and her milk spurted across the sky. Another legend said that the Milky Way was created when PHAETHON (2), son of Helios, the Sun-god, set the heavens on fire with his father's sun-chariot. Ovid (*Metamorphoses* 1.168–71) saw it as the highway of the gods, crossing the heaven and leading to the palace of Jupiter.

Mimas *see* GIANTS.

Minerva

Italian goddess of handicrafts, identified with the Greek ATHENA and so also a goddess of war. Together with JUPITER and JUNO she was one of the three great deities of the Capitoline Triad.

Minos

An early king of Crete. He was the son of ZEUS and EUROPA, and the brother of RHADAMANTHYS and (in all accounts after Homer) SARPEDON. Europa married the Cretan king, Asterius, who brought up the boys as his own sons. When they grew up, they quarrelled over the love of a beautiful youth, MILETUS, and Minos drove his brothers out of Crete. He married PASIPHAE, daughter of the Sun-god Helios, and had by her four sons, CATREUS, DEUCALION (2), GLAUCUS (2) and ANDROGEOS, and five daughters, ARIADNE, PHAEDRA, ACACALLIS, Xenodice and Euryale, the mother of ORION. When Asterius died childless and the kingship was in question, Minos declared that the gods supported his claim to the throne. To prove this, he prayed to POSEIDON to send him a bull from the sea, promising to sacrifice it when it appeared. The god answered his prayer. A magnificent white bull came out of the sea and Minos won his kingdom. But the bull was so beautiful that Minos could not bear to kill it, so he put it with his herds for breeding and sacrificed another in its place. The angry sea-god responded to this broken vow by inflicting on Pasiphae a passion for the bull. Nothing would satisfy her but to couple with the beast, so she persuaded the master-craftsman DAEDALUS to help her. He fashioned a hollow wooden cow, realistically covered with hide, and set it in a meadow. Pasiphae crouched waiting inside until the bull, completely taken in by so deft an imitation, mated with her. The fruit of their union was named Asterius but was better known as the MINOTAUR (*Minotauros*, 'Bull of Minos'), a monster with the body of a man and the head of a bull. Minos, appalled by his wife's deed and its freakish issue, commissioned Daedalus to build a vast underground maze called the Labyrinth, in which the creature could be shut away for ever. Pasiphae's passion and the birth of the Minotaur were dramatised in Euripides' tragedy *Cretans*, now lost, although we know from a fragment that Pasiphae defended her behaviour, arguing that such an extraordinary passion as hers must have been sent her by some god, angry with Minos himself. Thus she herself was not to blame.

Minos himself was hardly a faithful husband. He was attractive to women and fathered several illegitimate children, although his long pursuit of the Cretan goddess BRITOMARTIS proved unavailing. Eventually he had so many affairs that Pasiphae bewitched him (she was, after all, sister of the enchantress CIRCE). She drugged him in such a way that, whenever he had intercourse with a woman, he ejaculated snakes and scorpions. Despite this, he still persuaded Procris, the wife of CEPHALUS (2), to go to bed with him during her visit to Crete, though she too drugged him to ensure that he caused her no harm. In return for her favours, Minos rewarded her with the gifts of a javelin that never missed its mark and a hound, LAELAPS, that never failed to catch its quarry.

Minos' son Glaucus fell into a storage-jar of honey and was drowned (though he was brought back to life by the seer Polyidus); and his son Androgeos was killed while at Athens, after winning great distinction in the athletic contests at the Panathenaic festival. Minos responded by attacking Athens, but was unable to take the city, although he captured Megara thanks to the treachery of Scylla (*see* NISUS (1)).

The war with Athens lingered fruitlessly on, and eventually Minos prayed to his father Zeus that he might in some other way be avenged on the Athenians. Zeus sent a famine and a plague on the city, and when the Athenians enquired of an oracle how they could be saved, they were told that they should grant Minos whatever satisfaction he might choose. He chose a tribute of seven youths and seven girls to be sent to Crete, either annually or every nine years, as food for the Minotaur. This tribute came to an end only when the great Athenian hero THESEUS came to Crete as one of the sacrificial youths and killed the monster. Theseus left Crete together with Minos' daughter Ariadne, who had fallen in love with him and had provided him with the ball of thread that showed him his way back out of the Labyrinth.

It was Daedalus who had made this ball of thread, so when Minos learnt of Ariadne's flight with Theseus, and of Daedalus' involvement, he shut him up in the Labyrinth together with his son ICARUS. Daedalus, brilliant inventor that he was, built wings of wax and feathers with which they flew to freedom. Sadly, despite warnings from his father, Icarus flew too near the sun and fell to his death in the sea below; but Daedalus escaped safely to Sicily, where he stayed at the court of Cocalus, king of Camicus. Minos, meanwhile, was still intent on revenge and searched everywhere for him, taking with him a spiral seashell and promising a great reward to anyone who could pass a thread through it. He believed that no one but the clever Daedalus would be able to solve the problem, and sure enough, at the court of Cocalus, he was presented by the king with a threaded shell: Daedalus had bored a hole in it, then tied a thread to an ant and induced it to pass through the spiral. Minos at once demanded that Cocalus surrender his enemy to him, and the king promised to do so. But that night, while Minos was in the bath, he was scalded to death with boiling water (though some say pitch) by Cocalus' daughters, who flooded it through a system of pipes installed by Daedalus himself.

Despite his inglorious end, Minos was a great and respected king, famous for his vast sea-power. The Bronze-Age culture centred in Crete (*c.* 3500–1100 BC) has been called Minoan after him, a term coined by Sir Arthur Evans after his excavations at Knossos beginning in 1900. Like his brother Rhadamanthys, Minos was renowned for his wisdom and justice as a lawgiver, and after his death he became one of the judges over the souls of the dead in Hades, along with his brother and another just son of Zeus, AEACUS. In Dante's *Inferno*, Minos has been transformed into a demonic judge who twists his tail around his body, the number of times he girds himself being a sign of the circle of Hell to which the sinner must descend.

[Homer, *Odyssey* 11.568–71, 19.178–80; Bacchylides, *Ode* 17; Herodotus 1.171, 3.122, 7.170; Thucydides 1.4; Apollodorus 1.9.1, 3.1.1–4, 3.15.1, 3.15.7–8, *Epitome* 1.12–15; Diodorus Siculus 4.60.2–62.1, 4.77, 4.79.1–4, 5.78; Strabo 10.4.8–9, 16.2.38; Plutarch, *Theseus* 15–16; Pausanias 1.1.2, 1.1.4, 1.19.4, 1.27.9–10, 2.34.7, 7.4.6–7; Ovid, *Metamorphoses* 7.456–8, 8.1–176, *The Art of Love* 1.289–327. For Euripides' lost *Cretans*, see C. Collard, M. J. Cropp and K. H. Lee, *Euripides: Selected Fragmentary Plays* I (1995), pp. 53–78.]

Minotaur ('Bull of Minos')

A monster with the body of a man and the head and horns and tail of a bull, named Asterius at his birth. He was born to PASIPHAE, the wife of MINOS, king of Crete, from her coupling with the beautiful white bull that Poseidon sent from the sea. When the horrified Minos saw his wife's monstrous offspring, he employed the ingenious craftsman DAEDALUS to build the Labyrinth, a vast underground maze so cleverly devised that anyone going in would be quite unable to find the way out again. The Minotaur was consigned to its depths. The creature was fed on human flesh, supplied by the seven youths and seven girls whom Minos claimed as tribute from the Athenians, either annually or every nine years, in recompense for the death of his son ANDROGEOS. This tribute continued until the Athenian hero THESEUS came as one of the sacrificial youths and killed the rapacious Minotaur.

Theseus was helped by ARIADNE, Minos' daughter, who had fallen in love with him. She gave him a clew, a large ball of thread provided by Daedalus, one end of which Theseus tied at the entrance to the Labyrinth, then unwound the thread as he wended his way into the innermost depths of the maze. There he found the Minotaur. They fought, and the Minotaur died (fig. 93), though sources disagree as to how Theseus killed him. Apollodorus says that he used his bare fists, Ovid says a club. The many artistic representations from the seventh and sixth centuries BC, when the myth was at the height of its popularity, show Theseus fighting with sword, club and spear, while the Minotaur sometimes uses rocks to fight back. But always the outcome was the same, with the Minotaur dead (fig. 140) and Minos' cruel tribute ended. Theseus escaped from the Labyrinth by following his thread back to the entrance, then sailed away from Crete, taking Ariadne with him.

'Labyrinth' occurs in Linear B, and has been connected with the double axe (*labrys*), a powerful religious symbol depicted on many Minoan frescoes along with the 'horns of consecration' and scenes of ritual bull-leaping. These may have given rise to the legend of the Minotaur. A version of the story based on the discoveries of modern archaeology and anthropology is told in Mary Renault's novel *The King Must Die*. The figure of the Minotaur has been a great source of inspiration to artists in the twentieth century, particularly to Picasso, who has used the minotaur theme in many drawings and etchings, and to Michael Ayrton, whose bronzes of the Minotaur movingly suggest a man's mind miserably and irredeemably encased in the body of a beast.

[Apollodorus 3.1.4, 3.15.8, *Epitome* 1.7–9; Diodorus Siculus 1.61, 4.61, 4.77; Plutarch, *Theseus* 15–19; Pausanias 1.24.1, 1.27.10, 3.18.11, 3.18.16; Virgil, *Aeneid* 5.588–91, 6.20–30; Ovid, *Metamorphoses* 8.155–73, *Heroides* 10.101–2.]

Fig. 93 Theseus kills the Minotaur.

Minthe *see* MENTHE.

Minyas

The mythical founder of Orchomenus in Boeotia who gave his name to the Minyans, the clan to which the Argonauts were said to belong. Minyas was the father of Clymene (2), and through her the great-grandfather of JASON. He was also the father of three other daughters, Leucippe, Arsippe and Alcithoe (or Alcathoe), who were punished for refusing to honour the festival of DIONYSUS. Being industrious girls, they preferred to stay indoors all day, weaving at their looms, instead of going out and joining in the revels with the other women. In one version of the story, Dionysus himself appeared to them in the form of a young girl and advised them not to neglect the rites of the god. When they ignored him, he turned himself into a bull, a lion and a leopard, while milk and nectar flowed from their looms. The frightened sisters drew lots, and when Leucippe's lot came out they seized her son Hippasus and sacrificed him to Dionysus, then went outdoors to join the revelling MAENADS. Finally they were turned into a bat and two kinds of owl, or, in another version, a crow, a bat and an owl. In Ovid's version, they worked at their looms all day, contentedly telling stories to each other. Then suddenly at dusk their looms sprouted grape-vines and their threads vine-tendrils, the rooms glowed with fire, and the house was filled with smoke and the sound of wild beasts howling. The three girls fled in terror to remote corners of the house, where all three were turned into bats.

The 'treasury' of Minyas, a great Mycenean tholos tomb, was known at Orchomenus in the time of Pausanias, who thought it as fine a sight as the Egyptian pyramids or the huge walls of Tiryns (9.36.4–6). It still exists, though with the roof fallen in.

[Apollonius, *Argonautica* 1.229–33, 3.1091–5; Antoninus Liberalis, *Metamorphoses* 10; Aelian, *Historical Miscellany* 3.42; Ovid, *Metamorphoses* 4.1–415.]

Misenus

The warrior who gave his name to Cape Misenum in Campania. He was a comrade of HECTOR in the Trojan War, a courageous warrior and a fine trumpeter, who excelled at stirring the troops with his music and firing them to battle. When Hector was killed by Achilles, Misenus fought alongside AENEAS, and after Troy fell accompanied him to Italy. One day, while blowing into a sea-shell until the waves echoed with the sound, he became so carried away by his skill that he challenged the gods to play as well as he. The sea-god TRITON heard and jealously killed his rival, catching him up and drowning him in the surf among the rocks. When the Trojans found his body they mourned deeply for their comrade, then gave him a funeral with full honours, burying his bones on the headland that bears his name. They piled a huge grave-mound over him, setting on it the oars he had rowed with and the trumpet he had blown.

[Virgil, *Aeneid* 6.162–235.]

Mnemosyne ('Memory')

One of the TITANS, daughter of Uranus (Heaven) and GAIA (Earth). For nine nights she lay with ZEUS, and in the course of time she bore in Pieria, just north of Mount Olympus, nine daughters, the MUSES. Thus the goddesses of the arts were the daughters of Memory, an apt metaphor in a time before the invention of writing.

[Hesiod, *Theogony* 53–62, 135, 915–17.]

Mnesimache *see* DEXAMENUS.

Moirai *see* FATES.

Moliones or Molionides

Cteatus and Eurytus, twin sons of POSEIDON and Molione. They were also called the Actoriones after their stepfather Actor, the brother of AUGEAS, king of Elis. According to post-Homeric writers, the Molionides were Siamese twins, apparently imagined as each having one head, two arms and two legs, while sharing one torso between them. They were, not surprisingly, the strongest men of their generation. They also appear in the *Iliad*, where it is not quite clear whether Homer sees them as Siamese or

normal twins. Old NESTOR recounts that he would have killed them in battle, had not their father Poseidon saved them by shrouding them in a thick mist and carrying them off the battlefield (11.706–52). Although the twins were here still boys and not yet fully skilled in warfare, Nestor obviously sees this as a tremendous feat. But he was less successful against them at the funeral games of Amarynceus, where he won all the contests that he entered except for the chariot-race. This the Molionides won, with one twin holding the reins and the other lashing on the horses (23.638–42). Homer does not say outright that they were Siamese twins, but the fact that they both competed in an event where normally only one charioteer took part does indeed suggest that they were physically unable to compete singly. Certainly Siamese twins appear in Greek Geometric art of the eighth century BC, and we may be fairly sure that the Molionides are intended.

When HERACLES marched against Augeas because he had been refused payment for the cleansing of the Augean Stables, the Molionides fought on the side of their uncle. At first Heracles was ill and they were victorious, even mortally wounding his half-brother IPHICLES. But later Heracles ambushed and killed them at Cleonae as they were on their way to represent Elis at the Isthmian Games. Their tomb was seen at Cleonae centuries later by Pausanias (2.15.1). They had, however, married the twin daughters of Dexamenus, king of Olenus, and each left a son who fought in the Trojan War: Theraephone was wife of Eurytus and mother of THALPIUS, and Theronice wife of Cteatus and mother of AMPHIMACHUS.

[Homer, *Iliad* 2.620–1; Hesiod, *Catalogue of Women* fr. 17; Pindar, *Olympian* 10.26–34; Apollodorus 2.7.2; Pausanias 3.18.15, 5.1.10–5.2.3, 5.3.3, 8.14.9.]

Molorchus

The peasant who gave hospitality to Heracles when he was on his way to kill the NEMEAN LION.

Molossus *see* ANDROMACHE.

Momos ('Blame')

Son of NYX (Night), produced by her without the aid of a mate. He personified the spirit of disapproval and criticism. His only part in myth was in one of the stories of the events leading to the TROJAN WAR: we are told in the scholia that Momos advised Zeus to marry THETIS to a mortal and himself beget a beautiful daughter, so as to precipitate the war. A fragment of the Epic Cycle's *Cypria* tells us why this was necessary:

There was a time when the many tribes of men,
though they were wide-dispersed, weighed down

the broad and deep-bosomed earth. Zeus saw it
and took pity, and in his wisdom resolved
to lighten the all-nurturing earth of men
by causing the mighty strife of the Trojan War,
so that the load of death might empty the world.
And so the heroes died in Troy, and the plan
of Zeus was accomplished ...

On Momos' advice Zeus fathered on LEDA the beautiful
HELEN, for whom the Trojan War was fought, and married
the mortal PELEUS to Thetis, who then gave birth to
ACHILLES, the mightiest fighter at Troy.

[Hesiod, *Theogony* 214.]

Mopsus (1)

A Lapith seer, the son of Ampycus (or Ampyx). He fought
valiantly in the battle between the Lapiths and the
CENTAURS at the wedding of Peirithous, and sailed with
the ARGONAUTS, where he gave prophetic advice by interpreting the flight of birds. On their return journey he
died, bitten by a snake in Libya, and there his comrades
buried him.

[Hesiod, *Shield of Heracles* 181; Apollonius, *Argonautica*
1.65–6, 79–81, 1080–1106, 4.1502–36; Pausanias 5.17.10;
Ovid, *Metamorphoses* 8.316, 12.455–8.]

Mopsus (2)

Son of MANTO, either by APOLLO or by the mortal Rhacius.
Mopsus inherited the prophetic skills of his mother and
his grandfather, the blind seer TEIRESIAS. He took part in a
famous contest with the Greek seer CALCHAS, who lost
and died of a broken heart. Mopsus then joined forces
with AMPHILOCHUS (2), who was either another son of
Manto by the Argive Alcmaeon, or Alcmaeon's brother.
Together they founded the city of Mallus in Cilicia.
When Amphilochus went away for a while to Argos,
Mopsus was left in charge of the kingdom and refused to
give up any power on his partner's return. The two tried
to settle the matter by single combat and killed each
other. They were buried in graves that were out of sight
of each other, so that the rivals, who had fought each
other in life, might not scowl at each other in death.
Despite their rivalry, they afterwards shared a famous
oracle that Pausanias (1.34.3) calls the most trustworthy
of his day.

[Apollodorus, *Epitome* 6.2–4, 6.19; Strabo 14.1.27, 14.5.16.]

Mormo ('Frightful')

A hideous she-monster, said to bite little children and used
as a nursery-bogey to frighten them into good behaviour.

[Xenophon, *Hellenica* 4.4.17; Theocritus 15.40.]

Morpheus

A dream-god, the son of Hypnos ('Sleep') (*see* DREAMS).
Morpheus gathering sleepers into his arms has become a
commonplace of poetry.

Munippus *see* THYMOETES.

Munitus *see* LAODICE (1).

Musaeus ('He of the Muses')

A mythical singer often connected with ORPHEUS, the
supreme singer of myth, as son, follower or teacher. He
was a seer as well as a great musician, and was associated
with Eleusis, and with EUMOLPUS, one of the founders of
the Eleusinian Mysteries. Various poems of mystic inspiration are attributed to him.

[Diodorus Siculus 4.25; Strabo 10.3.17; Pausanias 1.14.3,
1.22.7, 1.25.8, 4.1.5, 10.5.6.]

Muses

Goddesses on whom poets and other creative artists,
thinkers and philosophers depended for their inspiration. According to the traditional account in Hesiod, the
Muses were nine in number and were the daughters of
ZEUS and the Titaness MNEMOSYNE ('Memory'); born in
Pieria at the foot of Mount OLYMPUS, they were often
known as the Pierides. Mount HELICON in Boeotia·was
also sacred to them, and it was here that they came to
Hesiod and gave him the gift of song. Hesiod allots to
each of them a name, but makes no further distinction
between them. Later their functions were differentiated,
with each Muse thought to preside over a specific area of
intellectual or creative endeavour (though these functions could vary). Usually they were: Calliope ('Lovely
Voice'), epic poetry (Hesiod says that Calliope was the
most important Muse because she had the tutelage of
kings); Clio ('Renown'), history; Euterpe ('Gladness'), flute-
playing; Thalia ('Good Cheer'), comedy; Melpomene
('Singer'), tragedy; Terpsichore ('Delighting in the Dance'),
choral lyric and dancing; Erato ('Loveliness'), lyric poetry;
Polymnia ('Many Songs'), hymns and pantomime; and
Urania ('Heavenly One'), astronomy. A different tradition
is recorded by Pausanias (9.29.1–6), who says that the
two Aloadae, OTUS and Ephialtes, were the first mortals to
sacrifice to the Muses and to say that Helicon was their
sacred mountain, but that they recognised only three
Muses instead of the later nine. These three were called
Melete ('Practice'), Mneme ('Memory') and Aoede ('Song').
In Rome, the Muses were identified with the rather
obscure Italian water-goddesses, the Camenae.

   The Muses lived on Olympus, near the dwellings of
the GRACES and HIMEROS (Desire). Presided over by APOLLO,

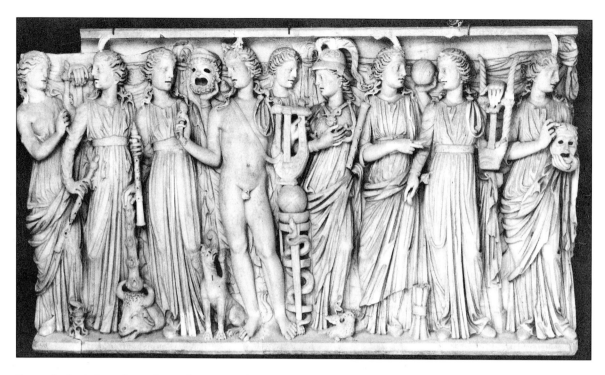

Fig. 94 Apollo, Athena and seven Muses.

the god of music and prophecy, they spent their time singing and dancing at the feasts of the gods. Sometimes they also came down to earth, as when they sang in mourning at the funeral of ACHILLES, or celebrated the marriages of men to goddesses PELEUS to THETIS, and CADMUS to HARMONIA. But on several other occasions their intercourse with mortals was less harmonious. PYRENEUS, a Thracian king, met his death when he tried to rape them. The Thracian bard THAMYRIS boasted that his skill at singing was greater than theirs, and they avenged this insult by blinding him and robbing him of his musicianship. DEMODOCUS, the Phaeacian bard in the *Odyssey*, was also blinded by one of the Muses, but she gave him the gift of song in recompense for his lost sight. The nine daughters of the Macedonian king PIERUS once challenged the Muses to a contest, with the nymphs as judges. When the Muses won, they punished the girls for their presumption by turning them into chattering magpies. Another contest was held when Hera persuaded the SIRENS to compete with the Muses in singing. Once again the Muses won, and they plucked out the Sirens' feathers to make crowns for themselves. They acted as judges in the musical contest between the Phrygian satyr MARSYAS and Apollo, after which the loser, Marsyas, was flayed alive. They also taught the SPHINX her famous riddle, by means of which she preyed on the Thebans, snatching up and devouring anyone who failed to give her the right answer.

Several of the Muses had famous children. The Sirens were said to be the daughters of either Melpomene or Terpsichore, HYACINTHUS the son of Clio, the CORYBANTES the sons of Thalia, ORPHEUS the son of Calliope, LINUS the son of either Calliope or Urania, and RHESUS the son of either Calliope or Euterpe. The Muses, either singly or in groups of varying sizes (fig. 94), appear frequently in poetry and art of all periods. A Museum (*Mouseion*) originally meant a 'seat of the Muses' and was a centre dedicated to learning and the arts. The Tenth Muse was a name first given to the Greek poetess Sappho, and more recently applied to other literary women, such as the English novelist and essay writer Hannah More (1745–1833).

[Homer, *Iliad* 2.594–600, *Odyssey* 8.63–4, 479–81, 24.60–1; Hesiod, *Theogony* 1–115, 915–17; Pindar, *Pythian* 3.86–92; Apollodorus 1.3.1–4, 3.5.8; Pausanias 5.18.4, 9.34.3.]

Mygdon (1) *see* LYCUS (3).

Mygdon (2) *see* COROEBUS (2).

Myrmidons

The Myrmidons were said to be born when AEACUS, the son of Zeus and Aegina, grew to manhood alone on the island of Aegina and was grieved by his solitude, whereupon Zeus transformed all the ants (*myrmekes*) into men and women. This race was the first to build ships and fit them with sails. They later migrated with Aeacus' son, PELEUS, to Phthia, and in due course Peleus' son, ACHILLES, led a Myrmidon army to the TROJAN WAR. We see them in action in the *Iliad*, when they go out under PATROCLUS' command to beat back the Trojans from the Greek ships (16.259–67):

> They came swarming out like wasps at the wayside
> when children are in the habit of making them angry,
> forever teasing them in their home by the roadside,
> as children will, and laying up harm for many.
> For if some passing traveller brushes, unknowing,
> against their nest, the wasps with valiant hearts
> all come flying out to defend their children.
> In spirit and fury like these the Myrmidons
> swarmed out from their ships, with ceaseless uproar.

[Hesiod, *Catalogue of Women* fr. 205.]

Myrrha or Smyrna

The mother of a son, ADONIS, born of her incestuous passion for her own father. She was usually said to be the daughter of CINYRAS, king of Cyprus, and Cenchreis, though sometimes of Theias, king of the Assyrians. It was APHRODITE who punished the girl by making her fall in love with her own father, either because Cenchreis had boasted that her daughter was more beautiful than the goddess, or because Myrrha herself had neglected Aphrodite's rites. Ovid *(Metamorphoses* 10.298–514) gives the best-known version of Myrrha's story. She was very beautiful and courted by many suitors, but the only man she desired was her father, and with a consuming passion. Animals mated indiscriminately with each other, she reasoned to herself, so why not humans? And yet she was ashamed of her love, knowing it to be wrong. At last, despairing, and seeing no possible ease from her torment, she decided to hang herself. But her horrified nurse caught her in the act and wrung the truth from her. Wishing only to ease her mistress' pain, she persuaded Cinyras to sleep with Myrrha by telling him that a young girl was in love with him and longed to share his bed. So he lay with her, not knowing in the darkness that this was his own daughter. For many nights she came to him in the dark, but at last he wanted to see her face and brought in a lamp. Appalled by the truth, he took his sword to Myrrha, but she escaped from him and fled far away from the palace.

She was pregnant, and for nine months she wandered the world in sorrow. At last, weary of life and yet afraid of death, she prayed to the gods to change her into something other than she was. They transformed her into a myrrh tree, and the drops of myrrh that flow from her trunk are thought to be her tears as she weeps for her sad fate. The goddess of childbirth brought forth her baby, Adonis, from the tree trunk, and the nymphs laid him on the soft grass and bathed him in his mother's tears.

Myrtilus

A son of HERMES. Myrtilus was the charioteer of OENOMAUS, king of Pisa in Elis, who was in the habit of challenging all his daughter's suitors to a chariot-race and killing them when they lost. Myrtilus betrayed his master and helped PELOPS to win his race with Oenomaus and the hand of Hippodameia. The precise details of the story vary (though the result was always the same, and Myrtilus died because of his treachery). Either Myrtilus himself was in love with Hippodameia, so he supported her cause after she had fallen in love with Pelops on sight; or he was bribed by Pelops, who promised him a share in the kingdom and a night in Hippodameia's bed; or bribed by Hippodameia herself with the promise of a night of love. Whatever his motive, he was persuaded to abet Pelops in his attempt to win the chariot-race, and he did this either by removing the bronze linchpins from the wheels of Oenomaus' chariot, or – perhaps more plausibly – by replacing them with pins of wax, so that the chariot foundered when the king was in hot pursuit of his (he hoped) latest victim. Oenomaus was killed, but with his dying breath he cursed his treacherous charioteer, wishing on him death at the hands of the man he had befriended.

This is exactly what happened. Pelops killed him in one version when he found him trying to rape Hippodameia; in another when Hippodameia falsely accused Myrtilus of rape; and in yet another to get out of paying the promised reward for his treachery. Whatever Pelops' motive, he murdered Myrtilus by hurling him into the sea, perhaps south of Attica where the waters were said to be named the Sea of Myrto after him. Then just as he himself had been cursed, Myrtilus cursed his own murderer with his last breath, a curse that was brought to fulfilment by his father Hermes among Pelops' descendants (*see* ATREUS). Hermes also immortalised his son in the stars as the constellation Auriga.

[Sophocles, *Electra* 504–15; Euripides, *Orestes* 988–1000; Apollodorus, *Epitome* 2.6–8.]

N

Naiads *see* NYMPHS.

Narcissus

The beautiful son of the river-god Cephissus and a nymph, Liriope. His story is memorably told by Ovid (*Metamorphoses* 3.339–510). When he was a baby, Liriope asked the blind prophet TEIRESIAS, then little-known, whether her son would live to a ripe old age, and he replied: 'Yes, if he never comes to know himself.' At the time this prophecy seemed inexplicable, but when years later it was proved true, Teiresias became famous and his reputation thereafter was assured. Narcissus reached his sixteenth year and was so beautiful that many fell in love with him, both youths and girls, but he scorned them all. Among these lovers was the nymph ECHO, but she had been punished by Hera for her talkativeness, and could now say nothing except repeat the last words spoken by others. Narcissus spurned her too, so that she wasted away until only her plaintive voice was left. Finally one of his rejected suitors prayed that Narcissus himself might fall in love unrequitedly, and NEMESIS heard, and granted the prayer.

There was a clear pool, with shining, silvery waters, where shepherds never came, nor goats, nor cattle. Its peace was undisturbed, and around it was a grassy sward, kept ever green by the waters. Sheltering woods encircled it and made it always cool, even in the fiercest sun. Here Narcissus came, wearied with hunting, and lay down to drink. When he saw his beauty reflected in the still surface of the pool, he fell in love with himself. Spellbound, he stayed stretched on the grass, gazing at his own image and falling more deeply in love as day followed day. Again and again he leaned down to clasp the beautiful image in his arms, but always it eluded him. He stayed there, caring nothing for food and drink, and slowly wasted away, until at last he laid down his weary head on the grass, and died. Even in Hades he kept looking at himself in the waters of the River Styx. Those who mourned him on earth prepared his funeral, but his body could nowhere be found. In its place grew a flower with a circle of white petals around a yellow centre.

Pausanias saw the pool of Narcissus on Mount Helicon, but declared the story that he fell in love with himself to be nonsense (9.31.6–9). He preferred a rationalised version of the myth: that Narcissus had been in love with his twin-sister who looked exactly like himself. Then she died, and afterwards he found consolation in looking into the pool at the reflection that was just like his lost love.

The fate of Narcissus has been of all Ovid's stories one of the most inspirational to postclassical artists. He has been frequently evoked in literature, particularly poetry, and has been painted by Tintoretto, Caravaggio, Poussin, Claude, and Turner, among many others. Cellini's famous statue shows him sitting on the edge of his pool. Freud found Narcissus, like Oedipus, a potent mythical figure, and produced a detailed study on the theme of 'narcissism', or self-adoration and self-absorption.

Nauplius (1) ('Seafarer')

The son of POSEIDON and AMYMONE, daughter of Danaus. He founded the city of Nauplia and became a famous navigator and slave-trader. When AUGE gave birth to Telephus after being seduced by Heracles, her father Aleus gave her to Nauplius to sell overseas, but he gave her instead to Teuthras, king of Teuthrania, who married her. When CATREUS learnt from an oracle that one of his children would kill him, he gave two of his daughters, AEROPE and Clymene, to Nauplius to sell abroad, but instead Nauplius gave Aerope to either Atreus or Pleisthenes, and himself married Clymene. She bore him three sons, PALAMEDES, OEAX and Nausimedon. Palamedes was falsely charged with treason and stoned to death by the Greeks at Troy, so Nauplius went there to protest against his son's unjust death. He was sent away by AGAMEMNON after achieving no kind of satisfaction, and returned home frustrated and embittered, planning his revenge. It was said that he visited the homes of the Greek leaders and turned three of their wives to adultery: Agamemnon's wife CLYTEMNESTRA with Aegisthus, IDOMENEUS' wife Meda with Leucus, and Aegialeia, wife of DIOMEDES (2), with Cometes. (We are not told how Nauplius achieved his aim – perhaps by tales of sexual infidelities at Troy.) Each of these three affairs led to exile or death for the cuckolded husband. It was sometimes said that Nauplius told Odysseus' mother, ANTICLEIA, that her son was dead, and she hanged herself in grief.

Nauplius also achieved a more general revenge on the Greeks. When they were sailing home from Troy at the end of the war, he rowed out alone to Cape Caphareus at the southern end of Euboea and there lit beacon fires. In the midst of a great storm sent by the gods (*see* AJAX (2)) these fires, promising safe harbour, lured the fleet to destruction on the cruel rocks. Nauplius himself killed any man who reached shore alive. Apollodorus adds that Nauplius made a practice of lighting beacon fires to wreck ships (presumably for their cargoes), and that he himself somehow died in the same fashion, deceived by a false light.

The foregoing events are attributed by ancient writers to the life of Nauplius (1), even though he lived some generations before the Trojan War. Apollodorus (2.1.5) explains the chronological discrepancy by saying that he lived to a great age. NAUPLIUS (2) would in fact more plausibly be 'Nauplius the Wrecker', but no classical writer seems to have thus identified him.

[Euripides, *Helen* 766–7, 1126–31; Apollodorus 2.1.5, 2.7.4, 3.2.2, *Epitome* 6.7–11; Pausanias 4.35.2; Seneca, *Agamemnon* 557–75.]

Nauplius (2)

One of the ARGONAUTS, a descendant of NAUPLIUS (1), and like him an expert seaman. Apollonius (*Argonautica* 1.133–8) gives the genealogy Nauplius (1) – Proetus – Lernus – Naubolus – Clytoneus – Nauplius (2).

Nausicaa

The young and lovely daughter of ALCINOUS and ARETE, king and queen of the Phaeacians on the fantasy-island of SCHERIA. She is the heroine of one of the most famous episodes in the *Odyssey*, when she helps the shipwrecked and destitute ODYSSEUS to get safely home to Ithaca (6.1–8.468). Influenced by Athena in a dream, Nausicaa goes with her maids down to the river-mouth to do the

Fig. 95 **Watched by Athena, Odysseus tries to cover his nakedness with a branch as he approaches Nausicaa.**

family washing, and while waiting for the clothes to dry they play ball. Their cries awaken Odysseus, who has been sleeping in the bushes and now comes out of hiding (fig. 95), naked but for the scanty covering given by a branch (6.130–9):

... like a mountain lion, trusting in his strength,
who goes on his way, buffeted by wind and rain,
his eyes blazing; he goes after cattle or sheep,
or after wild deer, and hunger drives him on
into a strong-built sheepfold to try for the flocks;
so Odysseus was ready to meet the lovely-haired girls,
even though naked, for he was in great need.
But to them he seemed fearsome, all encrusted with brine,
and they fled this way and that along the jutting shores.
Only Alcinous' daughter stood her ground ...

Odysseus charms Nausicaa with honeyed words, and she supplies him with clothes and food and drink, then takes him back to the city, telling him how to win the help of her parents. Alcinous and Arete entertain him royally in their palace, then give him many fine gifts and provide him with a Phaeacian ship to take him home to Ithaca. Nausicaa has fallen half in love with Odysseus and admits to herself that she would like to marry him. Alcinous too would be very happy to have him for a son-in-law. But Odysseus wishes only to return home to his dearly loved wife, PENELOPE. As he himself says to Nausicaa, 'There is nothing more steadfast or secure than when a man and woman of like mind share a home together'

Fig. 96 Heracles wrestles with the Nemean Lion, watched by Athena and Iolaus, who holds Heracles' weapons.

(6.182–4). He bids Nausicaa farewell, assuring her that he owes her his life and will remember her always.

Samuel Butler argued that the *Odyssey* was written by a woman, and that the figure of Nausicaa was her self-portrait, an idea that has been supported to some extent by Robert Graves (*Greek Myths*, vol. 2, p. 365).

Nausimedon *see* OEAX.

Nausinous and **Nausithous** *see* CALYPSO.

Neleus

Son of POSEIDON and TYRO, and twin-brother of PELIAS. After the babies were born their mother abandoned them in the wild, but they survived: it was said that Neleus was suckled by a bitch and Pelias by a mare until they were found by a horse-breeder, who took them in and brought them up. When they grew up they learnt their true identity and were reunited with their mother, then discovered that she was being treated with great cruelty by her step-mother, Sidero. The angry twins attacked Sidero, who fled for refuge into a sanctuary of Hera. Pelias slaughtered her on the very altars of the precinct. Later the brothers quarrelled, and Neleus, driven out of Iolcus by Pelias, went to Messenia. Here he was received kindly by his cousin APHAREUS, who gave him many of his coastal lands. Neleus settled in Pylos and made it one of the most flourishing cities in the Greek world. He married the beautiful CHLORIS (1), daughter of Amphion and Niobe, giving many gifts to win her. She bore him a daughter,

Pero (*see* MELAMPUS), and twelve sons including PERICLY-MENUS (2), the eldest, and NESTOR, the youngest.

When HERACLES killed Iphitus, he came to Pylos to be purified of the murder by Neleus, but Neleus refused to help because of his friendship for Iphitus' father, EURYTUS (1). Later Heracles came back with an armed force to exact his revenge, and in the ensuing battle he slaughtered Neleus and eleven of his twelve sons. Nestor was the sole survivor, and this only because he was away in Gerenia at the time. He became king of Pylos in his father's place.

From one of Nestor's long, rambling stories in the *Iliad* (11.670–761), it seems that, according to Homer, Neleus himself also survived the massacre, and as an old man fought the people of Elis and won a great many spoils from them. According to the Corinthians, Neleus died of disease in Corinth during the reign of SISYPHUS and was buried in a secret grave near the Isthmus.

[Hesiod, *Catalogue of Women* fr. 33a; Apollodorus 1.9.8–9, 2.6.2, 2.7.3; Pausanias 2.2.2, 4.2.5, 4.36.1–3, 6.25.2–3, 9.36.8.]

Nemean Lion

HERACLES' first Labour (*see* LABOURS OF HERACLES) for EURYSTHEUS was to bring him the skin of the Nemean Lion. This was no ordinary lion, but the monstrous offspring of monstrous parents: Hesiod names its mother as either ECHIDNA or the CHIMAERA (*Theogony* 326–32, with the pronoun at 326 being ambiguous) and its father as ORTHUS, the hound of Geryon; while Apollodorus (2.5.1) names its father as the monster TYPHON. HERA nurtured the beast and settled it in the foothills of Nemea in the Argolid, where it terrorised the neighbourhood, invincibly preying on the inhabitants and their herds.

On his way to Nemea Heracles lodged at Cleonae with Molorchus, a poor labourer, who wished to offer a sacrifice to honour his guest. Heracles, however, told him to wait for thirty days, and then to sacrifice either to Zeus the Saviour if he had safely returned from hunting the lion, or to Heracles himself if he had been killed.

Heracles tracked down the lion and shot an arrow at it, but realised, when the arrow bounced into the air, that its hide must be invulnerable to weapons. The lion took refuge in its lair, a cave with two mouths, so Heracles blocked up one entrance and went in by the other. He cast his arms around the lion's neck and choked it to death with his bare hands, then carried its body back to Mycenae. On his journey he once again passed through Cleonae. This being the last of the thirty days, he found Molorchus in the act of sacrificing to him, since he believed him dead. So Heracles sacrificed instead to Zeus the Saviour. He dedicated the Nemean Games in Zeus' honour before continuing on his way.

Eurystheus was so overcome by the sight of the immense lion and by the thought of Heracles' physical prowess that he ordered him never to enter Mycenae again, but to display his trophies outside the city gates. In his fear he even had a great bronze jar made and set in the earth so that he could hide in it if Heracles approached. After this the king employed COPREUS, a son of Pelops, to take his orders to Heracles, since he was too afraid to go in person.

Heracles skinned the lion's body by using its own claws to cut its otherwise impenetrable hide. Ever afterwards he wore its pelt as a trophy, with the beast's scalp serving as a helmet. The lion was immortalised and placed in the stars by Zeus as the constellation Leo, an eternal memorial of his son's first great task.

In ancient art the killing of the Nemean Lion (fig. 96) is the most popular of all Heracles' exploits, with hundreds of representations surviving. Some scenes depict him skinning the beast, and the metopes of the temple of Zeus at Olympia show him wearily resting after his victory. After about 600 BC the lion's pelt becomes his standard costume. Eurystheus' great jar also occurs in art: we see the king hiding inside it when Heracles delivers the Erymanthian Boar (fig. 57) and Cerberus (fig. 37), the monstrous hound of Hades.

[Homer, *Iliad* 15.639–40; Bacchylides, *Odes* 9.6–9, 13.46–54; Sophocles, *Women of Trachis* 1090–4; Diodorus Siculus 4.11.3–4; Pausanias 3.18.15, 5.11.5; Seneca, *The Madness of Hercules* 944–52.]

Nemesis

Daughter of NYX (Night), and goddess of retribution. She personifies the resentment felt (by gods or men) at anyone who violates the natural order of things, either by breaking a moral law, or by having an excess of some quality, such as riches or happiness or pride. Her best-known shrine was at Rhamnous, in Attica. Here there was a statue of the goddess, said to have been carved by Pheidias from a block of Parian marble once brought to Marathon by the Persians, who intended it to be made into a trophy commemorating their victory over the Greeks. Instead the Greeks were the resounding victors and the Persians' presumption was thereby punished. Nemesis' name is still used for an act of just retribution.

Nemesis would be little more than an abstraction, were it not for her part in the legend of HELEN of Troy. Although Helen was usually said to be the daughter, by ZEUS, of LEDA, there is also a rather different tradition, first found in the Epic Cycle's *Cypria*, in which her mother was Nemesis. Zeus pursued Nemesis with amorous intent, while she did her utmost to escape his embraces by changing her shape (Athenaeus 8.334b–d):

Over the earth and the black barren water
she fled, and Zeus pursued, for his heart longed
to have her. Now she took the form of a fish
and stirred the deep waters, speeding through
the waves of the loud-roaring sea, and now along
the river of Ocean, and the far ends of the earth,
and now across the furrowed land, becoming
such dread beasts as live there, trying to escape.

Apollodorus records the sequel (3.10.7): Nemesis changed into a goose, whereupon Zeus turned himself into a swan and mated with her. As a result of this union Nemesis laid an egg, which a shepherd found in a wood and presented to Leda. She put it carefully in a chest until it hatched, then brought up Helen as her own daughter. The story was in some way parodied in Cratinus' lost comedy, *Nemesis*, and it was probably known by Sappho, since she says in one of her fragments, 'They say that long ago Leda once found an egg, blue like a hyacinth.'

Perhaps Nemesis was said to be Helen's real mother because of all the grief and death that Helen brought on the Greeks by setting in train the war at Troy. Or it may be that it made a parallel with the mating of PELEUS and THETIS, where once again a goddess changed herself into many different shapes so as to avoid intercourse: one union generated the woman for whom the Trojan War was fought, and the other its greatest hero, ACHILLES.

[Homer, *Iliad* 3.156, 6.335, *Odyssey* 1.350, 2.136; Hesiod, *Theogony* 223–4; Herodotus 1.34; Sophocles, *Electra* 792, *Philoctetes* 601–2; Pausanias 1.33.2–8, 7.5.3.]

Neoptolemus

Son of ACHILLES and Deidameia, conceived while his father was living, disguised as a girl, at the court of LYCOMEDES on the island of Scyros. Achilles left to fight in the Trojan War, so the boy was brought up by his mother and grandfather and named Pyrrhus ('red-haired'). After Achilles' death at Troy, the Greeks learnt from the Trojan seer HELENUS the conditions necessary for capturing the city, two of which were the presence both of Pyrrhus and of PHILOCTETES, who owned the great bow and arrows of Heracles. ODYSSEUS and PHOENIX (3) journeyed to Scyros to fetch Pyrrhus, who willingly joined them and was renamed by Phoenix Neoptolemus, 'young warrior'. Odysseus presented him with the armour that had belonged to his dead father (fig. 97) and over which such dissension had raged between himself and AJAX (1). Neoptolemus then helped to fetch the wounded Philoctetes from the island of Lemnos.

The young man fought valiantly at Troy, killing many of the enemy including EURYPYLUS (2), the son of Telephus. True to Helenus' prediction, Troy soon fell to the

Greeks, with Neoptolemus being one of the warriors in the WOODEN HORSE, the instrument of the city's capture. He was also traditionally seen as one of the most ruthless of the Greeks who now put the Trojans to the sword, killing many, including old King PRIAM (figs. 27 and 123), Hector's little son ASTYANAX, and Priam's son POLITES (1). He also sacrificed Priam's daughter POLYXENA at the grave of Achilles (fig. 120), whose ghost demanded her as his war-prize.

Neoptolemus' own war-spoils were the seer Helenus and Hector's widow ANDROMACHE. He left Troy accompanied by Phoenix, but the old man died on the journey and Neoptolemus buried him. Thanks to the advice of either Helenus or his grandmother THETIS, he made a safe journey from Troy, avoiding the great storm at Cape Caphareus that destroyed most of the Greek fleet (*see* AJAX(2)). In one version he settled in Epeirus, where the people were called Molossians after his son by Andromache, Molossus, and the land was ruled for many generations by his descendants, one of whom was Olympias, the mother of Alexander the Great. According to Homer, Neoptolemus returned to his father's land of Phthia and married Menelaus' daughter HERMIONE. In one tradition, he saved the kingdom and the life of his grandfather PELEUS from the vengeful Acastus and his sons.

There are many different accounts of Neoptolemus' death. Either he went to Delphi to claim redress from APOLLO for killing his father, then in anger plundered the sanctuary and was killed by one of the god's priests, often named Machaereus. Or he went to Delphi to excuse his rashness in accusing the god of Achilles' death, or to dedicate some of the booty from Troy, or to enquire about Hermione's childlessness. While there he was killed in a squabble over sacrificial meat by the temple servants, or by Apollo himself, who was angry over his murder of Priam at the altar of Zeus; or he was slain by some Delphians through the treacherous instigation of Orestes, who wanted to marry Hermione, or by Orestes himself for the same reason. Many and varied are the motives and scenarios of his death, but it is generally agreed that he died by violence, and at Delphi. It is said that he was given the honour of burial under the threshold of Apollo's temple, then was later taken up and buried within the precinct. The traveller Pausanias saw his grave there in the second century BC, and tells us (10.24.6) that the Delphians still offered sacrifice to him every year as a hero.

[Homer, *Iliad* 19.326–33, *Odyssey* 3.188–9, 4.5–9, 11.505–40; Pindar, *Nemean* 7.34–48, *Paean* 6.98–121; Sophocles, *Philoctetes* 343–59; Euripides, *Trojan Women* 1126–30, *Orestes* 1656–7, *Andromache* 49–55, 1085–1165; Apollodorus 3.13.8, *Epitome* 5.10–11, 6.5, 6.12–14, 7.40; Strabo 9.3.9; Pausanias 1.4.4, 1.11.1, 1.13.9, 1.33.8, 2.5.5, 2.23.6, 4.17.4, 10.7.1, 10.24.4; Virgil, *Aeneid* 2.469–558. J. Fontenrose, *The Cult and Myth of Pyrros at Delphi* (1960).]

Nephele (1)

The first wife of ATHAMAS and mother of PHRIXUS and Helle.

Nephele (2)

The cloud that Zeus fashioned in the likeness of Hera to test IXION.

Neptune

Ancient Italian god of water whose festival was celebrated at the hottest and driest time of year, on 23 July. He was later identified with the Greek god of the sea, POSEIDON.

Nereids

Sea-NYMPHS; the fifty (occasionally in later accounts a hundred) daughters of the sea-god NEREUS and the Oceanid Doris. Varying lists of their names are given by Homer (*Iliad* 18.38–49), Hesiod (*Theogony* 240–64), the author of the *Homeric Hymn to Demeter* (417–24) and Apollodorus (1.2.7). Only four of the Nereids – AMPHITRITE, THETIS, PSAMATHE (1) (the only three Nereids to have children) and GALATEA (1) – had any individual role to play in myth, but we often hear of them appearing as a group. The poets picture their life in the sea, either living in its depths in their father's glorious palace, or sporting in the waves among other sea-creatures such as TRITONS and

Fig. 97 **Odysseus presents Neoptolemus with the arms of his dead father, Achilles.**

dolphins. They were renowned for their beauty, so much so that CASSIOPEIA, proud of her own attractions, boasted that she was even lovelier than the Nereids – which made the nymphs angry and POSEIDON send a sea-monster to ravage her land.

They helped the ARGONAUTS by bringing the *Argo* safely through the Wandering Rocks. According to Homer, they came with Thetis from the depths of the sea to mourn the death of PATROCLUS, then again at the death of ACHILLES, when they lamented for seventeen days before his funeral on the eighteenth. In Euripides' *Electra* (442–51), the Chorus sing that the Nereids brought armour made by HEPHAESTUS to Achilles before he set out to fight at Troy, a version of the story different from that of the *Iliad*, where Achilles' original armour came from his father Peleus and only its replacement, after Hector had stripped the first set of arms from the dead Patroclus, came from Hephaestus. But certainly in vase-paintings we see the Nereids, together with Thetis, delivering Achilles' arms, both when he is about to leave his father's house and later at Troy while he mourns Patroclus' death. (This later delivery of the replacement arms may well have been part of the action in Aeschylus' lost play, *Nereides*.) Sometimes the Nereids are shown carrying the armour while riding various forms of sea-life across the ocean.

We also see the Nereids in the background to such episodes as Heracles' wrestling match with their father Nereus; but they appear too in scenes unrelated to any specific story, often with a fish in their hands to denote their watery abode. They were also important figures in arts other than vase-painting, such as sculpture, where the skill and virtuosity of the sculptor can make their drapery seem transparent and the body beneath almost naked. They were popular figures in Roman mosaics and were commonly carved on the sides of Roman sarcophagi, perhaps as symbols of the soul's passing to the Islands of the Blest. The famous Mildenhall Dish in the British Museum (*c*. AD 350), a masterpiece of embossed silver, depicts Nereids with other sea-creatures, and provides a fine example of the grace and rhythm inherent in the sea-nymphs' flowing forms and draperies that would later be captured in Renaissance painting.

The Nereids were also important figures of popular religion (*see* Herodotus 7.191, where offerings are made to them to put an end to a storm); and indeed there is widespread belief in them in modern Greece, where they are still renowned for their beauty and are thought to prophesy the future.

See also fig. 143.

[Homer, *Iliad* 18.35–69, *Odyssey* 24.47–66; Apollonius, *Argonautica* 4.922–64; Apollodorus 2.4.3.]

Fig. 98 The sea-god Nereus rides a hippocamp, a sea-horse with the foreparts of a horse and the tail of a fish.

Nereus

An ancient sea-god, the eldest child of Pontus (Sea) and GAIA (Earth), thus belonging to the pre-Olympian generation of gods and older than the great sea-god, POSEIDON. By the Oceanid Doris, Nereus was the father of the NEREIDS, with whom he lived in the depths of the sea. He is given, along with PROTEUS and PHORCYS, the name of Old Man of the Sea. Hesiod describes him as 'truthful and honest ... trusty and gentle, never forgetting what is right in the sight of the gods, and ever thinking just and kindly thoughts' (*Theogony* 233–6). Like other sea-deities he had both the gift of prophecy and the ability to change his shape. HERACLES, needing to find out the way to the remote garden of the HESPERIDES, leapt on Nereus while he slept, then wrestled with him while the sea-god turned himself into many different shapes. But Heracles held on through all these transformations, refusing to release him until the Old Man told him what he needed.

Nereus occurs fairly frequently in ancient art and is depicted as both fish-tailed and fully human (fig. 98). He is shown wrestling with Heracles while changing his shape (snake, lion, fire), and looking on in other scenes of myth, such as Heracles wrestling with TRITON, or PELEUS wrestling with the Nereid THETIS. On the François Krater Nereus, as father of the bride, attends the wedding of Peleus and Thetis, bringing gifts.

[Homer, *Iliad* 1.357–9, 18.35–50; Apollodorus 2.5.11; Horace, *Odes* 1.15.]

Nessus

One of the CENTAURS. He acted as a ferryman at the River Evenus, and was killed there when he tried to rape DEIANEIRA in ferrying her across the river (figs. 46 and 99): HERACLES shot him with one of his unerring arrows,

Fig.99 Heracles is about to kill Nessus, grabbing him by the hair and planting his foot on his victim's back. The Centaur touches his chin, supplicating for mercy.

tipped with the poisonous blood that he had taken from another of his victims, the HYDRA OF LERNA. As Nessus lay dying, determined to get revenge on his killer, he told Deianeira that the blood from his wound would act as a powerful love-charm if it were ever needed. She took some, unaware that mixed with the blood was the Hydra's deadly venom. Years later she smeared it on a robe (often called the 'shirt of Nessus'), when she thought that she had lost Heracles' love to his new concubine, IOLE. When Heracles wore the robe, the poison ate into his flesh and he died in agony, so at last Nessus had his revenge.

Nestor

The youngest of twelve sons of NELEUS and CHLORIS (1), and the only one to survive the massacre by HERACLES at Pylos, apparently because Nestor was at that time in Gerenia, a town in Laconia where some say that he was brought up. We get our most vivid picture of Nestor from Homer's detailed and affectionate portrait of the old man in the *Iliad*: he is clearly one of the poet's favourite characters. Nestor is king of Pylos in the south-western Peloponnese. He has come to the TROJAN WAR, accompanied by his sons ANTILOCHUS and THRASYMEDES and bringing ninety ships, even though he is now a very old man, by far the oldest of the Greek leaders. Despite his great age he is still strong and he fights valiantly in battle, but he is most of all valued for his advice. This he is always ready

to give in any situation, and often at great length. But he is a persuasive speaker: 'From his tongue flowed words sweeter than honey', says Homer (1.248–9). Nestor tries to make peace between ACHILLES and AGAMEMNON in their furious quarrel, though in vain, and he later suggests the Embassy to Achilles, selecting the ambassadors and giving them many instructions. He also suggests the night-time spying-raid on the Trojans' camp in which DOLON is killed. He even offers to his son Antilochus much wordy advice on chariot-racing at the funeral games for Patroclus, admitting before he begins that what he has to say is superfluous.

His garrulity extends to an immense fondness for long, rambling stories of the distant past, rich in reminiscences of his own great achievements. He tells how he fought mightily against the CENTAURS, in the company of such fine heroes as THESEUS and PEIRITHOUS, and how he performed valorous deeds in war against the Epeians: 'I charged at them like a black hurricane, capturing fifty chariots, and from each one two men bit the dust, brought down by my spear' (11.747–9). He killed the Arcadian hero Ereuthalion (*see* LYCURGUS (2)), and almost killed the awesome MOLIONES. He performed outstandingly at the funeral games of Amarynceus, winning the boxing, the wrestling, the spear-throwing and the footrace: 'Here there was no man like me', he says, 'not among the Epeians, nor among the Pylians themselves, nor among the great-hearted Aetolians ...' (23.632–3). But however long-winded his stories or his advice, he is always heard out by his comrades with patience, and indeed with respect. Agamemnon says to him, 'By father Zeus, and Athene, and Apollo, I wish that I had ten such advisers among the Greeks, for then the city of Priam would soon fall beneath our hands, captured and sacked' (2.371–4). Thus Nestor is depicted as a highly respected elder statesman, the archetypal wise old man.

Nestor also appeared in epics other than the *Iliad*. In the lost *Cypria*, he went round Greece with MENELAUS at the start of the Trojan War, assembling leaders for the expedition. In the lost *Aethiopis*, his son Antilochus was killed by the great hero MEMNON, leader of the Ethiopians, who had come to help the Trojans after the death of Hector. Pindar adds (*Pythian* 6.28–42) that Antilochus died in saving the life of his father, whose chariot had foundered after one of its horses had been shot by Paris. In the *Odyssey*, the ghost of Agamemnon tells how Nestor, still the wise old adviser, stopped the Greeks from panicking at the death of Achilles, when Thetis and her sea-nymph attendants arose lamenting from the sea. Here too we see Nestor himself, now safely back at home in Pylos, where TELEMACHUS comes seeking news of his father Odysseus. Once again the old man is in reminiscent vein, telling of the homecoming of the surviving Greek heroes after the sack of Troy. He himself, he says, realised that some kind of disaster was imminent and sailed away ahead of most of the others, thus narrowly missing the tremendous storm that wrecked so much of the Greek fleet (*see* AJAX (2)).

At Troy Nestor had a concubine, Hecamede, who was given him as his prize of war when Achilles stormed Tenedos. He was married to Eurydice, the daughter of Clymenus (Homer), or to Anaxibia (Apollodorus), and was father of seven sons and two daughters, POLYCASTE and Peisidice. We are told nothing of how he eventually died, and must imagine him living out the rest of his life at Pylos, peacefully into extreme old age. He had ruled through three generations of men.

The huge Mycenean 'Palace of Nestor' has been excavated near Pylos. Its many rooms include a spacious throne room, some 12.90 m. by 11.20 m., with a great ceremonial hearth in the centre. Fragments of frescoes and many pots and Linear B tablets have been found. The 'Cup of Nestor' in the National Museum at Athens, a gold cup with a dove on each of its two handles, was in fact found at Mycenae and was so named because it resembles Nestor's cup described by Homer (*Iliad* 11.632–5): '... a magnificent cup which the old man had brought from home. Pierced with nails of gold, it had four handles, and on each handle two golden doves were feeding.'

[Homer, *Iliad* 1.247–84, 2.336–74, 591–602, 4.293–325, 8.80–158, 9.93–181, 10.73–253, 11.510–802, 14.1–134, 23.301–50, 615–50, *Odyssey* 3.4–485, 24.43–57; Apollodorus 1.9.9, 2.7.3; Pausanias 2.26.8–10; Quintus of Smyrna, *Sequel to Homer* 2.243–341; Ovid, *Metamorphoses* 8.365–9.]

Nicostratus

A son of MENELAUS and HELEN, perhaps born to them after the Trojan War. Pausanias says that he was the son of Menelaus by a slave-woman, and that he and his brother Megapenthes drove Helen out of Sparta after Menelaus' death, with the result that she died in Rhodes (*see* POLYXO (2)). The Spartan throne passed to Orestes.

[Hesiod, *Catalogue of Women* fr. 192; Apollodorus 3.11.1; Pausanias 2.18.6, 3.19.9.]

Nike

The goddess of Victory, daughter of the Titan PALLAS (2) and the Oceanid STYX. She and her siblings Zelus (Aspiration), Cratos (Power) and BIA (Might) were the constant companions of ZEUS, an honour accorded them after they and their mother supported Zeus in his battle with the

TITANS. Pheidias' colossal statue of Zeus at Olympia showed the god holding in his right hand a Nike, made of ivory and gold like the statue itself, and at the foot of his throne were several representations of the goddess dancing. In surviving art, Nike is shown winged and flying at great speed, with thin, swirling drapery. Perhaps her most famous portrayal is as the Winged Victory of Samothrace, a magnificent eight-foot high statue, dating from about 190 BC, now standing on the main staircase of the Louvre in Paris (fig. 100). The huge figure, with wings outstretched, originally showed Nike alighting on a ship's prow, and was set in the upper basin of a great fountain to commemorate a victory at sea.

[Hesiod, *Theogony* 383–403; Bacchylides, *Ode* 11.1–7; Pausanias 1.22.4, 3.15.7, 5.11.1–2.]

Niobe (1)

Daughter of PHORONEUS and the nymph Teledice. She was the first mortal woman with whom ZEUS had intercourse,

Fig. 100 **The Winged Victory (Nike) of Samothrace.**

and bore him ARGUS (2) and, according to Acousilaus, PELASGUS.

[Apollodorus 2.1.1.]

Niobe (2)

Daughter of TANTALUS (1), king of Sipylus in Lydia, and wife of AMPHION, king of Thebes, to whom she bore many children. The number varies from author to author, more often than not with the total figure made up of an equal number of males and females. Homer, for instance, said that there were twelve, six sons and six daughters; seven and seven said Aeschylus, Sophocles, Euripides, Apollodorus and Ovid; nine and nine said Sappho; ten and ten said Bacchylides and Pindar; while Hesiod said either ten and ten or nine and ten. But although the numbers varied, the aftermath was always the same: Niobe boasted that she was superior to the goddess LETO, who had only two children, whereupon the offended goddess sent her son and daughter to earth to avenge the insult. APOLLO shot all Niobe's sons while they were out hunting on Cithaeron, and ARTEMIS shot all her daughters in the house (though sometimes it was said that there were either one or two survivors – see Apollodorus 3.5.6, where the eldest girl, CHLORIS (1), who later married NELEUS, is said to have survived). Niobe, in her grief, went back to her father's land, and there she was turned into a rock on Mount Sipylus, an image of everlasting sorrow with water flowing down her face like tears.

The earliest mention of Niobe is in the *Iliad*, where ACHILLES uses her as an example to the grieving PRIAM of the need to eat, even in the midst of great sorrow (24.599–620). Homer seems to have adapted Niobe's story to suit Priam's situation, for he says that after her children were killed they lay unburied for nine days because Zeus had turned the people to stone, then on the tenth day the gods themselves buried them (just as the gods are concerned to have Priam's son, HECTOR, buried, after Achilles has for many days refused to release his body). Niobe ate, though she was 'worn out with weeping', just as Priam is being urged to eat by Achilles. Then, too, Priam will still lament his son on his return to Troy, just as Niobe continues to mourn.

Statius says that Niobe carried the ashes of her twelve children in twelve urns to be buried on Mount Sipylus, though Pausanias reports that the tomb of Niobe's children was to be seen at Thebes. He was also familiar with the rock that was Niobe, and says that this was a natural formation looking something like a woman.

Both Aeschylus and Sophocles wrote *Niobe* tragedies, now lost. Papyrus fragments of Sophocles' play make it clear that both Apollo and Artemis appeared on stage to hunt down the daughters (the sons having apparently been killed elsewhere), with Apollo pointing out to his sister one girl who is hiding and must not be allowed to escape. The dramatic impact of this must have been considerable. The deaths of the children and the grief of the mother are popular subjects in ancient art, especially in the many Roman copies of Hellenistic sculpture, and popular too in postclassical art. In Shakespeare, Hamlet describes his mother, grieving at his father's death, as 'like Niobe, all tears' (I. ii. 129). Niobe remains to this day a symbol of loss and grief.

[Hesiod, *Catalogue of Women* fr. 183; Sophocles, *Antigone* 822–32, *Electra* 150–2; Euripides, *Phoenician Women* 159–60; Diodorus Siculus 4.74; Pausanias 1.21.3, 2.21.9, 5.11.2, 9.16.7; Ovid, *Metamorphoses* 6.146–312; Statius, *Thebaid* 6.124–5.]

Nireus

The son of Charopus and Aglaia who led three ships from Syme, a small island north of Rhodes, to the TROJAN WAR. He was a weak and unwarlike man, and had few troops following him; but he was renowned for one special gift: after peerless ACHILLES, he was the handsomest man at Troy. He was killed there by EURYPYLUS (2), but became proverbial for his beauty.

[Homer, *Iliad* 2.671–5; Euripides, *Iphigeneia at Aulis* 204–5; Lucian, *Dialogues of the Dead* 5, 30; Quintus of Smyrna, *Sequel to Homer* 6.368–89, 7.1–16.]

Nisus (1)

Son of PANDION (2), the king of Athens who was exiled by the sons of Metion. After Pandion's death his own sons expelled the usurpers, and AEGEUS, as the eldest, took the throne of Athens, while Nisus became King of Megara. He is best known for having a daughter, Scylla, by whose treachery he died when MINOS, king of Crete, was waging war with his city. Nisus had in his hair either a red tress, or else a single red hair, on which his life depended. This was cut off by Scylla while he slept, either because she had fallen in love with Minos, or because she had been bribed with a Cretan necklace of gold. She expected gratitude from Minos, but instead he was filled with disgust at this betrayal of her father. He tied her to the stern of his ship and dragged her behind it until she drowned, or else he sailed away and she drowned while trying to swim after him. Nisus was turned into a sea eagle, and Scylla into a sea-bird pursued for ever by her vengeful father.

[Aeschylus, *Libation-Bearers* 612–22; Apollodorus 3.15.5–8; Pausanias 1.5.4, 1.19.4, 1.39.4–6, 2.34.7; ps.-Virgil, *Ciris*; Propertius 3.19.21–8; Ovid, *Metamorphoses* 8.6–151.]

Nisus (2)

Son of Hyrtacus, who was an ally of King Priam in the Trojan War. Nisus' legend stems from Virgil's account in the *Aeneid* (5.294–361, 9.176–445). Nisus survived the war and accompanied AENEAS to Italy. He was the constant companion of the beautiful youth Euryalus, whom he loved. Side by side the two went into battle together. They took part in the foot race at the funeral games for Anchises, and when Nisus fell, he ensured that his friend won the race by bringing down his chief competitor. They also took part together in a night raid against the sleeping enemy and left behind them many dead; but here the outcome was tragic, for as they returned to camp Euryalus lost his way in the woods and was captured by an enemy troop. Nisus ran to save his friend, but too late, and had to watch him brutally killed by the leader, Volcens (9.433–7):

> Euryalus rolled writhing in death, and the blood
> flowed over his lovely limbs, his neck drooped
> and his head sank on his shoulders, like a scarlet flower
> wilting and dying when cut by the plough, or like
> poppies that droop their heads on tired necks
> when rain weighs them down ...

Full of a lust for vengeance, Nisus fought his way through the thick of the enemy until face to face with Volcens, then killed him even as he himself died, falling on top of the dead body of his friend.

Notus

The warm and moist South Wind and its god. He was the son of EOS, goddess of Dawn, and the Titan Astraeus. Unlike his brothers BOREAS, the North Wind, and ZEPHYRUS, the West Wind, he has no particular mythological story associated with him.

[Hesiod, *Theogony* 378–80, 869–71.]

Numa Pompilius

The legendary second king of Rome, successor to ROMULUS. Numa traditionally ruled 715–673 BC, a long reign of peace. He was credited with the foundation of the Roman religious system and the reform of the Roman calendar, inspired, it was said, with wise advice from his lover, the water-nymph EGERIA.

[Dionysius of Halicarnassus 2.62–76; Plutarch, *Numa*; Livy 1.18–21.]

Numitor

A king of Alba Longa, deposed by his younger brother Amulius, but later restored to power by his grandsons ROMULUS AND REMUS.

Nycteus

Either the son of Chthonius, one of the 'Sown Men' of Thebes, or of Hyrieus and the nymph Clonia. Certainly he was the brother of LYCUS (1) and the father of ANTIOPE (1), who bore Amphion and Zethus to Zeus. Nycteus' daughter Nycteis married Cadmus' son Polydorus, the third king of Thebes, and bore him a son, LABDACUS. Nycteus became regent of Thebes when Polydorus died, Labdacus being still a child.

When Antiope became pregnant by Zeus, she fled from Nycteus' anger to Sicyon where the king, EPOPEUS (1), gave her refuge and married her. Either Nycteus led the Thebans against Sicyon and was mortally wounded during the ensuing battle, or he killed himself from shame and grief. Dying, he charged his brother Lycus with the task of punishing Antiope and Epopeus.

[Apollodorus 3.5.5, 3.10.1; Pausanias 2.6.1–4, 9.5.5.]

Nyctimene

Daughter of Epopeus, king of Lesbos. When her father had sex with her, she fled in shame to the woods, hiding herself away, so that Athena took pity on her and turned her into a night-bird (*nyct-*, night), the owl. This is why owls shun the daylight and only come out at night.

[Ovid, *Metamorphoses* 2.589–95.]

Nyctimus *see* LYCAON (1).

Nymphs (Greek *nymphe*, 'young girl', 'bride')

Female spirits of nature, either immortal or very long-lived, who dwelt in a particular place or natural phenomenon, usually in the countryside (though not always: there was, for instance, a fountain house sacred to the Nymphs in the Agora at Athens). They were visualised as beautiful young girls with an amorous disposition. There were several categories of nymphs, depending on where they dwelt. Oreads were mountain-nymphs (*oros*); Alseids were nymphs of groves (*alsos*); and Naiads were water-nymphs, living in springs, lakes or streams, and were often the daughters of the god of the river in which they lived. There were several kinds of tree-nymphs: Dryads, originally nymphs of oak trees (*drys*); Hamadryads, who were thought to live in a particular tree and to die with it; and Meliads, who were the nymphs of ash trees (*melia*) and were sprung from the drops of blood that fell on the earth when CRONUS hacked off the genitals of Uranus. NEREIDS were sea-nymphs, daughters of the Old Man of the Sea, Nereus; and OCEANIDS were the three thousand daughters of OCEANUS and Tethys, though were themselves only sometimes connected with the sea.

Nymphs had a widespread cult that continued into Roman times. Rather like the fairies of folklore, they had harmful as well as life-enhancing powers: HYLAS was drowned, DAPHNIS blinded, and HERMAPHRODITUS destroyed by nymphs for being unresponsive lovers. They themselves were often amorously involved (willingly or unwillingly) with gods or men: DAPHNE, ECHO, CALLISTO, SYRINX, AEGINA, CALYPSO and Eurydice, the wife of ORPHEUS, were all nymphs. Many a heroic genealogy has a nymph at its head as founder of the family.

Nymphs appear first in Homer, who calls them the daughters of ZEUS. In the *Iliad*, when Themis calls the gods to an assembly, all the nymphs of groves, springs and meadows are present. In the *Odyssey*, nymphs sport with ARTEMIS in the mountains, and flush out goats for ODYSSEUS and his men to catch; and Odysseus, when brought to Ithaca, is left sleeping in a cave of the nymphs, to whom he prays on waking. Thereafter nymphs appear frequently in literature and art, traditionally linked with the shepherds of ARCADIA and often associated with gods. They dance with PAN; they watch over the flocks with APOLLO and HERMES; they take part in the revel rout of DIONYSUS and consort with SATYRS AND SILENS; as virgins they hunt with Artemis in the wild. A vivid picture is given of their lives in the *Homeric Hymn to Aphrodite*, when the goddess tells ANCHISES that their son AENEAS will be reared by the nymphs who dwell on Mount Ida (259–72):

They rank neither with
mortals nor immortals:
long indeed do they live, eating the food
of heaven and dancing among the gods,
and the silens and watchful Hermes lie with them
in the depths of lovely caves. But at their time
of birth, pines or high-crowned oaks spring up
on the fruitful earth, trees beautiful and flourishing,

towering high on the high mountains,
and men call them precincts of the gods,
and never cut them down; but when
their allotted time of death is near at hand,
first these lovely trees wither upon the earth
and their bark shrivels up
and their branches fall away,
and then with the trees the souls of the nymphs
leave the light of the sun.

[Homer, *Iliad* 20.8–9, *Odyssey* 6.105–8, 122–4, 9.154–5, 13.103–4, 347–50, 355–60, 17.210–11, 240–6; Hesiod, *Theogony* 129–30, 184–7; *Homeric Hymn* 19.19–23, 26.3–10; Callimachus, *Hymn* 4.79–85; Pausanias 8.4.2; Ovid, *Fasti* 4.231–2.]

Nyx

The personification of Night, and its goddess. Homer (*Iliad* 14.256–61) makes it clear that she was an important divinity, whom even Zeus respected and dared not offend. In Hesiod's scheme of things in the *Theogony* (123–5), Nyx and her brother EREBUS (Darkness) were born of CHAOS, the primeval void. Then Erebus mated with Nyx – the very first sexual union – to produce AETHER (Brightness) and HEMERA (Day). From Nyx alone were born a whole series of powerful abstract forces (211–25): Moros (Fate), Ker (Doom), THANATOS (Death), HYPNOS (Sleep), the Oneiroi (DREAMS), MOMOS (Blame), Oizus (Misery), the HESPERIDES (Daughters of Evening), the Moirae (FATES), the KERES (Dooms), NEMESIS (Retribution), Apate (Deceit), Philotes (Tenderness), Geras (Old Age), and ERIS (Strife). Nyx lived in TARTARUS, the deepest and darkest part of the Underworld, from which she emerged each evening to bring night to the cosmos just as her daughter Hemera was returning.

Oceanids

Beneficent NYMPHS, the three thousand daughters of OCEANUS and Tethys (Hesiod, *Theogony* 346–66). 'They are scattered far and wide', says Hesiod, 'and everywhere alike they haunt the earth and the depths of the waters' (365–6). Their function, together with APOLLO and their three thousand brothers, all the rivers of the earth, was to care for the young. Few have any individual role to play in myth: they appear in a group, for instance, as the Chorus in Aeschylus' tragedy *Prometheus Bound*. Of the Oceanids named by Hesiod, those with the most significance (often for their role of wife and mother) are STYX, ELECTRA (1), DORIS, CLYMENE (1), CALLIRHOE (1), DIONE, PERSE, METIS and EURYNOME.

Oceanus or Ocean

The eldest of the TITANS, son of Uranus (Heaven) and GAIA (Earth), and god of the great river that was imagined by the early Greeks as completely surrounding the flat earth, marking its furthest bounds to north, east, south and west. (It was only much later that the geographers thought of Ocean as 'the ocean' in the usual sense.) On the far side of Oceanus were the strange and awesome places beyond mortal ken, like the home of the GORGONS, and Erytheia, the land of GERYON, and the garden of the HESPERIDES. HADES (2), the land of the dead, was sometimes thought to be there too, for according to Homer, Odysseus had to cross the river of Ocean to enter the Underworld. The Sun-god HELIOS lived near the banks of Oceanus in the east, every morning driving his chariot of light through the sky from east to west, and every night sailing home along the river of Ocean in a great golden bowl. It was this bowl which HERACLES borrowed when he needed to travel to Erytheia to steal the cattle of Geryon. Oceanus, Geryon's grandfather, sent huge waves to rock the bowl, until Heracles forced him to stop by frightening him with his drawn bow.

Oceanus married his sister-Titan TETHYS, and their three thousand sons were all the rivers that flow upon the earth, and their three thousand daughters the many nymphs of land and waters, the OCEANIDS. On the shield made for Achilles by Hephaestus and described in the *Iliad*, the river of Ocean was depicted on the rim running round the shield, surrounding all the pictures within, just as he surrounded the earth on which men and women worked out their lives. He also formed the rim of the shield in Hesiod's *Shield of Heracles:* 'and over him swans were soaring and crying out loudly, and many others were swimming on the surface of his waters, with shoals of fish surging nearby' (315–7).

In early mythology Oceanus was usually seen more as an element than a person, although he does appear as a character in Aeschylus' tragedy *Prometheus Bound*, sympathising with PROMETHEUS but advising submission to Zeus, and riding on a hippocamp, a sea-monster with the forelegs of a horse and the tail of a fish. He rarely appears in ancient vase-painting, but is depicted at the wedding of THETIS (his granddaughter) and PELEUS on the François Krater and on the Sophilos dinos in the British Museum. Here he has the torso and (horned) head of a man above a long, fishy tail, while Tethys, accompanying him, is shown as purely human. He often appears as a bearded god on Roman sarcophagi.

[Homer, *Iliad* 14.200–10, 246, 18.483–9, 607–8, 20.7–9, 21.193–9, *Odyssey* 11.13, 639, 12.1; Hesiod, *Theogony* 133, 337–70, 787–92; Apollodorus 1.1.3, 1.2.2.]

Ocnus

An industrious man with an extravagant wife who, work as hard as he might, at once spent everything that Ocnus earned. After death he was forced to endure in Hades an eternal task that reiterated his sufferings on earth: he continually plaited a rope, while by him stood a she-ass, eating the rope as fast as he could plait it.

[Diodorus Siculus 1.97.3; Pausanias 10.29.2; Propertius 4.3.21–2.]

Ocypete *see* HARPIES.

Odysseus (Latin Ulixes, hence Ulysses)

King of ITHACA, husband of the faithful PENELOPE, hero of Homer's *Odyssey*, and perhaps the most famous character in the whole of ancient myth. Not surprisingly he was always a popular figure with ancient artists, with the various episodes of his life frequently depicted on vase-paintings from as early as the seventh century BC.

1. THE EARLY YEARS

To Homer, Odysseus was the only son of LAERTES and ANTICLEIA, the daughter of AUTOLYCUS, though many later writers said that his father was the arch-trickster SISYPHUS, who seduced Anticleia after he had caught the master-thief Autolycus stealing his cattle. (This genealogy was felt better to explain Odysseus' cunning, for which he became proverbial.) It was Autolycus who gave Odysseus his name, choosing it because he himself had known much anger (*odussesthai*) in his life. Later, while visiting his grandfather's house and boarhunting with Autolycus' sons, Odysseus received a tusk wound in his leg, leaving the scar by which, many years later, the nurse EURYCLEIA would recognise him on his return to Ithaca after the TROJAN WAR. Another significant journey was to Messenia, where Odysseus was sent while still a boy to recover some stolen sheep. There he met Iphitus, son of the famous archer EURYTUS (1), the late king of Oechalia. The two became friends and exchanged gifts, with Iphitus giving Odysseus the great bow that had belonged to his father. With this bow Odysseus would slay the Suitors who years later invaded his home.

Odysseus joined the many suitors of HELEN, the beautiful daughter of King Tyndareos of Sparta, but he wasted no gifts on her since he was sure that the wealthy MENELAUS would be the chosen bridegroom. Instead he used the situation to win the wife of his choice, Penelope, the daughter of Tyndareos' brother ICARIUS (2). Tyndareos was afraid that violence would break out once one of the suitors was chosen, so he followed Odysseus' advice and made all the suitors swear an oath, vowing to support whoever should win Helen and to defend his marriage-rights. They did so willingly, and when Menelaus was duly chosen the disappointed suitors went peacefully home. Grateful for the good advice, Tyndareos interceded with Icarius on Odysseus' behalf and Penelope became his. But the fateful oath led in the course of time to the Trojan War, and would mean that Odysseus would be away from his home and dear wife for twenty years.

The couple settled on the island of Ithaca and the marriage was a very happy one. They had a son, TELEMACHUS, but while the boy was still a baby the Trojan War began. When Helen ran away to Troy with Paris, Menelaus and his brother AGAMEMNON called on all the rejected suitors to keep their vows and to help fetch her back. Envoys travelled round Greece marshalling troops, and it was the clever PALAMEDES who came to recruit Odysseus from Ithaca. Odysseus was ready for him, since he had learnt from a seer, HALITHERSES, that if he went to Troy he would not return home for twenty years, and then only after much suffering, so he hoped to avoid going to war by pretending to be mad. Palamedes found Odysseus wearing a madman's cap and ploughing his land with two different kinds of animals yoked together – a horse and an ox, or an ox and an ass – and sowing salt. But Palamedes realised that this was merely a ruse, and he proved that Odysseus was in his right mind by threatening little Telemachus: either he put the baby in front of the ploughshare, or he threatened him with his sword, at which Odysseus leapt to save his son. Then, having shown that he was sane, he was obliged to go to war. But he never forgave Palamedes, and in the course of time he had his revenge by contriving the death of the man who had forced him to leave his beloved Ithaca.

[Homer, *Odyssey* 19.392–466, 21.9–41; Hesiod, *Catalogue of Women* fr. 198; Apollodorus 3.10.8–9, *Epitome* 3.6–8.]

2. THE TROJAN WAR

Odysseus himself led twelve ships from Ithaca to fight at Troy, and he was also involved in various events early in the war that were crucial to the Greek cause. He gave immeasurable help to the Greek forces by recruiting the young ACHILLES, who would prove to be their greatest warrior. Achilles had been sent, dressed as a girl, to King LYCOMEDES on the island of Scyros, because his mother, Thetis, knew that he was fated to die if he fought at Troy. It was Odysseus who penetrated his disguise and carried him off to war. Later it was Odysseus who understood how to cure TELEPHUS' wound, with the result that he gratefully agreed to show the Greeks the way to Troy. Odysseus also fetched the young IPHIGENEIA from Mycenae to Aulis on the pretext of marriage to Achilles, and there at Aulis she was sacrificed to raise the winds that carried the Greek fleet on its long journey. The resultant war lasted for nine years, Troy being captured and destroyed in the tenth.

The *Iliad* recounts events during this tenth and final year, and here we see Odysseus in action, with Homer portraying him as one of the greatest of the Greek warriors. His eloquence and diplomacy are evident (if unsuccessful) when he goes with AJAX (1) and old PHOENIX (3) on the Embassy to Achilles in the hope of persuading him back to battle; as are his courage and resourcefulness in the many battle scenes, and also in the night-raid when he and his comrade DIOMEDES (2), after capturing and killing the Trojan spy DOLON (fig. 50), kill the Thracian king RHESUS (fig. 127) and steal his magnificent horses. We even gain a physical description of Odysseus: Priam comments that he is a head shorter than Agamemnon (who is himself by no means the tallest of the Greeks), but broader in the chest and across the shoulders, and he ranges among his men like a thick-fleeced ram among his flocks (3.191–8). The elder ANTENOR, recalling a time early in the war when Odysseus went on an embassy to Troy in the hope of recovering Helen by peaceful means, remembers that he was physically unimpressive, 'but when he let loose his great voice from his chest, and the words fell like winter snowflakes, then no man alive could rival Odysseus' (3.203–25).

When Achilles was killed by Paris, helped by Apollo, the Great Ajax carried his body off the battlefield (fig. 12) while Odysseus fought off the enemy. Then came a dispute as to who should receive Achilles' armour, with both Ajax and Odysseus staking their claims. The armour was awarded to Odysseus, and Ajax, raging at this slight to his honour, went mad and slaughtered the flocks that were to feed the army, all the while believing that he was torturing and killing the Greek leaders, and in particular his hated enemy Odysseus. When his madness left him and he realised what he had done, full of shame and despair he fell on his sword. Odysseus, with respect and compassion for his dead comrade, persuaded the angry Greeks to give Ajax' body honourable burial.

Odysseus was crucially involved in several undertakings that led to the fall of Troy and the final victory of the Greeks. He captured the Trojan seer HELENUS, who revealed to the Greeks the oracles, known only to himself, foretelling how they could take Troy: they must steal the PALLADIUM, the image of ATHENA, from her Trojan temple; they must bring the bones of PELOPS to Troy; and they must have fighting with them both NEOPTOLEMUS, the son of Achilles, and PHILOCTETES, who owned the bow and arrows of Heracles. Odysseus played a major part in achieving these ends. He went to Scyros and fetched Neoptolemus, to whom he gave the disputed armour that had belonged to Achilles (fig. 97). He led an embassy to Lemnos, where at his suggestion Philoctetes had been marooned at the beginning of the war, suffering from a foul-smelling snake-bite. Despite Philoctetes' hatred of Odysseus, he returned with him to Troy, bringing with him his bow. Together with Diomedes, Odysseus stole the Palladium

from Troy and escaped with it to the Greek camp. Finally, he conceived the idea of the WOODEN HORSE, the ploy by which the Greeks entered Troy. Many warriors hid in the hollow belly of the horse, which the Trojans, after much deliberation, dragged into the city. The Greeks waited for night to fall, then in the darkness left their hiding place and created carnage among the unsuspecting Trojans, slaughtering the now vulnerable enemy until Troy was at last theirs. Now Odysseus urged the murder of Hector's little son ASTYANAX, lest he grow up and take revenge for his father's death and the destruction of his city. Odysseus was awarded Priam's aged queen, HECUBA, as his slave, but she died and was transformed into a bitch.

[Homer, *Iliad* 2.631–7, 9.182–306; Sophocles, *Ajax*; Apollodorus, *Epitome* 3.22, 5.3–4, 5.9–23.]

3. THE RETURN TO ITHACA

It took Odysseus ten long years to return to his wife and son and the home he longed for, and when at last he arrived in Ithaca he had to take vengeance on the rapacious Suitors, the young men who had invaded his house during his absence, carousing at his expense and hoping to marry Penelope. These adventures are the subject of Homer's *Odyssey*. Homer depicts Odysseus as courageous, clever, and resourceful – indeed, his commonest epithets for his hero are *polutlas*, 'much-enduring', *polumetis*, 'man of many wiles', and *polumechanos*, 'man of great resource'. All of these characteristics would be sorely tested on Odysseus' long journey home.

Homer makes Odysseus himself, while he is among the Phaeacians at the court of King ALCINOUS on SCHERIA,

Fig. 101 **Odysseus, concealed beneath Polyphemus' ram, escapes from the cave of the Cyclops.**

relate the perils that he encountered during the early years of his return (Books 9–12). When his narrative opens, he has just left Troy with his twelve ships, which are driven by the wind to the land of the CICONIANS in south-western Thrace. He and his crew sack their city of Ismarus, killing all the men except for MARON, priest of Apollo, and capturing their women and possessions. Maron, in return for his life, gives Odysseus many gifts, including twelve jars of strong, honey-sweet wine which will later save his life in the cave of the Cyclops, POLYPHEMUS (2). But while the Greeks are lingering too long and feasting on their spoils, Ciconian reinforcements arrive, and in the subsequent battle six men out of each ship are killed before the survivors are able to set sail once again.

The ships survive a storm and arrive safely at Cape Malea, the south-eastern tip of the Peloponnese; but here the North Wind seizes them and drives them off-course for nine days. On the tenth day they land in the country of the LOTUS-EATERS. Here Odysseus almost loses the scouts who go ashore and taste the lotus, for it takes from them all desire to return home, and he has to drag them back to the ships by force and tie them down. Next they reach the land of the barbarous CYCLOPES, a race of giants who have only one eye in the middle of their foreheads. Odysseus and twelve of his men go ashore to explore, and find a cave which is full of lambs and kids, milk and cheeses. The men are alarmed and want to leave quickly, but Odysseus will not listen to them, since he hopes that the occupier of the cave will give him guest-gifts. They find to their cost that the cave belongs to the Cyclops Polyphemus, a murderous savage who traps Odysseus and his men in the cave by barricading the entrance with an immovable boulder, then eats six of them before the wily Odysseus can evolve a means of escape. He tells Polyphemus that his name is *Outis*, 'Nobody', then makes him drunk with the wine given by Maron. Once the monster is asleep they blind him with a red-hot stake (fig. 119), and none of the other Cyclopes bursts in to help him because he shouts out that 'Nobody' is killing him. When morning comes, Polyphemus pulls away the great boulder from the entrance to let out his flocks, and Odysseus and his six surviving men escape by clinging to the undersides of the sheep as they go out to pasture (fig. 101). Once safely back on board ship, he cannot resist shouting taunts at the Cyclops, who replies by flinging down an immense piece of rock that drives the vessel back to shore. The men escape only by rowing for their lives. Odysseus even shouts out his real name – a serious mistake, for the Cyclops tells his father POSEIDON of the harm that has been done him, and it will be Poseidon's

anger with Odysseus that will keep him, for all too many weary years, away from his longed-for Ithaca.

Their next port of call is the island of Aeolia, ruled by the guardian of the winds, AEOLUS (2), where for a month they are feasted royally. When the time comes for them to leave, Aeolus gives Odysseus all the boisterous winds sewn up in a leather bag, leaving outside only the gentle West Wind to blow him safely back to Ithaca. They sail for nine days, until on the tenth day they are actually in sight of the island. Then Odysseus falls asleep and his men open the leather bag, certain that it contains treasure which he does not intend to share with them. At once the winds burst out and sweep the ship violently all the way back to Aeolia. Odysseus, despairing, humbly begs Aeolus to help him once more, but Aeolus refuses, thinking it foolhardy to help a man so obviously hated by the gods.

For six days they sail on once more, then on the seventh day they come to a country inhabited by the LAESTRYGONIANS, a race of savage man-eating giants. The crews moor their ships within a quiet harbour, walled in with great cliffs, and Odysseus sends out three scouts to spy out the land. One of these scouts gets eaten by the king, Antiphates, but the other two escape and run back to the ships, followed by the entire bloodthirsty population. The Laestrygonians stand on the cliffs and fling boulders down on to the ships below, spearing the men like fish and carrying them off for eating. Only Odysseus' ship escapes, since he has cautiously anchored it right at the entrance to the harbour. He and his one remaining crew sail sorrowfully onwards.

They come next to Aeaea, the island of the enchantress CIRCE. Odysseus sends half of his men on a scouting party, led by his brother-in-law EURYLOCHUS who, when they come to Circe's home in the depths of a forest, has the sense to suspect danger and to wait outside when the rest of his party are welcomed indoors by the enchantress. When she bewitches the men, turning them into pigs, Eurylochus takes the news of their sorry fate back to the ship. Odysseus, with the help of HERMES, counters Circe's magic, for the god gives him a plant called moly that makes him immune to her spells. When she tries her magic on him, instead of becoming a pig as she intends, he rushes at her with a drawn sword (fig. 40). The defeated goddess suggests that they retire to bed and the pleasures of love, and Odysseus agrees, so long as she swears a solemn oath not to harm him. Afterwards he insists that she turns all his men back into human beings.

Odysseus and his men stay with the enchantress for a year, feasting on unlimited food and wine. At the end of that time, urged by his men, he is ready to be on his way once more, but Circe tells him that first he must go down to Hades, to seek advice about his journey from the shade of the Theban seer TEIRESIAS. So Odysseus and his men again set sail, and following Circe's directions accomplish the terrible journey to the Underworld. There they dig a trench and pour into it libations to the dead of milk and honey, wine and water, all sprinkled with white barley. Over this trench Odysseus sacrifices a young ram and a black ewe that Circe has given him, and as the blood runs down, the souls of the dead gather round. First he speaks to the shade of ELPENOR, a comrade who was accidentally killed on Circe's island and left unburied, and who now begs him to return to Aeaea and give his body proper burial. Odysseus promises to do so, then speaks to the shade of Teiresias who, after drinking blood from the trench, prophesies his future. Odysseus learns that Poseidon's anger will give him a hard journey home, but that he will eventually get there, so long as he is careful not to harm the cattle of the Sun-god HELIOS which are pastured on the island of Thrinacia. He learns that he will have to dispose of the Suitors who await him in his palace, and then leave home again, wandering further into a land far from the sea where he must sacrifice to Poseidon. Then he may return home once more, where he will at last die in peaceful and prosperous old age.

When the seer moves away, many other shades approach and drink the blood in turn, after which they are able to converse with Odysseus. He speaks with his mother Anticleia, then with many famous women such as Tyro, Antiope, Alcmene, Epicasta (mother of Oedipus, later called Jocasta), Chloris, Leda, Iphimedeia, Phaedra, Procris, Ariadne and Eriphyle. He speaks with some of the men who were his comrades at Troy: with Agamemnon, who tells of his murder at the hands of his wife Clytemnestra and her lover Aegisthus, and warns Odysseus to be careful when he too returns home; with Achilles and Patroclus and Antilochus; and with the Great Ajax, who still nurses his anger over the award of Achilles' arms and refuses to reply to his old enemy, stalking away in a proud silence.

Odysseus sees Minos, the judge of the dead, and the giant hunter Orion, and the tortures of Tityus, Tantalus and Sisyphus, and finally the great Heracles, before sailing back with his men to Aeaea. There he buries Elpenor, then at dawn sets off homeward to Ithaca, having learnt from Circe the many dangers of the journey ahead. First they pass by the land of the SIRENS, the singing enchantresses who lure men to their doom. The crew hear nothing of their magical songs, for Odysseus has filled their ears with wax; but he, bound tightly to the mast (fig. 132), can hear every intoxicating sound and struggles to

go to them. True to their orders, his men tie him the tighter until they are all safely out of hearing.

Next they must pass through a narrow strait in which two dangers lurk. On one side is the giant whirlpool CHARYBDIS, which will suck them all down to certain death if they go too near to her. They keep to the opposite side of the strait, but in so doing are attacked by the six-headed sea-monster SCYLLA (1), who lives in a cave high in a cliff. As they stare in terrified fascination at Charybdis, who is sucking down sea-water until the very bottom of the ocean is visible, Scylla swoops down her six long necks and seizes six of Odysseus' men. Too late he turns and sees them far out of reach, screaming and stretching out their hands to him in their death throes as Scylla devours them.

Soon they approach the island of Thrinacia where the cattle of the Sun-god Helios are pastured. Odysseus, remembering the warnings given him by both Teiresias and Circe, wishes to sail straight past, but his men, urged on by Eurylochus, persuade him to land. They swear to eat nothing but the generous provisions that Circe has given them, but these are soon consumed when adverse winds keep them on the island for a month. With their food gone, they hunt for fish and game. Finally, while Odysseus is away praying to the gods, Eurylochus persuades his shipmates to kill and eat some of the sacred cattle. When Odysseus returns, it is too late: the deed is done and the promised calamities are bound to follow. Helios hurries to Olympus and demands that Zeus punish the offenders, even threatening to leave the earth and take his light down among the dead men in Hades if he is refused. So when the men put to sea after six days of feasting on the forbidden meat, Zeus in anger sends a violent storm against them. The ship breaks up and only Odysseus, who took no part in the sacrilege, survives to tell the tale: 'My men were thrown into the water, and bobbing like sea-crows were carried away by the waves from around the black ship, and the god took away their homecoming' (12.417–19). Now, of the crews of the twelve ships that left Troy, there is only one man left alive.

Odysseus manages to lash together the broken keel and mast of his ship to form a kind of raft, and perched on this he is carried by a southerly wind all the way back to Scylla and Charybdis. This time his craft falls prey to Charybdis, who sucks it down deep to the ocean bottom, but Odysseus reaches out and hangs on to the overhanging branch of a fig tree until eventually the raft is spewed back up again. Now he sits astride it once more and paddles with his hands until he is out of danger. He is carried by the sea for nine days until he is washed up on the island of OGYGIA, the home of the goddess CALYPSO. She

seventeen days he sails onwards, but on the eighteenth day Poseidon returns from Ethiopia and sees his enemy once more travelling towards home. At once he lets loose a violent storm that breaks up Odysseus' raft. Odysseus almost drowns, but the sea-goddess Leucothea saves him, giving him a shawl which, tied round his chest, keeps him afloat. For two days he swims, until at last he reaches land and drags himself ashore at the mouth of a river. After flinging his life-preserving shawl back into the sea as Leucothea directed, he crawls into a thicket and falls asleep on a bed of leaves. He is on the magical island of Scheria, the land of the Phaeacians.

Next morning he encounters NAUSICAA, the daughter of Alcinous and ARETE, king and queen of the Phaeacians. Influenced by Athena in a dream, Nausicaa has come with her maids to the river-mouth to do the family washing. While waiting for the clothes to dry they play ball. Their cries awaken Odysseus and he comes out of the bushes (fig. 95), hiding his nakedness with a branch, a fearsome figure to all but Nausicaa, who stands her ground and offers him her help. She gives him clothes and food and drink, and takes him back with her to the city, telling him how to win the help of her parents. Alcinous and Arete welcome him to their palace as an honoured guest and promise to convey him home to Ithaca. They entertain him royally with games and a great feast at which the blind bard DEMODOCUS sings. Now Odysseus divulges his name and tells the long tale of his wanderings. Finally they give him many rich gifts and provide him with a Phaeacian ship to take him home. Odysseus sleeps on the journey, and the Phaeacian sailors deposit him, still sleeping, on the shore. After twenty long years he is at last in Ithaca once again.

4. IN ITHACA ONCE MORE

On waking he is surrounded by a thick mist and fails to recognise his island, but Athena appears and reassures him. She warns him about the rapacious Suitors in his palace, and disguises him as an old beggar so that he may go unrecognised among them and take his vengeance. She then travels to fetch back Telemachus from Sparta, where he has gone seeking news of his father. Odysseus meanwhile goes to the hut of his faithful swineherd EUMAEUS (fig. 102), pretending to be a Cretan who has fought at Troy and so has news of Odysseus. Eumaeus entertains the supposed stranger courteously. Telemachus later joins them there, and when Eumaeus has left on an errand Odysseus makes himself known to his son. The two are reunited joyfully, then together they plan the destruction of the Suitors.

The next morning Odysseus and Eumaeus set out for the palace, encountering the disloyal goatherd MELANTHIUS

Fig. 102 Odysseus with his faithful swineherd, Eumaeus, and pigs.

falls in love with him and keeps him as her lover for seven years, while all the time he longs to return home to rocky Ithaca. She even offers to make him immortal if only he will stay with her for ever, but Odysseus, despite the delights of the goddess' bed, would rather be at home with his mortal and ageing wife Penelope.

At the end of these seven years the gods intervene to release him. Athena, always Odysseus' champion, waits for a time when Poseidon, still implacably angry, is far away in Ethiopia. She appeals to Zeus, who responds by sending Hermes to tell Calypso that she must let Odysseus go. Sadly she bows to the inevitable. She gives Odysseus tools and materials to build a raft, then dresses him in fine clothing, supplies him with food and water and wine, and sends him on his way with a fair wind. For

on the way. They pass Odysseus' hound Argus, who is too old and weak to get to his feet when he recognises his master, but he wags his tail with joy, and dies. Inside the palace Odysseus finds the Suitors feasting as usual at his expense. He goes among them, begging, and they give him food, except for ANTINOUS, the most brutal and insolent of them all. He strikes Odysseus with a footstool and incites the (genuine) beggar IRUS to fight him. Odysseus fells Irus with a single bone-crushing blow. Penelope, prompted by Athena, appears among them and announces her reluctant intention of remarrying. She reproaches the Suitors for failing to bring her suitable presents, and at once, inflamed with passionate desire for her, they eagerly produce many rich gifts. Odysseus is delighted, both with Penelope's fidelity to him and her reluctance to remarry, and with her ability to extract gifts from the Suitors that help to compensate for their depredations. (Odysseus too has always been ready to acquire gifts in his wanderings wherever he can.)

Telemachus tells the Suitors to spend the night in their own homes, and when they have gone, he and Odysseus make their preparations for vengeance by stripping the hall of all its armour and weapons and shutting them away in a storeroom. Once Telemachus has retired for the night, Penelope comes down and speaks with the 'beggar'. She tells him how she succeeded in putting off the Suitors' demands for three years by pretending to weave her father-in-law's shroud, working at her loom by day and unravelling her work by night, until at last her trick was discovered. Odysseus responds by claiming to be the brother of Idomeneus, king of Crete, and to have once met Odysseus himself. Homer (19.204–12) says:

> He knew how to tell many lies that sounded true, and
> as she listened her tears streamed down and her body
> melted, as the snow melts on the tops of the moun-
> tains, when the East Wind melts it after the West Wind
> has piled it there, and as it melts the rivers run full in
> flood. Even so her lovely cheeks were streaming tears,
> as she wept for her husband who was sitting there by
> her side.

Odysseus, full of pity for her sorrow, is not yet ready to make himself known to her, but he reassures her by predicting his own imminent return. Penelope, doubting still, but comforted by her talk with the likeable stranger, calls for the nurse Eurycleia to wash her guest's feet. In so doing, Eurycleia recognises her master from an old scar on his leg once made by the tusk of a wild boar, but Odysseus stops her mouth with his hands before she can shout out the joyful news to her mistress. Before going to bed, Penelope tells Odysseus of her plan to hold an archery contest for the Suitors, to see which of them can string her husband's great bow and shoot an arrow through a row of double-headed axes. That man, she says, will win her as his wife. Odysseus urges her to hold the contest without delay.

The next day will be the Suitors' last. A great feast is held, at which the seer THEOCLYMENUS (1) solemnly warns them of their impending deaths, but they mock his words. After the banquet, Penelope brings out Odysseus' great bow and the twelve axes and announces the contest. Telemachus fixes the axes into the ground, and the Suitors, one by one, try unsuccessfully to string the bow. Meanwhile Odysseus slips away and makes himself known to his two faithful servants, the swineherd Eumaeus and the cowherd Philoetius, who greet their beloved master with tears of joy. On Odysseus' return to the hall, Penelope insists that he be given a try with the bow, and Telemachus, though he orders his mother back to her room where she cries herself to sleep, supports her decision. Eurycleia bars the doors from the outside, and within the hall Odysseus takes the bow and strings it with ease. With his right hand he plucks the bowstring, testing it, and it gives out a fine sound in response. The Suitors, now terribly alarmed, change colour. Zeus sends a portent by thundering loudly. Odysseus shoots an arrow through the axes, then stripping off his beggar's rags he turns to face the Suitors.

Now at last he can avenge himself on his enemies. He begins by shooting Antinous, the worst of them, and at first the others are angry, thinking that his shot was unintended. When Odysseus announces his identity, they soon realise their mistake and are overcome by fear. EURYMACHUS pleads on their behalf, but when this is of no avail he urges them all to fight and is himself the second to be shot. AMPHINOMUS is the third man to die, killed by the spear of Telemachus, who then runs to the storeroom to fetch arms and armour while Odysseus picks off the Suitors with his remaining arrows. Unfortunately Telemachus forgets to lock the room after him, and now the treacherous goatherd Melanthius helps the Suitors by bringing them weapons. Eumaeus and Philoetius catch him and tie him up, leaving him locked in the storeroom, then return to fight side by side with Odysseus and Telemachus. They are triumphant in the pitched battle that follows, even though they are four against many, since they are aided by Athena, disguised as MENTOR, who prevents all the Suitors' spear-casts from striking home. One by one the Suitors are relentlessly killed, and those still alive are terrified (22.298–309):

> Their minds gripped by panic, they stampeded
> about the hall like a herd of cattle, set upon
> and driven crazy by the darting gadfly

in the spring season when the days grow long.
The other men were like hook-taloned vultures
with curved beaks, who come down from the mountains
and swoop on smaller birds; fearful of the clouds,
these scatter over the plain, while the vultures
leap on them and do them to death, and they have
no defence or escape, and men enjoy the hunt;
so these men, storming about the house,
struck down the Suitors, one man after another,
and terrible cries rose up as their heads were broken,
and the floor was seething with blood.

At last all of the Suitors are dead, apart from PHEMIUS, the bard, and MEDON (4), the herald, both of whom served the Suitors against their will and so are spared. Now Odysseus is once more king of Ithaca, in a palace piled high with corpses.

They call in Eurycleia, who on seeing the slaughter begins to raise the cry of triumph until Odysseus silences her. On his instructions she fetches the twelve serving-women who have been disloyally sleeping with the Suitors, and these are set to carry the corpses of their dead lovers out into the courtyard, then to clean the blood-spattered hall. When all is done, Telemachus hangs them (*see* MELANTHO). Melanthius too is punished for his treachery: his nose, ears, hands, feet and genitals are cut off and thrown to the dogs, and he is left to die. Finally Odysseus fumigates the house and courtyard with burning sulphur. Now Penelope can be told the joyous news of her husband's return and triumph over the hated Suitors.

Eurycleia excitedly wakes her mistress and once again Penelope meets the stranger, who is now saying that he is Odysseus. At first she cannot believe him, and only when he describes the unique construction of their marriage-bed, built around an olive tree still rooted in the ground, does she accept that this is indeed her long-lost husband. Now at last husband and wife are reunited with great joy, and Athena lengthens the night for them by holding back EOS, goddess of Dawn, from bringing in the daylight until they have enjoyed each other to the full.

The next day Odysseus seeks out his aged father, Laertes, and finds him wearily toiling in his orchard, dressed in squalid clothes. The old man is overjoyed to have his son with him again and to learn of the Suitors' deaths. But many of the Suitors' relatives are planning a counter-attack, and soon they approach, urged on by Antinous' father Eupeithes. Laertes, Odysseus and Telemachus go out to meet them, aided by Eumaeus, Philoetius, and the faithful servant DOLIUS with his six sons. Athena breathes great strength into Laertes, so that he throws the first spear and kills Eupeithes. A pitched battle is about to break out when the goddess, shouting out a fearsome cry, separates the warring parties and re-establishes peace between Odysseus and the Ithacans. Thus ends the *Odyssey*.

5. AFTERMATH

Homer's conception of Odysseus' subsequent adventures is summarised in the predictions of Teiresias: he must go on a long journey, carrying with him an oar, until he reaches a place so far inland and a people so unfamiliar with the sea that a wayfarer thinks his oar is a winnowing-fan. There he must plant his oar in the ground and sacrifice to the angry Poseidon a ram, a bull and a boar, before returning home to Ithaca, reconciled with the god. In prosperous old age a gentle death will come to him from the sea.

Later ancient sources tell different and often contradictory stories about Odysseus' closing years: that he married CALLIDICE, the queen of Thesprotia, who bore him a son, Polypoetes; that Penelope bore him a second son, Ptoliporthes or Arcesilaus; that Odysseus killed Penelope for infidelity; that he was condemned to exile by Neoptolemus, arbitrating between him and the Suitors' kinsmen, and took refuge with THOAS (3), the king of Aetolia, married his daughter, and fathered on her a son, Leontophonus; that he met his death on Ithaca at the hands of his son by Circe, TELEGONUS.

[Homer, *Odyssey* 11.119–37; Apollodorus, *Epitome* 34–40; Pausanias 8.12.6.]

6. LATER ACCOUNTS

Odysseus, portrayed by Homer as brave, resourceful, intelligent and self-controlled, often becomes in the hands of later writers a much less likeable character. In Sophocles' *Ajax* he is noble and generous, but becomes in his *Philoctetes* an unscrupulous cynic; while Euripides gives the Homeric Odysseus a humorous treatment in his *Cyclops*, but makes him callous and cruel in his *Hecuba*. Virgil too depicts him as unscrupulous in his theft of the Palladium and his revenge on Palamedes, and he has often since been seen as an unprincipled rogue, though Shakespeare in his *Troilus and Cressida* reverts to a concept more in tune with Homer's heroic Odysseus.

His long journey home, beset by dangers, setbacks and temptations, has been seen in Christian terms as an allegory for man's experience on earth and preparation for heaven, and has given us our word 'odyssey' for any long and eventful journey. In James Joyce's *Ulysses*, the events of a single day, 16 June 1904, are modelled on the pattern of the *Odyssey*, with Leopold Bloom – in search of fulfilment, and in a sense a symbol of humanity – as Odysseus. Nikos Kazantzakis' *The Odyssey: a Modern Sequel* carries on from where Homer leaves off, with Odysseus travelling in his search for self-knowledge from Ithaca to Crete and down the length of Africa, to his death in Antarctica. This concept of Odysseus as the perpetual wanderer in search of knowledge begins with Dante, and is summed up in one of Tennyson's greatest poems, *Ulysses*. Here Odysseus is a man who yearns to travel, to explore. 'I cannot rest from travel; I will drink life to the lees', he says. 'How dull it is to pause, to make an end, / to rust unburnished, not to shine in use!' He and his fellow sailors are now old, and near to death, but the poem ends as Odysseus says to them:

> Come, my friends,
> 'Tis not too late to seek a newer world.
> Push off, and sitting well in order smite
> The sounding furrows; for my purpose holds
> To sail beyond the sunset, and the baths
> Of all the western stars, until I die.
> It may be that the gulfs will wash us down:
> It may be we shall touch the Happy Isles,
> And see the great Achilles, whom we knew.
> Tho' much is taken, much abides; and tho'
> We are not now that strength which in old days
> Moved earth and heaven; that which we are, we are;
> One equal temper of heroic hearts,
> Made weak by time and fate, but strong in will
> To strive, to seek, to find, and not to yield.

This has come a long way from Homer's Odysseus, who hates the sea and all the troubles it brings him, and hates the way it keeps him from his home in Ithaca. When, in the *Odyssey*, Calypso offers him immortality, Odysseus says to her (5.215–20):

> Lady goddess, do not be angry with me. I know all this for myself, that wise Penelope is never a match for you in beauty and stature, for she is a mortal, and you are immortal and ageless. But even so, what I want, and all my days I long for, is to go back to my house and to see the day of my homecoming.

[W. B. Stanford, *The Ulysses Theme* (2nd. edn. 1963); D. Page, *Folktales in Homer's Odyssey* (1973); W. B. Stanford and J. V. Luce, *The Quest for Ulysses* (1974); Tim Severin, *The Ulysses Voyage* (1987); Beaty Rubens and Oliver Taplin, *An Odyssey round Odysseus* (1989).]

Odyssey *see* ODYSSEUS.

Oeax

Son of NAUPLIUS (1) and Clymene, and brother of PALAMEDES and Nausimedon. Palamedes, framed by his enemy, Odysseus, was found guilty at Troy on a false charge of treason and stoned to death by the Greek army.

Oeax sent the news to their father by writing an account of his brother's death on a number of oar-blades, then throwing them into the sea in the hope that they would float to Greece. (This episode was dramatised in Euripides' lost tragedy *Palamedes*, and is parodied in Aristophanes' extant comedy *Women at the Thesmophoria*, 769–84.) One of these oar-blades was eventually washed up in Euboea, where their father found it, and read it, and avenged his son's death. Hyginus (*Fabula* 117) relates that Oeax took his own revenge on the Greek leader, AGAMEMNON, by telling his wife CLYTEMNESTRA that he would be bringing CASSANDRA back from Troy as his concubine. In this way he induced her, with the help of her lover AEGISTHUS, to kill her husband with an axe on his return home.

Oeax' hostility extended to Agamemnon's son ORESTES, since in his desire for revenge he urged the Argives to banish the boy for killing Clytemnestra. Oeax and his brother Nausimedon were also known, it seems, for supporting Agamemnon's enemy Aegisthus, since Pausanias (1.22.6) describes a fifth-century painting on the Acropolis showing 'Orestes killing Aegisthus, and PYLADES killing the sons of Nauplius, who had come to help Aegisthus'.

[Euripides, *Orestes* 431–3; Apollodorus 2.1.5, 3.2.2.]

Oedipus

The son of LAIUS, king of Thebes, and JOCASTA (Epicasta in Homer), and the hero of one of the best-known of all legends. From Greek tragedy we know him as the man who unwittingly killed his father, then married his mother and had four children by her; when the incest was discovered she committed suicide; he blinded himself, then wandered through the world as a polluted exile until his death. But originally Oedipus' story was very different. In Homer and the Epic Cycle he killed his father and married his mother – these are the immutable basics of his story – and his mother, when the truth was discovered, committed suicide. But Oedipus ruled on at Thebes, married again and had his four children by a second wife, EURYGANEIA. He died in battle while still active and in power, and was given splendid funeral games as the mark of respect due to a great hero. So originally there were no children born of incest, no self-inflicted blindness, no exile. This is all very different from the legend in Sophocles' seminal tragedy *Oedipus the King*, which gives the canonical version of Oedipus' story. This is certainly one of the most celebrated plays of all time, cited by Aristotle in his *Poetics* as a model of dramatic craftsmanship and overshadowing all other treatments.

Laius, king of Thebes, was married to Jocasta, but an oracle told him that if they had a son, that son would kill him. So when a son was born, the baby's ankles were pinned together and he was handed over to one of Laius' herdsmen, with instructions that he be cast out to die on Mount Cithaeron (fig. 103). The herdsman took pity on the helpless infant and gave him to a second herdsman, also pasturing his flocks on the mountain. This man took the baby back to his home city of Corinth. Here the infant was adopted by the childless king and queen, Polybus and Merope. They called him Oedipus ('Swollen Foot') because of the wounds in his feet.

Oedipus grew up fully believing that these were his true parents, but one day a drunken man taunted him with not being his father's child. Polybus and Merope reassured him, but doubts still gnawed at his mind, so he questioned the DELPHIC ORACLE in the hope of learning the truth. Instead of an answer to his query, the Oracle told him that he was destined to kill his father and marry his mother. Appalled at this prophecy, Oedipus determined never for the rest of his life to go back to Corinth. Instead he travelled towards Thebes. Near Daulis, at a narrow place where three roads met, a man in a chariot tried to force him off the road, striking at him with a

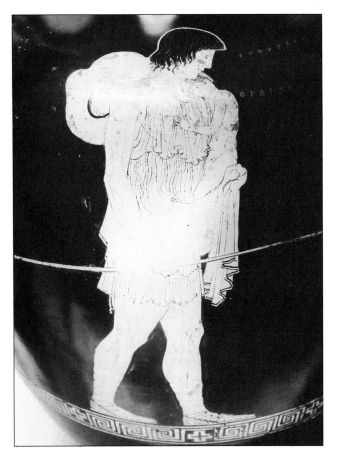

goad. Oedipus in anger killed the man, together with his attendants – except for one servant who managed to escape with his life. The man in the chariot was Oedipus' real father, Laius.

Oedipus went on to Thebes, where he found the monstrous SPHINX ravaging the city, devouring anyone who failed to answer her riddle correctly. The ruler, CREON (2), had ordained that anyone who could give a correct answer and rid the city of the monster would win the rule of the kingdom and the hand of the queen, Jocasta, recently widowed. Oedipus answered the riddle (fig. 133), at which the Sphinx hurled herself to her death. He was greeted as a hero, became king, and married his real mother. They had two sons, Eteocles and POLYNEICES, and two daughters, ANTIGONE (1) and ISMENE. Years later a terrible plague descended on Thebes.

This is the point at which *Oedipus the King* opens. Oedipus is determined to cure his afflicted city, so when he learns from the Delphic Oracle that the plague will end only when the man who murdered Laius has himself been killed or banished, he is set on discovering the murderer. He puts a solemn curse on the unknown killer; he questions Creon; he questions TEIRESIAS (a scene rich in irony, where the prophet, although physically blind, is aware of the facts, while Oedipus, although he can see, is mentally blind to the truth, and is too angry to listen to what Teiresias has to tell him). When Oedipus learns from Jocasta that Laius was killed at a place where three roads meet, he realises that he himself may well have been the murderer of the king. To find out the truth, he sends for the one servant of Laius who survived the massacre, and who has since lived far out in the Theban countryside. But there is worse knowledge to come. An old messenger arrives from Corinth to announce that Polybus is dead from old age, at first reassuring news, because it seems to mean that Oedipus did not after all kill his father. But the messenger also happens to be the very man who long ago carried the baby Oedipus to Corinth, and this he now reveals. So Oedipus now knows that Polybus and Merope are not his real parents, and he resolutely and optimistically sets out to learn whose child he really is. Jocasta has by now realised the whole truth and desperately tries to stop Oedipus from pursuing the matter. He refuses to listen and she goes indoors, where she will hang herself. Another old man arrives, the single eyewitness of Laius' murder, who proves to be none other than the herdsman who carried the baby Oedipus from the Theban palace out to his intended death on the

Fig. 103 **A herdsman, named Euphorbus, carries the infant Oedipus to his new home in Corinth.**

mountainside. Oedipus wrings the full truth from him, at the last minute guessing that what he is about to hear will be the worst possible knowledge. 'I am on the brink of terrible words', cries the herdsman. 'And I of terrible hearing', replies Oedipus. 'Yet I must hear' (1169–70). At last he learns that he himself is the unknown killer for whom he has been searching and, worse even than this, that Apollo's appalling oracle has come true. Distraught, he goes indoors, where he finds Jocasta dead by her own hand. He tears out the long golden pins from her robe and in his anguish gouges out his eyes, the eyes which had had sight, but which had nevertheless been blind to the truth. At the end of the play, a blind and broken man, he is ready to go into exile, leaving Thebes for ever, in obedience to the commands of Apollo.

The sequel to these events is recorded in Sophocles' tragedy *Oedipus at Colonus*, where Oedipus at last reaches the end of his sufferings in a moving death in which he is taken from earth by the gods. He has wandered as a blind outcast for many years, guided by his faithful daughter Antigone. Now he reaches the sacred precinct of the Eumenides at Colonus in Attica, which he knows from an oracle of Apollo is meant to be the place where he will die. King THESEUS gives him sanctuary, supporting him against Creon and Polyneices, both of whom try in vain to make him return to Thebes for their own selfish motives. In return Oedipus prophesies that the place of his death will forever bring blessings from the gods on Attica. (For Oedipus' curses on his sons, and the consequent troubles suffered by his family and his city, *see* POLYNEICES.) At the end of the play Oedipus' end is announced by peals of thunder. No longer needing guidance, the old blind man walks confidently into the depths of the sacred grove, and there the voice of a god rings out: 'Oedipus, Oedipus, why do we hesitate to go. Long indeed have you been made to wait' (1627–8). At a spot known only to Theseus, Oedipus mysteriously disappears from human sight; he has at last found the death he longed for.

There are of course many other accounts of Oedipus' story by other authors, often with minor variations. In 467 BC Aeschylus produced a tetralogy on the legend, the three tragedies *Laius*, *Oedipus* and *The Seven against Thebes*, and the satyr play *Sphinx*. Only the final tragedy is extant, dramatising the effects of Oedipus' curse on his sons, which results in the tragic and ultimately fatal conflict of the two brothers over the rule of Thebes. Fragments of the other plays remain and we know, for instance, that the oracle to Laius said that for his city's sake he must never have children, but that overcome by lust he fathered his doom-laden son. The scholia record a

version in which the baby Oedipus was put in a chest and cast out to sea; the chest floated to Sicyon, and there the baby was found and adopted by Polybus and his wife Periboea. In Euripides' lost *Oedipus*, Oedipus was blinded, not by his own hand, but by the servants of Laius; and in his *Phoenician Women*, Jocasta did not kill herself when she learnt about her incestuous marriage, but is alive in the play to try and make peace between Eteocles and Polyneices, who are fighting over the rule of Thebes. Here she dies only after her sons have killed each other, when in her grief she commits suicide over their corpses. Interesting as these variants are, it was Sophocles' version that became the definitive account of Oedipus' story and had by far the greatest influence on later works.

Seneca based his own *Oedipus* on that of Sophocles; as did Corneille his *Oedipe*, though he adds some mythological irrelevancies, as does Voltaire in his *Oedipe* of 1718. Cocteau, in his *Infernal Machine*, sees the story of Oedipus as an example of a cosmic joke, 'one of the most perfect machines constructed by the infernal gods for the mathematical annihilation of a mortal', and his Oedipus is brutally crushed by a hostile external world. Freud's interpretation of the myth is renowned: his 'Oedipus complex' is a boy's attraction to his mother and repressed hostility towards his father, who is seen by the child as a rival for his mother's love, all of which causes psychological problems later in life. Modern reworkings of the Oedipus legend which are influenced by Freudian theory, such as Pasolini's film *Oedipus Rex*, can be strikingly effective. Oedipus remains an eternal symbol of human self-deception.

[Homer, *Iliad* 23.677–80, *Odyssey* 11.271–80; Apollodorus 3.5.7–9; Diodorus Siculus 4.64–65.1; Pausanias 1.28.7, 1.30.4, 9.5.10–11, 10.5.3–4; Seneca, *Oedipus*, *Phoenician Women*. J. R. March, *The Creative Poet* (1987), pp. 121–54.]

Oeneus

Son of Porthaon and Euryte, and king of the Aetolians of Calydon. He married ALTHAEA, the daughter of Thestius, and had by her several sons and daughters, the best known of whom were MELEAGER, DEIANEIRA and GORGE, though Meleager was occasionally said to be the son of ARES, and Deianeira the daughter of DIONYSUS. Because of his name, Oeneus was sometimes linked with the story of wine (*oinos*) and was said to have been the first mortal to receive a vine from Dionysus (perhaps in thanks for the god's association with Althaea). *See* STAPHYLUS.(2).

Oeneus inadvertently brought a great scourge on Calydon. He once forgot to sacrifice to ARTEMIS and the angry goddess sent an immense wild boar against his land and people. This led to one of the great exploits of the ancient world, the CALYDONIAN BOARHUNT, in which heroes from all over Greece banded together to destroy the boar. It was finally killed by Meleager, but a fight ensued over the head and hide of the boar and he too lost his life. His sisters mourned for him so much that they were turned into guinea-hens (except for Deianeira, who married HERACLES, and Gorge, who married Andraemon). Althaea committed suicide.

After Althaea's death, Oeneus married again, his new wife being Periboea, the daughter of Hipponous. Various reasons are given for their union: either Oeneus won her as a gift of honour after he had sacked Olenus; or she was seduced by Hippostratus, the son of Amarynceus, and Hipponous sent her to Oeneus with instructions to kill her, but he married her instead; or he himself seduced her and made her pregnant, so her father insisted on the marriage. Their son TYDEUS was exiled for murder: he killed either Oeneus' brother Alcathous, or the sons of his brother Melas, because they were plotting to get hold of the kingdom, or even his own brother Olenias. He fled to Argos where he married Adrastus' daughter Deipyle and had a son by her, DIOMEDES (2). Deprived of Tydeus' support, Oeneus was deposed by the sons of another of his brothers, AGRIUS (2), who imprisoned him and gave his kingdom to their father. Tydeus was killed in the expedition of the Seven against Thebes, but in due course his son Diomedes came to help his grandfather, killing most of Agrius' sons and regaining the kingdom. By this time Oeneus was too old to rule, so he handed the throne of Calydon over to Andraemon, the husband of his daughter Gorge, and went with Diomedes back to the Peloponnese. But the two surviving sons of Agrius had the last word, for they ambushed the old man as he was passing through Arcadia and killed him. He was buried in the Argolid at Oenoe, a town named after him.

[Homer, *Iliad* 2.641–2, 6.216–9, 9.529–99, 14.115–8; Apollodorus 1.7.10–1.8.6, 3.7.5, *Epitome* 2.15; Diodorus Siculus 4.34.1–35.1; Pausanias 2.25.2, 4.35.1.]

Oenomaus

A king of Pisa in Elis. He was the son of ARES by the Pleiad STEROPE (1), though he was sometimes said to be Sterope's husband rather than her son. He had two children, a son, Leucippus, who loved the nymph DAPHNE, and a daughter, Hippodameia. She was pursued by many suitors, but Oenomaus murdered them all by forcing them to run a deadly chariot-race with him, until finally he was defeated and killed (*see* PELOPS).

[Apollodorus 3.10.1, *Epitome* 2.4–7; Pausanias 5.10.6.]

Oenone

A nymph, daughter of the river-god Cebren, who married PARIS while he was still a herdsman on Mount Ida near Troy. They had a son, CORYTHUS. Oenone had learnt from Rhea the art of prophecy, so she was able to warn Paris not to sail to Greece to fetch HELEN, since she knew what disasters would follow. Finding that she could not influence him, she told him to come to her if he were ever wounded, for she alone could heal him.

Paris sailed to Greece and eloped with Helen, thus setting in motion the Trojan War. He never returned to Oenone. Many years later, when he was mortally wounded by Philoctetes, he remembered her words and asked to be carried to Mount Ida. Still angry at his desertion of her, she refused to help him and he was carried back to Troy. Too late she changed her mind, hurrying to Troy with her healing drugs, but found Paris dead. She hanged herself from grief.

[Apollodorus 3.12.6; Quintus of Smyrna, *Sequel to Homer* 10.262–489; Ovid, *Heroides* 5.]

Oenopion

Usually said to be the son of DIONYSUS and ARIADNE, though sometimes of Ariadne and THESEUS. Oenopion became ruler of the island of Chios. He asked the giant hunter ORION to rid his island of wild beasts, promising him marriage to his daughter Merope as a reward, but he later went back on his bargain. When the frustrated Orion became drunk and raped Merope, Oenopion avenged his daughter by blinding him and driving him out of Chios. Orion returned after regaining his sight, intent on revenge, but the king had been safely hidden by his people in an underground house built by HEPHAESTUS. Orion departed, leaving Oenopion to rule on in peace.

[Apollodorus 1.4.3, *Epitome* 1.9; Diodorus Siculus 5.79.1; Plutarch, *Theseus* 20; Pausanias 7.4.8–9, 7.5.13.]

Oeonus

Son of LICYMNIUS and cousin of HERACLES. He was killed by the sons of HIPPOCOON for throwing a stone at their savage dog. Heracles avenged him by killing Hippocoon and all his sons.

Ogygia

The magical island of CALYPSO. Here she welcomed the shipwrecked ODYSSEUS and made him stay with her against his will for seven years. The cave where she lived was set in an idyllic spot (*Odyssey* 5.63–74):

> Around the cave there grew a flourishing wood,
> poplars and alders and fragrant cypresses.
> Here was the roosting place of long-winged birds,
> little owls and hawks and long-beaked choughs
> whose daily concerns take them down to the sea.
> There around the hollow cave there stretched
> a young, luxuriant vine, thick with grapes.

Nearby were four springs, flowing with bright water,
next to each other but running in different directions.
All around grew meadows, soft with violets
and parsley, and even a god who came to that place
would admire what he saw, his heart delighted within him.

But despite all this verdant beauty, Odysseus, 'sitting
weeping on the sea-shore, breaking his heart with tears,
lamentations and grief', still yearned continually to go
home to rocky Ithaca.

Olympus, Mount

The highest mountain in Greece, almost 10,000 feet high
and situated on and around the borders of Macedonia
and Thessaly. From early times Olympus was believed to
be the home of the gods ruled over by ZEUS, thus giving
them their familiar name of the Olympian gods. Gradually the concept of 'Olympus' became distinct from the
mountain itself, and the gods were rather nebulously
imagined as dwelling in the sky above Mount Olympus.
A gate of clouds kept by the HORAE, the Goddesses of the
Seasons, opened to allow the passage of the gods from
Olympus to earth. Homer describes their blessed abode
(*Odyssey* 6.42–6):

Here, they say, the dwelling of the gods
stands firm forever. No winds disturb it,
rains drench, nor does snow come near,
but the clear air stretches away, cloudless,
a bright radiance playing over it. Here
the blessed gods live all their days in bliss.

Omphale

A queen of Lydia, who took over the government of the
country on the death of her husband, Tmolus. When
HERACLES wished to be purified of the murder of Iphitus,
the son of EURYTUS (1), he was sentenced to be sold into
slavery and it was Omphale who bought him. He served
her for either one or three years. During this period he
performed many courageous feats: he killed the brigand
SYLEUS, captured the CERCOPES, killed a giant snake that
was plaguing the country, and sacked the city of Omphale's
enemies, the Itoni. But there was also a domestic side to
Heracles' period of servitude, for it was said that Omphale
wore his lionskin and brandished his club, while he himself wore women's clothes and helped his mistress and
her ladies with their spinning. He may have done this
under compulsion, but it may well be that he submitted
willingly to this treatment since (ever susceptible) he had
fallen in love with his queen. Certainly she bore him a
son, Lamus (or Agelaus according to Apollodorus), before
she set him free.

In ancient art Heracles appears in the company of
Omphale only occasionally (fig.104), but the story becomes

**Fig.104 Omphale and Heracles. Omphale is dressed
in Heracles' lion's skin and Heracles, exposing his
genitals, in her robe.**

far more popular in the postclassical arts, with paintings
by Cranach, Tintoretto, Rubens, Giordano, Boucher and
Goya, among many others.

[Sophocles, *Women of Trachis* 248–90; Apollodorus 2.6.3,
2.7.8; Diodorus Siculus 4.31.5–8; Ovid, *Heroides* 9.53–118,
Fasti 2.303–58; Seneca, *Hercules on Oeta* 371–7.]

Opheltes

The son of Lycurgus, king of Nemea, who was killed by a
snake (*see* HYPSIPYLE).

Ophion *see* EURYNOME.

Ophiuchus (The Serpent-holder)

A constellation most commonly thought to be the healer
ASCLEPIUS, holding one of his sacred snakes. Sometimes it
was said to be Heracles, killing a snake for the Lydian
queen OMPHALE; or PHORBAS, who was honoured for ridding the island of Rhodes of snakes; or the Thracian
king Carnabon, who in a jealous rage killed one of the
dragons drawing the chariot of TRIPTOLEMUS.

Ops

The Roman Goddess of Plenty, believed to be of ancient origin, who had her temple on the Capitol. She was identified with the Greek goddess RHEA (1), wife of Cronus, and was paired with Cronus' Roman equivalent, SATURN, as well as with Consus, a Roman god of the granary.

Orchamus

A Persian king whose daughter, Clytie, was loved by HELIOS.

Orcus

A Roman name for HADES (1) and his realm.

Oreads *see* NYMPHS.

Oreithyia *see* BOREAS.

Orestes

Son of AGAMEMNON and CLYTEMNESTRA, and brother of ELECTRA (3), IPHIGENEIA and CHRYSOTHEMIS. He killed his mother and her lover AEGISTHUS to avenge their murder of his father, but his vengeance was viewed rather differently down the centuries. Treated by Homer as an act of justice in response to an appalling crime, by the fifth century BC it was seen as rather more problematic, since Orestes was then said to be hounded by the FURIES of his dead mother in punishment for her shed blood.

According to the *Odyssey*'s version of the myth, Orestes returned to Mycenae eight years after Agamemnon's murder. He killed Aegisthus and, it is implied,

Clytemnestra as well, with his vengeance being depicted as an entirely praiseworthy deed for which he won an honoured reputation. The story is used as a moral example for the other characters of the epic: Telemachus is urged to confront and take revenge on the Suitors, just as Orestes did on the evil Aegisthus; and Penelope is drawn as the loyal and virtuous wife, in vivid contrast to the unfaithful and husband-killing Clytemnestra. Orestes is seen as a just and avenging hero, and there is no hint of any pursuit by his mother's Furies who later play so important a part in the legend. Her murderous treachery demanded punishment, and Orestes, as head of the family, would necessarily have been her judge and executioner. No mention is made of Electra, the sister who would later be reunited joyously with Orestes and would support him through the murders.

The lyric poet Stesichorus wrote a long *Oresteia*, now lost apart from a few fragments. We know, however, that Electra played a part in it, as did the Furies against whom APOLLO provided Orestes with a bow. But it is fifth-century tragedy, in which Orestes becomes a major figure, that provides the fullest details of his legend. At the time of Agamemnon's murder the young Orestes was taken for safety to STROPHIUS, king of Phocis and brother-in-law of Agamemnon, who brought the boy up with his own son, PYLADES. The two became firm friends, and in the vengeance plays Pylades accompanies Orestes when he returns secretly home to Mycenae, having learnt from Apollo's Delphic Oracle that he must avenge his father's death. Here he meets his sister Electra and they recognise each other with mutual joy. In Aeschylus' *Libation Bearers* (458 BC), this reunion occurs at the tomb of Agamemnon, and brother and sister join in an invocation to their father's ghost, urging him to support the vengeance. But the focus of this play is still mainly on Orestes as avenger, and Electra is not actively involved in the killings. Orestes gains admittance to the palace as a stranger, bringing news of his own death, and he kills first Aegisthus (fig. 7), then Clytemnestra. It is the murder of his mother which causes him the greatest anguish. Clytemnestra, face to face with her now recognised son, appeals to him (figs. 41 and 105) by the bond they shared when he was a baby (896–8): 'Stop, my son! Show pity, child, before this breast, where often you would lay your head in sleep, and with soft gums sucked in the milk that gave you life.' Orestes hesitates, appalled at what he is about to do, and turns for advice to Pylades, who (speaking for the first and only time in the play) reminds him of Apollo's

Fig. 105 Clytemnestra bares her breast and appeals for mercy to her son, Orestes, as he is about to kill her.

instructions and of the sacred nature of his vengeance. His confidence recovered, Orestes leads his mother into the palace and there kills her. He is at once hounded by her terrifying Furies (fig. 58), who form the Chorus of the following play, the *Eumenides*. Here Orestes is sent by Apollo to Athens, where he is tried by a jury of Athenians at the homicide court on the Areopagus, with Apollo acting as his advocate and the Furies as his prosecutors. When the jury's votes turn out to be equal, ATHENA gives the casting vote in Orestes' favour, on the grounds that a father takes precedence over a mother. He is acquitted. The Furies are propitiated by a new cult at Athens in which they are honoured in their new role as beneficent powers.

Electra's role in helping her brother is developed in the *Electra* plays of Sophocles and Euripides. In Sophocles' play she stands outside the palace door, while Orestes is inside killing their mother, and urges him on. In Euripides' *Electra* she is by far the more dominant figure of the pair while Orestes is weak and indecisive. He would prefer to let his mother go free, and it is Electra who plans how to kill Clytemnestra and drives Orestes on to do the deed, even grasping the sword with him when his own hand fails. Here in Euripides (quite unlike Sophocles) brother and sister are overcome with guilt and remorse as soon as the murder is accomplished. Here too (again unlike Sophocles, where the murder is seen as an act of justice rather as in Homer) the Furies will hound Orestes, though it is predicted by the DIOSCURI at the end of the play that he will again find freedom from his pursuers after trial at Athens.

In Euripides' unorthodox version of the aftermath of the vengeance in his *Orestes*, the Furies, instead of physically pursuing the murderer through Greece, are seen as imagined phantoms caused by Orestes' guilt at killing his mother. He is made to stand trial by Clytemnestra's father, TYNDAREOS. OEAX, who hated Agamemnon for letting his brother Palamedes be stoned to death, now urges Orestes' banishment. The verdict turns out to be worse than that, for Orestes and Electra are condemned to death by the Argive citizens. In an attempt to force MENELAUS to help them they, with Pylades, try (and fail) to kill HELEN, who is taken to safety and immortality by Zeus, and they seize HERMIONE as a hostage. Order is finally restored by Apollo, who rules that Orestes has only to suffer a year's exile from his city before being tried and acquitted, as usual, at Athens.

In Euripides' *Iphigeneia in Tauris*, Apollo has told Orestes that to gain his final release from the Furies he must fetch to Athens a holy image of Artemis from the land of the barbarian Taurians in the Cimmerian Cher-

sonese (Crimea). He and Pylades are captured on arrival by the natives and taken, on the orders of the savage king Thoas, to the priestess of Artemis' temple for sacrifice. This is the fate of all strangers who come to the land. At the last moment they discover that the priestess is Orestes' long-lost sister Iphigeneia, who is filled with joy at the thought of returning home to Mycenae with her dear brother. She tricks the Taurians into standing at a distance, while she pretends to wash away in the sea the stain of matricide from her two victims. All three sail swiftly away to safety, taking with them the statue of Artemis as instructed by Apollo. Athena intervenes to stop the furious king Thoas from pursuing them, and calmed by the goddess he even wishes them well. According to another version, which may originate from a play by Sophocles, the three fugitives were hotly pursued by Thoas. They came to the house of CHRYSEIS, who had borne a son to Agamemnon named Chryses. The boy, at first wishing to hand them over to Thoas, helped them instead to kill their pursuer when he found out that he was their half-brother. Orestes also plays a part in Euripides' *Andromache*, where Hermione, married to NEOPTOLEMUS, persecutes his concubine Andromache and her son Molossus. Orestes himself was betrothed to Hermione before the Trojan War, and he now saves her from her husband's wrath by carrying her off to Sparta, where he will marry her after Neoptolemus' death (here brought about at Delphi by Orestes himself).

Orestes took the throne of Mycenae and Argos, in one version first killing a usurper, his half-brother ALETES, the son of Aegisthus and Clytemnestra, and almost killing his half-sister ERIGONE (2) too. He also ruled Sparta on the death of Menelaus. He and Hermione had a son, TISAMENUS (1), who succeeded Orestes on his death.

Pausanias records several local traditions commemorating Orestes' cure from the madness brought on him by the Furies. At Athens there was an altar which he himself, it was said, set up to mark his freedom from the Furies granted by the court on the Areopagus, as in Aeschylus. There was a stone at Troezen on which he was purified by nine of the citizens, and another at Gythium where he was cured of madness. At a place near Megalopolis he was said to have bitten off one of his fingers in his frenzy, at which he became sane again and the Furies benign.

Oresthasium in Arcadia was reputedly the scene of Orestes' death in old age from a snake-bite, after which it was renamed Oresteium. He was buried at Tegea. Centuries later, according to Herodotus (1.67), when the Spartans were trying to capture Tegea, they were told by the Delphic Oracle that they would be victorious if they brought Orestes' bones back to Sparta. These, said the oracle obscurely, were at Tegea, at a place where two winds blew under strong constraint, where blow met blow and woe was laid upon woe. The place turned out to be a blacksmith's forge, the 'winds' being the two pairs of bellows, the 'blows and counterblows' the hammer and anvil, and the 'woe' the beaten iron, which, used for weapons, brings woe to mankind. Buried in the yard of the forge was found a coffin ten feet long, its whole length filled by a huge skeleton. The bones were taken to Sparta, and ever since that day the Spartans had the better of the Tegeans.

See also fig. 137.

[Homer, *Iliad* 9.141–3, *Odyssey* 1.29–46, 298–302, 3.193–200, 303–10, 4.546–7; Pindar, *Pythian* 11.15–37; Apollodorus, *Epitome* 6.14, 6.24–8; Pausanias 1.22.6, 1.28.5–6, 1.33.8, 2.16.7, 2.18.6, 2.29.9, 2.31.4, 3.3.5–6, 3.11.10, 3.22.1, 8.34.1–4; 8.54.4.]

Orion

A giant hunter who, after his death, was immortalised as one of the best-known constellations in the night sky. In the earlier tradition he was said to be the son of POSEIDON and Euryale, the daughter of MINOS, though a late account makes him the earth-born son of HYRIEUS. Poseidon granted Orion the ability to cross the sea with ease: either he could walk on water, or he was so tall that he could wade through the deepest ocean with his head and shoulders still clear of the waves. He was married to Side, a woman so lovely that she claimed to rival HERA, queen of heaven, in beauty. Hera punished this rash arrogance by casting Side into Hades. For the late story of Orion's daughters, Metioche and Menippe, *see* CORONIDES.

Orion crossed the sea to Chios and there wooed Merope, the daughter of King Oenopion, who promised him Merope's hand if he would rid the island of wild beasts. To Orion, the mightiest living hunter, this was no problem, but Oenopion then went back on his bargain. Orion, frustrated by the ever-delayed marriage, became drunk and raped Merope, and the angry king avenged his daughter by blinding Orion while he slept in his drunken stupor, then drove him out of Chios. Orion crossed the sea to Lemnos where HEPHAESTUS had his forge, and here the god took pity on him, giving him his servant Cedalion to act as his guide. Orion set the boy on his shoulders, telling him to lead him to the sunrise, and they travelled eastwards into the sun's rays until the Sun-god HELIOS restored Orion's sight. At once he returned to Chios, plotting revenge on Oenopion, but all to no avail, for the Chians had hidden their king in an underground house built by Hephaestus. Orion gave up his revenge and went to Crete, where he spent his time hunting wild animals in the company of ARTEMIS and LETO. So great was

his prowess that he boasted there was no animal on earth that he could not kill, and GAIA (Earth) in anger sent a giant scorpion that stung him to death. At the request of Artemis and Leto, Zeus immortalised Orion in the stars. The scorpion was made a constellation too because of his great service to the beasts of the earth.

There are other versions of Orion's death, but in every case he died violently. Either he fell in love with Artemis and tried to rape her, and it was the goddess who sent the lethal scorpion; or he was killed for daring to challenge Artemis to a discus match; or Artemis shot him for a variety of reasons: because he tried to rape the Hyperborean maiden Opis, or because he became the lover of EOS, goddess of the Dawn, or even accidentally. In this last case, Artemis enjoyed Orion's company so much that she was thinking of marrying him, so her brother Apollo, in alarm, tricked her into killing him. He pointed to an object far out to sea and challenged her to hit it with an arrow. She did so, and realised that the object had been Orion's head only when his corpse floated to shore.

Orion has been famous as a constellation from Homer onwards. He is said to be pursuing the PLEIADES, girls whom he had once loved when on earth. As a great hunter he is naturally accompanied by a dog, the constellation Canis Major, which includes the brilliant star Sirius, the Dog Star, and he has in his sights a Hare (Lepus) and a Bull (Taurus). A Bear (Ursa Major) keeps a watchful eye on him from a distance, and the Scorpion (Scorpio) is still in relentless pursuit of his old enemy.

[Homer, *Iliad* 18.486–9, *Odyssey* 5.121–4, 274, 11.572–5; Hesiod, *Works and Days* 619–20, *Catalogue of Women* fr. 148a; Apollodorus 1.4.3–5; Virgil, *Aeneid* 10.763–7; Ovid, *Fasti* 5.537–44. J. Fontenrose, *Orion* (1981).]

Orpheus

The supreme singer and musician of Greek myth, so skilled that he entranced the whole of nature with his song, taming savage beasts and moving even rocks and trees. As Shakespeare would put it (*Two Gentlemen of Verona* III. ii. 78–81):

> For Orpheus' lute was strung with poets' sinews,
> Whose golden touch could soften steel and stones,
> Make tigers tame, and huge leviathans
> Forsake unsounded deeps to dance on sands.

Orpheus accompanied the ARGONAUTS on their expedition to fetch the Golden Fleece, lulling the waves and soothing the crew with his music. He even saved their lives by drowning out the SIRENS' singing with his own, surpassing theirs in sweetness.

Orpheus was the son of one of the MUSES, usually said to be Calliope, by either APOLLO or the Thracian Oeagrus.

His best-known myth is his descent to the Underworld to fetch back his wife Eurydice. Our first reference to the story is in Euripides' *Alcestis* (357–62) of 438 BC, though it is only with Virgil and Ovid that the story is told in detail. Soon after Orpheus married the nymph Eurydice, she died of a snake-bite, perhaps while she was pursued by the amorous ARISTAEUS. Orpheus so mourned her death that he determined to bring her back from Hades. He passed through the entrance to the Underworld at Taenarum in Laconia and courageously made the long and lonely descent. He sang, and CHARON, the ferryman, and the watchdog CERBERUS were so charmed by his music that they allowed him to enter. Again he sang, and entranced the entire world of the dead. All the shades listened and wept. TANTALUS (1) forgot his hunger and thirst. The vultures stopped tearing at TITYUS' liver. SISYPHUS sat on his great stone to listen. The wheel of IXION stood still. Then, for the first time, the cheeks of the FURIES were wet with tears. Most important of all, HADES (1) and PERSEPHONE were delighted and said that he might take his Eurydice back to earth. Their only condition was that he must lead the way, and that he must not look back at her until they had regained the light of the sun. It may be that in the early, lost version of the myth, Orpheus succeeded in winning back his wife. But this is not so in the familiar, later version. They set off, Eurydice following her husband, and Orpheus was just reaching the end of the long ascent when, eager for sight of his wife and afraid that she might not be there behind him, he looked back. At once she melted away into the darkness, dying for the second time.

Orpheus tried to follow her, but this time his entrance to Hades was resolutely refused. Eventually he returned to Thrace and wandered through the land, mourning inconsolably and singing of his loss. Finally he was torn to pieces by Thracian women (or MAENADS). Various motives are given for their bloodthirsty act. Either they resented Orpheus for his fidelity to the memory of Eurydice, or for turning to the love of boys in his grief. Or they were driven to it by APHRODITE, resentful because of his mother Calliope's judgement in the dispute with Persephone over ADONIS; or by DIONYSUS, angry because Orpheus had failed to worship him, preferring HELIOS, the Sun-god. Or each of the women wanted Orpheus for herself, and they tore him apart in the resultant squabble. Whatever their motive, it resulted in a ghastly death for the world's finest singer.

The birds and the beasts, even the rocks and the trees, wept for Orpheus. His head was thrown into the River Hebrus and floated, still singing, down the stream. It was carried to Lesbos, where the people buried it and were rewarded with an especial skill in music and poetry. The Muses gathered up the scattered fragments of his body and buried them in Pieria, where the nightingale was said to sing more sweetly over his grave than anywhere else in Greece. His lyre was set by Zeus among the stars as the constellation Lyra. His shade passed once more to Hades, where he was reunited with his Eurydice, able now to walk with her and gaze his fill, no longer fearing to lose her by an incautious glance.

Orpheus was said to be the founder of the mystic cult of Orphism (*see* ZAGREUS) and was credited with the authorship of many poems and mystical books. He appears occasionally in ancient art (fig. 106); and Pausanias (9.30.4) tells us that there was a statue of him on Mount HELICON, home of the Muses, where he was surrounded by animals of stone and bronze, listening to his singing. His legend has been of tremendous inspiration in the postclassical arts, particularly to painters, dramatists and composers. Many operas have been based on the story of Orpheus and Eurydice, the most famous being Monteverdi's *Orpheus* (1607), Gluck's *Orpheus and Eurydice* (1762), and Offenbach's *Orpheus in the Underworld* (1858).

[Simonides, fr. 567; Pindar, *Pythian* 4.176–7; Aeschylus, *Agamemnon* 1629–30; Euripides, *Bacchae* 560–4, *Iphigeneia at Aulis* 1211–14, *Rhesus* 943–4; Plato, *Symposium* 179b–d; Apollonius, *Argonautica*; Apollodorus 1.3.2, 1.9.16, 1.9.25, 2.4.9; Diodorus Siculus 1.23, 1.96, 3.65, 4.25; Pausanias

Fig. 106 Thracians listen entranced to the music of Orpheus.

9.30.4–7, 10.7.2, 10.30.6; Virgil, *Georgics* 4.453–503, *Culex* 268–95; Ovid, *Metamorphoses* 10.1–85, 11.1–84. I. M. Linforth, *The Arts of Orpheus* (1941); C. Segal, *Orpheus: The Myth of the Poet* (1989).]

Orthus or Orthrus

The two-headed hound who guarded the cattle of GERYON. According to Hesiod he was the offspring of the monsters ECHIDNA and TYPHON and thus brother of CERBERUS and the HYDRA OF LERNA (*Theogony* 306–15). He fathered the Theban SPHINX and the NEMEAN LION on either Echidna or the CHIMAERA (*Theogony* 326–32, with the pronoun at 326 being ambiguous).

He was killed by HERACLES during his raid on Geryon's cattle. In ancient art Orthus is sometimes depicted in scenes of the combat, usually with arrows protruding from his body (fig. 60) although Apollodorus (2.5.10) says that he was clubbed to death. Sometimes he has two heads, sometimes one, and on one occasion three.

Osiris *see* DIONYSUS and ISIS.

Ossa, Mount

A mountain in Thessaly, one of three mountains piled up by the giants OTUS AND EPHIALTES in their attempt to scale the heavens and overthrow the gods.

Othryoneus *see* CASSANDRA.

Otus and Ephialtes

Twin giants, called the Aloadae after their nominal father Aloeus, but really the sons of POSEIDON. Aloeus was married to Iphimedeia, the daughter of his brother Triops, but she fell in love with the sea-god. She often went down to the sea and cupped the sea-water in her hands, pouring it over her body. One day Poseidon came to her and she bore him Otus and Ephialtes. The boys grew at an alarming rate. When Odysseus met the shade of Iphimedeia in Hades (*Odyssey* 11.305–20), she told him their story. They were the largest and handsomest of all mortals after the giant hunter Orion, and by the time they were nine years old they were over fifty feet (sixteen metres) tall. They threatened to do battle with the gods themselves, and to pile Mount Ossa on Mount Olympus, and Mount Pelion on Ossa, until they reached the very heaven. 'And they would have done it too', says Homer, 'if they had grown to manhood.' But before then Apollo killed them: 'before the down bloomed below their temples, or covered their chins with the blossom of youth'.

Apollodorus (1.7.4) says that they succeeded in piling Ossa on Olympus and Pelion on Ossa, and that when they reached the gods they shut ARES up in a bronze jar. The same strange story is told by Dione in the *Iliad* (5.385–91). Ares, god of war, was chained up in the jar for thirteen months, at the end of which time he was rescued in a state of great exhaustion by HERMES. Perhaps the Aloadae had aimed to weaken the gods militarily before they did battle with them. But Apollodorus also says that the twins wooed the goddesses HERA (Ephialtes) and ARTEMIS (Otus). After this presumption, Artemis killed them in Naxos by a trick. She turned herself into a deer and ran between them, upon which they each flung their spear at her, but missed and struck each other. So whether their intention was to make war or love with the gods, the outcome was the same, and they died.

Pausanias (9.22.6) saw the tomb of the Aloadae at Anthedon, on the coast of Boeotia. He says (9.29.1–2) that they founded Ascra in Boeotia, and were (surprisingly) the first mortals to sacrifice to the MUSES and to say that Helicon was their sacred mountain, recognising three Muses instead of the later nine. 'Piling Pelion on Ossa' has become proverbial for adding difficulty to difficulty.

Oxylus

Son of Andraemon or his grandson Haemon; an Aetolian who became king of Elis. Oxylus was banished from Aetolia for a year because he had accidentally killed a man while throwing the discus, either his brother Thermius or a man named Alcidocus. He took refuge in Elis. On his way home again at the end of a year, he met the HERACLIDS, on their way to conquer the Peloponnese. They had been advised by an oracle to take 'the three-eyed one' as their guide, and since Oxylus was riding a one-eyed horse, or driving a one-eyed mule, they saw in this combination the fulfilment of the oracle. Oxylus led them through the Peloponnese, but he was careful to stay away from fertile Elis, a land that he wanted for himself, and took them instead through mountainous Arcadia.

The Heraclids made themselves masters of the Peloponnese and divided it among themselves, but said that Oxylus might have Elis in return for his help. He still, however, had to overcome local resistance from the Elean king, Dius. Oxylus led a band of his Aetolian compatriots into Elis, where Dius proposed that the rule should be settled by single combat between two champions, his own Elean archer, Degmenus, and Oxylus' Aetolian slinger, Pyraechmes. Pyraechmes won and Oxylus became king of Elis, ruling the land in peace and prosperity.

[Apollodorus 2.8.3; Pausanias 5.3.5–5.4.5, 5.8.5.]

P Q

Paeon (1) (Sometimes **Paean**)

God of healing in the *Iliad*. He quickly cures ARES of the wound given him in battle by Diomedes; and Dione recounts how he once healed HADES (1), who left the Underworld and went for help to Olympus when painfully struck in the shoulder by one of Heracles' poisonous arrows. After Homer's time the name Paeon became an epithet of other gods associated with healing, of APOLLO and ASCLEPIUS, and of the final great healer, THANATOS (Death).

[Homer, *Iliad* 5.388–402, 899–904, *Odyssey* 4.232; Sophocles, *Oedipus the King* 154; Apollonius, *Argonautica* 4.1508–17.]

Paeon (2)

Son of ENDYMION, the king of Elis. Endymion made his three sons, Aetolus, Epeius and Paeon, run a race to determine who would inherit the throne. Epeius won and Paeon, angry at his defeat, travelled far away from Elis and settled north of Macedonia, naming the land Paeonia after himself.

[Pausanias 5.1.4–5.]

Palaemon

A sea-god, once the mortal Melicertes (*see* INO).

Palamedes ('The inventive one')

The proverbially ingenious son of NAUPLIUS (1) and CLYMENE (3), credited with the invention of writing, counting, weights and measures, and military tactics, as well as the games of draughts and dice with which he and his comrades whiled away the TROJAN WAR. At the beginning of the war, when he went with other envoys to enlist support for the expedition against Troy, he made an implacable enemy in ODYSSEUS by forcing him to serve against his will. He found Odysseus pretending to be mad, ploughing his land with two unlikely animals yoked together and sowing salt. But Palamedes realised that this was merely a ruse, and he foiled Odysseus'

scheme by offering some threat to his little son, TELEMACHUS. Either he put the baby in front of the ploughshare, or threatened him with his sword. Odysseus at once saved his son, proving that he was after all sane, and was then obliged to go to war. He never forgave Palamedes.

In due course Odysseus contrived his revenge. One version said that he and DIOMEDES (2) drowned Palamedes while he was fishing, another that they lowered him down a well where they claimed to have found gold, then threw down stones on top of him until he died. But according to the usual story, Odysseus forged a letter to Palamedes, purportedly from the Trojan king, Priam, promising a sum of gold if he would betray the Greeks. He then buried this same amount of gold in his victim's tent. The letter was either dropped in the camp, or planted on a Trojan captive. It soon came to the notice of AGAMEMNON, who read it, found the gold, and handed the apparently guilty Palamedes over to the army to be punished. They stoned him to death as a traitor. The irony of the inventor of writing being unjustly brought to death by a written message would become a powerful tragic theme in the hands of the fifth-century dramatists. Palamedes' brother OEAX and his father Nauplius were both consumed with hatred for the Greeks because of his unjustified murder, and they both did their best to avenge his death.

Palamedes was a vivid and important mythological figure to the Greeks, even though he may seem rather obscure to us because he is not much mentioned in extant literature. Aeschylus, Sophocles and Euripides all wrote *Palamedes* plays, and Sophocles in addition one (possibly two) *Nauplius* plays, dealing with Nauplius' revenge, and *The Mad Odysseus*, telling of Odysseus' recruitment by Palamedes on Ithaca. All of these plays are lost, but for fragments. Socrates, before he was put to death, felt a great sense of identity with Palamedes because of his unjust trial and murder, and looked forward to meeting him in the Underworld. The story of the false charge of treason does not occur in Homer, perhaps because he did not know of it (he makes no mention of Palamedes), perhaps because he wished to draw a sympathetic portrait of Odysseus and thus could not allow so discreditable a tale; but elsewhere Odysseus' hatred of Palamedes is notorious. Virgil has the Greek spy SINON win the Trojans' immediate confidence by pretending that Odysseus hated him because he had spoken out against his treatment of Palamedes. Pausanias (10.31.1–2) tells us that Polygnotus, in his painting of the Underworld, depicted Palamedes playing dice with AJAX (1) and THERSITES, all three of whom had suffered at Odysseus' hands.

[Epic Cycle, Proclus' summary of the *Cypria*; Xenophon, *Apology* 26; Plato, *Apology* 41b; Apollodorus 2.1.5, 3.2.2, *Epitome* 3.7–8, 6.8–11; Virgil, *Aeneid* 2.77–99; Ovid, *Metamorphoses* 13.34–62, 308–12. S. Woodford, 'Palamedes seeks revenge', *Journal of Hellenic Studies* 114 (1994), pp. 164–9.]

Palinurus

In Virgil's *Aeneid*, Palinurus is the helmsman of AENEAS' ship. In Book 5 (814–71), after the Trojans have encountered a violent storm, Poseidon reassures Venus that Aeneas will yet have a successful voyage to Italy. The life of one man only will be lost, and his death will ensure that the rest survive. Palinurus turns out to be that man. Somnus (Sleep) comes down to him while he is steering the ship through a clear night and induces him to go to sleep at the helm. He falls overboard, taking with him the tiller and part of the stern, and as he falls he wakes, and calls again and again to his comrades. But they are asleep and no one hears. Only later does Aeneas realise that his helmsman is lost, and grieves for him: 'You trusted too much in a clear sky and a calm sea, Palinurus', he says, 'and now your body must lie naked on an unknown shore' (870–1).

Palinurus is washed up alive on the Italian coast, but is there killed by a local tribe. In Book 6 (337–83) Aeneas, accompanied by the Sibyl, meets his shade in the Underworld among the sorrowing crowd of unburied dead who await passage over the Styx. The Sibyl reassures Palinurus that his bones will be laid to rest by the inhabitants of the place where he was killed, and that his name will be given to a local headland. 'And he rejoiced at the thought of the land that would be called after him', says Virgil (383). To this day, Cape Palinurus in south-western Italy bears his name.

Palladium

A statue of Pallas ATHENA, believed to have the power of keeping safe the city that possessed it. The statue, about four and a half feet long says Apollodorus, had its feet joined together, and one hand flourished a spear while the other held a spindle and distaff. When Zeus was amorously pursuing the Pleiad ELECTRA (1), she clung to the Palladium for safety and Zeus, in annoyance, flung it out of Olympus. It was at that moment that ILUS, king of Troy, prayed for a sign of approval from Zeus for his new city. The Palladium fell at his feet from the sky, and at the spot where it landed he built Troy's great temple of Athena to house it. It was believed that as long as the guardian statue was kept safely there, Troy would never fall.

In the tenth year of the Trojan War the Greeks captured the Trojan seer HELENUS, who revealed to them the oracles, known only to himself, foretelling how they could take Troy. One of the conditions of success was that they should steal the Palladium. This feat was undertaken by ODYSSEUS and DIOMEDES (2), although there are different versions of the way in which they achieved it. Either Odysseus left Diomedes on guard while he went to the temple alone, dressed in rags; HELEN recognised him and helped him to steal the sacred statue, and he transported it back to the Greek camp with Diomedes' help. Or Diomedes stood on Odysseus' shoulders to climb over the city walls, but refused to pull up his companion after him and alone won the glory of the successful theft. Or the two of them went into the city through a sewer and together brought out the Palladium. However the theft was achieved, the outcome was always the same and Troy fell to the Greeks.

The victorious Greeks took the statue away when they sailed, but various cities later claimed to possess it, including Athens, Sparta and Argos. The Romans too believed that an image in their temple of Vesta was the Palladium, either saved from the flames of Troy (the Greeks having stolen merely a copy) and brought to Italy by the Trojan AENEAS, or surrendered to them by Diomedes.

[Euripides, *Rhesus* 499–507; Apollodorus 3.12.3, *Epitome* 5.10–13; Dionysius of Halicarnassus 1.68–9, 2.66.5; Pausanias 1.28.8–9, 2.23.5; Virgil, *Aeneid* 2.162–79; Ovid, *Metamorphoses* 13.337–49, *Fasti* 6.417–36.]

Pallas (1)

Title of uncertain origin given to the goddess ATHENA, the virgin goddess of war. Suggested meanings include 'Brandisher' (of weapons) and 'Maiden'; or it may be derived from one of the GIANTS named Pallas, whom Athena slew during their war with the gods. She then flayed him and used his tough skin as a shield. Or (a late legend) she may have taken the name in memory of a playmate named Pallas whom she accidentally killed when young.

[Apollodorus 1.6.2, 3.12.3.]

Pallas (2)

A Titan, son of the TITANS CRIUS and EURYBIA, and father, by the river-goddess STYX, of Zelus (Aspiration), NIKE (Victory), Cratos (Power) and BIA (Might).

[Hesiod, *Theogony* 375–7, 383–8; Apollodorus 1.2.2–4; Pausanias 7.26.12.]

Pallas (3)

Son of PANDION (2), the deposed ninth king of Athens, and brother of AEGEUS, NISUS (1) and LYCUS (4). After their father's death, the brothers marched against Athens and drove out the sons of Metion, who had usurped Pandion's throne. Aegeus became king. For many years he was (as far as he knew) childless, but eventually he found that Aethra, the daughter of Pittheus, had borne him a son, THESEUS. When Aegeus publicly announced that Theseus would be his successor on the throne of Athens, Pallas and his fifty sons, who had hoped to inherit the kingdom on Aegeus' death and now felt that Theseus was a usurper, broke into open rebellion. Theseus crushed the revolt. After he had succeeded to the throne on his father's death, Pallas and his sons made a last desperate bid for power, but Theseus killed them all.

[Apollodorus 3.15.5–6, *Epitome* 1.11; Plutarch, *Theseus* 3, 13; Pausanias 1.22.2, 1.28.10.]

Pallas (4)

In the *Aeneid*, Pallas is the son of EVANDER who goes with AENEAS to fight the Latins. He is killed by TURNUS, to Aeneas' grief; and when Aeneas in turn wounds Turnus, it is the sight of his victim wearing Pallas' belt as a battle spoil that drives Aeneas, ablaze with anger, to kill him mercilessly.

[Virgil, *Aeneid* 8.102–607, 10.362–509, 11.1–99, 12.919–52.]

Pan

A god of shepherds and flocks – part-man part-goat – whose birth in ARCADIA is celebrated in the *Homeric Hymn to Pan*. HERMES fell in love with the (unnamed) daughter of Dryops, and for her sake spent his time tending her father's sheep. He won her love, and she bore him a most unusual son (35–47):

> ... who from his birth was a wonder to behold, with the feet of a goat and two horns – a noisy, laughing child. When the nurse saw his uncouth face and bearded chin, she was afraid and, springing up, she fled and left the boy. But Hermes the luck-bringer took him in his arms, and immeasurable joy filled his heart. He went quickly to the abodes of the immortal gods, carrying the child wrapped in the warm pelt of a mountain hare, and setting him down beside Zeus and the rest of the gods, he showed them his son. Then all

Fig. 107 **The pastoral god Pan pursues a youth, with the rustic herm behind him mirroring his excitement.**

the immortals were filled with rejoicing, especially Dionysus, and they called the child Pan ('All') because he delighted all their hearts.

Other genealogies were later supplied for Pan, one of the oddest making him the son of Hermes and PENELOPE, the wife of Odysseus, or – odder still – the fruit of Penelope's orgy with all 129 of her Suitors. Possibly the name of Dryops' daughter was Penelope, and she was later confused with the most famous Penelope in literature.

Pan was a god of the wild countryside, wandering the lonely reaches of mountain and forest, sleeping in the heat of the noontide (when it was thought very dangerous to disturb him), and playing soft and haunting melodies on the pipes of reed which he had himself invented (*see* SYRINX). In time Pan became so expert a musician on his panpipes that he and APOLLO held a musical contest. The judge, the mountain-god Tmolus, pronounced Apollo the winner, but MIDAS, king of Phrygia, was also listening and he favoured Pan. Angry at his intervention, Apollo gave him a pair of asses ears for his pains.

Pan had a lustful nature and was always pursuing NYMPHS who took his fancy. He desired ECHO, but she rejected him. He pursued PITYS, but she fled from his advances and was turned into a pine tree. He was more fortunate in the case of the moon-goddess, SELENE, for he won her favours with the gift of a fine fleece, luring her into the woods as she rode in her silver chariot. With such a nature Pan was thought to be responsible for the fertility of flocks and herds, and the animal domain in general. When a need was felt to encourage reproduction, his statue was beaten with squills to stimulate his powers of fertility.

In the fifth century, Pan's worship spread from ARCADIA into Attica and Boeotia, and from there to the rest of the Greek world. He showed particular favour to the Athenians, appearing to the runner Philippides on a mountain track, while he was running from Athens to Sparta to ask for help at the battle of Marathon (490 BC). Pan asked why the Athenians did not worship him, since he had often helped them in the past and would do so again in the future. After this he came to their aid at Marathon and the Athenians won a great victory. They dedicated to Pan the cave-shrine still to be seen on the slopes of the Acropolis and instituted sacrifices and torch races in his honour. Menander's comedy *The Bad-tempered Man* shows us a religious celebration in honour of Pan, held at the god's cave at Phyle in Attica. A sheep is sacrificed, a meal is enjoyed, and the happy and rowdy celebration lasts all night, with drinking and dancing in the presence of the god. At Rome, Pan was identified with the rustic gods Faunus and Silvanus.

A legend recorded by Plutarch recounts that during the reign of Tiberius (AD 14–37) the passengers of a ship sailing along the western coast of Greece heard a mysterious voice apparently calling to the pilot, a man called Thamus, that 'Great Pan (*Pan megas*) is dead'. This was most likely a misinterpretation of the title *pammegas* ('all-great') applied to the Syrian god Tammuz, identified with Adonis; but Christians took it to refer to the death and resurrection of Christ, and to signify the death of the pagan gods and the end of the pagan era. It was said that at the same time the responses of the pagan oracles ceased for ever. Despite this, Pan lives on, for his unseen presence is the cause of 'panic' (Greek, *panikos*), the overwhelming and irrational terror that can strike violently and unexpectedly, particularly in the silence (or the inexplicable sounds) of the lonely, rocky places where he dwells.

In ancient art Pan is at first depicted as all goat, but later his body and limbs become mainly human. He appears most notably on the Pan-painter's name vase in Boston (fig. 107), where he pursues a youth and is shown as a young man with a goat's head, a short goat's tail, and an erect phallus. He has been a favourite with pastoral poets from classical times onwards, the god of wild nature in an idealised Arcadia, and as such is a popular figure in postclassical painting. Because his name was often taken to mean 'all', he often appears in the company of Venus and Cupid, personifying the well-known saying 'Amor vincit omnia', 'Love conquers all'. For the same reason, he was sometimes seen as a universal god, of all life, the All.

[Herodotus 2.145, 6.105; Theocritus, *Idylls* 1.15–18, 7.106–8; Apollodorus 1.4.1, *Epitome* 7.38; Plutarch, *Moralia* 419b–d; Lucian, *Dialogues of the Gods* 2; Pausanias 1.28.4, 8.36.8, 8.38.11, 8.42.2–3, 8.54.6–7, 10.23.7; Virgil, *Georgics* 3.391–3.]

Pandareos

A king of Miletus. He offended the gods by stealing a wonderful golden guard-dog from the shrine of ZEUS on Crete, the very dog that had guarded the goat who suckled Zeus as a baby. This dog Pandareos left for safekeeping with TANTALUS (1), a king near Mount Sipylus in Lydia, but Tantalus decided to keep the precious beast for himself and thereafter swore that he knew nothing of the creature. Both men were punished. Zeus was said to have piled Mount Sipylus on top of Tantalus, while Pandareos and his wife were killed.

Their daughters were left orphaned, but the gods took pity on them. APHRODITE tended them and fed them on cheese and honey and wine. HERA granted them beauty and good sense, while ARTEMIS gave them stature and ATHENA taught them domestic crafts. One day, however, while Aphrodite was visiting Olympus to consult Zeus about their marriage, the girls were carried off by the HARPIES to be servants to the FURIES. One of Pandareos' daughters, AEDON, escaped this misfortune, for she was already married to Zethus, king of Thebes; but her fate was even more unhappy, for she accidentally killed her own son Itylus. In her grief she was turned into a nightingale, whose song forever laments her dead child.

[Homer, *Odyssey* 19.518–24, 20.67–78; Pausanias 10.30.1–2.]

Pandarus

A skilful archer, favoured by APOLLO. He was the son of Lycaon, the king of Zeleia at the foot of Mount Ida, and an ally of the Trojans. When he went to fight in the Trojan War, his father advised him to take his horses and chariots to Troy. But he was afraid that the horses would not have enough to eat, so he left them at home and fought as a foot-soldier. During a truce between the Greeks and Trojans, ATHENA came to him disguised as a Trojan, Laodocus, with the intention of stirring up trouble. She persuaded him that he would win great glory if only he could shoot MENELAUS dead, so with a prayer to Apollo, Pandarus took aim and shot. Athena deflected the arrow and Menelaus was merely wounded, but the truce was now broken and the war resumed. Soon afterwards Pandarus also wounded DIOMEDES (2), but was then killed by him while fighting alongside Aeneas.

In Chaucer's *Troilus and Criseyde* and Shakespeare's *Troilus and Cressida* (which in their incorporation of ancient characters make many violent changes to the old legends), Pandarus is made Cressida's uncle and is the go-between for the lovers, thus giving us the terms 'pander' and 'panderer' for a procurer.

[Homer, *Iliad* 2.824–7, 4.68–140, 5.95–105 and 166–296.]

Pandion (1)

The sixth mythical king of Athens, son of the snake-man ERICHTHONIUS (1) and the Naiad Praxithea. He married his mother's sister, Zeuxippe, who bore him twin sons, ERECHTHEUS and BUTES (2) (though in early myths Erechtheus was often said to be earth-born), and two daughters, Procne and Philomela. During a boundary dispute with LABDACUS, the king of Thebes, Pandion was aided by the Thracian Tereus and rewarded him with marriage to Procne. For the tragic sequel to this union, *see* TEREUS. When Pandion died, Erechtheus succeeded his father to the throne and Butes received the priesthoods of Athena and Poseidon. It was said that during Pandion's reign the worship of DIONYSUS was instituted in Attica, and perhaps of DEMETER too, though her advent is usually attributed to the reign of Erechtheus.

[Apollodorus 3.14.7–8; Pausanias 1.5.3–4.]

Pandion (2)

Son of CECROPS (2) and Metiadusa, and great-grandson of Pandion (1). After succeeding his father to the throne and becoming the ninth king of Athens, he was ousted by the sons of his uncle Metion. Pandion took refuge in Megara, where he married Pylia, the daughter of King Pylas, and had four sons by her, AEGEUS, NISUS (1), PALLAS (3) and LYCUS (4). When Pylas was exiled for killing his uncle Bias, Pandion took the throne. On his death, Nisus succeeded him to the throne of Megara, while his other sons returned to Athens and drove out the sons of Metion. Aegeus became king of Athens.

[Apollodorus 3.15.6; Strabo 9.1.6; Pausanias 1.5.3–4.]

Pandora ('All Gifts')

The first woman, created out of earth and water by HEPHAESTUS, and the cause of all mankind's woes. The earliest story of her creation can be found in Hesiod. (Though it should be borne in mind that Hesiod had no very high opinion of women: 'Don't be deceived by a wheedling, sweet-talking woman, flaunting her body', he says in his *Works and Days* (373–5), 'she's only after your barn. Anyone who trusts a woman is trusting a cheat.') PROMETHEUS displeased ZEUS by giving the boon of fire to mortals, so the great god decided to balance this blessing by giving men a bane to plague their lives. This bane was woman. On Zeus' instructions, Hephaestus fashioned her from clay in the likeness of the immortal goddesses. Athena dressed and adorned her, and taught her crafts, Aphrodite showered beauty over her, and Hermes put in her breast a nature of cunning and deceit. Then Zeus sent his beautiful but treacherous creation to the gullible Titan EPIMETHEUS, who forgot that he had been warned by his wise brother Prometheus never to take any gift offered by Zeus. Epimetheus, moved by Pandora's beauty, took her as his bride, and in so doing condemned mankind to a lifetime of suffering. For Pandora brought with her as dowry a great jar in which were stored sorrows and diseases and hard labour, previously unknown among men. When she opened the lid of her jar, these poured out and spread over all the earth, so that mortals would never again be free of them. Only hope remained in the jar, still in man's own control, to be some kind of consolation for all the troubles that Pandora had let loose on the world.

Pandora bore Epimetheus a daughter, Pyrrha, who married DEUCALION (1) and with him survived the Great Flood. In the postclassical arts Pandora's jar became confused with the box that PSYCHE was forbidden to open, so 'Pandora's box' became proverbial for a present that seems valuable but is in reality a curse. J. E. T. Rogers (*Economic Interpretations of History*) writes: 'The favours of Government are like the box of Pandora, with this important difference, that they rarely leave hope at the bottom.' Milton, in Book IV of *Paradise Lost*, draws the obvious comparison between Eve and Pandora, both being the root of all evil for mankind (*note*: Prometheus and Epimetheus were sons of Iapetus, here called Japhet):

> More lovely than Pandora, whom the gods
> Endowed with all their gifts; and O, too like
> In sad event, when to the unwiser son
> Of Japhet brought by Hermes, she insnared
> Mankind with her fair looks, to be avenged
> On him who had stole Jove's authentic fire.

[Hesiod, *Theogony* 570–612, *Works and Days* 47–105; Apollodorus 1.2.3, 1.7.2; Pausanias 1.24.7. D. and E. Panofsky, *Pandora's Box* (1962).]

Pandrosus ('Dewy') *see* AGLAURUS (2).

Panopeus and Crisus

Twin sons of PHOCUS (1). The boys shared a lifetime of hostility, for it was said that they fought each other even in their mother's womb. When Phocus was murdered in Aegina, Panopeus and Crisus emigrated to Phocis and founded towns named after them, Panopeus or Phanoteus and Crisa. Panopeus took part in the CALYDONIAN BOARHUNT and was an ally of AMPHITRYON in his raid on the Teleboans. He was the father of EPEIUS (2), who built the WOODEN HORSE.

Panopeus (called Phanoteus) is mentioned in Sophocles' *Electra* (45–6, 670) as being an ally of AEGISTHUS and CLYTEMNESTRA, while Crisus' son STROPHIUS was on the side of ORESTES and the murdered AGAMEMNON. Thus the hostility between the brothers persisted among their descendants.

[Homer, *Iliad* 23.665; Hesiod, *Catalogue of Women* fr. 58; Apollodorus 2.4.7; Pausanias 2.29.4; Ovid, *Metamorphoses* 8.312.]

Panthous

A Trojan elder, son of Othrys and priest of Apollo, who was killed by the Greeks at the sack of Troy. He was the father of three sons, all warriors in the Trojan War: POLYDAMAS, the comrade and prudent counsellor of Hector; EUPHORBUS, the man who first wounded Patroclus in his final, fatal battle and was then killed by Menelaus; and HYPERENOR (2), also killed by Menelaus. Menelaus says of them (*Iliad* 17.20–3):

> Not even so great is the fury of the panther, nor the lion's, nor the fury of the deadly wild boar, within whose breast the spirit is biggest and glares forth in the pride of his strength – none is so great as the pride within the sons of Panthous of the strong ash spear.

[Homer, *Iliad* 3.146–53; Virgil, *Aeneid* 2.318–35, 429–30.]

Paraebius

A poor man of Thrace who, however hard he laboured, grew steadily poorer. At last he asked the seer PHINEUS (2) for advice and learnt that he was paying the penalty for a past sacrilege of his father, who had chopped down an oak tree despite all the tears and pleas of the Hamadryad who lived within it. With her tree destroyed, the dying nymph wished future misery on him and his children. Phineus advised Paraebius now to sacrifice to the nymph, begging her to release him from her curse. He did so, and his luck changed. He was ever after grateful to Phineus and supported him when he was plagued by the monstrous HARPIES.

[Apollonius, *Argonautica* 2.456–89.]

Parcae *see* FATES.

Paris

A Trojan prince, the son of King PRIAM and HECUBA, also known as Alexander (*Alexandros*). When Paris was about to be born, Hecuba dreamed that she gave birth to a firebrand which burned the entire city of Troy. This ominous dream was interpreted by a seer, either AESACUS, Priam's son by another wife, or Priam's daughter CASSANDRA, as meaning that the child would bring utter destruction on Troy; so when Paris was born, Priam gave him to a

Fig. 108 **Paris runs from Menelaus, while Aphrodite (*left*) and Artemis look on.**

servant, Agelaus, to be cast out on Mount IDA to die. (For another tradition, *see* THYMOETES.) But the baby survived, for he was suckled by a bear for five days. When at the end of that time Agelaus found him alive and well, he took him home and brought him up on his farm as his own son.

Paris grew up to be an outstandingly handsome young man. He married the nymph OENONE and lived a rural life as a herdsman on Mount Ida. But before long this occupation would lead him to the truth about his birth. When Priam's servants came to carry off one of his favourite bulls, to be a prize at funeral games in honour of a son long-dead (none other than Paris himself), he was determined to get it back, so he went to Troy to compete in the games. He was so successful, defeating all comers including his own brothers, that he roused the anger of one of them, DEIPHOBUS, who drew his sword to attack him. Paris fled for sanctuary to the altar of Zeus, where his sister Cassandra saw him, and by her visionary powers recognised him as the long-lost son of the house; or according to Euripides' lost *Alexandros*, Hecuba herself, who had been urging Paris' murder, recognised him just in time and restrained Deiphobus. Priam and Hecuba welcomed Paris back into the family, with all thought of the old ominous dream forgotten.

But events had already been set in motion to fulfil Hecuba's prophetic dream. While Paris was tending his flocks on Mount Ida (fig. 81), he had been chosen by Zeus to judge which of three goddesses – HERA, ATHENA or APHRODITE – deserved to win the golden apple thrown down by ERIS at the wedding of Peleus and Thetis and inscribed with the words 'for the fairest'. They all offered Paris bribes: Hera offered him imperial power, Athena victory in battle, and Aphrodite the love of the most beautiful woman in the world, HELEN, wife of King MENELAUS of Sparta. Paris awarded the apple to Aphrodite (*see* JUDGEMENT OF PARIS). Now, as prince of Troy instead of a mere herdsman, he was in a position to visit Sparta and claim Aphrodite's promised reward. When he made known his intention of sailing to Greece, Cassandra and his brother HELENUS tried to dissuade him, as did his wife Oenone: all were seers, and knew just what disasters would follow. But he paid no attention, and set sail for Sparta.

Menelaus received Paris kindly and entertained him royally for nine days, while he responded by giving gifts to Helen. On the tenth day, after telling Helen to supply their guest with anything he might need, Menelaus sailed to Crete to bury his grandfather, Catreus. Influenced by Aphrodite, Helen succumbed to Paris' charms and went to bed with him, after which the couple eloped, taking

with them a good many treasures belonging to Menelaus. Once in Troy, where Helen was accepted by Paris' family and the Trojans, they formally celebrated their marriage. When Menelaus returned home to find that his guest had carried off his wife, he went for help to his brother AGAMEMNON and together they gathered a large army to fetch Helen back by force. Eventually all was ready and they set out for Troy. This was the beginning of the TROJAN WAR, which would lead irrevocably to the wholesale destruction of the city, as foretold in Hecuba's dream.

Homer's *Iliad* narrates events during the tenth year of the war, not long before it will come to an end. Here we see Paris in action. He is still physically beautiful, and there is no doubt that Helen is still in sexual thrall to him, for all that she keeps declaring how much she wishes she had never come to Troy. He is an attractive figure as he lightheartedly cavorts around the battlefield in his leopardskin, but his brother, the serious HECTOR, upbraids him for the trouble he has brought on Troy and for his cowardice (3.39–55):

> Evil Paris, beautiful, woman-crazy deceiver,
> better you had never been born, or had died unwed.
> Truly I would have wished it so. Better by far
> than for you to be a disgrace and a cause for scorn.
> Surely now the long-haired Achaeans laugh aloud,
> thinking you our bravest champion because of
> your beauty, while there is no strength, no courage
>   in your heart ...
> And would you not stand against warlike Menelaus?
> You would learn what kind of man he is, whose lovely
> wife you have taken. The lyre would not help you,
> nor the gifts of Aphrodite, nor your long hair,
> nor your beauty, when you lie low in the dust.

But Paris is far from the cowardly libertine that these lines might suggest. He stands up to Hector: 'Do not hold against me the lovely gifts of golden Aphrodite', he says. 'Glorious gifts of the gods' own giving must never be thrown away, even though a man would not take them by his own choice' (3.64–6). And to a later reproach from his brother, he responds by running gaily from Troy to the battlefield, obviously entirely happy to fight (6.506–14):

> As when a horse, stabled and corn-fed at the manger,
> breaks his rope and gallops in thunder over the plain
> to where he likes to bathe in a sweet-flowing river,
> exulting. He holds his head high and his mane
> streams over his shoulders; knowing his splendour,
> he is carried on swift knees to his loved pastures;
> so came Paris, son of Priam, from the high citadel,
> shining in all his armour like the shining sun,
> laughing aloud as his swift feet carried him.

He certainly has courage, for it is he who proposes his single combat against Menelaus, well aware that he is putting himself in serious danger (fig. 108). In fact he would have been killed by his opponent, had not Aphrodite saved him and spirited him away from the battlefield. But he can also fight effectively, as he does, for instance, against DIOMEDES (2), whom he wounds and puts out of action.

It was also Paris who finally killed ACHILLES, the greatest of the Greek warriors. This happened after the end of the *Iliad*, so we have no knowledge from Homer of exactly what occurred, just the dying Hector's prophecy that Achilles will be killed, for all his valour, 'by Paris and Phoebus Apollo at the Scaean Gate' (22.359–60). According to some late writers, Achilles was killed by Paris not in battle, but in the Thymbraean precinct sacred to Apollo while he was negotiating with Priam for POLYXENA's hand in marriage. Here Paris lay in wait and shot him.

Paris himself was soon afterwards mortally wounded by PHILOCTETES, using the great bow that had once belonged to Heracles. Paris remembered that Oenone had promised to cure any wound that he might have, so he asked to be carried to her on Mount Ida. But she was still angry at his long-ago desertion of her and refused to help him, so he was carried back to Troy. Too late, she changed her mind and hurried to Troy with her healing drugs. But she found Paris dead, and hanged herself from remorse.

[Homer, *Iliad* 3.15–447, 6.313–58, 503–29, 7.347–64, 11.369–83; Pindar, *Paeans* 8; Sophocles, (lost) *Alexandros*; Euripides, *Trojan Women* 919–44, *Iphigeneia at Aulis* 1284–1309, (lost) *Alexandros*; Apollodorus 3.12.5–6, *Epitome* 3.1–5, 5.3, 5.8; Ovid, *Heroides* 5, 16–17. R. A. Coles, 'A New Oxyrhynchus Papyrus: The Hyphothesis of Euripides' *Alexandros*', *BICS* Suppl. 32 (1974).]

Parnassus, Mount

One of the highest mountains in Greece, lying in the Pindus range, which had on its southern slopes APOLLO's famous oracle at Delphi, and nearby the Castalian Spring, whose waters were said to have the power of inspiration. Parnassus was thought in early myth to be the haunt of DIONYSUS and his revelling train of MAENADS, NYMPHS and SATYRS, while Helicon and Pieria were the favourite homes of the MUSES; but later it was Parnassus, more than any other place, that was seen as the home of Apollo and the Muses, and the seat of poetry and music. For this reason, Montparnasse was the name chosen for the low hill on the left bank of the Seine, where the university and the cultural centre of Paris were sited. Parnassus, with Apollo depicted as *musagetes*, leader of the Muses,

and with other classical figures symbolic of the arts, is a favourite scene of postclassical painting.

Parthenopaeus

One of the heroes who took part in the expedition of the SEVEN AGAINST THEBES. He was said in early epic to be a son of TALAUS and Lysimache, and thus a brother of ADRASTUS (1), the leader of the expedition; but later he was made son of the huntress ATALANTA and of either ARES, or MELEAGER, or Melanion. He was usually said to have been crushed to death at Thebes by a huge stone hurled down from the ramparts by PERICLYMENUS (1), but his killer has also been named as Amphidicus or Asphodicus. His son Promachus was one of the EPIGONI who avenged their fathers' deaths.

[Aeschylus, *Seven Against Thebes* 526–62; Euripides, *Phoenician Women* 1104–9, 1153–62, *Suppliant Women* 888–900; Apollodorus 1.9.13, 3.6.3–8, 3.7.2, 3.9.2; Pausanias 9.18.6.]

Pasiphae ('All-shining')

Daughter of the Sun-god HELIOS and the Oceanid Perse (or Perseis), and sister of AEETES, the king of Colchis who owned the Golden Fleece, and of the enchantress CIRCE. Pasiphae married MINOS, the king of Crete, and had many children by him, though she grew so angry at his promiscuity that she gave him noxious drugs which made him ejaculate snakes and scorpions during intercourse. She herself gave birth to the MINOTAUR after coupling with a beautiful white bull, sent by Poseidon from the sea. Pausanias (3.26.1) records that at Thalamae in Laconia she was worshipped as a Moon-goddess.

Pasithea *see* GRACES.

Patroclus

Son of MENOETIUS (2) and beloved comrade of ACHILLES (fig. 109). Indeed, it was Achilles' love for Patroclus that brought about his own death, as Homer movingly relates in the *Iliad*. When, during the last year of the war at Troy, Achilles stays in his tent, angry and refusing to fight because of the wrong that Agamemnon has done him by taking away his concubine BRISEIS, Patroclus and the rest of the MYRMIDONS stay out of the fighting too. Now the battle swings in favour of the Trojans, and the Greeks, with much loss of life, are beaten back to their ships. At the crucial moment when the triumphant Trojans are about to set fire to the ships, Patroclus learns from Nestor that many of the best Greek warriors are wounded and out of action – Diomedes, Odysseus, Agamemnon, EURYPYLUS (2). So Patroclus, urged on by Nestor, goes to Achilles in the hope of persuading him to rejoin the fighting and save the Greek cause. 'Pitiless, you are', he says to his friend. 'The horseman Peleus was never your father, nor Thetis your mother, but you were born of the grey sea and the high cliffs, so hard is the heart in you' (16.33–5). Or, he says, if Achilles himself will not fight, at least he should let Patroclus dress in his armour and lead out the Myrmidons, so that the enemy may think it is Achilles himself and give way in fear. 'So he spoke, begging this in his great ignorance', adds Homer, 'for this was his own death and sorrowful fate that he was asking for' (46–7).

The Trojans now succeed in firing one of the Greek ships and Achilles gives in to Patroclus' plea. He tells his friend to lead out the Myrmidons, and fight, and save the ships, but to be content with this. He must then come back to the camp and on no account advance against the walls of Troy. So Patroclus dresses in Achilles' armour and harnesses his horses, the divine XANTHUS and Balius and the mortal PEDASUS, and as he sets out with his men, Achilles pours a libation to Zeus, praying that he will make his friend's heart brave within him to drive the Trojans from the ships. He also prays for Patroclus' safety. Zeus answers his request in part only (249–52):

> He prayed, and all-wise Zeus heard him. The father
> granted one prayer, but the other he refused: he allowed
> Patroclus to beat back war and tumult from the ships,
> but refused to let him come safely back from the fighting.

For Patroclus disobeys Achilles' command. After he has beaten back the enemy from the ships, he carries on killing many Trojans and Trojan allies, including the great hero SARPEDON, son of Zeus himself, and then he goes against the walls of Troy (702–8):

> Three times Patroclus tried to mount the angle
> of the great wall, three times Apollo drove him back,
> pushing away his bright shield with immortal hands.
> But when for the fourth time Patroclus came on,
> like something more than human, the god cried out,
> threatening him with awesome words of command;
> 'Give way, lord Patroclus! It is not destined
> for this city of proud Trojans to fall to your spear.'

And Patroclus gives way. HECTOR draws near, urged on by APOLLO, and Patroclus kills his charioteer, CEBRIONES. Then he attacks more Trojans. Three times he charges against them, screaming, and three times he cuts down nine men. But when he charges for the fourth time, then Apollo comes against him once more. The god strikes the helmet from Patroclus' head, and splinters his great spear, and tears away his shield and breastplate. Patroclus stands bewildered, until he is struck, first by a spear-cast from EUPHORBUS, then mortally by a spear-thrust from Hector (823–8):

> As a lion overpowers a tireless boar in combat,

Fig. 109 Achilles has removed an arrow from Patroclus' arm and with careful concentration is binding the wound. Patroclus, bracing his left leg, bares his teeth in pain.

> and the two fight in their pride on a high mountain
> over a tiny spring of water, both longing to drink,
> and the lion beats down the boar as he fights for breath,
> so did Hector, son of Priam, with a close spear-thrust
> take the life of the mighty son of Menoetius,
> who had killed so many.

A long struggle takes place over Patroclus' corpse. Hector succeeds in stripping his armour, but MENELAUS and AJAX (1) save his body and carry it back to the ships. When Achilles learns of his dear comrade's death, he forgets his anger against Agamemnon and thinks only of taking revenge for his friend. Thus it is Patroclus' death that brings Achilles back into the fighting, for now, crazed with grief and rage and avenging fury, he goes into battle and massacres all the Trojans in his path until he comes face to face with Hector. He kills him too, even though he knows full well that he himself must die for it, since his own death is fated to come soon after Hector's.

Patroclus, vulnerable and compassionate, is one of the most sympathetic characters in the *Iliad*. After he is killed, Briseis says of him, 'I weep your death without ceasing, for always you were kind' (19.300), and Menelaus too sums up this special quality of tenderness: '... poor

Fig.110 Bellerophon, riding on Pegasus, attacks the Chimaera.

Pedasus

In Homer's *Iliad*, Pedasus is one of ACHILLES' three horses, the mortal trace-horse that he once won as booty and now harnesses alongside the immortal XANTHUS and Balius (16.148–54). When PATROCLUS borrows Achilles' chariot and drives it into battle at Troy, Pedasus runs long and courageously beside the immortal pair, until finally he is killed by the great hero SARPEDON with a spear-throw meant for Patroclus himself (16.463–9):

> Patroclus, throwing first, hit glorious Thrasymelus,
> the brave charioteer of lord Sarpedon, striking
> his lower belly and breaking the strength of his limbs.
> Sarpedon threw next and missed with his shining spear,
> but the spear struck the right shoulder of Pedasus
> the horse, who screamed and gasped out his life, falling
> into the dust with a moan, and his spirit fluttered from
> him.

Pegasus

A winged, immortal horse, offspring of POSEIDON and Medusa (*see* GORGONS), who sprang forth from his mother's neck when PERSEUS struck off her head. He was associated with waters, for he was said to be named Pegasus because he was born near the springs (*pegae*) of Ocean, and certainly the origins of two springs in Greece, both named HIPPOCRENE, 'Horse Spring', were attributed to the stamp of his hoof, one at Troezen, and the other more famous one on Mount Helicon, the haunt of the MUSES.

Pegasus belonged for a time to the mortal BELLEROPHON, who tamed him with the help of a golden bridle provided by Athena. Pegasus carried his master on the three life-threatening tasks set for him by King Iobates, and together horse and rider overcame the Chimaera, the Solymi and the Amazons. Pegasus was later the means by which Bellerophon took revenge on Iobates' wife, Stheneboea, for her own vengeful attempt to have him killed: he flew out over the sea with her, then flung her down to her death. Finally, however, Bellerophon tried to fly right up to the home of the gods on OLYMPUS, and ZEUS, angered by his presumption, sent a gadfly to sting his winged steed. Pegasus threw his rider back to earth and left the mortal world for ever. He flew to Olympus to dwell with the gods, and there drew the chariot that brought Zeus his thunder and lightning. Zeus immortalised him in the stars as the constellation Pegasus.

Pegasus appears with Bellerophon in ancient art from the early decades of the seventh century BC onwards (fig. 110). Later he became a symbol of immortality, and because of his links with Helicon and the Muses, of imagination and poetic vision. Keats damned the eighteenth-century

Patroclus, who was gentle, and knew how to be kindly to all men while he lived ...' (17.670–2). In some later writers, such as Aeschylus and his lost tragedy *The Myrmidons*, the bond between Patroclus and Achilles would be seen as homosexual love, but this is not so in Homer. Here their sexual relationships are with women, as at 9.663–8 when they both go to bed in their shared tent, but each with his own woman. In Homer their mutual love is the deep devotion of friends.

After Patroclus' death, Achilles holds funeral games in his honour and sacrifices twelve Trojan captives on his funeral pyre. Achilles' own death was narrated in the now lost *Aethiopis*, but we know from the *Odyssey* (24.71–84) that after he died his ashes were mixed with the ashes of Patroclus in a golden jar made by Hephaestus, and that the remains of the two friends were laid to rest with those of ANTILOCHUS, another dear comrade, and a grave mound was heaped high over them on a jutting headland there by the Hellespont. Patroclus was said to live for ever with Achilles and other heroes, all immortalised, on *Leuke*, the White Island, lying in the Black Sea at the mouth of the Danube.

[Homer, *Iliad* 1.337–45, 9.188–90, 11.598–847, 15.390–404, 16.2–18.355, 19.23–33, 23.4–897; Plato, *Symposium* 180a; Pausanias 3.19.13.]

Augustan poets by saying of them, 'They sway'd about upon a rocking horse, /And thought it Pegasus.' In post-classical art Pegasus is depicted with APOLLO and the Muses, often carrying a poet or even Apollo himself on his back. He is also (inaccurately) shown carrying Perseus as he rescues Andromeda.

[Hesiod, *Theogony* 274–86; Pindar, *Olympian* 13.60–92; Apollodorus 2.4.2; Strabo 8.6.21.]

Peirene

The name of a spring at Corinth and its nymph, the daughter of the river-god ACHELOUS.

Peirithous

A king of the Lapiths in Thessaly, famous for his friendship with the Athenian hero THESEUS and for his great battle with the CENTAURS. He was usually said to be the son of IXION and Dia, though Homer makes him the son of ZEUS. When he became king, his rule was challenged by the Centaurs, who claimed that as Ixion's grandsons they had a right to a share in the kingdom. At this stage the dispute was settled peaceably, and the Centaurs were given Mount Pelion as their territory.

Peirithous had heard of Theseus' great reputation for strength and courage, so he decided to put it to the test. He drove a herd of Theseus' cattle from the plain of Marathon, and when their owner pursued him he turned to fight. But as soon as they met face to face, the two were so struck with admiration for each other's person and courage that they joined hands and swore an oath of life-long friendship. They went on the CALYDONIAN BOARHUNT together, and Peirithous went with Theseus on his expedition against the AMAZONS and helped him to carry off the Amazon queen Antiope (fig.139). Peirithous himself married Hippodameia and invited many guests, including Theseus, to his wedding-feast. He also invited the Centaurs, now living peacefully on Mount Pelion. Unfortunately they were unused to wine and soon became thoroughly drunk and violent. They seized the Lapith women and a fierce battle broke out between Lapiths and Centaurs. Many were killed on both sides, but the Lapiths were the ultimate victors. They drove the Centaurs out of Thessaly and into the Peloponnese.

Peirithous had a son, POLYPOETES (1), by Hippodameia. Eventually she died, and since Theseus' wife Phaedra was also dead, the two widowers decided that they would each marry a daughter of Zeus. First they carried off the beautiful HELEN, daughter of Zeus and Leda. They drew lots for her, and Theseus won. Leaving her in the charge of Theseus' mother, Aethra, at Aphidnae in Attica, they set off together to win a bride for Peirithous. He chose PERSEPHONE, the daughter of Zeus and Demeter and the wife of HADES (1), so the two descended to the Underworld through the entrance at Taenarum, determined to carry Persephone back to earth. At first it seemed that all was going well, for Hades, feigning good cheer, greeted them with friendliness and invited them to take a seat. They did so, but unfortunately these were no normal seats. Once they were down, they found that they could no longer stand up again, either because the seats stuck to their flesh, or because they were at once bound in place with chains or snakes, or because these were seats of forgetfulness and they lost all will to move. There they stayed, and would both have stayed there for ever had not HERACLES come to the Underworld to fetch its guard-dog, CERBERUS, as his twelfth Labour for Eurystheus. Finding the two friends fast in their seats, he freed Theseus; but when he set about freeing Peirithous, the earth shook and he had to stop. So Theseus returned to the land of the living, though when he arrived there he found that he had fared no better than Peirithous in his choice of a bride, for Helen's brothers, the Dioscuri, had in his absence captured Aphidnae and taken her back to Sparta.

As for Peirithous' ultimate fate, he was occasionally said to have returned to earth at the same time as Theseus; but he was usually said to be fixed firmly on his seat in the Underworld for ever. It could have been worse: there exist traces of a version in which he was devoured by Cerberus.

[Homer, *Iliad* 2.740–4, 14.317–8, *Odyssey* 11.630–1; Apollodorus 1.8.2, 2.5.12, *Epitome* 1.24; Diodorus Siculus 4.26.1, 4.63; Plutarch, *Theseus* 30–1; Pausanias 1.2.1, 1.18.4, 2.22.6, 10.28.2, 10.29.9–10; Virgil, *Aeneid* 6.392–4; Horace, *Odes* 3.4.79–80, 4.7.27–8.]

Pelasgus

The man who gave his name to the Pelasgians, the supposed aboriginal inhabitants of Greece. They were said to have occupied several different regions, and Pelasgus is known as an early king in Arcadia, Argos and Thessaly. The Arcadians said that he had been born of the earth, and that in his reign he invented huts, and thought of making coats from sheepskins, and taught his people to live off acorns instead of grasses, leaves and roots. According to one genealogy he was the son of ZEUS and NIOBE (1). He himself had sons, TEMENUS (1) and LYCAON (1). Lycaon had fifty sons, who founded the cities of Arcadia, and a daughter, CALLISTO, who bore a son to Zeus, ARCAS, after whom Arcadia was named.

The Argive Pelasgus gave refuge to DANAUS and his fifty daughters when they were pursued by the fifty sons of Aegyptus. He also welcomed DEMETER during her long search for Persephone and built a temple in her honour called Demeter Pelasgis. His daughter Larissa gave her name to the citadel at Argos and to two Thessalian cities.

[Apollodorus 2.1.1, 3.8.1; Pausanias 1.14.2, 2.22.1, 2.24.1, 8.1.4–6, 8.2.1.]

Peleus

One of the great Greek heroes, who was granted the special privilege of marriage to a goddess and became the father of ACHILLES, the mightiest hero of the greatest war of ancient times.

Peleus was the son of AEACUS, king of Aegina, and ENDEIS, and brother of TELAMON. He and Telamon were exiled for killing their bastard half-brother PHOCUS (1), after which Peleus went to Phthia in Thessaly. Here he was purified of blood-guilt by the king, Eurytion, who also gave him a third-share of the kingdom and the hand in marriage of his daughter Antigone. She bore him a daughter, POLYDORA. Eurytion and Peleus sailed with the ARGONAUTS and went together to the CALYDONIAN BOARHUNT, but here Peleus accidentally killed his father-in-law with a spear-cast aimed at the boar, and was once again exiled. This time he went to Iolcus, where he was welcomed and purified by the king, ACASTUS, who had been a fellow-Argonaut. Peleus took part in the funeral games for Acastus' old father, Pelias, where he wrestled with the famous huntress ATALANTA and was defeated.

Unfortunately, Acastus' wife Astydameia (or Hippolyte) fell in love with him and tried to seduce him. Peleus honourably refused her advances, but was forced to pay a high price for his principles when the spiteful Asty-

dameia took her revenge: she sent a lying message to Antigone that Peleus was about to marry Acastus' daughter Sterope, and Antigone hanged herself in grief. Not content with this, Astydameia claimed to her husband that Peleus had tried to rape her. Acastus was unwilling to commit the impiety of killing a guest whom he himself had purified, so he tried to bring about his death indirectly. He took Peleus hunting on Mount Pelion, that haunt of wild CENTAURS, and challenged him to a contest to see who could catch the most game in a single day. Peleus was so successful that, to save the labour of carrying all his prey back to camp, he merely cut out the animals' tongues to prove his many kills. When at the end of the day he returned apparently empty-handed and was derided by Acastus and his men, he produced the tongues and proved his victory.

Peleus had survived the day unscathed, so during the night while he was asleep, Acastus stole his sword and hid it in a pile of cow dung, then left him alone and defenceless, hoping that either the hostile Centaurs or the wild beasts would kill him. His hope was almost fulfilled, for the Centaurs were about to attack Peleus when the wise Centaur CHEIRON came on the scene and saved him, giving him back his sword. (In another version, the gods provided him with a sword.) So Peleus escaped and in due course took his revenge. He returned to Iolcus with an armed force that included JASON and the DIOSCURI and sacked the city. He also killed Astydameia, cut her in two, and marched his army into Iolcus between the severed halves of her corpse. In some versions he killed Acastus as well.

Peleus now returned to Phthia where he became king. Because of his virtue he was awarded by the gods the extraordinary privilege of marriage to the sea-goddess THETIS. Like all sea-divinities she had the power of metamorphosis, so to win his bride Peleus had to wrestle with her while she changed into many different shapes – fire, water, wind, tree, bird, tiger, lion, snake and cuttle-fish. But through all these transformations he held her fast, until finally she became herself once more and consented to become his wife. The wedding took place on Mount Pelion, and the gods attended and brought gifts. Peleus was given a suit of fine armour, which Achilles later wore at Troy, and a stout ash spear, made from an ash tree that Cheiron felled. It was polished by ATHENA and had a blade wrought by HEPHAESTUS. POSEIDON gave the immortal horses XANTHUS and Balius; these also were later used at Troy by

Fig. 111 **Peleus wrestles with Thetis, undeterred by her metamorphoses into lion and snakes.**

Achilles. The MUSES sang in celebration. The only discordant note was introduced by ERIS, the goddess of Strife, who came to the wedding even though she had not been invited, and threw into the gathering a golden apple inscribed with the words 'for the fairest'. The rivalries which this provoked would lead to the JUDGEMENT OF PARIS, and in the course of time to the Trojan War – a war in which many would be killed, including Achilles, the only child of Peleus and Thetis.

When Achilles was born, Thetis tried to make him immortal by burning away the mortality that he had inherited from his father. She secretly put him in the fire by night, then anointed him with ambrosia during the day. But one night Peleus caught her in the act of putting their son in the fire and angrily interfered. At this, Thetis forsook both baby and husband and went back to live in the sea with the Nereids. Peleus gave Achilles to the Centaur Cheiron to rear and educate. According to Homer, although Cheiron taught Achilles about medicines, it was PHOENIX (3), a refugee whom Peleus had welcomed to his home and made king of the Dolopians, who helped to rear the young boy. Peleus also took in PATROCLUS, the boy who would become Achilles' life-long comrade and who would indirectly bring about his death.

Peleus' old age was sorrowful. Our image of him from the *Iliad* is of a sad old man, beset by his neighbours, desperately missing Achilles who is fighting at Troy, and too weak in his absence to protect himself. After Achilles' death Peleus was driven out of Phthia by the sons of Acastus, or else by Acastus himself, who thus avenged the destruction of Iolcus. Both Euripides and Sophocles wrote a (now lost) tragedy called *Peleus*; of Euripides' play we know almost nothing, but we know that Sophocles' play dealt with NEOPTOLEMUS' rescue of Peleus after he lost his kingdom. It is tempting to fill in here the details found in Dictys' *Diary of the Trojan War* (6.7–9), which sound as if they have come from a lost tragedy. When Neoptolemus heard of his grandfather's fate, he hurried to his aid and found him hiding in a cave on one of the Sepiades Islands. From here he would scan every passing ship, hoping that one of them would be bringing his grandson to his rescue. The sons of Acastus were hunting on the island, so Neoptolemus ambushed and killed them. He then lured Acastus himself to the cave and was about to kill him too when Thetis, coming from the sea to visit her husband, interceded. Acastus, happy to be spared, willingly restored the kingdom of Phthia to Neoptolemus and Peleus.

In Euripides' (extant) *Andromache*, Peleus has handed over the rule of Phthia to his grandson. In his absence, Peleus is able to protect Neoptolemus' concubine and son, ANDROMACHE and Molossus, from the plots of his wife, Hermione, and her father Menelaus. Despite this triumph, Peleus is stricken with grief when Neoptolemus is killed at Delphi through Orestes' treachery. At the end of the play, Thetis comes to announce that she will make Peleus immortal, and will take him to live with her for ever in the house of NEREUS.

Episodes from Peleus' early life were popular subjects in ancient vase-painting. We see him facing the boar at the Calydonian Boarhunt (fig. 34); wrestling at the funeral games of Pelias, most often with Atalanta; crouched in a tree with wild animals at its foot (presumably the episode with Acastus on Mount Pelion); wrestling with Thetis to win her (fig. 111), while she changes into different shapes to elude his grasp; at his wedding in the presence of the gods; and giving the young Achilles over to the Centaur Cheiron to rear (fig. 39). These confirm – better than his rather sporadic presence in the literature that has chanced to survive – just how important a hero Peleus was.

[Homer, *Iliad* 9.432–95, 11.830–2, 16.140–4, 18.83–5, 434–5, 23.82–90, 24.486–92, *Odyssey* 11.494–504; Pindar, *Olympian* 2.56–83, *Pythian* 3.86–103, *Nemean* 3.32–6, 4.54–68, 5.22–37; Euripides, *Andromache* 547–765, 1047–1283, *Trojan Women* 1123–30, *Iphigeneia at Aulis* 1036–79; Apollodorus 1.8.2, 3.9.2, 3.12.6–3.13.8; Catullus 64; Ovid, *Metamorphoses* 11.235–406. J. R. March, *The Creative Poet* (1987), pp. 3–26.]

Pelias

Son of POSEIDON and TYRO, and twin-brother of NELEUS. After the babies' birth, their mother abandoned them in the wild, but they survived: Peleus, it was said, was suckled by a mare and Neleus by a bitch until they were found by a horse-breeder, who took them in and brought them up. Pelias was given his name because of the livid mark (*pelion*) on his face where the mare had kicked him. When the boys grew up they learnt the truth about their birth and were reunited with their mother. They found that she was being treated with great cruelty by her stepmother, Sidero, so they attacked Sidero, who fled for refuge into a sanctuary of HERA. She was slaughtered by Pelias on the very altars of the precinct. Because of this sacrilege, and because throughout Pelias' long life he always ignored the honours due to Hera's divinity, the goddess became his enemy.

Later the brothers quarrelled, and Neleus settled in Messenia while Pelias stayed in Iolcus, marrying Anaxibia and having by her a son, ACASTUS, and several daughters including ALCESTIS, who became the wife of ADMETUS. Tyro, meanwhile had married Cretheus, the king of Iolcus, and had borne him three sons, AESON, AMYTHAON and PHERES (1). When Cretheus died, Aeson should have become king, but Pelias seized the throne. Aeson carried on living

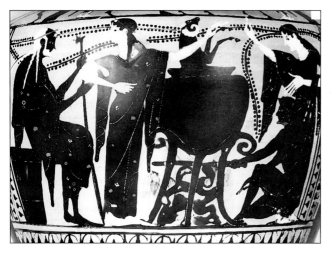

Fig.112 Medea demonstrates her magical rejuvenation of the ram to old Pelias. A man stokes the fire beneath the cauldron, and one of Pelias' daughters gestures in emotion.

in Iolcus and had a son, JASON, but from fear of Pelias he said that the boy had been born dead, then sent him in secret to be brought up by the wise Centaur Cheiron on Mount Pelion.

Pelias learnt from an oracle that he should beware of a man coming from the country and wearing a single sandal: this man would kill him. When Jason grew to manhood he returned to Iolcus, having lost a sandal as he was carrying Hera, disguised as an old woman, across the swollen River Anaurus – thus the goddess marked him as the instrument of Pelias' destruction. When Pelias saw Jason, he knew at once that this must be the man of doom. He asked Jason what he would do if he knew from an oracle that a certain man would kill him, and Jason replied that he would send such a man to fetch the GOLDEN FLEECE from the kingdom of AEETES in Colchis. So this is just what Pelias did. (For the long and eventually successful expedition, *see* ARGONAUTS.)

With Jason – or so he believed – disposed of, Pelias now forced Aeson to kill himself. Aeson's wife committed suicide too, and Pelias killed their infant son Promachus. Now he believed himself safe. But eventually Jason returned triumphant, bringing with him not only the Golden Fleece but the Colchian sorceress MEDEA, who was another of Hera's instruments and would bring about Pelias' death. Medea used her witchcraft to rejuvenate an old ram by cutting it up and boiling it in a cauldron with magic herbs (fig.112). When it emerged as a lamb, Pelias' daughters were persuaded that she could restore the

youth of their ageing father as well. So Pelias too was killed and cut up and boiled – and that was the end of him. 'And what his daughters received was not even enough to bury', says Pausanias tersely (8.11.3). Jason and Medea fled from Iolcus and took refuge with Creon, the king of Corinth.

Acastus held great funeral games in honour of his father. These were among the most famous of their kind that ever took place, with heroes coming from all over Greece to compete. They were a famous subject for ancient epic and vase-painting.

[Hesiod, *Theogony* 992–6; Pindar, *Pythian* 4.72–167; Apollonius, *Argonautica* 1.5–17; Apollodorus 1.9.8–10, 1.9.15–16, 1.9.27, 3.9.2; Pausanias 3.18.16, 5.17.9–11, 8.11.1–3, 30.10.8.]

Pelion, Mount

A mountain in Thessaly, the home of the CENTAURS, and one of the three mountains piled up by the giants OTUS and Ephialtes in their attempt to scale the heavens and overthrow the gods.

Pelopia

A daughter of Thyestes. *See* ATREUS.

Pelops

The son of TANTALUS (1), king of Lydia. His father killed him when he was a child, then cut him up and cooked him in a stew, which he served to the gods to test their omniscience. They realised what he had done and refused the food, all except DEMETER, who was grieving for her lost daughter Persephone and absentmindedly ate part of Pelops' shoulder. But all was well, for the gods brought the boy back to life and Demeter gave him a new shoulder made of ivory. In fact so beautiful was he that POSEIDON fell in love with him and carried him off to Olympus, where he stayed until returned to earth to grow into manhood.

Then Pelops began to think of marriage, and he resolved to win the hand of the beautiful Hippodameia, only daughter of Oenomaus, king of Pisa in Elis. This would be no easy task, for Oenomaus had no intention of letting his daughter marry: either he was in love with her himself, or he had been warned by an oracle that he would die by the hand of her husband. Many suitors had wooed her, but none had lived, let alone won the girl of their choice. It was Oenomaus' practice to challenge each of them to a chariot-race, starting from Pisa and finishing at the altar of Poseidon in faraway Corinth. The suitor would set out in his chariot with Hippodameia, her father giving them a start while he sacrificed a ram to Zeus. Then he too would set out, wearing armour and driving a chariot and immortal horses given him by his father ARES. Small wonder that he always caught up with the pair before they arrived at their destination, whereupon he would spear the unhappy suitor between the shoulder-blades and return home with his daughter.

When Pelops decided to try his skill, Oenomaus had already triumphantly nailed the heads of many defeated suitors over the door of his palace: perhaps twelve, or thirteen, or sixteen, or eighteen – quite enough to give Pelops pause. But with no hesitation the young man invoked the help of his old lover Poseidon, who supplied him with a chariot of gold drawn by winged horses. In one version, these were sufficient to bring Pelops to victory, so that he won his bride and killed her wicked father. But in the more usual tradition, he was helped to victory by Oenomaus' charioteer MYRTILUS, who was (to his own misfortune, as it turned out) open to bribery. Either Pelops bribed him with the promise of half the kingdom and a night in Hippodameia's bed, or the girl herself did so, having fallen in love with Pelops on sight. Myrtilus agreed to betray his master, and replaced the bronze linchpins in the wheels of Oenomaus' chariot with pins made of wax. The race began as usual and Pelops set off with Hippodameia; but when Oenomaus was in hot pursuit, his chariot foundered and he was dragged to his death in the reins. Dying, he cursed his treacherous charioteer, wishing on him death at the hands of the man he had helped.

This is exactly what happened. The victorious Pelops, loath to make good the promised bribes, killed Myrtilus by hurling him from his chariot into the sea. But he was not to be so easily rid of him, for with his last breath Myrtilus cursed his murderer, just as he himself had been cursed. Pelops set about nullifying any harm that this might do. He journeyed to the river of Ocean (*see* OCEANUS) at the far ends of the earth to be purified of the murder by HEPHAESTUS. He instituted the worship of HERMES, Myrtilus' father, throughout the land. He raised a mound in Myrtilus' honour beside the racetrack at Olympia, and some said that it was the charioteer's ghost who often terrified horses at that point during the Olympic Games, just as Oenomaus' mares had been scared by Myrtilus' destruction of the chariot (*see* TARAXIPPUS). But do what Pelops might, the curse remained and was a potent source of misery for his descendants (*see* ATREUS).

Pelops became a tremendously powerful ruler. Not only was he king of Elis, but he won the rule of most of the rest of southern Greece and renamed the entire region the Peloponnese (Pelops' Island). Arcadia withstood him for a while, but he finally won it by trickery: he pretended friendship for its king, STYMPHALUS, then killed him and scattered his mangled limbs over the land.

This treacherous deed brought the anger of Zeus and a prolonged drought on Greece, until the virtuous AEACUS interceded with the god for deliverance, and at last the rain came down. Pelops must have been forgiven, for Zeus provided him with a magnificent sceptre, made by Hephaestus, as a symbol of his authority, and this was passed from father to son down the generations.

After his marriage Pelops reburied Hippodameia's dead suitors, who had been shovelled into the earth anyhow by Oenomaus. He raised a monument to honour them with the intention of pleasing his wife, but also, no doubt, to add to his own honour by announcing to posterity the number and quality of the men defeated by Oenomaus, before the great Pelops came along in his turn and vanquished the evil king. Hippodameia herself instituted the Heraean Games at Olympia in gratitude to HERA for her marriage to Pelops. The couple had a large and powerful family. Their many sons included Atreus, THYESTES, PITTHEUS, and ALCATHOUS (1); and three of their daughters, Astydameia, Nicippe and Lysidice, married sons of PERSEUS, thus forming important political alliances. Pelops also had by a nymph an illegitimate but much-loved son, CHRYSIPPUS. He died young, either killing himself from shame after being abducted by LAIUS, or murdered by his half-brothers Atreus and Thyestes because they and their mother were afraid that Pelops, from affection, would make him his heir. When Pelops discovered the murder he exiled the two killers, and Hippodameia withdrew to Midea in the Argolid because of his anger.

Nothing is known of Pelops' death. He was afterwards one of the most renowned of Greek heroes, with a famous shrine at Olympia said to have been established by his even more renowned descendant HERACLES. Towards the end of the Trojan War, the Trojan seer Helenus predicted to the Greeks that they would take Troy only under certain conditions, one of which was that they should fetch the bones of Pelops from Elis. This they did. According to Pausanias, the Eleians parted with Pelops' shoulder-blade, but when this was being returned after the fall of Troy, the ship carrying it was wrecked and the bone lost off Euboea. Many years later a fisherman called Damarmenus brought up the bone in his net. Marvelling at its huge size, he enquired about it at Delphi. On the advice of the oracle he returned it to the Eleians, who repaid him by making him and his descendants the guardians of the bone.

The most famous mythical event connected with Pelops remains, however, the famous chariot-race. Both Sophocles and Euripides wrote tragedies on this theme (now lost) entitled *Oenomaus*. Pausanias saw the race depicted on the chest of Cypselus, with Pelops and Hippodameia together in the leading chariot, both drivers having two horses but Pelops' horses being winged. We have the famous sculptures from the east pediment of the temple of Zeus at Olympia, here showing the still moment before the race begins. In a fictional account, Apollonius describes the depiction of the race on Jason's robe, made for him by Athena. Here the final climactic moment was shown: Pelops with Hippodameia in the leading chariot, frenziedly shaking the reins, and close behind Oenomaus, his spear stretched out ready to thrust it into Pelops' back, with just at that very moment the linchpin giving way and the chariot about to topple sideways.

[Homer, *Iliad* 2.98–108; Pindar, *Olympian* 1.25–96; Apollonius, *Argonautica* 1.752–8; Apollodorus 2.4.5, 3.12.6, *Epitome* 2.3–10; Diodorus Siculus 4.73.1–6; Pausanias 5.8.2, 5.10.6–7, 5.11.5, 5.13.1–7, 5.14.6, 5.17.7, 6.20.7, 6.20.17–19, 6.21.3, 6.21.9–11, 6.22.1, 8.14.10–12; Pliny, *Natural History* 28.34.]

Pelorus
One of the SOWN MEN of Thebes.

Pemphredo *see* GRAEAE.

Penates, di
Roman household gods who protected the home. There were also state Penates (*Penates Publici*, protectors of Rome), whose cult was attached to the temple of VESTA. They were said to have been saved from the flames of Troy and brought to Italy by AENEAS.

[Dionysius of Halicarnassus 1.68; Virgil, *Aeneid* 1.378–9, 2.293–5, 717–20.]

Peneius *see* DAPHNE.

Peneleos
A Boeotian hero who sailed with the ARGONAUTS. He was one of HELEN's suitors, and with Leitus led a contingent of fifty ships from Boeotia to the TROJAN WAR. He fought fiercely, two of his victims being the Trojans Ilioneus and Lycon, but was himself finally killed by EURYPYLUS (2), the son of Telephus.

[Homer, *Iliad* 2.494 510, 14.486–507, 16.335–41, 17.597–600; Apollodorus 1.9.16, 3.10.8; Pausanias 9.5.14–15.]

Penelope
The wise and faithful wife of ODYSSEUS and the heroine of the *Odyssey*. She was the daughter of ICARIUS (2) and the nymph Periboea, and so much a favourite of her father that he would have preferred her not to marry. But Odysseus succeeded in winning her, either by wooing her with the support of Icarius' brother, Tyndareos, or by

defeating her other suitors in a footrace. The couple settled on the island of ITHACA.

The marriage was a happy one, and they had a son, TELEMACHUS. But while the boy was still a baby, the Trojan War began and Odysseus was called away to fight, leaving Penelope to manage affairs at home. Unlike many of the other Greek leaders' wives (most notably CLYTEMNESTRA, wife of Agamemnon), Penelope remained faithful to her husband through all the ten long years of the war; but this was not the end of her waiting. The other surviving Greeks sailed home, but Odysseus was kept from Ithaca for another ten years by the many tribulations of his journey and the wrath of Poseidon. Through all that time Penelope was faithful to the man she loved, even though she feared, and sometimes believed, that he was dead. When the *Odyssey* opens, at the end of those twenty years, Penelope is being harrassed by the rapacious Suitors, local nobles who have invaded Odysseus' house during his long absence, carousing at his expense and hoping to marry her. Unknown to everyone, Odysseus is about to return at last. He comes to the palace, disguised as a beggar by Athena's magical aid, and there meets with his beloved wife once more. She does not recognise him, but her heart warms towards this likeable stranger. Prompted by Athena, she sets up a contest to see who can string Odysseus' great bow and shoot an arrow through a row of double-headed axes. That man, she says, will win her as his wife.

After Penelope has cried herself to sleep in her bedchamber, Odysseus himself strings the bow, shoots through the axes, then kills all the Suitors. The nurse EURYCLEIA excitedly wakes her mistress, and once again Penelope meets the stranger, who now announces his true identity. But only after he describes the unique construction of their marriage-bed, built around an olive tree still rooted in the ground, does she accept that this is indeed her long-lost husband. Now at last husband and wife are reunited with great joy, and Athena lengthens the night for them by holding back EOS, goddess of Dawn, from bringing in the daylight until they have enjoyed each other to the full.

Homer depicts Penelope as a fit mate for his hero Odysseus, whom he describes as 'much-enduring' and 'a man of many wiles'. He hints at their similarity during their reunion (23.232–40). Odysseus

> wept, holding his lovely wife whose heart was loyal;
> and as when the land appears, a welcome sight,
> to men who are swimming, whose well-made ship
> Poseidon has wrecked at sea, pounding it with the wind
> and the massive waves, and only a few reach the land
> by swimming and escape the grey sea, their bodies

caked with salt, and joyfully they set foot on the land, escaping disaster – so welcome was her husband to her as she looked at him, and she would not let him go from the embrace of her white arms.

The simile here, of a shipwrecked sailor, is applied to Penelope, but describes Odysseus: he was the sailor, shipwrecked by Poseidon, who escaped on to the island of Scheria, caked with salt and joyful at escaping disaster. By making his simile refer to Penelope, who is as joyful as the sailor coming to safety, Homer gently emphasises the similarity of husband and wife.

Penelope has endured much over their twenty long years apart, just as Odysseus has; and like him too she is wily. She succeeded in putting off the Suitors' demands for three years by pretending to weave her father-in-law's shroud, as she explains to Odysseus (19.139–56):

> I set up a great loom in my palace, and began to weave
> a web of threads, long and fine. And I said to them:
> 'Young men, my Suitors now godlike Odysseus is dead,
> though you are eager to marry me, wait until I finish
> this web, so that my weaving will not be uselessly wasted,
> a shroud for the hero Laertes, for when he is laid low
> and taken by the destructive doom of death ...'
> So I spoke and their proud hearts obeyed me.
> Then every day I would weave the great web,
> and every night I undid it, lit by torchlight.
> For three years I kept my secret and convinced the Suitors,
> but when the fourth year came ... then at last
> they came on me and caught me, taking me to task,
> and I was forced against my will to finish it.

This is a trick worthy of Odysseus himself, that man of many wiles. Theirs is indeed a well-matched marriage. Odysseus said to NAUSICAA when he was among the Phaeacians, 'There is nothing more steadfast or secure than when a man and woman of like mind share a home together' (6.182–4), and Odysseus and Penelope are very much a man and woman of 'like mind'.

Other ancient sources add details to Homer's central story. It was sometimes said that Penelope had a second son, Ptoliporthes or Arcesilaus, by Odysseus after he came home from Troy. A lost epic poem, the *Telegony*, said that TELEGONUS, the son of Odysseus by the enchantress CIRCE, went to Ithaca in search of his father and unintentionally killed him. When Telegonus sorrowfully realised the identity of his victim, he carried Odysseus' corpse back to Circe's island of Aeaea, taking Penelope and Telemachus with

him as well. There he married Penelope, and Telemachus married Circe, who made all three of them immortal. According to Hyginus (*Fabula* 127), Telegonus and Penelope had a son, Italus, from whom Italy took its name.

A few minor ancient sources contradict the Homeric picture of Penelope as the patient and faithful wife. One account says that Odysseus drove her out after finding that she had taken lovers, and she died at Mantinea; another that he himself killed her after discovering that she had had an affair with the Suitor AMPHINOMUS. There is also an odd tradition that she was the mother of the pastoral god PAN, either by Hermes or after an orgy with all 129 of her Suitors. But it is the Homeric Penelope who has lived in legend until her name has become a symbol for a wife's fidelity to her husband. The term 'Penelope's web', born of the weaving trick with which she kept the Suitors at bay, has become proverbial for anything perpetually in process but never completed.

[Herodotus 2.145; Apollodorus 3.10.6, 3.10.8, *Epitome* 3.7, 7.26–39; Pausanias 3.12.1, 3.12.4, 3.20.10–11, 8.12.5–6; Ovid, *Heroides* 1. R. B. Rutherford, *Homer, Odyssey Books 19 and 20* (1992); N. Felson-Rubin, *Regarding Penelope* (1994).]

Penthesileia

One of the AMAZONS, daughter of ARES and the Amazon queen Otrere. She accidentally killed a fellow-Amazon, ANTIOPE (2), either in the battle during Theseus' marriage to Phaedra or while out hunting, and went to Troy to be purified of her blood-guilt by King PRIAM. She later led an army of Amazons to help him in the Trojan War after the death of his son Hector. She killed many Greeks, then

Fig. 113 Achilles kills the Amazon Penthesileia. Their eyes meet as he drives his spear through her neck.

was herself killed by ACHILLES and buried by the Trojans. The story went that, even as Achilles delivered the fatal blow, their eyes met and he fell in love with her; or that he fell in love with her corpse after he had stripped it of its armour. When THERSITES jeered at him (and, some say, gouged out the eyes of the dead Penthesilea), Achilles killed him with a single blow.

Achilles' slaughter of Penthesilea, with its romantic combination of love and death, was an inspiration to many ancient vase-painters (fig. 113) and sculptors. Achilles supporting the fallen Amazon was the subject of one of the panels painted by Panaenus around Pheidias' great statue of Zeus at Olympia.

[Epic Cycle, Proclus' summary of the *Aethiopis*; Apollodorus, *Epitome* 5.1–2; Diodorus Siculus 2.4.6; Pausanias 5.11.6; Quintus of Smyrna, *Sequel to Homer* 1.18–810.]

Pentheus

Son of Echion, one of the 'Sown Men' of Thebes, and of AGAVE, the daughter of CADMUS. Pentheus died young, punished by the god DIONYSUS for refusing to recognise his divinity. The most familiar version of Pentheus' legend is dramatised in Euripides' powerful tragedy *The Bacchae*. (There had been earlier plays on the subject, including a *Pentheus* by Aeschylus, but we know little about them.) Here in Euripides, Dionysus, disguised as one of his own devotees, has returned from his conquests in the East to Thebes, the scene of his birth, where he intends to institute Dionysiac worship. He is also intent on punishing his mother SEMELE's sisters, Agave, AUTONOE and INO, for claiming that she falsely named Zeus as the father of her child, and so was burnt up in the lightning flash as a punishment for her presumption. He has driven the three sisters mad, along with the other Theban women, and has sent them on to Mount Cithaeron where they are worshipping Dionysus as MAENADS. He now prepares to confront the scepticism of his cousin Pentheus. Old Cadmus has abdicated the throne of Thebes, and Pentheus is the new, young ruler who comes home to find all the women missing, and rumours of their licentious behaviour rife in the city. He is determined to stamp out completely this dangerous Dionysiac worship, despite various miraculous happenings that are brought to his notice, and despite the warnings of old Cadmus and the blind prophet TEIRESIAS. Finally Dionysus makes Pentheus mad, enticing him into maenad costume and leading him up the mountain to spy on the maenads. The god sets his victim in a perch high on a pine tree, then calls on the maenads to kill him. In a bacchic frenzy they uproot the tree and Pentheus falls to the ground, realising what ghastly fate awaits him (1114–28):

His mother first, as priestess, led the rite of death, and fell on him. He tore the headband from his hair, so that the wretched Agave might recognise him and not kill him, and he said, touching her cheek, 'Mother, it is I, your son Pentheus, whom you bore to Echion. Pity me, mother, and do not, for my mistakes, kill your own son.' But she was frothing at the mouth and rolling wild eyes; out of her right mind, she was possessed by Bacchus and paid no heed to her son. Grasping his right arm, she set her foot against his ribs and tore off the poor boy's arm at the shoulder.

The other maenads, including Autonoe and Ino, follow her lead, tearing at Pentheus' flesh. The mountain echoes and re-echoes with their cries, Pentheus shrieking as long as life is left in him and the women howling in triumph. Finally Agave picks up her son's head and carries it back to Thebes, proudly believing it to be the head of a mountain lion that she has killed with her bare hands. She calls for Cadmus to come and see her prey, and for Pentheus himself to nail up her magnificent trophy on the palace walls. The grief-stricken Cadmus gently brings her back to sanity, to see whose head it is that she holds in her arms. Aristotle says in his *Poetics* that an effective recognition scene is one of the key elements of a good tragedy. This scene in the *Bacchae*, where a mother recognises her dead son whom she herself has killed, has a good claim to be the most moving recognition scene in the whole of extant Greek tragedy.

Pentheus and the maenads are found occasionally in vase-paintings from the sixth century BC onwards, but they seem to reflect a different tradition in which an armed Pentheus went into battle against the women, and there is no hint of the transvestism which is so powerful a motif in Euripides' play. Nor, prior to Euripides, do we anywhere find Agave and her sisters specifically named or shown as Pentheus' murderers (and on one vase the leading maenad is named Galene). It is at least possible that these were Euripides' own innovations to the myth.

[Apollodorus 3.5.2; Pausanias 1.20.3, 2.2.7, 9.2.4; Ovid, *Metamorphoses* 3.511–733. J. R. March, 'Euripides' *Bakchai*: a Reconsideration in the Light of Vase-paintings', *BICS* 36 (1989), pp. 33–65.]

Perdix

An Athenian inventor. He was the nephew and apprentice of the brilliant craftsman DAEDALUS, but proved to be even more ingenious than his master. He is credited with three inventions: the iron saw, which he made by copying either the backbone of a fish or the teeth in a snake's jawbone, the geometrician's compasses, and the potter's wheel. Eventually Daedalus grew so jealous of Perdix' accomplishments that he killed him, flinging him to his death from the Acropolis. ATHENA, who had loved the boy for his skill, took pity on him and turned him into a partridge (*perdix*). This is why the partridge, remembering that terrible fall, always flies low and makes its nest on the ground. It was said that when Daedalus was sorrowfully burying his son ICARUS, also dead from a fall, a nearby partridge flapped its wings and uttered cries of joy.

For his crime Daedalus appeared before the court of the Areopagus and was exiled, moving on to Crete. In some accounts Perdix is called Talos or Calos, and the name Perdix is given to his mother, Daedalus' sister, who hanged herself in grief at her son's death.

[Apollodorus 3.15.8; Diodorus Siculus 4.76.4–7; Pausanias 1.21.4, 7.4.5; Ovid, *Metamorphoses* 8.236–59.]

Pergamus
Son of ANDROMACHE by Neoptolemus.

Periboea *see* OENEUS.

Periclymenus (1)
A son of POSEIDON who was a Theban champion in the war of the SEVEN AGAINST THEBES, where he killed PARTHENOPAEUS by hurling a great stone down on to his head from the city walls. He almost killed AMPHIARAUS too, for he was about to strike him with his spear when his intended victim was swallowed up (chariot, horses and all) by the earth.

[Pindar, *Nemean* 9.24–7; Euripides, *Phoenician Women* 1153–62; Apollodorus 3.6.8; Pausanias 9.18.6.]

Periclymenus (2)
The eldest son of NELEUS, king of Pylos, and CHLORIS (1); and one of the ARGONAUTS. His grandfather POSEIDON gave him the ability to change his shape at will. As Hesiod describes it (*Catalogue of Women*, fr. 33): 'At one time he would appear among the birds as an eagle; and then at another he would be an ant, a wonder to see; and then again a bright swarm of bees; and then a terrible relentless snake.' This ability was particularly useful in war, and when HERACLES and his followers attacked Pylos, Periclymenus changed his shape repeatedly during the battle that followed. Apollodorus (1.9.9) says that he became a lion, a snake and a bee, but none the less he was killed by Heracles, along with all the other sons of Neleus apart from Nestor. The Hesiodic fragment says that he died when he perched on the yoke of Heracles' chariot, planning how to bring his opponent down, and was shot by one of Heracles' unerring arrows – though the name of what transformation he had adopted at that particular time is (tantalisingly) missing from the surviving scrap of papyrus that tells the story. An eagle, a fly and a bee have all been suggested, though perhaps the eagle might seem the most likely, as in Ovid's version (*Metamorphoses* 12.556–72), where Periclymenus tears at Heracles' face with his talons, then soars high in the air. It is then that Heracles shoots him.

[Homer, *Odyssey* 11.281–6; Apollonius, *Argonautica* 1.156–60; Apollodorus 1.9.16.]

Perigune *see* SINIS.

Perimele *see* ACHELOUS.

Periphetes
The first of the many brigands killed by the young THESEUS on his journey from Troezen to Athens. Periphetes, the son of HEPHAESTUS, was called 'Club-bearer' because he habitually carried a bronze club with which he would beat to death travellers on the road through Epidaurus. Apollodorus adds that he was weak on his legs (like his father), so it may well be that he used his club as a crutch, hobbling along like a cripple, until he was within striking distance of his unsuspecting victims. Then, with a swift and sudden blow, he would fell them to the ground. However it may have been, he certainly accosted Theseus, who wrested the club from him and cracked open his skull. The club took Theseus' fancy, so he kept it with him, and just as Heracles always wore the skin of the Nemean Lion, the evidence of his first Labour, so Theseus carried the club of Periphetes as a reminder of his first trial of strength.

[Euripides, *Suppliant Women* 714–17; Apollodorus 3.16.1; Diodorus Siculus 4.59.2; Plutarch, *Theseus* 8; Pausanias 2.1.4.]

Pero
The beautiful daughter of NELEUS, king of Pylos, and CHLORIS (1). *See* MELAMPUS.

Perse or Perseis
An Oceanid, wife of the Sun-god HELIOS.

Persephone
Daughter of ZEUS and DEMETER, also known as Kore ('the Girl'), and as Proserpina to the Romans. She was carried off by HADES (1), her uncle, to be his wife and the queen of the Underworld. Zeus gave his permission for the match, but he was well aware that Demeter would not agree, so he intervened to assist Hades. One day, when Persephone was gathering flowers in a meadow with her companions, she wandered apart from the others and saw a glorious narcissus, covered with a hundred fragrant blooms, which Zeus had created to ensnare her. As she

reached out with both hands to pick the radiant flower, the earth gaped open and out sped Hades in his golden four-horse chariot. He snatched up the girl, caring nothing for her screams, and carried her down into his realm below. The water-nymph CYANE, who saw the abduction, tried to stop Hades, but in vain. In her sorrow she dissolved into the waters of her pool.

Demeter wandered the world searching unavailingly for her beloved daughter. In her grief and loss she withheld from mankind all her benefits, making the earth barren and inflicting famine on men. At last Zeus intervened once again, this time sending HERMES down to the Underworld to fetch Persephone back to the light of day (fig. 47). But before she left, she ate some pomegranate seeds, either because Hades had secretly given them to her, or of her own accord, an action that ASCALAPHUS (1), the son of the Underworld river-god Acheron, was only too happy to report – though to his cost, for he was turned into an owl by either Demeter or Persephone because of his tattling.

Mother and daughter were joyously reunited on OLYMPUS; but because Persephone had eaten while in the Underworld, she could not leave the place for ever and was obliged to spend part of every year with Hades (either four or six months). This was the cold winter period when seed lay dormant below the earth. In spring she came back once more to warmth and light, and the loving company of her mother. Her return to the living world, and the growth of the crops in spring, were celebrated in many rites shared by mother and daughter, most famously in the Eleusinian Mysteries and the festival of the Thesmophoria.

Thus Persephone had a dual nature: as queen of the dead (fig. 62), she was a dread and awesome goddess; and as Kore, living with her mother (fig. 142), she was a deity of joy and hope. But whenever she plays a part in the myths of others, it is always as the goddess of the Underworld. With her husband she listened to the entrancing music of ORPHEUS when he came down to win his wife, Eurydice, back from the dead. She quarrelled with Aphrodite over the possession of the beautiful young ADONIS, and was granted his company for a part of each year. She was the chosen bride of the mortal PEIRITHOUS, but when he and Theseus came down to kidnap her, they were trapped by Hades in seats from which they had no power to move. (Theseus was later rescued by Heracles, but Peirithous was fixed firmly in his seat forever.) According to Orphic myth, Persephone bore ZAGREUS to Zeus in the form of a snake. Apollodorus (1.3.1), uniquely, makes Persephone the daughter of Zeus and the Underworld river-goddess STYX, so presumably in this version

her home was always in Hades.

Various places are claimed as the scene of Persephone's abduction, including, in Ovid's version of the myth, Enna, in central Sicily. This is made the more memorable by Milton's haunting words in *Paradise Lost* (4.268–72, Demeter being given her Roman name of Ceres):

> that faire field
> Of Enna, where Proserpin gathring flours
> Her self a fairer Floure by gloomie Dis
> Was gatherd, which cost Ceres all that pain
> To seek her through the world.

[*Homeric Hymn to Demeter*; Hesiod, *Theogony* 767–74, 912–14; Apollodorus 1.3.1, 1.5.1–3; Diodorus Siculus 5.2–5; Ovid, *Metamorphoses* 5.346–571, *Fasti* 4.417–620.]

Persepolis *see* POLYCASTE.

Perses (1)
Son of the Titans CRIUS and EURYBIA, and father, by ASTERIA, of the goddess HECATE.

[Hesiod, *Theogony* 375–7, 409–11.]

Perses (2)
Son of HELIOS, the Sun-god, and the Oceanid Perse (sometimes called Perseis) and thus the brother of AEETES, the king of Colchis who owned the Golden Fleece. At some point after Jason's theft of the Fleece, Perses deposed Aeetes and made himself king of Colchis, but he was killed either by the sorceress MEDEA, Aeetes' daughter, or by Medea's son (*see* MEDUS (1)), whereupon Aeetes regained his throne.

[Apollodorus 1.9.1, 1.9.28; Diodorus Siculus 4.56.1.]

Perses (3)
Eldest son of PERSEUS and Andromeda.

Perseus
A great hero, son of ZEUS and DANAE. Perseus' grandfather Acrisius, king of Argos, had been warned by an oracle that he would be killed by Danae's future son, so he kept her shut away from all contact with men by imprisoning her in a bronze, underground chamber. Zeus came to her through a small aperture in the roof as a shower of golden rain, pouring down into her lap. Perseus was the result of their union, and Acrisius, refusing to believe that Zeus was the father, shut mother and baby into a wooden chest (fig. 45) and threw it into the sea. It drifted safely to the island of Seriphos where it caught in the fishing nets of Dictys, brother of the island's king, Polydectes. Dictys gave Danae and Perseus a home, and here the boy grew uneventfully to manhood. Then Polydectes fell in love with Danae, and finding that Perseus was a hindrance in

his attempts to woo her, he determined to be rid of him. He pretended that he wanted to marry Hippodameia, the daughter of the Pisan king, Oenomaus, and was collecting horses as contributions to the bride-gift. Perseus boasted that he would fetch the head of the Gorgon Medusa (*see* GORGONS) if necessary, and when he failed to provide the required horse Polydectes took him up on his offer, quite sure that he would not return alive, since the sight of the Gorgon could turn a man to stone.

Perseus was helped in his mission by ATHENA and HERMES. On their advice he went first to the three GRAEAE, and by taking possession of the one eye and the one tooth which they shared among themselves, he forced them to tell him the whereabouts of certain nymphs who would help him on his expedition. These nymphs provided him with winged sandals to carry him to Medusa, a cap of darkness belonging to Hades that would make him invisible, and a bag in which to carry the Gorgon's head. Added to these, Hermes gave him a scimitar of adamant with which to behead her. Perseus was now armed for his task.

Using his winged sandals he flew beyond the river of OCEAN to the land of the three Gorgons, the mortal Medusa and the immortal Stheno and Euryale. He found them all asleep. Because anyone who looked at them directly would be turned to stone, he was careful to gaze only at their reflection in Athena's shield of polished bronze, while the goddess helped him by guiding his hand that held the scimitar. Thus he beheaded Medusa, and from her severed neck were born two children by Poseidon, the winged horse PEGASUS and CHRYSAOR. Perseus thrust Medusa's head into his bag and flew away. His victim's two sisters tried to pursue him, but to no avail because he was wearing the cap of darkness, so they returned to mourn their sister. Perseus escaped safely and began to make his way home.

On his way he passed across the African continent. According to Ovid, he came to the land of the Hesperides and asked hospitality of ATLAS. When he was refused, he revealed Medusa's head and turned his recalcitrant host into Mount Atlas, who has ever afterwards held up the sky and all the stars. In Egypt Perseus paid a visit to Chemmis, the home of his ancestor DANAUS, with the result that in Herodotus' day the people of Chemmis still worshipped him, the only Egyptians to do so. He came next to the land of the Ethiopians where Cepheus was king, and saw there Cepheus' daughter ANDROMEDA chained to a rock on the sea-shore, waiting to be devoured by a sea-monster as a punishment for the boastfulness of her mother, Cassiopeia. He fell in love with Andromeda at first glance, and said that he would rescue her if he might

Fig. 114 Perseus, followed by Athena, escapes after beheading the Gorgon Medusa. He carefully averts his eyes from his victim's face, partially concealed in his bag, lest she turn him to stone.

marry her (fig. 17). Cepheus agreed, so Perseus killed the monster by flying up and attacking it from above with his scimitar, then set Andromeda free. But Andromeda had been betrothed to Cepheus' brother Phineus, who now tried to stop her marrying his rival. During a pitched battle, Perseus took Medusa's head from his bag and turned Phineus and all his supporters to stone. The marriage took place, and within the year Andromeda had given birth to their first son, Perses, who would become the ancestor of the Persian kings. Perseus then went back to Seriphos, taking his new wife with him but leaving their little son to be brought up by Cepheus, who had no male heir to succeed him.

Back in Seriphos, Perseus found his mother and Dictys forced to take refuge at the altars of the gods to escape persecution from Polydectes. Once again Medusa's head came into play. Perseus found the king and his retinue feasting within the palace and turned them all into stone. He made Dictys king in Polydectes' place. With his mission finally over, he gave the winged sandals and his other aids back to Hermes, but the Gorgon's head he gave to Athena, who put it in the centre of her *aegis*, a goatskin cloak fringed with snakes, or on her shield, as a threat to her enemies.

Perseus returned to Argos with Andromeda and Danae, intending to make himself known to his grandfather. But Acrisius had heard of his impending arrival and had left the city, still in fear of his life because of the sinister oracle. Perseus went on to Larissa to compete in the funeral games held by the local king, Teutamides, in honour of his father. But Acrisius was here too, and while throwing the discus Perseus accidentally struck and killed his grandfather. Thus was the oracle fulfilled.

Perseus was ashamed to succeed to his rightful inheritance of the throne of Argos, so he exchanged Argos for Tiryns, the kingdom of Megapenthes, son of Proetus. He also founded Mycenae, and it was here, according to Apollodorus, that Andromeda bore him more children: a daughter, Gorgophone (meaning 'killing of the Gorgon'), and five more sons, ALCAEUS (1), STHENELUS (1), ELECTRYON, Mestor and Heleius. Their great-grandson was the mighty hero HERACLES.

Aeschylus wrote a tetralogy on Perseus, now lost. Two of the tragedies seem to have told of his killing of the Gorgon (*The Children of Phorcys*) and his revenge on Polydectes (*Polydectes*), while the satyr play, the *Net-drawers*, treated Danae's arrival on Seriphus in the wooden chest. Perseus' adventures, particularly the killing of Medusa (fig. 114) and his flight from the pursuing Gorgons, are popular themes in ancient art from the seventh century BC. He is also a favourite subject among postclassical artists, with (to give just a few examples) paintings by Titian, Veronese, Rubens, Rembrandt, Tiepolo, Delacroix and Burne-Jones, sculptures by Canova and Rodin, and Cellini's famous bronze statue in Florence of Perseus holding up Medusa's severed head.

[Homer, *Iliad* 5.741, 14.319; Hesiod, *Theogony* 274–83, *Shield of Heracles* 216–37; Pindar, *Pythian* 12.6–21; Herodotus 2.91, 7.61; Apollodorus 2.4.1–5; Lucian, *Dialogues of the Sea Gods* 14; Pausanias 2.16.3; Ovid, *Metamorphoses* 4.605–5.249.]

Phaea

The wild sow of Crommyon killed by THESEUS on his journey from Troezen to Athens. This ferocious beast was the offspring of the monsters TYPHON and ECHIDNA, and was called Phaea ('Grey One') after the old woman who reared it (fig. 140). A late and rationalising tradition suggests that Phaea was instead a female brigand of Crommyon, a murderous and depraved woman, who was named The Sow because of her mode of life.

[Bacchylides, *Ode* 18.23–4; Apollodorus, *Epitome* 1.1; Plutarch, *Theseus* 9; Diodorus Siculus 4.59.4; Pausanias 2.1.3.]

Phaeacians *see* SCHERIA.

Phaedra

Daughter of MINOS, king of Crete, and PASIPHAE. She married THESEUS and bore him two sons, ACAMAS (1) and Demophon. At the core of her legend is her relationship with her stepson HIPPOLYTUS (2), Theseus' son by the Amazon Antiope (or Hippolyte). This was the subject of at least three Attic tragedies, two by Euripides entitled

Hippolytus and a *Phaedra* by Sophocles. In what seems to have been the traditional story, Phaedra was a shameless woman who fell in love with Hippolytus and tried to seduce him. When he rebuffed her, she took her revenge by declaring to Theseus that he had tried to rape her. Theseus cursed his son, calling on Poseidon to kill him, and the god answered his prayer by sending a bull raging from the sea to terrify Hippolytus' horses, which dragged him to his death. Phaedra, her treachery exposed, hanged herself. This seems to have been the plot in Euripides' first (lost) *Hippolytus*, where Phaedra propositioned her step-son actually onstage, causing him to cover his head in shame. It may also have been the plot in Sophocles lost *Phaedra*, though perhaps more justification was given to Phaedra here, for we know from the little that is left of the play that Theseus had been away for some years and was believed dead, so Phaedra's love was not originally adulterous in intent. But in Euripides' second and extant *Hippolytus* (428 BC), Phaedra is a virtuous woman and has been made to fall in love by APHRODITE. The goddess is getting her revenge on Hippolytus for ignoring her worship. Phaedra, ashamed, struggles to conquer her passion in silence, and is willing even to die before confessing it to her step-son. But eventually she is too weak to keep her love secret any longer, so she tells her nurse what ails her; and it is the nurse, anxious to ease her mistress' sufferings, who reveals her love to Hippolytus. He responds to these well-meant overtures with bitter rage against women in general and Phaedra in particular, and she, afraid that he will tell everything to Theseus, writes a letter to her husband accusing Hippolytus of rape, a slander designed to protect her children from a disgrace that they do not deserve. 'This day I shall die', she says, 'and bring pleasure to Aphrodite, my destroyer. I shall be the victim of a bitter love. But there is another whom I will hurt in dying ... ' Then she hangs herself from the rafters. Theseus returns to find his wife dead, to read the letter, and to curse Hippolytus to death by the bull from the sea.

In later dramatisations of the legend, Seneca in his *Phaedra* reverted to Phaedra's more shameless characterisation, while Racine says in the introduction to his masterpiece *Phèdre* that he owes much in his conception of Phaedra's character to Euripides – certainly a sense of guilt and predestination pervades his play. Pausanias tells us (10.29.3) that Polygnotus painted Phaedra seated in a swing, which is meant to suggest, he thinks, her suicide by hanging. He saw the graves of both Phaedra and Hippolytus at Troezen, and near them a myrtle tree, its leaves pierced with holes. These, it was said, had been made by Phaedra with her hair-pin when day after day, in an agony of frustrated love, she watched Hippolytus exercising on the race-course near by.

[Homer, *Odyssey* 11.321; Apollodorus, *Epitome* 1.17–19; Diodorus Siculus 4.62; Pausanias 1.22.1–2, 2.32.1–4; Ovid, *Heroides* 4.]

Phaethon (1) *see* CEPHALUS (1).

Phaethon (2)

Son of HELIOS, the Sun-god, and the Oceanid Clymene, wife of the Ethiopian king Merops. Our best-known version of Phaethon's fate is found in Ovid (*Metamorphoses* 1.750–2.380). When Phaethon wished to be reassured about his parentage, Clymene sent him to his father's palace in the far east, at the rising of the sun. Here Helios confirmed that Phaethon was indeed his son and promised to grant him anything he might desire. Phaethon asked to drive his father's sun-chariot across the sky for just one day. The god, fearful for his son's safety, tried to dissuade him, but nothing could quell Phaethon's enthusiasm and Helios was forced to stand by his word. With many anxious instructions from his father, Phaethon climbed into the chariot and the four horses set off, galloping into the air. All too soon they raced out of control, dragging the chariot and the terrified boy completely off course, now soaring up close to the stars, now hurtling down too near the earth. He set the heavens on fire, creating what we call the Milky Way. Scorched by the intense heat the earth caught fire too. Rivers dried up and the seas contracted. (It was because of this heat and drought that the skins of the Ethiopians were burnt black and North Africa turned into a desert.) To save the world from complete destruction, Zeus hurled Phaethon from his chariot with a thunderbolt, and his blazing corpse fell into the River Eridanus. Here his mourning sisters came, the Heliades, and as they stood weeping ceaselessly on the banks they were turned into poplar trees, and their tears into amber. CYCNUS (1), the musician-king of the Ligurians, also came to mourn for Phaethon. He wandered the banks singing of his loss until he was turned into a swan.

Ovid's version of Phaethon's story seems to have been similar in many respects to that of Euripides in his lost tragedy *Phaethon*, where the still-smoking body of the dead boy was carried onstage at the end of the play. Aeschylus also wrote a tragedy on the subject, *The Heliades*, where Phaethon's sisters made up the Chorus. Here, however, it seems likely that Phaethon was the acknowledged son of Helios, living in his father's palace. When his request to drive the chariot was refused by his father, the Heliades secretly yoked it for him. Thus they had even more reason to mourn when their brother met so terrible a death.

To commemorate his sad fate, Phaethon was after his death immortalised in the stars as the constellation Auriga, the Charioteer. The River Eridanus also became a constellation, stretching far through the sky to the west of Orion. Phaethon's tragic story would seem to cry out for visual treatment, but it was rarely illustrated in ancient art, and then only very late. It did, however, prove inspirational to many postclassical painters, and there are versions of 'The Fall of Phaethon' by Michelangelo (drawings), Tintoretto, Rubens and Jan Brueghel the Younger, among many others. Phaethon's name has been given to the phaeton, a light fast-moving open carriage, drawn by a pair of horses.

[Euripides, *Hippolytus* 737–41; Plato, *Timaeus* 22c; Apollonius, *Argonautica* 4.595–611; Diodorus Siculus 5.23.2–4; Pausanias 1.4.1; Virgil, *Aeneid* 10.187–93. James Diggle (ed.), *Euripides: Phaethon* (1970); C. Collard, M. J. Cropp and K. H. Lee, *Euripides: Selected Fragmentary Plays* I (1995), pp. 195–239.]

Phaethusa

Daughter of the Sun-god HELIOS.

Phegeus (1) *see* ALCMAEON.

Phegeus (2) *see* DARES.

Phemius

In Homer's *Odyssey*, Phemius is a bard in ODYSSEUS' household. He has been forced to sing for the Suitors in Odysseus' absence, as he tells his old master during the Suitors' massacre, pleading for his life: 'It was against my will, and through no wish of my own, that I served the Suitors here in your house and sang at their feasts, for they were too many and too strong, and they forced me to do it' (22.351–3). TELEMACHUS takes his part, and Odysseus spares his life.

Pheres (1)

Son of CRETHEUS, king of Iolcus, and TYRO, and brother of AESON and AMYTHAON. When their half-brother PELIAS usurped the throne of Iolcus from Aeson, Pheres founded a new city not far away, naming it Pherae after himself, while Amythaon, who had married Pheres' daughter Idomene, migrated to Messenia. Pheres and his two sons, ADMETUS and Lycurgus, later supported JASON in his confrontation with the usurper Pelias. Lycurgus became the king of Nemea, while Admetus succeeded to the throne of Pherae when his father abdicated in his favour.

When Apollo won for Admetus the extraordinary boon of a reprieve from his fated day of death, so long as he could find someone willing to die in his place, Admetus fully believed that his father would at once offer to be the substitute. Pheres soon disenchanted him, and the outcome is dramatised in Euripides' play *Alcestis*, named after Admetus' wife who has chosen to die for her husband. Here in a delightfully comic scene Admetus upbraids his father for his selfishness, and Pheres responds indignantly (690–704):

> Don't you die on my behalf, and I won't die on yours! You love to look on the daylight. Don't you think your father does too? As I see it, we shall be dead for a long time, while life is short and very sweet. You, with no shame at all, have taken pains enough to avoid dying ... So should you be abusing any relative of yours who

does not wish to die, when you are a coward yourself? Hold your tongue! Remember that if you love life, so do all men.

[Homer, *Odyssey* 11.259; Pindar, *Pythian* 4.125–7; Apollodorus 1.9.11, 1.9.14.]

Pheres (2) *see* MERMERUS.

Philammon

A famous musician, the son of APOLLO; his mother was usually said to be CHIONE (2) (sometimes Philonis), who bore AUTOLYCUS to Hermes on the same day. Philammon himself fathered the even more famous musician THAMYRIS on Argiope, a nymph of Mount Parnassus, and was said to be the second man to win the oldest contest at Delphi, the singing of a hymn to Apollo, while Thamyris was the third. Philammon was killed while leading a troop of Argives to defend Delphi from the attacking forces of PHLEGYAS, king of Orchomenus.

[Pausanias 2.37.2–3, 4.33.3, 9.36.2, 10.7.2.]

Philemon and Baucis

Two old Phrygian peasants who were rewarded by the gods for their kindness. ZEUS and HERMES, disguised as mortals, were travelling through Phrygia seeking a place to rest, but were turned away from a thousand homes. At last they came to a humble cottage on the side of a mountain. It was roofed with reeds and thatch and was poorly furnished, but here Philemon and Baucis had lived contentedly ever since they were married. Always they had been poor, and now they were old, but they welcomed Zeus and Hermes warmly and prepared a meal for them of good but simple fare. As the dinner went on, the old couple noticed that the wine jug kept refilling itself of its own accord, and they realised that they had been entertaining gods unaware. Awed and afraid, they made ready to kill their one and only goose in honour of their divine visitors. But the gods stopped them, then led the old people out of their cottage and up to the top of the mountain. When they looked down on the country-side below, they saw a land now drowned in water, sent by the gods to punish all the inhospitable mortals. Only the cottage of Philemon and Baucis was left standing. As they gazed in astonishment it was turned into a temple, with columns and floor of marble and roof of gold. The gods offered to grant the old couple any boon they chose, and they asked that they might serve in the temple as

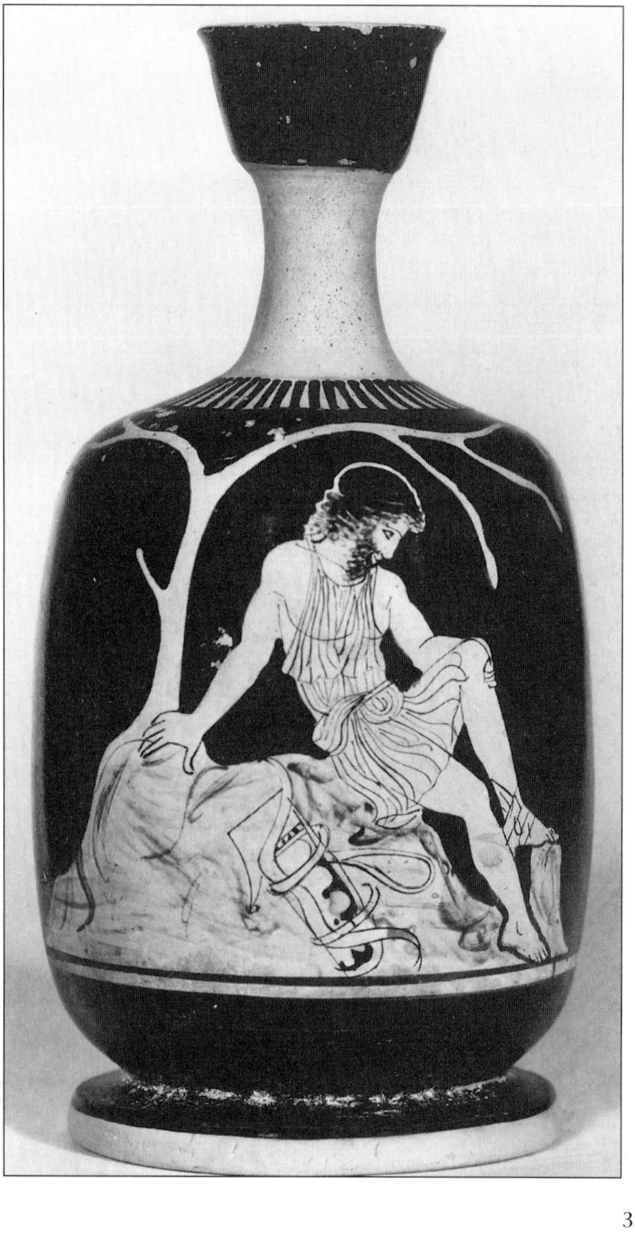

Fig. 115 **Philoctetes sits deserted, resting his wounded foot, his treasured bow on the ground beside him.**

priest and priestess for the rest of their lives, and that when the time came for death they might die at the very same instant, without grief. And so it came about. They looked after the temple as long as they lived, and one day, when they were very old, in the moment of their dying they were turned into trees, an oak and a linden, growing side by side and sharing a single trunk.

[Ovid, *Metamorphoses* 8.618–724.]

Philoctetes

Son of POEAS, king of Malis, and keeper of the great bow of HERACLES and its inescapable arrows, given by Heracles either to Philoctetes or to Poeas as a reward for setting light to his funeral pyre on Mount Oeta. Philoctetes was one of HELEN's suitors. Bound by the common oath to protect the marriage-rights of her chosen husband, he later led seven ships from Malis to fight in the TROJAN WAR. Unfortunately on the journey to Troy he suffered a snake-bite that refused to heal. There are various stories of how this came about. Either he was attacked by a deadly water-snake while the Greeks were feasting on the island of Tenedos; or they had stopped at the tiny island of Chryse, where a goddess of that name was worshipped, and the snake that bit Philoctetes was the guardian of her shrine; or HERA sent the snake to bite him because she resented his service in lighting Heracles' funeral pyre and thus helping him to immortality. In a quite different version, Philoctetes had promised Heracles that he would keep the place of his death a secret, but he later showed the Greeks the spot by wordlessly stamping on the ground with his foot, hoping thus to keep his oath. On the way to Troy, he had one of Heracles' arrows fall from its quiver and strike the offending foot. Whatever the cause of Philoctetes' wound, it festered incurably. On ODYSSEUS' suggestion, because of the unbearable stench of rotting flesh and Philoctetes' continual cries of agony, he was left behind by his comrades on the island of Lemnos while they sailed on to Troy. MEDON (3) took command of the seven ships from Malis.

The war at Troy dragged on for ten long years, during which Philoctetes suffered his wound and nursed his hatred for the Greeks, and most of all for Odysseus. He lived in a lonely cave, keeping himself from starving by shooting birds and animals. In the last year of the war, the Greeks learnt from a seer – either the captured Trojan HELENUS or the Greek CALCHAS – that Troy would not fall until they had Philoctetes fighting for them with Heracles' great bow. At once they sent an embassy to Lemnos to fetch their abandoned comrade. Sophocles' play *Philoctetes* dramatises the events on Lemnos, which he depicts as a completely uninhabited island, thus em-

phasising Philoctetes' long isolation (fig. 115). In other versions of the legend (and both Aeschylus and Euripides wrote a *Philoctetes*, now lost), DIOMEDES (2) was involved, usually with Odysseus, in fetching Philoctetes. Here it is Odysseus and (uniquely) the young NEOPTOLEMUS, son of the dead Achilles, who come to Lemnos. Not unnaturally, Philoctetes is loath to put himself out to help the army that abandoned him, but the unscrupulous Odysseus is prepared to go to any lengths of trickery or brute force to carry him off to Troy. Neoptolemus is also at first willing to trick Philoctetes, but eventually he is swayed by his own basic honesty and by his respect and compassion for the wounded man, and he decides instead to take him home to Greece. It is only the appearance of Heracles, as *deus ex machina* at the end of the play, that puts events back on course. He orders both Neoptolemus and Philoctetes to Troy.

Once there, Philoctetes' wound was cured by either MACHAON or Podaleirius and he returned to battle, where he killed PARIS. Soon afterwards Troy fell when the Greeks entered the city by means of the WOODEN HORSE, with Philoctetes one of the warriors inside it. According to the *Odyssey* (3.190), he returned safely home after the war, but some later accounts say that he journeyed to southern Italy and founded cities there. His wanderings over, he founded a sanctuary of Apollo and there dedicated his great bow.

[Homer, *Iliad* 2.716–28, *Odyssey* 8.219–20; Proclus' summaries of the *Cypria* and the *Little Iliad*; Pindar, *Pythian* 1.50–5; Apollodorus 2.7.7, 3.10.8, *Epitome* 3.14, 3.27, 5.8, 6.15b; Dio Chrysostom, *Orations* 52, 59; Pausanias 1.22.6, 8.33.4; Quintus of Smyrna, *Sequel to Homer* 9.325–479, 10.206–368; Virgil, *Aeneid* 3.401–2; Ovid, *Metamorphoses* 9.229–34, 13.45–55, 313–38; Hyginus *Fabula* 102.]

Philoetius

Odysseus' faithful cowherd on Ithaca. *See* EUMAEUS.

Philomela *see* TEREUS.

Philomelus *see* BOÖTES.

Philonoe (1) *see* BELLEROPHON.

Philonoe (2)

A daughter of TYNDAREOS and LEDA who was made immortal by ARTEMIS.

[Hesiod, *Catalogue of Women* fr. 23a; Apollodorus 3.10.6.]

Philonome *see* TENES.

Philyra ('Linden Tree')

Daughter of OCEANUS and Tethys, and mother of the Centaur CHEIRON by the Titan CRONUS, who mated with her in the form of a horse so as to deceive his jealous wife Rhea. This is why their son was born part man, part horse. Some say that Philyra so loathed the monster born of her that she prayed to the gods to change her into something other than she was, and they transformed her into a linden tree. But a happier version has her dwelling with Cheiron in his cave on Mount Pelion, and thus able to see her son become one of the wisest and most respected of living beings.

[Pindar, *Pythian* 4.102–3; Apollonius, *Argonautica* 2.1231–41; Apollodorus 1.2.4.]

Phineus (1)

Brother of CEPHEUS (1) and uncle of ANDROMEDA.

Phineus (2)

A blind seer-king of Salmydessus in Thrace, usually said to be the son of AGENOR (1), king of Tyre, though sometimes of Agenor's son PHOENIX (2). Phineus' story is told with many atrociously complicated variations. Several reasons are given for his blindness. Either he was blinded by Poseidon for showing PHRIXUS the way (presumably to Colchis), or the sons of Phrixus the way to Greece. Or the gods blinded him for revealing too much of the future to men. Or the Sun-god HELIOS blinded him when, offered the choice of long life or sight, he chose long life. Or BOREAS and the ARGONAUTS blinded him to avenge his cruel treatment of Boreas' two grandsons, which came about in the following way. Phineus' first wife was Cleopatra, Boreas' daughter. She bore him two sons (variously named), then died, or was abandoned, and Phineus took a second wife, Idaea (or Eidothea, or Eurytia). Now it was the boys who were blinded, either by Cleopatra, to punish Phineus for remarrying; or by Phineus himself, after Idaea accused her step-sons of rape; or Idaea blinded them out of resentment, using her shuttle as a dagger. In yet another version, the boys were simply locked up and whipped repeatedly. When the Argonauts visited Phineus they punished him by blinding him in his turn, or by killing him, and sent Idaea home to her father, who had her executed.

A quite different version told of a happier encounter with the Argonauts. When they visited Phineus on their way to Colchis, they found him not only blind but half-starved, because the pestilential HARPIES had been snatching his food (fig.63). Phineus foretold the dangers of the Argonauts' voyage, and in return the winged sons of Boreas, ZETES and Calais, chased off the Harpies and Phineus was able to live normally once again.

[Sophocles, *Antigone* 966–87; Apollonius, *Argonautica* 2.176–499; Apollodorus 1.9.21, 3.15.3; Diodorus Siculus 4.43.3–44.7.]

Phlegethon

One of the rivers of the Underworld, the River of Flame, flowing into the Acheron. Plato calls it the Pyriphlegethon and sees it as the source of the streams of lava that spout up at various places on earth.

The Phlegethon is one of Milton's 'four infernal rivers' in *Paradise Lost*: 'fierce Phlegethon / whose waves of torrent fire inflame with rage'.

[Homer, *Odyssey* 10.513; Plato *Phaedo* 113a–b; Virgil, *Aeneid* 6.265.]

Phlegyas

Son of ARES and Dotis (or Chryse), and father of Coronis, who bore ASCLEPIUS to APOLLO. Phlegyas was the king of Orchomenus and named his people Phlegyans after himself. He inherited his father's warlike nature, for he collected a fighting force of the best soldiers in Greece, then went on marauding expeditions through the neighbouring lands, carrying off crops and rustling cattle. At last he and his men even marched against Apollo's sanctuary at Delphi, where they destroyed the defending troop of Argives led by the bard PHILAMMON. But the god took his revenge, for he overthrew the Phlegyans with thunderbolts and earthquakes. According to another tradition, Phlegyas was killed by the brothers LYCUS (1) and Nycteus. In the *Aeneid* (6.618–20), Virgil depicts Phlegyas in the Underworld, eternally punished for his sins on earth and shouting out a lesson for all mankind: 'Be warned, learn to be just and not to slight the gods.'

[Homer, *Iliad* 13.298–303; Apollodorus 3.5.5; Pausanias 2.26.3–4, 9.36.1–4.]

Phobos and Deimos

Sons of ARES and APHRODITE. Their names mean 'Terror' and 'Fear', so they were suitable children for the war-god and often accompanied their father on the battlefield: 'They are terrible gods', says Hesiod (*Theogony* 935–6), 'who along with Ares, sacker of cities, put to rout the close-packed ranks of men in chilling war.'

[Homer, *Iliad* 4.439–40, 13.298–300, 15.119–20; Hesiod, *Shield of Heracles* 463–6.]

Phocus (1)

Bastard son of AEACUS, king of Aegina, by the Nereid Psamathe. He was given his name from *phoke*, 'seal', because his mother, being a sea-nymph with the gift of metamorphosis, changed herself into a seal in trying to escape intercourse with his father.

There are varying traditions about his death. He was killed by one or both of his half-brothers PELEUS and TELAMON, either accidentally, or because they were jealous of his athletic prowess, or because he was hated by their

318

mother Endeis, Aeacus' legitimate wife. Peleus and Telamon were sent into exile by their father, and Psamathe in anger sent a huge wolf to ravage Peleus' herds of cattle. Finally, however, her sister Thetis interceded on Peleus' behalf and the wolf was turned to stone.

Phocus is said to have given his name to the land of Phocis, where his sons by his wife Asteria, PANOPEUS and Crisus, settled; but sometimes he is confused with PHOCUS (2), who is also said to be the eponymous hero of Phocis.

[Apollodorus 3.12.6; Diodorus Siculus 4.72.6; Plutarch, *Moralia* 311e; Pausanias 2.29.2–10, 10.30.4; Ovid, *Metamorphoses* 11.346–406.]

Phocus (2)

Son of POSEIDON, or of Ornytion the son of SISYPHUS. He left Corinth and settled at the foot of Mount Parnassus, naming the land after himself. A generation later the sons of Phocus (1) settled there also, giving the name Phocis to a much larger area. It was said that ANTIOPE (1), driven mad by Dionysus, wandered to Phocis, where Phocus cured her and they were married. At their deaths they were buried together in a grave at Tithorea.

[Pausanias 2.4.3, 9.17.4, 10.1.1.]

Phoebe (1)

One of the TITANS, daughter of Uranus (Heaven) and GAIA (Earth). She married her brother-Titan Coeus and bore two daughters: LETO, who became the mother of APOLLO and ARTEMIS, and ASTERIA, who became the mother of HECATE. Aeschylus says that Phoebe gave to her grandson Apollo the site of his oracle at Delphi, and that he was afterwards called Phoebus, 'Shining One', in memory of her.

[Hesiod, *Theogony* 132–6, 404–10; Aeschylus, *Eumenides* 1–8; Apollodorus 1.1.3, 1.2.2.]

Phoebe (2) *see* HILAEIRA AND PHOEBE.

Phoebe (3)

A daughter of TYNDAREOS and LEDA. She is mentioned only once in early literature (Euripides, *Iphigeneia at Aulis* 49–51), but is named several times on Attic vases depicting Leda's family.

Phoebe (4)

A late name for ARTEMIS or DIANA, one often used by poets to refer to the moon.

Phoebus ('Radiant')

Name sometimes given to APOLLO.

Phoenix (1)

A fabulous bird, first mentioned by Herodotus in his description of Egypt, where he says that it was like an eagle in shape and size, but with splendid red and gold plumage. It lived for five hundred years, and its legend is principally concerned with its death and rebirth at the end of that time. Various accounts are given of what actually happened. In one version it flew to Heliopolis in Egypt, where it was burned to death on the altar of the Sun and a new phoenix miraculously arose from the ashes of the old. Or it made a nest of aromatic plants for its funeral pyre, where again it was consumed and reborn. Or it simply died on its fragrant nest, and a new phoenix at once arose who, when it grew strong enough, carried its dead parent to the temple of the Sun in Heliopolis, to be burned there by the priests. Whatever the details, the phoenix rising from the flames became an important symbol of death and resurrection for all believers in an afterlife.

[Herodotus 2.73; Nonnus, *Dionysiaca* 40.394–8; Ovid, *Metamorphoses* 15.392–409; Pliny, *Natural History* 103–5; Tacitus, *Annals* 6.28.]

Phoenix (2)

The son of AGENOR (1), king of Tyre or Sidon, who gave his name to Phoenicia. He was the brother of EUROPA, CADMUS, CILIX, PHINEUS (2) and THASUS, and along with his brothers he left home in search of Europa after she had been abducted by Zeus. When his quest failed, he chose not to return home but settled elsewhere in Phoenicia. The genealogies of this family are somewhat confused, and Phoenix was occasionally said to be the father of Europa, Cadmus, Phineus, CEPHEUS (1) and ADONIS.

[Homer, *Iliad* 14.321–2; Hesiod, *Catalogue of Women* frr. 138–141; Bacchylides, *Ode* 17.29–33; Apollodorus 3.1.1.]

Phoenix (3)

In the *Iliad*, Phoenix is the old tutor of ACHILLES who accompanies him to the TROJAN WAR. He was the son of AMYNTOR, the king of Eleon or of Ormenium at the foot of Mount Pelion. In youth he quarrelled irrevocably with his father and left home for ever. Amyntor had a favourite concubine, and his devotion to her made his wife so jealous that she begged Phoenix to make love to the girl, and by his youth and vigour win her affection away from the old man. This Phoenix did, and Amyntor was so angry that he called down the FURIES on his son, praying that he might never have children of his own – a prayer that was fulfilled. Phoenix too was now furious and came near to killing his father, but left home instead and went as a refugee to PELEUS, king of Phthia. Peleus made him king of the Dolopians.

Phoenix' conflict with his father was possibly the subject of Sophocles' lost tragedy *Phoenix*, but was certainly the subject of the lost *Phoenix* by Euripides, who seems to have given a different version of the story in which Amyntor's concubine tried to seduce Phoenix. In deference to his father he rejected her, so to get her revenge for the slight she accused him to Amyntor of attempted rape or seduction, and the king blinded his son. (We know from Aristophanes' reference to Euripides' play in his *Acharnians* (421) that here Phoenix was certainly blind.) Apollodorus (3.13.8) mentions this version, and adds that Peleus took the blind Phoenix to the wise Centaur CHEIRON, who gave him back his sight.

Phoenix could have no children of his own, but in Peleus' household he helped to bring up the young Achilles. In the *Iliad*, when Phoenix goes with ODYSSEUS and AJAX (1) on the Embassy to Achilles in the hope of persuading him to return to battle, the old man remembers those early days (9.485–7):

> I made you all that you are, godlike Achilles,
> loving you from my heart, for with no one else
> would you go to the feast or eat in your own halls
> until I had set you on my knees and cut your meat,
> giving you your fill and holding the wine to your lips.
> And many a time you soaked the front of my tunic
> by spitting out wine in your childish helplessness.
> So I have taken time and trouble over you,
> always knowing the gods would never grant me
> a child of my own. No, godlike Achilles,
> it was you I made my son, so that one day
> you would keep painful affliction away from me.
> So, Achilles, beat down your great anger.
> It is not in you to have a pitiless heart.

In the hope of further winning over Achilles, Phoenix goes on to tell the story of the great hero MELEAGER, who also refused to fight until it was too late and thereby lost

valuable gifts. But despite his obvious affection for the old man, Achilles still refuses to return to battle. Phoenix does, however, succeed in persuading him to sleep on his decision to leave Troy immediately and sail home. And in the morning Achilles stays at Troy.

Achilles' death at the hands of Paris and Apollo was recounted in the lost *Aethiopis*. After this Phoenix went with Odysseus to Scyros to fetch Achilles' son NEOPTOLEMUS to fight at Troy, and soon afterwards the city fell to the Greeks. After the sack of Troy, the old man set out for Greece with Neoptolemus, but he died on the journey and Neoptolemus buried him.

[Homer, *Iliad* 9.168–662, 16.196, 17.553–566, 19.310–13, 23.358–61; Sophocles, *Philoctetes* 343–7; Apollodorus, *Epitome* 4.3, 6.12; Propertius 2.1.60.]

Pholus

One of the CENTAURS, but unlike his fellows, who were descended from Ixion's son Centaurus, Pholus was the son of SILENUS by a Melian nymph. His nature, too, differed from the other Centaurs, and while they were savage and brutal (apart from the wise and humane Cheiron), he was civilised and hospitable. Unfortunately these better traits led to his death. When HERACLES was passing Pholus' home on Mount Pholoe during his pursuit of the Erymanthian Boar, the Centaur entertained him, putting roast meat in front of his guest. Heracles, a man of prodigious appetites, called for wine to go with the meat, but although Pholus possessed a great jar of wine, he hesitated to open it since it belonged to all the Centaurs in common. Heracles, however, insisted on broaching it. The smell from the open jar soon attracted the other Centaurs, who galloped up armed with rocks and fir-branches and tried to share it (fig. 116). A fight broke out, during which Heracles shot some of the beasts dead with his unerring arrows, tipped with the HYDRA OF LERNA's fatal venom, then chased the rest far away. Pholus meanwhile, drawing an arrow from one of the corpses, wondered that so small a thing could bring death to so large a creature. The arrow slipped from his hand and fell on his own foot, killing him at once. When Heracles returned, he found his host dead and sorrowfully buried him, then went on his way to catch the Erymanthian Boar. Pholus was immortalised among the stars as the constellation Centaurus.

[Apollodorus 2.5.4; Diodorus Siculus 4.12.3–8.]

Fig. 116 **Heracles draws wine from a great storage jar set in the ground, while the Centaur Pholus *(right)* gestures in alarm, and a second Centaur approaches with a drinking horn to demand his share.**

Phorbas

A Thessalian king, the son of Lapithes or Triopas, who emigrated to Rhodes on the invitation of the Rhodians and rid the island of snakes. After his death he was honoured as a hero, and according to some was immortalised in the stars as the constellation Ophiuchus.

[Diodorus Siculus 5.58.4–5; Hyginus, *Poetic Astronomy* 2.14.]

Phorcys

An ancient sea-god, the son of Pontus (the Sea) and GAIA (the Earth), and thus belonging to the generation of pre-Olympian divinities. He is sometimes given, along with NEREUS and PROTEUS, the name of Old Man of the Sea. According to Hesiod, Phorcys' sister, the sea-monster CETO, bore him the GRAEAE, the GORGONS, the monster ECHIDNA, and LADON, the snake who guarded the apples of the Hesperides. Homer makes him the grandfather of the Cyclops POLYPHEMUS (2), and Apollonius the father, by Crataeis, of SCYLLA (1).

Phorcys' monstrous children, and the monsters which they in turn generated, would prove to be a great test of metal for such heroes as HERACLES, PERSEUS, BELLEROPHON and ODYSSEUS; and Spenser appositely calls Phorcys in the *Faerie Queene* '... the father of that fatall brood / By whome those old Heroes wonne such fame'.

[Homer, *Odyssey* 1.68–74, 13.96, 345; Hesiod, *Theogony* 233–9, 270–336; Apollonius *Argonautica* 4.828–9.]

Phoroneus

A very ancient figure of Argive tradition, son of the river-god INACHUS and the Oceanid Melia, and king of the whole Peloponnese. By the nymph Teledice he had a son, APIS, and a daughter, NIOBE (1), who was the first earthly love of Zeus. Pausanias tells us that Phoroneus was the first man to gather together scattered families into cities, and that the Argives credited him, not Prometheus, with the discovery of fire, keeping an eternal flame burning in his memory.

[Apollodorus 2.1.1; Pausanias 2.15.5, 2.19.5.]

Phosphorus

The morning star (i.e. the planet Venus) which announces the approach of dawn. Like the other stars he was child of EOS, the Dawn, and the Titan Astraeus. He himself was father of Ceyx, the husband of ALCYONE (2), and of Daedalion, the father of CHIONE (2). His name means Light-bringer, as does the name of his Roman equivalent, Lucifer, and he was also called Eosphorus, Dawn-bringer. Homer tells of his daily appearance (*Iliad* 23.226–7):

The morning star passes over the earth,
harbinger of light, and after him
gold-robed Dawn is spread across the sea.

[Hesiod, *Theogony* 381; Apollodorus 1.7.4; Ovid, *Metamorphoses* 11.291–345.]

Phrixus and Helle

The son and daughter of ATHAMAS, king of Orchomenus in Boeotia, and his first wife Nephele. This marriage came to an end for some unspecified reason and Athamas married again, this time INO, one of Cadmus' daughters, who bore him two more sons, Learchus and Melicertes. Unhappily for Phrixus and Helle, their new stepmother resented their existence and secretly plotted Phrixus' death. First she persuaded the women of the land to roast the grain set aside for the next sowing, thus making it sterile. When this resulted in complete crop failure, Athamas, as Ino had guessed he would, sent messengers to consult the Delphic Oracle about the inevitable famine. Ino bribed them on their return to say that Phrixus must be sacrificed to Zeus. At first Athamas refused to perform such a sacrifice, but then gave in for his people's sake (though in one version, Phrixus volunteered to die). Just as he was about to cut Phrixus' throat a wondrous ram appeared, sent by Nephele. Given to her by HERMES, it could talk and fly, and its fleece was of spun gold. At the ram's command, Phrixus and Helle leapt on to its back and it flew away, carrying them to safety.

Other versions exist of Phrixus' near-sacrifice. In one version, a servant discovered Ino's wicked plot and reported it to Athamas. He condemned Ino and her younger son Melicertes to death, but the god DIONYSUS (Ino's nephew) wrapped them in a mist that allowed them to escape, then sent Phrixus and Helle mad. They were wandering lost in a forest when the wondrous ram arrived, sent by their mother. (This seems to have been the plot of one of Euripides' two lost *Phrixus* tragedies.) In another version, a certain Demodice (either the stepmother with a different name, or the wife of Cretheus, Athamas' brother) fell in love with the handsome Phrixus and tried to seduce him. When he repulsed her she accused him of rape, and Athamas ordered him to be executed for such an outrage. Once again the ram arrived just in time.

As the ram flew over the straits dividing Europe from Asia, Helle fell off its back and drowned in the sea below. It was named the Hellespont ('Helle's Sea') after her. The ram carried Phrixus further east and at last put him down at Aea, the capital of Colchis at the eastern end of the Black Sea. Here AEETES was king. He welcomed Phrixus and gave him the hand of one of his daughters, Chalciope, in marriage. In gratitude for his safe landing, and perhaps on the ram's own instructions, Phrixus sacrificed the beast to Zeus and gave its fleece to the king. Aeetes hung it in an oak tree in a grove of Ares and set a sleepless dragon to guard it. This would in due course be the motive for the long and arduous journey of JASON and the ARGONAUTS: the quest for the Golden Fleece. The earliest certain depictions of Phrixus and the ram in ancient art occur at around 500 BC.

Phrixus was usually said to have four sons by Chalciope – Argus, Melas, Phrontis and Cytissorus – though a fifth, Presbon, is also mentioned. In one version Phrixus lived to a prosperous old age in Colchis. In another, Aeetes learnt from an oracle that he was destined to be killed by a stranger from the race of Aeolus, so he murdered his son-in-law, who was Aeolus' grandson. Phrixus' sons escaped from Colchis with the Argonauts when they set off with the Golden Fleece, and it is said that both Cytorissus and Presbon were eventually united with their grandfather, Athamas. The ram was immortalised as the constellation ARIES.

[Apollonius, *Argonautica* 1.256–9, 2.1140–56, 1268–70, 3.190–1, 300–39, 584–8, 4.114–22; Apollodorus 1.9.1, 1.9.16, 1.9.21; Diodorus Siculus 4.47; Pausanias 1.24.2, 9.34.5.]

Phylacus

King of Phylace in Thessaly. He was the son of Deion, king of Phocis, and Diomede. He married Clymene (2), the daughter of Minyas, and she bore him a son, IPHICLUS (1), and Alcimede, who became the mother of JASON. Phylacus had a magnificent herd of cattle which were won from him by the seer MELAMPUS when he cured Iphiclus of impotence.

Phylas (1)

A king of the Thesprotian city of Ephyra. Soon after HERACLES married Deianeira, he helped his new father-on-law OENEUS, king of Calydon, by leading the Calydonians against their enemies the Thesprotians. He captured Ephyra and took Phylas' daughter, Astyoche, as his battle-prize. She bore him a son, TLEPOLEMUS.

[Apollodorus 2.7.6; Diodorus Siculus 4.36.1.]

Phylas (2)

A king of the Dryopes on Mount Parnassus (*see* DRYOPS). Because Phylas violated APOLLO's sanctuary at Delphi, HERACLES made war on him, defeating and killing the king and enslaving his people to Apollo. Phylas' daughter Meda bore Heracles a son, Antiochus.

[Diodorus Siculus 4.37.1; Pausanias 1.5.2, 4.34.9–11, 10.10.1.]

Phylas (3) *see* EUDORUS.

Phyleus

Son of AUGEAS, king of Elis. He married TIMANDRA, daughter of Tyndareos and Leda, when for love of him she deserted her first husband, Echemus. Phyleus supported HERACLES when Augeas refused to pay him for cleansing the 'Augean stables', and was banished from Elis by his father. He settled on the island of Dulichium, and returned there even after Heracles had made him king of Elis once Augeas had been killed. In the *Iliad*, NESTOR relates how he beat Phyleus in the spear-throwing contest at the funeral games of Amarynceus (23.630–7). Phyleus' son MEGES led forty ships from Dulichium to the Trojan War (2.625–9).

Phyllis *see* ACAMAS (1).

Phytalus

An Athenian who once gave hospitality to the goddess DEMETER, and in return was rewarded by her with the first fig tree. The traveller Pausanias (1.37.2–4) saw his grave, its inscription recording the honour in which Phytalus and his race were held because he had won such a rich gift for mankind.

Picus

An early king of Latium, the son of SATURN, the father of FAUNUS, and the grandfather of LATINUS. The enchantress CIRCE fell in love with Picus, then transformed him into a woodpecker (*picus*) when he spurned her advances, refusing to be unfaithful to his beloved wife CANENS. The woodpecker was Mars' sacred bird, thought to have prophetic powers, and it was sometimes said that in this guise Picus brought scraps of food to the abandoned twins ROMULUS AND REMUS.

[Strabo 5.4.2; Plutarch *Moralia* 268e–f; Virgil, *Aeneid* 7.47–9, 171, 187–91; Ovid, *Fasti* 3.37.]

Pielus

Son of ANDROMACHE by Neoptolemus.

Pierides

The name given both to the MUSES, because they were born in Pieria, and to the daughters of the Macedonian king PIERUS.

Pierus

A king of Pella in Macedonia, the son of Magnes, who gave his name to Pieria, the region north of Mount Olympus where the MUSES were born. His legend is closely associated with that of the Muses, for he is said to have introduced their cult into Thespiae in Boeotia, and to have been the father of HYACINTHUS by the Muse Clio. Oeagrus, Pierus' son by the nymph Methone, was according to one tradition the father of ORPHEUS by the Muse Calliope. Moreover Pierus' nine daughters (the Pierides) by his wife Evippe became so skilled at singing, and so proud of their expertise, that they challenged the Muses to a singing-contest with the NYMPHS as judges. The Muses were unanimously agreed the winners, but the girls resented their defeat. They went on hurling abuse at their victors until the Muses punished them by turning them into magpies. Even now, as birds, they retain their old style of speech, which is why magpies chatter long and harshly.

[*Contest of Homer and Hesiod* 314; Apollodorus 1.3.3; Pausanias 9.29.3–4; Ovid, *Metamorphoses* 5.293–331, 662–78.]

Pillars of Heracles (or **Hercules**)

The promontories on the northern and southern sides of the Straits of Gibraltar, Calpe (Gibraltar) and Abyla (Ceuta). HERACLES, on his quest for GERYON's cattle, set them up to mark how far he had travelled. There are two accounts of their formation: either the two continents were joined by an isthmus before the time of Heracles, and it was he who cut through the land and created the straits; or the straits were originally wider, and Heracles narrowed them to keep the monsters of the Atlantic from bursting into the Mediterranean. Whatever their origin, they were seen as the limits beyond which no man other than Heracles might sail. As Pindar says (*Olympian* 3.44–5): 'All places beyond are impassable by both the wise man and the fool.'

[Apollodorus 2.5.10; Diodorus Siculus 4.18.5.]

Pilumnus *see* DAUNUS (1).

Pisces (The Fishes)

A constellation commemorating the two fishes into which APHRODITE transformed herself and her son, EROS, to escape the immense and terrifying monster TYPHON.

Pittheus

Son of PELOPS and Hippodameia. Pittheus was king of Troezen in the Argolid and had a reputation for wisdom and the dispensing of justice. He had no sons, but through his cleverness and manipulation became the grandfather of the great hero THESEUS through his daughter, AETHRA. AEGEUS, the king of Athens, came to consult Pittheus about the Delphic Oracle's obscure reply when he enquired about his childlessness. 'Loose not the jutting neck of the wineskin, best of men, until you come again to the city of Athens', ordained the Oracle, meaning that he should not have intercourse with a woman until he returned home, and implying that the next time he did so, the union would bear fruit. Pittheus under-

stood at once, so he made his guest drunk and enticed him into sleeping with Aethra. The result was a son, Theseus (though it was often said that Poseidon was the boy's real father). Pittheus helped Aethra to bring up her son until he was of an age to travel to Athens and claim his birthright. Theseus later sent his own son HIPPOLYTUS (2) to live with Pittheus in Troezen, intending him to take over the throne on his great-grandfather's death. The boy died by his father's curse before he could do so.

In the time of Pausanias (second century AD), the Troezenians were still showing visitors the place where Pittheus taught the art of rhetoric, and the seats from which he and two fellow-judges dispensed justice. Pausanias himself had read a treatise on rhetoric purported to be by Pittheus.

[Euripides, *Medea* 667–87; Apollodorus 3.15.7, *Epitome* 2.10; Plutarch, *Theseus* 4; Pausanias 1.22.2, 2.30.8–9, 2.31.3–6.]

Pitys ('Pine-tree')

A nymph who was loved by the pastoral god PAN. She fled from his advances and was turned into a pine tree, which is why Pan often liked to decorate his brow with wreathes of pine leaves. In another version, Pitys was loved by both Pan and BOREAS, the god of the North Wind. She favoured Pan, and Boreas was so jealous that he blew her to her death from the top of a cliff. The Earth where her body landed took pity on her and turned her into a pine tree. Pitys can be heard weeping when Boreas blows through her branches.

[Lucian, *Dialogues of the Gods* 2; Nonnus, *Dionysiaca* 2.108, 118, 42.258–66.]

Pleiades

The seven daughters of the Titan ATLAS and the Oceanid Pleione, and half-sisters of Hyas and the HYADES. Six of the Pleiades bore children to gods: MAIA (1) was the mother of Hermes by Zeus, ELECTRA (2) of Dardanus and Iasion by Zeus, TAYGETE of Lacedaemon by Zeus, ALCYONE (1) of Hyrieus, Hyperenor and Aethusa by Poseidon, CELAENO (1) of Lycus by Poseidon, and STEROPE (1) of Oenomaus by Ares. The seventh sister, MEROPE (1), was the mother of Glaucus by a mortal, Sisyphus.

Two stories are told to account for the girls being immortalised in the night sky as the Pleiades, a cluster of seven stars also known as the Seven Sisters. One version says that when Hyas was killed while out hunting, the Hyades died of grief for him, and the Pleiades died in turn from mourning their half-sisters. Zeus out of pity put them all among the stars. In the second version he set the Pleiades in the sky to save them when they and their mother were pursued for five (or seven) years by the lustful giant ORION. Orion too was placed in the stars, immediately south of the constellation Taurus in which the Pleiades' star cluster lies, so he still pursues his old loves forever through the night sky. One of the seven stars shines more faintly than the rest, and this is said to be either Merope, hiding her head in shame for having married a mere mortal, or Electra, veiling her face in mourning for the death of her son Dardanus and the destruction of Troy.

[Homer, *Iliad* 18.486; Hesiod, *Works and Days* 383–4, 619–20, *Catalogue of Women* fr. 169; Pindar, *Nemean* 2.10–12; Apollodorus 3.10.1–3; Diodorus Siculus 3.60.]

Pleisthenes

Pleisthenes is a rather indeterminate character who plays a variety of parts in the legend of the house of ATREUS. Sometimes he is said to be the son of Atreus, the husband of Aerope (or Cleolla), and the father of Agamemnon, Menelaus and Anaxibia. He died young, and Atreus himself, now married to Aerope, brought up the children as his own. Pleisthenes is also named as a son of Atreus' brother THYESTES, who along with his own two brothers was cooked and served up by Atreus for Thyestes to eat. A third story, found in Hyginus (*Fabula* 86), says that Pleisthenes was the son of Atreus, but was brought up by Thyestes. As a result of the feud between the brothers, Thyestes sent Pleisthenes to kill Atreus, but instead Atreus killed the boy, discovering too late that he was in fact his own son. The origin of this last story sounds to have been a tragedy, just possibly Euripides' lost *Pleisthenes*.

[Hesiod, *Catalogue of Women* frr. 194–5; Apollodorus 3.2.2; Seneca, *Thyestes*.]

Pluto or Pluton

'Rich one', a euphemistic title of HADES (1), god of the Underworld, referring to his powers as a chthonic (earth) deity who enriched mankind with all the wealth that comes from the earth (fig.117). The Romans adopted the title from the Greeks, but also called the god Dis, a contraction of *dives*, 'rich'.

Plutus

The god of wealth, originally the wealth and fortune, both vegetable and mineral, that springs from the earth. He was born to IASION (1) and DEMETER after they made love in a thrice-ploughed field in Crete. Hesiod (*Theogony* 972–4) describes him as 'a kindly god, who goes everywhere over the earth and the broad back of the sea, and whoever finds him, and into whose hands he comes, that man he makes rich and bestows much fortune on him'. Plutus had an important part to play in the Mysteries of Eleusis, along with Demeter and PERSEPHONE, and he is depicted in art in their company, usually as a naked boy holding a cornucopia or a bunch of grain stalks.

In Aristophanes' comedy *Wealth*, Plutus has become the personification of wealth in general. He is an old man who has been blinded by Zeus so that he will distribute wealth impartially, visiting the good and the wicked alike; but in the play he regains his sight, and thereafter brings prosperity only to the deserving.

Podaleirius *see* MACHAON.

Podarces (1)

Son of IPHICLUS (1) of Phylace, and brother of PROTESILAUS. The two brothers were both suitors of HELEN, so bound by the common oath to defend the marriage-rights of her chosen husband, they took forty ships to fight in the TROJAN WAR, with Protesilaus as leader. An oracle had predicted that the first man to touch Trojan soil would be the first to die, so all the Greeks hesitated to land until Protesilaus took the initiative and leapt ashore. He killed a number of Trojans before being himself killed by Hector. Podarces then took command of the force from Phylace. He is still alive at the end of the *Iliad* when Hector is buried, but Quintus of Smyrna relates how, in fighting against the AMAZONS who had come soon afterwards to help the Trojans, he was killed by the Amazon queen, PENTHESILEIA. Many other Greeks were killed in this battle, but his comrades grieved for Podarces the most and gave him special burial (*Sequel to Homer* 1.814–22):

> Above the rest they mourned for brave Podarces,
> a man as mighty in battle as his hero-brother,
> the great Protesilaus, who, so long ago,
> had died at Hector's hands. So Podarces now
> had fallen to the spear of Penthesileia
> and brought on all the Greeks a bitter grief.
> but over him alone they laboured to heap up
> a burial mound, one to be seen from afar,
> to mark his splendid courage.

[Homer, *Iliad* 2.695–710; Hesiod, *Catalogue of Women* fr. 199; Apollodorus 1.9.12; Quintus of Smyrna, *Sequel to Homer* 1.230–46.]

Podarces (2)

The name given to PRIAM when he was young. He was renamed when his sister HESIONE ransomed him from Heracles (reputedly from *priamai*, 'to buy').

Podarge *see* HARPIES.

Poeas

A king of Malis, the son of Thaumacus and the father of PHILOCTETES. He sailed with Jason and the ARGONAUTS and was, according to some, the man who killed TALOS (1), the bronze man of Crete, by shooting him in his vulnerable ankle. Poeas was with HERACLES at his death, for he happened to pass by, looking for his sheep on Mount Oeta, while Heracles was lying in agony on his funeral pyre. No one until now had been willing to set light to the pyre, but Poeas agreed to do so and was rewarded with Heracles' great bow and unerring arrows. These he bequeathed to his son Philoctetes, though in some versions it was said to be Philoctetes himself who lit the pyre.

[Apollodorus 1.9.16, 1.9.26, 2.7.7.]

Polites (1)

Son of PRIAM, king of Troy, and HECUBA. He plays a minor part in the events of the TROJAN WAR detailed in the *Iliad*, acting as a scout for the Trojans and taking part in the fighting, where he kills Echius and saves the life of his wounded brother DEIPHOBUS. Virgil tells of Polites' death at the hands of NEOPTOLEMUS during the sack of Troy. Wounded, he runs from his attacker to where his parents have taken refuge at the palace altar, then dies in front of their eyes. Neoptolemus drags Priam through pools of his son's blood before slaughtering him too.

Virgil also mentions Polites' little son, a younger Priam, who survived the fall of Troy and took part in the funeral games held in honour of Anchises.

[Homer, *Iliad* 2.790–4, 13.526–39, 15.339–40, 24.250; Apollodorus 3.12.5; Virgil, *Aeneid* 2.526–53, 5.563–7.]

Polites (2)

In Homer's *Odyssey* (10.224–8), Polites is a companion of ODYSSEUS who is one of those turned into pigs by the enchantress CIRCE. His ghost was later said to haunt the town of Temesa in Italy (*see* EUTHYMUS).

Polybotes *see* GIANTS.

Polybus (1)

A king of Sicyon, the son of HERMES and Chthonophyle, daughter of the Sicyon after whom the place was named. Polybus inherited the throne from his grandfather. He married his daughter to Talaus of Argos, and years later the couple's son ADRASTUS (1) took refuge in Sicyon when driven out of Argos. When Polybus died without male children, Adrastus inherited his kingdom.

[Herodotus 5.67; Pausanias 2.6.6.]

Polybus (2)

King of Corinth and foster-father of the baby OEDIPUS.

Fig. 117 Hades/Pluto holds a cornucopia, symbolising all the riches that come from under the earth.

Polycaste

The youngest daughter of NESTOR, king of Pylos. In Homer's *Odyssey*, Polycaste gives TELEMACHUS his welcoming bath when he comes to Pylos in search of Odysseus (3.464–7):

> And when she had bathed him and smoothed him richly with oil, she put around him a splendid cloak and tunic, and he came from his bath looking like an immortal.

This clearly had its effect, for she was later said to have married him and borne him a son, Persepolis.

[Hesiod, *Catalogue of Women* fr. 221.]

Polydamas

Son of the Trojan elder PANTHOUS. He was born on the same night as HECTOR, but while Hector was the better warrior, Polydamas was the wiser man. In the *Iliad* he often offers prudent advice which the more reckless Hector, to his later regret, too often dismisses. Above all, after the furious ACHILLES has reappeared on the battlefield, Polydamas

sensibly recommends that the Trojans withdraw into their city at once and stay there during the following day, defending Troy from the walls and keeping their distance from the enemy. Hector's angry rejection of this wise counsel causes much unnecessary loss of life among the Trojans. The shame and sorrow that he feels because of his stubbornness, and the knowledge that he was wrong and Polydamas right, lead Hector to face Achilles alone outside the walls of Troy. He can, he reasons, despite shame and failure, at least die honourably. He does so.

Polydamas survives the *Iliad* and apparently the war.

[Homer, *Iliad* 12.60–90, 195–250, 13.723–57, 14.449–74, 15.339, 518–22, 18.249–313, 22.98–110.]

Polydectes *see* PERSEUS.

Polydeuces *see* DIOSCURI.

Polydora

The daughter of PELEUS by his first wife, Antigone. Polydora married Borus, the son of Perieres. She had by the river-god Spercheius a son, Menesthius, who became the leader of one of the Myrmidon battalions, under her half-brother ACHILLES, in the Trojan War.

[Homer, *Iliad* 16.173–8; Hesiod, *Catalogue of Women* fr. 213; Apollodorus 3.13.1.]

Polydorus (1)

Son of CADMUS and Harmonia, father of LABDACUS by Nycteis, and great-grandfather of OEDIPUS. Pausanias (9.5.3–4) says that Polydorus took the throne after Cadmus, but more usually the brief reign of PENTHEUS, Polydorus' nephew, is said to intervene.

[Hesiod, *Theogony* 978; Herodotus 5.59; Sophocles, *Oedipus the King* 267–8; Euripides, *The Phoenician Women* 5–9; Apollodorus 3.4.2, 3.5.2–5.]

Polydorus (2)

Son of HIPPOMEDON and one of the EPIGONI.

Polydorus (3)

In the *Iliad* Polydorus is the youngest son of PRIAM, king of Troy, by Laothoe, and the most beloved. For this reason his father forbids him to go into the fighting at Troy, but Polydorus disobeys, and as he dashes through the front rank of warriors, showing off the speed of his running, he is killed by ACHILLES with a spear thrown into his back.

The later, more familiar story is found in Euripides' tragedy *Hecuba*, which deals with the aftermath of the sack of Troy and is set in Thrace, where the Greeks are encamped with their Trojan captives. Polydorus is here the youngest son of Priam and HECUBA, who sent him for safety during the war to Polymestor, king of the Thracian Chersonese, and with him a large sum of gold. As the ghost of Polydorus relates at the beginning of the play, while Troy stood, he lived; but when the city fell, and HECTOR and Priam were dead, he was murdered by the treacherous Polymestor for the sake of the gold and his body thrown into the sea. During the course of the play, his corpse is found washed up on the shore and is brought to Hecuba. He had been her only surviving son, and the thought of him the only remaining joy in her present life of captivity. Now, with the discovery of his death, which has followed so soon upon the harrowing sacrifice of her daughter POLYXENA, Hecuba is changed from a figure of helpless grief and despair to one of raging, avenging fury. With the complicity of Agamemnon, Polymestor is summoned to the Greek camp. Together with his two little sons, Hecuba lures him into her tent with the promise of more gold. Here her serving women are waiting. Polymestor is quite at ease, thinking that he has nothing to fear from a crowd of mere women, but they overpower him with their sheer numbers. They stab his sons to death with his own weapons, then blind Polymestor himself by gouging out his eyes with their brooches. In this way Polydorus is avenged.

Virgil relates in the *Aeneid* (3.22–68) that after AENEAS left Troy he landed in Thrace, intending to found his new city there. As he was gathering branches for a sacrificial altar, he found that drops of blood fell from their broken ends. From below the earth came a voice from the corpse of Polydorus, telling Aeneas of his sad fate and warning him to leave such a cruel land. Aeneas and his men performed for the murdered boy the funeral rites that would give peace to his spirit, then departed.

Yet another version of Polydorus' fate is recounted by Hyginus (*Fabula* 109). Here he was sent as a little child to Polymestor, to be brought up by his wife Ilione, the eldest daughter of Priam and Hecuba, together with her own little boy of the same age, Deipylus. She exchanged the boys' identities, bringing up her brother Polydorus as Deipylus, and her son Deipylus as Polydorus. At the fall of Troy, the Greeks bribed Polymestor with the offer of marriage to Agamemnon's daughter Electra if he would only kill Polydorus. He was quite willing to do so, but of course killed Deipylus by mistake. The truth came out when Polydorus consulted an oracle of Apollo and was told that his city was in ashes and his mother enslaved. Hurrying home in alarm, he found Ilione just as he had left her and she told him the truth of his birth. Together they brought about the blinding and death of Polymestor.

[Homer, *Iliad* 20.407–18, 21.84–91, 22.46–51; Apollodorus 3.12.5; Ovid, *Metamorphoses* 13.429–575.]

Polyidus

A famous seer, son of Coeranus and descendant of MELAMPUS. He advised BELLEROPHON on how to tame the winged horse Pegasus; he purified ALCATHOUS (1) for the unintentional homicide of his own son Callipolis; and he brought GLAUCUS (2), the son of Minos, king of Crete, back to life after he was drowned in a storage-jar full of honey. He himself had a son, EUCHENOR, who died at Troy.

Polymede

A daughter of AUTOLYCUS who was sometimes said to be the wife of AESON and the mother of the great hero JASON.

Polymele *see* EUDORUS.

Polymestor

The king of the Thracian Chersonese who was blinded by HECUBA in revenge for murdering her son, POLYDORUS (3).

Polymnia or Polyhymnia *see* MUSES.

Polyneices ('Much Strife')

In early Greek epic, Polyneices was the son of OEDIPUS and his second wife EURYGANEIA; but in the more familiar version of fifth-century BC tragedy, he was born of the incestuous union between Oedipus and his wife and mother JOCASTA, as were his brother, Eteocles, and his two sisters, ANTIGONE (1) and ISMENE. Oedipus cursed his sons, either for their ill-treatment of him, or simply because they were polluted by their incestuous birth. Because of his curse, they were fated to divide their inheritance by the sword and to die by each other's hand.

The brothers fought over the rule of Thebes. With Oedipus no longer in power because of either death or exile, both brothers wished to be king. There are various accounts of how they attempted to settle the matter. Either they made a bargain that one of them would rule while the other left Thebes, taking a large share of the property, and when they came to draw lots it was Eteocles who won the kingship and Polyneices who left with many possessions, including the necklace and robe of his ancestress Harmonia, each to play a fateful part in the subsequent story (*see* ERIPHYLE); but Polyneices later went back on the bargain. Or the brothers agreed each to have alternately a year in power, then a year in exile, and Eteocles took the first year in power but refused to relinquish it when his turn was over. Or Eteocles simply took the throne and drove Polyneices out. Whatever the details, the end result was the same: Polyneices was exiled from his homeland and resolved to win the throne of Thebes by force.

Fig. 118 Polyneices bribes Eriphyle with the beautiful necklace of Harmonia.

He sought refuge with ADRASTUS (1), king of Argos, at the same time as another exile, Oeneus' son TYDEUS, banished from Calydon for murder. Adrastus married two of his daughters to the young men, Argeia to Polyneices and Deipyle to Tydeus, then promised to help his new sons-in-law to win back their lost kingdoms, and first of all Polyneices. This led to the fateful expedition of the SEVEN AGAINST THEBES. A large army was mobilised, though Polyneices was forced to win the support of the reluctant seer AMPHIARAUS by bribing his wife Eriphyle with the beautiful necklace of Harmonia (fig. 118). Amphiaraus had divined that the expedition was doomed to failure and its leaders, all but Adrastus, to death, and this is exactly what happened. Polyneices and Eteocles met in single combat at one of the gates of Thebes and each fell dead on the other's sword, thus fulfilling Oedipus' curse.

This dramatic story was a favourite with the Greek tragedians and we are fortunate to have several of the relevant plays extant. Eteocles appears in Aeschylus' *Seven Against Thebes*, where the tension steadily mounts as he hears who of the enemy is attacking each of the seven gates of Thebes and assigns, one by one, his best fighters to defend them. Finally he hears that at the seventh gate,

Fig.119 Odysseus and his men blind the Cyclops Polyphemus, who holds two human legs, the remnants of his last meal. The wine cup shows that he was first made drunk with Odysseus' potent wine.

the gate that he himself must defend, Polyneices waits. He knows that this confrontation must mean his death and the fulfilment of Oedipus' curse. Polyneices appears in Sophocles' *Oedipus at Colonus*, where he tries in vain to win the support of his old father, who has taken refuge with Theseus in Attica. Oedipus' bitter and implacable curses ring in Polyneices' ear as he hopelessly departs. Both brothers appear in Euripides' *Phoenician Women*, where Jocasta tries to make peace between her warring sons. She fails, and when the brothers have killed each other, she commits suicide over their corpses in her grief. Sophocles' *Antigone* dramatises the aftermath of the war, when Creon takes over the rule of Thebes on the brothers' deaths and refuses burial to all those who were killed while attacking the city. Antigone tries to give last rites to Polyneices and dies for her deed, as does Creon's son Haemon, who loves her, and Creon's wife Eurydice, out of grief for Haemon. Finally, in Euripides' *Suppliant Women* Theseus forces the Thebans to give up the Argive dead for burial.

Polyneices and Eteocles each left a son, THERSANDER and LAODAMAS. Thersander was one of the EPIGONI who avenged their fathers' deaths in a second successful attack on Thebes. Either Laodamas was killed during the battle

by Alcmaeon, or he led his surviving people to a new home in Illyria.

Polyphemus (1)

Son of the Lapith chieftain ELATUS (2). He was one of the Lapiths who fought in the famous battle against the CENTAURS. In Homer's *Iliad* (1.264) old Nestor speaks of him as one of the great warriors of earlier times. He sailed with Jason and the ARGONAUTS, when he was getting on in years but had a spirit as courageous as ever. During the journey he was accidentally left behind in Mysia while helping Heracles to find his lost lover HYLAS, and here he founded the city of Kios. But still he longed to rejoin his comrades, so he travelled far in search of them and finally died in the land of the Chalybes, on the Black Sea's southern coast. A tomb was built for him under a tall, white poplar, close to the edge of the sea.

[Apollonius, *Argonautica* 1.40–4, 1321–3, 4.1468–77; Apollodorus 1.9.16, 1.9.19.]

Polyphemus (2)

A Cyclops, the son of POSEIDON and the nymph Thoosa, daughter of Phorcys. Polyphemus lived an uncivilised life among other CYCLOPES on an island later identified as Sicily. Here they dwelt in caves and kept flocks, caring nothing about communal life, or about tilling the soil and growing crops. ODYSSEUS' encounter with Polyphemus, a barbarous giant with a single eye in the middle of his forehead, is the best-known episode of his adventures on the way home from Troy, recounted by him to the Phaeacians at the court of King Alcinous (*Odyssey* 9.105–566).

Odysseus goes ashore with twelve of his men and finds the Cyclops' cave, which is full of lambs and kids, milk and cheeses. His men are fearful and wish only to get away quickly, but Odysseus refuses to listen, since he hopes that the occupier of the cave will give him guest-gifts. (And indeed he will be granted a gift of a kind: a promise from the cannibalistic Cyclops that he himself will be eaten last.) The giant comes home, bringing into the cave all his sheep and goats for milking and blocking the entrance with a massive boulder. His response to Odysseus' plea for hospitality is to eat two of his men, seizing them in his great hands and dashing their brains out on the ground as if he were killing puppies, then washing down his meal of human flesh with draughts of milk. At last he sleeps, and now Odysseus thinks of killing him with his sword. But he realises that this would mean the death of them all, for they would never be able to budge the boulder at the cave-entrance. Another plan will have to be found.

In the morning the Cyclops breakfasts on two more of the men before going out to pasture his flocks, leaving his captives imprisoned. But now Odysseus knows what he must do. He sharpens an immense stake, hardening its tip in the fire, then hides it ready for evening. Polyphemus comes home as before, bringing all his flocks into the cave. Once again he blocks the entrance and dines on two more men, but now Odysseus can put his plan into action. He has with him the strong, honey-sweet wine once given him by MARON, and this he offers to the Cyclops, who gulps it down greedily. He asks Odysseus his name. 'My name is Nobody', comes the reply. At last the befuddled giant sleeps, and Odysseus and his men heat their stake in the fire until it is incandescent, then drive it into the Cyclops' single eye. Blinded and in agony he calls to all the other Cyclopes, who come running from their caves among the mountains to help him. But when he cries that 'Nobody' is harming him, they laugh and go away.

When the Cyclops pulls the boulder away from the entrance and the flocks go out to pasture, he carefully feels the animals' backs to make sure that no Greeks go with them. But Odysseus and his six remaining men escape by clinging to the undersides of the sheep. Now we see for a moment a more sympathetic side to the giant, as he talks to his favourite ram, the biggest of the flock and the last to leave (with Odysseus clinging on beneath). 'My dear old ram', he says, 'why are you the last of the sheep to leave the cave? Never before have you been left behind by the flock, but striding out, far ahead of the rest, you would be the first to pasture on grass and tender flowers, the first at running rivers, the first to come back eagerly to the sheepfold at evening. Now you are last of all. Perhaps you are grieving for your master's eye, which an evil man put out with the help of his wicked companions' (447–56).

Back safely at their ships, Odysseus and his men sail thankfully away, but Odysseus cannot resist one last display of bravado. He shouts to the Cyclops, taunting him and telling him his real name. He will pay dearly for this rashness, for Polyphemus calls on his father Poseidon to avenge his hurt, and the god's anger will keep Odysseus away from his home on Ithaca for many long, weary years.

Odysseus' encounter with Polyphemus, now a comic character, is the basis of Euripides' satyr play *Cyclops*. It is vividly retold by Virgil in the *Aeneid* (3.590–683), where again as in Homer the giant is depicted as bestial and cruel, but made a little more sympathetic by his affection for his sheep: 'they were the only delight he had left, his only comfort in distress' (660–1). Other later poetry makes Polyphemus (before his blinding) a would-be lover of the sea-nymph Galatea. In Theocritus' *Idyll* 11, the lovesick

Cyclops, rejected because of his grotesque appearance, consoles himself by singing. Ovid too relates the story of his unrequited passion (*Metamorphoses* 13.740–897). Polyphemus is on fire with love for Galatea, so much so that he neglects his herds and even forgets his savagery and love of killing. Instead he spends his time on his appearance, combing his bristling hair with a rake, trimming his shaggy beard with a scythe, and inspecting his looks in a pool of water – all to no avail, for Galatea loves the handsome Acis, the young son of Faunus and the river-nymph Symaethis, quite as much as she loathes the Cyclops. Lying in her lover's arms, she hears the song the giant sings to tempt her to him, accompanying himself on a set of pipes made from a hundred reeds. He offers her all the wealth of nature – apples, grapes, strawberries, cherries, plums, chestnuts – as well as the richness of his vast flocks. Pets he can give her too, not just ordinary ones like deer or hares or doves, but a pair of bear cubs that he has been saving just for her. He knows what he looks like, for he has seen his reflection in a pool, but he is *big*, and surely a body all covered in thick, bristling hair is becoming to a man. True, he has only one eye, but that one eye is as big as a shield.

Frustrated by his failure to lure Galatea to him, and furious as a bull whose cow has been taken away, the Cyclops strides through the island. Now he sees his hard-hearted love lying in Acis' arms. Overcome by rage, he heaves up a huge chunk of the mountainside and flings it at them. Galatea escapes to the sea, but her poor lover is crushed beneath the rock. She does for him the only thing she can, and changes him into a river that will ever afterwards bear his name.

Odysseus' blinding of Polyphemus (fig. 119) and the escape under the sheep's bellies (fig. 101) were popular subjects in ancient art from the seventh century BC, and we have some postclassical versions, including Turner's splendid *Ulysses Deriding Polyphemus* in London's National Gallery. But the episode that most caught the imagination of postclassical artists was the affair of Polyphemus, Acis and Galatea. Paintings exist by Carracci, Poussin, Claude and Giordano, among many others; and in the field of music, Handel's masque *Acis and Galatea*.

[Homer, *Odyssey* 1.68–75; Apollodorus, *Epitome* 7.3–9; Lucian, *Dialogues of the Sea-gods* 2; Ovid, *Metamorphoses* 14.160–220.]

Polyphontes (1) *see* MAEON.

Polyphontes (2) *see* CRESPHONTES (2).

Polypoetes (1)

Son of PEIRITHOUS, king of the Lapiths, and Hippodameia, conceived on the very day of their marriage, the day on which Peirithous led the Lapiths in their famous battle with the CENTAURS. Polypoetes too became a formidable warrior. We see him in action in the *Iliad*, where he has led forty ships to the TROJAN WAR together with his comrade Leonteus, the grandson of another great Lapith warrior, CAENEUS. They fight side by side in trying to beat back the Trojan attack on the Greek wall, and Homer likens them in their firmness to 'two high-crested oaks in the mountains, that stand and endure the wind and the rain day after day, their great roots fixed deep in the earth' (12.132–5); and in their aggression to 'two wild boars who await a rabble of men and dogs advancing upon them in the mountains, and charging sideways they tear at the trees around them, cutting them at the root, and the grinding of their tusks sounds clear, until someone strikes at them and takes the life from them' (146–50).

Despite this rather ominous simile, the two friends survived not only the Trojan attack (they later took part in the shot-putting contest at the funeral games for Patroclus, which Polypoetes won, and were together in the WOODEN HORSE), but the whole war.

[Homer, *Iliad* 2.738–46, 23.836–49; Epic Cycle, Proclus' summary of the *Returns*; Apollodorus 3.10.8, *Epitome* 6.2; Quintus of Smyrna, *Sequel to Homer* 12.318, 323.]

Polypoetes (2) *see* CALLIDICE.

Polyxena

The youngest daughter of PRIAM, king of Troy, and HECUBA, though she is first mentioned, not in the *Iliad*, but in fragments of the Epic Cycle: the *Cypria* said that she was mortally wounded at the fall of Troy by Diomedes and Odysseus, then buried by NEOPTOLEMUS; but the *Sack of Troy* told the more familiar version of her death, that she was sacrificed at ACHILLES' grave. Neoptolemus – appropriately, as Achilles' son – was her killer, as later writers

confirm, and as we see on a Tyrrhenian amphora of about 570 BC where three Greeks, Amphilochus, Antiphates and Ajax, hold her horizontal, while Neoptolemus cuts her throat and her blood streams down on to a burial mound (fig. 120).

Her death is given detailed and poignant treatment in Euripides' tragedy *Hecuba*, where the ghost of the dead Achilles has stilled the winds to stop the Greek fleet sailing home, and is demanding the sacrifice of Polyxena as his share of the spoils from Troy. Once she discovers that her sacrifice is inescapable, she goes to her death willingly and courageously. The herald TALTHYBIUS reports her dying words:

'Listen, you Greeks who sacked my city: I die willingly.
Let no one touch me, for I give my throat with gladness.
Let me go freely to my death, I beg you by the gods,
so I die free: born of royal blood, I shame to be called
a slave among the dead.' The crowd shouted assent,
and Agamemnon told the guards to loose the girl.
Hearing these words of authority, she seized her robe
and tore it open wide from shoulder to navel, showing
her breasts as lovely as a statue's. Then dropping
to her knees upon the earth, she spoke these brave
and pitiful words: 'Look, here, young man, if you
would strike my breast, strike here. But if you want my
    neck,
here is my throat, here and ready.' Then he, willing
and yet unwilling in pity for the girl, cuts her breath-pipe
with the iron sword, and streams of blood flow down.

In much later times, an erotic motive for Achilles' demand was imported into the story. He was said to have fallen in love with Polyxena while he still lived, perhaps when he saw her drawing water at the fountain where he came to ambush TROILUS (fig. 144), or when she accompanied Priam to ask for HECTOR's body. According to some late writers, Achilles met his death in the Thymbraean precinct sacred to Apollo while negotiating with Priam for Polyxena's hand in marriage. Here PARIS lay in wait and shot him.

In postclassical art, the emphasis has been on this love between Achilles and Polyxena, as well as on Polyxena's sacrifice and Hecuba's grief at her death.

[Sophocles' lost *Polyxena*; Euripides, *Trojan Women* 39–40, 260–71, 622–31; Apollodorus, *Epitome* 5.23; Quintus of Smyrna, *Sequel to Homer* 14.209–328; Ovid, *Metamorphoses* 13.439–505; Seneca, *Trojan Women* 938–44, 1118–64.]

Fig. 120 **Three warriors hold Polyxena's rigid body over the tomb of Achilles, as Neoptolemus plunges his sword into her throat.**

Polyxo (1)

The old nurse of Queen HYPSIPYLE of Lemnos, who urged the Lemnian women to accept the ARGONAUTS into their homes and have children by them.

Polyxo (2)

The widow of Heracles' son TLEPOLEMUS, the king of Rhodes, who was killed by Sarpedon in the war at Troy. It was said by Pausanias (3.19.9–10) that Polyxo laid the blame for her husband's death on HELEN, the cause of the Trojan War, and killed her in revenge. After Menelaus died, Helen was driven out of Sparta by Nicostratus and Megapenthes, his sons by a slave-woman. She sought refuge in Rhodes with her supposed friend Polyxo, who pretended to welcome her. But then Polyxo dressed her maids as FURIES and they hanged Helen from a tree. Thereafter she was worshipped in Rhodes as Helen *Dendritis*, 'Helen of the Tree'. This story is quite contrary to the usual tradition, which made Helen end her days peacefully at Sparta with Menelaus, and was probably invented to explain a cult practice in Rhodes of hanging Helen's image in a tree.

Pomona

The Roman goddess of fruits (*pomum*, 'fruit'). She was so devoted to her orchards that she spurned all suitors, until at last she was wooed and won by the god VERTUMNUS.

Pontus ('Sea') *see* GAIA.

Porphyrion

One of the GIANTS. According to Apollodorus (1.6.1), he and his brother ALCYONEUS were the strongest of them all. In the battle between the Gods and the Giants, ZEUS inspired Porphyrion with lust for HERA, and when he tried to rape her, smote him with a thunderbolt. HERACLES finished him off with his arrows. Pindar has a different version (*Pythian* 8.12–17): he calls Porphyrion the king of the Giants and says that it was APOLLO who shot him.

Portunus

The Roman god of harbours, identified with the Greek Palaemon (*see* INO).

Poseidon

One of the twelve great Olympian gods (fig. 148), Poseidon was the Greek god of the sea whose fearsome rage could bring violent storms and earthquakes on the world. Homer calls him *Gaieochos*, Earth-holder, and as lord of earthquakes, *Enosichthon* and *Ennosigaios*, Earth-shaker. He vividly depicts the mighty god as he journeys across his territory (*Iliad* 13.23–30):

He harnessed to his chariot his two bronze-shod horses,

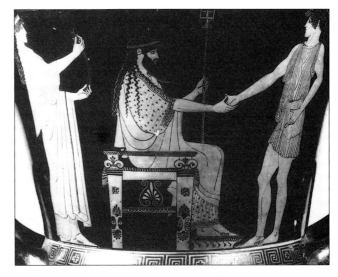

Fig. 121 Poseidon with his queen Amphitrite welcomes his son Theseus to his palace beneath the sea.

swift of foot, with long, streaming manes of gold.
Himself clothed in gold, he seized his well-wrought
golden whip, then climbing into his chariot he drove
across the waves. On every side, from the deeps of the sea,
came dolphins, playing in his path, acknowledging their
   lord,
and the sea parted in joy, cleaving a path before him.
So swiftly sped the horses that never once
was the axle of bronze beneath made wet with foam.

Poseidon was one of the six children of the Titans CRONUS and RHEA (1), swallowed and later regurgitated by his cannibalistic father. When Cronus had been defeated and his three sons divided the universe among themselves, they kept the earth and OLYMPUS as common property, while ZEUS took the heavens as his domain, HADES (1) the misty darkness of the Underworld, and Poseidon the seas. According to Homer, there was a time when Poseidon rebelled, conspiring with HERA and ATHENA to put Zeus in chains. But the sea-goddess THETIS saved him, sending Briareos (*see* HUNDRED-HANDERS) to release him.

Poseidon vied with APOLLO for the love of HESTIA, the goddess of the hearth, but she rejected both of them, swearing a vow of eternal chastity. He also vied with Zeus for the love of Thetis, but both gods withdrew their suit when they learnt that she was destined to bear a son mightier than his father. Poseidon's wooing of the Nereid AMPHITRITE came to a happier conclusion: with the help of a dolphin, who found her when she fled into hiding, he won her for his wife. With her he lived in a splendid golden palace in the depths of the sea (figs. 15 and 121). She bore him a son, the merman TRITON (fig. 143), and two daughters, RHODE and Benthesicyme. But Poseidon was one of the most prolific of the gods and fathered numerous children on many mistresses. He himself could be violent and vindictive, and some of his sons inherited his dangerous nature, such as the evil SCIRON, SINIS and CERCYON, killed by THESEUS; the boxer AMYCUS, killed by Polydeuces; and the Egyptian king BUSIRIS, killed by Heracles. Some of his formidable offspring were giants, such as the Siamese twins, the MOLIONES; OTUS AND EPHIALTES, who attempted to take over Olympus; the wrestler ANTAEUS, who was killed by Heracles; the great hunter ORION; Lamus, who founded the LAESTRYGONIANS, a race of man-eating giants; and perhaps best-known of all, the Cyclops POLYPHEMUS (2), who was blinded by ODYSSEUS.

Others of Poseidon's more famous children were the twins PELIAS and NELEUS, whom he fathered on TYRO, taking the shape of the river-god Enipeus; Libya's three sons, BELUS, AGENOR (1) and Lelex; EUMOLPUS, the son of CHIONE (1), who was thrown into the sea by his mother and reared by Poseidon's daughter Benthesicyme; the navigator NAUPLIUS (1), fathered on the Danaid AMYMONE while she was hunting for water in Argos; Hippothoon, the son of ALOPE, who was suckled by a mare and reared by shepherds after Alope was cruelly killed by her father; and of course the great Athenian hero, Theseus, borne to Poseidon by AETHRA (fig. 6).

Poseidon was also the god of horses, and in this guise was known as Poseidon *Hippios*, 'Horse Poseidon'. As a horse he mated with the goddess DEMETER, who bore him the divine horse, AREION, and a daughter, DESPOINA. Medusa (*see* GORGONS) was pregnant by him when she was killed by Perseus, and from her severed neck were born the winged horse, PEGASUS, and CHRYSAOR. Poseidon presented wondrous horses to favoured mortals, both to his lover PELOPS, to help him win the hand of Hippodameia, and to his son IDAS, to help him win the hand of MARPESSA. To PELEUS he gave as a wedding present the immortal horses XANTHUS and Balius, who were later taken by Achilles to fight at Troy.

The god showed his favour to other mortals in rather different ways. He raped Caenis while she was wandering alone on the seashore, then at her own request turned her into a man, CAENEUS, and made her invulnerable. He also made his son CYCNUS (3) invulnerable, and on his death at Achilles' hands turned him into a swan. He gave to his grandson PERICLYMENUS (2) and his mistress Mestra, daughter of ERYSICHTHON, the ability to change their shape at will. Like other sea-deities, Poseidon himself had

the power of changing his shape. He came to THEOPHANE as a ram, and fathered on her the flying, talking ram with the golden fleece which saved PHRIXUS and Helle from their wicked stepmother Ino, and which later became the motive for the long and arduous journey of Jason and the Argonauts. According to Ovid, Poseidon coupled with Canace, the daughter of Aeolus, as a bull, with Melantho, the daughter of Deucalion, as a dolphin, and with the Gorgon Medusa as a bird.

Being a mighty and formidable god, Poseidon sternly punished the mortals who offended him. He was furious with Odysseus for blinding the Cyclops Polyphemus, and kept him away from his homeland of Ithaca for many long, weary years; and he punished the Phaeacians, the people of SCHERIA, for helping Odysseus on his journey. When LAOMEDON, king of Troy, refused to pay Poseidon and Apollo the agreed wage for building his city walls, the sea-god sent a sea-monster against the land, which would have devoured Hesione, Laomedon's daughter, had she not been saved by Heracles. Laomedon's offence was the reason for Poseidon's resentment of the Trojans and his support for the Greeks during the Trojan War. He frequently intervened to help his favourites, even against the express command of Zeus. This did not stop him helping Athena to punish the Greeks at the end of the war for the rape of the Trojan prophetess Cassandra by AJAX (2): the sea-god sent violent storms that wrecked the Greek fleet off Cape Caphareus and brought death to many, including Ajax himself.

At the NEREIDS' request, Poseidon sent another sea-monster against the Ethiopians, to punish a vain boast made by their queen, Cassiopeia. This time the monster's victim was to be the queen's daughter, ANDROMEDA, but she was saved by Perseus. Poseidon was also associated with bulls: he brought death to HIPPOLYTUS (2), at the request of his father Theseus, by sending a bull from the sea that caused his horses to bolt and overturn his chariot. He sent as a gift to MINOS, king of Crete, a magnificent white bull from the sea, then punished the king for failing to sacrifice it by inflicting on his wife, Pasiphae, a passion for the bull that led to the birth of the MINOTAUR.

Poseidon came into conflict with some of the other gods over the patronship of certain lands. He and Athena contested the possession of Attica during the reign of CECROPS (1). Both demonstrated their divine powers, Poseidon by creating a well of sea-water on the Acropolis of Athens, Athena by planting an olive tree. Athena's was judged the greater benefit, so the land became hers. Poseidon in anger sent a flood to cover Attica. He also quarrelled with Hera over the possession of Argos. The river-gods INACHUS, Cephissus and Asterion judged the

dispute in favour of Hera, and Poseidon, angry once again, dried up their waters. He was more fortunate in the case of Corinth, which he disputed with the Sun-god, HELIOS. The Hundred-hander Briareos was called in as arbitrator, and he awarded the citadel of Acrocorinth to Helios and the Isthmus to Poseidon.

Poseidon was worshipped throughout the Greek world and from very early times: his name occurs on Mycenean Linear B tablets more frequently than that of any other divinity. At Rome he was identified with the sea-god Neptune. He is a popular subject in ancient art, easily recognised by his most famous attribute, the trident, though he sometimes holds a fish and is often accompanied by sea creatures. Occasionally he rides a hippocamp (a hybrid with the foreparts of a horse and the tail of a fish). Popular too in postclassical art, he   figures prominently in sea-triumphs with his wife Amphitrite and is a natural subject for fountain-figures, such as on the famous Trevi Fountain at Rome. His marble temple on the promontory of Sounion in Attica, built in the late fifth century BC, is still a landmark for sailors. In a modern poem, Roy Campbell epitomises Poseidon's dual nature as sea-god and god of horses in his *Horses on the Camargue*:

> ...
> I heard a sudden harmony of hooves,
> And, turning, saw afar
> A hundred snowy horses unconfined,
> The silver runaways of Neptune's car
> Racing, spray-curled, like waves before the wind.
> Sons of the Mistral, fleet
> As him with whose strong gusts they love to flee,

Fig. 122 Priam appeals to Achilles for the body of his son, Hector, lying dead beneath the couch. A woman (?Briseis) places a wreath on Achilles' head.

> Who shod the flying thunders on their feet
> And plumed them with the snorting of the sea ...
> ...
> But when the great gusts rise
> And lash their anger on these arid coasts,
> When the scared gulls career with mournful cries
> And whirl across the waste like driven ghosts:
> When hail and fire converge,
> The only souls to which they strike no pain
> Are the white-crested fillies of the surge
> And the white horses of the windy plain.
> Then in their strength and pride
> The stallions of the wilderness rejoice;
> They feel their Master's trident in their side
> And high and shrill they answer to his voice.
> With white tails smoking free,
> Long streaming manes and arching necks, they show
> Their kinship to their sisters of the sea –
> And forward hurl their thunderbolts of snow.

[Homer, *Iliad* 1.396–407, 7.442–63, 8.198–211, 12.1–33, 13.1–239, 14.355–401, 15.168–219, 20.13–352, 21.434–77, *Odyssey* 1.19–27, 68–79, 3.5–8, 4.500–11, 5.282–381, 9.528–36, 11.235–59, 13.125–87; Hesiod, *Theogony* 278–83, 453–506, 732–3; *Homeric Hymn to Poseidon*; Pindar, *Olympian* 1.23–88; Herodotus 7.129, 8.55; Euripides, *Trojan Women* 1–97; Apollodorus 1.1.5–1.2.1, 1.6.2, 1.7.4, 1.9.8, 2.1.4–5, 2.4.5, 3.10.1, 3.14.1–2, 3.15.4–7; Pausanias 1.26.5, 2.1.6,

2.15.5, 7.21.7, 8.7.2, 8.8.2, 8.14.5–6, 8.25.5–8, 8.42.1–2; Lucian, *Dialogues of the Gods* 1, 12, *Dialogues of the Sea-gods*, 2, 3, 5, 6, 8, 9, 13; Virgil, *Aeneid* 1.124–56, 5.779–826, *Georgics* 1.12–14; Ovid, *Metamorphoses* 6.115–20. W. Burkert, *Greek Religion* (1985), pp. 136–9.]

Priam

The most famous and the most powerful – but also the last – of the kings of TROY, ruling at the time of the TROJAN WAR. He was the son of LAOMEDON by Strymo, daughter of the river-god SCAMANDER, and was originally called Podarces. When HERACLES captured Troy because of Laomedon's refusal to pay the agreed reward for saving HESIONE from the sea-monster, he killed Laomedon and all his sons except for Podarces, who alone had advised Laomedon to honour his agreement. Hesione ransomed her brother Podarces with her veil, after which his name was changed to Priam (reputedly from *priamai*, 'to buy') and he took over the rule of Troy.

He had fifty sons (including HECTOR, PARIS, TROILUS, DEIPHOBUS, LYCAON (2), HELENUS, POLYDORUS (3), AESACUS and POLITES (1)) and at least fourteen daughters (including CASSANDRA, POLYXENA, LAODICE (1), CREUSA (3) and Ilione) by a number of wives, but his chief wife and consort was HECUBA. By her he had nineteen sons and several daughters. When she was pregnant with Paris, she had an ominous dream foretelling that this child would bring utter destruction on Troy. So when the boy was born, Priam gave him to a servant to be cast out to die. But Paris lived, and when he grew up he returned to Troy and

was welcomed back into the family. Going on a visit to Sparta, he abducted HELEN, the wife of King Menelaus, and carried her home with him. The Trojan War was the result, which did indeed bring destruction on Troy.

Our most memorable depiction of Priam comes from the *Iliad*, where it is now the tenth year of the war and both Priam and Hecuba are old. Priam is certainly too old to fight, and it is his son Hector who leads the Trojan forces and is the bulwark of the city's defence. Priam is the only Trojan whom the Greeks thoroughly trust, and they choose him to be present at the oath-taking before the duel between Menelaus and Paris. Homer depicts him as a kindly old man, honourable and dignified, and affectionate to Helen even though it was through her that this devastating war was brought on Troy. One by one he has seen his sons killed, many of them at the hands of ACHILLES, the greatest fighter on the Greek side; and in the course of the *Iliad* he has to watch Hector too slaughtered by Achilles, who is raging with fury and passion for revenge because Hector has killed his dear comrade PATROCLUS. Achilles massacres countless Trojans, and the rest flee in panic into the security of Troy, all except Hector, who alone stands his ground outside the walls and waits for his enemy. Priam and Hecuba plead

Fig.123 **Priam sits on an altar with the bleeding body of his grandson, Astyanax, on his lap, waiting in despair for the death that Neoptolemus is about to inflict on him.**

with him to come inside the city to safety, all to no avail. Hector waits, and fights, and dies, and Priam knows that with Hector dead, Troy must now fall.

Even though his greatest enemy is dead, however, Achilles' rage is in no way eased, and he refuses to give up Hector's body for burial. Instead he ties it to his chariot and drags it along in the dust behind him. This furious anger continues for eleven days, but the gods pity Hector and keep his body safe from harm, however much Achilles maltreats it. On the twelfth day they intervene and arrange for Hector to be ransomed. Zeus sends THETIS to Achilles, to say that it is time for Hector's body to be returned, and he sends IRIS to Priam, to tell him to go to the Greek camp by night, taking gifts, and to beg for the return of his son. Both obey the god's instructions, and the *Iliad* ends with a supremely moving scene of pity and reconciliation between these two enemies. Priam with great courage goes by night into the enemy camp, taking with him rich gifts in a wagon drawn by mules and driven by his herald, IDAEUS (1). HERMES, disguised as a young man, shows Priam the way to Achilles' tent (fig.122). The old man enters alone, finding Achilles there with two of his comrades.

> He came close beside Achilles, clasped hold of his knees, and kissed his hands, those terrible, murderous hands that had killed so many of his sons ... and Achilles was seized with wonder at the sight of godlike Priam, and the others wondered too, and looked at one another (24.477–84).

Priam urges Achilles to remember his father, Peleus, who is now grown old like Priam himself and will soon be bereaved of his son. Then he goes on to talk of his own pitiful fate (493–512):

> 'I have had the finest sons in far-spread Troy,
> but I say that not one of them is left to me.
> Fifty were my sons, the day the Greeks came here,
> nineteen born to me from a single mother,
> and the others born of women in my palace.
> Raging Ares brought down dead most of them,
> but one was left, who guarded my city and people,
> him you killed just now defending his country,
> Hector. Because of him I come to the Greek ships,
> to win him back from you, bringing untold ransom.
> Honour the gods, Achilles, and have pity on me,
> remembering your father. But I am yet more pitiable,
> suffering what no other man on earth has suffered:
> I have kissed the hands of the man who killed my son.'
> So he spoke, and roused in Achilles a passion
> of grief for his father. He took the old man's hand
> and gently pushed him away. Then the two of them

remembered. Priam, huddled at Achilles' feet,
wept loud for man-slaying Hector, and Achilles wept
for his own father, and now again for Patroclus,
and the house was filled with the sound of their grief.

At last Achilles' wrath is eased and replaced by pity. After they have wept together, Achilles raises the old man to his feet and seats him on a chair. He accepts Priam's gifts and prepares Hector's body for return to Troy with his father. Then the two so-called enemies, Greek and Trojan, share food together in peace, and sleep. When Priam wakes, he takes his son's body home. For eleven days there is a truce, agreed by Achilles, in which Hector is given the full honours of death. The *Iliad* ends with his funeral, the burial of a noble Trojan.

Troy did not fall immediately after Hector's death. Priam had other allies come to help him: the Amazon queen PENTHESILEIA came with her army of warrior-women. Priam's nephew, the great MEMNON, came with his Ethiopians. Both were killed by Achilles, not long before Achilles himself was killed by Paris and Apollo. Troy finally fell to the Greeks when they entered it by means of the WOODEN HORSE. They put the Trojan men to the sword and took the women and children as slaves. Priam himself had earlier foreseen the horrors that would come when he begged Hector not to risk his life – and his city – by fighting Achilles, not to leave his home and family to destruction and death, but to come to safety inside the walls (22.56–76):

> Come inside the walls, my son, that you may save
> the Trojan men and women, nor give great glory
> to Peleus' son, and yourself be robbed of your own life.
> And pity me, helpless, still alive, ill-starred,
> whom the father, Cronus' son, will bring to death
> on the threshold of old age by a grievous fate,
> when I have seen many evils, my sons destroyed
> and my daughters carried off captive, rooms laid waste,
> and little children dashed to the ground in the horror
> that is war, and the wives of my sons dragged off
> by the accursed hands of the Greeks. And myself
> last of all, ravening dogs will tear me at my gateway,
> when some man by thrust or throw of the sharp bronze
> has torn the life from my body – dogs that in my halls
> I reared at my table to guard my doors, maddened now
> will drink my blood and then lie down in my courts.
> All is seemly when a young man is slain in battle
> and torn with the sharp bronze, and he lies there dead,
> and though dead, everything about him is noble.
> But when an old man is killed, and the dogs disfigure
> the grey head and the grey beard and the parts
> that are private, this, for all sad humanity
> is the fate most pitiful.

Now, with the Greeks inside Troy, Priam's predictions became reality, and he himself, although he had taken refuge on the altar of Zeus in his own courtyard, was butchered by Achilles' son NEOPTOLEMUS.

The sack of Troy was a popular subject in archaic and classical art, with Priam's death on the altar the focus of the horrors perpetrated on the Trojans by the Greeks. Again and again his death is linked with that of Hector's little son ASTYANAX, with Neoptolemus attacking the old king while swinging the body of the child like a club (fig. 27). In the Kleophrades Painter's moving depiction of the scene on a hydria in Naples, Priam sits on the altar holding in his lap the dead child, while Neoptolemus looms above him, about to deliver the final blow (fig. 123). Priam's name, like that of his wife Hecuba, has become a symbol for someone who suffers extremes of fortune.

[Homer, *Iliad* 3.95–110, 146–313, 7.345–79, 22.25–92, 405–29, 24.143–804; Apollodorus 2.6.4, 3.12.3–5, *Epitome* 5.1, 5.21; Pausanias 2.24.3, 4.17.4, 10.27.2; Quintus of Smyrna, *Sequel to Homer* 13.220–50; Virgil, *Aeneid* 2.506–58.]

Priapus

A god of sexuality and fertility characterised by a grotesquely huge phallus. He was a latecomer to the Greek pantheon, originating in the Hellespont region and said to be the son of DIONYSUS and APHRODITE. Ashamed of his physical deformity, his mother abandoned him after his birth in the mountains and he was brought up by shepherds. Because of this he was always a rustic god, a guardian of orchards, gardens, bees and herds. His cult spread rapidly during the third century BC and he was later well known through most of the Roman Empire. His sacrificial animal was often the donkey, though various reasons are given for this choice. Either he had an argument with a donkey as to which of them had the biggest male appendage, and he lost. Or a donkey had interfered in his amorous pursuits, for as he was creeping up on the sleeping nymph Lotis, ready to have his way with her, she had been woken by a donkey's bray. Seeing what fate was almost upon her, she fled in panic, whereupon the gods took pity on her and turned her into a lotus tree. A similar story was told of Priapus' pursuit of the Roman goddess of the hearth, VESTA, who was woken at the crucial moment by a bray from Silenus' ass. Or perhaps donkeys were sacrificed to Priapus because they were believed to be the most lustful of the beasts, and so were deemed the most suitable offering for a god with such a tremendous sexual endowment.

[Diodorus Siculus 4.6; Strabo 13.1.12; Pausanias 9.31.2; Ovid, *Metamorphoses* 9.340–8, *Fasti* 1.391–440, 6.319–48.]

Procleia *see* TENES.

Procne *see* TEREUS.

Procris *see* CEPHALUS (2).

Procrustes

One of the many brigands dispatched by the young THESEUS on his journey from Troezen to Athens. Procrustes lived beside the road at Erineus, near Eleusis. His real name was Polypemon or Damastes, but he was nicknamed Procrustes, 'Beater', because of the way in which he dealt with the wayfarers whom he lured into his house on the promise of hospitality. He forced his victim to lie on one of his two beds, one of which was short and one long, then saw to it that they exactly fitted the bed. He put short men into the long bed and hammered them to length, tall men into the short bed and lopped off their extremities. (According to another version he had only one bed for all comers, and adjusted his visitors to it with either a hammer or a hand-saw.) Theseus, when invited indoors by Procrustes, dealt with his host in the same way. (It is not recorded which method Theseus needed to use on him, and on vase-paintings of the scene he sometimes wields an axe (fig. 140), sometimes a hammer.)

[Bacchylides, *Ode* 18.27–30; Apollodorus, *Epitome* 1.4; Diodorus Siculus 4.59.5; Plutarch, *Theseus* 11; Pausanias 1.38.5.]

Proetus

Son of Abas, king of Argos, and Aglaia, and twin-brother of ACRISIUS. The boys fought each other even in their mother's womb, and grew up to be as antagonistic to each other as ever. After their father's death they fought over the kingdom, until Acrisius drove Proetus out and took the throne of Argos. Proetus found refuge with IOBATES, king of Lycia, and married his daughter, who is usually called Stheneboea, though Homer calls her Anteia. Iobates provided Proetus with an army to attack Argos, but the twins then agreed to divide the Argolid between them. Acrisius ruled at Argos, and Proetus at Tiryns, which was traditionally said to have been fortified for him with huge blocks of stone by the CYCLOPES.

By Stheneboea Proetus had three daughters, Lysippe, Iphinoe and Iphianassa, and a son, MEGAPENTHES (1). The three daughters were unfortunately afflicted with madness, either by DIONYSUS because they refused his rites, or by HERA because they insulted her. In their frenzy they roamed over the whole country in a wild and unseemly fashion, divesting themselves of their clothes. Eventually they recovered: they were usually said to have been cured by MELAMPUS (whose price was a large part of Proetus' kingdom), though according to Bacchylides they recovered when Proetus prayed to ARTEMIS, promising her twenty red oxen, and the goddess was moved to intercede with Hera.

When BELLEROPHON sought sanctuary with Proetus at Tiryns, Stheneboea fell in love with him and tried to seduce him. He rejected her advances, so she vindictively accused him to her husband of attempted rape. Proetus, hesitating to kill a guest, sent the young man to Iobates in Lycia with sealed instructions that he should be killed on arrival. Iobates set Bellerophon three supposedly deadly tasks, but he survived them all with the help of the winged horse, PEGASUS, and married Iobates' daughter, Philonoe. Stheneboea died, either by taking poison when the truth about her machinations came to light, or by killing herself in chagrin when she learnt that Bellerophon had married her sister, or at the hands of the avenging Bellerophon himself, flung to her death into the sea from the back of Pegasus.

A late tradition, found in Ovid, said that at the end of his life Proetus drove Acrisius out of Argos, but was then killed by PERSEUS, Acrisius' grandson, who turned him to stone with the Gorgon Medusa's head.

[Bacchylides, *Ode* 11.40–112; Apollodorus 2.2.1–2.3.1; Pausanias 2.7.8, 2.16.1–2, 2.25.7–8; Ovid, *Metamorphoses* 5.236–41.]

Promachus (1)

Younger son of AESON who was murdered by PELIAS.

Promachus (2)

Son of PARTHENOPAEUS and one of the EPIGONI who avenged their fathers' deaths.

Prometheus ('Forethought')

One of the TITANS and the champion and benefactor of mankind, whose most important gift to mortals was that of fire. His myth first occurs in Hesiod, where he is the son of the Titan IAPETUS and the Oceanid Clymene, and the brother of Epimetheus ('Afterthought'), ATLAS and MENOETIUS (1). When gods and men were about to share a meal at Mecone (later Sicyon), it was given to Prometheus to serve them by dividing the meat of a great ox into two portions. He produced one portion consisting of the choice meat and entrails, but covered with the ox's stomach so that it looked unappealing, and another of the bones, but covered with rich and appetising fat. He told ZEUS to choose which of the two portions would be the gods' share, and Zeus, completely taken in, chose the fat-covered bones. (This set a precedent for the division of the meats in all later sacrifices, where men always took the best part for themselves and burned the bones for the gods.) Zeus was angry at being tricked and punished mankind by withholding from them the gift of fire. But Prometheus stole fire from heaven and carried it secretly down to earth in a fennel stalk (the pith of which burns slowly, thus making a convenient means of carrying fire from one place to another). Then Zeus was once more full of wrath, and this time he punished men by having HEPHAESTUS fashion the first woman, PANDORA, who was beautiful but deceitful, and would plague the lives of mankind by letting loose sorrows and sickness throughout the world. She was sent to Prometheus' gullible brother Epimetheus, and he, charmed by this vision of loveliness, took her as his bride.

Zeus also punished Prometheus himself: he had him chained to a cliff in the Caucasian Mountains and sent an eagle, offspring of the monsters TYPHON and ECHIDNA, to prey on him. Every day the eagle tore out Prometheus' liver, which every night grew whole again so that his torment might continue. Long ages passed before this daily agony ended, when Zeus' son HERACLES, on his way to fetch the golden apples of the Hesperides, shot the eagle and released the Titan. Zeus allowed this to happen, pleased that this feat increased the fame and honour of his son, and at last relinquished his long anger. Prometheus rewarded Heracles by telling him that he would obtain the golden apples if he sent Atlas to fetch them, while he himself held up the sky. Heracles did as Prometheus suggested and accomplished his difficult Labour successfully.

Fig. 124 **Hera and Prometheus.**

The chaining of Prometheus is dramatised in the tragedy *Prometheus Bound*, traditionally said to be by Aeschylus, which was the first (and only extant) play in a Prometheus trilogy. Here Zeus is depicted as a brutal tyrant, and Prometheus, son of THEMIS/Gaia, has done more for mankind than simply bring them fire: he has stopped Zeus from wiping out the human race when he wished to do so, and has taught men many useful skills, including architecture, agriculture, writing, medicine, the domestication of animals, the use of ships, mining for metals, and divination. Chained to his crag by Hephaestus, at the bidding of Cratos (Might) and BIA (Violence), he is comforted in his misery by a Chorus of OCEANIDS and by their father, OCEANUS. He is visited by IO, transformed into a cow by Zeus, and he predicts her future and his own eventual release by her descendant, Heracles. HERMES arrives, demanding to be told a secret that the Titan knows, vital to Zeus' safety, but in vain, and Prometheus continues to cry defiance at Zeus, fearless of his thunderbolts (1041–53):

> Let the twisted fork of lightning fire be flung
> against me: let the high air be stirred
> with thunderclaps and the convulsive fury
> of the winds: let earth to the roots of her foundations
> shake before the blasting storm: let it confound
> the waves of the sea and the paths of the heavenly stars
> in a wild turmoil, and let him raise
> my body high and dash it whirling down
> to murky Tartarus. He cannot make me die.

At the end of the play Zeus hurls Prometheus down to TARTARUS, rock and all.

We know something of the second play, *Prometheus Freed*, from fragments. Heracles killed the eagle, and Prometheus was reconciled with Zeus and set free in exchange for the secret told him by Themis: that the sea-goddess THETIS was destined to bear a son greater than his father. Zeus, who was at that time pursuing Thetis, was thus saved from being overthrown by a mighty son, the very fate that he had inflicted on his own father, Cronus. Thetis was later married off to Peleus, and the fruit of their union was Achilles, a son indeed greater than his father.

In later tradition Prometheus was sometimes said to have been not only the benefactor of the human race, but also its creator, fashioning it from clay. But mankind originated from him in another sense, for his son DEUCALION (1) married Pyrrha, the daughter of Epimetheus and Pandora, and when Zeus sent the Great Flood over the earth, Deucalion and Pyrrha were the sole survivors. On Prometheus' advice they built an ark, stocked it with food, and lived safely on it until the rain ceased. As the only mortals left alive, it was then their task to repopulate an empty world. On Zeus' instructions, brought to them by Hermes, they picked up stones from the earth and threw them over their shoulders. Deucalion's stones were transformed into men, and Pyrrha's into women. Thus, in one way or another, the human race owes its existence to Prometheus.

The Titan also plays a part in other myths. He (instead of Hephaestus) was occasionally said to have been the 'midwife' who split Zeus' head with an axe so that he might give birth to ATHENA. He was also said to have released the Centaur CHEIRON from endless suffering when he was wounded by one of Heracles' arrows. The immortal Centaur, in agony, longed in vain to die, so Prometheus offered himself to Zeus to be made immortal in Cheiron's place, and the Centaur gratefully died. This story implausibly ignores the fact that Prometheus, being a Titan, was already immortal.

Prometheus attacked by the eagle, with Heracles rescuing him, occurs in ancient art as early as the seventh century BC, and it was the subject of one of the panels painted by Panaenus around Pheidias' great statue of Zeus at Olympus. Prometheus was worshipped in several places in the ancient world, including Athens where his cult was celebrated by a torch race, commemorating his gift of fire to man. The Church Fathers later saw his agonies as a mystical symbol of the Passion, and Tertullian even wrote of Christ as the 'true Prometheus'. As the suffering champion of mankind, hurling defiance at Zeus' thunderbolts, Prometheus has been of tremendous inspiration in the postclassical arts, where he is often celebrated as a glorious symbol of the human spirit struggling against tyranny. His release in Shelley's *Prometheus Unbound* ushers in a golden age of love and beauty instead of hatred and oppression.

See also figs. 29 and 124.

[Hesiod, *Theogony* 507–616, *Works and Days* 47–105; Apollodorus 1.2.3, 1.3.6, 1.7.1–2, 2.5.4, 2.5.11, 3.13.5; Pausanias 1.30.2, 2.19.5, 2.19.8, 5.11.6, 10.4.4; Lucian, *Dialogues of the Gods* 5.]

Protesilaus

Son of IPHICLUS (1) of Phylace, and brother of PODARCES (1). Both brothers were suitors of HELEN, so bound by the common oath to protect the marriage-rights of her chosen husband, they later took forty ships to fight in the TROJAN WAR, with Protesilaus as leader. He left behind him a new bride and a home only half completed. An oracle had predicted that the first man to touch Trojan soil would be the first to die, so all the Greeks hesitated to land until Protesilaus took the initiative and leapt ashore. He killed a number of Trojans before being himself killed by HECTOR. His young wife LAODAMEIA (2) grieved so much that the gods allowed him to come back to earth for a short time. When he returned again to Hades, and she lost him for a second time, she killed herself.

In historical times Protesilaus was honoured as a hero at Phylace and elsewhere, but at the place where he was buried, Elaeus in the Thracian Chersonese, opposite the Troad, he was worshipped as a god. His grave was enclosed in a sacred precinct, and here his worshippers dedicated to him valuable gifts of gold, silver, bronze, and rich garments. These were all carried off by the Persians when Xerxes invaded Greece. Tall elms grew within his precinct and shadowed his grave, and it was said that the trees looking across the narrow sea to Troy came early into leaf, but their foliage soon faded and fell, like Protesilaus himself, while the trees facing away from Troy remained in leaf all season. It was also said that when an elm grew so high that Troy could be seen from it across the strait, the topmost boughs at once withered and died.

[Homer, *Iliad* 2.695–710; Epic Cycle, Proclus' summary of the *Cypria*; Herodotus 9.116–20; Apollodorus 3.10.8, *Epitome* 3.14, 3.29–30; Pausanias 1.34.2, 3.4.6; Quintus of Smyrna, *Sequel to Homer* 7.408–11; Catullus 68.73–130; Ovid, *Heroides* 13.]

Proteus

An ancient sea-god who was POSEIDON's sealherd and lived on the island of Pharos, off Egypt. Along with NEREUS and PHORCYS, he was often called the Old Man of the Sea, and like other sea-deities he had the skill of prophecy and the ability to change his shape at will (hence our adjective 'protean', meaning variable). The *Odyssey* (4.349–570) gives a vivid depiction of Proteus when he helps MENELAUS on his way home from Troy. When Menelaus is becalmed on Pharos, Proteus' daughter, the sea-goddess EIDOTHEA, tells him to seek out her father:

If somehow you could ambush him and catch him
he could tell you the way and the length of your journey
and how to make your way home over the fishy deeps ...
When the sun has climbed up to bestride the middle of
 the sky
the trusty Old Man of the Sea comes out of the water,
under the west wind blowing, with the dark sea rippling
 over him.
And when he comes out he sleeps, under the hollow caves,
and around him the seals, children of the fair sea's surge,
sleep all together, rising up out of the grey salt water
and shedding the sharp smell of the deep salt sea.

There I will take you myself when dawn appears,
and settle you down in a row, you and the three
 companions
you choose, the best from beside your well-built ships.
I will tell you all you need fear from the Old Man:
first he will go among his seals and count them,
but when he has seen them and finished counting their
 number
he will lie down in their midst like a shepherd among
 his sheep.
As soon as you see him asleep, then is the moment
for all your courage and strength: you must hold him
 there
all the time he frenziedly struggles, trying to escape.
He will try your strength by changing to all kinds of
 shapes,
all things that move on the earth, and water, and furious
 fire,
while you must hold him fast and squeeze him the harder.
But then when he questions you, looking the same
as when you saw him sleeping, then you must stay
your strength, hero, and set the Old Man free,
and ask him which of the gods makes life so hard for you,
and how to make your way home over the fishy deeps.

The next day Eidothea meets Menelaus and his three companions, bringing with her four sealskins, and hollows out four beds in the sand for them, as Menelaus himself recounts:

She settled us down in a row, and put a skin over each
 of us.
It was a most awful ambush, for the dire stench of the
 seals,
bred and brought up in the sea, oppressed us terribly.
For who would choose to lie down by a great
 sea-creature?
But the goddess came to our rescue and thought up a
 great help:
she brought ambrosia and put it by each man's nose,
where it smelled very sweet, and killed the creature's
 stench.
All morning we waited there with steadfast spirit, and
 the seals
came out of the salt sea-water and lay themselves down
along the edge of the sea. At noon the Old Man
came out of the water and found his well-fed seals.
He went among them all, counting up their number,
and counted us the first among his creatures,
with no idea of a trick. Then he himself lay down.
We with a shout leapt up, flinging our arms about him,
but the Old Man did not forget his cunning skills:
first he changed himself into a great maned lion,

and then to a snake, a panther, a massive boar.
He changed to running water, and then a towering tree.
But we kept hold of him firmly with steadfast spirit.

So Proteus gives in at last. He tells Menelaus how to get back home to Sparta, then dives back into the deep and swelling sea. This episode must have been the subject of Aeschylus' lost *Proteus*, the satyr play following his *Oresteia* trilogy.

Virgil tells a similar story in his *Georgics* (4.386–529), where ARISTAEUS ambushes Proteus in the same way (though here on the island of Carpathus instead of Pharos) to find out why his bees are dying. Virgil even keeps the detail of ambrosia being needed to overcome the awful stench of the seals.

Some time after Homer, Proteus appears as a benevolent king of Egypt, with a palace on Pharos, rather than as a sealherding sea-god; and in this later role he plays a part in the story of HELEN. The fullest details are given in the prologue of Euripides' play *Helen* (1–67), though we know from comments elsewhere that the tale first appeared in the lyric poet Stesichorus. Paris took only a phantom Helen to Troy, while the real and virtuous Helen was taken by Hermes for safekeeping to Proteus because he was the most honourable among men. Here she lived for the duration of the Trojan War, and for ten long years many men died quite needlessly.

Proteus is not himself a character in the *Helen*: when the play opens, the Trojan War is over and he himself is dead; but his two children by the Nereid PSAMATHE (1), Theoclymenus and Theonoe (once called Eido), take part in the action. This leads to the satisfying reunion of Menelaus with the real Helen, and the happy pair, with Theonoe's support, escape from Egypt and the cruel Theoclymenus who has himself been trying to marry Helen.

Herodotus (2.113–19) rationalises the story, saying that, according to the priests of Egypt, Paris brought Helen there on the way from Sparta to Troy. Proteus, here king of Memphis, was indignant when he learnt of the abduction. He drove Paris away, keeping Helen in safety; but the war still took place because the Greeks refused to believe that she was not with Paris in Troy. At the end of the war Proteus gave Helen back to Menelaus.

Psamathe (1)

A Nereid (*see* NEREIDS), daughter of the sea-god NEREUS and the Oceanid Doris. To AEACUS she bore a son, PHOCUS (1), so named because she had changed herself into a seal (*phoke*) in trying to avoid intercourse with his father. Phocus was brought up in Aeacus' household, but was later killed by his half-brothers, PELEUS and TELAMON.

Psamathe, in her anger, sent a huge wolf to ravage Peleus' herds of cattle, but her sister THETIS interceded on Peleus' behalf and the wolf was turned to stone.

Psamathe married PROTEUS, king of Egypt, and bore him a son, Theoclymenus, and a daughter, Theonoe (*see* EIDOTHEA).

[Hesiod, *Theogony* 260, 1004–5; Pindar, *Nemean* 5.11–13; Euripides, *Helen* 4–15; Apollodorus 1.2.7, 3.12.6; Ovid, *Metamorphoses* 11.346–406.]

Psamathe (2) *see* COROEBUS (1).

Psyche ('Soul')

The mortal love of Cupid (EROS, Amor), God of Love. Her story was first told by Apuleius in *The Golden Ass* (4.28–6.26, second century AD) with all the characteristics of a fairy-tale. A certain king and queen had three daughters, all of them beautiful, but the youngest, Psyche, quite breathtakingly lovely. The fame of her beauty spread far and wide, until the people stopped worshipping Venus (APHRODITE) and paid the girl divine honours instead. Venus naturally grew angry. She told her son Cupid to visit Psyche and inflame her with love for some completely worthless man, but when Cupid saw the girl's great beauty he fell in love with her himself. He arranged that Apollo should pronounce to Psyche's father an oracle saying that she must prepare to marry an evil spirit, feared even by the gods, who would come to fetch her as she stood on a lonely mountain top. In great sorrow, the king and queen obeyed the oracle's instructions, and the day came when Psyche was led to a craggy hilltop and left there, alone and afraid. But her fears were needless. She was wafted gently down into a flowery valley by Zephyrus, the West Wind, and there she found in the middle of a nearby wood a fairytale palace, full of unbelievable treasures. Here she was waited upon by unseen hands, until night came and it was time for bed. In the darkness Cupid came to her, and she lay in delight with this unseen, unknown husband, who stayed with her until just before dawn. And so the lonely days and the love-filled nights passed, with Cupid coming after dark and always leaving before the morning light.

Psyche, missing her family, at last persuaded Cupid to allow her sisters to visit her. He warned her urgently that they were likely to bring her great unhappiness, and that she must on no account listen if they tried to make her find out what he looked like. If she ever did so, he would leave her for ever. She promised that she would do just as he said, and on the sisters' first visit, after they had been carried down to her by Zephyrus, she kept her word. But the sisters were consumed with a violent envy of Psyche's good fortune and resolved to ruin her. On a subsequent visit they discovered that she had no idea what her husband looked like. They terrified her by saying that she must be married to a fearful monster, who would end up by devouring both her and the baby that she was now carrying. She had best kill him before she herself was killed.

So that night poor, credulous Psyche waited until Cupid slept after their lovemaking, then lit a lamp and approached him, armed with a sharpened carving knife. At once she recognised the beautiful Love-god and was overcome with wonder and desire. But a drop of scalding oil from the lamp fell on his shoulder and he was startled awake. At once he leapt up in pain, then seeing that his wife had broken her word he flew away from her, just as he had said he would. Psyche, in despair, searched everywhere for him, but in vain. On her travels she came to the cities where her sisters lived and told them what had happened. Each in turn, desirous of winning Cupid's love for herself, hurried to the crag from which Zephyrus had been wont to waft them down to the palace. They leapt confidently into the air, but no West Wind came for them, and each in turn was dashed to pieces on the rocks below.

Psyche continued her wanderings through country after country. She prayed for help at the temples of Ceres (Demeter) and Juno (Hera), but they could not help her for fear of offending Venus. At last she came to the palace of Venus herself. The goddess, furious that her son had not only failed to punish Psyche but had even made her pregnant, treated her cruelly and gave her formidable tasks to perform. First she had to sort out a vast heap of mixed grains into their separate kinds by nightfall, and did so only because a sympathetic colony of ants worked furiously to help her. Next Venus told her to fetch a hank of wool from a flock of murderous sheep. On the advice of a reed she waited until the beasts were asleep, then gathered up the loose wisps of wool clinging to the nearby briar bushes. Her third task was to fetch a jar full of ice-cold water from the River STYX, and this was fetched for her by an eagle who owed a debt of gratitude to Cupid. Lastly she had to go down to the Underworld to fetch a day's supply of Proserpina's store of beauty. Realising that she was being sent to her death, she climbed to the top of a high tower, intending to throw herself down and die. But the tower spoke to her, giving her detailed advice on how she could carry out Venus' command and still live. Psyche did exactly as the tower said, entering Hades by way of Taenarum in the Peloponnese. She carried two pieces of bread and two coins, and with these she appeased CERBERUS and CHARON both on the way in and the way out of the Underworld. She

avoided the various snares that Venus had set along her journey. When she reached Proserpina (PERSEPHONE), who offered her a chair and a meal, she was careful to sit on the ground and to eat only a crust of bread. The upshot was that she returned succesfully from her quest, carrying a sealed box filled for her by Proserpina. But she neglected to obey one of the tower's instructions: that on no account must she open the box. She allowed her curiosity to get the better of her and lifted the lid, intending to use a little of the beauty within on herself, so as to win back Cupid's love. Out stole a fatal sleep and overpowered her, and she fell to the ground as if she were dead.

Cupid, however, had been desperately missing his lost love, and he now flew to her aid and woke her. He went to plead his love with Jupiter (Zeus), who gave divine consent to his marriage with Psyche, and appeased Venus by making Psyche immortal so that the match was no disgrace. In the fullness of time Psyche's baby was born, a daughter called Voluptas (Pleasure).

In later times, Psyche's story came to be seen as an allegory of the soul's troublous journey through life towards a mystic union with the divine after death. The tale has proved highly inspirational in the postclassical arts: it has influenced musicians, playwrights (among them Molière) and many poets, and has been painted by innumerable artists including Correggio, Rubens (several versions), Claude, Boucher and Fragonard, and sculpted by (among others) Canova, Thorwaldsen and Rodin.

Pterelaus

Son of Taphius, and king of the Taphian islands near the mouth of the Gulf of Corinth. He was a descendant of PERSEUS' son Mestor, whose daughter Hippothoe had borne Taphius to POSEIDON. At Pterelaus' birth, the god put in his hair a single strand of gold that would keep him immortal as long as it remained there, but despite this gift Pterelaus lost his life. When ELECTRYON was ruling Mycenae, Pterelaus sent his six sons, together with a band of Taphians, to claim the land of Tiryns that had belonged to his great-grandfather Mestor. Electryon ignored their claim, so they set about raiding his cattle. In the ensuing battle all but one of both Electryon's and Pterelaus' sons were killed. In due course AMPHITRYON, who was betrothed to Electryon's daughter Alcmene, sailed with a band of allies to the Taphian islands to take revenge for the raid. Although they ravaged the islands, they could not take Pterelaus' own city, Taphos, while he still lived. But they were helped by his daughter Comaetho, who had fallen in love with Amphitryon: she pulled out the golden hair of immortality from her father's head and he died. Amphitryon was now able to subjugate all the islands, but if Comaetho expected gratitude, she had none. Amphitryon killed her for her treachery.

[Apollodorus 2.4.5–7.]

Pygmalion (1)

According to Apollodorus (3.14.3), Pygmalion was a king of Cyprus whose daughter Metharme married CINYRAS, an immigrant from Cilicia; but Ovid (*Metamorphoses* 10.243–97) tells the more familiar – and more romantic – story. When Pygmalion could find no living woman worthy of his love, he carved a wonderful ivory statue of a woman lovelier than any ever born. So beautiful was she that he fell passionately in love with her. At a festival of APHRODITE he prayed the gods to grant him a woman like his statue. But Aphrodite saw into his heart, and she granted him what he really wished: when he arrived home again, he found that his statue had come to life. He married her, and she bore him a daughter, Paphos, after whom the city of Paphos, the chief centre of Aphrodite's worship on Cyprus, was named.

The name Galatea was given to the statue-woman only in postclassical times. In W. S. Gilbert's comedy *Pygmalion and Galatea*, the sculptor is married, and his wife Cynisca is jealous of his animated statue. At last, after a great deal of trouble, Galatea returns to her original state. In G. B. Shaw's *Pygmalion*, the sculptor becomes Professor Henry Higgins, an expert in phonetics, and his Galatea is Eliza Doolittle, a Cockney flower girl, who is transformed by his education from a guttersnipe into an elegant woman. Shaw's version was adapted into the popular musical *My Fair Lady*.

Pygmalion (2) *see* DIDO.

Pygmies ('Fist-like Men')

A race of little men, who were thought to fight an annual battle with the cranes. The pygmies are first mentioned in Homer (*Iliad* 3.3–7), who locates them at the ends of the earth near OCEANUS. The cranes 'flee from winter and boundless rain, and clamorously wing their way to the streams of Ocean, bringing death and destruction to the pygmies; through the air they come to bring them baneful war'. The origin of this war was later accounted for in various ways, such as the transformation of a beautiful pygmy girl into a crane by HERA, angry because she had not received the worship she required. The girl, in her crane-form, tried desperately to get to her baby son who was still with the pygmies, but they drove her away with violence; and ever since this incident there has been hostility between cranes and pygmies. Perhaps in fact the story of the annual battle derived from a lost folk-tale, or simply from the sight of a vast flock of cranes flying south, uttering loud cries.

The battle between pygmies and cranes often occurs in ancient art, and first on the François Krater (*c.* 570 BC), where the pygmies are depicted as dwarfs, fighting with clubs, hooked sticks and slings, and riding on goats; later they often appear as podgy and grotesque (fig. 125), with enormous sexual organs. The idea of pygmies may well have been based on fact, for Herodotus had heard of little black men living in the heart of Africa, whose speech was unintelligible to travellers and who lived near a great river with crocodiles in it.

[Herodotus 2.32, 4.34; Antoninus Liberalis, *Metamorphoses* 16; Athenaeus 9.393e–f; Ovid, *Metamorphoses* 6.90–2; Pliny, *Natural History* 7.26–7.]

Pylades

Son of STROPHIUS, king of Crisa in Phocis, and Anaxibia, the sister of Agamemnon. Pylades was the faithful friend of his cousin ORESTES, accompanying him when he avenged his father's death and through all his subsequent exploits (fig. 58), and appearing in all the fifth-century dramas dealing with Orestes' adventures (though not always as a speaking character) except for Euripides' *Andromache*. Pylades married Orestes' sister, ELECTRA (3), and had two sons by her, Strophius and Medon.

Pylas

A king of Megara, variously named by Pausanias as Pylas, Pylus and Pylon. He gave refuge to PANDION (2) when he was driven from the throne of Athens by the sons of Metion, marrying him to his daughter Pylia. When Pylas was exiled for killing his uncle Bias, Pandion became king of Megara, while Pylas himself went to Messenia with a band of Lelegian followers and founded the city of Pylos.

Fig. 125 **A podgy pygmy attacks a crane.**

In due course he was driven from his city once again, this time by NELEUS, and emigrated to Elis where he founded a second Pylos.

[Apollodorus 3.15.5; Pausanias 1.39.4, 4.36.1, 6.22.5–6.]

Pyraechmes *see* OXYLUS.

Pyramus and Thisbe

Pyramus and Thisbe grew up living next door to each other. In the fullness of time they fell in love, but their parents forbade them to marry or even to meet. Luckily there was a chink in the wall between the two adjoining houses, through which they would spend hours whispering their love, and even kissing the wall between them since they could not kiss each other. At last they resolved to steal away at dead of night and meet at the tomb of Ninus, in the shade of a mulberry tree hung thick with snowy fruits, and close to a cool spring. Thisbe, her face veiled, arrived first and sat down beneath the appointed tree, but was startled away by the approach of a lioness who came, fresh from her kill, to drink at the spring. The girl fled for safety into a cave, but as she ran she dropped her veil, which the lioness seized and tore to pieces in her bloodied jaws. A little later Pyramus arrived, and saw the footprints of the lioness and the torn veil all stained with blood. Recognising the garment, and full of remorse for causing, as he thought, Thisbe's death, he killed himself with his sword. Thisbe returned and despairingly found her beloved's body. She joined him in death, stabbing herself with the same sword still warm from his own mortal wound. Their parents found their corpses. Moved too late by their children's love for one another, they buried their ashes in a single urn. The snowy fruit of the mulberry tree was coloured by all the spilt blood, and has ever since been a dark red.

This story was told by Chaucer in *The Legende of Goode Women*, and is of course the 'most Lamentable Comedy and most Cruel Death of Pyramus and Thisby' played by Bottom and his friends in *A Midsummer Night's Dream*, where the lovers meet at 'Ninny's tomb'. It is the subject of paintings by Cranach, Tintoretto, Poussin and Giordano, of drawings by Rembrandt, and of many operas, the best-known being Gluck's *Pyramo e Tisbe* (1746).

[Ovid, *Metamorphoses* 4.55–166.]

Pyreneus

A king of Daulis who intercepted the MUSES as they were journeying to Parnassus and invited them into his palace to shelter from the rain. When the storm blew over they began to make their departure, but Pyreneus fastened the doors and tried to rape them. They escaped by flying away, and the king, intent on following them, launched himself in a frenzy from one of the high battlements. He fell headlong to his death.

[Ovid, *Metamorphoses* 5.273–92.]

Pyrrha

The daughter of EPIMETHEUS and PANDORA. She married DEUCALION (1), the son of Prometheus, and became through him the mother of the human race after the Great Flood.

Pyrrhus *see* NEOPTOLEMUS.

Python

The monstrous she-dragon that inhabited Delphi before the coming of APOLLO and gave the place its first name, Pytho. She was usually thought to be the guardian snake of the original oracle there, belonging to GAIA (Earth) or THEMIS; though a late account says that Python was the (male) snake that tried to kill the pregnant LETO, knowing by his oracular powers that he was fated to perish at the hands of the goddess' son. The *Homeric Hymn to Apollo*, giving the serpent no name, says that she reared the monster TYPHON whom Hera had borne to challenge Zeus' power. She herself was a plague to mankind, ravaging the surrounding countryside and preying on flocks. When Apollo came to Delphi to establish his oracle he shot the great serpent dead. The place was named Pytho because her carcase rotted away (*pyth-*) in the sun beside the sacred spring, and the god was called Pythian Apollo. It was later said that he founded the Pythian Games to commemorate the dead serpent. She herself came to be called Python (though was thought of in most later accounts as male), and in memory of her original ownership of the oracle, Apollo's prophetess at Delphi was always known as the Pythia. The legend symbolises the victory of the celestial Olympian god over the dangerous chthonian forces of the earth.

[*Homeric Hymn to Apollo* 281–374; Euripides, *Iphigeneia among the Taurians* 1259–69; Pausanias 2.7.7, 2.30.3, 10.6.5–7; Ovid, *Metamorphoses* 1.438–47; Hyginus, *Fabula* 140.]

Quirinus

An early Roman god, claimed by the ancients to have been Sabine in origin, and from the third century BC identified with the deified ROMULUS.

[Plutarch, *Romulus* 29; Ovid, *Fasti* 2.475–80.]

R

Remus *see* ROMULUS AND REMUS.

Rhadamanthys

Son of ZEUS and EUROPA, and brother of MINOS and (in all accounts after Homer) SARPEDON. Europa married the Cretan king, Asterius, who brought up the boys as his own sons. When they grew up, they quarrelled over the love of a beautiful youth, MILETUS, and Minos drove his brothers out of Crete. Rhadamanthys went to rule over islands in the southern Aegean, where the people voluntarily put themselves under his control because of his reputation for justice. Later he married ALCMENE and lived with her at Ocaleae in Boeotia. Their tombs were shown at Haliartus.

Because Rhadamanthys was renowned for his wisdom and justice as a lawgiver, he went after death to ELYSIUM, where the most blessed mortals lived in bliss, and there became ruler and judge. (Sometimes he was said to have married Alcmene there, rather than on earth.) He was one of the judges of the dead in Hades, along with his brother Minos and another son of Zeus, AEACUS. Virgil (*Aeneid* 6.566–9) has him presiding over TARTARUS and punishing the wicked for their sins.

[Homer, *Iliad* 14.322, *Odyssey* 4.561–9; Hesiod, *Catalogue of Women* fr. 141; Pindar, *Olympian* 2.74–6, *Pythian* 2.73–4; Apollodorus 2.4.9, 2.4.11, 3.1.1–2; Diodorus Siculus 5.79.1–2; Plutarch, *Lysander* 28; Pausanias 8.53.4–5.]

Rhea (1) or Rheia

One of the TITANS, daughter of Uranus (Heaven) and GAIA (Earth). She married her brother-Titan CRONUS and bore him five children, HESTIA, DEMETER, HERA, HADES and POSEIDON. Cronus, however, had learnt from Gaia that he was destined to be overthrown by his own son, so he swallowed each baby as it was born. When Rhea was pregnant with her sixth child she turned to her mother for advice, and with good effect: ZEUS was taken at birth to Crete, while a stone wrapped in swaddling clothes was substituted for the baby (fig.126). Cronus, noticing nothing amiss, swallowed the stone. Zeus grew up in safety, eventually overthrowing his father, just as predicted, after forcing him to regurgitate his five eldest children. Pausanias (8.8.2–3) records an Arcadian legend saying that Poseidon too had been saved at birth, when Rhea put him in a flock of sheep to live with the lambs; she then told Cronus that she had given birth to a horse and gave him a foal to swallow. This equine birth would not have been entirely surprising, since Cronus also fathered the

Fig. 126 Rhea hands Cronus a large stone, wrapped like a baby in swaddling clothes.

344

Fig. 127 Diomedes slaughters Rhesus and his Thracian followers. Nearby are Rhesus' splendid horses.

Centaur Cheiron on the Oceanid Philyra, after transforming himself into a horse to deceive the jealous Rhea. (Pausanias adds: 'When I began to write this work, I was inclined to think these legends foolish, but on getting as far as Arcadia I grew to take a more considered view of the matter.')

Rhea came to be identified by the Greeks with the Phrygian mother-goddess CYBELE and thus was connected with the CORYBANTES. The Romans identified her with their Goddess of Plenty, Ops.

[Homer, *Iliad* 14.201–4, 15.187–8; Hesiod, *Theogony* 135, 453–506; Apollodorus 1.1.3–7, 1.2.4, 3.5.1, 3.12.6; Strabo 10.3.12; Pausanias 8.36.2–3.]

Rhea (2) *see* AVENTINUS.

Rhea (or **Rea**) **Silvia**

The daughter of Numitor who bore twin sons, ROMULUS AND REMUS, to the god Mars.

Rhesus

A Thracian king, the son of Eioneus according to Homer, but of the river-god Strymon and a MUSE (either Calliope or Euterpe) according to later writers. He was an ally of the Trojans, coming to help King PRIAM in the last year of the Trojan War, but was killed on the very night of his arrival at Troy. Homer recounts his death in the *Iliad* (10.432–514). During a night-raid on the Trojan camp, ODYSSEUS and DIOMEDES (2) intercept the enemy spy DOLON. Hoping to save his life, he points out to them the newly-arrived contingent from Thrace, all asleep from weariness. He points particularly to Rhesus' magnificent horses: 'They are the finest horses I ever saw, and the biggest', he says, 'they are whiter than snow, and they run with the winds' speed' (436–7). But for all his helpfulness, Dolon is killed by Diomedes, who then goes on to butcher thirteen of the sleeping Thracians, including

Rhesus himself, while Odysseus takes the horses (fig.127). They then escape safely back to the Greek camp. Although Homer makes no mention of it, a later tradition said that Troy was fated to remain invincible if ever Rhesus' horses drank the waters of the river SCAMANDER or grazed the grass on its banks. This prophecy seems to lie behind Virgil's brief mention of Rhesus' death (*Aeneid* 1.469–73).

The story of the night-raid and the slaughter of the Thracians is dramatised in the *Rhesus*, traditionally said to be by Euripides, although the attribution is doubtful. It is the only extant Greek tragedy whose plot is derived from the action of the *Iliad*. The play ends as Rhesus' mother, the Muse, is about to carry her son's body back to Thrace, where he will live on as a demi-god, an oracular spirit inhabiting a cave in the area of the Thracian silver mines.

Rhode or Rhodos ('rose')

The nymph who gave her name to the island of Rhodes. Her parents are variously named, and include POSEIDON and AMPHITRITE, ASOPUS, and APHRODITE. The Sun-god HELIOS claimed the island as his own when he saw it rising in beauty from the sea, and to him Rhode bore seven sons. One of these, Cercaphus, had sons after whom three of the island's chief cities were named: Ialysos, Cameiros and Lindos. Rhodes was an important centre for the worship of Helios. The islanders annually threw into the sea a chariot and four horses for the use of the Sun-god, thus replacing the weary steeds who had been bringing daily light to the world for a whole year.

[Pindar, *Olympian* 7.14, 54–76; Apollodorus 1.4.5; Diodorus Siculus 55–6; Strabo 14.2.8.]

Rhoeo *see* ANIUS.

Romulus and Remus

The mythical founders of Rome. Numitor, a descendant of AENEAS, was deposed from the rule of Alba Longa by his younger brother Amulius, who not only killed Numitor's sons but forced his only daughter, Rhea Silvia, to become a Vestal Virgin so that no children might be born of her. But he reckoned without the gods, for MARS lay with the girl and she bore him twin sons, Romulus and Remus. Flinging her into prison, Amulius ordered the babies to be thrown into the River Tiber, but the basket in which they lay floated safely to the shore near a fig tree, the Ficus Ruminalis, later held to be sacred. Here a she-wolf, hearing the infants' cries, came and suckled them, and a woodpecker fed them scraps of food. Both creatures were sacred to Mars. The royal shepherd, Faustulus, chanced by and saw the she-wolf tenderly licking the babies as if

they were her own young. Guessing the boys' royal parentage, he took them home, and he and his wife ACCA LARENTIA brought them up as their own. They grew into fine, strong young men who often led a band of young shepherds on daring exploits. One day Remus was captured and handed over to Numitor to be punished. Numitor suspected that Remus and his brother might be his lost grandsons and had his suspicions confirmed by Faustulus. Romulus and Remus, with the help of their loyal band of young men, attacked the palace and killed the usurper Amulius. Numitor once more became king.

The brothers now decided to found a city of their own. They chose a site not far from Alba Longa, and near the Tiber where they had been cast out to die. But now they quarrelled as to who should name the city and become its king. Since they could not know which twin was the elder, they left it to the gods to send a sign, with Remus taking up a position on the Aventine Hill and Romulus on the Palatine. Remus first saw six vultures, then Romulus saw twelve. Each of them was named king by their own followers, Remus on the grounds of priority, Romulus of quantity. In the brawl that followed, Remus was slain. In another version of his death, Remus spoke slightingly of the new city walls and jumped over them, at which he was killed either by Romulus or by his henchman Celer. Romulus declared in anger, 'So perish anyone else who shall leap over my walls.' Now he was left alone to found the city, which he called Rome after himself.

The city flourished. People flocked to live there, many of them outlaws and fugitives to whom Romulus willingly gave sanctuary, since they made Rome the stronger. Unfortunately the Romans were both feared and scorned by their neighbours and were refused marriage with the local women. Romulus overcame this problem by holding a great festival and inviting the families of the local tribes, including the Sabines. They came, but in the midst of the festivities the Romans drove off the men and carried away their daughters (the 'Rape of the Sabine Women'). At first the girls were terrified, but Romulus reassured them and their captors wooed them with words of love, so they soon accepted their new situation. Their fathers and brothers, meanwhile, rallied to win them back by force. Various small raids against Rome were unsuccessful, but finally the Sabines attacked in force under their king, Titus Tatius. They took the Roman citadel through the treachery of the commander's daughter, TARPEIA, and battle ensued between Sabines and Romans. At this the Sabine Women ran out into the thick of the fighting, begging their husbands and fathers not to kill each other. So Romans and Sabines made peace, agreeing to merge in a single federation, with Rome as their capital and Romulus and Titus Tatius their joint rulers. Soon afterwards Titus Tatius was killed in a quarrel with the people of Lavinium.

Romulus ruled for some forty years, during which time Rome grew and prospered. At the end of his life he left the earth in a mysterious fashion. He was holding a muster of troops in the Campus Martius (Field of Mars) when a storm blew up, and amid claps of thunder he was enveloped in a cloud so thick that he disappeared from view. When the cloud dispersed, he had vanished. The senators who had been nearest him declared that he had been caught up into heaven, and the soldiers, who loved Romulus, hailed him as a god. He was thereafter worshipped as the deity Quirinus. But according to Livy, there was a rumour that he had been murdered and torn to pieces by the senators, envious of his power.

The wolf appears on early Roman coins. The famous bronze she-wolf in the Capitoline Museum at Rome (fig.

128) dates to the fifth century BC, while the suckling twins were added in the sixteenth century.

[Dionysius of Halicarnassus 1.76–2.56; Plutarch, *Romulus*; Livy 1.3.10–1.17; Ovid, *Fasti* 2.381–421, 3.11–76, 179–228; Pliny, *Natural History* 15.77; Tacitus, *Annals* 13.58. J. N. Bremmer and N. M. Horsfall, *Roman Myth and Mythography* (1987), pp. 25–48.]

Fig. 128 **The bronze Capitoline Wolf, suckling the abandoned twins, Romulus and Remus.**

S

Sabines and **Sabine Women** *see* ROMULUS.

Sagitta (The Arrow)
A constellation representing the arrow used by HERACLES to kill the eagle that daily gouged out the liver of the Titan PROMETHEUS.

Sagittarius (The Archer)
A constellation immortalising the wise and kindly Centaur CHEIRON.

Salamis
A daughter of the river-god ASOPUS. She was carried off by POSEIDON to the island off the coast of Attica that would ever afterwards bear her name. There she bore the god a son, CYCHREUS, the island's first king.

[Apollodorus 3.12.7; Diodorus Siculus 4.72.4; Pausanias 1.35.2.]

Salmacis *see* HERMAPHRODITUS.

Salmoneus
Son of AEOLUS (1) and Enarete; husband of Alcidice, and father by her of a beautiful daughter, TYRO, who was seduced by Poseidon. Salmoneus left Thessaly, where he was born, and founded a city in Elis called Salmone. He thought himself the equal of ZEUS, and laid claim to divine honours for himself by ordering sacrifices to be made to him and not to the god. He even imitated Zeus' thunder and lightning by dragging dried hides and bronze pots behind his chariot and flinging lighted torches into the sky. He was not a popular ruler, for his people objected to having burning torches hurled at them by their king. But worse was to come, for Zeus in anger struck Salmoneus and his city with a genuine thunderbolt, and king and people were blotted from the face of the earth. As Virgil describes it, recounting Salmoneus' relegation to TARTARUS (*Aeneid* 6.592–4): 'Through thick clouds the almighty father hurled his missile – not for

him the smoky light from a pine torch – and savagely sent him spinning deep into the abyss.'

[Hesiod, *Catalogue of Women* fr. 30; Apollodorus 1.9.7–8; Diodorus Siculus 4.68, 6.6.4–6.7.3.]

Sarpedon
In the *Iliad*, Sarpedon is the son of ZEUS and Laodameia, daughter of BELLEROPHON, and with his cousin GLAUCUS (4) commands the Lycian contingent of PRIAM's allies in the TROJAN WAR. 'I have come from far away to be your ally', he says to HECTOR, 'from distant Lycia and the whirling waters of Xanthus. There I left my dear wife and my baby son, there I left my many possessions which a poor man might covet. Yet even so I spur on my Lycians, and myself strive to kill my man in battle, even though I own nothing here that the Greeks could carry off' (5.478–84). He is the mightiest warrior among the Trojan allies and takes a prominent part in the fighting. He kills TLEPOLEMUS, son of Heracles, and later leads a group of comrades on an assault against the fortifications around the Greek ships, resolved to breach the wall or die in the attempt (12.299–308):

> He went onwards like some mountain lion,
> one who for a long time has been without meat,
> and now his fearless heart urges him on
> to get inside a strong-built sheepfold
> and go for the sheepflocks. And even though
> he finds there herdsmen guarding their sheep
> with spears and with dogs, even so he will not
> be driven from the fold without some attack,
> and either he makes his spring and seizes a sheep,
> or is himself hit first by a spear from a quick hand.
> So now his spirit urged on godlike Sarpedon
> to rush at the wall and break apart its defences.

He succeeds, and makes the first breach in the wall: 'He opened a pathway for many', says Homer (12.399).

Finally Sarpedon is killed by PATROCLUS, for whom this

victory is the supreme achievement before his own death at Hector's hands. The two warriors meet: 'Like two hook-beaked, crook-clawed vultures fight, loud-screaming, above a rocky peak, so now these two, shouting aloud, rushed at each other' (16.428–30). Zeus watches the battle. Already he has fended death from his beloved son, and now, knowing that Sarpedon is destined to be killed by Patroclus, he pities him and wonders whether to save him yet again. Hera rebukes him bitterly, saying that he should not flout the laws of mortality. Zeus sorrowfully accepts his son's death. 'And he let fall to the ground a shower of bloody rain in honour of his dear son, whom Patroclus was about to kill on the rich earth of Troy, far from the land of his fathers' (16.459–61). Sarpedon dies, struck in the heart by Patroclus' spear (16.482–91):

> He fell, as when an oak tree falls, or a white poplar,
> or a tall pine, which carpenters in the mountains
> have hewn down with whetted axe to be a ship-timber.
> So he lay outstretched, in front of his horses
> and chariot, roaring, and clutching at the bloody dust.
> Like a proud and fiery bull that a lion kills
> when it comes amid a herd of shambling cattle,
> and he dies bellowing, brought down by the lion's jaws,
> so now before Patroclus the lord of the Lycian warriors
>   died raging ...

A bloody battle over Sarpedon's body ensues, with the Greeks striving to strip his armour and the Trojans striving to stop them, until 'no longer could a man, even a shrewd one, have recognised godlike Sarpedon, for he was covered completely from head to toe with weapons and blood and dust, while men still thronged about his corpse' (16.638–41). At last Zeus intervenes, and gives instruction to Apollo (16.667–75):

> Go now, beloved Phoebus, and lift Sarpedon
> out of range of the missiles, and cleanse him
> of the dark blood, then carry him far away
> and wash him in a running river, and anoint him
> with ambrosia, and fold him in godlike clothing.
> Then give him to be carried by swift messengers,
> Sleep and his twin brother Death, who soon
> will lay him down in the rich broad land of Lycia,
> where brothers and kinsmen will give him burial
> with grave and stone, the final honour to the dead.

Apollo does as Zeus bids. Sarpedon is lifted up by HYPNOS (Sleep) and THANATOS (Death) – a famous calyx krater by Euphronios depicts this very moment (fig. 75) – and is carried away from the Trojan battlefield to honourable burial in Lycia. Here in historical times there was a hero-cult of Sarpedon of great antiquity.

Writers after Homer give Sarpedon a different parent-age, making him one of the sons of Zeus and EUROPA, even though she lived some generations earlier than the events recounted in the *Iliad*. They explain the chrono-logical discrepancy, either by saying that Zeus allowed Sarpedon to live for three generations, or by making the Cretan Sarpedon the grandfather of the Iliadic hero. According to Apollodorus, after Europa had had her three children by Zeus she married the Cretan king, Asterius, who brought up Sarpedon and his brothers MINOS and RHADAMANTHYS. When these three were grown up, they all fell in love with the beautiful youth MILETUS and quar-relled over him. Minos drove his brothers out of Crete, and Sarpedon joined his mother's brother, CILIX, in south-ern Asia Minor, helping him to vanquish the Lycians then ruling over the land. Herodotus (1.173) adds that his people were then called the Termilae, but that their name was changed to Lycians when LYCUS (4), son of Pandion, was driven out of Athens and took refuge with Sarpedon.

[Homer, *Iliad* 2.876–7, 5.628–69, 6.198–9, 12.290–414, 16.419–683; Apollodorus 3.1.1–2; Diodorus Siculus 5.79.3.]

Saturn

An ancient Italian god identified with the Greek CRONUS. When Saturn was banished from his rule of Olympus by his son Jupiter, he became an early king of Latium, the father of PICUS, the grandfather of FAUNUS and the great-grandfather of LATINUS, who was ruling when AENEAS came to Italy. Saturn taught his people the arts of agri-culture and the blessings of civilisation, and his reign was a blissful Golden Age, when all men lived in peace and prosperity.

Saturn was worshipped together with the Goddess of Plenty, Ops, who was identified with Cronus' wife RHEA (1). His annual festival, the Saturnalia, was celebrated at the winter solstice and was the merriest time of the year. The festival was taken over in large part by our Christ-mas. Saturn gave his name to a day of the week, Saturday, and to those born under the influence of his planet, who had a 'saturnine' disposition and were gloomy, dull and morose.

[Dionysius of Halicarnassus 1.34; Virgil, *Aeneid* 6.792–4, 7.48–9, 8.314–27, 355–8, *Georgics* 2.536–40.]

Satyrs and Silens

Male creatures of the wild, primarily human in form but with some animal features, with a voracious appetite for sex and wine and a love of music and revelry. With NYMPHS and MAENADS they made up the riotous train of DIONYSUS. Satyrs are first mentioned by Hesiod as being 'hopeless at working and worthless', and Silens appear first in the *Homeric Hymn to Aphrodite* (262–3), making love to nymphs in the recesses of caves; but their names

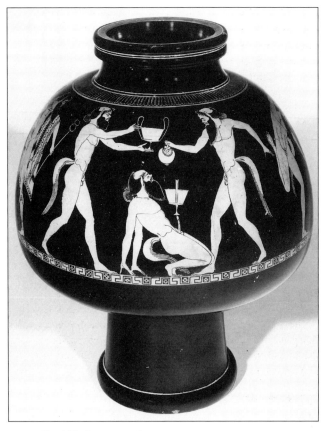

Fig. 129 **Satyrs at play.**

were often used interchangeably. Three labelled Silens appear on the François Krater, each with horses' ears, tails and hind legs, accompanying Dionysus as he brings Hephaestus back to Olympus. Their activities give a neat visual summary of their character: one carries a wineskin, one plays the double pipes, and one embraces a nymph. In later art satyrs more commonly have human legs and are usually depicted with rough hair, snub noses, horses' ears and tails, and perpetual proud erections. They are shown in typical satyrs' pursuits – making music, accompanying Dionysus, dancing, helping with the vintage, chasing nymphs or maenads, copulating with animals, and masturbating. The only individualised satyrs in myth are SILENUS and the Phrygian satyr MARSYAS.

At the Festival of Dionysus at Athens, in the fifth century BC, each tragedian wrote a satyr play that provided comic relief after his set of three tragedies. The chorus was composed of satyrs, accompanied by old Silenus, and the plot was taken from myth, sometimes with connections to the preceding trilogy. The only completely sur-

viving satyr play is Euripides' *Cyclops*, dramatising the famous story of Odysseus and Polyphemus, though about half of Sophocles' *Trackers* survives on papyrus, with the tale of the infant Hermes' wondrous growth and his theft of Apollo's cattle. There are many vases inspired by satyr plays, most notably the Pronomos vase which shows the entire cast of a victorious play. The actors dressed as satyrs wear shaggy trunks with an erect phallus and a horse's tail.

In Hellenistic and later art satyrs acquire goatish features, perhaps from their association with PAN. The Romans identified them with their native woodland spirits, the fauns. In postclassical art, satyrs and fauns are depicted with goats' legs and horns. They often appear in the type of revelling scenes familiar from antiquity, but also in family situations, with female fauns and baby satyrs.

See also figs. 67, 71, 79, and 129.

[Hesiod, *Catalogue of Women* fr. 123; Pausanias 1.23.5–6.]

Scamander

The chief river of the Trojan plain and its god, and like all river-gods the offspring of OCEANUS and Tethys. Scamander was the progenitor of the Trojan royal family, for his son TEUCER (1), born to the nymph Idaea, was the ancestor of the Trojan kings. His daughters too married into the Trojan royal house: Callirhoe became the wife of TROS, and Strymo the wife of LAOMEDON. Thus when the gods took sides during the Trojan War, Scamander naturally supported the Trojans.

In Homer's *Iliad*, after the death of Patroclus, ACHILLES slaughters Trojans in an avenging fury and flings their corpses into the waters of Scamander (called Xanthus by the other gods: 20.73–4). The river-god becomes enraged and cries out to Achilles in complaint (21.218–20):

> My lovely streams are crowded full with corpses,
> and I cannot pour my waters out to the bright sea,
> choked with the dead men you so ruthlessly kill.

But Achilles carries on attacking Trojans 'like something more than mortal' (227), so Scamander breaks his banks and rushes with great waves after Achilles, who runs away before them (251–69):

> Achilles leapt away the length of a spear-cast,
> with the swoop of a black eagle, the great hunter,
> who is the strongest and the swiftest of all birds.
> Like this he sped away, and on his chest
> the bronze armour clashed terribly as he fled,
> slipping away from under the rush of the waters,
> but the river came surging after with a mighty roar
> ... and every time swift-footed godlike Achilles
> would turn and try to fight the river ... so often

the great flood of the sky-fed river would strike his shoulders from above.

The river-god's rage swells even greater, and he calls for help to his brother-river and tributary SIMOEIS, then threatens Achilles with death (316–27):

'I say that never will his strength avail him, nor
his beauty, nor his lovely armour, which deep
in my waters will lie covered over with mud,
and him I shall wrap in sand, and on him shed
great heaps of shingle past all measuring,
nor will the Greeks know where to find his bones,
so vast a shroud of silt shall I heap on him.
Here shall be built his tomb – he will have no need
of a funeral mound and the Greeks to bury him.'
So he spoke, and rushed in tumult on Achilles,
raging on high and seething with foam and blood
and corpses. And the dark wave of the sky-fed river
rose towering up to overpower Achilles.

But Achilles is saved by the goddess HERA, who supports the Greek cause. She sends HEPHAESTUS, god of fire, to scorch the river with flame and dry it up. Scamander, his waters burning away, submits, and in fear makes a solemn vow to Hera (374–6):

Never will I ward from the Trojans the day of evil,
not even when all of Troy is burning with raging fire,
and the Greeks are doing the burning.

Thus, when the Greeks finally enter Troy, and sack the city, and put it to the torch, Scamander may not loose his lovely waters to save his descendants.

[Hesiod, *Theogony* 337–45; Apollodorus 3.12.1–3.]

Schedius *see* IPHITUS (2).

Scheria

Scheria (called Drepane by Apollonius in his *Argonautica*) is the fantasy-island of the Phaeacians, usually identified with Corfu. In Homer's *Odyssey* (6–8, 13.1–187), ODYSSEUS is shipwrecked here on his way home to Ithaca. ALCINOUS, the king, is married to ARETE, and they have five sons and a daughter, NAUSICAA. The Phaeacians enjoy a special relationship with the gods and live isolated from other communities, so they need have no fear of war or invasion. Their women are skilled at fine weaving, and their men at seamanship, with ships that find their own way miraculously over the sea without need of oars or steersmen. The people have a relaxed and luxurious way of life: 'We forever enjoy feasting', says Alcinous, 'and the lyre, and dances, and changes of clothing, and our warm baths and beds' (8.248–9).

Alcinous lives in a rich and splendid palace, which has bronze walls, silver pillars and doors of gold, and is guarded by gold and silver dogs fashioned by Hephaestus. Outside is a magical garden (7.114–21):

Here trees grow tall and abundant, pears
and pomegranates, trees shining with apples,
and sweet fig trees and flourishing olives.
And the fruit on these never dies or fails,
winter and summer, all the year round,
but always the breath of the west wind
makes some fruit grow, and ripens others.
Pear matures on pear, and apple on apple,
grape too upon grape, and fig upon fig ...

Scheria is for Odysseus a place of transition, which helps him to travel away from the mysterious world of nymphs and monsters, and back to the real world of home and family. He is carried back to Ithaca in one of the Phaeacians' miraculous ships, bringing to pass an earlier prophecy that their giving such help to strangers would one day earn them POSEIDON's wrath. The god is indeed angry that they have helped Odysseus, so when their ship returns to Scheria he turns it to stone and roots it to the bottom of the sea. No more will the hospitable Phaeacians escort travellers to their hoped-for destinations. Odysseus is their last passenger, and the Phaeacians now disappear for ever from the sight of men.

Schoeneus *see* ATALANTA.

Sciron

One of the many brigands dispatched by the young THESEUS on his journey from Troezen to Athens (figs. 130 and 140). Sciron, the son of either POSEIDON or PELOPS, haunted the Scironian Rocks on the coastal road of the Isthmus of Corinth, preying on passing travellers. He ordered them to wash his feet, then as they stooped to do so he kicked them into the sea below, where they were eaten by a giant turtle. When he tried his trick on Theseus he suffered the same fate as his victims, for Theseus caught him by the feet and flung him into the sea. The Megarians alone disagreed with this story, asserting that Sciron was a thoroughly respectable man, the foe of robbers and the friend of the virtuous, and connected by marriage to people of the highest quality. Their efforts to whitewash the villain met with little success.

Fraser (*Apollodorus: The Library*, vol. 2, p.130) describes the scene before its dangers were eliminated in the nineteenth century by the construction of a road and a railway: 'The Scironian Rocks are a line of lofty cliffs rising sheer from the sea; a narrow, crumbling ledge about half way up their face afforded a perilous foothold, from which the adventurous traveller looked down with horror on the foam of the breakers far below.'

Fig.130 Theseus, wearing a traveller's hat, flings the brigand Sciron to his death in the sea where a turtle waits to devour him.

[Apollodorus, *Epitome* 1.2–3; Diodorus Siculus 4.59.4; Plutarch, *Theseus* 10, 25; Pausanias 1.3.1, 1.39.6, 1.44.8; Ovid, *Metamorphoses* 7.443–7.]

Scorpio (The Scorpion)

A constellation representing the huge scorpion that killed the great hunter ORION. It was sent either by Gaia, angry at his boast that he would kill every animal on earth, or by Artemis, because he had tried to rape her. Both the scorpion and Orion were turned into constellations, so now the scorpion pursues Orion eternally through the night sky. When the scorpion rises, Orion sets.

Scylla (1)

A sea-monster who preyed on sailors passing through a narrow sea-channel traditionally thought to be the Straits of Messina, separating Italy from Sicily. Her lair was in a cave, half-way up a sheer cliff. In the sea on the opposite side of the strait was the giant whirlpool CHARYBDIS. In the *Odyssey*, the enchantress CIRCE forewarns ODYSSEUS of the perils facing him on his journey home to Ithaca: these will include a choice between the two evils of Scylla and Charybdis. She describes the horrors that lie in wait for him on Scylla's side of the strait (12.86–100):

Her voice is no more than a new-born puppy's,

but she herself is an evil monster. No one,
not even a god, could encounter her and be glad
at the sight. She has twelve feet, all waving in the air,
and six long necks with a frightful head on each,
all with three rows of teeth, packed close together
and full of black death. Her lower body is sunk
in a hollow cave, but she holds her heads outside
the terrible pit, and there she fishes, eagerly
peering round from her lookout, for dolphins
or dogfish to catch, or any bigger sea-monster,
so many of which live in the loud-moaning sea.
Never can sailors boast they have passed unharmed
in their ship, for with each of her heads she snatches
one man away from the dark-prowed vessel.

Despite this horrific danger, Scylla will be the lesser of the two evils, even though Odysseus may lose some of his crew to her, since to meet with Charybdis will mean certain destruction for the whole ship's company. His best plan will be to sail through the strait as fast as possible, invoking Scylla's mother Crataeis, who will stop her daughter from making more than one sally against them.

Despite Circe's advice, Odysseus plans to fight Scylla off if he can, so while he and his men sail through the strait he stands at the prow, fully armed, gazing up at the high sheer cliff until his eyes grow weary of watching. The ship comes near to Charybdis, and while all on board stare in terrified fascination at the great whirlpool, Scylla acts. Her six heads swoop down and she seizes six of Odysseus' men. Too late, he turns to look (12.248–59):

I saw their feet and their hands from below, already
lifted high above me, and they cried aloud to me,
calling me by name, the last time they ever did so,
in the sorrow of their hearts. As a fisherman on a rock,
using a very long rod, casts down food
as bait for the little fishes ... then hauls them up
and throws them out on land, gasping and struggling,
so they gasped and struggled as they were hauled
up the high cliff, and there at her door she ate them
as they screamed and stretched out their hands to me
in their terrible death throes. And this indeed
was the most pitiful thing my eyes ever looked upon
in all my sufferings sailing the cruel sea.

Later authors said that Scylla had originally been a beautiful nymph, the daughter of (most commonly) PHORCYS and Crataeis, said to be another name for HECATE. Being beautiful, Scylla was pursued by many suitors, all of whom she rejected. Finally the sea-god GLAUCUS (1) fell in love with her. He too was spurned, so he went to Circe for a love-potion. But Circe fell in love with him herself, and when he repulsed her, the jealous enchantress poisoned the water of the pool in which Scylla habitually bathed. When next Scylla slipped into the water, six ferocious dogs grew in place of her lower limbs, becoming the terrifying heads which thereafter preyed on her victims. In later times she was changed into a rock, and as such is still a terror to sailors.

The proverbial expression 'between Scylla and Charybdis' describes a situation with two equally hazardous alternatives.

[Homer, *Odyssey* 12.73–126, 222–59, 426–46; Apollonius, *Argonautica* 4.825–31; Apollodorus, *Epitome* 7.20–23; Virgil, *Aeneid* 3.420–32, 555–67; Ovid, *Metamorphoses* 13.730–14.74.]

Scylla (2) *see* NISUS (1).

Scythes

The hero who gave his name to the Scythians. According to Herodotus (4.8–10), when HERACLES was driving the cattle of Geryon back to Eurystheus at Mycenae, he somehow wandered to the land north of the Black Sea. Here he slept, and when he woke he found that his chariot-horses had mysteriously disappeared. He hunted for them all over the countryside until at last he came to a forest. In the forest he found a cave, and in the cave a woman who was a snake from the waist downwards. She was the queen of the land, and freely admitted to stealing Heracles' horses, but said that she would return them only if he made love to her. He did so, but still she kept him with her until he had given her three sons: only then did she give him back his horses. As he was leaving she asked what she should do with her sons when they grew up, and he gave her a bow and a belt, saying that her successor should be the son who could draw the bow and put on the belt in the way he showed her. If any of them failed, they would have to be exiled. When the three boys reached manhood, only the youngest, Scythes, was able to draw the bow and put on the belt, so he became king and gave his name to his people. The other two sons, Agathyrsus and Gelonus, were exiled and gave their names to two other powerful tribes.

Scythians *see* SCYTHES.

Selemnus

A river near Patrae in Achaea. Selemnus had once been a handsome shepherd-boy, loved by the sea-nymph Argyra. After a while the nymph tired of him, and Selemnus, deserted by his beloved, died of heartbreak. APHRODITE took pity on him and turned him into a river. But even as a river he still mourned for his lost love, so the goddess bestowed on him a further gift, forgetfulness.

The traveller Pausanias, who tells the story (7.23.1–3), reports that the river-water was used as a remedy for those hopelessly in love, for it was said that anyone who washed in it would forget their passion. 'If there is any truth in the story', he adds pithily, 'then the water of the Selemnus is of more value to mankind than great wealth.'

Selene

The Moon, and the goddess of the Moon, known to the Romans as Luna. She was the daughter of the Titan HYPERION and Theia, and sister of HELIOS, the Sun-god, and EOS, goddess of Dawn. Like her siblings, she was thought to drive a chariot through the sky to light the world, as the *Homeric Hymn* in her honour describes:

> From her immortal head a radiance from heaven
> embraces the earth, and great is the beauty that comes
> from her shining light. The dark air grows bright
> from her golden crown, and her rays fill the sky,
> when her fair skin is fresh from the waters of Ocean,
> and divine Selene dons her far-shining raiment,
> and yokes her lustrous horses, with their arching necks
> and glorious manes, and drives forward her team
> full speed, at eventime in the middle of the month,
> when her great orbit is full and her light is brightest.

This same hymn goes on to say that she bore Pandeia to ZEUS. Another lover was PAN, who won her favours with the gift of a fine fleece. But her best-known myth connects her with ENDYMION. She fell in love with his great beauty, and visited him every night in his eternal sleep.

When ARTEMIS (Diana) later came to be identified with the moon, Selene tended to recede into the background, but she is depicted in ancient and postclassical art in her moon-chariot. She appeared with her horses on the east pediment of the Parthenon, and the magnificent head of one of them is among the Elgin marbles in London's British Museum.

[Hesiod, *Theogony* 371–4; *Homeric Hymn to Hermes* 100; Pausanias 5.11.8; Virgil, *Georgics* 3.391–3.]

Semele

Daughter of CADMUS and HARMONIA, and mother by ZEUS of the god DIONYSUS. When HERA learnt that Semele was pregnant, she resolved to destroy her rival. She went to the girl disguised as her old nurse, Beroe, and sowed doubt in her mind as to whether her lover really was Zeus. She advised Semele to settle the question by asking him to appear to her in all his godlike glory, just as he appeared to Hera herself on Olympus. The credulous Semele did exactly this, and since Zeus had agreed to grant whatever boon she demanded, he had no choice but to carry out his promise. He came to her as the great storm-god, lord of the lightning, and she was burnt to ashes. But as she died, he snatched the unborn child from her womb and stitched him into a gash cut in his own thigh. Here Dionysus grew until he could be born full-term.

After Semele's death, her sisters AGAVE, INO and AUTONOE refused to believe that Zeus had been her lover, saying that she must have been made pregnant by some man, and that her painful fate was Zeus' punishment for her presumptuous lie. Their scepticism would in the course of time be severely punished (*see* PENTHEUS). Semele's tomb at Thebes continued to smoulder for years, and she herself was made immortal, fetched by Dionysus from Hades and taken to Olympus (fig. 131), where she was renamed Thyone.

Semele was occasionally depicted in ancient art, and Aeschylus wrote a now lost tragedy, *Semele*. It is possible that in early versions of the myth Zeus had a rival for Semele's love in her own nephew (*see* ACTAEON). Semele's story was popular in the postclassical arts, and she was painted by Tintoretto and Rubens, among others, and was the subject of several operas and music dramas, including a secular oratorio by Handel.

[Homer, *Iliad* 14.323–5; Hesiod, *Theogony* 940–2, 975–8; Pindar, *Olympian* 2.25–7, *Pythian* 11.1; Herodotus 2.146; Euripides, *Bacchae* 1–12, 24–31, 242–5, 286–97; Apollodorus 3.4.2–3, 3.5.3; Diodorus Siculus 3.64.3–4, 4.2.1–3, 4.25.4, 5.52.2; Lucian, *Dialogues of the Gods* 12; Pausanias 2.31.2, 3.19.3, 3.24.3, 9.2.3; Ovid, *Metamorphoses* 3.259–313.]

Serpent *see* DRACO.

Seven against Thebes

The heroes of one of the great expeditions of ancient mythology, when an army from Argos marched against

Thebes in an attempt to restore the throne to the exiled POLYNEICES, son of Oedipus. The attempt failed disastrously.

It all began when ADRASTUS (1), king of Argos, married two of his daughters to men exiled from their home-lands. Argeia married Polyneices, driven from Thebes because of a quarrel over the kingship with his brother Eteocles. Deipyle married Oeneus' son TYDEUS, banished from Calydon for murder. Adrastus agreed to help his new sons-in-law to recover their lost kingdoms. The first expedition would be against Thebes.

Adrastus mustered a large army of seven champions and their followers. There is no fixed canonical list of the Seven, and we are told by Pausanias (2.20.3) that originally there were more, and that it was Aeschylus who reduced the number to only seven warriors, one to fight at each of the seven gates of Thebes, though under the leadership of an eighth, Adrastus. Apollodorus (3.6.3) gives us a list of the nine champions who appeared in the varying sources, most being related by blood or marriage to Adrastus himself: his sons-in law Polyneices and Tydeus, his brother MECISTEUS, his brother-in-law AMPHIARAUS, his brother (or nephew) HIPPOMEDON, his nephew CAPANEUS, Capaneus' brother-in-law ETEOCLUS, and PARTHENOPAEUS, who was in early epic Adrastus' brother, and later an Arcadian chieftain, son of the huntress Atalanta.

All willingly joined Adrastus' force except for Amphiaraus: he was the greatest seer of his day, and could foretell that the expedition was doomed to failure and its leaders, all but Adrastus, to death. Not unnaturally he refused to join and tried to discourage the others. Old IPHIS (1), Eteoclus' father, now advised Polyneices that the situation could be resolved if he bribed ERIPHYLE, Amphiaraus' wife and Adrastus' sister, into supporting the campaign. Once, in a quarrel long before, Amphiaraus had agreed that any dispute he had with Adrastus should be settled by Eriphyle, so now Polyneices offered her, in return for her help, the beautiful necklace given by the gods to his ancestress Harmonia. Eriphyle took the necklace and forced her husband to join the expedition.

The army set out for Thebes, stopping at Nemea for water. Here they encountered HYPSIPYLE, formerly queen of Lemnos but now enslaved to the local king, Lycurgus, as the nurse of his baby son Opheltes. She showed them the way to a spring, meanwhile leaving the baby lying on a bed of parsley. They returned to find the child dead, bitten by a snake that had coiled itself around his little

Fig. 131 Dionysus takes his mother, Semele, to immortality among the gods on Olympus.

body. Amphiaraus interpreted this as an omen pointing to the failure of their expedition, so they killed the snake and buried the child under the name of *Archemoros*, 'Beginner of Doom'. They then held the first Nemean Games in his honour, at which Adrastus won the horse race, Eteoclus the footrace, Tydeus the boxing match, Amphiaraus the jumping and the discus throwing, Laodocus the javelin throwing, Polyneices the wrestling match, and Parthenopaeus the archery contest.

Despite this portent of disaster, the army continued on its way. When they drew near Thebes, they sent Tydeus ahead to demand that Eteocles surrender the throne to Polyneices. Tydeus delivered the message, then gave the Thebans a foretaste of his prowess by challenging all comers to single combat and defeating them. Despite this demonstration, Eteocles refused to pay any heed to Tydeus' demands and even sent out fifty armed men to ambush him as he left the city. He killed them all apart from MAEON, the son of Haemon. The Argive army now moved in against Thebes. Adrastus assigned one of his champions to attack each of the city's seven gates, and Eteocles stationed his best men to defend them. He also asked the blind prophet TEIRESIAS how best to overcome the enemy, and was told that Thebes would be saved if MENOECEUS (2), the unmarried son of Eteocles' uncle, CREON (2), were to offer himself freely as a sacrifice to the War-god Ares. Menoeceus willingly did so and the Thebans went confidently into battle.

They were right to be confident. Although accounts of the battle positions vary and the order of events during the fighting is confused, the outcome was never in question: the attackers were decisively routed. Some died in single combat. Capaneus, scaling the walls on a long ladder, boasted that not even the lightning of Zeus could stop him taking the city, but as he crested the wall a thunderbolt blasted him to his death. Parthenopaeus was crushed by a huge stone hurled down from the battlements by Periclymenus. Tydeus, a favourite of Athena, killed Melanippus, but had himself been mortally wounded by his foe. Athena approached Tydeus as he lay dying, meaning to make him immortal, but Amphiaraus divined her intention and intervened. He still bore a grudge against Tydeus for helping to initiate the expedition, so he now cut off Melanippus' head and gave it to the dying man, who savagely split open the head and began to gulp down his enemy's brains. Athena in disgust kept back her gift of immortality as Tydeus died a mortal's death. Amphiaraus met a unique end as he was fleeing in his chariot. Periclymenus was about to hurl a spear into the seer's back when Zeus split open the earth ahead of him with a thunderbolt, and Amphiaraus was swallowed up,

chariot, charioteer, horses and all. Finally the entire purpose of the expedition was brought to nothing when Polyneices and Eteocles met in single combat, and each fell dead on the other's sword. As Amphiaraus had foretold, Adrastus alone of all the champions survived, carried from the battlefield by his divine horse AREION.

With Eteocles dead, the rule of Thebes fell to Creon, who now, contrary to custom, refused to let Adrastus and the surviving Argives bury their dead. The reaction of Polyneices' sister ANTIGONE (1) to this command is the subject of Sophocles' famous tragedy *Antigone*, where she tries to give last rites to her brother and dies for her deed, as does Creon's son Haemon, who loves her, and Creon's wife Eurydice, out of grief for Haemon. In Euripides' *Suppliant Women*, THESEUS, king of Athens, in response to the supplications of Adrastus and the widows and children of the dead champions, leads an Athenian army against the Thebans and forces them to give up the corpses of the enemy dead. The bodies are brought back to Eleusis for burning and burial, and in a daring *coup de théâtre* Euripides has EVADNE (2), the wife of Capaneus, fling herself into the flames of her husband's funeral pyre.

Ten years after the attack by the Seven, the sons of the dead champions, the EPIGONI, made a second and successful expedition against Thebes to avenge their fathers' deaths.

[Homer, *Iliad* 4.376–410, 5.801–8, 10.285–90; Hesiod, *Works and Days* 161–3; Epic Cycle, *Thebaid* (lost but for a few fragments); Pindar, *Olympian* 6.12–17, *Nemean* 9.8–27, 10.7–9; Aeschylus, *Seven Against Thebes*; Sophocles, *Antigone* 100–54, *Oedipus at Colonus* 1291–1325; Euripides, *Phoenician Women*; Apollodorus 3.6–7; Plutarch, *Theseus* 29; Diodorus Siculus 4.65; Pausanias 1.39.2, 5.19.6, 8.25.4, 8.25.8, 9.5.10–14, 9.8.3–9.9.5, 9.25.2, 10.10.3; Statius, *Thebaid*.]

Sibyl or Sibylla

An inspired prophetess. She seems at first to have been a single prophetic woman, but in later times many places claimed to have their Sibyl and the term became generic. According to Pausanias, the most ancient Sibyl known was Herophile, who was born before the Trojan War since she prophesied that Helen of Sparta would bring destruction on the Troad. The most famous Sibyl was the Sibyl of Cumae in Campania, who told AENEAS how to pluck the talismanic Golden Bough that would give him entrance to the Underworld, then accompanied him on his fearsome journey. Tradition has it that she offered nine books of oracular utterances to the Roman king Tarquinius Superbus, asking a huge price for their purchase. When he refused, she burnt three books and offered him the remainder for the same sum. Again he refused, so she burnt three more, and finally sold the last three to him for the price that she had asked for the full nine. These books were identified with collections of oracles that in historical times were carefully preserved in the Roman temple of Capitoline Jupiter, to be consulted in national emergencies. They were burnt in a temple fire in 83 BC.

The Sibyl of Cumae had once been loved by APOLLO, who promised her any gift she might choose if she would take him as a lover. She asked for as many years of life as there were grains of dust in a pile of floor-sweepings, which numbered a thousand, but she forgot to ask for perpetual youth, and as the centuries passed she slowly shrivelled up (compare TITHONUS). Petronius' Trimalchio saw her in her cave at Cumae, hanging in a bottle, and when some children asked her what she wanted, she replied, 'I want to die.' In the second century AD, Pausanias saw on his travels a stone jar at Cumae said to contain her bones.

[Dionysius of Halicarnassus 4.62, 6.17; Pausanias 10.12; Virgil, *Aeneid* 6; Ovid, *Metamorphoses* 14.101–53; Petronius, *Satyrica* 48. H. W. Parke, *Sibyls and Sibylline Prophecy* (1989).]

Sicharbas *see* DIDO.

Side

Wife of the giant hunter ORION, and a woman so lovely that she claimed to rival HERA, queen of heaven, in beauty. Hera punished this rash arrogance by casting Side into Hades.

Sidero *see* TYRO.

Silens *see* SATYRS AND SILENS.

Silenus

The oldest and wisest and most drunken of the revel-rout of SATYRS accompanying DIONYSUS, and said to have been the young god's tutor. 'A drunken old man', says Ovid (*Metamorphoses* 4.26–7) 'who supports his tottering limbs with a staff, or clings unsteadily to his hump-backed donkey'. But intoxication inspired Silenus' wine-hazed mind with special knowledge and powers of prophecy. The Phrygian king MIDAS sought to share his wisdom, so he caught the old man by lacing the fountain at which he drank with wine. Silenus fell asleep after drinking, and the king's servants seized him and took him to their master (fig. 92). The philosophy which the satyr shared with Midas was pessimistic: that the best thing for man is not to be born at all, and the second best thing is to die as soon as possible. Virgil tells how Silenus was also captured by two shepherds, and regaled them with wondrous tales.

Silenus was the father, by a Melian nymph, of the Centaur PHOLUS. He himself was snub-nosed, thick-lipped, pot-bellied and bald, and Socrates was often compared to him, both for his ugliness and for his god-given wisdom. The old Satyr appears in most postclassical paintings of Bacchic revels, often shown slumped drunkenly on his donkey as in Ovid's description.

[Apollodorus 2.5.4; Pausanias 3.25.2–3; Virgil, *Eclogues* 6; Ovid, *Metamorphoses* 11.89–105; Cicero, *Tusculan Disputations* 1.48.114.]

Silvanus

A Roman god of the woods (*silvae*) and fields, and worshipped by shepherds as god of flocks. He was sometimes identified with the Greek god PAN, though he lacked Pan's wildness and was usually portrayed as a benign old man.

Silvius *see* LAVINIA.

Simoeis

A river of the Trojan plain, and its god, and like all river-gods the son of OCEANUS and Tethys. Simoeis had two daughters who married into the Trojan royal family: Astyoche became the wife of ERICHTHONIUS (2), and Hieromneme the wife of ASSARACUS. Thus when the gods took sides in the Trojan War, Simoeis supported the Trojans. In the *Iliad*, his brother-river SCAMANDER calls to him for help in his great battle with ACHILLES (21.311–15):

> Come to my aid with all speed, fill your streams
> with water from your springs, stir up all your torrents,
> stand high in a great wave, and rouse a mighty roar
> of timbers and rocks, so we stop this savage man
> who in his strength is raging like the gods.

But before Simoeis can respond, Hephaestus comes down from Olympus to save Achilles, subduing Scamander with flame.

In the *Aeneid*, Aeneas thinks of Troy as the place 'where fierce Hector lies, dead by Achilles' sword, where great Sarpedon lies, where Simoeis caught up so many shields and helmets and bodies of brave men, and rolled them down in his current' (1.99–101).

[Hesiod, *Theogony* 342; Apollodorus 3.12.2.]

Sinis

One of the many brigands killed by the young THESEUS on his journey from Troezen to Athens (fig. 140). Sinis, the son of either POSEIDON or Polypemon, haunted the Isthmus of Corinth and took advantage of his prodigious strength to prey on travellers. He was called the 'Pine-bender' because of the way in which he dispatched his victims. Either he bent down two pine trees and tied a man's arms to one tree, his legs to another, then let the trees spring up again so that they tore his victim in two. Or he forced a man to help him bend a pine tree to the ground, then released it so that his victim was catapulted high into the air and tumbled down again to his death. Theseus overcame Sinis and dealt him the fate that he had so often inflicted on others.

Sinis had a beautiful daughter called Perigune. When her father was killed, she ran away and hid in a bed of rushes and wild asparagus, vowing never to destroy such plants if they would only hide her now. But she emerged of her own accord once Theseus had promised to do her no harm. He took her to his bed and she bore him a son, MELANIPPUS (3). Afterwards Theseus married her to Deioneus, the son of Eurytus of Oechalia. Melanippus had a son, Ioxus, whose descendants, even though living far away in Caria, revered and honoured such plants as had once sheltered their ancestress.

[Bacchylides, *Ode* 18.19–22; Apollodorus 3.16.2; Diodorus Siculus 4.59.3; Plutarch, *Theseus* 8, 25; Pausanias 2.1.4; Ovid, *Metamorphoses* 7.440–2.]

Sinon

The Greek who persuaded the Trojans that the WOODEN HORSE would bring prosperity to Troy, when in fact it brought only death and destruction. The Greeks set fire to their camp and pretended to sail home, leaving behind them only the horse, its hollow belly filled with armed warriors, and Sinon. He allowed himself to be captured by the Trojans, then won their confidence by pretending to be a Greek deserter. He said that he had spoken out against Odysseus' treacherous murder of PALAMEDES, and that for this reason Odysseus hated him and had plotted with the prophet Calchas to destroy him. The seer had interpreted a supposed oracle from Apollo to mean that Sinon must be sacrificed to the gods for the Greeks to have a favourable return home, and he had only just escaped death. The Trojans, hearing this, believed that Sinon hated the Greeks as much as they did. He then went on to explain the purpose of the Wooden Horse: that it was an offering to ATHENA, built by the Greeks to appease her after they had stolen the PALLADIUM. They had deliberately made it too large to go through the gates

of Troy, because once inside it would gain for the city the goddess' protection. The Trojans were completely taken in. They let Sinon go, then breached their walls and dragged the horse into Troy. When night fell, Sinon let the warriors out of the horse, then signalled to the Greek fleet lying off Tenedos by raising a beacon-light on the grave of Achilles near the shore. This guided the ships as they landed in the dark. The Greeks massacred the sleeping, defenceless Trojans, and the city was finally theirs after a ten-year war.

[Apollodorus, *Epitome* 5.14–21; Virgil, *Aeneid* 2.57–198.]

Sinope

A daughter of the river-god ASOPUS. ZEUS pursued her, and to win her love he promised to give her whatever her heart desired. She cunningly asked that he allow her to remain a virgin, and the great god was forced to abide by his promise. He settled her on the shores of the Black Sea, where the city Sinope was named in her honour. She remained a virgin all her life, tricking APOLLO and the river-god Halys in the same way that she tricked Zeus (although another tradition says that she had a son by Apollo, Syrus, after whom the Syrians were named).

[Apollonius, *Argonautica* 2.946–54; Diodorus Siculus 4.72.2.]

Sirens

Singing enchantresses who lured men to their doom. In the *Odyssey*, CIRCE warns ODYSSEUS of the dangers they will offer him (12.39–46):

> First you will reach the Sirens who enchant all men,
> whoever comes their way. Anyone coming near,
> not knowing, and hearing the Sirens singing, never

Fig.132 Odysseus, tied to the mast of his ship, listens entranced to the Sirens' song, while his crew, their ears plugged with wax, row safely past. Because a mortal has heard their song, and lived, the Sirens now must die, and already one of the three plummets to her death.

will he go home to his wife and little children,
never will they delight in his return, but the Sirens
enchant him with the sweetness of their singing,
sitting in their meadow, with all around them
a great heap of bones from men rotting away
whose skins wither upon them ...

Circe advises Odysseus to stop the ears of his men with
beeswax, and to get them to bind him tightly to the
mast, forbidding them to release him, however much he
begs, until all danger is past. In this way Odysseus, alone
of all men, will have the joy of the Sirens' song, yet live.
He does so, and when he hears them singing their magical songs he does indeed wish to be released. But his
men merely tie him the tighter, and only when they have
gone far beyond the Sirens do they loose his bonds. Later
writers said that the Sirens were fated to die if anyone
successfully resisted their singing, so after Odysseus
heard them and passed by unharmed, they hurled themselves despairingly into the sea and were drowned.

Homer does not describe the Sirens, and there is nothing to suggest that for him they were anything other
than human. In later writers, however, they become bird-
women, with the faces and voices of women above feath-
ered, winged bodies, and this is how they appear in
vase-paintings (fig.132). In Homer there are two of them,
but most later writers speak of three, sometimes four.
Apollodorus says that one of them sang, while the other
two accompanied the singer on lyre and pipes. These
instruments are depicted in some of the vase-paintings.
The Sirens were usually said to be the daughters of the
River ACHELOUS by one of the MUSES, Melpomene or Terpsichore (small wonder that they knew how to beguile
men with their singing). They lived on an island called
Anthemoessa ('flowery'), traditionally located off the
west coast of Italy and not far from the straits where
SCYLLA (1) and CHARYBDIS lurked. The Sirens' name came
to be applied to any dangerous, alluring woman.

Although the Sirens' encounter with Odysseus is their
best-known story, they figure in other myths too. When
the ARGONAUTS sailed past Anthemoessa, ORPHEUS
drowned out their singing with the sound of his lyre, and
all were safe from the Sirens' spell except one, BUTES (3).
He heard their seductive song and plunged into the sea
to swim to them, but was saved by Aphrodite. According
to Ovid, the Sirens were not always half-bird, but had
once been the human companions of PERSEPHONE. When
she was abducted by Hades, they sought her in vain the
world over, then prayed to the gods for wings that they
might fly over the sea as well. The gods consented and
the Sirens' limbs became covered with golden plumage.
Others say that their transformation was a punishment

inflicted on them by DEMETER for allowing Hades to carry
off her daughter. Pausanias (9.34.3) says that HERA once
persuaded the Sirens to compete with the Muses in
singing, but the Muses won, and plucked out the Sirens'
feathers to make crowns for themselves.

[Homer, *Odyssey* 12.39–54, 158–200; Apollonius, *Argonautica*
4.891–921; Apollodorus 1.3.4, 1.7.10, 1.9.25, *Epitome*
7.18–19; Ovid, *Metamorphoses* 5.552–63.]

Siris *see* MELANIPPE (2).

Sirius

The Dog Star. *See* CANIS MAJOR.

Sisyphus

One of the four great sinners (along with IXION, TANTALUS
(1) and TITYUS) who after death endured eternal punishment for their transgressions on earth. Sisyphus was a
son of the powerful Thessalian king AEOLUS (1) and his
wife Enarete, and was himself the founder of the city of
Ephyra, later renamed Corinth. He was a great trickster,
famous for his cunning and ingenuity. When the master
thief AUTOLYCUS began to increase his herds by stealing
Sisyphus' cattle, Sisyphus suspected what was happening
and soon put a stop to it: he attached to his animals'
hooves lead tablets inscribed with the words 'stolen by
Autolycus', then followed their tracks. While visiting
Autolycus to reclaim his property, Sisyphus seduced his
daughter ANTICLEIA, with the result that he, rather than
her husband Laertes, was often said to be the father of the
wily ODYSSEUS.

Sisyphus married MEROPE (1), the daughter of Atlas,
and had four sons by her, including GLAUCUS (3), the
father of BELLEROPHON. At Corinth he instituted the Isthmian Games in honour of his dead nephew Melicertes,
whose body he found washed up on the shore (*see* INO).
He also fortified the high hill of the Acrocorinth as a
citadel, and acquired water for his city by doing a favour
for the river-god Asopus, whose daughter AEGINA had
been carried off by Zeus. Sisyphus had seen the abduction, and now promised to tell the girl's frantic father
what he knew, in return for a spring of fresh water. The
river-god at once granted him the spring of Peirene and
Sisyphus told him of Zeus' crime. Not surprisingly, Zeus
retaliated by sending THANATOS (Death) to take the informer
off to the Underworld, but Sisyphus was a match even for
Death. He tricked Thanatos and tied him up, so that for
a while no one at all could die. The gods were displeased
by this, and at last sent ARES to deal with the situation.
Ares released Thanatos and handed Sisyphus over to him
to meet his death. But the great trickster still had the
matter in hand, for before dying he had instructed his

wife Merope on no account to perform the customary funeral rites. This so affronted HADES (1) that he sent Sisyphus back to earth to reproach his wife and make the proper arrangements. Sisyphus, of course, did no such thing, but stayed happily on earth and lived to a ripe old age.

When he finally reached the Underworld at the end of his natural life, he was set an eternal punishment of perpetually rolling a great stone to the top of a hill, only to have it roll down again (and so a 'sisyphean task' is one demanding endless and frustrating labour). In Homer's *Odyssey*, Odysseus recounts what he saw when he visited Hades (11.593–600):

> I saw Sisyphus, suffering pains hard to bear.
> With both arms embracing a gigantic stone,
> pushing with hands and feet, he would thrust
> the stone to the top of a hill, but when it was about
> to go over the top, a mighty force turned it round,
> and the pitiless stone rolled back to the ground below.
> He strained once more to push it, and the sweat
> ran from his limbs, and dust rose from his head.

This punishment was given to Sisyphus for tale-telling on Zeus and for cheating Death; but perhaps most of all, simply as an endless task to keep the great trickster at last where he belonged.

Albert Camus, in his *Le mythe de Sisyphe: Essai sur l'absurde*, takes Sisyphus' efforts as a symbol for the absurdity of this life and the futility of man's endeavours, though happiness can still be found in the recognition of our condition and in the struggle to rise above it. He ends: 'I leave Sisyphus at the foot of the mountain. One always finds one's burden again. But Sisyphus teaches the higher fidelity that negates the gods and raises rocks. He too concludes that all is well ... The struggle towards the heights is enough to fill a man's heart. One must imagine Sisyphus happy.'

[Homer, *Iliad* 6.152–5; Pindar, *Olympian* 13.52; Apollodorus 1.7.3, 1.9.3, 3.4.3, 3.10.1, 3.12.6; Pausanias 2.1.3, 2.3.11, 2.5.1, 9.34.7, 10.30.5.]

Sleep *see* HYPNOS.

Smyrna *see* MYRRHA.

Solymi

A warlike tribe, enemies of the Lycians, whom BELLEROPHON fought singlehanded as one of the three fearsome tasks he faced for the Lycian king Iobates. He defeated them triumphantly, but years later his son Isander was killed while fighting them.

[Homer, *Iliad* 6.183–4, 203–4; Herodotus 1.173.]

Somnus

The Roman equivalent of the Greek HYPNOS, the personification of sleep. The DREAMS were his thousand sons.

Sosipolis ('Saviour of the State')

A divine child, worshipped by the people of Elis. The Arcadians had invaded the land of Elis, and the Eleans were drawn up to fight them, when a woman brought a baby to the Elean officers. She said that she was the child's mother, but had been told in her dreams to give him up so that he could fight for Elis. The officers took the baby and laid him on the ground, naked, in front of their army. When the Arcadians advanced, the child turned into a snake and they fled in terror, hotly pursued by the Eleans who won a resounding victory. The snake disappeared into the ground, and on that spot the Eleans built a sanctuary to the child under the name of Sosipolis.

[Pausanias 6.20.2–5.]

Sown Men (*Spartoi*)

Men born from dragon's teeth sown in the earth. When CADMUS killed the dragon, sacred to Ares, at the site of the city which the Delphic Oracle had instructed him to found, he followed the advice of Athena and sowed some of the monster's teeth in the earth. At once armed warriors sprang up, and when Cadmus flung a stone among them they turned and fought each other. Five men survived: Echion ('Snake-man'), the father of PENTHEUS; Udaeus ('From the Ground'), an ancestor of the prophet TEIRESIAS; Chthonius ('From the Earth'), the father of NYCTEUS and LYCUS (1); Hyperenor ('Superman'); and Pelorus ('Giant'). They helped Cadmus to found his city of Thebes, and they themselves became the ancestors of the Theban nobility.

A second crop of Sown Men sprang from the rest of the dragon's teeth, which Athena gave to AEETES, king of Colchis. When Jason came with the ARGONAUTS in search of the Golden Fleece, Aeetes set him the task of sowing the dragon's teeth and killing all the armed men that sprang up from the earth. Once again a pitched battle ensued between the warriors, but this time, with Jason hacking away with his sword in their midst, no Sown Men survived.

Sparta *see* LACEDAEMON.

Spartoi *see* SOWN MEN.

Sphinx ('Throttler')

A female monster with the head of a woman, the body of a lion, and the wings of a bird. Her father was either the monster TYPHON or the two-headed hound of Geryon, ORTHUS, and her mother either the three-headed CHIMAERA

Fig. 133 **Oedipus, in traveller's garb, sits on a rock, pondering the Sphinx's riddle.**

or the monster ECHIDNA; she herself was the sister of the fearsome NEMEAN LION. The Sphinx was particularly associated with the Theban legends centred on the House of OEDIPUS. She preyed on the people of Thebes, sent, it was said, by one of the gods, most commonly by HERA because the Thebans had dishonoured her, as goddess of marriage, when they failed to punish LAIUS for his abduction of Chrysippus. The Sphinx sat on Mount Phikion outside Thebes and challenged the Thebans who passed by to answer her famous riddle, given her by the MUSES: 'There is on the earth a two-footed, four-footed, three-footed thing with a single name; and alone of all creatures that travel on land or in the air or sea, it changes its form. But when it goes on most feet, then the speed of its limbs is weakest.' She snatched up and devoured anyone who failed to give the correct answer.

An oracle declared that the Thebans would be rid of the Sphinx as soon as her riddle was solved, so many men tried to answer it, and many were killed. The last victim was Haemon, the son of CREON (2) who was then ruling Thebes after the murder of King Laius. Creon ordained in desperation that whoever could give the right answer to the riddle would win the rule of the kingdom and the hand of Laius' widow, JOCASTA, in marriage. It was then that Oedipus arrived in Thebes, having recently killed a man at a place where three roads met. (His victim was Laius the king, and his own father, though he did not know it.) Oedipus answered the riddle correctly (fig. 133): a man is four-footed, two-footed and three-footed, for he crawls on all fours in infancy, walks erect when grown, and with the aid of a stick as a third leg in old age. The defeated Sphinx hurled herself down from the citadel to her death. Oedipus was rewarded with the kingship of Thebes and the hand of the widowed queen, thus unwittingly marrying his own mother.

Seneca puts into the mouth of his Oedipus a stirring account of the confrontation with the Sphinx (*Oedipus* 91–102):

> I faced that abominable witch, though her jaws dripped blood and the ground beneath was white with scattered bones. As she sat on her high crag with outstretched wings, waiting to seize her prey and lashing her tail like a lion, savage in her wrath, I asked her riddle. A terrible sound rang out from above and she snapped her jaws, tearing at the rocks, impatient to claw out my living heart, then spoke her cryptic words and set the baited trap. But the grim riddle of the monstrous bird I solved.

Sphinxes appear in Minoan and Mycenean art, probably inspired by Egyptian and Near Eastern sphinxes. They become popular figures in Greek art from the archaic period onwards, particularly in monumental and funerary contexts, though the first example of Oedipus facing the Sphinx and answering her riddle appears only towards the end of the sixth century BC. They gradually lost their aura of malevolence and were envisaged as mysterious and enigmatic beings, depicted in postclassical art with beautiful women's faces and breasts. Ingres painted three versions of Oedipus facing the Sphinx, one of which is in London's National Gallery, where she has full breasts and an outstretched lion's paw. A modern contrast to the bloodthirsty Sphinx of the ancient world is W. B. Yeats' haunting image in *The Double Vision of Michael Robartes*:

> On the grey rock of Cashel I suddenly saw
> A Sphinx with woman breast and lion paw,
> A Buddha, hand at rest,
> Hand lifted up that blest ...
> One lashed her tail; her eyes lit by the moon
> Gazed upon all things known, all things unknown,
> In triumph of intellect
> With motionless head erect.

[Hesiod, *Theogony* 326–9; Sophocles, *Oedipus the King* 130–1, 391–8; Euripides, *Phoenician Women* 45–54, 806–11, 1019–42, 1505–7; Apollodorus 3.5.8; Diodorus Siculus 4.64.3–4; Pausanias 5.11.2, 9.26.2–4. E. Vermeule, *Aspects of Death in Early*

Staphylus (1)

Usually said to be the son of DIONYSUS and ARIADNE, though sometimes of Ariadne and THESEUS. (Since his name means 'bunch of grapes', the god of wine is the likelier father.) Staphylus was one of the ARGONAUTS. His daughter Rhoeo bore ANIUS to Apollo.

[Apollodorus 1.9.16, *Epitome* 1.9; Diodorus Siculus 5.62; Plutarch, *Theseus* 20.]

Staphylus (2)

A herdsman in the service of OENEUS, king of the Aetolians of Calydon. Every day Staphylus took his flocks out to pasture, and one day noticed that one of his goats had taken to returning later than the others, and in a very frolicsome mood. On following it, he found it enjoying grapes from a vine, a fruit that he did not recognise. He picked some grapes for Oeneus, who squeezed the juice from them and made the first wine, which was then named after him (*oinos*).

Stentor

A Greek herald with a powerful voice who became proverbial after Homer described him as 'great-hearted Stentor of the brazen voice, who could shout as loud as fifty other men' (*Iliad* 5.785–6). The scholia tell us that he was killed for his presumption in claiming that he could shout as mightily as HERMES, the herald of the gods. His name has survived in 'stentorian', meaning 'uncommonly loud'.

Sterope (1)

Daughter of the Titan ATLAS and Pleione, and thus one of the seven PLEIADES. To ARES she bore OENOMAUS, who became the king of Pisa in Elis, though she was sometimes said to be Oenomaus' wife rather than his mother. Hesiod calls her Asterope.

[Hesiod, *Catalogue of Women*, fr. 169; Apollodorus 3.10.1; Pausanias 5.10.6.]

Sterope (2) *see* CEPHEUS (2).

Sterope (3)

Daughter of ACASTUS, king of Iolcus (*see* PELEUS).

Steropes *see* CYCLOPES.

Stheneboea *see* PROETUS.

Sthenelus (1)

Son of PERSEUS, king of Mycenae, and Andromeda. He married Nicippe, the daughter of PELOPS, who bore him a son, EURYSTHEUS, and two daughters, Alcyone and Medusa. When Sthenelus' brother ELECTRYON, the king of Mycenae, was accidentally killed by Amphitryon, Sthenelus seized the throne of both Mycenae and Tiryns, and installed ATREUS and Thyestes, his wife's brothers, on the throne of Midea. At his death Sthenelus was succeeded by his son Eurystheus, who was famous for imposing the twelve LABOURS OF HERACLES. When Eurystheus died, Atreus and Thyestes vied for the throne of Mycenae, and with it the rule of all Argos, in one of the most famous feuds in all mythology.

[Homer, *Iliad* 19.114–25; Apollodorus 2.4.5–6.]

Sthenelus (2)

A companion of HERACLES on his expedition to fetch the belt of HIPPOLYTE (1), queen of the Amazons. Apollodorus (2.5.9) says that Sthenelus and his brother Alcaeus, the sons of ANDROGEOS, were living on the island of Paros when Heracles put in there on his way to the land of the Amazons. Two of his men were killed by the inhabitants, so in their place he took Sthenelus and Alcaeus. At the end of his successful expedition, he subjugated the Thracians on the island of Thasos and gave it to the brothers as their kingdom.

Apollonius (*Argonautica* 2.911–29) makes Sthenelus a son of Actor, and says that he was killed on the way home from the Amazon campaign and buried at the mouth of the River Callichorus, on the Black Sea. When the ARGONAUTS were later sailing past his tomb, his ghost appeared to them, allowed back on earth for a short while by Persephone because he had begged to see his old companions once again. They beached the *Argo* and paid honour to Sthenelus with libations and sacrifices.

Sthenelus (3)

Son of CAPANEUS, one of the warriors killed in the expedition of the Seven against Thebes, and EVADNE (2), who died by flinging herself into her husband's funeral pyre. Sthenelus was a comrade of DIOMEDES (2) and accompanied him in the successful attack of the EPIGONI on Thebes. Then, as one of HELEN's suitors and bound by the common oath to protect the marriage-rights of her chosen husband, he went with his friend to the TROJAN WAR, taking eighty ships from Argos. There he acted as Diomedes' charioteer. We see him in action in Book Five of the *Iliad* where Diomedes performs feats of valour against the Trojans: Sthenelus supports his friend, driving him into the fighting and pulling the arrow from his shoulder when he is wounded by Pandarus, and on his instructions captures the splendid horses of Aeneas.

Sthenelus survived the war and was one of the warriors in the WOODEN HORSE, then returned to Argos with

Diomedes. They found that Sthenelus' son Cometes had, at the instigation of NAUPLIUS (1), seduced Diomedes' wife Aegialeia. Another son, Cylarabes, became king of the Argolid.

[Homer, *Iliad* 2.559–68, 4.367, 5.108–13, 241–50, 319–27, 835; Apollodorus 3.7.2–3, 3.10.8, *Epitome* 6.9; Pausanias 2.18.5, 2.22.8–9, 2.24.3, 2.30.10, 10.10.4; Quintus of Smyrna, *Sequel to Homer* 12.316.]

Stheno *see* GORGONS.

Strophius

Son of Crisus, and king of Crisa in Phocis. Through his wife Anaxibia he was the brother-in-law of AGAMEMNON. When Agamemnon was murdered, his young son ORESTES was sent for safety to Crisa, and Strophius brought him up along with his own son, PYLADES. The two boys became firm friends, and Pylades accompanied Orestes when he went back to Mycenae to avenge his father's death. Pylades' eldest son by ELECTRA (3) was also called Strophius.

[Aeschylus, *Agamemnon* 880–5; Euripides, *Iphigeneia among the Taurians* 915–21; Pausanias 2.16.7, 2.29.4.]

Strymo

Daughter of the river-god SCAMANDER, and wife of the Trojan king LAOMEDON.

Stymphalian Birds

HERACLES' sixth Labour for Eurystheus (*see* LABOURS OF HERACLES) was to get rid of the vast flocks of birds that infested the woods around Lake Stymphalus in Arcadia. Apollodorus (2.5.6) says that they had taken refuge there to avoid wolves, and that Heracles managed to flush them out by means of a bronze rattle, made by Hephaestus and given him by Athena. When the birds flew up in fright at the sound of the rattle, he shot them. Here they seem to be quite ordinary birds, which by their very numbers created a nuisance; but Pausanias (8.22.4) says that they were man-eating creatures with bronze beaks and as big as cranes.

The scene was not a popular one in ancient art. Apart from its occurrence in collective representations of the twelve Labours, almost all of the depictions left to us are from the sixth century BC. They show Heracles killing the birds with a variety of weapons – a stone and sling, a bow, even a club – and with no sign anywhere of a rattle (fig. 134).

[Apollonius, *Argonautica* 2.1052–7; Diodorus Siculus 4.13.2; Strabo 8.6.8; Quintus of Smyrna, *Sequel to Homer* 6.227–31.]

Stymphalus

A king of Arcadia, son of ELATUS (1) and grandson of ARCAS. The town of Stymphalus in north-eastern Arcadia was named after him, as was the lake of the same name, the home of the STYMPHALIAN BIRDS that provided HERACLES with his sixth Labour for Eurystheus (and it was said that Heracles had a son, Everes, by Stymphalus' daughter Parthenope). Stymphalus was treacherously murdered by PELOPS, king of Pisa in Elis, who was trying to gain control of the entire Peloponnese. Arcadia withstood him, so Pelops pretended friendship for Stymphalus, then killed him and scattered his mangled body over the land. This terrible deed brought the anger of Zeus and a prolonged drought on Greece, until the virtuous AEACUS prayed to the god for deliverance, and at last the rain came down.

[Apollodorus 2.7.8, 3.9.1, 3.12.6; Pausanias 8.4.6, 8.22.1–5.]

Styx ('Abhorrence')

The chief river of HADES (2) and its goddess, and like all rivers the offspring of OCEANUS and Tethys. Styx was married to the Titan PALLAS (2), and became mother of Zelus (Aspiration), NIKE (Victory), Cratos (Power) and BIA (Might). Because Styx and her children supported ZEUS in his war with the TITANS, Zeus honoured her by having her children accompany him always, and by decreeing that the most solemn oath the gods might swear would be by the waters of Styx. Whenever one of the gods needed to swear an oath, IRIS was sent with a golden jug to fetch some of Styx' icy water and the god would swear while making a libation. The oath was so strong and formidable that, if it were ever broken, the god would lie in a coma for a full year, and after that be cut off from the rest of the gods for another nine years. So severe were these penalties that we never hear of any broken oath, although we certainly hear of the gods swearing by Styx: in Homer, for instance, Hera swears by Styx to Hypnos and Zeus in the *Iliad* (14.271–80, 15.36–8), as does Calypso to Odysseus in the *Odyssey* (5.184–6).

The Styx was thought to be a branch of Oceanus, the great river that was imagined as completely surrounding the flat earth, with the Styx being only one ninth of the volume of its parent river. On leaving Oceanus, it dropped from a high, sheer cliff, then flowed down through the darkness beneath the earth (Hesiod, *Theogony* 786–92). At Nonacris in Arcadia there is a real-life Styx, so named at least as early as the sixth century BC, with waters cold from the snows that feed it and a waterfall as in Hesiod's description. Pausanias (8.17.6–18.6) records that its waters were instantly fatal, and that they broke or corroded all materials except the hooves of horses. There was even a rumour that Alexander the Great met his death by water from the Styx, sent to him in a mule's hoof. Conversely, there is a modern superstition that anyone who drinks

Fig.134 Heracles kills the Stymphalian Birds with a sling.

from the Arcadian Styx on the right day in the year may become immortal. This is akin to the ancient belief in the mythical Styx as an elixir of life, as in the late story of THETIS dipping Achilles into its waters, thus making him completely invulnerable except for the heel by which she held him.

[Hesiod, *Theogony* 361, 383–403, 775–806; Herodotus 6.74; Apollodorus 1.2.2–5; Plutarch, *Alexander* 77.]

Swan *see* CYGNUS.

Sychaeus *see* DIDO.

Syleus

A brigand killed by HERACLES during his period of servitude to OMPHALE, the Lydian queen. Syleus was in the habit of forcing passers-by to hoe his vineyard for him, but Heracles killed the outlaw with his own hoe when he tried to make him do the same. He then set fire to Syleus' vines and killed his daughter Xenodice, though a late story said that he became her lover, and when he went away she died of longing for him.

[Apollodorus 2.6.3; Diodorus Siculus 4.31.7.]

Symplegades

The 'Clashing Rocks' at the northern end of the Bosphorus, through which ships had to pass to enter the Black Sea; also called the Cyanean (Dark Blue) Rocks. They were not rooted in the sea-bed, so were constantly on the move, clashing together with tremendous force and crushing ships that tried to pass between them. The ARGONAUTS, as they journeyed to Colchis, were the first mortals ever to make the passage safely: as the rocks clashed together behind the *Argo*, just the tip of her stern-ornament was caught between them. After this the rocks posed no further dangers to man, for they were immovably locked together and rooted in one spot for ever.

On their way home from Colchis, the Argonauts passed through the Planctae, or 'Wandering Rocks'. These were located near to SCYLLA (1) and CHARYBDIS, who haunted the Straits of Messina separating Italy from Sicily. Once more the *Argo* made a safe passage, this time helped by Thetis and her sister-Nereids. The Planctae, despite their different location, were often conflated with the Symplegades and were thought to clash together in a similar manner. They are first mentioned in the *Odyssey* (12.59–72), when the enchantress CIRCE warns ODYSSEUS of the hazards that face him on his way home to Ithaca. Once again they are placed near the dangerous haunts of Scylla and Charybdis. Circe does not say that the rocks clash together, but speaks of terrible waves and storms of fire that destroy ships. Rather than brave these perils, Odysseus chooses to face Scylla and Charybdis and all the horrors that they entail.

[Pindar, *Pythian* 4.207–11; Herodotus 4.85; Euripides, *Medea* 1–2; Apollonius, *Argonautica* 2.317–40, 549–606, 4.926–64; Apollodorus 1.9.22.]

Syrinx

A nymph who lived in the mountains of Arcadia, spending her time in the chaste pursuit of hunting. Ovid (*Metamorphoses* 1.689–713) tells how she was desired by the pastoral god PAN, but she wished to keep her virginity, so she fled from him until she reached the River Ladon. Here she could go no further. Desperately she prayed to the river-nymphs to transform her, and just as Pan thought he had at last caught hold of her, he found that instead of the nymph's body he was holding a bunch of marsh reeds. He sighed with disappointment and the air blew through the reeds, producing a thin, haunting sound. Enchanted by so sweet a music, he cut the reeds into different lengths and joined them into the first set of panpipes, giving them the Greek name of *syrinx* after his lost love. Such panpipes are still played by shepherds.

Achilles Tatius (8.6) relates that near Ephesus there was a cave of Pan where the god put the very first syrinx, and this was used as a test for young girls who claimed that they were virgins. A girl would be shut inside the cave, and if she was indeed a virgin the pipes would sound melodiously, and the entrance to the cave would open of its own accord. If, however, she was not a virgin, the sound of a groan would be heard inside, and when the cave was opened on the third day, she would have disappeared.

Syrinx has been painted with Pan by many artists, including Rubens, Jordaens, Poussin, Giordano, Boucher and Fragonard; and her flight from Pan's pursuit is mimed in Ravel's ballet, *Daphnis et Chloé*. Elizabeth Barrett Browning used the myth, and the idea that poetic inspiration comes through possession by Pan's ecstatic powers, in her poem 'A Musical Instrument', beginning famously:

> What was he doing, the great god Pan,
>> Down in the reeds by the river?

He was of course making his pipes, cutting, and shaping, and blowing:

> Sweet, sweet, sweet, O Pan!
>> Piercing sweet by the river!
> Blinding sweet, O great god Pan!
>> The sun on the hill forgot to die,
>> And the lilies revived, and the dragon-fly
>> Came back to dream on the river.

He was also, half-beast that he was, 'making a poet out of a man', while:

> The true gods sigh for the cost and the pain –
> For the reed which grows nevermore again
>> As a reed with the reeds in the river.

Syrus, Syrians *see* SINOPE.

T

Talaus

Son of Bias and PERO (*see* MELAMPUS), who succeeded to his father's kingdom in the Argolid. He was one of the ARGONAUTS, but is most famous as the father of several children involved with the expedition of the SEVEN AGAINST THEBES. By his wife Lysimache, the daughter of Abas, he had sons, including ADRASTUS (1), MECISTEUS, PARTHENOPAEUS, and perhaps HIPPOMEDON, all of whom marched against Thebes, and a notorious daughter, ERIPHYLE, who was bribed into forcing her husband Amphiaraus to join the Seven.

[Apollodorus 1.9.12–13; Apollonius, *Argonautica* 1.118.]

Talos (1)

A bronze man who guarded Crete. Either he was the last survivor of the race of bronze and presented to EUROPA by Zeus when he won her love, or he was made by the god HEPHAESTUS and given to King MINOS. His task was to walk round the island three times a day on his untiring feet and get rid of strangers. Either he pelted them with huge rocks, or he made himself red hot and burnt them to death in a fiery embrace. His only weakness was a small spot at his ankle: a single vein containing ichor, the blood of the gods, ran all the way down from his neck and was sealed at the bottom with either a thin membrane of skin or a nail of bronze. It was this one weak place that brought about his death when the ARGONAUTS visited Crete. Either MEDEA uttered prayers and enchantments from a distance until Talos grazed his ankle on a sharp rock; or she came near, either promising to make him immortal or maddening him with drugs, then pulled out the bronze nail; or the Argonaut POEAS, a brilliant archer, shot him in the ankle. The result was the same: the ichor gushed from Talos' vein and he dropped lifeless to the ground.

[Apollonius, *Argonautica* 4.1639–88; Apollodorus 1.9.26.]

Talos (2) *see* PERDIX.

Talthybius

Talthybius and his comrade EURYBATES were the heralds of AGAMEMNON during the Trojan War. In the *Iliad*, when Agamemnon decides to take for himself Achilles' concubine BRISEIS, the two heralds go reluctantly to fetch her from Achilles' tent (fig. 3). In later writings, Eurybates is ignored while Talthybius continues to play his part, performing what are often disagreeable duties. It was his task to go with Odysseus to fetch IPHIGENEIA to Aulis: the pretext was her supposed marriage with Achilles, when in fact she was to be sacrificed to gain winds to take the Greek fleet to Troy. He plays a significant part in the action of Euripides' *Trojan Women*: it is Talthybius who carries off both CASSANDRA and little ASTYANAX to their fate, Cassandra to be Agamemnon's concubine, Astyanax to be flung to his death from the walls of Troy. The herald washes the child's broken body and cleans his wounds, then with compassion carries him to his grandmother, HECUBA, to be dressed for burial. At the end of the play Talthybius gives orders for Troy to be put to the torch. We see his compassion again in Euripides' *Hecuba*, when he describes to Hecuba the noble death of her daughter POLYXENA. A less painful errand was to CINYRAS, king of Cyprus, to recruit troops.

After the fall of Troy Talthybius returned to his native Sparta. Here Pausanias saw his tomb, though he also reports the existence of a second tomb at Aegium in Achaea. At Sparta a clan of heralds, the Talthybiadae, were named after him.

See also fig. 135.

[Homer, *Iliad* 1.318–48, 3.118–20, 4.192–209, 7.273–7; Herodotus 7.134–7; Apollodorus, *Epitome* 3.22; Pausanias 3.12.7, 7.24.1.]

Tantalus (1)

One of the four great sinners (along with IXION, SISYPHUS

Fig. 135 Talthybius restrains Clytemnestra as she leaps to the defence of her lover, Aegisthus (see fig. 8).

and TITYUS) who after death endured eternal punishment for their transgressions on earth. Tantalus was the son of ZEUS and a certain Pluto, whose name means 'Wealth' but who is otherwise unknown. Proverbial for his own wealth, he ruled the area around Mount Sipylus in Lydia and was the father of PELOPS, who settled in Elis in the Peloponnese; of BROTEAS, who carved the famous image of Cybele, the Phrygian Mother-goddess, on the side of Mount Sipylus; and of NIOBE (2), who married Amphion and had her many children killed by Apollo and Artemis.

Tantalus was a favourite of the gods, who shared with him at their tables on Olympus the nectar and ambrosia that granted immortality. But he offended them so much that he lost all his god-given benefits and was punished for eternity in Hades. His offences are variously defined. Either he invited the gods to a feast at which he served them the flesh of his own son Pelops, cut up and stewed, with the presumptuous intention of testing their omniscience. Or he divulged the gods' secrets to men. Or he stole some of their nectar and ambrosia to share with his mortal friends. There is also a story that when Pandareos, king of Miletus, stole a wonderful golden guard-dog from Zeus' shrine on Crete, he left it for safekeeping with Tantalus – who decided to keep the precious beast for himself and thereafter swore, to Hermes and to Pandareos

himself, that he knew nothing of the creature. Zeus was said to have piled Mount Sipylus on top of him in punishment.

Tantalus is best known, however, for his eternal punishment in the Underworld after death. In the *Odyssey*, Odysseus recounts what he saw when he visited Hades (11.582–92):

> I saw Tantalus, suffering pains hard to bear,
> standing in a lake with water up to his chin.
> Thirsty he was, but unable to quench his thirst,
> for every time the old man stooped, longing to drink,
> the water drained away and vanished, and black earth
> showed at his feet where the god dried it up.
> Above his head, fruit cascaded from towering trees,
> pears and pomegranates and shining apples,
> and sweet figs and ripened olives, but whenever
> the old man reached for them with his hands, a wind
> tossed them away towards the shadowing clouds.

Alternatively (or additionally), Tantalus was sometimes said to live in everlasting terror with a large rock suspended over him, threatening to fall and crush him, rather like the 'Sword of Damocles'.

The ghost of Tantalus is a character at the beginning of Seneca's tragedy *Thyestes*, where his crime has condemned the House of Pelops to a series of bloody feuds and murders from generation to generation. His punishment of unappeasable hunger and thirst gives us our verb to 'tantalise', to tease by holding out something desirable that cannot be obtained; and a 'tantalus' is a case in which bottles of wine and spirits may be locked with their contents tantalisingly visible.

[Pindar, *Olympian* 1.54–64; Euripides, *Orestes* 4–11; Plato, *Cratylus* 395d; Apollodorus, *Epitome* 2.1; Pausanias 2.22.3, 5.13.7, 10.31.12; Ovid, *Metamorphoses* 4.458–9, 6.172–6, 402–11.]

Tantalus (2)

A son of THYESTES. Seneca names him as one of the children murdered by ATREUS, who cooked Thyestes' sons and served them up to their father in a stew. But another tradition had Tantalus grow to manhood and marry CLYTEMNESTRA. They had a son, but AGAMEMNON murdered both Tantalus and his child, and took Clytemnestra for himself.

[Euripides, *Iphigeneia at Aulis* 1149–52; Apollodorus, *Epitome* 2.16; Diodorus Siculus 4.74.2–3; Pausanias 2.18.2, 2.22.2–3; Athenaeus 7.281b–c; Lucretius 3.980–1; Seneca, *Thyestes* 718.]

Taraxippus ('Horse-frightener')

A ghost that haunted the racecourse at Olympia and terrified the horses. An altar stood beside the track, and whenever horses reached this point in a race at the Olympic Games they were thrown into an unaccountable panic, so much so that chariots often crashed and their charioteers were injured or killed. Pausanias (6.20.15–18) gives various possible identifications of the ghost. It may have been that of Myrtilus, the charioteer of Oenomaus, haunting an empty mound raised in his honour by his murderer, Pelops; or of Oenomaus himself, whose mares had been scared by Myrtilus' trickery in the chariot-race which Pelops won; or of Alcathus, one of the unsuccessful suitors of Hippodameia, who had been killed by Oenomaus; or it may be that Pelops buried here a certain fearsome object which had frightened the mares of Oenomaus, as well as those of every charioteer since (for the myth behind these suggestions, *see* PELOPS). It may have been the ghost of a famous horseman called Olenius; or of a certain Dameon, who fought with Heracles against AUGEAS and the Eleans and was killed by Cteatus, one of the MOLIONES, then buried at Olympia together with his horse. Despite all these appealing suggestions, Pausanias thinks it most probable that Taraxippus was simply an epithet of POSEIDON, god of horses.

Taraxippus (2)

Pausanias (6.20.19) also mentions another Taraxippus who haunted the racetrack of the Isthmian Games at Corinth. This was the ghost of GLAUCUS (3) who had been devoured by his own horses.

Tarchon

A king of the Etruscans, said to have founded Tarquinii, the chief of the twelve cities of Etruria. Out of hatred for the exiled tyrant MEZENTIUS, Tarchon joined the allies of AENEAS in his war against the Italian tribes.

[Strabo 5.2.2; Virgil, *Aeneid* 8.503–7, 10.148–56, 11.725–59.]

Tarpeia

The Roman woman who was said to have given her name to the Tarpeian Rock, the precipice on the Capitoline hill at Rome from which murderers and traitors were flung to their death. Tarpeia's father was the commander of the Roman citadel when the Romans, under ROMULUS, were at war with the Sabines. In the usual story, Tarpeia accepted a bribe from the Sabine king, Titus Tatius, to let him and his men inside the fortress by night. She asked for her reward to be what the soldiers wore on their left arms, expecting golden armlets, but instead they repaid her treachery by crushing her to death beneath their shields.

Two variants suggest that Tarpeia was moved, not by greed, but either by love of the Sabine king, Titus Tatius, or by patriotism, since her intention was to disarm the Sabines and deliver them up defenceless to the Romans.

[Dionysius of Halicarnassus 2.38–40; Plutarch, *Romulus* 17–18; Livy 1.11.5–9; Ovid, *Fasti* 1.259–62; Propertius 4.4.]

Tartarus

A dark and horrible region far below the earth. According to the Greek creation myth of Hesiod's *Theogony*, Tartarus was one of the primal entities, along with GAIA (Earth) and EROS (Love). It was situated as far below the earth as heaven was above it, so that a bronze anvil dropped from heaven to earth, or from earth to Tartarus, would fall for nine days and arrive on the tenth. Surrounded by walls of bronze, and with great bronze gates, it was the prison of CRONUS and the other TITANS who had warred against Zeus. Here they were condemned to stay for ever in the gloomy dark, guarded by the HUNDRED-HANDERS; and here too, according to Homer, Zeus threatened to fling any god who opposed him. Apollo only just escaped this fate after killing the Cyclopes, when he was punished instead by being forced to spend a year in servitude to the mortal Admetus. Tartarus later came to be seen as the place which received all evil-doers after death, as in Virgil's powerful account. This had great influence on Christians who believed in the torments of Hell.

Tartarus mated with his sister Gaia to produce the terrifying monster TYPHON (who as the final challenger to Zeus' power ended up in his father's regions), and in some accounts the snaky monster ECHIDNA.

[Homer, *Iliad* 8.10–17, 478–81; Hesiod, *Theogony* 119, 713–35, 820–2; Apollodorus 1.1.4–5, 1.6.3, 2.1.2, 3.10.4; Virgil, *Aeneid* 6.548–627.]

Tatius, Titus

King of the Sabines. *See* ROMULUS AND REMUS.

Taurians see iphigeneia.

Taurus (The Bull)

A constellation commemorating the form that Zeus took when he carried off EUROPA.

Taygete

Daughter of the Titan ATLAS and Pleione, and thus one of the seven PLEIADES. She was a nymph of the Taygetus range of mountains west of Sparta. ZEUS desired her, and ARTEMIS transformed her for a time into a deer that she might escape his attentions – in vain, however, for he fathered on her LACEDAEMON. After Taygete resumed her normal form, she dedicated a hind to Artemis in gratitude for her help, and this became the hind with the golden horns, the CERYNEIAN HIND, that Heracles captured as his third Labour for Eurystheus.

[Pindar, *Olympian* 3.28–30; Apollodorus 3.10.1, 3.10.3; Pausanias 3.1.2, 3.18.10.]

Tecmessa

Daughter of Teleutas, a Phrygian king, and concubine of AJAX (1), who carried her off to Troy when he plundered her city. She bore him a son, EURYSACES.

In Sophocles' tragedy *Ajax*, which deals with the hero's madness and death, it is clear that Tecmessa truly loves Ajax. She realises that he sees suicide as the only possible course of action that will regain him his lost honour, and begs him not to kill himself, pleading their mutual attachment. But once he is dead, she is generous and loving enough to be glad for his sake. 'His death is bitter to me and sweet to his enemies', she says, 'but to him it is happiness, for he has won his great desire, the death he longed for.' It is she who discovers his body, and she covers it with her cloak, crying out (915–9):

> He must not be seen, so I shall cover him
> completely, with this enfolding cloak,
> since no one, loving him, could ever bear
> to see him with the black blood spurting up
> to his nostrils, out of the murderous wound
> he dealt with his own hand ...

A famous cup by the Brygos Painter depicts this very moment (fig. 136).

Teiresias

A blind Theban seer, son of the nymph CHARICLO (1) and of Everes, a descendant of Udaeus, one of the SOWN MEN of Thebes. Two stories are told to account for Teiresias' blindness. In the first, he chanced upon ATHENA bathing naked with his mother in a spring on Mount Helicon,

and at once the goddess struck him blind. But in reparation she gave him the gift of prophecy, the power to understand the speech of birds, and a staff with which he could guide himself as well as if he still had sight. She also promised him a long life, and after his death the retention of his mental powers undimmed among the dead. In the second version (although its details vary) Teiresias saw two snakes copulating, either on Mount Cithaeron near Thebes or on Mount Cyllene in Arcadia. He struck them and was turned into a woman. Later – Ovid says seven years later – he saw the same snakes copulating again. Again he struck them and this time was turned back into a man. These experiences obviously gave him a unique insight into the natures of male and female, so when ZEUS and HERA were arguing as to whether a man or a woman felt the greatest sexual pleasure, they turned to Teiresias for the answer. His reply was that a woman's delight was nine or ten times greater than a man's, which won Zeus the argument. The infuriated Hera at once struck Teiresias with blindness, but Zeus awarded him in consolation the gifts of prophecy and a long life.

Teiresias was said to have lived through seven generations, and he played a part in many myths. He first became famous when he prophesied that NARCISSUS would live to a ripe old age only 'if he never came to know himself', and in time his apparently inexplicable words were proved true. After this his reputation was assured. Amphitryon came to him to find out who had been sleeping with his wife ALCMENE, and Teiresias was able to reveal that her seducer was Zeus. Teiresias plays a part in several works of Greek literature, and perhaps for this reason he seems to us the most familiar of ancient seers. In the *Odyssey*, ODYSSEUS goes on CIRCE's advice to consult his shade in the Underworld. The seer drinks the blood of the ram and the black ewe sacrificed by Odysseus, then instructs him about his future: his journey home, the rapacious Suitors that await him in his palace, his necessary wanderings after the Suitors have been killed, and finally his return home to a peaceful old age.

Teiresias is also a (living) character in four extant Greek tragedies. In Euripides' *Bacchae*, when DIONYSUS attempts to bring his religion to Thebes in face of opposition by the young king PENTHEUS, Teiresias and CADMUS both join the god's revels and dress up as MAENADS – one of them blind and both of them old. Pentheus believes the new religion to be dangerous and their behaviour

Fig. 136 **Tecmessa spreads a cloak over the body of her dead lover, Ajax.**

appalling, and is quite unconvinced by Teiresias' arguments on behalf of the new god. As punishment for his disbelief, he is torn to pieces by a band of maenads led by his mother, Agave. In Sophocles' *Oedipus the King*, it is Teiresias who knows that OEDIPUS has killed his father and married his mother, and that the king is himself the polluter of Thebes, the very man for whom he is searching. He even tells Oedipus so, but Oedipus is too angry to pay his words serious attention and it is only later that he realises how the prophet, although blind in his eyes, yet saw the truth, while he himself, although his eyes had sight, has nevertheless been blind. In his anguish he puts out his own eyes. In Euripides' *Phoenician Women*, when the Seven are attacking Thebes, Teiresias reveals to CREON (2) that only the death of his virgin son, MENOECEUS (2), will save the city from their onslaught by appeasing Ares. Creon refuses to sacrifice his son. But Menoeceus willingly kills himself for the sake of Thebes, leaping from the battlements into the lair of the dragon that Cadmus once slew, and the city remains unvanquished. Finally in Sophocles' *Antigone*, the aftermath of the great battle is dramatised, and Creon forbids burial to the traitor Polyneices who brought the Seven against Thebes. ANTIGONE (1) disobeys him and gives her brother's body the sprinkling of earth that represents token burial. In punishment for this Creon imprisons her, leaving her to die. Teiresias warns him that he is wrong and Creon at last gives in, but too late, for Antigone has killed herself, and now Creon's son Haemon and wife Eurydice both commit suicide too.

There was a second and successful attack on Thebes by the EPIGONI, the sons of the Seven, ten years later. The ancient seer was forced to leave his home, either fleeing from the fallen city with his fellow-Thebans, or carried off by the enemy, together with his daughter MANTO, to be consecrated to Apollo at Delphi. On his journey he stopped near Haliartus at the spring TELPHUSA, and drank from it, and died. Pausanias says that he was buried nearby, though according to Proclus' summary of the Epic Cycle's *Returns* he was buried in Colophon in Asia Minor, and the great seer CALCHAS, with Leonteus and Polypoetes, travelled there overland from Troy to honour the old prophet.

[Homer, *Odyssey* 10.490–5, 11.84–151; Hesiod, *Melampodia* frr. 275–6; Apollodorus 2.4.8, 3.4.1, 3.6.7, 3.7.3–4; Diodorus Siculus 4.67.1; Pausanias 7.3.1, 9.33.1–2; Ovid, *Metamorphoses* 3.322–38.]

Telamon

Son of AEACUS, king of Aegina, and Endeis, and brother of PELEUS. He and Peleus were banished for killing their bas-

tard half-brother PHOCUS (1), after which Telamon settled in Salamis where King CYCHREUS bequeathed him his kingdom. He married Eriboea (or Periboea), daughter of Alcathous. When his great friend HERACLES prayed to Zeus to send him a brave son, an eagle appeared, showing the god's consent, so Telamon named the son born to him *Aias*, AJAX (1), after the eagle (*aietos*).

Telamon sailed with the ARGONAUTS and took part in the CALYDONIAN BOARHUNT. He also accompanied Heracles to fetch the belt of the Amazon queen, HIPPOLYTE (1), and according to Pindar, to defeat the tribes of the Meropes on Cos and to kill the giant ALCYONEUS. But his greatest exploit was to help Heracles sack Troy after King LAOMEDON refused to pay the agreed price for saving his city from a sea-monster. Telamon was the first to breach the walls and enter the city, a deed which Heracles would have taken as a deep insult to his own supremacy, if Telamon had not tactfully and immediately gathered up stones and built an altar to 'Heracles the Glorious Victor'. For his part in the sack of Troy Heracles gave Telamon Laomedon's daughter, HESIONE, as his concubine, and she bore him a son, TEUCER (2). Both Ajax and Teucer went to fight in the Trojan War, at the end of which old Telamon was still alive and king of Salamis.

Although Telamon plays only a small part in the ancient literature that survives, there is no doubt that he was one of the great Greek heroes. We get a glimpse of this in Sophocles' *Ajax*, where Ajax' greatest shame lies in his knowledge that he has brought dishonour on his father, who went to Troy and 'won by his valour the finest prize of honour of all the army, and came home from this land of Ida bringing all glory' (434–6). In the same play, Teucer gives a rather different little sketch of the old king: Teucer is afraid of his father's anger when he returns home without his brother, now dead, and he describes Telamon as 'a bad-tempered, harsh old man, who gets angry at nothing just for the pleasure of quarrelling' (1017–8). In fact his fear is justified, for when Teucer did at last go home, alone, Telamon sent him into exile.

In historical times, both Telamon and his son Ajax, together with the other sons of Aeacus, were invoked before the battle of Salamis in 480 BC to help the Greek cause.

[Pindar, *Isthmian* 6.26–54, *Nemean* 3.36–9, 4.25–30; Herodotus 8.64; Euripides, *Helen* 87–94; Apollodorus, 1.8.2, 1.9.16, 2.6.4, 3.12.6–7; Diodorus Siculus 4.32.1–5, 4.49.3–7; Plutarch, *Themistocles* 15; Pausanias 2.29.3–10.]

Telchines

Sorcerers who were the first inhabitants of the island of Rhodes. By their sorcery they could assume any form they chose and could bring on hail, rain and snow. It was said by some that they nursed the infant POSEIDON to keep him safe from his cannibalistic father, CRONUS. They invented the craft of metalwork and other useful arts, and they fashioned many wondrous things including Poseidon's trident, the sickle with which Cronus castrated his father, Uranus, and the first images of the gods. They also had malevolent powers: they killed animals and plants with a mixture of sulphur and water from the River STYX, and they could cast the evil eye on whatever, or whoever, they wished to harm. ZEUS grew to hate them and struck them with his thunderbolts, plunging them to the bottom of the sea.

[Callimachus, *Hymn* 4.30–1; Diodorus Siculus 5.55–6; Strabo 10.3.7, 10.3.19, 14.2.7; Ovid, *Metamorphoses* 7.365–7.]

Telegonus

Son of ODYSSEUS and the enchantress CIRCE. He does not appear in Homer's *Odyssey*, but he inspired an entire epic poem, the *Telegony*, attributed to Eugammon of Cyrene. This has been lost, but we know from Proclus' summary that Telegonus, when grown to manhood, went in search of his father. Landing on Ithaca he raided the island for food, then of course failed to recognise Odysseus when he came out to defend his country and wounded him mortally, striking him with his spear tipped with the deadly sting-ray. When he sorrowfully realised his victim's identity, he took his father's corpse, together with PENELOPE and TELEMACHUS, back to Circe's island of Aeaea. There he married Penelope, and Telemachus married Circe, who made all three of them immortal. According to Hyginus (*Fabula* 127), Telegonus and Penelope had a son, ITALUS. It is probable that Sophocles' lost tragedy *Odysseus Acanthoplex* told of Odysseus' death at Telegonus' hands.

[Hesiod, *Theogony* 1014; Apollodorus, *Epitome* 7.16, 7.36–7.]

Telemachus

The son of ODYSSEUS and PENELOPE. He plays a prominent part in Homer's *Odyssey*, where he develops from a timid youth, quite unable to control the unruly Suitors, to a self-confident and resourceful young man who helps his father to kill them.

Telemachus was only a baby when the Trojan War began, and Odysseus had no desire to fight but wished simply to stay at home with his family. When PALAMEDES came to recruit him to the Greek side, he pretended to be mad by ploughing his land with two unlikely animals yoked together and sowing salt. But Palamedes realised that this was merely a ruse, and put the little Telemachus in front of the ploughshare (or, in another version, threatened the baby with his sword). Odysseus at once

saved his son and gave himself away. He was then obliged to go and fight at Troy.

The city was at last taken in the tenth year of the war, but Odysseus' homecoming was delayed by the wrath of Poseidon. It was another ten long years before he returned to Ithaca. Meanwhile no one knew whether he was alive or dead, and as the years passed it seemed more and more likely that he had been killed. So while Telemachus was growing up, his mother was besieged by Suitors who were sure that her husband would now never return. They invaded Odysseus' house, behaving outrageously and carousing at his expense, and Telemachus was too weak and hesitant to eject them. But as the *Odyssey* opens, all this is about to change. In Books 1–4, often known as the *Telemachy*, ATHENA comes to him, disguised first as a Taphian visitor, Mentes, and later as MENTOR, the Ithacan noble whom Odysseus had left in charge of his house. She inspires Telemachus with courage and sends him off to seek news of his father. He first visits old NESTOR at Pylos, and then MENELAUS and HELEN at Sparta where he learns that Odysseus is still alive.

The Suitors lie in ambush to kill Telemachus on his return, but he sails home by a different route and evades them. Odysseus, meanwhile, has returned at last to Ithaca, disguised as a beggar, and father and son are movingly reunited in the hut of EUMAEUS the swineherd (16.4–219). 'I am your father', says Odysseus, 'and because of me you have been grieving, and suffering great pain, and enduring men's outrages.' Telemachus takes his father in his arms and they both weep for all the lost years since their parting, when Telemachus was only a baby (216–9):

> They cried loud and shrill, even more than the outcry
> of birds, eagles or vultures with hooked claws,
> whose children countrymen have taken away
> before they could fly. Such was their pitiful crying.

Reunited once more, father and son together plot the Suitors' destruction. From this point on, Telemachus is all courage and resourcefulness, keeping Odysseus' return a close secret, preparing for the vengeance by removing all the weapons from the palace hall (19.1–52), insisting to the Suitors that the 'beggar' has a chance to string the great bow (21.245–434), and fighting valiantly beside his father in the final massacre (22.1–478).

Later sources add further episodes to Telemachus' life. The Hesiodic *Catalogue of Women* had him marry Nestor's daughter, POLYCASTE, and have by her a son, Persepolis. In the lost *Telegony*, where Odysseus was killed by TELEGONUS, his son by CIRCE, Telemachus married Circe after his father's death and was made immortal by her. Hyginus

(*Fabula* 127) says that LATINUS was their son. But none of these accounts has the importance and centrality of Telemachus' adventures in the *Odyssey*.

Many postclassical treatments of Telemachus' legend derive from the well-known prose romance *Les aventures de Télémaque* by Fénelon, describing imaginary travels of Telemachus, accompanied by Minerva in the guise of Mentor, and including a famous meeting with CALYPSO on Ogygia. This has proved particularly inspirational in the field of opera. Telemachus is Stephen Dedalus in James Joyce's *Ulysses*, where the earlier episodes reflect Telemachus' quest in the *Telemachy* for news of his father.

Telemus

One of the CYCLOPES who, in Homer's *Odyssey* (9.506–12), lived with other Cyclopes on the island later identified as Sicily. He was a renowned seer, and predicted to his fellow-Cyclops POLYPHEMUS (2) that he would be blinded by ODYSSEUS. Polyphemus believed him, but failed to recognise Odysseus as the man in question when he arrived in the Cyclops' cave.

Telephassa *see* AGENOR (1).

Telephus

Son of HERACLES and AUGE, and said by Pausanias (10.28.8) to be of all that hero's sons the one most like his father. The usual version of Telephus' early days has him exposed as a baby on Mount Parthenion in Arcadia. Here he was suckled by a doe until he was found and brought up by shepherds. It was said that they named him Telephus after the doe (*elaphos*) and the teat (*thele*) that fed him. Only when grown to manhood did he learn from the oracle at Delphi that he must seek his true parents in Mysia. He found his mother married to Teuthras, the king of Teuthrania, and was adopted by him and made his heir to the throne.

When AGAMEMNON led the Greeks to fight in the Trojan War, they first landed in Mysia, believing it to be Troy, and began to pillage the land. Telephus and his countrymen pursued the Greeks back to their ships, slaughtering many, with Telephus killing, most notably, Polyneices' son THERSANDER. But when the mighty ACHILLES attacked Telephus, he fled, catching his foot in a grapevine as he ran. As he fell, Achilles wounded him in the thigh with a spear. (The scholia add that DIONYSUS caused his fall, angry with Telephus for depriving him of honours.) The Greeks then returned home to prepare for a second expedition. Telephus' wound, however, would not heal, and he learnt from an oracle that it could only be cured by the one that caused it. He went to Argos where the Greeks were reassembling their forces, and said that he would

Fig. 137 **The wounded Telephus, holding the infant Orestes, takes sanctuary at an altar and appeals to Agamemnon for help.**

show them the way to Troy if Achilles would heal him. Achilles denied any knowledge of medicine, but ODYSSEUS pointed out that the oracle meant the spear itself, and not the man wielding it, so Achilles rubbed some rust from his spear into the wound and Telephus was soon cured. He then showed the Greeks the way to Troy, while refusing to fight himself (he was married to PRIAM's sister Astyoche and so was naturally pro-Trojan). His son EURYPYLUS (2) later fought on the side of the Trojans and was killed by Neoptolemus.

Aeschylus, Sophocles and Euripides all wrote dramas on these travails of Telephus, all of which are now lost. We know most about Euripides' *Telephus*, where Telephus went as a beggar in rags to make his appeal to the Greeks. When his disguise was penetrated, on CLYTEMNESTRA's advice he seized Agamemnon's infant son, ORESTES, as a hostage, threatening to kill him if the Greeks refused to help. This last motif may have been dramatised by Aeschylus, for it begins to appear on vase-paintings in the second quarter of the fifth century BC (fig. 137). The rags were probably Euripides' innovation, for they are frequently parodied in Aristophanes, particularly in his *Acharnians*.

[Epic Cycle, Proclus' summary of the *Cypria*; Pindar, *Isthmian*

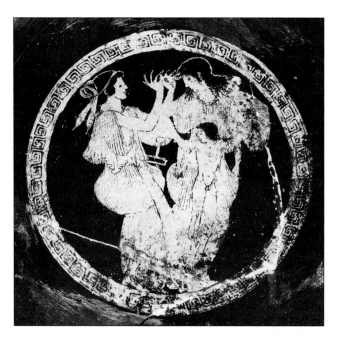

Fig.138 **Procne and Philomela are about to kill Itys.**

8.49–50; Apollodorus, *Epitome* 3.17–20, 5.12; Pausanias 1.4.6, 3.26.10.]

Tellus or Terra

The Roman goddess of the earth, 'Mother Earth', identified with the Greek goddess GAIA.

Telphusa

The nymph of a spring at Haliartus in Boeotia. When APOLLO was establishing his worship on earth, he came to Telphusa's spring, intending to found there his oracular shrine. Telphusa, having no wish to share her pleasant spot, persuaded the god to move on to Delphi, claiming that it would be far more peaceful there than at her spring, which was so often frequented by horses and mules. So Apollo settled at Delphi and there established his shrine. He found, however, that it was the lair of the monstrous she-dragon, PYTHON, who was plaguing the surrounding countryside and ravaging the flocks. He did battle with the great serpent and shot her dead, then returned to Haliartus to punish Telphusa for sending him into Python's lair and covered the nymph's spring with a great mound of rocks. It was said that TEIRESIAS, a seer inspired by Apollo, died after drinking Telphusa's waters: perhaps this was the nymph's revenge. The traveller Pausanias saw the seer's grave beside the spring.

[*Homeric Hymn to Apollo* 244–387; Apollodorus 3.7.3; Pausanias 9.33.1.]

Temenus (1)

A son of PELASGUS, living in the Arcadian city of Stymphalus, who, according to a local tradition related by Pausanias (8.22.2), brought up the goddess HERA. Temenus dedicated three sanctuaries in her honour: one as Child, while she was still young; a second as Wife, when she married ZEUS; and a third as Widow, when she returned to Stymphalus after one of her (not infrequent) quarrels with her husband.

Temenus (2)

Son of ARISTOMACHUS, brother of CRESPHONTES (1) and ARISTODEMUS, and one of the HERACLIDS who invaded and conquered the Peloponnese. Temenus, Cresphontes, and the two young sons of the dead Aristodemus, Procles and Eurysthenes, agreed to decide the ownership of its three chief regions by drawing lots, and Temenus won the Argolid. He married his daughter Hyrnetho to another Heraclid, DEIPHONTES, and made him his chief adviser. This made Temenus' own sons afraid that they might be disinherited, so they killed their father and seized the throne.

Tenes or Tennes

Son of CYCNUS (4), king of Colonae near Troy, and Procleia, although according to some he was the son of APOLLO. When Procleia died, Cycnus took a second wife, Philonome, who fell in love with Tenes. He rejected her advances, so she accused him to her husband of trying to seduce her, bringing forward a flute-player called Eumolpus as a so-called witness. Cycnus believed her, and putting Tenes and his sister Hemithea in a chest he launched it out to sea. The chest was washed up safely on the island of Leucophrys. Tenes settled there with his sister, and being made king by the inhabitants he renamed the island Tenedos after himself. Cycnus in due course learnt the truth about the supposed seduction. He stoned the flute-player to death and buried his wife alive in the earth, then sailed to Tenedos to ask his son's pardon. But Tenes was still furious at the treatment meted out to him. He cut the cables of his father's moored ship with an axe to prevent him from landing, thus setting him adrift just as Cycnus had done to him.

When the Greek army put in at Tenedos on the way to the war at Troy, THETIS warned ACHILLES that he must on no account kill Tenes, or else he himself would die at the hands of Apollo. Despite her warning Achilles killed him. In one version Tenes tried to ward off the Greek ships by bombarding them with stones, and Achilles attacked him with a sword. In another version, Achilles came across the beautiful Hemithea and pursued her, then killed Tenes when he tried to defend his sister from her would-be seducer. Thetis had commissioned one of the servants to remind her son of her warning, so when Achilles discovered his victim's identity, he killed that servant too for failing to warn him in time. He buried Tenes on the spot where a sanctuary was afterwards dedicated to his worship. No flute-player was ever allowed to enter, nor was the name of Achilles ever uttered within it.

Towards the end of the Trojan War Achilles was himself killed – by Paris and Apollo.

[Apollodorus, *Epitome* 3.23–6; Diodorus Siculus 5.83.4–5; Plutarch, *Moralia* 297d–f; Pausanias 10.14.1–4.]

Tereus

A son of ARES, and a king of either Thrace or Daulis. Tereus came to the help of PANDION (1), the king of Athens, in a boundary dispute with LABDACUS, the king of Thebes. When Athens proved victorious, Pandion in gratitude married his daughter Procne to Tereus. The resultant horrific story of Tereus, Procne and Philomela was famous in antiquity, and was notably dramatised in Sophocles' tragedy *Tereus* – sadly now lost, apart from fragments. But Ovid gives a moving account in his *Metamorphoses* (6.424–674) which must owe much to the earlier Greek version. Tereus and Procne were married, says Ovid (428–34):

> But neither the bridal goddess Juno, nor Hymen, nor the Graces were present at that wedding. Furies lit them on their way with torches stolen from a funeral, Furies prepared their marriage-bed, and the cursed screech-owl brooded over their house, perched on the roof above their wedding-chamber. Under this omen were Procne and Tereus married; and under this omen was their child born.

This child was their son, Itys.

When the couple had been married for five years, Procne asked Tereus to go to Athens and fetch her sister, Philomela, to visit her. He did so, but as soon as he saw Philomela's beauty, he was overcome by lust and plotted how to make her his own. She had no idea of the fate he had in mind for her, so she pleaded with her father to be allowed to visit her dear sister and Pandion agreed. They set off, but Tereus took Philomela, not back to his palace, but to a lonely dwelling in the depths of a dark forest. There he shut her in and raped her, and to stop her telling of what he had done, he cut out her tongue. Leaving her well guarded, he went home to his wife and told her that her sister was dead. Procne was deeply grieved.

A year passed by, during which Philomela wove a tapestry, a scarlet design on a white ground, telling in pictures the story of what she had suffered. This she sent by a servant to her sister. Procne read the sorry tale and went at once to fetch Philomela, smuggling her back to the palace. Then she set her mind on revenge. She stabbed her little son Itys to death, and the two sisters cut up his body and cooked his flesh (fig.138). Procne served it to Tereus, who ate heartily of what seemed a sumptuous meal and afterwards asked his wife where his son was. She presented him with Itys' bloody head, and realising the truth he leapt up with a roar of fury, intent on killing his son's murderers. But the gods intervened and turned all three of them into birds.

In the Greek version of the story, Procne became a nightingale, forever singing her son's name in mourning, *Itu!, Itu!*, while Philomela, having no tongue, became a swallow, who merely twitters inarticulately. Tereus was turned into a hoopoe (a royal, crested bird), continually uttering the question he asked his cruel wife just before his metamorphosis, *Pou!, Pou!* (Where? Where?). The Roman poets, oddly, reversed the fates of the two women, with Procne becoming the swallow and Philomela the nightingale. This is the version most often adopted in postclassical treatments, so that 'Philomel' has become a common poetic epithet for the nightingale.

Ovid, like many other writers, sets the story in Thrace. On the other hand, Thucydides (2.29) affirms that the tragedy took place in Daulis, a district of Phocis, and certainly Greek poets call the nightingale the Daulian bird. A final romantic judgement for Daulis comes from Fraser (*Apollodorus: The Library*, vol. 2, p. 99):

> No one who has seen the grey ruined walls and towers of Daulis, thickly mantled in ivy and holly-oak, on the summit of precipices that overhang a deep romantic glen at the foot of the towering slopes of Parnassus, will willingly consent to divest them of the legendary charm which Greek poetry and history have combined to throw over the lovely scene.

This legend is sometimes confused with that of AEDON, the wife of King Zethus of Thebes, who accidentally killed her son Itylus and was transformed by the gods into a nightingale, her song forever lamenting her dead child. Swinburne's poem *Itylus*, despite its title, refers to the Itys story and 'The woven web that was plain to follow / The small slain body, the flowerlike face', and memorably depicts the nightingale as bird of mourning:

> Sister, my sister, O fleet sweet swallow,
> Thy way is long to the sun and the south;
> But I, fulfilled of my heart's desire,
> Shedding my song upon height, upon hollow,
> From tawny body and sweet small mouth
> Feed the heart of the night with fire …

> O sister, sister, thy first-begotten!

the hands that cling and the feet that follow,
The voice of the child's blood crying yet,
Who hath remembered me, who hath forgotten?
Thou hast forgotten, O summer swallow,
But the world shall end when I forget.

[Apollodorus 3.14.8; Strabo 9.3.13; Pausanias 1.5.4, 1.41.8–9,
10.4.8–9.]

Terpsichore *see* MUSES.

Terra *see* TELLUS.

Tethys

One of the TITANS, daughter of Uranus (Heaven) and GAIA
(Earth). She married her brother-Titan OCEANUS, and they
lived together at the far ends of the earth. Their sons were
the three thousand rivers that flow upon the earth, and
their daughters were the OCEANIDS, the three thousand
nymphs of land and waters.

Tethys plays only a small part in the myths. When
AESACUS killed himself for love of a nymph, she had pity
on him and turned him into a water-bird, a diver. During
Zeus' war with the Titans, RHEA (1) entrusted her daughter
HERA to the care of Tethys, who grew to love her charge.
Later Hera became the wife of Zeus, and when he immortalised his lover CALLISTO in the stars as the Great Bear,
Tethys out of loyalty to Hera refused to let the constellation sink for rest into the waters of Ocean that surround
the earth. This is why the Great Bear never sets, but revolves eternally around the Pole Star, high in the heavens.

[Homer, *Iliad* 14.200–10; Hesiod, *Theogony* 136, 337–70;
Ovid, *Metamorphoses* 2.509–31, 11.784–95.]

Teucer (1)

Ancestor of the Trojan kings. According to the Greek tradition, he was the son of the river-god SCAMANDER and of
Idaea, a nymph of Mount Ida. He married his daughter
Bateia to the immigrant DARDANUS, who succeeded him as
king and changed the name of the people from Teucrians
to Dardanians. Teucer's great-grandson, TROS, gave his name
to Troy and the Trojans. According to Virgil, Teucer was
an immigrant to the Troad from Crete.

[Apollodorus 3.12.1; Virgil, *Aeneid* 3.107–10.]

Teucer (2)

Bastard son of TELAMON by HESIONE, daughter of King
Laomedon of Troy, and half-brother of AJAX (1) whom he
accompanied to the TROJAN WAR. As well as being an
expert spear-fighter, he was the best archer on the Greek
side. He often fought alongside Ajax, taking his stand in
the shelter of his great shield, then moving out to shoot
an opponent before darting back to its protection. In

this way he killed many of the Trojan enemy, wounded
GLAUCUS (4), and also SARPEDON, though not mortally
since Zeus intervened to save his son from death. He
even came close to killing the mighty HECTOR; but in one
confrontation Zeus broke his bowstring, and another
time Apollo diverted his arrow, whereupon Hector hit
Teucer with a rock and Ajax protected his brother until
he could be carried out of the battle.

In the archery contest at Patroclus' funeral games,
Teucer failed to pray to Apollo for success, so he came
only second to MERIONES; but later at the funeral games in
honour of Achilles he was the victor.

In Sophocles' *Ajax*, Teucer returns from a plundering
raid in Mysia only after his brother's suicide and in time
to grieve over his body (992–1001):

> Of all the sights I have ever seen
> this to my eyes is the saddest one;
> and of all the roads I ever walked,
> this one has brought my heart most pain,
> this one I walked to you,
> my dearest Ajax, when I heard
> your fate, and came to seek its truth ...
> I heard it from a long way off
> and groaned beneath a weight of grief,
> but, now that I have seen, I want to die.

But he is also in time to guard Ajax' body from the
vengeance of MENELAUS and AGAMEMNON so as to secure
for his brother honourable burial (1044–1417).

Teucer was one of the Greeks inside the WOODEN HORSE
at the sack of Troy. He returned home to Salamis, but
Telamon, angry that he had come back from Troy without Ajax, banished him (as Teucer himself had feared:
Ajax 1006–21). He is a character in Euripides' *Helen*,
where he meets HELEN in Egypt and tells her of events at
Troy and of his subsequent banishment (68–163). He
went on to Cyprus, where he became ruler, either because
he married the daughter of King CINYRAS, or because King
Belus of Syria conquered Cyprus and set him up there. In
Cyprus he founded a new Salamis.

In historical times, Teucer had a hero-cult in the area
of Phaleron. It was said that he was the first to appear at
the Peiraeus court of Phreattys, when he defended himself from on board ship against Telamon's accusations.

[Homer, *Iliad* 8.273–334, 12.387–405, 15.436–483, 23.859–83;
Sophocles' lost *Teucer*; Apollodorus, *Epitome* 5.5; Pausanias
1.3.2, 1.28.11, 8.15.6–7; Virgil, *Aeneid* 1.619–22.]

Teumessian Vixen

A fierce fox, fated never to be caught, which had been
sent by the gods to torment the people of Thebes. Its
name comes from its lair at Teumessus, a hill in Boeotia.

Every month, to appease the beast, a son of one of the Theban citizens was put out as its prey. AMPHITRYON undertook to rid the city of this pest, and to help him in his task he asked CEPHALUS (2) to bring to Thebes his hunting dog, LAELAPS, a hound that was fated never to miss its quarry. Cephalus did so, and the inescapable hound set off after the uncatchable fox. To put an end to what would clearly have been an everlasting pursuit, Zeus turned both animals to stone.

[Apollodorus 2.4.6–7.]

Teuthras *see* AUGE.

Thalia (1) *see* MUSES.

Thalia (2) *see* GRACES.

Thalpius

Son of Eurytus, one of the Siamese twins known as the MOLIONES. Thalpius led one of the Elean contingents of ten ships to the Trojan War.

[Homer, *Iliad* 2.615–24.]

Thamyris

A Thracian bard, son of PHILAMMON and the nymph Argiope. His mother had once lived on Parnassus, but when she was pregnant with Thamyris, Philammon refused to take her into his house so she settled in Thrace. Thamyris loved the beautiful young boy HYACINTHUS, but his love was unrequited, for Hyacinthus preferred the god Apollo.

The most famous story concerning Thamyris relates to his brilliant musicianship. He was so fine a musician, and so confident of his skill, that he boasted he could surpass the very MUSES in singing. As always, when a mortal challenges the gods, the results were disastrous and he was severely punished: 'The angry Muses maimed him', says Homer (*Iliad* 2.599–600). 'They took away his wondrous song and made him forget his lyre-playing.' Apollodorus (1.3.3) gives a few more details of this famous contest. They all agreed that if Thamyris won, he would be allowed to go to bed with each of the Muses in turn, but if he lost, they could deprive him of whatever they wished. Of course the Muses won, so they took away his sight and his musicianship. According to Pausanias (4.33.3), the Balyra river in Messenia was given its name after the blinded Thamyris threw (*ballein*) his lyre into it.

Sophocles wrote a *Thamyras* (Attic spelling), now lost. From Pollux (4.141) we learn that the stage mask for Thamyris was designed with odd eyes, one grey and one black. There are several examples in ancient vase-painting of his sad fate. Pausanias (10.30.8) tells us that in the great picture of the Underworld at Delphi, painted by Polygnotus, Thamyris was portrayed with long flowing hair and beard, blind, and sitting in utter dejection with a broken lyre at his feet. Pausanias also comments that in his view Thamyris lost his eyesight through disease, then forsook his art because of the consequent stress.

Thanatos

The personification of Death. 'Death and his brother Sleep' now form a literary commonplace, but they have been seen in this way ever since antiquity, when Hesiod (*Theogony* 211–12) made Thanatos and HYPNOS (Sleep) the sons of NYX (Night). The brothers dwelt in the depths of TARTARUS (758–66):

> There the sons of gloomy Night have their home,
> Sleep and Death, those terrible gods. The shining sun
> never looks upon them with his rays when he goes
> up to heaven, nor coming down again from heaven.
> Sleep roams the earth and the broad back of the sea,
> gentle and kind to men, but Death has a heart of iron,
> and in his breast is a spirit pitiless as bronze.
> Death holds fast to any man he catches,
> and is hated even by the immortal gods.

So Sleep was seen as travelling and scattering slumber something like the modern 'sand-man', while Thanatos was the angel of death, coming to mortals when their allotted timespan had run out and carrying them off irresistibly to Hades.

In Homer's *Iliad*, the twin brothers Sleep and Death, acting on the instructions of Zeus, carry the body of SARPEDON away from the Trojan battlefield and home to Lycia (fig. 75). Death also played a part in fifth-century Greek drama in the legend of Alcestis, who died to save the life of her husband ADMETUS. In Phrynichus' (lost) *Alcestis*, we know that Death appeared on stage with a sword and cut off a lock of Alcestis' hair, thus ritually sealing her fate. In Euripides' (extant) *Alcestis*, Death is again a character. Here, however, he loses his victim, for in this play HERACLES waits at Alcestis' tomb where Death will come to claim her, then wrestles with him and forces him to release her back to life.

Thus, despite his heart pitiless as bronze, Death could sometimes be defeated. Indeed, the arch-trickster SISYPHUS succeeded in binding Death, so that for a while no one on earth could die.

[E. Vermeule, *Aspects of Death in Early Greek Art and Poetry* (1979); R. Garland, *The Greek Way of Death* (1985); C. Sourvinou-Inwood, *'Reading' Greek Death* (1995).]

Thasus

Usually said to be the son of AGENOR (1) (sometimes of Cilix or Poseidon). He travelled in search of his abducted sister EUROPA, and finally colonised and gave his name to the island of Thasos.

Thaumas
Son of Pontus (Sea) and GAIA (Earth). Thaumas is a rather obscure figure of ancient myth. His brothers were the sea-deities NEREUS and PHORCYS, the 'Old Men of the Sea', so he too may have been thought of as a sea-god. On the other hand, his children by the Oceanid Electra were IRIS and the HARPIES, all as swift as the winds and very much creatures of the air. So obscure he must remain.

[Hesiod, *Theogony* 233–9, 265–9.]

Theano (1) *see* MELANIPPE (1).

Theano (2)
Wife of the Trojan elder ANTENOR.

Thebe
A Boeotian nymph, daughter of the river-god ASOPUS, who married AMPHION's brother, Zethus, and gave her name to the city of Thebes, previously called Cadmeia after its founder CADMUS.

Theia
One of the TITANS, the daughter of Uranus (Sky) and GAIA (Earth). She married her brother-Titan HYPERION, and bore HELIOS (Sun), SELENE (Moon) and EOS (Dawn). In the *Homeric Hymn to Helios*, Theia is called Euryphaessa.

[Hesiod, *Theogony* 135, 371–4.]

Theiodamas *see* HYLAS.

Themis
A goddess closely associated with justice, law and order. She was one of the TITANS, the daughter of Uranus (Heaven) and GAIA (Earth). She bore to ZEUS the three HORAE (Seasons) and the three FATES, all of whom personified aspects of order in the universe. With Zeus, she presided over divine assemblies on OLYMPUS, and according to the *Cypria* she planned with him the TROJAN WAR to remedy the overpopulation of the earth.

Like her mother, Themis had prophetic powers, and she was linked with Gaia as the owner of the original oracle at Delphi before Apollo arrived and killed PYTHON. Aeschylus equates Themis with Gaia and makes her the mother of the chained Titan PROMETHEUS, who is finally freed from his torment through knowledge gained from Themis' powers of prophecy.

[Homer, *Iliad* 15.87–95, 20.4–6, *Odyssey* 2.68–9; *Homeric Hymn to Apollo*, 123–5; Hesiod, *Theogony* 132–6, 901–6; Pindar, *Isthmian* 8.31–47; Aeschylus, *Eumenides* 1–8, *Prometheus Bound* 18, 211–15, 873–4; Euripides, *Iphigeneia among the Taurians* 1259–69; Apollodorus 1.1.3, 1.4.1, 3.13.5; Pausanias 10.5.6.]

Themiste *see* CAPYS (1).

Themisto
Daughter of the Lapith king Hypseus and the third wife of ATHAMAS, king of Orchomenus. For a tragic version of her marriage, *see* INO.

Themistonoe *see* CEYX (2).

Theoclymenus (1)
Descendant of the seer MELAMPUS, son of the seer Polypheides, and himself a seer. In Homer's *Odyssey* he is a fugitive from Argos, having killed a man, and TELEMACHUS gives him safe passage from Pylos to Ithaca (15.222–81, 508–38). Here he predicts that ODYSSEUS is not far away and is devising punishment for the Suitors (17.151–65). Later he solemnly warns the Suitors themselves of their impending deaths (20.346–72: words which would later have a powerful effect on Plato, since he quotes them in his dialogue *Ion*):

> Poor wretches, what is this evil you are suffering?
> Your heads and faces and limbs beneath are shrouded in night,
> Wailing blazes forth, and your cheeks are wet with tears,
> the walls are spotted with blood, and the lovely pillars.
> The porch is full of ghosts, full too the courtyard
> as they flock down to Hades, down into the darkness.
> The sun is lost from the sky, and an evil mist
> comes racing in ...

But the Suitors pay no attention and simply mock the seer.

Theoclymenus (2) *see* EIDOTHEA.

Theonoe *see* EIDOTHEA.

Theophane
The beautiful daughter of the Thracian king Bisaltes. POSEIDON desired her, and to get the better of her many suitors he carried her off to a distant island. The suitors discovered her whereabouts, and Poseidon's next attempt at foiling them was to turn Theophane and the rest of the islanders into sheep. The suitors began to kill and eat the sheep, and were turned into wolves by the god. He then turned himself into a ram and mated with Theophane. The fruit of their union was a lamb with a fleece of spun gold, which grew into the talking, flying ram that saved PHRIXUS and Helle from the wiles of their wicked stepmother Ino, and in due course became the motive for the long and arduous journey of Jason and the ARGONAUTS: the quest for the Golden Fleece.

[Ovid, *Metamorphoses* 6.117; Hyginus, *Fabula* 188.]

Theraephone *see* MOLIONES.

Theras

The man who gave his name to the island of Thera (Santorini). He was born a Theban, the son of King AUTESION and a fifth-generation descendant of OEDIPUS. His sister Argeia had married the Heraclid leader ARISTODEMUS, but was left a widow with two young sons, Procles and Eurysthenes, at the beginning of the successful invasion of the Peloponnese by the HERACLIDS. Theras became the boys' guardian and defended their rights to their father's share of the conquered territory. The boys won the rule of Sparta, and Theras ruled it on their behalf for many years.

When they came of age and took over the rule, Theras found that he resented being suddenly in a subordinate position. He emigrated, founding a colony on Calliste ('most beautiful'), the volcanic island to the north of Crete. At that time it was inhabited by Phoenicians, descendants of former companions of Theras' ancestor CADMUS, who had touched at the island during his search for his sister Europa. Theras took with him not only a party of Spartan colonists, but also a number of Minyans, descendants of the ARGONAUTS, who had been driven out of Lemnos and were living on Mount Taygetus. They had married Spartan women and been given a share in the land and the government, but the Spartans, resenting their increasingly arrogant behaviour, had imprisoned them. They were about to be put to death, when their Spartan wives visited them in prison and changed clothes with them, so they escaped disguised as women. Now many of them were only too glad to accompany Theras on his journey. Indeed, Calliste was an appropriate place of settlement for them, since according to one story, it was said to have grown from a clod of earth, given by the sea-god TRITON to the Argonaut EUPHEMUS – no doubt an ancestor of some of these present Minyans – and dropped by him into the sea on his homeward voyage.

Theras and his three ship-loads of Spartans and Minyans were welcomed in Calliste. Theras was awarded the rule of the island and its name was changed to Thera. The colony thrived, but sadly Theras' grandchildren in both Thera and Sparta died because of the avenging FURIES of LAIUS and Oedipus, still persecuting their descendants. The Furies were appeased only when a shrine was built and the appropriate observances made. Then the curse was lifted and the mortality ceased.

[Herodotus 4.145–9; Apollonius, *Argonautica* 4.1755–64; Pausanias 3.1.6–8, 3.15.6, 4.3.4–5, 7.2.2.]

Theronice *see* MOLIONES.

Thersander

Son of POLYNEICES and Argeia and grandson of Oedipus. Just as his father had bribed ERIPHYLE with the necklace of his ancestress Harmonia, so Thersander bribed her with Harmonia's beautiful robe, thus inducing her to persuade her son Alcmaeon to lead the EPIGONI against Thebes. The expedition was a success, Thebes was taken and Thersander became king. He sailed with the Greeks to the TROJAN WAR, but when they first landed mistakenly in Mysia, believing it to be Troy, he was killed by Heracles' son TELEPHUS (though in Virgil's account, he survived the war and was one of the warriors in the WOODEN HORSE). He was succeeded on the throne of Thebes by TISAMENUS (2), his son by Demonassa, the daughter of Amphiaraus and Eriphyle.

[Pindar, *Olympian* 2.43–5; Apollodorus 3.7.2–3, *Epitome* 3.17; Pausanias 9.5.14–15; Virgil, *Aeneid* 2.261.]

Thersites

The only man of low birth who plays a part in the *Iliad*. According to Homer he was the ugliest man at Troy, being lame, bandy-legged, hump-backed, and with a balding, pointed head. When he abused AGAMEMNON for stealing Briseis from Achilles, ODYSSEUS beat and threatened him until he collapsed in pain and fear, amid the laughter of the army.

Later sources gave him a noble pedigree, making him the son of Oeneus' brother AGRIUS (2), and thus cousin to the hero DIOMEDES (2). They add that when Achilles killed the Amazon PENTHESILEIA, Thersites jeered at him for falling in love with her (and, some say, gouged out her eyes), so Achilles struck him dead. This led to a quarrel among the Greeks, so Achilles went to Lesbos where he sacrificed to Apollo, Artemis and Leto, and was purified of the murder.

Because of his behaviour in abusing his superiors in the *Iliad*, Thersites' name is applied to any ill-willed, impertinent railer against authority. In Shakespeare's *Troilus and Cressida* he is 'a slave whose gall coins slanders like a mint'.

[Homer, *Iliad* 2.212–77; Epic Cycle, Proclus' summary of the *Aethiopis*; Apollodorus, *Epitome* 5.1; Quintus of Smyrna, *Sequel to Homer* 1.716–81.]

Theseus

The greatest Athenian hero, son of POSEIDON, or of AEGEUS, king of Athens. His mother was AETHRA, the daughter of PITTHEUS, king of Troezen. After Aegeus visited the Delphic Oracle to enquire about his childlessness, he called at Troezen to consult Pittheus about the Oracle's reply. Pittheus, wishing to have a grandson with Aegeus' royal blood in his veins, made his guest drunk and induced him to sleep with Aethra. Before leaving for Athens, Aegeus hid a sword and a pair of sandals beneath a great rock, telling Aethra that if she bore a son, who on reaching manhood was able to lift the rock, she should send him with these tokens of paternity to Athens. Aethra did indeed bear a son, Theseus; but it was said that Poseidon had visited her bed on the very same night as Aegeus, and that Theseus was really the son of the god.

1. THE EARLY YEARS

Theseus grew up in Troezen, in the care of Pittheus and Aethra. One story of his childhood foreshadows his future valour: when his kinsman HERACLES came to dinner, laying aside his lionskin to eat, the children of the palace thought it was a real lion and fled, shrieking, except for Theseus, who seized an axe and attacked it.

When Aethra judged that the time was right, she told Theseus of his parentage and showed him the rock. He lifted it with ease, then set out to walk to Athens with his father's sword and sandals. His mother and grandfather begged him to make a safe journey by sea, since the land-route was beset by ruffians and bandits. But Theseus was fired with a desire to emulate the courageous deeds of Heracles, and was ready to deal with anyone who offered him violence.

Near Epidaurus he met PERIPHETES, known as the 'Club-bearer' from his habit of beating travellers to death with a bronze club. Periphetes unwisely accosted Theseus, who responded by wresting the club from him and cracking open his skull. He kept the club and it became his emblem, a reminder of his first trial of strength, just as Heracles always wore the skin of the NEMEAN LION, the evidence of his first Labour.

On the Isthmus of Corinth Theseus encountered SINIS the Pine-Bender (fig. 140), a brigand who killed his victims either by helping them to bend a pine tree to the ground, then suddenly releasing it so that they were hur-

tled high into the air; or by fastening them to two pines that he himself had bent down which, when released, tore them in two. Theseus killed Sinis with his own pine trees. He found the brigand's beautiful daughter Perigune hiding in a bed of rushes and wild asparagus, and took her to his bed. In due course she bore him a son, MELA-NIPPUS (3).

After despatching PHAEA, the wild sow of Crommyon (fig. 140), he came to the Isthmus of Corinth and killed SCIRON (figs. 130 and 140), who haunted the rocky coastal road and forced passing travellers to wash his feet. As they stooped to do so, he kicked them into the sea below, where they were eaten by a giant turtle. Theseus pretended to comply with Sciron's command, but instead caught him by his feet and flung him down the cliffs to his death.

At Eleusis Theseus encountered CERCYON (fig. 140), who forced passing travellers to wrestle with him and always killed his opponent – until, that is, he wrestled with Theseus. This time Cercyon died. Soon afterwards Theseus was stopped by PROCRUSTES, an apparently kindly man who offered hospitality to wayfarers. He would then put them in one of two beds, a long bed if they were short, and a short bed if they were tall, and would adjust their size to fit the bed, either lopping off their extremities or hammering them out to length. Using whichever method was appropriate, Theseus dealt with his host in the same way (fig. 140).

Finally Theseus came to Athens and went to his father's palace. Aegeus was at that time living with the sorceress MEDEA, and although the king did not recognise his son, Medea immediately guessed his identity and determined to kill him. Because Aegeus was constantly fearful of the threat to his throne posed by his brother PALLAS (3) and his fifty sons, she had no trouble in sowing suspicion of the stranger. Aegeus sent Theseus to deal with the deadly MARATHONIAN BULL that was ravaging the countryside, thinking that he would never return alive. On his way, Theseus was given shelter by an old woman called HECALE, who promised to sacrifice in thanksgiving to Zeus if he returned safely the next day. Theseus successfully mastered the ferocious bull (figs. 87 and 140), but when he returned to Hecale's cottage, he found the old woman dead. Because of her kindness and hospitality, he later instituted a local ceremony to honour her memory. Back in Athens, he drove the bull alive through the city for everyone to see, before sacrificing it to Apollo.

Fig. 139 **Theseus, with the help of Peirithous, abducts the Amazon Antiope.**

378

Medea still cherished her murderous intentions, so she mixed a cup of poison and persuaded Aegeus to offer it to Theseus at a feast. At the last moment, Aegeus recognised the sword that Theseus was carrying and dashed the cup from his lips. Father and son embraced each other (fig. 6). Medea fled from Athens for ever.

Aegeus named Theseus as his successor on the throne of Athens, and the sons of Pallas, who believed that they had more right to inherit than he, broke into open rebellion. Theseus crushed the revolt.

2. THESEUS AND THE MINOTAUR

Soon afterwards the tribute owed by Athens to MINOS, king of Crete, for the death of his son ANDROGEOS, became due. Seven youths and seven girls were shipped to Crete, either every year or every nine years, and fed to the MINOTAUR in the Labyrinth. This time, on the third payment of tribute, Theseus made one of the company. Various reasons are given for his participation. Either he volunteered to go; or the selection was made by lot, and his name emerged; or Minos came in person to choose his victims, and picked Theseus out first of all because of his strength and beauty. Whichever the reason, Theseus set off with the firm intention of killing the Minotaur and putting an end to the tribute for ever. He promised his father that, if he survived, he would change the ship's black sail of mourning to a white or scarlet sail. Aegeus would then know at once, as the vessel sailed towards Athens, whether his son still lived.

On the outward journey one of the girls, Eriboea, took Minos' fancy. Theseus defended her from his advances, claiming that as a son of Poseidon he was Minos' equal and had every right to withstand him. Minos called for a sign from his own father, Zeus, who at once flashed down a thunderbolt. The king then flung his golden ring into the sea, Poseidon's domain, challenging Theseus to prove his paternity by retrieving it. Without hesitation Theseus dived into the water. While the ship sped onwards, dolphins carried him to his father's palace deep in the ocean (figs. 121 and 143). Here he recovered the ring, and AMPHITRITE, the sea-god's wife, presented him with a crimson cloak and a garland dark with roses. The dolphins swiftly carried him back to the ship, and to the amazement of Minos he emerged from the sea, triumphant. But he knew that his greatest challenge was awaiting him in Crete.

The Minotaur was a ferocious monster with the body of a man and the head and horns of a bull. It lived shut away in the Labyrinth, a vast underground maze built by the master-craftsman DAEDALUS, and so cleverly devised that anyone going in would be quite unable to find the way out again. Theseus was helped by Minos' daughter, ARIADNE, who fell in love with him on sight. She gave him a clew, a large ball of thread provided by Daedalus, that would bring him safely out of the Labyrinth if he survived his encounter with the monster. Theseus tied one end of this to the entrance, then unwound the thread as he made his way into the innermost depths of the maze, searching for the Minotaur. They fought, and the Minotaur died (figs. 93 and 140). Athens' cruel tribute was ended. Theseus followed the thread back to the entrance of the Labyrinth, then together with the other intended victims of the monster he sailed away from Crete, taking Ariadne with him.

They came to the island of Dia, later called Naxos, and there Theseus abandoned Ariadne. Some say that he did so from choice, perhaps because he had fallen in love with another girl (Plutarch mentions Aegle, the daughter of Panopeus); others say that he acted on the command of the gods. Whatever his motive, all was well for Ariadne in the usual version of the myth, for the god Dionysus arrived in his chariot and carried her off to be his wife, making her immortal. Theseus sailed onwards, stopping on the island of Delos to sacrifice in thanksgiving to Apollo. He and his companions danced for the first time the Crane Dance, the intricate patterns of which imitated the winding passages of the Labyrinth. This dance was still being performed by the Delians well into the historical period. From Delos Theseus sailed to Athens, but sadly he quite forgot his father's instructions to change the black sail of his ship to either white or scarlet. Aegeus, looking eagerly out to sea from a cliff, or from the heights of the Acropolis, saw in despair the black sail of mourning and flung himself down to his death.

3. THESEUS, KING OF ATHENS

Theseus was now the king of Attica, his greatest achievement as such being to unify the many small, independent communities of the land into one state, with Athens as the capital. He also instituted the festival of the Panathenaea, to be held every four years in honour of Athena; and at Corinth he reinstituted the Isthmian Games (initially founded by Sisyphus) in honour of his father Poseidon. Like the other great heroes of his generation, he went on the voyage of the ARGONAUTS and the CALYDONIAN BOARHUNT. With him went his dearest friend, PEIRITHOUS, the king of the Lapiths in Thessaly. The two had met while Peirithous was raiding a herd of Theseus' cattle, and had immediately been struck with mutual liking and admiration. At once they joined hands and swore an oath of life-long friendship. When Peirithous married Hippodameia, Theseus attended the wedding and fought alongside his friend in the famous battle between the Lapiths and the drunken CENTAURS, who were trying to rape all the women.

Theseus also went on an expedition against the AMAZONS (fig.14), either with Peirithous, or accompanying Heracles when he fetched the belt of HIPPOLYTE (1). Theseus carried the Amazon queen ANTIOPE (2) back to Athens as his mistress (fig.139), hotly pursued by the rest of the Amazons. A great army of these warrior-women pitched their camp in the city itself, but they were vanquished by the Athenians in a fierce battle and most of them were killed. Antiope stayed with Theseus, bearing him a son, HIPPOLYTUS (2), and was later deeply aggrieved when Theseus married PHAEDRA, the daughter of King Minos and thus the sister of the deserted Ariadne. Minos now being dead, his son and heir Deucalion arranged the match, so presumably he had forgiven Theseus' earlier abandonment of his sister. During the wedding celebrations Antiope led out her Amazons in arms, threatening to kill the assembled guests, but she herself was killed in the battle.

Phaedra bore Theseus two sons, ACAMAS (1) and Demophon, who would succeed him on the throne of Athens. Now the sons of Pallas made a final desperate attempt to depose Theseus, and he killed them all. Because of this kin-killing he was exiled from Athens for a year, so he took his wife and family to his other kingdom of Troezen, inherited from his grandfather Pittheus. Here his son Hippolytus was living. Phaedra fell in love with her stepson and tried to seduce him, but he spurned her advances. So she vengefully lied to Theseus that Hippolytus had tried to rape her, and Theseus cursed his son, calling on Poseidon to kill him. The god sent a bull from the sea to terrify Hippolytus' horses (fig 73), and he was thrown from his chariot and dragged to his death, entangled in the reins. Phaedra, her treachery exposed, hanged herself. (For Euripides' tragic version of the myth, *see* PHAEDRA.)

Hippodameia having also died, Theseus and Peirithous now agreed to help each other win new wives, worthy of their station, who were both daughters of Zeus. First they abducted HELEN of Sparta, the daughter of Zeus and Leda. They drew lots to see who should have her and Theseus won. Leaving her with Aethra at Aphidnae in Attica, they set off together down to the Underworld, where they planned to abduct PERSEPHONE, the daughter of Zeus and Demeter and now queen of Hades, as wife for Peirithous. In their absence, Helen was rescued by her two brothers, Castor and Polydeuces. They captured Aphidnae and took their sister back to Sparta, along with Aethra, who was made Helen's slave. Usually Helen was

thought to return home still a virgin, but in one version of the myth she was said to have borne IPHIGENEIA, generally known as the daughter of Agamemnon and Clytemnestra, to Theseus.

So Theseus and Peirithous had lost one of their chosen wives, and they fared no better with the other. On their arrival in the Underworld, HADES (1) made them welcome, urging them to sit and be comfortable. But once they did so, they were quite unable to stand up again, either because they found themselves bound with chains or snakes, or because the seats stuck to their flesh, or because these were seats of forgetfulness and they lost all will to move. Theseus was eventually freed by Heracles, when he visited Hades to fetch CERBERUS as his twelfth Labour for Eurystheus. But Peirithous had to stay there for ever.

4. AFTERMATH

When Theseus eventually returned to Athens, he found that MENESTHEUS, the great-grandson of Erechtheus, had been made king in his place, and that his own sons, Acamas and Demophon, had fled for refuge to Elephenor, king of the Abantes in Euboea. Theseus himself found refuge with LYCOMEDES, king of the island of Scyros. But Lycomedes, though pretending friendship, was Theseus' enemy, either because he was afraid of him, or because he secretly supported Menestheus. He took Theseus to the top of the island and pushed him to his death off a cliff.

Theseus was honoured at Athens as their greatest national hero, particularly from the last quarter of the sixth century BC, when we see a dramatic increase in his popularity in the visual arts. This may have been influenced by poetry, perhaps an epic *Theseid*, now lost, in which his deeds were memorably told and his connection with Athens celebrated, so that he was seen as a heroic symbol of the new Athenian democracy. Before about 520, only Theseus' battle with the Minotaur was depicted regularly in vase-paintings, but now whole cycles of his deeds appear, showing his exploits on the road from Troezen to Athens (fig. 140); and not only on vases, but in monumental sculpture, such as the Athenian Treasury at Delphi (*c.* 500) and the Hephaesteion in Athens (*c.* 450). During the Persian Wars, the Athenians were quite sure that they saw Theseus' apparition, clad in full armour and charging ahead of them against the barbarians, at their victorious battle of Marathon (490 BC). In 475 BC the Athenian general Cimon went to Scyros and brought back what he believed to be Theseus' bones, a skeleton of gigantic size that he had found buried with a bronze spear and sword. These were reinterred in the heart of Athens.

In fifth-century tragedy, Theseus appears as a heroic champion of justice, the strong and compassionate ruler of a great city. In Sophocles' *Oedipus at Colonus* he protects the old, blind OEDIPUS and his daughters and gives them sanctuary. In Euripides' *Suppliant Women*, dramatising the aftermath of the attack of the SEVEN AGAINST THEBES, Theseus forces the Thebans to give up the Argive dead for burial. In Euripides' *Madness of Heracles*, he befriends the broken, desperate Heracles after he has tragically murdered his wife and children, offering him refuge in Athens.

[Homer, *Odyssey* 11.321–5, 631; Bacchylides, *Odes* 17, 18; Thucydides 2.15; Apollodorus 2.6.3, 3.10.7, 3.15.6–*Epitome* 1.24; Diodorus Siculus, 4.16, 4.28, 4.59–63; Plutarch, *Theseus*; Pausanias 1.2.1, 1.3.1–3, 1.15.2, 1.17.2–6, 1.19.1, 1.20.3, 1.22.5, 1.24.1, 1.27.7–10, 1.41.7, 2.22.6–7, 2.31.1, 2.32.9, 2.33.1, 3.18.11, 5.11.4, 5.11.7, 8.45.6, 10.29.4, 10.29.9; Virgil, *Aeneid* 6.617–18; Ovid, *Metamorphoses* 7.404–52, 8.155–82, *Heroides* 4, 10. A. G. Ward (ed.), *The Quest for Theseus* (1970); C. Sourvinou-Inwood, *Theseus as Son and Stepson* (1979); J. Boardman, 'Herakles, Theseus and Amazons', in D. Kurtz and B. Sparkes (eds), *The Eye of Greece* (1982).]

Thespius

A king of Thespiae, west of Thebes, who had fifty daughters and who once entertained HERACLES. According to Apollodorus (2.4.9–10), Heracles was staying as Thespius' guest when, in his eighteenth year, he performed the first of his many and dangerous exploits, the killing of a lion that was roaming Mount Cithaeron and preying on the cattle of Thespius and Amphitryon. Heracles vanquished the great beast and skinned it, then wore its pelt like a cloak, with the scalp serving as a helmet. (Elsewhere it was said that ALCATHOUS (1) killed the Cithaeronian Lion, and that the pelt which Heracles always wore was that of the NEMEAN LION.)

Perhaps even more of a challenge to Heracles was that posed by Thespius' fifty daughters, for the king, wishing to have as many grandchildren as possible by such a hero, sent all fifty to have intercourse with him, either over fifty nights, or seven nights, or even just one night. Heracles fathered sons on them all, and twins on the eldest and youngest. When these boys grew up, most of them, on Heracles' instructions, went with IOLAUS to colonise Sardinia. Thespius remained Heracles' friend, and when he murdered his children by MEGARA, it was Thespius who purified him.

Pausanias (9.27.6–7) saw a sanctuary of Heracles at Thespiae. He records with disbelief the tradition that its first priestess was the only one of those fifty daughters who refused to sleep with Heracles, and because of the insult was condemned by him to remain a virgin and

Fig.140 The deeds of Theseus. He drags the dead Minotaur from the Labyrinth and *(clockwise from top)* deals with Cercyon, Procrustes, Sciron, the Marathonian Bull, Sinis and Phaea.

serve as his priestess for the rest of her life.

[Apollodorus 2.4.12, 2.7.6, 2.7.8; Diodorus Siculus 4.29; Pausanias 1.29.5, 7.2.2, 9.23.1, 10.17.5.]

Thessalus

The man who gave his name to the kingdom of Thessaly. His identity is uncertain, but the following are two possibilities:

Thessalus (1)

A son of JASON and MEDEA, said in one version to have survived his mother's murderous attack on her children. He fled to Iolcus, where he succeeded ACASTUS on the throne and gave his name to Thessaly.

Thessalus (2)

Son of HERACLES and Chalciope, the daughter of Eurypylus, king of Cos, fathered on her when Heracles sacked Cos on his way home from Troy. Thessalus had two sons, Antiphus and Pheidippus, who led the Coan contingent of thirty ships to the Trojan War. After the fall of Troy, Antiphus settled in the land which he called Thessaly after his father.

[Homer, *Iliad* 2.676–9; Apollodorus 2.7.8, *Epitome* 6.15; Strabo 9.5.23.]

Thestius

Son of ARES and Demonice, and king of Pleuron in Aetolia. His only claim to fame is as the father or grandfather of more famous descendants: his daughters were LEDA, the mother of HELEN, CLYTEMNESTRA and the DIOSCURI; Hypermestra, the mother of the seer AMPHIARAUS; and ALTHAEA, the mother of MELEAGER who killed the Calydonian Boar. Thestius also had a number of sons, two of whom were slain by Meleager during the fight over the spoils of the boarhunt. Althaea, incurably angry at the deaths of her brothers, responded by killing her own son.

[Apollodorus 1.7.7, 1.7.10, 1.8.2–3, 3.10.5–6; Strabo 10.2.24.]

Thetis

A sea-goddess, daughter of NEREUS and Doris, and the most famous of the NEREIDS, being the wife of the great hero PELEUS, and the mother of the even greater hero ACHILLES. ZEUS desired her, but she refused his advances out of loyalty to HERA, who had brought her up. POSEIDON too was a suitor; but when it was prophesied (*see* PROMETHEUS) that Thetis' son was destined to be greater even than his father, both gods gave up their pursuit and it was decided that Thetis should be married off to a mortal. Peleus was chosen as the worthiest, but still he had to win his bride, and since, like other sea-divinities, Thetis had the power of metamorphosis, he was forced to

wrestle with her while she changed into many different shapes – fire, water, wind, tree, bird, tiger, lion, snake and cuttle-fish. But stoutly he clung to her through all these transformations (fig.111), until at last she gave in.

The wedding was celebrated on Mount Pelion, and all the gods attended, bringing gifts – all, that is, except ERIS (Strife) who, being a disagreeable goddess, was not invited. Despite this she came, and threw into the gathering the 'Apple of Discord', a golden apple inscribed with the words 'for the fairest'. The rivalries which this provoked led to the JUDGEMENT OF PARIS, and eventually to the TROJAN WAR, and to the death of Peleus' and Thetis' as yet unborn son, Achilles.

Thetis naturally wished her children by Peleus to be immortal like herself. In one version of the myth, it was said that she had seven sons by Peleus, six of whom she killed in her attempts to make them immortal, so the seventh, Achilles, she simply let live, mortal that he was. But the more usual story was that Achilles was their only child, and Thetis tried to burn away his mortal part by secretly putting him in the fire at night, and anointing him with ambrosia during the day. But one night Peleus caught her in the act of apparently setting fire to their son, and was so angry with her that she deserted both husband and son and went back to live in the sea with the Nereids. A third, late version said that Thetis dipped the baby Achilles in the River STYX, holding him by the heel, and thus made him completely invulnerable except for the heel by which she held him. An arrow-shot in that one, weak heel would eventually bring about his death.

Without Thetis, Peleus had to have help in the rearing of Achilles. Both the Centaur CHEIRON and, according to Homer, PHOENIX (3) did much to rear and educate him. But Thetis too remained a constant support to her son, coming to him from her home with the Nereids whenever he needed her. When the Trojan War began, she knew that if Achilles went to fight, he was fated to die, so she dressed him as a girl and sent him instead to live with the women at LYCOMEDES' court. The secret, however, was in some way betrayed, and Odysseus penetrated Achilles' disguise, taking him as a recruit (and in fact an enthusiastic recruit) to the Greek army. On the way to Troy, Thetis warned Achilles that he must not kill TENES, the king of Tenedos, else it would lead to his own death at the hands of APOLLO, but despite this warning Achilles killed him. She also warned her son not to be the first

Fig. 141 The smith-god Hephaestus gives new armour to Thetis for her son, Achilles.

382

to land from the ships at Troy, because the first to land was fated to be the first to die. (It was Protesilaus who, disregarding this prophecy, leapt out first.)

In the *Iliad* we see Achilles in action at Troy and Thetis helping him in every way she can. He appeals to his mother when he retires from battle, angry that his concubine BRISEIS has been taken by Agamemnon, and she begs Zeus on her son's behalf to turn the tide of battle in the Trojans' favour, so that the Greeks will feel the lack of their mightiest warrior. Later, when Achilles' refusal to fight leads to the death of his dear comrade, PATROCLUS, Thetis comes from the sea to comfort him. She warns him that if he kills HECTOR in revenge, then he too must die, for his death is fated to come soon after Hector's. Achilles accepts this, since his great love for his friend demands that Patroclus be avenged, even at the cost of his own life. And Thetis accepts his decision, though with grief, because she loves him. She even has HEPHAESTUS make him new and splendid armour for his return to battle (fig. 141).

Achilles' death occurs after the end of the *Iliad*, but we know from the *Odyssey* that Thetis and her sister-Nereids came from the sea and lamented him for seventeen days, and on the eighteenth day his body was burnt. His ashes were mixed with the ashes of Patroclus, then laid in a golden jar, made by Hephaestus and once given to Thetis by DIONYSUS. (Perhaps the jar carried by Dionysus on the François Krater's depiction of the wedding of Peleus and Thetis is this very jar.) The remains of the two friends were laid to rest with those of ANTILOCHUS, another dear comrade, and a grave mound was heaped high over them. Great funeral games were held, and the Greeks competed for many beautiful prizes, provided by the gods at Thetis' request. Achilles, after all, became immortal, living for ever with Patroclus and other heroes on *Leuke*, the White Island, lying in the Black Sea at the mouth of the Danube.

Thetis played a small part in various other myths. She fetched Briareos (*see* HUNDRED-HANDERS) from Tartarus to save Zeus when Poseidon, Hera and Athena rebelled against him and plotted to tie him up. She sheltered Dionysus when he leapt into the sea, pursued by the non-believer LYCURGUS (1). When Hera flung Hephaestus out of Olympus and down into the sea, ashamed of him because he was crippled, Thetis and her sister Eurynome saved him and he stayed with them for nine years. Thetis interceded for Peleus when her sister PSAMATHE (1) sent a huge wolf to ravage his herds of cattle. During the voyage of the *Argo* she and her sister-Nereids helped the ARGONAUTS to pass the Wandering Rocks in safety.

The central and most important part of her myth,

however, remains her motherhood of Achilles. For all that she is a goddess, our most memorable image of Thetis is the *Iliad*'s humanised portrayal of the grieving mother, who knows full well that her son is doomed soon to die. 'I gave birth to a son peerless and brave', she says (18.55–60), 'one pre-eminent among men. He shot up like a young plant, and I nurtured him, like a tree grown in a rich orchard. Then I sent him away with the curved ships, to fight the Trojans in the land of Ilion. And never again shall I welcome him, come back home again to the house of Peleus.' Another unforgettable cry of grief comes from Thetis in a fragment of Aeschylus (350) from an unknown play, where she tells how, at her wedding, Apollo prophecied falsely that her son would have a long and happy life – Apollo, the very god who would bring about Achilles' death:

> He sang that I would be blest with a son
> who would live a long life, knowing no sorrow.
> He said all this, singing a paian in praise
> of my great good fortune, cheering my heart.
> And I believed the words of Apollo were true,
> rich as he is in holy, prophetic skill.
> But he who sang of this,
> he who was there at the feast,
> he who said these things –
> he it was who killed my son.

[Homer, *Iliad* 1.348–430, 493–533, 9.410–16, 18.35–148, 18.369–19.39, 24.74–142, *Odyssey* 24.36–94; *Homeric Hymn to Apollo* 316–21; Hesiod, *Theogony* 1003–7, *Catalogue of Women* fr. 210; Pindar, *Isthmian* 8.26–47, *Nemean* 4.62–8; Aeschylus, *Prometheus Bound* 790, 794, 952–4; Apollodorus 1.2.7, 1.3.5, 1.9.25, 3.5.1, 3.13.5–8, *Epitome* 3.26, 3.29; Apollonius, *Argonautica* 4.759–881, 922–64; Pausanias 5.18.5; Ovid, *Metamorphoses* 11.217–65.]

Thisbe *see* PYRAMUS.

Thoas (1)

Son of DIONYSUS and ARIADNE, and king of the island of Lemnos (*see* HYPSIPYLE).

Thoas (2) *see* EUNEUS.

Thoas (3)

Son of Andraemon and GORGE, succeeding his father as king of Aetolia. He was one of the many suitors of HELEN, offering sheep and oxen as his wedding gifts; and in due course, true to the oath taken by all the unsuccessful suitors, he led forty Aetolian ships to the TROJAN WAR. He fought valiantly throughout the hostilities and was well respected by his comrades. Surviving the war, he was one of the Greeks inside the WOODEN HORSE and returned safely home to Aetolia. His son Haemon was the father of OXYLUS, who guided the Heraclids through the Peloponnese and won the throne of Elis. According to one variant tradition, in conflict with the *Odyssey* and mentioned only by Apollodorus, ODYSSEUS took refuge with Thoas after being exiled from Ithaca, marrying his daughter and fathering on her a son, Leontophonus.

[Homer, *Iliad* 2.638–44, 4.527–35, 7.162–9, 13.214–39, 15.281–300; Hesiod, *Catalogue of Women* fr. 198; Apollodorus 1.8.6, *Epitome* 3.12, 7.40; Pausanias 5.3.6–7; Virgil, *Aeneid* 2.262.]

Thoas (4)

King of the Taurians, a barbaric tribe living in the Cimmerian Chersonese (Crimea), among whom Artemis installed IPHIGENEIA as priestess after her near-sacrifice by Agamemnon. Eventually ORESTES came to the land of the Taurians and rescued his sister from Thoas, taking her back home to Mycenae, and in one version killing Thoas himself.

Thoas (5)

One of the GIANTS (*see* AGRIUS (1)).

Thrace

A land lying to the east of Macedonia between the Aegean Sea and the Black Sea, regarded by the Greeks as being cold (it was the home of the violent North Wind, BOREAS) and barbaric. Myths associated with Thrace are often cruel and bloody. One of its kings, LYCURGUS (1), was driven mad as a punishment for opposing the god Dionysus, and while mad he killed his own son with an axe, and his wife too, then was himself either torn asunder by wild horses or devoured by panthers. DIOMEDES (1), who owned horses that he fed with human flesh, met an appropriate end at the hands of Heracles, devoured by his own animals. TEREUS raped his sister-in-law Philomela and cut out her tongue, then was tricked into eating the flesh of his murdered son, Itys. Demophon, too, unwittingly drank down the blood of his daughters, murdered by MASTUSIUS. RHESUS went to fight for King Priam in the Trojan War, but on the very night of his arrival was butchered, together with twelve of his Thracian followers, during a sortie from the Greek camp by Diomedes and Odysseus. Polymestor killed the young POLYDORUS (3) who had been left in his care, then had his eyes gouged out and his own sons murdered by the boy's vengeful mother, Hecuba.

Thrasymedes

One of the sons of NESTOR, king of Pylos. He went with his father and his brother ANTILOCHUS to the TROJAN WAR.

He has a minor part in the *Iliad*, often fighting alongside his brother. Antilochus was killed by the great Ethiopian hero MEMNON while saving Nestor's life, and Thrasymedes joined in the fight around his brother's body; but he himself survived the war and was among the warriors in the WOODEN HORSE. He returned with his father to Pylos, and there welcomed TELEMACHUS who had come in search of Odysseus. His tomb was to be seen near Pylos.

[Homer, *Iliad* 9.80–8, 10.196–7, 255–7, 14.9–12, 16.317–29, 17.377–83, 705, *Odyssey* 3.39, 442–50; Pausanias 4.36.2; Quintus of Smyrna, *Sequel to Homer* 2.260–344, 12.319.]

Thrinacia

The island where HELIOS, the Sun-god, pastured his cattle and sheep.

Thyestes

Son of PELOPS and Hippodameia, and brother of ATREUS, with whom he shared a bloody and implacable feud. Its starting-point was Thyestes' adultery with Atreus' wife Aerope, followed by the brothers' intense rivalry over the throne of Mycenae, and it led over the course of time to various hideous acts of blood-letting. The worst of these was the murder of Thyestes' sons by Atreus, after which he cooked and served them up to their father, who ate heartily of their flesh. Many of the ancient sources of this myth, in particular several fifth-century BC tragedies, have been lost, so our information about these sons is frustratingly partial. Three names are given, Aglaus, Orchemenus, and Callileon (or Caleus); Seneca (*Thyestes*) names only two, TANTALUS (2) and PLEISTHENES, with a third son unnamed. Sometimes the boys are the children of Thyestes and some woman other than Aerope, but in some versions they seem to have been born of Thyestes and Aerope herself, then brought up as the sons of Atreus. In the latter case, Atreus' fury at finding out the truth could perhaps be seen as a better motivation for his appalling revenge than simply kingship rivalry coupled with adultery. Vengeance for Thyestes' sufferings was later taken on Atreus, and on Atreus' son Agamemnon, by AEGISTHUS.

Thymoetes

A Trojan elder and adviser to King PRIAM. He was married to Cilla, who was either the daughter of Laomedon and thus the sister of Priam, or the sister of Priam's wife HECUBA. In a variant version of the events surrounding the birth of PARIS, Cilla bore a son, Munippus, on the same day that Paris was born to Hecuba. The seer AESACUS predicted that a child just born would grow up to bring destruction on Troy, and advised that both child and mother be put to death. Priam killed Cilla and Munippus (who was sometimes said to be Priam's own son by Cilla) rather than Hecuba and Paris, though it was Paris who was destined to set in motion the Trojan War and bring on Troy the promised destruction. Many years later Thymoetes was the first to urge that the WOODEN HORSE be brought into Troy – perhaps to take vengeance for that long-ago murder.

[Homer, *Iliad* 3.146; Apollodorus 3.12.3; Diodorus Siculus 3.67.5; Virgil, *Aeneid* 2.32–4.]

Thyone *see* SEMELE.

Tiberinus

The god of the River Tiber in central Italy. He was either the son of the god JANUS and a nymph, Camasene, or a descendant of AENEAS and king of Alba Longa. He was drowned in the river Albula, or killed on its banks, after which the river was renamed Tiber in his honour.

[Dionysius of Halicarnassus 1.71; Livy 1.3; Virgil, *Aeneid* 8.31–67; Ovid, *Fasti* 2.389–90, *Metamorphoses* 14.609–17.]

Timandra

A daughter of TYNDAREOS and LEDA. She married ECHEMUS, king of Arcadia, and bore him a son, Laodocus. Like her sisters HELEN and CLYTEMNESTRA, however, she was an unfaithful wife, and she deserted Echemus for PHYLEUS, king of Dulichium.

[Hesiod, *Catalogue of Women* frr. 23a and 176; Apollodorus 3.10.6; Pausanias 8.5.1.]

Timeas

A son of POLYNEICES and Argeia who, according to Pausanias (2.20.5), was one of the EPIGONI.

Tiphys

The original helmsman of the *Argo*, hailing from Boeotia. He piloted the ship through many dangers, including the SYMPLEGADES (Clashing Rocks), but to the ARGONAUTS' grief he was taken sick and died while they were among the Mariandyni, on the southern shore of the Black Sea. There he was buried, and his place at the helm was taken by ANCAEUS (2).

[Apollonius, *Argonautica* 1.105–10, 400–1, 2.851–63; Apollodorus 1.9.16; Pausanias 9.32.4.]

Tisamenus (1)

Son of ORESTES and HERMIONE. After his father's death, Tisamenus ruled the kingdoms of Argos and Sparta until the HERACLIDS invaded the Peloponnese and drove him off his throne. He offered to settle peacably among the Ionians, at Aegialus (later Achaea) in the northern Peloponnese, but they refused him, fearing that he would take over the rule of their land. He was killed in the ensu-ing battle and was buried at Helice. Later his bones were carried back to Sparta at the command of the Delphic Oracle. His grave there was still honoured in Pausanias' day.

[Apollodorus 2.8.2–3, *Epitome* 6.28; Pausanias 2.18.6–9, 7.1.7–8, 7.6.2.]

Tisamenus (2)

A king of Thebes, son of THERSANDER and Demonassa, and great-grandson of OEDIPUS. When his father was killed by Telephus at the beginning of the Trojan War, Tisamenus was too young to take his place, so the Boeotian contingent to Troy was led by Peneleos and Leitus. Peneleos was killed towards the end of the war by Telephus' son Eurypylus, and now Tisamenus became king of Thebes. After a quiet reign he left the rule to his son, AUTESION. When Autesion went with the Heraclids to invade the Peloponnese, the throne of Thebes passed to Damasichthon, the grandson of Peneleos.

Tisiphone (1) *see* FURIES.

Tisiphone (2)

A daughter of Alcmaeon and the prophetess MANTO.

Titans

The older generation of gods, the firstborn children of Uranus (Heaven) and GAIA (Earth). According to Hesiod they were twelve in all, six sons and six daughters: OCEANUS, COEUS, CRIUS, HYPERION, IAPETUS, CRONUS; and THEIA, RHEA (1), THEMIS, MNEMOSYNE, PHOEBE (1), and TETHYS. Some of their children were also regarded as Titans, most notably HELIOS, ATLAS, PROMETHEUS and LETO. The children of Cronus and Rhea, however, were members of the next generation of divinities, the Olympian gods who supplanted the Titans. For just as Cronus overthrew his father Uranus for his brutality, so Cronus in turn was overthrown by his own son ZEUS, in a great battle known as the *Titanomachia*. Cronus and those of the Titans (by no means all) who supported him were pitted against Zeus and his brothers and sisters, the Titans fighting from Mount Othrys and the gods from Mount Olympus. The battle lasted for ten years and shook the universe to its foundations, filling it with thunder and lightning, conflagrations, earthquakes, duststorms, and a tumult as great as if the whole heaven and earth crashed together. Finally Zeus summoned the CYCLOPES and the HUNDRED-HANDERS, and with his decisive aid he overcame the Titans and deposed Cronus. Now, reigning in his father's place, Zeus imprisoned Cronus and the hostile Titans in the depths of TARTARUS, setting the Hundred-handers to guard them, and punished Atlas by forcing him to hold up the sky for the rest of eternity.

According to a different tradition, the rule of the Titans was a blessed golden age in which men lived with carefree hearts and without toil or old age or grief (*see* CRONUS). For the part played by the Titans in the Orphic myth of Dionysus, *see* ZAGREUS. Our modern word 'titanic' derives from the prodigious size and power of the Titans.

[Homer, *Iliad* 14.277–9; Hesiod, *Theogony* 132–8, 207–10, 389–96, 617–735, 807–14; Aeschylus, *Prometheus Bound* 201–23; Apollodorus 1.1.2–1.2.5.]

Tithonus

One of the sons of LAOMEDON, king of Troy. In youth he had great beauty, and EOS, goddess of Dawn, fell in love with him. She carried him off to her home in Ethiopia, in the farthest East and by the river of Ocean. Here she bore him two sons, MEMNON and Emathion, who became kings, respectively, of Ethiopia and Arabia. And every morning 'Dawn arose from her bed, from the side of proud Tithonus, to carry light to the immortals and to men', as Homer puts it (*Iliad* 11.1–2, *Odyssey* 5.1–2). Because of her love for Tithonus, Eos asked Zeus to make him immortal and Zeus did so. The *Homeric Hymn to Aphrodite* (218–38) recounts the unhappy sequel: Eos had forgotten to ask that her lover might remain forever young, so as the years went by he grew older, and greyer, and more shrivelled. At first Eos looked after him, giving him food and ambrosia and rich clothing. But when he grew so old that he could no longer move, she shut his withered husk of a body away in his room and closed the shining doors on him, leaving him there to babble eternally. A different and happier ending to the story is given in the scholia: Eos changed him into a cicada, that most vocal of insects, so that she might have the joy of hearing her lover's voice forever sounding in her ears.

Tennyson's early poem 'Tithonus' keeps to the more melancholy version of the legend:

> The woods decay, the woods decay and fall,
> The vapours weep their burthen to the ground,
> Man comes and tills the field and lies beneath,
> And after many a summer dies the swan.
> Me only cruel immortality
> Consumes: I wither slowly in thine arms,
> Here at the quiet limit of the world,
> A white-hair'd shadow roaming like a dream
> The ever-silent spaces of the East,
> Far-folded mists, and gleaming halls of morn ...

[Homer, *Iliad* 20.236–8; Euripides, *Trojan Women* 847–58; Apollodorus 3.12.4.]

Tityus

A giant, and one of the four great sinners (along with IXION, TANTALUS (1) and SISYPHUS) who after death endured eternal punishment for their transgressions on earth. He was the son of ZEUS and Elara, though was often also called the son of GAIA (Earth), for Zeus hid the pregnant Elara in the earth from fear of Hera's jealousy and Tityus was in the course of time 'earth-born'. One day he tried to rape LETO as she journeyed through Panopeus to Delphi and was shot dead by her children, APOLLO and ARTEMIS. In the *Odyssey* (11.576–81), Odysseus sees Tityus' punishment in Hades for his crime: he is tied to the ground, sprawled over two acres, while two vultures squat on either side of him, tearing at his liver. The tissues always regrow, so his torment never ends. Elsewhere in the *Odyssey*, we hear of RHADAMANTHYS' voyage to see Tityus in Euboea (7.321–4). No reason is given for his journey, and we should perhaps see Rhadamanthys here in his role of the great law-giver, and his purpose to visit punishment on Tityus, condemning him to his eternal torment.

There was a cave in Euboea named Elarium after Tityus' mother, where Tityus himself had a shrine and was worshipped as a hero. The traveller Pausanias saw his vast grave-mound at Panopeus (10.4.5–6). He also tells us that Tityus' death at the hands of Apollo and Artemis was depicted on the Amyclae throne (3.18.15) and was the subject of a group of statuary at Delphi (10.11.1), and that Tityus was painted by Polygnotus in his famous picture of the Underworld as 'no longer being punished, but reduced to nothing by continuous torture, a dim and mutilated phantom' (10.29.3).

[Hesiod, *Catalogue of Women* fr. 78; Pindar, *Pythian* 4.90–2; Apollodorus 1.4.1; Strabo 9.3.14; Lucretius 3.984–94; Virgil, *Aeneid* 6.595–600; Ovid, *Metamorphoses* 4.457–8.]

Tlepolemus

A son of HERACLES, his mother being Astyoche, the daughter of PHYLAS (1), king of Ephyra in Threspotia, or, according to Pindar, Astydameia, the daughter of Amyntor. When Tlepolemus came of age, he killed his father's uncle LICYMNIUS, although sources disagree as to whether he did this accidentally, or in the course of a quarrel. He was exiled and sailed to Rhodes, where together with a large band of followers he settled the cities of Ialysos, Lindos and Cameiros. Zeus poured wealth on him and his people. He was one of the suitors of HELEN, and bound by the common oath to defend the marriage-rights of her chosen husband, he later led nine ships from Rhodes to the TROJAN WAR. His death is recounted in the *Iliad* (5.628–69). He came up against the great hero SARPEDON, a grandson of Zeus in combat with a son of Zeus. At first they attempted to intimidate each other with abusive speeches, and then:

... at the same moment the long spears shot
from their hands, and the shaft of Sarpedon
struck Tlepolemus in the middle of his throat,
the cruel spear driving straight through,
and dark night misted over his eyes,

while Sarpedon was merely wounded in the thigh, since
Zeus protected him from death. After the war, the surviving
Rhodians touched at Crete on their journey home,
then were driven off course by winds and settled in the
Iberian islands. It was said, in a late and unusual variant
of the legend of Helen, that Tlepolemus' wife POLYXO (2),
grieving for the loss of her husband at Troy, brought
about Helen's death to punish her for causing the Trojan
War.

[Homer, *Iliad* 2.653–70; Hesiod, *Catalogue of Women* fr. 232;
Pindar *Olympian* 7.20–38; Apollodorus 2.7.6, 2.7.8, *Epitome*
6.15.]

Tmolus

A mountain in Lydia and its god. Tmolus acted as judge
in the musical contest between Apollo and Pan (*see* MIDAS).

Triptolemus

The mortal from Eleusis in Attica whom the goddess
DEMETER chose to transmit her gift of grain and agriculture to the world. In the earliest version of the legend in
the *Homeric Hymn to Demeter* (153, 474), Triptolemus is
simply one of the leading citizens of Eleusis to whom the
goddess teaches her rites, but he is later said to be the
eldest son of the king, Celeus, and his wife METANEIRA, or
is even identified with their son, usually called Demophon,
whom Demeter tried to make immortal. Various other
parents are also given him, including Eleusis, the eponymous hero of the city, and OCEANUS and GAIA (Earth).

Demeter gave Triptolemus a supply of corn and a chariot drawn by winged dragons. In this he flew over all the
earth, scattering the corn and teaching the people how to
cultivate crops. A number of stories are told of his journeyings. He stayed for a while with Eumelus, the first
king of Patrae in Achaea, teaching him his skills. One
day, while Triptolemus was asleep, Eumelus' son Antheias
harnessed the dragons of his chariot, then flew up and

**Fig. 142 Triptolemus, holding stalks of grain, sits on
a wheeled, winged throne. Demeter *(left)* and
Persephone, holding torches, attend his departure to
spread knowledge of agriculture among mortals.**

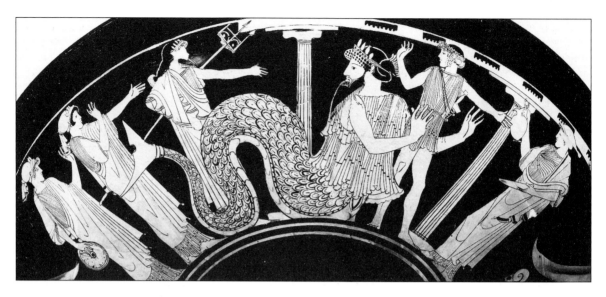

tried to sow the seed himself. But he fell to earth and was killed. Triptolemus and Eumelus founded a city and named it Antheia after the dead boy.

Triptolemus also visited Lyncus, a king of Scythia, and offered to teach him how to cultivate corn. The king welcomed him hospitably, but inwardly he was deeply jealous and wished that he himself could bestow such a rich gift on mankind. He decided to murder his guest and steal his corn and chariot. While Triptolemus slept he crept up on him with drawn sword, and was just about to strike when Demeter punished him by transforming him into a lynx. Carnabon was another king, this time of Thrace, who suffered a similar jealousy, welcoming Triptolemus but growing envious of his guest. He killed one of Triptolemus' dragons to prevent his escape, and would have killed him too had not Demeter come to her favourite's rescue. As a warning to the rest of mankind she set Carnabon among the stars, in the act of killing the dragon, as the constellation Ophiuchus, the Serpent-holder.

Sophocles wrote a *Triptolemus*, now lost, but we know that it mentioned the dragon-chariot, and that Demeter described the many places to which Triptolemus would travel in his agricultural mission. He is often depicted in ancient art, from the sixth century BC onwards, seated in his chariot and holding the ears of corn that Demeter has given him (fig. 142). Plato names Triptolemus as one of the judges of the dead, along with Minos, Rhadamanthys and Aeacus.

[Plato, *Apology* 41a; Apollodorus 1.5.2; Pausanias 1.14.1–3, 1.38.6, 7.18.2–3, 8.4.1; Ovid, *Metamorphoses* 5.642–61; Hyginus, *Poetic Astronomy* 2.14.]

Fig. 143 **The young Theseus in the palace of his father, Poseidon (holding a trident), at the bottom of the sea. The merman Triton prepares to carry him back to the surface, while Nereids bid him farewell.**

Triton

A minor sea-god, the son of POSEIDON and the Nereid AMPHITRITE. As we see from his many depictions in ancient art, he was a merman, with a human head and torso and a coiling, fishy tail (fig. 143). He is shown wrestling with HERACLES, though no trace of this episode survives in literature. He is also often shown blowing on his conch-shell horn. With this horn he had once, on his father's instructions, calmed the stormy seas and ordered the waters to retreat at the end of the Great Flood. So proud was he of his musical skill on this instrument, that when he heard the Trojan MISENUS boasting that he himself could play as well as any of the gods, the jealous Triton drowned his presumptious rival.

Triton played a part in the legend of the ARGONAUTS, appearing to them at Lake Tritonis in Libya, after they had been carried far inland by a tidal wave and were desperately seeking an outlet to the sea. At first he disguised himself as Eurypylus, a local king, and presented to one of their company, EUPHEMUS, a clod of earth as a gift of friendship. He himself received from the Greeks a golden tripod, brought from Delphi. Reverting to his true form, he swam beside the *Argo* and led the ship safely back to the Mediterranean. Euphemus dropped the clod of earth into the sea north of Crete, where it became the island of Thera.

In early literature there seems to be only one Triton, but later he becomes pluralised into a whole range of fishy beings who make up Poseidon's retinue. Pausanias, for instance, refers to several Tritons, one of whom attacked the women of Tanagra while they were bathing in the sea before sacrificing to Dionysus. They called on their god, who fought the Triton and defeated him. Another Triton was in the habit of plundering Tanagran cattle, and even attacking boats, until one day the towns-people left out a bowl of wine for him. Drawn by the smell, he drank the wine and fell asleep on the shore, at which a man of Tanagra approached and chopped off the Triton's head with an axe. Pausanias saw this headless Triton, and also a smaller one in Rome which, he reports, had hair on its head like that of marsh frogs, while the rest of its body was finely scaled like a shark. It had a man's nose, a wide mouth with animal teeth, hands with fingers and fingernails, but also gills and a dolphin's tail. Its eyes, adds Pausanias, seemed to be blue. He accurately describes several other unusual beasts, including rhino-ceroses ('Ethiopian bulls'), and comments (9.21.6): 'So no one should be over-hasty in their judgements, or in-credulous when considering rare creatures.'

In postclassical art, Tritons are often depicted sporting in the waves with NEREIDS, or in Poseidon's train, or in the sea-triumphs of Amphitrite, Galatea or Aphrodite. A Triton blowing his horn, raising the great shell to his bearded lips, has been a popular choice for fountain-figures, as on Bernini's Triton Fountain in the Piazza Barberini in Rome, and on Rome's famous Trevi Fountain. In Wordsworth's passionate sonnet 'The World is Too Much with Us', Triton becomes a symbol of a lost and less materialistic world:

> Great God! I'd rather be
> A Pagan suckled in a creed outworn;
> So might I, standing on this pleasant lea,
> Have glimpses that would make me less forlorn;
> Have sight of Proteus rising from the sea,
> Or hear old Triton blow his wreathed horn.

[Hesiod, *Theogony* 930–3; Pindar, *Pythian* 4.19–56; Herodotus 4.179, 188; Apollonius, *Argonautica* 4.1550–1622, 1731–64; Apollodorus 1.4.5, 3.12.3; Pausanias 3.18.10, 7.22.8, 8.2.7, 9.20.4–9.21.1, 9.33.7; Ovid, *Metamorphoses* 1.324–47.]

Troilus

Son of PRIAM, king of Troy, and HECUBA, though some-times said to be the son of APOLLO. He was killed by ACHILLES during the Trojan War, since it was said that Troy was destined never to fall if Troilus reached the age of twenty. References to the murder are few in literature, and none thoroughly explicit, so the details have to be pieced together from a variety of sources, including vase-paintings of the scene; but the story seems to have been that Achilles lay in wait for Troilus outside the walls of Troy, then pursued him and killed him in the Thym-braean sanctuary sacred to Apollo.

Despite the literary gaps this was clearly a very pop-ular story, since from the seventh century BC onwards it was a favourite subject in art, its most famous represen-tation being on the François Krater (*c.* 570 BC). From the different scenes depicted we can learn a little more about the murder. We see Achilles lying in ambush at a foun-tain house, where Troilus' sister POLYXENA comes to draw water, accompanied by her brother. Troilus is usually riding one horse and leading another. Achilles leaps out and pursues him, while he gallops away, and the water jar crashes to the ground as Polyxena too runs away in fear (fig. 144). Achilles outruns Troilus' horse ('swift-footed Achilles', as Homer calls him) and kills the boy on Apollo's altar. Some scenes even show Troilus brutally decapitated. Finally the Trojans attack Achilles over Troilus' mutilated body. In many scenes a violent con-trast is made between the huge attacking warrior and the small, defenceless boy (fig. 4).

Troilus seems always to have been associated with horses. In the only reference to him in Homer, where Priam simply mentions him as dead, he is described as 'delighting in horses' (*Iliad* 24.257). In art he is usually

Fig. 144 Troilus and Polyxena flee in terror from Achilles. Troilus rides one horse and leads another. Water pours from the broken jar that Polyxena has dropped in her fright.

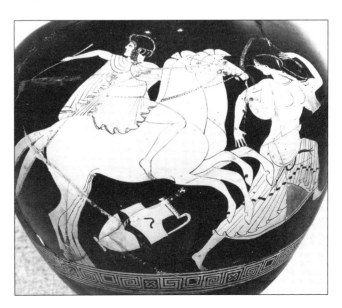

shown fleeing on horseback from Achilles pursuing on foot. In Sophocles' lost tragedy *Troilus*, we know that the boy was exercising his horses near Apollo's sanctuary when Achilles ambushed him. In Virgil (*Aeneid* 1.474–8) Troilus has a chariot, but his horses bolt and he is dragged along in the dust behind them, entangled in the reins.

Two quite different erotic motifs were later imported into the story. The first changed the motive for the murder, saying that Achilles fell in love with Troilus, who took refuge from his unwelcome suitor in Apollo's precinct. When the boy refused to come out, Achilles went in and killed him. The second was the romance between Troilus and Cressida (a corruption of CHRYSEIS), a medieval fiction developing from Benoit de Sainte-Maure's twelfth-century *Roman de Troie*, through Boccaccio's *Filostrato* and Chaucer's *Troilus and Creseyde*, to Shakespeare.

[Epic Cycle, Proclus' summary of the *Cypria*; Apollodorus 3.12.5, *Epitome* 3.32; Plautus, *Bacchides* 953–5.]

Trojan War

The greatest war in classical mythology, waged by an alliance of Greek cities against the Phrygian city of TROY. It all began at the wedding of the mortal Peleus with the sea-goddess Thetis, to which all the gods were invited except ERIS (Strife). She was annoyed at being excluded, so out of spite she threw into the midst of the gathering a golden apple inscribed with the words 'for the fairest'. The three goddesses Hera, Athena and Aphrodite argued as to who most deserved it, and to settle the dispute Zeus sent them to PARIS, the son of King PRIAM of Troy, as he tended his flocks on Mount Ida. He was to decide between them, a choice famously known as the JUDGEMENT OF PARIS (fig. 81). He chose Aphrodite, who had bribed him with the love of the most beautiful woman in the world, HELEN, wife of King MENELAUS of Sparta. Despite the warnings of his brother and sister, HELENUS and CASSANDRA, and of the nymph OENONE, all of whom were seers and knew just what disasters would follow, Paris set off for Sparta to claim Aphrodite's promised reward. Thanks to the goddess' influence, he easily won the love of Helen and carried her off to Troy, together with a good many treasures belonging to Menelaus.

The many suitors of the beautiful Helen had, before her marriage, sworn an oath to defend the marriage rights of her chosen husband. So now Menelaus and his more powerful brother, AGAMEMNON, reminded all the suitors of their old oath and mustered a large army to fetch Helen back by force, each of the suitors leading a contingent of ships and warriors. Not all came willingly. ODYSSEUS, king of Ithaca, hoped to avoid enlisting by pre-

tending to be mad, but his ruse was exposed by PALAMEDES. Accepting his fate, Odysseus then helped to recruit other leaders. It was he who enlisted the greatest of the Greek warriors, ACHILLES, who had been sent by his anxious mother to the court of LYCOMEDES, disguised as a girl, so as to avoid the coming war. Odysseus penetrated his disguise, and Achilles, even though he had been too young to be one of Helen's suitors and so had no duty to fight, eagerly joined the expedition. Other leading warriors were AJAX (1), the son of Telamon (fig. 145), who often fought alongside his namesake, AJAX (2), the son of Oileus; DIOMEDES (2), the son of Tydeus; and the highly respected, aged NESTOR.

The fleet mustered at Aulis. The seer CALCHAS predicted the length of the coming war when a snake climbed a plane tree and devoured a mother sparrow and her eight babies, and was then turned into stone by Zeus: he said this meant that the war would last for nine years, and that in the tenth year Troy would be taken. The fleet set sail. But the Greeks, not knowing the way to Troy, landed too far to the south in the land of MYSIA. Here they lost many men to a force led by the king of Teuthrania, TELEPHUS, who was himself wounded by Achilles. The Greeks, discouraged, returned home, followed by Telephus himself, who had learnt from an oracle that his wound could be cured only by the one that had caused it. This meant the spear that had wounded him, so Achilles rubbed some rust from his spear into the wound and Telephus was soon cured. Out of gratitude he agreed to show the Greeks the way to Troy. Once again the fleet mustered at Aulis, but now it was held back by unfavourable winds, or by no winds at all. Calchas interpreted another portent as meaning that Artemis was angry, and that Agamemnon's virgin daughter IPHIGENEIA must be sacrificed to appease the goddess. The girl was lured to Aulis on the pretext of marriage with Achilles, and there killed. The winds blew and the fleet sailed. This time, under Telephus' direction, it successfully reached the Troad.

Before the opening of hostilities, the Greeks sent Menelaus and Odysseus (in another version, ACAMAS (1) and Diomedes) as envoys to Troy in the hope of recovering Helen by peaceful means. The embassy failed, for the Trojans not only refused to give back Helen, but the more aggressive of them threatened to kill the envoys. Saved by the Trojan elder ANTENOR, Odysseus and Menelaus returned to their comrades with the news that war was now inevitable. An oracle had predicted that the first man to touch Trojan soil would be the first to die, so all the Greeks hesitated to land until PROTESILAUS took the initiative and leapt ashore. He killed a number of Trojans before being himself killed by the Trojan leader, HECTOR. Now the fighting started in earnest and many Trojans were killed, including the invulnerable CYCNUS (3), slain by Achilles. The Trojans retreated within their city and the Greeks held it under siege for nine years, meanwhile making forays against many other cities in the region to win food and plunder for the army. It was sometimes said that they were supplied by the daughters of ANIUS.

In the tenth year of the war (as recorded in Homer's *Iliad*), Achilles retired to his tent in anger because Agamemnon had taken his concubine BRISEIS (fig. 3). With Achilles out of action, the Trojans took heart and sallied forth from their city, fighting the Greeks on the plain and driving them back to their ships. Only the death of his dear comrade PATROCLUS brought Achilles back into battle. In a fury of vengeance he massacred the Trojans in vast numbers, and finally slew Hector, the man who had killed his friend. At first Achilles maltreated his victim's body, but then gave it back to Hector's father, Priam, when he came alone to the Greek camp, by night, to plead with his son's killer (fig. 122). There was an eleven-day truce in which Hector was given the full honours of death, then war resumed.

More allies came to help the Trojans. The Amazon queen PENTHESILEIA brought an army of female warriors, and herself killed many Greeks before being slain by Achilles (fig. 113). Even as Achilles delivered the fatal blow, their eyes met and he fell in love with her. Achilles also killed MEMNON, king of the Ethiopians, after which he routed the dispirited Trojans and rushed after them into Troy. Here he was killed by Paris and Apollo. The greatest Greek warrior, as well as Hector, the greatest of the Trojans, was now dead.

Odysseus captured the Trojan seer Helenus, who revealed the oracles, known only to himself, foretelling how the Greeks could take Troy: they must steal the PALLADIUM, the image of Athena, from her Trojan temple; they must bring the bones of PELOPS to Troy; and they must have fighting with them both NEOPTOLEMUS, the son of Achilles, and PHILOCTETES, who owned the great bow and arrows of the mighty Heracles. These conditions were fulfilled, but Troy did not yet fall. One more ploy was needed. The famous WOODEN HORSE was built and filled with the pick of the Greek warriors (fig. 147). The rest sailed away, leaving behind a spy, SINON. When the Trojans came out of their city to investigate, Sinon told them an elaborate story, convincing them that the horse would bring good fortune to Troy. They dragged it inside, deaf to the protests of the prophetess Cassandra and the priest of Apollo, LAOCOON (1). After celebrating the Greeks' departure and the end of the war, they slept, content, in

Fig. 145 During a lull in the fighting at Troy, Achilles *(left)* and Ajax play a board game. Achilles is winning.

their beds. Under cover of darkness, Sinon opened the Wooden Horse and let out the Greeks, then lit a beacon as a signal to the rest of the army to return. They attacked the sleeping, defenceless Trojans and a bloody massacre ensued. King Priam was murdered by Neoptolemus as he sought refuge at the altar of Zeus (figs. 27 and 123), and of the Trojan men, only AENEAS (fig. 35), the seer Helenus, and Antenor and his sons, escaped alive. The Greeks parcelled out the Trojan women as their slaves and concubines. They sacrificed Priam's daughter POLYXENA on Achilles' grave (fig. 120), as his share of the booty, and flung Hector's little son ASTYANAX from the walls of Troy. The Lesser Ajax dragged Cassandra away from the image of Athena to which she was clinging (figs. 27 and 35) and raped her, while the statue turned away its eyes in horror. Troy was put to the torch. But the Greeks too suffered vast losses, for Athena, vengeful because of Ajax' unpunished crime, wrecked the Greek ships in a tremendous storm at Cape Caphareus. Out of many, only few returned home.

[C. W. Blegen, *Troy and the Trojans* (1963); L. Foxhall and J. K. Davies (eds), *The Trojan War: Its Historicity and Context* (1984); D. F. Easton, 'Has the Trojan War been found?', *Antiquity* (1985), pp. 188–96; M. Wood, *In Search of the Trojan War* (1985); M. J. Mellink (ed.), *Troy and the Trojan War* (1986).]

Trophonius and Agamedes

Sons of the aged ERGINUS (1), king of the rich and powerful city of Orchomenus in Boeotia, though Trophonius was also said to be the son of APOLLO. Both brothers were famous as master-builders and were said to have built the footings of Apollo's temple at Delphi, the bridal chamber of ALCMENE at Thebes, and a sanctuary of POSEIDON near Mantineia. They also built the treasury of HYRIEUS at Hyria in Boeotia. This was supposedly robber-proof, but unknown to Hyrieus they had inserted in the walls a movable slab of stone, the secret of which only they knew. Hyrieus was amazed to find that his treasures kept disappearing, even though the treasury remained tightly sealed, so at last he set some kind of trap for the robbers. The next time the brothers came, Agamedes was caught in the snare and Trophonius, quite unable to release him and afraid that he would reveal his accomplice's name under torture, cut off his brother's head and ran off with it. The headless corpse thus remained unrecognised, but even though Trophonius escaped detection he did not escape death, for the earth at Lebadea suddenly opened and swallowed him up.

Another version of the myth relates that after the brothers had worked on Apollo's temple at Delphi, the god's oracle told them that they should live happily for six days, and on the seventh their reward would be given them. Six days passed in pleasures, and on the seventh day the brothers were found peacefully asleep in their beds.

At Lebadea the oracle of Trophonius was famous in historical times. Herodotus reports that it was consulted by the Lydian king Croesus and by the Persian general Mardonius. Pausanias visited it in person, and graphically describes for us the elaborate preliminary rituals and the final terrifying descent into the cave to confront Trophonius himself.

[*Homeric Hymn to Apollo* 296; Herodotus 1.46, 8.133–4; Euripides, *Ion* 300–2, 404–9; Plutarch, *Moralia* 109a; Pausanias 8.10.2, 9.11.1, 9.37.3–7, 9.39.1–9.40.2, 10.5.13.]

Tros

Son of ERICHTHONIUS (2), king of Dardania, and Astyoche, daughter of the river-god SIMOEIS. Tros' name was given to Troy, the Troad, and the Trojans. He married Callirhoe, daughter of the river-god SCAMANDER, and had by her a daughter, Cleopatra, and three sons, ASSARACUS, ILUS and GANYMEDE. Assaracus, succeeding his father, stayed in the city of Dardania on the slopes of Mount Ida, while Ilus built a new city, Ilium (Troy), nearer the coast. Ganymede was carried off because of his beauty to be the cupbearer of ZEUS, but Tros mourned so unceasingly for his lost son that Zeus pitied him, and recompensed him for his loss by giving him some magnificent horses. He also sent HERMES to tell Tros that his son would now be immortal among the gods. According to the *Homeric Hymn to Aphrodite* (215–7):

When Tros heard these tidings from Zeus,

he no longer mourned, but was glad in his heart,
and joyfully rode his storm-swift horses.

[Homer, *Iliad* 20.230–5; Apollodorus 3.12.2.]

Troy

A Phrygian city, also called Ilium, lying near the southern entrance to the Hellespont. This was the site of the TROJAN WAR, one of the greatest mythological stories ever told. Troy's beginnings lay in the union of the river-god SCAMANDER, the chief river of the Trojan plain, with Idaea, a nymph of Mount IDA. Their son TEUCER (1) became king of the area later named the Troad, calling his people Teucrians. He married his daughter Bateia to DARDANUS, an immigrant from Samothrace, who built a city on the slopes of Mount Ida and called it Dardania after himself. When Teucer died, Dardanus succeeded to the rule and renamed his people Dardanians. His son ERICHTHONIUS (2) married Astyoche, daughter of the river-god SIMOEIS, another important river near Troy, and their son TROS was to give his name to Troy, the Troad and the Trojans.

In the next generation Troy itself was founded. Tros married Callirhoe, another daughter of Scamander, and had three sons. One of these, GANYMEDE, was carried off to Olympus because of his beauty, to be the cupbearer of Zeus. Of the other two sons, ASSARACUS stayed ruling in Dardania after the death of Tros, while ILUS moved away. He won the wrestling match at games held by the king of Phrygia, for which his prize consisted of fifty youths and fifty young women. But the king, in obedience to an oracle, added to these a dappled cow, telling Ilus that he must follow the cow wherever it went, then found a city where it lay down. This Ilus did, and eventually the cow lay down on a hill, sacred to the goddess Ate, which rose from the broad plain between Mount Ida and the sea. Here Ilus built his city, naming it Ilium after himself. It was also called Troy after his father, Tros. When Ilus asked for a sign of approval from Zeus, the PALLADIUM, a wooden image of Athena, fell miraculously from the sky, and where it landed he built a temple to Athena to house the statue. It was said that while the Palladium stayed safe in Troy, the city would never fall.

Under the rule of Ilus' son, LAOMEDON, Troy was fortified, its great walls built by the gods POSEIDON and APOLLO, with the help, some say, of the mortal AEACUS. But soon after this Troy suffered its first assault by the Greeks. When Laomedon refused to pay HERACLES the agreed price for saving Hesione from the sea-monster, Heracles returned to Troy at the head of a large army. They breached the walls and killed Laomedon and all his sons but one. This survivor was PRIAM, the last king of Troy.

Priam was the most famous and the most powerful of

the Trojan kings, but during his rule Troy suffered a second assault by the Greeks and was utterly destroyed. When Priam's son PARIS carried off the beautiful HELEN, wife of King Menelaus of Sparta, and brought her back to Troy, a huge force of Greeks led by AGAMEMNON invaded the Troad. Here the Trojan War was fought for ten long years. At the end of that time, the Greeks entered Troy in the WOODEN HORSE. They fired the city, put the Trojan men to the sword, and took the Trojan women away as slaves. The only men who were allowed to live were ANTENOR and his sons, the seer HELENUS, and AENEAS. Priam himself was slaughtered on the altar of Zeus in the courtyard of his own palace. His many sons were already dead, including HECTOR, the bulwark of the Trojans, who had been killed by the great ACHILLES. Hector's little son ASTYANAX was flung from the city walls, and with him died the royal line of Troy.

It was Heinrich Schliemann who determined to prove the truth of the *Iliad* and first excavated the great mound of Hisarlik in the second half of the nineteenth century, rediscovering Troy – one of the greatest stories of archaeology. Of the nine levels which Schliemann defined, Troy VI, VIIa and VIIb are the cities that date from the Mycenean age. Fallen masonry and traces of fire show that Troy VI was violently destroyed around 1270 BC, and Troy VIIa around 1190 BC, though here traces of human bones too have been found in streets and houses.

Schliemann has been succeeded by other excavators, and indeed excavations at Troy are still continuing, though there have always been, and no doubt always will be, those who deny that Troy ever existed. Perhaps the last word can be left to Byron, writing in *Don Juan*:

> ... I've stood upon Achilles' tomb,
> And heard Troy doubted; time will doubt of Rome.

Turnus

Son of Daunus and Venilia; brother of the water-nymph JUTURNA; and king of the Rutulians of Ardea, in Latium, when AENEAS arrived in Italy with his Trojan followers. Turnus had been the favoured suitor of Lavinia, the daughter of King LATINUS and AMATA, but was rejected in favour of Aeneas. The *Aeneid* recounts the tragic aftermath of this rejection. Maddened by the Fury Allecto, sent by Juno, Turnus stirs up the Latins to fight the Trojans. In the bloody war that follows he acquits himself bravely as the Latin commander, killing many of the enemy, including PALLAS (4), Aeneas' young protégé. Finally the outcome is decided by single combat between Turnus and Aeneas. Turnus is wounded in the thigh and Aeneas, about to grant his victim's request to be carried back to his aged father Daunus, suddenly sees that Turnus is wear-

ing Pallas' belt as a battle spoil. 'Are you to escape me now, wearing spoils stripped from one I loved?', cries Aeneas (12.947–9). 'It is Pallas who with this blow makes sacrifice, Pallas who takes his vengeance for your crime.' And overcome with a mighty rage, Aeneas plunges his sword full into Turnus' heart, slaying him pitilessly.

[Dionysius of Halicarnassus 1.64; Livy 1.2.1–6; Virgil, *Aeneid* 7–12.]

Tyche

The goddess of Fortune, both good and bad, identified by the Romans with Fortuna. Tyche seems to have been unknown to Homer, but she later assumed a growing importance, particularly with the decline of belief in the traditional gods. Her cult spread widely from the fourth century BC, when momentous political changes encouraged a belief in the random and irrational workings of Fate.

Tydeus

Son of OENEUS, king of Calydon, either by his second wife Periboea or by his own daughter Gorge. Tydeus was banished from Calydon for murder and took refuge with ADRASTUS (1), king of Argos, at the same time as another exile, POLYNEICES, Oedipus' son from Thebes. Adrastus married two of his daughters to the young men, Deipyle to Tydeus and Argeia to Polyneices, then promised to help his new sons-in-law win back their lost kingdoms, and first of all Polyneices. This led to the fateful expedition of the SEVEN AGAINST THEBES.

During the final Argive attack on the city, the Theban MELANIPPUS (2) gave Tydeus a mortal wound before he too was killed. As Tydeus lay dying, his patron goddess ATHENA approached, intending to endow her favourite with immortality. AMPHIARAUS, who hated Tydeus for his part in initiating the expedition, cut off Melanippus' head and gave it to the dying man. Tydeus savagely split open the head and in his rage began to gnaw on his enemy's brains, a sight so barbaric that the disgusted goddess withheld her intended gift. Tydeus' son DIOMEDES (2) was one of the EPIGONI who avenged their fathers' deaths, and later fought in the Trojan War. It was sometimes said that Athena gave to him the immortality that she had intended for his father.

[Homer, *Iliad* 5.126, 6.222–3, 14.119–25; Aeschylus, *Seven Against Thebes* 377–416; Euripides, *Phoenician Women* 1119–21, 1165–8, *Suppliant Women* 901–2; Apollodorus 1.8.4–5, 3.6.1–8; Pausanias 3.18.12, 9.18.1–2.]

Tyndareos

A king of Sparta. His genealogy is in doubt, for his father may have been Perieres or Oebalus, and his mother

Gorgophone or Bateia. His brothers or half-brothers were LEUCIPPUS (1), APHAREUS, ICARIUS (1) and HIPPOCOON. Hippocoon drove Tyndareos out of Sparta and he took refuge with the Aetolian king THESTIUS, becoming his ally and marrying his daughter LEDA. But after Heracles had killed Hippocoon and his twelve (or twenty) sons, Tyndareos returned to Sparta and became king.

Tyndareos had several children by Leda, but she was also loved by Zeus, who seduced her in the form of a swan, and there is no absolute agreement as to who was the father of whom. Generally speaking, however, Zeus was thought to be the father of HELEN and Polydeuces (*see* DIOSCURI), and Tyndareos of Castor, CLYTEMNESTRA, TIMANDRA, PHILONOE (2) and PHOEBE (3). When the beautiful Helen came of an age to marry, suitors from all over Greece gave bride-gifts in the hope of winning her hand. Tyndareos was afraid of making powerful enemies by choosing one man above the rest, so on the suggestion of ODYSSEUS he made them all take an oath, vowing to support whoever should win Helen and to defend his marriage-rights. MENELAUS became Helen's husband. But the suitors' oath led in the course of time to the Trojan War, when Menelaus and his brother AGAMEMNON marshalled troops to fetch back Helen after she had run away to Troy with Paris. Tyndareos rewarded Odysseus for his helpful suggestion by gaining him his chosen bride, PENELOPE, the daughter of his brother Icarius. He married his own daughter Clytemnestra to Agamemnon, and helped him to regain the throne of Mycenae. He passed the rule of Sparta to Menelaus when his own sons, Castor and Polydeuces, were no longer living.

It was said that in sacrificing to the gods Tyndareos had neglected APHRODITE, so the goddess punished him by making three of his daughters unfaithful to their husbands. Helen ran off to Troy with Paris. Timandra deserted Echemus for Phyleus. Clytemnestra took a lover, Aegisthus, while Agamemnon was away at Troy, and she and her lover killed him on his return home. When ORESTES took revenge and in turn killed Clytemnestra, it was Tyndareos, according to Euripides in his *Orestes*, who brought the charge of matricide against him. Some said that Tyndareos was restored to life by the healer ASCLEPIUS.

[Hesiod, *Catalogue of Women* fr. 176; Apollodorus 1.9.5, 2.7.3, 3.10.3–3.11.2, *Epitome* 2.15–16, 6.25; Diodorus Siculus 4.33; Strabo 10.2.24; Pausanias 3.1.4–5, 3.17.4, 3.20.9.]

Typhon or Typhaon or Typhoeus

A vast and terrifying monster, the final challenger to the power of ZEUS, king of the gods. In the *Homeric Hymn to Apollo* (305–55), Typhon is said to have been a child of HERA alone, who was jealous when Zeus produced ATHENA from his head (and especially jealous since the child whom she herself had produced by parthenogenesis, HEPHAESTUS, was such a poor physical specimen). So Hera prayed to GAIA (Earth) for a son stronger than Zeus, striking the earth with her hand, and Gaia heard and fulfilled her prayer. Hera in due course gave her monstrous offspring to be reared by the snake PYTHON. But according to the more usual account narrated by Hesiod (*Theogony* 820–80), Typhon was the son of TARTARUS and Gaia. He had on his shoulders a hundred fearsome snake-heads, all with black tongues flickering and eyes flashing fire, and these heads were able to imitate every conceivable sound – the bellow of a great bull, the roar of a lion, the baying of a pack of hounds, the hissing of serpents. Apollodorus (1.6.3) adds that he was born in the Corycian cave in Cilicia, in south-eastern Asia Minor north of Cyprus. He was taller than all the mountains, and his head touched the stars. If he stretched out his arms, his one hand touched East and the other West, and instead of fingers he had a hundred snakes' heads. His mouth shot forth flames, his body was winged, and from the thighs down he was a mass of huge, coiling serpents. This monster challenged Zeus, who in Hesiod's version achieved supremacy without undue difficulty, responding with his mighty thunderbolts (839–56):

> The earth and the wide heaven above resounded with fearsome noise, and the sea, and the streams of Ocean, and the nethermost parts of the earth. Great Olympus trembled under the immortal feet of the king as he went forth, and the earth groaned in reply. A conflagration gripped the purple sea, from the god's thunder and lightning and the monster's fire, from the flaming bolt and tornado winds. The whole earth seethed, and the sea and the sky ... and Zeus leapt from Olympus and struck, scorching all the awesome heads on every side of the dreadful monster.

Typhon collapsed, crippled, and Zeus flung him into Tartarus. There Typhon became the father of all the irregular storm winds that bring harm to men and cause shipwrecks, thus giving his name to our word typhoon.

Apollodorus makes the conflict a more challenging one for Zeus, and indeed for the other gods too, who fled in terror to Egypt and changed themselves into various animals. (From other sources we know that Apollo became a hawk or a crow, HERMES an ibis, Ares and Aphrodite fishes, Artemis a cat, Dionysus a goat, Heracles a fawn, Hera and Hephaestus oxen, and Leto a mouse. This story was probably invented to explain the animal forms of

Egyptian gods whom the Greeks identified with their own deities. Typhon himself was identified with Seth, the enemy of Osiris, and Zeus was said to accompany the flight disguised as a ram with curling horns, to account for the cult of Zeus Ammon in ram-shape.) In this version, Zeus attacked Typhon with thunderbolt and sickle, chasing after him and finally grappling with him. But at close quarters Typhon wrested the sickle from Zeus and cut the sinews from his hands and feet, then carried the helpless god off to his cave in Cilicia. He hid the sinews in a bearskin and set the she-dragon DELPHYNE to guard them, but they were stolen by Hermes and AEGIPAN and refitted to Zeus' hands and feet. The god, his powers recovered, pursued Typhon once more with his thunderbolt. He was helped by the FATES, who fed Typhon weakening fruit, though pretending that it would strengthen him. Still the monster heaved whole mountains at Zeus in his flight. In Thrace one of these rebounded and wounded Typhon, thereafter being called Mount Haemus from his blood (*haima*) that spurted over it. Finally, when they came near Sicily, Zeus hurled Mount Etna on top of Typhon and crushed him beneath it.

Typhon left behind him various monstrous offspring born of another monster, ECHIDNA, most of them a bane to mankind. The volcano on Mount Etna is also his legacy, for there his anger pours forth in streams of fire as he struggles to free himself. Apollodorus, less dramatically, says that the flames are the remains of Zeus' thunderbolts. In ancient art Typhon tends, for practical reasons, to be depicted with a single human head, and a winged human torso attached at the waist to one or two great snakey coils (fig. 146).

[Homer, *Iliad* 2.782–3; Aeschylus, *Prometheus Bound* 351–72; Pindar, *Pythian* 1.15–28; Antoninus Liberalis, *Metamorphoses* 28; Ovid, *Metamorphoses* 5.321–58.]

Tyro

Daughter of SALMONEUS and Alcidice. She opposed her father's attempt to make himself equal to Zeus, so when Zeus in anger killed Salmoneus for his presumption, together with all his people, he spared Tyro and took her to her uncle, Cretheus, the king of Iolcus. Cretheus received her joyfully and brought her up.

In the *Odyssey*, when Odysseus meets Tyro's shade in Hades, we hear the story of her seduction by POSEIDON, who fathered on her twin sons (11.238–55):

> She fell in love with the river, divine Enipeus,
> most beautiful of rivers that flow upon the earth,
> and she would haunt Enipeus' lovely waters.
> So the god who holds the earth, the Earth-shaker,
> took his likeness, and lay with her at the mouth

Fig. 146 Zeus hurls a thunderbolt at the snake-tailed monster Typhon.

> of the swirling river, and a great dark wave,
> a mountain of water, curved up and around them
> and hid the god and the mortal woman. He loosed
> her virgin belt and drifted sleep upon her,
> then when he had ended his act of love, the god
> took her hand in his and said to her:
> 'Be happy, lady, in this love of ours, and when
> the year goes by you will bear splendid sons,
> for love with a god is never without issue.
> Take care of them and raise them. Now go home
> and hold your peace. Tell nobody my name.
> But I tell you, I am Poseidon, the Earth-shaker.'
> He spoke, and plunged back into the swelling sea.
> And she conceived, and bore Pelias and Neleus ...

The story continues in Apollodorus (1.9.7–11). Despite Poseidon's injunction, Tyro did not bring up her sons: she abandoned them in the wild and they were brought up by a horse-breeder. When they grew up they found their mother again, who was being treated with great cruelty by her stepmother, Sidero. There is some uncertainty as to whether this Sidero was the wife of Cretheus, Tyro's foster-father, or the second wife of Salmoneus, her real father; but, either way, PELIAS and NELEUS attacked the wicked stepmother, and Pelias killed her on the altars of a sanctuary of Hera. This recognition and revenge most likely formed the plot of one at least of Sophocles' two lost tragedies, *Tyro*, and according to Aristotle in the *Poetics* (16) the recognition occurred by means of the box in which the infants had been abandoned. Tyro's sad story ends happily, for she married Cretheus and had by him three sons, AESON, PHERES (1) and AMYTHAON.

[Homer, *Odyssey* 11.235–59; Hesiod, *Catalogue of Women* frr. 30, 31.]

U–Z

Udaeus

One of the SOWN MEN of Thebes.

Ulysses *see* ODYSSEUS.

Urania *see* MUSES.

Uranus

The divine personification of the sky (*ouranos*), whose main function in myth was to be the progenitor of a large number of children at the beginning of creation (*see* GAIA).

Ursa Major (The Great Bear)

A constellation in the northern sky immortalising the Arcadian huntress CALLISTO, who was transformed into a bear after being raped by Zeus. She bore the god a son, Arcas, who was also set among the stars (but not, as might be expected, as the constellation Ursa Minor, the Little Bear, which seems to have no particular myth attached to it). Arcas became the brilliant star Arcturus, 'Bear-guardian', in the nearby constellation Boötes, forever following his mother through the night sky. Ursa Major never sets, for Hera, jealous of her old rival and angry that Zeus had put her in the stars, asked the sea-gods Oceanus and Tethys never to allow her to sink for rest into the waters of Ocean that surround the earth. This is why the Great Bear revolves eternally around the Pole Star, high in the heavens.

The Greeks called the Great Bear *Arktos*, which gives us our name Arctic for the northern Polar region.

Venus

The Roman goddess of love and beauty, and the consort of the Roman war-god, MARS. She was identified with the Greek goddess of love, APHRODITE, and acquired Aphrodite's mythology as her own. She was the mother of AENEAS by the Trojan prince ANCHISES, and was thus claimed as ancestor, through Aeneas' son ASCANIUS/Iulus, by the emperors of the Julian line. To Lucretius (1.30–41), Venus was the supreme generative force.

The story of Aeneas' wanderings and his founding of a Trojan settlement in Italy, detailed in Virgil's *Aeneid*, was especially important to the Romans. Venus supported her son through his many trials, protecting him whenever she could from the violent hostility of JUNO. She helped him to escape from burning Troy, and arranged for DIDO, the queen of Carthage, to fall in love with him and give him a welcome refuge in her city. When Aeneas arrived in Italy and was involved in a war with the Latins, Venus had VULCAN make her son splendid new armour. She also helped him in his decisive battle with TURNUS, giving him back his spear, which had become immovably lodged in a tree trunk. With this spear Aeneas killed Turnus and won the war.

Vertumnus

The Roman god of the changing seasons (*vertere*, 'to change'), linked with the earth's fertility, and probably Etruscan in origin. He was able to change his shape at will, and by using this skill he wooed and won the goddess Pomona for his wife. By disguising himself as a haymaker, an ox-herd, a fisherman and suchlike, he found many ways of approaching his love and gazing at her beauty, but never did he catch her fancy, for she was devoted to her orchards and spurned all suitors. Finally he changed himself into an old woman, and pleaded his own cause so eloquently that, when he was changed back into his own shape, he found that at last she loved him with a passion equal to his own.

[Ovid, *Metamorphoses* 14.623–771.]

Vesta

The Roman goddess of the hearth, identified with the Greek goddess HESTIA. At Rome she was considered the guardian of the community. The priestesses who superintended her cult and kept an eternal fire burning on her altar, tending it night and day, were known as the Vestal Virgins. At her festival, the *Vestalia*, asses were adorned with necklaces of loaves and did no work, because Vesta was once saved by an ass from the amorous designs of PRIAPUS. After a feast of Cybele, where all the gods and nymphs and satyrs ate and drank their fill, Vesta fell asleep. Priapus saw her and desired her, and would have had her too if a bray from Silenus' ass had not woken her in time. So the goddess escaped a painful fate, and ever afterwards asses were honoured in her name.

[Ovid, *Fasti* 6.319–48.]

Virbius

A minor Italian god, whose cult was associated with the worship of DIANA at the goddess' sacred grove in Aricia, on the shores of Lake Nemi near Rome. He was said to be HIPPOLYTUS (2), who had been dragged to his death by his horses, then brought back to life again by the healer Asclepius. He was renamed Virbius from *vir* ('man') and *bis* ('twice'). Because of the manner of his death, no horses were allowed in the grove.

[Virgil, *Aeneid* 7.761–82; Ovid, *Metamorphoses* 15.497–546, *Fasti* 3.263–8, 6.735–56.]

Virgo (The Virgin)

A constellation usually thought to represent ERIGONE (1), the daughter of the Attic farmer Icarius who introduced Dionysus' gift of wine to his neighbours. Sometimes Virgo is said to represent some abstract concept such as Dike (Justice) or Tyche (Chance).

Volcens *see* NISUS (2).

Voluptas

Daughter of Cupid and PSYCHE.

Vulcan

Ancient Italian god of destructive, devouring fire, who was later identified with the Greek smith-god HEPHAESTUS. After this he too became the patron of smiths and other craftsmen who use fire for the good of mankind. Vulcan was the father of CAECULUS, who founded Praeneste, and of the fire-breathing monster CACUS, who lived on human flesh and was killed by Hercules.

Wandering Rocks *see* SYMPLEGADES.

Fig.147 **The Wooden Horse, on wheels, with the faces of the Greeks within visible through square portholes. Some Greeks have already climbed down from the horse, while others hand out their arms.**

White Island *see* ELYSIUM.

Wooden Horse

The famous stratagem by which the Greeks entered the otherwise impregnable city of Troy, thus achieving a triumphant end to the ten-year-long TROJAN WAR. The Wooden Horse was built by EPEIUS (2) on the suggestion of ATHENA or ODYSSEUS: a hollow image of a horse, huge enough to contain a group of armed men, and inscribed with the words, 'For their return home, the Greeks dedicate this thank-offering to Athena.' The Greeks sailed ostentatiously away, leaving armed warriors hiding silently within the horse while it was dragged into Troy. The men waited for night to fall, then in the darkness left their hiding place and created carnage, attacking the Trojans who lay asleep and unsuspecting, until the city was at last theirs.

Homer knows of the Wooden Horse: no mention is made of it in the *Iliad*, where its builder Epeius is mentioned simply as a champion boxer, but in the *Odyssey* the bard Demodocus at the court of King Alcinous sings of how the Greeks set fire to their camp and sailed away, while Odysseus and other warriors stayed in the horse. The Trojans dragged it as far as their acropolis, then argued as to whether they should cut it open, throw it down from a high place, or leave it as an offering to the gods. The last view prevailed, and by night the Greeks streamed out and sacked the city (8.492–520). Later Odysseus tells the shade of Achilles in the Underworld that his son NEOPTOLEMUS had been one of the warriors inside the horse, keeping his coolness and courage while the other Greeks were weeping and trembling (11.523–32). MENELAUS relates that when the horse had

been brought into Troy, HELEN walked around it with DEIPHOBUS, patting it and calling out the names of the Greek leaders while imitating the voices of their wives, and it was only Odysseus' quick thinking that prevented the men from answering, and the plan from coming to nothing (4.271–89). It sounds as though Homer did not imagine the horse as being unduly large. Later authors variously estimate the number of warriors inside: twenty three, thirty plus, fifty, a hundred, or even an unlikely three thousand have all been suggested, while Eustathius commenting on Homer (*Odyssey* 11.522) says – perhaps most plausibly – that they were twelve: Menelaus, Diomedes, Philoctetes, Meriones, Neoptolemus, Eurypylus, Eurydamas, Pheidippus, Leonteus, Meges, Odysseus and Eumelus.

Our most detailed account occurs in the *Aeneid* (2.13–267), with Virgil apparently taking many of his particulars from the lost Epic Cycle. The Greeks sail only as far as Tenedos, but the Trojans believe that they have gone home and come out of their city rejoicing. They find the horse, which in Virgil is immense, 'as big as a mountain', and debate what to do with it. LAOCOON (1) tries to stop them from dragging it into the city, realising that it is some kind of ploy and uttering the famous words, 'I fear the Greeks, especially when they bear gifts' (49). He casts his great spear into the horse's side to show that it is hollow. But the Greek SINON, pretending to be a deserter, persuades the Trojans that the horse has been built as an offering for Athena, and was made immense to prevent its being taken into Troy and bringing the goddess' favour to the city. The trap is laid and the Trojans fall into it. They are completely taken in by Sinon, and their belief in his words is further strengthened when two great snakes come swimming across the surface of the sea and seize Laocoon and his two sons in their coils, crushing them to death, apparently Laocoon's punishment for casting his spear at the goddess' offering. So the Trojans, full of confidence and rejoicing, breach their walls and take the horse into the heart of their city. CASSANDRA warns them that this means disaster, but – as ever – she is not believed, and the people of Troy spend their last, doomed day decking the shrines of the gods with garlands of thanksgiving. At night, when they are sleeping soundly and contentedly, Sinon opens the horse to release the warriors within. They kill the guards and throw wide the city gates, letting in the rest of the Greeks who have meanwhile sailed quietly back to Troy. The city is, as always, bloodily sacked.

The Wooden Horse first appears in ancient art on a bow fibula of about 700 BC, where it is shown with wheels instead of hooves. It is depicted perhaps most famously on a relief pithos from Mykonos of 675–650 BC (fig. 147), again with wheels, but here also with seven windows on its side, out of which peer seven Greek warriors. On the body of the pithos are scenes showing the brutality and carnage that the horse brought to the Trojans. Pausanias (1.23.8) describes a bronze horse on the Athenian Acropolis, whose inscribed base has since been found, that showed Menestheus, Teucer, Acamas and Demophon peeping out of it. In postclassical art the horse has been dramatically painted by Tiepolo, and two of his paintings in London's National Gallery show the building of the horse and the Trojans bringing it into Troy. James Joyce saw the Wooden Horse as the prototype of the tank: 'They are both shells containing armed warriors.'

[Epic Cycle, Proclus' summary of the *Little Iliad* and the *Sack of Troy*; Apollodorus, *Epitome* 5.14–21; Quintus of Smyrna, *Sequel to Homer* 12.23–13.60; Seneca, *Agamemnon* 612–58.]

Xanthus and **Balius**

In Homer's *Iliad*, Xanthus and Balius are the immortal horses 'Bay' and 'Dapple' who can run swift as the wind and belong to ACHILLES. One of the HARPIES, Podarge, conceived them to the West Wind, ZEPHYRUS, while she grazed in the form of a horse beside the river of Ocean. Poseidon gave them as a wedding present to Achilles' father PELEUS, and Achilles in due course took them to Troy. Homer tells how PATROCLUS borrows them (together with the mortal horse, PEDASUS, who is killed) when he leads the Myrmidons into battle. At his death the horses weep for him (17.426–40):

> The horses of Achilles standing apart from the battle
> wept, since first they learned how their charioteer
> had fallen in the dust at the hands of man-slaying
>   Hector ...
> They stayed as still as a gravestone set above
> the tomb of a dead man or woman, so they stood
> motionless, holding firm their lovely chariot,
> bowing their heads to the earth, and warm tears ran
> down from their eyes to the ground as they wept in
>   longing
> for their charioteer, their rich manes soiled with dust,
> streaming down both sides of the yoke from under the
>   collar.

Zeus pities them, regretting that they have ever been given to a mortal and thus grieved by mortal sorrows, and he breathes fresh energy into them to escape HECTOR and return safely to the Greek lines.

When Achilles himself returns to battle, passionate to kill Hector and thus avenge the death of Patroclus, Xanthus, given by Hera the power of human speech for a few brief moments, warns his master of his own imminent death which the horses will be unable to prevent (19.415–18):

> But we two could run swift as the breath of the West Wind which, men say, is of all winds the swiftest; yet still for you is a violent death fated at the hands of a god or a mortal.

But Achilles already knows that his death is fated to occur soon after the death of Hector, and he chooses to fight and avenge Patroclus, come what may.

[Homer, *Iliad* 16.148–51; Apollodorus 3.13.5.]

Xuthus

Ancestor of the Ionians and the Achaeans. Xuthus was the son of HELLEN and the nymph Orseis, and the brother of AEOLUS (1) and DORUS who were the ancestors of the Aeolians and the Dorians. After the death of Hellen, Xuthus was driven out of Thessaly by his two brothers for allegedly stealing family property. He went to Athens, where the king, ERECHTHEUS, gave him the hand of his daughter Creusa in marriage. He had by her two sons, ION and ACHAEUS. According to Pausanias, when Erechtheus died Xuthus was appointed judge to decide which of his sons should succeed him. He chose the eldest son, CECROPS (2), whereupon the other sons drove him out of Athens. With his own two sons he settled in Aegialus in the northern Peloponnese and lived there until his death. The land was later renamed Achaea after his son Achaeus, while Ion gave his name to the Ionians.

Xuthus is an important character in Euripides' *Ion*, where the family relationships are rather different. Aeolus and Dorus are no longer the brothers of Xuthus, for Aeolus is his father, and it is foretold at the end of the play that Dorus will be his son (along with Achaeus). Xuthus is the king of Athens, having himself succeeded Erechtheus, and Ion is the son of his wife Creusa and the god Apollo. Creusa abandoned Ion when he was born, but he was saved by Apollo and brought up at Delphi in the god's service, all the while believing himself to be an orphan. During the play Xuthus and Creusa come to Delphi to inquire about their childlessness, and Xuthus comes to believe that Ion is his son. Creusa, jealous and grieving for her own long-lost boy, tries unsuccessfully to poison Ion, but the truth comes out just as he is about to kill her in punishment. Mother and son are at last joyfully reunited, while Xuthus remains content in the belief that he is the boy's father. The family return in great happiness to Athens.

[Hesiod, *Catalogue of Women* fr. 9; Apollodorus 1.7.3; Strabo 8.7.1; Pausanias 7.1.1–3.]

Zagreus

A Greek god, identified with DIONYSUS, who was worshipped by those who practised the mystery religion of Orphism. Their story of his birth is the only significant divergence from the usual myth. ZEUS, they said, lay with PERSEPHONE in the form of a snake, and from their union Zagreus was born. Zeus intended this son to be his heir, but his jealous wife HERA persuaded the TITANS to kill the child. They distracted his attention with toys, then carried him off, tore him to pieces and devoured him, all but the heart, which Athena rescued and gave to Zeus. From this heart, still beating, Zeus refashioned his son in the body of his mortal love SEMELE. In due course the child was born a second time, though not without further intervention by the jealous Hera.

Zeus blasted the Titans to ashes with his thunderbolt, and from this residue was created mankind. This explained the mixture of good and evil in men, for they incorporated a tiny trace of divinity in a great deal of Titanic wickedness. The Orphics believed in the transmigration of souls, and in the possibility of stamping out man's inborn evil during three virtuous lives and intervening periods of purification in the Underworld. After this the believer would dwell in Elysium for ever.

[Diodorus Siculus 3.62, 3.64; Pausanias 7.18.4, 8.37.5; Nonnus, *Dionysiaca* 5.563–71, 6.155–205; Ovid, *Metamorphoses* 6.114.]

Zelus ('Aspiration') *see* BIA.

Zephyrus

The West Wind and its god. He was the son of the Titan Astraeus and EOS, goddess of Dawn, and was sometimes thought to have IRIS, the rainbow, as his wife. He fathered Achilles' immortal horses, XANTHUS AND BALIUS, on one of the storm-swift HARPIES, Podarge, while she grazed in the form of a horse beside the river of Ocean. (No doubt he himself took the form of a stallion, as did his brother, the North Wind BOREAS, when he coupled with the mares of ERICHTHONIUS (2), king of Troy.) Xanthus and Balius, as the offspring of such parents, could naturally run swift as the winds. Zephyrus also loved the beautiful youth HYACINTHUS and killed him out of jealous and unrequited love.

Zephyrus is often a stormy wind in Homer, and only in later literature is he seen as warm and gentle, with his name surviving in our word 'zephyr', meaning a soft and pleasant breeze. It was with this nature that he was seen as the lover of FLORA, goddess of spring and flowers, who was transformed from the nymph Chloris at his touch, just as the cold earth is transformed in spring at the warm touch of the West Wind. Shelley's Zephyrus, in 'Ode to the West Wind', is more like Homer's:

O wild West Wind, thou breath of Autumn's being,
Thou, from whose unseen presence the leaves dead
Are driven, like ghosts from an enchanter fleeing,
Yellow, and black, and pale, and hectic red,
Pestilence-stricken multitudes ...

[Homer, *Iliad* 16.148–51, 23.198–230, *Odyssey* 5.295, 12.289; Hesiod, *Theogony* 378–80, 869–71; Lucian, *Dialogues of the Sea-gods* 11 and 15; Ovid, *Metamorphoses* 1.108.]

Zetes and Calais

Twin sons of BOREAS, the North Wind, and his Athenian wife Oreithyia whom the wind-god swept up and carried off to Thrace. They were known as the Boreadae, and being winged like their father were the swiftest men on earth. Some said that their wings grew from their shoulders, some from their temples and their feet. They had long, dark hair that streamed behind them as they flew, dark as their father's storm-clouds.

They sailed with the ARGONAUTS to fetch the Golden Fleece. On the journey out, they saved the blind Thracian king PHINEUS (2) from persecution by the HARPIES, foul monsters who snatched up most of his food and left a loathsome stench over what little they left him, so that he almost starved to death. The Boreadae pursued the Harpies through the sky, and Phineus was never troubled by them again. In one version, Zetes and Calais were said to die during the pursuit, in another, to return to their comrades triumphant. But even in the latter case they had not long to live, for they were killed by HERACLES, angry because they had persuaded the rest of the Argonauts not to turn back when he was accidentally left behind in Mysia. He encountered the Boreadae on the island of Tenos on their return from the funeral games of Pelias. Here he killed them and piled earth over them, then set up two pillars on their grave, one of which swayed whenever their father the North Wind blew.

[Apollonius, *Argonautica* 1.211–23, 1.296–1308, 2.164–434; Apollodorus 1.9.21, 3.15.2–3; Ovid, *Metamorphoses* 6.711–21.]

Zethus *see* AMPHION.

Zeus

The king of the gods, known to the Romans as Jupiter or Jove. He was a weather-god, the sender of rain, hail, snow and thunderstorms. His weapon was the thunderbolt, the symbol of his invincible power over gods and men. In Homer he is called 'cloud-gatherer', 'thunderer on high', 'lord of the lightning', Zeus who 'delights in the thunder', the 'father of gods and men'. He was the protector of law and justice, with other epithets indicating the spheres over which he had jurisdiction: as the defender of the household (*Herkeios*), the hearth (*Ephestios*), prop-erty (*Ktesios*), friendships (*Philios*), oaths (*Horkios*), hospitality (*Xenios*), suppliants (*Hikesios*), and mankind in general (*Soter*, Saviour).

Zeus was the youngest son of CRONUS and Rhea. His five elder brothers and sisters had been swallowed at birth by their father, who knew that he was destined to be overthrown by his own son; but when Zeus was born, Rhea gave her husband a stone wrapped in swaddling clothes instead of the baby (fig. 126). Cronus, noticing nothing amiss, duly consumed the stone, while Zeus himself was taken safely to Crete, to a cave on either Mount Ida or Mount Dicte. Here he was brought up by the nymphs ADRASTEIA and Ida, and fed on milk from the she-goat AMALTHEIA. The CURETES (1) guarded the cave, making so much noise by dancing around the entrance, clashing their shields and spears, that no sound of Zeus' infant cries could reach his cannibalistic father.

When Zeus was fully grown, he challenged his father's power. First of all, helped either by his grandmother GAIA (Earth) or by METIS, he induced Cronus to disgorge the five children he had swallowed. These now fought on Zeus' side in a war against Cronus and some of his brother TITANS. After a violent battle that lasted ten years, Zeus and his brothers and sisters, aided by the gigantic CYCLOPES and HUNDRED-HANDERS, defeated and deposed Cronus. Zeus was now acknowledged as the king of the gods. He imprisoned his father and the hostile Titans in the depths of Tartarus and set the Hundred-handers to guard them.

With his brothers he divided up the universe. They kept the earth and OLYMPUS as common property, while POSEIDON took the seas as his domain, HADES (2) the misty darkness of the Underworld, and Zeus the heavens. Yet he still had to face other challenges to his supreme power. Gaia was angry because her children, the Titans, had been imprisoned in Tartarus, so she stirred up her offspring, the GIANTS, to fight against Zeus and the other gods. Another mighty battle ensued, and the gods, with the help of a mortal, HERACLES, killed all the Giants. Gaia, angrier than ever, gave birth to the fire-breathing monster TYPHON, covered in snakes, who was so tall that his head touched the stars, and if he stretched out his arms, his one hand touched East and the other West. Zeus, after a desperate struggle, overcame even this fearsome creature (fig. 146), and either flung him into Tartarus, or hurled Mount Etna on top of him, crushing him beneath it. After this Gaia accepted her grandson's supremacy as king of the gods, and there were no more serious challenges to his power.

In the *Iliad*, Homer mentions a time when there was a conspiracy between Poseidon, HERA and ATHENA to put

Zeus in chains, and the sea-goddess THETIS sent the Hundred-Hander Briareos to release him. But the overall impression of the Homeric Zeus is one who dominates by tremendous physical power. He once punished Hera for her persecution of Heracles by suspending her from Olympus, her hands bound with a golden chain, and with anvils tied to her feet. When HEPHAESTUS tried to help her, Zeus picked him up by his leg and flung him out of Olympus and down to earth. He was very ready to threaten any misbehaviour with physical violence, and he himself boasted to the other gods (8.19–27):

> If you hang down from heaven a chain of gold,
> and lay hold of it, all you gods and goddesses,
> you could never drag me down from heaven to earth,
> not Zeus the counsellor most high, not if you try
> full hard. But if I set my mind to drag you up,
> then I'd hoist you up together with earth and sea,
> and tie the chain around the peak of Olympus,
> leaving the whole world hanging in mid-air.
> By so much am I stronger than gods and men.

In the *Odyssey*, Homer depicts Zeus as rather more diplomatic. As time went by, he was seen more and more as a god who dominated, not by force and threats, but by wisdom and justice.

Zeus' wife and queen was his sister Hera. She bore him three children: ARES, the god of war, EILEITHYIA, the goddess of childbirth, and HEBE, the goddess of youth. Their fourth child, the smith-god Hephaestus, was sometimes said to have been born of Hera alone. But Zeus had many other children by other goddesses. His first wife had been Metis, but when she was pregnant with their first child, he learnt that her second child would be a son who would overthrow him, just as he had overthrown his own father, Cronus. At once he swallowed Metis, thus forestalling the birth of the dangerous son. When the time came for the first child to be born, Hephaestus split Zeus' head with an axe and out leapt Athena, fully armed (fig. 51).

THEMIS bore Zeus the HORAE and the FATES, EURYNOME the GRACES, and MNEMOSYNE the MUSES. LETO bore him the two great archer-deities, APOLLO and ARTEMIS. He visited MAIA (1) by night while Hera was asleep, and she bore the messenger-god, HERMES. DEMETER bore him PERSEPHONE, who became the queen of Hades. According to Homer, DIONE bore him the goddess of love, APHRODITE, though she was more usually said to be born from the sea.

Many mortal women too were seduced or raped by Zeus. Indeed, he was such an incorrigible philanderer that, according to a Hesiodic fragment (*Catalogue of Women*, fr. 124), after so many of his own lies to Hera he pardoned all false oaths made by mortals in the name of love

Fig. 148 **Bronze figure found in the sea off Cape Artemisium, representing either Zeus or Poseidon.**

(and as Shakespeare's Juliet would put it: '... at lovers' perjuries, they say, Jove laughs'). He often came to mortal women in disguise, both to trick his unwitting quarry, and to evade his jealous wife, who was always ready to suspect him of misbehaviour. He came to LEDA as a swan, and she bore him HELEN and Polydeuces, one of the DIOSCURI. DANAE was imprisoned by her father, Acrisius, so Zeus came to her through a chink in the roof as a shower of gold, and she bore him PERSEUS. He charmed EUROPA in the form of a beautiful, white bull and carried her off to Crete, where she bore him MINOS, RHADAMANTHYS and SARPEDON. To get close to the nymph CALLISTO he impersonated Artemis, then reassumed his own form and raped her. She bore him ARCAS, and was turned into a bear by Hera. To ALCMENE (fig. 13) he appeared in the guise of her own husband, Amphitryon, and she bore him Heracles. He raped ANTIOPE (1) in the form of a satyr, and she bore him twin sons, AMPHION and Zethus. Hera caused the death of his lover SEMELE, by suggesting that she ask Zeus to come to her in all his godlike glory. He appeared to her as the great storm-god, lord of the lightning, and she was burnt to ashes. But her baby DIONYSUS was saved. IO was turned into a cow (fig. 77) and otherwise persecuted, but eventually she regained her human form and bore Zeus EPAPHUS. AEGINA, the daughter of the river-god Asopus, bore him AEACUS. He had many other love affairs, and many other children, all too numerous to mention. He was also moved by male beauty, such as that of GANYMEDE (fig. 59), the son of the Trojan king Tros, who was snatched up from earth to be his cupbearer.

As the great god of law and justice, Zeus punished transgressors, but these also are too numerous to mention more than a few. He punished the Titan PROMETHEUS for giving fire to mankind by creating the first woman, PANDORA, and by chaining the Titan to a cliff in the Caucasian Mountains where an eagle tore continually at his liver. He blasted LYCAON (1) and his fifty sons with thunderbolts for serving him human flesh; and this was one of his reasons, apart from mankind's general wickedness, for his sending the Great Flood on the world (*see* DEUCALION (1)). The great healer ASCLEPIUS showed presumption in bringing the dead back to life, so Zeus killed him with a thunderbolt fashioned by the Cyclopes. When Apollo, Asclepius' father, killed the Cyclopes in revenge, Zeus forced him to serve a mortal, Admetus, for a year. SALMONEUS thought himself the equal of Zeus, so the great god struck him with a thunderbolt and hurled him into Tartarus. Four other great sinners also paid eternally

for their crimes by suffering in the Underworld: TANTALUS (1), IXION, SISYPHUS and TITYUS.

Zeus was worshipped from very early times, and several of his sanctuaries are named on Mycenean Linear B tablets. His famous oracle at DODONA was reputed to be the oldest Greek oracle. In ancient art he is a dignified, bearded figure (fig. 148), often holding a thunderbolt (fig. 146) and sometimes a long sceptre. He is sometimes accompanied by an eagle. Several of his metamorphoses are depicted: the bull (fig. 56), the swan (fig. 84) and the shower of gold. His most famous representation in antiquity was the colossal statue in gold and ivory, created by the artist and sculptor Pheidias for the god's great temple at Olympia. Although it has long been lost, we know a great deal about it from written descriptions, such as that of the traveller Pausanias (5.11). It was judged to be one of the Seven Wonders of the World.

[Zeus appears so constantly throughout Greek literature that no list of references is feasible. Sources for particular tales may be found in the cross-referenced entries. See also A. B. Cook, *Zeus: A Study in Ancient Religion*, vol. 1 (1914), 2 (1925), 3 (1940); H. Lloyd-Jones, *The Justice of Zeus* (1971, 1983); W. Burkert, *Greek Religion* (1985), pp. 125–31; K. Arafat, *Classical Zeus: A Study in Art and Literature* (1990).]

Zeuxippe

A Naiad (water-nymph) who married her nephew PANDION (1), the sixth king of Athens. She bore him two sons, ERECHTHEUS, who succeeded his father to the throne, and BUTES (2), and two daughters, Procne and Philomela, for whose tragic story *see* TEREUS.

Maps

Genealogies

Greek and Latin Authors

Select Bibliography

Illustrations

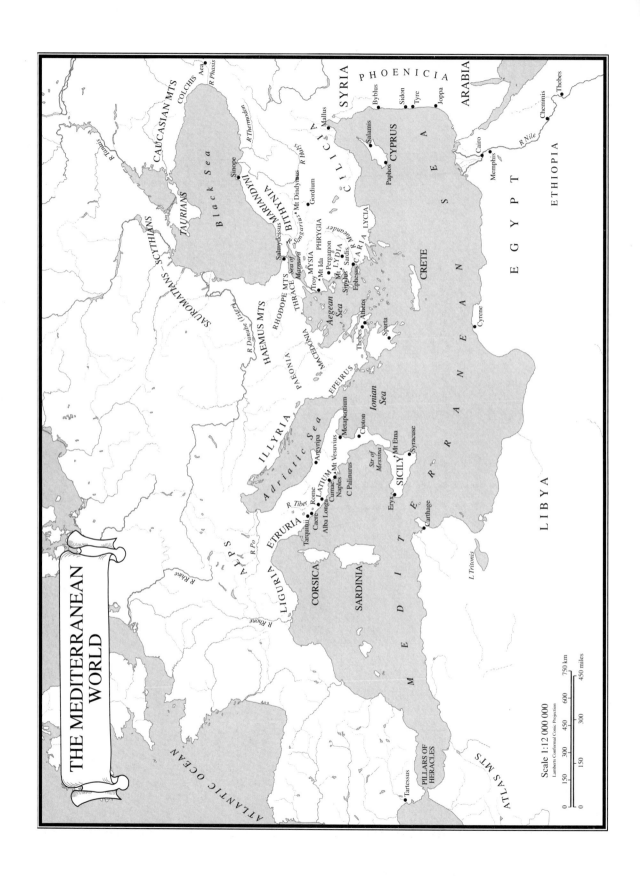

THE MEDITERRANEAN WORLD

Scale 1:12 000 000
Lamberts Conformal Conic Projection

0   150   300   450   600   750 km
0   150   300   450 miles

ATLANTIC OCEAN

PILLARS OF HERACLES

ATLAS MTS

Tartessus

CAUCASIAN MTS
COLCHIS   Aea
R Phasis
R Tropus

Black Sea

TAURIANS

SCYTHIANS

SAUROMATIANS

R Tanais (Don)

R Danube

HAEMUS MTS

RHODOPE MTS
THRACE

Sinope

MARIANDYNI
BITHYNIA
Salmydessus
Sea of Marmara
Mt Dindymus
R Sangarius
Gordium
PHRYGIA

Troy
Mt Ida
MYSIA
Pergamon
Mt LYDIA
Sardis
R Hermus
Ephesus
R Maeander
CARIA
LYCIA

R Halys
Mallus
CILICIA

SYRIA
PHOENICIA
ARABIA
Byblus
Sidon
Tyre
Joppa

Salamis
CYPRUS
Paphos

Thebes
Chemmis

Cairo
R Nile
Memphis

EGYPT

ETHIOPIA

CRETE

Aegean Sea
Athens
Thebes
Sparta

Cyrene

MEDITERRANEAN

LIBYA

L Tritonis

PAEONIA
MACEDONIA
EPEIRUS

ILLYRIA

Adriatic Sea

Ionian Sea

Metapontium
Croton
Argyripa
LATIUM
Mt Vesuvius
Cumae
Naples
C Palinurus

Str of Messina
Mt Etna
Syracuse
SICILY
Eryx

Carthage

Rome
R Tiber
Caere
Alba Longa
Tarquinii
ETRURIA

ALPS
R Po
R Athesis

LIGURIA

CORSICA

SARDINIA

R Rhône

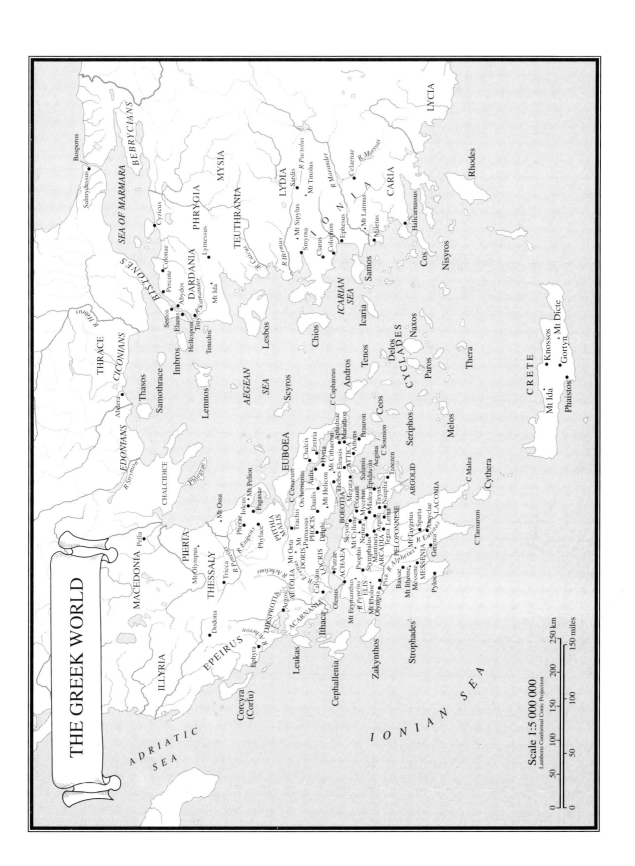

THE GREEK WORLD

Scale 1:5 000 000
Lamberts Conformal Conic Projection

ADRIATIC SEA

IONIAN SEA

ILLYRIA

MACEDONIA   Pella
PIERIA
MtOlympus
THESSALY   Tricca   R Peneius
EPEIRUS
THESPROTIA
Dodona
Ephyra   R Acheron
Corcyra (Corfu)

Leukas
Cephallenia
Ithaca
Zakynthos
Strophades

ACARNANIA
AETOLIA
Argos
Olenus
Calydon   R Achelous
Patrae   ACHAEA
Mt Erymanthus
R Peneius
Mt Pholoe   ELIS
Olympia   Pisa

Mt Ossa
Mt Pelion
Pherae   Iolcus   Pagasae
Phylace
PHTHIA   MALIS
R Enipeus
Mt Oeta   Trachis
DORIS   Parnassus
LOCRIS   Delphi   PHOCIS
Daulis
Orchomenus
C Cenaeum
Mt Helicon   Aulis
Sicyon   Corinth
Mt Cyllene   Nemea
Stymphalus   Cleonae
Mantineia   Mycenae
ARCADIA   Argos   Tiryns
Tegea   Lerna   R Alpheius
Bassae
Mt Ithome   Mt Maenalus
Messene   MESSENIA
Pylos   Gerenia   R Eurotas

EUBOEA
Chalcis
Eretria
Hyria
Mt Cithaeron   Marathon
Thebes   Eleusis   Aphidnae
Plataea   ATTICA
Megara   Athens   Brauron
Salamis   C Sounion
Aegina
Epidaurus
Nauplia   Troezen
ARGOLID
LACONIA
Amyclae
Sparta
Mt Taygetus
C Malea

C Caphareus

THRACE   CICONIANS
EDONIANS   R Strymon
CHALCIDICE
Phlegra
Abdera
Thasos   Samothrace
Imbros   Lemnos
Scyros

BEBRYCIANS
SEA OF MARMARA
Bosporos
Salmydessus
Cyzicus
Colonae
Percote
Abydos   DARDANIA
Sestos   Lymessus
Elaeus   Troy   R Scamander   Mt Ida
Hellespont   Tenedos
BISTONES
R Hebrus

PHRYGIA
MYSIA
TEUTHRANIA
R Caicus   R Hermus
LYDIA
Smyrna   Mt Sipylus
Sardis   R Pactolus   R Tmolus
Clarus   Mt Tmolus   R Maeander
Colophon   Ephesus   Mt Latmus
Celaenae   R Marsyas
CARIA
Miletus   Halicarnassus
LYCIA
Rhodes

IONIA

Lesbos
Chios
AEGEAN SEA
Tenos
Andros
Ceos
CYCLADES
Delos
Paros   Naxos
Seriphos
Melos
Thera
Samos
ICARIAN SEA
Icaria
Cos
Nisyros

Cythera

CRETE
Mt Ida
Knossos   Mt Dicte
Gortyn
Phaistos

C Taenarum

Scale bar:
250 km
150 miles
0   50   100   150   200
0   50   100

1: The First Gods

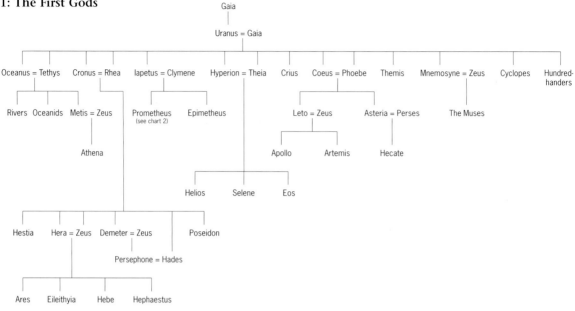

2: The Line of Prometheus

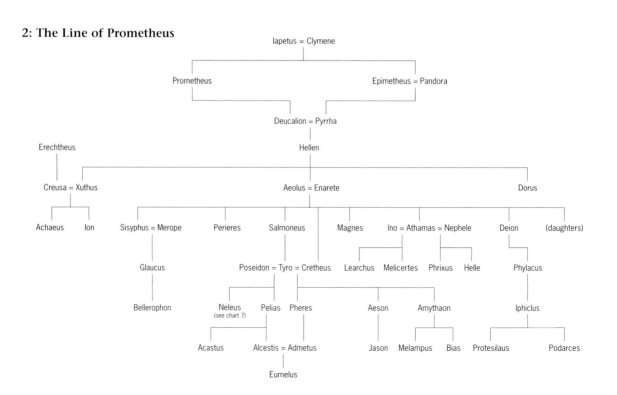

3: The Line of Io

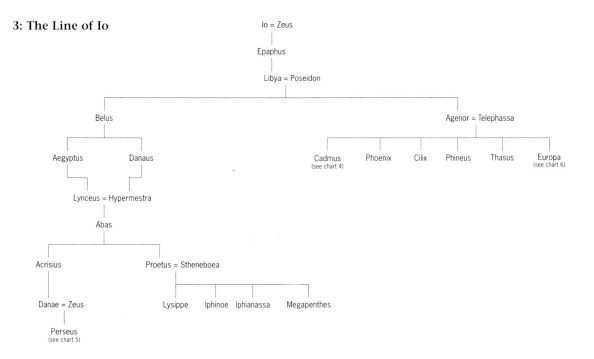

4: The Royal House of Thebes

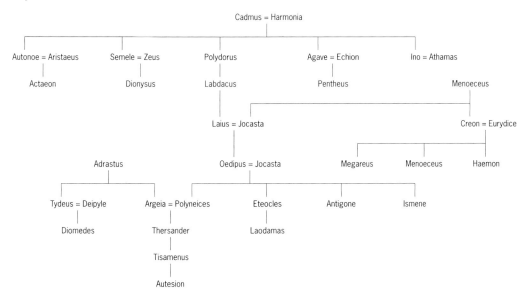

5: The Line of Danae

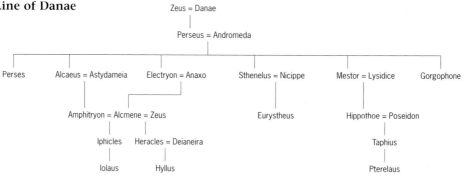

6: The Line of Europa

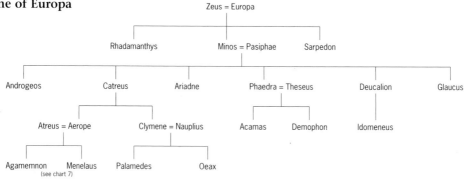

7: The Line of Tantalus

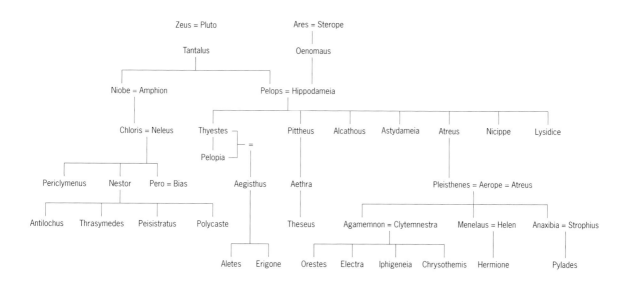

8: The Royal House of Athens

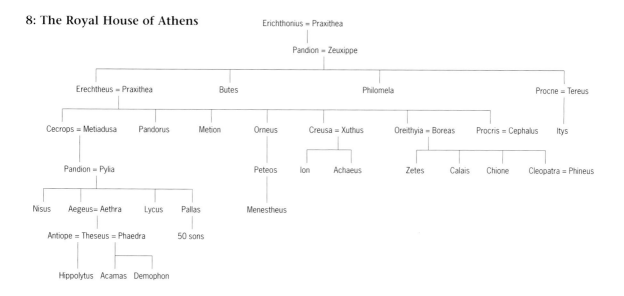

9: Trojans and Romans

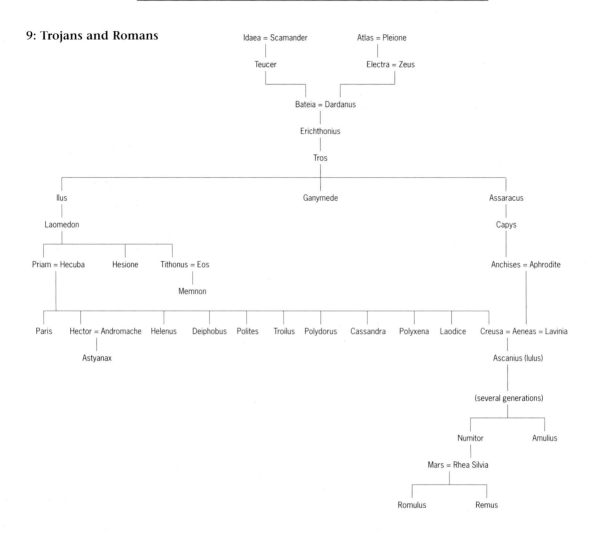

10: The Line of Aegina

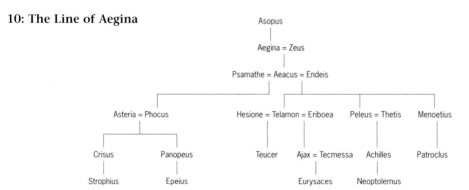

GREEK AND LATIN AUTHORS

Aelian Greek prose writer, born AD 165–170, died AD 230–235.

Aeschylus Greek (Athenian) tragic playwright, *c.*525–456 BC. Author of 70 to 90 plays, most lost but for fragments, but with seven extant works: *Persians*; *Suppliant Women*; *Seven against Thebes*; the *Oresteia* trilogy, made up of *Agamemnon*, *Libation Bearers*, and *Eumenides*; and (of disputed authenticity) *Prometheus Bound*.

Alcaeus Lyric poet from Lesbos, probably born *c.*625–620 BC

Antoninus Liberalis Greek mythographer, 2nd century AD. Author of a *Metamorphoses* based on Hellenistic sources.

Apollodorus Greek scholar, *c.*180–120 BC, whose name is conventionally given to the later (1st or 2nd century AD) handbook of Greek mythology known as the *Library* (*Bibliotheca*). It is composed of three books and a summary (the *Epitome*) of the remainder.

Apollonius of Rhodes Greek epic poet, 3rd century BC. Author of the *Argonautica*, which relates the story of the quest by Jason and the Argonauts for the Golden Fleece.

Apuleius Latin prose writer, born *c.*AD 125. Author of numerous works, including the *Metamorphoses*, more commonly known as *The Golden Ass*, the only Latin novel that survives complete.

Aristophanes Greek (Athenian) comic playwright, born 460–450 BC, died *c.*386. Extant works: *Acharnians, Knights, Clouds, Wasps, Peace, Birds, Lysistrata, Women at the Thesmophoria, Frogs, Assemblywomen, Wealth.*

Aristotle Greek philosopher, scientist and prose writer, 384–322 BC.

Arrian Greek historian, *c.*AD 86–160.

Athenaeus Greek prose writer of *c.*AD 200. Author of *The Learned Banquet* (*Deipnosophistai*), table talk on all manner of subjects relating to convivial occasions.

Bacchylides Greek lyric poet, *c.*520–450 BC.

Callimachus Greek poet and scholar, *c.*305–240 BC.

Catullus Latin lyric poet, *c.*84–54 BC.

Cicero Latin orator, philosopher, prose writer and poet, 106–43 BC.

Cratinus Greek comic playwight, 5th century BC. Author of more than two dozen comedies, all lost but for fragments.

Dio Chrysostom Greek orator and philosopher, born *c.*AD 40–50, died after AD 110.

Diodorus Siculus Greek (Sicilian) historian, writing *c.*60–30 BC. Author of a history from mythological times to 60 BC in forty books, fifteen of which (1–5, 11–20) survive complete.

Diogenes Laertius Greek philosophic writer, probably first half of the third century AD.

Dionysius of Halicarnassus Greek critic and historian, 1st century BC. Author of *Roman Antiquities* in twenty books, of which the first eleven survive complete, covering the period down to 441 BC.

Epic Cycle A collection of early Greek epic poems by poets other than Homer and Hesiod, lost but for meagre fragments, though in some cases there survive summaries by Proclus (perhaps a grammarian of the second century AD). They included a Trojan Cycle (*Cypria, Aethiopis, Little Iliad, Sack of Troy, Returns* and *Telegony*), a Theban Cycle (*Oedipodeia, Thebaid* and *Epigoni*) and a *Titanomachy*.

Euripides Greek (Athenian) tragic playwright, *c.*480–406 BC. Author of about 90 plays, most lost but for fragments, but with eighteen extant works: *Alcestis, Medea, Hippolytus, Children of Heracles, Hecuba, Electra, Andromache, Suppliant Women, Trojan Women, Helen, Ion, Phoenician Women, Orestes, Madness of Heracles, Iphigeneia among the Taurians, Iphigeneia at Aulis, Bacchae* and (satyr play) *Cyclops*. The *Rhesus* was traditionally said to be by Euripides, although the attribution is doubtful.

Hellanicus Greek historian and mythographer, *c.*480–395 BC.

Herodotus Greek historian (the 'father of history'), *c.*480–425 BC. Author of the *History*, a nine-book narrative of the Greek and Persian wars, with many digressions.

Hesiod Greek epic and didactic poet of around 700 BC. Author of the *Theogony* and the *Works and Days*, though several other epic poems were later attributed to him, such as the *Catalogue of Women* and the *Shield of Heracles*.

Homer Greek epic poet, second half of the eighth century BC. Author of the *Iliad* and the *Odyssey* (though some think that the poems were by different authors).

Homeric Hymns A collection of 33 Greek hymns in epic metre, addressed to various deities. In ancient times they were wrongly attributed to Homer, and were probably composed between the eighth and sixth centuries BC.

Horace Latin poet, 65–8 BC. Author of *Odes* (four books), *Epodes*, *Satires*, *Epistles* (two books) and *Secular Hymn*.

Hyginus Name given to the otherwise unknown author of two Latin works, the *Fabulae*, a handbook of mythology, and a *Poetic Astronomy*, both compiled from Greek sources probably in the second century AD.

Isocrates Greek orator, 436–338 BC.

Josephus Jewish historian writing in Greek, born AD 37/8.

Livy Latin historian, 59 BC–AD 17. Author of a History 'from the foundation of Rome' to his own times in 142 books, of which 35 survive.

Longus Greek author of the novel *Daphnis and Chloe*, probably late second or early third century AD.

Lucian Greek prose writer and philosopher, born c. AD 125–120, died after AD 180.

Lucretius Latin Epicurean philosopher and didactic poet, c. 94–51 BC. Author of *On the Nature of Things* in six books.

Musaeus Greek poet, probably of the late fifth or early sixth century AD. Author of a hexameter poem on Hero and Leander.

Nonnus Greek epic poet writing c. AD 450–470, whose extant works include the *Dionysiaca* in 48 books.

Ovid Latin poet, 43 BC–AD 17. Author of many works, including the *Metamorphoses* (fifteen books), *Amores*, *Heroides*, *Art of Love*, *Fasti* and *Tristia*. A number of minor poems are attributed to him.

Parthenius Greek poet and scholar, 1st century BC. Author of the *Love Romances*, a collection of prose summaries of esoteric love stories taken from Greek poets and prose writers.

Pausanias Greek traveller and writer, second century AD. Author of the *Description of Greece* in ten books.

Petronius Latin satirist, first century AD. Author of the *Satyrica*.

Pherecydes Greek prose writer, fifth century BC. Author of mythical and genealogical *Histories*, lost but for fragments.

Pindar Greek lyric poet, c. 518–438 BC. His only works to survive intact are his *Epinicia*, collections of choral lyric odes celebrating victories in the Games: *Olympic*, *Pythian*, *Nemean* and *Isthmian*.

Plato Greek (Athenian) philosopher and prose writer, c.

429–347 BC. Author of the *Apology*, vindicating Socrates who was put to death in 399, and of 25 dialogues, in most of which Socrates takes part. A number of letters and poems are also attributed to him.

Plautus Latin comic playwright, perhaps c. 254–184 BC. Twenty-one of his plays survive.

Pliny Latin prose writer, AD 23–79. Of his many and various works, the *Natural History* in 37 books survives.

Plutarch Greek philosopher and biographer, born before AD 50, died after AD 120. He was a prolific author and many of his works survive, including the *Moralia* ('moral essays') and 23 pairs of *Parallel Lives*, biographies of paired Greeks and Romans, both mythical and historical.

Pollux Greek scholar and rhetorician, 2nd century AD.

Proclus *see* Epic Cycle.

Propertius Latin elegiac poet, born 54–47 BC, died before 2 BC.

Quintus of Smyrna Greek epic poet of c. AD 400. Author of the *Sequel to Homer*, a long epic poem relating events from the end of the *Iliad* to the beginning of the *Odyssey*.

Sappho Lyric poet from Lesbos, born in the second half of the seventh century BC.

Seneca Latin philosopher and writer of both poetry and prose, c. 4 BC–AD 65. His extant works include nine tragedies: *Madness of Hercules*, *Trojan Women*, *Phoenician Women*, *Medea*, *Phaedra*, *Oedipus*, *Agamemnon*, *Thyestes* and *Hercules on Oeta*.

Simonides Greek lyric poet, c. 556–466 BC.

Sophocles Greek (Athenian) tragic playwright, c. 496–406 BC. Author of over 120 plays, most lost but for fragments, but with seven extant works: *Women of Trachis*, *Ajax*, *Antigone*, *Oedipus the King*, *Electra*, *Philoctetes* and *Oedipus at Colonus*.

Statius Latin epic poet, c. AD 45–96, whose extant works include the *Thebaid* and the unfinished *Achilleid*.

Stesichorus Greek lyric poet, active c. 600–550 BC. His works were collected in 26 books, but only fragments survive.

Strabo Greek historian and geographer, born c. 64 BC, died after AD 21. Author of the *Geographia* in seventeen books.

Tacitus Latin historian, c. AD 56–120.

Theocritus Greek pastoral poet, c. 310–250 BC.

Thucydides Greek historian, c. 460–400 BC. Author of the *History of the Peloponnesian War* in eight books.

Valerius Flaccus Latin epic poet, 1st century AD. Author of the *Argonautica*, which relates the story of the quest by Jason and the Argonauts for the Golden Fleece.

Virgil Latin poet, 70–19 BC. Extant works: the *Aeneid*, an epic poem in twelve books; the *Georgics*, a didactic poem on agriculture in four books; and the *Eclogues*, ten pastoral poems. A number of minor poems are attributed to him.

Xenophon Greek historian, c. 430-354 BC, and a prolific writer on a wide variety of subjects.

SELECT BIBLIOGRAPHY

J. N. Bremmer (ed.), *Interpretations of Greek Mythology* (1987).

J. N. Bremmer and N. M. Horsfall, *Roman Myth and Mythography*, BICS Suppl. 52 (1987).

W. Burkert, *Structure and History in Greek Mythology and Ritual* (1979).

W. Burkert, *Greek Religion* (1985).

R. Buxton, *Imaginary Greece* (1994).

Roberto Calasso, *The Marriage of Cadmus and Harmony* (1993).

R. Caldwell, *The Origin of the Gods* (1989).

T. H. Carpenter, *Art and Myth in Ancient Greece* (1991).

E. R. Dodds, *The Greeks and the Irrational* (1951).

K. Dowden, *The Uses of Greek Mythology* (1992).

P. E. Easterling and J. V. Muir (eds), *Greek Religion and Society* (1985).

L. Edmunds (ed.), *Approaches to Greek Myth* (1990).

R. B. Edwards, *Kadmos the Phoenician: A Study in Greek Legends and the Mycenean Age* (1979).

J. G. Fraser (ed.), *Apollodorus: The Library* (Loeb Classical Library), 2 vols (1921).

K. Friis Johansen, *The Iliad in Early Greek Art* (1967).

Timothy Gantz, *Early Greek Myth: A Guide to Literary and Artistic Sources* (1993).

R. L. Gordon (ed.), *Myth, Religion and Society* (1981).

F. Graf, *Greek Mythology: An Introduction* (1993).

M. Grant, *Myths of the Greeks and Romans* (1962).

M. Grant, *Roman Myths* (1971).

Robert Graves, *The Greek Myths* (1960).

Jane Henle, *Greek Myths: A Vase Painter's Notebook* (1973).

J. Herington, *Poetry into Drama* (1985).

R. Hinks, *Myth and Allegory in Ancient Art* (1939).

M. Jacobs, *Mythological Painting* (1979).

E. Kearns, *The Heroes of Attica*, BICS Suppl. 57 (1989).

G. S. Kirk, *Myth: Its Meaning and Function in Ancient and Other Cultures* (1970).

G. S. Kirk, *The Nature of Greek Myths* (1974).

Mary R. Lefkowitz, *Women in Greek Myth* (1986).

Lexicon Iconographicum Mythologiae Classicae (1981–1997).

H. Lloyd-Jones, *The Justice of Zeus* (1971).

Jennifer R. March, *The Creative Poet*, BICS Suppl. 49 (London, 1987).

Philip Mayerson, *Classical Mythology in Literature, Art, and Music* (1971).

M. P. Nilsson, *The Mycenean Origin of Greek Mythology* (1932).

H. J. Rose, *Handbook of Greek Mythology*, 6th edition (1958).

K. Schefold, *Myth and Legend in Early Greek Art* (1966).

K. Schefold, *Gods and Heroes in Late Archaic Greek Art* (1992).

M. Simpson, *Gods and Heroes of the Greeks: The Library of Apollodorus* (1976).

J.-P. Vernant, *Myth and Society in Ancient Greece* (1982).

J.-P. Vernant and P. Vidal-Naquet, *Tragedy and Myth in Ancient Greece* (1981).

P. Veyne, *Did the Greeks believe in their Myths?* (1988).

B. Vickers, *Towards Greek Tragedy* (1973).

M. L. West, *The Hesiodic Catalogue of Women* (1985).

Felicity Woolf, *Myths and Legends: Paintings in the National Gallery* (1988).

S. Woodford, *The Trojan War in Ancient Art* (1993)

LIST OF ILLUSTRATIONS

1 Attic red-figure calyx krater by Myson, *c.*500 BC. London, British Museum E 458.

2 Attic red-figure stamnos by Oltos, *c.*520 BC. London, British Museum E 437.

3 Attic red-figure cup by the Briseis Painter, *c.*470 BC. London, British Museum E 76.

4 Attic red-figure cup, signed by Euphronios as potter, *c.*510 BC. Perugia, Museo Civico.

5 Lucanian red-figure nestoris by the Dolon Painter, *c.* 390 BC. London, British Museum F 176.

6 Attic red-figure belly amphora by the Oianthe Painter, *c.*470 BC. London, British Museum E 264.

7 Attic red-figure pelike by the Berlin Painter, *c.*500 BC. Vienna, Kunsthistorisches Museum 3725.

8 Attic red-figure cup by the Brygos Painter, *c.*480 BC. Was Berlin, Staatliche Museen 2301.

9 Attic red-figure calyx krater by the Tyszkiewicz Painter, *c.*480 BC. Boston, Museum of Fine Arts 97.368.

10 Attic red-figure calyx krater by the Dokimasia Painter, *c.*470 BC. Boston, Museum of Fine Arts 63.1246.

11 Attic black-figure amphora by Exekias, *c.*540 BC. Boulogne, Musée Communal 558.

12 Handle of Attic black-figure volute krater, known as the François Krater, by Kleitias, *c.*570 BC. Florence, Museo Archeologico 4209.

13 Paestan red-figure bell krater by Python, *c.*340 BC. London, British Museum F 149.

14 Attic red-figure dinos from the Polygnotos Group, *c.* 450 BC. London, British Museum 99.7.21.5.

15 Attic red-figure stamnos by the Syleus Painter, *c.*470 BC. Toledo, Museum of Art 1956.24.

16 Lucanian red-figure hydria by the Amykos Painter, *c.*410 BC. Paris, Cabinet des Medailles 442.

17 Attic red-figure volute krater from the circle of the Sisyphus Painter, *c.*400 BC. Malibu, J. Paul Getty Museum 85.AE.102.

18 Attic red-figure volute krater by Euphronios, *c.*510 BC. Paris, Louvre G 103.

19 Late Hellenistic marble statue. Paris, Louvre MA 399.

20 Attic red-figure calyx krater by Myson, *c.*500 BC. London, British Museum E 458.

21 Marble statue, *c.*460 BC. Olympia Museum.

22 Attic red-figure cup by the Kleophrades Painter, *c.*490 BC. London, British Museum E 73.

23 Attic red-figure column krater by the Orchard painter, *c.*460 BC. New York, Metropolitan Museum of Art 1934.11.7.

24 Attic red-figure cup by Douris, *c.*470 BC. Rome, Vatican Museum 16545.

25 Attic black-figure amphora by the Towry Whyte painter, *c.*530 BC. London, British Museum B 168.

26 Attic red-figure amphora, *c.*500 BC. London, British Museum E 256.

27 Attic red-figure calyx krater by the Altamura Painter, *c.*465 BC. Boston, Museum of Fine Arts 59.178.

28 Attic red-figure pelike by the Syleus Painter, *c.*480 BC. Paris, Louvre G 233.

29 Laconian cup, *c.*560 BC. Rome, Vatican Museum 16592.

30 Bronze, 5th century AD. Florence, Galleria degli Uffizi.

31 Attic red-figure oinochoe by the Pan Painter, *c.*470 BC. London, British Museum E 512.

32 Attic red-figure pelike by the Pan Painter, *c.*460 BC. Athens, National Museum 9683.

33 Attic red-figure column krater by the Pan Painter, *c.* 460 BC. London, British Museum E 473.

34 Attic black-figure volute krater, known as the François Krater, by Kleitias, *c.*570 BC. Florence, Museo Archeologico 4209.

35 Attic red-figure hydria by the Kleophrades Painter, *c.* 480 BC. Naples, Museo Nazionale 2422.

36 Marble relief, 446–440 BC. London, British Museum.

37 Caeretan hydria, *c.*530 BC. Paris, Louvre E 701.

38 Attic black-figure amphora, *c.*540 BC. London, British Museum B 231.

39 Attic red-figure stamnos by the Berlin Painter, *c.*490 BC. Paris, Louvre G 186.

40 Attic red-figure calyx krater by the Persephone Painter, *c.*440 BC. New York, Metropolitan Museum of Art 41.83.

41 Paestan red-figure amphora, *c.*340 BC. Malibu, J. Paul Getty Museum 80.AE.155.1.